Case Studies and Boxes of Special Interest

		Page
Section 1-5	A Century of Business Cycles	12
Section 2-3	Where to Find the Numbers: A Guide to the Data	28
Section 2-10	Conflicting Measurements: Was the 2002–04 Recovery "Jobless" or Not?	47
Section 3-4	Why Did U.S. Saving Almost Vanish in 2004?	64
Section 4-7	How Monetary Policy Actually Worked in 2001–04	106
Section 5-3	The Government Budget in Historical Perspective	132
Section 5-6	How the Deficits Rejoined to Become "Twins"	145
Section 6-7	Asia Intervenes with Buckets to Buy Dollars and Finance the U.S. Current Account Deficit—How Long Can This Continue?	174
Section 7-10	What Caused the Great Depression?	221
Section 8-8	How Large Is the Sacrifice Ratio?	249
Section 8-11	The Goldilocks Economy—Why Inflation Was So Low in the Late 1990s	258
Section 9-3	*The Wizard of Oz* as a Monetary Allegory	290
Section 9-4	The Indexed Bond (TIPS) Has Arrived	294
Section 11-6	Uneven U.S. Growth Across Eras: Why Did U.S. Productivity Growth Slow Down and Then Revive?	368
Section 11-6	How the Great Inventions Created Economic Growth: Life in the "Bad Old Days"	374
Section 11-8	The Productivity Growth Contrast Between Europe and the United States	379
Section 12-5	Historical Behavior of the Debt-GDP Ratio Since 1790	395
Section 13-7	Why Interest Rates Were More Volatile in the 1980s and Less Volatile in the 1990s	439
Section 14-5	Was the Fed Responsible for the Decline in Economic Volatility?	461
Section 14-7	The Taylor Rule and the Changing Fed Attitude Toward Inflation and Output	467
Section 14-9	Should Monetary Policy Target the Exchange Rate?	473
Section 15-2	Main Features of U.S. Consumption Data	484
Section 15-6	Did Households Spend or Save the 2001 Tax Rebate?	499
Section 15-8	Did Soaring Household Assets Cause the Collapse in the Household Saving Rate?	506
Section 16-2	The Historical Instability of Investment	517
Section 16-4	The Simple Accelerator and the Postwar U.S. Economy	523
Section 16-7	Tobin's q: Does It Explain Investment Better Than the Accelerator or Neoclassical Theories?	530
Section 16-9	The Boom and Bust in "New Economy" Investment	533

Macroeconomics

Tenth Edition

The Addison-Wesley Series in Economics

Abel/Bernanke
Macroeconomics

Bade/Parkin
Foundations of Economics

Bierman/Fernandez
Game Theory with Economic Applications

Binger/Hoffman
Microeconomics with Calculus

Boyer
Principles of Transportation Economics

Branson
Macroeconomic Theory and Policy

Bruce
Public Finance and the American Economy

Byrns/Stone
Economics

Carlton/Perloff
Modern Industrial Organization

Caves/Frankel/Jones
World Trade and Payments: An Introduction

Chapman
Environmental Economics: Theory, Application, and Policy

Cooter/Ulen
Law and Economics

Downs
An Economic Theory of Democracy

Ehrenberg/Smith
Modern Labor Economics

Ekelund/Ressler/Tollison
Economics

Fusfeld
The Age of the Economist

Gerber
International Economics

Ghiara
Learning Economics

Gordon
Macroeconomics

Gregory
Essentials of Economics

Gregory/Stuart
Russian and Soviet Economic Performance and Structure

Hartwick/Olewiler
The Economics of Natural Resource Use

Hubbard
Money, the Financial System, and the Economy

Hughes/Cain
American Economic History

Husted/Melvin
International Economics

Jehle/Reny
Advanced Microeconomic Theory

Johnson-Lans
A Health Economics Primer

Klein
Mathematical Methods for Economics

Krugman/Obstfeld
International Economics

Laidler
The Demand for Money

Leeds/von Allmen/Schiming
Economics

Leeds/von Allmen
The Economics of Sports

Lipsey/Courant/Ragan
Economics

Melvin
International Money and Finance

Miller
Economics Today

Miller
Understanding Modern Economics

Miller/Benjamin
The Economics of Macro Issues

Miller/Benjamin/North
The Economics of Public Issues

Mills/Hamilton
Urban Economics

Mishkin
The Economics of Money, Banking, and Financial Markets

Parkin
Economics

Perloff
Microeconomics

Phelps
Health Economics

Riddell/Shackelford/Stamos/Schneider
Economics: A Tool for Critically Understanding Society

Ritter/Silber/Udell
Principles of Money, Banking, and Financial Markets

Rohlf
Introduction to Economic Reasoning

Ruffin/Gregory
Principles of Economics

Sargent
Rational Expectations and Inflation

Scherer
Industry Structure, Strategy, and Public Policy

Stock/Watson
Introduction to Econometrics

Studenmund
Using Econometrics

Tietenberg
Environmental and Natural Resource Economics

Tietenberg
Environmental Economics and Policy

Todaro/Smith
Economic Development

Waldman
Microeconomics

Waldman/Jensen
Industrial Organization: Theory and Practice

Weil
Economic Growth

Williamson
Macroeconomics

Macroeconomics

Tenth Edition

Robert J. Gordon

Stanley G. Harris Professor in the Social Sciences
Northwestern University

PEARSON

Addison
Wesley

Boston   San Francisco   New York
London   Toronto   Sydney   Tokyo   Singapore   Madrid
Mexico City   Munich   Paris   Cape Town   Hong Kong   Montreal

Publisher:	Daryl Fox
Editor in Chief:	Denise Clinton
Acquisitions Editor:	Roxanne Hoch
Assistant Editor:	Amy Fleischer
Editorial Assistant:	Julia Boyles
Managing Editor:	James Rigney
Senior Production Supervisor:	Nancy Fenton
Photo Researcher:	Beth Anderson
Supplements Production Coordinator:	Kirsten Dickerson
Media Producer:	Melissa Honig
Executive Marketing Manager:	Stephen Frail
Marketing Assistant:	Kate MacLean
Rights and Permissions Advisor:	Dana Weightman
Senior Manufacturing Buyer:	Carol Melville
Cover Design:	Gina Hagen Kolenda
Text Design, Production Coordination, Composition, and Illustrations:	Elm Street Publishing Services, Inc.

Cover image: Paul Klee. *Unstable Equilibrium*, 1922, 159. © Artists Rights Society (ARS), New York / VG Bild-Kunst, Bonn.

Photo credits: page **v** photo of Robert J. Gordon by Julie P. Gordon; Chapter 3, page **77** left: © Tim Sloan/AFP/Getty Images; page **77** right: © Kevin Fleming/CORBIS; Chapter 7, page **216**, ©Bettmann/CORBIS; Chapter 9, page **288**: © AP/Wide World Photos; page **290**: © The Kobal Collection; Chapter 10, page **328**: © AP/Wide World Photos; Chapter 11, page **366**: © Michael S. Lewis/CORBIS; page **374**: © Bettmann/CORBIS; Chapter 12, page **402**: Courtesy Robert J. Barro, Harvard University; Chapter 13, page **432**: Yale University Office of Public Affairs; page **436**: Digital Vision; Chapter 14, page **453**: PhotoDisc Blue; page **474**: Getty/Medio Images (RF); Chapter 15, page **493**: © Owen Franken/CORBIS; page **499**: PhotoDisc; Chapter 16, page **530**: © Tom Tracy, The Stock Connection; Chapter 17, page **549**: © Roger Ressmeyer/CORBIS; page **551** top: Photograph by Fournier; page **551** bottom: © Ralf-Finn Hestoft/CORBIS; Chapter 18, page **596**: © Reuters/CORBIS.

Many of the designations used by manufacturers and sellers to distinguish their products are claimed as trademarks. Where those designations appear in this book, and Addison-Wesley was aware of a trademark claim, the designations have been printed in initial caps or all caps.

Library of Congress Cataloging-in-Publication Data
Gordon, Robert J. (Robert James), 1940–
  Macroeconomics / Robert J. Gordon.—10th ed.
    p. cm.
  Includes bibliographical references and index.
  ISBN 0-321-27880-1 (alk. paper)
   1. Macroeconomics.   I. Title.
HB172.5.G67   2006
339—dc22   2005015268

Copyright © 2006 Pearson Education, Inc. All rights reserved. No part of this publication may be reproduced, stored in a retrieval system, or transmitted, in any form or by any means, electronic, mechanical, photocopying, recording, or otherwise, without the prior written permission of the publisher. Printed in the United States of America. For information on obtaining permission for use of material in this work, please submit a written request to Pearson Education, Inc., Rights and Contracts Department, 75 Arlington Street, Suite 300, Boston, MA 02116, fax your request to 617-848-7047, or e-mail at http://www.pearsoned.com/legal/permissions.htm.

1 2 3 4 5 6 7 8 9 10—QWT—09 08 07 06 05

About the Author
Robert J. Gordon

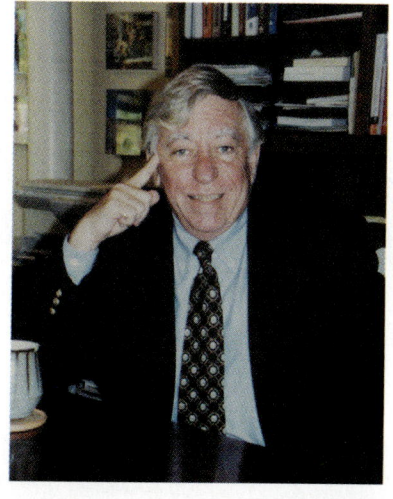

Robert J. Gordon is Stanley G. Harris Professor in the Social Sciences and Professor of Economics at Northwestern University. He did his undergraduate work at Harvard and then attended Oxford University in England on a Marshall Scholarship. He received his Ph.D. in 1967 at M.I.T. and taught at Harvard and the University of Chicago before coming to Northwestern in 1973, where he has taught for more than 30 years and was chair of the Department of Economics from 1992 to 1996.

Professor Gordon is one of the world's leading experts on inflation, unemployment, and productivity growth. His recent work on the rise and fall of the New Economy, the U.S. productivity growth revival, and the recent stalling of European productivity growth, have been widely cited. He is the author of *The Measurement of Durable Goods Prices,* which has become known as the definitive work showing that government price indexes substantially overstate the rate of inflation. His book of collected essays, *Productivity Growth, Inflation, and Unemployment,* was published in 2004. He is editor of *Milton Friedman's Monetary Framework: A Debate with His Critics, The American Business Cycle,* and *The Economics of New Goods.* In addition he is the author of more than 100 scholarly articles and more than 60 published comments on the research of others. In addition to his main field of macroeconomics, he is also a frequently quoted expert and author on the airline industry, and is the founder and president of an Internet chat group on airline management.

Gordon is a Research Associate of the National Bureau of Economic Research, a Research Fellow of the Centre for Economic Policy Research (London), a Guggenheim Fellow, a Fellow of the American Academy of Arts and Sciences, and a Fellow of the Econometric Society. He has served as the co-editor of the *Journal of Political Economy* and as an elected member of the American Economic Association. He serves currently as senior advisor to the Brookings Panel on Economic Activity and on the economic advisory panels of the Congressional Budget Office and the Bureau of Economic Analysis. He has served as a member of the Technical Panel on Assumptions and Methods of the Social Security Administration, and on the national "Boskin Commission" to assess the accuracy of the U.S. Consumer Price Index.

Gordon lives in Evanston, Illinois, with his wife Julie and their two dogs, Lucky and Toto.

with love, for Julie

Brief Contents

	Preface: To the Instructor	xvii
	Preface: To the Student	xxvi

PART ONE Introduction and Measurement — 1

- **CHAPTER 1** What Is Macroeconomics? — 3
- **CHAPTER 2** The Measurement of Income, Prices, and Unemployment — 25

PART TWO Income, Interest Rates, Policy, and the Open Economy — 55

- **CHAPTER 3** Spending, Income, and Interest Rates — 57
- **CHAPTER 4** Monetary and Fiscal Policy in the *IS-LM* Model — 94
- **CHAPTER 5** National Saving, the Government Budget, Foreign Borrowing, and the Twin Deficits — 130
- **CHAPTER 6** International Trade, Exchange Rates, and Macroeconomic Policy — 154

PART THREE Aggregate Demand, Aggregate Supply, Unemployment and Inflation — 195

- **CHAPTER 7** Aggregate Demand, Aggregate Supply, and the Self-Correcting Economy — 197
- **CHAPTER 8** Inflation: Its Causes and Cures — 232
- **CHAPTER 9** The Goals of Stabilization Policy: Low Inflation and Low Unemployment — 280

PART FOUR Macroeconomics in the Long Run: Growth and Public Finance — 317

- **CHAPTER 10** The Theory of Economic Growth — 319
- **CHAPTER 11** The Big Questions of Economic Growth — 349
- **CHAPTER 12** The Government Budget, the Public Debt, and Social Security — 387

PART FIVE — Stabilization Policy in an Open Economy — 415

CHAPTER 13 Money and Financial Markets — 417

CHAPTER 14 Stabilization Policy in the Closed and Open Economy — 449

PART SIX — Sources of Instability in the Private Economy — 481

CHAPTER 15 Instability in the Private Economy: Consumption Behavior — 483

CHAPTER 16 Instability in the Private Economy: Investment Behavior — 516

PART SEVEN — Debates at the Macroeconomic Frontier — 545

CHAPTER 17 New Classical Macro Confronts New Keynesian Macro — 547

CHAPTER 18 Conclusion: Where We Stand — 579

Appendixes — A-1
Glossary — G-1
Index — I-1

Contents

Preface: To the Instructor		xvii
Preface: To the Student		xxvi

PART ONE Introduction and Measurement 1

CHAPTER 1 What Is Macroeconomics? 3

1-1	How Macroeconomics Affects Our Everyday Lives	3
1-2	Defining Macroeconomics	5
1-3	Actual and Natural Real GDP	5
1-4	Macroeconomics in the Short Run and Long Run	9
1-5	CASE STUDY: A Century of Business Cycles	12
1-6	Macroeconomics at the Extremes	14
1-7	Taming Business Cycles: Stabilization Policy	19
1-8	The "Internationalization" of Macroeconomics	20
	International Perspective	
	How Does U.S. Economic Performance Stack Up?	21

CHAPTER 2 The Measurement of Income, Prices, and Unemployment 25

2-1	Why We Care About Income	25
2-2	The Circular Flow of Income and Expenditure	25
2-3	What Transactions Should Be Included in Income and Expenditure?	27
	Where to Find the Numbers: A Guide to the Data	28
2-4	Components of Expenditure	29
2-5	The "Magic" Equation and the Twin Deficits	33
2-6	How Much Income Flows from Business Firms to Households?	36
2-7	Nominal GDP, Real GDP, and the GDP Deflator	38
2-8	How We Measure Real GDP and the Inflation Rate	39
	How to Calculate Inflation, Real GDP Growth, or Any Other Growth Rate	44
2-9	Measuring Unemployment	45
2-10	CASE STUDY: Conflicting Measurements: Was the 2002–04 Recovery "Jobless" or Not?	47

PART TWO Income, Interest Rates, Policy, and the Open Economy 55

CHAPTER 3 Spending, Income, and Interest Rates 57

| 3-1 | Business Cycles and the Theory of Income Determination | 57 |

	3-2	Income Determination, Unemployment, and the Price Level	59
	3-3	Planned Expenditure	61
	3-4	**CASE STUDY: Why Did U.S. Saving Almost Vanish in 2004?**	**64**
	3-5	The Economy In and Out of Equilibrium	65
	3-6	The Multiplier Effect	70
	3-7	Sources of Shifts in Planned Spending	72
		International Perspective *How the United States and Japan Use Fiscal Policy*	**77**
	3-8	How Can Monetary Policy Affect Planned Spending?	78
	3-9	The Relation of Autonomous Planned Spending to the Interest Rate	79
	3-10	The *IS* Curve	83
		Learning About Diagrams: The *IS* Curve	**85**
	3-11	Conclusion: The Missing Relation	86
	APPENDIX TO CHAPTER 3: Allowing for Income Taxes and Income-Dependent Net Exports		91

CHAPTER 4 Monetary and Fiscal Policy in the *IS-LM* Model — 94

	4-1	Introduction: The Power of Monetary and Fiscal Policy	94
	4-2	Why People Use Money	95
	4-3	How the Fed Controls the Money Supply	97
	4-4	Income, the Interest Rate, and the Demand for Money	98
	4-5	The *LM* Curve	101
		Learning About Diagrams: The *LM* Curve	**103**
	4-6	The *IS* Curve Meets the *LM* Curve	104
	4-7	Monetary Policy in Action	105
		How Monetary Policy Actually Worked in 2001–04	**106**
	4-8	How Fiscal Expansion Can "Crowd Out" Investment	108
	4-9	Strong and Weak Effects of Monetary Policy	111
	4-10	Strong and Weak Effects of Fiscal Policy	114
	4-11	Using Fiscal and Monetary Policy Together	116
		International Perspective *Monetary and Fiscal Policy Paralysis in Japan's "Lost Decade"*	**118**
	APPENDIX TO CHAPTER 4: The Elementary Algebra of the *IS-LM* Model		126

CHAPTER 5 National Saving, the Government Budget, Foreign Borrowing, and the Twin Deficits — 130

	5-1	Introduction	130
	5-2	The Pervasive Effects of the Government Budget	131
	5-3	**CASE STUDY: The Government Budget in Historical Perspective**	**132**
	5-4	The Structural Budget	134

	5-5	National Saving and the Consequences of the Government Budget	139
	5-6	CASE STUDY: How the Deficits Rejoined to Become "Twins"	145
	5-7	Conclusion: Solutions to the National Saving Squeeze	147
		International Perspective Saving, Investment, and Government Budgets Around the World	148

CHAPTER 6 International Trade, Exchange Rates, and Macroeconomic Policy — 154

6-1	Introduction	154
6-2	The Current Account and the Balance of Payments	155
6-3	Exchange Rates	161
6-4	The Market for Foreign Exchange	163
6-5	Real Exchange Rates and Purchasing Power Parity	167
	International Perspective Big Mac Meets PPP	170
6-6	Exchange Rate Systems	170
6-7	CASE STUDY: Asia Intervenes with Buckets to Buy Dollars and Finance the U.S. Current Account Deficit—How Long Can This Continue?	174
6-8	Determinants of Net Exports	178
6-9	The Real Exchange Rate and Interest Rate	180
6-10	The *IS-LM* Model in a Small Open Economy	182
6-11	Capital Mobility and Exchange Rates in a Large Open Economy	187
	Summary of Monetary and Fiscal Policy Effects in Open Economies	188
6-12	Conclusion: Economic Policy in the Open Economy	189

PART THREE Aggregate Demand, Aggregate Supply, Unemployment and Inflation — 195

CHAPTER 7 Aggregate Demand, Aggregate Supply, and the Self-Correcting Economy — 197

7-1	Combining Aggregate Demand with Aggregate Supply	197
7-2	Flexible Prices and the *AD* Curve	198
7-3	Shifting the Aggregate Demand Curve with Monetary and Fiscal Policy	200
	Learning About Diagrams: The *AD* Curve	203
7-4	Alternative Shapes of the Short-Run Aggregate Supply Curve	203
7-5	The Short-Run Aggregate Supply (*SAS*) Curve When the Nominal Wage Rate Is Constant	205
	Learning About Diagrams: The *SAS* Curve	207

	7-6	How the Wage Rate Is Set	208
	7-7	Fiscal and Monetary Expansion in the Short and Long Run	210
		Summary of the Economy's Adjustment to an Increase in Aggregate Demand	213
	7-8	Classical Macroeconomics: The Quantity Theory of Money and the Self-Correcting Economy	214
	7-9	The Keynesian Revolution: The Failure of Self-Correction	216
	7-10	CASE STUDY: What Caused the Great Depression?	221
		International Perspective Why Was the Great Depression Worse in the United States than in Europe?	224

CHAPTER 8 Inflation: Its Causes and Cures — 232

	8-1	Introduction	232
	8-2	Real GDP, the Inflation Rate, and the Short-Run Phillips Curve	235
	8-3	The Adjustment of Expectations	238
		Learning About Diagrams: The Short-Run (*SP*) and Long-Run (*LR*) Phillips Curves	240
	8-4	Nominal GDP Growth and Inflation	240
	8-5	Effects of an Acceleration in Nominal GDP Growth	242
	8-6	Expectations and the Inflation Cycle	245
	8-7	Recession as a Cure for Inflation	247
	8-8	CASE STUDY: How Large Is the Sacrifice Ratio?	249
		International Perspective Did Disinflation in Europe Differ from That in the United States?	250
	8-9	The Importance of Supply Shocks	252
	8-10	The Response of Inflation and the Output Ratio to a Supply Shock	254
	8-11	CASE STUDY: The Goldilocks Economy—Why Inflation Was So Low in the Late 1990s	258
	8-12	Inflation and Output Fluctuations: Recapitulation of Causes and Cures	261
	8-13	How Is the Unemployment Rate Related to the Inflation Rate?	263
		APPENDIX TO CHAPTER 8: The Elementary Algebra of the *SP-DG* Model	272

CHAPTER 9 The Goals of Stabilization Policy: Low Inflation and Low Unemployment — 280

	9-1	The Costs and Causes of Inflation	280
	9-2	Money and Inflation	281
		International Perspective Money Growth and Inflation	284
	9-3	Why Inflation Is Not Harmless	285
		The Wizard of Oz as a Monetary Allegory	290

9-4	Indexation and Other Reforms to Reduce the Costs of Inflation	293
	The Indexed Bond (TIPS) Has Arrived	294
9-5	The Government Budget Constraint and the Inflation Tax	295
9-6	Starting and Stopping a Hyperinflation	299
9-7	Why the Unemployment Rate Cannot Be Reduced to Zero	302
9-8	Sources of Mismatch Unemployment	304
9-9	Turnover Unemployment and Job Search	307
9-10	Conclusion: Solutions to the Inflation and Unemployment Dilemma	311

PART FOUR Macroeconomics in the Long Run: Growth and Public Finance — 317

CHAPTER 10 The Theory of Economic Growth — 319

10-1	The Importance of Economic Growth	319
10-2	Standards of Living as the Consequence of Economic Growth	321
	International Perspective **The Growth Experience of Seven Countries over the Last Century**	322
10-3	The Production Function and Economic Growth	323
10-4	Solow's Theory of Economic Growth	327
10-5	Technology in Theory and Practice	331
10-6	Puzzles That Solow's Theory Cannot Explain	334
10-7	Human Capital, Immigration, and the Solow Puzzles	337
10-8	Endogenous Growth Theory: How Is Technological Change Produced?	339
10-9	Conclusion: Are There Secrets of Growth?	342
	APPENDIX TO CHAPTER 10: General Functional Forms and the Production Function	347

CHAPTER 11 The Big Questions of Economic Growth — 349

11-1	Answering the Big Questions	349
11-2	The Standard of Living and Concepts of Productivity	351
11-3	The Failure of Convergence	354
11-4	Human Capital and Technology	360
11-5	Political Capital, Infrastructure, and Geography	362
	International Perspective **Growth Success and Failure in the Tropics**	366
11-6	CASE STUDY: Uneven U.S. Growth Across Eras: Why Did U.S. Productivity Growth Slow Down and Then Revive?	368
	How the Great Inventions Created Economic Growth: Life in the "Bad Old Days"	374

xiv Contents

11-7	Labor Supply Shifts as a Source of Faster or Slower Productivity Growth	377
11-8	**CASE STUDY: The Productivity Growth Contrast Between Europe and the United States**	**379**
11-9	Conclusion on the Great Questions of Growth	382

CHAPTER 12 **The Government Budget, the Public Debt, and Social Security** — **387**

12-1	Introduction: The Government Budget and Long-Run Economic Growth	387
12-2	Long-Run Effects of Fiscal Policy on Economic Growth and Welfare	388
12-3	The Future Burden of the Government Debt	390
12-4	Will the Government Remain Solvent?	392
	International Perspective **The Debt-GDP Ratio: How Does the United States Compare?**	**394**
12-5	**CASE STUDY: Historical Behavior of the Debt-GDP Ratio Since 1790**	**395**
12-6	Why the Budget Deficit Disappeared Temporarily and then Reappeared	397
12-7	Alternative Views of Fiscal Policy: Supply-Side Economics	400
12-8	Alternative Views of Fiscal Policy: The Barro-Ricardo Equivalence Theorem	402
12-9	The Great Debate over Social Security	404
12-10	Long-Run Economic Growth and the Fiscal Debate	409

PART FIVE **Stabilization Policy in an Open Economy** — **415**

CHAPTER 13 **Money and Financial Markets** — **417**

13-1	Money in a World of Many Financial Assets and Liabilities	417
13-2	Financial Institutions, Markets, and Instruments	418
13-3	Definitions of Money	422
13-4	High-Powered Money and Determinants of the Money Supply	424
13-5	The Fed's Three Tools for Changing the Money Supply	428
13-6	Theories of the Demand for Money	432
	International Perspective **Cash Fades Out as Plastic Takes Over**	**436**
13-7	**CASE STUDY: Why Interest Rates Were More Volatile in the 1980s and Less Volatile in the 1990s**	**439**
13-8	Why the Federal Reserve "Sets" Interest Rates	442

CHAPTER 14 **Stabilization Policy in the Closed and Open Economy** — **449**

14-1	The Central Role of Demand Shocks	449
14-2	Stabilization Targets and Instruments in the Activists' Paradise	450
	Rules Versus Activism in a Nutshell: The Optimism-Pessimism Grid	**453**

14-3	Policy Rules	454
14-4	Policy Pitfalls: Lags and Uncertain Multipliers	456
14-5	**CASE STUDY: Was the Fed Responsible for the Decline in Economic Volatility?**	461
14-6	Time Inconsistency, Credibility, and Reputation	465
14-7	**CASE STUDY: The Taylor Rule and the Changing Fed Attitude Toward Inflation and Output**	467
14-8	Rules Versus Discretion: An Assessment	470
14-9	**CASE STUDY: Should Monetary Policy Target the Exchange Rate?**	473
	International Perspective **The Debate About the Euro**	474

PART SIX Sources of Instability in the Private Economy 481

CHAPTER 15 Instability in the Private Economy: Consumption Behavior 483

15-1	Consumption and Economic Stability	483
15-2	**CASE STUDY: Main Features of U.S. Consumption Data**	484
15-3	Background: The Conflict Between the Time-Series and Cross-Section Evidence	486
15-4	Forward-Looking Behavior: The Permanent-Income Hypothesis	489
15-5	Forward-Looking Behavior: The Life-Cycle Hypothesis	493
15-6	Rational Expectations and Other Amendments to the Simple Forward-Looking Theories	497
	Did Households Spend or Save the 2001 Tax Rebate?	499
15-7	Bequests and Uncertainty	501
	International Perspective **Why Do Some Countries Save So Much?**	502
15-8	**CASE STUDY: Did Soaring Household Assets Cause the Collapse in the Household Saving Rate?**	506
15-9	Why the Official Household Saving Data Are Misleading	509
15-10	Conclusion: Consumption and the Case For and Against Activism	511

CHAPTER 16 Instability in the Private Economy: Investment Behavior 516

16-1	Investment and Economic Stability	516
16-2	**CASE STUDY: The Historical Instability of Investment**	517
16-3	The Accelerator Hypothesis of Net Investment	519
16-4	**CASE STUDY: The Simple Accelerator and the Postwar U.S. Economy**	523
16-5	The Flexible Accelerator	525
16-6	The Neoclassical Theory of Investment Behavior	526
16-7	User Cost and the Role of Monetary and Fiscal Policy	528
	Tobin's q: Does It Explain Investment Better Than the Accelerator or Neoclassical Theories?	530

16-8	Business Confidence and Speculation	532
16-9	**CASE STUDY:** The Boom and Bust in "New Economy" Investment	533
	International Perspective **The Level and Variability of Investment Around the World**	**536**
16-10	Investment as a Source of Instability of Output and Interest Rates	538
16-11	Conclusion: Investment and the Case For and Against Activism	539

PART SEVEN   Debates at the Macroeconomic Frontier   545

CHAPTER 17   New Classical Macro Confronts New Keynesian Macro   547

17-1	Introduction: Classical and Keynesian Economics, Old and New	547
17-2	Imperfect Information and the "Fooling Model"	548
17-3	The Lucas Model and the Policy Ineffectiveness Proposition	551
17-4	The Real Business Cycle Model	555
17-5	New Classical Macroeconomics: Limitations and Positive Contributions	559
	International Perspective **Productivity Fluctuations in the United States and Japan**	**560**
17-6	Essential Features of the New Keynesian Economics	563
17-7	Why Small Nominal Rigidities Have Large Macroeconomic Effects	565
17-8	Coordination Failures and Indexation	568
17-9	Long-Term Labor Contracts as a Source of the Business Cycle	570
17-10	"Real" Sources of Wage Stickiness	572
17-11	Assessment of the New Keynesian Model	574

CHAPTER 18   Conclusion: Where We Stand   579

18-1	The Evolution of Events and Ideas	579
18-2	The Reaction of Ideas to Events, 1923–47	580
18-3	The Reaction of Ideas to Events, 1947–69	583
18-4	The Reaction of Ideas to Events, 1970–2004	587
18-5	The Reaction of Ideas to Events in the World Economy	593
18-6	Macro Mysteries: Unsettled Issues and Debates	595
	International Perspective **How Does Macroeconomics Differ in the United States and Europe?**	**596**

APPENDIXES

A:	Time Series Data for the U.S. Economy: 1875–2004	A-1
B:	International Annual Time Series Data for Selected Countries: 1960–2004	A-9
C:	Data Sources and Methods	A-15
Glossary		G-1
Index		I-1

Preface: To The Instructor

Every time we teach macroeconomics, the business and political climate changes from what it was in last year's class and from the last textbook edition. Current debates include whether higher oil prices will rekindle inflation and derail the economic recovery, why and whether the post–2001 economic recovery in the U.S. has been "jobless," how and whether to reform Social Security, and how economic growth in China and India are changing the global economic landscape.

This book stems from the belief that all macroeconomic questions relate to a core set of basic macro puzzles, and that those puzzles have solutions. This text guides students to the most direct solution of each puzzle and implements that approach by introducing a few basic models. These models are then applied immediately in Case Study sections and International Perspective boxes.

I have found it most effective to begin the course with business cycles and inflation because my students relate to what is happening today, and what will happen in the near future. Later in the course, we turn to a unified discussion of growth theory, the failure of many poor nations to achieve economic growth, and take a closer look at policy and the sources of economic instability.

Economics has become increasingly empirical, and it is critical that students learn to interpret data and use it to evaluate macroeconomic questions. This text uses two strategies to reinforce the connection between theory and data. First, the text includes a unique set of data that provide capsule illustrations of how recent research explains, or challenges, the macro puzzles. The data set goes far beyond what is available on government data Web sites, was developed exclusively for this text, and is available online for use in your course. Second, I am delighted to point out that, for the first time, the text appears in full color. Color is used strategically to reinforce macroeconomic theory by linking theoretical models to the corresponding real-world data.

Guiding Principles of the Text

This text has been guided by five organizing principles since its inception, and the tenth edition develops them further.

1. **Macro questions have answers.** The use of traditional macro models can be enormously fruitful in developing answers to macro puzzles. Unlike other texts, this book introduces the natural level of output and natural rate of unemployment in the first few pages of Chapter 1. Students learn from the beginning that the output and unemployment gaps move in opposite directions, and that to understand why output is so low is the same as understanding why unemployment is so high. Similarly, the fully developed dynamic inflation model of Chapter 8 shows that we have an answer to the puzzle of why inflation was so high in the 1970s and so low in the 1990s.

When an economic model fails, this is not swept under the rug, but rather is used to highlight what the model misses, as in the lively treatment in Chapter 10 of "Puzzles That Solow's [Growth] Theory Cannot Explain" (see pp. 334–39). The Solow failure opens the way to a unique treatment of the debate between the new institutional economics, and the exponents of a tropical geography explanation of the failure of poor countries to converge to the income level of rich countries (pp. 354–69). This is a departure from other intermediate macro texts, which barely mention the theory's failures or the modern research that takes us beyond these failures.

2. **Up-front treatment of business cycles and inflation.** Students come to the macro classroom caring most about today's issues, starting with how they and their family members can avoid unemployment. Responding to this basic curiosity of students, a core principle of this book is that students should be taught about business cycles first, instead of beginning the text with the dry abstractions of classical economics and growth theory. This allows us to begin with topical issues that interest students, such as the jobless 2002–04 recovery, the aggressive monetary and fiscal expansion to combat the jobless recovery, the continuing slump in Japan, and high unemployment in Europe.

Accordingly, this text introduces the *IS-LM* model immediately after the first two introductory chapters, with a goal in each edition of having the *IS* and *LM* curves cross by p. 100 (it happens on p. 104 of this edition). An integrated treatment covers monetary and fiscal policy stabilization, fiscal and foreign deficits and national saving, and the interplay between the balance of payments and exchange rates. The *AS-AD* model then allows an in-depth treatment of the Great Depression, and a dynamic version of the *AS-AD* model directly implies the Phillips Curve and the sources of high and low inflation. By the end of Chapter 9, students have learned the core theory of business cycles and inflation, and the text then turns to basic growth theory, the puzzles that Solow's theory cannot explain, and the big issues of economic growth and the non-convergence of so many poor countries.

3. **Integration of models.** The challenge many instructors face is that most intermediate macro texts overload the simple models, offering a new model every chapter or two without telling students how the models connect and work together. This book adopts the core distinction between short-run macro devoted to explaining business cycles and their prevention, and long-run macro dedicated to explaining economic growth and the long-run consequences of debt and deficits.

This text is unique in its focused, cohesive presentation of the macro concepts. The aggregate demand curve is explicitly derived from the *IS-LM* model (pp. 198–203), and then the short-run Phillips Curve is explicitly derived from the short-run aggregate supply curve (pp. 235–37). In discussing the biggest question of economic growth—why so many nations are still so poor—the text provides an integration of the production function in the Solow growth theory with the added elements of human capital, political capital (i.e., legal systems and property rights), geography, and infrastructure (pp. 362–68).

4. **Simple graphs can convey important research results.** The graphs in this book go beyond those in the typical macro textbook in several dimensions, including the use of original data, the double-stacking of graphs plotting related concepts (see pp. 233 and 252), the extensive use of shading be-

tween lines to convey concepts like a positive and negative output gap, and the integrated use of color. A unique feature of this text is its use of graphs on the natural level of real GDP and the natural rate of unemployment to illustrate the key concepts like the output and unemployment gaps (pp. 5–14), the Okun's Law relation linking the gaps (pp. 263–66), the structural budget deficit (pp. 134–38), the role of supply shocks and demand shocks in causing the diametrically opposite behavior of inflation in the 1970s and 1990s (pp. 257–63), and why the natural rate of unemployment declined in the 1990s (pp. 309–10).

Research results and data transformations are also used to illustrate changes in monetary policy lags and efficacy over time (pp. 457–60), apparent changes in the Fed's weights applied to inflation and output in the context of the Taylor Rule (pp. 467–70), the contradiction between the official measure of the U.S. saving rate and the vast increase in the wealth of U.S. households (pp. 506–12), and the role of computer price changes in amplifying the high-tech boom and bust of the late 1990s (pp. 533–38).

5. **The economy is open from the start.** Students come to their macroeconomics classroom concerned about the open economy. They carry iPods made in China, and they worry about whether their future jobs will be out-sourced to India and whether a further slump in the dollar will make future trips to Europe unaffordable. This text avoids the false distinction between the closed and open economy. As early as pp. 34–35, the linkage between saving, investment, government budget, and foreign lending or borrowing is emphasized by the label "magic equation" to dramatize the importance of a basic accounting identity. In the *IS-LM* model of aggregate demand, net exports can be a source of instability (pp. 72–73). Fiscal deficits can be financed by foreign borrowing, but international crowding out and growing international indebtedness reduce the future standard of living (pp. 138–45).

The emphasis on international macro is reinforced by International Perspective boxes which explore policy paralysis in Japan in the past decade, the motivation for massive dollar accumulation by Asian central banks, why the Great Depression was more severe in the U.S. than in Europe, how the euro eliminates monetary policy autonomy and constrains fiscal policy for individual European nations, and numerous other topical international comparisons.

A Tour of the Highlights

Introduction and Measurement

There are three strong points of the introductory Chapter 1. First is the unifying kick-off with the three major concepts of macro, followed by the early introduction of the concept of natural real GDP and the natural rate of unemployment linked to data on the past century. Finally, the section "Macroeconomics at the Extremes" illustrates the Great Depression, the German hyperinflation, and the growth explosion of Korea compared to the Philippines. Chapter 2 on measurement includes several flow diagrams with consistent use of color, a Case Study on the jobless recovery, and a useful topic box (p. 44) that shows how to calculate the annual growth rate of *anything* over any period, ranging from one day to five centuries.

The *IS-LM* Model and the Open Economy

Chapters 3 and 4 introduce the Keynesian expenditure model and the *IS-LM* model. The usefulness of the *IS-LM* model is motivated by a box on policy paralysis in the long slump in Japan (pp. 118–19). Chapters 5 and 6 discuss fiscal debt and deficits, national saving, and the links between international deficits, national saving, and the exchange rate. A centerpiece of Chapter 6 is the unifying idea of the "trilemma."

Inflation and Unemployment

The next section covers flexible prices and the determinants of inflation. Chapter 7 derives the *AD* curve from the *IS-LM* model and motivates the short-run and long-run *AS* curves. The *AD-AS* model is then applied to controversies surrounding the Great Depression, including a new box on why the U.S. suffered a much deeper slump than Europe or Japan. Chapter 8 begins with an explicit derivation of the short-run Phillips Curve (*SP*) from the *AD-AS* model, and then builds a dynamic inflation model to illustrate the effects of demand and supply shocks, supported by case studies and examples. A core strength of the text since its inception has been the explicit *SP-DG* model of inflation, which is capable of explaining all the ups and downs of postwar inflation. This is presented using graphs in the body of Chapter 8 and as an explicit algebraic model in the Appendix to Chapter 8. The costs of inflation and unemployment in Chapter 9 conclude this section.

The Long Run

Chapter 10 on growth theory goes beyond traditional expositions by emphasizing the "puzzles that Solow's theory cannot explain," leading the way in Chapter 11 to explore more modern explanations of the failure of many poor nations to converge to the living standards of rich nations. This chapter also includes unique material on the U.S. productivity slowdown of 1973–95, the subsequent revival and "explosion" of productivity growth in 1995–2005, and the failure of Europe to grow in the past decade. The section on long-run issues concludes with a treatment of the public debt, theories of fiscal policy, and the debate about Social Security.

Stability and Instability in an Open Economy

Stabilization policy is the focus of Chapters 13 and 14, including basic material on money supply and theories of money demand, and an updated discussion of monetary policy discretion, rules, and the recent debate about inflation targeting vs. Taylor Rules that target both inflation and the output gap. The sources of *IS*-curve instability are then examined in Chapter 15 on consumption and Chapter 16 on investment. A novel feature of the consumption chapter is its focus on the contrast between the low U.S. saving rate and rising household wealth, and the investment chapter examines the role of instability in high-tech investment as a cause of the boom of the 1990s and slump after 2000.

Debates at the Macro Frontier

The book concludes with a two-chapter part on where we stand today. Chapter 17 on doctrinal disputes begins with the Friedman-Phelps-Lucas model of "fooling" or incorrect expectations and the real business cycle model. These are criticized and contrasted with various new Keynesian models based on menu costs, efficiency wages, and other ideas. Chapter 18 explores "the effect of events on ideas," tracing the economy's evolution since 1923 and the effects of major events like the Great Depression, postwar inflation, and the twin peaks of inflation and unemployment on the rise and fall of alternative theories. The book concludes with a summary of what we know and the remaining puzzles.

New to the Tenth Edition

The Tenth Edition is the most substantive revision in years and reflects today's macroeconomic debates and controversies. It features organizational improvements, the latest data, myriad new case studies and boxes, and an innovative full-color design.

Organizational and Substantive Changes

The chapters are in the same order as in previous editions, but there have been considerable changes within chapters. My goal has been to provide a more cohesive discussion of models so that students understand how the concepts relate to one another, and to motivate the discussion by providing more examples in the chapter introductions.

The most important organizational change is to move the derivation of the *IS* curve forward, from Chapter 4 to Chapter 3, so that its common elements with the Keynesian cross model can be emphasized. Chapter 4 begins with a new section explaining how the Fed controls the money supply (pp. 97–98) and develops the *IS-LM* model and its policy implications, including the strong and weak effects that were previously in Chapter 5. (The previous Appendix to Chapter 5 has been moved to Chapter 4.) Chapter 5 includes a new treatment of the theoretical links between the fiscal and foreign deficits, showing the effects of an increased fiscal deficit on domestic investment, domestic saving, and foreign borrowing in a small and large open economy on an investment-saving diagram.

Chapter 8 continues to develop a graphical model of the inflation-output tradeoff (amplified in algebraic form in the Appendix to Chapter 8). This is supplemented with a new concluding section showing how the inflation-output tradeoff directly implies the unemployment–inflation tradeoff, through the intermediate relation of Okun's Law (the data graph on Okun's Law is moved from Chapter 2 to Chapter 8, p. 265). The first half of Chapter 9 on the effects of inflation has been reorganized and rewritten for clarity, and the discussion of the causes of the decline in the natural rate of unemployment has been moved from Chapter 8 to Chapter 9 (pp. 309–10).

Greater emphasis is placed on connecting concepts across chapters. For instance, when discussing the standard Keynesian assumption of fixed prices, students see a connection between the *IS-LM* model when the assumption is adopted (Chapter 3, pp. 57–60) and the model when the fixed price assumption is abandoned in favor of flexible prices (Chapter 7, pp. 197–98).

Finally, chapters have been substantially updated to reflect the latest debates and issues, such as Social Security reform (pp. 404–09) and the ongoing debate between adherents of inflation targeting and Taylor-type Rules (Chapter 14).

New Case Studies, Boxes, and Applications

The following four elements reinforce the connection between theory and real-world applications.

- *Data graphs* are updated to provide vivid illustrations of the basic concepts, such as the volatility of real GDP growth (p. 58) and the relation between inflation and the output ratio (p. 233).
- *Case Studies* apply the theory immediately after it is introduced, for instance the definition that national saving must equal the sum of domestic and foreign investment (pp. 145–46).
- *International Perspective* boxes compare economic performance in the United States with selected foreign nations, including policy paralysis in Japan (pp. 118–19), and why the Great Depression was worst in the United States (pp. 224–25).
- *Topic boxes* provide illustrations that are not explicitly international, such as a new topic box on monetary policy in 2001–04 (p. 106), and the empirical performance of Tobin's q model (pp. 530–31).

New examples appear frequently throughout the book, a few of which include:

- Pages 263–68. This new section applies Okun's Law to show that the correlations between inflation and the output ratio derived earlier in the chapter work in the same way but in opposite directions for inflation and unemployment. The twin peaks of inflation and unemployment in 1974–81 and the valley of inflation and unemployment in 1997–99 are illustrated and explained.
- Pages 357–58. The failure of many poor nations to converge is illustrated on a new graph and in a new table updated from 1960–90 to 1960–2000, based on the latest Penn World Tables.
- Pages 467–70. A new Case Study asks whether the Fed's monetary policy during 1980–2005 resembled that predicted by a Taylor Rule. The surprising result is that the Fed's behavior implies a sharp change in the late 1980s from a high weight on avoiding inflation to a high weight on stabilizing output.

Pedagogy

New: The Use of Full Color

This is the first intermediate text to integrate color in a way that links theory to data in a meaningful way. This book has always been unique in its use of double-framed data graphs to show related concepts like inflation and the output ratio, or inflation and oil prices. Now, graphs throughout the book use shading in consistent colors to connect macro concepts and discussions.

This can be seen as early as the first chart on p. 6, where real GDP is red, as is any component of expenditure including consumption and investment. Accordingly, red denotes the *IS* curve and periods when actual output is above natural output (or actual unemployment is below natural unemployment). Blue is used to show the unemployment rate, as well as periods of depressed economic activity. Later, the initial *IS* curve (p. 84) uses red shading for the area showing an excess demand for commodities and blue shading for an excess supply.

The use of color strengthens conceptual ties throughout the book. The supply curve of money, the *LM* curve, and plots of short-term interest rates are always shown in green. Government expenditures are red and revenues are green, a government surplus is shown by green shading and a deficit by red shading. The government debt and long-term interest rates appear in purple. Data on inflation and the *AD* curve are plotted in orange. The *SAS* and *SP* curves are plotted in blue. Long-run "natural" concepts like natural real GDP, the natural rate of unemployment, the *LAS* curve, and the *LP* curve are all plotted in black.

Color is also used consistently for country-specific data. The U.S. is always red, the U.K. (or EU) is blue, Canada is grey, Japan is orange, Germany is black, France is purple, and Italy is green.

Continuing Pedagogical Features

The Tenth Edition retains the main pedagogical features of the previous editions that aid student understanding.

- *Key terms* are introduced in bold type, defined in the margin, and listed at the end of each chapter.
- *Self-Test questions* appear at intervals within each chapter, so that students can immediately determine whether they understand what they have read.
- *Learning about Diagrams boxes*. Each of these boxes covers on a single page every aspect of the key schedules—*IS*, *LM*, *AS*, *AD*, and *SP*—and discusses why they slope as they do, what makes them rotate and shift, and what is true on and off the curves.
- *End-of-Chapter elements* include a summary, a list of key terms, a revised set of questions and problems, and answers to the self-test questions.
- The *Glossary* at the end of the book lists definitions to every key term, with a cross-reference to the sections where they are first introduced.
- *Data Appendixes* provide annual data for the U.S. back to 1875, quarterly data back to 1947, and annual data since 1960 for other leading nations. New to this edition, this data can now be downloaded from the book's Companion Web site for use in your course. Appendix C lists data sources and Web sites that offer the latest data on key macroeconomic variables.
- *Data diagrams* have been replotted electronically to ensure accuracy, to incorporate the 2004 revisions in the National Income and Product Accounts, and to include annual and quarterly data to the end of 2004 and in some cases to March 2005.

Supplements

With each edition, the supplements get more robust with the aim of helping you to prepare your lectures and your students to master the material.

- *Instructor's Manual Online.* Jan Ondrich (Syracuse University) revised the manual for this edition, providing chapter outlines, chapter overviews, a discussion of how the Tenth Edition differs from the Ninth Edition, answers to the end-of-chapter questions and problems, and additional questions that instructors may wish to use for homework assignments, classroom discussion, or essay examination questions. The manual is available on the secure Addison-Wesley Web site (www.aw-bc.com/econ, keyword = Gordon).

- *Test Bank: Print and Computerized.* Completely revised by Andrew Foshee (McNeese State University), the Test Bank offers more than 2,000 questions specific to the book. Instructors can create tests using the bank of questions in a Word document, or by using the Computerized Test Bank software. Both versions are available on the Instructor's Resource Disk or the secure Addison-Wesley Web site (www.aw-bc.com, keyword = Gordon).

- *PowerPoint Files and Transparency Masters.* PowerPoint files contain the figures in the text. Instructors can use these to create PowerPoint lectures, or they can print out the slides for use as transparency masters. The PowerPoint files are available on the Instructor's Resource Disk or on the secure, Addison-Wesley Web site (www.aw-bc.com/econ, keyword = Gordon).

- *Study Guide.* Prepared by Andrew Foshee (McNeese State University), this manual breaks each chapter into a series of key questions, with each question covering a specified topic. Students test their understanding by answering short-answer, numerical, and short essay questions, and problems that ask students to draw graphs and use current data.

- *Companion Web site.* The open-access Web site offers two new important resources. First, instructors and students can now download the robust data set that was created explicitly for this text, including the historical data and natural level of output. Second, students can now find online quizzes to practice the major concepts in every chapter. These questions were written by the author of the *Study Guide,* Andrew Foshee. In addition, the Web site offers an online glossary review and links to related sites for macroeconomic data and research. (www.aw-bc.com/Gordon)

Acknowledgments

I remain grateful to all those who gave thoughtful comments on this book over the years. In recent years, these colleagues include:

    Terence J. Alexander, *Iowa State University*
    Jeffrey H. Bergstrand, *University of Notre Dame*
    William Branch, *University of California, Irvine*
    John P. Burkett, *University of Rhode Island*
    Henry Chen, *University of West Florida*
    Peter Daw, *Northwestern University*
    David DeJong, *University of Pittsburgh*
    Robert Driskill, *Vanderbilt University*
    James Eaton, *Bridgewater College*
    Sherman Folland, *Oakland University*
    Andrew Foshee, *McNeese State University*
    Donald E. Frey, *Wake Forest University*
    Edward Gamber, *Lafayette College*
    John Graham, *Rutgers University*
    William Harris, *Georgetown University*
    Luc Hens, *Vesalius College, Vrije Universiteit Brussel*
    Tracy Hofer, *University of Wisconsin, Stevens Point*

Barney Hope, *California State University, Chico*
Brad R. Humphreys, *University of Maryland, Baltimore County*
Alan G. Isaac, *American University*
Thomas Kelly, *Baylor University*
Barry Kotlove, *Edmonds Community College*
Devashish Mitra, *Syracuse University*
Khan A. Mohabbat, *Northern Illinois University*
Hong Nguyen, *University of Scranton*
Nicholas Noble, *Miami University, Oxford*
Norman Obst, *Michigan State University*
Jan Ondrich, *Syracuse University*
Chris Papageorgiou, *Louisiana State University*
Rati Ram, *Illinois State University*
Michael Reed, *University of Kentucky*
Charles F. Revier, *Colorado State University*
David Ring, *State University of New York, Oneonta*
Wayne Saint Aubyn Henry, *University of the West Indies*
Subarna K. Samanta, *The College of New Jersey*
Joseph Santos, *South Dakota State University*
Manly E. Staley, *San Francisco State University*
Mark Thoma, *University of Oregon*
Kristin Van Gaasbeck, *California State University, Sacramento*
Ky-hyang Yuhn, *Florida Atlantic University*

Above all, I am grateful to Jan Ondrich of Syracuse University for his many contributions to the Tenth Edition, the most obvious of which was as the author of the *Instructor's Manual*. But Jan's contribution goes far beyond that. He reviewed the manuscript for accuracy and consistency and suggested many changes. He also suggested improvements in many of the end-of-chapter questions and problems.

An expanded set of questions and problems was provided by David Ring of SUNY at Oneonta. In addition, the book contains a great deal of data, some of it originally created for this book, both in the text and Data Appendix. Jared Rector created all the data, tables, and graphs, as well as the Data Appendix. Ian Dew-Becker helped by developing some of the original data, including the natural rate of unemployment and the productivity growth trend.

Many thanks go to the staff at Addison-Wesley. I am extremely grateful to Denise Clinton for suggesting and then implementing the conversion of the book to four colors. Roxanne Hoch radiated enthusiasm at every stage and motivated me to live up to her high expectations. Amy Fleischer handled the initial stage of having the previous edition reviewed and then of nagging me for manuscript as I fell behind schedule. The final stages of handling proof and other pre-publication details were managed efficiently, with new heights of tact and courtesy in nagging the author to overcome his endless delays, by Nancy Fenton of Addison-Wesley and Ingrid Mount of Elm Street Publishing Services.

Finally, thanks go to my wife Julie for putting up with the overwhelming litter of manuscript and proofs that often spilled out of my home office onto kitchen counters and the kitchen table. As always, her unfailing encouragement and welcome diversions made the book possible.

Robert J. Gordon
Evanston, IL
May 2005

Preface: To the Student

Macroeconomics is one of the most important topics for you as a college student because the health of the economy will have an influence on your whole life. The overall level of employment and unemployment will determine the ease with which you find a job after college and with which you will be able to change jobs or obtain promotions in the future. The inflation rate will influence the interest rate that you receive on your savings and that you pay when you borrow money, and also the extent to which the purchasing power of your savings will be eroded by higher prices.

This macroeconomics text will equip you with the principles you need to make sense out of the conflicting and contradictory discussions of economic conditions and policies in newspapers and news magazines. You will be better able to appraise the performance of the President and Congress, and to predict the impact of their policy actions on your family and business.

You will also be able to understand why people your age in many other countries are so poor, and why some poor countries succeed in the transition to being like the rich countries, while many others fail.

Who Should Read This Book?

Most college students taking this course will have taken a course in economic principles. But this book has been written to be read by *all* students, even those who have not previously enrolled in an economics course. How is this possible? In Chapters 1–3 we review material covered in every principles course. By the end of Chapter 3, all students will have learned the concepts essential to understanding the new material to be developed.

This book has been carefully designed to look and read like a principles text. The entire presentation is graphic, with simple algebra used only in the review of elementary ideas. Examples are used frequently. Most chapters have at least one Case Study that gives you a breather from the analysis and shows how the ideas of the chapter can be applied to real-world episodes. "International Perspective" boxes show you how U.S. economic performance compares with that in other nations, such as Germany and Japan. To help with vocabulary problems, new words are set off in boldface type and defined both in the margins and in the Glossary in the back of the book. Many end-of-chapter questions provide numerical examples for you to solve in order to cement your understanding of the theory. Finally, end-of-chapter appendixes for Chapters 3, 4, 8, and 10 provide optional algebraic treatments of the theory, available for assignment by instructors or for those students who want to do independent work that will deepen their command of the material.

A unique feature of this textbook is the set of Self-Test questions. These questions, which appear three or four times in each chapter, test your understanding of the main point of the preceding section. Write down your answers on a sheet of paper and compare them with those provided at the end of each chapter. You will quickly see whether you have understood what you have been reading, or whether you need to review the material.

How to Read This Book

Each chapter begins with an introduction linking it to previous chapters and ends with a summary. When you begin a chapter, first read the introduction to make sure you understand how the chapter differs from the previous ones. Then plan to read each chapter twice. On the first reading, use the Self-Test questions and answers to check whether you understand what you have been reading. Then, after completing your first reading of the chapter, study the Summary and try to answer the end-of-chapter questions, marking those points you do not understand. Finally, go back for a second reading, paying attention to the discussion of issues you may not have grasped fully at first.

Always try to write out answers to the questions and problems. Those who have purchased the accompanying *Study Guide* find that the path to greater comprehension has been laid out for you in detail.

If you should get lost in the course of reading the text, remember that there are built-in study aids to help, in addition to the Self-Test questions. If you don't understand a particular section, turn to the Summary at the end of the chapter. If you forget the meaning of a word, turn to the Glossary. (The Glossary will also help you tackle any outside readings assigned by your instructor.) A Guide to Symbols on the back inside covers of the book will help you with the alphabetical symbols that are used in equations or in diagrams as labels.

Optional Material

Footnotes and chapter appendixes have been provided as a place to put more difficult or less important material. Your instructor will decide whether an appendix is to be assigned, but even if not assigned, tackle it on your own when you have mastered the ideas in the chapter. Footnotes contain qualifications, bibliographical references (valuable if you ever need to write a term paper on these topics), and cross-references to related material and diagrams in the book.

Notice that tables in the appendix contain historical data starting with 1875 and updated to 2004. These figures can help you determine what was going on in periods not covered by the case studies or can be used in outside assignments and term papers. Don't forget possible applications in history, political science, and sociology courses.

The World Wide Web has made it much easier for you to locate recent data to update the graphs and tables in this book. For information on using the Web to find data, turn to page 28 and several specific Web sites listed in Appendix C.

Finally, I would value any feedback from you in the form of comments, suggestions, corrections, and questions at rjg@northwestern.edu.

Supplements

This text includes two resources to help you prepare for your exams and projects.

- *Study Guide*. Students praise the unique format of this *Study Guide* because it helps them focus on the concepts that are most important. Prepared by Andrew Foshee (McNeese State University), this manual breaks each chapter into a series of key questions you need to understand in that chapter. In addition, each chapter includes short-answer, numerical, and short essay questions, and problems that let you draw graphs and use current data.
- *Companion Web site*. The open-access Web site offers two new important resources. First, students can test their understanding by taking the new online quizzes that cover every chapter. Second, for projects and assignments, students can now download the data set created explicitly for this text, including the historical data and natural level of output. The Web site also offers an online glossary review and links to related sites for macroeconomic data and research. (www.aw-bc.com/Gordon)

PART ONE

Introduction and Measurement

CHAPTER 1 What Is Macroeconomics?

CHAPTER 2 The Measurement of Income, Prices, and Unemployment

CHAPTER 1

What Is Macroeconomics?

Business will be better or worse.
—Calvin Coolidge, 1928

1-1 How Macroeconomics Affects Our Everyday Lives

Macroeconomics is concerned with the big economic issues that determine your own economic well-being as well as that of your family and everyone you know. Each of these issues involves the overall economic performance of the nation rather than whether one particular individual earns more or less than another.

> **Macroeconomics** is the study of the major economic totals, or aggregates.

The nation's overall macroeconomic performance matters, not only for its own sake but because many individuals experience its consequences. For instance, the economy experienced a recession in the year 2001, and more than two million people lost their jobs. They were among the victims of the downturn in the overall economy. Other victims besides job losers were students who found it difficult to find a summer job or a good job after graduation. Macroeconomic performance can also determine whether inflation will erode the value of family savings, and whether today's students in their future lives will have a higher standard of living than their parents.

The "Big Three" Concepts of Macroeconomics

Each of these connections between the overall economy and the lives of individuals involves a central macroeconomic concept introduced in this chapter—unemployment, inflation, and economic growth. The basic task of macroeconomics is to study the causes of good or bad performance of these three concepts, why each matters to individuals, and what (if anything) the government can do to improve macroeconomic performance. While there are numerous other less important macroeconomic concepts, we start by focusing just on these, which are the "Big Three" concepts of macroeconomics:

1. **The unemployment rate.** The higher the overall unemployment rate, the harder it is for each individual who wants a job to find work. College seniors who want permanent jobs after graduation are likely to have fewer job offers if the national unemployment rate is high, as in 2001–03, than low, as in 1999–2000. All adults fear a high unemployment rate, which raises the chances that they will be laid off, be unable to pay their bills, have their cars repossessed, lose their health insurance, or even lose their homes through

> The **unemployment rate** is the number of persons unemployed (jobless individuals who are actively looking for work or are on temporary layoff) divided by the total of those employed and unemployed.

3

mortgage foreclosures. In "bad times," when the unemployment rate is high, crime, mental illness, and suicide also increase. It is no wonder that many people consider unemployment to be the single most important macroeconomic issue. And this is nothing new. Robert Burton, an English clergyman, wrote in 1621 that "employment is so essential to human happiness that indolence is justly considered the mother of misery."

2. **The inflation rate.** A high inflation rate means that prices, on average, are rising rapidly, while a low inflation rate means that prices, on average, are rising slowly. An inflation rate of zero means that prices remain essentially the same, month after month. In inflationary periods, retired people, or those about to retire, lose the most, since their hard-earned savings buy less as prices go up. Even college students may lose as the rising prices of room, board, and textbooks erode what they have saved from previous summer and after-school jobs. While a high inflation rate harms those who have saved, it helps those who have borrowed. It is this capricious aspect of inflation, taking from some and giving to others, that makes people dislike inflation. People want their lives to be predictable, but inflation throws a monkey wrench into individual decision making, creating pervasive uncertainty.

> The **inflation rate** is the percentage rate of increase in the economy's average level of prices.

3. **Productivity growth.** "Productivity" is the average output per hour of work that a nation produces in total goods and services; it was about $49 per worker-hour in the United States in 2005. The faster average productivity grows, the easier it is for each member of society to improve his or her standard of living. If productivity were to grow at 3 percent from 2005 to the year 2025, U.S. productivity would rise from $49 per worker-hour to $89 per worker-hour. When multiplied by all the hours worked by all the employees in the country, this extra $40 per worker-hour would make it possible for the nation to have more houses, cars, hospitals, roads, schools, and airplane trips, without the need for cutting spending elsewhere.

> **Productivity** is the average output produced per hour.

But if the growth rate of productivity were zero instead of 3 percent, U.S. productivity would remain at $49 in the year 2025. To have more houses and cars, we would have to sacrifice by building fewer hospitals and schools. Such an economy, with no productivity growth, has been called the "zero-sum society," because any extra good or service enjoyed by one person requires that something be taken away from someone else. Many have argued that the achievement of rapid productivity growth and the avoidance of a zero-sum society form the most important macroeconomic challenge of all.

The first two of the "Big Three" macroeconomic concepts, the unemployment and inflation rates, appear in the newspaper every day. When economic conditions are poor, daily headlines announce that one large company or another is laying off thousands of workers. In the past, sharp increases in the rate of inflation have also made headlines, as when the price of gasoline jumped during 2004. The third major concept, productivity growth, has received widespread attention in the past decade as a source of an improving American standard of living compared to that in Europe and Japan.

Macroeconomic concepts also play a big role in politics. Incumbent political parties benefit when unemployment and inflation are relatively low, as in the landslide victories of Lyndon Johnson in 1964 and Richard Nixon in 1972. Incumbent presidents who fail to gain reelection often are the victims of a sour economy, as in the cases of Herbert Hoover in 1932 and Jimmy Carter in 1980.

The recession of 1990–91 and the weak recovery of 1992 helped Bill Clinton defeat George H. W. Bush in the presidential election of 1992. The defeat of Al Gore by George W. Bush in 2000 was an exception since the strong economy of 2000 should have helped Gore's incumbent Democratic party win the presidency. Rapid GDP growth in 2003–04 helped to reelect George W. Bush, restoring the tradition that a strong economy favors the election of the incumbent party.

1-2 Defining Macroeconomics

How Macroeconomics Differs from Microeconomics

Most topics in economics can be placed in one of two categories: macroeconomics or microeconomics. *Macro* comes from a Greek word meaning large; *micro* comes from a Greek word meaning small. Put another way, macroeconomics deals with the totals, or **aggregates**, of the economy, and microeconomics deals with the parts. Among these crucial economic aggregates are the three central concepts introduced in the last section.

An **aggregate** is the total amount of an economic magnitude for the economy as a whole.

Microeconomics is devoted to the relationships among the different *parts* of the economy. For example, in micro we try to explain the wage or salary of one type of worker in relation to another. For example, why is a professor's salary more than that of a secretary but less than that of an investment banker? In contrast, macroeconomics asks why the total income of all citizens rises strongly in some periods but declines in others.

Economic Theory: A Process of Simplification

Economic theory helps us understand the economy by *simplifying complexity*. Theory throws a spotlight on just a few key relations. Macroeconomic theory examines the behavior of aggregates such as national income and the unemployment rate while ignoring differences among individual households. It reaches striking conclusions by pretending that there is just one interest rate, instead of the many rates reported in daily newspapers.

It is this process of simplification that makes the study of economics so exciting. By learning a few basic macroeconomic relations, you can quickly learn how to sift out the hundreds of irrelevant details in the news in order to focus on the few key items that foretell where the economy is going. You also can begin to understand which national and personal economic goals can be attained and which are "pie in the sky." You can learn when it is fair to credit a president for strong economic performance or blame a president for poor performance.

1-3 Actual and Natural Real GDP

We have learned that the "Big Three" macroeconomic concepts are the unemployment rate, the inflation rate, and the rate of productivity growth. Linked to each of these is the total level of output produced in the economy. The higher the level of output, the lower the unemployment rate. The higher the level of output, the faster tends to be the rate of inflation. Finally, for any given number of hours worked, a higher level of output automatically boosts output per hour, that is, productivity.

6   Chapter 1 • What Is Macroeconomics?

Gross domestic product is the value of all currently produced goods and services sold on the market during a particular time interval.

The official measure of the economy's total output is called **gross domestic product** abbreviated GDP. As you will learn in Chapter 2, real GDP includes all currently produced goods and services sold on the market within a given time period and excludes certain other types of economic activity. As you will also learn, the adjective "real" means that our measure of output reflects the quantity produced corrected for any changes in prices.

Actual real GDP is the value of total output corrected for any changes in prices.

Actual real GDP is the amount an economy actually produces at any given time. But we need some criterion to judge the desirability of that level of actual real GDP. Perhaps actual real GDP is too low, causing high unemployment. Perhaps actual real GDP is too high, putting upward pressure on the inflation rate. Which level of real GDP is desirable, neither too low nor too high? This intermediate compromise level of real GDP is called "natural," a level of real GDP in which there is no tendency for inflation to accelerate or decelerate.

Figure 1-1 illustrates the relationship between actual real GDP, natural real GDP, and the rate of inflation. In the upper frame the red line is actual real GDP. The lower frame shows the inflation rate. The thin dashed vertical lines connect the two frames. The first dashed vertical line marks time period t_0. Notice in the bottom frame that the inflation rate is constant at t_0.

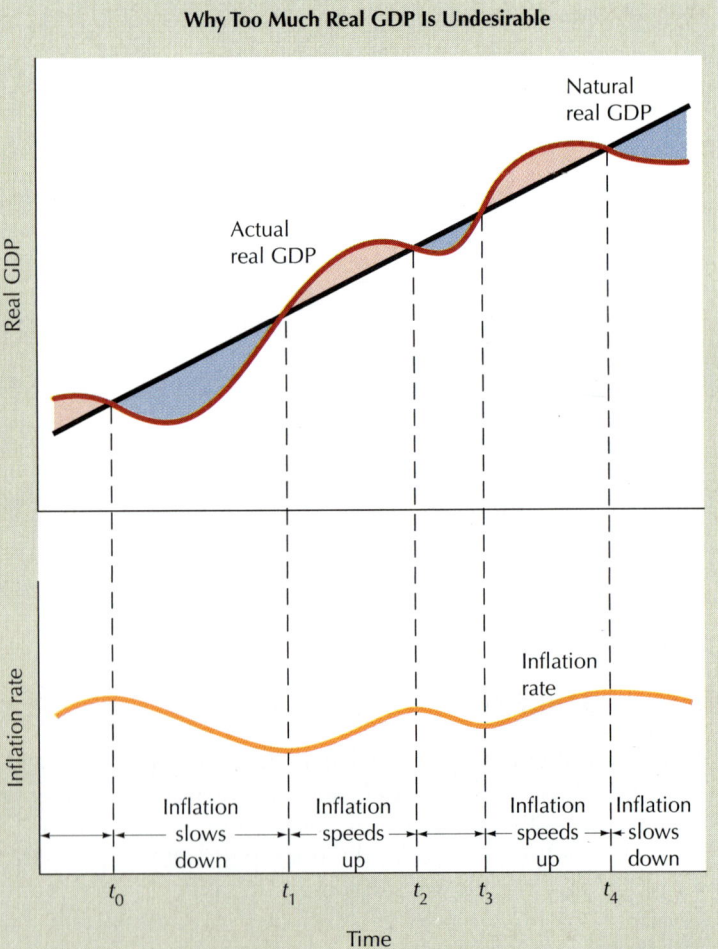

Figure 1-1 The Relation Between Actual and Natural Real GDP and the Inflation Rate

In the upper frame the solid black line shows the steady growth of natural real GDP—the amount the economy can produce at a constant inflation rate. The red line shows the path of actual real GDP. In the blue region in the top frame, actual real GDP is below natural real GDP, so the inflation rate, shown in the bottom frame, slows down. In the region designated by the red area, actual real GDP is above natural real GDP, so in the bottom frame inflation speeds up.

By definition, **natural real GDP** is equal to actual real GDP when the inflation rate is constant. Thus, in the upper frame, at t_0 the red actual real GDP line is crossed by the black natural real GDP line. To the right of t_0, actual real GDP falls below natural real GDP, and we see in the bottom frame that inflation slows down. This continues until time period t_1, when actual real GDP recovers until once again it is equal to natural real GDP. Here the inflation rate stops falling and is constant for a moment before it begins to rise.

This cycle repeats again and again. *Only when actual real GDP is equal to natural real GDP is the inflation rate constant.* For this reason, natural real GDP is a compromise level to be singled out for special attention. During a period of low actual real GDP, designated by the blue area, the inflation rate slows down. During a period of high actual real GDP, designated by the shaded red area, the inflation rate accelerates.

Natural real GDP designates the level of real GDP at which the inflation rate is constant, with no tendency to accelerate or decelerate.

Unemployment: Actual and Natural

When actual real GDP is low, many people lose their jobs, and the unemployment rate is high, as shown in Figure 1-2. The top frame duplicates Figure 1-1

Unemployment Cycles Are the Mirror Image of Real GDP Cycles

Figure 1-2 The Behavior over Time of Actual and Natural Real GDP and the Actual and Natural Rates of Unemployment

When actual real GDP falls below natural real GDP, designated by the blue shaded areas in the top frame, the actual unemployment rate rises above the natural rate of unemployment as indicated in the bottom frame. The red shaded areas designate the opposite situation. When we compare the blue shaded areas of Figures 1-1 and 1-2, we see that the time intervals when unemployment is high (1-2) also represent time intervals when inflation is slowing down (1-1). Similarly, the red shaded areas represent time intervals when inflation is speeding up and unemployment is low.

exactly, comparing actual real GDP with natural real GDP. The blue line in the bottom frame is the actual percentage unemployment rate, the first of the three central concepts of macroeconomics. The thin vertical dashed lines connecting the upper frame and lower frame show that whenever actual and natural real GDP are equal in the top frame, the actual unemployment rate is equal to the **natural rate of unemployment** in the bottom frame.

The definition of the natural rate of unemployment corresponds exactly to natural real GDP, describing a situation in which there is no tendency for the inflation rate to change. When the actual unemployment rate is high, actual real GDP is low (shown by blue shading in both frames), and the inflation rate slows down. In periods when actual real GDP is high and the economy prospers, the actual unemployment rate is low (shown by red shading in both frames) and the inflation rate speeds up.

Figures 1-1 and 1-2 summarize a basic dilemma faced by government policymakers who are attempting to achieve a low unemployment rate and a low inflation rate at the same time. If the inflation rate is high, lowering it requires a decline in actual real GDP and an increase in the actual unemployment rate. This happened in the early 1980s, when inflation was so high that the government deliberately pushed unemployment to its highest level of the past 65 years. If, to the contrary, the policymaker attempts to provide jobs for everyone and keep the actual unemployment rate low then the inflation rate will speed up, as occurred in the 1960s and late 1980s.

> The **natural rate of unemployment** designates the level of unemployment at which the inflation rate is constant, with no tendency to accelerate or decelerate.

Real GDP and the Three Macro Concepts

The total amount that the economy produces, actual real GDP, is closely related to the three central macroeconomic concepts introduced earlier in this chapter. First, as we see in Figure 1-2, the *difference* between actual and natural real GDP moves inversely with the *difference* between the actual and natural unemployment rates. When actual real GDP is high, unemployment is low, and vice versa.

The second link is with inflation, since inflation tends to speed up when actual real GDP is higher than natural real GDP (as in Figure 1-1). The third link is with productivity, which is defined as actual real GDP per hour; data on actual real GDP are required to calculate the level or growth rate of productivity.

Each of these links with the central macroeconomic concepts requires that actual real GDP be compared with *something else* in order to be meaningful. It must be compared to natural real GDP to provide a link with unemployment and inflation, or it must be divided by the number of hours worked to compute productivity. Actual real GDP by itself, without any such comparison, is not meaningful, which is why it is not included on the list of the three major macro concepts.

Self-Test

1. When actual real GDP is above natural real GDP, is the actual unemployment rate above, below, or equal to the natural unemployment rate?
2. When actual real GDP is below natural real GDP, is the actual unemployment rate above, below, or equal to the natural unemployment rate?
3. When the actual unemployment rate is equal to the natural rate of unemployment, is the actual rate of inflation equal to the natural rate of inflation?

1-4 Macroeconomics in the Short Run and Long Run

Macroeconomic theories and debates can be divided into two main groups: (1) those that concern the "short-run" stability of the economy, and (2) those that concern its "long-run" growth rate. Much of macroeconomic analysis concerns the first group of topics involving the short run, usually defined as a period lasting from one year to five years, and focuses on the first two major macroeconomic concepts introduced in Section 1-1, the unemployment rate and the inflation rate. We ask why the unemployment rate and the inflation rate over periods of a few years are sometimes high and sometimes low, rather than always low as we would wish. These ups and downs are usually called "economic fluctuations" or **business cycles**. Much of this book concerns the causes of these cycles and the efficacy of alternative government policies to dampen or eliminate the cycles.

The other main topic in macroeconomics concerns the long run, which is a longer period ranging from one decade to several decades. It attempts to explain the rate of productivity growth, the third key concept introduced in Section 1-1, or more generally, **economic growth**. Learning the causes of growth helps us predict whether successive generations of Americans will be better off than their predecessors, and why some countries remain so poor in a world where other countries by contrast are so rich.

> **Business cycles** consist of expansions occurring at about the same time in many economic activities, followed by similarly general recessions and recoveries that merge into the expansion phase of the next cycle.
>
> **Economic growth** is the topic area of macroeconomics that studies the causes of sustained growth in real GDP over periods of a decade or more.

The Short Run: Business Cycles

The main short-run concern of macroeconomists is to minimize fluctuations in the unemployment and inflation rates. This requires that fluctuations in real GDP be minimized.

Figure 1-3 contrasts two imaginary economies: "Volatilia" in the left frame and "Stabilia" in the right frame. The black "natural real GDP" lines in both frames are *absolutely identical.* The two economies differ only in the size of their business cycles, shown by the size of their **real GDP gap**, which is simply the difference between actual and natural real GDP.

In the left frame, Volatilia is a macroeconomic hell, with severe business cycles and large gaps between actual and natural real GDP. In the right frame, Stabilia is macroeconomic heaven, with mild business cycles and small gaps between actual and natural real GDP. All macroeconomists prefer the economy depicted by the right-hand frame to that depicted by the left-hand frame. But the debate between macro schools of thought starts in earnest when we ask how to achieve the economy of the right-hand frame. Active do-something policies? Do-nothing, hands-off policies? There are economists who support each of these alternatives, and more besides. But everyone agrees that Stabilia is a more successful economy than Volatilia. To achieve the success of Stabilia, Volatilia must engage in "gap-closing," that is, eliminating its large real GDP gap.

> The **real GDP gap,** sometimes called the *output gap,* is the percentage difference between actual and natural real GDP.

Business Cycle Concepts

The hallmark of business cycles is their pervasive character, which affects many different types of economic activity at the same time. This means that they occur again and again but not always at regular intervals, nor are they the

Figure 1-3 Business Cycles in Volatilia and Stabilia

The left frame shows the huge business cycles in a hypothetical nation called Volatilia. Short-run macroeconomics tries to dampen business cycles so that the path of actual real GDP is as close as possible to natural real GDP, as shown in the right frame for a nation called Stabilia.

The **peak** is the highest point reached by real output in each business cycle.

The **trough** is the lowest point reached by real output in each business cycle.

The **recession** is the interval in the business cycle between the peak and the trough.

The **expansion** is the period in the business cycle between the trough and the peak.

---

same length. Business cycles in the past have ranged in length from one to twelve years.[1]

Figure 1-4 illustrates two successive business cycles in real output. The high point in real output in each cycle is called the business-cycle **peak**. The low point is called the **trough**. The period between peak and trough is called a **recession**. After the recession comes the **expansion**, which continues until the following peak.[2]

Although a simplification, Figure 1-4 contains two realistic elements that have been common to most real-world business cycles. First, the expansions last longer than the recessions. Second, the two business cycles illustrated in the figure differ in length. Since World War II, business-cycle expansions have been as short as one year (July 1980 to July 1981) and as long as ten years (March 1991 to March 2001). The record-setting 1991–2001 expansion raises a question to which we return often in this book—why was the expansion so long and why did it end?

---

[1] A comprehensive source for the chronology of and data on historical business cycles, as well as research papers by distinguished economists, is Robert J. Gordon, ed., *The American Business Cycle: Continuity and Change* (Chicago: University of Chicago Press, 1986). A discussion of the 2001 recession and contrasts with previous recessions can be found at www.nber.org/cycles/main.html.

[2] The first part of the expansion is sometimes called the recovery. The recovery begins when the economy reaches the trough and continues until the level of real GDP exceeds its value at the previous peak.

A Succession of Cycles

Figure 1-4 Basic Business-Cycle Concepts

The real output line exhibits a typical succession of business cycles. The highest point reached by real output in each cycle is called the *peak* and the lowest point the *trough*. The *recession* is the period between peak and trough; the *expansion* is the period between the trough and the next peak.

The Long Run: Economic Growth

For a society to achieve an increasing standard of living, total output per person must grow, and such economic growth is the long-run concern of macroeconomists. Look at Figure 1-5, which contrasts two economies. Each has mild business cycles, like Stabilia in Figure 1-3. But in Figure 1-5, the left frame presents a country called "Stag-Nation," which experiences very slow growth in real GDP. In contrast, the right-hand frame depicts "Speed-Nation," a country with very fast growth in real GDP. If we assume that population growth in each country is the same, then growth in output per person is faster in Speed-Nation. In Speed-Nation everyone can purchase more consumer goods, and there is plenty of output left to provide better schools, parks, hospitals, and other public services. In Stag-Nation people must constantly face debates, since more money for schools or parks requires that people sacrifice consumer goods.

Over the past decade, countries like Stag-Nation include Germany and Japan. Countries like Speed-Nation include China and India. The United States has been between these extremes.

How do we achieve faster economic growth in output per person? In Chapters 10–12 we study the sources of economic growth and the role of government policy in helping to determine the growth in America's future standard of living, as well as the reasons why some countries remain so poor.

Self-Test

Indicate whether each item in the following list is more closely related to short-run (business cycle) macro or to long-run (economic growth) macro:

1. The Federal Reserve reduces interest rates in a recession in an attempt to reduce the unemployment rate.

Economic Failure and Success in Another Dimension

(a) Stag-Nation

(b) Speed-Nation

Figure 1-5 **Economic Growth in Stag-Nation and Speed-Nation**
In both frames the business cycle has been tamed, but in the left frame there is almost no economic growth, while economic growth in the right frame is rapid. For Speed-Nation there can be more of everything, while Stag-Nation in the left frame is a "zero-sum society," in which an increase in one type of economic activity requires that another economic activity be cut back.

2. The federal government introduces national standards for high school students in an attempt to raise math and science test scores.
3. Consumers cut back spending because news of layoffs makes them fear for their jobs.
4. The federal government gives states and localities more money to repair roads, bridges, and schools.

1-5 Case Study

A Century of Business Cycles

This section examines U.S. macroeconomic history since the late nineteenth century. You will see that unemployment, as bad as it was in the early 1980s, early 1990s, and in 2001–04, did not come close to the extreme crisis levels of the 1930s.

Real GDP

Figure 1-6 is arranged just like Figure 1-2. But whereas Figure 1-2 shows hypothetical relationships, Figure 1-6 shows the actual historical record. In

Figure 1-6 Actual and Natural GDP and Unemployment, 1900–2004

A historical report card for two important economic magnitudes. In the top frame the black line indicates natural real GDP. The red line shows actual real GDP, which was well below natural real GDP during the Great Depression of the 1930s and well above it during World War II. In the bottom frame the black line indicates the natural rate of unemployment, and the blue line indicates the actual unemployment rate. Actual unemployment was much higher during the Great Depression of the 1930s than at any other time during the century. Notice how periods of high actual unemployment like the 1930s, designated by blue shaded areas in the bottom frame, occur simultaneously with periods of low actual real GDP in the top frame. Red shaded areas indicate times when the economy was "overheated," with high actual real GDP and low unemployment.

the top frame the solid black line is natural real GDP, an estimate of the amount the economy could have produced each year without causing acceleration or deceleration of inflation.

The red line in the top frame plots actual real GDP, the total production of goods and services each year measured in the constant prices of 2000. Can you pick out those years when actual and natural real GDP are roughly equal? Some of these years were 1900, 1910, 1924, 1963, 1977, 1987, 1995, and 2001.

In years marked by blue shading, actual real GDP fell below natural real GDP. A maximum deficiency occurred in 1933, when actual real GDP was only 64 percent of natural GDP; about 36 percent of natural real GDP was thus "wasted," that is, not produced. Before 1929 and since 1950, these intervals of substantial output deficiency have been much less serious than in the Great Depression but nevertheless have added up to billions in lost output.

In some years actual real GDP exceeded natural real GDP, shown by the shaded red areas. This occurred mainly in wartime, particularly during World War I (1917–18), World War II (1942–45), the Korean War (1951–53), and the first half of the U.S. involvement in the Vietnam War (1965–69).

Unemployment

In the bottom frame of Figure 1-6, the blue line plots the actual unemployment rate. By far the most extreme episode was the Great Depression, when the actual unemployment rate remained above 10 percent for ten straight years, 1931–40. The black line in the bottom frame of Figure 1-6 displays the natural rate of unemployment, the minimum attainable level of unemployment that is compatible with avoiding an acceleration of inflation. The red shaded areas mark years when actual unemployment fell below the natural rate, as in 1917–19 and 1966–69. The blue shaded areas mark years when unemployment exceeded the natural rate.

Notice now the relationship between the top and bottom frames of Figure 1-6. The blue shaded areas in both frames designate periods of low production, low real GDP, and high unemployment, such as the Great Depression of the 1930s and the "Great Recessions" of 1975 and 1981–82. The red shaded areas in both frames designate periods of high production and high actual real GDP, and low unemployment, such as World War II and other wartime periods.

1-6 Macroeconomics at the Extremes

Most of macroeconomics treats relatively normal events. Business cycles occur, and unemployment goes up and down, as does inflation. Economic growth registers faster rates in some decades than in others. Yet there are times when the economy's behavior is anything but normal. The normal mechanisms of macroeconomics break down, and the consequences can be dire. Three examples of unusual macroeconomic behavior involving our "Big Three" concepts are the Great Depression of the 1930s, the German hyperinflation of the 1920s, and the stark difference in economic growth between two Asian nations over the past 45 years.

Unemployment in the Great Depression, 1929–40

The first of our "Big Three" macroeconomic concepts is the unemployment rate. The most extreme event involving unemployment in recorded history was the Great Depression of the 1930s. As is clearly visible in Figure 1-6 in the previous section, real GDP collapsed between 1929 and 1933, and the unemployment rate soared. A closer look at the decade of the 1930s is provided in Figure 1-7. For contrast with the 1930s, the blue line displays the unemployment rate from 1992 to 2004, which fell as low as 4.0 percent during the prosperity year of 2000 and was never higher than 7.5 percent, the rate reached in 1992. The unemployment rate during the Great Depression behaved quite differently, as shown by the purple line, soaring from 3.2 percent in 1929 to 25.2 percent in 1933, and never falling below 10 percent until 1941.

In the United States, the Depression caused many millions of jobs to disappear. College seniors could not find jobs. Stories of job hunting were

Figure 1-7 **The Unemployment Rate from 1929–41 Compared with 1992–2004**

The purple line displays the unemployment rate from 1992 to 2004, which was never higher than 7.5 percent or lower than 4.0 percent. In contrast the blue line exhibits the unemployment rate during the Great Depression; this never fell below 14 percent during the ten years from 1931 to 1940.

unbelievable but true. For example, men waited all night outside Detroit employment offices so they would be first in line the next morning. An Arkansas man walked 900 miles looking for work. So discouraged were Americans of finding jobs that for the first (and last) time in American history, there were more emigrants than immigrants. In fact, there were 350 applications per day from Americans who wanted to settle in Russia. Since there was no unemployment insurance, how did people live when there were no jobs? Wedding rings were sold, furniture pawned, life insurance borrowed against, and money begged from relatives. Millions with no resources moved aimlessly from city to city, sometimes hopping on freight cars; some cities tried to keep the wanderers out with barricades and shotguns.[3]

The Great Depression affected most of the industrialized world but was most serious in the United States and in Germany. The Great Depression in Germany led directly to Hitler's takeover of power in 1933 and indirectly caused the 50 million deaths of World War II. What caused the disastrous depression and what could have been done to avoid it? We need to study basic macroeconomics first, and then we can examine the causes of the Great Depression in Chapter 7.

The German Hyperinflation of 1922–23

A *hyperinflation* can be defined as an inflation raging at a rate of 50 percent or more *per month*. If a Big Mac cost $2 in January, a 50 percent monthly inflation would raise the price to $3 in February, $4.50 in March, $6.75 in April, and onward until it reached $173 in December. There were several examples of hyperinflation in the twentieth century, most of them involving the experience of European countries after World Wars I and II. The best known is the German hyperinflation, which proceeded at 322 percent per month between August 1922 and November 1923; in its final climactic days in October 1923, it rose at 32,000 percent per month! Figure 1-8 displays the German price level from 1920 to 1923. The price level goes from slightly above 1.0 in 1920 and early 1921 to 550 by the end of 1922 and about 100,000,000,000 at the end of 1923.

The basic cause of the German hyperinflation was the Versailles Peace Treaty which ended World War I and required payment of massive reparations by Germany to Britain and France. The Germans were unwilling to obtain funds to pay the reparations by raising taxes, so instead they ran huge government budget deficits financed by printing paper money. When people realized the implications of these deficits, they became less willing to hold money; it was both the rapid increase in the supply of money and the ever-declining demand for money that combined to fuel the hyperinflation.[4]

The inflation decimated the savings of ordinary Germans. A farmer who sold a piece of land for 80,000 marks as a nest egg for his old age could barely buy a sandwich with the money a few years later. Elderly Germans can still recall the days in 1923 when:

> People were bringing money to the bank in cardboard boxes and laundry baskets. As we no longer could count it, we put the money on scales and weighed it. I can

---

[3] Details in this paragraph are from William Manchester, *The Glory and the Dream: A Narrative History of America, 1932–72* (Boston: Little-Brown, 1973), pp. 33–35.

[4] Data from Philip Cagan, "The Monetary Dynamics of Hyperinflation," in Milton Friedman, ed., *Studies in the Quantity Theory of Money* (Chicago: University of Chicago Press, 1956), Table 1, p. 26.

When Sausages Cost 100 Billion Marks

Figure 1-8 **The German Price Level, 1920–23**
The orange line shows the German price level, which increased from a little above 1 in 1920 and 1921 to 550 at the end of 1922 and to 100,000,000,000 in November 1923.

still see my brothers coming home Saturdays with heaps of paper money. When the shops reopened after the weekend they got no more than a breakfast roll for it. Many got drunk on their pay because it was worthless on Monday.[5]

Just as the Great Depression helped to create resentments about the existing government that turned voters to Hitler's Nazi party, so bitter memories of lost savings in the hyperinflation ten years earlier added to Hitler's growing support. We will return to the causes and effects of rapid inflation in Chapter 9.

Fast and Slow Growth in Asia

Neither the Great Depression nor the German hyperinflation had any significant effect on the American or German standard of living a decade or two later. For effects that really matter over the decades, we need to look at the third of our "Big Three" macroeconomic concepts: productivity growth. Differences in growth rates that may appear small can compound over the decades and create

---

[5] Alice Siegert, "When Inflation Ruined Germany," *Chicago Tribune,* November 30, 1974.

18 Chapter 1 • What Is Macroeconomics?

South Korea Leaves the Philippines in the Dust

Figure 1-9 Per-Capita Real GDP, South Korea and the Philippines, 1960–2005

Per-capita real GDP in the Philippines barely grew from 1960 to 2005; the growth rate between those years was only 1.4 percent per annum. In contrast, the growth rate in Korea was 5.7 percent, enough to boost per-capita real GDP to a level fully 13 times the 1960 value.

Source: 1950–92, from Angus Maddison, *Monitoring the World Economy,* converted from 1990 U.S. PPP prices to 2004 U.S. prices, and extended from 1992 to 2005 using population data from the U.S. Census Bureau and real GDP data (both actual and forecast) from the International Monetary Fund.

enormous differences in the standard of living of any economic unit, from individuals to nations. A classic example of the importance of rapid growth is illustrated in Figure 1-9, which displays real GDP per capita in South Korea and the Philippines over the period 1960 to 2005.

In 1960, real GDP per capita in the Philippines was actually 14 percent higher than in South Korea, with values of $1,975 and $1,728, respectively. But between 1960 and 2005, real GDP per capita grew at 5.7 percent per year in South Korea compared to only 1.4 percent in the Philippines. Figure 1-9 shows the wide gap that opened up between the Korean and Philippine standards of living, with 2005 values of only $3,632 for the Philippines and $22,918 for South Korea. As a result of its superior economic growth record, the average Korean in 2005 could save or consume more than six times as much as the average citizen of the Philippines. Stated another way, the Korean could consume everything enjoyed by the Philippine citizen and then have five times as much left over. This extra output in Korea is shown by the orange shading in Figure 1-9.

The outstanding achievement of South Korea has been duplicated in several other countries in East Asia, notably Hong Kong, Singapore, and Taiwan, and for a shorter period in the past two decades by China. What secrets have the Koreans learned about economic growth that the Philippine government and population have not learned? The story of growth successes and failures is a fascinating one that awaits us in Chapters 10 and 11.

1-7 Taming Business Cycles: Stabilization Policy

Macroeconomic analysts have two tasks: to analyze the causes of changes in important aggregates and to predict the consequences of alternative policy changes. In policy discussions the group of aggregates that society cares most about—inflation, unemployment, and the long-term growth rate of productivity—are called goals, or **target variables**. When the target variables deviate from desired values, alternative **policy instruments** can be used in an attempt to achieve needed changes. Instruments fall into three broad categories: **monetary policies**, which include control of the money supply and interest rates; **fiscal policies**, which include changes in government expenditures and tax rates; and a third, miscellaneous group, which includes policies to equip workers with skills they need to qualify for jobs.

How are target variables and policy instruments related to the three central macroeconomic concepts introduced at the beginning of this chapter? All three concepts—the unemployment rate, inflation rate, and productivity growth—are the key target variables of economic policy, the goals society cares most about.

The goal of policymakers regarding productivity growth is simple—just make productivity growth as fast as possible. There are no negatives to rapid productivity growth, and virtually every country in the world admires the growth achievement of South Korea (and some other East Asian countries) displayed in Figure 1-9 in the previous section. However, the goal of policymakers regarding the unemployment rate is not so simple. An attempt to reduce unemployment to zero would be likely to cause a significant acceleration of inflation, and moderation of inflation may be impossible if policymakers attempt to maintain the unemployment rate too low. A compromise goal for policymakers is to try to set the actual unemployment rate equal to the natural unemployment rate, since this would tend to maintain a constant inflation rate that neither accelerates nor decelerates.

Target variables are aggregates whose values society cares about.

Policy instruments are elements that government policymakers can manipulate directly to influence target variables.

Monetary policy tries to influence target variables by changing the money supply or interest rate or both.

Fiscal policy tries to influence target variables by manipulating government expenditures and tax rates.

The Role of Stabilization Policy

Macroeconomic analysis begins with a simple message: Either type of **stabilization policy**, monetary or fiscal, can be used to offset undesired changes in private spending. The effects of monetary and fiscal policy on the price level and on real GDP are the main subjects of Parts Two and Three of this book.

There are many problems in applying stabilization policy. It may not be possible to control aggregate demand instantly and precisely. A policy stimulus

A **stabilization policy** is any policy that seeks to influence the level of aggregate demand.

intended to fight current unemployment might boost aggregate demand only after a long and uncertain delay, by which time the stimulus might not be needed. The impact of different policy changes may also be highly uncertain. These and other limitations of policy "fine-tuning" or "activism" are central themes in the consideration of monetary and fiscal policy in Part Five.

Most policy disagreements stem from the incompatibility of worthy economic goals. Most people would like the price level to be stable and the unemployment rate to be close to zero. But this state of nirvana cannot be achieved instantly, if ever. Macroeconomics, like economics in general, is the science of *choice* in the face of limitations for each of the possible alternatives. Choices emphasized in this book include whether to reduce the inflation rate at the cost of higher unemployment during a transition period that may last five years or longer and whether to boost investment and economic growth at the cost of higher tax rates.

> **Self-Test**
>
> 1. Is it the task of stabilization policy to set the unemployment rate to zero? Why or why not?
> 2. Is it the task of stabilization policy to set the inflation rate to zero? Why or why not?
> 3. What are the two big problems in applying stabilization policy to control aggregate demand?

1-8 The "Internationalization" of Macroeconomics

More than ever before, macroeconomics is an international subject. The days are gone when the effects of U.S. stabilization policy could be analyzed in isolation, without consideration for their repercussions abroad. This old view of the United States as a **closed economy** described reality in the first decade or so after World War II. In the 1940s and 1950s, trade accounted for only about 5 percent of the U.S. economy, exchange rates were fixed, and financial flows to and from other nations were restricted.

A **closed economy** has no trade in goods, services, or financial assets with any other nation.

An **open economy** exports goods and services to other nations, imports from them, and has financial flows to and from foreign nations.

The United States has increasingly become an **open economy**. Imports now equal 15 percent of U.S. GDP. The exchange rate of the dollar has been flexible since 1973 and has fluctuated far more widely than anyone had predicted prior to that time. International financial flows are massive and often instantaneous, with computers sending messages to buy or sell stocks and bonds at the speed of light among the major financial centers of Tokyo, London, New York, and Chicago.

As the economy has become internationalized, so has macroeconomic analysis. For instance, during the years of persistent government deficits (1980–97 and 2001–05), the depressing effect of government deficits on private domestic investment was partly offset by capital inflows from abroad, as foreigners purchased U.S. stocks, bonds, factories, and hotels. Further, in an open economy there are additional impacts of monetary and fiscal policy to consider. When it reduces interest rates, the Federal Reserve Board must take into account the likelihood that the value of the dollar will decline, which

International Perspective

How Does U.S. Economic Performance Stack Up?

One result of the internationalization of macroeconomics is an increased attention to the comparative economic performance of the United States. The figure shows how the United States compares with Japan and the major European nations in its unemployment, inflation, and productivity growth rates. The data are presented as a set of bar graphs, with the unemployment performance displayed in the top frame, inflation in the middle frame, and productivity growth in the bottom frame. Three bars are grouped together in each frame for each region, showing performance during the years 1960–73, 1973–87, and 1987–2005.

Above all, one startling fact stands out. Despite its recent problems, the economic performance of Japan is superior to both the United States and Europe in most periods. Japan had a lower unemployment rate in all three periods and a much lower inflation rate in the most recent period. Japanese productivity growth was faster than that in the United States in all three periods. Compared to Europe, the United States did better on both unemployment and inflation in the second two periods. The clear failing of the United States was in its productivity growth in the first two periods, much slower than in Europe or Japan. However, in the third period, productivity growth in the United States revived to a faster rate than in Europe, and in the shorter period since 1995, U.S. productivity growth has far outpaced that in either Europe or Japan, as we shall learn in Chapter 11.

How the United States Compares

tends to boost U.S. exports and stimulate the economy while also causing inflation to accelerate.

Along with a new analysis of fiscal and monetary policy and of the determinants of inflation, the internationalization of macroeconomics brings new attention to American efficiency and competitiveness. If the U.S. economy is doing so well, why are we so "hooked" on imports of foreign goods? As we shall see early in the book, America's current account deficit may be more of a reflection of its low private saving rate and persistent government deficits than of any unique enthusiasm for foreign goods and services.

Summary

1. The three central macroeconomic concepts are those that most affect everyday lives. They include the unemployment rate, inflation rate, and productivity growth.

2. Macroeconomics differs from microeconomics by focusing on aggregates that are summed up over all the economic activities in the economy. Theory in macroeconomics is a process of simplification that identifies the most important economic relationships.

3. Gross domestic product (GDP) is a measure of the overall size of the economy. While it does not affect everyday life directly, the behavior of GDP helps us to understand the behavior of the three central macroeconomic concepts that do influence everyday life.

4. Neither too much nor too little real GDP is desirable. The best compromise level is called natural real GDP and is consistent with a constant inflation rate. When the economy is operating at its natural level of real GDP, it is also by definition operating at its natural rate of unemployment.

5. The topic of "business cycles" studies short-run phenomena in macroeconomics over a period of one to five years. The topic of "economic growth" studies long-run phenomena over a period lasting a decade or more.

6. While most macroeconomic analysis concerns relatively normal events, a challenge for macroeconomists is to explain how extreme and unusual events can occur. Two of these were the Great Depression of the 1930s and the German hyperinflation of 1922–23. Another challenge is to understand how the rate of economic growth can be so different between two countries like South Korea and the Philippines that are located in the same region of the world.

7. In this century, U.S. inflation has fluctuated widely but was worse during wars and between 1965 and 1991. Periods of high unemployment have coincided with those of low real GDP. The Great Depression clearly scored worst on both counts.

8. The three central macroeconomic aggregates, (unemployment rate, inflation rate, and productivity growth) are the main targets of stabilization policy. Stabilization policy may not be effective in improving well-being if both unemployment and inflation are too high, and stabilization policy may operate with a long delay or have effects that are highly uncertain.

9. Macroeconomics is now an international subject. International repercussions influence the way fiscal and monetary policy work and how the inflation process operates. The current account deficit raises new concerns about U.S. competitiveness.

Concepts

macroeconomics
unemployment rate
inflation rate
productivity
aggregate
gross domestic product
actual real GDP
natural real GDP

natural rate of unemployment
business cycles
economic growth
real GDP gap
peak
trough
recession
expansion

target variables
policy instruments
monetary policy
fiscal policy
stabilization policy
closed economy
open economy

Questions

1. Read either an entire week of the *Wall Street Journal* or a business-oriented weekly magazine such as *Business Week* or *The Economist*. Identify three stories that deal with topics related to microeconomics and another three stories that discuss topics related to macroeconomics. Explain why you have put each story in either the microeconomics or macroeconomics category.
2. Using the quarterly data in Table A-2 (Appendix A), attempt to identify the recession phases of the basic business cycle depicted in Figure 1-4 for the period 1947–2001.
3. How are the natural real GDP and the natural real unemployment rates related to the rate of inflation?
4. Between January and December 1994, U.S. unemployment fell from 6.6 percent to 5.5 percent of the labor force. The Federal Reserve, the nation's monetary policymaking authority, took active measures beginning in February 1994 to raise short-term interest rates. What might have motivated policymakers to raise interest rates and what were they hoping to accomplish?
5. In April 2000, the seasonally adjusted unemployment rate was 3.8 percent. By June 2001, the unemployment rate had increased to 4.5 percent. Yet the measures by the Federal Reserve to reduce short-term interest rates were taken in stages, and in fact the unemployment rate continued to rise. What might have motivated the policymakers' cautious behavior?
6. (a) The "big three" concepts of macroeconomics are the unemployment rate, the inflation rate, and productivity growth. Discuss which of these concepts are primarily to evaluate the behavior of the economy (i) in the short run and (ii) in the long run.
   (b) Using Figures 1-3 and 1-5 as guides, discuss how natural real GDP is used to evaluate the behavior of the economy in both the short run and the long run.
7. Using the information contained in the "Case Study: A Century of Business Cycles," discuss when in its history the U.S. economy most resembled the economies of Volatilia and Stabilia depicted in Figure 1-3.
8. Explain why productivity growth not only allows a society to have higher living standards in the form of more goods and services, but also allows it to increase what percentage of an average person's life is spent in school, on vacation, in retirement, or in other non-work related activities.
9. Explain how the value of real GDP relative to natural real GDP can be used by policymakers to decide how to change the values of the target variables.
10. How does the performance of the U.S. economy compare and contrast with the performance of the Japanese and European economies since 1960?

Problems

1. (a) Suppose that real GDP is currently $97 billion per year and natural real GDP is currently $100 billion. Measured as a percentage, what is the real GDP gap?
   (b) Suppose natural real GDP is growing by $4 billion per year. By how much must real GDP have risen after two years to close the real GDP gap?
2. Using the data contained in Table A-2 of Appendix A, compute the output gaps at the beginning and end of the following recessions: (a) 1973–75; (b) 1981–82; (c) 1990–91; (d) 2001. What do the declines in the output gaps tell you about the relative severity of these four recessions?
3. The sum of exports and imports as a percent of gross domestic product is sometimes used as a measure of how open an economy is. In particular, the greater is the percentage, the more open is the economy. Using the following data, compute this measure of the openness of the United States economy in 1960, 1970, 1980, 1990, and 2000. Discuss what the data show in terms of the "internationalization" of the United States economy since 1960.

	1960	1970	1980	1990	2000
GDP	2,501.8	3,771.9	5,161.7	7,112.5	9,817.0
Exports	90.6	161.4	323.5	552.5	1,096.3
Imports	103.3	213.4	310.9	607.1	1,475.8

Self-Test Answers

p. 8 (1) When actual real GDP is above natural real GDP, the actual unemployment rate is below the natural unemployment rate. (2) In this opposite case, the actual unemployment rate is above the natural unemployment rate. (3) There is no such thing as the natural rate of inflation. When the economy is operating at its natural rate of unemployment, the inflation rate does not change. But it does not change from whatever level is inherited from the past, and this could be zero, 10 percent per year, or 100 percent per year.

pp. 11–12 (1) short-run, (2) long-run, (3) short-run, (4) both (the money can create jobs during a recession but also will stimulate long-run productivity growth).

p. 20 (1) Stabilization policy cannot set the unemployment rate to zero or any other rate below the natural rate of unemployment without causing accelerating inflation. (2) Stabilization policy can set the inflation rate to zero only at the cost of a recession and a substantial cost in terms of lost output. (3) The two big problems are lags and uncertainty. A policy change may affect aggregate demand only after a long and uncertain delay, and the impact of different policy changes may also be highly uncertain.

CHAPTER 2

The Measurement of Income, Prices, and Unemployment

It has been said that figures rule the world; maybe. I am quite sure that it is figures which show us whether it is being ruled well or badly.
—Johann Wolfgang Goethe, 1830

Our first task is to develop a simple theoretical model to explain real output (gross domestic product, or GDP) and the price level. Before we can turn to theory in Chapter 3, however, we must stop in Chapter 2 for a few definitions. What are GDP and the price level? How are they measured? What goods and services are included in or excluded from GDP? How are private saving, private investment, the government deficit, and the current account deficit related to one another? How are the inflation rate and unemployment rate measured?

2-1 Why We Care About Income

In Chapter 1 we identified two key links between real GDP and the three central concepts of macroeconomics. First, in Figure 1-2 we noted that movements in the unemployment rate (the first central concept) are closely related to the parallel movements of the gap between actual and natural real GDP. Thus the key to understanding changes in unemployment is the change in actual real GDP.

Second, the level and growth rate of our standard of living are measured by productivity (the third central concept), defined as the ratio of output to the number of hours worked. Output is the same as real GDP. Thus any discussion of U.S. productivity performance in comparison with the country's history or with other nations requires an understanding of the data on real GDP.

This chapter begins by asking what is included in GDP and why. We then learn about the different sectors of the economy that purchase portions of the total GDP and how that GDP is the source of different types of income. We learn how the price level and rate of inflation are measured. Finally, we learn how the unemployment rate is measured and how the unemployment rate is related to real GDP.

2-2 The Circular Flow of Income and Expenditure

We begin with a very simple economy, consisting of households and business firms. We will assume that households spend their entire income, saving

Figure 2-1 The Circular Flow of Income and Consumption Expenditures

Circular flow of income and expenditure in a simple imaginary economy in which households consume their entire income. There are no taxes, no government spending, no saving, no investment, and no foreign sector.

A Simple Imaginary Economy

nothing, and that there is no government.[1] Figure 2-1 depicts the operation of our simple economy, with households represented by the box on the left and business firms by the box on the right. There are two kinds of transactions between the households and the firms.

First, the firms sell goods and services (product)—for instance, bread and shoes—to the households represented in Figure 2-1 by the lower orange line, labeled product. The bread and shoes are not a gift, but are paid for by a flow of money (C), say $1,000,000 per year, represented by the solid red line, labeled **consumption expenditures**.

Second, households must work to earn the income to pay for the consumption goods. They work for the firms, selling their skills as represented by the upper purple line, labeled labor services. Household members are willing to work only if they receive a flow of money, usually called wages, from the firms for each hour of work. Wages are the main component of income (Y), shown by the upper green line.

Since households are assumed to consume all of their income, and since firms are assumed to pay out all of their sales in the form of income to households, it follows that income (Y) and consumption expenditures (C) are equal. For the same reason, the labor services provided in return for income are equal to the goods and services (product) sold by the firms to households in return for the money flow of consumption expenditures:

$$\begin{aligned} \text{income } (Y) &= \text{labor services} \\ &= \text{consumption expenditures } (C) \\ &= \text{product} \end{aligned}$$

Consumption expenditures are purchases of goods and services by households for their own use.

---

[1] Because households do no saving, there is no capital or wealth, and all household income is in the form of wages for labor services.

Self-Test

1. Imagine that a student named Eric purchases a haircut, priced at $10, with a $10 bill. Describe in words how the student's haircut will be included in each of the four flows of Figure 2-1.
2. Imagine that a student named Alison obtains a job as a lifeguard at a summer camp paying $8 per hour for July and August, and that the camp obtains the money to pay Alison from fees paid by parents for their children to go to the camp. Describe in words how the fees and the lifeguard job will be included in each of the four flows of Figure 2-1.

Each of the four elements in the preceding equation is a **flow magnitude**—any money payment or physical good or service that flows from one economic unit to another. A flow of expenditure, just like a flow of water through a pipe, can be measured only if we first specify the length of time over which the flow is measured. Thus U.S. GDP (= income = expenditure = factor services) in 2004 was roughly $11,600 billion *per year*. Most flow magnitudes in the United States are measured at annual rates. If the flow of GDP in a quarter-year is $2,900 billion, this amounts to $11,600 billion at an annual rate.

A flow is distinguished from a **stock**, which is the economic magnitude of a single unit at a particular moment of time. A stock of money or savings accounts or business equipment or government debt can be measured by adding up its value at a given point in time—for instance, midnight on December 31, 2005. Measuring a stock is like taking a flash snapshot. It requires specifying a particular date, not a time interval.

*A **flow magnitude** is an economic magnitude that moves from one economic unit to another at a specified rate per unit of time.*

*A **stock** is an economic magnitude in the possession of a given economic unit at a particular point in time.*

2-3 What Transactions Should Be Included in Income and Expenditure?

The **National Income and Product Accounts** (also called NIPA, or national accounts, for short) is the official U.S. government accounting of all the millions of flows of income and expenditure in the United States. Historical data for GDP and other macro concepts are listed in Appendix A for the United States and in Appendix B for other major nations. A guide to government data sources is provided in the box on p. 28.

National Income and Product Accounts is the official U.S. government economic accounting system that keeps track of GDP and its subcomponents.

Defining GDP

In our free market economy, the fact that a good or service is sold is usually a sign that it satisfies certain human wants and needs; otherwise, people would not be willing to pay a price for it. So by including in the GDP only things that are sold through the market for a price, we can be fairly sure that most of the components of GDP do contribute to human satisfaction. There are three major requirements in the rule for including items in the total **final product**, or GDP:

Final product consists of all currently produced goods and services that are sold through the market but not resold during the current time period.

Final product includes all currently produced goods and services that are sold through the market but are not resold.

Currently produced. The first part of the rule—*to be included in final product, a good must be currently produced*—obviously excludes sales of any used items

Where to Find the Numbers: A Guide to the Data

The first place to look for macroeconomic data is the appendixes in the back of this textbook. There you will find annual data covering more than a century (from 1875 on) and quarterly data since 1947 on major macroeconomic concepts. Also included are several important annual data series for Japan, Canada, and the major European nations for the period since 1960.

Time Passes and Revisions Occur: How to Cope

The appendixes are unlikely to satisfy all of your data needs for any of three reasons: (1) you may want to find a data series that does not appear in the appendixes; (2) you may need data for quarters and years not included in the appendixes (which are current through 2004); and (3) some of the data in the appendixes may have been revised. Whether you are curious about more recent developments or need to complete a class assignment, you need to know where to look.

You are unlikely to find what you need at the newsstand or college bookstore; instead, head to the Internet. There you can find the most recent and comprehensive sources of economic data.

The "Big Three" Agencies

Using the Internet is by far the easiest way to gather economic data; whether it be rather simple data, such as real GDP or the most recent Consumer Price Index, or more detailed data, such as the unemployment rate for males aged 20–24, productivity in the electric utility industry, or how much U.S. consumers spend on funerals, there is no better place to search than online. For these and many other series, turn to one of the Web sites of the specialized government agencies that actually produce the data. The three most important of these agencies are the Bureau of Economic Analysis (BEA, a branch of the Commerce Department), the Bureau of Labor Statistics (BLS, a branch of the Labor Department), and the Federal Reserve Board (usually called by its nickname, the Fed).

BEA: National Income Data All the data on GDP, and related income and product series, are produced by the BEA in an organized system of tables called the National Income and Product Accounts (NIPA). These extend back to 1929 for annual data and to 1947 for quarterly data and are updated regularly on the BEA Web site www.bea.gov. Here you can find not only NIPA tables, but recent news releases, industry data, and international and regional series.

BLS: Labor Market, Price, And Wage Data While the BEA mainly reprocesses data originally produced by other agencies, the BLS is a primary producer of data on employment, unemployment, consumer and producer prices, and wage rates. The BLS runs a large survey, contacting thousands of families each month to learn about their employment and unemployment experience and contacting thousands of retail outlets to track price changes. All of the BLS data series are available at www.bls.gov.

The Fed: Financial Market Data The Federal Reserve compiles data on interest rates, the money supply, and other figures describing the banking and financial system. One of the regional Feds, the Federal Reserve Bank of St. Louis, supports an online database known as FRED (www.research.stlouisfed.org/fred). This database provides historical U.S. economic and financial data, including daily interest rates, monetary and business indicators, exchange rates, balance of payments and select regional economic data. The Federal Reserve Board of Governors Web site (www.federalreserve.gov) is also useful.

The preceding list does not even include the grandfather of all statistics agencies, the Bureau of the Census, which conducts the decennial Census of Population and, every five years, economic censuses of business establishments. The Census data form the raw material for much of the BEA's work in creating the national accounts, not to mention much research by economists on both macro and micro topics. See www.census.gov.

International Web Sites to Know:
 Org. for Economic Cooperation and Development
  www.oecdwash.org
 United Nations Statistics Division
  www.unstats.un.org/unsd/default.htm
 World Bank
  www.worldbank.org/data

Many more sites are available through such search engines as google.com, yahoo.com, and ask.com.

The opening screen of the Bureau of Labor Statistics Web site.

such as houses and cars, since they are not currently produced. It also excludes any transaction in which money is transferred without any accompanying good or service in return. Among the **transfer payments** excluded from national income in the United States are gifts from one person to another and "gifts" from the government to persons, such as Social Security, Medicare, and unemployment benefits. Also excluded are capital gains accruing to persons as the prices of their assets change.

> **Transfer payments** are those made for which no goods or services are produced in return.

Sold on the market. The second part of the rule—*goods included in the final product must be sold on the market and are valued at market prices*—means that we measure the value of final product by the market prices that people are willing to pay for goods and services. We assume that a Mercedes gives 10,000 times as much satisfaction as a package of razor blades for the simple reason that it costs about 10,000 times as much. Excluded from GDP by this criterion is the value of personal time spent engaged in activities that are not sold on the market (time spent commuting, baking a cake, and so on). Also excluded is any allowance for the costs of air pollution, water pollution, acid rain, or other by-products of the production process for which no explicit charge is made.

But not resold. The third part of the rule—*to be included in final product, a good must not be resold in the current time period*—further limits the inclusion of items. The many different goods and services produced in the economy are used in two different ways. Some goods, like wheat, are mainly used as ingredients in the making of other goods, in this case, bread. Any good resold by its purchaser, rather than used as is, goes by the name **intermediate good**.

The opposite of an intermediate good is a **final good,** one that is not resold. Bread sold at the grocery is a final good, used by consumers, as are shoes, clothes, haircuts, and everything else the consumer buys directly. Only final goods are included in final product; intermediate goods like the leather bought by the shoemaker are not included.

> A **final good** is part of final product, whereas an **intermediate good** is resold by its purchaser either in its present form or in an altered form.

2-4 Components of Expenditure

Types of Investment

The goods and services produced by business firms, which are not resold as intermediate goods to other firms or consumers during the current period, qualify by our rule as final product. But the business firm does not consume them. Final goods that business firms keep for themselves are called **private investment** or private capital formation. These goods add to the nation's stock of income-yielding assets. Private investment consists of *inventory investment* and *fixed investment*.

> **Private investment** is the portion of final product that adds to the nation's stock of income-yielding physical assets or that replaces old, worn-out physical assets.

Inventory investment. Bread purchased by the grocer but not resold to consumers in the current period stays on the shelves, raising the level of the grocer's inventories. Since all the bread that is produced is included in GDP, we must define expenditure so as to include the bread, whether it is sold to consumers and is part of consumption, or whether it remains unsold on the shelf. *By including the change in inventories as part of expenditure, we guarantee that GDP (that is, total product) by definition equals total expenditure.*

> **Inventory investment** includes all changes in the stock of raw materials, parts, and finished goods held by business.

> ### Self-Test
> Imagine that a grocer has 10 loaves of bread at the close of business on December 31, 2004. Valued at the wholesale baker's price of $0.80, the value of the grocer's inventory is $8.00. At the close of business on March 31, 2005, the grocer has 15 loaves or $12.00 of bread on the shelves.
> 1. What is the level of the grocer's inventory on December 31, 2004, and on March 31, 2005?
> 2. What is the change in the grocer's inventories in the first quarter of 2005?
> 3. What is the implication of these numbers for the contribution of the grocer's inventories to GDP in the first quarter of 2005?

Fixed investment includes all final goods purchased by business that are not intended for resale.

Fixed investment. Fixed investment includes all final goods purchased by business, other than additions to inventory. The main types of fixed investment are structures (factories, office buildings, shopping centers, apartments, houses) and equipment (cash registers, computers, trucks). Newly produced houses and condominiums sold to individuals are also counted as fixed investment—a household is treated in the national accounts as a business firm that owns the house as an asset and rents the house to itself.[2]

Relation of Investment and Saving

Figure 2-1 described a simple imaginary economy in which households consumed their total income Figure 2-2 introduces investment into that economy. Total expenditures on final product are the same as before, but now they are divided into consumption expenditures by households (C) and business purchases of investment goods (I). Households spend part of their income on purchases of consumption goods and save the rest.

Personal saving is that part of personal income that is neither consumed nor paid out in taxes.

The portion of household income that is not consumed is called **personal saving**. What happens to income that is saved? The funds are channeled to business firms in two basic ways:

1. Households buy bonds and stocks issued by the firms, and the firms then use the money to buy investment goods.
2. Households leave the unused income (savings) in banks and other financial institutions. The banks then lend the money to the firms, which use it to buy investment goods.

In either case, business firms obtain funds to purchase investment goods. The box labeled "capital market" in Figure 2-2 symbolizes the transfer of personal saving to business firms for the purpose of investment.

In other words, saving is a "leakage" from the income used for consumption expenditures. This leakage from the spending stream must be balanced by an "injection" of nonconsumption spending in the form of private investment.

---

[2] An individual who owns a house is treated as a split personality in the national accounts: as a business firm *and* as a consuming household. My left side is a businessperson who owns my house and receives imaginary rent payments from my right side, the consumer who lives in my house. The NIPA identifies these imaginary rent payments as "Imputed rent on owner-occupied dwellings," which makes rent payments the most important exception to the rule that a good must be sold on the market to be counted in GDP.

Figure 2-2 Introduction of Saving and Investment to the Circular Flow Diagram

We begin with the simple imaginary economy (Figure 2-1) but now assume that households save 20 percent of their income. Business firms' investment accounts for 20 percent of total expenditure. Again, we are assuming that there are no taxes, no government spending, and no foreign sector.

Saving Leaks Out of the Spending Stream but Reappears as Investment

Income (Y = $1,000,000)
Households
Personal saving (S = $200,000)
Capital market
Business firms
Private investment (I = $200,000)
Consumption expenditures (C = $800,000)

Net Exports

Exports are expenditures for goods and services produced in the United States and sent to other countries. Such expenditure creates income in the United States but is not part of the consumption or investment spending of U.S. residents. **Imports** are expenditures by U.S. residents for goods and services produced elsewhere and thus do *not* create domestic income. For instance, an American-made Chevrolet exported to Canada is part of U.S. production and income but is Canadian consumption. A German-made Mercedes imported to the United States is part of German production and income but is U.S. consumption. If income created from exports is greater than income spent on imported goods, the net effect is a higher level of domestic production and income. Thus the difference between exports and imports, **net exports**, is a component of final product and GDP.

Another name for net exports is **net foreign investment**, which can be given the same economic interpretation as domestic investment. Why? Both domestic and foreign investment are components of domestic production and income creation. Domestic investment creates domestic capital assets; net foreign investment creates U.S. claims on foreigners that yield us future flows of income. An American export to Japan is paid for with Japanese yen, which can be deposited in a Japanese bank account or used to buy part of a Japanese factory. The opposite occurs as well. When the United States imports more than it exports, as it has in every year since 1981, net foreign investment is negative. U.S. payments for imports provide dollars that foreign investors use to buy American factories, hotels, and other assets including bank accounts in the United States.

GNP Versus GDP

Until 1991, the main aggregate in the national income accounts was **gross national product (GNP)**, not gross domestic product (GDP). The two terms

Exports are goods produced within one country and shipped to another.

Imports are goods consumed within one country but produced in another country.

Net exports and **net foreign investment** are both equal to exports minus imports.

Gross national product (GNP) is goods and services produced by labor and capital supplied by U.S. residents, whether the actual production takes place within the borders of the United States or in a foreign country.

differ only in their geographical coverage. GDP covers goods and services produced within the borders of the United States, whereas GNP covers goods and services produced by labor and capital supplied by U.S. residents, whether the actual production takes place within the borders of the United States or in a foreign country. To convert GDP into GNP, we must add in elements, such as the income of American residents earned abroad and dividends that McDonald's receives from sales of its hamburgers in London and Tokyo, and then subtract income that we pay to foreigners, such as profits earned by Honda on its auto plant in Ohio.

Since the additions are slightly smaller than the subtractions, GNP is a bit smaller than GDP. For example, GNP was 0.3 percent smaller than GDP in 2004. In recent years GNP has grown slightly more slowly than GDP, since negative net foreign investment means that foreign income from American production has been growing faster than American income earned on foreign production.

The Government Sector

Up to this point we have been examining an economy consisting only of private households and business firms. Now we add the government, which collects taxes from the private sector and makes two kinds of expenditures. Government purchases of goods and services (tanks, fighter planes, schoolbooks) generate production and create income. The government can also make payments directly to households. Social Security, Medicare, and unemployment compensation are examples of these transfer payments, given the name *transfer* because they are "gifts" from the government to the recipient without any obligation for the recipient to provide any services in return. As you learned in Section 2-3, transfer payments are not included in GDP.

Figure 2-3 adds the government (federal, state, and local) to our imaginary economy of Figures 2-1 and 2-2. A flow of tax revenue (R) passes from the households to the government.[3] The government buys goods and services (G). In addition the government sends transfer payments (F), such as welfare payments, to households, leaving a deficit that must be financed. To do this, the government sells bonds to private households through the capital market, just as business firms sell bonds and stock to households to finance their investment projects.

Also shown in Figure 2-3, in the bottom right corner, is the foreign sector. Imports are already included in consumption and investment spending, so imports are shown as a leakage by the blue arrow pointing down toward the foreign sector box. Exports are spending on domestic production, as shown by the red arrow going from the foreign sector to the business firms. To keep the diagram simple, exports equal imports.[4]

---

[3] In the real world, both households and business firms pay taxes. Here we keep things simple by limiting tax payments to personal income taxes.

[4] If imports exceed exports, there is a flow equal to the difference going from the foreign sector box to the capital market box. This is the inflow of foreign capital available to finance private investment or the government deficit.

The Government Surplus or Deficit Balances the Requirements of the Capital Market and the Government Sector

Figure 2-3 Introduction of Taxation, Government Spending, and the Foreign Sector to the Circular Flow Diagram

Our simple imaginary economy with the addition of a government collecting $100,000 in tax revenue, paying households $100,000 in transfer payments, and purchasing $100,000 of goods and services. Its total expenditures ($200,000) exceed its tax revenues ($100,000), leaving a $100,000 deficit that is financed by selling government bonds to the households.

2-5 The "Magic" Equation and the Twin Deficits

The relationships displayed in Figure 2-3 can be summarized in a simple relationship that we call the "magic" equation because of its versatility in explaining central macroeconomic concepts. The **magic equation** helps us understand the relationships among investment, private saving, the government surplus or deficit, and the surplus or deficit of exports versus imports.

A central phenomenon of the current U.S. economy is that the government is running a large deficit, with government expenditures far in excess of tax revenue. At the same time, the U.S. economy imports far more than it exports, implying a large international deficit (negative net exports). How are these "twin deficits" financed? What difference would it make if the government ran a surplus while the international deficit remained the same? What would happen if the international deficit were zero while the government deficit remained large? The magic equation can help us to answer these questions.

The **magic equation** states that private saving plus net tax revenue must by definition equal the sum of private domestic investment, government spending on goods and services, and net exports.

Implications of the Equality Between Income and Expenditures

By definition total income created (Y) is equal to total expenditure on final product (E). Why is this true by definition? Because income is created from total production, and expenditures include both the production that is sold to final users, as well as the production that is not sold (i.e., the change in inventories). We can indicate that this relationship is true by definition by using the three-bar equals sign, otherwise known as the "identity sign":

$$Y \equiv E$$

There are four types of expenditure on final product: consumption expenditures (C); private domestic investment (I); government purchases of goods and services (G); and net exports (NX):

$$E \equiv C + I + G + NX \qquad (2.1)$$

The total personal income that households receive consists of the income created from production (Y) and transfer payments from the government (F). This total ($Y + F$) is available for the purchase of consumption goods (C), saving (S), and the payment of taxes (R):

$$Y + F \equiv C + S + R$$

An equivalent expression is obtained if we subtract F from both sides:

$$Y \equiv C + S + R - F \qquad (2.2)$$

Transfer payments (F) can be treated as negative taxes. Thus there is no reason to distinguish tax revenues from transfers. Instead, we define net tax revenue (T) as taxes (R) minus transfers (F), converting equation (2.2) into the simpler expression:

$$Y \equiv C + S + T \qquad (2.3)$$

Leakages and Injections

Since $Y \equiv E$, the right side of equation (2.3) is equal to the right side of equation (2.1), and we obtain:

$$\begin{array}{c c} C + S + T \equiv & C + I + G + NX \\ -C & -C \\ \hline S + T \equiv & I + G + NX \end{array} \quad \text{(subtracting C from both sides)} \qquad (2.4)$$

The bottom line of (2.4) can be translated to a general rule:

> Since income is equal to expenditure, the portion of income not consumed (saving plus net taxes) must be equal to the nonconsumption portion of expenditure on final product (investment plus government spending plus net exports).

Leakages describe the portion of total income that flows to taxes or saving rather than into purchases of consumer goods.

Injections is a term for nonconsumption expenditures.

In other words, **leakages** out of the income available for consumption goods ($S + T$) must be exactly balanced by **injections** of nonconsumption spending ($I + G + NX$).

Equation (2.4) is one of the most important relationships in macroeconomics and reappears often in the next few chapters. We call it the magic equation. Its more technical name is the leakages–injections identity. The importance of this relationship is that it shows how some of the most basic concepts in macroeconomics—private saving, government spending and taxes, domestic investment, and net exports—are connected *by definition*. As we see in the next section, for instance, the fact that the government is running a budget deficit ($T - G$ less than zero) implies that investment plus net exports must be less than saving ($I + NX - S$ less than zero). Subsequently in Chapters 5 and 6 we shall return to the magic equation and learn that any change in the sum of private and government saving requires a change in the sum of domestic and foreign investment, and how changes in foreign borrowing alter the balance between domestic saving and investment.

The Government Budget and the Twin Deficits

The magic equation shows how the funds resulting from a government budget surplus are used, and it is equally useful in showing how the government finances a budget deficit. We can arrange equation (2.4) to show the uses of a government budget surplus:

$$T - G \equiv (I + NX) - S \qquad (2.5)$$

On the left side of this definition is the government budget surplus. If the left side is negative, the government is running a budget deficit. Shown on the right side is the excess of total investment, both domestic (I) and foreign (NX), over private savings (S). The definition indicates that there are three ways that a government budget surplus can be used. First, a budget surplus allows private saving to decline without any need for a decline in total investment. Second, a government budget surplus can stimulate domestic investment. Third, a government budget surplus can boost foreign investment or, if foreign investment is negative, reduce the amount of borrowing from foreigners.

If government spending is greater than net tax revenue, the government is running a deficit, and equation (2.5) shows that there are three possible implications. First, the government budget deficit could make domestic investment (I) smaller than otherwise. Second, the government budget deficit requires that private saving must rise to avoid any downward pressure on the sum of domestic and foreign investment ($I + NX$). Third, if there is no increase in private saving, then to avoid a decline in domestic investment there must be more borrowing from foreigners (larger negative NX) or a decline in lending to foreigners.

We can use a numerical example from recent years to illustrate how the right-hand side of equation (2.5) changed as the government shifted from its 1993 deficit to its surplus in 2000 and then back to deficit in 2004:

	$T - G$	$\equiv$	$(I + NX)$	$- S$
1993	-1.8	$\equiv$	$(17.6 - 1.0)$	$- 18.4$
2000	4.4	$\equiv$	$(20.8 - 4.0)$	$- 12.4$
2004	-4.6	$\equiv$	$(15.9 - 4.9)$	$- 15.6$

In 1993, there was a budget deficit equal to -1.8 percent of GDP. This was financed by foreign borrowing (negative NX) of -1.0 percent of GDP, requiring that domestic saving (18.4 percent) be larger than domestic investment (17.6 percent). In contrast, in the year 2000 there was a budget surplus equal to 4.4 percent of GDP, together with even greater foreign borrowing of -4.0 percent of GDP. The funds from the government surplus together with the large amount of foreign borrowing allowed domestic investment to be much larger (20.8 percent) than domestic saving (12.3 percent). By 2004, the government budget had returned to deficit (-4.6 percent). In effect, foreign borrowing (-4.9 percent) allowed domestic investment (15.9 percent) to be slightly in excess of domestic saving (15.6 percent).

The magic equation (2.4 or 2.5) can be rearranged in several additional ways, as we shall see in Chapter 5. Because it is true by definition, it does not identify the direction of causation among the interrelated variables. For instance, in the year 2000 did the government run a budget surplus because domestic investment was so strong, or was investment so strong because the government ran a surplus? Did the sharp decline in investment between 2000 and 2004 cause the government to run a deficit, or did the government deficit occur for other reasons?

During most of the period since 1980, the United States has experienced "twin deficits," with a government budget deficit accompanied by foreign borrowing (negative NX). The example of the year 2000, with its budget surplus accompanied by foreign borrowing, was the exception rather than the rule, but that year 2000 shows that the deficits are not guaranteed to be "twins." Is the experience of the United States unusual? Turn to the box on pp. 148–49 to see how the magic equation operates in Europe and Japan.

2-6 How Much Income Flows from Business Firms to Households?

Income, Leakages, and the Circular Flow

An important lesson of circular flow diagrams like Figure 2-3 (see p. 33) is that the expenditures on GDP (consumption, investment, government spending, and net exports) create income, and this income is available to be spent on another round of expenditure. Households receive only part of the GDP generated by business firms; the rest leaks out of the circular flow in the form of tax revenue for government and saving that provides funds to the capital market. Recall from equation (2.4) that total leakages (taxes and saving) must by definition equal total nonconsumption spending, also called *injections*.

Table 2-1 provides a concise summary of the steps by which income travels from business firms to households. Down the left-hand side are the various concepts of total income; these differ depending on which tax and saving leakages are included. The three remaining columns identify the major types of saving and tax leakages, as well as transfer payments (which work like taxes in reverse).

Depreciation (consumption of fixed capital) represents the part of the capital stock used up due to obsolescence and physical wear.

Net domestic product (NDP) is equal to GDP minus depreciation.

Line 1 starts with GDP, the total amount of income created by domestic production. The first leakage, on line 2, is for **depreciation**, sometimes called consumption of fixed capital, which is the amount that business firms must set aside to replace structures and equipment that wear out or become obsolete (like old jet aircraft that still work but use too much fuel or make too much noise). Since depreciation deductions are not counted as corporate profits, such deductions do not count as income. What remains after depreciation deductions appears on line 3, and is called **net domestic product (NDP)**. This represents how much we produce each year after setting aside enough to replace worn-out and obsolete capital.

In economics, **gross** refers to the inclusion of depreciation; **net** refers to the exclusion of depreciation.

The terms **gross** and **net** in economics usually refer to the inclusion or exclusion of depreciation. Thus the difference between "gross investment" and "net investment," or between "gross saving" and "net saving," is exactly the same type of distinction as that between GDP and NDP.

2-6 How Much Income Flows from Business Firms to Households? 37

Table 2-1 Households Get What Remains After All the Leakages

Concept	Leakage into saving	Leakage into taxes	Transfers from government
1. Gross domestic product (11,814.9)			
2. Less:	→ Depreciation (consumption of fixed capital, 1497.9)		
3. Equals: Net domestic product (10,317.0)			
4. Less:		→ Indirect business taxes (799.6)	
5. Equals: Domestic income (9,517.4)			
6. Less:	→ Undistributed profits (440.7)	→ Social Security and corporate taxes (1,089.3)	
7. Plus:			← Transfer payments and interest (1,713.0)
8. Equals: Personal income (9,700.4)			
9. Less:		→ Personal income taxes (1,048.9)	
10. Equals: Personal disposable income (8,651.5)			
Divided among:	→ Personal saving (63.4)		
11. Personal consumption expenditure (8,282.5)			
12. Interest and personal transfer payments (305.6)			

Note: 2004:Q3 amounts in $ billions are shown in parentheses. Several minor items are included with larger items.
Source: www.bea.gov, NIPA tables 1.7.5, 1.12, and 2.1.

Next, line 4 in Table 2-1 deducts indirect business taxes, which include state and local sales and property taxes. These tax payments are not available as income to households or business firms. Only what is left over, called **domestic income** (line 5), is available to provide net income to the domestic factors of production (labor and capital) that produce current output.

By far the most important portion of domestic income is compensation paid to employees (which includes wages, salaries, and fringe benefits). Next in order of importance are net interest income, proprietors' income (from small businesses like farms and shops), corporate profits, and rental income.

Domestic income is the earnings of domestic factors of production, computed as net domestic product, minus indirect business taxes, which are taxes levied on business sales.

From Domestic Income to Personal Income

Not all of domestic income is paid out to households as personal income, and personal income also includes some receipts by households that are not

38 Chapter 2 • The Measurement of Income, Prices, and Unemployment

counted in GDP or domestic income. Lines 6 and 7 in Table 2-1 explain these differences. First, part of domestic income is kept by corporations in the form of undistributed profits—that is, the part of corporate profits that is not paid as dividends to stockholders or as corporate taxes to the government. Undistributed profits are a type of saving leakage, providing funding for the capital market to finance investment spending.

Next, large amounts flow to the government in the form of corporate and Social Security tax payments, then back from the government to households in the form of transfer payments like Social Security and unemployment benefits. Government funds also are paid out for interest on the national debt. Adjusting domestic income for these deductions and additions yields **personal income**, the sum of income payments to households (line 8). Personal income represents the current flow of purchasing power to households coming from *both* the productive activities of business firms *and* transfers from the government sector.

All personal income is not available to households to spend, first because they must pay personal income taxes to the government (line 9). What remains is one of the most important concepts in national income accounting, **personal disposable income** (line 10). This is available for households to use in the three ways shown at the bottom of Table 2-1: consumption expenditure, personal interest and transfer payments, and personal saving (lines 11 and 12).

The total saving and tax leakages (with transfers treated as a negative tax) are symbolized as $S + T$ in equation (2.4) on p. 34 which shows that, by definition, they must be equal to nonconsumption spending (injections), symbolized by $I + G + NX$. This is the leakages–injections identity, for which we use the easy-to-remember name, the magic equation.

Personal income is the income received by households from all sources, including earnings and transfer payments.

Personal disposable income is personal income minus personal income tax payments.

2-7 Nominal GDP, Real GDP, and the GDP Deflator

Thus far, all the terms and relationships of national income accounting apply to a particular time period (a quarter or a year) and are measured at the prices actually paid by households and firms. Any economic magnitude measured at the prices actually paid is described by the adjective **nominal**. For instance, **nominal GDP** is the total amount of current product valued at the prices actually paid on the market.

Nominal is an adjective that modifies any economic magnitude measured in current prices.

Nominal GDP is the value of gross domestic product in current (actual) prices.

Real and Nominal Magnitudes

Nominal amounts are not very useful for economic analysis because they can increase either when people buy more physical goods and services—more cars, steaks, and haircuts—or when prices rise. An increase in my nominal spending on consumption goods from $20,000 in 2004 to $25,000 in 2005 might indicate that I became able to buy more items, or it could simply mean that I had to pay higher prices in 2005 for the same items purchased in 2004.

Are we better off if we spend more money? Or have price increases chewed up all our higher spending, leaving us no better off than before? Changes in nominal magnitudes cannot answer these questions; they hide more than they reveal. So economists concentrate on changes in real magnitudes, which eliminate the influence of year-to-year changes in prices and reflect true changes in the number, size, and quality of items purchased.

Real GDP and Real Output

To focus on changes in production and eliminate the influence of changing prices, we need a measure of real gross domestic product, or real GDP. Like any real magnitude, real GDP is expressed in the prices of an arbitrarily chosen base year. The official measures of GDP in the United States currently use 2000 as the base year. Real GDP for every year, whether 1929 or 2005, is measured by taking the production of that particular year expressed at the constant prices of 2000. For instance, 2005 real GDP measured in 2000 prices represents the amount that the actual 2005 production of goods and services would have cost if each item *had been sold at its 2000 price.*

Since prices usually increase each year, nominal GDP is higher than real GDP for years after 2000. Similarly, nominal GDP is lower than real GDP for years before 2000. You can see this regular pattern in Figure 2-4, which displays nominal and real GDP for each year since 1900. Only in 2000 are nominal and real GDP the same.

The ratio of nominal GDP to real GDP is a price index called the **implicit GDP deflator**, and this is displayed as the orange line in Figure 2-4. The implicit GDP deflator measures the ratio of the prices actually paid in a particular year to the prices paid in the base year 2000. For instance, in 1959 nominal GDP was about one-fifth of real GDP, indicating that prices actually paid in 1959 were about one-fifth of the prices that would have been paid in 2000 for the same goods and services.

Later on we will consider other real magnitudes, such as real consumption and the real money supply. An alternative label for real magnitudes is constant-dollar; in contrast, nominal magnitudes are usually called current-dollar. To summarize:

> The **implicit GDP deflator** is the economy's aggregate price index and is defined as the ratio of nominal GDP to chain-weighted real GDP.

Alternative labels for magnitudes			
Items measured in prices of a single year	Constant-dollar	or	Real
Items measured in actual prices paid in each separate year	Current-dollar	or	Nominal

Self-Test

Without looking at Figure 2-4, you should now be able to answer the following:

1. Is the implicit GDP deflator greater or less than 1.00 in every year before 2000? In every year after 2000?
2. In what year is the implicit GDP deflator equal to exactly 1.00?

2-8 How We Measure Real GDP and the Inflation Rate

Clearly, nominal GDP is of no interest by itself. We must find some way of separating its movements into those caused by changes in real GDP and those caused by inflation. Only if we succeed in making this "split" of nominal GDP changes will we be able to identify separately the growth rate of total output, or real GDP, and the inflation rate.

40 Chapter 2 • The Measurement of Income, Prices, and Unemployment

Nominal GDP Always Grows Faster than Real GDP When Prices Rise

Figure 2-4 Nominal GDP, Real GDP, and the Implicit GDP Deflator, 1900–2004

Notice how the nominal GDP line lies below the real GDP line before 2000 but lies above the real GDP line after 2000. This reflects the fact that before 2000 the current prices used to measure nominal GDP were lower than the 2000 prices used to measure real GDP. After 2000, the current prices used to measure nominal GDP were higher than the 2000 prices used to measure real GDP. Notice how the nominal GDP line crosses the real GDP line in 2000, the same year that the GDP deflator attains the value of 1.0.

Source: Appendix Table A-1.

Why We Care About Real GDP and Inflation

As we learned at the beginning of this chapter, we care about real GDP because its movements create a mirror image movement in the opposite direction in the unemployment rate, one of the three key macroeconomic concepts introduced in Chapter 1. Further, we care about accurate measurements of real GDP, since they are essential to measuring productivity, or output per hour, the third of our central macro concepts.

The inflation rate is the second of our three central macroeconomic concepts. Very fast inflation can destroy a society, as in the German hyperinflation of 1922–23 (see pp. 16–17). Repeated bouts of rapid inflation in several Latin American countries have been a major hindrance in achieving economic growth and development. Even in the United States, inflation was so rapid, particularly in the 1970s and early 1980s, that draconian measures were taken to stop the inflation, including unprecedented levels of interest rates that decimated the construction and auto industries. Fast inflation is bad because of the direct harm it causes, and because of the indirect harm done by measures taken to stop it.

How We Calculate Changes in Real GDP

Real GDP cannot be observed directly. No one can see, feel, or touch it. There's an old saying that "you can't add apples and oranges." Real GDP carries that saying to its limit, since real GDP consists not just of apples and oranges, but also computers, electricity, haircuts, restaurant meals, and thousands of other goods and services that can't be added directly. The only way to combine the different products is to place a value on each component of GDP, and that requires using the prices of the goods and services produced. However, since prices are constantly changing, our measure of real GDP and its changes will depend on which time period we choose to take the prices for this essential valuation of the components of GDP.

Table 2-2 shows how the change in real GDP between year 1 and year 2 differs, depending on the prices that are used. Lines 1 and 2 show the hypothetical prices and quantities of oranges and apples used in this imaginary two-good economy. Notice that the price of oranges doubles between year 1 and year 2, while the price of apples goes up only 25 percent (from $0.20 to $0.25). As a result, the consumption of oranges drops in year 2 while the consumption of apples doubles. As you will see, the change in measured real GDP between years 1 and 2 depends on the importance we assign to the big decline in orange consumption and the big increase in apple consumption.

One approach, which was used until recently to calculate real GDP in the United States, was to hold the value of all products fixed over all years at the prices of a single year. The actual dollars spent on oranges, apples, and total fruit are shown on line 3 of the table. The expenditures, measured in fixed year 1 prices, are shown on line 4.a. This yields an increase in real GDP in year 2 (measured in the constant prices of year 1) of 20 percent, since the ratio of year 2 expenditures to year 1 expenditures ($6.00/$5.00) is 1.20. This gives us line 6.a, showing that real GDP, using year 1 prices, increases from 1.00 in year 1 to 1.20 in year 2.

But we get a different answer if we measure constant-dollar expenditures in each year using fixed year 2 prices. As shown on line 4.b, expenditures in year 2

Table 2-2 Calculation of Fixed-Weight and Chain-Weighted Real GDP and GDP Deflators in an Imaginary Economy Producing Only Oranges and Apples

	Year 1	Year 2
1. Prices		
a. Oranges	$0.10	$0.20
b. Apples	0.20	0.25
2. Quantities		
a. Oranges	30	20
b. Apples	10	20
3. Current-dollar expenditures		
a. Oranges (1.a times 2.a)	$3.00	$4.00
b. Apples (1.b times 2.b)	2.00	5.00
c. Total: Nominal GDP	5.00	9.00
4. Constant-dollar expenditures each year		
a. At fixed year 1 prices	$5.00	$6.00
b. At fixed year 2 prices	8.50	9.00
5. Expenditures each year		
a. At fixed year 1 quantities	$5.00	$8.50
b. At fixed year 2 quantities	6.00	9.00
6. Real GDP (index, year 1 = 1.00)		
a. At fixed year 1 prices	1.00	1.20
b. At fixed year 2 prices	1.00	1.06
c. Chain-weighted (geometric mean, 6.a and 6.b)	1.00	1.13
7. GDP deflator (index, year 1 = 1.00)		
a. At fixed year 1 quantities	1.00	1.70
b. At fixed year 2 quantities	1.00	1.50
c. Chain-weighted (geometric mean, 7.a and 7.b)	1.00	1.60
8. Additional indexes, year 1 = 1.00		
a. Nominal GDP (3.c)	1.00	1.80
b. Implicit GDP deflator (8.a/6.c)	1.00	1.59

Sources, by line, for Table 2-2:
4.a. Year 1 same as 3c. Year 2 ($.10 \times 20 + .20 \times 20 = 6.00$)
4.b. Year 2 same as 3c. Year 1 ($.20 \times 30 + .25 \times 10 = 8.50$)
5.a. Year 1 same as 3c. Year 2 ($.20 \times 30 + .25 \times 10 = 8.50$)
5.b. Year 2 same as 3c. Year 1 ($.10 \times 20 + .20 \times 20 = 6.00$)
6.a. Year 2 divided by year 1 from line 4a, $6.00/5.00 = 1.20$
6.b. Year 2 divided by year 1 from line 4b, $9.00/8.50 = 1.06$
6.c. Year 2 is geometric mean of year 2 from the two lines above, $\sqrt{1.20 \times 1.06}$
7.a. Year 2 from line 5a, $8.50/5.00 = 1.70$
7.b. Year 2 from line 5b, $9.00/6.00 = 1.50$
7.c. Year 2 is geometric mean of year 2 from the two lines above, $\sqrt{1.70 \times 1.50}$

increase from $8.50 to $9.00. This yields an increase in real GDP in year 2 (measured in the constant prices of year 2) of 6 percent, since the ratio of year 2 expenditures to year 1 expenditures ($9.00/$8.50) is 1.059. Why does this second method give us a lower estimate of the increase in real GDP? This occurs because year 2 prices are relatively lower for apples compared to oranges, and using year 2 prices places a lower importance on the big jump in apple consumption.

This example shows a general tendency—that choosing the prices of a later year tends to give us a lower increase in real GDP, since the later year places a lower valuation on the quantities that have increased most rapidly. This is particularly important in recent years in actual calculations of real GDP, since the prices of some goods, such as personal computers, TV sets, and telephone equipment, have been declining rapidly in contrast to continuous increases in the prices of many other goods and services.

The Chain-Weighted Calculation of Real GDP

Which is the correct measure of the increase in real GDP in this example? Is 20 percent correct or is 6 percent? The startling fact is that *there is no single answer to this question*, because the prices of each year are equally valid as alternative ways to value the quantities actually produced. A reasonable compromise is to average the two answers together. To do this, economists have long known that the best type of average is a geometric average, which is obtained by multiplying the two answers together and then talking the square root, that is:

$$\sqrt{1.20 \times 1.06} = 1.13.^5$$

The United States now calculates real GDP using this technique of geometric averaging across hundreds of different types of products. The outcome is called **chain-weighted real GDP**, because the weights move forward from year to year. For instance, the percentage change in real GDP between 2004 and 2005 uses a geometric average of 2004 and 2005 price weights. Then the percentage change in real GDP between 2005 and 2006 shifts to a geometric average of 2005 and 2006 price weights. The resulting percentage changes are chained together into an index of real GDP, moving forward and backward from the base year of 2000.

Chain-weighted real GDP is calculated by valuing changes in quantities by the average of prices charged at the beginning and end of the period of change.

The Implicit Deflator and the Chain-Weighted Deflator

The method illustrated in line 6.c. of Table 2-2 yields the chain-weighted measure of real GDP. There are two different GDP deflators. One, the implicit GDP deflator, is simply the ratio of nominal GDP to chain-weighted real GDP.

The implicit deflator which is plotted in Figure 2-4 on p. 40, tells us the ratio of prices actually charged in any single year (say, 1959) to the prices charged in the base year 2000. For instance, the implicit GDP deflator in 1959 was 0.208, the ratio of actual nominal GDP ($506.6 billion) to spending for the same year measured in 2000 prices ($2,441.3 billion):

$$\frac{\text{implicit GDP}}{\text{deflator for 1959}} = 0.208 = \frac{506.6 \text{ billion}}{2{,}441.3 \text{ billion}} = \frac{\text{nominal GDP}}{\text{real GDP}}$$

In words, this equation states that the implicit GDP deflator in 1959 was 0.208 because 1959 nominal GDP was 20.8 percent of the value of the 1959 real GDP. This percentage in turn reflects the fact that the average level of prices in 1959 was about one-fifth of the level of the base year 2000.

---

[5] Take a scientific calculator and check the answer for yourself. Multiplying 1.20 by 1.06 and then taking the square root yields an answer of 1.128. An alternative method to arrive at exactly the same answer is to take the natural logarithms of 1.20 and 1.06, which are 0.1823 and 0.0583, respectively, add them together (0.2406), divide by 2 (0.1203), and then take the antilogarithm (e^x) of the answer, yielding 1.128.

How to Calculate Inflation, Real GDP Growth, or Any Other Growth Rate

Often you will want to calculate a percentage growth rate, whether of the U.S. rate of inflation, real GDP, or even your own income over a period of years. In this section we will learn a very simple formula that will allow you to calculate the growth rate of *anything* over any period, no matter how long or short, and convert it to an annual rate.

In this book we will use lowercase letters, say x, to designate the growth rate of a variable, the level of which is called the same uppercase letter X. Let's say that we have been given the value of the GDP deflator for 1974 as 34.7 and for 1975 as 38.0, and we have been asked to calculate the inflation rate for 1975. (You will find GDP deflator data for these and many other years in Appendix Table A-1 in the back of this book.)

The general formula to calculate the percentage annual growth rate of any variable X at a time period t from another period s years earlier (call this $t-s$) is as follows:

General Form
$$x_t = 100\, LN(X_t/X_{t-s})/s$$
Numerical Example
$$9.08 = 100\, LN(38.0/34.7)/1.0$$

Here LN means "natural logarithm" and is a function found on any scientific calculator. The answer to the example is found simply by taking the ratio $38.0/34.7 = 1.0951$ and then pushing the "LN" button, which yields 0.0908 and finally multiplying that result by 100.

Exactly the same formula can be used to calculate the annual rate of inflation between two adjacent quarters. Let us take the level of the GDP deflator for the first quarter of 2004, abbreviated "2004:Q1" from Appendix Table A-2, which is 107.31. The value for the next quarter, 2004:Q2 is 108.17. What is the annual rate of inflation between those two quarters?

General Form
$$x_t = 100\, LN(X_t/X_{t-s})/s$$
Numerical Example
$$3.19 = 100\, LN(108.17/107.31)/0.25$$

The method is exactly the same. The only difference is that now we are comparing two adjacent quarters rather than two adjacent years, and so $s = 0.25$ instead of $s = 1$ as before.

Our final exercise is to calculate the average annual growth rate of U.S. real GDP from 1875 to 2004, using the data in Appendix Table A-1:

General Form
$$x_t = 100\, LN(X_t/X_{t-s})/s$$
Numerical Example
$$3.47 = 100\, LN(10{,}842/123)/129$$

Again, this is exactly the same formula, now with $s = 129$ since there are 129 years between 1875 and 2004. Despite the fact that real GDP in 2004 was 88.1 times larger than in 1875, such a long period elapsed between those two years that the annual growth rate was a mere 3.47 percent.

The extremely useful formula discussed in this box can be used for any calculation involving growth rates, not just for such macroeconomic concepts as the price level or real GDP, but to calculate the annual rate of return of an investment over any period of time, even for a single day.

The second type of GDP deflator is calculated directly from the prices and quantities of the goods and services in the economy. Returning to the example of oranges and apples in Table 2-2, we can calculate in line 5.a and 5.b the expenditures in each year using *actual prices* of each year but the *fixed quantities* of either year. Line 5.a shows that expenditures using actual prices, but fixed year 1 quantities, increase from $5.00 in year 1 to $8.50 in year 2, an increase of 70 percent. Accordingly, this method yields a price index in year 2 of 1.70, when year 1 is used as a base of 1.00; these indexes are shown separately on line 7.a. Likewise, using year 2 quantities gives us a price index in year 2 of 1.50 (line 7.b).

Once again, neither answer is correct. The best approximation is to take a geometric average; this results in a price index of 1.60, as shown in line 7.c. This is the method used to construct the **chain-weighted GDP deflator**. Normally, the implicit and chain-weighted deflators give very close to the same answer. For instance, in our example the implicit deflator in year 2 is 1.593 (line 8.b), while the chain-weighted deflator is 1.60 (line 7.c).

The rate of inflation is simply the percentage growth rate of the chain-weighted GDP deflator. The box on p. 45 explains how to calculate the growth rate of any magnitude.

The **chain-weighted GDP deflator** is calculated by weighting price changes by the average of quantities sold at the beginning and end of the period of change.

2-9 Measuring Unemployment

The unemployment rate is the first of the central macro concepts introduced in Chapter 1. Families dread the financial and emotional disruption caused by layoffs, so news of an increase in the unemployment rate creates public concern and plummeting popularity ratings for incumbent politicians. Because of widespread public awareness, the unemployment rate is generally considered the most important of the central macro concepts (although slow growth in productivity may have a greater impact on the lives of more people in the long run). In this section we learn how the unemployment rate is measured.

The Unemployment Survey

Many people wonder how the government determines facts such as "the teenage unemployment rate in February 2005 was 17.5 percent," because they themselves have never spoken to a government agent about their own experiences of employment, unemployment, and time in school. It would be too costly to contact everyone in the country every month; the government attempts to reach each household to collect information only once each decade when it takes the decennial Census of Population. However, it would not be enough to collect information just once every ten years, because then policymakers would have no guidance for conducting current policy.

As a compromise, each month 1,500 Census Bureau workers interview about 60,000 households, or about 1 in every 1,400 households in the country. Each month one-fourth of the households in the sample are replaced, so that no family is interviewed more than four months in a row. The laws of statistics imply that an average from a survey of a sample of households of this size comes very close to the true figure that would be revealed by a costly complete census.

Questions asked in the survey. The interviewer first asks each separate household member, "What were you doing most of last week—working, keeping house, going to school, or something else?" Anyone who has done any work at all for pay during the past week, whether part-time (even one hour per week), full-time, or temporary work, is counted as employed.

For those who say they did no work, the next question is, "Did you have a job from which you were temporarily absent or on layoff last week?" If the person is awaiting recall from a layoff or has obtained a new job but is waiting for it to begin, he or she is counted as unemployed.

If the person has neither worked nor been absent from a job, the next question is, "Have you been looking for work in the last four weeks, and if so, what have you been doing in the last four weeks to find work?" A person who has not been ill and has searched for a job by applying to an employer, registering with an employment agency, checking with friends, or other specified job-search activities is counted as unemployed. The remaining people who are neither employed nor unemployed, mainly homemakers who do not seek paid work, students, disabled people, and retired people, fall in the category of "not in the labor force."

Definitions based on the interview. Despite the intricacy of questions asked by the interviewer, the concept is simple: People with jobs are employed; people who do not have jobs and are looking for jobs are **unemployed**; people who meet neither labor-market test are not in the labor force. The **total labor force** is the total of the civilian employed, the armed forces, and the unemployed. Thus the entire population aged 16 and over falls into one of four categories:

> The **unemployed** are those without jobs who either are on temporary layoff or have taken specific actions to look for work.

> The **total labor force** is the total of the civilian employed, the armed forces, and the unemployed.

1. Total labor force
   a. Civilian employed
   b. Armed forces
   c. Unemployed
2. Not in the labor force

> The **unemployment rate** is the ratio of the number unemployed to the number in the labor force, expressed as a percentage.

The actual **unemployment rate** is defined as the ratio

$$U = \frac{\text{number of unemployed}}{\text{civilian employed + unemployed}}$$

Example: In February 2005 the BLS reported an unemployment rate of 5.4 percent. This was calculated as the ratio

$$U = \frac{\text{number of unemployed}}{\text{civilian employed + unemployed}} = \frac{7{,}988{,}000}{140{,}144{,}000 + 7{,}988{,}000}$$

or

$$U = 5.4 \text{ percent}$$

The labor force participation rate is the ratio of the total labor force (civilian employed, armed forces, and the unemployed) to the population aged 16 or over. Those who do not participate in the labor force include those above age 15 who are in school, retired individuals, people who do not work because they are raising children or otherwise choose to stay at home, and those who cannot work because they are ill, disabled, or have given up on finding jobs. In February 2005 this rate was 65.8 percent.

Flaws in the definition. The government's unemployment measure sounds relatively straightforward, but unfortunately it disguises almost as much as it reveals:

1. *The unemployment rate by itself is not a measure of the social distress caused by the loss of a job.* Each person who lacks a job and is looking for one is counted as "1.0 unemployed people," whether the person is the head of a household responsible for feeding numerous dependents or a 16-year-old looking only for a 10-hour-per-week part-time job to provide pocket money. Only a minority of the unemployed can be described as workers who have lost one job and are looking for another.

2. *The government's unemployment concept misses some of the people hurt by a recession.* Some suffer a cut in hours, being forced by their employers to shift from full-time to part-time work. Still counted as employed, these "involuntary part-time" workers never enter the unemployment statistics.

3. *A person lacking a job must have performed particular specified actions to look for a job during the past four weeks.* What about people who have looked and looked and have given up, convinced that no job is available? They are not counted as unemployed at all. They simply disappear from the labor force, entering the category of "not in the labor force." Those out of the labor force who would like to work but have given up on the job search are sometimes called "discouraged workers" or the "disguised unemployed."

Do the flaws matter? Since the official concept of the unemployment rate omits those who are involuntarily working part-time when they would prefer full-time employment, and also omits the discouraged workers, it is generally agreed that the official concept understates the total amount of unemployment. Yet this does not turn out to be very important, since a broader measure of unemployment, which includes the effect of involuntary part-time work as well as the discouraged workers, exhibits cyclical fluctuations similar to those of the official concept of the unemployment rate. Recessions and expansions occur at the same time. The primary impediment to achieving low unemployment, which is the tendency of the economy to generate accelerating inflation when the unemployment rate becomes too low, is completely independent of the particular unemployment measure that is used.

2-10 Case Study

Conflicting Measurements: Was the 2002–04 Recovery "Jobless" or Not?

A frequent point of contention in the 2004 presidential election campaign between George W. Bush and John Kerry was whether the economy was strong or weak. While real GDP had grown at a relatively rapid rate of 3.4 percent per annum during the first three years after the 2001 recession, employment had not, or at least one measure of employment had not.

The previous section describes the "household" survey of the government's Bureau of Labor Statistics (BLS). The same survey that collects data on the unemployment rate also, through the same set of questions, obtains an estimate of the total level of employment. The result of the BLS household survey is shown as the blue line in Figure 2-5. This measure of "household employment" was very weak in the first two years of the economic recovery that began in early 1991, then grew rapidly until early 2001, fell until early 2002, and then began a steady recovery. By 2004:Q4, household employment was 1.9 million (or about 1.4 percent) *higher* than in the quarter when the recession began, 2001:Q1.

A different story is told by the orange line, the employment total developed from the BLS "payroll employment survey," hence the nickname "payroll

48 Chapter 2 • The Measurement of Income, Prices, and Unemployment

Conflicting Views of Employment Growth

[Graph showing two lines from 1990 to 2004. Y-axis: Employment as a percentage of 2001:Q1 value, ranging from 80 to 105. Household survey (blue line) and Payroll survey (orange line).]

Figure 2-5 Employment from the Household and Payroll Survey, 1990–2004

The blue line displays total employment as measured by the household survey (the same survey that is the source for the unemployment rate). The orange line displays total employment as measured by the payroll survey. Both series are set equal to 100 in the first quarter of 2001 in order to highlight that the payroll measure grew faster in the 1990s but grew more slowly after 2001.

Source: Bureau of Labor Statistics.

employment." The payroll employment survey is often considered more reliable than the household survey, simply because its sample is much larger. In contrast to the household survey, with its survey of 60,000 households, the payroll survey is based on 400,000 establishments that submit more than 8 million records of employees.

In Figure 2-5 the orange payroll employment line grew much faster than the blue household employment line from 1992 to the economic peak in early 2001. Afterward, its behavior went in the opposite direction. Even as late as 2004:Q4, payroll employment was still 0.2 million *below* its peak of early 2001, in contrast to the 1.9 million *increase* in the household survey.

This discrepancy occupied center stage during the 2004 presidential election. Democrats argued that the pessimistic record of the payroll survey was more accurate, whereas Republicans supported the more optimistic verdict of the household survey. Who was right? A nonpartisan verdict was rendered by the Chair of the Federal Reserve Board, who believed that the payroll survey was more accurate.

There is at least one systematic reason why the household survey could register a faster increase in employment during the recovery from a recession, as in 2002–04. First, many employees of large firms who were laid off or fired during the 2001 recession went into business for themselves as consultants. By moving from establishments covered by the payroll survey to self-employment, they could have been missed by the payroll survey yet included in the household survey. Second, it is well known that the payroll survey is based on a sample of business establishments that becomes increasingly obsolete over time as some businesses fail and new ones are started up before the survey finds out about them.

Overall, the big discrepancy between the payroll and household surveys had not been reconciled as of early 2005. The payroll survey is revised each year as new data become available, and it is possible that the "truth" about employment in 2002–04 will look something like the *average* of the blue and orange lines in Figure 2-5.

Summary

1. This chapter is concerned with the definition and measurement of national income—what is included and excluded, and why, as well as with the measurement of real GDP, inflation, and the unemployment rate.

2. A flow magnitude is any money payment, physical good, or service that flows from one economic unit to another per unit of time. A flow is distinguished from a stock, which is an economic magnitude in the possession of an individual or firm at a moment of time.

3. Final product (GDP) consists of all currently produced goods and services sold through the market but not resold during the current time period. By counting intermediate goods only once, and by including only final purchases, we avoid double-counting and ensure that the value of final product and total income created (value added) are equal.

4. Leakages out of income available for consumption spending are, by definition, exactly balanced by injections of nonconsumption spending. This equality of leakages and injections is guaranteed by the accounting methods used.

5. In the same way, by definition, total income (consumption plus leakages) equals total expenditure (consumption plus injections). Injections of nonconsumption spending fall into three categories—private domestic investment (on business equipment and structures, residential housing, and inventory accumulation); foreign investment or net exports; and government spending on goods and services. The definitions require private saving to exceed private investment (domestic and foreign) by the amount of the government deficit.

6. GNP includes all income received by U.S. residents, whereas GDP includes only economic production within the borders of the United States.

7. Net domestic product (NDP) is obtained by deducting depreciation from GDP. Deduction of indirect business taxes from NDP yields domestic income, the sum of all net incomes earned by domestic factors of production in producing current output. If we deduct corporate undistributed profits, corporate income taxes, and Social Security taxes, and add in transfer payments, we arrive at personal income, the sum of all income payments to individuals. Personal disposable income is simply personal income after the deduction of personal income taxes.

8. Chain-weighted GDP is calculated by valuing changes in quantities by the average of prices charged at the beginning and end of the period of the change.

9. The chain-weighted GDP deflator is calculated by weighting price changes by the average of quantities sold between the beginning and end of the period of the change.

10. The implicit GDP deflator is defined as nominal GDP in actual current prices divided by chain-weighted real GDP.

11. Those aged 16 and over are counted as unemployed if they are temporarily laid off or want a job, and take specified actions to find a job. The unemployment rate is the number of unemployed expressed as a percent of the total number of persons employed and unemployed.

Concepts

consumption expenditures
flow magnitude
stock
National Income and Product Accounts
final product
transfer payments
final good
intermediate good
private investment
inventory investment
fixed investment
personal saving

exports
imports
net exports
net foreign investment
gross national product (GNP)
magic equation
leakages
injections
depreciation (consumption of fixed capital)
net domestic product
gross
net

domestic income
personal income
personal disposable income
nominal
nominal GDP
chain-weighted real GDP
chain-weighted GDP deflator
implicit GDP deflator
unemployed
total labor force
unemployment rate

Questions

1. Explain the difference between a stock magnitude and a flow magnitude. Label each of the following as either a stock or a flow:
   (a) depreciation
   (b) saving
   (c) wealth
   (d) government debt
   (e) government deficit
   (f) current account deficit
   (g) savings
   (h) money supply
   (i) labor force
   (j) labor services
   (k) net exports
   (l) net taxes

2. Decide whether each of the following transactions is included in GDP. If the transaction is included, determine which component of final spending it represents. If the transaction is excluded from GDP, explain why.
   (a) Your local ice cream maker buys peaches to make peach ice cream.
   (b) Your local ice cream maker buys a new and improved ice cream maker.
   (c) Your buy peach ice cream from your local ice cream maker.
   (d) Your local ice cream maker sells peach ice cream to a restaurant that serves peach smoothies.
   (e) Your cousin in Canada buys peach ice cream from your local ice cream maker.
   (f) You buy a used book to learn how to make peach ice cream.
   (g) You buy peaches to make peach ice cream for yourself.
   (h) You buy a new ice cream maker to make peach ice cream for yourself.
   (i) You give some of your peach ice cream to your cousin when she visits from Canada.

3. Explain whether each of the following would be included in GDP, GNP, or both of the United States.
   (a) The salary of an American who is working in Japan for Honda (a Japanese company).
   (b) The profits that Honda earns from its production of cars in Ohio.
   (c) The value of the software that Microsoft sells to Honda for use in its corporate headquarters in Japan.

4. Explain why the value of goods and services purchased by Europeans vacationing in the United States would be considered U.S. exports and the money that Americans spend traveling overseas are considered part of U.S. imports.

5. Assume that the GDP of the United States is eight times as large as the GDP of China. Can you conclude, based on this information, that the average individual in the United States is eight times as well off as the average individual in China? Why or why not?

6. The term "underground economy" encompasses economic activity that people do not report because it is illegal or because they hope to avoid paying taxes.

Though the size of the underground economy is unknown, it may be a sizable fraction of the nation's GDP. How does the underground economy affect the accuracy of official measures of GDP, unemployment, and productivity, and complicate the tasks of policymakers?

7. If all other things remain equal in the current period (GDP, G, T, S, C, etc.), what do you predict will happen to the level of domestic investment if the exchange rate between the dollar and the yen appreciates? Explain how it is possible for consumption (C) to remain constant in this situation. What do you predict will happen to GDP in the next period?

8. (a) Savings and taxes are called leakages. From what do they leak? Where do they go? Imports are also a leakage. From what do they leak? Where do they go?
   (b) Private domestic investment and government purchases of goods and services are called injections. What are they injections into? From where do they come? Exports are an injection. What are they injections into? From where do they come?

9. When the government runs a budget deficit, funds flow from capital markets to the government as the government borrows from capital markets by selling bonds. Explain how funds flow from the government to the capital markets when the government runs a budget surplus.

10. In the national income and product accounts, personal income is calculated by subtracting from national income any income earned but not received and adding back in any income received but not earned. Explain.

11. Four hundred tires are produced by a tire manufacturer and sold for $75 each to General Motors in December 2004. In February 2005, General Motors puts the tires on 100 newly produced cars and sells each car for $30,000. What is the contribution made to GDP in 2004 and 2005 by the transaction described? (Assume all other components of the cars are produced in 2005.)

12. Starting from the situation depicted in Figure 2-3, assume that business firms produce an additional $500,000 worth of goods, of which only $450,000 are bought during the current year. What are the new values for the following categories?
   (a) income
   (b) consumption expenditure
   (c) personal saving
   (d) investment

13. Suppose that the amount of private saving declines. Explain why at least one of the following must occur: Government saving must increase, private domestic investment must decrease, or net foreign investment must decrease.

14. If you learn that nominal GDP for 2005 is greater than nominal GDP for 2004, what do you know about changes in the level of output during this period? Changes in prices during this period? Would your answer change if it were real GDP that had increased in 2005?

15. In late 2003 and early 2004, the Federal Reserve was concerned about the possibility of deflation, which is a general fall in prices. If deflation occurs, explain which grows faster, nominal GDP or real GDP.

16. How do chain-weighted real GDP and the chain-weighted GDP deflator differ from the calculations that government statisticians used formerly to measure aggregate output and inflation? Why were the chain-weighted measures adopted?

17. If the government suddenly decided to include the noncivilian employed, i.e., the armed forces, together with the civilian employed in the denominator of the unemployment rate, what would happen to the unemployment rate?

18. Due to a recession, ABC Enterprises's sales decline. In order to reduce losses, ABC lays off 10 percent of its labor force, including Don, Ellen, and Frank. ABC indicates that it will hire all its workers back within two months. In each of the following cases, explain if the person is employed, unemployed, or not in the labor force.
   (a) Don decides he is going to use the two months to go fishing in Montana.
   (b) Ellen questions whether ABC will really hire her back. She quickly finds another job.
   (c) Frank's wife decides she wants to go back to work, but urges him to go back to school. He agrees and resigns his position at ABC. He also decides to devote all of his efforts to school. His wife starts looking for a job to support them.

Problems

1. Use the following data to answer the following questions (all figures are in billions of dollars):

Item	Amount
Government purchases of goods and services	$1,721.6
Exports	1,096.3
Receipts of factor income from the rest of the world	382.7
Depreciation (consumption of fixed capital)	990.8
Net fixed investment	688.2
Corporate income taxes	265.2
Consumption expenditures	6,739.4
Indirect business taxes	664.6
Imports	1,475.8
Payments of factor income to the rest of the world	343.7
Inventory change	56.5
Social Security contributions	702.7
Undistributed corporate profits (retained earnings)	130.3
Government transfer and interest payments	1,366.3
Personal interest payments	286.2
Personal taxes	1,235.7

   (a) What is gross domestic product?
   (b) What is gross national product?
   (c) What is net domestic product?
   (d) What is domestic income?
   (e) What is personal income? (*Hint:* Personal interest payments are part of the category "transfer payments and interest" in Table 2-1.)
   (f) What is disposable personal income?
   (g) What is personal saving?

2. Assume that gross private domestic investment is $800 billion and the government (state, local, and federal combined) is currently running a $400 billion deficit. If households and businesses are saving $1,000 billion, what is the value of net exports? Use equation (2.5) to explain your answer.

3. You are given the following information:

Year	Private Savings	Net Taxes	Government Purchases Goods and Services	Private Domestic Investment	Net Exports
1997	—	1,575.9	1,594.0	1,387.7	−104.6
1998	1,223.2	1,721.5	1,624.4	—	−203.8
1999	1,186.1	1,847.2	1,686.9	1,642.6	—

   (a) Compute the amount of government saving for the years 1997, 1998, and 1999.
   (b) Using the magic equation and your answer to part a, compute the amount of private saving in 1997.
   (c) Using the magic equation and your answer to part a, compute the amount of gross private investment in 1998.
   (d) Using the magic equation and your answer to part a, compute the amount of net exports in 1999.

4. Assume that a country produces only two goods, automobiles and fast PCs. In year 1, automobiles cost $20,000 each and the PCs cost $3,000 each; 1,000 automobiles and 10,000 PCs are produced. In year 2, the price of automobiles has increased to $22,000; because a new, even faster type of PC is about to be introduced, the price of fast PCs has fallen to $700. In year 2, 1,000 automobiles and 15,000 PCs are produced.
   (a) Fill in the following table.

	Year 1	Year 2
Nominal GDP (Total of current-dollar expenditures)		
Constant-dollar expenditures		
(i) at fixed year 1 prices		
(ii) at fixed year 2 prices		
Expenditures		
(i) at fixed year 1 quantities		
(ii) at fixed year 2 quantities		

   (b) Using the technique of chain-weighting, calculate the percentage change in real GDP between year 1 and year 2.
   (c) Letting year 1 = 1.0, calculate the chain-weighted GDP deflator for year 2.
   (d) Compare the values of the implicit and chain-weighted real GDP deflators for year 2.

5. If nominal GDP is $10,608 and chain-weighted real GDP is $10,400, what is the value of the implicit GDP deflator?

6. Suppose that the implicit GDP deflator equals 1 and real GDP equals 10,000. Calculate the value of nominal GDP.

7. Suppose that the implicit GDP deflator equals 1.025 and nominal GDP equals 11,200. Calculate the value of real GDP.

8. Calculate percentage annual growth rates using the data that follow.

(a) Productivity growth measures increase in output per hour of work. Output per hour was 75.7 in the first quarter of 1973, 103.7 in the first quarter of 1996, and 132.8 in the first quarter of 2004 (1992 = 100). Calculate the average annual rates of productivity growth between 1973 and 1996 and between 1996 and 2004. Using your answers, explain during which of these two periods living standards rose more quickly.

(b) The Consumer Price Index was 53.8 in 1975, 82.4 in 1980, 107.6 in 1985, 130.7 in 1990, 152.4 in 1995, and 172.2 in 2000 (1982–84 = 100). During which five-year interval was the annual inflation rate the highest? During which interval was the average annual inflation rate the lowest? What was the trend in inflation over the last quarter of the twentieth century? (*Hint:* The inflation rate is the annual percentage change in the price index.)

(c) In the second quarter of 2000, real GDP (measured in billions of 2000 dollars) was 9,847.9. In the second quarter of 2001, real GDP was 9,905.4, and in the third quarter of 2001, it was 9,871.1. Calculate the percentage annual growth rates between the second quarters of 2000 and 2001, and the second and third quarters of 2001. Interpret your results.

9. How long will it take real GDP to double if it grows at the following rates?
   (a) 4 percent per year
   (b) 6 percent per year
   (c) 8 percent per year

10. In 2003, civilian employment was 137,736,000, and unemployment was 8,774,000. What was the unemployment rate?

Self-Test Answers

p. 27 (1) The payment of the $10 bill to the barber is a flow of money shown by the red line labeled consumption expenditure. The provision of the haircut by the barber for the student is shown by the orange line labeled product. The barber's income of $10 is shown by the green line labeled income and the barber's provision of labor services to perform the haircut is shown by the purple line labeled labor services. (2) Alison provides labor services, shown by the purple line, to the summer camp, in return for which she receives income ($8 per hour for each hour she works) from the summer camp, shown by the green line. The camp fees paid by parents are part of consumer expenditures, shown by the red line, and the camp services are part of product, shown by the orange line.

p. 30 (1)(2) Included in GDP for the first quarter of 2005 is the change in the value of the grocer's inventories between December 31, 2004 and March 31, 2005. This is $12.00 minus $8.00, or $4.00. If the level of inventories had fallen, instead of rising as in the example, inventory investment would have been negative. (3) The grocer's inventory charge contributes $4.00 to GDP in the first quarter of 2005.

p. 39 (1) Less than 1.0 in every year before 2000; greater than 1.0 in every year after 2000. (2) Equal to 1.0 in 2000.

PART TWO

Income, Interest Rates, Policy, and the Open Economy

CHAPTER 3 Spending, Income, and Interest Rates

CHAPTER 4 Monetary and Fiscal Policy in the *IS-LM* Model

CHAPTER 5 National Saving, the Government Budget, Foreign Borrowing, and the Twin Deficits

CHAPTER 6 International Trade, Exchange Rates, and Macroeconomic Policy

CHAPTER 3

Spending, Income, and Interest Rates

An honest man is one who knows that he can't consume more than he has produced.
—Ayn Rand, 1966

Our introduction to macroeconomics in Chapter 1 distinguished two main groups of issues: those that concern *short-run* business cycles or economic fluctuations and those that concern the economy's *long-run* growth rate and the sources of differences in the standard of living of rich and poor nations. This chapter begins a two-part unit, spanning Chapters 3–9, that develops the theory of business cycles and examines the potential role of monetary and fiscal policy in dampening the amplitude of these cycles. Thus we will be concerned with the *short-run* behavior of the economy for the next several chapters and will return to the sources of *long-run* growth starting in Chapter 10.

3-1 Business Cycles and the Theory of Income Determination

As we learned in Chapter 1, a business cycle refers to the alternation of periods of rapid or slow growth in real GDP. Figure 1-3 contrasts two hypothetical nations to demonstrate the importance of minimizing fluctuations in real GDP, with "Volatilia" showing large swings in real GDP, and "Stabilia" showing much smaller swings because of its more stable economy. Figure 1-4 defines the key terminology of business cycles, describing an economy that starts from a trough in real GDP, proceeds through an expansion that usually lasts several years until real GDP reaches its peak, followed by a recession that only lasts a few quarters until the next trough. In this chapter we start to learn about the origins of business cycles; we put together into a simple economic model the numerous factors that contribute to economic volatility.

The Reduced Volatility of Business Cycles

The goals of monetary and fiscal policy are to dampen business cycles and move toward an ideal world in which real GDP grows steadily from one quarter to the next. The real world as shown in Figure 3-1 is far from that ideal world. Plotted along the red line are changes in real GDP compared with the same quarter one year earlier. Since 1950, the four-quarter growth rate of real GDP has been as high as 12.6 percent and as low as −3.1 percent. Over the

58 Chapter 3 • Spending, Income, and Interest Rates

A History of Volatility in Real GDP Growth

Figure 3-1 Real GDP Growth in the United States, 1950–2004
The shading shows that the growth in real GDP (plotted as the change from four quarters ago) can be divided up into three types of performance. The shaded red periods are when the actual growth rate was faster than the 55-year average of 3.45 percent. The shaded light blue periods are when the actual growth rate was slower than 3.45 percent but greater than zero. The shaded darker blue periods indicate periods of negative real GDP growth and identify recessions.

more recent period since 1980, the range has been between a high of 8.1 percent and a low of −2.8 percent.

A notable feature of Figure 3-1 is that real GDP was much more volatile before 1985 than after. In fact, real GDP growth showed remarkable steadiness between 1992 and 2000, with most quarters relatively close to the 1950–2004 average growth rate of 3.5 percent. Why did real GDP growth become less volatile? What forces dampened the business cycle? These questions help to motivate our study of a simple model showing how real GDP is determined and how monetary and fiscal policy can be used to offset other "shocks" that can raise or lower real GDP growth.

We use this model of income determination in Chapters 3 and 4 to help us distinguish several hypotheses regarding the improved stability of the economy since 1985. We learn that unstable ups and downs of real GDP can be caused by changes in consumer confidence, business optimism, government spending, and foreign events that influence U.S. exports and imports. These shocks to **aggregate demand** (also known as **demand shocks**) are the basic source of business cycles and economic volatility. One possible reason for the improved performance since 1985 might be that demand shocks have become smaller and less important. Another reason might be that monetary and fiscal policy have become more effective, countering demand shocks without delay. A third reason might be some change in conditions that makes monetary and/or fiscal policy more powerful. Our model of income determination allows for all of these possibilities. We learn how demand shocks have a multiplier effect, exacerbating the impact of any given demand shock on real GDP. We learn that the stabilizing impact of monetary and fiscal policy can be strong or weak, depending on particular relationships in the economy.

> **Aggregate demand** is the total amount of desired spending expressed in current (nominal) dollars.
>
> **A demand shock** is a significant change in desired spending by consumers, business firms, the government, or foreigners.

3-2 Income Determination, Unemployment, and the Price Level

We learned at the beginning of this book that the three central macroeconomic concepts are unemployment, inflation, and productivity growth. Yet our theory in this chapter concerns the level of real GDP and real income, not the unemployment rate, inflation, or productivity growth. We postpone our treatment of the determinants of productivity growth as part of our examination of long-run economic growth later in the book, also we postpone our treatment of inflation until Chapters 7–9. Finally, we do not need a separate theory of fluctuations in the unemployment rate, since unemployment is the mirror image of business cycles in real GDP, or more precisely of changes in the difference (gap) between actual and natural real GDP (see Chapter 1, Figure 1-2). When that gap rises into positive territory as the economy expands, the unemployment rate falls; when that gap becomes negative as the economy slides into a recession, the unemployment rate rises. *Thus the key to understanding the causes of fluctuations in unemployment is to develop a theory of fluctuations in real GDP.*

Income Determination and the Price Level

Shocks to aggregate demand can change either real GDP, the price level (GDP deflator), or both. Later we will learn that the division of changes in aggregate demand between changes in real GDP and the price level depends both on shocks to aggregate demand and to **aggregate supply**, the amount that firms are willing to produce at a given price level. Changes in aggregate supply depend on such factors as the costs of production for business firm, including wages and the prices of raw materials such as oil. It makes sense to discuss changes in aggregate demand and in aggregate supply separately. We cover aggregate demand in Chapters 3 and 4 and aggregate supply in Chapters 7 and 8.

> **Aggregate supply** is the amount that firms are willing to produce at any given price level.

As we have learned, economic theory is a process of simplification that allows us to study parts of a problem, one at a time, and then bring together those parts into a more complete model of the economy. In order to focus on changes in aggregate demand, we will make a bold but extremely useful simplifying assumption: *The price level is fixed in the short run.* Because the price level is fixed, *all changes in aggregate demand automatically cause changes in real GDP by the same amount in the same direction.*

$$\text{Changes in Real GDP} = \frac{\text{Changes in Aggregate Demand}}{\text{Fixed Price Level}} \tag{3.1}$$

Many features of the real world support our assumption that the price level is fixed in the short run and that changes in aggregate demand are translated directly into changes in real GDP. Prices in restaurants are printed on menus that are expensive to reprint. Price labels for many products on supermarket shelves are changed infrequently. Prices in mail-order catalogues are set for the entire season until the next catalogue is printed. The most important cost for many business firms is the cost of the wages and salaries paid to workers, and the wage or salary level usually changes only once each year, and some wages are set by labor union contracts that last for as long as three years.

True, the prices of vegetables at the supermarket and of gasoline at the pump can change from day to day, but we gain insight by adhering to the useful simplification that all prices are like those in mail-order catalogues, fixed for a set period of time. Once we have used this simplification to learn about shocks to aggregate demand and the potential role of monetary and fiscal policy in stabilizing the economy, we then will be ready to turn to the role of aggregate supply in determining the division of aggregate demand changes between changes in real GDP and in the price level.

What We Explain and What We Take as Given

Any theoretical model in economics sets limits on what it tries to explain. The limited number of variables to be explained are called **endogenous variables**. The large number of variables that are taken as given and are not explained are called **exogenous variables**.

Endogenous variables are those explained by an economic theory.

Exogenous variables are those that are relevant but whose behavior the theory does not attempt to explain; their values are taken as given.

In macroeconomic theory we begin with a short list of endogenous variables and treat most as exogenous. Gradually, we move some from the exogenous list to the endogenous list as our theory becomes more realistic. In the first part of Chapter 3, we develop a simple model that explains only two endogenous variables, consumption and real GDP. All the other important macroeconomic variables are not explained, that is, they are treated as exogenous variables. This includes not just the price level, which is treated as fixed (as discussed in the previous section), but also investment and interest rates. In the last part of Chapter 3, we move investment to the list of endogenous variables. Then in Chapter 4 a more complete model shifts the interest rate to the list of endogenous variables. In Chapter 7, we complete our process of model building by shifting the price level to the list of endogenous variables.

Throughout our study of business cycles in Chapters 3–9, the key instruments of monetary and fiscal policy will continue to be treated as exogenous, or taken as given. These include the money supply, government spending, and tax rates. Also taken as exogenous is the real GDP of foreign nations that determine the quantity of U.S. exports, as well as potential causes of demand shocks, such as changes in the confidence of consumers about future incomes and jobs and the confidence of business firms about future sales and profits. Now we turn to the simplest version of the theory of income determination that treats only consumption and income (or real GDP) as endogenous and everything else as exogenous.

3-3 Planned Expenditure

Our study of national income accounting in Chapter 2 identified four types of expenditure on GDP. By definition, total expenditure on GDP (E) is equal to the sum of these four components: consumption (C), investment (I), government spending on goods and services (G), and net exports (NX).

$$E \equiv C + I + G + NX \tag{3.2}$$

The Consumption Function

At the beginning, we treat only consumption spending (C) as endogenous, or explained by the theory, and treat the other three types of planned spending as exogenous. An obvious way to explain consumption is that people spend more when their incomes go up and vice versa. The income that matters for consumption decisions is income after taxes, or **disposable personal income**. This can be written as total real income (Y) minus personal taxes paid (T), or $Y - T$.[1]

How do households divide their disposable income between consumption and saving? Households consume a fixed amount that does not depend on their disposable income, plus a fraction of each dollar of disposable income:

General Linear Form
$$C = C_a + c(Y - T) \tag{3.3}$$

The fixed amount is called **autonomous** consumption, abbreviated (C_a), and this is completely independent of disposable income. The amount by which consumption expenditures increase for each extra dollar of disposable income is a fraction called the **marginal propensity to consume**, abbreviated (c). This equation (3.3) says in words that consumption spending (C) equals autonomous consumption (C_a) plus the marginal propensity to consume times disposable income [$c(Y - T)$]. Another name for this last term is **induced consumption**.

The *consumption function* is any relationship that describes the determinants of consumption spending. This function can be written as a general expression, as in equation (3.3), or as a numerical example. For instance, if we choose $500 billion to be the value of autonomous consumption and 0.75 to be the value of the marginal propensity to consume, the consumption function can be written

Numerical Example
$$C = 500 + 0.75\,(Y - T)$$

Either way of writing the consumption function, either in the general version of equation (3.3) or in the specific numerical example, states that total consumption is the sum of autonomous consumption and induced consumption.

The consumption function can also be shown graphically, as in Figure 3-2. The thick red line shows on the vertical axis the amount of consumption for alternative values of disposable income (measured along the horizontal axis).

An **autonomous** magnitude is independent of the level of income.

The **marginal propensity to consume** is the dollar change in consumption expenditures per dollar change in disposable income.

Induced consumption is the portion of consumption spending that responds to changes in income.

---

[1] The notation T in this chapter continues, as in Chapter 2, to mean "total taxes minus transfer payments."

Figure 3-2 A Simple Hypothesis Regarding Consumption Behavior

The red line passing through F and D illustrates the consumption function. It shows that consumption is 75 percent of disposable income plus an autonomous component of $500 billion that is spent regardless of the level of disposable income. The blue shaded area shows the amount of positive saving that occurs when income exceeds consumption; the pink area shows the amount of negative saving (dissaving) that occurs when consumption exceeds income.

How Disposable Income Is Divided Between Consumption and Saving

When disposable income is zero, total consumption consists just of the autonomous component ($500 billion). For each extra $1,000 billion of disposable income, as we move to the right on the graph, the red consumption function line rises by $750 billion, since its slope (the marginal propensity to consume) is 0.75. For instance, at point D disposable income is $8,000 billion and total consumption is $6,500 billion (consisting of $6,000 billion of induced consumption and $500 billion of autonomous consumption).

> **Self-Test**
>
> 1. If a person's disposable income is zero, what is that person's level of consumption spending in the general linear form of equation (3.3)? In the numerical example?
> 2. How can that person consume a positive amount with a zero disposable income? Think of yourself—what options are open to you to buy something even if you had no income?

Induced Saving and the Marginal Propensity to Save

The simplest way to show the amount of saving is to use a graph like Figure 3-2. The thick green line shows the amount of disposable income in both a horizontal and a vertical direction; this line is often called the "45-degree" line. Since the thick red line shows the consumption function, the distance between the two lines indicates the total amount of saving.

To the right of point F, total saving is positive because disposable income exceeds consumption; this is indicated by the blue shading. To the left of point F, total saving is negative because consumption exceeds disposable income; this is indicated by the pink shading. How can saving be negative? Individuals can consume more than they earn, at least for a while, by withdrawing funds from a savings account, by selling stocks and bonds, or by borrowing. Negative saving is quite typical for many students who borrow to finance their education.

The blue shaded vertical distance between the green and red lines represents saving (S), that is, the difference between disposable income and consumption:

General Linear Form

$$S = Y - T - C = Y - T - C_a - c(Y-T)$$
$$= -C_a + (1-c)(Y-T)$$

Numerical Example

$$S = Y - T - C = Y - T - 500 - 0.75(Y-T)$$
$$= -500 + 0.25(Y-T) \qquad (3.4)$$

This *saving function* starts with the definition of saving as personal disposable income minus consumption; then it substitutes the consumption function from equation (3.3). The last line simplifies the saving function, which now states that personal saving equals minus the amount of autonomous consumption ($-C_a$) plus the **marginal propensity to save** $(1 - c)$ times disposable income $(Y - T)$.

Notice the three points in Figure 3-2 marked with letters corresponding to different levels of disposable income. At H, disposable income is zero, so consumption is C_a, or 500, and saving from equation (3.4) is $-C_a$, or -500. At F, disposable income and consumption are equal, so saving is zero. At D, consumption of 6,500 is less than disposable income of 8,000, so saving is a positive 1,500.

Marginal propensity to save is the change in personal saving induced by a $1 change in personal disposable income.

Self-Test

1. Can you derive a general expression showing how the level of consumption and disposable income at point F depend on autonomous consumption (C_a) and the marginal propensity to consume (c)?
2. If disposable income is 5,000 rather than 8,000, the economy in Figure 3-2 will be at a point between points F and D. Calculate the values of consumption (C) and saving (S) when disposable income is 5,000.

Autonomous Consumption, the Interest Rate, and the Stock Market

Thus far we have seen that the total amount of consumption spending will change if there is a change in income, but also if any factor causes a change in autonomous consumption (C_a). What are these factors? One of the most important is the interest rate; as we learn in the last part of this chapter; autonomous consumption rises when the interest rate falls. Low interest rates in 2001–04 stimulated consumption of automobiles, TV sets, stereos, computers, and many other products, and these low interest rates (working through their stimulus to autonomous consumption) help to explain why the recession of 2001 was so mild.

The other major factor affecting autonomous consumption is **household wealth**. This consists of all the assets of households, particularly the market value of houses, stocks, bonds, and bank accounts, minus any mortgage loans, credit card balances, or other liabilities. When wealth increases, households can spend more even if their income is fixed, thus boosting autonomous consumption and reducing saving. As discussed in the next section, the boom in the

Household wealth is the total value of household assets, including the market value of homes, possessions such as automobiles, and financial assets such as stocks, bonds, and bank accounts, minus any liabilities, including outstanding mortgage and credit card debt, automobile loans, and other loans.

stock market in the late 1990s raised household wealth and helps to explain why the household saving rate decreased so much. The collapse in the stock market in 2000–03 did not cause a reversal of the household saving rate, because household wealth was held up by a boom in house prices and thus in the component of wealth consisting of the value of houses minus the value of mortgage debt.

3-4 Case Study

Why Did U.S. Saving Almost Vanish in 2004?

Figure 3-3 is arranged exactly like Figure 3-2 and shows the actual values of disposable income and consumption spending in the United States during the years 1929–2004. As in Figure 3-2 the amount of personal saving[2] is shown by the light blue shaded area between the green and red lines.

Four major conclusions can be drawn from the evidence. First, consumption increased as disposable income grew during the years since World War II. Second, in the worst years of the Great Depression, in 1932 and 1933, households consumed more than their entire disposable incomes, so the fraction saved was negative (−1.0 percent in 1932 and −1.5 percent in 1933). Third, these usual peacetime relationships were interrupted during World War II (1942–45), when consumer goods were unavailable or rationed. In that period, households were forced to consume much less and save much more than is normal in peacetime, fully 26 percent of disposable income in 1944. After the war, consumers rushed out to spend their accumulated savings, helping to maintain prosperity.

The fourth conclusion is quite surprising. In the late 1980s and throughout the 1990s, real personal saving decreased, from 11.2 percent of personal disposable income in 1982, to 4.8 percent in 1994, to 1.2 percent in 2004. The gradual shrinking of saving in the 1990s was generally attributed to the long stock market boom following 1982, during which the average value of stock prices increased tenfold. Consumers were able to raise their consumption relative to their disposable income by selling some of their stocks that had enjoyed large capital gains.

The saving rate stayed low after 2000 even though the boom in the stock market collapsed, with a decline of 32 percent in the Standard and Poor's 500 stock price index between 2000 and 2003. Why didn't the saving rate recover after the stock market collapse? The most important reason was the sharp decline in interest rates achieved by monetary policy. Many households took advantage of low interest rates to refinance the mortgages on their homes. Because low interest rates imply lower monthly payments, households could use the money released by lower monthly payments to boost their consumption relative to their income. Further, many households "took cash out" in the refinance, boosting the amount financed from, say, $150,000 to $200,000. The extra $50,000 could be used to pay off credit card or other high-interest debt, in which case it would

---

[2] Be careful to distinguish between "savings" (with a terminal "s"), which is the *stock* of assets that households have in savings accounts or under the mattress, from "saving" (without a terminal "s"), which is the *flow* per unit of time that leaks out of disposable income and is unavailable for purchases of consumption goods. It is the flow of *saving* that is designated by the symbol S.

Figure 3-3

Consumption, Saving, and Disposable Income, 1929–2004

In 2004, saving was barely positive and amounted to a mere 1.2 percent of disposable income. Saving was unusually high during World War II because consumer goods were rationed. Since 1950, personal saving as a percentage of disposable income ranged from 1.2 to 11.2 percent.

Chart title: How Actual U.S. Disposable Income Has Been Split Between Consumption and Saving. Area indicates disposable income minus consumption, or personal saving. Labels: Saving almost disappears in 2004; World War II saving bulge. Data points: 1929, 1933, 1944, 1950, 1960, 1970, 1980, 1990, 2000, 2004.

---

have no impact on the personal saving rate. But any households that spent part or all of that $50,000 on consumption goods and services reduced the personal saving rate, since their consumption increased without any change in their disposable income.

3-5 The Economy In and Out of Equilibrium

Until now, we have seen that the level of consumption spending depends on disposable income. But so far we have no idea what the level of income will actually be. $5,000 billion? $10,000 billion? We need an extra element, besides the consumption function, to construct our theory of income determination.

This extra element is that expenditure is not always what is desired or planned, and if some expenditure is unplanned, business firms will adjust production until the unplanned component of expenditure is eliminated. The total amount of spending that people want to do includes only the planned component, called **planned expenditure** (E_p). The rest of expenditure ($E - E_p$) is *unplanned* and *undesired*. To simplify, we assume that investment (I) is the only component of total expenditure that can contain an unplanned component, whereas consumption (C), government spending (G), and net exports (NX) are always equal to the planned amount.

$$E_p = C + I_p + G + NX \tag{3.5}$$

The four components of expenditure are exactly the same as in equation (3.2), except that we use a subscript p for investment. We do not need a subscript p for C, G, or NX, since the actual amount of spending is always the amount planned.

The next step is to combine the consumption function from equation (3.3) with the definition of planned expenditure from equation (3.5):

$$E_p = C_a + c(Y - T) + I_p + G + NX \tag{3.6}$$

In words, this states that planned expenditure equals autonomous consumption, plus the part of consumption that depends on disposable income (induced consumption), plus the fixed values of planned investment, government spending, and net exports.

The word **parameter** means something that is taken as given, including not only exogenous variables but also fixed elements of a function. In the case of the consumption function, there are two such fixed elements (C_a and c), and we will take both as given. In addition, the three components of planned expenditure other than consumption (I_p, G, and NX) can be considered as both exogenous variables and parameters.

A **parameter** is a value taken as given or known within a particular analysis.

Autonomous Planned Spending

It helps to simplify the subsequent analysis if we take all the elements of equation (3.6) that do not depend on total income (Y) and call them *autonomous planned spending* (A_p):

General Linear Form

$$A_p = E_p - cY = C_a - cT_a + I_p + G + NX \tag{3.7}$$

In words, this states that autonomous planned spending consists of all the components of planned spending that do not depend on income, that is, excluding only induced consumption (cY). To summarize, the five components of autonomous planned spending are autonomous consumption (C_a), the effect of autonomous taxes in reducing consumption ($-cT_a$), planned investment (I_p), government spending (G), and net exports (NX). In comparing equations (3.6) and (3.7), notice that we have replaced the tax component (T_a), reflecting our assumption that all taxes are autonomous.[3]

As our numerical example, we will continue to assume that autonomous consumption (C_a) equals 500 and the marginal propensity to consume (c) equals 0.75, and add assumed values of 1,200 for planned investment (I_p) and −200 for net exports (NX). Government spending and autonomous taxes are set to zero. These imply that autonomous planned spending is equal to a total of 1,500:

Numerical Example

$$A_p = 500 - 0.75(0) + 1{,}200 + 0 - 200 = 1{,}500$$

---

[3] We exclude only cY rather than $c(Y - T)$ because we assume that all tax revenues are autonomous (now designated T_a) and do not depend on income.

Overall, we have learned that total planned expenditure (E_p) has two parts, autonomous planned spending (A_p) and induced consumption (cY).

General Linear Form	Numerical Example	
$E_p = A_p + cY$	$E_p = 1{,}500 + 0.75Y$	(3.8)

When Is the Economy in Equilibrium?

A basic lesson of Chapter 2 was that *actual* expenditure (E) and total income (Y) are always equal by definition. But there is no reason for income (Y) always to equal *planned* expenditure (E_p). Only when the economy is in **equilibrium** is income equal to planned expenditure. Only then do households, business firms, the government, and the foreign sector want to spend exactly the amount of income that is being generated by the current level of production.

Equilibrium is *a situation in which there is no pressure for change*. When the economy is *out of equilibrium*, production and income are out of line with planned expenditure, and business firms will be forced to raise or lower production. When the economy is *in equilibrium*, production and income are equal to planned expenditure, and on the average, business firms are happy to continue the current level of production.

This idea is illustrated in Figure 3-4. The thick green line, as in Figure 3-2, has a slope of 45 degrees; everywhere along it the level of income plotted on the horizontal axis is equal to the level of expenditure plotted on the vertical axis. Hence the green line is labeled $E = Y$. The red line is the total level of planned expenditures (E_p) given by equation (3.8), namely, 1,500 plus 0.75

Equilibrium is a state in which there exists no pressure for change.

Figure 3-4 How Equilibrium Income Is Determined

The economy is in equilibrium at point B, where the red planned expenditure (E_p) line crosses the 45-degree income line. At any other level of income, the economy is out of equilibrium, causing pressure on business firms to increase or reduce production and income.

times income (Y). Only where the green and red lines cross at point B is income equal to planned expenditure, with no pressure for change. Households and business firms want to spend $6,000 billion when income is $6,000 billion. And this amount of income is created by the $6,000 billion of production of the goods and services that households and business firms want to buy.[4]

What Happens Out of Equilibrium?

The economy is out of equilibrium at all points other than B along the 45-degree line. For instance, at point J, income is $8,000 billion. How much do households and business firms want to spend when income is $8,000 billion? The two components of planned expenditure are:

$$\begin{aligned}\text{autonomous planned spending } (A_p) &= 1{,}500 \\ \underline{\text{induced consumption } (0.75Y)} &= \underline{6{,}000} \\ \text{planned expenditure } (E_p) &= 7{,}500\end{aligned}$$

Thus at an income level of $8,000 billion, planned expenditure (E_p) is only $7,500 billion (point H on the E_p line), leaving business firms with $500 billion of merchandise that nobody wants to purchase.

The $500 billion of unsold production is counted as inventory investment in the official national income accounts. But businesses do not desire this inventory buildup (if they did, they would have included it in their planned investment, I_p). To bring inventories back to the original desired level, businesses react to the situation at J by cutting production and income, which moves the economy left toward point B. In the diagram, the distance between points J and H, amounting to $500 billion, is labeled I_u, which stands for **unintended inventory investment**.

The distance JH measures the excess of income over planned expenditure—that is, the positive value of I_u. Production and income will be cut until this discrepancy disappears and the unwanted inventory buildup ceases ($I_u = 0$). This occurs only when the economy arrives at B. Only at B are businesses producing exactly the amount that is demanded.

Unintended inventory investment is the amount business firms are forced to accumulate when planned expenditure is less than income.

Self-Test

1. What happens in Figure 3-4 when income is only $4,000 billion?
2. Describe the forces that move the economy back to equilibrium at B.

At point J, as in every situation, income and actual expenditure are equal by definition:

$$\begin{aligned}\text{income } (Y) &\equiv \text{expenditure } (E) \\ &\equiv \text{planned expenditure } (E_p) + \\ &\quad \text{unintended inventory investment } (I_u)\end{aligned} \quad (3.9)$$

By contrast, the economy is in equilibrium only when unintended inventory accumulation or decumulation is equal to zero ($I_u = 0$). When we substitute ($I_u = 0$) into the equation (3.9), we obtain the economy's equilibrium situation:

$$Y = E_p \quad (3.10)$$

---

[4] Note that the horizontal axis in Figure 3-4 is income (Y) rather than disposable income ($Y - T$) as in Figure 3-2. This reflects our assumption that taxes are autonomous and are included in A_p on the vertical axis.

Table 3-1 Comparison of the Economy's "Always True" and Equilibrium Situations

	Always true by definition	True only in equilibrium
1. What concept of expenditure is equal to income?	Actual expenditure including unintended inventory accumulation	Planned expenditure
2. Amount of unintended inventory investment (I_u)	Can be any amount, positive or negative	Must be zero
3. Which equation is valid, (3.9) or (3.10)?	(3.9) $Y = E = E_p + I_u$	(3.10) $Y = E_p$
4. Where does the economy operate in Figure 3-4?	Any point on 45-degree income line (example: point J)	Only at point B where E_p line crosses 45-degree income line
5. Numerical example in Figure 3-4 of nonequilibrium and equilibrium situations.	At point J, $Y(8,000) = E(8,000)$ $= E_p(7,500) + I_u(500)$	At point B, $Y(6,000) = E_p(6,000)$

Table 3-1 summarizes the differences between what is always true and what is true only in equilibrium.

Determining Equilibrium Real GDP

How do we calculate the equilibrium level of real GDP? We start by taking the definition of equilibrium in equation (3.10) and subtract induced consumption (cY) from both sides of that equation:

$$Y - cY = E_p - cY$$

We can replace $E_p - cY$ on the right-hand side by its equivalent, autonomous planned spending, A_p (Why? See equation 3.7):

$$(1 - c)Y = A_p \qquad (3.11)$$

Because the marginal propensity to save equals 1.0 minus the marginal propensity to consume ($s = 1 - c$), we can rewrite (3.11) as

General Linear Form	Numerical Example	
$sY = A_p$	$0.25Y = 1,500$	(3.12)

Describing these equations in words, we start in equation (3.10) with the definition that equilibrium occurs when actual real GDP (Y) equals planned expenditure (E_p). Then, subtracting induced consumption (cY) as in equation (3.11), we obtain the statement that real GDP minus induced consumption, which is the same as **induced saving** (sY) equals planned expenditures minus induced consumption, which is the same as autonomous planned spending (A_p). Since we obtained equation (3.12) from the definition of equilibrium income, we can solve for equilibrium income simply by dividing both sides of equation (3.12) by the marginal propensity to save (s):

Induced saving is the portion of saving that responds to changes in income.

General Linear Form	Numerical Example	
$Y = \dfrac{A_p}{s}$	$Y = \dfrac{1,500}{0.25} = 6,000$	(3.13)

In the numerical example, $6,000 billion of income is required to generate the $1,500 billion of induced saving needed to balance $1,500 billion of autonomous planned spending.

3-6 The Multiplier Effect

Our conclusion thus far that equilibrium income equals $6,000 billion is absolutely dependent on our assumption that autonomous planned spending (A_p) equals $1,500 billion. Any change in autonomous planned spending will cause a change in equilibrium income. To illustrate the consequences of a change in A_p, we shall assume that business firms become more optimistic, raising their guess as to the likely profitability of new investment projects. They increase their investment spending by $500 billion, boosting A_p from $1,500 billion to $2,000 billion. In each situation where a change is described, a numbered subscript is used to distinguish the original from the new situation. Thus A_{p0} denotes the original level of A_p ($1,500 billion), and A_{p1} denotes the new level ($2,000 billion).

Calculating the Multiplier

We can use equation (3.13) to calculate the equilibrium level of income in the new and old situations. Note that only A_p changes; there is no change in the marginal propensity to save (s).

	General Linear Form	Numerical Example	
Take new situation	$Y_1 = \dfrac{A_{p1}}{s}$	$Y_1 = \dfrac{2{,}000}{0.25} = 8{,}000$	
Subtract old situation	$Y_0 = \dfrac{A_{p0}}{s}$	$Y_0 = \dfrac{1{,}500}{0.25} = 6{,}000$	
Equals change in income	$\Delta Y = \dfrac{\Delta A_p}{s}$	$\Delta Y = \dfrac{500}{0.25} = 2{,}000$	(3.14)

The top line of the table calculates the new level of income when A_{p1} is at the new value of 2,000. The second line calculates the original level of income when A_{p0} is at the old value of 1,500. The change in income, abbreviated ΔY, is simply the first line minus the second. The **multiplier** (k) is defined as the ratio of the change in income (ΔY) to the change in planned autonomous spending (ΔA_p) that causes it:

> The **multiplier** is the ratio of the change in output to the change in autonomous planned spending that causes it. It is also 1.0 divided by the marginal propensity to save.

	General Linear Form	Numerical Example	
multiplier (k) =	$\dfrac{\Delta Y}{\Delta A_p} = \dfrac{1}{s}$	$\dfrac{\Delta Y}{\Delta A_p} = \dfrac{1}{0.25} = 4.0$	(3.15)

In Figure 3-5 we can see why the multiplier (k) is $1/s$, or 4.0. Figure 3-5 reproduces from Figure 3-4 the original situation, with A_p at its original value of $1,500 billion.

The $500 billion increase in A_p causes the E_p line to shift upward by $500 billion and to intersect the 45-degree line at point J. Because only 25 percent of

The Multiplier Effect in Action

Figure 3-5 The Change in Equilibrium Income Caused by a $500 Billion Increase in Autonomous Planned Spending

The increase in autonomous planned spending (A_p) by $500 billion is shown by the increase in the vertical intercept of the red planned expenditures line from $1,500 billion to $2,000, as shown in the lower left corner of the diagram. The upward shift in the red line moves the equilibrium position where the red planned expenditures line crosses the green 45-degree line from point B to point J. This $500 billion change in A_p has a multiplier effect, raising real income by $2,000 billion.

extra income is saved, income must rise by $2,000 billion to generate the required $500 billion increase in induced saving. In terms of the line segments:

$$\text{multiplier } (k) = \frac{\Delta Y}{\Delta A_p} = \frac{RJ}{RB} = \frac{1}{s} \left(\text{since } s = \frac{RB}{RJ} \right)$$

Example of the Multiplier Effect in Action

How does the magic of the multiplier work? One answer is given by Figure 3-5, which is based on the initial definition of equilibrium, that real income (Y) must be equal to planned expenditure (E_p). If planned expenditure rises, as from the lower red dashed line to the upper red line, then real income must rise by an amount equal to $1/s$ as much, or in this example $1/0.75 = 4.0$. Thus the $500 billion increase in planned autonomous spending (A_p) boosts real income (Y) by $500 billion times 4.0, or $2,000 billion. This is exactly the same answer that we get in equation (3.15) above.

A real-life example provides another answer. An example of an increase in planned investment is the decision by Southwest Airlines in 2004 to purchase $4 billion of Boeing 737 aircraft. Initially the $4 billion of new investment spending would raise income by the $4 billion earned by Boeing workers in Seattle, where the aircraft plant is located. But, using our example of a marginal propensity to consume (c) of 0.75, the Boeing workers would soon spend 0.75 of the $4 billion, or $3 billion, on goods and services at Seattle stores. The stores would have to reorder $3 billion of additional goods, causing production and income to rise at plants all over the country that supply the goods to the stores in Seattle. Workers at these supplying plants also have a marginal propensity to consume of 0.75, adding another $2.25 billion of spending and income. So far, in the first three rounds of spending, income has gone up by $4.0 plus $3.0 plus $2.25 billion, or $9.25 billion. But the process continues, as induced consumption is increased in each successive round of spending. Eventually, the total increase in income will be four times the initial increase in planned investment, or $16 billion (= $4 billion times 1/0.25), just as in Figure 3-5.[5]

3-7 Sources of Shifts in Planned Spending

Is a multiplier expansion or contraction of output following a change in autonomous planned spending desirable or not?

Assume that the *desired* level of real GDP is $8,000 billion. In Figure 3-5, a level of autonomous planned spending (A_p) of $2,000 billion would be perfect, for it would bring about an equilibrium level of actual real GDP of $8,000 billion at point J, the desired level. On the other hand, a decline in A_p by $500 billion would cut equilibrium income to $6,000 billion at B and would open up a gap of $2,000 billion between *actual* and the *desired* level of real GDP.

What might cause actual real GDP to decline below the desired level? A drop in planned investment, a major component of A_p, can be and has been a major cause of actual real-world recessions and depressions. In the Great Depression, for instance, fixed investment dropped by 81 percent, and this contributed to the 27 percent decline in actual real GDP between 1929 and 1933.

The most important point of this section is that there are five components of autonomous planned spending, as in equation (3.7), and any of these can change. Real GDP can increase or decrease through a multiplier response to changes in autonomous consumption, planned investment, and net exports, an example of the "demand shocks" that create instability, business cycles, and recessions. At least in principle, if it can act fast enough, the government can

---

[5] It is possible to use an algebraic trick to prove that the sum of ΔA_p plus the induced consumption at each round of spending is exactly equal to the multiplier $\frac{1}{1-c}$ times ΔA_p. The first round of consumption is $c\Delta A_p$. The second is c times the first, $c(c\Delta A_p)$, or $c^2 A_p$. Thus the total ΔY is the series of all the infinite number of rounds of spending:

$$\Delta Y = \Delta A_p + c\Delta A_p + c^2 \Delta A_p + \cdots + c^\infty \Delta A_p \tag{a}$$

Factor out the common element ΔA_p on the right-hand side of equation (a):

$$\Delta Y = \Delta A_p (1.0 + c + c^2 + \cdots + c^\infty) \tag{b}$$

Multiply both sides of equation (b) by $-c$:

$$-c\Delta Y = \Delta A_p (-c - c^2 - \cdots - c^\infty) \tag{c}$$

The difference between lines (b) and (c) is

$$(1 - c)\Delta Y = \Delta A_p \tag{d}$$

We can neglect the c^∞ term, since any fraction raised to the infinity power is zero. Dividing both sides of equation (d) by $(1 - c)$, we obtain the familiar:

$$\Delta Y = \frac{\Delta A_p}{1 - c} = \frac{\Delta A_p}{s}$$

offset any undesirable shift in autonomous consumption, planned investment, or net exports by creating an offsetting movement in autonomous planned spending *in the opposite direction* through its control over government spending and autonomous taxes. In this section, we focus on the effects of changes in government spending and autonomous taxes, but remember that exactly the same changes in real GDP can be created not just by government actions but by the actions of consumers, business firms, and a changing demand for U.S. exports and imports emanating from foreign countries.

Government Spending and Taxation

The government can adjust its expenditures on goods and services as well as its tax revenues in an attempt to offset fluctuations in real GDP caused by movements in autonomous consumption, in planned investment, and in net exports. Our definition of autonomous planned spending (A_p) in equation (3.7) already includes government spending (G) and the effect of autonomous taxes (T_a) on consumption. For convenience we repeat equation (3.7):

General Linear Form
$$A_p = C_a - cT_a + I_p + G + NX \tag{3.7}$$

Self-Test

1. Why is I_p written with a p subscript, but the other components of autonomous planned spending (C_a, $-cT_a$, G, and NX) are not?
2. Why does the (cT_a) term appear with a minus sign but all the other sums appear with a plus sign?
3. Why is T_a multiplied by c but the other terms are not?

Equation (3.7) states that autonomous planned spending equals the sum of five components. It also implies that the *change* in autonomous planned spending equals the sum of the *change* in each of the same five components. We can state this idea as an equation if we insert the "change" symbol, Δ, in front of each element in equation (3.7). The only remaining element without a Δ symbol is the marginal propensity to consume (c), which we are assuming to be fixed throughout this discussion:

$$\Delta A_p = \Delta C_a - c\Delta T_a + \Delta I_p + \Delta G + \Delta NX \tag{3.16}$$

In sum, the five causes of changes in A_p are:

1. A $1 change in autonomous consumption (C_a) changes A_p by $1 in the same direction.
2. A $1 change in autonomous tax revenue (T_a) changes A_p by c (the marginal propensity to consume) times $1 *in the opposite direction*.
3. A $1 change in planned investment (I_p) changes A_p by $1 in the same direction.
4. A $1 change in government spending (G) changes A_p by $1 in the same direction.
5. A $1 change in net exports (NX) changes A_p by $1 in the same direction.

Once the change in A_p has been calculated from this list, our basic multiplier expression from equation (3.14) determines the resulting change in equilibrium income:

$$\Delta Y = \frac{\Delta A_p}{s} \qquad (3.14)$$

> **Self-Test**
>
> 1. Notice that there is no Δ in front of the *c* in equation (3.16). Why?
> 2. Notice that there is no Δ in front of the *s* in equation (3.14). Why?
> 3. How is *s* defined in terms of *c*?

Fiscal Expansion

To provide an example of a situation in which higher government spending can expand real income, let us assume that initially the level of autonomous planned spending (A_p) is 1,500. This means that the level of real income will be 6,000, as shown at point B in Figure 3-5. This is unsatisfactory, because we have assumed that the desired level of real GDP is at the higher level of $8,000 billion. Thus point B represents a situation in which actual real GDP and real income are $2,000 billion lower than desired. How can government fiscal policy correct this situation through its control over the level of government expenditure?

It is clear from our basic income-determination formula (3.14) that the required $2,000 billion increase in real income and real GDP can be achieved by any action that raises autonomous planned spending (A_p) by $500 billion. Two possibilities are (1) a $500 billion increase in G (government spending on goods and services) and (2) a $667 billion reduction in autonomous tax revenue.[6]

The $500 billion change in government spending ($\Delta G = 500$) in Figure 3-5 has exactly the same effect on income as any other $500 billion increase in A_p. The economy reaches a new equilibrium at point J. The multiplier (*k*) for ΔG is also the same, already given by equation (3.15) in the preceding section.

The Government Budget Deficit and Its Financing

Any change in government expenditure or tax revenue has consequences for the government's budget. The government budget surplus has already been linked to other key magnitudes in Section 2-4 on p. 34 as the magic equation. Tax revenue minus government expenditure $(T - G)$, by definition equals investment plus net exports minus private saving.[7]

$$T - G \equiv I + NX - S$$

---

[6] Why $667 billion? Because according to equation (3.16), a reduction in taxes raises A_p by *c* times the reduction. If $c = 0.75$, as in our numerical example, then

$$\Delta A_p = -c\Delta T_a = -0.75(-667) = 500$$

Recall that transfer payments (Medicare, Social Security, and unemployment benefits) are equivalent to negative taxes, so that a $667 billion *reduction* in taxes has the same impact on A_p as a $667 billion *increase* in transfer payments.

[7] See equation (2.5) on p. 35. This page 35 also provides examples of the real-world values of the magic equation for the years 1993, 2000, and 2004.

Similarly, the change in the left side of the equation must balance the change in the right side:

$$\Delta T - \Delta G \equiv \Delta I + \Delta NX - \Delta S \qquad (3.17)$$

When the government boosts its spending by 500, the movement in Figure 3-5 from point B to point J assumes that autonomous consumption, investment, and net exports are fixed ($\Delta C_a = \Delta I = \Delta NX = 0$) and that tax revenue remains at zero ($\Delta T = 0$). Thus the only elements of (3.17) that are changing are ΔS and ΔG. The value of ΔG is the fiscal stimulus of 500. But what is the value of ΔS? Recall from the saving function shown in equation (3.4) that saving changes by the marginal propensity to save times the change in disposable income, $\Delta S = s(\Delta Y - \Delta T)$. Using this expression for saving, we can substitute the numbers for this example into equation (3.17) and obtain:

$$\Delta T - \Delta G = \Delta I + \Delta NX - s(\Delta Y - \Delta T)$$
$$0 - \Delta G = 0 + 0 - s(\Delta Y - 0)$$
$$0 - 500 = 0 + 0 - 0.25(2{,}000) = -500$$

The $2,000 billion increase in output induces $500 billion of extra saving. Each extra dollar of saving is available for households to purchase the $500 billion of government bonds that the government must sell to finance its $500 billion government budget deficit. The payoff of this government deficit is the $2,000 boost in income needed to raise income to its desired amount.

The Tax Multiplier

As an alternative to stimulating the economy by raising government spending by $500 billion, it could choose to reduce autonomous taxes by $667 billion. As we have seen, these two actions have exactly the same effect, which is to boost autonomous planned spending by $500 billion and to raise income through the multiplier effect by $2,000 billion.

How is the multiplier for a change in autonomous taxes stated? As before, the change in income (ΔY) is equal to the change in autonomous planned spending (ΔA_p) divided by the marginal propensity to save (s):

General Linear Form   Numerical Example

$$\Delta Y = \frac{\Delta A_p}{s} = \frac{-c \Delta T_a}{s} \qquad \Delta Y = \frac{-(0.75)(-667)}{0.25} = \frac{500}{0.25} = 2{,}000 \qquad (3.18)$$

Here we replace (ΔA_p) by the effect of autonomous taxes on autonomous planned spending ($-c\Delta T_a$).

The multiplier for an increase in taxes is the income change in equation (3.18) divided by ΔT_a.

General Linear Form   Numerical Example

$$\frac{\Delta Y}{\Delta T_a} = \frac{\Delta A_p}{s \Delta T_a} = \frac{-c \Delta T_a}{s \Delta T_a} = \frac{-c}{s} \qquad \frac{\Delta Y}{\Delta T_a} = \frac{-0.75}{0.25} = -3.0 \qquad (3.19)$$

Financing a Tax Cut

When the government decides to stimulate the economy with a tax cut, as did the Bush administration in 2001, then the reduction in tax revenues raises the government budget deficit. In fact, to achieve the same degree of stimulus, enough to raise income by $2,000 billion, the government must cut taxes by $667 billion and run that amount of extra deficit, more than is needed when the economy is stimulated by the alternative method of boosting government spending by $500 billion.

To see how this larger government budget deficit is financed, we use the same equation (3.17) as before and substitute the example of a $667 billion tax cut:

$$\Delta T - \Delta G = \Delta I + \Delta NX - s(\Delta Y - \Delta T)$$
$$-667 - 0 = 0 + 0 - 0.25[2{,}000 - (-667)]$$
$$-667 = -0.25(2{,}667) = -667$$

The $2,000 billion increase in output plus the $667 billion tax cut boosts disposable income by $2,667 billion, thus inducing 0.25 times 2,667 or $667 billion in extra saving. Each extra dollar of saving is available for households to purchase the $667 billion of government bonds that the government must sell to finance its $667 billion government budget deficit.

Self-Test

1. If government spending is reduced by $500 billion and the rest of the example in the text is retained, how much does saving change?
2. What is the government doing when it runs a surplus, and how do private savers react?
3. If taxes are raised by $667 billion and the rest of the example in the text is retained, how much does saving change? How do private households pay for the higher taxes?

The Balanced Budget Multiplier

In the previous example, the government could boost income by $2,000 billion either by raising government spending by $500 billion or by cutting taxes by $667 billion. Yet either method would create a large increase in the government deficit, which may be undesirable. Yet, surprisingly, the government can stimulate the economy even if it needs to maintain a balanced budget. To see this, we simply add the multipliers for government spending ($k = 1/s$) and that for a change in taxes (*tax change multiplier* $= -c/s$):

$$\text{Balanced budget multiplier} = \frac{1}{s} + \frac{-c}{s} = \frac{1-c}{s} = 1.0 \qquad (3.20)$$

This states that the multiplier for a balanced-budget fiscal expansion is always 1.0, no matter what the value of c! Why? The positive multiplier occurs because one dollar of government spending raises autonomous planned expenditure by exactly one dollar, whereas the extra dollar of taxes only reduces autonomous planned expenditure by c times one dollar, and c (the marginal propensity to consume) is normally substantially less than unity. Thus, the government can achieve any desired increase in income and real GDP by a sufficiently large increase in government spending accompanied by exactly the same increase in tax rates.[8]

---

[8] The appendix to this chapter shows that this simple expression for the balanced budget multiplier does not apply to a more realistic world in which tax revenues and imports depend on income.

International Perspective

How the United States and Japan Use Fiscal Policy

One method to stabilize the economy by reducing the amplitude of business cycles is to use "countercyclical" fiscal policy. Such a policy operates "counter" or "against" the business cycle by using fiscal stimulus (higher spending or lower taxes) when the economy is weak and using the reverse when the economy is strong. However, fiscal policy in practice runs up against major problems. If government spending is used, then government spending on what? If the government takes a long time to develop plans for projects such as highways, hospitals, or schools, the economy's condition in the meantime may have changed from too weak to too strong. If tax cuts are used, they may be delayed by political debates, and households may decide to save the tax cut money rather than spending it.

Countercyclical fiscal policy in the United States has primarily used tax changes, and spending changes have rarely been used since the New Deal era of the 1930s. Tax reductions were used to stimulate the economy in 1964–65, for restraint in 1968, and again for stimulus in 1975 and 1981–83. However the tax cuts of the early 1980s left the government budget mired in persistent deficits until the late 1990s, and this experience gave fiscal policy a bad name.

This changed in 2001 when Congress ratified the Bush administration's proposal for significant cuts of income tax rates to be spread over the next half-decade, starting with checks of $300 (for single filers) or $600 (for joint returns) sent in the mail to American taxpayers in the summer of 2001. Skepticism seemed to be warranted when the personal saving rate jumped, indicating that a substantial fraction of the payments had been saved rather than spent. Further tax cuts occurred in 2003 and were extended in 2004.

Since the early 1990s, the Japanese economy has been depressed, and numerous forms of fiscal stimulus have been employed as the Japanese government struggles to find a route back to prosperity. In contrast to the United States, the Japanese place much more emphasis on public works projects. To avoid time lags in starting new projects, the Japanese have a set of plans ready and vary fiscal expenditures to speed up or slow down completion of particular projects. For instance, the 115-mile Tokyo Coastal Bay Expressway was under construction for two decades. Many observers are skeptical of the usefulness of many of these public works projects, pointing to roads that lead nowhere and a report that 60 percent of the Japanese coastline is encased in concrete. However, the Chapter 3 multiplier for government spending does not require that the spending must be useful to stimulate spending, and recent evidence has supported that textbook view.

Although tax cuts have also been introduced in Japan, these have been ineffective, as they have been announced as temporary and have soon been followed by even larger tax increases. Overall, Japanese policymakers continue to struggle to extricate their economy from its 15-year slump. In 2003–04, the Japanese economy seemed to be reviving somewhat, but this mainly reflected increased demand for Japanese exports from the United States and China, rather than any new-found potency of fiscal policy. We return in Chapter 5 to a deeper look at the Japanese policy dilemma, and at some of the mistakes and misconceptions that have plagued policymakers.

3-8 How Can Monetary Policy Affect Planned Spending?

Thus far fiscal policy seems to be the only tool that the government can use to fight against demand shocks caused by changes in autonomous consumption, planned investment, and net exports. Where does monetary policy fit in? Now we are ready to drop our simplifying but unrealistic assumption that autonomous consumption and planned investment are exogenous, taken as given and not explained by the model. In the next two sections we learn how and why interest rates can influence planned autonomous spending, raising spending when interest rates are low as in years such as 2001–04 and cutting spending in years when interest rates are high such as 1981 and 1989.

How then does monetary policy control the interest rate? We delay our discussion of that crucial question for Chapter 4. Now we will simply take the interest rate as given, while converting autonomous consumption from an exogenous into an endogenous variable. In the next chapter the interest rate joins the list of endogenous variables, and our model of income determination will be able to provide a balanced examination of the effects of both fiscal and monetary policy.

Functions of Interest Rates

While in the real world there are many different interest rates, here we simplify by assuming that there is only a single interest rate. Savers receive this rate as a return on their savings accounts and holdings of bonds. And both business firms and consumers pay this interest rate when they borrow from financial institutions.

Interest rates help the economy allocate saving among alternative uses. For savers, the interest rate is a reward for abstaining from consumption and waiting to consume at some future time. The higher the interest rate, the greater the incentive to save. For borrowers, the interest rate is the cost of borrowing funds to invest or buy consumption goods. At a higher interest rate, people will borrow fewer funds and purchase fewer goods. Thus if the desire to borrow exceeds the willingness to save sufficient funds, the interest rate tends to rise.

Interest rates are central to the role of monetary policy. Since the government, through the Federal Reserve Board (the Fed), can influence the interest rate, it can affect the cost of borrowed funds to private borrowers.

Types of Interest Rates

Banks offer a variety of interest rates on checking and savings accounts. Some types of accounts allow customers to earn interest instantly; others require customers to leave funds on deposit for a year or more. The phrase "short-term interest rate" refers to interest that is paid on funds deposited for three months or less; "long-term interest rate" refers to interest on funds deposited for a year or more.

In addition to short-term interest rates on bank deposits, there are short-term interest rates that apply to funds borrowed by the government (the Treasury bill rate), by businesses (the commercial paper rate), and by banks (the federal funds rate). Similarly, in addition to long-term rates on bank deposits, there are long-term interest rates that apply to funds borrowed by the government (the Treasury bond rate), by businesses (the corporate bond rate), and by households (the mortgage rate). The business sections of most local newspapers and *The Wall Street Journal* publish the daily values of these rates.

The hallmark of a good theory is its ability to spotlight important relationships and to ignore unnecessary details. For most purposes, the differences between alternative interest rates fall into that category of detail, in contrast to the important overall *average* level of interest rates. Thus "the" interest rate discussed in this chapter can be regarded as an average of all the different interest rates listed in the previous paragraph.

3-9 The Relation of Autonomous Planned Spending to the Interest Rate

We begin by asking why planned investment (a component of autonomous planned spending) depends on the interest rate. Business firms attempt to profit by borrowing funds to buy investment goods—office buildings, shopping centers, factories, machine tools, computers, airplanes. Obviously, firms can stay in business only if the earnings of investment goods are at least enough to pay the interest on the borrowed funds (or to attract enough investors to warrant a new issue of stock).

Example of an Airline's Investment Decision

American Airlines calculates that it can earn $10 million per year from one additional Boeing 757 jet airliner after paying all expenses for employee salaries, fuel, food, and airplane maintenance—that is, all expenses besides interest payments on the borrowed funds. If the 757 costs $50 million, that level of earnings represents a 20 percent **rate of return** ($10,000,000/$50,000,000), defined as annual earnings divided by the cost of the airplane. If American must pay 10 percent interest to obtain the funds for the airplane, the 20 percent rate of return is more than sufficient to pay the interest expense.

The **rate of return** on an investment project is its annual earnings divided by its total cost.

In the top frame of Figure 3-6, point *A* shows that the 20 percent rate of return on the first 757 exceeds the 10 percent interest rate on borrowed funds. The steplike red line in the top frame of Figure 3-6 shows the rate of return on the first through fifth planes. The green area between point *A* and the 10 percent interest rate represents the annual profit rate made on the first plane. Point *B* for the second plane also indicates a profit. Point *C* shows that purchase of a third extra 757 earns only a 10 percent rate of return, or $5 million (10 percent of $50 million) in extra earnings after payment of all noninterest expenses.

Why do the second and third planes earn less than the first? The first plane is operated on the most profitable routes; the second and third must fly on routes that are less likely to yield full passenger loads. A fourth plane (at point *D*) would have an even lower rate of return, insufficient to pay the interest cost of borrowed funds. How many planes will be purchased? The third can pay its interest expense and will be purchased, but the fourth will not. If the interest cost of borrowed funds were to rise above 10 percent but remain below 15 percent, American would purchase two planes instead of three. If the interest rate were to fall to 5 percent or below, then American would purchase four planes.

Figure 3-6 The Payoff to Investment for an Airline and the Economy

The red steplike line in the top frame shows the rate of return to American Airlines for purchases of additional 757s. If the interest rate is 10 percent, a profit is made by purchasing the first two planes, and the company breaks even by buying the third plane. Purchase of a fourth or fifth plane would be a mistake, because the planes would not generate enough additional profit to pay for the cost of borrowing the money to buy them. The bottom frame shows the same phenomenon for the economy as a whole.

An Increase in Planned Private Spending Reduces the Rate of Return

The Interest Rate and the Rate-of-Return Line

The interest rate not only influences the level of business investment but also affects the level of household consumption. For instance, households deciding whether to purchase a dishwasher or a second automobile will consider the size of the monthly payment, which depends on the interest rate. In the bottom frame of Figure 3-6, the rate-of-return line shows that the return on planned investment and autonomous consumption spending ($I_p + C_a$) declines as the level of spending increases. As for American Airlines, each successive investment good purchased by business firms is less profitable than the last. Similarly, each successive consumption good purchased by households provides fewer services than the last (for instance, a family's second car is less important and useful than its first car).

Determination of the level of $I_p + C_a$ is a two-step process. First we plot the rate-of-return line representing firms' and consumers' expectations of the benefit of additional purchases. Second, we find the level of $I_p + C_a$ at the point where the rate-of-return line crosses the interest rate level.

When the interest rate is 10 percent, as in Figure 3-6, autonomous planned spending ($I_p + C_a$) will be $1,500 billion at point C, as long as the level of business and consumer optimism remains constant. A decrease in the interest rate will increase purchases ($I_p + C_a$); for instance, a decrease from 10 percent to 5 percent moves autonomous planned spending from $1,500 billion at C to $2,000 billion at D.

Business and Consumer Optimism

Can purchases ever change when the interest rate is held constant at 10 percent? Certainly—an increase in business and consumer optimism about the expected payoff of additional purchases can shift the entire rate-of-return line to the right, as indicated by the red "new rate-of-return line" in Figure 3-7. This shifts to the right (to point F) the intersection of the rate-of-return line with the fixed horizontal interest rate line.

As an example, the events of September 11, 2001, caused a sharp decline in business and consumer confidence, shifting the rate of return line to the left. Among the initial effects were massive cancellations by airlines of their previous orders for new aircraft.

Summarizing, we can show the amount of $I_p + C_a$ spending that would occur at different interest rates and different levels of confidence.

	Demand for $I_p + C_a$	
Interest rate	Original rate-of-return line (pessimistic expectations)	New higher rate-of-return line (optimistic expectations)
15	1,000 (at B)	1,500
10	1,500 (at C)	2,000 (at F)
5	2,000 (at D)	2,500

The left-hand column (pessimistic expectations) is plotted as the "original rate-of-return line" (red dashes) in Figure 3-7. The right-hand column (optimistic expectations) is plotted as the solid red "new rate-of-return line."

Figure 3-7 Effect on Autonomous Planned Spending of an Increase in Business and Consumer Confidence

The dashed red "original rate-of-return line" is an exact copy of the solid red "rate-of-return line" in Figure 3-6. If the level of business and consumer confidence were to increase, the spending schedule would shift rightward to the solid red "new rate-of-return line." If the interest rate were to stay constant at 10 percent, then autonomous planned spending (A_p) would increase from $1,500 billion at point C to $2,000 billion at point F.

The Demand for Autonomous Planned Spending

You learned earlier that there are five components of autonomous planned spending (A_p): planned investment, autonomous consumption, government spending, the effect of autonomous taxes on consumption, and net exports. We have already seen that planned investment and autonomous consumption both depend on the interest rate; both types of spending are stimulated by a lower interest rate.

In Figure 3-8 we plot the relationship of the components of autonomous planned spending on the horizontal axis to the interest rate on the vertical axis. The negative relationship between the interest rate and both planned investment and autonomous consumption ($I_p + C_a$) is copied from Figure 3-7. The other three components of autonomous spending do not depend on the interest rate. Accordingly, the total amount of government spending, the effect of autonomous taxes on consumption, and net exports ($G - cT_a + NX$) are plotted as a black vertical line in Figure 3-8.

Total autonomous planned spending also consists of autonomous consumption (C_a) and planned investment (I_p), both of which depend negatively on the interest rate, so *the amount of these two components added to the first three depends on the interest rate*. The lower the interest rate, the larger C_a and the larger I_p. The total of all five components is shown by the line on the right labeled "A_p demand schedule." This schedule shows that the total of all autonomous planned spending depends on the interest rate.

Shifts in the A_p Demand Schedule

As before, government spending, taxes, and net exports are given exogenous amounts. A change in any of these will shift the A_p demand schedule. As you previously learned, a shift of business expectations toward optimism and confidence will boost planned investment at any given interest rate, so such attitudes will also shift the A_p demand schedule. Finally, an improvement in consumer confidence will raise autonomous consumer spending and shift the schedule in the same way to the right from the initial position shown by the downward sloping red line in Figure 3-8.

Figure 3-8 Relation of the Various Components of Autonomous Planned Spending to the Interest Rate

The vertical black line shows that three components of autonomous planned spending do not depend on the interest rate. These are government spending (G), the effect of autonomous taxes ($-cT_a$), and net exports (NX). The sloped line shows that autonomous consumption (C_a) and planned investment (I_p) depend inversely on the interest rate. Hence, the total demand for autonomous planned spending, as shown by the "A_p demand schedule," also depends inversely on the interest rate.

Self-Test

Explain how the A_p demand schedule will shift to the left, right, or not at all in response to the following events:

1. A reduction in auto imports from Japan as the quality of American-built cars improves.
2. The stimulus to housing given by lower mortgage interest rates.
3. Higher taxes levied by the government in an attempt to reduce the budget deficit.
4. Higher government spending on security at airports.
5. A reduction in consumer confidence after the September 11, 2001, attacks.

3-10 The IS Curve

As shown in Figure 3-8, autonomous planned spending (A_p) depends on the interest rate. And Figure 3-5 has shown that real GDP and real income depend on autonomous planned spending. Now, if we put these two relationships together, we conclude that real GDP and real income must depend on the interest rate. In this section we derive a graphical schedule that shows the different possible combinations of the interest rate and real income that are compatible with equilibrium, given the state of business and consumer confidence, the marginal propensity to save, and the level of government spending, taxes, and net exports. This schedule is the **IS curve**.

> The **IS curve** is the schedule that identifies the combinations of income and the interest rate at which the commodity market is in equilibrium; everywhere along the IS curve the demand for commodities equals the supply.

How to Derive the IS Curve

The left frame of Figure 3-9 displays the "A_p demand schedule." This shows the demand for autonomous planned spending at different levels of the interest rate and is copied from the "original rate-of-return line" in Figure 3-7. Notice that at a 10 percent interest rate (point C), A_p will be $1,500 billion, just the same as (at point C) in Figure 3-7. To simplify the discussion, initially we assume that there are no government spending, tax revenue, or net exports, so total autonomous spending consists simply of the two components, $I_p + C_a$, both of which depend negatively on the interest rate.[9]

What will be the equilibrium level of real income if A_p equals $1,500 billion? We answer this question, just as we did earlier in the chapter, by using a multiplier of 4.0. When we are at point C in the left frame with A_p equal to $1,500 billion, then in the right frame real GDP is plotted at point C with a value of $6,000 billion (4 times $1,500 billion).

Two other possibilities are shown in Figure 3-9. At point B, the interest rate is 15 percent. As shown in the left frame by the A_p demand schedule, this high interest rate cuts autonomous planned spending back from $1,500 billion at

---

[9] The equation of the A_p demand schedule in the lower left quadrant of Figure 3-9 is:

$$2{,}500 - 100r$$

Thus, when the interest rate is at 10 percent, the level of autonomous planned spending along the A_p demand schedule is $2{,}500 - (100 \times 10) = 1{,}500$.

84 Chapter 3 • Spending, Income, and Interest Rates

Why Equilibrium Real Income Depends on the Interest Rate

Figure 3-9 Relation of the *IS* Curve to the Demand for Autonomous Spending

In the left frame, the "A_p demand schedule" is copied from the dashed red line in Figure 3-7. It shows that the demand for autonomous planned spending depends on the interest rate. For instance, at a 10 percent interest rate the level of A_p is $1,500 billion at point C. Because the multiplier (k) is 4.0, the equilibrium level of income is $6,000 billion and is plotted in the right frame at point C, opposite the 10 percent interest rate that we assumed at the beginning.

point C to $1,000 billion at point B. Since the multiplier is 4.0, real GDP is 4.0 times $1,000 billion, or $4,000 billion as shown in the right frame at point B. Similarly, at the low interest rate of 5 percent, real GDP in the right frame is $8,000 billion at point D.

Self-Test

1. What interest rate is compatible with an $8,000 billion level of equilibrium real income?
2. At what point does this equilibrium occur in the right frame of Figure 3-9?

Because A_p depends on the interest rate, equilibrium income does also. The *IS* curve in Figure 3-9 plots the values of equilibrium real income when the marginal propensity to save is 0.25 and the multiplier is 4.0, as we have assumed throughout this chapter. Notice that points B, C, and D along the *IS* curve are all plotted at a horizontal distance exactly 4.0 times the value of the A_p line in the left-hand frame.

Learning About Diagrams: The *IS* Curve

Since the *IS* curve is so important and useful, we pause here to study it more closely. (A full algebraic treatment of the *IS-LM* model is given in the appendix to Chapter 4.)

Diagram Ingredients and Reasons for Slope

The vertical axis is the interest rate and the horizontal axis is the level of income.

The *IS* curve takes information from two other graphs, the A_p demand schedule and the equilibrium between induced saving and autonomous planned spending. Because A_p depends on the interest rate, and because equilibrium income is a multiple (k) of A_p, equilibrium income becomes a negative function of the interest rate.

The horizontal position (equilibrium income) along the *IS* curve is equal to the horizontal position along the A_p demand schedule times the multiplier k.

The *IS* curve slopes down because income is a multiple of A_p, and A_p depends negatively on the interest rate.

The *IS* curve becomes flatter, the more responsive is A_p to the interest rate, and the larger the multiplier.

The *IS* curve becomes steeper, the less responsive is A_p to the interest rate, and the smaller the multiplier.

What Shifts and Rotates the *IS* Curve?

The *IS* curve is equal to the interest-dependent level of A_p times the multiplier (k). Anything that shifts the A_p demand schedule will shift the *IS* curve in the same direction. The factors that shift the *IS* curve to the right include an increase in business or consumer confidence, an increase in government spending or net exports, and a decrease in taxes (or increase in transfers). Opposite changes will shift the *IS* curve to the left.

A rightward shift in the A_p demand schedule causes a rightward shift in the *IS* curve by an amount equal to the A_p shift times the multiplier.

The multiplier (k) transforms the A_p demand schedule into the *IS* curve. An increase in the multiplier (due, for instance, to a smaller marginal propensity to save) rotates or twists the *IS* curve outward around its intercept on the vertical interest rate axis. Thus the higher the multiplier, the flatter the *IS* curve.

Anything that makes investment or consumption demand less sensitive to the interest rate (for instance, a tendency for firms to pay for investment goods with internal funds rather than borrowed funds) rotates or twists the *IS* curve upward around its intercept on the horizontal income axis. Thus the less sensitive the response of autonomous spending to the interest rate, the steeper the *IS* curve.

What Is True of Points That Are off the *IS* Curve?

The entire area to the left of each *IS* curve is characterized by too low a level of production and income for the economy to be in equilibrium. There is undesired inventory decumulation (negative unplanned investment, I_u).

The entire area to the right of each *IS* curve is characterized by too high a level of production and income for the economy to be in equilibrium. There is undesired inventory accumulation (positive unplanned investment, I_u).

At any point off the *IS* curve there is pressure for business firms to adjust production until the economy returns to the *IS* curve.

What the *IS* Curve Shows

The *IS* curve shows all the different combinations of the interest rate (r) and income (Y) at which the economy's market for commodities (goods and services) is in equilibrium, which occurs only when income equals planned expenditures. At any point off the *IS* curve the economy is out of equilibrium.

It will be convenient to have a label for the horizontal position of the A_p line, since this in turn will affect the horizontal position of the *IS* curve.[10] Let us define A'_p as the value of autonomous planned spending that would take place at an

---

[10] We call the *IS* schedule a "curve," even though we have drawn it as a straight line, because in the real world the relationship might be a curve. Also the term "*IS* curve" has been familiar to generations of economists since its invention by the late Sir John Hicks in a classic article, "Mr. Keynes and the Classics: A Suggested Interpretation," *Econometrica*, vol. 5 (April 1937), pp. 147–159.

interest rate of zero. In Figure 3-9, the A_p line intersects the horizontal axis at $2,500 billion, so our label for this A_p line will be $A'_{p0} = 2,500$. The *IS* curve always lies at a horizontal distance 4.0 times the A_p line, because the multiplier (k) is 4.0. Notice in Figure 3-9 that the *IS* curve intersects the horizontal axis at $10,000 billion, exactly 4.0 times the level of $A'_{p0} = 2,500$.

3-11 Conclusion: The Missing Relation

The *IS* curve is like a menu, providing us with innumerable combinations of interest rates and income that are consistent with equilibrium in the commodity market. But which item on the menu should we choose? There is not enough information here to make a choice. We need to find another relationship to link income and the interest rate in order to tie down the economy's position along the *IS* curve. In the familiar language of elementary algebra, we have two unknowns but only one equation. In the next chapter, we supply the missing equation and arrive at a complete theory of how income and the interest rate are determined.[11]

The missing relation between real income and the interest rate (in addition to the *IS* curve, occurs in the "money market," a general expression for the financial sector of the economy. The operation of the money market provides the crucial missing link that explains how the interest rate is determined. At the beginning of the next chapter, we will learn how the money market creates a second, positively sloped relationship between real income and the interest rate. We will learn that the Fed, through its control of the money supply, can shift this positive relationship back and forth and offset some or all of the effects of the demand shocks (such as changes in business and consumer confidence) that shift the position of the *IS* curve. We will also learn how monetary and fiscal policy can be used together to determine both the interest rate and the level of real income

Summary

1. This chapter presents a simple theory for determining real income. Important simplifying assumptions include the constancy of the price level.
2. Disposable income is divided between consumption and saving. Throughout the chapter consumption is assumed to be a fixed autonomous amount, $500 billion in the numerical example, plus 0.75 of disposable income. Saving is the remaining 0.25 of disposable income minus the $500 billion of autonomous consumption.
3. During the twentieth century, U.S. consumption was a roughly constant fraction of disposable income. Exceptions were during World War II, when rationing prevented households from obtaining the goods they desired and forced them to save an abnormal fraction of their income, and in the period after 1997 when saving almost vanished.
4. Output and income (Y) are equal by definition to total expenditures (E), which in turn can be divided up between planned expenditure (E_p) and unintended inventory accumulation (I_u). We convert this definition into a theory by assuming that business firms adjust production whenever I_u is not zero. The economy is in equilibrium, with no pressure for production to

---

[11] Despite its name, the *IS* curve has no unique connection with investment (I) or saving (S). It shifts whenever there is a shift in the A_p demand schedule, which can be caused by a change in government spending, in taxes or transfers, or in net exports, as well as by changes in business and consumer confidence.

change, only when there is no unintended inventory accumulation or decumulation ($I_u = 0$).
5. Autonomous planned spending (A_p) equals total planned expenditure minus induced consumption. The five components of autonomous planned expenditure are autonomous consumption (C_a), planned investment (I_p), government spending (G), net exports (NX), and the effect on consumption of autonomous tax revenue ($-cT_a$).
6. Any change in autonomous planned spending (ΔA_p) has a multiplier effect: An increase raises income and induced consumption over and above the initial boost in A_p. Income must increase until enough extra saving has been induced ($s\Delta Y$) to balance the injection of extra autonomous planned spending (ΔA_p). For this reason, the multiplier, the ratio of the change in income to the change in autonomous planned spending ($\Delta Y / \Delta A_p$), is the inverse of the marginal propensity to save ($1/s$).
7. The same multiplier is valid for a change in any component in A_p. Thus, if private spending components of A_p are weak, the government can raise its spending (G) or cut taxes (T) to maintain stability in A_p and thus in real output.
8. Interest rates allocate the supply of funds available from savers to alternative borrowers. Not only do private households and firms borrow in order to buy consumption and investment goods, but the government also borrows to finance its budget deficit.
9. Private autonomous planned spending (A_p) depends partly on the interest rate. The higher the interest rate, the lower is A_p.
10. Private autonomous planned spending (A_p) also depends on the optimism or pessimism of investors and consumers about the future. An increase in optimism tends to raise A_p for any given level of the interest rate.
11. The *IS* curve indicates all the combinations of the interest rate and real income at which the economy's commodity market is in equilibrium. At any point off the *IS* curve, the commodity market is out of equilibrium.

Note: Asterisks designate Concepts, Questions, and Problems that require the Appendix to Chapter 3.

Concepts

aggregate demand
demand shock
aggregate supply
endogenous variables
exogenous variables
autonomous magnitude
marginal propensity to consume

induced consumption
marginal propensity to save
household wealth
parameter
equilibrium
unintended inventory investment
induced saving

multiplier
rate of return
IS curve
*marginal leakage rate
*automatic stabilization

Questions

1. Explain the distinction between exogenous variables and endogenous variables. Explain the distinction, if any, between a parameter and an exogenous variable. For the most complete model used in this chapter, which of the following variables are endogenous? Which are exogenous?
    (a) autonomous taxes
    (b) consumption
    (c) marginal propensity to consume
    (d) exports
    (e) net exports
    (f) GDP
    (g) price level
    (h) interest rate
    (i) investment
    (j) tax revenue
    (k) disposable income
    (l) saving
    (m) foreign trade surplus (deficit)
    (n) government budget surplus (deficit)
2. Why do we distinguish between autonomous consumption and induced consumption?
3. Explain why inventories would tend to rise just before the start of a recession and again tend to rise once businesses become more confident that the economy is expanding.
4. What moves the economy toward equilibrium when unintended inventory investment is positive? negative?
5. Assume that there is an increase in autonomous investment of $100 billion. Will the effect on the level of equilibrium real GDP be greater with a relatively high

or a relatively low marginal propensity to consume? Explain.

6. Explain why government action that increases the deficit is expansionary fiscal policy. What about action that decreases the surplus?

7. Explain why the IS curve slopes down and to the right. Explain the difference between a movement along the IS curve and a shift of the IS curve.

8. Explain how each of the following will shift the IS curve.
   (a) The decline in sales of American agricultural products to foreign countries resulting from a strong U.S. dollar in the early-to-mid 1980s.
   (b) The collapse in consumer confidence that occurred in the fall of 1990 following the rapid rise in energy prices after Iraq's invasion of Kuwait in August 1990.
   (c) The decline in the personal saving rate from 4.8 percent in 1994 to 1.2 percent in 2004.
   (d) The drop in business confidence following the collapse of the stock market and the Internet bust in 2000.

9. One of the hypotheses for the increased stability of the United States economy since 1985 is that demand shocks have become smaller and less important. Explain why a demand shock can be thought of as a shift of the IS curve. Then discuss the hypothesis concerning demand shocks and the increased stability of the U.S. economy in terms of shifts of the IS curve.

The following four questions assume knowledge of the Appendix to Chapter 3.

*10. Given a consumption function of the form $C = C_a + c(Y - T)$ and $T = T_a + tY$, write the formula for the expanded consumption function. Write the formula for the expanded saving function that is implied by the stated consumption function.

*11. How would your answer in question 5 change if the alternatives read with a relatively high or with a relatively low marginal leakage rate? Explain.

*12. Explain the effect of each of the following scenarios on the values of the marginal leakage rate and the multiplier.
   (a) The marginal propensity to consume decreases.
   (b) The tax rate decreases.
   (c) The share of imports in GDP decreases.

*13. When all taxes and net exports are autonomous, the balanced budget multiplier is one. Find the balanced budget multiplier when all taxes are autonomous, but net exports have an autonomous and induced component. Is this new balanced budget multiplier less than, greater than, or equal to one?

Problems

1. Consider an economy in which all taxes are autonomous and the following values of autonomous consumption, planned investment, government expenditure, autonomous taxes, and the marginal propensity to consume are given:

   $C_a = 1{,}400 \quad I_p = 1{,}800 \quad G = 1{,}950 \quad T_a = 1{,}750 \quad c = 0.6$

   (a) What is the level of consumption when the level of income (Y) equals $10,000?
   (b) What is the level of saving when the level of income (Y) equals $10,000?
   (c) What is the level of planned investment when the level of income (Y) equals $10,000? What is the level of actual investment? What is the level of unintended inventory investment?
   (d) Show that injections equal leakages when income (Y) equals $10,000.
   (e) Is the economy in equilibrium when income (Y) = $10,000? If not, what is the equilibrium level of income for the economy described in this question?

2. $C = C_a + c(Y - T_a)$
   where:

   $C_a = 2{,}200 \quad I_p = 2{,}400 \quad T_a = 1{,}900$
   $NX = -100 \quad c = 0.5 \quad G = 1{,}850$

   (a) Determine the equilibrium levels of GDP, consumption, saving, and taxes.
   (b) What is the value of the marginal propensity to save?
   (c) Is there a surplus or deficit in the government budget? How much?
   (d) Show that leakages equal injections.
   (e) What is the new equilibrium level of GDP if government spending increases by $140 billion?

3. You are given the following values for the marginal propensity to consume, c, the income tax rate, t, and the share of imports in GDP, nx: $c = 0.85$, $t = 0.2$, $nx = 0.08$.
   (a) Compute the values of the marginal propensity to save, the marginal leakage rate, and the multiplier.
   (b) Suppose the marginal propensity to consume decreases to 0.75. Compute the new values of the marginal propensity to save, the marginal leakage rate, and the multiplier.

(c) Suppose the share of imports in GDP increases to 0.1, given $c = 0.75$, and $t = 0.2$. Compute the new values of the marginal leakage rate and the multiplier.

(d) Suppose that the income tax rate increases to 0.25, given $c = 0.75$, and $nx = 0.1$. Compute the new values of the marginal leakage rate and the multiplier.

(e) Based on your answers to b–d, explain how the values of the marginal leakage rate and the multiplier change with changes in the marginal propensity to consume, the income tax rate, and the share of imports in GDP.

*4. Assume an economy in which the marginal propensity to consume, c, is 0.8, the income tax rate, t, is 0.2, and the share of imports in GDP, nx, is 0.04. Autonomous consumption, C_a, is 660; autonomous taxes, T_a, are 200; autonomous net exports, NX_a, are 300; planned investment, I_p, is 500; and government spending, G, is 500.

(a) What is the value of autonomous planned spending (A_p)?
(b) What is the value of the multiplier?
(c) What is the equilibrium value of income (Y)?
(d) What is the value of consumption in equilibrium?
(e) Show that leakages equal injections.
(f) Suppose government expenditures decline by 150. Describe the economic process by which the new equilibrium value of Y is attained.
(g) What is the new equilibrium value of Y?

5. Consider an economy in which taxes, planned investment, government spending on goods and services, and net exports are autonomous, but consumption and planned investment change as the interest rate changes. You are given the following information concerning autonomous consumption, the marginal propensity to consume, planned investment, government purchases of goods and services, and net exports: $C_a = 1{,}400 - 15r$; $c = 0.5$; $I_p = 2{,}350 - 35r$; $G = 1{,}940$; $NX = -200$; $T_a = 1{,}600$.

(a) Compute the value of the multiplier.
(b) Derive the equation for the autonomous planned spending schedule, A_p.
(c) Derive the equation for the IS curve, $Y = kA_p$.
(d) Using the equation for the IS curve, calculate the equilibrium levels of income at interest rates equal to 0, 2, and 4.
(e) Using your answers to part d, calculate the slope of the IS curve, $\Delta r / \Delta Y$.
(f) Suppose that autonomous consumption rises by $40 billion dollars, so that $C_a = 1{,}440 - 15r$. Explain whether this increase in autonomous consumption is caused by a rise or fall in consumer confidence. Derive the new equation for the IS curve.

(g) Using the equation for the new IS curve, calculate the new equilibrium levels of income at interest rates equal to 0, 2, and 4.
(h) Using your answers to parts d and g, explain whether the IS curve shifts to the left or right when autonomous consumption rises. Explain why the horizontal shift of the IS curve equals the multiplier times the change in autonomous planned spending.

6. The purpose of this problem is to study how the slope of the IS curve changes as the multiplier changes and the responsiveness of autonomous planned spending to interest rate changes. Initially, use the same information as given in problem 5.

(a) Suppose that the marginal propensity to consume increases from 0.5 to 0.6. Compute the new value of the multiplier.
(b) Derive the equation for the new autonomous planned spending schedule, A_p.
(c) Derive the equation for the new IS curve, $Y = kA_p$.
(d) Using the equation for the new IS curve, calculate the new equilibrium levels of income at interest rates equal to 0, 2, and 4.
(e) Using your answers to part d, calculate the slope of the new IS curve, $\Delta r / \Delta Y$.
(f) Given that $c = 0.6$, suppose that the equation for planned investment expenditures is now $I_p = 2{,}350 - 45r$. Derive the equation for the new autonomous planned spending schedule, A_p.
(g) Derive the equation for the new IS curve, $Y = kA_p$.
(h) Using the equation for the new IS curve, calculate the new equilibrium levels of income at interest rates equal to 0, 2, and 4.
(i) Using your answers to part h, calculate the slope of the new IS curve, $\Delta r / \Delta Y$.
(j) Using your answers to part e of problem 5, and parts e and i of this problem, explain whether the IS curve gets flatter or steeper as (1), the multiplier increases, and (2), the responsiveness of autonomous planned spending to the interest rate increases.

*7. Consider an economy in which consumption, taxes, and net exports all change as income changes. In addition, consumption and planned investment change as the interest rate changes. You are given the following information concerning autonomous consumption, the marginal propensity to consume, planned investment, government purchases of goods and services, and net exports: $C = C_a + 0.85(Y - T)$; $C_a = 225 - 10r$; $I_p = 1{,}610 - 30r$; $G = 1{,}650$; $NX = 700 - 0.08Y$; $T = 100 + 0.2Y$.

(a) Compute the value of the multiplier.
(b) Derive the equation for the autonomous planned spending schedule, A_p.
(c) Derive the equation for the IS curve, $Y = kA_p$.

(d) Using the equation for the *IS* curve, calculate the equilibrium level of income at an interest rate equal to 3.

(e) At the equilibrium level of income at an interest rate of 3, show that leakages equal injections.

Self-Test Answers

p. 62 (1) $C = C_a$ in the general linear form, $C = 500$ in the numerical example. (2) Your options are to borrow, reduce your savings account, and to sell stocks, bonds, or any other assets you may own.

p. 63 (1) At point F consumption and disposable income are equal. Thus consumption, $C_a + c(Y - T)$, equals disposable income, or $Y - T$. Setting these two equal, we can subtract $c(Y - T)$ from $Y - T$ to obtain $C_a = (1 - c)(Y - T)$. Dividing by $1 - c$, we obtain the answer that disposable income $(Y - T)$ is equal to $C_a/(1 - c)$ and so is consumption. Thus at point F consumption equals $500/0.25$, or $2{,}000$, while saving equals zero. (2) When disposable income is $5{,}000$, consumption $C = 500 + 0.75(5{,}000) = 4{,}250$. Saving $= Y - T - C = 5{,}000 - 4{,}250 = 750$.

p. 68 (1) When income is only $4{,}000$, planned expenditure is equal to autonomous spending $(1{,}200 + 500 - 200)$ plus induced consumption (0.75 times $4{,}000 = 3{,}000$), for a total of $4{,}500$. Thus planned expenditure exceeds income, forcing firms to reduce their inventories in order to meet demand. (2) Unintended inventory investment is -500, and firms raise production in order to provide goods to meet planned expenditures; this increase in production moves the economy toward the equilibrium income level of $6{,}000$.

p. 73 (1) We write planned investment as I_p with a p subscript, to reflect our assumption that *consumers, the government, and exporters and importers are always able to realize their plans*, so that there is no such thing as autonomous unplanned consumption, autonomous unplanned tax revenues, unplanned government spending, or unplanned net exports. Only business firms are forced to make unplanned expenditures, as occurs when investment (I) is not equal to what they plan (I_p), but also includes unplanned inventory (I_u). (2) cT_a appears with a minus sign because an increase in taxes will reduce, rather than increase, autonomous planned spending by the amount of the tax times the fraction of the tax that would have been consumed rather than saved. (3) T_a is multiplied by c because taxes are not part of GDP. A change in taxes only alters GDP if it alters consumption. The effect on consumption is given by $-T_a$ times the marginal propensity to consume.

p. 74 (1) We are assuming that the marginal propensity to consume does not change. (2) When we assume the marginal propensity to consume does not change, the marginal propensity to save will not change either.[a] (3) $s = 1 - c$.

p. 76 (1) Income will decline by $2{,}000$ and saving will decline by one quarter of $2{,}000$, the exact amount of the decline in government expenditures. (2) Tax revenues exceed government spending. Private savers no longer purchase government bonds. Saving will equal the amount that total investment exceeds the surplus. (3) If taxes are raised by \$667 billion, saving declines by exactly \$667 billion. Private households pay for the higher taxes by reducing their level of saving.

p. 83 (1) A reduction of imports raises net exports and shifts the A_p demand schedule to the right. (2) A change in interest rates moves the economy *along* the schedule but does not shift it. (3) Higher taxes reduce consumption and thus shift the A_p demand schedule to the left. (4) Higher government spending shifts the A_p demand schedule to the right. (5) A reduction in consumer confidence shifts the A_p demand schedule to the left.

p. 84 (1) An interest rate of 5 percent is compatible with a \$8,000 billion level of equilibrium real income. (2) This occurs at point D on the *IS* curve in the right-hand frame of Figure 3-9.

---

[a] Using the calculus formula for the change in a ratio, the change in income when both A_p and s are allowed to change is
$$\Delta Y = \Delta A_p/s - A_p \Delta s/s^2$$
Equation (3.14) in the text simply sets Δs equal to zero in this expression.

Appendix to Chapter 3
Allowing for Income Taxes and Income-Dependent Net Exports

Effect of Income Taxes

When the government raises some of its tax revenue (T) with an income tax in addition to the autonomous tax (T_a), its total tax revenue is:

$$T = T_a + tY \quad (1)$$

The first component is the autonomous tax, for which we continue to use the symbol (T_a). The second component is income tax revenue, the tax rate (t) times income (Y). Disposable income ($Y - T$) is total income minus tax revenue:

$$Y_D = Y - T = Y - T_a - tY = (1 - t)Y - T_a \quad (2)$$

Leakages from the Spending Stream

Following any change in total income (Y), disposable income changes by only a fraction ($1 - t$) as much. For instance, if the tax rate (t) is 0.2, then disposable income changes by 80 percent of the change in total income. Any change in total income (ΔY) is now divided into induced consumption, induced saving, and induced income tax revenue. The fraction of ΔY going into consumption is the marginal propensity to consume disposable income (c) times the fraction of income going into disposable income ($1 - t$). Thus the change in total income is divided up as shown in the following table.

Fraction going to:	General Linear Form	Numerical Example
1. Induced consumption	$c(1 - t)$	$0.75(1 - 0.2) = 0.6$
2. Induced saving	$s(1 - t)$	$0.25(1 - 0.2) = 0.2$
3. Induced tax revenue	t	0.2
Total	$(c + s)(1 - t) + t$ $= 1 - t + t = 1.0$	1.0

As in equation (3.10) on p. 68, the economy is in equilibrium when income equals planned expenditures:

$$Y = E_p \quad (3)$$

As before, we can subtract induced consumption from both sides of the equilibrium condition. According to the preceding table, income (Y) minus induced consumption is the total of induced saving plus induced tax revenue. Planned expenditure (E_p) minus induced consumption is autonomous planned spending (A_p). Thus the equilibrium condition is

induced saving + induced tax revenue = autonomous planned spending (A_p) (4)

From the table just given, equation (4) can be written in symbols as:

$$[s(1 - t) + t]Y = A_p \quad (5)$$

The term in brackets on the left-hand side is the fraction of a change in income that does *not* go into induced consumption—that is, the sum of the fraction going to induced saving $s(1 - t)$ and the fraction going to the government as income tax revenue (t). The sum of these two fractions within the brackets is called the **marginal leakage rate**. The equilibrium value for Y can be calculated when we divide both sides of equation (5) by the term in brackets:

The **marginal leakage rate** is the fraction of income that is taxed or saved rather than being spent on consumption.

General Linear Form	Numerical Example
$Y = \dfrac{A_p}{s(1-t)+t}$	$Y = \dfrac{2{,}000}{0.25(0.8)+0.2} = \dfrac{2{,}000}{0.4} = 5{,}000 \qquad (6)$

The numerical example shows that if autonomous planned spending (A_p) is $2,000 billion, income will be only $5,000 billion, rather than $8,000 billion as in the example used previously in Chapter 3. Why? A greater fraction of each dollar of income now leaks out of the spending stream—0.4 in this numerical example—than occurred due to the saving rate of 0.25 by itself. This allows the injection of autonomous planned spending ($A_p = 2{,}000$) to be balanced by leakages out of the spending stream at a lower level of income.

Income Taxes and the Multiplier

The change in income (ΔY) is simply the change in autonomous planned spending (ΔA_p) divided by the marginal leakage rate:

$$\Delta Y = \frac{\Delta A_p}{s(1-t)+t} \qquad (7)$$

The multiplier ($\Delta Y/\Delta A_p$) is simply 1.0 divided by the marginal leakage rate. The multiplier was $1/s$ when there was no income tax. Now, with an income tax:

$$\text{multiplier} = \frac{1}{\text{marginal leakage rate}} = \frac{1}{s(1-t)+t} \qquad (8)$$

In Chapter 3, where the income tax rate is assumed to be zero, the numerical example of the multiplier was 4. This was a special case of equation (8), valid when $t = 0$, so that the marginal leakage rate equals simply s, or 0.25.

Now that we have introduced an income tax rate of 0.2, the marginal leakage rate is 0.4 [see equation (6)] and the multiplier is 1/0.4 or 2.5. Thus raising the income tax rate reduces the multiplier and vice versa. This gives the government a new tool for stabilizing income. When the government wants to stimulate the economy and raise income, it can raise income in equation (6) and the multiplier in equation (8) by cutting income tax rates. This occurred most recently in 2001 and again in 2003. And, when the government wants to restrain the economy, it can raise income tax rates, as occurred most recently in 1993.

The Government Budget

The government budget surplus is defined as before; it equals tax revenue minus government spending, $T - G$. Substituting the definition in equation (1), which expresses tax revenue (T) as the sum of autonomous and induced tax revenue, we can write the government surplus as:

$$\text{government budget surplus} = T - G = T_a + tY - G \qquad (9)$$

Automatic stabilization is the effect of income taxes in lowering the multiplier effect of changes in autonomous planned spending.

Thus the government budget surplus automatically rises when the level of income expands. This consequence of the income tax is sometimes called **automatic stabilization**. This name reflects the automatic rise and fall of income tax revenues as income rises and falls. When income rises, income tax revenues rise and siphon off some of the income before households have a chance to spend it. Similarly, when income falls, income tax revenues fall and help minimize the drop in disposable income. This is why the presence of an income tax makes the multiplier smaller.

Autonomous and Induced Net Exports

The theory of income determination in equation (6) states that equilibrium income equals autonomous planned spending (A_p) divided by the marginal leakage rate. When the United States trades with nations abroad, U.S. producers sell part of domestic output as exports. Households and business firms purchase imports from abroad, so part of U.S. expenditure does not generate U.S. production.

How do exports and imports affect the determination of income? We learned in Chapter 2 that the difference between exports and imports is called net exports and is part of GDP. When exports increase, net exports increase. When imports increase, net exports decrease. Designating net exports by NX, we can write the relationship between net exports and income (Y) as:

$$NX = NX_a - nxY \qquad (10)$$

Net exports contains an autonomous component (NX_a), reflecting the fact that the level of exports depends mainly on income in foreign countries (which is exogenous, not explained by our theory) rather than on domestic income (Y). Net exports also contains an induced component ($-nxY$), reflecting the fact that imports rise if domestic income (Y) rises, thus reducing net exports. The meaning of nx can be stated as "the share of imports in GDP."

Because we now have a new component of autonomous expenditure, the autonomous component of net exports (NX_a), we can rewrite our definition of A_p as the following in place of equation:

$$A_p = C_a - cT_a + I_p + G + NX_a \qquad (11)$$

Because imports depend on income (Y), the induced component of net exports ($-nxY$) has exactly the same effect on equilibrium income and the multiplier as does the income tax. Imports represent a leakage from the spending stream, a portion of a change in income that is not part of the disposable income of U.S. citizens and thus not available for consumption. The fraction of a change in income that is spent on net exports (nx) is part of the economy's marginal leakage rate.

Types of leakages	Marginal leakage rate
Saving only	s
Saving and income tax	$s(1 - t) + t$
Saving, income tax, and imports	$s(1 - t) + t + nx$

Full Equations for Equilibrium Income and the Multiplier

When we combine equation (6), equation (11), and the table, equilibrium income becomes:

$$Y = \frac{A_p}{\text{marginal leakage rate}} = \frac{C_a - cT_a + I_p + G + NX_a}{s(1 - t) + t + nx} \qquad (12)$$

The change in income then becomes

$$\Delta Y = \frac{\Delta A_p}{\text{marginal leakage rate}},$$

where $\Delta A_p = \Delta C_a - c\Delta T_a + \Delta I_p + \Delta G + \Delta NX_a$ and the marginal leakage rate is the same as the denominator of equation (12).

The Balanced Budget Multiplier

The balanced budget multiplier may be generalized from equation (3.20) in Chapter 3 by replacing s in the denominator by the marginal leakage rate:

$$\text{balanced budget multiplier} = \frac{1 - c}{\text{marginal leakage rate}}.$$

CHAPTER 4

Monetary and Fiscal Policy in the *IS-LM* Model

Money is always there, but the pockets change.
—Gertrude Stein

4-1 Introduction: The Power of Monetary and Fiscal Policy

The last chapter examined the determinants of the demand for commodities, that is, the goods and services that make up total real GDP. We learned that the economy is in equilibrium when total output or real GDP is equal to what households, business firms, the government, and foreigners want to buy, that is, planned expenditures. When any of the determinants of planned expenditures change, business firms will react by raising or reducing output, and the economy will experience business cycles rather than smooth and steady growth of real GDP.

Equilibrium real GDP is equal to autonomous planned spending times the multiplier.[1] The primary causes of business cycles are changes in autonomous planned spending, which has five components, any of which can change and thus cause equilibrium real GDP to move up or down. Three of the five components, namely government spending, autonomous tax revenue, and the demand for exports, are set by the government and by foreigners, and these three components do not depend on the interest rate. However, the remaining two of the five components, namely autonomous consumption and planned investment, depend on the interest rate.

The last chapter summarized the relationship between equilibrium real GDP and the interest rate in a downward-sloping graphical schedule called the *IS* curve. Everywhere along the *IS* curve, the commodity market is in equilibrium and there is no unplanned inventory accumulation or decumulation. The position of the *IS* curve depends on the components of planned autonomous spending and the multiplier, and its slope depends on the multiplier and the responsiveness of planned spending to changes in the interest rate. However, this single graphical schedule, the *IS* curve, cannot determine two unknown

---

[1] In the text of Chapter 3, the multiplier (k) is equal to the inverse of the marginal propensity to save ($k = 1/s$). In the Appendix to Chapter 3, we expand the concept of "leakages" to include not just saving, but also the government's revenues from the income tax, as well as the leakage out of the spending stream when part of a change in GDP is spent on imports from foreign countries rather than on domestic production. Denoting the income tax rate as t and the share of GDP spent on imports as nx, our expanded concept of the multiplier is the inverse of the marginal leakage rate, that is, $k = 1/MLR = 1/[s(1 - t) + t + nx]$.

variables: real GDP and the interest rate. We cannot determine real GDP without knowing the value of the interest rate, and the reverse is true as well: We cannot determine the interest rate until we have determined real GDP.

To determine *both* real GDP and the interest rate simultaneously, we need a second, separate relationship between them. This second relationship, called the *LM* curve, is provided by the money market, where the supply of money controlled by the Federal Reserve Board interacts with the demand for that money by households and business firms. The economy's equilibrium real GDP and its equilibrium interest rate are simultaneously determined at the intersection of the *IS* curve and the *LM* curve, where both the commodity market and money market are in equilibrium.

This *IS-LM* Model allows us to understand more fully the sources of business cycles and what can be done by the government to dampen or, ideally, to eliminate business cycles. Monetary policy, controlled by the Federal Reserve Board, can be used to change interest rates and hence equilibrium real GDP. Fiscal policy, controlled by Congress and the President, can also be used to change equilibrium real GDP and the interest rate by means of changes in government spending, autonomous tax revenue, and the income tax rate. We will learn that both the level of real GDP and the interest rate can be affected by monetary and by fiscal policy, working separately or in combination.

This chapter greatly improves our understanding of the determination of real GDP and the causes of business cycles, going well beyond Chapter 3 in which there was no monetary policy and no indication of how the interest rate is determined. In this chapter we can begin our investigation of the key questions at the heart of recent debates:

1. How does monetary policy work? By what mechanism did the Federal Reserve Board (the Fed) reduce the interest rate from 6.5 to 1.0 percent between late 2000 and late 2002?

2. What difference did it make that the federal government ran persistent budget deficits from 1980 to 1997, followed by budget surpluses during 1998–2001, followed by deficits in 2002–05? Why did this shift from deficit to surplus back to deficit occur?

3. Does the multiplier effect of fiscal policy, previously examined in Chapter 3, depend on the conduct of monetary policy? Does the multiplier effect of monetary policy depend in turn on the conduct of fiscal policy?

4. If real GDP is higher or lower than desired, so that a policy action restraining or stimulating the economy is needed, should that policy action be carried out in the form of monetary or fiscal policy, or by a combination of the two?

4-2 Why People Use Money

The money market is a general expression for the financial sector of the economy. In reality, the financial sector consists of many assets in addition to money, including short-term debt of corporations and the government, as well as bonds, stocks, and mutual funds. In this chapter we will limit our attention to the segment of the financial sector generally referred to as "money."

The **money supply** (M^s) consists of two parts: currency and checking accounts at banks and thrift institutions. At this stage in the book, the money supply may be considered to be a policy instrument that the Fed can set

The **money supply** consists of currency and transactions accounts, including checking accounts at banks and thrift institutions.

exactly at any desired value, just as we have been assuming that the government can precisely set the level of its fiscal policy instruments—that is, its purchases of goods and services and tax revenues. Later, in Chapter 13, we will learn how the Fed achieves its control over the money supply in actual practice.

The theory developed in this chapter establishes a link between the money supply, income, and interest rates. In order to understand the hypothesis underlying the demand for money, we begin by examining the three traditional functions of money: its roles as a medium of exchange, a store of value, and a unit of account.

A Medium of Exchange

The most important function that differentiates money from other assets is its role as a **medium of exchange**. Money is one of the most important inventions in human history because it has allowed society to rise above the cumbersome method of exchange known as the barter system. With barter, one good or service is exchanged directly for another. If, as a professor, I want a leaky faucet fixed, I must find a plumber who wants to learn about economics. It might take weeks or months to find such a plumber, since the matching of services requires a "double coincidence of wants."

A barter society remains primitive because people have to spend so much time arranging exchanges that they have little time remaining to produce efficiently. As a result, to avoid arranging exchanges they must become self-sufficient (I would have to fix my own leaking faucet), thus failing to take advantage of the essential role of specialization in the development of an advanced economic system. Money eliminates the need for barter and the double coincidence of wants.

Which types of assets serve as a medium of exchange? Thirty years ago almost all exchanges in the United States involved coins, currency, or checking accounts that paid no interest. Gradually other methods of exchange have developed, including interest-bearing checking accounts, savings accounts, and money market mutual funds against which checks can be written. The requirements for an asset to qualify as a medium of exchange include ready acceptability, protection from counterfeiting, and divisibility (ability to use for small transactions).

A **medium of exchange** is used for buying and selling goods and services and is a universal alternative to the barter system.

A Store of Value

People do not always spend the entirety of their income the instant they receive it. Some receipts may be spent a day or two later, but others may be saved for a substantial period of time. People need some way of storing the purchasing power of their receipts until a later time. Any asset that performs this function is called a **store of value**. There are many financial instruments that serve as a store of value but not as a medium of exchange, including passbook savings accounts that do not provide check-writing services, as well as bonds and stocks. Money can be used both as a medium of exchange and as a store of value.

A **store of value** is a method of storing purchasing power when receipts and expenditures are not perfectly synchronized.

A Unit of Account

Money is also used for accounting purposes. How much your employer will pay you in wages, how much you owe the bank, how much a firm has earned, and how much a bond is worth are all recorded in some **unit of account**. This unit is called dollars in the United States, pounds sterling in the United Kingdom, yen in Japan, euro in twelve western European nations, and so on.

A **unit of account** is a way of recording receipts, expenditures, assets, and liabilities.

The dollars entered on accounting records do not physically exist, in the sense that no coin or piece of currency corresponding to each one exists in a particular location. Some dollars that serve as bookkeeping entries can also serve as a medium of exchange without any piece of paper actually changing hands, as in wire transfers between bank accounts.

4-3 How the Fed Controls the Money Supply

In this section we use a simple definition of the money supply that includes only currency and checking accounts. Subsequently in Chapter 13 we will discover that there are several alternative definitions of the money supply, some of which include assets other than currency and checking accounts. The Fed controls the supply of currency through its control over the printing press (pull out a dollar bill and notice that over the photo of George Washington is a label "Federal Reserve Note"). The Fed controls the total amount in checking accounts by requiring the banks keep a certain fraction, say 10 percent, of their checking account deposits in a special account at the Fed called "bank reserves."

The Fed's Balance Sheet

A commercial bank has two main kind of assets, the bank reserves it holds on deposit at the Fed and the loans that it grants to households and business firms; these earn interest for the bank. The main liability of a commercial bank are the deposits that households and business firms entrust to the bank. By paying a lower interest rate on deposits than it receives on its loans, the bank has enough left over to pay its employees, cover its other expenses, and earn a profit.

Likewise, the Fed has a balance sheet, as illustrated in Table 4-1. The Fed's main asset consists of its holdings of government bonds. The Fed has two main types of liabilities. The first is the currency that it has printed and that it is obligated to redeem at any time, hence a liability. The second type of Fed liability is the total of bank reserves that it holds on deposits for the commercial banks. As shown in Table 4-1, in this example the Fed owns $400 billion of government bonds, and its liabilities consist of $200 billion of currency and $200 billion of bank reserves. The total of its liabilities is called "the monetary base," which is $400 billion in this example.

What Action by the Fed Will Raise the Money Supply?

The Fed's liabilities are not the same as the money supply. The money supply consists of currency ($200 billion in Table 4-1) and checking deposits at banks.

Table 4-1 A Simplified Version of the Fed's Balance Sheet (all values in $ billions)

Assets		Liabilities	
		Currency	200
Government Bonds	400	Bank Reserves	200
Total Assets	400	Total Liabilities = Monetary Base	400

Since the banks are required to hold 10 percent of their checking deposits as reserves at the Fed, we know that the $200 billion of bank reserves in Table 4-1 must be supporting $2,000 billion of checking deposits (in this simplified example we ignore saving deposits, certificates of deposits, and other types of bank deposits). Thus the total money supply is the total of $200 billion of currency and $2,000 billion of checking deposits, a total of $2,200 billion.

The money supply (M^s) is equal to the monetary base times the money multiplier:

$$M^s = \text{money multiplier} \times \text{monetary base} \qquad (4.1)$$

or, in this example

$$\$2{,}200 \text{ billion} = 5.5(\$400 \text{ billion}).^2$$

But the Fed may not always be satisfied with a money supply of $2,200 billion. Let us say that the Fed has decided that real GDP is too low, and to stimulate more planned spending, the Fed needs to raise the money supply by $550 billion. To do this, the Fed must raise the monetary base by $100 billion. As we learn in Chapter 13, the Fed can raise the monetary base by $100 billion by purchasing $100 billion worth of government bonds. In Table 4-1, this would raise its assets by $100 billion. What about its liabilities? The Fed pays for the $100 billion in government bonds by writing a check to the seller of the bonds. The seller deposits the Fed's check in the seller's bank account, and that bank sends the check back to the Fed, receiving credit to its bank reserve account at the Fed, which rises by $100 billion. Thus both the Fed's assets and liabilities have risen by $100 billion, and because the money multiplier in equation (4.1) above is 5.5, the total money supply increases by $550 billion, just as the Fed desires.

In the real world, the Fed is constantly buying and selling government securities. Sometimes this occurs because the Fed wants to raise or lower the money supply, but sometimes the Fed must act to maintain a given money supply if the money multiplier changes. For instance, if the money multiplier suddenly were to drop from 5.5 to 5.0, to maintain the original money supply of $2,200, the Fed would would have to raise the monetary base from $400 billion to $440 billion by buying $40 billion of government bonds.

Now that we understand the method by which the Fed controls the money supply, it is time to introduce the money supply into our model of income determination. Whatever the money supply that the Fed chooses, the equilibrium level of real GDP and the interest rate will adjust to keep the commodity and money markets in equilibrium. The resulting amount of real GDP may be too high or too low, and then monetary policy and/or fiscal policy will need to adjust to push real GDP toward the desired amount.

4-4 Income, the Interest Rate, and the Demand for Money

The hypothesis that links the money supply, income, and the interest rate states that *the amount of money that people demand in real terms depends both on income and on the interest rate.* Why do households give up interest earnings to hold

---

[2] In Chapter 13 we learn that the money multiplier is 1.0 plus the ratio of currency to deposits (0.1 in this example) divided by the sum of the reserve-to-deposit ratio (also 0.1) and the ratio of currency to deposits (0.1). Thus the money multiplier in this example is 1.1 divided by 0.2, or 5.5.

money balances that pay no interest? The main reason is that at least *some* holding of money is necessary to facilitate transactions, due to the role of money as a medium of exchange.

Income and the Demand for Money

Funds held in the form of stocks or bonds pay interest but cannot be used for transactions. People have to carry currency in their pockets or have money in their bank accounts to back up a check before they can buy anything. (Even if they use credit cards, they need money in their bank accounts to keep up with their credit card bills.) Because rich people make more purchases, they generally need a larger amount of currency and larger bank deposits. Thus the demand for **real money balances** increases when everyone becomes richer—that is, when the total of real income increases.

Real money balances equal the total money supply divided by the price level.

Changes in real income alter the demand for money in real terms—that is, adjusted for changes in the price level. Let us assume that the demand for real money balances (M/P) equals half of real income (Y):

$$\left(\frac{M}{P}\right)^d = 0.5Y$$

The superscript d means "the demand for."

If real income (Y) is $8,000 billion, the demand for real money balances ($M/P)^d$ will be $4,000 billion, as shown in Figure 4-1 by the vertical line (L') drawn at $4,000 billion. The line is vertical because we are assuming initially that the demand for real balances ($M/P)^d$ does not depend on the interest rate (r).

How Income and the Interest Rate Determine the Demand for Real Balances

Figure 4-1 The Demand for Money, the Interest Rate, and Real Income

The vertical line L' is drawn on the unrealistic assumption that the demand for real balances is equal to half of real income ($8,000 billion in this case), but does not depend on the interest rate. The L_0 curve maintains income at $8,000, but it allows the demand for real balances to decrease by $1,000 billion for each 5 percent increase in the interest rate. The shaded area shows the amount shifted into other assets, an amount that grows as the interest rate rises, leaving a smaller and smaller amount to be held as money.

The Interest Rate and the Demand for Money

The L' line is unrealistic, however, because individuals will not hold as much money at a 10 percent interest rate as at a zero interest rate. Why? Because the interest rate plotted on the vertical axis is paid on *assets other than money*, such as bonds and savings certificates. The higher the reward (r) for holding interest-earning financial assets (that are not money), the less money will be held.

If the interest rate (r) paid on nonmoney assets were less than the interest paid on money, there would be no point in holding them. Individuals would hold all of their financial assets in the form of money to take advantage of its convenience. But if the interest rate on them were higher than the interest paid on money, individuals would cut down on their average money holding in order to earn the higher interest available on alternative assets. They would consider these higher interest earnings sufficient compensation for the nuisance of periodically converting these assets into money.

In Figure 4-1 the downward slope of the L_0 line through points F and D indicates that when real income is $8,000 billion and the interest rate is zero, the demand for real balances is $4,000 billion. But when the interest rate rises from zero to 5 percent, people suffer inconvenience to cut down their money holdings from $4,000 billion to $3,000 billion (point D). When the interest rate is 10 percent, only $2,000 billion of money is demanded (point F). The new L_0 line can be summarized as showing that the real demand for money $(M/P)^d$ is half of income minus $200 billion times the interest rate:

$$\left(\frac{M}{P}\right)^d = 0.5Y - 200r$$

A change in the interest rate moves the economy up and down its real money demand schedule, whereas a change in real output (Y) shifts that

Figure 4-2 Effect on the Money Demand Schedule of a Decline in Real Income from $8,000 to $6,000 Billion

A Drop in the Level of Income Shifts the Money Demand Schedule to the Left

The L_0 line is copied from Figure 4-1 and shows the demand for real balances at different rates of interest, assuming that real income is $8,000 billion. A $2,000 billion drop in the level of income to $6,000 billion causes the demand for real balances to drop by half as much, or $1,000 billion, at each interest rate level. For instance, at an interest rate of 10 percent the demand for real balances falls from $2,000 billion at point F to $1,000 billion at point C.

schedule to the left or right, as shown in Figure 4-2. At any given interest rate, the change in the amount of money demanded is given by

$$\Delta\left(\frac{M}{P}\right)^d = 0.5\Delta Y$$

Between points F and C, the interest rate is the same, output falls by 2,000, and the demand for money declines by $1,000.

> **Self-Test**
>
> 1. What are the two determinants of the real demand for money?
> 2. What is the effect of each determinant on the real demand for money?
> 3. Does a change in either determinant shift the *IS* curve?

4-5 The *LM* Curve

Thus far we have learned that the supply of money (M^s) is controlled by the Fed, and that the real quantity of money demanded by households $(M/P)^d$ depends on both income and the interest rate. Now we can tie these two relationships together by assuming that the money market is always *in equilibrium* (a situation where there is no pressure for change), with the real supply of money equal to the real demand for money. This equilibrium condition for the money market allows us to derive a relationship called the *LM curve*, just as we previously derived an equilibrium condition for the commodity market called the *IS curve*. To achieve equilibrium in the money market, the real supply of money (M^s/P) must equal the demand for real money $(M/P)^d$:

$$\frac{M^s}{P} = \left(\frac{M}{P}\right)^d = 0.5Y - 200r \qquad (4.2)$$

If the amount of money supplied by the government is $2,000 billion and the price index (P) is set at a constant value of 1.0, then M^s/P equals $2,000 billion. To simplify the analysis, we assume that the supply of money does not depend on the interest rate, so M^s/P is drawn in the left frame of Figure 4-3 as a vertical line at a level of $2,000 billion for every interest rate. The two money demand schedules, L_0 and L_1, are copied from Figure 4-2.

How to Derive the *LM* Curve

The sloped money demand line L_0, drawn for an income of $8,000 billion, crosses the M^s/P line at point F, where the interest rate is 10 percent. The demand for money at F is $2,000 billion, and the supply of money is also $2,000 billion. Because the two are equal, the money market is in equilibrium when $Y = 8,000$ (assumed in drawing the L_0 line) and $r = 10$ percent. This equilibrium combination of values is plotted at point F in the right frame of Figure 4-3.[3]

---

[3] Thus, in equation (4.2)

$$\begin{aligned}2,000 &= 0.5(8,000) - 200(10) \\ &= 4,000 - 2,000 \\ &= 2,000\end{aligned}$$

102 Chapter 4 • Monetary and Fiscal Policy in the *IS-LM* Model

A Fixed Money Supply Is Consistent with Many Different Levels of Income

Figure 4-3 Derivation of the *LM* Curve

In the left frame the L_0 and L_1 schedules are copied from the previous figure. The vertical M^s/P line shows the available supply of money provided by the government. The money market is in equilibrium where the supply line (M^s/P) crosses the demand line (L_0 or L_1). When income is $8,000 billion, equilibrium occurs at point F, plotted again in the right frame. When income is $6,000 billion, equilibrium occurs where L_0 crosses M^s/P at point G, also plotted in the right frame. The *LM* curve or schedule shows all combinations of Y and r consistent with equilibrium in the money market.

If income is $6,000 billion instead of $8,000 billion, the demand for money is shown by schedule L_1 passing through points C and G in the left frame of Figure 4-3. Now the demand for real money balances can be equal to the fixed real supply of money only at point G, where the interest rate is 5 percent. Thus Y = 6,000 and r = 5 is another combination consistent with equilibrium in the money market, and this is plotted at point G in the right frame of Figure 4-3.[4]

What the *LM* Curve Shows

The line connecting points G and F in the right-hand frame of Figure 4-3 is called the **LM curve**. The *LM* curve represents all combinations of income (Y) and interest rate (r) where the money market is in equilibrium—that is, where the real supply of money equals the real demand for money.

At any point off the *LM* curve, say point D, the money market is not in equilibrium. The problem at D and all other points in the purple shaded area is

The **LM curve** is the schedule that identifies the combinations of income and the interest rate at which the money market is in equilibrium; on the *LM* curve the demand for money equals the supply of money.

---

[4] Thus, in equation (4.2)

$$2,000 = 0.5(6,000) - 200(5)$$
$$= 3,000 - 1,000$$
$$= 2,000$$

Learning About Diagrams: The *LM* Curve

The *LM* curve is as important and useful as the *IS* curve, introduced in Section 3-10. This box explains the slope of the *LM* curve and what makes it shift and rotate its position.

Diagram Ingredients and Reasons for Slope

The vertical axis is the interest rate and the horizontal axis is the level of income (same as the *IS* curve).

The *LM* curve shows the different combinations of the interest rate and income consistent with setting the demand for money equal to a *fixed* supply of money. Since the demand for money is fixed everywhere along the *LM* curve, but income increases as we move to the right, "something" must happen to offset the higher demand for money that results from higher income. That something is the higher interest rate, which induces people to shift out of money into nonmonetary assets, freeing up more of the fixed available money to be used for the higher level of transactions.

Along any given *LM* curve, the level of real money balances (M^s/P) is fixed, but real income (Y) varies. The ratio of real income to real balances is called the *velocity* of money (V):

$$\text{velocity } (V) = \frac{Y}{M^s/P} = \frac{PY}{M^s}$$

The right-hand expression states that velocity is also equal to nominal income (PY) divided by the nominal money supply (M^s). The higher the interest rate, the higher is velocity. Why? If r increases, people want to hold less money. But the money supply is fixed. To maintain equilibrium in the money market, there *must be an increase in income* to induce households to hold the fixed existing quantity of money. Anything that can cause the economy to move up and down along a fixed *LM* curve achieves a change of velocity by altering Y while M^s/P is fixed.

What Shifts and Rotates the *LM* Curve?

The *LM* curve is drawn for a fixed real supply of money (M^s/P). A higher nominal supply of money (M^s) will shift the *LM* curve to the right, and a lower nominal supply of money will shift the *LM* curve to the left. An increase in the price level (P) will shift the *LM* curve to the left, and vice versa.

Anything that makes the demand for money less sensitive to the interest rate makes both the money demand schedule, $L(Y)$, and the *LM* curve steeper (rotating it upward around its horizontal intercept). Anything that makes the demand for money less responsive to changes in income will make the *LM* curve flatter and also shift it outward.

What Is True of Points That Are off the *LM* Curve?

The entire area to the left of the *LM* curve has an excess supply of money because income is lower than that needed to create a sufficient demand for money to match the supply.

The entire area to the right of the *LM* curve has an excess demand for money because income is higher than required to match the demand for money to the fixed supply.

At any point off the *LM* curve there is pressure for interest rates to change. For instance, when there is an excess demand for money, people try to obtain money by selling bonds and other financial assets, and this pushes up the interest rates on bonds and other financial assets.

---

that the demand for real money exceeds the available supply. At point *C* and all other points in the green shaded area there is an excess supply of money that exceeds the demand.

How does the economy adjust to guarantee that the given supply of money created by the government is exactly equal to the demand when the money market is out of equilibrium, as at point *D*? One possible adjustment, a reduction in the price level, will be considered later. In this chapter we continue to assume that the price index (P) is fixed at 1.0. Without changing prices, the economy might achieve money market equilibrium from point *D* by increasing the interest rate from 5 to 10 percent. This would move it to point *F*, cutting the demand for money. Or, instead, income might fall from $8,000 billion to $6,000 billion while the interest rate remains fixed. This would cause a movement to point *G* and would also cut the demand for money. Or some other combination might occur, with a partial drop in income and a partial increase in the interest rate. Which of these possibilities actually occurs depends on the slope of the *IS* curve, as we see in the next section.

> ### Self-Test
>
> 1. By how much does the demand for money change when the economy moves from point *D* to point *F* in Figure 4-3?
> 2. From point *D* to point *G*?
> 3. From point *C* to point *F*?
> 4. From point *C* to point *G*?

4-6 The *IS* Curve Meets the *LM* Curve

Now we are ready to examine the economy's general equilibrium, which takes account of behavior in both the commodity and money markets. We do this by bringing together the IS_0 curve from Figure 3-9 and the LM_0 curve from Figure 4-3.

Equilibrium in the commodity market occurs only at points on the *IS* curve. Figure 4-4 copies the IS_0 schedule from Figure 3-9 drawn for a value of $A'_{p0} = 2,500$. At any point off the IS_0 curve, for instance *G* and *F*, the commodity market is out of equilibrium. *C*, *D*, and E_0 all represent different combinations of income and the interest rate that are compatible with commodity-market equilibrium. At which equilibrium point will the economy come to rest? The single IS_0 schedule does not provide enough information to determine *both*

Figure 4-4 The *IS* and *LM* Schedules Cross at Last

The IS_0 schedule is copied from Figure 3-9, the LM_0 schedule is copied from Figure 4-3. Only at the point E_0 is the economy in general equilibrium, with the conditions for equilibrium attained in both the commodity market (along *IS*) and the money market (along *LM*). At points *U*, *V*, *G*, and *F*, the commodity market is out of equilibrium. At points *U*, *V*, *C*, and *D*, the money market is out of equilibrium.

The Economy's "General" Equilibrium

income and the interest rate. *Two* schedules are needed to pin down the equilibrium values of *two* unknown variables.

The *LM* curve provides the necessary additional information, showing all combinations of income and the interest rate at which the money market is in equilibrium for a given real money supply—in this case, $2,000 billion. Figure 4-4 copies the LM_0 schedule from Figure 4-3 drawn for a value of $M^s/P = 2,000$. At any point off the LM_0 curve, for instance points C and D, the money market is out of equilibrium. At D income is too high and the real demand for money exceeds the real supply. At C income is too low and the real demand for money is below the real supply. Equilibrium in the money market occurs only at points such as G, F, and E_0, each representing combinations of income and the interest rate at which the real demand for money is equal to a real money supply of $2,000 billion.

How does the economy arrive at its **general equilibrium** at point E_0 if it starts out at the wrong place, such as at points U or V? If the commodity market is out of equilibrium and involuntary inventory decumulation or accumulation occurs, firms will step up or cut production, pushing the economy in the direction needed to reach E_0. If the money market is out of equilibrium, there will be pressure to adjust interest rates, since people will have to sell stocks and bonds if they cannot otherwise satisfy their demand for money. Either way the economy arrives at E_0.

General equilibrium is a situation of simultaneous equilibrium in all the markets of the economy.

4-7 Monetary Policy in Action

The *IS-LM* model uses two relations (or schedules) to determine the two endogenous variables, real income and the interest rate. The exogenous variables, which the model does not explain, are the level of business and consumer optimism, the single instrument of monetary policy (the money supply), the two instruments of fiscal policy (government spending and tax revenues), and net exports. Whenever there is a change in one of the exogenous variables, the result will be a change in either or both of the two endogenous variables, real income (or GDP) and the interest rate. In this section we will see that a decision by the Fed to change the money supply will normally lead to a change in both real GDP and the interest rate.

What level of real GDP does the Fed desire? We shall assume that the desired level of income, natural real GDP, is $8,000 billion. In Figure 4-4 the equilibrium level of real income (GDP) at point E_0 is only $7,000 billion. Thus there is a $1,000 billion gap between actual and natural real GDP that needs to be filled. What should the Fed do?

To raise GDP by the required $1,000 billion, the Fed must increase the money supply. This action is called an **expansionary monetary policy**. Conversely, if natural real GDP is lower than actual real GDP, the Fed can decrease the money supply. This is an example of a **contractionary monetary policy**.

An **expansionary monetary policy** is one that has the effect of lowering interest rates and raising GDP.

A **contractionary monetary policy** is one that has the effect of lowering GDP and raising interest rates.

Normal Effects of an Increase in the Money Supply

Will an increase in the money supply increase real income, reduce the interest rate, or both? If the *IS* and *LM* curves have the "normal" shapes displayed in Figure 4-4, the answer is both.

How Monetary Policy Actually Worked in 2001–04

Monetary policy is carried out by the Federal Reserve System (or the "Fed" for short). Roughly every five weeks, an important meeting is held by the Federal Open Market Committee (FOMC). At precisely 2.15 P.M. Eastern time, an announcement is issued as to whether the FOMC has decided to raise, reduce, or leave unchanged the federal funds rate, an interest rate that banks charge each other for lending or borrowing bank reserves (see Chapter 13). In 2001 and early 2002, the FOMC responded to perceived weakness in the economy with unprecedented speed, cutting the federal funds rate at eleven straight meetings from 6.5 percent at the end of 2000 to 1.75 percent in January 2002, as shown by the quarterly average plotted by the green line in the figure. In subsequent meetings the federal funds rate was further reduced to 1.0 percent by June 2003. Only in June 2004 did the Fed begin to reverse itself by starting to raise the federal funds rate, reaching a level of 3.0 percent by May 2005.

In our textbook model of Chapters 3 and 4, there is only one interest rate. In reality, there are two major interest rates, the federal funds rate controlled by the Fed, and the rate of 10-year government bonds, shown by the purple line in the figure. The 10-year bond rate is set in a daily auction at the Chicago Board of Trade and is only indirectly influenced by the Fed, but is extremely important as it is the basis on which interest rates on home mortgages are set. The traders who set the 10-year bond rate are influenced by their *expectations* about the future course of Fed policy; the longer the traders expect the Fed to keep the federal funds rate at a low level, the lower the 10-year bond rate will go. The lowest monthly rate reached by the 10-year bond rate was in early June 2003, just before the Fed made its final reduction in the federal funds rate to 1.0 percent.

In the text, a reduction in the interest rate achieved by the Fed stimulates spending, as the *LM* curve moves rightward along the downward-sloping *IS* curve, as in Figure 4-5. In reality, the decline in the federal funds rate in 2001–03 allowed auto companies to offer lower interest rates on auto loans, and a unique type of incentive for auto purchases called "zero-rate financing" an amazingly low interest rate of zero on auto loans. While the auto companies lost money on zero-rate financing because their cost of obtaining money was above zero, they would not have been able to afford zero-rate financing if the Fed had not kept the federal funds rate so low. In response, auto purchasers raced to showrooms to buy cars at a zero interest rate on their car loans, and economists were surprised that auto sales reached record levels in the fall of 2001, despite the traumatic effect on consumer confidence of the September 11, 2001, attacks, and auto sales continued at relatively high levels throughout 2002, 2003, and 2004.

As bond traders watched the Fed lower the federal funds rate, the 10-year bond rate responded (as shown by the purple line in the figure), falling from 6.7 percent in January 2000, to 3.3 percent in June 2003. This interest rate is the basis for setting interest rates on home mortgage loans and home equity loans. Lower mortgage rates allowed more home buyers to qualify for mortgages, or allowed them to buy bigger homes, stimulating new home construction, a part of real GDP.

A remarkable new phenomenon, which had not occurred in previous periods of falling interest rates, was the refinancing of mortgage interest rates. American financial institutions give homeowners a good deal, guaranteeing that the interest rate on a fixed-rate mortgage will stay the same for as long as 30 years, but allowing homeowners to obtain a new mortgage at a lower interest rate when mortgage interest rates decline. The boom in refinancing of mortgage rates, called "re-fi's," in 2001–03 allowed millions of homeowners to lower their monthly payments (leaving more money for other purchases), and/or to increase the balance of the mortgage in order to obtain extra cash.

The effect of lower interest rates on consumption expenditures is one of four "channels" by which the Fed influences total spending. And the potent impact of lower

---

Figure 4-5 repeats the LM_0 curve of Figure 4-4, drawn on the assumption that the real money supply is $2,000 billion. Also repeated is the IS_0 curve of Figure 4-4, which assumes that $A'_{p0} = 2,500$ and $k = 4.0$. The economy's general equilibrium, the point where both the money and commodity markets are in equilibrium, occurs at point E_0.

Assume that the Fed now raises the nominal money supply from $2,000 billion to $3,000 billion. As long as the price level stays fixed at 1.0, the real money supply increases by the same amount. The *LM* curve shifts to the right by $2,000 billion. Now, at the new, higher real money supply of $3,000 billion, interest rates on consumption spending in 2001–04 suggests that this first channel was operating with great efficacy. However, there are three other channels of monetary influence, and none of these was operating normally.

The second channel is the influence of lower interest rates on planned investment. The 2001 recession had been caused primarily by a collapse in high-tech investment, particularly investment in computers, software, and telecommunications equipment. Lower interest rates did not stimulate spending on those products because the economy was awash in excess high-tech equipment; if a firm owns 100 computers and is only using 50 of them, lower interest rates will not induce the firm to buy more computers.

The third channel of monetary influence works through the stock market. Normally lower interest rates boost stock prices, thus stimulating both consumption and investment spending. But stock prices fell from mid-2000 until early 2003.

The fourth and final channel works through the exchange rate. As we will learn in Chapter 6, lower interest rates cause the exchange rate of the dollar to depreciate, making U.S. exports cheaper for foreigners to buy, thus boosting net exports. Instead of depreciating, the dollar appreciated (became more expensive) throughout 2001 but it then depreciated during 2002–04.

The first channel of monetary influence, the effect of lower interest rates in stimulating consumption, was clearly a very important reason why the recession of 2001 was so mild. But, nevertheless, the recovery remained weak and employment continued to fall until mid-2003. Some commentators have described monetary policy in 2001–04 as "a four-cylinder engine running on only one cylinder."

---

there is an "excess supply of money" of $1,000 billion. How can the economy generate the $1,000 billion increase in the real demand for money needed to balance the new higher supply?

Finding themselves with more money than they need, individuals transfer some money into savings accounts and use some to buy stocks, bonds, and commodities. This raises the prices of bonds and stocks and reduces the interest rate. The lower interest rate raises the desired level of autonomous consumption and investment spending, requiring an increase in production. Only at point E_1, with an income level of $8,000 billion and interest rate of 5 percent,

Figure 4-5 The Effect of a $1,000 Billion Increase in the Money Supply with a Normal *LM* Curve

The real money supply rises from $2,000 billion along the old LM_0 curve to $3,000 billion along the new LM_1 curve. In order to maintain equilibrium in both the commodity and money markets here, two effects occur: equilibrium income rises and the interest rate declines, as indicated by the movement from E_0 to E_1.

A Higher Money Supply Boosts Income and Cuts the Interest Rate

are both the money and commodity markets in equilibrium. Compared to the starting point E_0, the increase in the real money supply has caused both an *increase* in real income and a *reduction* in the interest rate.

Monetary policy works exactly the same in reverse. If the desired level of real income was not $8,000 billion but rather $7,000 billion, the Fed could move the economy leftward from point E_1 in Figure 4-5 to point E_0, simply by reducing the real money supply from $3,000 billion to $2,000 billion. As a result, the LM_1 curve would shift leftwards to LM_0, and income would decline from $8,000 billion to $7,000 billion.

4-8 How Fiscal Expansion Can "Crowd Out" Investment

In the last section we examined the effects on real income and the interest rate of changes in monetary policy by shifting the *LM* curve along a fixed *IS* curve. Now we shall do the reverse and shift the *IS* curve along a fixed *LM* curve. The original *IS* curve is copied from Figure 4-4 and is labeled in Figure 4-6 as the "old IS_0 curve"; it is drawn on the assumption that the amount of autonomous planned spending that would occur at a zero interest rate (A'_{p0}) is equal to $2,500 billion.

Expansionary Fiscal Policy Shifts the *IS* Curve

An expansionary fiscal policy taking the form of a $500 billion increase in government purchases shifts the *IS* curve to the right. Note that the horizontal distance between the old and new *IS* curves is not $500 billion but $2,000 billion,

4-8 How Fiscal Expansion Can "Crowd Out" Investment

The Crowding Out Effect Cuts the Fiscal Multiplier

Figure 4-6 The Effect on Real Income and the Interest Rate of a $500 Billion Increase in Government Spending

Along the original IS_0 curve, the autonomous spending desired at a zero interest rate (A'_{p0}) is 2,500 and the economy's equilibrium occurs at point E_0. A $500 billion increase in government spending boosts spending from $A'_{p0} = 2,500$ to $A'_{p1} = 3,000$, and shifts the IS curve rightward to IS_1. The economy's equilibrium slides up the LM curve from point E_0 to E_3. In contrast to Chapter 3's multiplier of 4.0, now the government spending multiplier is only 2.0. But, since income increases from E_0 to E_3, crowding out is partial, not complete.

since the horizontal shift of IS is $500 billion times the multiplier, still assumed to be 4.0.

Figure 4-6 demonstrates that the effect of an expansionary fiscal policy on real income is not indicated by our original Chapter 3 multiplier ($k = 4.0$) once the money market is taken into consideration. The full fiscal multiplier of $k = 4.0$ would move the economy horizontally from the initial equilibrium position at E_0 to point E_2, where income is $2,000 billion higher. At E_2, however, the money market is not in equilibrium, because E_2 is off the LM_0 curve. Income is higher than at E_0, raising the demand for money, but the real supply of money remains unchanged at the original assumed value $M^s/P = 2,000$. There is an excess demand for money.

To cut the demand for money back to the level of the fixed supply, the interest rate must rise. But an increase in the interest rate makes point E_2 untenable by reducing planned consumption and investment expenditures. *Only at point E_3 are both the commodity and money markets in equilibrium.* Real income does not increase by the full $2,000 billion, but only by half as much, $1,000 billion.

The higher interest rate accounts for the fact that the fiscal policy multiplier is 2.0, rather than 4.0, when the requirement for money market equilibrium is taken into account. The increase in the interest rate from 7.5 to 10 percent cuts private autonomous planned consumption and investment spending by $250 billion, fully half of the $500 billion increase in government spending. Thus fully half of the original multiplier of 4.0 is "crowded out."

Comparison of Equilibrium Positions E_0 and E_3

	Initial E_0	New E_3
Interest rate (r)	7.5	10.0
Private autonomous spending ($I_p + C_a = 2{,}500 - 100r$)	1,750	1,500
Government spending (G)	0	500
Total autonomous spending ($A_p = I_p + C_a + G$)	1,750	2,000
Income ($Y = 4.0 A_p$)	7,000	8,000

The Crowding Out Effect

The crowding out effect describes the effect of an increase in government spending or a reduction of tax rates in reducing the amount of one or more other components of private expenditures.

Some economists and journalists use the phrase **crowding out effect** to compare points such as E_2 and E_3 in Figure 4-6. The $1,000 billion difference in real income between points E_2 and E_3 results from the investment and consumption spending crowded out by the higher interest rate. Point E_2, used in calculating the size of the crowding out effect, is a purely hypothetical position that the economy cannot and does not reach. Actually, far from being crowded out, total private spending is higher in the new equilibrium situation at E_3 than at the original situation at E_0—real income has increased by $1,000 billion, of which only $500 billion represents higher government purchases, leaving the remaining $500 billion for extra private expenditures. The composition of private spending changes, however, as a result of the higher interest rate. Induced consumption spending increases, but autonomous private spending decreases. Expenditures are divided up as follows in the two situations:

	At E_0	At E_3
Government purchases	0	500
Autonomous private spending ($I_p + C_a$)	1,750	1,500
Induced consumption	5,250	6,000
Total real expenditures	7,000	8,000

Can Crowding Out Be Avoided?

The fundamental cause of crowding out is an increase in the interest rate that is required whenever income rises and the supply of money is fixed while the demand for money responds positively to an increase in income. To offset the increase in the demand for money caused by higher income, it is necessary for the interest rate to rise by enough to offset the effects of higher income on the demand for money.

The simplest way to avoid crowding out would be for the Fed to increase the money supply, thus allowing the LM curve to shift rightward by the same amount as the IS curve. Another possible exception to crowding out would be if the demand for money did not depend on income. Other hypothetical situations in which crowding out would be avoided are when the IS curve is vertical (that is, the interest responsiveness of spending is zero) or when the *LM* curve is horizontal (that is, the interest responsiveness of the demand for money is infinite).

In the next section we will examine some of these situations in which monetary policy and fiscal policy are unusually strong or weak, then study interactions among monetary and fiscal policy. Using monetary and fiscal policy together, the government can achieve the desired (natural) level of real GDP at any level of the interest rate.

4-9 Strong and Weak Effects of Monetary Policy

The *IS-LM* model that we have developed shows how real income (or GDP) and the interest rate are determined. Previously, in Figure 4-5, we examined the "normal" effects of an increase or decrease in the money supply. With the assumed *IS* curve and the *LM* curve labeled LM_0 (which assumes a real money supply of $2,000 billion), the economy's equilibrium occurred at a real income of $7,000 billion and was labeled E_0.

We repeat the same assumed equilibrium point E_0 in Figure 4-7. The diagram differs from those in previous sections of this chapter, however, by dropping specific numbers from the vertical and horizontal axes. Now that we have learned how the *IS-LM* model works, we can simplify our analysis by labeling each point with alphabetical symbols rather than specific numbers. For in-

Figure 4-7 The Effect of an Increase in the Money Supply with a Normal *LM* Curve and a Vertical *LM* Curve

The top frame shows the normal effect of an increase in the real money supply, which is to raise real income and to reduce the interest rate. In the bottom frame, the *LM* curve is vertical, and the same increase in the real money supply leads to a greater drop in the interest rate and a greater increase in real income.

stance, in Figure 4-7 the equilibrium level of income along the initial LM_0 curve is labeled Y' and the equilibrium interest rate is labeled r'.

Now we will ask how much will real income increase if the Fed raises the money supply enough to shift the LM curve from the old LM curve to the new LM curve? We do not need to calculate the exact numerical value of the change in income and the interest rate, since we will be interested in answers to two simple questions. First, following an increase in the real money supply, does real income increase by a lot, a little, or not at all? Second, does the interest rate decline by a lot, a little, or not at all?

Strong Effects of Monetary Expansion

The answer to these questions depends on the slopes of both the IS and LM curves. With the normal slopes shown in the top frame of Figure 4-7, the economy moves from point E_0 to point E_1. The higher money supply boosts income from Y' to Y_1 and lowers the interest rate from r' to r_1. The economy's equilibrium moves from E_0 to E_1, just as in Figure 4-5. Higher income and lower interest rates suffice to boost the demand for money by the amount needed in order to match the assumed higher supply of money that the Fed has created.

What would it take for the impact of the same increase in the money supply to differ from this normal case? In one variant, monetary expansion has an unusually strong effect on income. This occurs when the LM curve is steep (due to a low interest responsiveness of the demand for money). Shown in the bottom frame of Figure 4-7 is the same starting place at E_0, and exactly the same IS curve as in the top frame. But now the old and new LM curves are vertical, indicating the extreme case of a zero interest responsiveness of the demand for money. The same increase in the money supply as in the top frame moves the LM curve to "new LM" (note that the horizontal shift in the LM curve in both the top and bottom frames is the identical distance marked from E_0 to E_2). As a result, the economy moves from point E_0 to point E_4 in the bottom frame. Income increases twice as much in the bottom frame as in the upper frame, while the interest rate falls twice as much.

Why does monetary policy exert a greater stimulus in the bottom frame? In both frames the money supply increases by the same amount, and so does money demand. But in the bottom frame the demand for money is totally insensitive to a reduction in the interest rate, *so all the "work" of boosting money demand must be achieved by higher income.* Since the lower interest rate offers no help in boosting money demand, income must rise further than in the top frame. And, to maintain commodity-market equilibrium along the fixed IS curve, a greater drop in the interest rate is needed to achieve the required boost in income.

Weak Effects of Monetary Policy

The Fed boosts the money supply when it believes that income is too low. But in some circumstances the effects of monetary policy are so weak that the policy cannot boost real income sufficiently to reach the desired level Y_1. This section reviews two such cases. First, changes in the interest rate may have only weak effects on autonomous planned spending (A_p). Second, money demand might be extremely sensitive to changes in the interest rate, which weakens the Fed's ability to reduce the interest rate.

4-9 Strong and Weak Effects of Monetary Policy

Figure 4-8 Effect of the Same Increase in the Real Money Supply with a Zero Interest Responsiveness of Spending and with a High Interest Responsiveness of the Demand for Money

In the top frame, the higher money supply does not stimulate expenditures because expenditures are assumed to be independent of the interest rate—that is, the *IS* curve is vertical. In the bottom frame, the *LM* curve is so flat that the same increase in the money supply (as in the top frame of this figure and in both frames of Figure 4-7) hardly reduces the interest rate at all, and so real income hardly increases at all.

Two Examples of Impotent Monetary Policy

Vertical IS curve implies monetary policy is impotent

Flat LM curve implies monetary policy is impotent

Steep *IS* curve. The first case is shown in the top frame of Figure 4-8. The zero interest responsiveness of A_p implies that the *IS* curve is vertical. This situation occurs when business firms are so pessimistic about the future that they choose not to boost investment spending in response to lower interest rates. As a result, a lower interest rate does not raise equilibrium income. Income is "stuck" at point Y' in response to the same rightward shift in the *LM* curve that occurs in the top frame of Figure 4-7. The only effect of the higher money supply in the top frame of Figure 4-8 is a lower interest rate as the economy moves from point E_0 down vertically to point E_5. Since real income is stuck at Y', all the work of boosting money demand now must be achieved by a lower interest rate.

Flat *LM* curve. The second case of weak monetary policy occurs when the demand for money is extremely responsive to the interest rate, which makes the *LM* curve very flat, as shown in the bottom frame of Figure 4-8. Once again, the money supply goes up by the same amount as before, and the *LM* curve shifts horizontally by the distance shown between E_0 and point E_2. But now, because the *LM* curve is so flat, the economy's equilibrium position hardly moves at all, from E_0 to E_6. Before the interest rate falls enough to stimulate an increase in autonomous planned spending, it is already low enough to boost money demand and falls no further. In the extreme case of a horizontal *LM* curve, the Fed loses control over both output and the interest rate, which remain unchanged in response to a higher money supply. This case is called the **liquidity trap**, signifying a loss of control by the central bank over the interest rate. Some economists have suggested that Japan experienced a liquidity trap in 1998–2002.[5]

The **liquidity trap** is a situation in which the central bank loses its ability to reduce the interest rate.

> ### Self-Test
> 1. If the demand for money is independent of the interest rate, is the *LM* curve vertical or horizontal?
> 2. Does an increase in the money supply have strong or weak effects when the *LM* curve is steeper than normal?
> 3. When it is flatter than normal?

4-10 Strong and Weak Effects of Fiscal Policy

As with monetary policy, the effect of a fiscal policy stimulus on real income depends on the slopes of the *IS* and *LM* curves. Fiscal policy is strong when the demand for money is highly interest-responsive, as illustrated in the top frame of Figure 4-9. With this extreme case of a horizontal *LM* curve, the multiplier becomes just the simple multiplier (k) of Chapter 3. There is no crowding out effect, since the interest rate remains constant.

The opposite situation occurs when the interest responsiveness of money demand is zero, which makes the *LM* curve vertical. An increase in government spending shifts the *IS* curve to the right in the bottom frame of Figure 4-9, exactly as in the top frame by the identical distance from E_0 to E_2, but real income cannot increase without throwing the money market out of equilibrium. Why? An increase in real income would raise the demand for money above the fixed money supply.

But because of the zero interest responsiveness of money demand, no increase in the interest rate can keep money demand in balance with the fixed money supply and a higher level of income. Thus as long as the money supply is fixed, real income cannot be any higher than its initial position at Y'. In this case the only effect of a fiscal stimulus is to raise the interest rate. The crowding out effect is complete, with the higher interest rate cutting autonomous *private* spending by exactly the amount by which government spending increases, leaving total autonomous spending unchanged.

Which diagram is the most accurate depiction of the effects of expansionary fiscal policy with a fixed real money supply—the "normal" case depicted in Figure 4-6 or the extreme cases shown in Figure 4-9? Numerous historical

---

[5] Normally an increase in the money supply reduces the interest rate because people try to get rid of the excess money by purchasing bonds and other financial assets, thus raising the price of bonds and other financial assets and reducing the interest rate. In an extreme (and hypothetical) case of the "liquidity trap," people are convinced that the prices of bonds and other financial assets are unusually high and are likely to fall, so they hold on to the extra money and refuse to buy any financial assets. As a result, the Fed (or the Bank of Japan) loses control of the interest rate, and the *LM* curve becomes a horizontal line that no longer shifts its position in response to a higher money supply. For a discussion of policy weakness in Japan, see pp. 118–19.

Figure 4-9 Effect of a Fiscal Stimulus When Money Demand Has an Infinite and a Zero Interest Responsiveness

In the top frame, an infinite interest responsiveness means that the interest rate is fixed, and no crowding out can occur. In contrast, the same fiscal stimulus has no effect on income when the interest responsiveness is zero (bottom frame), because then a higher interest rate releases no extra money to support higher income, and the income level is completely determined by the size of the real money supply. Since the fiscal stimulus causes no growth at all in income from E_0 to E_8, crowding out is complete.

episodes suggest that the original analysis of Figure 4-6 is accurate—the crowding out effect is partial rather than complete or nonexistent. Furthermore, statistical evidence shows that the interest responsiveness of the demand for money is neither zero nor infinity. For this reason we should regard Figure 4-6 as giving a reliable example of the effects of expansionary fiscal policy, while Figure 4-9 depicts two artificial and extreme cases rather than realistic possibilities.

Summary of Crowding Out

The fundamental cause of crowding out is an increase in the interest rate caused by a fiscal policy stimulus. Crowding out can be avoided only if there is no upward pressure on the interest rate when the IS curve shifts rightward; with a fixed money supply this requires a horizontal LM curve as in the top frame of Figure 4-9. In this frame, there is zero crowding out.

Crowding out can be either partial or complete. If there is any increase in real income in response to the fiscal policy stimulus, crowding out is partial, as is shown in Figure 4-6. If there is no increase in income at all in response to the fiscal policy stimulus, then crowding out is complete. This occurs in the bottom frame of Figure 4-9, where there is absolutely no increase in income at the new point E_8, as compared with the initial point E_0.

> ### Self-Test
> Indicate whether crowding out is zero, partial, or complete in the following cases:
> 1. Zero interest responsiveness of autonomous planned spending.
> 2. Zero interest responsiveness of the demand for money.
> 3. Infinite interest responsiveness of the demand for money.

4-11 Using Fiscal and Monetary Policy Together

So far we have used the *IS-LM* model to examine, first, the effects of a monetary expansion and, second, the separate effects of a fiscal expansion. Yet the two types of policy do not always work in isolation. The Fed's monetary policy, formed on the "west side" of Washington, may strengthen or dampen the fiscal policy formed on the "east side" of Washington.[6] An important application of this section is the recent history of Japan, where the potential for fiscal expansion to reinforce monetary expansion, and vice versa, has until recently been ignored.

The Fiscal Multiplier Depends on the Monetary Response

How does the response of income to a fiscal policy stimulus (the fiscal multiplier) depend on the Fed? The basic idea is simple: The more the Fed *expands* the money supply, the larger is the fiscal multiplier; the more the Fed *contracts* the money supply, the smaller is the fiscal multiplier. If the Fed contracts the money supply enough, the fiscal multiplier could even be negative.

Three cases are shown in Figure 4-10. In the upper left frame, we repeat the standard case from Figure 4-6. When the Fed holds the money supply constant, the *LM* curve remains at its original position. A fiscal stimulus consisting of either an increase in government spending or a tax cut shifts the *IS* curve rightward to the "new *IS* curve." Because the money supply is fixed, the higher demand for money created by rising income forces interest rates higher, crowding out some investment and consumption spending. The economy goes from point E_0 to E_3 just as in Figure 4-6.

In the upper right frame is a second possibility. If the Fed's goal is to keep the interest rate fixed, the money supply must be allowed to change passively whenever there is a shift in the *IS* curve (due not only to fiscal policy but also to changes in consumer and business confidence and to changes in net exports). If the Fed allows the money supply to change by the amount needed to keep the interest rate constant at r', it must shift the *LM* curve rightward. The result of the fiscal stimulus is now the same as the Chapter 3 multiplier (k), which ignored the money market and the impact of interest rate changes. The economy goes from E_0 to E_2, the same as the new equilibrium position in the top frame of Figure 4-9. When trying to stabilize the interest rate and allowing the money

---

[6] Monetary policy is formulated in the Federal Reserve building, about seven blocks west of the Washington Monument. Fiscal policy is formulated not just in the White House (near the Washington Monument) but in the Capitol and nearby Senate and House office buildings, which are about fifteen blocks east of the Washington Monument.

Figure 4-10 The Effect on Real Income of a Fiscal Stimulus with Three Alternative Monetary Policies

In the top left frame, the real money supply is held constant and the stimulus of fiscal policy on real income is partly crowded out (as in Figure 4-6). In the top right frame, the Fed maintains a fixed interest rate, which eliminates the crowding out effect (as in the top frame of Figure 4-9). In the bottom left frame, the Fed attempts to maintain a constant level of real income by shifting LM to the left whenever IS shifts to the right, implying complete crowding out; in this case, fiscal policy influences only the interest rate, not real income.

supply to respond passively to any change in the *IS* curve, the Fed is said to "accommodate" fiscal policy. In effect, the east side of Washington has taken control of the west side.

The upper right frame of Figure 4-10 is critical in understanding the recent policy dilemma of Japan. Japanese policymakers tended to view monetary and fiscal policy in isolation. A fiscal stimulus had the defect that it would raise the interest rate, as in the upper left frame of Figure 4-10. Monetary policy had the

International Perspective

Monetary and Fiscal Policy Paralysis in Japan's "Lost Decade"

The decade long economic slump in Japan is one of the most remarkable macroeconomic phenomena of the postwar era. As shown in the graph, economic growth in Japan in the 1980s was so rapid that per-capita real GDP in Japan grew from 74 percent of the U.S. level in 1980 to 86 percent in 1991. But then the great slump began just as the U.S. economy began to take off. Between 1991 and 2004, growth in per-capita real GDP in Japan was a mere 1.1 percent per year, contrasted with 2.1 percent per year in the United States.

How could an economy that had been so successful suddenly cease its growth? The key to understanding the Japanese situation is to recognize the paralysis on the part of monetary and fiscal policymakers. Monetary policymakers believed that there was nothing left for them to do, because interest rates were close to zero. Fiscal policymakers believed that there is nothing left for them to do, because the public debt in Japan is excessive, well over 100 percent of GDP, and to cut taxes or boost spending would cause a further increase in the already-excessive debt.

Interest Rates: Japan in the 1990s and the United States in the 1930s

The low level of interest rates in Japan has a historical precedent in the low level of U.S. interest rates in the 1930s. This similarity is shown in the next pair of graphs. The Japanese short-term interest rate fell below 1 percent after 1995 and was less than 0.3 percent in 1999–2004. In the United States, the short-term interest rate fell below 1 percent after 1931 and was less than 0.05 percent in 1938–40.

The economist Paul Krugman of Princeton has called attention to the similarity between these episodes. Krugman claims that the Japanese situation exhibits a liquidity trap, a situation (as defined on p. 114) in which the nominal interest rate is near zero, and monetary policy is rendered ineffective because it loses its power to reduce the interest rate further.

A liquidity trap is a situation in which, because the nominal interest rate obtainable on short-term assets other than money is close to zero, investors are indifferent whether they hold money or these short-term assets. As a result of this indifference, the interest responsiveness of the demand for money is infinite, and the *LM* curve is a horizontal line like that depicted in the top frame of Figure 4-9, except that this horizontal line would be plotted very close to the horizontal axis (at roughly 0.2 percent for the Japanese case of 1999–2004 and at 0.05 percent for the United States in 1938–40).

If monetary policy is impotent because it cannot reduce the interest rate any further, a fiscal stimulus is

Source: IMF and OECD.

required to end the slump and bring real GDP back to its desired level. This fiscal stimulus occurred in the United States in 1940–41 as exports and military expenditures increased.

The Japanese Policy Dilemma and the *IS-LM* Model
The low level of the Japanese interest rate created a policy dilemma in Japan. Monetary policy could not push interest rates appreciably lower, yet fiscal policymakers felt constrained in achieving a large fiscal stimulus by the high existing level of the fiscal deficit in Japan and by the fact that the public debt in Japan had exceeded 100 percent of real GDP.

However, the *IS-LM* model suggests a way out of the Japanese policy dilemma. As shown in the top right frame of Figure 4-10 on p. 117 a *combined* monetary and fiscal policy stimulus that shifts the *LM* and *IS* curves rightward by the same amount can boost real GDP without any need for a decline in interest rates. Also, with such a combined policy there is no need for a further increase in the national debt held by the public, since to achieve its monetary expansion, the central bank can buy the government bonds issued as a result of the increased fiscal deficit.

Despite the implication of the *IS-LM* model that monetary and fiscal expansion should be undertaken together, it took until 2003–04 for Japanese policymakers to realize that this was an option. Why did the Bank of Japan resist what seemed to be the obvious solution, which was that the Bank buy up the government bonds issued as a result of the fiscal stimulus? This solution, sometimes called "monetizing the debt," would be the real-world equivalent of shifting the *LM* curve rightward along with the *IS* curve.

The traditional reason for the historic reluctance of central bankers to monetize the debt and conduct a simultaneous monetary and fiscal expansion has been fear of inflation. Yet Japan's problem was deflation, not inflation. In fact, Krugman's solution for the Japanese dilemma was that the Bank of Japan should buy up so much Japanese government debt that it would convince the public that there would be a steady inflation in the foreseeable future. Further, monetization of the debt would tend to depreciate the foreign exchange rate of the Japanese yen, which would stimulate Japanese net exports.

Only after 2002 did Japan begin to recover from its decade-long slump. While the prescription of the *IS-LM* model in favor of a combined monetary-fiscal expansion seemed clear, implementing this policy recommendation was blocked by the reluctance of the Bank of Japan to give up its historic commitment to maintaining price stability, for example, zero inflation. As Princeton economist Kenneth Rogoff concluded, "The real problem is that the Bank of Japan does not have the big picture right. It does not realize that a good conservative central bank should be willing to let the price level rise on a rainy day—and Japan is experiencing a typhoon."[a]

---

[a]The best source is Kenneth N. Kuttner and Adam S. Posen, "The Great Recession: Lessons for Macroeconomic Policy From Japan," *Brookings Papers on Economic Activity*, no. 2 (2001), pp. 93–160. A briefer summary of the main issues is contained in the conference discussion of this paper, pp. 161–75.

Source: Bank of Japan and Federal Reserve Board.

defect that interest rates were already very low, and the Bank of Japan was reluctant to boost the money supply in the belief that it was difficult, if not impossible, to reduce the interest rate. Yet, as shown in the upper right frame of Figure 4-10, a *combined* monetary and fiscal policy stimulus could avoid both of these drawbacks. When combined with a fiscal stimulus that causes the IS curve to shift rightward, a monetary stimulus *does not require a decline in the interest rate*. Similarly, when combined with a monetary stimulus that causes the LM curve to shift rightward, a fiscal stimulus *does not require an increase in the interest rate*. Working together, monetary and fiscal policy could achieve in Japan (or elsewhere) a policy stimulus much more potent than either policy tool could achieve working separately.

The Japanese dilemma discussed in the box on pp. 118–19 shows that there is another advantage to using monetary and fiscal stimuli together—that the required fiscal deficit can be financed by money creation, thus avoiding any need for an increase in the national debt held by households, banks, and business firms.

The Monetary-Fiscal Mix and Economic Growth

Returning to Figure 4-10, the bottom left frame shows that the *IS-LM* model contains an important lesson about economic growth. By changing the mix of monetary and fiscal policy, government policymakers can alter the interest rate without any need for a change in real income. In general, the lower the interest rate for any given level of real income or real GDP, the larger the fraction of that real GDP that will consist of real investment and the smaller the fraction that will consist of real consumption. Higher investment tends to boost economic growth.

Let us see in the bottom left frame of Figure 4-10 how the government can cause the interest rate to vary without changing the level of real income from its initial level Y'. If the Fed wants to maintain income at Y', it can respond to a fiscal stimulus *by moving the* LM *curve in the opposite direction from the movement in the* IS *curve*. Thus, if government spending is increased, the Fed must reduce the money supply. In the bottom left frame of Figure 4-10, the economy moves from E_0 to E_8 (the same position shown in the bottom frame of Figure 4-9). When the Fed behaves this way, fiscal policy no longer has any control over the level of income and affects only the interest rate. The effect of fiscal policy is to raise the interest rate from r' to r_8, because the Fed has reduced the money supply by enough to maintain the initial level of income Y'.

This illustrates an important point about monetary and fiscal policy. Once the government has decided on the desirable level of income, say Y', it can achieve that level of income with many different interest rates, of which r' and r_8 are only two examples. We can assume that points E_0 and E_8 share not only the same level of output, but also the same level of employment and unemployment. What are the differences?

Point E_8 offsets the fiscal policy stimulus, assumed to be a higher level of government spending, by reducing the money supply. In contrast, point E_0 has a higher real money supply (shown by the fact that the LM curve is farther to the right) but a tighter fiscal policy (shown by the fact that the IS curve is farther to the left). The higher interest rate at E_8 crowds out planned investment and autonomous consumption below that at point E_0, in order to make room for a higher level of government spending.

The two points E_0 and E_8 are said to differ in the mix of monetary and fiscal policy. Point E_0 has a **policy mix** of "easy money, tight fiscal," while point E_8 has

The **policy mix** refers to the combination of monetary and fiscal policy in effect in a given situation. A mix of tight monetary and easy fiscal policy leads to high interest rates, while a mix of easy monetary and tight fiscal policy leads to low interest rates.

the opposite policy mix of "tight money, easy fiscal." Which mix should society prefer? At E_0, investment is higher; thus the economy is building for the future, and its future level of productivity growth will be higher. At E_8, government spending is higher than at E_0, and investment is lower. Should society prefer the faster output growth of point E_0 or the higher level of public services of point E_8?

This is a central question of macroeconomics to which we return in Chapters 10–12. Its solution depends on whether the government spending consists largely of government consumption (national defense, police, and fire protection) or government investment (highways and school buildings). If the extra government spending at point E_8 consists of government consumption, then the choice between points E_8 and E_0 depends on society's taste for present consumption of goods and services (at E_8) versus future consumption, since a high investment strategy at E_0 yields higher consumption only in the future. If the extra government spending at E_8 consists of government investment, then the choice depends on whether there is a higher payoff for society from government investment (of which there is more at E_8) as compared with private investment (of which there is more at E_0). The same criteria are relevant if the fiscal stimulus takes the form of a tax cut that can stimulate either private investment or consumption, depending on the types of taxes that are cut.

Summary of Monetary-Fiscal Interactions

By working together, monetary and fiscal policy can be more effective than if they are operated independently. A fiscal stimulus accompanied by a monetary expansion is more effective than a fiscal stimulus carried out in the presence of a fixed or shrinking money supply. This can be seen in the difference between the upper left and upper right frames of Figure 4-10, where the crowding out evident on the left is eliminated on the right by the increase in the money supply. Stagnation in Japan over the decade 1992–2002 (discussed in the box on pp. 118–19) is ample evidence that both monetary and fiscal policy can be paralyzed when they ignore the possibility of working together.

Further, by working together, monetary and fiscal policy can keep real GDP at the desirable natural level of real GDP, while choosing the level of the interest rate. Policies that lead to a government deficit and promote consumption imply a high interest rate, while policies that lead to a government surplus and promote private saving imply a low real interest rate that encourages domestic investment and reduces foreign borrowing.

Summary

1. The main functions of money are its use as a medium of exchange, a store of value, and a unit of account.
2. The real quantity of money that people demand depends both on real income and on the interest rate. Equilibrium in the money market requires that the real supply of money equal the demand for real money balances.
3. The *LM* curve represents all the combinations of real income and of the interest rate where the money market is in equilibrium.
4. An increase in the money supply raises real income and reduces the interest rate when the *IS* curve has its normal negative slope and the *LM* curve has its normal positive slope.
5. A fiscal expansion raises real income and the interest rate, causing crowding out if the money supply is held constant and both the *IS* and *LM* curves have their normal slopes.
6. Monetary policy has a relatively strong effect on real income when the interest responsiveness of the demand for money is relatively low (steep *LM* curve). Monetary policy is weak when the interest responsiveness of the demand for money is very high (flat *LM* curve), or when the interest responsiveness of

autonomous planned spending is very low (steep *IS* curve).
7. The normal effect of a fiscal policy stimulus, consisting either of an increase in government spending or a reduction in tax rates, is to raise both real income and the interest rate. The fiscal multiplier is lower than the Chapter 3 multiplier (k) due to partial crowding out of planned investment and autonomous consumption.
8. A fiscal stimulus has a relatively strong effect on real income when the interest responsiveness of the demand for money is relatively high (flat *LM* curve) or the interest responsiveness of autonomous spending is relatively low (steep *IS* curve). A fiscal stimulus has a relatively weak effect with the opposite pattern of interest responsiveness (steep *LM* curve or flat *IS* curve).
9. The effect of a fiscal stimulus on income (fiscal multiplier) is greatest, and there is no crowding out effect, if the Fed is attempting to stabilize interest rates, since this requires that the money supply passively accommodate the fiscal stimulus (the *LM* curve must move to the right by exactly the same distance as the *IS* curve).
10. An intermediate fiscal multiplier, with partial crowding out, occurs when the Fed maintains a constant real money supply, the original case of Figure 4-6.
11. The fiscal multiplier is zero when the Fed stabilizes real income, moving the *LM* curve in the opposite direction from the *IS* curve.
12. By varying the monetary–fiscal mix, government policymakers can maintain a given level of real income with many different interest rates. An "easy money, tight fiscal" mix yields a low interest rate and stimulates private investment. A "tight money, easy fiscal" mix yields a higher interest rate, less private investment, and some combination of additional government consumption, government investment, or private consumption, depending on the particular fiscal policy chosen.

Note: Asterisks designate Concepts, Questions, and Problems that require the Appendix to Chapter 4.

Concepts

money supply
medium of exchange
store of value
unit of account
real money balances
LM curve
general equilibrium
expansionary monetary policy
contractionary monetary policy
crowding out effect
liquidity trap
policy mix

Questions

1. Explain how the determinants of the demand for money, income, and the interest rate are related to the uses of money as a medium of exchange and a store of value.
2. Describe the automatic adjustment that will take place in the economy when the current position of the economy is off the *IS* curve.
3. Describe the automatic adjustment that will take place in the economy when the current position of the economy is off the *LM* curve.
4. Why is the distinction between autonomous expenditure and induced expenditure crucial to an understanding of the crowding out effect?
5. Under what circumstances could government spending (federal, state, and local) be crowded out? Do you think this is likely to be the case?
6. What happens to the velocity of money (defined in the box on p. 103) when the economy moves along a given *LM* curve? Why does velocity behave this way?
7. Use Figure 4-4 to identify a point where each of the following situations occurs and how the economy will adjust:
   (a) planned spending exceeds income and there is an excess supply of money
   (b) unintended inventory investment is positive and the real demand for money is less than the real supply of money
   (c) unintended inventory investment is negative and there is an excess demand for money
   (d) planned spending is less than income and the real demand for money exceeds the real supply of money
8. What are the four channels through which monetary policy influences total spending? Discuss the relative importance of each during 2001–04. (See the box on pp. 106–107.)
9. A change in which of the following would cause the *LM* curve to shift? To rotate? To both shift and rotate? Which do not affect the position or slope of the *LM* curve? (See the box on p. 103.)

(a) nominal money supply (M^s)
(b) responsiveness of the demand for money to the interest rate
(c) responsiveness of the demand for money to income
(d) business and consumer confidence
(e) interest rate (r)
(f) price level (P)

10. During the 1980s, the size of the federal government debt became so large that servicing the interest payments became a significant portion of total federal expenditure. In response, many representatives and senators felt that the federal deficit needed to be reduced. If government spending (G) becomes negatively sensitive to changes in the interest rate, what effect does this have on the amount of autonomous consumption and planned investment that is crowded out? If autonomous taxes (T_a) become positively sensitive to changes in the interest rate, what effect does this have on the amount of autonomous consumption and planned investment that is crowded out?

11. Suppose that private sector spending is highly sensitive to a change in the interest rate. Compare the effectiveness of monetary and fiscal policy in terms of raising and lowering real GDP.

12. Suppose that the demand for money is highly insensitive to a change in the interest rate. Compare the effectiveness of monetary and fiscal policy in terms of raising and lowering real GDP.

13. Suppose Congress raises autonomous taxes. How will this tax increase affect real income? The interest rate? Consumption? Planned investment?

14. If the A_p demand schedule shifts to the right, what happens to the real interest rate? Does the change in real interest rate amplify or dampen the swings in income that result from changes in A_p?

15. Suppose that the Fed is not worried about inflation, but is convinced that unemployment is too high. Use the IS-LM model to explain what actions the Fed is likely to take to ensure that very little private sector spending is crowded out by a tax cut aimed at reducing unemployment.

16. You learned in Chapter 1 that inflation speeds up when actual real GDP exceeds natural real GDP. Suppose that policymakers believe actual real GDP exceeds natural real GDP and fear that inflation will rise. Compare the effects on private sector spending of the following two policies: (a) only monetary policymakers are able to take actions to bring actual and natural real GDP in line with one another; (b) monetary and fiscal policymakers are able to jointly adopt a "tight money, tight fiscal" policy mix in an effort to reduce actual real GDP relative to natural real GDP.

17. Assume that the Federal Reserve Board has decided to maintain the level of real GDP at the current level. If Congress passes a $50 billion decrease in personal taxes, what action, if any, would the Fed have to take? Describe the effect of the actions of Congress and the Fed on:
    (a) the interest rate
    (b) the composition of output
    (c) the future growth rate of the GDP

18. Evaluate the following argument using the IS-LM model: When consumer and business confidence are high and the economy is booming, the interest rate is high. Therefore, during a recession the Fed could promote a higher level of income if it used monetary policy to raise the interest rate.

Problems

1. Assume the commodity market and the money market for an economy are described by the following IS and LM curves.

   IS: $Y = 11{,}000 - 250r$;   LM: $Y = 8{,}000 + 250r$.

   (a) Compute the equilibrium interest rate (r) and equilibrium real output (Y).
   (b) Suppose that fiscal policymakers raise taxes and cut government spending. As a result, the IS curve shifts left to $Y = 10{,}000 - 250r$. Compute the new equilibrium interest rate (r) and new equilibrium real output (Y).
   (c) Suppose that there is no change in fiscal policy, so that the IS curve is $Y = 11{,}000 - 250r$. Instead monetary policymakers take action to reduce the money supply so that the LM curve shifts left to $Y = 7{,}000 + 250r$. Compute the new equilibrium interest rate (r) and new equilibrium real output (Y).

2. Suppose that the commodity market is described by the IS curve given in problem 1. On the other hand, the money market is described by the LM curve $Y = 8{,}600 + 150r$.
   (a) Explain whether the LM curve is flatter or steeper compared to the LM curve of problem 1. For which of the two LM curves is the demand for money more responsive to the interest rate? Verify that the equilibrium interest rate (r) and equilibrium real output (Y) are the same as in part a of problem 1.
   (b) Suppose that fiscal policymakers again take action to reduce real GDP so that the IS curve shifts left to $Y = 10{,}000 - 250r$. Compute the new

equilibrium interest rate (r) and new equilibrium real output (Y).

(c) Suppose that there is no change in fiscal policy, so that the IS curve is $Y = 11{,}000 - 250r$. Instead monetary policymakers take action to reduce the money supply, which shifts the LM curve left to $Y = 7{,}600 + 150r$. Compute the new equilibrium interest rate (r) and new equilibrium real output (Y).

(d) Compare your answers to parts b and c of this problem with those of problem 1. Are they consistent with what the text says concerning the effectiveness of monetary policy?

3. Suppose that the money market is described by the LM curve given in problem 1. On the other hand, the commodity market is described by the IS curve $Y = 10{,}400 - 150r$.

(a) Explain whether the IS curve is flatter or steeper compared to the IS curve of problem 1. For which of the two IS curves is autonomous planned spending more responsive to the interest rate? Verify that the equilibrium interest rate (r) and equilibrium real output (Y) are the same as in part a of problem 1.

(b) Suppose that fiscal policymakers again take action to reduce real GDP so that the IS curve shifts left to $Y = 9{,}400 - 150r$. Compute the new equilibrium interest rate (r) and new equilibrium real output (Y).

(c) Suppose that there is no change in fiscal policy, so that the IS curve is $Y = 10{,}400 - 150r$. Instead monetary policymakers take action to reduce the money supply, which shifts the LM curve left to $Y = 7{,}000 + 150r$. Compute the new equilibrium interest rate (r) and new equilibrium real output (Y).

(d) Compare your answers to parts b and c of this problem with those of problem 1. Are they consistent with what the text says concerning the effectiveness of fiscal policy?

*4. Assume the following equations summarize the structure of an economy.

$$C = C_a + 0.85(Y - T)$$
$$C_a = 260 - 10r$$
$$T = 200 + 0.2Y$$
$$(M/P)^d = 0.25Y - 25r$$
$$M^s/P = 2{,}125$$
$$I_p = 1{,}500 - 30r$$
$$G = 1{,}700$$
$$NX = 500 - 0.08Y$$

(a) Compute the value of the multiplier.
(b) Derive the equation for the autonomous planned spending schedule, A_p.
(c) Derive the equation for the IS curve.
(d) Calculate the slope of the IS curve, $\Delta r/\Delta Y$. (Hint: Use the equation of the IS curve to compute $\Delta Y/\Delta r$. Then use the fact that the slope of the IS curve, $\Delta r/\Delta Y$, equals the inverse of $\Delta Y/\Delta r$.)
(e) Derive the equation for the LM curve.
(f) Calculate the slope of the LM curve, $\Delta r/\Delta Y$. (To do this, use the same hint as in part d.)
(g) Compute the equilibrium interest rate (r).
(h) Compute the equilibrium real output (Y).

*5. Using the information given in problem 4, compute the new equilibrium real output and interest rate

(a) if government spending increases by 160. What is the amount of autonomous spending that is crowded out by this expansionary fiscal policy?
(b) if G equals 1,700 but the real money supply increases by 100.

*6. Using the information given in problem 4, compute by how much the Fed must increase the money supply if it wishes to avoid the crowding out of the expansionary fiscal policy described in part a of problem 5. What will be the new value of real GDP? Suppose that the money multiplier is 5. How much of a bond purchase would the Fed have to make in order to achieve its desired increase in the real money supply?

*7. Assume that the economy is initially in equilibrium at a level of real output (Y) of $9,000 and an interest rate (r) of 5 percent. Suppose that government spending increases by $500 and the economy moves to a new equilibrium at $Y = 9{,}600$ and $r = 8$ percent. Given that $k = 3$, calculate how much Y is crowded out. How much autonomous spending is crowded out? What is the value of the coefficient for the interest-rate responsiveness of the IS curve? Of the A_p demand schedule?

*8. Suppose that the real demand for money in the economy changes to $(M/P)^d = 0.2Y - 75r$ and the real money supply changes to $M^s/P = 1{,}875$ but the structure of the commodity market is the same as in problem 4.

(a) Derive the equation for the new LM curve and verify that the equilibrium interest rate and real output are the same as you computed in parts 4g and 4h, respectively.
(b) Calculate the slope of the new LM curve, $\Delta r/\Delta Y$.
(c) Compared to the money demand curve given in problem 4, has money demand become more or less responsive to a change to the interest rate? Is the LM curve steeper or flatter as a result? How does this change in the interest responsiveness of money demand alter the amount by which real output will change following an expansionary change in fiscal or monetary policy?
(d) Compute the new equilibrium interest rate and real output if government spending increases by 160.
(e) Compute the new equilibrium interest rate and real output if G equals 1,700 but the real money supply increases by 100.

(f) How and why do the answers in parts d and e differ from problem 5a and 5b, respectively? Is your prediction in part c confirmed?

*9. Suppose that autonomous consumption and planned investment in the economy described in problem 4 change to $C_a = 470 - 15r$ and $I_p = 1{,}700 - 60r$. All other aspects of the structure of the commodity and the money markets are as described in problem 4.
 (a) Derive the equation for the new IS curve and verify that the equilibrium interest rate and real output are the same as you computed in parts 4g and 4h, respectively.
 (b) Calculate the slope of the new IS curve, $\Delta r/\Delta Y$.
 (c) Compared to problem 4, have autonomous consumption and planned investment become more or less responsive to a change in the interest rate? Is the IS curve steeper or flatter as a result? How does this change in the interest responsiveness of autonomous spending alter the amount by which real output will change following an expansionary change in fiscal or monetary policy?
 (d) Compute the new equilibrium interest rate and real output if government spending increases by 160.
 (e) Compute the new equilibrium interest rate and real output if G equals 1,700 but the real money supply increases by 100.
 (f) How and why do the answers in parts d and e differ from problem 5a and 5b, respectively? Is your prediction in part c confirmed?

*10. Assume the following equations summarize the structure of an economy.

$$C = C_a + 0.8(Y - T)$$
$$C_a = 260 - 10r$$
$$T = 200 + 0.2Y$$
$$(M/P)^d = 0.25Y - 25r$$
$$M^s/P = 2{,}000$$
$$I_p = 1{,}900 - 40r$$
$$G = 1{,}800$$
$$NX = 700 - 0.14Y$$

 (a) Derive the equation for the IS curve.
 (b) Derive the equation for the LM curve.
 (c) Compute the equilibrium interest rate (r) and real output (Y).
 (d) Suppose consumer and business confidence decline, resulting in decreases in the amounts of autonomous consumption and planned investment by 40 and 60, respectively. Derive the new equation for the IS curve and compute the new equilibrium interest rate (r) and real output (Y).
 (e) Suppose that natural real GDP equals the amount of real output that you computed in part b. Compute the amount of a cut in autonomous taxes that would be necessary in order to overcome the declines in consumer and business confidence and restore real output to natural real GDP.
 (f) Suppose that instead of fiscal policy, monetary policy is used to restore real output to natural real GDP. Compute by how much the Fed would have to increase the money supply in order to do so.
 (g) Compute the amounts of autonomous consumption and planned investment associated with each of the policies described in parts e and f. Explain which policy is likely to result in a higher rate of growth in real output over the long run.

Self-Test Answers

p. 101 (1) The levels of income (Y) and the interest rate on assets other than money (r) are the two determinants of the real demand for money, $(M/P)^d$. (2) An increase in Y raises the real demand for money, and an increase in the interest rate reduces the real demand for money. (3) Neither determinant shifts the IS curve, because the axes of the IS curve diagram are these very determinants, Y and r.

p. 104 (1) In going from D to F, the interest rate rises from 5 to 10 percent, and the demand for money decreases by the interest responsiveness (200) times the change in the interest rate (5)—that is, by 1,000. (2) In going from D to G, the level of real income falls from 8,000 to 6,000. The demand for money decreases by the income responsiveness (0.5) times the change in real income (2,000)—that is, by 1,000. (3) This is the reverse of Part (2); the demand for money increases by 1,000. (4) This is the reverse of Part (1). The demand for money increases by 1,000.

p. 114 (1) If the demand for money is independent of the interest rate (the variable on the vertical axis), then the LM curve is vertical. (2) An increase in the money supply has strong effects when the LM curve is steeper than normal, as occurs in the bottom frame of Figure 4-7. (3) An increase in the money supply has weak effects when the LM curve is flatter than normal, as occurs in the bottom frame of Figure 4-8.

p. 116 (1) Zero crowding out, because the increase in the interest rate caused by a fiscal policy expansion does not have any effect in reducing planned investment or autonomous consumption; (2) complete crowding out, the case shown in the bottom frame of Figure 4-9; (3) zero crowding out, the case shown in the top frame of Figure 4-9.

Appendix to Chapter 4

The Elementary Algebra of the *IS-LM* Model

When you see an *IS* curve crossing an *LM* curve, as in Chapter 4, you know that the equilibrium level of income (Y) and the interest rate (r) occurs at the point of crossing, as at point E_0 in Figure 4-4. But how can the equilibrium level of income and the interest rate be calculated numerically without going to the trouble of making careful drawings of the *IS* and *LM* curves? Wherever you see two lines crossing to determine the values of two variables such as Y and r, exactly the same solution can be obtained by solving together the two equations describing the two lines.

In the Appendix to Chapter 3, we found that equilibrium income is equal to autonomous planned spending (A_p) divided by the marginal leakage rate, so that the autonomous spending multiplier (k) is equal to the inverse of the marginal leakage rate ($k = 1/\text{MLR}$).

$$\text{multiplier} = k = \frac{1}{\text{marginal leakage rate}} = \frac{1}{\text{MLR}} \tag{1}$$

In this appendix we shall continue using the same example as in the graphs of Chapters 3 and 4, namely $k = 4.0$.

Once we have determined the multiplier from equation (1) above, we can write real income simply as:

General Linear Form | Numerical Example
$Y = kA_p$ | $Y = 4.0 A_p$ (2)

In Section 3-9, the assumption was introduced that autonomous planned spending A_p declines when there is an increase in the interest rate (r). If the amount of A_p at a zero interest rate is written as (A_p'), then the value of A_p can be written:

General Linear Form | Numerical Example
$A_p = A_p' - br$ | $A_p = A_p' - 100r$ (3)

Here b is the interest responsiveness of A_p; in our example there is a $100 billion decline in A_p per one percentage point increase in the interest rate. Substituting (3) into (2), we obtain the equation for the *IS* schedule:

General Linear Form | Numerical Example
$Y = k(A_p' - br)$ | $Y = 4.0(A_p' - 100r)$ (4)

Thus if A_p' is 2,500 and $r = 0$, the IS_0 curve intersects the horizontal axis at 10,000.

The *LM* curve shows all combinations of income (Y) and the interest rate (r) where the real money supply (M^s/P) equals the real demand for money ($M/P)^d$, which in turn depends on Y and r. This situation of equilibrium in the money market was previously written as equation (4.1) in the text:

General Linear Form | Numerical Example
$\left(\frac{M^s}{P}\right) = \left(\frac{M}{P}\right)^d = hY - fr$ | $\left(\frac{M^s}{P}\right) = 0.5Y - 200r$ (5)

In this example, where h is the responsiveness of real money demand to higher real income, 0.5 here, and f is the interest responsiveness of real money demand, there is a $200 billion decline in real money demand per one percentage point increase in the interest rate. Adding fr (or $200r$) to both sides of (5), and then dividing by h (or 0.5), we obtain the equation for the *LM* schedule when M^s/P is 2,000:

General Linear Form

$$Y = \frac{\frac{M^s}{P} + fr}{h}$$

Numerical Example

$$Y = \frac{2{,}000 + 200r}{0.5} \qquad (6)$$

We are assured that the commodity market is in equilibrium whenever Y is related to r by equation (4) and that the money market is in equilibrium whenever Y is related to r by equation (6). To make sure that both markets are in equilibrium, both equations must be satisfied at once.

Equations (4) and (6) together constitute an *economic model*. Finding the value of two unknown variables in economics is very much like baking a cake. One starts with a list of ingredients, the *parameters* (or knowns) of the model: A'_p, M^s/P, b, f, h, and k. Then one stirs the ingredients together using the recipe instructions, in this case equations (4) and (6). The outcome is the value of the unknown variables, Y and r. The main rule in economic cake-baking is that the number of equations (the recipe instructions) must be equal to the number of unknowns to be determined. In this example, there are two equations and two unknowns (Y and r). There is no limit on the parameters, the number of ingredients known in advance. Here we have six parameters, but we could have seven, ten, or any number.

To convert the two equations of the model into one equation specifying the value of unknown Y in terms of the six known parameters, we simply substitute (6) into (4). To do this, we rearrange (6) to place the interest rate on the left side of the equation, and then we substitute the resulting expression for r in (4). First, rearrange (6) to move r to the left side:[1]

$$r = \frac{hY - \frac{M^s}{P}}{f} \qquad (6a)$$

Second, substitute the right side of (6a) for r in (4):

$$Y = k(A_0 - br) = k\left[A'_p - \frac{bhY}{f} + \frac{b}{f}\left(\frac{M^s}{P}\right)\right] \qquad (7)$$

Now (7) can be solved for Y by adding $kbhY/f$ to both sides and dividing both sides by k:

$$Y\left(\frac{1}{k} + \frac{bh}{f}\right) = A'_p + \frac{b}{f}\left(\frac{M^s}{P}\right)$$

Finally, both sides are divided by the left term in parentheses:

$$Y = \frac{A'_p + \frac{b}{f}\left(\frac{M^s}{P}\right)}{\frac{1}{k} + \frac{bh}{f}} \qquad (8)$$

---

[1] First multiply both sides of (6) by h:

$$hY = \frac{M^s}{P} + fr$$

then subtract M^s/P from both sides:

$$hY = \frac{M^s}{P} = fr$$

Now divide both sides by f:

$$\frac{hY - \frac{M^s}{P}}{f} = r$$

Equation (6a) is then obtained by reversing the two sides of this equation.

Equation (8) is our master general equilibrium income equation and combines all the information in the *IS* and *LM* curves together; when (8) is satisfied, both the commodity market and money market are in equilibrium. It can be used in any situation to calculate the level of real income by simply substituting into (8) the particular values of the six known right-hand parameters in order to calculate unknown income.[2]

Because we are interested primarily in the effect on income of a change in A'_p or M^s/P, we can simplify (8):

$$Y = k_1 A'_p + k_2 \left(\frac{M^s}{P} \right) \qquad (9)$$

All we have done in converting (8) into (9) is to give new names, k_1 and k_2, to the multiplier effects of A'_p and M^s/P on income. The definitions and numerical values of k_1 and k_2 are:

General Linear Form

$$k_1 = \frac{1}{\frac{1}{k} + \frac{bh}{f}}$$

Numerical Example

$$k_1 = \frac{1}{\frac{1}{4.0} + \frac{100(0.5)}{200}} = 2.0 \qquad (10)$$

$$k_2 = \frac{b/f}{\frac{1}{k} + \frac{bh}{f}} = \left(\frac{b}{f}\right) k_1$$

$$k_2 = \frac{100(2.0)}{200} = 1.0 \qquad (11)$$

Using the numerical values in (10) and (11), the simplified equation (9) can be used to calculate the value of real income:

$$Y = k_1 A'_p + k_2 \left(\frac{M^s}{P}\right)$$
$$= 2.0(2,500) + 1.0(2,000)$$
$$= 7,000 \qquad (12)$$

This is an example of how the value of income can be calculated for a specific numerical example. With this equation it is extremely easy to calculate the new value of Y when there is a change in A'_p caused by government fiscal policy or by a change in business and consumer confidence, and when there is a change in M^s/P caused by a change in the nominal money supply. Remember, however, that the definitions of k_1 and k_2 in (10) and (11) do depend on particular assumptions about the value of parameters b, f, h, and k.

The main point of Sections 4-9 and 4-10 is that changes in fiscal and monetary policy may have either strong or weak effects on income, depending on the answers to these questions.

1. How does the effect of a change in A'_p on income, the multiplier k_1, depend on the values of b and f (the interest responsiveness of the demand for commodities and money)?
2. How does the effect of a change in M^s on income, the multiplier k_2, depend on the values of b and f?

You should work through these sections to see if you can derive each of the diagrammatic results by substituting the appropriate definition of k_1 and k_2 into the simplified general equilibrium equation (9).

---

[2] A parameter is taken as given or known within a given exercise. Parameters include not just the small letters denoting the multiplier (k), and the interest and income responsiveness of planned autonomous expenditures and money demand (b, h, and f), but also autonomous planned expenditures at a zero interest rate (A'_{p0}) and the real money supply (M^s/P). Most exercises involve examining the effects of a change in a single parameter, as in A'_{p0} or in M^s/P.

Example: The top frame of Figure 4-7 shows the effects of raising the money supply. In our example let us raise M^s/P from 2,000 to 3,000. We know, using (10), that the value of k_1 is 2.0. Using (11), the value of k_2 is 1.0. Thus using equation (9), income in the new situation at point E_1 in the top frame of Figure 4-7 is

$$Y = k_1 A'_p + k_2 \left(\frac{M^s}{P}\right)$$
$$= 2.0(2,500) + 1(3,000)$$
$$= 8,000$$

Using equation (6a), we learn that the interest rate in the new situation is

$$r = \frac{[(0.5)(8,000) - 3,000]}{200} = 5.0$$

In the bottom frame, $f = 0$, and so

$$k_1 = \cfrac{1}{\cfrac{1}{k} + \cfrac{bh}{f}} = \cfrac{1}{\cfrac{1}{4} + \cfrac{100(0.5)}{0}} = 0$$

$$k_2 = \cfrac{b}{\cfrac{f}{k} + bh} = \cfrac{100}{\cfrac{0}{4} + 100(0.5)} = 2.0$$

Thus in the bottom frame of Figure 4-7, the new equilibrium situation at point E_4 is as follows when the real money supply rises from 3,500 along the old LM line to 4,500 along the new LM line:

$$Y = k_1 A'_p + k_2 \left(\frac{M^s}{P}\right) = 0(2,500) + 2.0(4,500) = 9,000$$

We cannot solve for the interest rate using (6a), since the denominator (f) is zero. Instead, we can use equation (4) to solve for the interest rate along the IS curve. When (4) is solved for the interest rate, we obtain the general expression:

$$r = \frac{A'_p - Y/k}{b} = \frac{2,500 - 9,000/4}{100} = \frac{250}{100} = 2.5$$

This lower interest rate is depicted by point E_4 in the lower frame of Figure 4-7.

CHAPTER 5

National Saving, the Government Budget, Foreign Borrowing, and the Twin Deficits

Any jackass can draw up a balanced budget on paper.
—Lane Kirkland, 1980

5-1 Introduction

We have now learned how to use the *IS-LM* model to determine the value of both real income (GDP) and the interest rate. We have also learned that there is a desirable level of real GDP, which we call "natural real GDP." When the economy is operating with actual real GDP equal to natural real GDP, there is no need for monetary or fiscal policy actions to boost or restrain the level of actual real GDP.[1] But sometimes actual real GDP may not be at its desired level, most notably in the U.S. Great Depression of the 1930s or Japan's slump of the past decade, and actions by monetary and fiscal policymakers are needed to stimulate the economy.

More recently the U. S. economy slumped into recession in 2001 as a result of the collapse of the late 1990s' boom in the stock market and in high-tech investment, and a strong response by stimulative monetary and fiscal policy offset most of the decline in real GDP that otherwise would have occurred. We have already reviewed on pp. 106–107 the strong stimulative impact of monetary policy, which by sharply reducing interest rates in 2001–02 boosted interest-sensitive spending, particularly auto and home sales. Without this monetary stimulus, the recession would have been a serious downturn but instead was one of the mildest of the postwar era.

We have learned that in certain conditions monetary or fiscal policy may be ineffective. However, the conditions that make monetary policy ineffective tend to make fiscal policy effective, and vice versa. Thus the two types of policy should be coordinated rather than used separately. We also learned at the end of the last chapter that the use of monetary and fiscal policy can be coordinated in order to obtain the desired or "natural" level of real GDP together with a wide range of possible interest rates, either high or low, depending on the importance of stimulating private investment with low interest rates.

In this chapter we take a closer look at fiscal policy. We learn that changes in the government budget surplus or deficit reflect not just the decisions of policymakers, but feedback from the economy itself in raising or reducing tax revenues. The budget influences real GDP, but real GDP also influences the

---

[1] *Review:* "Natural" real GDP and the "natural" rate of unemployment are defined in Section 1-3 on pp. 5–8.

budget. For instance, economic prosperity in the late 1990s explains part of the shift from a budget deficit to surplus, and the 2001 recession and its aftermath explain part of the shift back from surplus to deficit after 2001. We examine the role of the weak economy and of the Bush administration tax cuts and spending increases as explanations of this turnaround from the government budget surplus into deep deficits.

A second major theme in this chapter is the interaction of the government budget with net exports and foreign lending or borrowing. When net exports (NX) are positive, the nation lends to foreigners, whereas negative NX implies borrowing from foreigners. We learn how the government budget and foreign borrowing are interconnected through the magic equation initially introduced in Chapter 2. This states that national saving (the sum of the government budget surplus and private saving) must be equal to the sum of domestic and foreign investment. Thus when the government budget shifts from surplus to deficit, one way to balance the magic equation is for foreign investment to become more negative, that is, for borrowing from foreigners to increase, causing the government budget deficit to be joined by a foreign trade deficit, the so-called twin deficits. But other outcomes are possible as well, including an increase in private saving and/or a decline in domestic investment. A simple theoretical graph displaying the government surplus, private saving, domestic investment, and foreign borrowing helps us to understand which combination of these alternative outcomes will occur. Finally, we ask how long the twin deficits can continue and what are their likely long-run effects on interest rates and economic growth.

5-2 The Pervasive Effects of the Government Budget

In this section we examine several adverse effects of persistent deficits that in the early 1990s eventually created the political will to end the deficits and push the government budget into surplus. However, persistent deficits returned in 2002–05, making this analysis as relevant to the current decade as to the 1980s and early 1990s.

Crowding Out of Net Exports

The *IS-LM* model in Chapter 4 emphasized that a fiscal expansion, taking the form of an increase in government spending or a reduction in tax rates, is likely to crowd out domestic private investment. But, in addition, a fiscal expansion may crowd out net exports. We can review the magic equation (2.5) in Chapter 2 (here renumbered as equation 5.1) to see why one or the other type of crowding out must occur:

$$T - G \equiv (I + NX) - S \tag{5.1}$$

On the left-hand side of this definition is the government budget surplus $(T - G)$. On the right-hand side is the excess of total investment, both domestic (I) and foreign (NX), over private saving (S). This means that a government surplus is available to finance an excess of domestic investment over private saving $(I - S)$ or to lend to foreigners (positive NX).

When the quantity on the left-hand side is negative (T smaller than G), the government is running a deficit. Then equation (5.1) indicates that there are only three ways for the government deficit to be financed. First, private saving can go up. Second, domestic private investment can go down; this is the crowding out effect that we examined in Figure 4-6 on p. 109. Third, foreign investment can go down, and if it drops far enough and becomes negative, we call it foreign borrowing.

Impact on Future Generations

Persistent government budget deficits have another implication as well. A deficit raises the public (or national) debt, while a surplus reduces the public debt. Future generations, including current college students reading this book, will be obliged to pay higher taxes than otherwise would be necessary so the government can pay interest on its debt incurred as a result of the deficits incurred in 1980–97 and 2002–05.

Clearly, a persistent budget deficit has pervasive consequences on domestic investment, foreign investment or borrowing, and the wealth of citizens in the future. A persistent surplus reverses these effects. However, it will take many years of surpluses to offset fully the impact of the deficits that have already occurred. This is ample motivation to study closely in the remainder of this chapter the causes and effects of the budget deficit.

5-3 Case Study

The Government Budget In Historical Perspective

Throughout history the largest government budget deficits have been incurred as a result of wars, when government expenditures increased more than government tax revenues. Governments choose not to pay the full cost of wars through taxation for fear that heavy taxes will demoralize citizens when their utmost efforts are needed for war production.

The top frame of Figure 5-1 plots U.S. government real expenditures (including transfer payments) and revenues as a percentage of natural real GDP, for the century between 1900 and 2004. The difference between expenditures and revenues is shaded: red shading indicates a government budget deficit and green shading indicates a government budget surplus. Included is not just the federal government budget but also the budgets of the state and local governments.

Wars and the Increasing Size of Government

Five facts stand out in the top frame of Figure 5-1. First, government expenditures exhibit a marked spike in war years, with World War II having a much greater impact than World War I. Second, tax revenues also exhibit a spike in wartime, but a smaller spike than expenditures, so deficits increase in wartime. Third, the size of government has increased in the years since World War II, as compared with the years before 1930, with real expenditures averaging about 30 percent of natural real GDP and edging up to about 33 percent in 1992, after which there was a slight decline back to 30 percent in 1998–2004. Fourth, expenditures increased more than revenues during the 1980s, leading to a persistent budget deficit that temporarily ended in 1997. Fifth, revenues were stable at 28 to 30 percent during the 1980s and 1990s before briefly soaring to 33 percent in 2000 and then plummeting to 25 percent in 2004.

Figure 5-1 Real Government Expenditures, Real Government Revenues, and the Real Government Budget Deficit, 1900–2005

The top frame compares real government expenditures and revenues (for federal, state, and local government) as a share of natural GDP, and shows the dramatic effects of wars and also the gradual increase in the expenditure share in the 1970s and 1980s and its decline in the 1990s, followed by the temporary bulge of revenue in 1999–2000 and its collapse in 2002–04. The middle frame shows the government budget surplus and deficit for the century, and the bottom frame is a blowup of the experience of the 1955–2004 period, calling attention to the unusual 1980–97 and 2002–05 deficits.

The middle frame shows the government budget deficit and surplus. The areas in red and green shading in the middle frame are identical to the corresponding areas in the top frame. Here the tendency of wars to create deficits is even more evident. The 1980–97 and 2002–05 deficits pale in comparison with the gigantic deficit of World War II. To compare more clearly the recent deficits, the period 1955–2005 is magnified in the bottom frame.

The Effect of Recessions

During a recession, government revenues decline and transfer payments increase. Notice in the bottom frame how deficits occurred during or soon after the recessions of 1958, 1970, 1975, 1982, 1990–91, and 2001.

If government deficits had frequently been associated with recessions in the past, why did the deficits of 1980–97 and 2002–05 create so much controversy? The answer is visible in the bottom frame of Figure 5-1. Each previous recession deficit episode has a sharp V shape, and the government budget deficit quickly went to zero as the economy recovered after the recession. But 1980–97 was different. As the economy recovered after the 1982 recession, the *government budget deficit did not disappear but remained relatively large*. The large budget deficits after 1982 occurred in peacetime, not in wartime, and in a situation of economic recovery and expansion rather than recession.

Similarly, after the 2001 recession the recovery of the economy did not lead to the elimination of the budget deficit. During 2002–04, despite robust growth of real GDP, *the government deficit did not disappear but grew ever larger and in 2004 exceeded that of 1992 as a share of natural real GDP*. In the next section we turn to the causes of the growing deficits after 2001. How much of the turnaround in the government budget can be attributed to the Bush administration tax cuts, how much to the Iraq war and homeland security, and how much to other factors?

5-4 The Structural Budget

In this section we distinguish between two types of change in the government budget deficit. The first type, called the **cyclical surplus** or **cyclical deficit** occurs *automatically* as a result of the business cycle. Recessions cause government revenues to shrink and the cyclical deficit to grow; this condition is followed by recoveries and expansions that cause government revenues to grow and the cyclical deficit to shrink. The second type is called the **structural surplus** or **structural deficit**; this is the surplus or deficit that remains after the effect of the business cycle is separated out. The structural surplus or deficit is calculated by assuming that current levels of government spending and tax rates remain in effect, but that the economy is operating at natural real GDP rather than the actual observed level of real GDP.

The **cyclical deficit** is the amount by which the actual government budget deficit exceeds the **structural deficit**, which in turn is defined as what the deficit *would be* if the economy were operating at natural real GDP. The **cyclical surplus** and **structural surplus** are the same as the deficit concepts with the signs reversed.

Automatic Stabilization

Recall from Chapters 2 and 3 that the symbol T stands for "net" tax revenues, that is, total tax revenues minus government transfer payments. If net tax rev-

Figure 5-2 The Relation Between the Government Budget Surplus or Deficit and Real Income

How the Economy Influences the Budget

In the green area, the government budget is in surplus, while in the red area, the government budget is in deficit. The budget line BB_0 shows all the levels of the government budget surplus or deficit that are compatible with a given level of government expenditures (G_0) and tax rates (t_0). The BB line slopes upward to the right, because as we move rightward from B to A, the higher real income (Y) raises tax revenues ($t_0 Y$), thus increasing the surplus or reducing the deficit by the amount $t\Delta Y$.

enues (T) rise when income is high and fall when income is low, we can express net tax revenue as equal to the average net tax rate (t) times real income (Y):[2]

$$T = tY \qquad (5.2)$$

This implies that the government budget can be written as

$$\text{budget surplus} = T - G = tY - G \qquad (5.3)$$

The government budget deficit is simply a negative value of the surplus, as defined in (5.3). The purpose of writing the government budget surplus or deficit in this way is to distinguish two main sources of change in the surplus or deficit: (1) **automatic stabilization** through changes in Y, and (2) **discretionary fiscal policy** through changes in G and t.

When real GDP increases in an economic expansion, the government surplus automatically rises as more net tax revenues are generated (that is, gross tax revenues rise and transfer payments such as unemployment benefits fall). The higher surplus (or lower deficit) helps to stabilize the economy, since the extra net tax revenues that are generated by rising incomes leak out of the spending stream and help restrain the boom. Similarly, tax revenues drop and transfers rise in a recession, cutting the leakages out of the spending stream and helping dampen the recession.

The automatic stabilization effect of real income or GDP (Y) on the government surplus or deficit is illustrated in Figure 5-2. The horizontal axis is real income and the vertical axis is the government budget surplus and deficit. In the green area above the zero level on the vertical axis, the government runs a surplus, with tax revenues exceeding expenditures. In the red area below zero, the government runs a deficit, with expenditures exceeding tax revenues. Along the horizontal line separating the green and red areas, the government budget is balanced, with expenditures exactly equal to tax revenues.

Automatic stabilization occurs because government tax revenues depend on income, causing the economy to be stabilized by the leakage of tax revenues from the spending stream when income rises or falls.

Discretionary fiscal policy alters tax rates and/or government expenditures in a deliberate attempt to influence real output and the unemployment rate.

---

[2] Note that t is now the average ratio of total tax revenue to GDP, whereas in the Appendix to Chapter 3 the same symbol t was used for the marginal income tax rate.

The budget line shows the government budget surplus or deficit at different levels of real income.

The purple upward-sloping BB_0 schedule is the **budget line**, which illustrates the automatic stabilization relationship between the government budget and real income when other determinants of the budget in equation (5.3) are constant, that is, at the assumed values G_0 and t_0. The budget line BB_0 has a slope equal to the tax rate t_0. In Figure 5-2 the budget line BB_0 is drawn so that the government runs a balanced budget at point A, when real income is equal to natural real GDP (Y^N). If the economy were to fall from Y^N to Y_0, the economy would move from point A to point B, where the government is running a deficit because its tax revenues have fallen by $t_0 \Delta Y$.

Discretionary Fiscal Policy

The second source of change in the government budget deficit comes from alterations in government spending (G) and in the tax rate (t). It is evident from equation (5.3) that a decline in government spending (G) reduces the budget deficit, while a decrease in the tax rate (t) raises the deficit. How do such discretionary changes affect the budget line? Figure 5-3 copies the budget line BB_0 from Figure 5-2. The initial budget line BB_0 is drawn on the assumption that government spending is G_0. An increase in government spending from G_0 to G_1 shifts the purple budget line downward for any given level of real income, since at a given level of income the government spends more and has a higher deficit at G_1 compared with the original spending level G_0. The new budget line is shown in the position BB_1.

Find point C along the new budget line BB_1. This shows that at the new higher level of government spending (G_1), the budget would have a large deficit at a real income level of Y_0. There are three ways to reduce the deficit. One way, shown by a movement from C to D, would be to increase real income to Y^N. The second way, shown by a movement from C to B, would be to reduce government spending. A third way, not shown separately, would be to increase the tax rate (t_0), which would also shift the budget line

Figure 5-3 Effect on the Budget Line of an Increase in Government Expenditures

The upper budget line BB_0 is copied from Figure 5-2 and assumes a value for government spending of G_0. The lower budget line BB_1 assumes that the level of government spending has increased to G_1, thus reducing the government budget surplus or increasing the government budget deficit at every level of real income.

Does the Budget Influence the Economy, or Does the Economy Influence the Budget?

upward.[3] Changes in the actual budget deficit provide no indications of specific discretionary fiscal policy actions (that is, changes in government spending and the tax rate), since the actual budget deficit can also change as real income increases or decreases with no change in tax rates or government expenditures, as from C to D or B to A.

The Natural Employment Surplus or Deficit

Since the actual budget surplus or deficit cannot identify discretionary fiscal policy changes, how can we summarize the effect of fiscal policy on the economy? In Figure 5-3 the more expansionary budget line BB_1 has a *lower* vertical position than the original budget line BB_0. Thus its expansionary effect can be summarized by describing the vertical position of the budget line at some standard agreed-upon level of real income, for instance, when real income is equal to natural real GDP (Y^N).

The budget surplus or deficit at the natural level of real GDP is called the **natural employment surplus (NES)** or the **natural employment deficit (NED)**. It is defined as the government budget deficit that *would occur if* actual real GDP (Y) were equal to natural real GDP (Y^N). If we substitute natural real GDP (Y^N) for actual real GDP in equation (5.3), we can define the natural employment surplus as:

$$\text{natural employment surplus} = tY^N - G \qquad (5.4)$$

The natural employment deficit is simply a negative value of the surplus in (5.4) and changes when there is a change in government spending (G), the tax rate (t), or natural real GDP (Y^N) itself.

In Figure 5-3 there is a different natural employment surplus or deficit for each of the two budget lines shown. For the original budget line BB_0, the natural employment deficit is abbreviated NED_0. The value of NED_0 is zero, since along BB_0 the government budget is in balance at Y^N. For the new budget line BB_1, the natural employment deficit is NED_1 and is shown by the distance AD, since along BB_1 the government deficit is the amount AD when the economy is operating at Y^N.

We can now review the major budget concepts with the help of Figure 5-3. The actual budget deficit is shown by the economy's actual position along the appropriate BB line in the figure, for instance at points like B or C. The natural employment deficit is the deficit along each budget line measured at the natural level of real GDP, as at points like A and D. *Structural deficit* is another name for the natural employment deficit. The structural deficit changes whenever there is a change in government expenditures or tax rates. The cyclical deficit is the difference between the actual deficit and the natural employment deficit, the vertical distance between A and B along budget line BB_0, and the vertical distance between D and C along budget line BB_1. Automatic stabilization is represented by the slope of the budget line, since higher tax revenues and lower transfer payments cause a greater amount of real income to leak out of the spending stream whenever real income expands.

The **natural employment surplus** or **deficit** is government expenditures minus a hypothetical figure for government revenue, calculated by applying current tax rates to natural real GDP rather than actual real GDP.

---

[3] An increase in the tax rate *rotates* the budget line about its fixed vertical intercept, shifting it upward while making it steeper. A reduction in the tax rate rotates the budget line down, making it flatter.

Self-Test

How would the following be shown in Figure 5-3 and what effect would each of these have on the natural employment deficit?

1. More spending for highway repair?
2. An increase in the Social Security tax rate?
3. An increase in Social Security benefits?
4. A recession that increases the unemployment rate from 5 to 10 percent?

The Actual and Natural Employment Deficits: Historical Behavior

How have actual and natural employment deficits differed over the past 40 years? The purple line in Figure 5-4 displays the actual government budget

Only Clinton Achieved a Natural Employment Surplus

Figure 5-4 **A Comparison of the Actual Budget and the Natural Employment Budget, 1960–2004**

The orange "natural employment surplus" line lies above the purple "actual surplus" line in years when the economy is weak and lies below when the economy is strong. A natural employment deficit occurred in all years except in 1998–2001.

Source: Congressional Budget Office.

outcome. The natural employment surplus or deficit is shown by the orange line.[4]

The orange line isolates the structural component of the budget deficit. The distance between the purple and orange lines represents the cyclical component of the deficit. When the purple line is underneath the orange line, as in 1975–77, 1980–85, 1991–93, and 2002–04, the economy is weak, as shown by the blue shading. When the purple line is above the orange line, the economy is prosperous, with actual real GDP greater than natural real GDP, as shown by the red shading.

The purple line in Figure 5-3 shows that the government ran a natural employment deficit (NED) in every year between 1960 and 2004 except the four years 1998–2001. However, there were several periods when the NED was particularly large. First, the NED reached a peak of −4.4 percent of GDP in 1966, largely as the result of Vietnam War spending. Second, the NED was at −3.0 or larger negative numbers during the entire period 1981–91 as the result of the Reagan-era tax cuts and military buildup. The brief disappearance of the NED in 1998–2001 was the result of a booming economy, a temporary upsurge of stock market prices that generated unprecedented government revenue from the capital gains tax, and an increase of income tax rates for high-income earners legislated by President Clinton and Congress in 1993.

5-5 National Saving and the Consequences of the Government Budget

We have now learned that there is a distinction between the actual budget surplus or deficit and the structural budget surplus or deficit that corrects for the impact of the business cycle on government revenues and expenditures. In this section we study the impact of the government budget on the nation's total saving, which determines its ability to finance total investment.

Fiscal Policy and National Saving

In order to invest, a nation must save. Its total saving is called **national saving (NS)** and consists of private saving (S) plus government saving, which is the same thing as a government budget surplus ($T - G$). A government budget deficit reduces national saving. In turn, national saving is the amount available to finance domestic investment (I) and net foreign investment, which is the same as net exports (NX). The relation between national saving and the two types of investment is summarized in the following equation, which is a simple rearrangement of the magic equation (5.1) on p. 131.

National saving is the sum of private saving (by both households and business firms) and government saving. In turn, government saving is the government budget surplus; a government budget deficit subtracts from national saving.

$$S + (T - G) \equiv I + NX, \text{ or } NS \equiv I + NX \quad (5.5)$$

In words, this equation states that national saving (NS) on the left-hand side must equal the sum of domestic and foreign investment ($I + NX$) on the right-hand side.

---

[4] The actual deficit in Figure 5-4 refers only to the federal government and this differs slightly from Figure 5-1, which also includes state and local governments.

Crowding Out in a Closed Economy

We have learned that an increase in government spending (G) or a reduction in taxes (T) reduces national saving (NS). Figure 5-5 provides a simple graphical representation of the working of the magic equation in a "closed economy" that has no exports or imports, that is, where $NX = 0$. Subsequently we will use the same graph to interpret the effects of fiscal policy in an open economy that exports to and imports from the rest of the world.

In Figure 5-5, the vertical axis is the interest rate, just as in the graphs of the *IS-LM* model in Chapter 4. However, the horizontal axis is now the amount of investment (I) and of national saving (NS). As in the *IS-LM* model, the demand for investment (I^d) depends negatively on the interest rate, as indicated by the red downward sloping I^d line. This represents the same negative effect of the interest rate on investment spending as we have already studied in Figures 3-7 and 3-8 on pp. 81–82.

National saving (NS), as in equation (5.4) consists of two components, private saving (S) and the government budget surplus $(T - G)$. The government component of national saving does not depend on the interest rate. But the pri-

Figure 5-5 National Saving and Domestic Investment in a Closed Economy
The downward sloping investment demand (I^d) line reflects the negative effect of higher interest rates on investment, just as in Figures 3-7 and 3-8. The upward sloping national saving (NS) line reflects the positive effect of higher interest rates on private saving, a component of national saving. The economy's equilibrium is at point E_0.

vate component of saving does depend on the interest rate. As we learned in Figure 3-8 on p. 82, autonomous consumption (C_a) depends negatively on the interest rate, just as does investment. But if autonomous consumption falls when the interest rate increases, then for any given amount of disposable income, private saving (which is disposable income minus consumption) must *rise* when the interest rate increases. The sum of government saving (which does not depend on the interest rate) and private saving (which depends positively on the interest rate) is national saving, and the *NS* line in Figure 5-5 is a positively sloped line reflecting the positive dependence of private saving on the interest rate. The economy's equilibrium is at point E_0 where the red I^d line crosses the blue *NS* line.

What happens when government spending is increased by an amount ΔG? As shown in Figure 5-6, this causes the national saving line to shift leftward from NS_0 to NS_1; the amount of the leftward shift is shown by the distance between points A and E_0. The new equilibrium is at point E_1, and the decline of investment between I_0 and I_1 demonstrates again the crowding-out effect of a fiscal policy expansion. This is the same crowding-out effect as was previously

Fiscal Deficits Cause Domestic Crowding Out

Figure 5-6 Effect of a Fiscal Expansion in a Closed Economy
The downward sloping investment demand (I^d) line and upward sloping national saving (*NS*) lines are the same as in Figure 5-5. An increase in government spending (or a reduction in tax revenue) shifts the NS_0 line leftward to NS_1 and the equilibrium point northwest from E_0 to E_1.

displayed in Figure 4-6 on p. 109; the only difference is that in that graph we plotted the impact of the fiscal policy expansion on real GDP, whereas here we plot the decline of investment that accompanies the fiscal expansion. The increase in the interest rate that occurs in the two diagrams is the same.[5]

Notice that the decline in national saving between points E_0 and E_1 (which is also indicated by ΔNS along the horizontal axis) is less than the increase in government spending. This is the result of the positive slope of the NS line; the increase in the interest rate not only crowds out private investment but also stimulates additional private saving (ΔS), shown by the horizontal distance between points A and E_1. The change in national saving is equal to the change in private saving minus the change in government spending ($\Delta NS = \Delta S - \Delta G$).[6]

Fiscal Policy in a Small Open Economy

Now we relax the restriction in the previous section that the economy is closed, with no foreign trade. But in reality every country is an **open economy** that sells exports to and buys imports from foreign countries, and experiences inflows and outflows of capital to and from other nations. Many economies (Belgium or Costa Rica, for example) are called small open economies because changes in their domestic policies have no influence on the world interest rate. The interest rate in these countries (r) is equal to the interest rate in foreign countries (r^f) and is unaffected by a change in domestic fiscal policy. For these countries, an increase in government spending or decrease in tax rates that reduces national saving has no effect on the interest rate or on investment; net exports decline by the exact amount of the decrease in national saving. Using equation (5.4) we can write the change in national saving as:

$$\Delta NS = \Delta I + \Delta NX \tag{5.6}$$

and when there is a change in national saving in a small open economy with a fixed interest rate, we can solve for the change in net exports as

$$\Delta NX = \Delta NS \tag{5.7}$$

where the change of investment is zero because the interest rate is fixed ($\Delta I = 0$). The top frame of Figure 5-7 illustrates the adjustment to a decline in national saving (ΔNS) caused by the same increase in government spending that occurred in Figure 5-6. Now the interest rate is fixed at the foreign interest rate ($r = r^f$), and thus there is no crowding out of domestic investment ($\Delta I = 0$). The economy's new equilibrium point E_1 is at the same point as the original equilibrium point E_0 and investment is unchanged. The increase in government spending is exactly balanced by a decline in national saving that equals the decline in net exports ($\Delta G = -\Delta NS = -\Delta NX$). The decline in net exports is the same thing as an increase in foreign borrowing, so intuitively *it is borrowing from foreigners that allows domestic investment (I) to remain unchanged despite a decline in national saving.* Comparing the top frame of Figure 5-7 with Figure 5-6, notice that the decline in national saving is smaller in

---

An **open economy** sells exports to other nations, buys imports, and experiences capital flows consisting of purchases and sales of foreign assets by domestic residents and purchases and sales of domestic assets by foreign residents.

---

[5] In Figure 5-6 we simplify the analysis by ignoring the effect of changes in real GDP on private saving.

[6] As before, we simplify the analysis by ignoring the effect of changes in real GDP on private saving, and we also assume that all tax revenue is autonomous, not depending on income.

5-5 National Saving and the Consequences of the Government Budget

Figure 5-7 Effect of a Fiscal Expansion in an Open Economy

The downward sloping investment demand (I^d) line and upward sloping national saving (NS) lines are the same as in Figure 5-6. An increase in government spending (or a reduction in tax revenue) shifts the NS_0 line leftward to NS_1. The top frame depicts the adjustment for a small open economy in which the interest rate is fixed at the level of the foreign interest rate ($r = r^f$). Because the interest rate does not increase, there is no crowding out of investment, and the funds to maintain domestic investment unchanged at I_0 are provided by borrowing from foreigners (that is, a decline in net exports). The bottom frame depicts the adjustment in a large open economy where changes in domestic policy influence the world interest rate. The interest rate is shown as increasing by half the amount as in Figure 5-6. The fiscal policy stimulus causes three changes. There is a decline in investment, as shown by the horizontal distance between point E_0 and point E_1. There is a decline in net exports (increase in foreign borrowing), as shown by the horizontal distance between point E_1 and point B. And there is an increase in private saving, as shown by the horizontal distance between point A and point B.

Figure 5-6, because the increase in the interest rate between the initial equilibrium at E_0 and the new equilibrium at E_1 causes an increase in private saving (along the positively sloped NS line) that partially offsets the decline in government saving. In contrast, in the top frame in Figure 5-7 there is no increase in private saving because there is no increase in the interest rate.

Fiscal Policy in a Large Open Economy

A large open economy like the United States differs from a small open economy because changes in domestic monetary and fiscal policy are capable of altering the foreign interest rate (r^f). A fiscal policy stimulus in the United States will put upward pressure on the foreign interest rate, but if fiscal policy is unchanged in other countries, then the interest rate will not increase as much as if the United States were a closed economy. For instance, in a simple case where the world consisted half of the United States and half of foreign countries, then the interest rate would increase by half as much following a U.S. fiscal stimulus as it would in a closed economy.

The bottom frame of Figure 5-7 continues to assume that the domestic interest rate equals the foreign interest rate $(r = r^f)$. Now, however, a domestic fiscal stimulus causes an increase in the foreign interest rate by half as much following a domestic fiscal stimulus as in the closed-economy example of Figure 5-6. The economy moves from its initial equilibrium point E_0 to the new point E_1 and investment falls from I_0 to I_1. There is partial crowding out, but not as much as in the closed economy case of Figure 5-6. The decline in national saving caused by the increase in government spending is partially offset as before by an increase in private saving (the horizontal distance between points A and B), and now foreign borrowing (a decline in net exports) allows the decline of investment to be smaller than the decline in national saving.

To summarize this analysis, we can return to the first line of equation (5.4), the magic equation, and rewrite it as in equation (2.5) on p. 35 with the government surplus on the left and its other components on the right, but now we include the Δ symbol to focus on the change in the components of the magic equation:

$$\Delta(T - G) \equiv \Delta I + \Delta NX - \Delta S \qquad (5.8)$$

In the bottom frame of Figure 5-7, an increase in government spending causes the government surplus to decline by the distance between point E_0 and point A. The decline in investment is shown by the horizontal distance between point E_0 and point E_1. The decline in net exports is shown by the horizontal distance between point E_1 and point B. And the increase in private saving is shown by the horizontal distance between point A and point B.

In general, a fiscal policy stimulus causes a combination of three events—a decline in domestic investment, a decline in net exports (increase in foreign borrowing), and an increase in private saving. The balance between these three outcomes depends on the responsiveness of private saving and domestic investment to a higher interest rate, and the responsiveness of the world interest rate to events within a large open economy like the United States. These three outcomes work in reverse when there is a restrictive change in fiscal policy caused by a decline in government spending or an increase in tax revenue.

Self-Test

1. In a small open economy following a *decline* in government spending, is there an increase or decrease in net exports? In foreign borrowing? In private saving? In domestic investment?
2. In a large open economy following a *decline* in government spending, is there an increase or decrease in net exports? In foreign borrowing? In private saving? In domestic investment?

5-6 Case Study

How the Deficits Rejoined to Become "Twins"

In the middle of this decade, widespread attention has focused on the large government budget deficit and the large foreign trade deficit (i.e., negative net exports), and as indicated at the beginning of this chapter, these are often called the twin deficits. As is clear from Figure 5-7 and from the magic equation itself, there is no reason why a government budget deficit should be accompanied by a foreign trade deficit of the same size. Rearranging equation (5.5), we can express the relationship between the government deficit $(G - T)$ and the foreign trade deficit $(-NX)$:

$$G - T \equiv -NX + (S - I) \tag{5.9}$$

Thus the government budget deficit $(G - T)$ is equal to the foreign trade deficit $(-NX)$ only if private domestic saving is equal to domestic investment $(S = I)$. Yet there is no reason why this should be true, and in most periods private domestic saving is not equal to domestic investment. In fact, in the late 1990s domestic investment was so much larger than private domestic saving that a foreign trade deficit was accompanied by a government budget surplus rather than a government budget deficit.

The history of the components of equation (5.9) is shown in Figure 5-8 for the period 1960–2004. All data are expressed as a percentage of GDP, and a horizontal black line is drawn at zero. The distance between the horizontal line and the purple line at the bottom of the graph is the government budget deficit plotted as a negative number $(T - G)$, and this is the same as the government budget number shown by the purple line in Figure 5-1 (it includes the state and local governments as well as the federal government). The red line plots domestic investment (I) and the blue line plots national saving $(NS = S + T - G)$. The orange shaded difference between the I and NS lines represents negative net exports (foreign borrowing), since we can rearrange the magic equation (5.9) to solve for foreign borrowing $(-NX)$:

$$-NX \equiv I - (S + T - G) \equiv I - NS \tag{5.10}$$

Stated another way, the sum of foreign borrowing and national saving $(-NX + NS)$ represents the amount available to finance domestic investment. Finally, the blue-shaded distance between national saving (NS) and the government surplus $(T - G)$ equals private saving (S). For instance, in the year 2000 the blue NS line is plotted at 7.7 percent of GDP, which represents the sum of the

146 Chapter 5 • National Saving, the Government Budget, Foreign Borrowing, and the Twin Deficits

Figure 5-8 Components of Net Saving and Investment, 1960–2004

The bottom purple line is the government budget surplus and is the same as the purple line in Figure 5-1. The blue line is national saving, and the blue-shaded area between those lines is domestic private saving. The red line represents domestic private investment and the orange-shaded area represents foreign borrowing. Thus the chart shows how in 1980–2004 domestic private investment was partly financed by national saving and partly by foreign borrowing. Before 1980 both private and national saving were higher. The gray area shows foreign investment. In 1997–98, a shift toward budget surplus was accompanied by an increase in domestic investment, while borrowing from abroad increased as well, and after 2000 the government budget shifted to a deficit, national saving and domestic investment fell, and foreign borrowing increased further.

government surplus of 2.6 percent and private saving of 5.1 percent. A different situation is shown in the year 2004, when the blue *NS* line is plotted at a much lower 2.5 percent of GDP, representing the sum of the government surplus of −3.4 percent and private saving of 5.9 percent. While private saving (consisting not just of household saving but also of corporate saving) remained relatively constant during 2000–04, the shrinking blue shaded area shows that private saving has fallen by almost half since before 1995. The average ratio to GDP of private saving was 9.4 percent in 1960–92 but fell to only 5.1 percent during 2000–04.

To summarize, the government budget deficit and the foreign deficit were "twins" over the period 1983–97. After a brief period of government budget surplus in 1998–2001, the twin deficits were rejoined in 2002–04.

5-7 Conclusion: Solutions to the National Saving Squeeze

To the extent that domestic private investment is the source of future economic growth, then the reduction in national saving depicted in Figure 5–8 is bad news for future generations of U.S. citizens, including today's college students. The only way that domestic private investment can exceed national saving is through foreign borrowing. But foreigners do not send investment funds to the United States as a gift. Instead, they expect to receive interest and dividends on their investment. To the extent that the after-tax return on domestic private investment is just sufficient to pay interest and dividends to foreigners, domestic residents do not benefit from this investment (except to the extent that the government collects sales, Social Security, and corporate profits taxes from the foreign firms that make the investment).

Since foreign borrowing is no solution, what other options remain to increase national saving in order to stimulate domestic investment and long-run economic growth? The two obvious solutions are (1) to increase private saving, and (2) to increase government saving.

Raise the private saving rate. Many economists believe that the low U.S. household saving rate is unsustainable. To them, Americans are behaving irrationally, living beyond their means. They believe that as households realize how much debt they are in, they will reduce their spending and raise their saving. But these economists neglect an important fact. The U.S. household saving rate is low because households have enjoyed rapid appreciation of real estate and financial assets for the past two decades. Even after the stock market decline of 2000–02, housing prices continued to increase. We will return in Chapter 15 to a further analysis of household consumption and saving behavior.

Raise the government saving rate. The basic solution to the inadequate national saving rate in the United States is to raise the government saving rate. This requires some combination of a decrease in government spending and an increase in tax rates, exactly the opposite policies from those pursued by the Bush administration in 2001–04.

While the Bush tax cuts were supported as necessary to stimulate the economy, we have seen (pp. 106–107) that monetary policy moved very quickly to reduce interest rates. These interest rate reductions stimulated spending on automobiles, housing, and other forms of consumption. Households that refinanced mortgages at lower interest rates were able to reduce their monthly payments and/or increase the principal value of their mortgage (receiving "cash back" in the amount of the new mortgage balance minus the old mortgage balance).

Because of the strong effects of monetary policy in 2001–04, some critics argued that the Bush tax cuts were not necessary and reduced national saving when there was no reason to do so. Other critics focused explicitly on the distributional impact of the tax cuts. In the year 2004, the tax cuts gave a boost in disposable income of $90 billion to the bottom 80 percent of the income distribution, $90 billion to households in the top 2 to 20 percent of the income distribution, and another $90 billion to households in the top 1 percent of the income distribution. Evidence shows that the marginal propensity to consume is much lower in the top 1 percent of the income distribution than in the bottom 80 percent.

International Perspective

Saving, Investment, and Government Budgets Around the World

We have seen that the U.S. government budget was in persistent deficit from 1980 to 1997 and again after 2000. How was the government able to finance this deficit? Do other major industrial nations run budget deficits, and how do they finance theirs?

The figure covers the period since 1980. It shows the workings of the magic equation (5.9), which states that the government budget deficit equals private saving minus total investment (domestic and foreign). When the government runs a deficit, total investment $(I + NX)$ must be smaller than private saving (S). For the United States in the top frame, saving (S, the blue line) exceeded total investment ($I + NX$, the red line) in all years but 1998–2000. The shaded red area between the two lines represents the government budget deficit. In the bottom frame, the European Community also ran persistent budget deficits, which began to narrow only at the end of the period. Japan had a budget surplus between 1987 and 1992 but a budget deficit before and after.

How were budget deficits financed? In the United States, saving (S) declined slowly and thus did not help finance the pre-1998 budget deficits at all. Instead, total investment declined. Domestic investment (I) and foreign investment (NX), while not shown separately in the figure, are listed separately in the table for three periods: 1978–80, before the large budget deficits began; and two more recent periods, 1988–90 and 2000–02.

In all three periods, the United States ran a government budget deficit. In the first two periods, private saving roughly equaled domestic investment, so foreign borrowing was needed to finance the government budget deficit. In the third period, foreign borrowing increased, because domestic investment surged far more than private saving.

For Japan each period is different. In the first, a large budget deficit was financed by an excess of private saving over domestic investment. In the second period, the budget ran a surplus that was sent abroad as foreign investment. Finally, in the third period the excess of private saving over private investment was so large that it was sufficient to finance both a large government deficit and substantial foreign investment.

In Europe the story is simpler. In all three periods there were government deficits and negligible foreign investment, financed by a large excess of private saving over private investment.

The figure and table reveal several similarities and differences among the regions. In Japan both private saving and domestic investment declined from one period to the next, while in Europe there was an investment rebound in the third period. In the United States both private saving and domestic investment declined from the first period to the second and then both rebounded in the third. In all three periods the United States had the lowest rate of private saving, but in the third period it had the highest rate of domestic investment.

How the Government Budget Deficit Was Financed in the United States, Japan, and the European Union, Selected Intervals (all figures are expressed as percentages of GDP)

		$T - G$	=	$(I$	+	$NX)$	−	S
U.S.	1978–80	−0.4	=	17.1	+	−0.1	−	17.6
	1988–90	−3.2	=	14.8	+	−1.4	−	16.6
	2000–02	−0.7	=	21.6	+	−4.0	−	18.4
Japan	1978–80	−4.9	=	31.7	+	−0.1	−	36.5
	1988–90	1.6	=	33.1	+	2.1	−	33.6
	2000–02	−6.9	=	17.4	+	2.5	−	26.7
EU	1978–80	−4.2	=	22.1	+	0.3	−	26.6
	1988–90	−4.2	=	17.6	+	−0.2	−	21.7
	2000–02	−2.2	=	20.9	+	0.5	−	23.6

5-7 Conclusion: Solutions to the National Saving Squeeze 149

Source: OECD *Economic Outlook,* December 2004.

Thus, if the goal of the tax cuts was to create a multiplier stimulus of real GDP, as in the *IS-LM* model, then all of the tax cuts should have gone to the bottom 80 or 90 percent of the income distribution, where households spend most of each extra dollar of disposable income. From the point of view of economic stimulus, the $90 billion provided to the top 1 percent of households was wasted, since they spent little on extra consumption.

Some have argued that tax reductions for the richest Americans are justified in order to stimulate investment. But the main conclusion of this chapter is that the sum of domestic and foreign investment is equal to national saving. And a tax cut cannot increase national saving. The tax cut must reduce national saving unless the marginal propensity to consume is zero. The top 1 percent of the income distribution received $90 billion of tax cuts in 2004; even if they consumed only 20 percent of their tax cut benefit and saved the other 80 percent, national saving still was reduced by $18 billion. Why? The $90 billion tax cut reduced national saving and the hypothetical $72 billion increase in private saving (=0.8 × 90) offset only part of the decline in national saving caused by the larger government deficit.

Subsequent chapters. We return in subsequent chapters to issues related to the effect of fiscal policy on national saving, domestic investment, and foreign borrowing. In Chapter 6, we take a closer look at international economic relationships and at the foreign borrowing that is indirectly caused by fiscal deficits. In Chapter 12, we return to the long-run consequences of fiscal deficits and the related problems of large future anticipated deficits in funding Social Security and Medicare.

Summary

1. An increase in the government budget deficit can crowd out domestic private investment and/or require foreign borrowing to maintain the initial level of domestic private investment.

2. Over the past century, the government has run a budget deficit in most years, primarily because of wars and recessions. The budget deficits of 1983–97 and 2002–04 were unusual because they were not caused by wars or recessions.

3. The actual budget surplus or deficit is what actually occurs. The natural employment surplus or deficit is the hypothetical level of the budget surplus if the economy were operating at its natural level of output. The natural employment surplus changes whenever there is a change in government spending and/or tax rates, and these changes are called discretionary fiscal policy.

4. For any given level of government spending and tax rates, the government budget surplus rises if GDP is high and falls if GDP is low. Thus the economy changes the budget surplus or deficit, just as discretionary fiscal policy can change the economy through the multiplier effect of Chapters 3 and 4.

5. A closed economy is one without foreign trade, lending, or borrowing. In such an economy, a fiscal policy stimulus raises the interest rate, crowds out investment, and raises private saving. The decline in national saving is less than the decline in the fiscal surplus (or increase in the fiscal deficit), due to the positive response of private saving to a higher interest rate.

6. A small open economy cannot influence its interest rate, which is set equal to the interest rate in the rest of the world. In such an economy, a fiscal policy stimulus does not crowd out investment but rather causes a reduction in foreign lending or increase in foreign borrowing.

7. A large open economy can partially influence its interest rate. The most likely result of a fiscal policy stimulus is an increase in private saving, an increase in foreign borrowing, and a reduction in domestic investment.

8. In the 1960s and 1970s, domestic investment was mainly financed by private saving. In the 1980s and 1990s, domestic investment was financed by a combination of private saving and foreign borrowing, and a persistent fiscal deficit required additional foreign borrowing. After a brief respite when the government budget was in surplus in 1998–2001, during 2002–04 domestic investment was limited by sharply lower national saving, because the government budget went from surplus to deficit and because private saving remained low.

Concepts

cyclical surplus
cyclical deficit
structural surplus
structural deficit

automatic stabilization
discretionary fiscal policy
budget line
natural employment surplus (NES)

natural employment deficit (NED)
national saving (NS)
open economy

Questions

1. You have heard that the actual government deficit for the current year is going to be $30 billion greater than in the past year. Based on this projection, what conclusions can you make regarding the government's fiscal policy?
2. Explain the distinction among the following concepts:
   (a) cyclical deficit
   (b) structural deficit
   (c) natural employment deficit
   (d) actual deficit
3. Government deficits and surpluses are expressed throughout this chapter as percents of natural real GDP. Explain why it is necessary to express government deficits and surpluses in this manner in order to compare them over time.
4. Respond to the following statements about an economy where the government budget deficit has increased during a recession.
   (a) The increase in the budget deficit indicates that policymakers have implemented expansionary fiscal policies to bring the economy out of recession.
   (b) The increase in the budget deficit indicates that fiscal policymakers have been irresponsible. They should enact restrictive policies, such as tax hikes or spending cuts, to reduce the deficit.
5. Explain whether each of the following results in a change in the cyclical deficit, or a change in the natural employment deficit, or both.
   (a) A cut in the tax rate aimed at reducing unemployment.
   (b) The rise in taxes that occurs during an expansion.
   (c) The higher defense spending associated with the Iraq war.
   (d) The increase in unemployment compensation due to a rise in the unemployment rate.
6. During the 1983–95 period and again in 2002–04, the behavior of the government budget deficit was quite different from that of other recent post-recession periods. Explain in what way the budget deficit differed and why this difference occurred.
7. Explain why you would expect the actual government deficit to be larger than the natural employment deficit when the economy is weak.
8. The combination of tax increases, tighter spending controls, and a very strong economy helped move the U.S. government budget from deficit to surplus by the end of the 1990s. Explain how these events led from budget deficit to surplus and relate them to the concepts of discretionary fiscal policy, automatic stabilization, budget line, cyclical deficit, and natural employment deficit.
9. Compare and contrast the effect of a tax increase on private saving, domestic investment, net exports, and foreign borrowing in (a) a closed economy, (b) a small open economy, and (c) a large open economy.
10. If expansionary fiscal policy is enacted during a recession, fiscal policy should turn contractionary as the economy expands. Evaluate this statement. In addition, discuss the political difficulties associated with changing fiscal policy from being expansionary to contractionary.
11. Compare and contrast how the United States, Japan, and the European Union have financed government budget deficits since 1980.

Problems

1. Assume $Y^N = 11{,}250$, $t = 0.2$, and $G = 2{,}120$.
   (a) Compute the amount of taxes at natural real GDP.
   (b) Explain whether there is a natural employment surplus or deficit and compute the amount of the natural employment surplus or deficit.
   (c) Suppose the average tax rate is cut by 10 percent. Compute the new average tax rate and amount of taxes at natural real GDP.
   (d) Explain whether there is now a natural employment surplus or deficit and compute the amount of the natural employment surplus or deficit.
   (e) Suppose the average tax rate is 0.2, but government spending increases by 10 percent. Is there now a natural employment surplus or deficit? How large is it?

2. Assume $Y^N = 10{,}900$, $Y = 10{,}600$, $t = 0.16$, and $G = 1{,}890$.
   (a) Compute the amount of taxes at natural real GDP and actual real GDP.
   (b) Compute the amount of the natural employment deficit.
   (c) Compute the amount of the actual deficit. Is there a cyclical surplus or deficit? How large is it?
   (d) Suppose that fiscal policy is used to increase actual real GDP to natural real GDP. This fiscal expansion requires the average tax rate to be cut to 0.14. Compute the new amount of taxes at natural real GDP.
   (e) Compute the new amount of the natural employment deficit. Why are the natural employment deficit and actual deficit now equal? Why is there neither a cyclical surplus nor a cyclical deficit?
   (f) Suppose that instead of fiscal policy, monetary policy is used to increase actual real GDP to natural real GDP. What are the actual and natural employment deficits? Why are these answers different from part e?

3. You are given the following information for the equations for investment demand, private saving, and the government's deficit: $I^d = 2{,}400 - 125r$, $S = 1{,}750 + 75r$, $T - G = -350$. Suppose that this is a closed economy. The equilibrium interest rate is the one at which national savings and investment demand are equal.
   (a) Derive the equation for national saving.
   (b) Compute the equilibrium interest rate. Compute the amounts of investment demand, private saving, and national saving at the equilibrium interest rate.
   (c) Suppose that the government budget deficit is cut by $200 billion. Compute the new equilibrium interest rate. Compute the values of investment demand, private saving, and national saving at the new equilibrium interest rate.
   (d) Compare and contrast your answers to parts b and c.

4. Given the information at the beginning of question 3, assume we have a small open economy and that the foreign interest rate is 4.8 percent.
   (a) Compute the amounts of investment demand, private saving, national saving, net exports, and net foreign borrowing at the foreign interest rate.
   (b) Suppose that the government budget deficit is cut by $200 billion. Compute the new values of investment demand, private saving, national saving, and net exports. Is the economy now borrowing from the rest of the world or lending to the rest of the world?
   (c) Suppose that instead of a small open economy, we have a large open economy, and that initially the domestic and foreign interest rates are both 4.8 percent. The government budget deficit is cut by $200 billion. As a result, the domestic and foreign interest rates both decline to 4.4 percent. Compute the new amounts of investment demand, private saving, national saving, net exports, and foreign borrowing (lending) at the new domestic and foreign interest rates.
   (d) Explain why your answers to parts b and c differ.

Self-Test Answers

p. 138 (1) More spending for highway repair shifts the budget line *BB* down (raises the natural employment deficit, NED). (2) An increase in the Social Security tax rate moves *BB* up (reduces NED). (3) An increase in Social Security benefits moves *BB* down (raises NED). (4) A recession moves the economy leftward down a fixed *BB* schedule (no change in NED).

p. 145 (1) Increase in net exports; decrease in foreign borrowing; no change in private saving; no change in domestic investment. (2) Increase in net exports; decrease in foreign borrowing; decrease in private saving; increase in domestic investment.

CHAPTER 6

International Trade, Exchange Rates, and Macroeconomic Policy

Trade is the mother of money.
—Thomas Draxe, 1605

6-1 Introduction

Throughout this book we have treated the economy as "open" to trade in goods and services, as well as capital flows. We learned in Chapter 2 that foreign trade contributes to overall economic activity. GDP includes exports minus imports, which we call net exports. When net exports rise, GDP increases. When net exports decline, GDP decreases.

An economy with positive net exports must lend to foreigners ("foreign lending" or "foreign investment"), while an economy like the United States with negative net exports must borrow from foreigners ("foreign borrowing"). In the last chapter we learned that a government budget deficit can be financed partially or completely by foreign borrowing, depending on the size of the economy. A small open economy cannot influence the world interest rate and therefore can borrow the entire amount of the government budget deficit without crowding out private investment, whereas a large open economy influences the world interest rate, which will rise in response to a government budget deficit and thus crowd out private investment.

What We Learn in This Chapter

This chapter begins with the balance of payments, which records the main elements of a nation's foreign transactions, including its exports, imports, and capital flows. We learn how a persistent surplus in a nation's current account tends to be balanced by outflows of capital. This causes a buildup of net international assets, such as U.S.-owned plants making Ford automobiles and Heinz catsup in foreign countries. The opposite can also occur, since a persistent deficit in a nation's current account causes a decline in net international assets and ultimately a buildup of net international indebtedness. Over the past two decades, assets in the United States owned by foreigners, such as Sony Pictures and the Mercedes automobile plant in Alabama, have outweighed American investments abroad, leading to a large increase in American international indebtedness.

The foreign exchange rate of the dollar responds to imbalances in flows of exports, imports, and capital movements. We shall study the determinants of the foreign exchange rate and its interrelationship with monetary policy and interest rates. Later in the chapter we shall apply Chapter 4's *IS-LM* model to the analysis of the open economy. We shall learn that the effects of monetary and fiscal policy differ greatly, depending on whether the foreign exchange rate is fixed or flexible.

The "Trilemma"

A unifying theme of this chapter is the international **"trilemma"**—that it is impossible for any nation to maintain simultaneously (1) independent control of domestic monetary policy, (2) fixed exchange rates, and (3) free flows of capital with other nations ("perfect capital mobility"). Thus fixed exchange rates and capital mobility create a new reason why domestic monetary policy may be impotent beyond those factors that we studied in Chapter 4. For instance, Europe's common currency (the euro) has stripped member nations of their ability to conduct an independent domestic monetary policy and has led to a persistent economic slump in some European nations, particularly Germany.

How is the United States affected by the trilemma? By adopting flexible exchange rates, the United States is free to pursue an active domestic monetary policy despite keeping its borders open to perfect capital mobility. But, while the United States may want to keep its exchange rate flexible, it cannot prevent foreign nations, particularly China and Japan, from keeping their exchange rates relatively or totally fixed to the dollar. Ordinarily, the tendency of the United States to run a large foreign trade deficit would cause the U.S. dollar to depreciate, but this tendency for the dollar to become weaker can be prevented when a foreign central bank, like that of China, buys up dollars to prevent the dollar from depreciating and to prevent the Chinese currency from appreciating.

In this decade, the United States has been running extraordinarily large foreign trade deficits, financed in part by the desire of China, Japan, and other countries to keep their currencies from strengthening against the dollar. Another main theme of this chapter is to ask whether the United States can continue to live beyond its means, borrowing more and more from foreign private companies, households, and governments. Why are these foreign countries accumulating so many dollars, can this situation last forever, and will foreigners, particularly Asians, soon change their behavior and cause the dollar to crash?

> The **trilemma** is the impossibility for any nation of maintaining simultaneously (1) independent control of domestic monetary policy, (2) fixed exchange rates, and (3) free flows of capital with other nations.

6-2 The Current Account and the Balance of Payments

Throughout this book we have treated net exports (*NX*) as a part of GDP. In this section, we introduce a more comprehensive measure of the nation's international transactions called its **current account**, which equals net exports plus two additional components that are *not* part of GDP. The first of these is the net flow of international investment income, the amount Americans earn on their investments abroad minus the amount foreigners earn on their investments in the United States. Earnings such as Procter and Gamble's profits on a soap factory in France add to net investment income, while earnings such as Toyota's profits on its factory in Kentucky subtract from net investment income.

Net earnings on investments abroad do not represent production in the domestic economy and hence are not included in GDP; they are included in an

> The **current account** records the nation's current international transactions, including exports and imports of goods and services, income from foreign investments, and transfers to and from other countries.

alternative concept of overall production called Gross National Product (GNP), a concept previously introduced on pp. 31–32. The second component of the current account beyond net exports is net international transfers, such as the remittances that Mexican immigrants send home to their families in Mexico. Net international transfers are included in the current account but not in GDP; just like any transfer payment they are excluded from GDP because they do not represent production of goods and services.

Throughout the past two decades, the U.S. current account has been negative and since 2001 has grown to become an ever-larger share of GDP. To balance the perpetually negative current account, the United States must borrow from foreign firms and households, foreign governments, or both. Foreign borrowing builds up the total indebtedness of the United States to foreign nations and implies that some part of U.S. economic growth in the future is mortgaged to pay the interest payments on this debt.

The Current Account and the Capital Account

The foreign trade surplus or deficit is part of the official data on the international transactions of the United States. Like any nation, the United States has a balance of payments that records these transactions. The **balance of payments** is divided into two main parts.

> The **balance of payments** is the record of a nation's international transactions, and includes both credits (which arise from sales of exports and sales of assets) and debits (which arise from purchases of imports and purchases of assets).

1. The first part is the current account, which records the types of flows that matter for current income and output. The main components of the current account are exports and imports of goods and services, receipts and payments of investment income, and transfer payments. Just as purchases and sales of assets are excluded from GDP, so too are they excluded from the current account.

> The **capital account** is the part of the balance of payments that records capital flows, which consist of purchases and sales of foreign assets by domestic residents, and purchases and sales of domestic assets by foreign residents.

2. The second part of the balance of payments is the **capital account**, which records purchases and sales of foreign assets by U.S. residents and purchases and sales of American assets by foreign residents.

Any category of the balance of payments can generate a *credit* or a *debit*. To keep these terms straight, think of flows of money. Any international transaction that creates a payment of money to a U.S. resident is a credit. Included are exports of goods and services, investment income on U.S. assets held in foreign countries, transfers to U.S. residents, and purchases of U.S. assets by foreigners. Debits are the opposite of credits and result from payments of money to foreigners by U.S. residents. Debits are created by imports of goods and services, investment income paid on foreign holdings of assets within the United States, transfer payments by U.S. residents to foreigners, and purchases of foreign assets by U.S. residents.

The Balance of Payments Outcome

When total credits are greater than total debits, the United States is said to run a balance of payments surplus. When this occurs, we receive more foreign money from the credits than the sum of dollars we pay out for the debits. The opposite situation, when we pay out more dollars for the debits, is called a balance of payments deficit. The overall balance of payments surplus or deficit is the sum of the balance for the current account and the capital account.

$$\text{Current account balance} + \text{capital account balance} = \text{balance of payments outcome} \qquad (6.1)$$

Since the early 1980s, the United States has run a persistent current account deficit, because it has consistently run a deficit on its trade in goods and services and a deficit on its transfer payments as well. In the same time period, the United States has also run a persistent capital account surplus that has partly offset the current account deficit. When a nation runs a capital account surplus, households, firms, and the government *are engaged in net borrowing from foreigners* (borrowing from foreign central banks is counted not in the capital account but in the overall balance of payments surplus or deficit).

The U.S. balance of payments outcome for four different years (1970, 1980, 1990, and 2004) is presented in Table 6-1. In both 1970 and 1980, the current account was in surplus, but the capital account was in deficit by a greater amount, so the overall balance was negative. In 1990 and 2004, the situation was reversed. The current account registered a large deficit, which was partly but not entirely offset by a surplus in the capital account. As a result, the balance of payments was negative in 1990 and 2004, just as it was in 1970 and 1980.

The balance of payments outcome in the most recent year, 2004, is particularly interesting, because the capital account surplus covered less than one-half of the current account deficit. The rest of the current account deficit was financed by massive borrowing from foreign governments, as reflected in the balance of payments outcome. Several Asian countries, particularly China and Japan, increased their foreign official reserves at a very rapid rate in order to keep their currencies from strengthening against the dollar. In effect, China and Japan willingly lent hundreds of billions of dollars to the United States to allow it to import much more than it exported in 2004.

How is the balance of payments related to the foreign trade concepts introduced earlier, namely, net exports (NX) and the current account deficit? Net exports are the same as the balance of trade in goods and services, shown on line

Table 6-1 The U.S. Balance of Payments, Selected Years

	1970	1980	1990	2004
1. Current Account	2.3	2.3	−79.0	−665.9
a. Trade in goods and services	2.3	−19.4	−80.9	−617.1
b. Net investment income	6.2	30.1	28.6	24.1
c. Transfer payments	−6.2	−8.3	−26.7	−72.9
2. Capital Account	−5.9	−24.8	42.9	313.4
3. Balance of Payments Outcome (row 1 + row 2)	−3.6	−22.5	−36.1	−352.5

Note: Balance on current account given in source. Balance of payments is the sum of the increase in foreign official assets minus the increase in U.S. official reserve assets. The capital account on line 2 is then calculated as line 3 minus line 1.

Source: www.bea.gov, U.S. International Transactions, Table 1.

1a of Table 6-1. The additional items on lines 1b and 1c make the current account deficit differ somewhat from net exports. The items on lines 2 and 3 show how the current account deficit was financed, mainly by a massive inflow of capital from foreigners. Part of this inflow came from the private sector of foreign countries—that is, foreign households and business firms—and is counted as the capital account surplus on line 2. The remaining inflow involved foreign central banks and is counted on line 3 as the financing that allowed the United States to run a balance of payments deficit in all years shown.

Self-Test

How much is the United States borrowing from (or lending to) foreign central banks in the following three situations?

1. Current account deficit of 100 and capital account surplus of 70.
2. Current account surplus of 100 and capital account deficit of 70.
3. Current account surplus of 70 and capital account deficit of 100.

Foreign Borrowing and International Indebtedness

A current account deficit must be financed either by net borrowing from foreign firms, households, and governments (counted as a capital account surplus), or from foreign central banks (counted as a balance of payments deficit). Either way, a country experiencing a current account deficit *automatically* must increase its indebtedness to foreigners in the private sector, to foreign governments, or to foreign central banks. Similarly, a current account surplus implies a reduction in foreign indebtedness or an increase in a country's net investment surplus. This relationship can be expressed in the following simple equation:

$$\text{Change in net international investment position} = \text{current account balance} \quad (6.2)$$

Figure 6-1 illustrates the workings of equation (6.2) for the United States during the period since 1975. The top frame displays the U.S. current account, showing its shift into large deficits during 1982–87, its recovery back to balance in 1991, and then its steady descent into unparalleled deficits exceeding −5 percent of GDP by 2004.[1] The bottom frame displays the U.S. **net international investment position.** This shows a shift in the net investment position from surplus during 1975–85 to a deficit that grew slowly between 1985 and 2000, and then has grown precipitously during 2001–04.

A nation's **net international investment position** is the difference between all foreign assets owned by a nation's citizens and domestic assets owned by foreign citizens.

How does this shift in the international investment position affect U.S. residents? The steady downward plunge of the international investment position shown in the bottom frame of Figure 6-1 illustrates that the assets owned by foreigners in the United States are steadily becoming larger relative to the assets owned by U.S. residents in foreign countries. These foreign-owned assets

---

[1] The current account was only briefly balanced in 1991, in contrast to persistent deficits during every other year in the interval 1983–2004. Why? Three reasons have been suggested: (1) Most important, foreign governments made large contributions to pay for the 1991 Gulf War, converting the transfer payment item in Table 6-1, line 1c, into a temporary positive item instead of the usual negative item, (2) the U.S. was in a recession in 1991, which reduced imports and made net exports less negative than usual, and (3) the 1990–91 reunification of Germany created a temporary economic boom in Europe that boosted U.S. exports.

6-2 The Current Account and the Balance of Payments 159

Figure 6-1 The U.S. Current Account Balance and Its Net International Investment Position, 1975–2004

The top frame shows the persistent U.S. deficit on current account after 1981. The bottom frame shows that the net investment position fell in most years after 1982. Overall, the net investment position fell by more than 35 percent of GDP (more than $4 trillion in today's economy) between 1982 and 2004.

in the U.S. must be generating ever-greater interest and dividend income for foreigners, relative to the interest and dividend income earned by U.S. residents on their holdings of foreign assets. *Thus we would expect that U.S. net investment income* (line 1b in Table 6-1) *would become an ever-larger negative amount, as foreign investment earnings* (a negative item on line 1b) *grow relative to U.S. investment earnings abroad* (a positive item on line 1b).

The Startling Ability of the United States to Generate Net Investment Income

U.S. net investment income (line 1b of Table 6-1) expressed as a percentage of GDP has indeed declined as the net international investment position has deteriorated. The share in GDP of U.S. net investment income was 1.1 percent in 1980, and this fell to 0.5 percent in 1990 and 0.2 percent in 2004. But this is actually a startling set of numbers! If the U.S. international investment position had grown by 2004 to −25 percent of GDP, how could U.S. investment income remain positive? There is only one answer to this question: *The United States must earn a much higher rate of return on the assets that U.S. residents own abroad than foreigners earn on their assets owned in the United States.*

Why does this occur? The most straightforward answer is that about half of the negative U.S. international investment position shown in the bottom frame of Figure 6-1 is accounted for by foreign holdings of international reserves. These are the amounts that the Bank of China, Bank of Japan, and other foreign central banks hold in U.S. dollars with the intention of stabilizing their own exchange rates. Typically, these amounts are held in very short-term U.S. government debt or in U.S. bank accounts, typically in 2002–04 yielding an interest rate of 1 to 2 percent. In contrast, the U.S. government holds virtually no assets in foreign countries.

The relatively high rate of return on U.S. assets held in foreign countries also can be explained by the greater propensity of U.S. investors to build factories in foreign countries and buy foreign corporations, as when Wal-Mart bought discount retailers in Britain and Germany. While foreigners also buy U.S. factories and U.S. corporations (as when British Petroleum bought the major Chicago-based oil company Amoco), a relatively greater share of foreign investment in the United States takes the form of relatively low-yielding bonds and stocks. Overall, most economists are very surprised that the −25 percent international investment position of the United States shown in the bottom frame of Figure 6-1 has not yet implied large negative investment income entries into line 1b of Table 6-1.

The International Investment Position and the U.S. Standard of Living

Even though the United States earns higher returns on its assets held in foreign countries than foreigners earn on their assets held in the United States, the inexorable arithmetic of continuing current account deficits implies a future effect on the U.S. standard of living. If the current account were to continue at the 2004 ratio of 5 percent of GDP, then the international investment position of the United States would deteriorate by another 50 percent of GDP over the next decade. Even if the United States were to pay an interest rate to foreigners of only 5 percent on this extra 50 percent of indebtedness, that would imply that fully 2.5 percent (0.05 × 50 percent) of U.S. GDP would need to be diverted to foreign countries over that decade. If the growth rate of the U.S. standard of living would otherwise be 2.0 percent per year, then one-eighth of that diversion, or 0.25 percent per year, would be unavailable for Americans to enjoy. The decline in the U.S. international investment position over the next decade would reduce the growth rate in the U.S. standard of living from 2.0 to 1.75 percent per year. Continuing large U.S. current account deficits (as shown in

Figure 6-1) must inevitably impair the ability of Americans to enjoy the fruits of their economic growth.

6-3 Exchange Rates

Nations trade goods and services within their own borders using a particular currency. Within the United States, of course, the U.S. dollar is used for transactions. Canada uses the Canadian dollar, the United Kingdom uses the pound, Japan uses the yen, Germany and France use the euro, and so on for all the other countries of the world. When an American wants to purchase a Japanese car, he or she wants to pay in dollars but the Japanese producer wants to be paid in yen.

How Exchange Rates Are Quoted

To make the preceding transaction possible, there must be a price of yen in terms of dollars, and a price of dollars in terms of yen. This price is called the **foreign exchange rate**. The foreign exchange rate of the dollar is quoted separately for every currency in the world, and these quotes are reported every day in many newspapers, as shown in Table 6-2.

To take an example, look at the first column at the line labeled Japan (Yen). The foreign exchange rate of the yen is shown two ways, first as dollars per yen and second as yen per dollar. The first listing shows that the price of one yen is $0.009434, or less than one cent. This price rose slightly from the previous day (in this case from Wednesday to Thursday). The next listing shows that $1.00 is worth 106.00 yen. These quotations are exactly equivalent—$0.009434 per yen is the same as 106.00 yen per dollar, since $1/106 = 0.009434$.

It is conventional to express the foreign exchange rate of the dollar as units of foreign currency per dollar, that is, 106.00 yen per dollar, rather than the other way around. However, there are two exceptions. First, the foreign exchange rate of the dollar with the British pound is always quoted as dollars per pound. This treatment of Britain as different goes back to the period before World War I when Britain rather than the United States was the center of the world monetary system.

The second exception is the exchange rate of the dollar versus the euro, which is the common currency of 12 nations, created in 1999. This exchange rate is always quoted as dollars per euro, or $1.2872 as shown on the very last line of the table. The opposite quote was that one euro was worth $0.7769 on the Thursday shown in the table.

*The **foreign exchange rate** for a nation's currency is the amount of one nation's money that can be obtained in exchange for a unit of another nation's money.*

Changes in Exchange Rates

It is very important that we pay attention to the way exchange rates are quoted. When the exchange rate is quoted as foreign currency per dollar, as in the case of the Japanese yen and most other currencies, then a higher number means that the dollar experiences an **appreciation**. For instance, in Table 6-2 the British pound/dollar rate went went from 0.5411 to 0.5423, indicating an appreciation. But other important currencies in the table moved in the

*An **appreciation** is an increase in the value of one nation's currency relative to another nation's currency. When the dollar can buy more units of a foreign currency, say the euro, the dollar is said to appreciate relative to that foreign currency.*

162 Chapter 6 • International Trade, Exchange Rates, and Macroeconomic Policy

Table 6-2 Daily Quotations of Foreign Exchange Rates

Exchange Rates — November 4, 2004

The foreign exchange mid-range rates below apply to trading among banks in amounts of $1 million and more, as quoted at 4 p.m. Eastern time by Reuters and other sources. Retail transactions provide fewer units of foreign currency per dollar.

Country	U.S. $ EQUIV. Thu	U.S. $ EQUIV. Wed	CURRENCY PER U.S. $ Thu	CURRENCY PER U.S. $ Wed
Argentina (Peso)-y	.3378	.3380	2.9603	2.9586
Australia (Dollar)	.7574	.7557	1.3203	1.3233
Bahrain (Dinar)	2.6526	2.6524	.3770	.3770
Brazil (Real)	.3549	.3535	2.8177	2.8289
Canada (Dollar)	.8282	.8272	1.2074	1.2089
1-month forward	.8278	.8268	1.2080	1.2095
3-months forward	.8270	.8260	1.2092	1.2107
6-months forward	.8260	.8249	1.2107	1.2123
Chile (Peso)	.001663	.001658	601.32	603.14
China (Renminbi)	.1208	.1208	8.2781	8.2781
Colombia (Peso)	.0003927	.0003909	2546.47	2558.20
Czech. Rep. (Koruna) Commercial rate	.04090	.04079	24.450	24.516
Denmark (Krone)	.1732	.1725	5.7737	5.7971
Ecuador (US Dollar)	1.0000	1.0000	1.0000	1.0000
Egypt (Pound)-y	.1609	.1603	6.2150	6.2399
Hong Kong (Dollar)	.1286	.1285	7.7760	7.7821
Hungary (Forint)	.005239	.005219	190.88	191.61
India (Rupee)	.02217	.02208	45.106	45.290
Indonesia (Rupiah)	.0001101	.0001097	9083	9116
Israel (Shekel)	.2253	.2251	4.4385	4.4425
Japan (Yen)	.009434	.009412	106.00	106.25
1-month forward	.009450	.009429	105.82	106.06
3-months forward	.009487	.009466	105.41	105.64
6-months forward	.009545	.009522	104.77	105.02
Jordan (Dinar)	1.4114	1.4104	.7085	.7090
Kuwait (Dinar)	3.3972	3.3932	.2944	.2947
Lebanon (Pound)	.0006603	.0006603	1514.46	1514.46
Malaysia (Ringgit)-b	.2632	.2632	3.7994	3.7994
Malta (Lira)	2.9830	2.9757	.3352	.3361
Mexico (Peso) Floating rate	.0876	.0874	11.4181	11.4403
New Zealand (Dollar)	.6908	.6898	1.4476	1.4497
Norway (Krone)	.1575	.1572	6.3492	6.3613
Pakistan (Rupee)	.01656	.01656	60.387	60.387
Peru (new Sol)	.3019	.3016	3.3124	3.3156
Philippines (Peso)	.01773	.01775	56.402	56.338
Poland (Zloty)	.2999	.2978	3.3344	3.3580
Russia (Ruble)-a	.03479	.03477	28.744	28.760
Saudi Arabia (Riyal)	.2667	.2666	3.7495	3.7509
Singapore (Dollar)	.6040	.6003	1.6556	1.6658
Slovak Rep. (Koruna)	.03224	.03211	31.017	31.143
South Africa (Rand)	.1642	.1646	6.0901	6.0753
South Korea (Won)	.0008997	.0008981	1111.48	1113.46
Sweden (Krona)	.1416	.1414	7.0621	7.0721
Switzerland (Franc)	.8420	.8380	1.1876	1.1933
1-month forward	.8430	.8390	1.1862	1.1919
3-months forward	.8452	.8412	1.1832	1.1888
6-months forward	.8486	.8445	1.1784	1.1841
Taiwan (Dollar)	.03005	.02995	33.278	33.389
Thailand (Baht)	.02442	.02430	40.950	41.152
Turkey (Lira)	.00000068	.00000068	1470588	1470588
U.K. (Pound)	1.8440	1.8481	.5423	.5411
1-month forward	1.8399	1.8438	.5435	.5424
3-months forward	1.8320	1.8357	.5459	.5448
6-months forward	1.8210	1.8252	.5491	.5479
United Arab (Dirham)	.2723	.2723	3.6724	3.6724
Uruguay (Peso) Financial	.03690	.03670	27.100	27.248
Venezuela (Bolivar)	.000521	.000521	1919.39	1919.39
SDR	1.5040	1.4963	.6649	.6683
Euro	1.2872	1.2823	.7769	.7798

Special Drawing Rights (SDR) are based on exchange rates for the U.S., British, and Japanese currencies. Source: International Monetary Fund.

a-Russian Central Bank rate. b-Government rate. y-Floating rate.

Source: "Exchange Rate" table, *The Wall Street Journal*, November 5, 2004, Copyright 2004. Permission conveyed through Copyright Clearance Center.

A **depreciation** is a decline in the value of one nation's currency relative to another nation's currency. When the dollar can buy fewer units of a foreign currency, say the British pound, the dollar is said to depreciate relative to that foreign currency.

opposite direction. A lower number means that the dollar experiences a **depreciation.** For instance, in the table the yen/dollar rate changed from Wednesday to Thursday from 106.25 to 106.00, and so we say that "on Thursday the dollar depreciated against the Japanese yen." Similarly, the euro/dollar rate declined from 0.7798 to 0.7769, indicating a depreciation of the dollar against the euro.

From day to day, changes in exchange rates may seem trivial. But changes can mount up to very large magnitudes over a few months or years. For the dollar, the most notable change in the last three years has been its depreciation against the euro. When Table 6-2 in the last edition of this textbook is compared to Table 6-2 in the current edition, the euro/dollar rate skidded from 1.1410 on February 19, 2002, to the value of 0.7769 shown in this section. This represents a depreciation in the value of the dollar of 32 percent. Alternatively, the dollar-to-euro ratio changed from $0.8764 to $1.2872, representing an appreciation of the euro against the dollar of 47 percent.

6-4 The Market for Foreign Exchange

When a U.S. tourist steps into a taxi at the Zurich airport, the driver will expect to be paid in Swiss currency, not U.S. dollars. To obtain the needed Swiss currency, the tourist must first stop at the airport bank and buy Swiss francs in exchange for U.S. dollars. Banks that have too much or too little of given types of foreign money can trade for what they need on the foreign exchange market. Unlike the New York Stock Exchange or the Chicago Board of Trade, where the trading takes place in a single location, the foreign exchange market consists of hundreds of dealers who sit at desks in banks, mainly in New York, London, and Tokyo, and conduct trades by phone and by computer keystrokes.

The results of the trading in foreign exchange are illustrated for four foreign nations in Figure 6-2. Each section of the figure illustrates the exchange rate, expressed as units of foreign currency per U.S. dollar. The data plotted are quarterly, so they do not show additional day-to-day and month-to-month movements. As is obvious from each section of the figure, major changes occurred during the years plotted. The exchange rates of the dollar against these four currencies have truly been flexible, rising and falling—often substantially—during each quarter.

The factors that determine the foreign exchange rate and influence its fluctuations can be summarized on a demand–supply diagram like those used in elementary economics to analyze many problems of price determination. In Figure 6-3, the vertical axis measures the price of the dollar expressed in Swiss francs. The horizontal axis shows the number of dollars that would be demanded or supplied at different prices.

Why People Hold Dollars and Swiss Francs

Currencies such as the U.S. dollar and the Swiss franc are held by foreigners who find dollars or Swiss francs more convenient or safer than their own currencies. For instance, sellers of goods or services may be willing to accept payment in dollars or Swiss francs, but not in the Argentine peso or the Malaysian ringgit. Thus a change in the preference by holders of money for a currency such as the dollar will shift the demand curve for dollars and influence the dollar's exchange rate.

All currencies have a demand that is created by a country's exports and a supply generated by a country's imports. For instance, purchases of U.S. exports automatically create a demand for the dollar. So, too, do funds paid by foreigners who invest in U.S. factories, who repay previous loans, who send to the United States dividends and interest payments on U.S. overseas investments, and who are attracted to put money into U.S. savings accounts and government securities. Thus the demand curve for dollars D_0 in Figure 6-3 is labeled with two of the items that create the demand (U.S. exports, capital inflows). In the same way, the supply curve of dollars S_0 depends on the magnitude of the items that generate payments by U.S. citizens to foreigners—mainly U.S. imports and capital outflows.

What explains the slopes of the demand and supply curves as drawn in Figure 6-3? The demand curve D_0 will be vertical only if the price elasticity of Swiss demand for U.S. imports is zero, that is, completely insensitive to changes in price. If the price elasticity of demand is negative, then the demand curve will be negatively sloped, as shown. For instance, consider a U.S. machine costing $10,000, which would require Swiss buyers to pay 20,000 Swiss

Since 1970 the Dollar has Zigzagged Up and Down Against Other Currencies

Figure 6-2 Foreign Exchange Rates of the Dollar Against Four Major Currencies, Quarterly, 1970–2005

Each foreign exchange rate is expressed as units of foreign currency per dollar. Note that each rate displays quarter-to-quarter fluctuations together with a trend that lasts several years or more. Against the Canadian dollar, the U.S. dollar experienced a major appreciation between 1976 and 1986, followed by a depreciation until 1992, another appreciation between 1992 and 2002, and a sharp depreciation from 2002 to 2004. Against the British pound, the U.S. dollar has displayed erratic behavior, with major appreciations in 1975–76 and 1980–85. Against the Swiss franc, the U.S. dollar displayed a major appreciation in 1980–85 and to a lesser extent in 1995–2002. Against the Japanese yen, the dollar has displayed a long-run tendency over the entire period to depreciate, especially between 1985 and 1995.

The Exchange Rate of the Dollar Depends on the Law of Supply and Demand

Figure 6-3 Determination of the Price in Swiss Francs of the Dollar
The demand curve D_0 slopes downward and to the right, reflecting the increased demand for dollars induced by depreciation (a lowering in the dollar's price). The supply curve S_0 is assumed to slope upward, although this does not always occur (see text). The equilibrium price of the dollar in the diagram is assumed to be SF 1.50, at the crossing point of the D_0 and S_0 curves.

francs (SF) if the exchange rate were SF 2 per dollar (as at point A in the figure). If the exchange rate were to drop to SF 1.50 per dollar (as at point E_0), the cost of the same machine would drop to SF 15,000. If the Swiss demand for such machines were to increase from 10 machines to 11 in response to the lower price, the Swiss demand for dollars would increase from $100,000 to $110,000 (since the price in dollars is still unchanged, $10,000). In short, a depreciation in the dollar along the demand curve from A to E_0 boosts the demand for dollars (plotted on the horizontal axis) and accounts for the negative slope of the demand curve.

The analysis for the supply curve S_0 is different. Here the supply curve will be vertical if the price elasticity of the U.S. demand for Swiss imports is −1.0. Only in this situation are U.S. expenditures on imports in dollars independent of the exchange rate.[2] Only if the price elasticity is greater than unity (in absolute value) will the supply curve slope positively, as drawn in Figure 6-3.

---

[2] The price elasticity of demand, a concept used in every elementary economics course, is defined as

$$\text{elasticity} = \frac{\text{percentage change of quantity}}{\text{percentage change of price}}$$

When the elasticity is −1.0, the percentage change of quantity is equal to and opposite in sign from the percentage change of price, so that revenue (= price × quantity) does not change. A depreciation of the dollar causes a given percentage increase in the price of Swiss machines imported into the United States, provided the Swiss price in SF does not change. If the number of machines purchased drops by the same percent, then total dollar expenditures do not change, and the supply curve is vertical.

Self-Test

For each of the following events, state whether there is a shift in the supply or demand curve for dollars in Figure 6-3, and whether the curve shifts to the left or right:

1. An increase in the desire of Swiss households to buy videotapes of old Hollywood movies.
2. Popularity of French cheese reduces U.S. purchases of Swiss cheese.
3. American Airlines discontinues a flight from Zurich to Chicago that attracts mainly Swiss passengers.
4. U.S. citizens start producing imitation Swiss beer, which displaces imports of the real thing.

How Governments Can Influence the Foreign Exchange Rate

The foreign exchange rate is determined where the demand curve D_0 crosses the supply curve S_0 in Figure 6-3. As the curves are drawn, the equilibrium exchange rate is SF 1.50 per dollar at point E_0. At a higher exchange rate, say SF 2.00 per dollar, the supply of dollars exceeds demand by the distance AB. The supply of dollars created by U.S. imports and by capital outflows exceeds the demand for dollars created by U.S. exports and capital inflows. In order to induce foreigners to accept U.S. dollars, U.S. citizens will have to accept a lower exchange rate, SF 1.50 per dollar.

But, as we have learned, some countries are not willing to accept a depreciation in the dollar from SF 2.00 at point A to SF 1.50 at point E_0. Some countries want to maintain an exchange rate that prevents this depreciation of the dollar, since this would mean an appreciation of their currencies, making their exports more expensive to sell to the rest of the world. How do foreign governments manipulate the exchange rate of the dollar to prevent an appreciation of their own currencies and a depreciation of the dollar?

Let us imagine in Figure 6-3 that the Swiss government wants to maintain the exchange rate at SF 2.00 per dollar instead of allowing the dollar to decline to the equilibrium exchange rate of SF 1.50. A more expensive dollar (at 2.00) would imply a cheaper Swiss franc, allowing Switzerland to sell more exports to the rest of the world. What the Swiss government must do to maintain an exchange rate of SF 2.00 per dollar is to buy dollars, adding its own demand by an amount AB to the market demand for dollars shown at point A. How does Switzerland purchase the needed number of dollars shown by the distance AB? It sells Swiss francs. Switzerland, like any government, has the ability to create an unlimited amount of its own currency. In short, a government that wants to prevent a depreciation of the dollar (and a corresponding appreciation of its currency against the dollar) must buy dollars. This is the real-world situation today in which China and Japan are buying massive numbers of dollars to keep their currencies from appreciating. As we have seen, this is recorded as the negative balance of payments item for the United States in the bottom line of Table 6-1 on p. 157.

6-5 Real Exchange Rates and Purchasing Power Parity

Nominal and Real Exchange Rates

For most issues in macroeconomics, we adjust variables for the effects of inflation. Real GDP is a more meaningful gauge of economic activity than nominal GDP. The level of saving and investment are related to the real interest rate, not to the nominal interest rate. Similarly, we shall see that it is the **real exchange rate** that determines net exports, not the nominal exchange rate.

The real exchange rate is equal to the nominal foreign exchange rate adjusted for the difference in inflation rates between two countries. The definition can be written as a formula, where we express the real exchange rate (e) as equal to the nominal exchange rate (e') times the ratio of the domestic price level (P) to the foreign price level (P^f):

$$e = e' \times P/P^f \qquad (6.3)$$

Real exchange rate = nominal exchange rate × ratio of domestic price level to foreign price level

The **real exchange rate** is equal to the average nominal foreign exchange rate between a country and its trading partners, with an adjustment for the difference in inflation rates between that country and its trading partners.

To understand this relationship, let us assume that in 2005 the nominal and real exchange rates of the Mexican peso are both 10 per dollar, and the price level in both countries is 100:

$$10 \text{ pesos}/\$ = 10 \text{ pesos}/\$ \times (100/100)$$

Real exchange rate = nominal exchange rate × ratio of domestic price level to foreign price level

Then, let us assume that in 2006, the Mexican economy experiences a rapid inflation, causing the Mexican price level to double from 100 to 200, while the U.S. price level remains fixed at 100. If the nominal exchange rate were to remain at 10 pesos per dollar, the real exchange rate would fall by half:

$$5 \text{ pesos}/\$ = 10 \text{ pesos}/\$ \times (100/200)$$

In such a case, we would say that the dollar has experienced a *real depreciation* against the peso, since one dollar buys only half as many pesos when adjusted for differences in national price levels. The opposite would be true as well; the Mexican peso would have experienced a *real appreciation*.

Normally, countries that experience unusually high inflation, as in this example, find that their nominal exchange rate depreciates while their real exchange rate remains roughly unchanged. For the real exchange rate to remain unchanged in this example, the nominal exchange rate of the peso would have to jump from 10 to 20 pesos per dollar (this is a nominal appreciation of the dollar and a nominal depreciation of the peso).

$$10 = 20 \times 100/200$$

This final example is quite realistic. Usually countries with unusually rapid inflation, as has been experienced by Mexico, Argentina, Brazil, and other Latin American countries at various times over the past several decades, witness a nominal depreciation of their currency without any major change in the real exchange rate. (We return to the causes and consequences of rapid inflation in Chapter 9.)

We care about the real exchange rate, not the nominal exchange rate, because it is a major determinant of net exports. When the real exchange rate appreciates (that is, there is a real appreciation), imports become cheap for domestic residents to purchase, while exports become expensive for foreigners to purchase. The result is a squeeze on domestic profits and layoffs of domestic workers. In the opposite situation, when the real exchange rate depreciates, domestic profits improve and companies are eager to hire workers. As we shall see, fluctuations in the real exchange rate help to explain fluctuations in the U.S. current account balance plotted in Figure 6-1.

> ### Self-Test
>
> Assume that the price level in 2005 in both the United States and Switzerland is 100, and that both the real and the nominal exchange rates of the Swiss franc are 1.5 SF per dollar. Now imagine that in the year 2006 the U.S. price level has increased from 100 to 110, while the Swiss price level remains fixed at 100, and the nominal exchange rate changes to 1.3 SF per dollar.
>
> 1. What is the real exchange rate of the dollar in the year 2006?
> 2. Has the dollar experienced a real appreciation or depreciation?
> 3. Following this change what would you expect to happen to U.S. exports to Switzerland? To U.S. imports from Switzerland?

The Theory of Purchasing Power Parity

The most important determinant of exchange rates is the fact that in open economies the prices of traded goods should be the same everywhere after adjustment for customs duties and the cost of transportation. This is called the **purchasing power parity (PPP) theory** of the exchange rate.

The **purchasing power parity (PPP) theory** holds that the prices of identical goods should be the same in all countries, differing only by the cost of transport and any import duties.

This theory implies that the real exchange rate (e) should be constant. We can set the real exchange rate at a constant value of unity in equation (6.3) above:

$$1 = e' \times P/P^f \tag{6.4}$$

Fixed real exchange rate = nominal exchange rate × ratio of domestic price level to foreign price level

By swapping the left-hand and right-hand sides of equation (6.4), and solving for e', we emerge with the PPP theory of exchange rates:

$$e' = \frac{P^f}{P} \tag{6.5}$$

This states that if the foreign price level (P^f) increases faster than the domestic price level (P), there is an increase in P^f/P and the nominal exchange rate must appreciate if PPP is to prevail.

PPP and Inflation Differentials

Another way of writing equation (6.5) is to express the exchange rate and the two prices in terms of rates of growth.[3]

---

[3] The growth rate of a ratio such as P^f/P is equal to the growth rate of the numerator (p^f) minus the growth rate of the denominator (p).

$$\Delta e'/e' = p^f - p \qquad (6.6)$$

Growth rate of nominal exchange rate = growth rate of foreign price level − growth rate of domestic price level

Here the term $\Delta e'/e'$ is positive when there is an appreciation of a currency. The same term is negative when there is a depreciation of a currency. The term $p^f - p$ is the **inflation differential** between foreign and domestic inflation. When this differential is positive, the PPP theory of exchange rates expressed in equation (6.6) states that $\Delta e'/e'$ is positive and the exchange rate of the domestic currency appreciates.

The PPP theory contains an essential kernel of truth: Nations that allow their domestic inflation rate (p) to exceed the world rate will experience a depreciation of their exchange rate, and vice versa. But there are numerous exceptions to the relationship, because the demand for and supply of foreign currency depend on factors other than the simple ratio of domestic and foreign aggregate price indexes.

> The **inflation differential** is foreign inflation minus domestic inflation; the PPP theory of exchange rates predicts that when this differential is positive the domestic country's nominal exchange rate appreciates and when this differential is negative the nominal exchange rate depreciates.

Why PPP Breaks Down

The "Big Mac" International Perspective box in this section shows that the PPP equation relating the change in the exchange rate to the inflation differential does not work well for most industrialized nations; for example, in 2004, the dollar was overvalued against most currencies. There are numerous reasons why PPP breaks down. They all have a single fact in common—for any given inflation differential between two nations, there are numerous factors that can cause major appreciations and depreciations in the exchange rate without altering the inflation differential. Some of these factors are:

1. A nation may invent new products that other countries want to import, such as the Internet software developed by U.S. firms in the 1990s. Such inventions may cause the dollar to appreciate without any change in the inflation differential.

2. A nation may discover new deposits of raw materials that it can sell to other nations, thus raising the demand for its currency. For instance, in the late 1970s the British began producing oil from the North Sea, causing the exchange rate of the pound to appreciate.

3. The exchange rate depends not just on exports and imports but on the demand for a currency by foreigners. Customers from all over the world send funds to Switzerland and other countries for deposit in banks and other financial institutions, often to avoid taxes or to hide the proceeds from criminal activity. The higher demand for the Swiss franc and other such currencies causes them to appreciate.

4. The theory of PPP is based on the comparison of the exchange rate with an economywide price index in two countries, but that price index may include types of economic activity that are not traded (for example, building construction and retail services). There is no mechanism that forces prices of nontraded goods and services to be the same across countries.

5. For any given inflation differential, government policy can cause a currency to depreciate when the government makes large foreign transfers. Governments can also interfere with free trade by subsidizing exports or

International Perspective

Big Mac Meets PPP

If PPP worked perfectly, goods would cost the same in all countries after conversion into a common currency. An interesting test of PPP has been constructed by the *Economist* magazine, which for many years has collected data on the prices of Big Mac hamburgers in the United States and in numerous foreign countries. In the month covered by the table, the Big Mac cost an average of $2.90 in four American cities. According to PPP, the cost in other countries should be $2.90 times the exchange rate of the other currency per dollar. To understand this table taken from *The Economist*, we will take the example of a single country, Sweden. We need to know one important fact not listed in the table, that the *actual* exchange rate of the Swedish kroner was 7.58 kroner per dollar. Multiplying the American cost of $2.90 by the actual exchange rate of $7.58, a Big Mac in Sweden should have cost 22 kroner. However, the actual cost in Sweden was 30 kroner, not 22.

Stated another way, if the relative prices of Big Macs in Sweden and the United States were representative of all goods, a dollar has the purchasing power of 10.3 kroner (Big Mac Swedish price of 30 kroner divided by U.S. price of $2.90), not the 7.58 kroner available on the foreign exchange market. The foreign exchange market appears to undervalue the dollar by 36 percent $(10.30 - 7.58)/7.58$.

As shown in the right-hand column of the table, the dollar is overvalued (+) against some countries and undervalued (−) against others. The dollar tends to be undervalued against the relatively rich countries of western Europe, including the euro zone, Britain, Denmark, Sweden, and Switzerland. The dollar is overvalued against all other countries, including countries with such widely differing standards of living as Japan and Indonesia. The dollar is overvalued by more than 50 percent against some countries that have a dollar price of the Big Mac that is less than half of the $2.90 U.S. price, including China, Malasia, and the Philippines.

The extent of over- or undervaluation of the U.S. dollar changes through time. As shown in Figures 6-2 and 6-4, the dollar appreciated from 1995 to 2001 against most currencies and then depreciated between 2002 and 2004. When the dollar was at its peak in 2001, it was overvalued relative to the euro area. By 2004, the depreciation of the dollar shifted the Big Mac comparison with the euro area from an overvaluation of 11 percent (in April 2001) to an undervaluation of 13 percent as shown in the accompanying table. We explore reasons for the 1995–2001 appreciation of the dollar and its 2002–04 depreciation in subsequent sections of this chapter.

---

taxing imports. Finally, a government may try to prevent its currency from appreciating by buying foreign currency, as did Japan and China in this decade (see pp. 174–77).

As we shall see later in Figure 6-4, the U.S. real exchange rate has not remained constant, as assumed in the PPP equation (6.4), which suggests that PPP is not a good description of U.S. exchange rate behavior.

6-6 Exchange Rate Systems

A balance of payments deficit like the one experienced by the United States in 2004 means that more dollars are flowing abroad as a result of the current account deficit than are coming back in the form of capital inflows from foreign private investors. As a result, there is a net outflow of dollars. Two basic systems have been developed to handle a surplus or deficit in the balance of payments, like the deficit that the United States ran in 2004 (Table 6-1, line 3). The difference between these systems lies in whether the foreign exchange rate of the dollar is allowed, month after month, year after year, to change freely (say, from 1.5 Swiss francs per dollar this month to 1.2 Swiss francs per dollar next month) or is held fixed (at, say, 1.5 Swiss francs per dollar).

The Hamburger Standard

	Big Mac price in dollars	Implied PPP exchange rate of the dollar	Under (−)/ over (+) valuation of the dollar, %
United States	2.90	—	—
Argentina	1.48	1.50	49
Australia	2.27	1.12	22
Brazil	1.70	1.86	41
Britain	3.37	1.54	−16
Canada	2.33	1.10	20
Chile	2.18	483	25
China	1.26	3.59	57
Czech Rep.	2.13	19.5	27
Denmark	4.46	9.57	−54
Euro area	3.28	1.06	−13
Hong Kong	1.54	4.14	47
Hungary	2.52	183	13
Indonesia	1.77	5,552	39
Japan	2.33	90.3	20
Malaysia	1.33	1.74	54
Mexico	2.08	8.28	28
New Zealand	2.65	1.50	8
Peru	2.57	3.10	11
Philippines	1.23	23.8	57
Poland	1.63	2.17	44
Russia	1.45	14.5	50
Singapore	1.92	1.14	34
South Africa	1.86	4.28	36
South Korea	2.72	1,103	6
Sweden	3.94	10.3	−36
Switzerland	4.90	2.17	−69
Taiwan	2.24	25.9	23
Thailand	1.45	20.3	50
Turkey	2.58	1,362,069	11
Venezuela	1.48	1,517	29

Notes: (1) PPP exchange rate is calculated as actual exchange rate multiplied by the ratio of the actual price expressed in dollars to the U.S. price of $2.90. (2) The U.S. price is the average of New York, Chicago, San Francisco, and Atlanta. (3) The exchange rates of Britain and the euro area are expressed as dollars per unit of foreign currency. All other exchange rates are expressed as units of foreign currency per dollar.

Source: From "The Hamburger Standard," *The Economist*, May 27, 2004. *The Economist* Newspaper. Reprinted with permission. More recent versions of the Big Mac index can be found at www.economist.com.

Flexible vs. Fixed Exchange Rates

Flexible exchange rate system. Under a "pure" version of the **flexible exchange rate system**, an outflow of dollars would act just like an excess supply of any commodity—the price would go down until an equilibrium price is established. The balance of payments deficit would be eliminated by a decline in

In a **flexible exchange rate system** the foreign exchange rate is free to change every day in order to establish an equilibrium between the quantities supplied and demanded of a nation's currency.

the foreign exchange rate of the dollar sufficient to raise exports and cut imports, as occurred in the United States following the huge 1985–87 decline in the value of the dollar. In addition, for reasons explained later, a decline in the exchange rate tends to stimulate larger private capital inflows. Although the exchange rates have varied widely since 1973, the current system of flexible exchange rates still is not a pure one. If it were, the United States could not run a balance of payments deficit as it did in 2004, as shown in Table 6-1. Instead, today's system is a mixture of flexible and fixed exchange rates.

Fixed exchange rate system. During the post–World War II era prior to 1973, most major countries maintained a **fixed exchange rate system**. Under this system, central banks agreed in advance to finance any surplus or deficit in the balance of payments. To do this, central banks maintained foreign exchange reserves, mainly in gold and dollars. The banks stood ready to buy or sell dollars as needed to maintain the foreign exchange rate of their currencies.

> In a **fixed exchange rate system,** the foreign exchange rate is fixed for long periods of time.

Workings of the Fixed Exchange Rate System

In the 1950s and 1960s, the German central bank (Bundesbank) maintained a rate of 4.0 marks per dollar. If an excess supply of dollars entered Germany (due, for instance, to higher U.S. imports of Volkswagens) and threatened to put downward pressure on the rate to, say, 3.5 marks per dollar, the Bundesbank could intervene by purchasing the excess dollars and adding them to its **foreign exchange reserves**. Similarly, if an excess demand for dollars (due, for instance, to exports of Boeing jet planes to Lufthansa, the German airline) put upward pressure on the rate to, say, 4.5 marks per dollar, the Bundesbank could intervene by selling dollars from its reserves, thus satisfying the excess demand for dollars.

Clearly, there is a flaw in this system. What if a country were to keep increasing its imports, paying for them by drawing down its reserves? Eventually it would run out of reserves, like a family whose bank balance has fallen to zero. Under the fixed exchange rate system, such an event would cause a crisis, and the country would be forced to reduce, or **devalue**, its exchange rate. An example occurred in 1994, when Mexico was forced to devalue the peso, thus making it less valuable in relation to the dollar. By doing so, Mexico intended to make Mexican exports less expensive and more attractive to foreign purchasers, thus increasing the demand for the peso. An example in the opposite direction occurred in 1969 when Germany's reserves of dollars were growing rapidly, and it decided to **revalue** the mark (that is, increase the value of the mark) by 5 percent.

> **Foreign exchange reserves** are government holdings of foreign money used under a fixed exchange rate system to respond to changes in the foreign demand for and supply of a particular nation's money. Such reserves are also used for intervention under a flexible exchange rate system.
>
> Under the fixed exchange rate system, a nation **devalues,** or reduces the value of its money in terms of foreign money, when it runs out of foreign exchange reserves. A nation **revalues,** or raises the value of its money, when its foreign exchange reserves become so excessive that they cause domestic inflation.

Characteristics of the Flexible Exchange Rate System

Under the old, fixed exchange rate system, changes in the exchange rate were very infrequent. The word *devaluation* was used for a decline in the value of a country's currency and the word *revaluation* was used for an increase in the value of a country's currency. In today's flexible exchange rate system, different terms are used. A *depreciation* of the foreign exchange rate occurs when a country's currency decreases in value in terms of other currencies. An *appreciation* in the foreign exchange rate occurs when a country's currency increases in value in terms of other currencies.

The current system is not a pure flexible exchange rate system because the Fed and foreign central banks do not allow the dollar to fluctuate with complete freedom. The system is not pure because central banks have practiced **intervention**. Foreign central banks, particularly those of China and Japan, have "propped up" the value of the dollar by buying massive amounts of it,

> **Intervention** occurs under the flexible exchange rate system when domestic or foreign central banks buy or sell a nation's money in order to prevent unwanted variations in the foreign exchange rate.

thus artificially inflating the demand for dollars and keeping the dollar's foreign exchange rate higher than it otherwise would have been. In the period 1986–2004, foreign central banks increased their dollar reserves by more than $1 trillion as a result of their intervention.

Other terms are used to describe flexible exchange rate systems. A "clean" system is one that is pure, without any intervention by central banks. A "dirty," or "managed," flexible exchange rate system is one with frequent intervention by central banks. Why is the current system so dirty? Central banks in China and Japan fear a possible collapse of the dollar, which would make American exports more competitive and reduce the American demand for imports. Such circumstances would create layoffs and factory closings in foreign countries, something governments want to avoid.

The Exchange Rate of the Dollar Since 1970

Since the flexible exchange rate system began in 1973, the dollar has experienced substantial volatility. Figure 6-4 shows the changes in both the nominal and real exchange rates of the dollar since 1970. Displayed is the effective exchange rate of the dollar, which weights the dollar's exchange rate against

Figure 6-4 Nominal and Real Effective Exchange Rates of the Dollar, 1970–2004

Except for a minor difference in the late 1990s, the real and nominal exchange rates for the United States followed essentially the same path. This means that the inflation differential between the United States and other nations was very small compared to the highly variable ups and downs of the nominal exchange rate. This implies that the real exchange rate should have mimicked the movements of the nominal exchange rate, which it did. By far the most dramatic movement of both the nominal and real exchange rates was the sharp appreciation of 1980–85, the equally sharp depreciation of 1985–87, the more recent appreciation of 1995–2001 and subsequent depreciation of 2002–04.

Source: www.frb.gov.

an average of the euro, British pound, Japanese yen, and other currencies, with each country weighted in proportion to its importance in American foreign trade. The base year for the effective exchange rate is 1980, so any period (such as 1985) with an exchange rate greater than 100 indicates that the dollar was stronger than in 1980. Any period with an exchange rate less than 100 (such as 1995) indicates that the dollar was weaker than in 1980.

Let us first examine the nominal exchange rate of the dollar, the black line in Figure 6-4. The transition to the flexible exchange rate system in 1971–73 involved a substantial depreciation of the dollar, and the dollar took another dip in 1977–80. Then, from 1980 to 1988, international economics was dominated by the effect of the enormous appreciation of the dollar, which peaked in February 1985, and the depreciation of equal magnitude that followed in 1985–87. The strong dollar exacerbated the U.S. recession of 1981–82 and slowed the pace of economic recovery in 1984–85.

From 1988 to 1995, the dollar fluctuated within a relatively narrow range but then began a sharp appreciation against most currencies after 1995. This strength of the dollar was the counterpart of the weakness of several currencies, particularly in Asia during the late 1990s and the weakness of the euro from its inception in early 1999 until early 2002. Then, in 2002–04, the dollar depreciated again and by late 2004 was almost back to its 1995 level in nominal terms, although not yet in real terms.

Has the real exchange rate behaved differently than the nominal effective exchange rate? As shown in Figure 6-4, between 1995 and 2001 the real exchange rate appreciated somewhat more rapidly than did the nominal exchange rate, indicating that during this interval the U.S. price level increased more than the foreign price level. Otherwise, the real exchange rate has mimicked virtually every movement of the nominal exchange rate since 1973, indicating that the U.S. and foreign price levels have increased at about the same rate.

Self-Test

1. As a college student planning a trip to Europe this summer, do you hope for an appreciation or a depreciation of the dollar?
2. Looking at the plot of the effective exchange rate in Figure 6-4, would you have preferred to travel to Europe in 1995 or 2001?
3. If a German student had the same choice, when would he or she have preferred to travel to the United States?

6-7 Case Study

Asia Intervenes with Buckets to Buy Dollars and Finance the U.S. Current Account Deficit— How Long Can This Continue?

The United States escapes the ironclad logic of the trilemma that no nation can simultaneously operate an independent domestic monetary policy while maintaining fixed exchange rates and allowing perfectly mobile international capital movements. The United States escapes this logic by maintaining flexible exchange rates with its trading partners, including the euro area, Britain, Japan, and many other nations. But the U.S. cannot *force* other nations to maintain flexible exchange rates between their currencies and the dollar. Instead, other nations can subvert the U.S. intention to maintain flexible exchange rates *by taking actions to fix the value of their currencies to the dollar*.

China is the world's leading example of a country that can unilaterally convert the flexible exchange rate with the dollar into a fixed exchange rate. How does China do this? The equilibrium value of its exchange rate is below the current rate; that is, to reach the equilibrium value, the ratio of the Chinese yuan to the dollar must decline from the current rate of 8.24 to a lower number. The dollar must depreciate and the yuan must appreciate, since the demand for dollars by China to purchase U.S. exports is much lower than the supply of dollars provided by U.S. residents to buy imports made in China.

To avoid this depreciation of the dollar and parallel appreciation of the yuan, the Bank of China must purchase vast quantities of dollars, adding to the demand for dollars just enough to maintain the 8.24 yuan/dollar exchange rate. Why does China pursue this policy? By fighting against an appreciation of the yuan, China receives all the benefits of any currency that has a relatively low exchange rate. Chinese exporters can sell their goods at cheaper prices in the U.S. market, and higher volumes of exported goods allow Chinese business firms to employ more workers, helping to propel the remarkable economic growth of China that we explore further in Chapter 11. Like China, Hong Kong also achieves a fixed exchange rate against the U.S. dollar by purchasing dollars. Several other Asian countries, particularly Japan and Taiwan, buy dollars to keep their currencies from appreciating, even if they do not keep their currencies exactly fixed against the dollar from day to day.

A remarkable aspect of this situation is that the United States is uniquely positioned to take advantage of the willingness of other nations to finance its current account deficit. The United States has been called "the country in the center" due to the attractiveness of U.S. dollars as the currency in which most nations prefer to hold their international reserves. Despite the depreciation of the dollar and appreciation of the euro in 2002–04, Asian nations continue to keep most of their international reserves in dollars. Thus, in essence, the United States can "print money" that Asians willingly hold in order to finance its U.S. current account deficit. Ironically, it was this same ability to print international money in the 1960s under the former Bretton Woods system that led to the breakdown in 1971 of fixed exchange rates. Many commentators are worried that the current system is equally unsustainable and must inevitably lead to a collapse of the U.S. dollar exchange rate at some point in the future—the near future according to pessimists and the far future according to optimists.

How Large are the Reserves and Which Countries Hold Them?

Figure 6-5 displays foreign official holdings of dollars as a percent of U.S. GDP. These are the dollar reserves of nations such as China, Japan, and other countries (mainly in Asia).[4] As of 1995, these reserves were little more than 5 percent of

---

[4] These data show the increase in the official balances that finance the U.S. balance of payments deficit. They take foreign official holdings of dollar assets and subtract U.S. holdings of official international reserves.

Figure 6-5 Foreign Official Holdings of Dollar Reserves as a Percent of U.S. GDP

Shown is the percentage ratio of foreign official holdings of dollar reserves to U.S. GDP. The rapid growth of these reserves since 1995 is the counterpart of the decline in the U.S. international investment position shown in the bottom frame of Figure 6-1. Almost half of the U.S. negative investment position is accounted for by foreign official holdings of dollar reserves.

U.S. GDP, little more than in 1978. But then the dollar reserves began to explode, soaring to almost 8 percent in 1998 and then to almost 14 percent in 2004.

The dollar reserves are held primarily by Asian central banks. In February 2004, the top four Asian central banks held $1.5 trillion of dollar reserves, of which $741 billion were held by Japan, $403 billion by China, $207 billion by Taiwan, and $157 billion by South Korea. This is double the amount that these countries owned only two years earlier. Asian central banks continued to purchase bucketfuls of dollars throughout 2004; as shown in line 3 of Table 6-1, less than half of the U.S. current account deficit in 2004 was financed by capital account inflows, and the rest had to be financed by purchases of dollars by mainly Asian central banks.

Why Do the Asians Subject Themselves to Disastrous Capital Losses?

The U.S. government views this buildup of Asian dollar reserves with an attitude of "benign neglect." Why not, since the huge purchases of dollar securities, much of which is U.S. government debt, helps to support the U.S. stock and bond markets and allows the U.S. federal government to support tax cuts and expenditure increases without the sharp increase in domestic U.S. interest rates that would otherwise occur. But for Asian countries this is a raw deal, because the hundreds of billions of dollars that the Asians are spending of their own currencies to buy dollars could be used to raise the living standards of millions of their own inhabitants through investment in their domestic economies.

The Asian central banks are pouring their own funds into a currency, the dollar, on which they make capital losses. While China can buy enough dollars to keep its yuan/dollar exchange rate fixed, it cannot prevent the flexible exchange rate between the dollar and other currencies (such as the euro, the British pound, and the Swiss franc) from depreciating. Thus the buying power of Chinese and Japanese dollar reserves in the world economy sink each year that the dollar depreciates, as it did between 2002 and 2004.

The Asian strategy of stabilizing their currencies against the dollar creates an economic dilemma for the twelve European nations in the euro area. Since early 2002, the euro has appreciated by almost 50 percent against the dollar, making European exports more expensive and causing a slump in European economic growth. But the Asian policies make the European dilemma worse. If China keeps its currency pegged to the dollar, and the euro appreciates by 50 percent against the dollar, then *automatically* the euro appreciates by 50 percent against the Chinese yuan. Cheap Chinese exports flood not only the United States but also Europe, costing not just American but also European jobs.

Is There an Exit Strategy for the Asians?

The Asians keep buying dollars because they need to keep their own currencies low and the dollar strong in order to create jobs in China and Japan and avoid domestic unrest and unemployment. Policies of the U.S. government adopted during 2002–04 surprised the Asians by boosting the U.S. government budget deficit and increasing the amount that Asians had to finance. As one Japanese policymaker stated, "The U.S. government's procurement of funds for the Iraq war, and a huge tax cut, resulted in a sharp rise in U.S. debt, so if Japan cuts purchases of U.S. government bonds, the U.S. must raise interest rates, which could seriously harm world markets." Thus, from the Japanese point of view, the United States seems to be able to force Japan to finance its own government budget deficit.

Can this situation continue? The Asian nations and the United States both seem to be trapped into a symbiotic relationship. One journalist drew an analogy with a small shopkeeper:

> This is an absurd situation, like a shopkeeper lending ever larger amounts of money to an important customer who is also a profligate spender, so that he can maintain consumption. The customer signs ever-increasing amounts of IOUs, and the shopkeeper has decreasing faith in these. But he cannot sell them so long as he retains his dependence on keeping the customer happy.[5]

---

[5] Quotes in this section are from Kathy Wolfe, "Asia Ponders Exit Strategy from the Dollar," *Executive Intelligence Review*, February 20, 2004.

6-8 Determinants of Net Exports

Now we are ready to fit the foreign exchange rate into the *IS-LM* model of income determination developed in Chapters 3–5. The analysis proceeds in two steps. First, we allow net exports, previously assumed to be exogenous, to depend both on income and on the exchange rate. Second, we allow the exchange rate to depend on the interest rate. The combined effect of these two steps is to introduce an additional channel by which interest rates affect total expenditures.

Net exports (NX), as we learned in Chapter 2, is an aggregate that equals exports minus imports, and it is a component of total expenditure in GDP, along with consumption (C), investment (I), and government spending (G):

$$E = C + I + G + NX \tag{6.7}$$

A $200 billion increase in net exports provides just as much of a stimulus to income and employment as a $200 billion increase in consumption, investment, or government spending. A $200 billion decrease in net exports can offset much of the stimulus to expenditures provided by expansionary monetary and fiscal policy.

Net Exports and the Foreign Exchange Rate

Clearly fluctuations of net exports play an important role in the fluctuations of total real expenditures. Determining the ups and downs of net exports are real income and the foreign exchange rate.

Effect of real income. We can indicate the dependence of net exports (NX) on income as

$$NX = NX_a - nxY \tag{6.8}$$

Here, NX_a is the autonomous component of net exports (determined mainly by foreign income), nx is the fraction of a change in income that is spent on imports, and Y is real income.[6] If we ignored changes in the foreign exchange rate, then equation (6.8) would adequately explain net exports. For the given level of foreign income that determines the autonomous component (NX_a), net exports would be low in economic expansions when income is high, causing a large volume of imports, and net exports would be high in recessions when income is low, causing a small volume of imports.

Effect of the foreign exchange rate. When the exchange rate appreciates against foreign currencies, U.S. exports become more expensive in terms of foreign currencies, so exports tend to decline. Also, the lower dollar prices of imports attract American customers, and the quantity of goods imported into the United States rises. With exports down and imports up, the appreciation of the foreign exchange rate causes a drop in net exports. This is just what happened in the United States during 1995–2001. The appreciation of the dollar and the collapse of net exports are shown in Figure 6-6.

The striking fact that stands out in Figure 6-6 is the strong negative relationship between net exports and the real exchange rate. When the real ex-

---

[6] This equation is identical to equation (10) in the Appendix to Chapter 3, p. 93.

A Mirror Image?

Figure 6-6 U.S. Real Net Exports and the Real Exchange Rate of the Dollar, 1970–2004

The two lines display a striking mirror-image relationship, indicating that an appreciating dollar tends to reduce net exports, and vice versa.

change rate was low in the late 1970s, U.S. net exports rose, peaking in 1980. The rise in the real exchange rate between 1980 and 1985 was accompanied by a continuous decline in net exports. The 1985–88 depreciation of the dollar led to a sharp jump in net exports after 1987, and the 1996–2001 appreciation contributed to the collapse of net exports in 1998–2001. The failure of U.S. net exports to rise in 2003–04 in response to the dollar's depreciation is an important but rare exception.

To reflect this negative relationship, we amend equation (6.8) to allow net exports (NX) to depend not just on income but also on the real exchange rate (e), which is expressed as a percentage of a base year (for instance, 1980 = 100).

$$\text{General Linear Form} \qquad\qquad \text{Numerical Example}$$
$$NX = NX_a - nxY - ue \qquad NX = 1{,}000 - 0.1Y - 2e \qquad (6.9)$$

This equation states in words that net exports are equal to autonomous net exports (NX_a), minus a parameter (nx) times real income (Y), minus another parameter (u) times the real exchange rate (e). For any given level of income, an appreciation of the real exchange rate (as happened in the United States between 1995 and 2001) reduces net exports. For instance, if the economy is operating with actual real income at the natural real GDP level of $8,000 billion, and the real exchange rate is 100, then net exports are zero [=1,000 − (0.1 × 8,000) − 2 × 100)]. An appreciation in the real exchange rate from 100 to 150 would reduce net exports in the example to −$100 billion [=1,000 − (0.1 × 8,000) − (2 × 150)].

6-9 The Real Exchange Rate and Interest Rate

The foreign exchange rate is set in the foreign exchange market. This is not a single room like the floor of the New York Stock Exchange but consists of bank employees all over the world buying and selling different currencies by telephone and online computer networks. When the demand for a currency like the dollar rises relative to the supply of dollars, these bank employees (foreign exchange traders) bid up the value of the dollar, causing it to appreciate. When the demand for dollars falls, its value falls, or depreciates.

The Demand for Dollars and the "Fundamentals"

The demand for dollars stems from two sources: the desire to buy American products and the desire to buy financial assets denominated in dollars (like bank deposits, U.S. government bonds, and the bonds issued by U.S. corporations). Changes in the worldwide desire to buy American products tend to occur gradually. Among the factors, sometimes called fundamentals, that might create such changes are the invention of new American products, like personal computers. A fundamental factor that could *reduce* the desire to hold dollars might be the development of new products in other countries, like Japanese VCRs or camcorders. Higher expected inflation in the United States than in other countries would also reduce the desire to hold dollars.

Because the fundamental factors tend to change slowly, they cannot account for much of the highly volatile movements evident in Figure 6-6 in the dollar's real exchange rate. Instead, these sharp up and down movements can be attributed to the second main source of the demand for dollars, the desire by foreigners to buy securities denominated in dollars. When U.S. securities become more attractive, the demand for dollars increases and the foreign exchange traders bid up the dollar's value. Similarly, when foreign securities become more attractive to Americans, U.S. residents supply extra dollars to the foreign exchange traders to obtain the foreign currencies they need to buy foreign securities and the dollar's value goes down.

The **interest rate differential** is the average U.S. interest rate minus the average foreign interest rate.

The relative attractiveness of U.S. and foreign securities depends on the **interest rate differential**, defined as the average U.S. interest rate minus the average foreign interest rate. When the U.S. interest rate increases and the foreign interest rate remains unchanged, the interest rate differential increases. Foreigners find U.S. securities attractive; they demand additional dollars to buy them, and the foreign exchange rate of the dollar is bid up by the foreign exchange traders.

This section has suggested that an increase in the U.S. interest rate should cause an appreciation of the dollar, and a decrease in the U.S. interest rate should cause a depreciation of the dollar. The relationship between the U.S. interest rate and the value of the dollar is demonstrated in Figure 6-7, which plots the two together for the period since 1970. The real exchange rate of the dollar is copied from Figure 6-6. The periods in the 1970s of the lowest real interest rates coincided with periods when the dollar was low. The period of high interest rates after 1980 was accompanied by an appreciation of the dollar. The 1984 peak in the real interest rate came shortly before the 1985 peak in the real exchange rate. The decline in the real interest rate during 1984–89 coincided with the decline in the real exchange rate from 1985 to 1989.

The positive relationship between the real interest rate and the real exchange rate appears to have broken down after 1995. The real exchange rate ap-

Figure 6-7 The U.S. Real Corporate Bond Rate and the Real Exchange Rate of the Dollar, 1970–2004

The real exchange rate is copied from Figure 6-6. A positive relationship between the two lines is evident, with movements in the interest rate appearing to occur prior to movements in the exchange rate. The relationship changed after 1995 as discussed in the text.

preciated by almost as much as it did in 1980–85, but the real interest rate was virtually unchanged. This new relationship reflects the role of the late 1990s U.S. stock market boom in attracting foreign capital inflows, which pushed up the value of the dollar, even though the real interest rate did not rise. After 2000, when the stock market collapsed, foreign investors pulled some of their funds out of the United States and the dollar fell.

Self-Test

Assume that you are an American student traveling to Europe next summer. Which would you prefer?

1. A boom in the U.S. stock market?
2. A collapse in the U.S. stock market?

Interest Rates and Capital Mobility

The mechanism by which interest rates affect the exchange rate involves flows of capital between countries. **Perfect capital mobility** occurs when a resident of one country can purchase any desired assets in another country immediately, in unlimited amounts, with very low commissions and fees. The crucial implication of perfect capital mobility is that interest rates in one country are tightly linked to interest rates in other countries. Why? An American investor faced with a choice of a return of 6.0 percent at home and 6.6 percent in Germany would immediately choose to buy financial assets in Germany. This reduction in the supply of funds in the United States would

Perfect capital mobility occurs when investors regard foreign financial assets as a perfect substitute for domestic assets, and when investors respond instantaneously to an interest rate differential between domestic and foreign assets by moving sufficient assets to eliminate that differential.

raise the U.S. interest rate, and the increase in the demand for German securities would reduce the German interest rate. Interest rates in the two countries would converge at the same level, say 6.3 percent.

The implication of perfect capital mobility is profound. *Any event in one country that tends to change its interest rate (r) relative to the interest rate in foreign countries (r^f) will generate huge capital movements that will soon eliminate the interest rate differential ($r - r^f$).* As an example, a monetary expansion that reduces the domestic interest rate will generate a huge capital outflow that will bring the interest rate back to its original level. A fiscal expansion that raises the domestic interest rate will generate a huge capital inflow that will bring the interest rate back to its original level.

The Two Adjustment Mechanisms: Fixed and Flexible Rates

Perfect capital mobility implies that domestic monetary and fiscal policy do not affect the domestic interest rate. With fixed exchange rates, a stimulative monetary policy will not reduce the domestic interest rate, but will instead cause the country to lose international reserves as the capital account in the balance of payments is thrown into deficit. In a pure flexible exchange rate system (in which there are no international reserves), the monetary policy stimulus generates an excess supply of dollars, and the exchange rate of the dollar drops until supply and demand are once again in balance.

In short, perfect capital mobility implies that both monetary and fiscal policy lose control over the interest rate. With fixed exchange rates, a monetary stimulus causes a loss of reserves and a fiscal stimulus causes an increase in reserves. With flexible exchange rates, a monetary stimulus causes a depreciation of the exchange rate and a fiscal stimulus causes an appreciation of the exchange rate. The reverse events occur with a monetary policy contraction or a fiscal policy contraction.

Is Perfect Capital Mobility Relevant for the United States?

A **small open economy** with perfect capital mobility has no power to set its domestic interest rate at a level that differs from foreign interest rates.

As an analytical tool, perfect capital mobility is most relevant for a **small open economy**, too small to influence the world level of interest rates (r^f). In such an economy, because of perfect capital mobility, the small domestic capital market is swamped by capital inflows whenever there is even a minor increase in the domestic interest rate above the world interest rate (and capital outflows for even a minor decrease in the domestic interest rate).

The United States is too large to be considered a small open economy, and even under perfect capital mobility its own domestic capital market is too large for capital movements to bring its domestic interest rate into perfect equality with the foreign interest rate. We examine the case of the **large open economy** in Section 6-11, after first studying how monetary and fiscal policy work in a small open economy with perfect capital mobility. We already have had a preview of the effects of fiscal deficits in open economies on pp. 142–44.

A **large open economy** can influence its domestic interest rate. A high domestic interest rate generates a steady stream of capital inflows that are not great enough to eliminate an interest rate differential between the domestic and foreign interest rate; a low domestic interest rate generates a steady stream of capital outflows.

6-10 The *IS-LM* Model in a Small Open Economy

The assumption of perfect capital mobility introduces a new element into the *IS-LM* model of income determination. This is the assumption that the differential between domestic and foreign interest rates ($r - r^f$) must remain at zero.

Any small change in the domestic interest rate caused by shifts in monetary and fiscal policy (or in shifts in the *IS* curve due to different levels of consumer and business optimism) will generate capital flows that will quickly bring the domestic interest rate into line with the unchanged foreign interest rate.

The *BP* Schedule

Because perfect capital mobility implies that the interest rate differential must remain at zero, the balance of payments can be in equilibrium only at a single domestic interest rate (r) equal to the foreign interest rate (r^f). Any higher interest rate will lead to unlimited capital inflows, causing a huge balance of payments surplus. Any lower interest rate will lead to unlimited capital outflows, causing a huge balance of payments deficit. The balance of payments is in equilibrium, equal to zero, only along the horizontal line *BP* in Figure 6-8, drawn at the position where the domestic and foreign interest rates are equal ($r' = r^f$).

Anywhere along the horizontal *BP* line the overall balance of payments is in equilibrium (equal to zero) and both the capital and current account balances are zero as well. Why? With a zero interest rate differential ($r - r^f = 0$), capital flows are zero, implying that the capital account is zero. But to make the overall balance of payments equal to zero, the current account balance must be zero as well. In such an economy, along the horizontal *BP* line, Table 6-1 on p. 157 would show a zero on lines 1, 2, and 3.

The Analysis with Fixed Exchange Rates

Now we will examine the effects of a monetary and then a fiscal expansion in a small open economy with fixed exchange rates. Throughout, we will assume that the price level is fixed. These results remain valid, even if the price level is allowed to change, as long as changes in the price level occur more slowly than the speed at which capital flows in and out of the small open economy.

Figure 6-8 Effect of an Increase in the Money Supply with Fixed Exchange Rates

The increase in the real money supply initially shifts the *LM* curve rightward, from LM_0 to LM_1. However, the decline in the interest rate at point E_1 causes capital outflows and a loss of foreign exchange reserves. This reaction reduces the money supply, which continues until the *LM* curve shifts back to LM_0 and the economy moves back to point E_0.

Monetary expansion. Initially, the monetary expansion depicted in Figure 6-8 raises the nominal money supply. Since the price level is fixed, the real money supply also increases, and this shifts the *LM* curve rightward from schedule LM_0 to LM_1. The *IS* curve is assumed to be unchanged. We previously found that such an expansion would move the economy from point E_0 to point E_1. But now the reduction of the interest rate to r_1, which is below the initial level r', generates huge capital outflows and losses of international reserves. To prevent this movement, the central bank must boost the interest rate back up to the initial level by reversing the monetary stimulus. The LM_1 curve shifts back to LM_0, and the economy returns to E_0. Because international capital flows move so quickly, all this would happen so fast that the economy would never actually get to point E_1.

In short, with fixed exchange rates the central bank is impotent in a small open economy. It can neither reduce the interest rate nor expand output. It cannot carry out a contractionary policy either, since it would be swamped with capital inflows that would force it to carry out an offsetting policy expansion. Thus our analysis is consistent with the trilemma, which states that independent monetary policy cannot coexist with fixed exchange rates and perfect capital mobility.

Fiscal expansion. With fixed exchange rates, the only way domestic policymakers can alter the level of real income is to use fiscal policy, as is shown in Figure 6-9. Here the initial situation is the same, point E_0. A fiscal expansion that shifts IS_0 rightward to IS_1 tends to move the economy to point E_2. But the increase in the interest rate attracts capital inflows, swamping the central bank with reserves. Under a fixed exchange rate system, the bank must respond by allowing the money supply to rise until the interest rate returns to its initial level. The money supply must be increased enough to shift LM_0 to LM_1.

Figure 6-9 Effect of a Fiscal Policy Stimulus with Fixed Exchange Rates

An increase in government spending or a reduction in tax rates shifts the *IS* curve rightward to position IS_1. The economy initially moves toward point E_2, but the higher interest rate creates a capital inflow and an increase in foreign exchange reserves, which in turn raises the money supply and shifts the *LM* curve rightward to LM_1. The economy winds up at point E_3.

Fiscal Policy Gains Control Over Monetary Policy Under Fixed Exchange Rates

Instead of going to E_2 as would occur in a closed economy without capital inflows, the economy moves to point E_3.

Clearly, capital mobility with fixed exchange rates makes fiscal policy very effective. Point E_3 is exactly the same outcome that we reached with fiscal expansion in Chapter 4 under two situations, the first of which was a horizontal *LM* curve (top frame of Figure 4-9 on p. 115) and the second of which was accommodating monetary policy (top right frame of Figure 4-10 on p. 117). *Perfect capital mobility with fixed exchange rates forces monetary policy to be accommodative; in effect, fiscal policy gains control of monetary policy.*

The Analysis with Flexible Exchange Rates

In the previous section we learned that a fixed exchange rate system makes monetary policy impotent and fiscal policy very effective in changing the level of real income. In this section we learn that the opposite is true with flexible exchange rates. Monetary policy becomes extremely effective, whereas fiscal policy becomes ineffective.

When exchange rates are flexible, the central bank does nothing to prevent an exchange rate appreciation or depreciation. Thus any event that reduces the domestic interest rate will cause a capital outflow, raising the supply of domestic currency on the foreign exchange market and causing the exchange rate to depreciate. In an *IS-LM* diagram like Figure 6-10, the exchange rate depreciates whenever the economy moves below the *BP* line and appreciates whenever the economy moves above the *BP* line.

Figure 6-10 Effect of a Monetary and Fiscal Policy Stimulus with Flexible Exchange Rates

An increase in the real money supply shifts the *LM* curve rightward to LM_1. The reduction in interest rates at point E_1 causes the exchange rate to depreciate, which in turn boosts net exports and shifts the *IS* curve rightward to IS_1. The economy winds up at point E_3. Starting again from E_0, a fiscal policy stimulus shifts the *IS* curve rightward to position IS_1. The economy initially moves toward point E_2, but the higher interest rate causes the exchange rate to appreciate, which in turn cuts net exports and shifts the *IS* curve back to IS_0. This movement cancels out the impact of the fiscal stimulus on both real income and the interest rate.

The new ingredient in the *IS-LM* model implied by flexible exchange rates was introduced in equation (6.9). An exchange rate appreciation reduces net exports and hence shifts the *IS* curve to the left (since net exports are a component of autonomous planned spending, and any change in autonomous planned spending shifts the *IS* curve). Similarly, an exchange rate depreciation raises net exports and shifts the *IS* curve to the right.

Monetary expansion. In Figure 6-10, as before, a monetary expansion shifts LM_0 rightward to LM_1. Capital outflows lead to a depreciation of the exchange rate. In equation (6.9), this depreciation boosts net exports at any given level of income. The higher level of net exports shifts the initial IS_0 schedule to the new position IS_1. Once the economy arrives at E_3, the exchange rate stops depreciating and the economy is in full equilibrium; the balance of payments is in equilibrium along the *BP* line, and the economy is also on its current *IS* and *LM* schedules. The level of real income has increased because a depreciated exchange rate has boosted net exports for any given level of income, shifting *IS* to the right.

However, as also shown in equation (6.9), higher income boosts imports. As a result, when the economy arrives at its new equilibrium point E_3, the boost to net exports from the depreciated exchange rate is offset exactly by the reduction in net exports caused by higher income. The current account is in balance and, because the domestic interest rate is equal to the foreign interest rate, the capital account is also in balance, thus balancing the overall balance of payments as required along the *BP* schedule.

Fiscal expansion. The effects of a fiscal expansion in the form of higher government spending can also be shown in Figure 6-10. The normal effect of a fiscal expansion is to shift *IS* rightward and boost the domestic interest rate to a point like E_2. But now, with flexible exchange rates, fiscal expansion causes the exchange rate to appreciate. Domestic exports are made less competitive, and domestic residents start buying more imported goods. Net exports fall, and this continues until the *IS* curve shifts back to the left to its initial position, returning the economy to the original point E_0. In this example the *LM* curve does not shift. *Domestic crowding out is replaced by international crowding out, and international crowding out is complete*. The domestic interest rate and income are the same as they were initially at E_0; thus, so are domestic investment and saving. The increase in the fiscal deficit caused by the higher level of government spending is exactly offset by the decline in net exports, and the higher fiscal deficit is totally financed by foreign borrowing. *The twin deficits are identical*, and the cause of the foreign trade deficit is the fiscal deficit. To summarize these different cases:

1. With fixed exchange rates, fiscal policy is highly effective and the central bank is forced to accommodate fiscal policy actions. Monetary policy is impotent, since any increase in the money supply immediately flows abroad and fails to stimulate the domestic economy.
2. With flexible exchange rates, monetary policy is highly effective. The Fed can control the money supply and can stimulate the economy by causing the exchange rate to depreciate. This action boosts net exports until income has grown so much that (due to income-induced growth in imports) net exports return to their original level. With flexible exchange rates, fiscal policy is impotent and international crowding out is complete.

6-11 Capital Mobility and Exchange Rates in a Large Open Economy

In the last section we examined the effects of monetary and fiscal policy in a small open economy, one that has no control at all over its own interest rate. In such an economy, perfect capital mobility causes the domestic interest rate to equal the foreign interest rate.

How a Large Open Economy Differs from a Small Open Economy

In contrast to a small open economy, a large open economy like the United States has substantial control over its domestic interest rate. Its large size relative to the rest of the world means that capital flows are not sufficiently powerful to push its domestic interest rate into exact equality with the world interest rate. Capital mobility is imperfect. When the domestic interest rate rises above the foreign interest rate by a fixed amount, say 0.5 percent, only a limited inflow of foreign capital will occur, not enough to eliminate the interest rate differential.

In the previous section, we examined the effects of monetary and fiscal policy in a small open economy, using the *BP* curves. How does this analysis differ in a large open economy? The main difference involves the *BP* curve, as shown in Figure 6-11. Recall that at every point along the *BP* curve the balance of payments is in equilibrium, so any current account surplus is offset by a capital account deficit, or vice versa.

For a small open economy, the *BP* curve is a horizontal line. In contrast, in a large open economy there can be a continuing capital inflow if the domestic interest rate is high enough and a continuing capital outflow if the domestic interest rate is low enough. As a result, the distinguishing characteristic of a large open economy is that the capital account is in surplus when the domestic interest rate is high and in deficit when the domestic interest rate is low. To achieve an overall balance of payments of zero, any surplus in the capital account must

Figure 6-11 The *BP* Line in a Small and Large Open Economy

The *BP* line shows the different combinations of the domestic interest rate and real income that are consistent with balance of payments equilibrium, that is, a zero total balance of the current account plus the capital account. The *BP* line is positively sloped for a large open economy. At a point like *A*, the interest rate is low, the capital account is in deficit, and the current account is in surplus due to low imports. At a point like *C*, the interest rate is high, the capital account is in surplus, and the current account is in deficit due to high imports.

be offset by a deficit of exactly the same amount in the current account; this requires a high level of real income at a point like C in Figure 6-11, so that imports (which depend on income) are large and the current account is in deficit. The opposite occurs at a point like A; the deficit in the capital account is offset by a current account surplus, caused by low income that in turn reduces imports. In short, the BP line slopes up for a large open economy, because capital inflows *depend positively on the interest rate*. At a high interest rate, capital inflows are large; at a low interest rate, capital outflows are large.

Monetary and Fiscal Policy with Fixed and Flexible Exchange Rates

Once we adopt the positively sloped BP curve for a large open economy, the previous analysis of monetary and fiscal policy remains valid with only minor adjustments.

We previously concluded that with fixed exchange rates monetary policy was impotent, regardless of the slope of the BP curve. Thus monetary policy is equally impotent in both a small and a large open economy. Fiscal policy is effective, but somewhat less so than in a small open economy, since the effects of a fiscal policy stimulus are divided between an increase in real income and in the domestic interest rate, instead of being entirely directed toward an increase in real income.

With flexible exchange rates, fiscal policy is impotent in a large open economy, just as in a small open economy. The prompt collapse of net exports following the 1981 shift to fiscal deficits provides a perfect example of the impotence of fiscal policy in a large open economy. Monetary policy is highly effective with flexible exchange rates, as in a small open economy. However, since higher income is accompanied by higher interest rates (due to the upward sloping BP curve), there is some crowding out of domestic expenditure, and this must be offset by a larger stimulus to net exports than in a small open economy,

Summary of Monetary and Fiscal Policy Effects in Open Economies

Small open economy, perfect capital mobility

	Fixed exchange rates	Flexible exchange rates
Monetary policy	Impotent, no independent effect, consistent with trilemma	Strong, exchange rate impact augments direct effect of policy on domestic spending
Fiscal policy	Strong, fiscal policy gains control over money supply	Impotent, international crowding out augments domestic crowding out

Large open economy, imperfect capital mobility

	Fixed exchange rates	Flexible exchange rates
Monetary policy	Impotent, same as in small open economy	Strong, with more exchange rate effect than in small open economy
Fiscal policy	Strong, but not as effective as in small open economy	Impotent, as in small open economy

requiring an even larger exchange rate depreciation. To summarize these contrasting cases:

1. With fixed exchange rates, fiscal policy is highly effective, but a fiscal stimulus does not increase real income as much in a large open economy as in a small open economy. Monetary policy is impotent in both a large and a small open economy.
2. With flexible exchange rates, monetary policy is highly effective and boosts income even more in a large open economy than in a small open economy. With flexible exchange rates, fiscal policy is impotent in both a large and a small open economy. International crowding out is complete.

6-12 Conclusion: Economic Policy in the Open Economy

We have learned in this chapter that there are interactions among monetary and fiscal policy, the current account balance, and the foreign exchange rate. A unifying theme is the international trilemma, which states that countries cannot simultaneously maintain an independent monetary policy, fixed exchange rates, and free unfettered international capital movements. The implications of this analysis differ for the United States, Europe, and Asia.

The Trilemma, the United States, and the Euro

The United States has chosen to keep its exchange rate flexible and to leave to other countries the decision of whether to tie their currencies to the dollar or to let their currencies float. This means that the United States has been able to maintain control over domestic monetary policy and also has allowed free inflows of private capital that largely financed the huge increase in the U.S. current account deficit that occurred in 1998–2004. Another important factor in financing the U.S. deficit has been the willingness of foreign central banks, especially in Asia, to accumulate large stocks of dollar reserves, thus lending to the United States the remaining funds needed to pay for its current account deficit.

By adopting a single currency (the euro) in 1999, twelve nations in Europe chose to emulate the United States by having a fixed exchange rate within the borders of the twelve nations while allowing the exchange rate of the euro to float against other currencies. The trilemma implies that the twelve nations have thereby given up a traditional aspect of national sovereignty, the ability to maintain independent control of domestic monetary policy. Instead, they have ceded control over monetary policy to the European Central Bank, which now plays a role analogous to that of the U.S. Federal Reserve System. We return to issues raised by the introduction of the euro in Chapter 14.

Finally, we have learned that the United States and the major Asian countries, especially China and Japan, have entered into a mutually reinforcing relationship of codependence. The United States relies on Asia to finance its ever-growing current account deficit. Asian countries willingly accumulate dollar reserves in order to prevent their currencies from appreciating, thus preventing a slump in their exports and potential unemployment. The United States maintains flexible exchange rates, thus escaping from the constraints of the trilemma, while the Asian countries are in a trap in which they continue to accumulate dollar assets that not only earn an interest rate barely above zero, but also decline in value as the dollar depreciates against currencies in other regions of the world, especially against the euro.

Summary

1. The balance of payments consists of the current account (the balance of exports, imports, net investment income, and transfers) and the capital account (which registers purchases and sales of foreign assets by U.S. residents and of U.S. assets by foreigners). For most of the past four decades, the United States has run a current account deficit, which has been only partly offset by a capital account surplus, thus resulting in a persistent balance of payments deficit.

2. A current account deficit must be financed by borrowing from foreigners. Borrowing from foreign households, firms, and governments is classified as a capital account surplus, while borrowing from foreign central banks is treated as a balance of payments deficit. A current account deficit thus increases net indebtedness to foreigners.

3. In a flexible exchange rate system, the foreign exchange rate is free to move every day. An increase in the amount of foreign currency that can be bought per unit of domestic currency is called an appreciation, and a decrease is called a depreciation.

4. In the absence of government intervention, the foreign exchange rate tends to appreciate when there is increased demand for a currency due to higher exports or capital inflows. The exchange rate tends to depreciate when there is an increased supply of a currency due to higher imports or capital outflows.

5. The real exchange rate remains constant if changes in the nominal exchange rate are exactly offset by the differential between domestic and foreign inflation. The purchasing power parity theory of long-run exchange rate determination predicts that the real exchange rate will remain constant.

6. The real exchange rate can change for many reasons not taken into account by the PPP theory. These include differences between nations in the rate of technological change, their comparative rates of discovery of natural resources, and the balance of flows of capital and government transfer payments between them.

7. Exchange rates between nations were largely fixed until 1973. Since then there has been a mixed "impure" flexible exchange rate system, under which central banks practice intervention to prevent undesired movements in exchange rates. Some countries, especially in Asia, have attempted to fix their exchange rates versus the U.S. dollar and have accumulated large quantities of U.S. dollars in the form of international reserves, thus allowing the United States to run a larger current account deficit than would otherwise have been possible.

8. Net exports, the difference between exports and imports, depend both on income and on the real exchange rate. In turn, the real exchange rate depends on the real interest rate. An increase in the real interest rate causes an appreciation of the real exchange rate, as foreign investors find domestic securities more attractive and bid up the exchange rate in order to buy them.

9. In a small open economy with fixed exchange rates, fiscal policy is highly effective and monetary policy is completely impotent. With flexible exchange rates the policy roles are reversed, since monetary policy is highly effective and fiscal policy is impotent.

10. In a large open economy with fixed exchange rates, monetary policy is impotent, but fiscal policy is effective (although less so than in a small open economy). With flexible exchange rates monetary policy is highly effective (even more so than in a small open economy), but fiscal policy is impotent.

Concepts

trilemma
current account
balance of payments
capital account
net international investment position
foreign exchange rate
appreciation
depreciation
real exchange rate
purchasing power parity (PPP) theory
inflation differential
flexible exchange rate system
fixed exchange rate system
foreign exchange reserves
devalue
revalue
intervention
interest rate differential
perfect capital mobility
small open economy
large open economy

Questions

1. Explain the difference between a credit and a debit in the balance of payments.
2. Distinguish between the current account and the capital account in the balance of payments.
3. Four international transactions are listed below. For each, determine whether it is a credit or a debit in the U.S. balance of payments, whether it is a current account or capital account transaction, and whether it increases or decreases the size of the U.S. balance of payments deficit.
   (a) Japan buys rice from the U.S.
   (b) Ford Motor Company builds an automobile plant in Russia.
   (c) A German insurance company buys U.S. government bonds.
   (d) U.S. residents vacation in Asia.
4. Figure 6–1 shows that the United States' net international borrowing has become a larger percentage of GDP since 1990. Yet net investment income from the rest of the world has remained a positive, though declining, share of output. Explain how this is possible.
5. What are the ways that a country can adjust to an imbalance between international receipts and expenditures?
6. Under what conditions is the demand for foreign exchange negatively sloped?
7. Under what conditions is the supply of foreign exchange positively sloped? Negatively sloped?
8. What is a "dirty" flexible exchange rate system, and what incentives exist to transform a "clean" system into a "dirty" one?
9. What is the relationship between a country's foreign exchange rate and its net exports? Why?
10. What is the relationship between a country's interest rate and its foreign exchange rate? Why?
11. Suppose an economy's productivity growth rate increases, causing the prices of its exports to fall, the quantity of its exports to rise, and its current account balance to move from a deficit to a surplus. Using a supply and demand diagram, explain the effect of this increase in productivity growth on the country's foreign exchange rate. If the country's policymakers want to maintain the foreign exchange rate at its current value, what actions must they undertake?
12. Despite the fall of the dollar against the Euro in 2004, the Japanese government was willing to buy American dollars in order to keep the value of the yen from appreciating relative to the dollar. Suppose that instead of slow growth, the Japanese economy had experienced rising inflation over the past decade. Discuss how rising inflation might have changed the Japanese government's willingness to help finance the United States' current account deficit.
13. What is the *BP* schedule? Why is the *BP* line horizontal for a small open economy but positively sloped for a large open one?
14. "Perfect capital mobility with fixed exchange rates forces monetary policy to be accommodative; in effect, fiscal policy gains control of monetary policy." Explain.
15. Fiscal policymakers in a large open economy are reluctant to raise taxes or cut spending. If actual real GDP currently exceeds natural real GDP, will the Central Bank be able to curtail inflation? Under what circumstances?
16. For a large open economy in a pure flexible exchange rate system, it is expansionary monetary policy rather than expansionary fiscal policy that will have a negative long-term effect on private investment. Evaluate.

Problems

1. Suppose a country has net exports of 40, transfer payments of 20, net investment income of −15, and a balance of payments surplus of 10. Find this country's current account balance and capital account balance.
2. In 2004, the current account deficit was approximately five percent of output. Suppose that there are three alternative paths for the current account over the next ten years: (a) the current account deficit remains at five percent of GDP, (b) the current account deficit declines steadily so that in ten years it is only 2.5 percent of GDP, or (c) the current account deficit declines steadily so that it is 0 in ten years. In addition, there are three alternative returns that foreigners could demand for continuing to buy our debt, namely 2, 5, or 10 percent.
   (a) Under each of the alternative paths for the current account deficit, calculate the additional accumulated debt held by foreigners as a percent of GDP at the end of the 10-year period.
   (b) Suppose the U.S. hopes that foreigners buy its additional debt. For each possible rate of return and each path for the current account deficit, calculate the percentage of GDP that will be paid in interest to foreigners holding the additional debt.

3. Suppose the Swiss demand for a U.S. machine is given by the following equation:

$$q = 200{,}000/p$$

Here q is the quantity of U.S. machines bought by the Swiss and p is the price, in Swiss francs (SF), of the U.S. machine.
   (a) If the exchange rate is 2 SF per dollar and the dollar price of the machine is $10,000, what is the SF price of the machine?
   (b) According to the demand function just given, how many machines would the Swiss buy?
   (c) If the dollar price of the machine remained unchanged but the exchange rate fell to 1 SF per dollar, what would the SF price of the machine now be?
   (d) Now how many machines would the Swiss buy?
   (e) At the exchange rate of 2 SF per dollar, what is the quantity demanded of dollars by the Swiss?
   (f) At the exchange rate of 1 SF per dollar, what is the quantity demanded of dollars by the Swiss?
   (g) If this machine were the only U.S. export to Switzerland, draw the Swiss demand curve for dollars. Put dollars demanded on the horizontal axis and the SF/$ exchange rate on the vertical axis.
   (h) At the exchange rate of 2 SF per dollar (or $0.50/SF), what is the quantity supplied of Swiss francs by the Swiss?
   (i) At the exchange rate of 1 SF per dollar (or $1/SF), what is the quantity supplied of Swiss francs by the Swiss?
   (j) If this machine were the only U.S. export to Switzerland, draw the Swiss supply curve of Swiss francs. Put SF supplied on the horizontal axis and the $/SF exchange rate on the vertical axis. (Note the inversion of the exchange rate. Although there are exceptions, it is customary to express a country's exchange rate as the number of units of foreign currency that exchange for one unit of the domestic currency.)

4. Fill in the missing information in each of the following examples.

Example	Real Exchange Rate	Nominal Exchange Rate	Domestic Price Level	Foreign Price Level
(a)		6	100	100
(b)		6	110	100
(c)		6	100	110
(d)	6		110	100
(e)	6		100	110

What conclusions regarding real and nominal exchange rates do these examples suggest?

5. In addition to its Big Mac index, *The Economist*[1] magazine started to publish a PPP index based on the price of a tall latte at Starbucks coffee shops around the world. This problem is intended to show how to use such an index to determine whether a currency is over- or undervalued. You are given the following information:

Country	Coffee price in U.S. dollars	Actual exchange rate
United States	1.50	
Javaland	1.20	2.35
Uppercaffina	2.25	6.00
Isle of Roast	2.70	1.65
Erewhon	.90	4.35

Calculate the implied purchasing power parity (PPP) exchange rate for each of the fictional countries and explain which currencies are over- or undervalued.

6. Suppose that the domestic price level P grows at the rate of 2 percent per quarter for five years, while the foreign price level P^f grows at the rate of 1 percent per quarter for five years. At what rate must e' change for PPP to hold?

7. Assume the following equations summarize the structure of a small open economy with a flexible exchange rate system.

$$C = C_a + 0.85(Y - T)$$
$$C_a = 200 - 8r$$
$$T = 200 + 0.2Y$$
$$(M/P)^d = 0.25Y - 25r$$
$$M^s/P = 2{,}250$$
$$I_p = 1{,}700 - 32r$$
$$G = 1{,}800$$
$$NX = 870 - 0.08Y - 200e$$

   (a) Initially let foreign and domestic interest rates be equal, so that $r = r^f$, and let the foreign exchange rate (e) equal 2.
      1. Derive the equation for net exports, NX.
      2. Compute the value of the multiplier.
      3. Derive the equation for the autonomous planned spending schedule, A_p.
      4. Derive the equation for the *IS* curve.
      5. Derive the equation for the *LM* curve.
      6. Compute the equilibrium domestic and foreign interest rates (r and r^f).
      7. Compute equilibrium real output (Y).
   (b) We now let the small economy's domestic interest rate diverge temporarily from the foreign interest rate. Suppose that the monetary authority

[1] *The Economist*, January 17, 2004, p. 67, The Starbucks Index.

attempts to reduce output by decreasing the real money supply, M^s/P, by 50 to 2,200.
1. Derive the equation for the new *LM* curve.
2. Compute the new equilibrium domestic interest rate (r).
3. Compute the new (temporary) equilibrium real output (Y).
4. Given the decrease in the real money supply, compute the level of real output that equalizes domestic and foreign interest rates.
5. Find the foreign exchange rate that equalizes domestic and foreign interest rates. (*Hint:* Calculate the change in net exports required to reduce output to the level that equalizes domestic and foreign interest rates. Then calculate the change in the foreign exchange rate required to change net exports by that amount.)

(c) Again we let the domestic interest rate diverge temporarily from the foreign interest rate. Suppose that fiscal policymakers decrease government spending (G) by 80 to 1,720. Assume that the value of the real money supply equals 2,250.

1. Derive the equation for the new autonomous planned spending schedule, A_p.
2. Derive the equation for the new *IS* curve.
3. Compute the new equilibrium domestic interest rate (r).
4. Compute the new (temporary) equilibrium real output (Y).
5. Given that there has been no change in the real money supply, compute the level of real output that equalizes domestic and foreign interest rates.
6. Find the foreign exchange rate that equalizes domestic and foreign interest rates. (*Hint*: Calculate by how much must autonomous planned spending change to equalize in domestic and foreign interest rates. Then calculate the change in the foreign exchange rate required to change in net exports by that amount.)

(d) Based on your answers to parts b and c, compare and contrast the effectiveness of monetary and fiscal policy in a small open economy with a flexible exchange rate system.

Self-Test Answers

p. 158 (1) Balance of payments deficit of 30, which requires borrowing 30 from foreign central banks; (2) balance of payments surplus of 30, which requires lending 30; (3) same as (1).

p. 166 (1) Shifts the demand curve for dollars to the right. (2) No effect on the supply curve of dollars (people from the United States shift some of the supply of dollars from Switzerland to France). (3) Shifts the demand curve for dollars to the left. (4) Shifts the supply curve of dollars to the left.

p. 168 (1) The real exchange rate in the year 2006 is $1.3 \times (110/100) = 1.43$ SF per dollar. (2) Since the real exchange rate was 1.5 SF per dollar in 2005, the dollar has experienced a real depreciation. (3) U.S. exports to Switzerland should rise and imports should fall.

p. 174 (1) A college student going to Europe (like anyone buying foreign goods or services) hopes for an appreciation of the dollar. (2) Other things remaining the same, you would have preferred traveling to Europe in 2001 when the dollar's foreign exchange value was approximately 41 percent higher than it was in 1995. (3) For the German student, the situation is the opposite. He or she would prefer to travel to the U.S. when the dollar is weaker, as was the case in 1995.

p. 181 College students going to Europe prefer a strong dollar. This means that they prefer a booming stock market that attracts capital investment into the United States.

PART THREE

Aggregate Demand, Aggregate Supply, Unemployment, and Inflation

CHAPTER 7 Aggregate Demand, Aggregate Supply, and the Self-Correcting Economy

CHAPTER 8 Inflation: Its Causes and Cures

CHAPTER 9 The Goals of Stabilization Policy: Low Inflation and Low Unemployment

CHAPTER 7
Aggregate Demand, Aggregate Supply, and the Self-Correcting Economy

The price of commodities in the market is formed by means of a certain struggle which takes place between the buyers and the sellers.
—Henry Thornton, 1802

We have now completed Part Two of the book, comprised of Chapters 3–6. We have studied the determinants of aggregate demand, and we have seen that changes in any of these determinants create demand shocks.[1] Among the demand shocks introduced in Chapter 3 were changes in autonomous consumption, planned investment, net exports, and fiscal policy (i.e., changes in government spending and tax rates). We learned that changes in consumer confidence, in stock market prices, and in housing prices can alter autonomous consumption, and that changes in business optimism and expectations of future profits can alter planned investment. Added in Chapter 4 as a source of demand shocks was the money supply, which induces changes in interest rates that lead to changes in such interest-sensitive components of spending as autonomous consumption and planned investment. Then in Chapter 6 we learned that changes in the exchange rate constitute yet another source of demand shocks. All demand shocks can create multiplier effects of response in the total economy, and the size of the multiplier depends on the fraction of an extra dollar of income that leaks out of spending into saving, income taxes, and imports.

The economy's chief line of defense against demand shocks is monetary and fiscal policy. We have learned that these policies under some conditions can have strong or weak effects, and we have learned that their impact is quite different when exchange rates are fixed than when exchange rates are flexible.

7-1 Combining Aggregate Demand with Aggregate Supply

In principle, shocks to aggregate demand can change either real GDP, the price level (GDP deflator), or both. Up until now, in order to focus on changes in aggregate demand, we have made a bold but useful simplifying assumption: *that the price level is fixed in the short run.* This has implied that all changes

---

[1] *Review:* The concepts "aggregate demand" and "demand shocks" were first defined in Chapter 3 on p. 59, and these definitions are also found in the glossary in the back of the book.

in aggregate demand automatically cause changes in real GDP by the same amount in the same direction. Repeating from equation (3.1) on p. 60:

$$\text{Changes in Real GDP} = \frac{\text{Changes in Aggregate Demand}}{\text{Fixed Price Level}} \quad (7.1)$$

Now it is time to drop the unrealistic assumption that the price level is fixed. Recall that the price level is measured by an aggregate price index like the GDP deflator. When the prices of most goods are rising, the aggregate deflator (P) increases, and we have inflation. When the prices of most goods are falling, P decreases, and we have deflation. How can we determine whether changes in aggregate demand create changes in real GDP, the price level, or both?

This chapter introduces two new elements to answer that question. First, we introduce a negatively sloped schedule relating real GDP to the price level, called the **aggregate demand (AD) curve**. We have already learned in Chapters 3–6 all the reasons why the *AD* curve shifts its position; here the only new element is the curve has a negative slope, reflecting the fact that a higher price level reduces the real money supply and hence reduces aggregate demand.

But the *AD* curve by itself cannot determine two unknowns, real GDP and the price level. The needed extra relationship is the **short-run aggregate supply (SAS) curve**, a positively sloped relationship between real GDP and the price level. Whereas the *AD* curve shows how much people want to buy, the *SAS* curve shows how much business firms are willing to sell at each price level. When the price level increases, while the costs of labor and other factors of production remain stable, then business profits will increase and firms will produce more real GDP. Both real GDP and the price level are determined at the point where the *AD* and *SAS* curves intersect. We shall learn that the reason for the positive slope of the *SAS* is inherently temporary, that prices adjust while labor costs (the nominal wage) do not. Once the nominal wage rate is free to adjust in proportion to the price level, the **long-run aggregate supply (LAS) curve** becomes vertical.

This chapter begins by deriving the *AD* and *SAS* curves, explaining why they are sloped as they are, and what causes them to shift their position. Subsequently, we use both curves to examine differing views of economists regarding the causes of business cycles and the effectiveness of monetary and fiscal policy. We use the distinction between aggregate demand and supply to examine the causes of the Great Depression, which involve the causes of the leftward shift in the *AD* curve, the slope of the *SAS* curve, and the determinants of shifts in the *SAS* curve.

The **aggregate demand (AD) curve** shows different combinations of the price level and real output at which the money and commodity markets are both in equilibrium.

The **short-run aggregate supply (SAS) curve** shows the amount of output that business firms are willing to produce at different price levels, holding constant the nominal wage rate.

The **long-run aggregate supply (LAS) curve** shows the amount that business firms are willing to produce when the nominal wage rate has fully adjusted to any changes in the price level.

7-2 Flexible Prices and the *AD* Curve

In this section we develop the *AD* curve, which summarizes the effect of changing prices on the level of real GDP. The *AD* curve summarizes the *IS-LM* model of Chapter 4; the only new element is that the price level is now allowed to change instead of being fixed as in Chapters 3–6.

Effect of Changing Prices on the *LM* Curve

We already know that the *LM* curve shifts its position whenever there is a change in the *real* money supply. Until now, every *LM* shift has resulted from a change in the *nominal* money supply, while the price level has been fixed. The price level has been treated as a parameter, or a known variable, allowing us to concentrate on the determination of the two unknowns, real income (Y) and the interest rate (r).

However, the LM curve can shift *in exactly the same way* when a change in the real money supply M^s/P is caused by a change in the price level P, while the nominal money supply M^s remains fixed at a single value, say M_0^s. The top frame of Figure 7-1 illustrates three LM curves drawn for three values of P and M^s/P, each assuming the same nominal money supply, M_0^s. Initially the economy is at point E_0, where the IS curve crosses the LM_0 curve, drawn for the initial assumed price level P_0. The economy is in equilibrium with income level Y_0 and interest rate r_0. So far, everything is the same as in Chapter 4.

Now we consider something new, a change in the price level. If the price level were *lower* than P_0, say P_1, the real money supply would be *larger* (M_0^s/P_1). To maintain equilibrium in the money market, the interest rate would have to fall to r_1. This change would boost planned expenditures and cause real GDP to grow to the larger amount Y_1, so that the economy's equilibrium position would move from E_0 to point H. The reverse is true as well. A higher price level, say P_2, would reduce the real money supply and cause real GDP to shrink to the lower level Y_2, and the economy's equilibrium position would move to point J.

Figure 7-1 Effect on Real Income of Different Values of the Price Level

In the top frame, three different LM curves are drawn for three different hypothetical values of the price level. Corresponding to the three levels of the price level are three positions of equilibrium, J, E_0, and H. These three points are drawn again in the lower frame with the same horizontal axis (real income), but with the price level for the vertical axis. A drop in the price index from point J to E_0, and then to H, raises the *real* money supply and stimulates real output along the aggregate demand curve AD_0.

The bottom frame of Figure 7-1 presents the relationship between equilibrium real GDP (Y) and the assumed price level. The horizontal axis (real GDP) is the same as that in the top frame, but the vertical axis plots the price level. Points J, E_0, and H in the bottom frame plot the three different assumed price levels and the corresponding level of real GDP from the top frame. In this example, price level P_2 is twice as high as P_0, and P_0 is twice as high as P_1.

In the bottom frame, the aggregate demand curve (AD_0) connecting points J, E_0, and H shows all the possible combinations of P and Y consistent with the assumed level of the *nominal* money supply (M_0^s) and also with the assumed IS_0 curve. If the price level is higher, then real spending and real GDP are low, and vice versa. Because the level of real GDP along the AD curve is always at a point where the IS and LM curves cross in the upper frame, *everywhere along the AD curve both the commodity and money markets are in equilibrium.*

Why is the AD curve a curved line instead of a straight line? The shape results from the fact that a given percentage decline in the price level boosts the real money supply by an ever greater percentage, the lower is the price level, hence raising real GDP by more at a low price level than at a high price level. For instance, let us assume that the nominal money supply is 1,000. Reducing the price level from 2 to 1.5 will raise the real money supply from 500 to 667, an increase of 33 percent. Reducing the price level from 1.5 to 1.0 will raise the real money supply from 667 to 1,000, an increase of 50 percent. Reducing the price level from 1.0 to 0.5 will raise the real money supply from 1,000 to 2,000, an increase of 100 percent.

7-3 Shifting the Aggregate Demand Curve with Monetary and Fiscal Policy

Effects of a Change in the Nominal Money Supply

The AD curve is fixed in position by the assumed value of the nominal money supply and the assumed position of the IS curve, which in turn depends on consumer and business confidence, fiscal policy, and net exports. A change in any of these assumed conditions will shift the position of the AD curve and thus change the amount of spending and real GDP at any given price level.

To understand the factors that shift the AD curve, we begin with a doubling of the nominal money supply, from M_0^s to M_1^s. The economy starts out at point E_0, the same as in Figure 7-1. In the top frame of Figure 7-2 this doubling shifts the LM curve rightward to the new position LM_1. Since the price level has not changed, in the bottom frame the economy remains at the same vertical position as at point E_0 but moves horizontally to point H', which lies directly below point H' in the upper frame. The economy's real GDP is exactly the same at point H and H'.

But, since we drew the initial AD_0 curve on the assumption that price level P_1 is half of P_0, it follows that the price level at H' is double its value at H in the bottom frame. Similarly, every point along the new, higher AD_1 curve is twice as high as along the original AD_0 curve. *The general rule is that an increase in the nominal money supply by a given percentage shifts the AD curve vertically by the same percentage.*[2] Why? The price level must shift upward by

---

[2] The proportional vertical movement in the AD schedule requires that all forms of real wealth double when the nominal money supply doubles.

Figure 7-2 The Effect on the AD Curve of a Doubling of the Nominal Money Supply

In the top frame, a doubling of the nominal money supply from M_0^s to M_1^s moves the LM curve rightward from LM_0 to LM_1 and moves the economy's general equilibrium (where IS crosses LM) from point E_0 to point H'. In the lower frame, we remain at a vertical distance of P_0, since nothing has happened to the price level. The higher money supply raises real income and causes the economy's equilibrium position in the bottom frame to be at point H' rather than at point E_0. Notice that the new AD_1 curve running through point H' lies everywhere twice as high as the old AD_0 curve.

the same percent as the nominal money supply in order to leave the real money supply unchanged, and the position of the LM curve depends on the real money supply.

Self-Test

1. Would a steeper IS curve make the AD curve steeper or flatter?
2. Would a steeper LM curve make the AD curve steeper or flatter?

Effects of a Change in Autonomous Spending

In the last section, the IS curve remained fixed at its original position but an increase in the nominal money supply shifted the LM and AD curves. Now we reverse what is fixed and what changes. We hold fixed the nominal money supply but allow a drop in planned spending to shift the IS curve to the left. This change might occur because of a decline in consumer or business confidence, a decline in government spending, an increase in tax rates, an increase in autonomous net taxes, or a drop in the autonomous component of net exports.

When the IS curve shifts leftward in the top frame of Figure 7-3, the economy's equilibrium position shifts southwest from point E_0 to point F, at the

Figure 7-3 The Effect on the AD Curve of a Decline in Planned Autonomous Spending

Any event that reduces planned autonomous spending by shifting the *IS* curve leftward also creates a parallel leftward shift in the *AD* curve. If the price level remains stable at P_0, the economy shifts leftward to point *F* and real income drops to Y_3. Another possibility is that the price level could drop to P_3, moving the economy down to point *G* and allowing real income to remain at the original Y_0. A drop in the price level to P_3 would increase the real money supply and shift the *LM* curve to the right in the top frame to a position that intersects the IS_1 line directly above Y_0.

crossing point of the new *IS* curve and the unchanged *LM* curve, drawn for the unchanged nominal money supply (M_0^s) and a given price level (P_0). In the bottom frame, if the price level remains at P_0, the economy shifts from point E_0 to point *F*. Real GDP falls from Y_0 to Y_3. The drop in planned spending creates a leftward shift in the *AD* curve.

Comparing the bottom frames of Figures 7-2 and 7-3, we note that the shifts in the *AD* curve are different. A change in the nominal money supply, as in Figure 7-2, shifts the *AD* curve up or down *vertically*. However, a change in autonomous spending in Figure 7-3 shifts the *AD* curve to the left or right *horizontally*. The decline in real GDP in the bottom frame that results from a given leftward shift in the *IS* curve is exactly the same, no matter whether the initial price level is low or high.

Will the reduction in planned spending reduce real income and leave the price level unchanged? Or will the reduction in planned spending reduce the price level and leave real income unchanged? Which outcome will occur? Figure 7-3 cannot tell us, because the *AD* curve by itself does not contain enough information to pin down both the price level and real income. To ascertain where the economy will come to rest along the numerous possible positions along the *AD* curve, we must find another schedule to intersect the *AD* curve. This is the *SAS* curve initially defined on p. 198.

Learning About Diagrams: The AD Curve

The aggregate demand (AD) curve, as drawn in the bottom frames of Figures 7-1 to 7-3, summarizes everything we have already learned about the IS-LM model and adds a single new ingredient, the ability of the price level to change instead of remaining fixed (as in Chapters 3–6).

Diagram Elements and Reasons for Slope

The vertical axis is the price level and the horizontal axis is the level of real GDP.

The AD curve shows all the possible crossing points of a single IS commodity-market equilibrium curve with the various LM money-market equilibrium curves drawn for each possible price level. Everywhere along the AD curve *both* the commodity (IS) and money (LM) markets are in equilibrium (as shown in Figure 7-1).

The AD curve slopes downward because a lower price level (P) raises the real money supply, thereby lowering the interest rate and stimulating planned expenditures. This stimulus requires an increase in actual real GDP (Y) to keep the commodity market in equilibrium. The steeper the IS curve, the steeper the AD curve.

What Shifts the AD Curve?

The AD curve is drawn for a fixed nominal supply of money (M^s) and a fixed set of determinants of the IS curve (business and consumer confidence, government spending, tax rates, autonomous net taxes, and the autonomous component of net exports).

A given percentage increase in the nominal money supply will shift the AD curve *vertically* upward by a similar percentage. Why? A vertical shift means that real GDP is fixed. This requires that the LM curve must remain fixed, since nothing occurs to shift the IS curve. The price level must shift upward by the same percent as the nominal money supply in order to leave the real money supply unchanged, and a fixed real money supply is required for a fixed LM curve.

Anything that shifts the IS curve creates a parallel *horizontal* shift in the AD curve in the same direction. The *amount* of the horizontal shift of the AD curve is usually less than that of the IS curve, because of the crowding out effect.[a]

What Is True of Points That Are off the AD Curve?

The entire area to the right of the AD curve has an excess supply of commodities; too much is being produced relative to the demand for goods and services at that price level.

The entire area to the left of the AD curve has an excess demand for commodities; too little is being produced relative to the demand for goods and services at that price level.

At any point off the AD curve, there is pressure for change. For instance, at a point with excess production to the right of the AD curve, there is unplanned inventory accumulation, which places downward pressure on production. There is also downward pressure on prices as firms attempt to boost sales with lower prices.[b]

---

[a] For details, see equation (10) in the Appendix to Chapter 4. For any given change in, say, government spending, the IS curve shifts in the same direction by the multiplier k, while the AD curve shifts in the same direction by the multiplier k_1, defined in equation (10).

[b] The equation of the AD curve is the income equation (9) in the Appendix to Chapter 4.

$$Y = k_1 A'_P + k_2 \frac{M^s}{P}$$

7-4 Alternative Shapes of the Short-Run Aggregate Supply Curve

The short-run aggregate supply schedule shows how much business firms are willing to produce at different hypothetical price levels. Such a schedule of business firms' behavior can have several possible shapes. Depending on the shape, the implications of a shift in the AD curve are quite different. In Figure 7-4 we show a rightward shift in the AD curve from AD_0 to AD_1.

Figure 7-4 Effect of a Rightward Shift in the *AD* Curve with Three Alternative Short-Run Aggregate Supply Curves

The horizontal supply curve at the price level P_0 reflects the "fixed price" assumption of Chapters 3–6. An increase in aggregate demand that shifts the AD_0 curve to AD_1 will move the economy from its initial position E_0 to new position E_1. In contrast, if the supply curve is vertical, higher aggregate demand pushes the economy from point E_0 to E_3. An intermediate possibility is that both output and prices rise *in the short run* to a point such as E_2, and that *in the long run* the *boost* in real GDP gradually disappears until we arrive at E_3.

The Reaction of Real GDP and the Price Level to Higher Aggregate Demand Depends on the Shape of the Aggregate Supply Curve

How will the increase in aggregate demand be divided between a higher level of real GDP and a higher price level? Three hypothetical answers, corresponding to three hypothetical aggregate supply curves, are shown in Figure 7-4. In Chapters 3–6 we assumed that the price level always remains fixed; thus we assumed that the economy moved from its initial position E_0 directly rightward to a higher level of real GDP at point E_1 along the horizontal aggregate supply curve. Thus throughout Chapters 3–6 we were assuming a horizontal aggregate supply curve like that shown in Figure 7-4.

A second possibility is that real GDP is always fixed at the level of natural real GDP. If so, the same increase in aggregate demand would have no effect at all on real GDP. Instead, business firms would simply raise the price level from P_0 to a higher price level at point E_3 along the vertical aggregate supply curve in Figure 7-4, leaving their level of production (Y) unchanged. As we shall see, natural real GDP is the only output level consistent with equilibrium in the labor market.

A third possibility is shown by the line labeled "positively sloped aggregate supply curve." If this curve were valid, then the rightward shift in the *AD* curve would cause business firms to raise *both* their prices and their level of production, moving the economy to a point like E_2. As we shall see, a point like E_2 is likely to be achieved only temporarily.

The choice among the three shapes of the aggregate supply curve in Figure 7-4 has created decades of controversy in macroeconomics. The horizontal supply curve that was assumed in our fixed-price analysis of Chapters 3–6 is very convenient but unrealistic, since it cannot explain why the inflation rate is not always zero. The vertical supply curve is a convenient shortcut for analyzing periods of very rapid inflation, since it implies that changes in the money supply mainly or entirely affect the inflation rate with minor or negligible effects on real output. The third, positively sloping alternative seems more realistic, at least for the short run.

In the next section, we shall see that the positively sloped line in Figure 7-4 is the short-run aggregate supply (*SAS*) curve introduced at the beginning of this chapter. It is valid only in the short run, a period short enough for the price level

7-5 The Short-Run Aggregate Supply (SAS) Curve When the Nominal Wage Rate Is Constant

We are now ready to learn why aggregate demand shocks, taking the form of changes in the nominal money supply or in any of the factors that can shift the *IS* curve, will change *both* real GDP and the price level. Will a demand shock change the price level more than it changes real GDP, or will the demand shock change real GDP more than the price level? The answer depends on the slope of the *SAS* curve.

In this section we show how the upward-sloping *SAS* curve can be derived from the behavior of firms in the labor market. We assume that the nominal wage rate is fixed and postpone until the next section the question of how long the wage rate is fixed and what factors cause it to change.

The Labor Demand Curve

Distinguishing the nominal and real wage rates. We first encountered the distinction between nominal and real variables in Chapter 2, where we introduced nominal and real GDP. The nominal wage rate is simply the actual wage rate paid (W). Initially, the nominal wage rate is assumed to be fixed at a particular amount (W_0). The real wage rate (W/P) is the nominal wage rate (W) divided by an aggregate price index, such as the GDP deflator.

The left-hand frame of Figure 7-5 plots the real wage (W/P) on the vertical axis and the level of employment (N) on the horizontal axis. Since the real wage is the price that firms pay to hire workers, the downward-sloping labor demand curve (N_0^d) states that a decrease in the real wage will induce firms to hire more workers, and vice versa. Any given labor demand curve holds constant other factors of production that work together with labor, for example, land, capital, technology, materials, and energy. The vertical position of the labor demand curve represents the marginal product of labor; the labor demand curve slopes downward because the marginal product of labor declines as additional workers are hired to work with a fixed quantity of land, capital, technology, materials, and energy.[3] An increase in any of these nonlabor factors of production will shift the N^d curve upward.

Firms hire workers up to the point that the real wage equals their marginal product. For instance, at point *B* in the left-hand frame of Figure 7-5, a real wage of W_0/P_0 induces firms to hire N_0 workers. To hire workers beyond that point, say to hire N_1 workers at point *C*, would mean hiring workers having a marginal product of labor less than the assumed real wage of W_0/P_0, causing firms to lose money on those extra workers.

---

[3] The decline in the marginal product as one factor of production is added while the quantity of other factors remains fixed is called the law of diminishing returns, and is introduced in every elementary economics textbook.

Figure 7-5 The Labor Demand Curve and the Short-Run Aggregate Supply Curve

The left-hand frame displays the labor demand curve, which shows that a decline in the real wage induces firms to hire additional workers. The right-hand frame shows that a higher price level (by reducing the real wage and inducing firms to hire additional workers) raises real GDP.

The Short-Run Aggregate Supply (SAS) Curve

Now we can examine the relationship between employment and real GDP at different price levels. For instance, point B in the left frame shows that N_0 workers will be hired if the price level is P_0 and the real wage is W_0/P_0. Looking directly to the right, we see that at point B the same price level (P_0) will induce a production level of Y_0, the amount that N_0 workers can produce.

The line connecting points A, B, and C in the right frame is the *SAS* curve. It slopes upward because a higher price level reduces the real wage and induces firms to hire more workers, which in turn raises real GDP. Notice that all three points in both the left and right frames—A, B, and C—share exactly the same nominal wage rate (W_0). For this reason, the *SAS* curve is labeled with the wage rate assumed in drawing it, W_0. Only the price level differs among the three points. Because a change in the price level also changes the real wage, it changes employment and real GDP.

For instance, at point C in the right frame of Figure 7-5, the price level is at P_1, a higher level than P_0. Since the nominal wage rate is assumed to be fixed at W_0, the real wage at point C in the left frame is W_0/P_1, a lower value of the real wage that induces firms to higher number of workers N_1 who can produce the higher value of output Y_1 at point C in the right frame. Similarly, point A shows that a lower price level P_2 in the right frame implies a higher real wage at point A in the left frame, and a lower level of employment N_2 and lower level of output Y_2.

The slope of the *SAS* curve determines how much real GDP responds to a demand shock, and how much the price level responds. As drawn in Figure 7-5,

Learning About Diagrams: The SAS Curve

The short-run aggregate supply curve, abbreviated *SAS*, depicts the amount of output that business firms are willing to produce at different alternative price levels.

Diagram Elements and Reasons for Slope

The *SAS* curve is plotted with the same vertical and horizontal axes as the *AD* curve; the aggregate price level is on the vertical axis and real GDP is on the horizontal axis. Examples are shown in the right frame of Figures 7-5 and 7-6 on pp. 206 and 208.

The *SAS* curve slopes up because, with a fixed nominal wage rate, a higher price level makes it profitable for business firms to increase output. Since increasing output requires adding more workers, each of whom is less productive than the last, the real wage must decline for firms to be willing to produce more output, and hence the price level must increase.

The greater the decline in worker productivity as additional workers are added, the steeper is the *SAS* curve.

What Shifts the SAS Curve?

The *SAS* curve is drawn for a fixed nominal wage rate and a fixed set of determinants of the labor demand curve. These are the factors of production other than labor—land, capital, technology, materials, and energy.

A given percentage change in the nominal wage rate will shift the *SAS* curve upward by the same percentage. When the nominal wage rate and the price level (drawn on the vertical axis) increase by the same percentage, the real wage is fixed, employment and output are fixed, and we remain at the same horizontal position in the diagram.

Anything that shifts the production function will also shift the *SAS* curve. Larger inputs of capital, technology, materials, or energy will shift the production function up and the *SAS* curve to the right, allowing more output to be produced at a given price level. The reverse is also true; an event like a sharp increase in oil prices can reduce nonlabor inputs like energy, shifting the *SAS* curve to the left.

What Is True of Points That Are off the SAS Curve?

Since the *SAS* curve shows the different combinations of output and the price level consistent with profit maximization by business firms, any point off the *SAS* curve would not be chosen by these firms.

A point to the right of the *SAS* curve indicates that firms are producing too much, hiring workers whose marginal product is below their real wage. Firms could boost profits by reducing output.

A point to the left of the *SAS* curve indicates that firms are producing too little, since additional workers could be hired who produce more than their real wage. Firms could boost profits by raising output.

---

the response of real GDP and of the price level to a demand shock will be in roughly the same proportion. For the *SAS* curve to be much steeper than shown, the labor demand curve in the left frame of Figure 7-5 would have to be steep, indicating that the addition of extra workers causes a sharp decline in the productivity of workers. Similarly, for the *SAS* curve to be relatively flat, the labor demand curve would also need to be relatively flat.

Self-Test

Which of the following causes a movement *along* the short-run aggregate supply (*SAS*) curve, and which causes a shift in the curve? If the curve shifts, does it shift up or down?

1. A union concession that reduces the wage rate to help a firm survive foreign competition.
2. A discovery of a giant oil field in Missouri that reduces the price of oil.
3. An increase in the money supply.
4. An increase in the GDP deflator.

7-6 How the Wage Rate Is Set

So far we have seen that the aggregate supply curve slopes upward for any *given* nominal wage rate. But surely the wage rate will not stay at the same level forever. If the wage rate increases, the *SAS* curve will shift up, and its intersection point with the economy's aggregate demand curve (*AD*) will shift as well. *Thus the determinants of the actual wage rate paid have a crucial effect on the nature of the economy's response to a change in aggregate demand.*

The Equilibrium Real Wage Rate

In Figure 7-5 we can see in operation the distinction between the nominal and real wage rates. As long as the labor demand curve is at the fixed position N_0^d, an increase in employment from N_0 to N_1 requires a decrease in the real wage rate from W_0/P_0 to W_0/P_1. Since the nominal wage rate W_0 remains fixed, then this required decline in the real wage rate *must* be accomplished by an increase in the price level. When P increases and W remains fixed, employment increases to N_1 in the left frame of Figure 7-6 and output increases to Y_1 in the right frame.

But the nominal wage rate is unlikely to stay fixed forever. If it shifts up to W_1, then the aggregate supply curve will shift up from SAS_0 to SAS_1. In

A Higher Nominal Wage Rate Shifts the SAS Curve Up

Figure 7-6 The Short-Run Aggregate Supply Curve for Two Different Values of the Wage Rate, W_0 and W_1

The labor demand curve and aggregate supply curve SAS_0 are identical to those drawn in Figure 7-5. So also are points B and C, the quantities N_0 and Y_0, and the price levels P_0 and P_1. The new ingredient here is a higher wage rate W_1, which shifts the aggregate supply curve up from SAS_0 to SAS_1. The higher wage rate shifts the SAS curve because at a given price level, workers are more costly, and so firms hire fewer workers and produce less output. Points B and B' in the left frame are identical, because we assume that the percentage difference between W_1 and W_0 is the same as between P_1 and P_0. Thus point B' lies directly above point B in the right frame.

Figure 7-6 we assume that W_1 exceeds W_0 by the same percentage as P_1 exceeds P_0, so

$$\frac{W_1}{P_1} = \frac{W_0}{P_0}$$

Thus the real wage rate W_1/P_1 at point B' along the new SAS_1 line is exactly the same as the real wage rate W_0/P_0 at point B. Hence, the level of employment and real GDP (N_0 and Y_0) must be identical at points B and B'. Indeed we see in the left frame of Figure 7-6 that points B and B' coincide because the real wage rate is identical at points B and B' in both the left and right frames of Figure 7-6.

Determinants of the equilibrium real wage rate. Equilibrium is a situation in which there is no pressure for change. The key insight into understanding aggregate supply behavior is the concept of the **equilibrium real wage rate**, which is determined by the intersection of labor demand and supply curves. In Figure 7-7 we have copied our previous labor demand curve (N_0^d), which shows the marginal product of additional labor input.

The supply of labor is also assumed to depend on the real wage, and in Figure 7-7 labor supply is represented by a labor supply curve that slopes upward. This indicates that a higher real wage rate would induce a higher quantity of labor supplied. For instance, a higher real wage rate might induce homemakers to take outside jobs by increasing their willingness to put up with the inconvenience of commuting and arranging day care for their children. A higher real wage rate might also make people more willing to moonlight, sacrificing leisure and sleep to take second jobs.

The position of the labor supply curve can shift if anything occurs that makes people more or less willing to take jobs at a given real wage rate. For instance, an increase in the working-age population, due to immigration or a high birth rate, will tend to shift the labor supply curve to the right. Factors that make jobs less attractive—for instance, the availability of generous unemployment or

The **equilibrium real wage rate** is the real wage rate for the point at which the labor supply and demand curves intersect, so there is no pressure for change in the real wage.

Figure 7-7 Determination of the Equilibrium Real Wage Rate

Here the labor demand curve (N_0^d) is the same as in Figures 7-5 and 7-6. But now we add a labor supply curve (N_0^s). This slopes upward, indicating that more people will be willing to take jobs at a higher real wage rate. Whenever an event pushes the economy away from point B, there is pressure for the real wage rate to change, as shown by the arrows.

welfare benefits for those not working—will tend to shift the labor supply curve to the left.

The equilibrium real wage rate is simply the real wage rate located where the labor demand curve crosses the labor supply curve. Such an intersection occurs at point B in Figure 7-7, with an equilibrium level of employment (N_0) and an equilibrium real wage (W_0/P_0). The diagram poses a dilemma for firms, however. If firms are to raise employment from N_0 to N_1, the real wage rate must be reduced, as shown at point C. But point C does not lie on the labor supply curve.

Employers need to find some factor that will make workers willing to provide more work than shown by their labor supply curve. Otherwise, we would never observe changes in employment, nor changes in real GDP, over the business cycle.

Labor contracts and wage bargaining. Labor contracts are one factor that would explain the fixity of the nominal wage in the short run. Labor unions negotiate contracts with business firms, and often these contracts set the wage rate for as long as three years, or even longer. Unions and firms agree to such contracts as a way of minimizing time spent on negotiating, arguing, and to reduce the disruption caused by strikes that may occur when the two sides to the wage negotiation fail to agree. Many workers do not belong to labor unions but have their wages or salaries set for one year at a time. For instance, most college professors earn a fixed salary during the academic year from September to August of the next year, and sometime in the spring they learn what their salary increase will be for the following academic year.

When the economy operates with an employment and output level above the levels of N_0 and Y_0 that are consistent with labor-market equilibrium, firms and workers know that the real wage is reduced below the equilibrium amount W_0/P_0 only temporarily. When the next wage change occurs, perhaps a year or even three years later, there will be upward pressure on the nominal wage rate to restore the equilibrium real wage rate. Similarly, in periods of weak aggregate demand when the economy is operating below the equilibrium levels of employment and output (N_0 and Y_0), the real wage is temporarily above the equilibrium amount W_0/P_0, and there will be downward pressure on the nominal wage rate to restore the equilibrium real wage rate.

7-7 Fiscal and Monetary Expansion in the Short and Long Run

In Chapter 4 we examined the effect of a fiscal stimulus, assuming that the price level was fixed, and we found that the fiscal stimulus normally raised real output. Now we learn that the fiscal stimulus causes both output and the price level to increase in the short run, but in the long run only increases the price level without increasing output.

In Figure 7-8, we begin in equilibrium at point B, with an actual price level equal to P_0. This is exactly the same as point B in Figures 7-5 and 7-6.

Initial Short-Run Effect of a Fiscal Expansion

Now a fiscal stimulus is introduced, in the form of an increase in government purchases that shifts the aggregate demand curve rightward from AD_0 to AD_1.

7-7 Fiscal and Monetary Expansion in the Short and Long Run 211

A Fiscal Expansion Raises Both the Price Level and Real GDP in the Short Run

Figure 7-8 Effects on the Price Level and Real Income of an Increase in Planned Autonomous Spending from AD_0 to AD_1

Higher planned autonomous spending shifts the economy's equilibrium position from the initial point B to point C, where both the price level and the real output have increased. Point C is not a sustainable position, however, because the real wage rate has fallen below the equilibrium real wage rate. Only at point E_3 does the actual real wage rate return to its initial equilibrium value.

Where do we find the new equilibrium levels of output and the price index? If the price level were to remain constant, we would move straight to the right from point B to point L. But the price level cannot remain fixed, because firms will insist on an increase in the price level in order to reduce the real wage and induce an increase in employment sufficient to raise the level of real GDP. In short, point L is not a point at which firms will be willing to produce.

Point C is at the intersection of the new AD_1 schedule and the SAS_0 schedule. The increase in government purchases has simultaneously raised the price level to P_1 and increased output to Y_1. This shift has occurred because higher aggregate demand has raised prices, stimulating business firms to produce more, at least as long as the wage rate fails to adjust.

Note that output has not increased by the full Chapter 4 multiplier based on a fixed price level, the horizontal distance between B and L. Instead, point C lies northwest of the constant price point L, because the higher price level at C reduces the real money supply and hence the demand for commodities. The situation illustrated in Figure 7-8 at point C would result from any stimulative factor that raises aggregate demand—not only an increase in government purchases, but also cuts in tax rates or increases in transfer payments, business and consumer confidence, net exports, or the money supply. As long as the SAS curve slopes upward to the right, any of these changes will shift the AD curve rightward and simultaneously raise both output and prices to point C.

The Rising Nominal Wage Rate and the Arrival at Long-Run Equilibrium

Point C is not the end of the adjustment of the economy to the higher level of government purchases. Business firms are satisfied but workers are not because the price level has risen from P_0 to P_1, while the nominal wage rate is still stuck at W_0. The real wage rate has decreased to W_0/P_1.

Each *SAS* curve assumes that the nominal wage rate is fixed at a particular value, which is W_0 for the supply curve SAS_0. Once workers learn that the actual price level has risen, they will discover to their dismay that the real wage rate has fallen. To achieve a return of their real wage to the original level, at the next round of wage bargaining, workers will insist on an increase in the nominal wage rate to W_1. Just as in Figure 7-6, the new aggregate supply schedule SAS_1 shows the consequences of an increase in the nominal wage rate from W_0 to W_1.

Clearly the economy now moves to point D, with a higher price level P_2. But at point D workers are upset once again. The real wage rate is W_1/P_2, lower than the equilibrium real wage rate. Again they insist on an increase in the nominal wage rate. Eventually the economy must slide up the AD_1 line to point E_3. Why? Because only at the initial level of real GDP (Y_0) and employment (N_0) is the real wage rate at its equilibrium value (W_0/P_0). Any time the economy is operating in the area to the right of Y_0, there is upward pressure on the nominal wage rate, and *SAS* will shift up.

The Long-Run Aggregate Supply Curve

The vertical line rising above the original real GDP level (Y_0) is called the long-run aggregate supply (*LAS*) curve. Only at this one level of output, also called natural real GDP (Y^N), is the labor market in equilibrium at the original real wage (W_0/P_0). This is the only level of output where there is no pressure for change in the real wage, since this is the only level of output (and employment) where business firms are willing to produce and where workers are content with the real wage rate. This point of equilibrium in the labor market is where the labor supply and demand curves cross (in Figure 7-7). *Thus, only at the natural level of real GDP (Y^N) is the actual real wage rate equal to the equilibrium real wage rate.* The vertical *LAS* line shows all the possible combinations of the price level (P) and natural real GDP (Y^N). It was initially defined on p. 198.

Short-Run and Long-Run Equilibrium

Short-run equilibrium occurs at the point where the aggregate demand curve crosses the short-run aggregate supply curve.

The economy is in **short-run equilibrium** when two conditions are satisfied. First, the level of output produced must be enough to balance the demand for commodities. This first condition is satisfied at any point along the appropriate *AD* curve. Second, the price level *P* must be sufficient to make firms both able and willing to produce the level of output specified along the *AD* curve. This can happen only along a short-run supply (*SAS*) curve specified for a particular nominal wage rate (W_0).

Long-run equilibrium is a situation in which labor input is the amount voluntarily supplied and demanded at the equilibrium real wage rate.

The economy is in **long-run equilibrium** only when all the conditions for a short-run equilibrium are satisfied, and, in addition, the real wage rate is at its equilibrium value. In Figure 7-8, long-run equilibrium occurs only where all three schedules—*AD*, *SAS*, and *LAS*—intersect. The reason why the economy does not move immediately to its new long-run equilibrium following an *AD*

Summary of the Economy's Adjustment to an Increase in Aggregate Demand

Is the Economy in Short-Run (SR) or Long-Run (LR) Equilibrium in Figure 7-8 on p. 211?

Point	AD curve, initial or new?	Price level	Wage level	Output level	In SR or LR equilibrium?
B	Initial	P_0	W_0	Y^N	SR, LR
C	New	P_1	W_0	Y_1	SR
D	New	P_2	W_1	Above Y^N, Below Y_1	SR
E_3	New	P_3	W_3	Y^N	SR, LR

shift is that adjustment takes time and there are time lags in the response of wages and prices.

Self-Test

If the economy is to remain in long-run equilibrium, what must happen to the price level, the wage level, and the level of real GDP when the following events occur?

1. An increase in government-financed highway construction.
2. An increase in Japanese GDP that boosts U.S. net exports.
3. An increase in the U.S. money supply.
4. An increase in productivity caused by more use of computers (while the money supply is constant).

Interpretations of the Business Cycle

The preceding theory of price and output adjustment relies on an asymmetry between price and wage adjustment. In the short run, prices are flexible while the nominal wage rate is fixed. A realistic explanation of this asymmetry is that the nominal wage or salary for many types of jobs is changed only infrequently, sometimes only once per year, and in labor union contracts not for three years or more. The assumed short-run fixity of the nominal wage rate together with the flexibility of the price level implies a **countercyclical** movement of the real wage; that is, a movement in the real wage in the opposite direction from the movement in real GDP. However, statistical studies of data for the United States do not show a strong or consistent countercyclical movement of the real wage. In reality, movements in the real wage are relatively minor compared to the volatile movements of real GDP over the business cycle (see Figure 3-1 on p. 58).

An alternative view of the theory is that *both* prices and wages are fixed in the short run, and that the *SAS* curve is relatively flat. Just as the nominal wage rate is set by labor contracts and customs that alter wages only infrequently, so many prices remain the same for long periods of time. Prices for many products are set in advance, including prices on restaurant menus and in mail-order catalogs. Firms buy supplies at prices that are fixed for long periods of time. We return to theories of wage and price rigidity in Chapter 17. There we will learn that there are good reasons for both prices and wages to adjust only slowly over time. When real GDP rises above equilibrium (or natural) real GDP, a process is set in motion that causes *both* prices and wages to rise, and

*A **countercyclical variable** moves over the business cycle in the opposite direction from real GDP.*

there is inflationary pressure until the economy returns to a point along the *LAS* curve like point E_3 in Figure 7-8.

7-8 Classical Macroeconomics: The Quantity Theory of Money and the Self-Correcting Economy

The classical economists who predated Keynes's *General Theory*, including Adam Smith, David Ricardo, John Stuart Mill, Alfred Marshall, and Arthur C. Pigou, believed that the economy possessed powerful **self-correcting forces** that guaranteed full employment and prevented actual real GDP (Y) from falling below natural real GDP (Y^N) for more than a short time. These forces consisted of flexible wages and prices, which would adjust rapidly to absorb the impact of shifts in aggregate demand. Because the classical economists did not believe that business cycles in real output or in unemployment were problems, they saw no need for the government to engage in stabilization policy.

> The economy's **self-correcting forces** refer to the role of flexible prices in stabilizing real GDP under some conditions.

The Quantity Equation and the Quantity Theory of Money

The most important macroeconomic model developed by classical economists is the famous "quantity equation," relating the nominal money supply (M^s) and velocity (V) to the price level (P) and real GDP (Y).

$$M^s V \equiv PY \tag{7.2}$$

The quantity equation is true by definition, simply because velocity is *defined* as $V \equiv PY/M^s$.

To convert the quantity equation into a theory, classical economists assumed that any change in M^s or V on the left-hand side of the equation would be balanced by a proportional change in P on the right-hand side of the equation, with no change in real GDP (Y). Primary emphasis in this theory, called the **quantity theory of money**, was placed on the idea that changes in the money supply (M^s) cause proportional changes in the price level P. Why did the theory focus on M^s rather than V? Velocity (V) was regarded as being relatively stable and primarily determined by changes in payment methods (for instance, cash versus checks) that gradually evolved over time. Over shorter periods of two to five years, business cycles were attributed mainly to changes in the money supply.

> The **quantity theory of money** holds that actual output tends to grow steadily, while velocity is determined by payment practices such as the use of cash versus checks; as a result, a change in the money supply mainly affects the price level and has little or no effect on velocity or output.

Any theory can be analyzed in terms of the quantity equation (7.2). For instance, the *IS-LM* model of Chapter 4 examines the effect of a change in government spending, which causes a shift in the *IS* curve but not in the *LM* curve, reflecting the assumption that changes in government spending do not change the money supply. Since both M^s and P are fixed, higher government spending raises V on the left-hand side of equation (7.2) and raises Y on the right-hand side. In this sense, the analysis of shifts in planned spending in the fixed-price *IS-LM* model is the opposite of the quantity theory, linking changes of V to changes in Y, unlike the quantity theory that links changes in M^s to changes in P.

Self-Correction in the Aggregate Demand-Supply Model

The approach of the old classicists, whose analytical model primarily relied on the quantity theory of money, can be translated into the aggregate demand and

Figure 7-9 Effect of a Decline in Planned Spending When the Price Level Is Perfectly Flexible

A Business Cycle in Prices, Not in Real GDP or Unemployment

The economy never moves far from the LAS line

The classical economists assumed that the price level would decline whenever a drop in aggregate demand occurred. Starting from point E_0, a drop in planned spending would shift the AD curve from AD_0 to AD_1 and move the economy straight down to point E_1. The level of real GDP remains at Y^N, because the lower price level raises the level of real balances (M_0^s/P) by exactly enough to offset the decline in planned spending. A shift back to AD_0 would raise the price level and return the economy to the original position E_0.

supply model developed in this chapter. Figure 7-9 has the same elements as Figure 7-8 but lacks a short-run aggregate supply (SAS) curve.

The classical economists assumed that the economy would not operate away from the long-run aggregate supply curve (LAS). For instance, if a decline in demand caused the AD curve to shift downward from AD_0 to AD_1 in Figure 7-9, the classical economists would predict that the economy would move from the initial point E_0 to the new point E_1 with only a brief interval (shown by the curved arrow on the left) during which actual real GDP would decline below natural real GDP. The price level would fall from its initial level at P_0 to the new level P_1.

The classical economists took the same view of the economy's behavior in response to an increase in aggregate demand. With Y above Y^N, firms would raise nominal wage rates and prices. Wage and price increases would continue until production fell back to the Y^N level.

Because the downward and upward movement of the economy from E_0 to E_1 and back again would not involve any significant movement of real GDP (Y) away from natural real GDP (Y^N), *no business cycle in real GDP would occur*. Yet there would be a business cycle in the price level, from P_0 down to P_1 and back to P_0, and it was this movement in the price level that the classical economists attempted to explain in their early theories of the business cycle. However, classical economists did not view price movements as sufficiently undesirable to warrant the intervention of government monetary or fiscal policy.

Classical View of Unemployment and Output Fluctuations

We have seen that classical economists did not believe that real GDP could remain for more than a short period below natural real GDP (Y^N). How, then, did they explain the unemployment that occurs in real-world modern economies when people are laid off and production is cut back? Jobless individuals were sometimes written off as irresponsible, having an insufficient desire to work. Any normal person would be compelled by hunger to seek work, some classical economists thought. And most believed that if there were not enough jobs to go around, competition among workers would reduce the real wage rate until an equilibrium was obtained in the labor market.

Although some journalists and a few isolated economists (including Karl Marx and Friedrich Engels) began to suggest that unemployment was an inevitable by-product of the newly emerging industrial society of England in the mid-nineteenth century, most classical economists dismissed unemployment as a transitory, self-correcting condition of only minor social importance. In fact, the term *unemployment* did not exist until the early twentieth century.

Ironically, some governments outside the United States developed unemployment insurance before classical economists were willing to recognize the existence of prolonged unemployment. The world's first unemployment insurance system was introduced in the United Kingdom by Winston Churchill in 1911; only afterward, in 1913, was the first important book by a classical economist (Arthur C. Pigou) written on the subject of unemployment.[4] The book attributed such unemployment as existed to the failure of wages to adjust fast enough to maintain equilibrium in the labor market. Suggested cures for unemployment involved remedies for wage stickiness rather than any suggestion that there was a role for the government to intervene and stimulate aggregate demand through expansionary monetary or fiscal policy.

7-9 The Keynesian Revolution: The Failure of Self-Correction

The Great Depression began with the stock market crash in late 1929 and by 1932 real GDP had declined by one-third and unemployment had spiraled upward beyond 20 percent. Classical economists were caught flat-footed, without any explanation for the severe and prolonged unemployment beyond the claim that for some reason real wages were too high. Economics had lost its intellectual moorings, and it was time for a new diagnosis. In this atmosphere, it was perhaps not surprising that the 1936 publication of Keynes's *The General Theory of Employment, Interest, and Money* was eagerly awaited. Its publication transformed macroeconomics, and only one year later John R. Hicks published an article in which he set out the *IS-LM* model of Chapter 4 as an interpretation of what Keynes had written.

Monetary Impotence and the Failure of Self-Correction in Extreme Cases

We can use the aggregate demand and supply curves to illustrate Keynes's analysis of the high unemployment that bedeviled the world's economy in the 1930s. For Keynes, the economic problem could be divided into two categories: one concerning demand and one concerning supply. The demand problem was the possibility of **monetary impotence**, while the supply problem was that of **rigid wages**.

John Maynard Keynes (1883–1946)

His *The General Theory of Employment, Interest, and Money* (1936) is one of the most influential works in economics in the twentieth century.

Monetary impotence is the failure of real GDP to respond to an increase in the real money supply.

Rigid wages refers to the failure of the nominal wage rate to adjust by the amount needed to maintain equilibrium in the labor market.

---
[4] This was Arthur C. Pigou's *Unemployment*. The description of the views of the classical economists in this section is taken from the much more detailed and fully documented treatment in John A. Garraty, *Unemployment in History: Economic Thought and Public Policy* (New York: Harper & Row, 1978), pp. 70–145.

Figure 7-10 The Lack of Effect of a Drop in the Price Level When There Is a Failure of Self-Correction

The conditions of a failure of self-correction are either (1) a vertical IS curve that lies to the left of Y^N, or (2) a normal IS curve that intersects a horizontal LM curve to the left of Y^N. With a failure of self-correction, the aggregate demand schedule is a vertical line like AD', in contrast to the normally sloped AD_0 curve. Because of a failure of self-correction, the higher real money supply is unable to stimulate the economy; thus, a decline in the price level just moves the economy down from F to F' to F''.

Unresponsive expenditures: The vertical IS curve. As we learned in Section 4-9 on pp. 111–14, increases in the real money supply (M^s/P) can have either strong or weak effects, depending on the shapes of the IS and LM curves. One case of monetary impotence occurs when the IS curve is vertical. Any change in the nominal money supply shifts the LM curve up and down along the vertical IS curve, leaving real GDP unaffected. Just as important, any decline in the price level (P) that raises the real money supply (M^s/P) leaves real GDP unaffected.

We examined a vertical IS curve in Figure 4-7; now, in Figure 7-10, we observe its implications for the aggregate demand curve. If IS is vertical at an income level like Y', then a decline in P has no power to raise real GDP above Y', so the aggregate demand curve is the vertical line AD' in Figure 7-10. Shown for contrast in Figure 7-10 is a normally sloped AD_0 curve, copied from Figure 7-8.

The liquidity trap: A horizontal LM curve. The same problem of a vertical AD' curve may occur if there is a horizontal LM curve and *if the* IS *curve intersects this horizontal* LM *curve to the left of* Y^N (a nearly horizontal LM curve was illustrated in the bottom frame of Figure 4-8). In this case, an increase in M^s/P does not shift the LM curve down. Real GDP is stuck at, for example, point Y', where the horizontal LM curve crosses the normally sloped IS curve. Again, the aggregate demand curve is vertical, as in Figure 7-10.

Monetary impotence and a failure of self-correction arise when there is a vertical IS or horizontal LM curve.[5] In either case, the classical cure-all of deflation cannot remedy a cyclical recession or depression. In Figure 7-10, the price

---

[5] A more precise definition of the conditions necessary for monetary impotence and a failure of self-correction is as follows: There must be (1) no effect of a change in M^s/P on the IS curve, and (2) the interest rate along the IS curve, where actual real GDP equals natural real GDP (Y^N) and that we can call r^N, lies below the minimum attainable interest rate along the LM curve, which we can call r_{min}. When the LM curve is not horizontal, r_{min} is zero, and condition 2 is satisfied whenever r^N is negative or whenever IS is vertical and lies left of Y^N (as in the top frame of Figure 4-8). When there is a liquidity trap, the LM curve is horizontal at the level of r_{min} and condition 2 is satisfied even with a normally sloped IS curve, as long as r^N is less than r_{min}.

level can fall continuously, from P_0 to P' to P'', yet real GDP remains stuck at Y'. The economy just moves downward vertically from point F to F' to F'', without any rightward motion.

Fiscal Policy and the Real Balance Effect

The crucial problem that makes the AD' curve in Figure 7-10 lie to the left of natural real GDP (Y^N) is low business and consumer confidence. How can confidence be revived? All problems disappear if planned spending can be raised far enough to make the IS curve intersect LM at or to the right of Y^N. For this reason, Keynes believed that fiscal policy, which can shift the IS curve, is the obvious antidepression tool to use.

In theory, however, government action may not be necessary. A. C. Pigou originally pointed out that the Keynesian dilemma illustrated by the vertical AD' curve in Figure 7-10 may not be a dilemma at all. Why? The demand for commodities may depend directly on the level of real money balances (M^s/P). This would make the IS curve shift rightward whenever P falls, thus raising M^s/P and *guaranteeing a negative slope for the* AD *curve*. The **Pigou Effect** or **real balance effect** occurs when an increase in M^s/P influences the demand for commodities *directly*, without requiring a reduction in interest rates. With the real balance effect, the AD curve is *always* negatively sloped, like AD_0, and a price deflation can achieve any desired real GDP level if prices fall far enough. The AD curve *cannot be vertical* in the presence of a real balance effect.

The **Pigou** or **real balance Effect** is the direct stimulus to aggregate demand caused by an increase in the real money supply and does not require a decline in the interest rate.

Why is the real balance effect so powerful when the price level is flexible? Imagine yourself owning only a $10 bill. You would not be able to consider purchasing a $70,000 Mercedes. But there is some price level at which your money would have more impressive buying power. If the price index were to decline from 1.0 to 0.0001, the price of the Mercedes would fall from $70,000 to $7.00, and your $10 would be more than ample to buy the Mercedes, leaving $3.00 in change! Although the numbers in this illustration are extreme, they forcefully illustrate the logic of the real balance effect. A fixed nominal amount of money buys more when the price level falls, so that individuals are bound to find some portion of their previous money balances excessive and to spend more on real commodities.

When the price level is perfectly flexible and the real balance effect is in operation, no monetary or fiscal policy is necessary. The Federal Reserve governors and the President's Council of Economic Advisers can "go fishing," confident that the AD curve crosses the LAS curve, as in Figure 7-8.

We have now identified two stimulative effects of price deflation:

The **Keynes Effect** is the stimulus to aggregate demand caused by a decline in the interest rate.

1. The **Keynes Effect** is the stimulus to aggregate demand (both consumption and investment) due to a decline in the interest rate, which in turn is brought about by an increase in the nominal money supply (M^s) or decrease in the price level (P), both of which increase the real money supply (M^s/P). It is the Keynes Effect that can be thwarted by a vertical AD curve as in Figure 7-10.

2. The Pigou (or real balance) Effect is the direct stimulus to consumption spending that occurs when a price deflation causes an increase in the real money supply; this stimulus does not require a reduction in the interest rate. The Pigou Effect guarantees that the AD curve cannot be vertical.

Destabilizing effects of falling prices. Unfortunately, the stimulative effects of price deflation are not always favorable, even when the Pigou or real balance Effect is in operation. There are two major unfavorable effects of deflation:

1. The **expectations effect**. When people expect prices to continue to fall, they tend to postpone purchases as much as possible to take advantage of lower prices in the future. This decline in the demand for commodities may be strong enough to offset the stimulus of the Pigou Effect.

2. The **redistribution effect** may be more important than the expectations effect. An unexpected deflation causes a redistribution of income from debtors to creditors. Why? Debt repayments are usually fixed in dollar value so that a uniform deflation in all prices, which was not expected when the debts were incurred, causes an increase in the real value of mortgage and installment repayments from debtors to creditors (banks and, ultimately, savers).[6] This redistribution reduces aggregate demand, since creditors tend to spend only a relatively small share of their added income, while debtors have nothing to fall back on and are forced to reduce their consumption to meet their higher real interest payments.

> The **expectations effect** is the decline in aggregate demand caused by the postponement of purchases when consumers expect prices to decline in the future.
>
> The **redistribution effect** is the decline in aggregate demand caused by the effect of falling prices in redistributing income from high-spending debtors to low-spending savers.

During the Great Depression deflation of 1929–33, for instance, the GDP price deflator declined by 24 percent. Yet the interest income of creditors hardly fell at all, from $4.7 to $4.1 billion (current dollars). Farmers were hit worst by falling prices—their current-dollar income fell by two-thirds, from $6.2 to $2.6 billion—and many lost their farms through foreclosures as a result of this heavy debt burden. Although many factors were at work in the collapse of real autonomous spending during the Great Depression, it appears that the negative expectations and redistribution effects of the 1929–33 deflation may have dominated the stimulative Keynes and Pigou Effects. The box looks further into the puzzle of why the Great Depression was worse in the United States than in other nations.

The expectations and redistribution effects are not just ancient fossils relevant only to the 1930s. In the early and mid-1980s, falling prices of farm products, farmland, and oil reduced the income of farmers, oil producers, and employees of farms and oil companies. Many of these people were severely hurt by falling prices, especially because in the 1970s some (especially farmers) had incurred a heavy burden of debt to buy high-priced farmland.

Self-Test

Not only do falling prices and a depressed economy affect aggregate demand, but so do rising prices and prosperity.

1. Explain whether the Pigou (real balance) Effect stabilizes or destabilizes the economy when aggregate demand is high.
2. How does this effect occur?
3. Similarly, explain whether the expectations and redistribution effects stabilize or destabilize the economy when prices are rising.
4. Describe how these effects occur.

---

[6] A concise discussion of the consequences of these effects on the economy's self-correcting mechanism is contained in James Tobin, "Keynesian Models of Recession and Depression," *American Economic Review* (May 1975), pp. 195–202. See also Axel Leijonhufvud, *On Keynesian Economics and the Economics of Keynes* (New York: Oxford University Press, 1968), pp. 315–31.

Nominal Wage Rigidity

Keynes attacked the classical economists on two fronts. As we have seen, his first line of attack was the possibility of a vertical AD' line that fails to intersect the LAS line, creating monetary impotence and a failure of self-correction. His second line of attack was simply that deflation would not occur in the necessary amount because of rigid nominal wages. And if little or no deflation occurred, *the debate about the relative potency of the Keynes, Pigou, expectations, and distribution effects would become irrelevant.*

Figure 7-11 shows the effects of rigid nominal wages. In the right-hand frame the two aggregate demand curves, AD_0 and AD_1, are copied from Figure 7-9. They have the normal negative slopes. AD_1 lies to the left of AD_0 because consumer and business pessimism lowers the assumed amount of planned spending. The short-run aggregate supply curve SAS_0 is fixed in position by the fixed nominal wage rate (W_0). Starting at point E_0, the leftward shift in aggregate demand moves the economy to point A, where the new AD_1 curve intersects the aggregate supply curve SAS_0.

Keynes pointed out that the economy would remain stuck at point A even with the normally sloped aggregate demand curve AD_1. Why? If the nominal wage is completely rigid and never changes from the value W_0, then the supply

Unemployment in the Original Keynesian Model

Figure 7-11 Effect of a Decline in Planned Spending When the Nominal Rate Is Fixed at W_0

The short-run aggregate supply curve SAS_0 in the right frame is fixed in position by the assumption of a rigid nominal wage rate, W_0. The decline in planned spending shifts the aggregate demand curve in the right frame leftward from AD_0 to AD_1, and the economy moves southwest from point E_0 to point A. In the left frame, the reduction in the price level raises the real wage from the original W_0/P_0 to the new W_0/P_2, and the economy moves from point E_0 to point A. Unemployment is represented by the distance between N_2 and N_0.

curve is fixed as well at the position SAS_0. The price level would not fall below P_2. Hence the economy would not move from point A to point E_1, as required in the analysis of the classical economists.

Failure to attain equilibrium in the labor market. Keynes's assumption of a rigid *nominal* wage differs from the description of the economy's adjustment toward long-run equilibrium in Sections 7-6 and 7-7, which assumed that there is an equilibrium *real* wage rate that equates demand and supply in the labor market.

Keynes's assumption of nominal wage rigidity fails to explain how or why the wage remains rigid. Its only virtue is that it provides an explanation of **persistent unemployment**, as at point A in the left frame of Figure 7-11, without requiring any special shape for the aggregate demand curve. But the arbitrariness of the assumption raises three important questions that will concern us in the next section as well as in Chapter 17.

1. Is the nominal wage rigidity assumption realistic? Did the aggregate supply curve in the Great Depression remain at a fixed position like SAS_0, or did it steadily shift downward and bring the economy to long-run equilibrium, as the classical economists would have predicted?

2. Is it possible to devise a convincing theory of business cycles without relying on either a vertical *AD* curve or rigid nominal wages? The Keynesian rigid nominal wage "story" raises a basic puzzle: Why do markets "fail to clear"? That is, why does the economy not operate continuously at the intersection of the labor supply and demand curves? Several prominent economists, particularly Milton Friedman, Robert Lucas, and Edward Prescott, have attempted to revive classical economics in a way that is consistent with observed business cycles yet allows for **market-clearing**, in contrast to the Keynesian tradition of **non–market-clearing**. We turn to these models in Chapter 17.

3. How do labor unions and current practices of wage negotiation relate to the Keynesian assumption of wage rigidity? Do they justify his assumption of non–market-clearing and support his explanation of persistent unemployment? This question is addressed in Chapter 17.

Persistent unemployment is a situation in which a high level of unemployment can last for many years, as in the United States from 1929 to 1941 and from 1980 to 1985.

A **market-clearing model** or theory holds that the economy is always in equilibrium at the intersection of the supply and demand curves, particularly in the labor market.

A **non–market-clearing model** holds that the economy can be pushed off its supply and demand curves in the labor market and sometimes in other markets.

7-10 Case Study

What Caused the Great Depression?

This case study investigates several important aspects of the Great Depression years of 1929 to 1941. Three topics are given primary emphasis. First, why was aggregate demand so low? Is there evidence to support monetary impotence or a failure of self-correction? Second, did the economy's aggregate supply curve shift downward to provide self-correction, or did it remain stationary as it does in the right-hand frame of Figure 7-11 when the nominal wage is rigid? Third, was the nominal wage rigid, and did real wages fluctuate countercyclically?

Table 7-1 exhibits several important features of the period between 1929 and 1941. This twelve-year period is distinguished most by the unemployment figures shown in column 7, especially by the extraordinarily high level reached by the unemployment rate (25.2 percent in 1933), and the long duration of high unemployment (ten straight years from 1931–40 with unemployment above 10 percent). An obvious puzzle is why the economy was so weak, especially between 1934 and 1939. In 1939, *the real money supply* (column 2) *was 48 percent higher than in 1929*. Yet in 1939 real GDP (column 3) *was only 10 percent higher than in 1929*. In 1939 the unemployment rate was still 17.2 percent.

Explanations of Weak Aggregate Demand

The Keynesian interpretation that the *IS* curve shifted far to the left is supported in Table 7-1 by column 4, which shows the collapse of real fixed investment from $14.9 billion in 1929 prices in 1929 to $3.9 billion in 1933, *a decline of 74 percent*. Also shown is the incomplete recovery of real fixed investment, with a value in 1939 that was still 27 percent below the 1929 level. The failure of investment to recover fully to the 1929 level, despite a 53 percent increase in the real money supply since 1929, is consistent with either a vertical *IS* curve or a horizontal *LM* curve. Which diagnosis is more realistic?

For the *IS* curve to be vertical, a decline in the interest rate must fail to stimulate autonomous planned spending, which chiefly consists of fixed investment. As shown in Table 7-1, the interest rate declined substantially from 1934 to 1941, and yet real fixed investment in 1939 and 1940, was still below its 1929 level.

For the *LM* curve to be horizontal, an increase in the real money supply must fail to reduce the interest rate. Yet the long-term interest rate fell fairly steadily from 3.7 percent in 1932 to 2.0 percent in 1941. Thus the observations between 1934 and 1941 seem consistent with the hypothesis that the demand for money depends inversely on the interest rate. There is no sign that the interest rate hit a minimum level at any time during the latter half of the Great Depression decade.

What pushed the *IS* curve to the left? There was a sharp decline in both consumption and investment spending from 1929 to 1930. Part of the decline in consumption reflects the working of the multiplier, as induced consumption fell in response to a decline in autonomous planned spending. Autonomous consumption contributed to this decline in planned spending, as the crash of the U.S. stock market in October 1929 wiped out a significant proportion of the wealth of households. A decline in real wealth works the same way as the real balance effect introduced in this chapter on p. 218; higher real wealth raises autonomous consumption and lower real wealth as in 1929–30 reduces autonomous consumption.

The collapse of fixed investment documented in Table 7-1 reflects in part a hangover from excessive investment in the 1920s, particularly of residential and nonresidential structures. Excessive optimism created too much construction, much like the investment boom of the late 1990s, which endowed the economy with an excess supply of high-tech and telecommunications equipment. The weakness of investment throughout the 1930s reflected the influence of overbuilding in the 1920s—why should firms build new factories and office buildings when their existing factories and office buildings were half vacant?[7]

---

[7] See Robert J. Gordon and James A. Wilcox, "Monetarist Interpretations of the Great Depression: An Evaluation and Critique," in Karl Brunner, ed., *Contemporary Views of the Great Depression* (Hingham, MA: Martinus Nijhoff, 1981), pp. 49–107.

Table 7-1 Money, Output, Unemployment, Prices, and Wages in the Great Depression, 1929–41

Year	Money supply ($ billions)	Real money supply ($ billions, 1929 prices)	Real GDP ($ billions, 1929 prices)	Real fixed investment ($ billions, 1929 prices)	Output ratio (Y/Y^N) (percent)	GDP deflator (1929=100)	Unemployment rate (percent)	Long-term interest rate	Average hourly earnings (dollars)	Average real hourly earnings (1929 dollars)
	(1)	(2)	(3)	(4)	(5)	(6)	(7)	(8)	(9)	(10)
1929	26.0	26.0	103.7	14.9	102.8	100.0	3.2	3.6	.563	.563
1930	25.2	26.1	94.8	11.4	90.8	96.3	8.9	3.3	.560	.581
1931	23.5	26.7	88.7	8.0	82.1	86.3	16.3	3.3	.532	.605
1932	20.6	25.5	77.2	4.5	69.0	76.2	24.1	3.7	.485	.600
1933	19.4	24.4	76.1	3.9	65.7	74.1	25.2	3.3	.457	.575
1934	21.4	26.0	84.3	5.2	70.4	78.3	22.0	3.1	.512	.623
1935	25.3	30.4	91.9	6.7	74.1	79.8	20.3	2.8	.524	.630
1936	28.8	34.4	103.7	8.9	80.8	80.7	17.0	2.7	.534	.637
1937	30.2	35.0	109.2	11.0	82.2	84.2	14.3	2.7	.566	.656
1938	29.8	35.3	105.4	9.1	76.7	81.7	19.1	2.6	.576	.681
1939	33.4	39.8	114.0	10.9	80.1	80.7	17.2	2.4	.583	.695
1940	38.8	45.8	123.7	13.2	84.0	81.9	14.6	2.2	.597	.705
1941	45.4	51.1	144.9	15.5	95.0	87.4	9.9	2.0	.655	.737

Sources: See Appendix A. The interest rate is series B-72 in *Long-Term Economic Growth* (U.S. Department of Commerce, 1970). Average hourly earnings are from Martin N. Baily, "The Labor Market in the 1930s," in James Tobin, ed., *Macroeconomics, Prices, and Quantities* (Brookings Institution, 1983), Table 1, p. 23.

The role of domestic and international monetary policy. In 1927–29 the Fed pursued a restrictive monetary policy in order to cool down the stock market boom as well as the overheated construction boom. Further, the Fed's policy tightening was transmitted to foreign countries, causing an even more drastic tightening of monetary policy in those countries. As other countries fell into recession and depression, their demand for U.S. exports declined, amplifying the declines in autonomous consumption and planned investment. Starting in 1930, banks began to fail (closing their doors without enough money in the vaults to redeem deposits), and households lost their life savings.[8] After the middle of 1931, most economists agree that the primary cause of the severity of the Great Depression was restrictive monetary policy; the

---

[8] The classic account stressing bank failures, the collapse of the money supply, and Federal Reserve policy errors as the root causes of the Great Depression is Milton Friedman and Anna J. Schwartz, *A Monetary History of the United States, 1867–1960* (Princeton University Press for NBER, 1963), Chapter 7. A more recent account that emphasizes international factors is Barry Eichengreen, *Golden Fetters: The Gold Standard and the Great Depression, 1919–1939* (New York: Oxford University Press, 1992). Other assessments of the role of monetary and nonmonetary factors are Barry Eichengreen, "The Origins and Nature of the Great Slump Revisited," *Economic History Review*, vol. 45, no. 2 (May 1992), pp. 213–39, and Christina D. Romer, "The Nation in Depression," *The Journal of Economic Perspectives*, vol. 7, no. 2 (Spring 1993), pp. 19–39.

International Perspective

Why Was the Great Depression Worse in the United States than in Europe?

The text reviews the basic causes of the Great Depression, which combined a downward shift in planned investment in response to excessive building during the 1920s with a downward shift in autonomous consumption following the stock market crash of October 1929. Augmenting these demand shocks that pushed the *IS* curve leftward was a decline in exports, due both to trade restrictions (tariffs and quotas) levied by each nation against their trading partners, and also due to declining foreign demand for exports as foreign central banks tightened monetary policy. The leftward *IS* shifts were greatly exacerbated by the perversely restrictive monetary policy pursued by the Fed, which allowed thousands of banks to fail and allowed the nominal money supply to decline by 25 percent between 1929 and 1933.

The figure shows the evolution of real GDP per person between 1920 and 1941 in the United States compared with Germany, Japan, and the United Kingdom. Real GDP per person is expressed as a percent of the 1929 value in each country. Thus, in 1933 real GDP per person had fallen to 70 percent of the 1929 value in the United States, in contrast to 86 percent in Germany, and 94 percent in both the United Kingdom and Japan. Other countries exceeded their 1929 value by 1934 in the case of the United Kingdom and Japan and by 1935 for Germany. In contrast, the United States just barely equaled the 1929 value by 1937, fell back into a recession in 1938, and finally exceeded the 1929 value only in 1939, fully ten years later.

Three factors help to explain why the other three countries experienced economic slumps that were less severe and shorter in duration than in the United States. These are exchange rate policy, fiscal policy, and policy toward wages and prices. The clearest contrast was in exchange rate policy. In September 1931, the United Kingdom abandoned the gold standard that fixed its exchange rate with that of the dollar. The devaluation of the British pound sterling boosted British exports and cut British imports, thus shifting the British *IS* curve to the right and initiating the recovery shown by the blue line during 1932–34. The U.S. government did not reduce the value of the dollar until 1933, and in the interval of 1931–33, the world demand for exports shifted from the United States to the United Kingdom and other countries that had devalued their currencies in 1931.

The contrast between Germany and the United States lies both in fiscal policy and wage policy. The 1929–32 slump in Germany was almost as severe as in the United States, but its recovery starting in 1933 was much faster. The new German government of Adolf Hitler took control on January 30, 1933. Soon after, the government began an ambitious policy of fiscal expansion, raising government spending drastically and financing this spending largely through budget deficits rather than higher taxes. While most of the government spending went for rearmament as Germany built its military machine that conquered most of Europe in 1939–42, some of the government spending went for housing construction and for the Autobahn, a system of limited access multi-lane freeways that anticipated the U.S. interstate highway construction of the 1950s and 1960s. By 1938, the German economy had reached a level of income per person fully 30 percent above the 1929 level. Rearmament in Japan, which invaded Manchuria in 1931 and China in 1937, caused the path of the Japanese economy to resemble that of Germany.

Not only was fiscal expansion in the United States much more timid than in Germany or Japan, but the nominal money supply was allowed to decline by 25 percent between 1929 and 1933 (Table 7-1, column (1)).

Prices and the Output Ratio in the Great Depression

Does the behavior of output and the price level in the Great Depression support the Keynesian assumption of rigid nominal wages or the classical interpretation of a self-correcting economy? If the classicists are correct, we should find evidence of the economy's self-correcting forces at work through price

United States also pursued policies that attempted to push wages and prices up, therefore causing the *SAS* curve to shift upward and offset some of the impact of the recovery in aggregate demand. In contrast, the German government restricted the growth of wages. Because labor was cheap, employment grew much faster in Germany than in the United States during the 1930s.

Despite its disastrous policies that caused World War II and the Holocaust, in the narrower realm of economic policy, Germany must be given credit for its fiscal expansion that began in 1933 and implemented Keynesian economics even before Keynes's book was published. The rapid recovery of the U.S. economy in 1939–41 provides another example of the strong expansionary effects of a rightward shift in the *IS* curve (caused by higher government spending, exports, and fixed investment) when increases in nominal wages are relatively modest.

deflation. Turning back to the right frame of Figure 7-11, we would expect that when price deflation works in a stabilizing direction, the economy would slide down an *AD* curve to the southeast, as from point *A* to point E_1.

Now compare this theoretical diagram to a graph of the actual data plotted in the top frame of Figure 7-12. The horizontal axis is measured as the ratio of actual to natural real GDP. Starting to the right of the vertical *LAS* schedule in 1929, with a price index of 100 (on a 1929 base), the economy moved rapidly to the southwest until 1933. Then a recovery to the northeast began, interrupted briefly in 1938.

Figure 7-12 The Price Level (P) and the Ratio of Actual to Natural Real GDP (Y/Y^N) During the Great Depression, 1929–41

The upper frame illustrates the actual values of the implicit GDP deflator (P) and an estimate of the ratio of actual to natural real GDP during the Great Depression era, 1929–41. The remarkable fact in the top frame is that the economy returned almost to natural output in 1941 with a price level that was only modestly below that in 1929, despite the intervening decade that should have pushed the price level much lower. The bottom frame illustrates a hypothetical interpretation of what happened.

(Source: Appendix A.)

The Economy Traveled Down and Up the SAS Curve in the 1930s

Absence of self-correction.
The story of the Great Depression appears to lie in shifts in the AD curve to the left and then back to the right. There is no evidence at all of a movement southeast along a given AD curve, as would have occurred had price deflation played a major role in stimulating the recovery. Particularly important is the fact that there was no deflation between 1936 and 1940, even though Y/Y^N remained at or below 86 percent throughout that five-year interval.

Despite the absence of perfect price flexibility, the price level was not rigid during the Great Depression and did drop 26 percent between 1929 and 1933. The path from northeast to southwest to northeast reflects a regularity, as if the AD curve were following a well-marked highway. The bottom frame of Figure 7-12 represents a hypothetical interpretation of what happened. The AD curve in 1929 was close to the vertical LAS schedule, but by 1933 it had moved well to the left as business and consumer confidence collapsed. The actual location of the economy in 1933 suggests that the economy's aggregate supply schedule looks like SAS_0 of Figure 7-11, and so we have drawn in a positively sloped SAS_0 curve in the bottom frame of Figure 7-12.

Behavior of nominal and real wage rates.
The interpretation of the Great Depression contained in Figure 7-12 raises an obvious question: Why did the aggregate supply curve fail to shift downward to bring the economy to its long-run equilibrium level of output along the vertical LAS line at a lower price

level? A fixed *SAS* curve requires a rigid nominal wage rate. Data on the nominal wage rate are included in Table 7-1, column 9.

By 1937, the nominal wage rate was back to the 1929 level, despite an unemployment rate of 14 percent. Thus, it is an exaggeration for the Keynesian model to treat the nominal wage rate as absolutely rigid. A decline did occur in 1931–33. But the nominal wage rate did not exhibit the continued decline after 1933 that would have been necessary to bring the economy back to natural real GDP through the classical mechanism of self-correction.

Policy failures after 1932. As we have seen, there was a profound failure of monetary policy in 1929–33, as banks were allowed to fail and as the nominal money supply was allowed to decline. And, as shown in the box, the failure to devalue the dollar in response to the British devaluation of 1931 prolonged the U.S. depression, in constrast to the rapid recovery of the British economy.

But policy failures did not stop with the inauguration of President Franklin D. Roosevelt in 1933. The government could have pursued an aggressive fiscal expansion but did not. It failed to understand the difference between actual and structural budget deficits, as explained in Figures 5-2 and 5-3 on pp. 135-37. It was inhibited in raising government spending and cutting taxes by its fear of budget deficits, yet these deficits were caused by the weakness of the economy, not by fiscal expansion.

Just as serious an error was the failure to understand the role of falling wages and prices in promoting a recovery; the *SAS* curve needed to shift down but instead the government tried to push the *SAS* curve up. During 1934 and 1935 the National Industrial Recovery Act (NIRA) explicitly attempted to raise wages and prices. Although the NIRA was declared unconstitutional in 1935, it was succeeded in the next several years by alternative legislation aimed at boosting prices and particularly wages.

Summary

1. The aggregate demand curve shows the different combinations of real output and the price level that are consistent with equilibrium in the commodity and money markets. The position of the aggregate demand curve depends on planned spending and on the money supply.
2. A shift in aggregate demand may change the level of real output, the price level, or both. With a horizontal aggregate supply curve, only real output changes. With a vertical aggregate supply curve, only the price level changes. With a positively sloped aggregate supply curve, both real output and the price level change.
3. The short-run aggregate supply curve slopes upward because a higher price level reduces the real wage. This induces firms to hire more workers, and the resulting increase in output raises real GDP.
4. The equilibrium real wage rate is located where the labor supply and demand curves cross. If a shift in demand changes the price level, and hence pushes the real wage rate away from the equilibrium real wage rate, there is pressure for change in the nominal wage rate.
5. The position of the short-run aggregate supply curve for the economy depends on the nominal wage rate. When changing demand conditions raise the nominal wage rate, the short-run aggregate supply curve shifts up.
6. In the short run, a fiscal or monetary expansion raises both real output and the price level. However, the short-run change in real output puts pressure for change on the nominal wage rate and causes the short-run aggregate supply curve to shift. This pressure for change is eliminated only when real output returns to the value that occurred prior to the fiscal or monetary expansion.
7. The economy is in long-run equilibrium only at a single level of natural real GDP, where there is no upward or downward pressure on the nominal wage rate. In the long run, any change in aggregate demand changes the price level without causing a change in real GDP.

8. Classical economists believed that cycles in aggregate demand mainly affected the price level, not real output. The economy's self-correcting forces of price flexibility protected real output from fluctuations.
9. Keynes criticized the classical economists on two grounds. The first was that the aggregate demand curve might be vertical rather than negatively sloped, due to a failure of planned spending to respond to the interest rate (vertical IS curve), or to a failure of a higher real money supply to lower the interest rate (horizontal LM curve), or both. Pigou countered that falling prices raise wealth and spending, guaranteeing a negatively sloped aggregate demand curve.
10. Keynes also criticized the classical economists because he believed that nominal wages were rigid, preventing prices from adjusting sufficiently to return real GDP to the level of natural real GDP.

Concepts

aggregate demand curve
short-run aggregate supply curve
long-run aggregate supply curve
equilibrium real wage rate
short-run equilibrium
long-run equilibrium

countercyclical variable
self-correcting forces
quantity theory of money
monetary impotence
rigid wages
Pigou or real balance Effect

Keynes Effect
expectations effect
redistribution effect
persistent unemployment
market-clearing model
non–market-clearing model

Questions

1. Explain the difference between the aggregate demand curve developed in this chapter and the demand curve for a product (for example, movies) used in microeconomics.
2. How will the AD curve be affected if, all other things remaining equal, (a) the interest responsiveness of the demand for money becomes larger? (b) the income responsiveness of the demand for money becomes larger?
3. All other things remaining equal, which of the following changes would cause the AD curve to shift to the right? To the left? Make it flatter? Make it steeper? Leave it unchanged (that is, cause a movement along the AD curve)? (Hint: Explain how each change affects the IS or LM curves that lie behind the AD curve.)
   (a) an increase in the nominal money supply
   (b) an increase in autonomous exports
   (c) an increase in the marginal tax rate
   (d) an increase in the marginal propensity to consume
   (e) a decrease in the responsiveness of investment to changes in the interest rate
   (f) an increase in the price level
   (g) an increase in government spending
   (h) a decrease in the exchange rate
4. Explain the importance of the assumption of fixed *nominal* wages in the determination of the short-run aggregate supply curve.
5. Each point along the short-run aggregate supply (SAS) curve corresponds to a point on the labor demand curve. Using the SAS and Figure 7-7, explain whether workers are working more or less than they would like at points along the SAS where (a), actual real GDP is less than natural real GDP and (b), actual real GDP is greater than natural real GDP.
6. Describe whether the following variables increase or decrease when real GDP (Y) increases above Y_0 in Figure 7-5.
   (a) the price level
   (b) the nominal wage rate
   (c) the real wage rate
   (d) the level of employment
   (e) the demand for labor
   (f) the quantity of labor demanded
7. Explain whether the labor demand curve or labor supply curve shifts and how the equilibrium real wage rate changes for each of the following:
   (a) Concerns over homeland security reduce the amount of immigration by workers willing to work for less than present American workers.
   (b) Improvements in education raise labor productivity.
   (c) Higher oil prices force companies to switch to equipment and structures that save energy but simultaneously reduce labor productivity.
   (d) The government cuts unemployment benefits in order to reduce its budget deficit.

8. Explain with words and diagrams how each of the following events affects the SAS curve.
   (a) technology improves
   (b) the nominal wage rate decreases
   (c) the quantity of nonlabor inputs declines
9. Explain why relatively flat, as opposed to relatively steep, labor demand and short-run aggregate supply curves are more consistent with the empirical observation that there are relatively minor changes in the real wage rate over the course of the business cycle.
10. Assume that the aggregate demand curve shifts to the right through increased government spending. Assuming that the position of the AD curve changes, how does this event affect the government budget deficit and the foreign trade deficit?
11. Predict, with the aid of the IS-LM and the AS-AD models, the short-run and long-run results of each of the following:
   (a) a decrease in the nominal money supply
   (b) an increase in net exports that results from a depreciation of the dollar.
   (Hint: Both models measure real GDP on the horizontal axis, so aligning the diagrams vertically will help you to see how they are related. Assume the economy is initially in long-run equilibrium at the natural real GDP [Y^N]. Also, remember that changes in the price level shift the LM curve.)
12. Is sustainable long-run equilibrium always reached when the AD and SAS curves intersect? Why or why not?
13. According to the view of the classical economists, there should have been a movement down the AD curve during the 1930s. Explain why this type of movement would require a shifting SAS curve. Did the SAS curve shift during the Great Depression in the way expected by the classical economists?
14. What is meant by the term *monetary impotence*? According to Keynes, what two conditions could lead to monetary impotence? Were either of these conditions present during the Great Depression?
15. Use the AD-AS model to explain how differences in exchange rate policy, fiscal policy, and policy toward wages and prices made the Great Depression worse in the United States than it was in the United Kingdom or Germany.
16. Explain the role played by the interest rate in the Pigou Effect.
17. Why does the existence of a potent Pigou Effect guarantee a negatively sloped AD curve?
18. If policymakers were trying to decrease output in a period of continuing inflation, would the existence of the Pigou Effect have any impact? Can you explain, under these circumstances, how the redistribution effect and the expectations effect might affect the economy?
19. Given the existence of a Pigou, or real balance, Effect, what do you predict will happen to the IS and AD curves if the economy experiences an unexpected increase in autonomous exports? (Assume that the economy begins in a long-run equilibrium position where AD crosses LAS.)
20. The whole controversy regarding the location of the IS curve and the potency of the real balance effect becomes irrelevant if nominal wages are rigid downward. Why is this so? Use the AD-SAS model to explain your answer.

Problems

1. The IS and LM curves for the economy have the following equations:

   $$IS: Y = k(A'_p - 200r)$$
   $$LM: Y = 5(M^s/P) + 500r$$

   where $k = 2.5$, $A'_p = 5,200$, $M^s = 1,800$, and $P = 1.0$.
   (a) Find the equilibrium level of output and the equilibrium interest rate.
   (b) What are the equilibrium real output and equilibrium interest rate when the price level equals 0.8? When it is 1.2? When it is 2.0? Plot the aggregate demand curve based on these answers.
   (c) Suppose that natural real output [Y^N] equals 11,000. Given the aggregate demand curve from part b, determine long-run equilibrium real output, the interest rate, and the price level.
   (d) Suppose that autonomous spending increases by 600 billion so that $A'_p = 5,800$. What are the equilibrium levels of real output and the interest rate when the price level equals 0.8, 1.0, 1.2, and 2.0? Plot the new aggregate demand curve.
   (e) Assuming an upward-sloping SAS curve that intersects the original AD curve at $Y = 11,000$ and $P = 1.0$. What will happen in the short-run to actual real output, the price level, and the real wage rate as a result of the increase in aggregate demand?
   (f) Given the increase in aggregate demand, determine the new long-run equilibrium real output, equilibrium interest rate, and equilibrium price level. Explain what will happen to the nominal wage rate and the SAS curve as the economy adjusts to the new long-run equilibrium.

230 Chapter 7 • Aggregate Demand, Aggregate Supply, and the Self-Correcting Economy

2. The *IS* and *LM* curves for the economy have the following equations:

$$IS: Y = k(A'_p - 250r)$$
$$LM: Y = 4(M^s/P) + 500r$$

where $k = 2$, $A'_p = 6{,}400$, and $M^s = 2{,}400$. The equation for the short-run aggregate supply curve is $Y = 10{,}400 - 25W + 1{,}000P$, where W is the nominal wage rate.

(a) Find the short-run equilibrium level of output and the equilibrium interest rate when the price level equals 0.8. When it is 1.0. When it is 1.2. When it is 2.0. Plot the aggregate demand curve based on these answers.

(b) Suppose that natural real output $[Y^N]$ equals 10,400. Compute the value of the equilibrium real wage rate. (*Hint*: Remember that the *SAS* and *LAS* curves intersect where the real wage rate equals the equilibrium real wage rate.)

(c) Given that the nominal wage rate, W, equals 48, calculate real output when the price level equals 0.8, 1.0, 1.2, and 2.0. Plot the *SAS* curve on the same graph as you drew your *AD* curve in part a.

(d) Given the *AD* curve from part a and the *SAS* curve from part c, determine short-run equilibrium, real output, equilibrium interest rate, and price level.

(e) Suppose that the nominal money supply decreases by 400 billion from 2,400 to 2,000. What are the new equilibrium levels of real output and the interest rate when the price level equals 0.8, 1.0, 1.2, and 2.0? Plot the new aggregate demand curve on the same graph that you used for parts a and c.

(f) Use your graph of the new *AD* curve and the *SAS* curve, given *W* equals 48, to find the new short-run equilibrium actual real output and price level.

(g) Given the decrease in the nominal money supply, determine the new long-run equilibrium real output, equilibrium interest rate, and equilibrium price level. What will happen to the nominal wage rate and the *SAS* curve as the economy adjusts to the new long-run equilibrium? Calculate the value of the nominal wage rate at the new long-run equilibrium.

3. You are given the following labor demand and labor supply curves for the economy.

$$N^d = 250 - 2(W/P)$$
$$N^s = 3(W/P)$$

(a) Calculate the equilibrium real wage rate and the equilibrium quantity of labor.

(b) Suppose that the nominal wage rate equals 60. In the short-run, aggregate demand and aggregate supply are equal at a price level of 1.0. Compute the real wage rate. Explain where actual real output is relative to natural real output. Suppose that policymakers change aggregate demand so that in long-run equilibrium, the nominal wage rate stays at 60. What is the long-run equilibrium price level? Explain whether policymakers took actions that increased or decreased aggregate demand.

(c) Suppose that the nominal wage rate equals 56. In the short-run, aggregate demand and aggregate supply are equal at a price level of 1.4. Calculate the real wage rate. Where is actual real output relative to natural real output? Given the aggregate demand curve, suppose that in long-run equilibrium the price level equals 1.6. Calculate the value of the nominal wage rate that equates the demand for and supply of labor. How does the nominal wage rate changes and the *SAS* curve shift as the economy adjusts from its current short-run equilibrium to the new long-run equilibrium?

4. A Pigou Effect is introduced into an economy similar to problem 1 by allowing A'_p to become price-dependent. We now have:

$$IS: Y = k(A'_p - 200r)$$
$$LM: Y = 5(M^s/P) + 500r$$

where $k = 2.5$, $A'_p = 4{,}600 + 600/P$, $M^s = 1{,}800$, $P = 1.0$. As with parts a and b of problem 1, this problem aims to derive the *AD* curve.

(a) Find the equilibrium level of output and the equilibrium interest rate.

(b) What are the equilibrium real output and equilibrium interest rate when the price level equals 0.8? When it is 1.2? When it is 2.0? Plot the aggregate demand curve based on these answers.

(c) Is the *AD* curve flatter or steeper than the *AD* curve of part b of problem 1.

Self-Test Answers

p. 201 (1) When the *IS* curve is steep, an increase in the real money supply causes output to increase less than when the *IS* curve is flat, implying a steeper *AD* curve. (2) When the *LM* curve is steep, an increase in the real money supply causes output to increase more than when the *LM* curve is flat (compare the top and bottom frames of Figure 4-7). Thus, when the *LM* curve is steep, a given price reduction (which raises the real money supply) leads to a greater output increase and a *flatter AD* curve than when the *LM* curve is flat.

p. 207 (1) A union concession shifts the *SAS* curve down. (2) A discovery of a giant oil field shifts the *SAS* curve down. (3) An increase in the money supply shifts the aggregate demand *(AD)* curve upward and thus causes a movement *along* the *SAS* curve. (4) An increase in the price level causes movement *along* the *SAS* curve.

p. 213 (1)–(3) All these events cause an upward shift in the aggregate demand *(AD)* curve. In long-run equilibrium, the price level and nominal wage level must increase by the same percentage, while the level of real GDP does not change. (4) This causes a rightward shift in both the *LAS* and *SAS* downward along the fixed *AD* curve, reducing the long-run equilibrium price level and raising real output.

p. 219 (1) The Pigou Effect stabilizes the economy when demand is high. (2) rising prices reduce the value of real balances and real wealth, which in turn reduce consumption. (3) The expectations and redistribution effects destabilize the economy. (4) The expectations effect causes people to spend sooner, since they expect future prices to be higher. This boosts demand when demand is already high. Similarly, the redistribution effect causes income to be redistributed from savers who spend little to borrowers who spend much, thus boosting demand when demand is already high.

CHAPTER 8

Inflation: Its Causes and Cures

Why is our money ever less valuable? Perhaps it is simply that we have inflation because we expect inflation, and we expect inflation because we've had it.
—Robert M. Solow[1]

8-1 Introduction

Explaining the Inflation Rate

Throughout Chapters 3–6 the price level was assumed to be fixed, implying that the inflation rate was zero. In Chapter 7 for the first time the price level was allowed to rise or fall, responding to shifts in the aggregate demand (*AD*) curve and in the short-run aggregate supply (*SAS*) curve. The *AD-SAS* model implies that any event that causes a *single upward shift* in the economy's *AD* curve will cause a *single upward jump* in the price level. But **inflation** is a continuous increase in the price level, not a single jump. Thus sustained inflation requires a *continuous increase* in aggregate demand. To focus on the causes of a sustained inflation, in this chapter we will alter our *AD-SAS* model to explain the inflation rate (designated as lowercase *p*), instead of explaining the price level (designed as uppercase *P*) as in Chapter 7.

In this chapter we learn that an acceleration or deceleration of inflation can be caused either by shifts in aggregate demand ("demand shocks") or in aggregate supply ("supply shocks"). When supply shocks are absent, shifts in aggregate demand are the main cause of swings in real GDP and in the rate of inflation. Any attempt to sustain a level of real GDP above the natural level of real GDP will cause continuously accelerating inflation. The unfortunate corollary is that a reduction of inflation requires a transition period of recession in which actual real GDP falls below natural real GDP. It is a central goal of the Fed to restrain inflation, and on repeated occasions during the postwar era, the Fed has been sufficiently concerned about accelerating inflation to institute restrictive policies that raise interest rates, in order deliberately to create a recession as needed to reduce the inflation rate. The impact of higher aggregate demand in creating inflation forces the Fed into a constant state of vigilance, to make sure that aggregate demand does not become excessive and to always be prepared to move to a restrictive monetary policy when needed.

The Volatile History of the Inflation Rate

The price level (*P*) is measured by the GDP deflator. The rate of inflation (*p*) is measured by the *percentage rate of change* of the GDP deflator, and this is plotted

Inflation is a sustained upward movement in the aggregate price level that is shared by most products.

---
[1] *Technology Review* (December/January 1979), p. 31.

in the top frame of Figure 8-1. There we see that the inflation rate in the United States since 1960 has ranged from low values of around 1 percent per year in the early 1960s and again briefly in 1998, to high values of 10 percent per year in 1975 and again in 1982. How can these volatile ups and downs in the inflation

Figure 8-1 The Inflation Rate and the Output Ratio, 1960–2004

The top frame displays the inflation rate, measured as the percentage rate of change of the GDP deflator over the previous four quarters. The bottom frame displays the output ratio, that is, the percentage ratio of actual real GDP to natural real GDP. The high output ratio of 1965–69 caused inflation to accelerate during the late 1960s, and the same pattern is evident in the late 1980s. The low output ratio observed in the 1982–83 period explains part of the sharp drop in the inflation rate between 1981 and 1984. But sometimes the inflation rate and output ratio moved in opposite directions, as in 1974–75, 1979–81, and 1995–98.

rate be explained? One promising hypothesis is suggested by Chapter 7, where we learned that an increase in aggregate demand raises the price level permanently, and it also raises actual real GDP temporarily above natural real GDP. We begin our search for the causes of inflation in this chapter by examining the relationship between the inflation rate and the ratio of actual real GDP to natural real GDP.

How is Inflation Related to the Output Ratio?

The central theme of this chapter is that there is no unique relationship between inflation and the **output ratio**, that is, the ratio of actual real GDP to natural real GDP. The output ratio exceeds 100 percent when actual real GDP exceeds natural real GDP. The output ratio falls short of 100 percent when actual real GDP is less than natural real GDP.

The volatile history of the output ratio is plotted in the bottom frame of Figure 8-1. There we see five periods when the output ratio soared above 100 percent (i.e., the percentage amount by which actual real GDP exceeded natural real GDP). The longest period with the highest output ratio was the Vietnam-era expansion of 1966–69, and the output ratio reached its second-highest peak at the end of the economic boom of the late 1990s. Smaller values of the output ratio above 100 percent are observed in 1972, 1978, and 1988–90. Sustained periods when the output ratio was below 100 percent are observed in the early 1960s, 1974–75, and especially 1982–83. The output ratio barely dipped below 100 percent in the recession periods of 1990–91 and 2001.

> The **output ratio** is the ratio of actual real GDP to natural real GDP. In the absence of supply shocks, the inflation rate remains constant when the output ratio is 100 percent, accelerates when the output ratio is above 100 percent, and decelerates when the output ratio is below 100 percent.

Demand Shocks and Supply Shocks

Sometimes inflation and the output ratio rise or fall together. The economy's response to an upward shift in aggregate demand has already been examined in Figure 7-8; an increase in aggregate demand raises the price level and also raises the output ratio above 100 percent, but only temporarily. Soon the nominal wage rate begins to increase, and the output ratio gradually declines back to 100 percent, ending its temporary increase.

In this chapter we are interested in changes in the growth rate of aggregate demand, which we will call a **demand shock**.[2] When a positive demand shock occurs, inflation increases and the output ratio rises temporarily. The most important of these demand shocks occurred in the late 1960s, due primarily to Vietnam War spending, and in the bottom frame of Figure 8-1 we can clearly see the effect of the sustained high ratio in causing a steady acceleration of inflation between 1965 and 1970 in the top frame. A milder example of the same pattern appears in the late 1980s, when the output ratio increased above 100 percent, causing an acceleration of inflation. A negative demand shock can cause the inflation rate to fall, most notably in 1982–83 when the deepest recession of the postwar era caused a sharp reduction of the inflation rate.

> A **demand shock** is a sustained acceleration or deceleration in aggregate demand, measured most directly as a sustained acceleration or deceleration in the growth rate of nominal GDP.

We learn in this chapter that there is a second reason why inflation might be accompanied by a decline, rather than an increase, in the output ratio. An adverse **supply shock** can boost inflation while causing the output ratio to decline, as occurred when there were sharp jumps in the price of oil in 1974–75 and 1979–81. A beneficial supply shock can reduce inflation while causing the output ratio to increase, as occurred in 1986 and in the late 1990s. The central

> A **supply shock** is caused by a sharp change in the price of an important commodity (e.g., oil) that causes the inflation rate to rise or fall in the absence of demand shocks.

---

[2] The term "demand shock" was previously defined in Section 3-1 on p. 59.

goal of this chapter is to use a unified model to explain why inflation sometimes is positively correlated and sometimes is negatively correlated with the output ratio.

We use the model of this chapter to explain the real-world relationship of inflation and the output ratio during the major episodes of U.S. economic history since 1960. Sometimes inflation accelerated when aggregate demand was strong, as in the 1960s and late 1980s. Sometimes inflation failed to accelerate when aggregate demand was strong, as in the late 1990s. Sometimes inflation accelerated when aggregate demand was weak, as in 1974–75 and 1980–81.

8-2 Real GDP, the Inflation Rate, and the Short-Run Phillips Curve

A *continuous* increase in demand pulls the price level up *continuously*. This kind of inflationary process is sometimes called demand-pull inflation, describing the role of rising aggregate demand as the factor "pulling up" on the price level. This type of inflation can be caused by large government budget deficits and excessive rates of growth of the money supply.

We see how demand-pull inflation works in Figure 8-2. Here the top frame repeats the aggregate demand and supply schedules from Chapter 7, with minor changes: For expositional simplicity, we have drawn both curves as

How a Continuous Increase in Aggregate Demand Causes Continuous Inflation

Figure 8-2 Relationship of the Short-Run Aggregate Supply (*SAS*) Curve to the Short-Run Phillips (*SP*) Curve

In the top frame, the economy starts in long-run equilibrium at point E_0. When aggregate demand shifts up from the AD_0 curve to the AD_1 curve, the price level moves to point E_1. The economy can stay to the right of the *LAS* line only if aggregate demand shifts up continuously from AD_1 to AD'_1 to even higher levels of aggregate demand. The nominal wage rate adjusts upward whenever the economy is in the area to the right of *LAS*. Aggregate demand must keep ahead of the upward adjustment of the nominal wage rate, shown by the vertical path marked by black arrows. This continuous inflation of 3 percent per period is represented directly below in the lower frame at point E_1.

straight lines, and we have introduced specific numbers on the vertical and horizontal axes. The horizontal axis now plots the output ratio, that is, the ratio of actual to natural real GDP. When the output ratio is 100 percent, the economy is producing actual real GDP at the level of natural real GDP. The economy initially is assumed to be at point E_0, where the AD_0 and SAS_0 curves cross. The initial values of the price index (P_0) and an index of the nominal wage rate (W_0) are both 1.0. The real wage rate (W_0/P_0) is initially at its equilibrium value of 1.0. The output ratio is 100 percent.

The short-run aggregate supply (*SAS*) curve has a positive slope, meaning that a higher level of output raises the price level. Each *SAS* curve is drawn for a particular nominal wage rate, shifting upward when the nominal wage rate increases, just as in Chapter 7. The long-run aggregate supply (*LAS*) curve is a vertical line at the point when the output ratio is 100 percent (i.e., when actual real GDP equals natural real GDP). As we learned in Chapter 7, there is upward pressure for an increase in the wage rate (and thus for an upward shift in the *SAS* curve), whenever the output ratio exceeds 100 percent. This occurs whenever the economy operates to the right of the vertical *LAS* curve.

Effects of an Increase in Aggregate Demand

An increase in aggregate demand shifts the *AD* curve upward from AD_0 to AD_1 in Figure 8-2. The economy moves initially to point E_1, where the price level is 1.03. The higher price level puts upward pressure on the nominal wage rate to rise. Everywhere to the right of the *LAS* curve, including point E_1, there is upward pressure on the nominal wage rate, so gradually the *SAS* curve will shift up. When this occurs, we move to the new SAS_1 curve, which assumes that the nominal wage rate is 3 percent higher than it was along the original SAS_0 curve.

How Continuous Inflation Occurs

What happens to the output ratio and the price level as the result of the upward shift from SAS_0 to SAS_1? There are two possibilities, both illustrated in the top frame of Figure 8-2.

A one-shot increase in aggregate demand. The first possibility is that aggregate demand remains at the level indicated by the AD_1 schedule. Then the upward shift of the supply curve to SAS_1 shifts the economy from E_1 northwest to point *D*. What must happen to prevent the output ratio from declining? The aggregate demand schedule *AD* must shift upward by exactly the same amount as the supply schedule *SAS*. Thus if the nominal wage rate increases from 1.00 to 1.03, shifting supply up from SAS_0 to SAS_1, output can remain fixed *only if the demand curve shifts up* again, this time from AD_1 to AD'_1. Once again the price level of 1.06 at point E'_1 has raced ahead of the wage rate of 1.03, and there will again be upward pressure on the nominal wage rate.

A continuous increase in aggregate demand. To keep the output ratio from declining, aggregate demand must increase continuously; the economy will move straight upward along the path depicted by the black arrows in the top frame. The bottom frame shows the same process in a much simpler way. The horizontal axis is the same as in the top frame, but now the vertical axis measures not the price level but its rate of change, the inflation rate. Thus in the top frame when the price level is fixed in long-run equilibrium, as at point E_0, the percentage rate of change of prices (or inflation rate) in the bottom frame is zero, as at point E_0. The vertical axis measures the zero rate of inflation occurring at point E_0 as $p = 0$.

The maintenance of a high output ratio requires a continuous increase in aggregate demand and in the price level, as depicted by the vertical path of the black arrows in the top frame. This same process of continuous inflation in the bottom frame is illustrated by *the single point E_1*, where in each period the rate of change of the price level is 3 percent (just as in the top frame the price level rises by 3 percent between points E_1 and E_1').

The *SP* Curve

The bottom frame of Figure 8-2 differs from the top frame only by plotting the *inflation rate* rather than the price *level* on the vertical axis. In the bottom frame, the upward-sloping line connecting points E_0 and E_1 is called the *SP* line. It shows that to maintain the output ratio above 100 percent, aggregate demand must be raised *continuously* to create a *continuous* inflation (3 percent at point E_1).

Thus point E_1 in the lower frame and indeed all points with an output ratio above 100 percent share the characteristic that the economy is not in a long-run equilibrium, because the price level is constantly racing ahead of the nominal wage rate. The reason for the continuous upward pressure for higher wages is that labor contracts fail to *anticipate further inflation, and, as a result, they fail to specify in advance the wage increases needed to keep up with inflation*. Such wage contracts are said to have an **expected rate of inflation** of zero. This is abbreviated $p^e = 0$ and is included as a label on the *SP* line.

The term *SP curve* is used as an abbreviation for the term **short-run Phillips (SP) Curve**, which is named after A. W. H. Phillips, who first discovered the statistical relationship between real GDP and the inflation rate.[3] The *SP* curve slopes upward for the same reason that the *SAS* curve slopes up in Chapter 7. There are additional reasons for the upward slope of the *SP* curve. As output increases, the economywide inflation rate tends to rise, due to the sensitivity of raw materials prices to higher aggregate demand, and due to the tendency of business firms to boost prices more rapidly when aggregate demand is high.

The position of the *SP* curve is fixed by the rate of inflation that was expected at the time current wage contracts were negotiated (p^e), assumed in Figure 8-2 to be zero. Because the position of the *SP* curve depends on expectations, it is sometimes called the **expectations-augmented Phillips Curve**.

The **expected rate of inflation** is the rate of inflation that is expected to occur in the future.

The schedule relating real GDP to the inflation rate achievable given a fixed expected rate of inflation is the **short-run Phillips (SP) Curve**.

The **expectations-augmented Phillips Curve** (another name for the *SP* curve) shifts its position whenever there is a change in the expected rate of inflation.

---

[3] Phillips showed that over 100 years of British history, the rate of change of wage rates was related to the level of unemployment. Because the change in wage rates, in turn, is related to inflation, and unemployment is related to real GDP, the research of Phillips popularized the idea, depicted by the *SP* curve in Figure 8-2, that a high level of output is associated with a high inflation rate. See A. W. H. Phillips, "The Relation Between Unemployment and the Rate of Change of Money Wage Rates in the United Kingdom, 1861–1957," *Economica* (November 1958), pp. 283–299. The curve should actually be called the Fisher Curve, since the relationship between the unemployment and inflation rates had been pointed out much earlier in Irving Fisher, "A Statistical Relation Between Unemployment and Price Changes," *International Labour Review* (June 1926), pp. 785–792, reprinted in *Journal of Political Economy* (March/April 1973), pp. 596–602.

Self-Test

From what you have learned so far, try to generalize about the accuracy of the expected rate of inflation in the bottom frame of Figure 8-2.

1. In what area is actual inflation greater than expected inflation?
2. In what area is actual inflation less than expected inflation?
3. Where in the diagram does the expected rate of inflation turn out to be exactly right?

8-3 The Adjustment of Expectations

The remarkable thing about the inflation process illustrated in Figure 8-2 is that it presupposes that people never learn to *anticipate* inflation when they negotiate their labor contracts. Each period, the price level races ahead of the nominal wage rate along the path shown by the upward-pointing arrows, but people fail to build this inflation into their labor contracts *ahead of time*.

Changing Inflation Expectations Shift the *SP* Curve

Once negotiators anticipate inflation in advance, the short-run Phillips Curve shifts upward, as illustrated in Figure 8-3. There the lower SP_0 short-run Phillips Curve is copied directly from the bottom frame of Figure 8-2. Everywhere along the SP_0 curve, no inflation is expected. At point E_0 the actual inflation rate is just what is expected—zero—and the economy is in a long-run equilibrium position with the price level completely fixed. At point E_1, no inflation is expected ($p^e = 0$) either, but the actual inflation rate turns out to be 3 percent.

When an expected 3 percent inflation occurs ($p = p^e = 3$), the long-run equilibrium position occurs at point E_2. The entire short-run Phillips Curve has

Figure 8-3 Effect on the Short-Run Phillips Curve of an Increase in the Expected Inflation Rate (p^e) from Zero to 3 Percent

The lower SP_0 curve is copied directly from the bottom frame of Figure 8-2 and shows the relation between output and inflation when no inflation is expected ($p^e = 0$). But when people begin fully to expect the 3 percent inflation, the 3 percent actual inflation yields only the level of real GDP at E_2. The short-run Phillips Curve has shifted upward by exactly 3 percent, the amount by which people have raised their expected inflation rate. The vertical *LP* line running through points E_0 and E_2 shows all the possible positions of long-run equilibrium where the actual and expected inflation rates are equal ($p^e = p$).

The Relation Between the Output Ratio and Inflation Depends on the Rate of Expected Inflation (p^e)

shifted upward by exactly 3 percent, the degree of adjustment of the expected inflation rate. The rise of the output ratio above 100 percent has led firms to raise their prices, and workers have obtained larger wage increases in newly negotiated contracts. Now an output ratio above 100 percent cannot be achieved along the new SP_1 schedule unless the actual inflation rate exceeds 3 percent, in which case the actual inflation rate would again exceed the expected inflation rate.

The economy is in long-run equilibrium only when there is no pressure for change. Point E_1 certainly does not qualify, because the actual inflation rate of 3 percent at point E_1 exceeds the zero inflation rate expected along the SP_0 curve. There is pressure for people to adjust their erroneous expectation ($p^e = 0$) to take account of the continuing inflation. At point E_2, the pressure for change ceases, because expected inflation has been boosted enough ($p^e = 3$). Wage agreements allow *in advance* for a 3 percent inflation. This keeps employment and output unaffected by inflation.

Thus point E_2 qualifies as a point of long-run equilibrium, because expectations turn out to be correct, just as does point E_0. The only difference between points E_0 and E_2 is the inflation rate that is correctly expected, zero at E_0 versus 3 percent at E_2. Otherwise the two points share the correctness of expectations and the same output ratio of 100 percent.

The *LP* "Correct Expectations" Line

The black vertical *LP* line connects E_0 and E_2 and shows all possible points where the expected inflation rate turns out to be correct. The term *LP line* stands for *Long-run Phillips Curve* and can be thought of as the "correct expectations" line. Everywhere to the right of the *LP* line, inflation turns out to be higher than expected, and the expected inflation rate will be raised. Everywhere to the left, inflation turns out to be lower than expected, and the expected inflation rate will be reduced. The vertical *LP* line showing all possible positions of long-run equilibrium is analogous to the vertical *LAS* long-run supply schedule of Chapter 7. Its message is the same: Real GDP (Y) cannot be pushed permanently away from its long-run natural level (Y^N), and the output ratio cannot be permanently raised above 100 percent.

What important message does the vertical *LP* line send to policymakers? It tells them that the best way to stabilize the economy is to adopt policies to keep the output ratio equal to 100 percent. If the output ratio is too high, inflation is likely to accelerate (as between points E_0 and E_1 in Figure 8-3). The appropriate response is that policymakers adopt restrictive policies that reduce back to 100 percent. Similarly, if the output ratio is to the left of the *LP* line, then output is needlessly being wasted and jobs are being destroyed, and policymakers should adopt stimulative policies to spur a recovery in the output ratio that pushes the economy rightward, back to the *LP* line.

Self-Test

Assume that the economy is initially at point E_2 in Figure 8-3. There is a decline in aggregate demand, and the output ratio declines from 100 to 94 percent.

1. What happens subsequently to the expected inflation rate?
2. What happens to the position of the *SP* curve?
3. What happens to the position of the *LP* curve?

Learning About Diagrams: The Short-Run *(SP)* and Long-Run *(LP)* Phillips Curves

The Phillips Curve depicts the relationship between inflation and the output ratio.

Diagram Elements and Reasons for Slope

Both the *SP* curve and *LP* curve are plotted with the output ratio on the horizontal axis and with the inflation rate on the vertical axis.

The *SP* curve slopes upward because higher output boosts inflation through the same mechanisms that cause the short-run aggregate supply curve to slope upward in Chapter 7.

The *LP* curve shows the level of output when inflation is accurately anticipated ($p^e = p$). The *LP* curve is a vertical line, because accurate anticipations can occur only when the output ratio is 100 percent, that is, when actual and natural real GDP are equal ($Y = Y^N$).

What Shifts the *SP* Curve and *LP* Curve?

The crossing point of the *SP* curve with the *LP* curve shows the rate of anticipated inflation (p^e). An increase in p^e will shift the *SP* curve up, and a decrease in p^e will shift the *SP* curve down.

The *LP* curve does not shift its position. If there is an increase in natural real GDP, then actual real GDP must increase by the same amount for the output ratio to remain at 100 percent.

What Is True at Points off the Curves?

A point below the *SP* curve represents an inflation rate below that anticipated by firms and workers. A point above the *SP* curve represents the opposite.

A point to the right of the *LP*, curve but on the *SP* curve represents a situation in which actual inflation exceeds expected inflation. In such a situation, there is upward pressure on the expected rate of inflation. A point to the left of the *LP* curve but on the *SP* curve represents a situation in which actual inflation is less than expected inflation, putting downward pressure on expected inflation.

8-4 Nominal GDP Growth and Inflation

Once we have determined the value of p^e, the average inflation rate expected at the time contracts were negotiated, we know which *SP* curve applies to today's economy. But we still have a major question remaining if we are to understand the determination of the output ratio and the inflation rate: *Where will the economy's position be along the current SP curve?* For instance, along SP_0, will the economy be at point E_0, point E_1, or some other point?

The *SP* curve is a single relationship between the inflation rate and the output ratio. We need to find an additional relationship, because two separate relations between inflation and the output ratio are needed to pin down the values of these two unknown variables.

Our model of inflation in this chapter uses a single variable to represent the growth rate of aggregate demand, and this is the growth rate of nominal GDP. First we review the relationship between the *levels* of nominal GDP, real GDP, and the GDP deflator. Then we introduce the relationship between the *growth rates* of nominal GDP, real GDP, and the GDP deflator (the growth rate of the GDP deflator is the same thing as the inflation rate).

Starting with the *levels* of these variables, we recall from Chapter 2 that nominal GDP (X) is defined as the price level (P) times real GDP (Y):

$$X = PY \tag{8.1}$$

Just as real GDP is determined in the *IS-LM* model of Chapter 4 by such factors as real government spending and the real money supply, so nominal GDP is determined by nominal government spending and the nominal money supply. In addition, nominal GDP is determined by any other *shock* to aggregate demand discussed in the preceding chapters, including changes in tax rates, autonomous net taxes, the autonomous component of net exports, real wealth, and shifts in business and consumer optimism.[4]

In this chapter we are interested in the *growth rate* of the price level, that is, the rate of inflation, and its relation to the *growth rate* of nominal GDP. The growth rate of any product of two numbers, such as P times Y in equation (8.1), is equal to the sum of the separate growth rates of the two numbers.[5] Writing the growth rates of variables in equation (8.1) as, respectively, x, p, and y, implies

$$x = p + y \quad (8.2)$$

In words, this equation says that the growth rate of nominal GDP (x) equals the inflation rate (p) plus the growth rate of real GDP (y).

If the level of nominal GDP starts out at 100, as in period 0 in Table 8-1, then a growth rate of 6 percent will bring the level to 106 in period 1. As shown in Table 8-1, several different combinations of inflation and real GDP growth are compatible with a 6 percent growth rate for nominal GDP ($x = 6$). The lesson we learn from Table 8-1 is that for any given growth rate of nominal GDP, the rate of real GDP growth will vary inversely with the inflation rate.

For instance, alternative B shows that if inflation is 6 percent, higher prices will absorb all of the 6 percent growth of nominal GDP so that nothing will remain for real GDP growth. Real GDP remains constant, then, at its initial level of 100. Inflation "uses up" all of nominal GDP growth.

In contrast, alternative C shows that if inflation is only 3 percent, then half of the 6 percent growth in nominal GDP will remain for real GDP to grow by 3 percent, from 100 initially to 103 in period 1. Here inflation uses up only half of nominal GDP growth.

Finally, alternative A on the top line of Table 8-1 shows that if inflation is 9 percent, then nominal GDP growth of 6 percent will not be sufficient to maintain real GDP constant at 100. Real GDP growth must be *minus* 3 percent,

---

[4] We can take our basic equation for the aggregate demand (*AD*) curve, developed in the Appendix to Chapter 4 as equation (9) on p. 128, and repeat it here:

$$Y = k_1 A'_p + k_2 M^s / P$$

This states that real GDP (Y) equals an autonomous spending multiplier times the value of *real* autonomous planned spending at a zero interest rate (A'_p), plus a monetary multiplier times the real money supply (M^s/P). When multiplied through by the price level (P), this becomes an expression that determines nominal GDP (X) as equal to the autonomous spending multiplier times *nominal* autonomous spending at a zero interest rate (PA'_p), plus a monetary multiplier times the nominal money supply (M^s).

[5] The formal way to show this is to take the logarithm of the product of two terms, such as PY:

$$\log X = \log P + \log Y$$

Then the derivative of both sides is taken with respect to time:

$$\frac{d \log X}{dt} = \frac{d \log P}{dt} + \frac{d \log Y}{dt}$$

This is the same as the equality in equation (8.2), since x is defined as $(d \log X)/dt$ and likewise for p and y.

Table 8-1 Alternative Divisions of 6 Percent Nominal GDP Growth Between Inflation and Real GDP Growth

		Level of variable			Growth rate of variable between periods 0 and 1		
	Period	Nominal GDP (X)	Real GDP (Y)	GDP deflator (P)	Nominal GDP (x)	Real GDP (y)	GDP deflator (p)
Alternative A:							
Inflation at 9 percent	0	100	100	1.00	6	−3	9
	1	106	97	1.09			
Alternative B:							
Inflation at 6 percent	0	100	100	1.00	6	0	6
	1	106	100	1.06			
Alternative C:							
Inflation at 3 percent	0	100	100	1.00	6	3	3
	1	106	103	1.03			

forcing the level of real GDP to fall from 100 in period 0 to 97 in period 1. Here inflation uses up more than the available rate of nominal GDP, forcing real GDP to fall.

Example: When inflation is less than the growth rate of nominal GDP, real GDP must rise, just as in alternative C. When inflation is greater than the growth rate of nominal GDP, real GDP must fall, just as in alternative A.

		x	$=$	p	$+$	y
Years like Alternative C	1977	10.7	=	6.2	+	4.5
	1984	10.6	=	3.7	+	6.9
	2004	6.5	=	2.0	+	4.5
Years like Alternative A	1974	8.1	=	8.6	+	−0.5
	1982	4.0	=	5.9	+	−1.9
	1991	3.3	=	3.4	+	−0.1

8-5 Effects of an Acceleration in Nominal GDP Growth

The basic theme of this chapter is that the inflation rate can be either positively or negatively correlated with the output ratio, depending on the evolution of demand shocks and supply shocks. The role of supply shocks is examined later in this chapter. Now we are concerned with the role of demand shocks, that is, shifts in aggregate demand due to such factors as changes in the real money supply, business and consumer optimism, real wealth, government spending, tax rates, and foreign events that determine net exports. In this chapter we

The Impact on Inflation and the Output Ratio of Faster Nominal GDP Growth

Figure 8-4 The Adjustment Path of Inflation and the Output Ratio to an Acceleration of Nominal GDP Growth from Zero to 6 Percent When Expectations Fail to Adjust

The economy initially is at point E_0 with actual and expected inflation of 0 percent. A 6 percent acceleration in nominal GDP growth moves the economy in the first period to point F. If the expected rate of inflation ($p^e = 0$) fails to respond to faster actual inflation (an unrealistic assumption), the economy eventually arrives at point E_3. Once we allow expectations to adjust, the economy will move to point E_4, which is both on the LP line and allows inflation to be equal to nominal GDP growth.

measure demand shocks by a single variable, that is, changes in the growth rate of nominal GDP (x).

How do changes in nominal GDP growth (x) affect real GDP (Y) and the inflation rate (p)? We shall assume that initially the economy is in a long-run equilibrium in Figure 8-4 at point E_0. The actual and expected inflation rates are both zero ($p = p^e = 0$). Thus the SP curve that applies is SP_0, which assumes $p^e = 0$, and is copied from Figure 8-3.

If nominal GDP growth is also zero ($x = 0$), then the economy can stay at point E_0, since $x = p$. Why? As we can see by subtracting p from both sides of equation (8.2), when $x = p$, the growth rate of real GDP (y) must be zero:

$$y = x - p \tag{8.3}$$

$$0 = 0 - 0 \text{ (the specific values at point } E_0\text{)}$$

As long as $x = 0$, point E_0 is a long-run equilibrium, meeting the three conditions (1) that the economy is on the SP curve, (2) that $x = p$ (so $y = 0$), and (3) that expectations are accurate ($p^e = p$).

In order to link equation (8.3) to Figure 8-4, we need to assume that the growth rate of natural real GDP is zero ($y^N = 0$). Then positive growth in actual real GDP ($y > 0$) will cause an increase in the output ratio, because actual real GDP, which is the numerator of the output ratio (Y/Y^N), will increase while natural real GDP, which is the the denominator of the output ratio, will remain unchanged. Likewise, negative growth in output ($y < 0$) will cause a decrease in the output ratio.[6]

Now let us assume that nominal GDP growth (x) accelerates permanently from 0 to 6 percent. What happens? The economy can no longer stay at E_0,

---

[6] The Appendix to Chapter 8 loosens this assumption that the growth rate of natural real GDP is zero and allows for any rate of change of natural real GDP.

because it is no longer true that $x = p$. Instead, the 6 percent value of x exceeds the 0 percent initial value of p, and real GDP must grow. With no price increases at all, firms respond to rising expenditures by producing more goods and services, so the *growth rate* of real GDP (y) becomes positive and the output ratio rises. Equation (8.3) teaches us the following key rule about the adjustment of real GDP and inflation: *Real GDP must grow; that is, the growth rate of real GDP is positive* ($y > 0$), *whenever nominal GDP growth exceeds the inflation rate* ($x > p$).

Starting from E_0, an acceleration in nominal GDP growth from zero to 6 percent will slide the economy up the fixed positively sloped schedule SP_0, since people initially expect an inflation rate of zero ($p^e = 0$). This extra 6 percent of nominal GDP growth is divided between inflation and output growth, according to equation (8.3). In this example, two percentage points of the total six percentage point acceleration in x are devoted to higher inflation at point F, and the remaining four percentage points are devoted to output growth, that is, raising the output ratio from 100 to 104. Point F is a position of *short-run equilibrium*, since it is on the SP_0 curve and it also satisfies equation (8.3).

The continuing adjustment. What happens next? The economy cannot stay at point F, because *F is not a position of long-run equilibrium*. It violates two of the three requirements stated earlier for long-run equilibrium—that $x = p$ and that expectations be accurate. First, if nominal GDP growth is 6 percent forever, and the inflation rate is only 2 percent at point F, then equation (8.3) tells us that real GDP growth must be positive and the output ratio must increase, moving us to the right of point F in Figure 8-4. This means that the economy cannot stay at point F. Second, *expectations have turned out to be incorrect*. Instead of the zero inflation expected along the SP_0 curve, inflation has turned out to be 2 percent.

Let us deal with the first of these issues. Real GDP grows whenever nominal GDP growth exceeds the inflation rate. This means that $y > 0$ when $x > p$ as in equation (8.3). Since we have assumed that nominal GDP growth has accelerated permanently to 6 percent, this means that *real GDP must keep growing until inflation "uses up" all of nominal GDP growth*, that is, until inflation rises enough so that $p = x = 6$. This occurs only at point E_3, where the inflation rate (plotted on the vertical axis) is equal to 6 percent, the same as the assumed permanent growth rate of nominal GDP.

But point E_3 is not satisfactory, because it fails to satisfy the second condition for long-run equilibrium—that expectations be accurate. The economy cannot stay at E_3 because this point has inflation racing along at 6 percent, while expectations of inflation (p^e) remain at zero. It is inevitable that labor contract negotiations will take the ongoing 6 percent inflation into account. As the rate of wage increase is raised to take account of the unfortunate reality of 6 percent inflation, the SP curve will shift upward. Thus point E_3 is not a position of long-run equilibrium.

The SP curve will stop shifting upward only when the economy reaches a long-run equilibrium, satisfying the three requirements that (1) the economy is on the SP curve, (2) $x = p$ (so the output ratio stops growing), and (3) expectations are accurate ($p^e = p$). While the first two conditions are met at point E_3, the third is satisfied only along the vertical LP line. And where along the LP line do we satisfy the second condition, $x = p$? Given the assumed growth rate of nominal GDP ($x = 6$), this occurs only at point E_4, where $x = p = 6$. Why? Only when $x = p$ does the output ratio stop growing, with $y = 0$.

8-6 Expectations and the Inflation Cycle

Forward-Looking, Backward-Looking, and Adaptive Expectations

How high can real GDP be pushed by the acceleration in nominal GDP growth, and for how long? Everything depends on the speed at which p^e (the average rate of inflation expected when current wage and price contracts were negotiated) responds to higher inflation. This speed of adjustment depends on several factors.

Forward-looking expectations. First, are expectations forward-looking or backward-looking? **Forward-looking expectations** attempt to predict the future behavior of an economic variable, like the inflation rate, using an economic model that specifies the interrelation of that variable with other variables. Contract negotiators with forward-looking expectations might reason, for instance, that an acceleration of nominal GDP growth from zero to 6 percent implies 6 percent inflation in the long run, and immediately raise the expected rate of inflation to 6 percent. The growth rate of the nominal wage rate would speed up by 6 percent, and this would shift the *SP* curve directly upward by 6 percent. The economy would move *immediately* from point E_0 to point E_4, without any period at all with the output ratio greater than 100 percent.

Forward-looking expectations attempt to predict the future behavior of an economic variable, using an economic model that specifies the interrelationship of that variable with other variables.

The rationality of backward-looking expectations. Another alternative, **backward-looking expectations**, does not attempt to calculate the implications of economic disturbances *in advance*, but simply adjusts to what has *already* happened. For instance, the backward-looking approach bases expectations of inflation on the past behavior of inflation, without any attempt to guess the future path of nominal GDP growth or its implications. There are two important reasons why rational workers and firms may form their expectations by looking backward rather than forward:

Backward-looking expectations use only information on the past behavior of economic variables.

1. People may have no reason to believe that an acceleration in nominal GDP growth will be permanent. Nominal GDP growth has fluctuated before, making individuals reluctant to leap to the conclusion that the change is permanent. They may prefer just to wait and see what happens.

2. Even if the acceleration of nominal GDP growth were permanent, the existence of long-term wage and price contracts and agreements, both formal and informal, would prevent *actual* inflation from responding immediately. Since people know about these contracts and agreements, they know that changes in wages and prices will adjust *gradually* to the acceleration in nominal GDP. The exact speed of adjustment cannot be predicted in advance, since it depends on many factors, including the average length of wage and price contracts and agreements. Further, *one* set of contract negotiators may have no idea whether *other* negotiators expect future nominal GDP growth to be 6 percent, 0 percent, or some other number.

The most popular form of backward-looking expectations, and one that has been widely studied and verified, is called **adaptive expectations**.[7] The idea is simply that when people find that actual events do not turn out as they

Adaptive expectations base expectations for next period's values on an average of actual values during previous periods.

---

[7] The idea of adaptive expectations was first used in macroeconomics in a classic paper, Phillip Cagan, "The Monetary Dynamics of Hyperinflation," in Milton Friedman, ed., *Studies in the Quantity Theory of Money* (Chicago: University of Chicago Press, 1956), pp. 25–117.

were expected to, they adjust their expectations to bring them closer to reality. Here is a particularly simple example of adaptive expectations. Assume that the expected inflation rate is always set equal to what actually happened last period. In Figure 8-4, the acceleration of nominal GDP growth from zero to 6 percent, which raises actual inflation from zero to 2 percent as the economy moves from point E_0 to point F, would cause the next period's expected inflation rate to rise by the same amount, to 2 percent. Here is the simple relation to remember: *This period's expected inflation rate equals last period's actual inflation rate, or $p^e = p_{-1}$.*

Adjustment Loops

The economy's response to higher demand growth depends on the adjustment of expectations. In Figure 8-5, two responses are plotted. The blue line moving straight northeast from point E_0 through point F to E_3 duplicates Figure 8-4. Expectations do not adjust at all, and the economy remains on its original SP_0 curve.

The orange line shows full adjustment with a one-period lag. In each period the SP curve shifts upward by exactly the previous period's increase in actual inflation. Because actual inflation increases by two percentage points in going from E_0 to point F, then in the next period the SP curve shifts upward by two percentage points and takes the economy northward from F to H. But then expectations adjust upward again, because at H inflation has risen above the 2 percent people expected. Eventually, after looping around the long-run equilibrium point E_4, the economy arrives there. (The appendix to this chapter shows how to calculate the exact location of the economy in every time period along this path.)

The orange path exhibits several basic characteristics of the inflation process:

1. An acceleration of demand growth (as in Figures 8-4 and 8-5) raises the inflation rate and the output ratio in the short run.

2. In the long run, if expectations adjust to the actual behavior of inflation, the inflation rate (p) rises by exactly the same amount as x, and any increase in the output ratio along the way is only temporary. The economy eventually arrives at point E_4.

Figure 8-5 Effect on Inflation and Real GDP of an Acceleration of Demand Growth from Zero to 6 Percent

When expectations do not adjust at all, the economy follows the black path northeast from E_0 to E_3, exactly as in Figure 8-4. When expectations adjust fully to last period's actual inflation, the economy moves upward along the orange path going northwest from point H toward the long-run equilibrium at point E_4.

Higher Nominal GDP Growth Raises Inflation Permanently But Raises the Output Ratio Only Temporarily

3. Following a permanent increase in nominal GDP growth (x), inflation (p) always experiences a temporary period when it overshoots the new growth rate of nominal GDP. For instance, in Figure 8-5, x increases from 0 to 6, and eventually inflation settles down to 6 percent at point E_4. But along the adjustment path the final equilibrium value of 6 percent inflation is temporarily exceeded. Along the orange path, for instance, inflation reaches 8 percent in periods 4 and 5. Overshooting occurs along this path because the economy initially arrives at its long-run inflation rate ($p = 6$) in period 3 before expected inflation has caught up with actual inflation. The subsequent points that lie above 6 percent reflect the combined influence on inflation of (1) the upward adjustment of expectations and (2) the continued upward demand pressure that raises actual inflation above expected inflation whenever the economy is to the right of its LP line.

Self-Test

Look at the orange adjustment loop in Figure 8-5. Why is the line from point 1 to point 2 steeper than from E_0 to point 1?

8-7 Recession as a Cure for Inflation

How to Achieve Disinflation

In the theoretical model summarized in Figure 8-5, an increase in nominal GDP growth causes an acceleration of inflation. Now we need to find out how to achieve **disinflation**, that is, a marked deceleration in the inflation rate. It seems obvious that the most straightforward way of eliminating inflation would be *to set in reverse* the process that created the inflation. By causing demand growth (x) to slow down, the government can cause inflation to decelerate.

Disinflation is a marked deceleration in the inflation rate.

The "Cold Turkey" Remedy for Inflation

The response of inflation to a slowdown in nominal GDP growth is explored in Figure 8-6. This figure is identical to Figure 8-4, except that here we begin with 10 percent inflation. On the horizontal axis, we plot the output ratio. Expected inflation is assumed to be 10 percent along the SP_2 line, and the economy is initially at point E_5.

In Figure 8-6, we assume that the government introduces a policy, sometimes called **cold turkey**, that suddenly reduces demand growth (x) from 10 to 4 percent. If the position of the SP_2 curve remains fixed, with people expecting inflation of 10 percent because inflation last period was 10 percent, then the economy will move initially to point K. The government's policy cuts inflation from 10 percent at point E_5 to 8 percent at K, but at the cost of a recession, as the output ratio falls from 100 to 96.

The **cold turkey** approach to disinflation operates by implementing a sudden and permanent slowdown in nominal GDP growth.

Notice that the move from E_5 to point K in Figure 8-6 represents an exact reversal of the adjustment from E_0 to point F in Figure 8-4. In both cases, the initial reaction of the economy to the 6 percent change in nominal GDP growth is divided into two percentage points of adjustment of inflation and four percentage points of adjustment in real GDP.

Figure 8-6 Initial Effect on Inflation and Real GDP of a Slowdown in Nominal GDP Growth from 10 Percent to 4 Percent

Initially the economy is in a long-run equilibrium at point E_5 with expected inflation (p^e) equal to the actual inflation rate (p) of 10 percent. When nominal GDP growth slows down suddenly and permanently from 10 percent to 4 percent, the economy initially moves to point K in the first period. Eventually the economy will reach long-run equilibrium at point E_6.

Slowing Nominal GDP Growth Initially Causes a Recession

The Process of Adjustment to the New Long-Run Equilibrium

The process of adjustment finally comes to an end when inflation is equal to the new growth rate of nominal GDP ($p = x = 4$), and when the expected inflation rate has declined to its long-run equilibrium value ($p^e = 4$). Recall that the vertical LP line shows all the different combinations of inflation and real GDP when expectations are correct. One such point on LP is E_6, where inflation is 4 percent and thus is compatible in the long run with a nominal GDP growth of 4 percent.

The downward spiraling loop. In Figure 8-7 the economy starts at point E_5, the same point as in the previous diagram. Nominal GDP growth, actual inflation, and expected inflation are all 10 percent at point E_5 ($x = p = p^e$). The orange loop running southwest from point E_4 shows what would happen if the rate of nominal GDP growth (x) were suddenly slowed down from 10 percent in 1980 and prior years to 4 percent in 1981 and all future years. The economy's initial reaction is to go to the point marked 1981, with inflation of 8 percent and an output ratio that falls from 100 to 96 percent. *The point marked 1981 is exactly the same as point K in Figure 8-6.*

For 1982 and the following years, the economy follows the orange path. This downward spiraling loop, which shows the effects of a permanent deceleration of x from 10 to 4, is the *mirror image* of the upward spiraling loop in Figure 8-5, which showed the effects of a permanent acceleration of x from 0 to 6. The economy overshoots, with inflation falling temporarily below the 4 percent permanent growth rate of nominal GDP (x).

Self-Test

1. If the slope of the *SP* curve were flatter than assumed in Figures 8-6 and 8-7, would the economy's adjustment to lower nominal GDP growth be slower or faster?

2. If the slope of the *SP* curve were steeper, would the economy's adjustment be slower or faster?

Figure 8-7 Adjustment Path of Inflation and Real GDP to a Policy That Cuts Nominal GDP Growth from 10 Percent in 1980 to 4 Percent in 1981 and Thereafter

The orange line between 1980 and 1981 traces exactly the same path as between E_5 and K in Figure 8-6 and shows what happens in subsequent years. The particular shape of the adjustment path assumes that nominal GDP growth suddenly slows from 10 percent to 4 percent in 1981 and remains at 4 percent forever.

The Output Cost of Disinflation

The path depicted in Figure 8-7 displays the cold turkey approach to disinflation, that is, a sudden drop in nominal GDP growth from 10 percent in 1980 to 4 percent forever afterward. The cost of disinflation is a slump in output. What policy would avoid this decline in output? One alternative would be to do nothing and live with inflation. This would require that the economy stay permanently at point E_5 in Figure 8-7.

The sacrifice ratio. The model that generates the disinflation loop of Figure 8-7 can be used to assess the costs and benefits of a cold turkey policy compared to a policy of living with inflation. With a cold turkey policy, over the five years 1981–85, the total amount by which the output ratio falls below 100 percent is 16.3 percent. A convenient measure of the cost of disinflation is the **sacrifice ratio**, the ratio of the *cumulative* output lost to the permanent reduction in the inflation rate created by a disinflationary policy like the cold turkey approach shown in Figure 8-7. With the cold turkey policy, the sacrifice ratio is a loss of output of 16.3 percent to obtain a permanent reduction of inflation of 6 percent, or a sacrifice ratio of 2.7 (16.3/6).

The issue addressed by the sacrifice ratio is "how important is it to reduce the inflation rate permanently?" Would citizens endorse a policy of permanently reducing the inflation rate by 1 percent if they knew this would require a loss of output equal to 2.7 percent of one year's GDP, which amounts to about $325 billion?

The **sacrifice ratio** is the cumulative loss of output incurred during a disinflation divided by the permanent reduction in the inflation rate.

8-8 Case Study

How Large Is the Sacrifice Ratio?

The preceding section concluded that the sacrifice ratio is 2.7 in our theoretical model, which arbitrarily assumes that the slope of the short-run Phillips Curve (SP) is one-half.

International Perspective

Did Disinflation in Europe Differ from That in the United States?

Most industrial nations have experienced relatively low rates of inflation since the early 1990s. But before this, inflation rates were much higher and differed widely among the major nations.

The figure compares the inflation rate for the United States, beginning in 1975, with the four largest European nations—France, Germany, Italy, and the United Kingdom. Until the 1990s, Germany had the lowest inflation rate of all, and its inflation rate rose relatively little during the time of the 1979–81 oil shock. Germany's success in maintaining relatively low inflation is attributable to the relatively tight monetary policy conducted by the German central bank, the Deutsche Bundesbank.

During the early 1980s, the other three European countries had higher inflation rates than the United States and more than double the inflation rate experienced by Germany. These countries did not follow the same tight monetary policy as did Germany; instead, monetary and fiscal policies were much looser, allowing nominal GDP to rise much faster than in Germany. In 1980, the inflation rate in Italy reached 20 percent per year; in the United Kingdom, the inflation rate was almost as high.

Clearly, something important changed after 1980. While the United States achieved a substantial disinflation between 1981 and 1986 (as shown in Figures 8-1 and 8-9), the amount by which the inflation rate fell was even greater in Italy and the United Kingdom. The key ingredient in the European disinflation was the establishment of the European Monetary System (EMS) in 1979. Member nations attempted to maintain their exchange rates within a relatively narrow band around that of the German currency, the deutsche mark, or DM.

At first, the British and Italian exchange rates could not be held fixed for very long, since their inflation rates were so much higher than Germany's. At a fixed exchange rate, high inflation meant that British and Italian export prices rose rapidly compared to German prices, and these countries became uncompetitive. Hence, the EMS allowed for periodic adjustments of exchange rates for nations with high inflation rates. But the U.K. and Italy committed themselves to reducing inflation, primarily through tight monetary policies (aided by the decline in the real price of oil as displayed in Figure 8-9). By 1987 they had made sufficient progress and could commit to maintaining their exchange rates within a narrow band relative to the deutsche mark. However, the price of this progress was that unemployment rose to levels that were much higher than those in the United States. For instance, the unemployment rate in France never fell below 9 percent after 1985 and was above 12 percent in 1996–97.

The era of fixed exchange rates for the major European nations within the EMS lasted from 1987 to 1992, when it broke down. Italy, the United Kingdom, and several other countries, including Spain and Sweden, devalued their exchange rates relative to the DM, while France and several other countries maintained parity with it.

The divergence of exchange rates in Italy and the United Kingdom after 1992 helps to explain why in

---

However, in the real world, the speed of adjustment of inflation, and thus the value of the sacrifice ratio, depends on the actual slope of the Phillips Curve, not the assumptions of textbook authors. To compare the predictions of the textbook model with the real world, we can plot the inflation rate against real output with actual data in Figure 8-8 and compare the real-world adjustment path with the theoretical path in Figure 8-7. The plot in both diagrams starts in 1980 and extends through 1995 (it stops in 1995 in order to capture the two disinflation episodes of 1981–86 and 1990–95).

Comparing the two diagrams, we see that the real world behaved very similarly to the predictions of the theoretical model. The main difference is that in the real world nominal GDP growth was not held at 4 percent forever but was allowed to increase sharply in 1983–84; this explains why inflation did not decelerate as much in the real world (Figure 8-8) as in the theoretical model (Figure 8-7).

1994–97 inflation in those countries was substantially above that in France and Germany. However, the introduction of a single currency (the euro) in 1999 tied the exchange rate of Italy to that of France and Germany, leading to the near-convergence of Italy's inflation rate with those two countries. The United Kingdom (which refused to join the euro) maintained the same inflation rate as Italy during 2000–05.

Source: OECD *Economic Outlook*, December 2004.

How large was the real-world sacrifice ratio? The cumulative loss of output (the amount by which the output ratio fell below 100 percent) during 1980–86 was 28.2 percent. Since inflation fell by about six percentage points (from 9 to 3), the sacrifice ratio was 28.2/6, or 4.7. This is higher than the sacrifice ratio of 2.7 that we calculated from the theoretical adjustment path in Figure 8-7.[8]

The recession of the early 1990s achieved a further reduction of inflation from 3.8 percent in 1990 to 2.2 percent in 1995. The cumulative loss of output during 1991–95 was 7.9 percent, so the sacrifice ratio was 7.9/1.8, or 4.4, which is almost identical to that in the early 1980s.

---

[8] This estimate of the real-world sacrifice ratio is based on data for Y/Y^N and the GDP deflator contained in Appendix Table A-2.

Figure 8-8 The Inflation Rate and the Output Ratio, 1980–95

Notice how slower growth in nominal GDP was divided between slower inflation and slower real GDP growth. The output ratio fell from 97.8 percent in 1981:Q1 to 90.5 percent in 1982:Q4. A revival in demand growth allowed the output ratio to increase between 1983 and early 1989. The inflation rate decelerated during 1981–86, accelerated during 1987–90, and decelerated again as the output ratio fell in 1990–92. Inflation stayed low during the 1992–95 expansion because the output ratio did not exceed 100 percent during those years. Compare this graph with the same data as plotted in Figure 8-1 on p. 233.

Overall, our simple model of inflation appears to predict quite well the economy's adjustment to a "cold turkey" disinflation in which nominal GDP growth is reduced. The real-world sacrifice ratio is slightly higher than in the theoretical model, suggesting that the real-world *SP* curve may be slightly flatter than is assumed in the theoretical model of Figures 8-6 and 8-7.

Up until now we have deliberately omitted any discussion of inflation in the 1970s and in the most recent period, 1995–2004. These episodes illustrate the role of supply shocks, another determinant of inflation that operates quite differently from the demand shocks that we have been studying up to this point in the chapter.

8-9 The Importance of Supply Shocks

Demand inflation is a sustained increase in prices that is preceded by a permanent acceleration of nominal GDP growth.

So far in this chapter, we have studied **demand inflation**, which is inflation caused by an acceleration of the growth rate of nominal aggregate demand—that is, nominal GDP. Demand inflation can be caused by changes in any of the demand factors studied earlier in the book—consumer and business confidence, the money supply, real wealth, government spending, tax rates, transfers, and net exports. These same factors can also cause a deceleration in nominal GDP that leads to the adjustment paths of deflation depicted in Figures 8-7 and 8-8.

Now we turn to a second reason for changes in the inflation rate, that is, **supply inflation**. As we see in the top frame of Figure 8-9, during the decade between 1971 and 1981 the U.S. inflation rate exhibited volatile accelerations and decelerations that can be attributed to supply inflation. Shifts in supply inflation also help us understand why inflation was so low in 1986, and why it was again so low in 1995–98.

Supply inflation is an increase in prices that stems from an increase in business costs not directly related to a prior acceleration of nominal GDP growth.

8-9 The Importance of Supply Shocks   253

Jumps in Real Oil Prices Explain the Twin Peaks of Inflation

Figure 8-9 Four-Quarter Growth Rate of the GDP Deflator and the Level of Nominal and Real Oil Prices, 1970–2004

The top frame displays the inflation rate since 1970; this is the same series as was plotted in Figure 8-1. In the bottom frame, the nominal price of oil is compared with the real price of oil, using 1972 as a base year. Notice the upsurge in inflation in the top frame at the times of the two oil shocks in the bottom frame, that is, in 1974 and 1979–80. Notice also the low point of inflation in 1986 when oil prices tumbled, and also the low level of inflation and oil prices in 1998.

Types of Supply Shocks

Supply inflation stems from sharp changes in business costs that are not related to prior changes in nominal GDP growth. The most important single cause of supply inflation in the 1970s and early 1980s in most industrialized countries in the world was a sharp increase in the price of oil, shown in the bottom frame of Figure 8-9. A sharp decline in the price of oil in 1986 reversed some of the earlier harm done by supply inflation. The rise in the real price of oil during 1990, in 1999–2000, and again in 2004 are other examples of an adverse supply shock, while the decline during 1996–98 provides a recent example of a beneficial supply shock. Supply inflation can also result from an increase in the prices of other raw materials, particularly farm products, if they are sufficiently important.

Sometimes the *weather* causes supply shocks, as in the case of a crop failure that causes a sharp increase in farm prices. Usually supply shocks caused by the weather are *temporary*, lasting only a year or two, after which conditions return to normal. The OPEC oil shocks, however, were considered *permanent*, causing an increase in the real price of oil that lasted from 1974 to 1986.

Supply shocks can be either *adverse* or *beneficial*. An adverse supply shock is one that makes inflation worse while causing real GDP to fall, as in the case of sharp increases in oil in the 1970s. A beneficial supply shock is one that reduces inflation while causing real GDP to rise, as in the case of the sharp decline in oil prices in 1986.

Whether adverse or beneficial, supply shocks pose a difficult challenge for the makers of monetary and fiscal policy. Adverse supply shocks impose unpleasant choices on policymakers, who can avoid extra inflation only at the cost of lower real GDP, or vice versa. But even beneficial supply shocks may require policymakers to make choices.

Supply Shocks, the "Twin Peaks," and the "Valleys"

If demand shocks were the only cause of inflation, then we would observe periods after an acceleration of nominal GDP growth during which the output ratio would rise and the inflation rate would rise. Yet in other periods, the relationship between inflation and the output ratio would not be positive but rather negative. In the next section, we will learn to understand the source of this negative correlation as due to supply shocks that cause inflation to move sharply higher or lower, followed by a subsequent movement of the output ratio in the opposite direction. This explains the "twin peaks" of inflation in the periods 1974–75 and 1979–81. It also explains the "valleys" of low inflation in 1986 and 1997–98, both periods when the output ratio was using.

8-10 The Response of Inflation and the Output Ratio to a Supply Shock

In Figure 8-9 we examined the relationship between oil price shocks and the U.S. inflation rate. There we saw that increases in the *level* of the real price of oil caused a change in the aggregate *rate of inflation*. How can this response of the rate of inflation be explained in terms of the *SP* diagram?

Figure 8-10 The Effect on the Inflation Rate and the Output Ratio of an Adverse Supply Shock That Shifts the *SP* Curve Upward by 3 Percent

The economy is initially at point E_4, with an output ratio of 100 percent and both actual and expected inflation rates of 6 percent. The supply shock shifts the *SP* curve upward to SP_3. The movement of the economy depends on the policy response. With an accommodating policy, the economy moves from E_4 to point N, with a neutral policy to point L, and with an extinguishing policy to point M.

Supply Shocks and the Short-Run Phillips (*SP*) Curve

To see how supply shocks can shift the *SP* curve, we use Figure 8-10. The SP_2 curve in Figure 8-10 assumes that the expected rate of inflation is 6 percent. The vertical axis plots the aggregate rate of inflation, while the horizontal axis plots the output ratio.

Supply shocks shift the *SP* schedule. As long as the real price of oil remains constant, the only factor that could make the *SP* curve shift would be a change in the expected rate of inflation (p^e). But if a supply shock changes the real price of oil, then we have a second reason why the *SP* curve might shift up.

Point E_4 in Figure 8-10 depicts a situation of long-run equilibrium. Actual inflation is 6 percent, and initially the rate of nominal GDP growth is assumed to be 6 percent. Since SP_2 assumes that expected inflation (p^e) is 6 percent, the condition $p^e = p$, required for long-run equilibrium, is satisfied.

Now let us assume that oil producers suddenly double the price of oil over the course of a year, as occurred in 1979, and let us assume that its action is sufficient *to add three extra percentage points to the inflation rate at any given level of the output ratio.* The three extra points of inflation are reflected in the upward shift of the *SP* schedule from SP_2 to SP_3. Where will the economy move along the new SP_3?

Policy Responses to Supply Shocks

The response of the economy to the adverse permanent supply shock depicted in Figure 8-10 *depends on the response of nominal GDP growth*. The government can implement policy measures to alter nominal GDP growth. These policy actions determine where the economy moves along the new SP_3 schedule.

256 Chapter 8 • Inflation: Its Causes and Cures

Neutral, accommodating, and extinguishing policy responses. There are three possible policy responses. The first is called a **neutral policy**. Such a policy would attempt to keep nominal GDP growth unchanged from the original rate (6 percent). This is shown by point L in Figure 8-10. Since real GDP growth, by definition, must be equal to nominal GDP growth minus the inflation rate ($y = x - p$), *a neutral policy makes the output ratio decline by the same amount as inflation increases*. Thus, at point L, the output ratio falls by 2 percent (from 100 to 98) and inflation rises by 2 percentage points (from 6 to 8 percent).[9] The sum of −2 and +2 is precisely zero, the assumed zero change in the growth rate of nominal GDP.

> Following a supply shock, a **neutral policy** maintains nominal GDP growth so as to allow a decline in the output ratio equal to the increase of the inflation rate.

Does the government have any way to escape the simultaneous worsening of inflation and decline in the output ratio shown at point L? It can keep the output ratio fixed only if it is willing to accept more inflation. Or, it can keep inflation from accelerating above 6 percent only if it is willing to accept a greater decline in the output ratio.

An **accommodating policy** attempts to maintain the output ratio intact at point N. To do this, inflation must be allowed to rise by the full extent of the vertical shift in SP, so that inflation jumps from 6 to 9 percent per year. This acceleration of inflation requires an acceleration of nominal GDP growth from 6 to 9 percent per year.

> Following a supply shock, an **accommodating policy** raises nominal GDP growth so as to maintain the original output ratio.

An **extinguishing policy** attempts to eliminate entirely the extra inflation caused by the supply shock. This requires cutting nominal GDP growth by 6 percent to zero, which is enough to take the economy to point M, where the inflation rate is 6 percent, but the output ratio has fallen from 100 to 94 percent (instead of to 98 percent at point L). Why is the extra four-point decline in the output ratio necessary? To extinguish the extra two percentage points of inflation that occur at L compared to M, the output ratio must be cut by four percentage points, since the slope of the SP curve is assumed to be 1/2 (two units in a vertical direction for each four units in the horizontal direction).

> Following a supply shock, an **extinguishing policy** reduces nominal GDP growth so as to maintain the original inflation rate.

What Happens in Subsequent Periods

If the hypothetical supply shock occurs for just one period, then in Figure 8-10 the SP curve shifts down to its original position (SP_2) after one period at position SP_3. The economy would then be free to return to the original output ratio and the original inflation rate. The indirect effect on the output ratio (Y/Y^N) and on the rate of inflation would last for just one period.

But *the SP curve returns to position SP_2 only if the expected inflation rate remains at 6 percent*. The expected inflation rate must not respond to the one-period increase in the actual inflation rate that occurs at points L and N in Figure 8-10. Is this plausible? The response of the expected inflation rate depends on whether people view the supply shock as temporary or permanent and on whether labor contracts incorporate cost-of-living agreements (COLAs) that automatically boost wages by a percentage that is related to the inflation rate.

Why are COLAs crucial? Without COLAs, contract negotiators will recognize that it is possible for the economy to return to its original position (point E_4 in Figure 8-10) after the one-period effect of the supply shock. But with COLAs, the one-period increase of inflation (to point L or N) will be incorporated auto-

---

[9] The text discussion of the graphical example in Figure 8-10 ignores the decline in Y^N that is likely to occur. The precise definition of a neutral policy is one involving no change in the excess of nominal GDP growth over the growth rate of natural real GDP from its initial value, assumed to be 6 percent ($x - y^N = 6$). This more precise definition is developed in the appendix to this chapter.

matically into a faster growth of nominal wage rates *next period*. Contract negotiators in subsequent periods will see that COLAs have raised the rate of change of the nominal wage and will realize that this makes it impossible for the economy to return to point E_4. Their expected rate of inflation will shift up above the original 6 percent, and the SP curve will shift to a position above the original SP_2 in subsequent periods.

The policy dilemma. Thus we see that COLAs create a dilemma for the makers of monetary policy. COLAs imply that a permanent supply shock will permanently raise the inflation rate *unless an extinguishing policy response to the initial impact of the supply shock prevents any increase at all of inflation and thus prevents any increase at all in the rate of change of nominal wage rates.*

What should the Fed do when presented with this dilemma? It faces the classic trade-off between inflation and lost output. With even partial COLA protection for workers, a permanent adverse supply shock will permanently raise the inflation rate in the absence of an extinguishing policy. But this does not mean that the Fed should actually pursue such an extinguishing policy. The social costs of the loss in output may be severe, as Y/Y^N declines to point M in Figure 8-10, while the social costs of permanently higher inflation following a neutral or accommodating policy response may be relatively small. We examine those social costs in the next chapter.[10]

Why Beneficial Supply Shocks Help Us Understand the 1990s

The great macroeconomic puzzle about U.S. economic performance in the 1990s, especially in 1996–2000, is why the economy performed so well. By early 2000, the unemployment rate had reached a lower level than in any calendar quarter since 1969, while in 1997–98 the inflation rate was lower than at any time since 1961. How could both unemployment and inflation be so low at the same time? Our analysis of supply shocks provides the answer.

The policy options in response to beneficial supply shocks like those in the late 1990s are the same as for adverse supply shocks like those of the 1970s and early 1980s. A neutral policy maintains constant nominal GDP growth, thus causing the benefits of the supply shock to be split between lower inflation and higher real GDP. An accommodating policy requires a reduction in nominal GDP growth, so that the entire impact of the beneficial shock reduces the inflation rate and none spills over to boost the output ratio. In contrast, the third policy option, an extinguishing policy, would keep the inflation rate constant and allow the full impact of the shock to boost the output ratio.

Preview: A Graphical Summary of the Role of Supply Shocks

The evolution of the U.S. economy was dominated by the effects of supply shocks in 1974–75, 1979–81, 1986, and again in 1996–2000. In the first two episodes, the supply shocks operated in an adverse direction, primarily due to sharp jumps in oil prices but also due to increases in non-oil import prices in response to a decline in the foreign exchange rate of the dollar. Accordingly, the

---

[10] The analysis of supply shocks in this chapter was introduced in two papers. See Robert J. Gordon, "Alternative Responses of Policy to External Supply Shocks," *Brookings Papers on Economic Activity*, vol. 6, no. 1 (1975), pp. 183–206, and Edmund S. Phelps, "Commodity Supply Shocks and Full-Employment Monetary Policy," *Journal of Money, Credit, and Banking*, vol. 10 (May 1978), pp. 206–21. The separate models in these two papers were merged and summarized in Robert J. Gordon, "Supply Shocks and Monetary Policy Revisited," *American Economic Review Papers and Proceedings*, vol. 74 (May 1984), pp. 38–43.

Figure 8-11 **Effect of Adverse Supply Shocks in the 1970s and Beneficial Supply Shocks in the 1990s**

The black *SP* line shows the relationship between the inflation rate and the output ratio if there are no supply shocks. Adverse supply shocks, primarily increases in the real price of oil, moved the economy in an undesirable direction in the 1970s, with an acceleration of inflation and decline in the output ratio. Beneficial supply shocks, as discussed in the text, moved the economy in a desirable direction in the late 1990s, with a deceleration of inflation and an increase in the output ratio.

main response of the economy was for inflation to increase and for the output ratio to decline, as shown by the arrow marked "1970s" in Figure 8-11.

As we shall see in the next section, several supply shocks operated in the opposite (beneficial) direction during the late 1990s. As a result, the main response of the economy was for inflation to decrease and for the output ratio to increase, as shown by the arrow marked "1990s" in Figure 8-11. We now turn to the key question: What were these beneficial supply shocks that help to explain the outstanding economic performance of the U.S. economy in the late 1990s?

Self-Test

Imagine that the real price of oil falls by half within a single year and exhibits no change thereafter.

1. With what policy response will the inflation rate be reduced by this event in the year of the change?
2. With what policy response will the output ratio increase in the year of the change?
3. With what policy response will there be no change in the inflation rate? No change in the output ratio?

8-11 Case Study

The Goldilocks Economy—Why Inflation Was So Low in the Late 1990s

The American economy of the late 1990s was a source of pride for the United States, a source of envy for foreigners trying to learn the secret of the U.S. success, and a source of puzzlement for macroeconomists. Many observers had believed as the output ratio reached 100 percent in 1994 (see the bottom frame of Figure 8-1 on p. 233), inflation was sure to accelerate. Indeed, the output ratio continued to increase and in 1999–2000 reached its highest values since the late 1960s. Yet inflation refused to accelerate and instead fell in early 1998 to its lowest rate observed since the early 1960s (although inflation did finally accelerate in 1999–2001).

Some called this macroeconomic achievement the "miracle economy," while others called it the "Goldilocks" economy after the story of Goldilocks and the three bears, whose three bowls of porridge were "too hot," "too cold," and "just right."[11] Clearly, the deceleration of inflation in 1997–98 was at the heart of this achievement. Since inflation did not accelerate, there was no need for the Fed to pursue a restrictive monetary policy; indeed the Fed felt free to reduce interest rates in late 1998. Freed from the restraint of restrictive monetary policy that had choked earlier expansions, the miracle economy charged ahead, real GDP growth exceeded all previous estimates of what was possible, and the stock market tripled between 1995 and 2000.

While some observers attributed the miracle economy to the Fed's brilliant monetary policy, it was clear that the true heroine of the drama was the deceleration of inflation, and the basic challenge for economists was to explain that deceleration. In this section we interpret the decline in inflation as the result of several beneficial supply shocks that occurred simultaneously during the mid-to-late 1990s. Because there were multiple shocks working together, they had more impact than any single shock operating by itself.

The Four Beneficial Supply Shocks of the 1990s

We have learned in the previous two sections that beneficial supply shocks push the economy's *SP* curve downward and to the right, thus allowing policymakers the happy choice between lower inflation, a higher output ratio, or both. The story of the 1990s was not simply the reverse of the 1970s, when higher oil prices caused poor macroeconomic performance. Instead, in the 1990s, lower oil prices were only one of four supply shocks that all moved in the beneficial direction at roughly the same time.

1. **Lower real price of energy.** Energy prices fell between 1996 and early 1999, providing the first of the four beneficial supply shocks to the economy. Part of the decline in energy prices can be traced to a financial crisis in Asia during 1997–98. Weaker demand in several Asian economies reduced the demand for oil relative to the supply of oil and put downward pressure on the price of oil.

2. **Lower real price of imports.** By far the most important of the beneficial supply shocks was the declining relative price of imported products other than oil. From 1992 to 1999, the real price of imports declined cumulatively by a total of 20.5 percent. This key ingredient in the "Goldilocks economy" reflected the continuing appreciation of the U.S. dollar that occurred from

---

[11] The analysis in this section is based in part on Robert J. Gordon, "Foundations of the Goldilocks Economy: Supply Shocks and the Time-Varying NAIRU," *Brookings Papers on Economic Activity*, no. 2, (1998), pp. 297–333, and subsequent unpublished research that updates this article.

1995 to 2001 (see Figure 6-6 on p. 179). Any tendency of the dollar to appreciate makes imports cheaper, helping to explain why the real price of imports fell so much in the late 1990s.[12]

Overall, the combined effect of lower real energy and import prices was to hold down inflation by about 1.5 percent compared to what would have happened with a constant level of energy and import prices. Changes in the real prices of energy and imports are the "traditional" supply shocks, which operated in an adverse direction in the 1970s and a beneficial direction in the 1990s. In addition, two new types of supply shocks that played little, if any, role prior to the 1990s both operated in a beneficial direction in the 1990s.

3. **Faster decline in the real prices of computers**. The price of computers has declined continuously since the earliest mainframe computers in the 1950s. The role of computer prices as a beneficial supply shock in the late 1990s reflects a sharp acceleration in their rate of annual price decline, which went from an average annual rate of −14 percent during 1987–95 to −32 percent during 1995–99. This shift to a faster rate of price decline subtracted about 0.3 percent from the rate of inflation that would have otherwise occurred in 1995–99.

4. **Slower inflation in medical care**. Medical care is a major sector in the economy, making up 17 percent of personal consumption expenditures and 12 percent of total GDP. During the late 1980s and early 1990s, inflation in this sector was running at a rate almost twice as fast as the rest of the economy, but after 1993, medical care inflation slowed down to roughly the same rate as the rest of the economy. Much of this decline in medical care inflation has been attributed to the spread of health maintenance organizations (HMOs) and other types of managed medical care. The slowdown in medical care inflation between 1993 and 1998 reduced inflation by another 0.3 percent. After 1999, medical care inflation speeded up again, helping to explain the acceleration of inflation in 1999–2000 evident in the top frame of Figure 8-9.

Taking these four factors together, they combined to produce a significant downward shift in the SP curve during the late 1990s. And their effect lingered even after they began to be reversed, as when oil prices increased after early 1999 and medical care inflation resumed after 1998. Because inflation had been so low in 1997–98, the expected rate of inflation (p^e) was also much lower than if the beneficial supply shocks had never happened. A low expected rate of inflation helped to minimize the acceleration of inflation in 1999–2000.

After 2000, the economy fell into a recession, and the output ratio was below 100 percent throughout the period 2001–04 (as shown in Figure 8-1 on p. 233). The low output ratio caused the inflation rate to decline in 2001–02 and then to remain relatively stable in 2003–04 despite another sharp increase in oil prices and the beginning of a depreciation in the dollar, which raised import prices and put upward pressure on the prices of import-competing goods.

---

[12] A lower real price of imports directly reduces the price deflator for consumer expenditures, part of which is spent on imported goods and services. In addition, competition from imported goods and services puts downward pressure on the prices of import-competing goods and services produced within the United States and hence also reduces the GDP deflator.

8-12 Inflation and Output Fluctuations: Recapitulation of Causes and Cures

In this chapter, we have learned that an acceleration of inflation can be caused by excessive nominal GDP growth and by adverse supply shocks. Supply inflation and demand inflation are interrelated because the extent and duration of the acceleration of inflation following a supply shock depends on the response of nominal GDP growth, which is controlled in part by policymakers.

A Summary of Inflation and Output Responses

Figure 8-12 provides a highly simplified summary of our analysis in this chapter. The figure presents four cases corresponding to (a) demand shifts alone, (b) supply shifts alone, (c) demand and supply shifts in the same vertical direction, and (d) demand and supply shifts in opposite directions. In our discussion we identify examples from U.S. history that illustrate the four cases.

Case A: Demand shifts alone. When we observe a marked increase in the output ratio with a modest or small increase in the rate of inflation, we can infer that there has been an acceleration of nominal aggregate demand growth with little if any shift in the *SP* curve. Expectations of inflation (p^e) remain roughly constant, and there are no supply shocks. The economy exhibited this type of response during 1963–66, when tax cuts and the beginning of Vietnam War spending, supported by monetary accommodation, boosted nominal GDP growth. A similar movement to the northeast occurred in 1987–89. Examples of a shift in a southwestern direction, with a deceleration of nominal GDP growth, occurred in the first few quarters of the 1981–82 recession, when there was a sharp decline in the output ratio with little downward response of the inflation rate, and a milder repeat of this episode in 1990–91 and 2001–02.

Case B: Supply shifts alone. The United States experienced a straight northwestward movement in 1973–74, when food and energy supply shocks sharply boosted the inflation rate, with a relatively small change in the rate of nominal GDP growth. As a result, the inflation rate and the output ratio moved in opposite directions and by about the same amount. In 1979 and 1980, a second supply shock had roughly the same impact. The most important examples of a southeast movement were caused by the 1986 collapse in the price of oil and by the beneficial supply shocks of 1996–2000 reviewed in the previous section.

Case C: Demand and supply shifts in the same vertical direction. When we observe the economy move straight north on the diagram, with an acceleration of inflation but little change in the output ratio, we can infer that there is a simultaneous demand and supply shift. For instance, between 1967 and 1969 nominal GDP growth accelerated while the *SP* curve shifted upward in response to accelerating inflationary expectations. As a result of this, inflation accelerated while the output ratio remained constant.

Case D: Demand and supply shifts in opposite directions. The economy can move straight to the right when nominal GDP growth accelerates and cancels out the effect of a downward *SP* shift. This occurred in 1984, when the effect of falling inflation expectations in holding down the inflation rate was offset by rapid nominal GDP growth. A leftward movement can occur when

A Summary of Inflation and Output Responses

Case A: Aggregate demand shift
- Fixed SP
- Acceleration of nominal GDP growth
- Deceleration of nominal GDP growth

Case B: Supply shock
- Adverse SP shift with neutral nominal GDP response
- Beneficial SP shift with neutral nominal GDP response

Case C: Simultaneous demand and supply shifts in same direction
- Adverse SP shift with nominal GDP growth accommodation
- Beneficial SP shift with nominal GDP growth accommodation

Case D: Simultaneous demand and supply shifts in opposite direction
- Nominal GDP growth extinguishes adverse SP shift
- Nominal GDP growth extinguishes beneficial SP shift

Figure 8-12 Responses of the Inflation Rate (p) and the Output Ratio (Y/Y^N) to Shifts in Nominal GDP Growth and in the *SP* Curve

In Case A, an aggregate demand shift moves the economy to the southwest, or to the northeast if there is no supply shift. In Case B, a supply shift moves the economy to the northwest, or to the southeast when nominal GDP growth is unchanged (a neutral policy response). Case C illustrates the northward or southward movement that occurs with an accommodative policy response to a supply shift. Case D illustrates the westward or eastward movement that accompanies a supply shift with an extinguishing supply response.

nominal GDP growth decelerates while the *SP* curve is shifting upward. This occurred during the 1969–70 recession, when nominal GDP growth slowed while the *SP* curve was shifting upward as the expected inflation rate (p^e) continued its slow and delayed adjustment to the acceleration of actual inflation during 1966–69. This interpretation helps us understand why inflation in early 1971 was still as rapid as in 1969 despite an intervening decline in the output ratio. The same pattern was repeated in 1989–90.

Self-Test

In Figure 8-12, which plots the inflation rate against the output ratio, it is possible for the economy to move in any direction. Can you explain why the economy would move in each possible direction:

1. North?
2. Northeast?
3. East?
4. Southeast?
5. South?
6. Southwest?
7. West?
8. Northwest?

Cures for Inflation

Just as excessive nominal GDP growth and adverse supply shocks are the fundamental causes of inflation, the basic cure for inflation is to turn these causes on their head. The reverse of fast nominal GDP growth is obviously slow nominal GDP growth. A decision to reduce the inflation rate by restricting the growth rate of nominal GDP can be both effective and costly, as in 1981–82 or, to a lesser extent, in 1990–92. Inflation can be cut markedly, but only at the cost of a substantial and prolonged slump in the output ratio and a substantial increase in the number of jobless workers.

But government policy against inflation is not limited to creating a deceleration of nominal GDP growth. Whether there are adverse supply shocks or not, the government can attempt to create beneficial supply shocks by eliminating or weakening price-raising or cost-raising legislation, and by creative tax and subsidy policy.

Sometimes government policymakers are just plain lucky, as when a beneficial supply shock occurs. The decline in oil prices in 1986 was one example of such a beneficial shock, and so was the role of several beneficial supply shocks in 1996–2000. In these episodes, it is important for policymakers to recognize their good luck and to prepare for a possible reversal in the sources of the beneficial shocks.

8-13 How Is the Unemployment Rate Related to the Inflation Rate?

Economists frequently discuss the "tradeoff between unemployment and inflation." Is there such a tradeoff? In this section we learn that there is a strong negative correlation between the unemployment rate and the *output ratio*, and so: *Everything we have learned in this chapter about the relationship between the output ratio and the inflation rate is true in the reverse direction for the relationship between the unemployment rate and the inflation rate. Since the relationship between the output ratio and the inflation rate can be positive, negative, vertical, or horizontal, the same is true for the relationship between the unemployment rate and the inflation rate. In short, there is no systematic negative relationship between the unemployment rate and the inflation rate.*

Changes in the Unemployment Rate are the Mirror Image of Changes in Real GDP

At the beginning of this book, we learned that the unemployment rate and inflation rate are two of the most important concepts in macroeconomics. What have we learned thus far about the unemployment rate? Beginning in Chapter 1 (see Figure 1-2 on p. 7) we learned that the unemployment rate is *inversely related* to real GDP, or more precisely, to the *output ratio* (the ratio of actual real GDP to natural real GDP). Thus we can discuss the economy's prosperity as described either by *low* unemployment or a *high* output ratio. We can describe the opposite conditions of weak aggregate demand, recessions, and job loss either by *high* unemployment or a *low* output ratio.

Throughout Chapters 3–6 of this book, we have focused on explaining business cycles in real GDP, caused primarily by the ups and downs in aggregate demand. *We have not required a separate theory to explain unemployment, simply because unemployment is inversely related to the output ratio.* Any factor that raises aggregate demand—whether events in the private sector of the economy such as business and consumer optimism or an increase in foreign income that raises net exports, or an event in the government sector such as higher government spending, lower tax rates, or a higher money supply—all of these both boost the output ratio and reduce unemployment. In this section, we will take a closer look at the mirror image relationship between the unemployment rate and the output ratio.

The Unemployment Rate, the Output Ratio, and Okun's Law

The close relationship between the unemployment rate and the output ratio is illustrated in Figure 8-13. The unemployment rate is plotted on the vertical axis, and the average unemployment rate since 1965 is indicated at a vertical level of 6.0 percent. The output ratio is plotted on the horizontal axis, and the long-run equilibrium value of the output ratio is marked at 100 percent.

In Figure 8-13 we notice the cluster of prosperous years, 1965–69 and 1999–2000, in the lower right corner, with values of the output ratio well above 100 percent and unusually low unemployment rates. The contrasting situation in the upper left corner occurred in the recession years 1975, 1982, and 1983, when massive layoffs caused the output ratio to fall and unemployment to rise. The negative slope of the blue line going through the points in Figure 8-13 just reflects common sense. When sales slump, workers are laid off and the jobless rate rises. But when sales boom and the output ratio is high, some of the jobless are hired and the unemployment rate declines.

The close negative connection between the unemployment rate (U) and the output ratio was first pointed out in the early 1960s by Arthur M. Okun, who was chairman of the Council of Economic Advisers in the Johnson administration. Because this theory has held up so well, the relationship is known as **Okun's Law**. U tends to follow the major movements in the output ratio; in addition, the percentage-point change in the unemployment rate tends to be roughly 0.5 times the percentage change in the output ratio, in the opposite

Okun's Law is a regular negative relationship between the output ratio (Y/Y^N) and the gap between the actual unemployment rate and the average rate of unemployment.

8-13 How Is the Unemployment Rate Related to the Inflation Rate? 265

A High Output Ratio Goes with Low Unemployment, and Vice Versa

Figure 8-13 The U.S. Ratio of Actual to Natural Real GDP (Y/Y^N) and the Unemployment Rate, 1965–2004

This diagram illustrates that unemployment (U) moves inversely with the output ratio (Y/Y^N). In prosperous years, such as 1965–69 and 1999–2000, the observations are in the lower right corner, with a high output ratio and low unemployment. The opposite extreme occurred in 1982, with the observation plotted at the upper left corner. A recession occurred, the output ratio fell, and workers were laid off. The negatively sloped blue line expresses the relationship between U and Y/Y^N, sometimes called Okun's Law.

(*Source*: Appendix Table A-1.)

direction. For instance, the downward-sloping Okun's Law line is drawn so that an output ratio of 100 percent corresponds to an average actual unemployment rate of 6.0 percent. A drop in the output ratio by 4 percentage points, from 100 to 96, would correspond to an increase in the unemployment rate of 2.0 percentage points, as indicated by the Okun's Law line going through 8.0 percent unemployment on the vertical axis and 96 percent on the horizontal axis.

Recall that the output ratio is defined as the ratio of actual to natural real GDP. When the output ratio is equal to 100 percent, the actual unemployment rate is equal to the natural rate of unemployment. Throughout much of the period plotted in Figure 8-13, the natural unemployment rate was very close to the average unemployment rate of 6.0 percent. In periods like 1965–69, the output ratio was well above 100 percent and the actual unemployment rate was well below the natural rate of unemployment. In periods like 1975 and 1982–83, the output ratio was well below 100 percent and the actual unemployment rate was well above the natural rate of unemployment.[13]

Interpreting the Postwar History of Unemployment and Inflation

The analysis of this chapter now allows us to interpret the history of unemployment and inflation since 1960, as displayed in Figure 8-14. We have already learned that when supply shocks are absent, an increase in aggregate demand boosts the output ratio and the inflation rate. Because unemployment declines when the output ratio rises, an increase in aggregate demand creates a *negative tradeoff* between unemployment and inflation. It is this negative tradeoff that restrains the Fed from allowing aggregate demand to increase so much that the unemployment rate is pushed substantially below the natural rate of unemployment.

When is the unemployment rate too low? This occurs whenever the output ratio rises above 100 percent, implying that the actual unemployment rate falls substantially below the natural rate of unemployment. As shown in Figure 8-14 by the blue line, the unemployment rate fell to its lowest level of the entire period during 1965–69, and the orange line shows the acceleration of inflation that occurred between 1965 and 1970. This was the classic period of the negative tradeoff between unemployment and inflation, but once inflation expectations and wages began to ratchet upward in response to accelerating inflation, the Fed introduced restrictive policies that reduced aggregate demand, and the unemployment rate shot up in 1970–71.

A similar and milder episode of relatively low unemployment in 1988–89 also pushed up the inflation rate in 1988–90 and again elicited a restrictive response by the Fed that reduced aggregate demand and led to the recession of 1990–91. The negative tradeoff between unemployment and inflation is also evident in the periods when high unemployment brought the inflation rate down, as in 1975–76, 1982–83, 1991–92, and 2001–02.

A central theme of this chapter has been that demand shocks and supply shocks have opposing effects on the relationship between the output ratio and inflation—demand shocks create a positive relation and supply shocks create a negative relationship. The same thing is true of the relationship between unemployment and inflation, but in reverse. There is a *negative tradeoff* between unemployment and inflation created by demand shocks, and a *positive relation* between unemployment and inflation created by supply shocks. This is evident in the 1970s, when sharp increases in oil prices in 1974–75 and 1979–81 created the "twin peaks" of unemployment and inflation. In each case, inflation soared first, which pushed the economy into recession. In 1975, the peak of unemployment came about six months after the peak of inflation; in 1982, the peak of unemployment came about 18 months after the peak of inflation. Thus inflation created these recessions, just as in the theoretical model of Figure 8-10 on p. 255.

Beneficial supply shocks also created a positive relation between unemployment and inflation in the late 1990s. By making possible a decline of infla-

---

[13] *Review*: Natural real GDP and the natural rate of unemployment are both defined as a situation consistent with a constant inflation rate. See Section 1-3, pp. 5–8.

8-13 How Is the Unemployment Rate Related to the Inflation Rate? 267

The Peaks and the Valleys

Figure 8-14 The Unemployment Rate and the Inflation Rate, 1960–2004
During 1963–70 and 1986–90, the inflation–unemployment relation was negative, as falling unemployment indicated a positive demand shock that boosted inflation. But in 1973–75, 1979–81, and 1997–98, the unemployment–inflation relation was positive, as an autonomous upward or downward movement of the inflation rate caused by supply shocks was followed by a movement of the unemployment rate in the same direction.

tion in 1997–98 despite high aggregate demand, supply shocks made it possible for the Fed to keep interest rates relatively stable, and as a result unemployment declined steadily from 1992 to 1999.

Implications of the Unemployment–Inflation Tradeoff

As we can see from Figure 8-14, unemployment is sometimes negatively related to inflation because of demand shocks and sometimes positively related because of supply shocks. In the absence of supply shocks, however, the negative unemployment–inflation tradeoff is the primary constraint that prevents the Fed from allowing aggregate demand to grow without limit. When the unemployment rate falls below the natural rate of unemployment, the Fed must raise interest rates in order to restrain the growth of aggregate demand and prevent an acceleration of inflation. Often the Fed's restrictive policies create a recession, as in 1969–70, 1981–82, and 1990–91, and the recession raises the unemployment rate and reverses the acceleration of inflation, working through the negative unemployment–inflation trade-off.

The unemployment–inflation tradeoff suggests that the unemployment rate cannot be maintained below the natural rate of unemployment for any substantial length of time. To achieve a lower unemployment rate permanently, something must happen to reduce the natural rate of unemployment itself. Indeed, in the 1990s the natural rate of unemployment fell from roughly 6 percent to roughly 5 percent. In the next chapter, we will learn about both the costs of inflation and the determinants of the natural rate of unemployment, and about some of the factors that reduced the natural rate of unemployment in the 1990s.

Summary

1. The fundamental cause of demand inflation is excessive growth in nominal GDP. In long-run equilibrium, when actual inflation turns out to be exactly what people expected when they negotiated their labor contracts, the pace of that inflation depends only on the growth rate of nominal GDP.

2. In the short run, actual inflation may be higher or lower than expected, and real GDP can differ from long-run equilibrium natural real GDP. An acceleration of nominal GDP growth in the short run goes partially into an acceleration of inflation, but also partly into an increase in the output ratio, that is, the ratio of actual to natural real GDP. When expectations of inflation catch up to actual inflation, the economy will return to its level of natural real GDP.

3. The response of inflation to an acceleration in demand growth depends on the slope of the short-run Phillips Curve (SP) and the speed with which expectations of inflation respond to changes in the actual inflation rate. The flatter is the SP curve, the longer it takes for inflation to respond to faster nominal GDP growth, and the longer the temporary expansion of the output ratio.

4. A permanent end to inflation requires that nominal GDP growth drop to the growth rate of natural real GDP, assumed in the text to be zero. But this will cause a temporary recession in actual real GDP, the length and intensity of which will depend on the slope of the SP curve.

5. The highly variable inflation experience of the United States since the 1960s cannot be explained solely as the consequence of previous fluctuations in the growth rate of nominal GDP. Instead, supply shocks caused inflation to accelerate and decelerate independently of the influence of nominal GDP growth.

6. The main effect of an adverse supply shock is the impact on the inflation rate and on the output ratio. Policymakers cannot avoid a worsening of inflation, a decline in the output ratio, or both. An accommodating policy keeps real GDP at its previous level, but causes inflation to accelerate by the full impact of the supply shock; an extinguishing policy attempts to cancel out the acceleration of inflation, but at the cost of a reduction in real GDP.

7. Accommodation would be an attractive policy if the upward shift in the SP curve were expected to be temporary, and if expectations of inflation did not respond to the temporary jump in the inflation rate. But accommodation may cause a permanent increase of inflation if wage contracts have cost-of-living adjustment clauses that incorporate the supply shock into wage growth.

8. The low inflation rate experienced by the United States in the late 1990s reflected in part the role of beneficial supply shocks, created by favorable developments in the medical care and computer industries, as well as the falling real prices of energy and imports.

9. Demand shocks create a negative tradeoff between unemployment and inflation, and supply shocks create a positive relation between unemployment and inflation. The negative tradeoff created by demand shocks explains why the Fed has used restrictive policy in several episodes to create recessions in order to control inflation.

Concepts

inflation
output ratio
demand shock
supply shock
expected rate of inflation
short-run Phillips Curve
expectations-augmented Phillips Curve
forward-looking expectations
backward-looking expectations
adaptive expectations
disinflation
cold turkey
sacrifice ratio
demand inflation
supply inflation
neutral policy
accommodating policy
extinguishing policy
Okun's Law

Questions

1. Use Figure 8-1 to discuss when, since 1960, the output ratio and the inflation rate moved in the same direction and when they moved in opposite directions.
2. In what ways are the *SAS* curve and the *SP* curve similar? In what ways do they differ?
3. Explain whether each of the following events causes a movement up or down along the *SP* curve or an upward or downward shift of the *SP* curve.
   (a) an increase in the rate of money supply growth
   (b) an increase in the inflation rate expected by workers and business firms
   (c) a decrease in production costs resulting from technological improvements
   (d) a decrease in nominal GDP growth
4. If the equilibrium real wage remains constant, what happens to the nominal wage when the actual inflation rate exceeds the expected inflation rate?
5. What are the three conditions for long-run equilibrium? What happens if each of the conditions is violated?
6. In Figure 8-4, why can't the economy move from point E_0 to point D in Figure 8-4 when the level of real GDP increases?
7. Distinguish between forward-looking and backward-looking expectations. Which type of expectations would rational workers and firms be most likely to use? Explain why.
8. Suppose that when nominal GDP growth changes, workers and firms immediately adjust their inflation expectations so that $p^e = x$. Is this an example of forward-looking or backward-looking expectations? How does it alter the adjustment loops in Figures 8-5 and 8-7? How does it affect the output cost of disinflation?
9. Suppose that workers and business firms believe that the Fed will take action to prevent demand shocks from causing a permanent change in the inflation rate.
   (a) Will the short-run Phillips Curve shift when a change in the output ratio changes the inflation rate?
   (b) For workers and business firms to continue to hold these expectations, explain what actions the Fed must take when there is a positive demand shock and when there is a negative demand shock.
10. Assume that the output ratio initially equals 100 and that natural real GDP grows by 3 percent per year. If p^e remains constant and actual real GDP rises, what happens to the rate of inflation?
11. Explain the role played by the slope of the *SP* curve in determining the path taken by the economy when there is a deceleration of nominal GDP growth.
12. What data suggest that the fluctuations in the inflation rate that took place during the 1970s were not examples of demand inflation?
13. What differentiates accommodating, extinguishing, and neutral policy responses to an adverse supply shock? What happens to the rate of inflation and the real output ratio in each of the three cases?
14. Under what conditions would a permanent supply shock cause a temporary increase in the inflation rate? If these conditions exist, are there any permanent effects of the supply shock on the economy?
15. Compare and contrast the causes and effects of the beneficial supply shocks of 1986 and 1995–2000.
16. Identify the combination of changes in nominal GDP growth and supply shocks that could account for each of the following observed changes in inflation and the output ratio.
    (a) Inflation and the output ratio both increase.
    (b) Inflation increases and the output ratio decreases.
    (c) Inflation is constant and the output ratio decreases.
    (d) Inflation decreases and the output ratio is constant.
17. In each of the following cases, explain whether the policymakers' response to a beneficial supply shock was accommodating, extinguishing, or neutral.
    (a) The inflation rate fell, but the unemployment rate did not change.
    (b) The inflation and the unemployment rates both fell.
    (c) The unemployment rate fell, but the inflation rate did not change.

Note: Asterisks designate Problems that require the Appendix to Chapter 8.

Problems

1. Suppose that natural real GDP is constant. For every 1 percent increase in the rate of inflation above its expected level, firms are willing to increase real GDP by 4 percent. The purpose of this problem is to learn how to draw the short-run Phillips Curve and to understand how either a change in the expected rate of inflation or a supply shock causes it to shift.
   (a) Given that the output ratio is initially 100 and the expected inflation rate equals 3.2 percent, calculate the rate of inflation if real GDP grows by 3.2 percent.
   (b) Given that the output ratio is initially 100 and the expected inflation rate equals 3.2 percent,

calculate the rate of inflation if real GDP grows by 5.6 percent.
(c) Given that the output ratio is initially 100 and the expected inflation rate equals 3.2 percent, calculate the rate of inflation if real GDP declines by 2.4 percent.
(d) Given that the output ratio is initially 100 and the expected inflation rate equals 3.2 percent, calculate the rate of inflation if real GDP declines by 4.4 percent.
(e) Use your answers to parts (a)–(d) to draw the short-run Phillips Curve, given that the expected inflation rate equals 3.2 percent.
(f) Given that the output ratio is initially 100 and the expected inflation rate equals 1.4 percent, calculate the rate of inflation if real GDP grows by 2.8 percent.
(g) Given that the output ratio is initially 100 and the expected inflation rate equals 1.4 percent, calculate the rate of inflation if real GDP grows by 5.2 percent.
(h) Given that the output ratio is initially 100 and the expected inflation rate equals 1.4 percent, calculate the rate of inflation if real GDP declines by 1.6 percent.
(i) Given that the output ratio is initially 100 and the expected inflation rate equals 1.4 percent, calculate the rate of inflation if real GDP declines by 6.4 percent.
(j) Use your answers to parts (f)–(i) to draw the short-run Phillips Curve, given that the expected inflation rate equals 1.4 percent.
(k) Suppose that a beneficial supply shock lowers the inflation rate by 1.2 percentage points at any output ratio. Use your answers to parts (f)–(i) to draw the short-run Phillips Curve, given the beneficial supply shock.

*2. Suppose that natural real GDP is constant. The growth rate of nominal GDP, x, equals the rate of inflation, p, plus the growth rate of real GDP, y. The equation for the short-run Phillips Curve is $p = p^e + 0.5(\text{output ratio} - 100)$. Finally, the expected rate of inflation in the current period equals the actual rate of inflation in the previous period, that is, $p^e = p_{-1}$.
(a) Show that the equation for the short-run Phillips Curve describes Figure 8-3 in the sense that points E_0, E_1, and E_2 in Figure 8-3 all satisfy the equation for the short-run Phillips Curve.
(b) Initially assume that the nominal GDP growth rate, the expected rate of inflation, and the actual rate of inflation all equal 2 percent, and that the output ratio equals 100. The following table gives the nominal GDP growth rate, x, over the next ten periods.

Time period	1	2	3	4	5	6	7	8	9	10
x	5.0	6.0	5.5	4.8	4.4	3.1	2.6	2.8	3.0	3.2

For each of these time periods, derive the short-run Phillips Curve and calculate the rate of growth of real GDP, the output ratio, and the rate of inflation.
(c) Explain why the rates of inflation and the output ratio for time periods 5 and 10 are on the long-run Phillips Curve.

3. The purpose of this problem is to study the sacrifice ratio. Suppose that initially actual and natural real GDP both equal 11,000 and that the rate of inflation is 3.5 percent. Natural real GDP grows by 3 percent per year over the next five years. Actual real GDP decreases by 2 percent in the first year, but then grows by 4 percent in the second year, 5.5 percent in the third year, 4.2 percent in the fourth year, and 3.5 percent in the fifth year. Inflation in years 1–5 equals 3.1 percent, 2.2 percent, 1.6 percent, 1.3 percent, and 1.1 percent, respectively.
(a) Calculate natural real GDP for years 1–5.
(b) Calculate actual real GDP for years 1–5.
(c) Calculate the output ratio for years 1–5.
(d) Calculate the cumulative loss of output for years 1–5.
(e) Calculate the sacrifice ratio.

4. Suppose that natural real GDP is constant. For every 1 percent increase in the rate of inflation above its expected level, firms are willing to increase real GDP by 2 percent. The output ratio is initially 100 and the inflation rate equals 2 percent.
(a) Based upon the preceding information, draw the short-run Phillips Curve.
(b) What is the growth rate of nominal GDP in the economy?
An adverse supply shock raises the inflation rate associated with every output ratio by 3 percentage points.
(c) Draw the new short-run Phillips Curve.
(d) The government chooses to follow a neutral policy in response to this shock. What will be the growth rate of nominal GDP? What will be the new rate of inflation? What will be the output ratio?
(e) If the government chose to follow an accommodating policy, what would be the new inflation rate? The output ratio? The growth rate of nominal GDP?
(f) If the government chose to follow an extinguishing policy, what would be the new inflation rate? The output ratio? The growth rate of nominal GDP?

5. This problem uses Okun's Law to study how the unemployment and inflation rates change when there are demand shocks. Assume that the relationship between the output ratio and the unemployment rate,

U, is given by the equation $U = 6.0 - 0.5(\text{output ratio} - 100)$.

(a) Compute the unemployment rate for each of the 10 periods in problem 2d.
(b) When and why were the inflation and unemployment rates negatively correlated? When and why were the inflation and unemployment rates positively correlated?
(c) Explain why there is no long-run unemployment–inflation tradeoff.

Self-Test Answers

p. 238 (1) Everywhere to the right of 100 percent actual inflation is greater than expected inflation (for instance, actual inflation of 3 percent at E_1 is greater than expected inflation of $p^e = 0$ along the SP_0 line). (2) Everywhere to the left of 100 percent actual inflation is less than expected inflation. (3) Only at 100 percent is expected inflation correct.

p. 239 (1) A decline in aggregate demand moves the economy to the left of point E_3, down along the SP_1 curve. (2) When real GDP declines from 100 to 94, the actual inflation rate drops to zero, and is now below the 3 percent inflation rate expected everywhere along the SP_1 curve. Eventually the expected inflation rate will decline as well, shifting the SP curve downward. (3) The LP curve remains fixed.

p. 247 Why in Figure 8-5 is the orange line from point 1 to 2 steeper than the blue line from E_0 to point 1? The line is steeper because inflation is higher at point 2 than at point 1, because the expected rate of inflation (p^e) has shifted up in response to the actual inflation that occurred at point 1. And, since nominal GDP growth (x) is the same at point 1 and point 2, but inflation (p) is higher, the growth of real GDP ($y = x - p$) must be less from 1 to 2 than from E_0 to point 1. Similarly, since inflation is even higher at point 3, real GDP growth must be even lower, and in fact is negative, going from point 2 to point 3.

p. 248 (1) The slope of the SP curve determines how a slowdown in nominal GDP growth is divided between a decline in the inflation rate (p) and a decline in real GDP growth (y). The flatter the SP curve, the larger is the decline in real GDP and the smaller is the decline in actual inflation. With backward-looking (adaptive) expectations, a smaller decline in the actual inflation rate produces a smaller decline in the next period's expected inflation rate. Smaller declines in expected inflation make the economy's adjustment path longer: It takes more time for the economy to return to long-run equilibrium. (2) Conversely, the economy's adjustment path is shorter the steeper the SP curve and the faster the decline in actual and, hence, in expected inflation.

p. 258 (1) The inflation rate will fall in the year of the decline in the relative price of oil, except in the case of an extinguishing policy that raises nominal GDP growth sufficiently to cancel out the oil price effect. And, if the inflation rate declines in the first year, it will also decline in subsequent years if the expected rate of inflation declines and/or if COLA agreements cause lower inflation in the first year to cause lower wage changes in subsequent years. (2) The output ratio will increase unless there is an accommodating policy that cuts nominal GDP growth by the amount of the supply stock. (3) An extinguishing policy response will prevent a change in the inflation rate. An accommodating policy response will prevent a change in the output ratio.

p. 263 *North:* an adverse supply shock accommodated by an increase in nominal GDP growth. *Northeast:* an acceleration of nominal GDP growth, causing inflation during the period prior to the adjustment of expectations. *East:* a beneficial supply shock extinguished by an increase in nominal GDP growth. *Southeast:* a beneficial supply shock accompanied by an unchanged rate of nominal GDP growth. *South:* a beneficial supply shock accommodated by a reduction in nominal GDP growth. *Southwest:* a deceleration of nominal GDP growth, causing disinflation prior to the adjustment of expectations. *West:* an adverse supply shock extinguished by a reduction in nominal GDP growth. *Northwest:* an adverse supply shock accompanied by an unchanged rate of nominal GDP growth.

Appendix to Chapter 8

The Elementary Algebra of the *SP-DG* Model

Throughout Chapter 8, we have located the short-run equilibrium rate of inflation and level of real GDP along an *SP* curve, as at point E_4 of Figure 8-10. Now we learn how to draw a second line—the *DG* line—which shows where the economy will operate along the *SP* schedule. We also learn how to calculate the inflation rate and level of real GDP without going to the trouble of making drawings of the *SP* and *DG* lines. We do this by solving together the equations that describe the *SP* and *DG* lines, just as we did in the appendix to Chapter 4, where we learned the equivalent in algebra to the *IS* and *LM* curves. We use *SP-DG* diagrams to show that either the algebraic or graphical method leads to the same answer.

The centerpiece of our model in this appendix is the deviation of the output ratio from 100 percent. One way to write this deviation is:

$$100(Y/Y^N) - 100$$

This deviation is zero when the output ratio (Y/Y^N) equals 1.0, which occurs when actual output (Y) equals natural output (Y^N).

Calculations in the model are more accurate and straightforward when we use natural logarithms. Since the natural logarithm of 1.0 is zero, the natural log of the output ratio is zero when the output ratio is unity. Thus a second way of expressing the deviation of the output ratio from 100 percent is the "log output ratio" expressed as a percentage.

$$\hat{Y} = 100[LN(Y/Y^N)]$$

The following table shows that $\hat{Y}$ is very close in value to the deviation $100(Y/Y^N) - 100$:

Y/Y^N	$100(Y/Y^N) - 100$	$\hat{Y}$
0.90	−10	−10.5
1.00	0	0.0
1.05	5	4.9

In the rest of this appendix, a value of $\hat{Y}$ of zero corresponds to 100 on the horizontal axis of those diagrams in Chapter 8 that plot the output ratio against the inflation rate.

Equation for the *SP* Curve

The *SP* curve can be written as a relationship between the actual inflation rate (p), the expected inflation rate (p^e), and the log output ratio $(\hat{Y})$.

General Linear Form   Numerical Example

$$p = p^e + g\hat{Y} + z \qquad\qquad p = p^e + 0.5\hat{Y} \qquad (1)$$

Here the z designates the contribution of supply shocks to inflation, and initially in the numerical example we assume that the element of supply shocks is absent $(z = 0)$, so that we can concentrate on demand inflation. The numerical example also assumes that the slope of the *SP*, designated g in the general linear form, is 0.5 in the numerical example. Thus $g = 0.5$ indicates that the *SP* line slopes up by 1 percentage point in extra inflation for each 2 percentage points of extra real GDP relative to natural real GDP. We also note that when $\hat{Y} = 0$, the economy is on its vertical *LP* line where actual and expected inflation are equal $(p = p^e)$.

In order to understand what makes the *SP* curve shift, we assume the expectations of inflation (p^e) are formed adaptively as a weighted average of last period's actual inflation rate (p_{-1}) and last period's expected inflation rate (p^e_{-1}), where j is the weight on last period's actual inflation rate (j must be between 0 and 1).

General Linear Form   Numerical Example

$$p^e = jp_{-1} + (1 - j)p^e_{-1} \qquad\qquad p^e = p_{-1} \qquad (2)$$

The numerical example assumes that $j = 1$; that is, that expected inflation depends simply on what the inflation rate actually turned out to be last period, with the subscript -1 indicating "last period." This was also assumed in drawing Figures 8-5 and 8-7.

When we substitute (2) into (1), we obtain a new expression for the *SP* line that depends on two current-period variables ($\hat{Y}$ and z) and two variables from last period (p_{-1} and p^e_{-1}):

General Linear Form   Numerical Example

$$p = jp_{-1} + (1-j)p^e_{-1} + g\hat{Y} + z \qquad\qquad p = p_{-1} + 0.5\hat{Y} \qquad (3)$$

Equation for the *DG* Line

But we need more information than that contained in (3) to find both current inflation (p) and the current log output ratio ($\hat{Y}$). In other words, we have two unknown variables and one equation to determine their equilibrium values. What is the missing equation? This is the *DG* line and is based on the definition that nominal GDP growth (x) equals the inflation rate (p) plus real GDP growth (y), all expressed as percentages:

$$x \equiv p + y \qquad (4)$$

In the theoretical diagrams of Chapter 8, the natural level of real GDP (Y^N) is constant. But now we want to be more general and allow Y^N to grow, as it does in the real world. We subtract the growth rate of natural real GDP (y^N) from each side of equation (4):

$$x - y^N \equiv p + y - y^N \qquad (5)$$

Let us give a new name, "excess nominal GDP growth" ($\hat{x}$), to the excess of nominal GDP growth over the growth rate of natural real GDP ($\hat{x} = x - y^N$). We can also replace the excess of actual over natural real GDP growth ($y - y^N$) with the change in the log output ratio ($\hat{Y}$) from its value last period ($\hat{Y}_{-1}$).[1]
When these replacements are combined, (5) becomes

$$\hat{x} \equiv p + \hat{Y} - \hat{Y}_{-1} \qquad (6)$$

Combining the *SP* and *DG* Equations

Now we are ready to combine our equations for the *SP* line (3) and *DG* line (6). When (6) is solved for the log output ratio $\hat{Y}$, we obtain the following equation for the DG line:

$$\hat{Y} \equiv \hat{Y}_{-1} + \hat{x} - p \qquad (7)$$

---

[1] This replacement relies on the definition of a growth rate from one period to another as the change in logs (here we omit the "100" that changes decimals to percents):

$$y = \log(Y) - \log(Y_{-1})$$
$$y^N = \log(Y^N) - \log(Y^N_{-1})$$

Subtracting the second line from the first, we have

$$y - y^N = \log(Y) - \log(Y^N) - [\log(Y_{-1}) - \log(Y^N_{-1})] = \hat{Y} - \hat{Y}_{-1}$$

This says that the *DG* relation between $\hat{Y}$ and p has a slope of -1 and that the relation shifts when there is any change in $\hat{Y}_{-1}$ or $\hat{x}$. Now (7) can be substituted into the *SP* equation (3) to obtain:

$$p = jp_{-1} + (1-j) p^e_{-1} + g(\hat{Y}_{-1} + \hat{x} - p) + z \tag{8}$$

This can be further simplified if we factor out p from the right-hand side of (8).[2]

General Linear Form   Numerical Example

$$p = \frac{1}{1+g}[jp_{-1} + (1-j) p^e_{-1} + g(\hat{Y}_{-1} + \hat{x}) + z] \qquad p = [\tfrac{2}{3}p_{-1} + 0.5(\hat{Y}_{-1} + \hat{x})] \tag{9}$$

Now we are ready to use equation (9) to examine the consequences of any event that can alter the inflation rate and log output ratio in the short run and long run. One focus of Chapter 8 was the consequences of accelerations and decelerations in nominal GDP growth (*x*), so let us use equation (9) to reproduce the path of adjustment plotted in Figure 8-5 following an acceleration in *x* from zero to 6 percent per annum. Now, however, we shall perform the analysis for adjusted nominal GDP growth ($\hat{x}$), thus allowing it to remain valid for any value of y^N.

Example when $\hat{x}$ Rises from Zero to 6 Percent

We start out initially with zero inflation and with an output ratio of 100 percent, as at point E_0 in Figure 8-5. This means that the log output ratio ($\hat{Y}$) is zero. We also assume that there are no supply shocks ($z = 0$). Thus our initial situation begins with:

$$p_{-1} = p^e_{-1} = \hat{x} = \hat{Y}_{-1} = 0$$

Substituting into the numerical example version of (9), we can confirm that these values are consistent with an initial value of zero inflation:

$$p = \tfrac{2}{3}[0 + 0.5(0 + 0)] = 0$$

Now there is an assumed sudden jump in $\hat{x}$ to 6 percent per year. What happens to inflation in the first period? Substituting $\hat{x} = 6$ into the numerical example, we have:

$$p = \tfrac{2}{3}[0 + 0.5(0 + 6)] = \tfrac{2}{3}(3) = 2$$

The new log output ratio can be found by using equation (7):

$$Y = \hat{Y}_{-1} + \hat{x} - p = 0 + 6 - 2 = 4$$

Thus we have derived the combination of p and $\hat{Y}$ plotted at point F in Figure 8-5—that is, inflation of 2 percent and a log output ratio of 4.[3]

The adjustment continues in future periods. We can compute the values of p and $\hat{Y}$ in the next few periods by substituting the correct numbers into the numerical example version of (9), using a pocket calculator. These values correspond exactly to the path labeled "Path with one-period lag in adjustment of expectations" in Figure 8-5:

Period	p_{-1}	$\hat{Y}_{-1}$	$\hat{x}$	p	$\hat{Y}$
0	0.00	0.00	0	0.00	0.00
1	0.00	0.00	6	2.00	4.00
2	2.00	4.00	6	4.67	5.33
3	4.67	5.33	6	6.89	4.44
4	6.89	4.44	6	8.07	2.37

---

[2] To obtain (9) from (8), add gp to both sides of equation (8). Then divide both sides of the resulting equation by $1 + g$.

[3] In Figure 8-5 we assumed for simplicity that natural real GDP was not growing. Thus any change in real GDP became simply a shift in the output ratio, in this case a 4 percent increase from 100 to 104 in Figure 8-5.

Exercise 1: Using the same numerical example, calculate what happens for the first four periods when the economy is in an initial long-run equilibrium at point E_5 in Figure 8-6, with $x = p = p^e = 10$ and $\hat{Y} = 0$, and suddenly the adjusted growth rate of nominal GDP ($\hat{x}$) falls to a new permanent value of zero. How is your answer changed if the coefficient of adjustment of expectations is assumed to be $j = 0.25$ instead of $j = 1.0$?

[*Hint:* This requires that you substitute $j = 0.25$ and $g = 0.5$ into the General Linear Form version of equation (9).]

Learning to Shift the *SP* Curve and *DG* Line

In this section we learn how to draw graphs in which the *SP* curve and *DG* lines are accurately shifted, so that the economy's adjustment path can be traced out. In an example we will see how to trace out the path in Figure 8-5 marked "Path with one-period lag in adjustment of expectations," showing how the economy reacts to a permanent 6-percentage-point acceleration in nominal GDP growth.

Shifting the *SP* Curve

The two *SP* curves plotted in the left frame of Figure 8-15 are based on the Numerical Example of equation (1), repeated here for convenience:

$$p = p^e + 0.5\hat{Y} \qquad (1)$$

The lower SP_0 curve assumes that $p^e = 0$. Thus it shows that inflation (p) is zero when $\hat{Y} = 0$. When $\hat{Y}$ is 4, inflation is 2 percent. In our numerical example, the inflation rate in period 1 is shown by point F on SP_0. If $j = 1$, so the expected rate of inflation always equals last period's actual rate of inflation ($p^e = p_{-1}$), then there is an easy rule for drawing the new *SP* line for the subsequent period:

Rule for shifting *SP* when $j = 1$: If the economy is at point F in period 1, then the *SP* curve for period 2 can be drawn as intersecting the *LP* line at the same vertical coordinate as point F, shown by the point F'.

Figure 8-15

Thus in the example the *SP* curve for period 2 is SP_1, shown as having the same slope as SP_0, but intersecting *LP* at point F'. The vertical coordinate of the point where *SP* intersects *LP* tells us what expected rate of inflation (p^e) is being assumed along that *SP*. Along SP_1, for instance, p^e must be 2 percent, since the vertical coordinate of point F' is 2 percent.

Shifting the *DG* Line

The *DG* lines plotted in the right frame of Figure 8-15 are based on equation (7), repeated here for convenience:

$$\hat{Y} = \hat{Y}_{-1} + \hat{x} - p \tag{7}$$

Since p and $\hat{Y}$ are on the two axes, to plot a *DG* line we need to know the values of $\hat{x}$ and $\hat{Y}_{-1}$. The DG_1 line in the right frame of Figure 8-15 assumes that $\hat{x} = 6$ and $Y_{-1} = 0$. This line has a slope of minus 45 degrees, sloping down 1 percentage point vertically for every percentage point in the horizontal direction.

When the economy is at point F in period 1 in our example, with an inflation rate of 2 percent and an output ratio of $\hat{Y} = 4$, we must draw a new *DG* line for period 2. To develop a general rule for shifting *DG*, we draw a horizontal line, *CY*, which stands for "constant output." The *CY* line is always horizontal, and its vertical coordinate is the assumed growth rate of $\hat{x}$, in this case 6 percent. It shows that if inflation were equal to $\hat{x}$, then by equation (7) the output ratio would be constant, $\hat{Y} = \hat{Y}_{-1}$, hence the name constant output, or *CY* line. Now we can write a general rule for shifting *DG*:

> **Rule for shifting *DG*:** Start from the economy's position in period 1, point F in this example. Then draw a horizontal *CY* line at a vertical coordinate corresponding to the assumed value of $\hat{x}$, in this case 6 percent. Then the *DG* line for period 2 will be a line with a slope of minus 45 degrees intersecting the *CY* line at the same horizontal coordinate as point F. This point of intersection is labeled point F'' in the right frame of Figure 8-15.

Thus in the example the *DG* line for period 2 is DG_2, shown as parallel to the DG_1 line but intersecting *CY* at point F''. Note that the rule also applies to the DG_1 line. Since the economy in the previous period (period 0) was at a log output ratio of 0, the DG_1 line intersects the *CY* line at point E_3 which has a horizontal coordinate of 0.

Another, equivalent way to remember the rule for shifting the *DG* line is simple. When $\hat{x}$ increases, the *DG* line shifts up *vertically* by the amount of the change in $\hat{x}$, for example, up by 6 percentage points to the line DG_1. But when $\hat{Y}_{-1}$ increases, the *DG* line shifts to the right *horizontally* by the amount of the change in Y_{-1}, for example, by 4 percentage points between the lines DG_1 and DG_2.

Tracing the Economy's Adjustment with Shifts in *SP* and *DG*

Now we are prepared to draw a graph tracing the economy's adjustment to a permanent 6 percent acceleration in $\hat{x}$, from an initial value of zero to a new value of 6. In Figure 8-16, the economy starts at point E_0 on SP_0 drawn for the initial assumed expected rate of inflation ($p^e = 0$), and on the DG_0 line drawn for $\hat{x} = 0$ and an output ratio last period ($\hat{Y}_{-1}$) of 0.

The permanent acceleration of $\hat{x}$ fixes the *CY* line at a vertical position of 6. We draw a new DG_1 line intersecting *CY* directly above point E_0. The *SP* does not shift in period 1, because expectations of inflation adjust with a one-period lag. Thus in period 1 the economy moves from E_0 to F, with an inflation rate (p) of 2.0 percent and an output ratio ($\hat{Y}$) of 4.0 percent. Then in period 2 both *SP* and *DG* shift. We draw the new SP_1 line, as in Figure 8-16, as intersecting the *LP* line at the same vertical coordinate as point F. We draw a new DG_2 line, as in Figure 8-16, as intersecting the *CY* line at the same horizontal coordinate as point F. The two new lines, SP_1 and DG_2, intersect at point H, where the inflation rate (p) is 4.67 percent and the log output ratio is 5.33 percent. This is the same as the economy's position in period 2, calculated by the algebraic method in the preceding section.

Figure 8-16

The adjustment in period 3 is also shown in Figure 8-16. A new SP_2 curve is drawn as intersecting the LP at the same vertical coordinate as point H. A new DG_3 line is shown as intersecting the CY line at the same horizontal coordinate as point H. The economy's new position in period 3 is at the intersection of the SP_2 curve and DG_3 labeled in Figure 8-16 as point I. Inflation has now risen to 6.89 percent and the log output ratio has fallen to 4.44 percent.

The general principles developed in this section can be used to show the economy's adjustment to either a shift in $\hat{x}$ or a supply shock. General characteristics of the adjustment process, shown in the example of Figure 8-16, are as follows:

> The SP line always shifts up in the subsequent period when the economy's position in the current period is to the right of LP, and it shifts down when the economy is to the left of LP. The DG line always shifts to the right in the subsequent period when the economy's current position is below the CY line, that is, when inflation is less than $\hat{x}$. And the DG line shifts to the left in the subsequent period when the economy is above the CY line. Thus, in the example of Figure 8-16, the DG line drawn for period 4 would intersect the CY line at the same horizontal coordinate as point I and thus would be to the left of the DG_3 line.

The Consequences of a Supply Shock

We have examined the effect on inflation of an acceleration of growth in nominal GDP. But another source of inflation may be a supply shock, such as an increase in the relative price of food or energy. Let us assume that we start in long-run equilibrium at point E_3 in Figure 8-10, with $\hat{x} = p = p^e = 6$ and $\hat{Y} = 0$. Initially the supply-shock variable z is equal to zero. But now let us assume there is a jump in the relative price of oil that boosts z to a value of 3 for two periods, followed by a return after that to z = 0.

The discussion of supply shocks emphasized that two crucial factors determine how the economy reacts to a supply shock. First, is $\hat{x}$ increased, decreased, or left the same by policymakers following the shock? Second, do expectations adjust to the temporary shock? Cost-of-living adjustment clauses in wage contracts are equivalent to an adjustment of expected inflation for the influence of the supply shock.

The simplest case to analyze is one in which there is no response of either demand growth ($\hat{x}$) or expected inflation (p^e). To trace the path of inflation and the log output ratio, we simply use the general formula (9) with $\hat{x}$ assumed to be permanently fixed at 6, and $j = 0$ (representing the failure of expectations to respond at all to actual inflation). The general form for this case becomes:

$$p = \frac{1}{1+g}[p^e_{-1} + g(\hat{Y}_{-1} + \hat{x}) + z] \qquad (10)$$

$$= \frac{2}{3}[p^e_{-1} + 0.5(\hat{Y}_{-1} + \hat{x}) + z]$$

Now, starting in the initial situation, we substitute the required elements into this formula for each period in succession.

Period	p^e_{-1}	$\hat{Y}_{-1}$	$\hat{x}$	z	p	$\hat{Y}$
0	6	0.00	6	0	6.00	0.00
1	6	0.00	6	3	8.00	−2.00
2	6	−2.00	6	3	7.33	−3.33
3	6	−3.33	6	0	4.89	−2.22
4	6	−2.22	6	0	5.26	−1.48
5	6	−1.48	6	0	5.51	−0.99

This adjustment path shows what would happen to the economy with a two-period supply shock of $z = 3$, with a neutral aggregate demand policy that maintains steady excess nominal GDP growth, and with no response of expectations to the effects of the supply shock. A good example of this is the temporary 1990–91 oil shock after the Iraqi invasion of Kuwait. In period 1 the inflation rate jumps from 6 to 8, exactly duplicating the movement from point E_3 to point L in Figure 8-10. In the next period, inflation diminishes somewhat, since the position of the DG line depends on the current period's starting value of $\hat{Y}$, which has fallen from 0 to −2. Thus the intersection of DG and SP slides southwest down the stationary SP_3 line to $p = 7.33$ and $\hat{Y} = -3.33$. Then the supply shock ends, z returns to its original zero value, and the economy gradually climbs back up the SP_2 line to its long-run equilibrium position, $p = 6.0$ and $\hat{Y} = 0$.

Exercise 2: What rate of adjusted nominal growth should policymakers choose if they want to pursue an accommodating policy? An extinguishing policy? (*Hint:* An accommodating policy means that $\hat{Y}$ remains fixed at 0, which requires that $\hat{x} = p$. Substitute p for $\hat{x}$ in equation (10) and, in addition, note that $\hat{Y}_{-1} = 0$, thus obtaining $p = p^e_{-1} + z$. For an extinguishing policy, take (10) and set the left-hand side (p) equal to 6; then solve for the required $\hat{x}$.)

Exercise 3: For a neutral policy response, calculate the adjustment path of inflation and $\hat{Y}$ in the first four periods when expectations respond fully to the extra inflation caused by the supply shock. That is, assume now that $j = 1$ instead of $j = 0$ as in the previous exercise. Next, maintaining the assumption that $j = 1$, calculate the same adjustment path when the policy response is accommodative. (See the hint for Exercise 2.) How would you describe the disadvantages of an accommodative policy when $j = 1$?

The Behavior of the Unemployment Rate

The unemployment rate (U) is very closely related to the log output ratio ($\hat{Y}$), as we learned from Okun's Law and Figure 8-13 on pp. 264–66. Corresponding to the natural level of real GDP (Y^N), defined as the level of real GDP at which expectations of inflation turn out to be accurate, there is a natural rate of unemployment (U^N). When real GDP is above Y^N, and inflation is accelerating, we also find that the actual unemployment rate (U) is below the natural rate of unemployment (U^N). This relationship can be written.[4]

General Linear Form	Numerical Example	
$U = U^N - h\hat{Y}$	$U = U^N - 0.5\hat{Y}$	(11)

How is this relationship to be used? First, we must determine the value of the natural rate of unemployment. In the United States in the 1980s this appeared to be approximately $U^N = 6.0$ percent. Then we take alternative values for $\hat{Y}$ and substitute these values into equation (11). Here are two examples:

Example 1: $\hat{Y} = -6$
Since $U^N = 6.0$, we use (11) to determine the unemployment rate:
$$U = 6.0 - 0.5(-6) = 9.0$$
In other words, there is an unemployment rate of 9.0 percent.

Example 2: $\hat{Y} = 6$
$$U = 6.0 - 0.5(6) = 3.0$$

The unemployment rate is 3.0 percent. Thus we see that for every 6 percentage points by which $\hat{Y}$ exceeds 0, the unemployment rate lies 3 percentage points below U^N, the natural unemployment rae of 6.0 percent. And for every 6 percentage points by which $\hat{Y}$ falls short of 0, the unemployment rate lies 3 percentage points above the natural unemployment rate of 6.0 percent.

There is also a simple short-cut way of calculating the *change* in the unemployment rate from last period (U_{-1}) to this period (U).[5]

General Linear Form	Numerical Example	
$U = U_{-1} - h(y - y^N)$	$U = U_{-1} - 0.5(y - y^N)$	(12)

Thus, starting with $U_{-1} = 6.0$, a value of $y - y^N$ of 1.0 will cause the unemployment rate to fall to $U = 5.5$ percent.

Exercise 4: Go back through the previous exercises and calculate the unemployment rate for each period corresponding to that period's value of $\hat{Y}$.

---

[4] *Caution:* In the Appendix to Chapter 4 we used h to designate the income responsiveness of the demand for money. In Chapter 17, h designates the slope of the Lucas-Friedman supply curve. There is no connection between these different uses of "h," just a shortage of alphabetical letters.

[5] How can (12) be derived from (11)? Let us write down (11) and then subtract from it the value of (11) for last period:
$$U = U^N - h\hat{Y}$$
$$-U_{-1} = -U^N_{-1} - (-h\hat{Y}_{-1})$$
If there is no change in U^N from one period to the next, then this difference is:
$$U - U_{-1} = -h(\hat{Y} - \hat{Y}_{-1})$$
But now we can substitute $y - y^N$ into this expression
$$U - U_{-1} = -h(y - y^N)$$
To see why this substitution is valid, look back at footnote 1 in this appendix on p. 273.

CHAPTER 9

The Goals of Stabilization Policy: Low Inflation and Low Unemployment

The government fighting inflation is like the Mafia fighting crime.
—Laurence J. Peter

This book began by introducing three major concepts of macroeconomics—unemployment, inflation, and growth in per person output—that are linked to the three major goals of macroeconomic policy, namely, to achieve low unemployment, low inflation, and rapid growth in per person output. In Chapter 1 we learned why growth in output per person is desirable; simply put, more is better, allowing society to have everything it now produces (and more) without the need to sacrifice something currently produced.

Now we inquire into the two other major goals of economic policy, beginning with low inflation in the first part of this chapter and ending with low unemployment in the last part. As we learned in Chapter 8, in order to achieve a lower inflation rate by restrictive monetary or fiscal policies, policymakers must be willing to accept a transition period during which the output ratio is lower and the unemployment rate is higher. Is the goal of achieving lower inflation worth the cost of lost jobs in the period during which inflation is reduced? This depends on the costs of inflation—just what is it that society loses if inflation proceeds at a rate of 5 percent per year instead of 2 percent?

In the last part of the chapter we inquire into the costs of unemployment. Is unemployment of a teenager seeking a part-time job as costly to individuals and society as unemployment of an adult head of household? Why can't the unemployment rate be pushed down to zero percent? Why are some people unemployed even in a prosperous economy?

9-1 The Costs and Causes of Inflation

Inflation is widely viewed as a social evil, although the degree of its seriousness is debated. At one extreme, inflation is considered as serious a problem as unemployment. This view was popularized by Arthur Okun, who defined the "misery index" as the sum of the inflation and unemployment rates. This index implies that the social value of a reduction of inflation by one percentage point (say from 3 to 2 percent) exactly offsets the social cost of an increase in the unemployment rate by one percentage point (say from 6 to 7 percent), leaving the economy with an unchanged level of "misery."

Others think that the harm done by inflation is minimal. James Tobin has written that "inflation is greatly exaggerated as a social evil." As we learned in

Chapter 8, policymakers desiring to reduce the inflation rate must reduce the growth rate of nominal GDP, and such action is likely to cause a temporary drop in the output ratio and an increase in unemployment. Many economists like Tobin do not regard the benefits of lower inflation as worth the sacrifice of lost output and jobs necessary to achieve it.

In Chapter 8 we also learned that the basic cause of inflation is excessive growth in nominal GDP. In this chapter we ask why governments inflate; that is, why they allow excessive nominal GDP growth to occur. We then examine the costs of inflation, asking whether they are serious enough to warrant stopping inflation, even though doing so may require policies that cut output and cause millions to lose their jobs.

Any debate about the costs of inflation must distinguish between moderate (crawling) inflation and extreme inflation, usually called **hyperinflation**. One traditional definition of hyperinflation is an inflation rate of 50 percent per month, or 12,975 percent per year.[1] We shall use as our definition an inflation rate of 1,000 percent per year or above; a rate of 1,000 percent per year (or 22 percent per month) afflicts a society with all the problems usually associated with hyperinflation. Argentina, Brazil, Nicaragua, Peru, and Poland all suffered from inflation rates of over 1,000 percent per year for one or more years in the late 1980s or 1990s.[2]

Everyone agrees that hyperinflation is a severe plague, and we will learn how economic policymakers have managed to stop hyperinflations in several specific cases. Before turning to hyperinflation, we will examine the social costs of moderate inflation, such as that experienced by the United States. We will see that there are quite different costs associated with an inflation that is fully anticipated (crawling along at roughly the same rate year after year) and of an inflation that is a "surprise," changing in an unpredictable way.

Hyperinflation is a very rapid inflation, sometimes defined as a rate of more than 22 percent per month, or 1,000 percent per year, experienced over a year or more.

9-2 Money and Inflation

In Chapter 8 our model of inflation showed that a permanent increase in the growth rate of nominal GDP would lead to a permanent increase in the inflation rate. Since nominal GDP growth is so important in determining the inflation rate, we need to understand its determinants.

Definitions Linking Money, Velocity, Inflation, and Output

A convenient starting point for understanding the determinants of inflation is provided by the quantity equation of Section 7-8:

$$M^s V \equiv X \equiv PY \qquad (9.1)$$

---

[1] Why is a 50 percent monthly inflation equivalent to an annual rate of 12,975 percent? This occurs because of compounding. Starting at 100, after one month prices are up to 150, after two months they are at 225, after three months they are at 338, and after twelve months they are at 12,975. Although these simple geometric changes are widely cited in the literature, they become increasingly misleading at high rates of inflation; a better measure is the logarithmic price change, which in this example is 40.5 percent per month, or 487 percent per year. See problems 1 and 2 at the end of the chapter.

[2] The 1,000 percent cutoff for episodes of "extreme" inflation is suggested in R. Dornbusch et al., "Extreme Inflation: Dynamics and Stabilization," *Brookings Papers on Economic Activity*, 1990, no. 2, pp. 1–84.

This equation is familiar; it duplicates equation (7.2) on p. 214. The right side of the equation states that nominal GDP (X), by definition, is equal to the price index, or the GDP deflator (P), multiplied by real GDP (Y). The left side states that nominal GDP is also equal, by definition, to the money supply (M^s) multiplied by velocity (V).[3] Thus nominal GDP must rise if there is an increase in either the money supply or in velocity.

Equation (9.1) is a good beginning, but it concerns the price *level*. How can we convert equation (9.1) into a relationship that shows the determinants of the rate of *inflation*, that is, the rate of change of the price level? As we learned in Chapter 8, the growth rate of any product of two numbers, such as P times Y in equation (9.1), is equal to the sum of the separate growth rates of the two numbers. This allows us to take equation (9.1), a relationship among *levels* (written as uppercase letters), and restate it as a relationship among *growth rates* (written as lowercase letters):

$$m^s + v \equiv x \equiv p + y \qquad (9.2)$$

In words, this states that the growth rate of the money supply (m^s) plus the growth in velocity (v) equals the growth rate of nominal GDP (x), which in turn is divided between the inflation rate (p) and the growth rate of real GDP (y). The formula immediately allows us to classify the determinants of inflation, when we rewrite equation (9.2) with inflation on the left side:

$$p \equiv x - y \equiv m^s + v - y \qquad (9.3)$$

If we are interested in the long-run determinants of inflation, we can assume that the growth rate of real output (y) is fairly constant, roughly fixed by the growth rate of the population and of productivity. This leads to the same conclusion that we reached in Chapter 8: *In the long run, the inflation rate equals the excess growth rate of nominal GDP, that is, the difference between nominal GDP growth and the long-run growth rate of real GDP.*

The right-hand terms in equation (9.3) provide additional insight into the causes of inflation. In the long run, the inflation rate must equal the excess growth rate of money plus velocity, relative to the long-run growth rate of real GDP.[4]

Thus, to understand the determinants of inflation, we need to know what determines the excess growth of money plus velocity. The growth rate of the money supply is controlled by the central bank (in the United States by the Federal Reserve, in Canada by the Bank of Canada, and by similar institutions in other countries). Velocity changes whenever there is a change in real GDP relative to the real money supply (M^s/P). In Chapter 4 we learned that anything that shifts the *IS* curve will change velocity, including changes in busi-

---

[3] Why is the left side true by definition? As we learned in Chapter 4 in the box on p. 103, velocity is defined as $V \equiv PY/M^s$, or $V \equiv Y/(M^s/P)$. This definition is repeated in Chapter 7 on p. 214.

[4] In the Appendix to Chapter 8, we subtracted the long-run growth rate of natural real GDP (y^N) explicitly from both nominal and real GDP growth. Applying the same subtraction to equation (9.3), we have

$$p \equiv (x - y^N) - (y - y^N) \equiv (m^s + v - y^N) - (y - y^N)$$

This states that in the long run when $y - y^N$ is zero, inflation equals the excess growth of nominal GDP relative to that of natural real GDP, and inflation also equals the excess growth of money plus velocity relative to that of natural real GDP.

ness and consumer confidence, government spending, tax rates, autonomous net taxes, autonomous net exports, or the foreign exchange rate. Further, if the demand for money changes for reasons independent of changes in income, then velocity will change. For instance, velocity could change following the introduction of credit cards that allow households to economize on their holdings of money.

While the growth rate of velocity can be highly volatile in the short run, over the long run velocity growth tends to be quite stable. For the United States, the average annual growth rate of velocity has been almost exactly zero over the past four decades.[5] Thus if we assume $v = 0$ in equation (9.3), the determinants of inflation become extremely simple: *In the long run, the inflation rate equals the excess growth rate of the money supply, that is, the difference between the growth rate of the money supply and the long-run growth rate of real GDP. If the central bank allows the money supply to grow rapidly, rapid inflation will result. The key to attaining zero inflation is for the central bank to allow the money supply to grow no faster than the long-run growth rate of real output.*

Self-Test

Assume that over a decade the growth rate of the money supply is constant at 5 percent per year, and the growth rate of velocity is constant at 3 percent per year. In the first half of the decade, the growth rate of output is 4 percent per year; then, because of a slowdown in productivity growth, it is only 2 percent for the last half of the decade. The growth in money and in velocity are not affected by the productivity growth slowdown.

1. What is the inflation rate in the first half of the decade?
2. What is the inflation rate in the last half of the decade?
3. What is the nominal GDP growth rate in the first half of the decade?
4. What is the nominal GDP growth rate in the last half of the decade?

Why Do Central Banks Allow Excessive Monetary Growth?

The previous section identified excessive monetary growth as the fundamental cause of inflation *in the long run*. If the growth rate of velocity is zero in the long run, then excessive nominal GDP growth and excessive monetary growth are identical. Why do governments and central banks allow excessive monetary growth to occur?

Four basic factors examined below can lead to excessive nominal GDP and monetary growth. As shown in Chapter 8, a permanent increase in nominal GDP growth leads to a *temporary* increase in output along with a permanent increase in the inflation rate. A permanent decrease in nominal GDP growth leads to a *temporary* decrease in output along with a permanent decrease of the inflation rate. This analysis underlies the first reason governments cause inflation.

Reason 1: Temptation of demand stimulation. Governments and central banks may set off inflation when they attempt to raise output and reduce unemployment. While Chapter 8 indicated that such policies can boost inflation

---

[5] The velocity of the money supply concept M2 (defined in Chapter 13) was 1.73 in 1960 and 1.87 in 2004, for an annual growth rate of 0.2 percent.

International Perspective

Money Growth and Inflation

Equation (9.3) in the text ($p \equiv m^s + v - y$) states that the inflation rate (p) is equal to the rate of monetary growth (m^s) plus the difference between velocity growth and real GDP growth ($v - y$). If this difference is positive, then inflation exceeds the rate of monetary growth, and vice versa.

The graph plots the inflation rate over the period 1990–2002 against the rate of monetary growth for 15 countries. The diagonal 45-degree line shows all the points with equal rates of inflation and monetary growth, that is, with $v = y$. In most of the low-inflation countries, the plotted points lie below the 45-degree line, indicating that velocity growth was less than real GDP growth. For instance, in the United States, velocity growth was roughly zero, less than output growth of about 3.3 percent per year. These plotted points illustrate that the relationship between inflation and monetary growth is relatively close, supporting the theme of the text that the key to understanding inflation is to understand why some governments choose much higher rates of monetary growth than others.

The scale in the graph is logarithmic, and two of the countries plotted (Brazil and the Ukraine) had an inflation rate of almost 1,000 percent per year over the period. In some years Brazil and other countries had inflation rates of 2,000 percent or more. Later in this chapter, we look more closely at the causes of high inflation and its basic cause, rapid monetary growth.

Inflation vs. Money Growth, 1990–2002

with only a temporary benefit to output, governments may think (erroneously) that the benefits of higher output will last forever or (perhaps correctly) at least long enough to benefit the government at the next election. In some countries, the central bank is controlled directly or indirectly by the government. Even in the United States, with its relatively independent central bank, it is widely believed that the Fed boosted monetary growth in 1972 to help reelect President Nixon.

Reason 2: Fear of recession and job loss. The corollary to the first reason is the fact that stopping inflation usually causes a temporary drop in output and loss of jobs. Thus an implication of the first reason for higher inflation is that governments are reluctant to stop inflation once it gets started: An economy must sacrifice a substantial amount of lost output in order to reduce the inflation rate permanently. The size of this output sacrifice (measured by Chapter 8's sacrifice ratio) is highly controversial and differs among countries. One estimate (pp. 250–51) for the United States is that a permanent decrease in the inflation rate of one percentage point would require a one-time loss of 4.7 percent of a year's GDP, or about $560 billion. The sacrifice required in some countries may be higher, in others lower. Politicians and central banks may be reluctant to impose this sacrifice on citizens, and as a result inflation tends to persist year after year.

Reason 3: Adverse supply shocks. Chapter 8 also introduced adverse supply shocks as a cause of higher inflation. When higher food or oil prices raise business costs, the inflation rate rises unless the central bank introduces an extinguishing policy that offsets the extra inflation with a massive recession. Any sharp increase in the price of oil, such as those that occurred in 1973–74 and 1979–80, poses a distasteful choice for central banks. An extinguishing policy reaction can offset extra inflation only at the cost of extra unemployment. An accommodative policy calls for the central bank to "print the extra money to pay for the inflation," and this is likely to create a permanent upsurge of inflation following an adverse supply shock. Even a neutral policy, which leaves the growth rate of nominal GDP and the money supply unchanged, will cause a temporary upsurge of inflation.

Reason 4: Financing government deficits by printing money. In our analysis of the *IS-LM* model of Chapter 4, we learned that governments can run deficits (by boosting expenditures or cutting taxes) in two ways. First, they can hold the real money supply steady and issue bonds to pay for the deficit, which usually requires an increase in the interest rate. Or they can hold the interest rate steady by raising the money supply sufficiently, a policy previously described as monetary accommodation of a fiscal stimulus. However, many countries lack markets in which the government can sell bonds; in such countries virtually the only source of finance for government deficits is an increase in the money supply (often called financing deficits by "printing money"). Thus governments with excessive spending or insufficient tax revenues can cause inflation (p), according to equation (9.3), by boosting the growth rate of the money supply (m^s).

In summary, we have learned that the basic reasons why central banks allow excessive monetary growth are the temptation of demand stimulation together with the related fear of recession and output loss, the partial or complete accommodation of adverse supply shocks, and the effect of government deficits in boosting monetary growth.

9-3 Why Inflation Is Not Harmless

If a temporary period of lost output and higher unemployment must be experienced in order to reduce inflation, then policymakers need to be convinced that it is harmful for them to allow inflation to continue. At first glance, worry about inflation may appear misplaced. When inflation is zero, wages may increase at 2 percent a year. When inflation proceeds at 6 percent annually, wages may grow at 8 percent annually. Workers have little reason to be bothered about the inflation rate (p) if the growth in their wages (w) always stays the same distance ahead, as in this example:

	No inflation	6 percent annual inflation
Growth rate of nominal wages (w)	2	8
Growth rate of price deflator (p)	0	6
Growth rate of real wages (w − p)	2	2

However, even if real wage growth is unaffected by inflation, it is still possible for inflation to impose substantial costs on society. Inflation is felt primarily by owners of financial assets. The distinction between surprise and fully anticipated inflation is central to understanding the costs of inflation and the suggested methods for reducing those costs. In this section we distinguish between nominal expected real and actual real interest rates. Using this distinction, we will learn that four conditions required for inflation to be harmless, and why all four conditions are unrealistic.

Nominal and Real Interest Rates

Even in countries with moderate inflation, people learn the difference between nominal and real interest rates, even if they have not been taught the following economists' jargon: *The **nominal interest rate** (i) is the rate actually quoted by banks and negotiated in financial markets. The **expected real interest rate** (r^e) is what people expect to pay on their borrowings or earn on their savings after deducting expected inflation ($r^e = i − p^e$). The expected real interest rate is what matters for investment and saving decisions. The **actual real interest rate** is the nominal interest rate minus the actual rate of inflation (r = i − p).*

The **nominal interest rate** is the market interest rate actually charged by financial institutions and earned by bondholders.

The **expected real interest rate** is the nominal interest rate minus the expected rate of inflation.

The **actual real interest rate** is the nominal interest rate minus the actual inflation rate.

The nominal interest rate can differ greatly in two countries with different inflation rates, or in one country at different moments in history. But investment and saving decisions will be the same in the two situations as long as the expected real interest rate is the same, and as long as all other determinants of investment and saving besides the expected real interest rate are held constant.

Consider two situations, both with a real expected interest rate (r^e) of 3 percent. In the first situation, expected inflation is zero and the nominal interest rate is 3 percent:

General Form   Numerical Example

$$r^e = i − p^e \qquad r^e = 3 − 0 = 3 \qquad (9.4)$$

In the second situation, there is an expected inflation rate of 6 percent and a nominal interest rate of 9 percent. The real interest rate is the same value, 3 percent:

General Form   Numerical Example

$$r^e = i − p^e \qquad r^e = 9 − 6 = 3 \qquad (9.5)$$

Why is the incentive to save and invest the same in each situation? In the second situation, savers face the prospect that one year later prices will be higher by 6 percent, but they receive an interest rate on their saving of 9 percent, of which 3 percent compensates them for their willingness to save (just as in the zero-inflation situation), while the additional 6 percent compensates them for inflation, that is, the fact that goods they plan to consume with their saving will be 6 percent more expensive one year later. Investors react similarly; the fact that they can sell their products for 6 percent more after one year of 6 percent inflation compensates them for having to pay a nominal interest rate of 9 percent.

Four Conditions Necessary for Inflation to be Harmless

The above example creates the impression that inflation does not matter, since the nominal interest rate will adjust to maintain the same incentives for savers and investors at a 6 percent inflation rate as at a zero inflation rate. However, the example makes several important assumptions, none of which is validated in the real world:

1. Inflation is universally and accurately anticipated.
2. An increase in the expected inflation rate raises the market nominal interest rate (i) for both saving and borrowing by exactly the same number of percentage points.
3. All savings are held in bonds, stocks, or savings accounts earning the nominal interest rate (i); no one holds money in accounts with an interest rate held below the market nominal interest rate.
4. Only real (not nominal) interest income is taxable, and only the real cost of borrowing is tax deductible.

Violation of Condition 1: Interest Rates in a Surprise Inflation

Now let us violate condition 1 in the preceding summary list of four conditions, that is, that inflation is accurately anticipated. In several episodes in the United States, such as in 1966–69, 1973–74, 1978–80, and 1987–90, the actual inflation rate accelerated well above the rate expected by most people.

Now imagine that at the beginning of the year, everyone expects zero inflation and savers are offered an interest rate of 3 percent, but at the end of the year, the price of goods jumps by 6 percent. Savers' hopes have been dashed, because their savings have been eroded by an **unanticipated inflation**.

When actual inflation (p = 6 percent in the example) differs from expected inflation (p^e = 0 in the example), the actual real interest rate differs from that which was expected. In the example, a 3 percent real interest rate was expected (r^e = 3), but after the fact (*ex post facto*) the actual real interest (r) turned out to be much less:

Unanticipated inflation occurs when the actual inflation rate (p) differs from the expected (or anticipated) inflation rate (p^e).

General Form	Numerical Example	
$r = i - p$	$r = 3 - 6 = -3$	(9.6)

Deflation hurts debtors. The basic case against unanticipated inflation, then, is that it redistributes income from creditors (savers) to debtors without their knowledge or consent. Conversely, an unanticipated deflation does just the opposite, redistributing income from debtors to creditors, as we learned in Section 7-9 on p. 219. Throughout history, farmers have been an important group of debtors who have been badly hurt by unanticipated deflation. The interest income of savers hardly fell at all between 1929 and 1933, but farmers, badly hurt by a precipitous decline in farm prices, saw their nominal income fall by two-thirds, from $6.2 to $2.1 billion. Because their nominal income fell by so much but their nominal interest payments did not fall, many farmers were unable to purchase seed, fertilizer, and other necessities. As a result, many lost their farms through foreclosures of their mortgages.

Gainers from surprise inflation. Clearly, all savers lose from a surprise inflation. Who gains? The gainers from unanticipated inflation are those who are heavily in debt but have few financial assets, owning mainly physical assets whose prices rise with inflation. Private individuals who have just purchased houses with small down payments are among the classic gainers from an unanticipated inflation.

Violation of Condition 2: Expected Inflation and the Fisher Effect

We have previously defined the expected real interest rate (r^e) as the nominal interest rate (i) minus the expected inflation rate (p^e). The same relation can be rearranged to show that the nominal interest rate is the sum of the expected real interest rate and the expected inflation rate:

$$i = r^e + p^e \qquad (9.7)$$

Thus the nominal interest rate can rise either if the expected real interest rate rises or if the expected inflation rate rises.[6] Among a group of nations that have roughly the same expected real interest rate, we would expect those that have a history of rapid inflation to have high nominal interest rates. This relation between expected inflation and the nominal and real interest rate is called the **Fisher equation**, so named for the famous Yale University economist Irving Fisher (1867–1947).[7] The implication that a one percentage point increase in the expected inflation rate causes a one percentage point increase in the nominal interest rate is called the **Fisher Effect**.[8] The corollary to the Fisher Effect is that the expected real interest rate is independent of changes in the expected inflation rate. *The Fisher analysis predicts that nations with rapid monetary growth will experience both rapid inflation and high nominal interest rates.*

The second condition for inflation to be harmless stated that an increase of the inflation rate by a given number of percentage points raises the nominal interest rate by the same number of percentage points. Restated, the real interest rate must not be affected by the inflation rate. If the Fisher Effect was always a realistic description of the real world, then the real interest rate would be independent of the inflation rate, and the second condition would be valid.

However, in the real world, the Fisher Effect is frequently violated. Figure 9-1 plots the nominal interest rate on 10-year Treasury bonds against an estimate of the expected rate of inflation, a three-year average of the rate of change of the GDP deflator, expressed as an annual rate. The green shad-

Irving Fisher (1867–1947)

Fisher, a pioneering mathematical economist, developed theories on interest rates, intertemporal choice, and money and prices. His work forms the basis of much of today's macroeconomics.

The **Fisher equation** states that the nominal interest rate equals the expected inflation rate plus the expected real interest rate.

The **Fisher Effect** predicts that a one percentage point increase in the expected inflation rate will raise the nominal real interest rate by one percentage point, leaving the expected real interest rate unaffected.

---

[6] The *IS-LM* model of Chapter 4 showed how real output and the real interest rate were determined. Recall that in the *IS-LM* model, the real interest rate rises as a result of any event that shifts the *IS* curve to the right (higher government spending, lower tax rates, etc.) or any event that shifts the *LM* curve to the left (a reduction in the supply of money or an increase in the demand for money).

[7] Fisher also popularized other important ideas in economics, including the theory that deflation feeds on itself, by cutting the buying power of debtors (for example, farmers in the Great Depression).

[8] More sophisticated analyses show that an increase in the inflation rate tends to reduce the real interest rate, so that the nominal interest rate does not rise one-for-one with the inflation rate. This is sometimes called the "Mundell Effect," stemming from a famous paper by 1999 Nobel Prize winner Robert Mundell, "Inflation and Real Interest," *Journal of Political Economy*, vol. 71 (June 1963), pp. 280–83.

Figure 9-1 The 10-year Treasury Bond Rate and the Expected Rate of Inflation

The purple line plots the 10-year Treasury bond rate, the same interest rate as was plotted in the box on page 107. The orange line plots an estimate of the expected rate of inflation, the average annual change over three years in the GDP deflator. The green shading between the two lines shows the expected real interest rate. Notice that in 1975–76 the expected inflation rate soared but the interest rate barely responded, pushing the expected real interest rate down to zero. In contrast, the expected real interest rate rose in the 1980s when the expected inflation rate was decreasing.

ing between the two lines shows the implied expected real interest rate. Clearly, the expected real interest rate changes when there is a sudden increase or decrease in expected inflation, implying that the second condition for inflation to be harmless is violated in the real world. This is especially evident in 1975–76, when the nominal interest rate failed to respond to an upsurge of expected inflation, driving the real interest rate to zero. The opposite occurred in the early 1980s, when the nominal interest rate increased by more than the upsurge of inflation, due partly to the tight monetary policy pursued by the Fed in 1980–82 in order to bring down the rate of inflation. This was the cold turkey policy discussed in Chapter 8, pp. 247–49.

Violation of Condition 3: Money Does Not Pay Interest

The third condition for inflation to be harmless is that all assets pay the nominal interest rate. But there are many assets and many interest rates, and a significant number of assets pay an interest rate below the interest rate on 10-year Treasury bonds displayed in Figure 9-1. At the extreme is currency, which pays

The Wizard of Oz as a Monetary Allegory

The famous movie *The Wizard of Oz*, originally produced in 1939 and an annual television ritual for several decades, is based on a 1900 book (*The Wonderful Wizard of Oz*) by L. Frank Baum. Recently, economists have recognized that the book is an allegory for the major economic and political issues in the late nineteenth-century United States, the battle over free silver, which involved a debate about whether deflation or inflation was desirable.[a]

The three decades after the Civil War (1865–95) were characterized by a steady deflation that reduced the overall price level by about 40 percent and the price of farm products by about 55 percent. As we have learned in this chapter, inflation benefits borrowers at the expense of savers, and deflation does the opposite, benefiting savers at the expense of borrowers. Some of the losers from the 1865–95 deflation were farmers (who not only were debtors but also were particularly hard hit by the decline in farm prices).

The main cause of the deflation was slow monetary growth, which in turn was due to the gold standard (which essentially limited the growth in the money supply to growth in the supply of gold). Farmers and other borrowers supported the free coinage of silver, which, if adopted, would have boosted the money supply and, perhaps, converted the deflation into an inflation. The gold standard was seen as benefiting the eastern United States, home of the creditors and savers.

What are some of the references in the book? Dorothy represents America; her dog Toto represents the Prohibition Party (the name is short for "teetotaler"); and Oz is the abbreviation for ounce (as in ounce of gold or silver). Dorothy's house lands on the Wicked Witch of the East (stronghold of the gold standard), who dries up completely, leaving only her silver shoes (symbolizing the triumph of silver, but changed to ruby slippers in the movie); the yellow brick road (symbol of the gold standard) leads to the Emerald City (Washington, D.C.). The Scarecrow is the western farmer; the Tin Woodsman is the workingman whose joints are rusted due to unemployment in the depression of the 1890s; and the Cowardly Lion is William Jennings Bryan, leader of the free-silver movement (a lion, as the symbol of one of America's greatest orators; a coward, because he later retreated from support of free silver after economic conditions improved in the late 1890s). In the end, the Wicked Witch of the West melts when Dorothy pours a bucket of water on her, symbolizing the power of water (rain) in solving the problems of the western farmers, and the Wizard is unmasked as an ordinary man who, like a dishonest politician, has been fooling the people.

[a]This box is a very brief summary of Hugh Rockoff, "The 'Wizard of Oz' as a Monetary Allegory," *Journal of Political Economy*, vol. 98 (August 1990), pp. 739–60. Readers interested in the full richness of the references in the *Wizard of Oz* should consult this fascinating article. An easy introduction to the movie and the late nineteenth century references can be found at www.uno.edu/~coba/econ/projects/oz.

no interest at all, and checking accounts, which pay virtually no interest. Since currency and checking accounts represent a basic definition of the money supply, we will explore in this section the consequences of the fact that money pays no interest, thus violating the third condition.

The market rate of interest is not paid on money for three main reasons. First, currency pays no interest. Second, banks earn no interest on the reserves (deposits) they are required to keep at the Federal Reserve banks, so banks cannot afford to pay the market rate of interest on deposits. Third, bank deposits enjoy the protection of deposit insurance, and customers are willing to accept lower interest rates on deposits because they are protected from loss by deposit insurance. The fact that the market rate of interest is not paid on money has several consequences for society.

People demand money for its convenience services. The main reason that a fully anticipated creeping inflation imposes welfare costs on society is that people do not desire money for itself, but rather for the **extra convenience services** that it provides. Inflation causes people to hold less money, so they suffer inconvenience. Money provides convenience to the consumer because purchases can be made instantly. If no money were held (that is, no currency and no checking accounts), then the consumer would have to suffer the inconvenience of going to the bank to make a savings deposit withdrawal, or—even less convenient—to sell a stock or bond before the purchase could be made.[9]

> The **extra convenience services** of money are the services provided by holding one extra dollar of money instead of bonds.

People hold currency even though it pays no interest. The reason they are willing to hold currency paying zero interest, instead of holding a certificate of deposit paying 5 percent interest, *must be* that the money provides them with at least 5 percent more convenience services than the certificate. How is this related to inflation? When the inflation rate increases, the nominal interest rate on all assets other than currency tends to increase. If the inflation rate rose by 5 percent, then the nominal interest rate on certificates would rise from 5 percent to 10 percent, that is, to a rate 5 percent higher than before. Thus people would cut back on their money holdings until the extra convenience services of money rose from 5 to 10 percent. They would hold less cash in their pockets, retain cash only for those expenditures where only cash is accepted (as for taxi rides and cash-only restaurants), and would hold less cash for nonessential purposes.

The "shoe-leather cost" of inflation. The effect of higher inflation and higher interest rates in causing people to hold less cash is sometimes called the "shoe-leather cost" of inflation. Why? Higher interest rates cause people to hold less cash in their pockets at any given moment, so they must go more often to the bank or nearest cash machine to obtain cash by making withdrawals from savings accounts and other interest-paying assets. The inconvenience and loss of productive time that people suffer while making these trips to the bank figuratively wear out their shoes, hence the saying shoe-leather cost.

Financial deregulation has allowed the banking system to pay interest on most types of checking accounts. Thus it is only currency (and the nonpayment of interest on bank reserves at the Federal Reserve banks) that accounts for money's shoe-leather costs. Taking account of the payment of interest on bank checking accounts, it has been estimated that the value of convenience services lost from a 10 percent inflation in the United States is just 0.25 percent of GDP, or about $30 billion at 2005 prices. This loss is very small in comparison to the costs of the recession that would be needed to eliminate permanently a 10 percent fully anticipated inflation, which has been estimated at 4.7 percent of GDP per 1 percent permanent reduction of inflation, or 4.7 percent of GDP for a 10 percent permanent reduction of inflation (see the discussion of the "sacrifice ratio" on pp. 250–51). And the cost of reducing inflation could be lowered even further if the Federal Reserve System paid interest on bank reserves.

---

[9] While credit cards are an alternative to currency and checking accounts for many purchases, there are still many small purchases that require the use of currency and many large purchases that require the use of checks.

> **Self-Test**
>
> Assume that financial deregulation occurs and allows payment of interest on checking accounts.
>
> 1. What effect does this event have on the shoe-leather costs of fully anticipated inflation?
> 2. What effect does this have on holdings of money per dollar of nominal GDP?
> 3. What effect does it have on velocity?

Violation of Condition 4: Taxes Are Levied on Nominal Interest, Not Real Interest

The fourth condition for inflation to be harmless is that only real interest is taxable. But in every nation, tax rules are based on nominal interest, both interest earned as part of income and interest paid that is tax deductible (e.g., home mortgages). The following example shows how inflation (p) reduces the after-tax real interest rate when nominal interest rate is taxed, even if the nominal interest rate obeys the Fisher Effect and rises by as much as the inflation rate.

We consider an example with a tax rate (t) of 30 percent, or 0.3. Initially, the inflation rate is zero and the nominal interest rate is 3 percent, so the real interest rate is 3 percent. But when the inflation rate jumps to 10 percent, even if the nominal interest rate jumps to 13 percent, the real interest rate after tax declines rather than staying constant.

General Form

After-tax real interest = after-tax nominal interest − inflation rate

After-tax real interest = $i(1 - t) - p$

Numerical example

(a) $2.1 = 3(1 - 0.3) - 0$

(b) $-0.9 = 13(1 - 0.3) - 10$

In this example, line (a) shows that the after-tax real interest rate with zero inflation is 2.1 percent, that is, the nominal interest rate of 3 percent, times the 0.7 fraction that the saver is allowed to keep after the tax rate of 0.3 is paid, minus the zero percent rate of inflation. Line (b) shows that when inflation rises from zero to 10 percent, the after-tax real interest rate falls to *minus* 0.9 percent, that is, the nominal interest rate of 13 percent, times the 0.7 fraction that the saver is allowed to keep, minus the 10 percent rate of inflation. Comparing the two examples, an increase in the inflation rate from zero to 10 percent reduces the after-tax real interest rate from 2.1 percent to *minus* 0.9 percent. Thus, the fourth condition for inflation to be harmless, that inflation has no effect on the real after-tax interest rate, is violated. As a result, savings and investment decisions are distorted by inflation, which encourages people to borrow more and save less.[10]

---

[10] A recent article argues that the cost of high inflation working through the failure of the tax system to tax real returns and the real cost of borrowing is much higher than the traditional shoe-leather cost of inflation working through the failure to pay interest on money. See James B. Bullard and Steven Russell, "How Costly Is Sustained Low Inflation for the U.S. Economy?" Federal Reserve Bank of St. Louis *Review*, May/June 2004, vol. 86, no. 3, pp. 35–67.

9-4 Indexation and Other Reforms to Reduce the Costs of Inflation

There is a strong case for the institution of reforms that can cut substantially the costs imposed by inflation. These reforms fall into three categories: the elimination of government regulations that redistribute income from savers to borrowers, the creation of an indexed bond to give savers a secure place to save, and a restatement of tax laws to eliminate the effects of inflation on real tax burdens. The first two of these reforms have already been achieved, the third has not.

Decontrol of Financial Institutions

Much of the distortion caused by the U.S. inflation of the 1970s resulted from federal government-imposed interest rate ceilings on commercial banks and savings institutions. Financial deregulation solved this problem. By 1985 all regulations on the payment of interest on checking, savings, and time-deposit accounts had been lifted. Since then, inflation has a smaller redistributive effect than in the past, since all individuals, rich and poor alike, are able to receive a return close to the market rate of interest on their savings accounts. Checking accounts still pay a very low rate of interest to compensate banks for the cost of clearing checks.

Even if all checking and savings accounts paid a nominal interest rate that included a full inflation premium, savers would still suffer an erosion of purchasing power on their pocket cash. Inflation would still cause people to incur shoe-leather costs as they work harder to keep their cash balances at a minimum.

Indexed Bonds

Even though the lifting of government interest rate ceilings on savings and checking accounts has substantially cut the costs of inflation, many economists recommended that the government issue an indexed bond that would fully protect savers against any unexpected movements in the inflation rate. Finally, in early 1997, the U.S. government responded to these recommendations by issuing an indexed bond, called *TIPS*, which stands for "Treasury Inflation-Protected Securities."

An **indexed bond** protects savers from unexpected movements in the inflation rate by paying a fixed real interest rate (r_0) plus the actual inflation rate (p). Thus the saver's nominal interest rate would be

> An **indexed bond** pays a fixed real interest rate; its nominal interest rate is equal to this real interest rate plus the actual inflation rate.

General Form	Numerical Example
$i = r_0 + p$	(a) $3 = 3 + 0$
	(b) $13 = 3 + 10$

In numerical example (a), savers would receive a 3 percent return if the inflation rate were zero. If inflation suddenly accelerated to 10 percent, as in example (b), savers would find that the nominal return (i) rose to 13 percent, and they would be just as well off as if there had been no inflation. The box discusses the performance of TIPS since they were introduced in 1997.

Indexed Tax System

Another important reform made effective in 1985 is the partial indexation of the personal income tax system. This now raises the dollar amounts of tax credits, exemptions, standard deductions, and tax rate brackets each year by

The Indexed Bond (TIPS) Has Arrived

Following the lead of Canada, the United Kingdom, and other countries, the U.S. Treasury introduced inflation-indexed bonds to investors in 1997. These bonds protect the savings of investors from being eroded by unanticipated increases in the inflation rate. The indexed bond introduced in the United States is called TIPS, for Treasury Inflation-Protected Securities.

Unlike a conventional bond, an indexed bond promises to pay its holder a fixed real rate of return. An indexed bond maintains its promised real rate of return even if inflation suddenly accelerates by 5, 10, or even 20 percent relative to the inflation rate that was expected when the saver purchased the bond.

The U.S. Treasury's 10-year indexed bond is structured like a similar bond available since 1991 in Canada. Semiannual interest payments are calculated by adjusting the principal for inflation (using the Consumer Price Index or CPI) and applying the fixed real interest rate (determined at the auction at which the bonds were first issued) to the inflation-adjusted principal.

The benefits for the U.S. Treasury are several. Indexed bonds can reduce the risk premium that the government must pay to savers who fear that their returns on bonds will be eroded by future unanticipated inflation. By eliminating the risk of loss from future unanticipated inflation, the Treasury can reduce its average borrowing costs, thus reducing the interest component of the federal government deficit. An additional benefit is that the process of issuing indexed bonds provides information about the inflation expectations of investors, measured as the difference in market-determined interest rates on conventional and indexed bonds of the same maturities.

The figure in this box plots the 10-year Treasury bond (which is not inflation-protected) and the 10-year TIPS. The green shading shows the real interest rate based on the expectations of those who buy TIPS, and the orange shading shows the inflation rate expected by those investors. In 2003–04, there was a drop in the expected real interest rate and an increase in the implied expected inflation rate. The implied expected inflation rate in 2004 was about 2.6 percent, somewhat higher than the average annual inflation rate of the CPI in the three years ending in October 2004, which was 2.4 percent. Why were TIPS investors pessimistic about future inflation?

Financial journalists cautioned investors during 2004 that the market for TIPS was "overbought," meaning that investors had pushed up the prices of TIPS bonds too high, making their yields too low. Or, perhaps the sharp increase in oil prices that occurred during 2004 made investors pessimistic about the future course of inflation.

the amount of inflation that has been experienced. Without an indexed tax system, inflation would raise individual incomes and push taxpayers into higher tax brackets.

But the government must do more than index credits, exemptions, deductions, and tax brackets in order to achieve a fully inflation-neutral tax system. It must end present rules that discriminate against savers and favor borrowers by taxing real rather than nominal interest and capital gains. Just as savers should be taxed only on real interest income and real capital gains, borrowers should be allowed to deduct from their taxable income only the real portion of the interest they pay on loans. These reforms would eliminate the present effect of inflation in the U.S. tax system of discouraging saving and encouraging borrowing and spending.

9-5 The Government Budget Constraint and the Inflation Tax

At the beginning of this chapter we identified excessive money creation as the primary cause of inflation in the long run, and the International Perspectives box on p. 284 illustrated the close correlation between money creation and inflation in several nations that experienced rapid inflation over the 1990–2002 period. Now we return to the puzzle of why governments allow excessive money creation to occur. In countries such as the United States that have experienced modest rates of inflation, the primary answer is that the government was tempted to raise monetary growth in order to create a temporary increase in output at the cost of inflation that would be experienced by the electorate after the election was over. Also, the government was reluctant to stop an inflation, once started, for fear of the temporary period of high unemployment that would be a by-product of the effort to stop inflation, as occurred during 1982–83.

But in countries that have experienced rapid inflation or hyperinflation, the reason for excessive money creation is almost always large government deficits. By definition, government spending must be financed by some combination of tax revenues, bond creation, or money creation. When there are political obstacles to raising sufficient tax revenue, and in countries that do not have active bond markets, the government has no option other than money creation, that is, turning on the printing press.

A household must withdraw its savings or borrow if its expenditures exceed its income; the same is true of the government. The options open to the government for financing its expenditures are summarized in the **government budget constraint**. This divides government spending into two parts, spending on goods and services (G) and spending on interest payments (iB), where i is the nominal interest rate on government bonds and B is the dollar amount of government bonds outstanding. Government revenue sources are tax revenue net of transfer payments (T), the issuance of additional bonds (ΔB), and the issuance of additional government monetary liabilities (ΔH). Government monetary liabilities, which consist of currency held by the public and bank reserves, are often called high-powered money and are abbreviated H. Both B and H are part of the government debt; the only difference is that bonds pay interest and high-powered money does not.

The **government budget constraint** relates government spending to the three sources available to finance that spending: tax revenue, creation of bonds, and creation of money.

The Government Budget Constraint Equation

The government budget constraint can be expressed in a simple formula:

$$\underbrace{G - T}_{\text{basic deficit}} + \frac{iB}{P} = \frac{\Delta B}{P} + \frac{\Delta H}{P} \qquad (9.8)$$

Here $G - T$ is called the *basic deficit*, that is, the deficit that the government would run excluding its interest payments on outstanding bonds. In the last few years in the United States, the federal government has run both a basic deficit and a basic surplus. Compare the following four situations. In the first, the federal government ran a basic deficit. In the second, it ran a basic surplus, that is, a negative basic deficit, but a positive total deficit. In the third, it ran a basic and a total surplus, that is, a negative basic deficit and a negative total deficit. In the fourth, it returned to the 1992 situation by running both a basic and total deficit. As in equation (9.8), the data are expressed in real terms (in billions of dollars at 2000 prices):

	Basic Deficit	+	Interest Cost	=	Total Deficit
1992	73.3	+	217.1	=	290.4
1996	−171.5	+	279.0	=	107.5
2000	−519.7	+	283.3	=	−236.4
2004	174.0	+	238.6	=	412.6

Stated another way, the basic deficit in 2004 was less than half of the total deficit; more than half of the total deficit was accounted for by the interest cost.

Bond Creation Versus Money Creation

Despite the fact that the U.S. federal government moved into surplus between 1998 and 2001, it moved back into deficit after 2001; for many years before 1998, it ran a deficit. Most other industrialized countries have run a government budget deficit rather than a surplus throughout the past two decades, without the interruption of a surplus as the United States enjoyed in 1998–2001. How are governments able to finance these deficits? There are two methods. These are the issuance of additional government bonds, represented by ΔB, and the issuance of additional high-powered money, represented by ΔH. When the government raises H, the total nominal money supply (M) increases.

An increase in H raises aggregate demand more than an increase in B, because a higher H raises the money supply and eliminates the crowding out effect of Chapter 4. Because a deficit financed by H is more stimulative to the economy, the government may want to finance its budget deficit by issuing more H when the economy is weak and by issuing more B when the economy is strong.

In the United States, the size of the government deficit is determined by the administration and Congress, while the choice between bond and money creation is made by the Federal Reserve. Since the Fed controls ΔH, and since there is a large, well-organized market for government bonds, the Fed can respond to a larger government deficit by raising ΔH, reducing ΔH, or leaving ΔH unchanged. However, not every nation is able to choose between bond and monetary finance of government deficits. Developed nations such as the United States, Japan, Canada, and the more prosperous European nations have sophisticated capital markets where the government can sell bonds. But less developed nations lack these markets, so their governments have little latitude to finance their government deficits by selling bonds. As a result, in many countries a higher government deficit *automatically* requires raising ΔH, which boosts the growth rate of the money supply and (according to equation (9.3) on p. 282) the rate of inflation.

Effects of Inflation

Inflation may seem to aggravate the government's problem of financing its basic deficit, since according to the Fisher Effect, inflation raises the nominal interest rate (i) that appears on the left-hand side of equation (9.8). However, inflation also eases the government's problem. This is not evident in equation (9.8), where the inflation rate (p) does not appear. However, we can slightly rearrange equation (9.8) by multiplying the first term on the right-hand side by B/B and the second term by H/H. This converts (9.8) into:

$$G - T + \frac{iB}{P} = \frac{\Delta BB}{BP} + \frac{\Delta HH}{HP} \qquad (9.9)$$

The term $\Delta BB/BP$ is the percentage change in bonds ($\Delta B/B$) times the amount of real bonds outstanding (B/P), and ($\Delta HH/HP$) is the percentage change in high-powered money ($\Delta H/H$) times the amount of real high-powered money (H/P) outstanding. Clearly, if B/P and H/P are to remain stable, then the percentage growth rate of B, represented by a lowercase b, and the growth rate of H, designated by a lowercase h, will each have to equal the inflation rate (p):

$$\Delta B/B = b = \Delta H/H = h = p \qquad (9.10)$$

This equation says simply that the growth rate of bonds (b) and the growth rate of high-powered money (h) equal the rate of inflation. If that is true, then the real value of bonds (B/P) and the real value of high-powered money (H/P) will remain fixed. That is, the numerator of each ratio (B/P and H/P) will grow at the same rate as the denominator when $b = h = p$.

Why Inflation Is Tempting to Governments

Our aim is to determine the nature of the government's budget constraint that would keep the real value of bonds and high-powered money fixed. Since equation (9.10) gives the condition ($b = h = p$) that will allow this situation to persist, we need to substitute the inflation rate (p) into equation (9.9), replacing the term there for the growth rate of bonds ($\Delta B/B$) and also replacing the term for the growth rate of high-powered money ($\Delta H/H$). In arriving at this final statement of the government budget constraint, we also move the term representing real interest payments (iB/P) from the left-hand side of equation (9.9) to the right-hand side of equation (9.11):

$$G - T = \frac{pH}{P} - \frac{(i-p)B}{P} \qquad (9.11)$$

$$\text{basic deficit} = \text{seignorage} - \text{real interest}$$
$$\text{or} \qquad \text{on bonds}$$
$$\text{inflation tax}$$

The first term on the right-hand side of equation (9.11), namely (pH/P), represents the inflation rate times real high-powered money, that is, the revenue that the government receives when it creates just enough H to maintain fixed the real quantity of high-powered money (H/P). This revenue that the government gets from inflation is called **seignorage**. From the point of view of private households and firms that must add to their nominal quantity of H enough to keep real H/P constant, this same revenue is called the **inflation tax**.

Stated simply, if pH/P were the only term on the right-hand side of equation (9.11), it would indicate the amount of the deficit that the government could run by creating the right amount of nominal high-powered money (H) that would be consistent with keeping the real quantity of high-powered money constant. If the inflation rate is not zero, then this amount is not zero, and the government can run a deficit and still maintain real high-powered money constant. Subsequently we will see that the inflation tax is a cost of inflation to households, the exact counterpart of the benefit that inflation provides to the government.

Inflation does not eliminate the government's obligation to pay interest on its outstanding bonds held by private households and firms. But the second right-hand term $[(i - p)B/P]$ in equation (9.11) illustrates that the government only has to worry about paying the *real* interest expense of servicing the bonds. While it pays bond holders the nominal interest rate (i), bond holders have to give part of i back to the government to purchase sufficient additional bonds to keep their real bond holdings (B/P) constant.

An Example Showing That the Government Gains

To see how this works in an example, imagine that we start with $100 of bonds, a 5 percent inflation rate per year, an 8 percent nominal interest rate, and a 3 percent real interest rate. The government must pay $8 in interest. But, to keep the real quantity of bonds (B/P) constant, the government sells $5 in new bonds to the public, raising the value of outstanding bonds to $105. The government's net interest expense is just $3 (the real interest rate of 3 percent times the original $100 of bonds). Why? Because the government *pays* $8 in interest but *receives* $5 as a payment by the public for the new bonds.[11]

Thus the government benefits from inflation in two ways. First, it obtains an extra source of revenue, called seignorage or the inflation tax. The government can then lower ordinary taxes or increase spending more than it could otherwise. Second, the government may gain if inflation raises the nominal interest rate by less than inflation itself. Sharp increases of inflation, particularly such as those during the oil shock periods of the 1970s, are often accompanied

---

Seignorage is the revenue the government receives from inflation and is equal to the inflation rate times real high-powered money.

The **inflation tax** is the revenue the government receives from inflation and is the same as seignorage, but viewed from the perspective of households.

---

[11] To simplify the presentation, both equation (9.11) and the numerical example in this paragraph neglect the taxation of interest earnings, which further reduces the government's net real interest expense.

by an increase in the nominal interest rate of less than one-for-one, thus reducing the real interest rate. And, as shown in equation (9.11), it is the real interest rate that matters for government finance.

> **Self-Test**
>
> Assume that after centuries of a zero budget deficit and a zero debt, the nation of Abstinia runs a one-year deficit equal to 1 percent of GDP, which it finances by creating H/P equal to 1 percent of GDP.
>
> 1. If inflation over the next decade occurs at 5 percent per year, what must be true of the basic deficit and the level of H for Abstinia to end the decade with the same level of H/P equal to 1 percent of GDP?
>
> 2. What is the answer to the same question if the inflation rate over the next decade is 10 percent per year?

9-6 Starting and Stopping a Hyperinflation

We have already defined hyperinflation as an inflation rate of 1,000 percent or more per year. If an inflation of 1,000 percent per year were to occur in the United States, a Big Mac would increase in price from around $2.50 to $2500! Clearly, such an inflation rate would be disruptive if wages and salaries did not grow as rapidly, and if interest rates on savings accounts were less than the inflation rate.

As shown in Table 9-1, in 1986–90 three of the listed countries experienced annual inflation rates that average over 1,000 percent per year. In all of those countries, inflation was more rapid than it had been in the previous period. In fact, all of these countries (excepting Argentina) had inflation rates below 100 percent in the first period shown, 1975–80.

Table 9-1 Annual Rates of Inflation in Selected High Inflation Countries, 1975–2005

	1975–80	1980–86	1986–90	1990–95	1995–2000	2000–2005
Argentina	206	300	829	119	0.5	10
Bolivia	16	1,969	68	13	7	3
Brazil	57	148	1,077	1,419	17	9
Israel	61	177	24	14	7	2
Mexico	20	61	76	19	22	5
Nicaragua	23	150	4,749	1,827	11	8
Peru	46	95	2,343	1,342	8	2
Poland	9	29	188	132	15	3

Sources: International Monetary Fund, World Economic Outlook 2004, and http://www.imf.org/external/pubs/ft/weo/2005/01/pdf/statappx.pdf.

In the next period (1990–95) three of these countries—Nicaragua, Brazil, and Peru—continued to experience an annual inflation rate above 1,000 percent, while in Argentina the inflation rate fell to 119 percent per year. In sharp contrast was the period 1995–2000 in which none of the countries had inflation rates above 25 percent per year, and an even more dramatic event occurred in the most recent period, 2000–05, when none of the countries had an inflation rate above 10 percent. Clearly, macroeconomic policies improved markedly after 1995, and each country succeeded in limiting growth in its money supply, thus preventing hyperinflation.

Since there are more than 100 countries for which records are available, the fact that only four countries experienced inflation rates greater than 1,000 percent per year over the periods shown in Table 9-1 suggests that hyperinflations are unusual events. But, like the Great Depression of the 1930s, such unusual events are nevertheless worth studying for what they can teach us about macroeconomic behavior, and because the memory of these events may continue to influence economic theories and the beliefs of policymakers.

Costs of an Anticipated Hyperinflation

We have previously reviewed the inconvenience (or shoe-leather) cost of inflation that occurs because the interest rate paid on money is zero. The inconvenience cost of inflation becomes much larger in a hyperinflation, like that which occurred in Germany in 1922–23. In 1919 a farmer sold a piece of land for 80,000 marks as a nest egg for old age. All he got for the money a few years later was a woolen sweater. As the following account reveals, elderly Germans can still recall the terrible days in 1923.

> People were bringing money to the bank in cardboard boxes and laundry baskets. As we no longer could count it, we put the money on scales and weighed it. I can still see my brothers coming home Saturdays with heaps of paper money. When the shops reopened after the weekend they got no more than a breakfast roll for it. Many got drunk on their pay because it was worthless Monday.[12]

How a Hyperinflation Begins

What factors cause a hyperinflation to take off?[13] The first factor is familiar from Chapter 8. There we learned that accommodation of an adverse supply shock by more rapid nominal GDP growth can cause inflation to accelerate. What converts a mild acceleration into a hyperinflation is frequent (for example, monthly) **wage indexation**. Such indexation sets off a rapid inflationary spiral in which wage indexation leads to wage increases, which set off further price increase, which make a nation's goods less attractive to foreigners, in turn reducing the demand for its currency and causing a depreciation of the exchange rate, which in turn raises import prices and acts as a further supply shock. For instance, Argentina, Brazil, and Israel all had experienced relatively rapid inflation in the late 1970s and had in place systems involving frequent wage indexation. This system facilitated the countries' transition to more rapid inflation in the 1980s (although Israel never reached the hyperinflation stage).

Wage indexation calls for an automatic increase in the wage rate in response to an increase in a price index. It is the same as cost-of-living agreements (see Section 17-9).

---

[12] Alice Segert, "When Inflation Buried Germany," *Chicago Tribune*, November 30, 1974.

[13] This section summarizes several of the important conclusions of the Dornbusch et al. source cited in footnote 2.

The combination of supply shocks, monetary accommodation, and frequent wage indexation is an "unholy trinity" that can lead to hyperinflation. In a hyperinflation, wage indexation occurs more frequently, aggravating the destructive power of the unholy trinity.

The other classic cause of hyperinflation is deficit financing, particularly as a result of wars (when government spending rises far more than revenues from conventional taxes). Hyperinflations do not generally occur while wars are being fought, since price controls are often used to suppress the inflationary pressure caused by deficit financing (a situation called "repressed inflation").[14] But when price controls are lifted after wars, the consequence of deficit finance can cause an explosion of monetary growth. Classic postwar hyperinflations far exceeded the rate of 1,000 percent per year, or 22 percent per month, that defines a hyperinflation. The average *monthly* inflation rate during the German hyperinflation of 1922–23 was 322 percent, while the "mother of all hyperinflations" occurred in Hungary between August 1945 and July 1946, when the average monthly inflation rate was 19,800 percent! (See pp. 16–17 for more on the 1922–23 German hyperinflation.)

In thinking about hyperinflations, we should not be satisfied with the simple conclusion that a supply shock or a government budget deficit causes hyperinflation, as if the supply shock or budget deficit was totally exogenous. Instead, the essence of a hyperinflation is its cumulative dynamic character, best characterized as a vicious circle. Hyperinflation can create continuous supply shocks if there is a flight from a nation's currency by causing a real exchange rate depreciation. Hyperinflation can cause the real budget deficit to worsen by giving citizens a strong incentive to delay tax payments as long as possible. Government must then finance the growing budget deficit by an ever-increasing rate of monetary growth. The labor market also adapts to hyperinflation by increasing the frequency of wage indexation, pouring more fuel on the inflationary fire.

How to End a Hyperinflation

The steps a government must take to end a hyperinflation are sometimes called a stabilization strategy. The key ingredient is to achieve a sharp reduction in the budget deficit by cutting government expenditures and subsidies and by raising taxes. In countries where tax evasion is a tradition, this fiscal reform may involve shifting to a broad-based tax that is easy to enforce, like the value-added tax.[15] At least in the short run, it is necessary to cut through the wage-price spiral by introducing some type of controls on wages, often called an **incomes policy**. This policy may involve reducing the frequency of wage indexation or obtaining an agreement between firms and workers to reduce real wages.

One by one, the nations that have experienced hyperinflation have achieved successful stabilizations, including Bolivia in 1985, Argentina in

Incomes policy is an attempt by policymakers to moderate increases in wages and other income, either by persuasion or by legal rules.

---

[14] However, during the U.S. Civil War prices doubled in the North and toward the end of the war rose at a near-hyperinflationary rate in the South.

[15] A value-added tax, which does not exist in the United States, is common in Europe and was introduced in Canada in 1991. This tax has the same effect as a universal sales tax on all goods and services and is collected on the value that is added at each stage of production, that is, a firm's sales minus its expenditures on materials and supplies (which have already been taxed).

Credibility is the extent to which households and firms believe that an announced monetary or fiscal policy will actually be implemented and maintained as announced.

1991–92, and Brazil, Nicaragua, and Peru in 1995–96. The successive failures of past attempts at reform, particularly in the cases of Argentina and Brazil, suggest that stopping a hyperinflation is a complex and difficult task. Much depends on the **credibility** of the government, that is, the public's belief that budget deficits and monetary growth are really going to stop. It may take several dramatic actions all at once to achieve credibility. The monumental achievement of stopping inflation in Argentina in 1991 required a drastic plan that combined every possible ingredient—fiscal correction, suspension of indexation, a fixed exchange rate, and international support. Unfortunately, Argentina's achievement was only temporary; as a result of poor control of fiscal deficits, by 2002 Argentina was once again a land of crisis, with a devalued currency and a soaring inflation rate of 26 percent. This inflation rate was brought down to 5 percent in 2004, only as a result of a catastrophic recession that reduced real GDP by 20 percent between 2000 and 2002.

9-7 Why the Unemployment Rate Cannot Be Reduced to Zero

Thus far in this chapter we have concentrated on the causes and costs of inflation. The other major goal of macroeconomic policy (besides achieving as high as possible a growth rate in output per person) is to maintain the unemployment rate as low as possible. The analysis of unemployment appears to be simpler than that of inflation, because everyone agrees that more jobs are better. The only obstacle to reducing the unemployment rate to zero, according to our analysis of Chapter 8, is that too high an output ratio (which causes too low an unemployment rate) would cause the inflation rate to accelerate, thus exacerbating the costs of inflation.

In the rest of this chapter, we learn some of the other reasons (besides higher inflation) why maintaining too low an unemployment rate is undesirable. There are good reasons why the overall unemployment rate is not zero, and these emerge from the efficient operation of a well-functioning economy.

The Actual and Natural Rates of Unemployment

At the beginning of the book, we were introduced to the concept of the natural rate of unemployment. The word "natural" describes exactly the same situation for unemployment as it does for output, an economy with a constant rate of inflation in the absence of supply shocks (see Section 1-3 on pp. 5–8). When the actual and natural rates of unemployment are equal, so also are the actual and natural levels of real GDP equal, and the output ratio is 100 percent.

Figure 9-2 plots the actual and natural rates of unemployment since 1970. The actual and natural rates of unemployment were roughly equal in 1972, 1978, 1987, 1991, 1994–95, and 2001. When the actual unemployment rate was above the natural rate, especially in 1975–77, 1981–84, 1991–94, and 2001–04, the inflation rate tended to decrease. When the actual unemployment rate was below the natural rate, especially in 1988–90 and 1997–2000, the inflation rate tended to increase, although in the late 1990s there was hardly any increase in the inflation rate due to the effect of beneficial supply shocks.

Figure 9-2 The Actual Unemployment Rate and the Natural Rate of Unemployment, 1980–2004

The actual unemployment rate was above the natural rate of unemployment in 1980–86, 1991–94, and after 2001. The actual unemployment rate was below the natural rate of unemployment during 1987–90 and 1996–2001. The natural rate of unemployment declined from 6.3 percent in 1985 to 5.0 percent after the year 2000.

Between the early 1980s and the late 1990s, the natural rate of unemployment (the black line in Figure 9-2) declined from more than 6 percent to roughly 5 percent. Later in this chapter we will examine some of the reasons for this decline. By the year 2000 it was possible to maintain the actual unemployment rate at 5 percent without creating pressure for higher inflation, whereas in 1985 the unemployment rate would need to be maintained at about 6.3 percent to avoid pressure for higher inflation. This improvement is good for everyone, but still we must explain why it is not possible for the natural rate of unemployment to be zero instead of five percent.

Distinguishing the Three Types of Unemployment

The difference between the actual rate of unemployment and the natural rate of unemployment, designated in Figure 9-2 by red and blue shading, is called **cyclical unemployment**. In Figure 9-2, cyclical unemployment is negative and the economy is prosperous when the shading is red, and cyclical unemployment is positive and the economy lacks job openings when the shading is blue. You will find the same color shading in Figure 1-6 on p. 13, which displays the

Cyclical unemployment is the difference between the actual unemployment rate and the natural rate of unemployment.

actual and natural unemployment rates for a much longer period going back to 1900.

Why is the natural rate of unemployment a number like 5.0 percent, rather than zero? When the economy is operating at the natural rate of unemployment, it experiences two types of unemployment. One is called **turnover unemployment**, sometimes also called frictional unemployment. Turnover unemployment occurs in the normal process of job search by individuals who have voluntarily quit their jobs, are entering the labor force for the first time, or are reentering the labor force. Any economy can expect to have a moderate amount of turnover unemployment, and we shall see that there are good reasons for the United States to have more turnover unemployment than some other countries.

Mismatch unemployment is the second component of the natural rate of unemployment. Sometimes also called structural unemployment, it occurs when there is a mismatch between the skill or location requirements of job vacancies and the present skills or location of members of the labor force. For an unemployed individual, mismatch unemployment tends to last much longer than turnover unemployment, since more time is required for people to learn new skills or to move to new locations.

To summarize, the actual unemployment rate is divided up into cyclical, turnover, and mismatch unemployment. When the actual unemployment rate is equal to the natural rate of unemployment, then cyclical unemployment is zero and all unemployment is accounted for by the turnover and mismatch components. Cyclical unemployment can be eliminated by stimulative monetary or fiscal policy that expands the economy when cyclical unemployment is positive and by restrictive monetary or fiscal policy that reduces aggregate demand when cyclical unemployment is negative. In the remainder of this chapter, we are concerned with the remaining two types of unemployment, turnover and mismatch, and the factors that tend to make them high or low.

Turnover unemployment is another name for frictional unemployment. It is one of the two components of the natural rate of unemployment.

Mismatch unemployment is another name for structural unemployment. It is one of the two components of the natural rate of unemployment.

9-8 Sources of Mismatch Unemployment

Vacancies and Unemployment in an Imaginary Economy

We can better understand the mismatch component of the natural unemployment rate (U^N) if we think of an imaginary society in which U^N is zero. All jobs are completely identical in their skill requirements, and all are located at exactly the same place. All workers are completely identical, with skill requirements perfectly suited for the identical jobs, and all workers live in the same location as the jobs. We can imagine a 10-mile-high combined factory-office-apartment skyscraper with very fast elevators at the corner of State and Madison streets in Chicago.

In this imaginary economy it is impossible for vacancies and unemployment to exist simultaneously. Why? Imagine that initially some workers are unemployed, and that the government pursues expansive monetary and fiscal policies that stimulate aggregate demand. Additional jobs open up, but the unemployed workers are in exactly the right place and possess the right skills, so that they instantly zoom up or down the speedy elevators in the 10-mile-high skyscraper to the job's location. Each job vacancy disappears immediately, and unemployment disappears instantly.

Quickly all the unemployed find jobs. Any further job vacancies caused by an additional demand stimulus will not disappear because there are no available jobless people to fill them. Further aggregate demand stimulus will just expand the number of job vacancies.

Skill differences among jobs can cause structural unemployment. To be slightly more realistic, let us now assume that there are two types of jobs and workers in the 10-mile-high skyscraper, typists and computer programmers. As the economy expands, it gradually uses up its supply of trained computer programmers. Once all the computer programmers have jobs, all of the unemployment consists of jobless typists. If the government further stimulates aggregate demand, we assume that an equal number of job vacancies is created for programmers and typists. The typist vacancies disappear immediately as available typists are carried by elevator to fill the job openings. But there are no computer programmers left, and so the programmer job openings remain. *Vacancies and unemployment exist simultaneously because firms refuse to hire typists to fill programmer vacancies.* The costs of training are just too high.

In reality, the actual economy is divided into numerous separate labor markets that differ in location, working conditions, and skill requirements. Any increase in aggregate spending generates job openings in some labor markets, while many people remain unemployed in other markets. Some unemployed are able to fill developing job vacancies. But others are prevented from qualifying by the cost of moving to the locations of the job openings, by the cost of acquiring the required skills, and even by the "cost of information" involved in finding out what jobs are available.

Vacancies and upward pressure on wage rates. In the imaginary economy, with all jobs and workers alike and located at the same place, policymakers could use aggregate demand stimulus to push the unemployment rate to zero. There would be no job vacancies and no tendency for firms to boost wage rates to fill empty job slots. Thus it would be possible to experience zero unemployment without upward pressure on wages.

But in the real-world economy, with numerous separate labor markets, vacancies and unemployed workers can coexist. There may be unfilled job openings for hotel workers in Iowa, while aircraft factory workers may be unemployed in Seattle. Structural or mismatch unemployment exists. Any attempt to use aggregate demand policy to push the total unemployment rate to zero will create numerous job vacancies for the types of skills that are in short supply and in the locations where labor is scarce. Firms will be desperate to fill these job vacancies and will boost wage rates, hoping to steal workers away from other firms. Higher wages will raise business costs and cause price increases. *Thus a situation with a low unemployment rate and lots of job vacancies maintained by rapid demand growth is one in which the inflation rate will continuously accelerate.*

Causes of and Cures for Mismatch Unemployment: Mismatch of Skills

All groups in the labor force, including adult men, adult women, and teenagers, are victims of mismatch between their own skills and locations and the skill and location requirements of available jobs. Why does this worker-job mismatch occur? We begin with causes of skill mismatch, add some suggested policy remedies, and then turn to the causes of and remedies for location mismatch.

Lack of job training. Vacant jobs often have specific skill requirements. Sometimes firms are willing to train workers when the skills are specific to the particular job; for example, an administrative assistant needs to know the filing system in a particular office. But some training, for example, how to use a personal computer, is general in nature. Firms may be unwilling to train employees in general skills for fear that the employees will quit before the firm's training investment can be repaid. Yet schools may not be able to provide the training because they lack either the equipment or properly trained instructors.

Solutions for low skills fall into three basic categories—better public education, subsidies for firms to train workers, and government-financed training programs. Better public education is essential, particularly for students from disadvantaged backgrounds, since training subsidies and programs will not work if teenagers and young adults cannot read or perform arithmetic.

Inflexibility of relative wages. Elementary economics teaches that a surplus of a commodity develops when its price is too high. In the same way, high unemployment of some groups, particularly teenagers, signals an excessive real wage for that group. In the United States there is a uniform minimum wage for both adults and teenagers, but teenage unemployment is higher than adult unemployment, and some people have proposed a lower minimum wage for teenagers.

Discrimination. Some employers will not hire women, minorities, or teenagers. Much discrimination stems from long-standing customs and from social pressure. We observe that most administrative assistants, secretaries, elementary school teachers, and nurses are women, and that minority workers are sometimes pushed into relatively unpleasant occupations. Despite the gains of the civil rights movement and antidiscrimination legislation, less-educated women and minority individuals are still in many cases prevented from entering unions in blue-collar trades.

Several Western European nations have helped to reduce discrimination against women by subsidizing maternity leaves and providing subsidized child care, thus allowing women with children to maintain more stable job records. A case could be made for similar subsidies in the United States. Some barriers, particularly the limitation of many blue-collar craft unions to white males, may require legal rather than economic remedies.

Causes of and Cures for Mismatch Unemployment: Mismatch of Location

Often job vacancies and unemployment are very unequally distributed across regions of the United States. Several solutions, other than a better employment service, have been proposed to reduce the locational source of mismatch unemployment. One suggestion is subsidies to help unemployed workers pay the costs of relocating to areas with ample job openings. Another suggestion is to establish enterprise zones, a system of tax incentives or similar incentives to induce manufacturers to move their factories to depressed areas. The states of Alabama and South Carolina paid major subsidies to induce Mercedes-Benz and BMW to build automobile plants in their states.

9-9 Turnover Unemployment and Job Search

We have now examined the sources of mismatch unemployment, one of the two components of the natural unemployment rate. A second component is turnover unemployment. What is the difference between mismatch and turnover unemployment? The barriers that stand between vacant jobs and workers unemployed due to mismatch are serious and require substantial investments in training or moving to eliminate. But the barriers that stand between vacant jobs and those unemployed due to turnover are much more minor, involving the costs of job search for a relatively short period in the local community for a suitable job.

One way of differentiating mismatch and turnover unemployment is the length of unemployment episodes ("spells"). In a year like 1996, when the economy was operating close to the natural rate of unemployment, half of all weeks of unemployment occurred in spells of at least three months' duration. Thus some of the unemployed found jobs quite rapidly, in a month or two, suggesting turnover unemployment. Many other individuals took much longer, suggesting mismatch unemployment. Thus turnover and mismatch unemployment are not in conflict; both occur at the same time, to different people.

Reasons for Turnover Unemployment

As we learned in Section 2-9 on pp. 44–47, Census Bureau workers ask a number of questions in order to determine whether individual household members are unemployed. These questions allow the unemployed to be broken down into five groups:

1. Persons laid off who can expect to return to the same job.
2. Persons who have lost jobs to which they cannot expect to return.
3. Persons who have quit their jobs.
4. Reentrants who are returning to the labor force after a spell of neither working nor looking for work.
5. New entrants who have never worked at a full-time job before but are now seeking employment.

Turnover unemployment consists primarily of individuals in categories 3, 4, and 5, although reentrants and new entrants may spend a long time in futile search if their skills and location are mismatched with job vacancies.

Some reasons for unemployment are concentrated in particular demographic groups. For instance, job loss tends to be most concentrated among adult males. Reentry unemployment is felt mainly by adult females, teenagers, and college students. New entry unemployment, of course, is mainly experienced by teenagers and college-age youth.

Table 9-2 shows how the types of unemployment are divided among the major demographic groups. The month illustrated is November 2004, when the economy was operating at an unemployment rate of 5 percent, close to the natural rate of unemployment. To simplify the table, the categories of temporary and permanent job loss are consolidated. Overall, perhaps the most striking contrast is between the large percentage of adult male unemployment caused by the "lost job" category (64.7 percent on line 1) as opposed to the small share of teenage unemployment caused by job loss (13.7 percent). Thus in a year like 2004

Table 9-2 Unemployment Rates by Reason, Gender, and Age in November 2004

	Unemployment Rate				Percentage of Group Unemployment			
	Adult Men	Adult Women	Teenagers	All Groups	Adult Men	Adult Women	Teenagers	All Groups
Job losers	3.1	2.2	2.2	2.6	64.7	48.2	13.7	50.9
Job leavers	0.5	0.6	1.2	0.6	10.9	12.7	7.3	11.0
Reentrants	1.0	1.6	6.4	1.5	21.6	35.6	39.1	29.5
New entrants	0.1	0.2	6.5	0.4	2.9	3.5	39.8	8.6
Total for group	4.7	4.6	16.3	5.1	100.1	100.0	99.9	100.0

Source: Bureau of Labor Statistics, November 2004, Table A-31; ftp://ftp.bls.gov/pub/suppl/empsit.cpseea31.txt.

it would be fair to conclude that adult males experience mostly mismatch unemployment, while teenagers experience mostly turnover unemployment as they enter the labor force for the first time and reenter between periods in school.

The economics of job refusal. The basic reason for turnover unemployment is explained by the theory of "search" unemployment, which develops the idea that an unemployed person may sometimes do better to refuse a job offer than accept it! Why? Imagine a teenager who quits school and begins to look for her first job. She walks down the street and soon encounters a restaurant displaying a sign "Dishwasher Wanted." An inquiry provides the information that the dishwasher opening is available immediately and pays $7.00 per hour. Will the teenager accept the job without further search? Refusal may benefit the teenager if she is able to locate a job with higher pay, say $9.00 per hour, or better working conditions.

Job search theory treats unemployment as a socially valuable, productive activity. Unemployed individuals "invest" in job search. The cost of their investment is the cost of the search itself plus the loss of wages that could be earned by accepting a job immediately. The payoff to their investment is the prospect of earning a higher wage and/or better working conditions for many months or years into the future. Because people do not always want the first available job and prefer to search, the only ways for the government to bring down turnover unemployment are (1) to provide better employment agencies that provide information that shortens the period of job search; (2) to lessen job search by reducing the motivation for quitting, reentry, and initial entry; or (3) to change the economic incentives that unnecessarily prolong the search, particularly unemployment benefits and high taxes on the income of the employed, both of which cut the net earnings of taking a job immediately rather than remaining unemployed. The invention of Internet job-finding services have helped to reduce the cost of search and hence reduce the natural rate of unemployment.

Effects of unemployment compensation. Some economists blame the government for making turnover unemployment higher than necessary and advocate measures to reduce the duration in weeks of an average episode (spell) of unemployment, as well as reducing the number of episodes per worker.

The incentive for temporary layoffs given by the unemployment compensation system occurs not only in recessions but also when the economy is operating at its natural rate of unemployment. The economy may be in equilibrium, with no tendency for inflation to accelerate or decelerate, yet a firm may find that its sales have dropped temporarily. The unemployment compensation system provides an incentive for the firm to adjust by laying off workers rather than by cutting hours per employee or simply by allowing inventories to grow.

Self-Test

Would the following events raise or lower the amount of turnover unemployment?

1. A change in rules allowing the unemployed to earn unemployment benefits for one year instead of the present six months.
2. A reduction in the personal income tax rate.
3. A decrease in the fraction of the working-age population consisting of teenagers.
4. An increase in the price of telephone calls.

The Human Costs of Recessions

In assessing the costs of reducing inflation by creating a temporary recession, we need to consider not only the hundreds of billions of dollars of lost output, but also the human costs of recessions. The basic difference between the costs of unemployment and inflation is that the unemployment of a household head hits the family like a hammer, whereas the costs of inflation are milder and spread more broadly across the entire population.

The human costs of unemployment are tragic. Researchers have found that with every 1 percent increase in the U.S. unemployment rate, 920 more people commit suicide, 650 commit homicide, 500 die from heart and kidney disease and cirrhosis of the liver, 4,000 are admitted to state mental hospitals, and 3,300 are sent to state prisons. In total, a 1 percent increase in unemployment is associated statistically with 37,000 more deaths, including 20,000 heart attacks. Unemployed workers are also more likely to experience dizziness, rapid heart beat, troubled sleep, back and neck pain, and high blood pressure.[16]

Common among the psychological costs of unemployment is a sense of being condemned to uselessness in a world that worships the useful. Just as serious are the long-term consequences. Many people have been deprived of medical insurance as a consequence of unemployment, since such insurance is a job benefit typically paid in part or wholly by employers. Physical and mental health deteriorates, and this is exacerbated by alcoholism. The health of children also suffers, particularly when parents take out their frustration and rage on their children in the form of child abuse.

Just as recessions and high unemployment create social and health problems, so a sustained period of low unemployment can alleviate some of these same problems. The prosperity of the U.S. economy in the late 1990s and the reduction of the unemployment rate to the lowest levels in 30 years revealed numerous examples of what the late Arthur M. Okun called the "high pressure"

---

[16] Barry Bluestone and Bennett Harrison, *The Deindustrialization of America* (New York: Basic Books, 1982), Chapter 3.

economy.[17] Among the most notable beneficiaries of the high-pressure economy of the late 1990s were young black men with little education and few skills. In the low-unemployment economy of the late 1990s, many black men aged 16 to 24 with a high school education or less, and many saddled with prison records, were working in greater numbers, earning bigger paychecks, and committing fewer crimes than in the early 1990s. Thus beneficiaries of the prosperous economy were not only the young black men themselves, but also—because of the decline in the crime rate—those who might otherwise have become the victims of crimes that did not occur. In fact, studies showed that crime dropped most in those cities where unemployment was the lowest.[18]

Why Did the Natural Rate of Unemployment Decline in the 1990s?

Figure 9-2 on p. 303 showed that the natural unemployment rate declined from 6.3 percent in the mid-1980s to 5.0 after the year 2000. This decline contributed to the prosperity of the late 1990s, because a given actual unemployment rate created less inflationary pressure than would have occurred a decade earlier. In addition, the beneficial supply shocks discussed in Chapter 8 (see pp. 259–60) held down the inflation rate despite the fact that the actual unemployment rate dipped below the natural rate of unemployment during 1996–2001. Together, the decline in the natural rate and the beneficial supply shocks prevented the inflation rate from rising and thus allowed the Fed to keep interest rates at relatively low levels without any need for the sharp increases in interest rates that had occurred in the 1980s.

Several factors worked together to bring down the natural rate of unemployment in the 1990s. First, teenagers and young adults always have higher unemployment rates than older workers, because they spend time looking for work between periods in school. The fraction of teenagers in the total population fell in the 1980s and 1990s. This factor can explain perhaps one-third of the decline in the natural rate of unemployment since the late 1980s.[19] Second, by 2000 the population of inmates in prison, mostly young males, had quadrupled since 1985, and some of these inmates would have been unemployed if they were not in prison.

Third, the growth of temporary help agencies in the 1990s helped firms fill vacancies faster and helped workers find jobs faster, reducing both turnover and mismatch unemployment. Fourth, the invention of the World Wide Web made it easier for the labor market to match vacancies and job seekers. Taken together, these and other factors operating in labor markets help to explain why the natural rate of unemployment declined in the 1990s, allowing the economy to remain prosperous without rising inflation that would have forced the Fed to raise interest rates more than it did.

---

[17] Arthur M. Okun, "Upward Mobility in a High-Pressure Economy." *Brookings Papers on Economic Activity*, vol. 4 (1973, no. 1), pp. 207–52. See also Lawrence F. Katz and Alan B. Krueger, "The High-Pressure U.S. Labor Market of the 1990s," *Brookings Papers on Economic Activity*, vol. 30 (1999, no. 1), pp. 1–65.

[18] Sylvia Nasar with Kristen B. Mitchell, "Booming Job Market Draws Young Black Men into Fold," *New York Times*, May 23, 1999, p. 1.

[19] See Lawrence F. Katz and Alan B. Krueger, "The High-Pressure U. S. Labor Market of the 1990s," *Brookings Papers on Economic Activity*, 1999, no. 1, pp. 1–65.

9-10 Conclusion: Solutions to the Inflation and Unemployment Dilemma

Both inflation and unemployment are costly, but economists differ widely in their assessment of the relative costs. All agree that a steady inflation is less costly than a highly variable surprise inflation. And all agree that a hyperinflation is far more costly than a steady creeping inflation of, say, 3 percent per year. But there the agreement stops. Some economists consider it important to reduce the inflation rate to zero, whereas others consider the costs of a steady 3 percent inflation to be trivial.

As we have seen also in this chapter, the costs of turnover unemployment are quite low, and turnover unemployment usually lasts only a few weeks. But the costs of mismatch unemployment can be very large, leading to family breakdown, mental illness, loss of health insurance, and an erosion of job skills. For this reason many economists believe that the costs of mismatch unemployment swamp the costs of a steady creeping inflation of, say, 3 percent.

We have learned that four options are available to reduce the costs of inflation: (1) restrictive monetary and fiscal policies that reduce output and raise unemployment temporarily, (2) price and wage controls, (3) cost-reducing policies such as reducing the burden of financial regulation, and (4) issuance of an indexed bond like TIPS and reform of the tax system to make it inflation-neutral.

What are the corresponding options to reduce the unemployment rate? There is little need for policies to reduce turnover unemployment. Responsibility for the avoidance of cyclical unemployment lies mainly with the Fed. This leaves mismatch unemployment, which results from a mismatch of job openings and available unemployed workers by skill and location. Research suggests that migration of workers between states and regions quickly eliminates unusually high or low unemployment rates in particular states without the need for government intervention.

Thus the main focus for policymakers is reducing the natural rate of unemployment by reducing the mismatch of jobs and workers by skill. Numerous programs have been suggested to help reduce the job-worker skill mismatch. Among these are widely available student loans for college (to be repaid by subsequent earnings or community service), adult learn-to-read programs, better prenatal care, improved funding of such programs as Operation Headstart, and national standards and testing to raise the overall educational level of U.S. schools. The choice among such programs goes beyond macroeconomics, into such disciplines as labor economics, sociology, and political science.

Summary

1. In the long run the inflation rate equals the excess growth rate of nominal GDP, that is, the difference between nominal GDP growth and the long-run growth rate of real GDP.
2. Money growth equals the growth rate of nominal GDP minus the growth rate of velocity. Since velocity is not greatly affected by inflation, the long-run inflation rate equals the growth rate of the money supply minus the long-run growth rate of real GDP.
3. Governments allow excessive monetary growth for several reasons: (1) the temptation to boost demand before an election, (2) the output loss required to stop inflation, (3) adverse supply shocks require extra monetary growth if higher unemployment is to be avoided, and (4) inflation provides the government an added opportunity to finance expenditures without resorting to unpopular taxes.

4. The costs of unanticipated inflation are primarily felt by savers, while the benefits of such inflation primarily accrue to borrowers. Unanticipated deflation works in the opposite direction, benefiting savers while hurting borrowers.

5. The Fisher Effect is the one-for-one increase in the nominal interest rate in response to an increase in the expected rate of inflation, implying that the real rate of interest is unaffected by inflation.

6. In an ideal world, with inflation-neutral taxes and an operative Fisher Effect, fully anticipated inflation would affect only holders of money earning less than the market interest rate, particularly holders of currency. The struggle by such holders to reduce their holdings of money is the shoe-leather cost of inflation and becomes particularly important in a hyperinflation.

7. In practice the Fisher Effect has not been validated, so that the real interest rate tends to drop even when inflation accelerates over a sustained period. This implies that even an anticipated inflation redistributes income and wealth from savers to borrowers.

8. The government budget constraint states that government spending and interest payments on government bonds must be financed by some combination of conventional taxes, money finance (the inflation tax), and bond finance. In many countries, bond finance is not feasible, so that an upsurge of expenditures or a decline in conventional tax revenues implies increased reliance on money finance, implying a higher inflation rate.

9. A hyperinflation can begin with the unholy trinity of adverse supply shocks, monetary accommodation, and frequent wage indexation. A hyperinflation can also result from a shock that sharply boosts government spending or cuts conventional tax revenue.

10. Reforms to reduce the cost of inflation include decontrol of financial institutions (which had largely occurred in the United States by the mid-1980s), indexed bonds, and an indexed tax system.

11. The main reason for high unemployment in the United States is that the natural rate of unemployment is not zero but in the vicinity of 5.0 percent. Roughly half of the natural unemployment rate consists of turnover unemployment; the rest consists of mismatch unemployment.

12. Mismatch unemployment is caused by an imbalance between the high skill requirements of available jobs and the low skills possessed by many of the unemployed. In an economy with flexible relative wages, the unskilled would be able to find jobs more easily but would receive lower wage rates. Any real cure for the problems of the unskilled—whether high unemployment, or low wages, or both—requires an increase in their skills and better matching of their locations with the locations of available job openings.

13. Turnover unemployment is another component of the natural rate. The barrier that maintains turnover unemployment is the absence of perfect information, making necessary an investment in job search to locate job openings that offer higher wage rates or better working conditions.

14. Policy solutions to reduce turnover unemployment include an improved employment service to provide better information, as well as changes in the present system of unemployment compensation, which provides a subsidy to workers who turn down job offers and continue to search or to remain at home awaiting recall to their old jobs.

Concepts

hyperinflation
nominal interest rate
expected real interest rate
actual real interest rate
unanticipated inflation
Fisher equation

Fisher Effect
extra convenience services
indexed bond
government budget constraint
seignorage
inflation tax

wage indexation
incomes policy
credibility
cyclical unemployment
turnover unemployment
mismatch unemployment

Questions

1. What is the misery index? What major criticism or criticisms can you make of it?
2. Distinguish between a hyperinflation and a moderate (crawling) inflation.
3. Do you agree that, as measures of the inflation rate, simple percentage changes become increasingly misleading at high rates of inflation? Why or why not?
4. What does "excess nominal GDP growth relative to natural real GDP growth" mean? Under what conditions is it equal to the inflation rate?
5. What are the four main reasons for inflation? Explain how each results in an excessive growth rate of nominal GDP.
6. Explain the distinction among the following: the nominal interest rate, the expected real interest rate, and the actual real interest rate. Which of these interest rates is the most relevant to saving and investment decisions? Which of the rates has the greatest impact on determining the distribution of income?
7. What determines the winners and losers in an unanticipated inflation? Using your answer as a starting point, explain why the major redistributional effect of unanticipated inflation is to transfer real wealth from the rich to the middle class.
8. How is the nominal interest rate affected in each of the following cases?
    (a) The money supply growth rate slows.
    (b) Velocity rises.
    (c) The expected real interest rate falls.
    (d) Real GDP growth rises.
9. Distinguish between the Fisher equation and the Fisher Effect. Which one is true by definition, and which one provides a testable hypothesis? Use Figure 9-1 and the figure in the box on p. 294 to explain whether the data support or refute the hypothesis.
10. Explain why taxing real interest and real capital gains as opposed to nominal interest and nominal capital gains, but allowing the deduction of nominal interest rather than real interest, would still result in too little saving and too much borrowing and spending.
11. Explain term by term the government budget constraint of equation (9.8).
12. "In the steady state, the government benefits from inflation." Explain.
13. What are the two ways of financing a government deficit? Explain the conditions under which the financing of the deficit would be inflationary.
14. Explain the relationship between wage indexation and hyperinflation.
15. What should a government do to stop a hyperinflation?
16. Explain why people want to hold money up to the point where extra convenience services are equal to the nominal interest rate. How can this observation help us understand the net social loss to society of an inflation?
17. "Policymakers may reduce temporarily the natural rate of unemployment by pursuing an expansionary monetary policy." Do you agree with this statement? Explain your answer.
18. How can vacancies and unemployed workers coexist? If policymakers pursue an expansionary policy to increase real GDP, what will happen to the number of unemployed workers? What will happen to the number of vacancies as real output increases?
19. Explain how your answer to question 18 helps us understand why wages tend to rise faster as real output increases (that is, why the SP curve is upward sloping).
20. Explain why the length of unemployment episodes is one way of distinguishing between mismatch and turnover unemployment.
21. Explain the benefits of turnover unemployment. Compare and contrast the difficulty of reducing unemployment due to a mismatch of skills as opposed to a mismatch of location. Finally, discuss what impact being able to obtain information concerning employment opportunities over the Internet is likely to have on turnover unemployment, unemployment due to a mismatch of skills, and unemployment due to a mismatch of locations.
22. During the 1990s, the natural rate of unemployment fell and a higher productivity growth rate resulted in a faster rate of growth of natural real GDP. With no change in either the velocity of money or the growth rate of the money supply, what would indicate to the monetary authority that the natural rate of real GDP had declined and/or the growth rate of natural real GDP had increased?

Problems

1. Let P_0 be the initial price level (say, a price index such as the CPI). Let p be the inflation rate per period.
   (a) If P_t is the price at the end of period t, show that
   $$P_t = P_0(1 + p)^t$$
   (b) If $P_0 = 1.00$ and $p = 50$ percent per month, calculate P_{12}.
   (c) Given P_{12}, calculate the percentage change from P_0, that is, the annual rate of inflation when the monthly rate is 50 percent.

2. If inflation is a continuous process (that is, prices rising daily or even hourly, as in a hyperinflation), calculating inflation rates at discrete intervals (such as months, quarters, and years) may be misleading. We desire a continuous analogue to the equation in problem 1. In
   $$P_t = P_0 e^{pt}$$
   let e represent the base of natural logarithms, p the instantaneous rate of inflation, and the other variables remain as defined earlier.
   (a) Prove that p is the instantaneous rate of inflation in the preceding equation. *Note:* This requires the use of calculus. You're trying to prove the following:
   $$p = (1/P_t)(dP_t/dt).$$
   (b) The logarithmic price change is given by
   $$p = (\ln P_t - \ln P_0)/t.$$
   Derive this equation from the immediately preceding one.
   (c) If $P_0 = 1.00$, $P_{12} = 129.75$, and the time interval between these periods is twelve months, find p, using the log price change formula.
   (d) For (c), you should have gotten $p = 40.5$ percent per month. Now calculate the instantaneous rate of inflation *per year* equivalent to the instantaneous rate of inflation of 40.5 percent per month. *Hint:* Use the equation for log price change, but this time let $P_1 = 129.75$ and $t = 1$.

3. Suppose that the growth rate of the money supply is 5 percent per year, the velocity of money is constant, and that natural real GDP grows by 3 percent per year. Finally assume that in the long run, actual and natural real GDP grow at the same rate.
   (a) What is the rate of inflation in the long run?
   (b) Suppose that the growth rate of natural real GDP increases to 3.5 percent per year. Given no change in the growth rate of the money supply in the long run, what is the new rate of inflation in the long run?
   (c) Again, suppose that the growth rate of natural real GDP increases to 3.5 percent per year. If the monetary authority wishes to maintain the inflation rate in the long run at the same level as in part (a), what action do they need to take?
   (d) Given the increase in the growth rate of natural real GDP, what is an argument in favor of maintaining the growth rate of the money supply at 5 percent and what is an argument in favor of maintaining the inflation rate at a constant level?

4. Bill borrows $200,000 for three years from Larry and agrees to pay Larry 8 percent interest, compounded annually. The entire amount of the loan plus interest will be paid at the end of the third year. The price level at the time of the loan is 1.00.
   (a) What is the amount that Larry will receive at the end of the third year? If the price level is 1.00 at the end of the third year, what is the real value of the payment received by Larry?
   (b) Assume that the inflation rate in the economy is 3 percent per year for each of the three years. What is the price level at the end of the third year? What is the real value of the payment received by Larry?
   (c) Again, assume that the inflation rate in the economy is 3 percent per year for each of the three years. In this case, however, Larry had indexed the loan to protect himself from inflation. What would be the nominal interest rate for each year of the loan? What is the nominal amount of the payment received by Larry at the end of the third year? What is the real value of the payment?

5. Suppose that the nominal interest rate before taxes equals 8 percent, the rate of inflation equals 3 percent, and the tax rate equals 25 percent.
   (a) Suppose that nominal interest is taxed. What are the after-tax nominal and real interest rates?
   (b) Suppose that the inflation rate increases to 6 percent. What is the new nominal interest rate necessary to maintain the same after-tax real interest rate as in part a?
   (c) Suppose that the tax system is reformed so that real interest is taxed. What is the real interest rate before taxes that yields the same after-tax real interest rate as in part a?
   (d) Suppose that Fisher Effect holds. What are the nominal interest rates, given that real interest is taxed and the inflation rates equal 3 and 6 percent?

6. Suppose the relationship between H/P and p is given by
   $$H/P = 8 - 0.8p$$

Here, H/P is real high-powered money, in billions of dollars, and p is the rate of inflation, in percent. Define the inflation elasticity of real high-powered money, η, as

$$\eta = -\%\Delta(H/P)/\%\Delta p = -(p/[H/P])(\Delta[H/P]/\Delta p)$$

(a) If the current rate of inflation is 5 percent, what are H/P, pH/P, and η?
(b) If p falls to 4 percent, what are H/P, pH/P, and η?
(c) If p rises to 6 percent, what are H/P, pH/P, and η?
(d) On the basis of these calculations, can you formulate a relationship between pH/P and η?

7. Suppose that the amounts of real government spending, G, equals 700, real high-powered money, H/P, equals 1,500, and real government bonds, B/P, equals 2,000. The rate of inflation equals 5 percent and the nominal interest rate equals 7.5 percent.
(a) What is the amount of seignorage (inflation tax)?
(b) What is the real interest rate?
(c) What is the real interest on bonds?
(d) Using equation (9.11), what is the amount of taxes that keeps the real value of bonds and high-powered money fixed?
(e) Suppose that rate of inflation decreases to 4 percent. What is the new amount of seignorage?
(f) Suppose that the Fisher Effect holds. Given the lower inflation rate, what is the amount taxes must be raised or the amount government spending must be cut in order to keep the real value of bonds and high-powered money fixed?

8. Suppose that the natural rates of unemployment for adult males is 4.8 percent, 4.5 percent for adult females, and 13.4 percent for teenagers. Fifty-five percent of the labor force consists of adult males, 30 percent is made up of adult females, and the rest consists of teenagers.
(a) What is the natural rate of unemployment for the entire labor force?
(b) Suppose that portion of the labor force that consists of adult females rises from 30 to 40 percent, but the adult male and the teenage portions decrease to 50 and 10 percent, respectively. What is the new natural rate of unemployment for the entire labor force and why has it changed?
(c) Suppose that government policies, a reduction in discrimination, the development of the Internet employment services, as well as other factors reduce the natural unemployment rates for adult males, adult females, and teenagers to 4.3 percent, 4.0 percent, and 12.5 percent respectively. What is the new natural rate of unemployment for the entire labor force?

Self-Test Answers

p. 283 (1) The inflation rate in the first half of the decade is 4 percent per year. (2) For the last half it is 6 percent per year. (3) Nominal GDP growth is 8 percent in the first half and (4) also 8 percent in the last half.

p. 292 (1) Financial deregulation, which allowed the payment of interest on checking accounts, made the demand for money (that is, checking accounts plus currency) less responsive to an increase in the interest rate. Hence an increase in the nominal interest rate caused by higher inflation causes less shifting away from money than prior to deregulation, thus reducing the shoe-leather cost of fully anticipated inflation. (2) It raises the ratio of the money supply to nominal GDP. (3) It reduces velocity (PY/M^s).

p. 299 (1) If inflation occurs at 5 percent per year for a decade, then the price level grows at 5 percent per year. To keep H/P constant, H must grow at 5 percent per year. Seignorage, the pH/P term in equation (9.11), is equal to 5 percent ($p = 0.05$) times 1 percent of GDP ($H/P = 0.01$ times GDP), or 0.05 percent of GDP. Thus the government must run a basic deficit of 0.05 percent of GDP in order to end the decade with a fixed level of H/P. (2) The basic deficit must be 0.10 percent of GDP.

p. 309 (1) An extension of the time to earn unemployment benefits would reduce the cost of refusing a job and hence would extend the period of search and raise the turnover unemployment rate. (2) A reduction in the personal income tax rate would raise the cost of refusing a job, since it would increase the after-tax pay for any given pretax wage rate, and hence would reduce the period of search and the turnover unemployment rate. (3) Fewer teenagers would imply less turnover, since teenagers often engage in search unemployment when they look for after-school or summer employment, or work during years off from school (4) A higher price of phone calls would raise the cost of search and hence would reduce the amount of search and reduce the turnover unemployment rate.

PART FOUR

Macroeconomics in the Long Run: Growth and Public Finance

CHAPTER 10 The Theory of Economic Growth

CHAPTER 11 The Big Questions of Economic Growth

CHAPTER 12 The Government Budget, the Public Debt, and Social Security

CHAPTER 10

The Theory of Economic Growth

In essence the question of growth is nothing new but a new disguise for an age-old issue, one which has always intrigued and preoccupied economics: the present versus the future.
—James Tobin[1]

10-1 The Importance of Economic Growth

As we learned in Chapter 1, a fundamental task of macroeconomics is to determine the sources of economic growth. By economic growth we usually mean the growth rate of real GDP per person (or per capita). The achievement of rapid economic growth is one of the most (if not *the* most) important distinguishing features of a successful economy. The fact that the U.S. economy grew more rapidly than those of the industrialized nations of Europe during the century between 1850 and 1950 allowed Americans to enjoy a higher standard of living than most residents of Europe throughout the postwar era.

Welfare Gains from Growth

The profound importance of growth comes from the power of compound arithmetic. Even apparently small differences in growth rates make a huge difference in the standard of living over, say, a period of fifty years. Consider an average income of $40,000 in 2005. At a growth rate of 2 percent, that income would grow over fifty years to $108,700 in the year 2055. At a growth rate of 2.5 percent, that income would grow to $139,600 in 2055, a difference of $30,900, or more than three-quarters of the initial income level!

Thus the welfare gains resulting from even minor increases in the rate of economic growth are enormous. In the oft-quoted words of Nobel Prize–winning University of Chicago economist Robert E. Lucas, Jr., "the consequences for human welfare are simply staggering. Once one starts thinking about them, it is hard to think of anything else."[2] This is true because small differences in the rate of economic growth can make a huge difference in the welfare of the average citizen when compounded over 50 or 100 years.

The newly industrializing countries of Southeast Asia (Korea, Taiwan, Hong Kong, and Singapore) are widely admired for their success in achieving very rapid economic growth over the past forty years. Although Korea had about the same level of real income per capita as the Philippines in 1965, by

---

[1] "Economic Growth as an Objective of Government Policy," *American Economic Review*, vol. 54 (May 1964), p. 1.

[2] Robert E. Lucas, Jr., "On the Mechanics of Economic Development," *Journal of Monetary Economics*, vol. 22 (July 1988), p. 5.

2004 (thanks to its stunning achievement of rapid economic growth), Korea's real income per capita was *six times* that of the Philippines.[3] Other Asian economies, including China, Thailand, and Malaysia, also grew very rapidly and steadily improved the standard of living of their citizens.

The Great Questions of Economic Growth

By far the most important reason to study economic growth is the great and growing chasm between standards of living in the world's rich and poor countries. By "rich" we mean North America, much of Europe, Japan, some of the successful Asian countries, and Australasia. By "poor" we mean many of the rest. In between, there are middle-income countries like most former members of the Soviet Bloc, which are neither rich nor poor. As is illustrated by the contrast between Korea and the Phillipines, only a few decades of fast growth were necessary for Korea to leave the ranks of the poor and come close to joining the rich nations, while the Phillipines remains mired in poverty. What secrets did the Koreans discover? What kept the Phillipines from benefiting from the same methods? After we learn about the theory of growth in this chapter, we turn in the next chapter to the puzzle of rich versus poor.

A less cosmic question, but one of great interest to citizens of a single nation like the United States, is what explains the ebb and flow of economic growth? American growth in productivity, or output per hour, was much slower during 1972–95 than before 1972 or since 1995. The average American is roughly one-quarter poorer today because growth was so slow in 1972–95. What explains that dismal period of slow productivity growth? Why did productivity growth accelerate after 1995, and was that revival of more rapid growth a temporary event or is it likely to continue through the next decade? This topic, which is of great importance for the future American standard of living as well as for the country's ability to sustain the Social Security system and provide improved medical care, is also treated in the next chapter.

The Next Three Chapters

Economic growth has always been a central topic in macroeconomics. We now begin a three-chapter discussion of economic growth and other issues related to the long-run evolution of the economy. In this chapter we examine the simple theory of economic growth and its relation to growth in population and in the capital stock. To address puzzles that the simple theory cannot explain, we broaden the approach to include other types of investments that tend to favor growth, including education, research, and development.

Chapter 11 begins by taking a closer look at the success of rich nations and the failure of poor nations. Simple growth theory suggests that poor nations should grow more rapidly, yet some succeed while others fail. Why? We introduce the role of political and other noneconomic factors that may promote or retard growth, including crime, corruption, absence of property rights and a reliable legal system, and the geographical disadvantages suffered by some nations. We also examine the past century of U.S. economic growth and ask whether the unusually rapid productivity growth of the 1995–2004 period can be sustained in the future.

---

[3] See Figure 1–9 on p. 18.

A key source of growth is saving and investment; the total amount of investment is boosted when the government runs a budget surplus and is reduced when the government runs a budget deficit. Chapter 12 examines the long-run effects of the government budget. How big can a government deficit become before there is a danger that the public debt will explode, becoming an ever larger percentage of GDP? If the government runs a deficit instead of a surplus, does this threaten future economic growth? Does it drain funds from future Social Security benefits? What ideas have been suggested to reform Social Security, and what are their long-run advantages and disadvantages?

10-2 Standards of Living as the Consequence of Economic Growth

The Poor United Kingdom

In 1870, average real GDP per person in the United Kingdom was about 61 percent higher than in the United States. But by 2004 average real GDP per person in the United States was 49 percent higher than that in the United Kingdom. How was this possible? Faster **economic growth**, meaning a higher average annual growth rate of natural real GDP per person, allowed the United States to overtake the United Kingdom in 1916 and to move ahead by a growing distance between 1916 and 1950. Although the United Kingdom kept pace with the United States after 1950, the United Kingdom was never able to close the gap. This was a race between the tortoise and the hare, in which the tortoise never caught up.

In economics, **economic growth** is the study of the causes and consequences of sustained growth in natural real GDP per person.

The gap between the average real GDP per person in the two countries makes an enormous difference in their relative standards of living. The comparisons are made in a way that holds constant the prices of goods and services in the two countries.[4] Thus the average American can purchase all the goods and services bought by the average U.K. resident and still have 49 percent more left over for additional spending. And this difference is the result of a seemingly puny and insignificant difference in the U.S. economic growth rate between 1870 and 2002: 2.05 percent per year for the United States as compared to 1.40 percent for the United Kingdom. *Minor differences in economic growth rates sustained over a long period build up into substantial differences in relative living standards.*

Economic Growth: Something for Nothing?

It is easy to see why economic growth is such a fascinating topic. High rates of economic growth make it possible to have more of everything—higher health

---

[4] The "bible" for comparisons of living standards across nations, as in the table and figure in the International Perspective box in this section, is an immense body of data collected by economists at the University of Pennsylvania. See Robert Summers and Alan Heston, "The Penn World Table (Mark 5): An Expanded Set of International Comparisons, 1950–88," *Quarterly Journal of Economics* (May 1991), pp. 1–41. The latest version of the data is available at http://pwt.econ.upenn.edu/. As a simple example of what the Penn project involves, let us assume that if Japanese output is translated from yen to dollars at today's exchange rate, Japanese output per person is $60,000 while U.S. output is just $40,000. If every good in Japan costs twice as many dollars to buy as the same goods in the United States, then the true Japanese standard of living must be divided by 2 and becomes $30,000 ($60,000/2), or just 0.75 of the U.S. standard of living. The Penn project makes such comparisons of the cost of living for many different goods in more than 100 countries over a long period of time and can easily be accessed at the Web site listed above. Another excellent source of economic growth data is http://www.ggdc.net/index-dseries.html.

International Perspective

The Growth Experience of Seven Countries over the Last Century

The accompanying figure shows the level of per person GDP in seven leading industrial countries for selected years over the past 135 years. The figures are expressed in 2004 U.S. dollars and are based on a careful study that bases the prices actually paid by inhabitants of other countries on the average paid in all industrialized countries. The table summarizes some of the most important information contained in the figure, including the values, in 2004 U.S. prices, of per person GDP in both 1870 and 2005, as well as the growth rates of per person GDP during selected intervals. In the table, countries are listed in order of 2005 per person GDP. Several major conclusions can be drawn from an inspection of the figure and companion table:

1. All nations have enjoyed substantial growth in per person GDP: in the United States it increased by a factor of almost 16, from $2,564 in 1870 to $40,952 in 2005.
2. The figure is plotted on a logarithmic scale. This means that the slope of each line indicates the economic growth rate; a steep line means fast growth

spending and welfare benefits, with plenty left over for more private consumption of goods and services. In contrast, a society with a low rate of economic growth suffers continual strife as difficult choices must be made about the allocation of a slow-growing pie. In this unfortunate "zero-sum" society, more spending on health or education may mean higher taxes or a cut in Social Security benefits. No wonder that exploration of economic growth has moved to the forefront as a central topic of macroeconomics.

and a flat line indicates slow growth. For all countries except the United States, 1955–73 was the period of fastest growth, and all countries have experienced a growth slowdown since 1973.
3. Differing growth rates among countries have led to changes in relative positions. Japan had the most rapid growth, particularly between 1955 and 1973, when it reached the incredible rate of 8.1 percent per annum. Japan overtook Italy in 1970 and the United Kingdom in 1980.
4. The United Kingdom's loss of relative position has been continuous over the entire century. From 1870 to 1955, the United Kingdom had a growth rate at the bottom of the group. The United Kingdom was overtaken by the United States in 1916, by France and Germany in 1960, and by Japan in 1980.
5. The United States is something of a "has-been" in the growth race, owing its high living standard to its superior growth performance before 1950. In particular, the United States gained an advantage in its freedom from wartime destruction as compared to some European nations. While the other nations grew faster in 1955–73, since 1973 the United States has again widened the gap, growing faster than the other nations, except for Japan and Italy.

Types of Economic Change

The figure displays not only the process of economic growth that raises the standard of living decade after decade, but two types of shorter-term movements. The first of these is wartime destruction, which is clearly visible in the sharp drop in the living standards of Germany and Japan from 1940 to 1950. Making up for wartime destruction explains much of the rapid economic growth in these two countries in the 1950s and early 1960s.

The second type of short-term economic change is the business cycle. The data for each country are annual, so the alternation of business recessions and expansions is visible, most notably during the depression years of the 1930s. The figure also highlights the unique nature of the Great Depression in the United States and Canada, where per person real GDP declined much more than in the other countries, as discussed in the box on pp. 224–25.

Level and Growth Rate of per Capita Real GDP in 2004 Dollars for Seven Countries, 1870–2004

	Level in 2004 U.S. dollars		Average annual growth rate in percent				
	1870	2005	1870–2005	1870–1913	1913–1955	1955–1973	1973–2005
United States	2,564	40,952	2.05	2.01	2.15	2.14	1.93
Canada	2,326	30,693	1.91	2.01	1.47	2.94	1.78
Japan	1,058	30,469	2.49	1.48	1.31	8.07	2.23
Germany	2,009	29,947	2.01	1.62	1.65	3.88	1.53
France	2,515	28,684	1.80	1.46	1.28	4.35	1.51
United Kingdom	4,135	27,540	1.40	1.00	1.09	2.48	1.75
Italy	2,443	25,509	1.74	1.31	4.57	2.05	1.95

10-3 The Production Function and Economic Growth

The traditional theory of economic growth (often called the "neoclassical" theory) has filled many academic journals with highly mathematical articles. Yet the basic ideas are very simple. The theory divides output growth into two categories: (1) growth of **factor inputs**, such as labor and capital, and (2) growth in

The economic elements that directly produce real GDP are **factor inputs.**

output relative to growth in factor inputs. Thus the theory converts the question of how to achieve faster output growth into two subquestions: how to achieve faster growth in factor inputs, and how to achieve faster growth in output relative to inputs.

Throughout most of this book we have examined the causes and consequences of changes in the ratio of actual real GDP to natural real GDP, which we have called the output ratio (Y/Y^N). But now we are interested in changes in economic conditions over long periods during which the output ratio may be expected to be roughly constant. Thus our theory of economic growth refers to the growth of natural real GDP.

The Production Function

How much real GDP (Y) can be produced at any given time? This depends on the total available quantity of the two main factor inputs, capital (K) and labor (N), and also the behavior of output per average available factor input, which the neoclassical theory calls A (for the "autonomous" growth factor).[5]

The **production function** states the relationship between Y, A, K, and N:

$$Y = AF(K, N) \tag{10.1}$$

In words, real GDP (Y) equals an autonomous growth factor (A), expressed as an index, multiplied by a function of an index of capital input (K) and labor input (N). The appendix to this chapter provides background information on the general functional form used in equation (10.1) and a popular numerical example often used to illustrate the workings of the production function.

The **production function,** a relationship usually written algebraically, shows how much output can be produced by a given quantity of factor inputs.

Output per person and the capital-labor ratio. We need to isolate those factors that determine the increase in per person real GDP, which can be written as follows when the production function is divided through by the amount of labor input (N).[6]

$$\frac{Y}{N} = Af\left(\frac{K}{N}\right) \tag{10.2}$$

This important relationship states that there are just two sources of growth in the standard of living, or real GDP per person (Y/N). These are the autonomous growth factor (A), and the ratio of capital to labor input (K/N), or "capital per person." (In this chapter we simplify by treating "persons" and

---

[5] The use of the symbol A in this context and the decomposition of real GDP growth into growth in labor, capital, and the "residual" A date back to the seminal paper by Robert M. Solow, "Technical Change and the Aggregate Production Function," *Review of Economics and Statistics*, vol. 39 (August 1957), pp. 312–20. The symbol A stands for autonomous growth factor and should not be confused with A_p, the symbol for autonomous planned spending in Chapters 3–7.

[6] How can equation (10.2) be derived from equation (10.1)? There are two intermediate steps. First, we multiply and divide K by N in equation (10.1):
$$Y = AF(NK/N, N) \tag{10.1'}$$
If the function F displays constant returns to scale (see appendix to this chapter), then there is a unit elasticity of Y with respect to a given percentage increase in both N and K. This fact allows us to factor out the N term and rewrite equation (10.1') as follows:
$$Y = ANf(K/N, 1) \tag{10.1''}$$
Notice here that we have given a new name (f) to the function. Equation (10.2) in the text is obtained by dividing through both sides of (10.1") by N.

"employment" as synonyms, ignoring changes in the ratio of employment to the population.)

Equation (10.2) is the per person version of the production function. It is illustrated in Figure 10-1. This production function is drawn by assuming that the autonomous growth factor is fixed at A_0. Like the production functions presented in Chapter 7, which plotted output against labor input, this one exhibits diminishing returns. Thus each successive addition to the per person stock of capital (K/N) yields less and less of an increase in per person output (Y/N). In the diagram, point B represents one possible level of production, with capital input per person $(K/N)_0$ producing output per person $(Y/N)_0$.

Self-Test

1. Why is the production function a curved line instead of a straight line?
2. What happens to the ratio of output to capital (Y/K) as more capital per person is accumulated?
3. What happens to Y/K if the level of capital per person declines?

The production function in Figure 10-1 is just a start toward an adequate theory of economic growth. So far our analysis tells us simply that the main sources of growth in the standard of living are an autonomous factor (A) and growth in capital per person (K/N). But this does not explain why these two sources of growth differ among countries or among historical eras. We do not yet know why the autonomous growth factor in Figure 10-1 is A_0 rather than some other amount, nor do we know what determines the level of K/N.

Our study of what determines the autonomous growth factor is deferred until later. Here, we focus on the determinants of growth of capital per person

Figure 10-1 A Production Function Relating per Person Output to per Person Capital Input

The production function shows how much output per person can be produced by different amounts of capital per person. One possible position for the economy is point B, but other positions are possible as well. We cannot tell from this diagram how large the economy's per person capital stock will be. The slope of the production function is the marginal product of capital ($\Delta Y/\Delta K$), showing the extra amount produced by raising capital, when the amount of labor is held constant.

(K/N). We begin by reviewing the basic relationships between investment, the growth in capital, and saving.

Saving, Investment, and the Growth in Capital per Person

How is growth in K/N related to total national saving? This relationship is important, since it represents the link between the government's fiscal policy and the long-run growth of output per person. The concept of saving (S) that matters for economic growth is not the household saving of Chapter 3, but rather total national saving, *including the saving of households, corporations, and the government*. If we assume that net exports are zero, total *national* saving (S) equals private investment (I).[7]

$$S = I \qquad (10.3)$$

Our task is to determine how the growth in capital is related to investment, and hence to total national saving (S).

The basic link between investment and the growth in capital is simple. Spending on investment goods (I) either causes the capital stock to grow (ΔK) or it replaces old capital that wears out or becomes obsolete (dK):

$$I = \Delta K + dK \qquad (10.4)$$

Here we make the assumption that replacement investment can be represented by a fixed depreciation rate (d) times the capital stock (K). The depreciation rate indicates what fraction (say, 0.06) of the capital stock is replaced each year due to wear and tear or to obsolescence.

We want to know how saving and investment are related to the rate of change of the capital stock ($\Delta K / K$). To express equation (10.4) in terms of the growth rate of capital, we multiply and divide ΔK by K, as follows:

$$I = \frac{K \Delta K}{K} + dK = \left(\frac{\Delta K}{K} + d \right) K \qquad (10.5)$$

In words, this states that investment equals the growth rate of capital ($\Delta K/K$) plus the depreciation rate, both times the capital stock.

Saving and Investment in the Steady State

A **steady state** is a situation in which output and capital input grow at the same rate, implying a fixed ratio of output to capital input.

A **steady state** occurs when output (Y) and capital input (K) grow at the same rate, implying a fixed ratio of output to capital. A particularly simple case occurs when the autonomous growth factor (A in equation 10.2) is constant, so that the economy stands still at a point like B in Figure 10-1. This occurs when the growth of both Y and K are equal not only to each other but also to the growth in labor input (N), implying that the economy stands still at a fixed value of the vertical axis (Y/N) and of the horizontal axis (K/N).

---

[7] We can repeat here a version of the "magic equation," equation (5.5) on p. 139, which shows the relation of national saving ($S + T - G$) to private investment (I) and net exports (NX):

$$S + (T - G) = I + NX$$

When S is redefined to include both private saving and government saving, we have:

$$S = I + NX$$

This is the same as equation (10.3) in the text, where NX is set equal to zero.

As in previous chapters, we use lowercase letters to designate growth rates, including the growth rate of output ($y = \Delta Y/Y$), the growth rate of capital ($k = \Delta K/K$), and the growth rate of labor input ($n = \Delta N/N$). Thus the condition for a steady state, in which capital per person (K/N) is constant, can be written as

$$k = n \qquad (10.6)$$

In commonsense terms, equation (10.6) states the condition necessary for the economy to stand still at a point like B in Figure 10-1. Since we already have a relationship between investment and the growth of capital ($\Delta K/K$) in equation (10.5), we can represent the behavior of investment in a steady state by replacing the growth of capital in equation (10.5) by the growth of labor input (n):

$$I = (n + d)k \qquad (10.7)$$

Since saving equals investment from (10.3), we can set saving equal to the right-hand side of equation (10.7):

$$S = (n + d)K$$

This implies that

$$s\frac{Y}{K} = n + d \qquad (10.8)$$

To obtain equation (10.8), we redefine total national saving (S) as the ratio of national saving to output ($s = S/Y$) times output (Y), and then divide both sides of the equation by K. In words, the final line of equation (10.8) states that saving per unit of capital must equal the sum of the growth rate of labor input and the depreciation rate, which in turn is the amount of steady-state investment per unit of capital.

Self-Test

There are four components of equation (10.8): s, Y/K, n, and d.

1. Which of these components changes its value as we move to the left or right along the production function in Figure 10-1?
2. For those components that do not change, suggest at least one factor that determines the value of that component.

10-4 Solow's Theory of Economic Growth

Can an increase in the ratio of national saving to output (s) create a permanent increase in the growth rate of output? The answer is no. This was the most surprising result of the "neoclassical" theory of economic growth originally developed in the 1950s by MIT's Robert M. Solow,[8] a theory for which he was awarded the Nobel Prize in 1987. We have already developed the major building blocks of Solow's theory. These are the per person production function of equation (10.2) and Figure 10-1, and the relationship between saving and steady-state investment in equation (10.8).

---

[8] Robert M. Solow, "A Contribution to the Theory of Economic Growth," *Quarterly Journal of Economics*, vol. 70 (February 1956), pp. 65–94.

Solow's Insight

The algebra of equation (10.8) had been worked out in the 1940s by Sir Roy Harrod, an English economist, and Evsey Domar, who later taught at MIT. In their Harrod-Domar model of economic growth, all of the elements of equation (10.8) are constant. But then, why does the left side of equation (10.8) equal the right side? This equality seems an unlikely coincidence, since the elements of equation (10.8) depend on totally unrelated factors. The ratio of national saving to output (s) on the left-hand side of the equation is determined by the saving decisions of households, business firms, and the government, while the ratio of output to capital (Y/K) is determined by technological factors. And the growth rate of labor input (n) and depreciation rate (d) on the right-hand side of equation (10.8) are determined by totally different considerations—birth rates, death rates, immigration, and the rate at which old capital wears out or becomes obsolete. In Solow's words, describing a simple version of equation (10.8) in which d is omitted:

> Discomfort arose because ... all three of the key ingredients—the saving rate, the rate of growth of the labor force, and the capital-output ratio—were given constants, facts of nature. The saving rate was a fact about preferences; the growth rate of labor supply was a demographic-sociological fact; the capital-output ratio was a technological fact.... The possibility of steady growth would be a miraculous stroke of luck. Most economies, most of the time, would have no equilibrium growth path. The history of capitalist economies should be an alternation of long periods of worsening unemployment and long periods of worsening labor shortage.[9]

In Solow's words again, "I began tinkering with the theory of economic growth, trying to improve on the Harrod-Domar model ... I thought first about replacing the constant capital-output (and labor-output) ratio by a richer and more realistic representation of the technology."

What Solow did, in short, was to marry the per person production function of equation (10.2) to the saving-investment relation in equation (10.8). To do this, we simply multiply both sides of equation (10.8) by K and divide both sides by N:

$$s\frac{Y}{N} = (n + d)\frac{K}{N} \tag{10.9}$$

On the left-hand side, we have total national saving per person, which is the national saving rate (s) times output per person (Y/N), and this, in turn, is given by the per person production function of equation (10.2). On the right-hand side of equation (10.9), we have the amount of steady-state investment per person, that is, the amount of investment needed to equip each new population member with the same capital per person as the existing population, and to replace worn-out or obsolete capital.

The Solow Model in Pictures

The two sides of equation (10.9) can be plotted separately, as in Figure 10-2. In the left frame, the upper red line is a copy of the per person production function from Figure 10-1, plotting the output-labor ratio (Y/N) as a function of the capital-labor ratio (K/N). When we multiply this line by the fixed saving rate (s), we obtain the blue line, national saving per person (sY/N). The

---

Robert M. Solow (1924–)

Solow, 1987 Nobel Prize winner, invented both the modern theory of economic growth and the standard method for empirically distinguishing the roles of capital and technological change in the growth process.

---

[9] Robert M. Solow, "Growth Theory and After," *American Economic Review*, vol. 78 (June 1988), p. 307.

Figure 10-2 Output, Saving, and Steady-State Investment per Person

The upper curved red line in the left frame copies the per person production function from Figure 10-1. Multiplying it by the saving rate (s) produces the lower curved blue line showing per person saving. Consumption per person is the distance between the two lines. The right frame shows steady-state investment per person, the amount needed to replace old capital and equip new workers for each capital-labor ratio (K/N).

distance between the two lines indicates consumption per person. The right-hand frame plots steady-state investment per person, which rises steadily to the right, since a larger K/N raises the amount of investment needed to equip new population members and replace worn-out and obsolete capital.

Now in Figure 10-3 we put together the two parts of Figure 10-2, omitting for clarity the per person production function. The steady state occurs at point E_0, where the capital-labor ratio is $(K/N)_0$. Why is this a steady state? At any point to the left of E_0, say point C, saving and investment are higher than the investment required to maintain (K/N) at a fixed level. This extra investment makes (K/N) grow, moving the economy rightward from point C to the steady-state equilibrium E_0. Similarly, starting at point D, saving and investment are below the required amount, meaning that not enough is being invested to equip new members of the population and replace worn-out and obsolete capital. Hence starting from point D, the economy moves leftward back down the red line to the steady-state equilibrium at point E_0.

Effects of a Higher Saving Rate

To understand the startling implication of the Solow growth model that a change in the ratio of national saving to output does not create a permanent change in the growth rate of output, let us see how an increase in the saving rate affects the economy. In Figure 10-4 we begin by copying the steady-state investment line (which remains unchanged in the examples of Figures 10-2, 10-3, and 10-4, but could change as in the self-test on p. 330) and the "old saving line" directly from Figure 10-3. The economy's initial position is at point E_0, just as it was in that figure.

Figure 10-3 Equilibrium of Saving and Investment in the Solow Growth Model

This figure superimposes the two frames of Figure 10-2. The saving line crosses the steady-state investment line at point E_0. At any point to the left, like C, saving and actual investment exceed steady-state investment (the amount needed to keep K/N constant), and accordingly K/N grows until the economy reaches point E_0. At any point to the right, like D, saving and actual investment are less than steady-state investment and K/N shrinks back to E_0. Only at E_0 is per person saving just the right amount to equip new members of the population with $(K/N)_0$ and replace worn-out and obsolete capital.

There Is Pressure for K/N to Move Toward the Steady-State Equilibrium

Now in Figure 10-4 we introduce a sudden increase in the saving rate from s_0 to s_1, which shifts the blue saving line up. The distance between point F along the new blue saving line and point E_0 along the old blue saving line represents *additional saving available to fuel growth in per person capital*. The economy moves to the right up the new saving line, since there is extra saving available to equip new members of the population with a higher capital-labor ratio, and as well to provide for the added depreciation of old capital at that higher ratio. Eventually the economy arrives at point E_1 along the new saving line. But once at E_1, the capital-labor ratio is fixed at the new higher ratio, per person saving and output are fixed, and the growth in output is once again equal to the growth rate of labor input (at E_1 as at E_0, $y = k = n$).

Thus the saving rate matters, but not as people had believed prior to the development of Solow's model. An increase in the saving rate raises the standard of living, since the higher capital-labor ratio at E_1 produces a higher output-labor ratio. To achieve this higher standard of living, the growth rate of output is *temporarily* raised above the growth rate of N. But the higher saving rate does not create a permanently higher growth rate of output, which depends only on population growth. In the steady state Y/N is fixed, so that Y and N must grow at the same rate. Intuitively, the extra saving finances only a higher *level* of the capital stock per person (K/N), not continuing *growth* in the capital stock per person. The extra saving is "eaten up" by the extra replacement investment implied by the higher capital stock, and the extra net investment required to equip each worker with the higher level of capital stock per person.

Self-Test

Explain the effect of a reduction in the rate of population growth (n) on the following:

1. The growth rate of output.
2. The capital-output (K/Y) ratio.
3. The capital-labor (K/N) ratio.

Figure 10-4 The Effect of a Higher Saving Rate on Capital and Income per Person

The lower "old saving line" is copied from Figure 10-3. A higher saving rate implies the higher "new saving line." The economy's position immediately jumps from E_0 to F. Now saving and actual investment are above steady-state investment, and so K/N grows until the economy reaches point E_1.

One aspect of this theory may seem puzzling. We learned in Chapter 3 that an increase in the saving rate (s) depresses the economy by reducing consumption spending. How can we be so sure here that an increase in the saving rate will stimulate the growth of per person capital? The answer is that *the Solow model is intended for long-run analysis* (decades, not months or years) *and assumes continuous full employment and flexible prices*. Thus, when the saving rate rises in this model, consumption and the price level both decline. The interest rate falls by enough to stimulate sufficient investment to guarantee that saving and investment will remain equal along the economy's path between E_0 and E_1.

10-5 Technology in Theory and Practice

At first glance, the Solow growth model seems to contain a major flaw. As presented thus far, the model implies that the permanent growth rate of output should be the same as the growth rate of the population, and that the standard of living (Y/N) should be fixed. How, then, does the theory explain the sharp increase in the standard of living shown in the box on pp. 322–23 that has occurred over the last century in each of the major industrialized nations?

Two Types of Technological Change

Solow used two methods to make the model consistent with history. Both methods introduce an added element into the story: growth in technology in all its forms, including better schooling, improved organization, better health care, and all the fruits of innovation and research. The two methods for introducing technological change into the Solow growth model are to assume (1) that technology makes each worker more efficient, and (2) that technology shifts the production function relating per person output to per person capital.

Labor-augmenting technological change. This approach leaves our previous discussion of the Solow growth model, including the diagrams, completely intact. We simply need to adopt a broad definition of growth in "labor input." Instead of just counting the number of bodies at work, we count effective labor input, taking into account improved education and the storehouse of technology that makes today's workers more efficient than workers a century ago. We now interpret N as effective labor input, and n as the growth rate of effective labor input. In the steady state, output can grow at 3 percent ($y = 3$) if effective labor input grows at 3 percent ($n = 3$), leaving the ratio of output to effective labor input (Y/N) fixed. Now K/N remains fixed if the capital stock grows at 3 percent. Effective labor input growth of 3 percent exceeds population growth of, say, 1 percent, allowing the standard of living (Y per person) to grow at 2 percent.[10]

Neutral technological change. One problem with the first approach is that it assumes that technology only makes workers more efficient, with no impact on capital input. A more realistic assumption is that technology makes *both* labor and capital input more efficient. This "neutral" type of technological change simply means that the autonomous growth factor (A) in equations (10.1) and (10.2) grows over time. Here we copy equation (10.2) and renumber it for convenience:

$$\frac{Y}{N} = Af\left(\frac{K}{N}\right) \qquad (10.10)$$

If education, innovations, and research raise the value of A every year, then per person GDP can increase steadily. The growth rate of per person GDP ($y - n$) is

General Form Numerical Example
$$y - n = a + b(k - n) \qquad y - n = a + 0.25(k - n) \qquad (10.11)$$

Here a is the growth rate of the autonomous growth factor, and b is the elasticity of output with respect to capital input, assumed to be 0.25 in the numerical example. An economy might, for instance, have values of $a = 1.5$ and $k - n = 2$, which would be consistent with a steady state in which

$$y - n = a + b(k - n) = 1.5 + 0.25(2) = 2.0$$

In this example, there is a steady state, because per person output and per person capital are growing at the same rate, allowing Y/K to remain fixed. After introducing neutral technological change into the diagrams of the Solow growth model, the production function shifts upward steadily, thus shifting the saving line up and to the right along a fixed steady-state investment line. Y/N and K/N rise in the steady state, but at the same rate.

---

[10] Labor-augmenting technical change can be introduced into our original production function from equation (10.1) by defining effective labor input as a technological factor (A) times the population:

$$Y = F(K, AN)$$

When A enters in this form, it is sometimes called "Harrod-neutral" technical change.

Self-Test

Calculate the percentage growth rate of real GDP per person ($y - n$) from the numerical example of equation (10.10), assuming that b always equals 0.25, for the following combinations of the rates a, k, and n:

a	k	n	y − n
0	0	4	____
0	4	4	____
4	0	0	____
4	4	4	____

The "Solow Residual"

Soon after Solow developed his theory of growth, he applied the theory to the measurement of the autonomous growth factor (a) in equation (10.10). His idea was to turn equation (10.10) around so that a could be calculated from the other components:

$$a = (y - n) - b(k - n) \qquad (10.12)$$

Since data were available on the growth rates of output (y) and of both capital and labor input (k and n), the only trick in determining the value of a was to identify the elasticity b. Here Solow's idea was to apply the theory of profit maximization in a competitive firm. Solow pointed out that such firms would also set the return on capital equal to the marginal product of capital, which implies that the elasticity b can be measured by the share of capital income in total GDP.[11]

Solow's finding was controversial. Fully seven-eighths of the growth in output per hour of work ($y - n$) over the period he studied (1909–57) was attributed to "technical change in the broadest sense," including education, research, innovations, and other improvements, while only the remaining one-eighth was attributed to growth in the capital stock per hour of work ($k - n$). But this is not a very satisfactory outcome. Knowing that some mysterious a factor was important in the growth process does not tell us, for instance, what caused a to grow more slowly during 1973–95 or more rapidly after 1995.

Some skeptics believe that a should not be given a name like "technological change," which implies we know precisely what determines a. They suggest that we call a instead the **residual** or, more frankly, "the measure of our ignorance." Government agencies like the U.S. Bureau of Labor Statistics, which now routinely calculate a, describe a as the growth in **multifactor productivity**, or **total factor productivity**. In recent years macroeconomists have come to describe a as **Solow's residual**.

The simplified version of Solow's growth model summarized in the previous section (Figures 10-2, 10-3, and 10-4) illustrated one key implication of his model, that a change in the saving rate would cause only a temporary, rather than a permanent, increase in the growth rate of output per unit of labor input. That simplified version could not explain steady growth of output—a defect that we have remedied in this section by introducing technological change. And we have seen that Solow's own empirical research identified technological change (broadly defined) as a much more important source of economic growth than

> The **residual** is the amount that remains after subtracting from the rate of real GDP growth all of the identifiable sources of economic growth.
>
> The growth in **multifactor productivity,** or **total factor productivity,** is the growth rate of output per hour of work, minus the contribution to output of the growth in the quantity of other factors of production per hour of work, notably capital but sometimes including energy, raw materials, or other factors of production.
>
> **Solow's residual** is the same as growth in multifactor productivity.

---

[11] Let r be the rate of return to capital. Then competitive firms will set r equal to the marginal product of capital (MPK). The share of capital in GDP is rK/Y, which competitive firms will set equal to $(MPK)(K/Y)$, which is equal to the elasticity of output with respect to capital, $(dY/dK)(K/Y) = (dY/Y)(dK/K)$.

increases in capital input per unit of labor input. In the past decade, however, the Solow growth model has received substantial criticism. In the next section we identify several puzzles that his model cannot explain, and in the following section, we learn about recent developments in growth theory.

10-6 Puzzles That Solow's Theory Cannot Explain

In recent years economists have become increasingly dissatisfied with Solow's neoclassical theory of economic growth, for two primary reasons. First, the theory makes economic growth depend primarily on "Solow's residual," which remains unexplained. Thus we are left with very little understanding of why the world's standard of living stagnated until the industrial revolution that occurred around the year 1800, why it grew rapidly from then until the early 1970s, and why in some countries like the United States the standard of living grew slowly in the 1970s and 1980s but then accelerated after 1995. Second, we are left with little understanding of differences among nations—why some are rich and some remain poor, and why some grow rapidly while others stagnate.

The critics of neoclassical growth theory go beyond claiming that the theory provides an inadequate explanation of growth. They point to widely observed phenomena in the world that *conflict* with the predictions of the theory. In this section we review these conflicts.

Conflict 1: Income per Capita Varies Too Much Across Countries

Real income per capita in a rich country like the United States is more than ten times as high as in a poor country like India or Bangladesh. Yet this fact conflicts with the neoclassical theory. Why? The theory states that there are only two reasons for differences in per capita income. One reason could be a difference in saving rates, since, as shown in Figure 10-4, an increase in the saving rate raises income per capita (Y/N). Another could be a difference in the slope of the steady-state investment line $(n + d)$. However, even very large differences in the saving rate or rate of population growth cause only small variations in per capita income, not the large variations observed in the world. To take one example, quadrupling the saving rate and reducing the rate of population growth by two-thirds would boost per capita income only from 1.0 to 1.7, whereas in the real world we observe countries differing in per capita income by magnitudes on the order of 1.0 to 10.0.[12]

---

[12] To see this, let us combine equation (10.9) with the Cobb-Douglas production function (explained in the appendix to this chapter):

$$s\left(\frac{Y}{N}\right) = (n + d)\left(\frac{K}{N}\right) \qquad \text{(i)}$$

$$\left(\frac{Y}{N}\right) = \left(\frac{K}{N}\right)^b \qquad \text{(ii)}$$

By solving equation (ii) for (K/N), substituting into equation (i), and simplifying, we obtain:

$$\left(\frac{Y}{N}\right) = \left(\frac{s}{n+d}\right)^{\frac{b}{1-b}} \qquad \text{(iii)}$$

Using as examples $s = 0.1$, $n = 0.03$, $d = 0.07$, and $b/(1 - b) = 1/4$, we can calculate that $Y/N = 1^{1/3} = 1$. Quadrupling the saving rate to 0.4 would raise Y/N from 1 to $4^{1/3} = 1.59$. Reducing the rate of population growth from 0.03 to 0.01 (assuming the saving rate remains at 0.4) would raise Y/N further from 1.59 to $(0.4/0.08)^{1/3} = 1.7$.

A flaw in the neoclassical theory is to assume that all countries have the same production function (equation 10.2). Poor countries are assumed to operate at the same level of technology and knowledge as rich countries. To see that the production function is at fault, consider a specific version of equation (10.2) called the Cobb-Douglas production function (see the appendix to this chapter).

General Form   Numerical Example

$$Y/N = (K/N)^b \qquad Y/N = (K/N)^{0.25} \qquad (10.13)$$

Here we set the autonomous growth factor (A) equal to unity to simplify the exposition.

To see what difference in K/N would be needed to explain a ten-fold difference in per capita income, we can solve for K/N:

General Form   Numerical Example

$$K/N = (Y/N)^{1/b} \qquad K/N = (Y/N)^{1/0.25} \qquad (10.14)$$

Let us take the value of Y/N for the poor nation to be 1 and the value of Y/N for the rich nation to be 10. Substituting 10 for the rich nation's Y/N in the numerical example, we see that the rich nation's K/N must be equal to $(Y/N)^{1/0.25}$ or 10^4, which is 10,000. Yet there is no evidence of such huge differences among nations in K/N. In fact, a regular feature of real-world economies is a roughly constant ratio of K/Y, not ratios of K/Y that are hugely greater in rich countries than poor countries (by 10,000/10 or 1,000 times greater in the example).

Conflict 2: Poor Countries Do Not Have a Higher Rate of Return on Capital

The neoclassical theory describes the difference in per capita income between poor countries and rich countries simply as a result of differing levels of per capita capital, which in turn result from differences in the three parameters that appear in equation (10.9)—the saving rate (s), population growth rate (n), and depreciation rate (d). As shown in Figure 10-5 a poor country is at a position like point P, with a low capital-labor ratio $(K/N)_P$, while a rich country is at a position like point R, with a high capital-labor ratio $(K/N)_R$.

But this leads to an unrealistic implication. The slope of the per person production function in Figure 10-5 is the marginal product of capital ($\Delta Y/\Delta K$), and this is much higher on the left side of the diagram for the poor country than on the right side of the diagram for the rich country. A simple numerical example shows that the marginal product of capital should be as much as 4,000 times higher in a poor country as in a rich country when per capita income is ten times as high.[13] The implied high marginal product of capital in the poor country implies that the rate of return on capital in poor countries should be much higher than in rich countries, *and that there should be massive flows of capital from rich countries to poor countries to earn this higher rate of return.* Yet we do not observe high rates of return on capital, or massive capital inflows, in many of

---

[13] With the Cobb-Douglas production function, the marginal product of capital (*MPK*) is

General Form   Numerical Example

$$MPK = b(K/N)^{b-1} \qquad MPK = 0.25(K/N)^{-0.75}$$
$$\quad = b(Y/N)^{(b-1)/b} \qquad MPK = 0.25(Y/N)^{-3.0}$$

Thus, if Y/N is ten times greater in a rich country, the marginal product of capital in the numerical example would be 0.25 times 10^{-3} or 1/4,000 times smaller.

Figure 10-5 A Production Function Relating per Person Output to per Person Capital Input

Why the Marginal Return to Capital Should Be Higher in Poor Countries

The per person production function is the same as in Figures 10-1 and 10-2. The poor country has a capital-labor ratio of $(K/N)_P$ and produces at point P. The rich country has a capital-labor ratio of $(K/N)_R$ and produces at point R. The marginal product of capital is given by the slope of the production function, $\Delta Y/\Delta K$. Because of the curvature of the per person production function, this slope is clearly larger for the poor country than for the rich country. The text discusses reasons why this diagram makes the erroneous prediction that the marginal return to capital is higher in poor countries than in rich countries.

the poorest countries of the world. Some less-developed countries enjoy substantial inflows, but others do not.

How can we explain why the rate of return on capital in very poor countries is not substantially higher than in rich countries? The poor countries may not be operating on the same production function as the rich countries, unlike the single production function drawn in Figure 10-5.

Conflict 3: Convergence Has Not Been Uniform

The neoclassical model predicts that poor nations should "converge" to the income levels of the rich. That is, nations that are initially poor should have faster growth rates than nations that are initially rich. This occurs for three reasons. First, nations that are below their steady-state growth paths (for instance, at point F in Figure 10-4) will grow faster until they reach the steady state (at point E_1 in Figure 10-4). Second, as noted, the neoclassical model predicts that the rate of return is much higher in poor countries, causing capital to flow from rich to poor countries and thus boosting the capital stocks of poor countries. Third, whatever the barriers that prevent poor countries from fully utilizing the production technology, the passage of time should allow poor countries to learn how to use the productive techniques of the rich countries.

Economists have devoted much attention in recent years to the issue of convergence, and the subject is controversial.[14] There has been convergence among

---

[14] A pioneering study of cross-country differences in growth rates is Robert J. Barro, "Economic Growth in a Cross Section of Countries," *Quarterly Journal of Economics*, vol. 106 (May 1991), pp. 407–33. Another influential study is N. Gregory Mankiw, David Romer, and David N. Weil, "A Contribution to the Empirics of Economic Growth," *Quarterly Journal of Economics*, vol. 107 (May 1992), pp. 407–37. A less technical introduction is contained in Robert J. Barro, *Determinants of Economic Growth: A Cross-Country Empirical Study* (Cambridge, Mass.: MIT Press, 1997), Chapter 1.

the major industrialized countries; for example, Japan has caught up substantially to the per capita income levels of Europe and the United States, as shown in the box on pp. 222–23. There has also been convergence among the income levels of states within the United States and among regions within Western Europe. However, in the world at large convergence has not been uniform. Many nations of Africa and some of the poorer nations of Asia have fallen further behind the advanced countries over the past fifty years, and the relative income levels of major Latin American nations have fallen relative to Western Europe and the United States. We need to go beyond neoclassical growth theory to understand the persistent differences between rich and poor nations.

10-7 Human Capital, Immigration, and the Solow Puzzles

If the neoclassical model cannot explain differences in per capita income by observed differences in capital per person, then what explanation remains? One of the most promising is to recognize that most of the income that labor receives in the rich countries is not a reward to "pure" labor (that is, just the fact that someone is alive) but rather to the education that people have acquired. Education makes a tremendous difference in the incomes that people receive. Management consultants with an MBA degree are typically paid double the salary earned by those with no more than an undergraduate degree, who in turn receive double or more the typical earnings of high school graduates, who in turn earn substantially more than high-school drop-outs.

What Is Human Capital?

Economists use the term **human capital** to refer to the value over one's lifetime of the extra earnings made possible by education. A 20-year-old planning to work for 45 years might be able to make $6 million in the future with an MBA degree, but someone of that age might be limited to a lifetime income of only $600,000 if he or she drops out of school with only an elementary-school education, thus limiting the available job options to menial jobs like digging ditches and washing dishes. The difference between $6 million and $600,000, or $5.4 million, is said to be the "human capital" that the MBA degree-holder has accumulated. Another person who stops his or her education with an undergraduate degree might be expected to make $3 million in the future and to acquire $2.4 million in human capital (the difference versus the alternative of a mere elementary-school education). For society as a whole, the value of human capital is the sum of the human capital of each inhabitant.

The name "human capital" was given to the value of education in order to reflect the parallels between investing in education and investing in physical capital, that is, structures and equipment like computers and forklifts. Investment in physical capital requires that money be spent in order to earn a future return, in the form of the extra profits that can be made after the structure is built or the equipment is purchased. Similarly, investment in human capital requires an expenditure of money on education and the sacrifice of income that could otherwise be earned by working instead of going to school. This expenditure is made in order to earn a higher income in the future, and the rate of return on the cost of education can be stated on a percentage basis in just the same way as the rate of return on the cost for a firm of buying a new computer.

Human capital is the value, for a person or for society as a whole, of the extra future earnings made possible by education.

How Does Human Capital Raise Total Output?

An economy like the United States that contains many educated people can produce more output and a higher standard of living than an economy like many in Africa where most inhabitants have had little education. Thus human capital (H) becomes a factor of production, just like physical capital (K), and the production function, instead of using equation (10.1), can be written as:

$$Y = A F(K, H, N) \tag{10.15}$$

In words, this states that real GDP (Y) equals an autonomous growth factor (A), expressed as an index, multiplied by a function of an index of physical capital (K), human capital (H), and labor (N). Now labor is interpreted as the productive capability of the population *if* everyone had dropped out of school after elementary school (sometimes called "brute force" labor, capable only of digging ditches), while all the extra earnings of the population above that educational level are included in human capital input (H).

Human Capital and the Solow Puzzles

The inclusion of human capital goes a long way toward repairing the inability of the Solow neoclassical model to explain differences between the rich and poor countries. Let us write the per person production function in the Cobb-Douglas form of equation (10.13), making only a single change, namely, to add human capital per person (H/N) as an extra determinant of output per person (Y/N):

General Form	Numerical Example
$Y/N = (K/N)^b (H/N)^c$	$Y/N = (K/N)^{0.25}(H/N)^{0.65}$

This states that output per person equals physical capital per person (K/N) raised to the power b, which is 0.25 as before, and human capital raised to the power c, which is assumed to be 0.65. Instead of labor making a contribution to output of $(1 - b)$ or 0.75, the contribution of uneducated labor (N) is now $1 - b - c$, or only 0.10 (which equals 1.0 minus 0.25 minus 0.65).

As we saw in the preceding discussion of equations (10.13) and (10.14), the basic reason that the Solow neoclassical model cannot explain observed differences between rich and poor nations is that the exponent on capital ($b = 0.25$) is so small. If capital is so unimportant, then why should poor countries lag so far behind rich countries? But now we have introduced human capital as an additional difference between rich and poor countries, and the sum of the exponents on the two types of capital ($b + c$) is now 0.9, not 0.25. If we replace 1/0.25 in equation (10.14) by 1/0.9, we find that a rich nation having 10 times the per person income (Y/N) as a poor nation needs to have only $10^{1/0.9}$ or about 12.6 times as much combined physical and human capital as the poor nation. This is much more plausible than the implication of equation (10.14) in the model without human capital that the rich nation needed to have 10,000 times as much physical capital as the poor nation.[15] In the same way, if the exponent on total capital is 0.9 rather than 0.25, it is no longer necessary for the rate of return on investment in capital (both physical

---

[15] This insight is one of the contributions of the article by Mankiw, Romer, and Weil cited in the previous footnote.

The Immigration Puzzle

Thus the addition of human capital to the Solow neoclassical growth theory goes a long way toward explaining the conflicts introduced in the previous section. Rich countries differ from poor countries not just because they have many more structures and lots more equipment, but because their inhabitants are much better educated than those in poor countries. Yet the human capital explanation runs into a problem when we consider the immigration of an unskilled person from a poor country to a rich country. To be specific, let us consider a poorly educated Guatemalan who crosses the Rio Grande and soon finds a job in the United States paying, say, $10 per hour in contrast to the $1 per hour that he made in Guatemala. Yet the first day on the job, there has been no change in the former Guatemalan's human capital. What is it about the process of production in a rich country that allows a recent immigrant to have a much higher marginal product and earn a much higher wage than was previously possible in Guatemala?

Let us say that the Guatemalan's new job is with a landscaping service that mows the lawns of well-to-do Americans. The task of mowing the lawn (using physical capital consisting of a gas-powered lawn mower) takes virtually no education. What enables the Guatemalan to earn $10 per hour is that there are Americans who themselves are rich enough to be able to afford to pay to have their lawn mowed instead of mowing it themselves. Thus the immigration puzzle comes down to this: *every factor* that makes the United States a richer country than Guatemala contributes to the ability of the new immigrant to earn much more. As we will see in the next chapter, there are many factors not included in a production function like equation (10.15) that help to explain the immigration puzzle—differences between rich and poor countries include additional factors beyond physical and human capital, among them cultural attitudes toward work, climate and geography, how well the legal system protects property rights, the presence or absence of crime and corruption, and infrastructure in the form of highways, airports, and a well-functioning electricity supply and telephone system.

10-8 Endogenous Growth Theory: How Is Technological Change Produced?

Ever since the development of Solow's neoclassical growth model in the 1950s, economists have been uneasy about several of its implications. We have now reviewed several implications of the model that conflict with important facts about the real world. As we have seen, a primary problem is that technical

---

[16] Go back to footnote 13 on p. 335 and substitute $b = 0.9$ in place of $b = 0.25$. The bottom line of the numerical example becomes:

$$MPK = 0.9(Y/N)^{-0.1/0.9}$$

If Y/N in the rich country is 10 times higher, then the marginal product of capital in the rich country should be 0.9/1.29 or about 0.7 times that in the poor country, not 1/4,000 as in the example of footnote 13 based on $b = 0.25$.

change (*a*, the autonomous growth factor) is *exogenous*, dropping from the sky totally unexplained. Thus a nation desiring to boost its growth rate of output gains no insight into how to achieve *A*.

Since the late 1980s there has been an explosion of activity in what is now called "endogenous growth theory," so named because it attempts to explain technical change as the outcome of market activity in response to economic incentives rather than just assuming that technical change drops exogenously from the sky. The chief inventors of endogenous growth theory are Paul Romer of Stanford University and his Ph.D. thesis adviser at the University of Chicago, Robert E. Lucas, Jr. (also the inventor of the new classical macroeconomics and pictured in Chapter 17). Much of the writing on endogenous growth theory is highly technical; here we summarize some of the main ideas at a nontechnical level.[17] As the early ideas of Romer and Lucas continue to be subjected to critical reviews and reconsidered, the theory is still evolving.

The Production of Ideas

Endogenous growth theory begins from the awkward fact that, as we have seen, the standard of living in many advanced countries is as much as ten times higher than that in many less-developed countries. But if technical change is freely available to all nations, then *all* of this huge superiority in standards of living must be attributable to a capital-labor ratio that is higher by a factor of 10,000. This would imply very little capital in less-developed countries and a huge rate of return to additional investment, since this would be guaranteed to bring these countries up toward the level of advanced nations. As a consequence, we should observe massive flows of capital from advanced countries to poor countries, but in fact we do not.

As we have seen, one solution to this puzzle is to introduce human capital as a key source of difference between rich and poor nations. But consideration of immigration leads to basic problems for the human capital approach, as it does for the concept of "effective labor" in the neoclassical model. Both of these models imply that immigrants to a rich country from a poor country with, say, 1/10 the output per person and 1/10 the human capital per person, upon arrival in the rich country should earn only 1/10 as much as native citizens. But many immigrants to the United States and other rich countries soon achieve the same high average standard of living as native residents.

Endogenous growth theorists thus have been led to focus on what are the characteristics of a rich society that not only make its native residents rich but also seem automatically to equip immigrants from poor countries with much higher incomes than they earned before. They have built models in which the key to growth is the development of ideas for new goods. To solve the incentive problem of how these ideas get produced, the models rely on monopoly power that is reinforced by patents and copyrights. International trade also plays an important role, since each country can concentrate on developing the

---

[17] Frequently cited academic papers include Paul M. Romer, "Increasing Returns and Long-Run Growth," *Journal of Political Economy*, vol. 94 (1986), pp. 1002–37; the same author's "Endogenous Technological Change," *Journal of Political Economy*, vol. 98 (1990), pp. S71–103; and Robert E. Lucas, Jr., "On the Mechanics of Economic Development," *Journal of Monetary Economics*, vol. 22 (1988), pp. 3–42. The summary in this section is partly based on Paul M. Romer, "Increasing Returns and New Developments in the Theory of Growth," in W. A. Barnett, et al., eds., *Equilibrium Theory and Applications* (Cambridge University Press, 1991), pp. 83–100.

ideas to produce a few new goods and then trade them with other countries, so that consumers can enjoy all of the new goods produced anywhere in the world. For instance, American households enjoying DVD rental movies are benefiting from early research that took place in Europe and the United States, together with product development in Japan and Korea that made the DVD player inexpensive to buy and relatively repair-free.

When the concept of ideas is applied broadly, it helps explain not only the introduction of new goods but also the development of better production techniques and higher quality in older goods like automobiles and household appliances. Rich countries use ideas and techniques that produce more and better goods per person. Furthermore, most of these ideas won't work without associated investment in physical capital and human capital. Even if a poor country like Bangladesh obtained piles of instruction manuals for making automobiles and personal computers, these manuals would be useless without educated people, factories, and equipment. This approach simultaneously explains why poor people clamor to migrate to rich countries, and also why poor nations are so eager for foreign investment by companies from rich countries, companies that can bring with them the required equipment and educated engineers and managers.

Empirical Studies and Policy Implications

As endogenous growth theory has developed, so has research on a wide variety of rich and poor countries, looking for correlations between growth rates and other variables. The conclusion is that faster growth is associated with a higher rate of investment by either the private or government sector, a lower share in GDP of government consumption spending, higher school enrollment rates, greater political stability, and lower fertility (that is, fewer children per female of childbearing age). And if the influence of all these factors is taken into account, a poor country tends to grow more rapidly than a rich country.

Unfortunately, all these factors are not the same in rich and poor countries. Poor countries have lower rates of investment, lower school enrollment rates, higher fertility rates, and less political stability. The implication of this research is that government policies can affect growth rates by taxing consumption, subsidizing investment and research, and shifting resources from government consumption to government investment.

Overall, endogenous growth theory has taken economists a long way from the original Solow model, with its pessimistic implications that a higher national saving rate alters economic growth only temporarily, and that technological change is exogenous, falling from the sky with no potential for policy effects.[18] However, endogenous growth theory is incomplete, because still omitted are numerous additional factors that contribute to growth and help to explain the growing gap between the rich and poor countries. We return to these additional factors, some of them noneconomic, in the next chapter.

---

[18] Readable overviews of endogenous growth theory are provided in a symposium in the Winter 1994 issue of the *Journal of Economic Perspectives*. See especially Paul Romer, "The Origins of Endogenous Growth," pp. 3–32, and Robert M. Solow, "Perspectives on Growth Theory," pp. 45–54.

10-9 Conclusion: Are There Secrets of Growth?

The theory of economic growth has come a long way since the original Solow growth model, which tended to minimize the role of capital accumulation and maximize the role of an unexplained rate of technological change. An important development in the new growth theory has been to broaden the definition of capital, so that it includes research and development and human capital (that is, education). In the next chapter we will broaden the concept of capital further to include government-financed infrastructure (for example, highways and airports), and more generally, the "capital" needed to protect liberty and property rights.

Despite these developments, however, much remains unexplained. Those studying the success of some fast-growing nations and the failure of other nations find it difficult to tie a record of success to particular economic theories. Columbia economist Joseph Stiglitz argues that it is necessary to go far beyond traditional economic theories and into political science to understand what happened in the successful countries of East Asia and elsewhere:

> No single policy ensured success, nor did the absence of any single ingredient ensure failure. There was a nexus of policies, varying from country to country, sharing the common themes that we have emphasized: governments intervened actively in the market, but used, complemented, regulated, and indeed created markets, rather than supplanted them. Governments created an environment in which markets could thrive. Governments promoted exports, education, and technology; encouraged cooperation between government and industry and between firms and their workers; and at the same time encouraged competition. The real miracle of East Asia may be political more than economic: Why did governments undertake these policies? Why did politicians or bureaucrats not subvert them for their own self interest? . . . The recognition of institutional and individual fallibility gave rise to a flexibility and responsiveness that, in the end, must lie at the root of sustained success.[19]

The verdict of Stiglitz in the preceding quote is humbling for economists, because it implies that the successful countries had a particular talent for "just doing the right thing," and the definition of the right thing varied across countries.

We take a more systematic look in the next chapter at the key sources of economic growth.

---

[19] Joseph E. Stiglitz, "Some Lessons from the East Asian Miracle," *World Bank Research Observer*, vol. 11, no. 2 (August 1996), pp. 151–77.

Summary

1. Divergences between the economic growth rates of individual nations, sustained over long periods of time, can create substantial differences in living standards. Although Britain had the highest level of real GDP per capita in 1870 among the major industrialized nations, by 1996 Britain was at the bottom as a consequence of its slow rate of economic growth in the twentieth century.
2. The production function explains real GDP as depending on the quantity of factor inputs (capital and labor) and on an autonomous growth factor that reflects the influence of research, innovation, and other factors. An increase in the growth rate of real GDP per person requires either an increase in the growth rate of capital per person or an increase in the growth rate of the autonomous growth factor.
3. National saving is the sum of government saving (which equals the government surplus or deficit) plus private saving. National saving equals private investment, which is equivalent to the change in the capital stock plus the investment expenditures required to replace capital goods that wear out or become obsolete.
4. An equilibrium called the "steady state" occurs when output, capital, and labor input are all growing at the same rate. If per person saving exceeds steady-state investment per person, the capital-labor ratio will grow until the per person steady-state investment is high enough to halt the growth in the capital-labor ratio. At this point, the economy reaches a new steady state with a constant capital-labor ratio.
5. In the Solow model of economic growth, the economy's growth rate of output in the long run depends only on its rate of population growth or, more broadly, on the growth rate of "effective" labor input (which takes account of improvements in education, skills, and technology). An increase in the saving rate does not change the economy's steady-state growth rate of output.
6. There are three facts that conflict with the predictions of the Solow growth theory. First, income per capita varies too much across countries. Second, poor countries do not have a higher rate of return on capital as the theory predicts. Third, poor countries have not uniformly converged to the income level of rich countries, as the theory predicts.
7. These facts that conflict with the Solow theory are partially eliminated when human capital, that is, the value of education, is introduced as an additional source of differences in output per capita between rich and poor countries. Yet human capital raises an additional question as to why immigrants to rich countries are able to earn so much more than in poor countries when their educational attainment is not altered by the act of immigration.
8. Endogenous growth theory emphasizes the interactions between the production of ideas, investment in physical capital, and investment in human capital (education) to explain why poor countries cannot instantly boost their standard of living up to the level of rich countries. It takes many years of investment in physical and human capital for the ideas developed in the rich countries to benefit the poor countries.
9. Solow's growth model states that an increase in the national saving rate cannot permanently boost the growth rate of output, but there are two reasons to believe that this theoretical result is misleading. First, the strong relationship between saving rates and growth rates in different countries over long periods of time suggests that saving and growth are related in a way not explained by the Solow growth model. Second, endogenous growth theory suggests several ways in which a higher rate of saving and investment might generate faster growth in ideas, human capital, and physical capital.

Concepts

economic growth
factor inputs
production function
steady state
residual
multifactor productivity/total factor productivity
Solow's residual
human capital

Questions

1. In terms of the great questions of economic growth discussed at the beginning of this chapter, why do the presented theories of economic growth concentrate on the growth of output per person as opposed to total output?
2. If the production function is characterized by constant returns to scale, what happens to real GDP (Y), capital per person (K/N), the ratio of output to capital (Y/K), and output per person (Y/N) when labor and capital inputs both double? What happens when labor and capital inputs double and the autonomous growth factor (A) also doubles?
3. What is the "steady state" in the Solow growth model? How is it reached from some other initial situation in which the conditions required for the steady state are not satisfied?
4. Explain what an increase in the depreciation rate, d, means. Using a graph like Figure 10-3, explain the effect of an increase in the depreciation rate on the steady-state capital-labor ratio and steady-state income per person. Again using a graph like Figure 10-3, explain how the savings rate must change in order for a rise in the depreciation rate to have no effect on the steady-state capital-labor ratio and steady-state income per person. Finally, discuss why your explanations make intuitive sense.
5. Assuming the autonomous growth factor (A) remains unchanged, explain why the gains in output per worker associated with an increase in the capital-labor ratio inevitably fall following increases in the level of investment.
6. What is the most important implication of the Solow growth model? Does it imply that an increase in the rate of private saving is useless as a means to increase the standard of living in the long run?
7. Explain why, in spite of the suggested steady-state outcome of Solow's model, the national saving rate is treated in this chapter as playing such an important role in determining the rate of economic growth.
8. Many people advocate policies to raise the U.S. national saving rate (s). According to the Solow growth model, should a low saving rate be a matter of national concern? What policies might be implemented to raise it?
9. Explain the difference between labor-augmenting technological change and neutral technological change. Explain into which category of technological change each of the following examples falls:
   (a) Development of a new microprocessor that allows for faster computers that enable architects to design buildings in less time.
   (b) A new operating system that enables programmers to use their existing computers to write and test programs in less time.
10. The record of economic growth in the leading industrialized countries over the past century hardly represents the steady state described and predicted by the Solow model. Explain what the "Solow residual" is and how it is used to account for the long-term improvement in output per person in these countries over the past century. Explain what problem the "Solow residual" presents for economic growth theory.
11. Explain the difference between productivity as defined on p. 4 in Chapter 1 and multifactor productivity as defined in this chapter. Explain why productivity as defined in Chapter 1 must increase if multifactor productivity rises and why productivity can increase without an increase in multifactor productivity.
12. The three big problems with the Solow model can be labeled *exogeneity*, *incentives*, and *nonconvergence*. Carefully explain each italicized term.
13. What is endogenous growth theory? What weaknesses of the Solow growth model led to its development?
14. Distinguish between *human capital* and *physical capital*. Why are both important to a country's economic growth?
15. "According to endogenous growth theory, government policy has little effect on a nation's economic growth rate." Is this statement true, false, or uncertain? Explain your answer.

Problems

1. (a) Using the data presented in the International Perspective box (pp. 322–23), compute the per capita real GDP of Germany, Japan, Canada, France, the United Kingdom, and Italy relative to the United States in 1870 and 2005.
   (b) For the country whose per capita real GDP rose relative to the United States between 1870 and 2005, discuss when the increase occurred.
   (c) For each of the countries whose per capita real GDP fell relative to the United States between 1870 and 2005, discuss when the gap between standards of living, as measured by per capita real GDP, narrowed and when it widened.
2. You are given the following information concerning the relationship between the capital-labor ratio and output per person in eight situations:

Capital-labor ratio							
A	B	C	D	E	F	G	H
0	10,000	20,000	22,000	23,512	25,000	30,000	30,260

Output per person							
A	B	C	D	E	F	G	H
0	19,102	23,518	24,200	24,688	25,416	26,560	26,629

(a) Suppose that the savings rate, s, equals 0.1; the population growth rate, n, equals 0.01; and the depreciation rate, d, equals 0.1. Calculate the amounts of savings per person and steady-state investment per person at each of the capital-labor ratios given in the table above. Calculate the values of the steady-state capital-labor ratio and steady-state output per person.

(b) Suppose that the population growth rate, n, decreases to 0.005, but there are no change in the savings and depreciation rates. Calculate the new amount of steady-state investment per person at each of the capital-labor ratios given in the table above. Calculate the new steady-state values of the capital-labor ratio and output per person.

(c) Suppose that the savings rate, s, increases to 0.125, but the population growth and depreciation rates are the same as in part (a). Compute the new amount of savings per person at each of the capital-labor ratios given in the table above. Then explain the new steady-state values of the capital-labor ratio and output per person.

3. Assuming that the United States' output is characterized by a Cobb-Douglas production function with constant returns to scale and that the elasticity of output with respect to the capital input equals 0.25, consider the following five cases, where n equals the growth rate of labor, k equals the growth rate of capital, and a equals the growth rate of the autonomous growth factor.

Case I: $n = 1\%$ $k = 3\%$ $a = 2.5\%$
Case II: $n = 2\%$ $k = 3\%$ $a = 0.75\%$
Case III: $n = 1\%$ $k = 4\%$ $a = 2.4\%$
Case IV: $n = 3\%$ $k = 3\%$ $a = 0\%$
Case V: $n = 0\%$ $k = 0\%$ $a = 3\%$

(a) In each case, what is the rate of growth of output?
(b) In each case, what is the rate of growth of per person output?
(c) Assuming that the autonomous growth factor is a "neutral" type of technological change, which case or cases are consistent with steady state growth?

4. Using equation (10.10), derive a formula for the steady-state growth rate of income per person and the capital-labor ratio in terms of the autonomous growth factor, a, and elasticity of output with respect to the capital input, b. (*Hint*: let c equal the steady-state growth rate of income per person and the capital-labor ratio and solve equation (10.10) for c in terms of a and b.) Use this formula to discuss how the steady-state growth rate of income per person and the capital-labor ratio change due to an increase in (i), the autonomous growth factor, and (ii), the elasticity of output with respect to the capital input.

5. Suppose that the elasticity of output with respect to the capital input, b, equals 0.3. If a country's income has been growing at 3.1 percent per year over the past 25 years, while the labor input has been growing at 1.5 percent per year and the capital input has been growing at 2.5 percent per year, what part of the total growth is accounted for by autonomous growth factors? Suppose that over the next 25 years, the growth of income increases to 4.1 percent per year, while the growth rates of labor and capital decrease and increase, respectively, by 0.5 percent per year. What is the annual rate of increase in the autonomous growth factor over the next 25 years?

6. Consider an economy characterized by the following production function: $Y = AK^{1/3}N^{2/3}$, with a capital stock of $3,000 billion and current net investment of $120 billion.
(a) If the growth rate of autonomous factors is zero and the growth rate of labor is 1 percent, what is the current growth rate of per person output? Is this a steady-state situation?
(b) If the government wanted to increase the growth rate of per person output by an extra percentage point through tax and subsidy policies that affected capital growth alone, by what percentage would it have to raise investment?
(c) In the unlikely event that the government successfully stimulated the required investment, at what rate of growth in output would the economy arrive in the steady state according to the implications of the Solow growth model? Does the text accept this assumption? Why or why not?

7. You are given the production function, $Y = AK^{1/3}N^{2/3}$, where $A = 4$.
(a) Convert the production function to a function relating Y/N to K/N.
(b) Consider two countries that have access to the same technology and have the same quality of labor and capital, as well as the same production function, given above. Suppose that one country has per-person output 10 times as high as the second country. To what factor is the difference attributable? Quantify the difference between the countries with respect to that factor.

8. You are given the production function $Y = AK^{1/4}H^{1/4}N^{1/2}$, where $A = 4$. The population growth rate n is 0.025, the depreciation rate d is 0.075 (both physical and human capital depreciate at the same

rate), and the growth rate of autonomous factors is zero. Investment I is the sum of two components, investment in physical capital I_K and investment in human capital I_H. The fraction of GDP that goes to physical capital investment is $s_K = 0.05$ and the fraction of GDP that goes to human capital investment is $s_H = 0.05$.

(a) Convert the production function to a function relating Y/N to both K/N and H/N.

(b) Consider two countries that have access to the same technology and have the same quality of labor and capital, as well as the same production function, given above. Suppose that one country has per-person output 10 times as high and a physical capital-labor 100 times as the second country. To what other factor is the difference attributable? Quantify the difference between the countries with respect to that factor.

(c) Find the steady-state physical capital-labor ratio and the steady-state human capital-labor ratio.

(d) Find the steady-state per person output.

9. Suppose that the production function for an economy is given by $Y = AK^b H^c N^{1-b-c}$. The marginal product of physical capital, MPK, is given by the formula $bAK^{b-1}H^c N^{1-b-c}$ and the marginal product of physical capital, MPH, is given by the formula $cAK^b H^{c-1} N^{1-b-c}$. It is assumed that each unit of each factor is paid its marginal product. Find the shares of both physical and human capital in GDP (in each case the total payment to the factor divided by output).

Self-Test Answers

p. 325 (1) Y/K declines as K/N increases. This result follows from diminishing returns to capital per person in the per person production function (equation 10.2). Because additions to output per person decrease in size with constant increases to capital per person, output per person grows more slowly than capital per person, and the ratio of output to capital declines. This can be seen by drawing a straight line from the origin (lower-left corner) of Figure 10-1 to point B. The slope of this line is the Y/K ratio. As K/N increases, we move to the right along the production function, and the slopes of lines from the origin to points on the production function decrease. (2) Y/K declines as K/N increases. (3) Y/K rises as K/N declines.

p. 327 (1) Only Y/K varies as we move along the production function in Figure 10-1, which plots Y/N against K/N. The other parameters s, n, and d, are all held constant and are not introduced into the graphical analysis until Figure 10-2. (2) The saving-income ratio (s) is related to the interest rate and wealth; the population growth rate (n) depends on fertility decisions, health, and immigration; the depreciation rate (d) depends on the longevity of capital.

p. 330 (1) A decline in the growth rate of population (n) causes the growth rate of output (y) to decline by exactly the same amount, after which the economy reaches a new steady state. But the lower rate of population growth raises the standard of living (Y/N). Be sure that you can explain why: Start from point E_0 in Figure 10-3, assume that the old saving line remains valid, and rotate the steady-state investment line downward to the right, as required by the decline in the growth rate of population (n). (2) As the steady state investment line shifts downward, K rises relative to Y, and (3) K rises relative to N.

p. 333 The following are the growth rates of real GDP per person ($y - n$) corresponding to the four blanks: -1.0, 0.0, 4.0, 4.0.

Appendix to Chapter 10

General Functional Forms and the Production Function

Until this point, we have used only "specific linear" forms for the behavioral equations. For instance, the demand for money in the Appendix to Chapter 4 on p. 126 was written as:

$$\left(\frac{M}{P}\right)^d = hY - fr$$

This equation can be stated in words as: The real demand for money $(M/P)^d$ is equal to a positive number (h), times real GDP (Y), minus another number (f), times the interest rate (r). The equation tells specifically how the real demand for money depends on real GDP and the interest rate.

The production function can also be written in a specific form called the Cobb-Douglas production function.[1]

General Linear Form	Numerical Example
$Y = AK^b N^{1-b}$	$Y = AK^{0.25} N^{0.75}$

In words, this states that real GDP (Y) is equal to an autonomous growth factor (A), multiplied by a geometric weighted average of an index of capital (K) and of labor (N). The weights, b and $1-b$, represent the elasticity (or percentage response) of real GDP to an increase in either factor.[2] For instance, in our numerical example if all variables are indexes initially at 1.0, a 4 percent increase in labor input will cause a 3 percent increase in real GDP. Initially:

$$1.0 = 1.0(1.0^{0.25} 1.0^{0.75})$$

After a 4 percent increase in labor input:

$$1.03 = 1.0(1.0^{0.25}\, 1.04^{0.75})$$

Thus the elasticity of real GDP with respect to a change in labor input is $0.75 (= 3/4)$.

Several other characteristics of the production function are evident. First, an equal percentage increase in both factors, capital and labor, raises real GDP by the same percentage. This characteristic, called *constant returns to scale*, occurs because the sum of the weights (b and $1-b$) is unity. When both factor inputs increase by 4 percent, we have

$$1.04 = 1.0(1.04^{0.25}\, 1.04^{0.75})$$

after a 4 percent increase in both K and N.

A second characteristic is the direct one-for-one response of real GDP to the autonomous growth factor A. If A increases by 4 percentage points, while capital and labor input remain fixed at 1.0, real GDP increases by the same four percentage points

$$1.04 = 1.04(1.0^{0.25}\, 1.0^{0.75})$$

after a 4 percent increase in A.

---

[1] The function is named after an Amherst mathematics professor, Charles W. Cobb, and a University of Chicago economics professor (later U.S. senator), Paul H. Douglas, and is described in a book by the latter, *The Theory of Wages* (New York: Macmillan, 1934), especially Chapter V.

[2] *Elasticity* is a term introduced in most elementary economics courses and refers to the percentage change in one variable in response to a 1 percent change in another variable.

348 Chapter 10 • The Theory of Economic Growth

The Cobb-Douglas production function is only one of many ways in which real GDP might be related to A, K, and N. Often in economics we want to make the simple statement that "Y is related to A, K, and N," but without restricting the particular form of the relationship. To accomplish this, we sometimes use a *general functional form*. An example of such a general form for the production function is:

$$Y = F(A, K, N)$$

In words, this states simply that real GDP (Y) depends on an autonomous growth factor (A), an index of capital input (K) and an index of labor input (N). The capital letter F and the parentheses mean *depends on*, and any alphabetical letter can be used.

Why is it interesting to know simply that one variable depends on others? By writing an alternative equation, one could state the *alternative hypothesis* that there is no role for an autonomous growth factor:

$$Y = F(K, N)$$

This states that real GDP depends *only on* capital and labor input.

Sometimes it is desirable to make a specific assumption about the form in which one variable enters, but not the others. This occurs in equation (10.1) on p. 324 in the text, which states that the elasticity of real GDP with respect to the autonomous growth factor is unity, but does not restrict the form of the relationship between real GDP and the other inputs, capital and labor:

$$Y = A F(K, N)$$

Without further information one cannot look at these general functional forms and learn whether the assumed relationship is positive or negative. The positive relationship between real GDP and both capital and labor inputs can be written in either of two ways:

$$\text{Method 1: } Y = A F(K, N)$$
$$(+)(+)$$

$$\text{Method 2: } Y = A F(K, N); \quad F_K > 0, F_N > 0.$$

The terms to the right of the semicolon in method 2 can be put into these words: The response of real GDP to a change in capital input (F_K) and in labor input (F_N) is positive (>0).

Exercise: Consider a general functional form for the demand for money:

$$\left(\frac{M}{P}\right)^d = L(Y, r)$$

State in words what this function states about the relationship between the real demand for money $(M/P)^d$ and real GDP (Y) and the interest rate (r). Use both methods 1 and 2 to write down the facts that the real demand for money depends positively on real GDP and negatively on the interest rate.

CHAPTER 11
The Big Questions of Economic Growth

Few problems are more fascinating, more important, or more neglected than the rates at which development proceeds in successive generations in different countries.
—Wesley Mitchell, 1927

11-1 Answering the Big Questions

More than half of the world's population lives on less than $2,800 per year, one-tenth of the $28,000 average level of per-person consumption in the United States. This startling level of inequality of the average income level across countries is much greater than the degree of inequality within a single country like the United States. Many theoretical models, like the Solow neoclassical growth model examined in the last chapter, predict that poor countries would steadily *converge* to the income levels of the rich countries. But this has not happened; the ratio of income per person in the richest countries to that of the poor countries has barely changed in the past 40 years.

Why Are We So Rich and They So Poor?

There is no more important question in economics than understanding the success of some countries in becoming relatively rich and the failure of other countries that have remained so poor. As expressed by Harvard economist David Landes, "Why Are We So Rich and They So Poor?"[1] Some countries, like the United States, Britain, and France, have remained at or near the frontier of income per person throughout the past half-century. Some other countries, like Asia's "Four Tigers" (Korea, Taiwan, Hong Kong, and Singapore), have achieved very rapid growth and within only one generation have transformed themselves from a group of poor nations to a group of rich nations, achieving the convergence predicted by the Solow growth model. But a third group of countries, including India, Bangladesh, and numerous countries in Africa and Latin America, have failed to converge. In many cases, their income per-person was below 10 percent of the U.S. level in 1960 and remains there today.

The Solow growth model of Chapter 10 provides a partial answer to the first basic question about economic growth. Countries with a higher level of income per person have a higher level of capital per person, which they achieve by saving and investing. The weakness of the Solow model is that it predicts differences between rich and poor nations in both capital per person and the rate of return on capital that are several orders of magnitude greater than is true in

---

[1] David S. Landes, "Why Are We So Rich and They So Poor?" *American Economic Review Papers and Proceedings* (May 1990), pp. 1–13.

the data. This weakness is partially remedied, as we have seen on pp. 337–39, by including human capital as well as physical capital in the analysis and by assuming that much of the income earned by labor is actually a reward to human capital rather than pure physical exertion. Yet even then we are left with questions, starting with the need to explain why an immigrant from a poor country to a rich country is able to achieve such a big jump in income without any immediate change in his human capital (i.e., educational attainment).

A bigger question is why some countries are so much more productive than others in using the capital that they have. In this chapter we broaden our investigation of the sources of economic growth in several directions. We will see that people will not start businesses or invest in those businesses if they cannot earn a decent return on their investment. Economic growth requires a political environment that creates incentives for investment, requiring a legal system that protects property rights and protection of ordinary citizens against corruption, bribery, theft, and confiscation of the returns on their investments. Even in a crime-free environment, political decisions can influence the incentives to invest and the productivity of those investments, including regulations on the trading of securities, on the protection of ideas through patent rights, and on the costs and difficulty of hiring and firing workers. Growth also requires investment in **infrastructure**, including some types of capital that benefit society as a whole and are often provided by government investment, including highways, airports, telephone systems, and electricity supply.

Infrastructure consists of types of capital that benefit society as a whole, including highways, airports, trains, waterways, ports, telephone networks, and electricity grids.

What Creates a Growth Miracle?

We have divided nations into the rich, the poor that have remained poor, and an intermediate group of countries, including Asia's Four Tigers, that have sprinted ahead from the ranks of the poor to the ranks of the rich. The experience of such countries that have sustained growth rates of 5 percent or more for several decades—often called a "growth miracle"—is illustrated by the comparison of Korea versus the Philippines on pp. 17–19. Such sustained rates of growth create unbelievable changes in the standard of living of ordinary citizens; for instance, a 5 percent growth rate sustained for four decades is sufficient to boost per-capita real income by a factor of 7.4, from $2,500 to $18,500.

The Solow theory suggests that all nations should eventually converge to the level of the world's technological leader, which for most of the past century has been the United States. The achievements of the fast-growing miracle economies could simply be dismissed as an automatic process if it were not for the fact that their achievements are so unusual; in fact, many other countries that started out poor 40 years ago are still just as poor, with income levels less than one-tenth of the United States. We can learn a great deal by studying the experience of the miracle nations as well as those countries that failed, especially by contrasting them as in this chapter.

The Mechanism of Growth

In addition to questions about the success or failure of poor countries in catching up to the technological frontier established by the rich countries, there is the separate question of the frontier itself. What determines the rate at which the frontier advances? Is it saving and investment, technological change, education, or other factors? As we shall see, growth would grind to a halt without a continuing stream of new inventions, and maintaining the flow of inventions and new ideas requires incentives to inventors to make the large, up-front investments needed to create new computer chips, software, medical technology, drugs, and other novel products.

What Caused the Worldwide Growth Slowdown and Subsequent Revival?

Growth at the frontier, that is, the level of per-capita income enjoyed by the leading rich country, is not smooth or steady. Much of this book has been devoted to understanding the business cycles that cause periods of prosperity to alternate with shorter periods of recession and high unemployment. But even disregarding the recessions and averaging over the entire business cycle, growth proceeds at an uneven pace. The period of most rapid growth in the United States was the entire half-century between 1913 and 1973; in Europe and Japan the period of rapid growth was compressed into the shorter interval between 1948 and 1973, part of which consisted of making up for wartime destruction.

The last sections of this chapter examine the pace of economic growth in the rich countries, particularly the United States, over the past century. Why was growth fastest in the middle of the twentieth century, and why did it slow down after 1973? A new event to examine is the revival of productivity growth in the United States after 1995. Why did this revival occur, and what made it occur in the United States but not, at least so far, in Europe or Japan? Does the return of rapid U.S. productivity growth in 1995–2005 at rates similar to 1913–73 indicate that the slowdown period of 1973–95 is a historical oddity, never to be repeated?

11-2 The Standard of Living and Concepts of Productivity

In Chapter 10 we used the concepts of "output per person," "productivity," and "output per hour" interchangeably, using the symbol Y/N. As before, the growth rate of a ratio is the difference between the growth rates of the numerator and denominator, so the growth rate of these concepts was designated as $y - n$.

Distinguishing the Standard of Living from Labor Productivity

However, it is possible for the growth rate of the population to differ from the growth rate of labor input. To maintain intact our previous development of the Solow growth model, we will continue to use the symbol N (growing at rate n) for labor input or hours of work, and we will introduce the new symbol q for the rate of population growth. Factors that could cause work hours to grow faster than the population ($n > q$) include a movement of women into the labor force, as happened in the 1970s and 1980s, or a decline in the birthrate that initially reduces growth in the number of children and only later reduces growth in the workforce, defined as those aged 16 and older. Factors that could cause work hours to grow more slowly than the population ($n < q$) include a move to an earlier age of retirement and to longer vacations, as well as factors causing higher unemployment or a lower labor-force participation rate.[2]

The **standard of living** is real GDP per member of the population, or "real output per capita."

Labor productivity is real GDP per hour of work, or "real output per hour."

Economic growth refers to an improvement in the **standard of living**, defined as output per capita or member of the population (Y/Q). **Labor productivity** is defined as output per hour of work (Y/N), using the same definition of output. The growth rate of the standard of living is $y - q$, while the growth rate of labor productivity is $y - n$. Thus the difference between the growth rate of the standard of living and that of labor productivity is

$$y - q - (y - n) = n - q \tag{11.1}$$

Therefore, whenever hours grow faster than the population $(n > q)$, the standard of living grows faster than labor productivity, and vice versa.

The distinction between q and n is worth making when examining differences between the United States and other countries. As shown in the figure on p. 322, European countries still lag well behind the United States in their output per capita, but several of the leading European nations have caught up to the United States in their level of labor productivity, or output per hour. The reason that productivity in Europe has grown faster than the standard of living is clear from equation (11.1)—hours of work in Europe have grown more slowly than the population. Over the past few decades, Europeans have chosen to take longer vacations than are typical in the United States, their average unemployment rate has risen, and their labor-force participation rate has declined. Europeans retire at earlier ages than Americans. These events prevent the European standard of living from catching up to the United States even as the productivity gap has vanished for some European nations. We return to contrasts between Europe and the United States in the last section of this chapter.

Multifactor Productivity (Solow's Residual)

A second concept of productivity is important in the study of economic growth. Already defined in Chapter 10, this is multifactor productivity (MFP), which is sometimes called "Solow's residual" after Robert M. Solow, the Nobel-prize winning inventor of neoclassical growth theory. The concept of MFP differs from labor productivity in that it expresses the amount of output produced relative to *both* labor and capital inputs; in contrast, labor productivity expresses the amount of output produced relative to labor input only. The contribution that capital makes to output is measured by the elasticity of output to capital (b), which we will continue, as in Chapter 10, to assume is 0.25 in our numerical examples. The elasticity of output to capital and labor input together is unity (1.0), and so the elasticity of output to labor is the remaining amount not attributable to capital $(1 - b)$, or 0.75 in the numerical example.

The growth rate of MFP (for which we use, as before, the symbol a) can be written as the growth rate of output (y) minus the contribution of capital (bk) minus the contribution of labor hours $[(1 - b)n]$:

$$a = y - bk - (1 - b)n \tag{11.2}$$

---

[2] The labor force, defined on p. 46, is the sum of employment plus unemployment. The labor-force participation rate is the ratio of the labor force to the working-age population, aged 16 and older. The labor-force participation rate in the United States in March 2005 was 65.8 percent.

11-2 The Standard of Living and Concepts of Productivity

Thus, to measure the growth rate of multifactor productivity, we need to know four facts—the growth rates of output, capital, and labor (y, k, and n), and the elasticity of output with respect to capital (b). As Robert Solow showed in the 1950s in part of the work that earned him the Nobel Prize in economics, this elasticity can be measured by the share of capital in national income, including corporate profits, depreciation, rent, interest, and the portion of the income of the self-employed that is attributable to capital.[3]

How are the growth rates of multifactor productivity (a) and labor productivity ($y - n$) related to each other? Equation (11.2) can be rearranged to show their relationship.[4]

General Form	Numerical Example	
$a = (y - n) - b(k - n)$	$2.25 = (4 - 1) - 0.25(4 - 1)$	(11.3)

In words, the growth rate of multifactor productivity is equal to the growth rate of labor productivity minus b times the growth in the ratio of capital input to labor input.[5] Since growth in the ratio is almost always positive, the growth of MFP is almost always slower than that of labor productivity.

Self-Test

The definition of MFP growth in equation (11.3) has five elements: y, a, k, n, and b.

1. Assuming that b always equals 0.25, any of the four remaining elements can be calculated if the other three are known. Fill in the blanks:

y	a	k	n
—	4	4	1
4	3	4	—
3	0	—	1

2. For each example in the table above, which is higher: labor productivity growth or MFP growth? Why should this be the case?

How the Real Wage Is Related to Productivity

If labor productivity (Y/N) grows slowly, the real wage (W/P) tends to grow slowly. We have already learned in equation (11.2) that an ingredient in the measurement of multifactor productivity (MFP) is labor's share in national income ($1 - b$). This central concept, called labor's share, can be defined in a way that connects labor productivity with the real wage:

$$\text{Labor's share} = 1 - b = \frac{WN}{PY} = \frac{W/P}{Y/N} \quad (11.4)$$

The first expression states that labor's share is equal to the total compensation of labor [the nominal wage rate (W), times the quantity of labor input (N)], divided by total income in nominal terms (PY). The second expression states that this is exactly the same as the real wage divided by labor productivity.

---

[3] Solow's idea of linking the elasticity of output to capital with capital's share in national income is explained in Chapter 10, footnote 11, on p. 333.

[4] Equation (11.3) is identical to equation (10.12) on p. 333.

[5] The growth of the ratio of capital input to labor input is often called "capital deepening."

Equation (11.4) helps us see that if labor's share in national income is constant, then the real wage must grow at the same rate as labor productivity. As usual, we employ lowercase symbols to represent growth rates, and we can use the familiar relationship that the growth rate of any ratio equals the growth rate of the numerator minus the growth rate of the denominator. This implies that the growth rate of labor's share equals the growth rate of the real wage $(w - p)$, minus the growth rate of labor productivity $(y - n)$:

$$\text{Growth rate of labor's share} = (w - p) - (y - n) \tag{11.5}$$

This leads us to a very important conclusion about the growth rate of the real wage. If labor's share is constant (so that the growth rate of labor's share is zero), then *the growth rate of the real wage must be exactly equal to the growth rate of productivity.*

Condition if the growth rate of labor's share is zero

$$w - p = y - n \tag{11.6}$$

Labor's share of national income in the United States has been virtually constant for the past 30 years. As a result, the real wage has grown at the same rate as labor productivity.

11-3 The Failure of Convergence

If half of the world's population still lives in countries with output per capita that is less than one-tenth the level of the United States, then this implies that these countries have failed to converge to the U.S. standard of living. Yet convergence is just what is predicted to occur by the Solow neoclassical growth model studied in the last chapter. First, let us review why the Solow model predicts convergence; then we will look at the facts.

The Theoretical Prediction of Convergence

The simple Solow model with no technical change does not actually explain economic growth. It predicts that a country with a given per-person production function and given saving rate (s) will have a fixed level of labor productivity (Y/N) and capital per worker (K/N). For instance, in Figure 11-1 we have copied the equilibrium in the Solow model from Figure 10-3, where the economy operates at point E_0 with a capital stock per hour of $(K/N)_0$ and a level of saving equal to $s(Y/N)_0$. How does the Solow model explain how a poor nation might be operating at point P with a much lower level of capital per hour $(K/N)_P$ and level of saving $s(Y/N)_P$?

Clearly, such an economy must not be in its long-run equilibrium, because its level of saving per person at point P exceeds its investment requirements shown at point A, that is, the amount of investment $(n + d)(K/N)_P$ needed to provide for population growth and depreciation. Since actual investment equals saving and is in excess of investment requirements, the capital-labor ratio will grow steadily until the economy reaches long-run equilibrium at point E_0. According to the Solow model, the only difference between rich nations and poor nations is that the poor nations have a lower capital-labor ratio K/N. Since there is no difference in the per-person production function between rich and poor nations, the process of saving in excess of investment requirements

Figure 11-1 Saving, Investment, and Capital per Hour in Long-Run Equilibrium for a Poor Nation

The blue saving line and black investment requirements line are copied from Figure 10-3. The long-run equilibrium point is shown at E_0. The only reason given by the Solow growth model for the low output per hour $(Y/N)_P$ of poor nations is their low level of capital per hour $(K/N)_P$, and their economies operate at the point labeled P. Because their saving and investment per hour at P exceed their investment requirements for population growth and depreciation, shown at A, there is sufficient excess investment to boost the K/N ratio up to the equilibrium value $(K/N)_0$.

will automatically cause the poor nations to converge to the same equilibrium point E_0 as the rich nations.

Does technological change alter the convergence prediction of the Solow model? No, because technology is assumed to be freely available to all countries. Thus the model continues to assume that the only reason for nations to be poor is that they start at a level of the capital-labor ratio (K/N) that is well below the equilibrium value. As shown in Figure 11-2, the equilibrium level of labor productivity (Y/N) can steadily increase, but the Solow model predicts that rich countries and poor countries alike will eventually converge to the same equilibrium value. The rich countries reach the equilibrium value earlier because they started with a higher capital-labor ratio and thus required a shorter period of saving and investment.

A key empirical prediction of the Solow model is that the poorer the nation, that is, the lower its labor productivity (Y/N) in an initial period of time, the faster the growth of its labor productivity. We can see this in Figure 11-2, where the arrow labeled "Poor nations" rises at a steeper slope than the arrow labeled "Rich nations." Thus the Solow model would predict that there would be a *negative* relationship between a nation's initial level of Y/N and its subsequent growth rate $(y - n)$. In short, poor nations should uniformly exhibit faster growth rates of labor productivity and per-capita output than rich nations. After rich and poor nations converge to the long-run equilibrium path, their growth rates should be identical.

Facts About Convergence

Data on rich and poor countries refer to output per person. Extensive research has been carried out by Robert Summers and Alan Heston of the University of Pennsylvania to improve the comparability of real output data across countries. The Summers-Heston data measure real output per person at a common set of prices for all nations, and this tends to improve the standing

Figure 11-2 Output per Hour of Rich and Poor Nations During the Period of Convergence

Both the rich and poor nations are assumed to start off with an equilibrium level of capital per hour (K/N) that is below equilibrium, but the poor nations begin much below the rich nations. Because all nations initially have investment in excess of requirements for population growth and depreciation, they all grow faster than the equilibrium path until they catch up. Since the poor nations start further back, it takes them more time to converge to the equilibrium path, and their growth rates are faster during this time period.

Poor Nations Grow Faster while they Are Converging

of poor nations markedly compared to the crude alternative of comparing GDP across nations using foreign exchange rates.[6]

Despite these corrections for common prices, many nations remain very poor. This is shown in Figure 11-3, which has one dot for each of 104 nations. The horizontal position of each dot represents real output per worker in 1960 as a percentage of the United States, and the vertical position represents the growth rate of real output per worker from 1960 to 2000. The extent of worldwide poverty in 1960 is shown by the number of dots to the left of 10 percent on the horizontal axis; in each of these nations (28 of the 104), real output per worker in 1960 was less than 10 percent of the U.S. level. Among these poor countries, those that grew slower than the U.S. after 1960 are shown by red dots. *These are the poor countries that failed to converge.*

Recall that the Solow model predicts faster growth in poor nations than in rich nations, indicating that the slope of the dots in Figure 11-3 should be negative, slanting downward from left to right. Indeed, there are green dots at the upper left corner of the diagram; among the fast growing nations that started out relatively poor in 1960 are Korea, Singapore, Hong Kong, and Taiwan (the Four Tigers), together with Japan. These five nations all registered growth rates in the vertical direction of 5.0 percent or higher. The next group of nations with growth rates around 4.0 to 4.5 percent include Cyprus, Greece, Portugal, and Thailand.

However, the overall correlation of the dots in Figure 11-3 is zero. There are almost as many countries having growth rates below the U.S. rate, shown by

---

[6] Robert Summers and Alan Heston, "The Penn World Table (Mark 5): An Expanded Set of International Comparisons, 1950–1988," *Quarterly Journal of Economics*, vol. 106 (May 1991), pp. 327–68. The latest data are available at http://pwt.econ.upenn.edu/php_site/pwt61_form.php.

Figure 11-3 Output per Worker Relative to the United States in 1960 and the Growth of Output per Person, 1960–2000

The convergence hypothesis suggests that the poorest nations, those on the left of the diagram, will have the fastest rates of growth. The dots should slope downward to the right and all dots should be above the horizontal line, which represents the growth rate of the United States. The low correlation of the growth rates and levels and the substantial number of red dots, showing poor countries with growth rates below that of the United States, are evidence contradicting the convergence hypothesis.

Source: Robert Summers and Alan Heston, "The Penn World Table (Mark 5): An Expanded Set of International Comparisons, 1950–1988," *Quarterly Journal of Economics*, vol. 106 (May 1991), pp. 327–68. The latest data are available at http://pwt.econ.upenn.edu/php_site/pwt61_form.php.

the red and blue dots, as having growth rates above the U.S. rate, shown by the green dots. There are even a few rich nations that failed to converge. Among these, shown in the second section of Table 11-1, are New Zealand, Venezuela, and Argentina. The next section of the table lists Japan and two of the Four Tigers, nations that were initially poor but converged rapidly. Poor nations that slipped back, the opposite direction of convergence, included Ghana, Cameroon, and Mali in sub-Saharan Africa. Any country with an average growth rate below the U.S. growth rate of 2.5 percent per year wound up with an average level of output per person relative to the United States that was *worse* in 2000 than in 1960, the opposite of convergence. About one-third of the nations plotted in Figure 11-3 experienced the opposite of convergence. Some

Table 11-1 Examples of Countries Displaying Convergence, Anti-Convergence, or Neither (Levels and Growth Rates in Percent)

	Output per person relative to the United States		Growth rate of output per person, 1960–2000	
Country	2000	1960	Actual	Relative to U.S.
Rich countries that converged				
Austria	71	60	2.9	0.4
Italy	65	56	2.9	0.4
France	67	64	2.6	0.1
Rich countries that failed to converge				
New Zealand	57	94	1.2	−1.3
Venezuela	19	64	−0.5	−3.0
Argentina	33	60	1.0	−1.5
Poor countries that converged				
Hong Kong	80	25	5.4	2.9
Japan	74	37	4.2	1.7
South Korea	48	12	5.9	3.4
Poor countries that fell back				
Ghana	4	7	1.1	−1.4
Cameroon	6	14	0.5	−2.0
Mali	3	8	−0.0	−2.5
Poor countries that made no progress				
Morocco	11	11	2.6	0.1
India	7	7	2.7	0.2

Source: Robert Summers and Alan Heston, "The Penn World Table (Mark 5): An Expanded Set of International Comparisons, 1950–1988," *Quarterly Journal of Economics*, vol. 106 (May 1991), pp. 327–68. The latest data are available at http://pwt.econ.upenn.edu/php_site/pwt61_form.php.

others, including the examples shown in the bottom section of Table 11-1, made no progress, exhibiting roughly the same growth rates as the United States over the 1960–2000 period.

While the prediction of convergence seems to be a failure of the Solow model, this verdict needs to be qualified. Among the rich nations, the required negative correlation between the initial income level and subsequent growth rate was quite strong, with few exceptions. This verdict is valid either for the 1960–2000 period examined in Figure 11-3 or the longer 1885–1994 period.[7] What seems to go wrong with the prediction of convergence refers to the poor countries. When the poor countries are included, as in Figure 11-3, the negative correlation disappears, and there appears to be no systematic relationship

---

[7] See Charles I. Jones, *Introduction to Economic Growth*, 2d ed. (New York: Norton, 2001), Chapter 3.

Figure 11-4 The Effect of a Low Saving Rate or High Rate of Population Growth on Output per Person

The upper blue line shows the long-run equilibrium growth path for the rich nations. Two factors could cause the long-run path to be lower for the poor nations—either a lower saving rate (s) or a faster rate of population growth (n).

between the initial 1960 level of real GDP relative to the United States and the subsequent growth rate.

Solutions Suggested by the Solow Model

The reason the Solow model suggests convergence is that it assumes unrealistically that all nations have the same per-person production function, saving rate, growth rate of the population, and depreciation rate. We have already seen in Figure 10-4 on p. 331 the Solow model's prediction that an increase in the saving rate can temporarily *raise* the growth rate of output and capital per person. In the same diagram, an increase in the rate of population growth (n) would *reduce* the growth rate of output and capital per person.[8] Thus one valid explanation for the failure of poor countries to converge is that, with either a lower saving rate (low s) or higher rate of population growth (high n), their equilibrium growth path is not the single path depicted by the blue line in Figure 11-2 but rather is a lower path as shown by the lower blue line in Figure 11-4. Thus the puzzle of why some poor countries do not fully converge to the output per person level of the rich nations can be explained by any combination of lower saving rates or faster rates of population growth.

Does the empirical evidence support the Solow model's prediction that a higher investment rate allows nations to achieve a higher standard of living? The relationship between the investment rate (the share of investment in GDP)

---

[8] Turn back to Figure 10-4 on p. 331. Imagine tilting the black investment requirements line labeled $(n + d)(K/N)$ upward. This will cause the equilibrium point E_0 to move downward and to the left, reducing the equilibrium levels of Y/N and K/N. Thus an increase in the rate of population growth (n) will reduce the equilibrium levels of Y/N and K/N, just as an increase in the saving rate (s) will have the opposite effect.

and the standard of living across many nations is very weak. Poor countries have investment ratios ranging all the way from 2 percent to 25 percent. Similarly, rich countries have investment rates ranging from 12 to 30 percent. Thus the Solow model ultimately fails in explaining the failure of at least half of the poor countries to converge over the past few decades. We turn in the next two sections to alternative explanations of the continuing gap between the rich and poor countries.

> ### Self-Test
>
> The Solow growth model makes predictions both about the level of per-person output and its growth rate.
> 1. What is the long-run effect of an increase in the saving rate on the level of per-person output and capital?
> 2. What is the long-run effect of an increase in the saving rate on the growth rate of output per capita?
> 3. What is the long-run effect of an increase in the rate of population growth on the level of per-person output and capital?
> 4. What is the long-run effect of an increase in the rate of population growth on the growth rate of output per capita?

11-4 Human Capital and Technology

The Solow model as developed in Chapter 10 cannot explain the relationship between the levels and growth rates of output per capita, as displayed in Figure 11-3. While the Solow model, as in Figure 11-4, can allow the saving rate and population growth rate to differ, thus yielding a lower equilibrium level of output per capita for poor nations, it seems to assume much more likeness between poor and rich nations than is true in fact. In particular, its assumptions that the per-person production function and the rate of technological change are identical across poor and rich countries seem dubious. Also, the Solow model as treated so far in this chapter neglects the role of human capital, previously introduced in Section 10-7 on pp. 337–39.

Human Capital and Economic Growth

Perhaps the most basic flaw in the simple Solow model is to assume that labor input is identical across rich and poor countries. In fact, educational attainment (the number of years of education achieved by an average member of the population) is vastly different between rich and poor countries. Studies of economic growth usually find that poor nations fall short in every measure of factors that tend to promote growth, including insufficient physical capital, human capital, and saving rates, as well as excessive rates of population growth. But, to use an old phrase, "correlation does not imply causation." Perhaps the sources of low growth are themselves *endogenous*, that is, caused by low growth itself. Poor countries simply cannot afford to engage in high levels of investment in physical and human capital. Further, for poor countries to achieve the lower fertility rates needed to achieve lower rates of population growth may require education, the crucial growth factor that poor nations cannot afford.

Does Technological Change Require Human Capital?

The Solow model assumes that the rate of technological change is the same in every country, *and that the best available technology is freely available to all countries*. This explains why in Figure 11-2 we have drawn the upper blue long-run equilibrium line as the same for rich and poor countries alike. The different levels for rich and poor countries of the blue long-run equilibrium lines, in Figure 11-4 are caused solely by different saving rates and rates of population growth, not different growth rates of technological change.

Yet this is surely an unrealistic assumption in the Solow model. Modern technology often requires modern equipment and software. Thus both investment and technological change require educated workers, that is, a previous investment in human capital. If workers are illiterate, can they use personal computers and the Internet as fruitfully as in countries where all workers can read and write, and where most workers are familiar with personal computers? As a skeptic suggested, "If you unloaded a pile of Dell computers and Microsoft software on a pier in Bangladesh, would that create the long-awaited convergence of the Bangladeshi standard of living to the level of the United States?" Bangladesh and many other poor countries do not have sufficient numbers of educated workers who know how to use modern computers and software, rendering modern technology inaccessible in contrast to the assumption of the Solow model that it is freely available everywhere.

Importing Technological Change Through Foreign Investment

Most research and development takes place in the rich countries, especially in the United States, western Europe, and Japan. Poor countries are unable to afford large investments in research and development activities, so what can they do to acquire the technical knowledge being developed by the rich nations? Three main methods are available. First, engineers in poor countries may try to copy modern products made in rich countries. However, this is very difficult and often impossible for the most advanced products, including computer chips. A second method is to purchase imported machinery that embodies the latest technology. Developing nations have been importing the latest technology since the early nineteenth century, when American firms imported British steam engines. A third method is to obtain investment by foreign firms, which open factories in the poor country based on the latest technology. Mexican economic growth has been spurred in the past decade by American investment, and Singapore's inclusion as one of Asia's four fast-growing "tigers" has been heavily dependent on foreign investment, mainly by Japanese and American companies. More recently, rapid economic growth in China has been propelled by foreign investment, not just from Japan and the United States, but from neighboring Hong Kong and Taiwan.

"Not so fast," economics ministers in many poor countries might respond if shown this list of three channels by which they might obtain modern technology. "Our people are not sufficiently educated to copy the latest techniques, we cannot afford to pay for imported modern machinery, and our countries are not attractive as locations for foreign investment." This hypothetical comment from the poor countries brings us to the heart of the development problem that they face. Everything depends on everything else, and some countries are in a "vicious" circle in which they are too poor to improve the educational level of their citizens or to obtain modern technology, two prerequisites to growth.

The view that "everything is endogenous" and that some poor countries are caught in a "poverty trap" makes the prospects for growth seem hopeless for many poor countries. Yet this ignores the fact that many other poor nations have succeeded in launching themselves on the path to convergence, as shown by the many green dots in Figure 11-3 on p. 357. Perhaps not every growth-inducing factor is endogenous, and there are some other factors that governments can influence, that is, convert into an exogenous growth-promoting influence. The next section discusses two important factors that governments can influence, the political/legal environment and infrastructure investment, and one that they cannot influence, the geographical location of their countries.

11-5 Political Capital, Infrastructure, and Geography

Recently economists have made substantial progress toward identifying fundamental, underlying sources of growth that help us understand why some countries "take off" on a path toward convergence, while other countries remain mired at extremely low levels of income. The most basic of these sources is the legal and political environment. The free market system requires that entrepreneurs who are taking risks by starting a new business have a high probability of making a decent profit to reward them for their effort and for the risk they are taking that their business may fail. The legal system must protect the right to own property and must protect it from thieves; the tax system must be fairly administered; and the opportunity to start a business must be open, not limited to relatives or cronies of corrupt dictators. The second major factor that involves government decisions is infrastructure investment in such crucial factors of production as highways, airports, ports, telephone networks, and electricity systems. Unfortunately, a third factor, geography, impairs the growth opportunities of some nations but cannot usually be influenced by government policy.[9]

Political and Legal Determinants of Costs and Returns

In most countries, permits must be purchased in order to start a business and construct a building. In advanced countries like the United States, these permits are easily obtained, and their price is only a small fraction of the overall cost of starting the business. But in other countries, the permits may be very expensive, there may be long delays in obtaining them, and, more important, officials may expect bribes. In Russia some investors have reported that as many as ten different agencies each expected a bribe in order to grant permission for new projects. In another example, the cost of starting a small business in Peru was estimated to be 32 times the monthly minimum wage, an impossible sum for an average worker or even a relatively well-off citizen. Not surprisingly, Peru is one of the growth failures shown in Figure 11-3 that barely registered

---

[9] Parts of this section are based on Charles I. Jones, *Introduction to Economic Growth*, 2d ed. (New York: Norton, 2001), Chapter 7. See also Robert E. Hall and Charles I. Jones, "Why do Some Countries Produce So Much More Output per Worker than Others?" *Quarterly Journal of Economics*, vol. 114 (February 1999), pp. 83–116.

positive growth in output per person during 1960–2000, and its output per person fell back from 26 percent of the U.S. level in 1960 to 14 percent in 2000. Over the entire period from 1975 to 2000, output per person in Peru registered a negative growth rate.

There are a wider variety of factors that can influence the expected returns from starting a business in a foreign country. First, the country must have relatively free trade so that products manufactured in that country can be exported. Governments obtain access for their exports to other countries by having relatively low barriers to trade for imports into their countries. Just as important is what has been called "diversion," which includes the problem of theft (both "outside" robberies and theft by managers or workers), very high levels of taxation levied by governments, or "protection money" like that paid to the Mafia in gangster movies. Any kind of diversion reduces the expected profits on a business investment both directly and indirectly, by forcing business firms to invest in such anti-diversion activities as security systems.

The amount of diversion in a country is determined by government policy and the type of legal system that is provided by a country's constitution. Sometimes the diversion is created by the government itself, as when dictators in Indonesia and some African countries give lucrative contracts to businesses owned by a dictator's relatives. Not only must diversion be minimized, but government policies must also be *predictable*. Countries with reputations for frequent changes in government, whether by political coups or constitutional changes, will have low expected returns to investment due to the high risks of locating a business there.

Why Do Governments Tolerate and Even Engage in Diversion?

It seems obvious that theft and corruption would impede economic growth by reducing the expected returns to investment, both by domestic citizens and foreign firms, which can chose from a wide variety of countries for the location of investment projects. Why then do governments tolerate these forms of diversion, and why do some governments engage directly in diversion through bribe taking and corruption? Douglas North, the 1993 Nobel prizewinner in economics, points out that government officials may want to maximize their own power and their own monetary incomes rather than being "benevolent social planners" who attempt to maximize the welfare of everyone in society. North's notion takes one step further the conventional economic precept that individuals try to maximize utility and firms try to maximize profits. Government bureaucrats may deliberately take bribes and tolerate theft by Mafia-type organizations in order to maximize income and power or minimize the nuisance of trying to get rid of offenders.[10]

MIT economist Daron Acemoglu and Berkeley economist James Robinson attempt to go further and determine the political environment that encourages or discourages government activities that minimize diversion:

> Political elites may block technological and institutional development, because of a political replacement effect. Innovations often erode elites' incumbency advantage, increasing the likelihood that they will be replaced. Fearing replacement, political elites are unwilling to initiate change, and may even block economic

---

[10] Douglass C. North, *Structure and Change in Economic History* (New York: Norton, 1991).

development. . . . It is only when political competition is limited and also their power is threatened that elites will block development.[11]

Empirically, the presence or absence of diversion helps explain not only economic growth but also the values of other determinants of growth like investment rates and education.[12] Just as education is often called "human capital," as in the analysis of Chapter 10, in the same way we can refer to a healthy political and legal environment that discourages diversion as "political capital." Since it is a key ingredient both in growth and in fostering other growth-inducing factors like investment in physical capital and human capital, the presence of political capital may be the key to understanding why some countries succeed and others fail at achieving economic growth.[13]

Physical Infrastructure

The capital of Costa Rica, a country in Central America, is San Jose, which is located in the center of the country. To reach either the Atlantic or Pacific Ocean from San Jose, it is necessary to drive on two-lane winding roads, and it often takes three hours or more to drive 60 miles. American tourists sometimes return from Costa Rica by changing planes at the Dallas–Fort Worth International Airport, where outside their airplane window they see seven runways and many miles of taxiways and surrounding multilane expressways. In the immediate vicinity of this airport, there are probably more cubic yards of concrete than in all of Costa Rica.

Infrastructure is any type of capital not owned by the individual business firm that makes the firm's production more efficient. Good highways allow trucking firms to produce more output with the same number of trucks; airports with multiple runways allow airlines to minimize delays; fast railways provide a better transport option than airplanes over distances shorter than 200 miles; ports with many docks help shipping firms to avoid waiting time; well-functioning telephone networks help people communicate easily without waiting for dial tones or having their phone calls interrupted; and a grid providing ample amounts of electricity avoids the inefficiency created by blackouts and brownouts.

Countries differ in how much of their infrastructure is financed by the government. In France, the highways, airports, ports, railroads, telephone network, and electricity grid are all entirely or partly owned by the government. In the United States, infrastructure is owned by a mix of private companies and governmental organizations.

How is physical infrastructure related to growth? In some poor countries, the value of a business investment is reduced by poor highways and airports, by the absence of railroads, by telephone systems in which it takes months for a telephone to be installed and in which dial tones may be delayed, and by electricity systems that have inadequate capacity. Like political capital,

---

[11] Daron Acemoglu and James A. Robinson, "Economic Backwardness in Political Perspective," NBER Working Paper 8831 (March 2002). See also Daron Acemoglu, Simon Johnson, and James Robinson, "Institutions as the Fundamental Cause of Long-run Growth," NBER Working Paper 10481 (May 2004).

[12] See the article by Hall and Jones cited in footnote 9. See also Jeffrey D. Sachs and Andrew Warner, "Economic Reform and the Process of Global Integration," *Brookings Papers on Economic Activity*, 1995, vol. 26, no. 1, pp. 1–95.

[13] A comprehensive introduction to the problem of low economic growth in poor countries is William Easterly, *The Elusive Quest for Growth* (Cambridge, MA: MIT Press, 2002).

physical infrastructure is crucial for growth, and its quantity can be influenced by government decisions.

Geography

If income per capita is plotted on a map of the world, it quickly becomes apparent that rich countries lie in temperate zones and many poor countries lie in tropical zones. Of the 30 economies classified as high income, only two (Hong Kong and Singapore, two of the Asian Four Tigers) lie in the tropical zone, and these two small countries have only 1 percent of the total population of the rich countries. Otherwise, all of the rich countries, including those in North America, Western Europe, Northeast Asia, the Southern Cone of Latin America, and Australasia, are located outside the tropics. In addition to being located in the tropics, another predictor of poverty is lack of access to sea-based trade. Countries that are both tropical and landlocked, including Chad and Mali in Africa (both appear as nonconverging countries in Table 11-1 on p. 358), are among the very poorest in the world.

The leading scholar of the role of geography in economic development is Jeffrey Sachs of Columbia University. Sachs proposes four hypotheses regarding the role of geography in the growth performance of poor countries.[14]

1. Technologies developed in the temperate zones may not be applicable to tropical areas, where insects may transmit different diseases than are common in the temperate zones, and where the soil and weather are not suitable for agricultural techniques common in rich countries.

2. Technological innovation in any region often involves high development costs and low production costs, as in the case of Microsoft Windows, where hundreds of millions may be spent in development, but producing each copy costs only a few cents. Thus the bigger the market, the quicker the initial investment will be recouped and the higher the total profits will be. Small economies in tropical regions may be too small to justify any significant investment in technological innovation.

3. Poor productivity in rural agriculture in tropical countries and the prevalence of tropical diseases directly affect population growth—recall in the Solow model that a lower rate of population growth boosts the standard of living and stimulates a transition to a higher capital-labor ratio. As rich countries developed, the rapid growth of agricultural productivity produced a surplus of food and encouraged families to move from farm to city, where the cost of raising children was higher. This encouraged a "demographic transition" to lower birth rates, lower death rates, and a lower rate of population growth.

4. Most tropical countries were conquered and included in the empires of temperate-zone countries like Britain, France, Germany, and Belgium. Colonial domination impeded the process of economic growth by neglecting the formation of human capital through primary and higher education and by limiting economic activity to agriculture and mining, where most of the profits enriched landlords and absentee owners of the colonial power.

---

[14] This section is based on Jeffrey D. Sachs, "Tropical Underdevelopment," NBER Working Paper 8819 (February 2001). His five hypotheses regarding tropical underdevelopment have been reduced to four to simplify the exposition.

International Perspective

Growth Success and Failure in the Tropics

The text examines Jeffrey Sachs's hypothesis that geography is an important determinant of success in achieving economic growth. A tropical location is associated with poor health and low productivity in agriculture. These disadvantages are compounded when a country is landlocked, with no border on a seacoast. Most of the world's nations that are landlocked and located in the tropics are among those that have failed to begin the process of growth that leads to convergence with the rich countries. Ghana and Mali, listed in Table 11-1, are among those plotted in the lower left corner of Figure 11-3 (see pp. 357–58).[a]

Yet one of the fastest growing countries in the past three decades has been Botswana, an African country that is both tropical and landlocked. What are the secrets of Botswana's success? The text stresses the importance of political capital, minimizing diversionary activities that reduce the returns to private investment and raise the costs of setting up new business firms. A positive influence of the government on the process of economic growth requires a benevolent attitude by the political elite rather than a self-serving attempt to enrich themselves. In turn, as argued by MIT's Daron Acemoglu and several co-authors, it helps if the political elite is secure rather than worried about being replaced through a revolution or coup.

In Botswana one political party is dominant. This, together with a legacy of laws and contract procedures dating back to the British colonial period, has allowed the political elite to pursue sensible policies. Foreign investment, mainly by mining companies, is encouraged. Bribery and political corruption have not been a problem. Botswana's biggest problem is a disease that is not limited in its effects to the tropics—around 30 percent of its adults are infected with HIV, the virus that causes AIDS. Through its success in achieving economic growth, Botswana is able to provide free AIDS drugs to anyone who needs them. Overall, Botswana's experience supports the importance of political capital as a key ingredient in economic growth.

Other success stories among tropical nations include Singapore, Thailand, Malaysia, and Hong Kong. These nations have the advantage of not being landlocked, and both Singapore and Hong Kong have the best natural ports in the region. Sachs singles out two common features of these tropical success stories. First, these nations all stressed the improvement of public health early in the development process. Singapore and Hong Kong have the advantage of being islands, where control of tropical diseases is easier. Second, these nations adopted policies to encourage activities other than agriculture. Their governments adopted policies to attract foreign firms to establish manufacturing plants oriented toward exporting most of their output. The explosive growth in manufacturing was concentrated not just in traditional industries like textiles but also in such modern industries as electronic machines and semiconductors.

Unfortunately, the examples of Botswana and the successful nations of Southeast Asia are of only limited relevance for the poorest countries in sub-Saharan Africa. In these countries, the conditions of rampant disease and poor agricultural land are so severe that substantial foreign aid is needed from the rich countries, especially to provide drugs that help control both AIDS and diseases like malaria that are specific to the tropics.

[a]This box is based on Jeffrey D. Sachs, "Tropical Development," NBER Working Paper 8119 (February 2001), and on "Economics Focus: The Tropical Exception," *Economist* (March 30, 2002).

The four factors suggested by Sachs do not imply that economic growth for tropical countries is impossible, but the barriers to a growth "take-off" are surely raised by the impediments that he mentions. The box on p. 366 looks further into the puzzle of why some countries in the tropical zone are growth success or "miracle" stories and many others are not.[15]

Integrating the Exogenous Factors in Economic Growth

We can use the phrase "exogenous factors" as a common label for political capital (minimizing theft-like sources of diversion), infrastructure capital, and geography. These factors are exogenous not in the sense that they are fixed and immutable but rather that they are external to the decision-making process of individual households and firms. How should we integrate these exogenous factors into the theories of economic growth studied in Chapter 10?

After we added human capital (H) to the production function linking output (Y) to physical capital (K), labor input (N), and an autonomous growth factor (A) representing technological change, we obtained equation (10.15) on p. 338, rewritten here:

$$Y = AF(K, H, N) \qquad (11.7)$$

Here we interpret labor (N) as "brute force" labor, earning the kinds of wages of people doing unskilled jobs suitable for those with an eighth-grade education, while all the extra earnings of the population above that education level are included in human capital (H). In this section we have introduced three new exogenous determinants of growth: political capital (P), infrastructure capital (R), and geography (G). The three new factors enter into the production process in different ways. Infrastructural capital is just like physical capital and enters in the same way. Political capital affects the productivity of the entire production process and enters as a determinant of the previously autonomous growth factor A, as does geography. Technology (T) is also a determinant of A.

Putting these ideas together, our "final" equation that explains the puzzles of economic growth is

$$Y = A(G, P, T)F(K, R, H, N) \qquad (11.8)$$

This states in words that output depends on two functions, A and F. The first function (A) depends on the positive or negative role of geographical location (G), the amount of political capital in a country (P), and the level of technology (T). This function (A) is multiplied by the traditional production function (F), which depends on physical capital (K), infrastructure capital (R), human capital (H), and labor input (N).

The more comprehensive theory of growth depicted in equation (11.8) helps us to understand many of the puzzles involving the continuing inability of poor nations to take off on a sustainable growth path that would ultimately lead to convergence with the rich countries. The geographical factor suggests that some poor countries may never converge; the political factor helps explain why some countries are not attractive locations for foreign investment; and the

---

[15] A delightfully readable introduction to the role of geography in economic development is David S. Landes, *The Wealth and Poverty of Nations* (New York: Norton, 1998), Chapter 2.

technological factor itself depends on a set of determinants that are not included in the equation.

One of the growth puzzles posed in Chapter 10 asked about the "immigration puzzle." Without any change in his or her educational attainment *(H)*, an immigrant to the United States from Guatemala can obtain a wage at least ten times higher. This difference is too high to be explained simply by differences in physical capital per person. But now we have learned that there is a long list of factors that allow everyone in the United States to be more productive than in Guatemala—geography, political capital, and infrastructure. Further, even though the immigrant's human capital does not change simply through the act of immigration, the *average* level of human capital of other members of the population is much higher in the new country (the United States) than in the original country (Guatemala). Because the United States has much larger quantities of these factors that favor economic growth, the mere act of moving from one country to another can drastically change the demand for the labor of the unskilled Guatemalan. In the United States, many people have incomes sufficiently high to make them willing to pay $10 per hour for lawn-mowing services, while in Guatemala, almost no one has an income high enough to pay anything to have his or her lawn mowed.

11-6 Case Study

Uneven U.S. Growth Across Eras: Why Did U.S. Productivity Growth Slow Down and Then Revive?

Up to this point, the chapter has focused on the need to explain why some nations remain so poor while the standard of living in rich countries is many times higher and continues to advance. For citizens of rich countries like the United States, a question closer to home is why the pace of economic growth varies so much over eras. In particular, why was productivity growth relatively fast between 1913 and 1972, why did growth slow down so much after 1973, and why did growth revive after 1995?

The Three Eras of Postwar U.S. Productivity Growth

The rapid advance in the U.S. standard of living in the first half of the twentieth century was fueled by growth in labor productivity that averaged slightly below 2 percent per year. In this section we focus on the more recent history since 1960. The red line in Figure 11-5 shows the annual growth rate of actual labor productivity over the period since 1960. Because growth in actual productivity is so erratic, zigging and zagging up and down every few years, we also display as a green line the "trend" in labor productivity growth that smooths out the zigzags.

The green trend line shows that the productivity trend in the 1960s was considerably better than the 2 percent historical average achieved in the half-century before 1950. The trend reaches almost 3 percent in 1961–62 and then steadily slows down to only 1.3 percent in 1980. The period of relatively slow productivity growth, between 1.3 and 1.8 percent, extends over the two decades between 1975 and 1995. Then beginning in 1995 the trend exhibits a

The Three Eras of Postwar Productivity Growth

Figure 11-5 Growth Rate of Labor Productivity in the United States, 1960–2004

The zigzag red line shows the annual growth rate of labor productivity in the U.S. nonfarm private business sector in the previous eight quarters. The green line shows the long-term trend in productivity growth, smoothing out the zigzags in order to give a smoother estimate of the average performance of productivity growth over different eras. The green productivity growth trend was high, nearly 3 percent in the early 1960s, and then slowed down gradually to a low barely above 1 percent by 1980. The productivity growth trend stagnated around 1.5 percent from 1980 to 1995 and then soared continuously upward, reaching 3.5 percent in 2003 and 2004.

---

strong revival, soaring by 2003–04 to 3.5 percent, well beyond the growth rate of the early 1960s.

We can simplify the evidence in Figure 11-5 by referring to three eras of productivity growth since 1960, described simply as "fast," "slow," then "fast." Economists and policymakers in the mid-1960s took for granted that productivity would grow at close to 3 percent per year forever, and they were perplexed and dismayed as the growth rate deteriorated throughout the 1970s. Economists devoted reams of research to attempts to explain the "productivity growth slowdown," yet no consensus emerged as to its causes. Pessimistic views took over, and by 1995 economists had given up on the idea that productivity growth of 3 percent could ever be achieved again for any substantial period of years.

Yet, as shown by the green line in Figure 11-5, good news began to arrive, as actual productivity growth moved solidly above 2 percent after 1995 and above 3 percent after 2002. The average growth rate of labor productivity between 1996 and 2004 was 3.0 percent, and the green trend line reached 3.5 percent in 2003–04. Our discussion in this section is divided into two main topics—what caused the dismal years of slow productivity growth between 1974 and 1995 and what caused the revival in productivity growth after 1995?

Causes of the 1973–95 Productivity Growth Slowdown

In assessing alternative hypotheses, we need to remember that the productivity growth slowdown lasted for two decades, and it was concentrated outside of the manufacturing sector. The growth rate of labor productivity in manufacturing did not experience a slowdown and indeed was somewhat faster during 1973–95 than before 1973. Here we review some of the leading explanations, starting with those that center on slower growth in inputs. Then we turn to hypotheses that try to explain the slowdown in MFP, the Solow residual, represented by the lowercase letter a in equations (11.2) and (11.3) above.

1. **Measured capital per labor hour.** The growth of measured capital per labor hour slowed in the United States after 1973, both because the growth of the capital stock slowed down and because the growth of labor hours increased. The real wage rate in the United States declined substantially in response to the supply shocks of 1973–74 and 1979–80. As a result, labor was relatively cheap in the United States after 1973, so lots of workers were hired for unskilled jobs, and productivity growth fell.

2. **Raw materials and energy.** The late Michael Bruno of Hebrew University in Jerusalem and Jeffrey Sachs of Columbia University argued that the worldwide character of the productivity slowdown after 1973 suggests the likelihood of a common cause. Bruno and Sachs stressed the direct effect of the higher relative prices of energy and raw materials, together with restrictive macroeconomic policies that were introduced in response to those increases in relative prices.[16] More recent research by William Nordhaus of Yale University identifies particular energy-dependent industries that bore the brunt of the slowdown, including oil and gas extraction, motor vehicles, electricity generation, pipelines, and air transportation.[17]

3. **Decline in labor quality.** The role of labor quality in the productivity slowdown is still debated. The percentage of teenagers and adult women in the labor force rose after 1973, yet their average wages were lower than those of adult men. Consequently, analysts who measured the relative productivity of groups of workers by their relative wages concluded that the quality of the workforce declined as its age-gender composition shifted toward a greater share of adult female workers and teenagers of both genders. However, other economists believed that the low relative wages of women reflected, at least in part, the effects of discrimination rather than lower productivity.

4. **Infrastructure.** Section 11-5 and equation (11.8) on p. 367 included infrastructure capital as an important source of growth. Rich nations differ from poor nations by having more spending on education, sewers, highways,

---

[16] Michael Bruno and Jeffrey Sachs, *Economics of Worldwide Stagnation* (Cambridge, MA: Harvard University Press, 1985).

[17] William D. Nordhaus "Retrospective on the 1970s Productivity Slowdown," NBER Working Paper 10950 (December 2004)

railroads, airports, and other types of infrastructure investment. Inadequate public investment in infrastructure has been cited as a major cause of the 1973–95 productivity slowdown in the United States.[18] However, this conclusion is controversial, and another study over a longer historical time period and comparing a number of industrialized nations finds little systematic relationship between productivity growth and the share of output devoted to infrastructure investment.[19]

5. **Problems of Particular Industries.** Several industries that suffered from poor productivity growth during the 1973–95 slowdown period were those cited above by Nordhaus as being related to energy use and thus affected by the oil price shocks of the 1970s. Productivity growth fell in the mining and electric utility industries, yet there were other causes beyond high energy prices. The problem in the mining industry was that the United States was running out of oil reserves; old oil wells were drying up faster than new oil resources could be discovered, and the expense of finding new oil skyrocketed. The problems of electric utilities went beyond higher oil prices also. Government-imposed air pollution regulations required firms to buy pollution abatement equipment and to hire new workers to run and maintain this equipment, directly reducing productivity (because the benefit of clean air is not included in GDP). Further, doubts about the safety of nuclear power caused expensive plants to be shut down, wasting resources. Construction was another problem industry, but its slow productivity growth was chronic, beginning back in the early 1960s and not directly related to high energy prices.

Running Out of Resources and Ideas

Because the 1973–95 productivity growth slowdown was so pervasive and long-lasting, some economists believed that the fundamental cause went beyond slower growth in factor inputs. William Nordhaus helped popularize the depletion hypothesis, which is a much more pessimistic approach than those reviewed earlier in this section.[20] One aspect is the depletion of natural resources, in particular the decline in the rate of finding new productive oil wells in the United States, already discussed above.

Perhaps the more rapid productivity growth prior to 1973, dating back to the early twentieth century, was the direct effect of ideas developed back in the late nineteenth century. These great inventions included the electric motor, motor transport, air transport, radio, television, plastics, and other petrochemicals. This was the era that saw the emergence of the suburb, the supermarket, and the superhighway, not to mention indoor plumbing and central heating. Perhaps the economy had finished exploiting most of the benefits of the great inventions and was short on new ideas to replace them.

Overall, there is no simple answer to the puzzle posed by the productivity growth slowdown. There is probably an element of truth to several of the ideas that have just been explored, including the role of energy prices, the depletion

---

[18] See David A. Aschauer, "Is Public Expenditure Productive?" *Journal of Monetary Economics*, vol. 23 (March 1989), pp. 177–200.

[19] See Robert Ford and Pierre Poret, "Infrastructure and Private-Sector Productivity," *OECD Economic Studies*, no. 17 (Autumn 1991), pp. 63–89.

[20] The Nordhaus approach is set out in William D. Nordhaus, "Economic Policy in the Face of Declining Productivity Growth," *European Economic Review*, vol. 18 (May/June 1982), pp. 131–58.

hypothesis, and the problems experienced by specific industries. The absence of a single simple answer to the puzzle is perplexing to policymakers, because the lack of a single explanation makes it hard to devise government policies to boost productivity growth.

The Post–1995 Revival of Productivity Growth

The historical record in Figure 11-5 on p. 369 shows how strongly productivity growth revived after 1995. Gradually economists abandoned the pessimism of the 1973–95 slowdown period and began to debate the causes of the revival. In this section, we ask what caused the revival and if it will continue.

As recently as 1997–98, economists had been struggling to explain "Solow's paradox" as set forth a decade earlier by Robert M. Solow (the inventor of the Solow growth model): "We can see the computer age everywhere except in the productivity statistics." But by 1999 and 2000, economists suddenly looked up from their word processors to discover that before they had satisfactorily explained Solow's paradox, it had been rendered obsolete by the post–1995 productivity revival. Suddenly the economy was awash not only in computers, but also in productivity growth.

The New Economy and the Delay Hypothesis

Commentators universally adopted the phrase "New Economy" to describe what appeared to be a new era in macroeconomics. Since the period of the productivity revival coincided with the spread of the Internet and cellular phones as well as the invention of the World Wide Web (WWW) and e-commerce, it was natural to suppose that the basic cause of the productivity growth revival was both the production and use of high-tech equipment. The New Economy label was applied not just to personal computers and peripheral equipment like printers and monitors but also to all of the routers and switchers that made the Internet possible, plus telecommunications equipment and fiber-optic cable, as well as the software that made computers and cellular phones easy to use.

A widespread consensus emerged that the New Economy represented a fundamental transformation in macroeconomics. Among the leaders of the technological enthusiasts was the Fed's chairman Alan Greenspan, who stated, "A perceptible quickening in the pace at which technological innovations are applied argues for the hypothesis that the recent acceleration in labor productivity is not just a cyclical phenomenon or a statistical aberration, but reflects, at least in part, a more deep-seated, still developing, shift in our economic landscape."[21]

The sudden revival of productivity growth, after years in which Solow's paradox accurately captured the lack of productivity payoff from computers, appeared to vindicate Stanford economist Paul David, who had predicted that the benefits of computers were being delayed, but after some period would finally begin to boost economywide productivity. His "delay hypothesis" was based on the historical example of electricity, which was invented in the 1880s but had its big productivity payoff four decades later in the 1920s. Enthusiasts treated the New Economy as a fundamental industrial revolution as great or greater in importance than the concurrence of inventions, particularly electricity and the internal combustion engine, that transformed the world at the turn of the last century.

---

[21] This statement is from a speech given by Alan Greenspan at the Federal Reserve Bank of Chicago, May 6, 1999.

Causes of the Productivity Growth Revival

Analysts were unanimous in their belief that the production and use of high-tech equipment was a fundamental cause of the productivity revival.[22] Starting in 1995, as shown in Figure 16-5 on p. 534, there was an acceleration in the rate at which the prices of computers were declining, from a decline of roughly 15 percent per year to more than 30 percent per year. As households and firms rushed to purchase new, ever-cheaper computers, software innovations like Windows 95 and Windows 98, together with the invention of the World Wide Web and Web browsers, created new uses for all these computers. Real investment in computer equipment accelerated from an annual growth rate of 20 percent to 40 percent, and this directly translated into faster growth in output per hour of those employees making the computers, since it took only a few extra employees to make the additional computers.

Initially it appeared that most of the productivity growth revival could be explained by the production of computers and other high-tech equipment, but by 1999–2000 the productivity revival had continued long enough and was big enough to require additional explanations. It appeared that productivity growth had increased not just in firms *producing* the high-tech equipment but also in several sectors of the economy that were heavy *users* of the equipment, including the securities industry (where daily trading totals of four billion shares per day became commonplace) as well as wholesale and retail trade.

Why Did Productivity Growth Explode after the High-Tech Investment Boom Collapsed?

The post–1995 period can be divided into two parts. From 1995 to 2000, the stock market boomed and high-tech investment grew rapidly to an unusually high level relative to total GDP. Those who had attributed most of the explanation of the post–1995 productivity revival to New Economy high-tech investment predicted that productivity growth would decline once the investment boom ended. Indeed, the stock market collapsed starting in early 2000, many new "dot.com" Internet companies went out of business, and growth in high-tech investment turned from strongly positive to strongly negative. What was the response of productivity growth?

The answer is given in Figure 11-5 on p. 369. After a brief pause in 2001, actual productivity growth soared in 2002–04, and the green line showing the productivity growth trend rose to 3.5 percent, higher than at any time in the postwar era. How could productivity growth explode upward while high-tech investment was collapsing? Economists searching for answers pointed to several unusual aspects of the 2001–04 period.[23]

1. The 2001 recession was characterized by a much steeper decline in profits than in the previous mild recession of 1990–91. Also, the decline in the stock market was much steeper than a decade earlier. Part of the reason for

---

[22] A separate analysis of the New Economy investment boom and bust appears in Section 16-9. The major papers analyzing the causes of the productivity revival are listed in Chapter 16, footnote 14, on p. 537.

[23] This section summarizes part of Robert J. Gordon, "Exploding Productivity Growth: Context, Causes, and Implications," *Brookings Papers on Economic Activity,* no. 2 (2003) pp. 207–98.

How the Great Inventions Created Economic Growth: Life in the "Bad Old Days"

It was the "second Industrial Revolution" of the late nineteenth century that created the golden age of productivity growth that began around 1910. Indeed, MFP grew at a snail's pace in the nineteenth century; as Brad DeLong of the University of California at Berkeley observed, "Compared to the pace of economic growth in the 20th century, all other centuries—even the 19th . . .—were standing still."[a] To understand the profound sense in which the great inventions of the second Industrial Revolution altered the standard of living of the average American resident during the golden age, we begin with a brief tour of some of the less desirable aspects of living in the late nineteenth century.

Life in the "Bad Old Days"

An eye-opening introduction to the conditions of that era is provided by Otto Bettman, the founder of the famed Bettman photographic archive.[b] Bettman divides the horrors of the past into eleven categories, which for brevity are condensed into four here.

Air, Food, Drink, and Health. The urban streets of the 1870s and 1880s were not just full of horses but also teemed with pigs, which roamed the streets and were tolerated because they ate garbage. In Kansas City, the confusion and stench of patrolling hogs were so penetrating that Oscar Wilde observed, "They made granite eyes weep." The steadily increasing production of animal waste caused the more pessimistic observers to fear that American cities would disappear like Pompeii—but not under ashes. Added to that was acrid industrial smog, as well as sidewalks piled high with kitchen slops, coal dust, and dumped merchandise, which became stirred together in slime after a rain. All of this was made worse in the summer, which was almost as unbearable outdoors as inside, especially with the heavy clothes of the day. Rudyard Kipling said of Chicago, "Having seen it, I desire urgently never to see it again. Its air is dirt." Added to putrid air was the danger of spoiled food—imagine meat and poultry hung unrefrigerated for days, spoiled fruit, bacteria-infected milk, and virtually all types of food suspected of adulteration. Epidemics included yellow fever, scarlet fever, and smallpox. The pain and lack of sanitation in surgery were endemic, and many hospitals were deathtraps.

Motive Power. Before the invention of electricity, urban streets were a chaotic jungle of horse trolleys and horse-drawn conveyances of all types, made even more congested in the winter by horse-drawn snowplows that did little more than move the snow out of the way of the trolleys by dumping it on the sidewalks. Rural life was also no picnic; among its features were isolation, loneliness, and the drudgery of fireplace cooking and laundry done by muscle-power. Travel between cities on railroads was surprisingly dangerous; in 1890 railroad-connected accidents caused 10,000 deaths. Emigrants traveled west on wooden benches in worn-out boxcars attached to freight or cattle trains.

Housing. In 1882, only 2 percent of New York City's houses had water connections. Urban apartments were crowded, damp, airless, and often firetraps. Even middle-class apartment buildings were little more than glorified tenements; families were shelved in layers, with no insulation from the neighbors' cooking smells or babies' squallings. In the slums as many as eight persons shared a single small room.

Working Conditions. Those who have seen the movie "Titanic" may have shared my momentary shock at the working conditions of the sweating laborers shoveling coal into the huge mouths of the ship's boilers. Coal miners, steel workers, and many others worked 60-hour weeks in dirty and dangerous conditions, exposed to suffocating gas and smoke. Danger was not confined to mines or mills; in 1890, one railroad employee was killed for every 300 employed. Sewing in a sweatshop might have been the most oppressive occupation for women but was not as dangerous as soap-packing plants or the manual stripping of tobacco leaves.

The Great Inventions

The transition from these often abysmal living conditions to today's much easier and more pleasant life resulted from the complex interaction of ideas, inventions, and the feedback from growing wealth that allowed poor families to live as well or better than the wealthy did one hundred years earlier. While there were many individual inventions, it helps to group them together into five "clusters" or groups. Each of these clusters had a primary breakthrough invention that occurred during the period 1860–1900.

1. The first great invention in the "Group of Five" is electricity (including electric lights and electric motors), which dates from the simultaneous invention of the electric light bulb in 1879 by Thomas A. Edison in the United States and by Joseph W. Swan in England, and the first power station in 1882. Electricity drastically reduced the price of a lumen of light. Electric motors revolutionized manufacturing by decentralizing the source of power and making possible flexible and portable tools and machines. After a somewhat longer lag, electric motors embodied in consumer appliances eliminated the greatest source of drudgery, manual laundry; through refrigeration, food spoilage was virtually eliminated; and through air conditioning, summers became enjoyable and the southern United States was opened for modern economic development.

2. Sharing the title with electricity for the most important invention that had its main diffusion in the twentieth century is the internal combustion engine, which made possible personal autos, motor transport, and air transport. Grouped in this category are such derivative inventions as the suburb, highway, and supermarket. Gradually eliminated or greatly reduced were many of the ills of the late nineteenth century, from manure to unplowed snow to rural isolation.

3. The third group of great inventions includes petroleum, natural gas, and various processes that "rearrange molecules," including chemicals, plastics, and pharmaceuticals. Some of these inventions were spontaneous, and others were induced by the demands of motor and air transport. They helped to reduce air pollution created by industrial and heating uses of coal, and they made possible many new and improved materials and products, including those that conquered illness and prolonged life. Unlike the discontinuity created by the revolutionary impact of electricity and the internal combustion engine, the development of petroleum, chemicals, and their derivative industries was more of a continuous process dating from the mid-nineteenth century onward.

4. The fourth cluster of great inventions consists of the complex of entertainment, communication, and information innovations that were developed before World War II. This set of inventions that made the world smaller (in a more profound sense than the Internet) can be traced back to the telegraph (1844) and includes the telephone (1876), phonograph (1877), popular photography (1880s and 1890s), radio (1899), motion pictures (1881 to 1888), and television (1911). Television is the only one of these innovations that was diffused into the popular marketplace after World War II. Otherwise, all the rest were well established before World War II and created a quantum leap in the standard of living when a year such as 1939 is compared with a year 50 years earlier.

5. Perhaps the most tangible improvement in the everyday standard of living, besides electric light, came through the rapid spread after 1880 of running water, indoor plumbing, and urban sanitation infrastructure.

The "Group of Five" inventions, in turn, created an increase in per-capita income and wealth during the golden years of productivity growth (1913–72) that allowed an improvement in living standards even in those aspects of consumption where inventions did not play a major role; this was seen particularly in the ability of families to afford many more square feet of shelter (and in the suburbs, more land surrounding that shelter) than in 1880.

[a]Quoted in "A Century of Progress," *Economist* (April 15, 2000), p. 86.
[b]Based on material from Otto Bettman, *The Good Old Days— They Were Really Terrible!* (New York: Random House, 1974).

the sharp decline in both profits and stock prices was a string of accounting and corruption scandals involving corporations such as Enron, Tyco, and Worldcom that had significantly overstated their profits. Because of the sharp downward pressure on profits, business firms embarked on an unprecedented attack on their costs, laying off millions of employees. The resulting "jobless recovery" had as its counterpart sharply rising productivity, as firms learned that they could produce the same amount of output with many fewer employees. We previously introduced the jobless recovery in Figure 2-5 on p. 48, where the "payroll survey" measure of employment (this is the measure used in computing the productivity statistics) exhibits a decline until the end of 2003, fully two years after the end of the recession in output.

2. But how did business firms succeed in producing more output with so many fewer employees? In addition to the profit squeeze and associated cost cutting, another hypothesis centers on *intangible capital*, types of investment that are not included in the measured totals of fixed investment in the GDP data. According to this hypothesis, the investment boom of the late 1990s produced unmeasured intangible capital in the form of improvements of business practices and training of employees to understand and use computers and the Internet. When the high-tech investment boom was over, the intangible capital remained, and the improved business practices and better understanding of what computers and the Internet could do explain how business firms could produce more output with fewer employees.[24]

By the year 2005, the revival in productivity growth had continued for a full decade. Skeptics who had initially dismissed the revival as a temporary phenomenon were silenced, and the debate turned to how long the revival would last and whether the long-run trend in productivity growth would remain as high as the 3.5 percent registered in 2003–04 or would settle back down to 2.5 or 3.0 percent, still very high numbers from the perspective of the 1973–95 slowdown period. If the explosion of productivity growth in 2002–04 was caused by savage corporate cost cutting in reaction to collapsing profits, then the recovery of business profits should bring an end to the jobless recovery, a return to more normal hiring of employees, and a retreat of productivity growth from the superheated performance of 2002–04. Time would tell, but the benefits of the productivity explosion in raising the American standard of living were likely to persist.

Self-Test

Explain how each of the following contributed to the 1973–95 slowdown in labor productivity growth:

1. The increase in women's labor force participation rate.
2. The increase in energy prices during the 1970s.
3. The construction of the interstate highway system in the 1958–85 period.

---

[24] See Susanto Basu et al., "The Case of the Missing Productivity Growth, or Does Information Technology Explain Why Productivity Accelerated in the United States but not in the United Kingdom?" *NBER Macroeconomics Annual 2003*, pp. 9–63.

11-7 Labor Supply Shifts as a Source of Faster or Slower Productivity Growth

We are interested in productivity growth because it is the fundamental cause of increases in the standard of living and of real wages over long periods of time. It is frequently assumed that the problem of slow real wage growth in the United States during the 1973–95 period must have been caused by slow productivity growth during the same period. Indeed, we can use the standard labor market diagram, first introduced in Figure 7-7 on p. 209, to illustrate this assumption.

An Adverse Productivity Shock Reduces the Real Wage, Hours, or Both

The top frame of Figure 11-6 plots the real wage on the vertical axis and the level of labor input (measured in hours) on the horizontal axis. The initial labor demand curve is shown as the dashed line (N_0^d) and slopes downward, reflecting the decline in the marginal product of labor that occurs when more labor input is added while the quantity of other factors of production (not just capital, but also energy and imported materials) remains constant.

Instead of staying in its initial position, two events could cause the labor demand curve to shift downward to a position like N_1^d. First, this shift could occur if the quantity of the other factors of production (in addition to labor) were to decline instead of staying constant. Second, such a downward shift could occur even if the quantity of these other factors of production remained constant—for example, if MFP were to decline (that is, if less output were produced by a given quantity of factors of production). In either case, the new lower labor demand curve is shown by the solid line in the top frame of Figure 11-6. The original level of employment (N_0) could be maintained only at point Z, where the real wage is shown to fall in the same proportion as the vertical downward shift in the labor demand curve.

Is there any escape from the logic that an autonomous decline in labor productivity must cause an equiproportionate decline in the real wage rate, as occurs at point Z? If for some reason the real wage were completely rigid, as at point X, employment could not be maintained at point N_0 but instead would decline to point N_1. Some analysts believe that this outcome occurred in Europe during the 1970s and early 1980s at the time of the adverse supply shocks, and that this helps to explain why unemployment increased so much in Europe relative to the United States during that period.

The Possibility of Feedback from Low Real Wages to Low Productivity

The top frame of Figure 11-6, as we have seen, shows how an adverse shock to labor productivity can cause a decline in the real wage. However, the relation can work in reverse. The bottom frame of Figure 11-6 shows a fixed labor demand curve, which assumes a fixed quantity of factors of production (other than labor) and a fixed level of MFP. Now let us assume that there is an outward shift in the labor supply curve.

What factors might cause such a downward shift? This could be caused by any event that increases the supply of labor, such as a larger workforce

Figure 11-6 The Effect on the Labor Market of an Adverse Productivity Shock and a Downward Shift in Labor Supply

In the top frame, the economy is initially at point B. An adverse productivity shock shifts the labor demand curve downward. If the amount of labor input remains unchanged, the economy moves to point Z, where the real wage is lower than at point B. Another possibility is that the real wage is held fixed, possibly by union contracts, in which case the economy goes to point X, and labor input falls to point N_1. In the bottom frame, a downward shift in the labor supply curve, for reasons suggested in the text, would move the economy from point B to point C along a fixed labor demand curve. Labor input would rise from N_0 to N_2, while the real wage would fall from $(W/P)_0$ to $(W/P)_1$. The marginal product of labor is lower at point C than at point B, implying that average labor productivity is lower as well.

caused by more immigration. Another factor causing such a shift would be any event that reduces the wage at which a given quantity of labor input is willing to work, including a reduction in the power of unions or a reduction in the real minimum wage (which may tend to depress wages for unskilled workers). Increased anxiety workers about job security might also cause such a shift.

If the labor supply curve shifts downward along the labor demand curve, the real wage will decline, but so also will labor productivity.[25] The economy will shift from point B to point C, and the decline in both the real wage and productivity will have been caused by a shift in the labor supply curve rather than a shift in the labor demand curve.

While Figure 11-6 shows why a downward shift in the *levels* of labor productivity and the real wage are related, caused either by a downward shift in labor supply or labor demand, the same logic applies to the growth rates of labor productivity and the real wage. For instance, growth in labor productivity and the real wage could be held down by inadequate growth in capital input, whether that takes the form of slow growth in physical capital, in forms of human capital such as education and training, or in government-financed infrastructure such as highways and airports.

Similarly, any event that stimulates the *growth* of labor supply can hold down the growth rates of labor productivity and the real wage, including steady growth in the labor force caused by immigration, or a shift in labor's bargaining position resulting from a decline in the strength of labor unions. Some observers interpret the steady increase in foreign trade, sometimes called the globalization of the world economy, as having the effect of creating competition between foreign workers and domestic U.S. workers, thus weakening the position of U.S. workers. This would directly slow the growth of the real wage and indirectly, as in the bottom frame of Figure 11-6, slow the growth rate of productivity.

> **Self-Test**
>
> For each of the following events, indicate whether it shifts the labor demand curve or the labor supply curve, and whether the shift is to the left or right. In addition, how does each event affect labor productivity and real wages?
>
> 1. College tuition becomes more expensive, causing some students to drop out and look for work.
> 2. Tighter rules prevent immigration of unskilled workers.
> 3. The real price of oil declines.
> 4. A tax on equipment investment makes it more expensive to purchase equipment.

11-8 Case Study

The Productivity Growth Contrast Between Europe and the United States

American travelers to several of the more prosperous European countries, including France, Germany, and Sweden, notice interesting differences. For instance, it is much less common in Europe for supermarkets to employ baggers

---

[25] The labor demand curve is drawn on the assumption that the real wage equals the marginal product of labor. When the marginal product of labor declines, as from point B to point C in the bottom frame of Figure 11-6, the average product of labor (Y/N) declines as well. In the special case of the Cobb-Douglas production function, the change in the average product of labor is proportional to that of the marginal product.

in addition to checkout cashiers. Parking lots are more likely to be fully automated than to employ attendants. Valet parking services are nowhere to be seen. The bus boy occupation—clearing and setting tables—that is so prevalent in American restaurants at the middle-price and high-price level is largely absent in similar restaurants in these European countries.

These observations are symptoms of a broader set of differences in the evolution of the economies of the United States and leading European nations over the last two decades. While the United States lagged behind Europe in the growth of real wages and in productivity during the 1973–95 period, the United States had a much superior record in achieving growth in jobs and maintaining a relatively low unemployment rate.

Europe Catches Up, Then Falls Back

Figure 11-7 displays the *level* of productivity in Europe and in the United States. During the long period when American productivity was growing slowly, Europe caught up from 71 percent of the American level in 1973 to 93

Figure 11-7 Level of Labor Productivity in Europe and the United States, 1970–2004

The level of productivity in the United States is displayed as an index number with 1995 = 100. The level of productivity in the 15 members of the pre–2004 European Union is displayed as an index number with 1995 = 93, based on evidence that in 1995 European productivity was roughly 7 percent below that of the United States. The level of productivity of Europe had almost caught up to that in the United States by 1995, but after 2001 the level of productivity in Europe slipped back relative to the United States.

percent in 1995. During this period, as we learn in this section, Europeans emphasized policies that made labor expensive to employ, as shown along the initial labor supply curve in the bottom frame of Figure 11-6. As a result, in Europe employment grew slowly but productivity grew rapidly as firms tried to minimize their use of labor input to avoid its high cost. The United States during this period was operating along the new labor supply curve in the bottom frame of Figure 11-6, pursuing policies that made it cheap for firms to hire unskilled labor, leading to many low-wage jobs but also leading to the slow productivity growth.

After 1995, productivity growth in the United Stated revived, as we learned in Section 11-6. This occurred not because the United States changed its labor market policies, and indeed immigration increased steadily throughout the 1990s. What changed in the United States was an upward shift in the labor demand curve, due to the productivity enhancing effects of high-tech investment in computer and telecommunications hardware and software. Despite the influence of this New Economy investment, Europe's level of productivity grew at the same rate, and so in 2001 Europe still achieved a productivity level equal to 93 percent of that of the United States.

However, during 2001–04, productivity growth in the United States was much faster than in Europe, and so the level of European productivity in Figure 11-7 fell back from 93 to 89 percent. Europe did not experience the drastic decline in profits and in the stock market, or the collapse of high-tech investment, that occurred in the United States. The jobless recovery of the U.S. economy, which combined rising output with falling employment, did not occur to the same extent in Europe.

Different Institutions in Europe and the United States

The long period during 1973–95 of slow productivity growth and rapid employment growth in the United States compared to Europe reflected systematic differences in institutions and policies. The United States has relatively weak labor unions, a relatively low and declining real minimum wage, and substantial competition for low-skilled jobs from legal and illegal immigrants. In some countries like France it is very expensive to hire low-skilled workers, because of a high minimum wage and high payroll taxes that finance government-supported medical care and old-age pensions.

As these differences in labor market policies fostered a catching up of European productivity toward the U.S. level in 1973–95, Europe suffered from the lack of employment growth that was the counterpart of a strong productivity performance. Employment stagnated, unemployment was high, the average duration of unemployment was much longer than in the United States, job prospects for young people were bleak, labor force participation languished, and many workers were encouraged to retire at young ages compared to the United States. Europeans also reacted to the scarcity of jobs by taking longer vacations than in the United States, in effect spreading the available work among more people.

How Could Europe Be So Productive Yet So Poor?

As a result, the European standard of living did not catch up toward the U.S. level, despite the catching up of productivity. Why did this occur? We come full circle back to the first equation in this chapter, repeated here for convenience:

$$y - q - (y - n) = n - q. \tag{11.1}$$

Here the growth rate of output is y, the growth rate of labor hours is n, and the growth rate of the population is q. The reason that the European standard of living $(y - q)$ grew more slowly than labor productivity $(y - n)$ is that labor hours per member of the population $(n - q)$ experienced negative growth. Long vacations, high unemployment, low labor force participation, and early retirement meant that Europeans worked many fewer hours per member of the population than occurred in the United States.

Since 1995 and especially since 2001, the United States has enjoyed a revival of productivity growth. Until 2001 Europe maintained the same pace of productivity growth, but since 2001 the United States has pulled away. What factors explain the failure of Europe to achieve the 2002–04 U.S. productivity explosion? We pointed above to European labor market institutions making it expensive to employ low-skilled workers. A different set of European institutions appears to contribute to Europe's poor productivity performance in the first part of this decade.

Much of the U.S. productivity revival has occurred in wholesale and retail trade, and within those industries the big productivity gains have been achieved by large new stores (so-called big boxes) in suburbs and at freeway interchanges operated by Wal-Mart, Target, Home Depot, Best Buy, and other nationwide retailers. The European retailing industry has not participated in this productivity boom to the same extent, because of differing European institutions. European zoning or land use regulations are much more restrictive than in the United States, and there is substantial political pressure in Europe to preserve small, inefficient stores in the city center. More generally in Europe, differences in national customs and languages make it harder for retailers to expand across all of Europe, and regulations make it more difficult to start new businesses.

To summarize, during the 1973–95 period Europe's productivity level almost caught up with the United States, but the same factors that made productivity high caused labor input per member of the population to be low, causing the European standard of living to stagnate relative to the United States. More recently since 2001, Europe has failed to emulate the United States productivity growth explosion, and its standard of living has started to decline as a percentage of the United States level.

11-9 Conclusion on the Great Questions of Growth

This chapter takes us considerably further toward an understanding of economic growth than did the simple theories examined in Chapter 10. We have learned that the achievement of economic growth requires more than simply saving and investment in physical capital and then sitting back to wait for the fruits of exogenous and automatic technological progress. Economies do not obtain technical progress for free, but only through a costly process of research, development, and invention. Without a continual stream of important inventions since the year 1800, continuing investments in steam engines and wooden plows would have left productivity little better than it was in that year. Most of today's standard of living relies on inventions of products and processes, including the railroad, internal combustion engine, and electricity, that did not exist in 1800.

Poor countries can obtain technological innovations that originated in rich countries by copying the innovation, by importing it, or by encouraging investment by foreign firms that bring technology with them. But some poor nations are better able than others to obtain technology through these channels. We have seen that governments can encourage growth by promoting education, by building political capital that minimizes diversion (including theft, bribes, and corruption), and by developing infrastructure capital. Yet even the most enlightened governments still face special obstacles to growth if their countries are located in the tropics. This makes the growth achievement of such tropical East Asian countries as Thailand and Singapore especially impressive.

Closer to home, American students may sympathize with the continuing struggle of poor nations, but they also are interested in the outlook for their own standard of living. Will their standard of living stagnate or double within a single generation? For two decades between 1973 and 1995, the growth in U.S. productivity was much slower than before 1973, and growth in real wages stagnated. While some explanations of this productivity slowdown period are unconvincing, it appears that differing labor market institutions constitute a unifying theme explaining faster productivity growth in Europe than in the United States over 1973–95, combined with slower European growth in employment and hours of labor input.

The post–1995 U.S. productivity revival has occurred despite labor market institutions that make it easy for American firms to hire low-skilled labor. The first phase of the revival through the year 2000 represented the beneficial effects on productivity of the New Economy boom in high-tech computer and telecommunications investment. The surprising American explosion in productivity growth in 2002–04, despite the collapse of New Economy investment, is still not clearly understood. Part of the explanation stresses a collapse in profits that unleashed unusually savage cost cutting as firms were forced to produce more output with fewer workers. Another related explanation is that many new business practices were made possible by the pervasive spread of computers and invention of the World Wide Web, and that learning by business firms made possible by high-tech investment in the 1990s carried over to make possible faster productivity growth during 2002–04.

Summary

1. The big questions of economic growth are the continuing income gap between the rich and poor countries, the sources of growth "miracles" of formerly poor countries, and the cause of productivity growth slowdowns and revivals within the group of rich nations.

2. The standard of living is output per person or per capita, labor productivity is output per hour, and multifactor productivity is output per weighted input of labor and capital together. The growth rates of labor productivity and of the real wage are equal if labor's share in the national income remains constant.

3. While convergence of poor countries to the income levels of rich countries is predicted by the Solow growth model of Chapter 10, it has not happened in fact for many poor countries. While the Solow model predicts that poor nations should grow faster than rich nations, fully half of the poor nations in 1960 grew more slowly than the United States from 1960 to 1990.

4. Poor countries typically invest a smaller share of their incomes than rich countries and have low amounts of human capital. Yet low investment in physical and human capital may be as much a consequence of poverty as a cause of it. Low levels of education prevent the poorest countries from utilizing advances in technology developed by the rich nations.

5. Poor countries can obtain modern technology by copying it, by importing machinery embodying modern technology, or by attracting foreign investment by firms that bring modern technology with them. Each of these methods confronts obstacles, since modern technology is hard to copy, some countries are too poor to import it, and some countries are unattractive as locations for foreign investment.
6. Impediments to growth that handicap many poor countries include "diversion" (crime, bribery, corruption), inadequate infrastructure (poor highways, inadequate telephone systems), and geographical handicaps, particularly location in the tropics and lack of access to ports on an ocean.
7. The post–1973 productivity growth slowdown remains a puzzle. Among the explanations that do not adequately explain the slowdown are slower growth in capital per hour, higher prices of energy, a decline in labor quality, slower growth of infrastructure, running out of resources and ideas, and problems of measurement in the service sector.
8. The post–1995 productivity growth revival in the United States was initially caused by a faster rate of decline in computer prices and the invention of new ways to use computers, particularly the Internet and the World Wide Web. But, the productivity growth revival continued in 2002–04 even after computer investment stopped growing, suggesting that some of the benefits of high-tech investment in the late 1990s were having delayed favorable impacts several years later.
9. Slower growth in both productivity and the real wage rate can be caused either by adverse shocks to productivity or shocks to labor supply that have the effect of reducing the wage rate at which people are willing to work. Such shocks to labor supply include the declining influence of unions, a declining real minimum wage, low-skill immigration, and the role of global competition.

Concepts

infrastructure   standard of living   labor productivity

Questions

1. What is the significance of the modifier "multi-factor" in "multi-factor productivity"?
2. Under what conditions will labor's share of national income grow? Decline? Remain constant over time?
3. Does the empirical evidence validate the predictions of the Solow model regarding convergence? Explain.
4. Is it true that a high investment rate is a precondition for convergence?
5. What is the relationship between real wages and labor productivity? How would real wages and labor productivity be affected by:
   (a) an increase in the quantity of other productive factors (such as capital, energy, and raw materials) used in production;
   (b) a decline in the size of the workforce resulting from lower rates of population growth and immigration?
   Is the cause-and-effect relationship between real wages and productivity the same in each case? Explain in terms of shifts in the labor demand and labor supply curves.
6. Explain what is meant by *diversion*. Discuss why governments tolerate or engage in diversion.
7. Explain how political capital, infrastructure, and geography affect growth in per-capita income.
8. "Because each factor of production is paid its marginal product, the fraction of the population engaged in research and development is economically optimal." Comment.
9. This chapter discusses a number of explanations offered for the 1973–95 productivity growth slowdown. For each one, analyze whether the explanation offered affected the growth rate of inputs or multi-factor productivity.
10. Discuss how the reasons for the post–1995 revival of productivity growth were different for the 1995–2000 period as contrasted to the 2000–04 period.
11. Explain what is meant by *intangible capital* and what it has in common with and how it differs from human capital.
12. Explain why the rise in per-capita income that resulted from the "great inventions" underestimates the improvement in the quality of life that they caused.
13. "Restrictive monetary policy will lower the rate of labor productivity growth. Restrictive fiscal policy, on the other hand, will raise it." Is this statement true, false, or uncertain? Explain.
14. Convinced that strong measures must be taken to stimulate productivity growth, Senator Progrowth in-

troduces a bill to increase federal government spending on education by $150 billion. Why might those who agree with the senator about the importance of economic growth nonetheless question the wisdom of this legislation?

15. Discuss how the contrast between Europe and the United States in terms of growth in productivity and standards of living is due to differences in:
    (a) shifts in the demand for and supply of labor,
    (b) institutions and policies.

Problems

1. Calculate the growth rates of output (y) and labor productivity ($y - n$) in each of the following scenarios. Assume that the share of capital in total income (b) is 0.25.

(a)

y	a	k	n	$y - n$
—	2.5	2	1	—
—	2.0	2	1	—
—	1.5	2	1	—
—	1.0	2	1	—

(b)

y	a	k	n	$y - n$
—	2.5	2.0	1	—
—	2.5	1.5	1	—
—	2.5	1.0	1	—
—	2.5	0.5	1	—

(c)

y	a	k	n	$y - n$
—	2.5	2.0	1.0	—
—	2.5	2.0	1.5	—
—	2.5	2.0	2.0	—
—	2.5	2.0	2.5	—

Based on your calculations, what happens to output growth and labor productivity growth as MFP growth declines, capital input growth declines, and labor input growth increases, holding the other variables constant? Are these the results you would expect? Why or why not?

2. Suppose that in Country 1 the growth rates of multifactor productivity (a), capital (k), and labor (n) are 2.5, 3, and 1 percent per year, respectively, and that capital's share of output (b) equals 0.25. Initially output per hour equals 40 in Country 1 and 10 in Country 2.
   (a) Calculate the labor productivity growth rate in County 1.
   (b) Calculate output per hour in Country 1 at the end of 10, 20, and 30 years.
   (c) Suppose that the labor productivity grows 4 times as fast in Country 2 as it does in Country 1 for the first 10 years, 3 times as fast for the second 10 years, and twice as fast for the third 10 years. Calculate output per hour in Country 2 at the end of 10, 20, and 30 years.
   (d) Calculate Country 2's output per hour as a percentage of Country 1's output per hour at the end of 10, 20, and 30 years. Are these calculations consistent with the predictions of the Solow growth model?

3. (a) Suppose labor productivity and the GDP deflator are growing at 2 percent per year. For labor's share of income to remain constant, how fast must nominal wages be increasing?
   (b) Suppose that labor productivity growth declines to 1.2 percent per year. What happens to labor's share of income if the growth rates in nominal wages and the GDP deflator are unchanged? Suppose that the Fed keeps the rate of inflation constant. What must the new growth rate of nominal wages be for labor's share of income to remain constant?
   (c) Suppose that labor productivity growth improves to 3 percent per year. What happens to labor's share of income if the rates of growth in nominal wages and the GDP deflator are unchanged? Suppose that the Fed keeps the rate of inflation constant. What must the new growth rate in nominal wages be for labor's share of income to remain constant?

4. A business firm has a choice of two countries in which to undertake a project. The governments of Country 1 and Country 2 are honest and corrupt, respectively, in the sense that unlike Country 2, there is no diversion in Country 1. The startup costs of the two projects are $2 million and $2.1 million in Country 1 and Country 2, respectively. Neither project will yield any profits this year. The profits in Country 1 over the next two years equal $1.050 million and $1.764 million. The profits in Country 2 over the next two years equal $1.260 million and $1.9845 million. The interest rate equals 5 percent.
   (a) Show that the firm is better off undertaking the project in Country 2 if there is no diversion there.
   (b) For the firm to continue to undertake the project in Country 2, what is the maximum amount of diversion that Country 2 can force the firm to pay?

5. You are given the production function $Y = AK^{1/5}R^{1/5}H^{1/5}N^{2/5}$, where K represents physical capital, R represents infrastructure capital, and H represents human capital. Convert this to a function relating Y/N to K/N, R/N, and H/N. Now consider two countries that have access to the same information on technology, the same quality and quantity of labor and capital of each type, as well as the same production function given above. Both countries are geographically similar. However, the first country, Country 1, has per person output 10 times as high as the second country, Country 2. The only relevant difference between the two countries is that the same fraction of the capital of each type in Country 2 is diverted to unproductive activity, while there is no diversion in Country 1. Find the fraction of the per person capital of each type that is being diverted.

6. Suppose that in Country 1 the growth rates of multifactor productivity (a), capital (k), labor (n), and population (q) are 3, 3.4, 1, and 1 percent per year, respectively, and that capital's share of output (b) equals 0.25. The growth rates of capital (k), labor (n), and population (q) are 3.8, 1, and 2 percent per year, respectively, in Country 2, while capital's share of output (b) is the same as in Country 1.
   (a) Calculate the growth rates of labor productivity, output, and output per capita in County 1.
   (b) If Country 2 is to have the same growth rate of output per capita as Country 1, calculate Country 2's growth rates of multifactor productivity, labor productivity, and output. (*Hint:* What must the growth of output be in Country 2 for it to have the same rate of growth in output per capita as Country 1?)

Self-Test Answers

p. 353 $y = 5.75; n = 0; k = 9$. In each case labor productivity growth ($y - n$) exceeds MFP growth (a), because in each case the growth of capital per worker ($k - n$) is positive. The growth of capital per worker increases the growth of output relative to labor input, which is what labor productivity growth measures, but it does not increase the growth of output relative to *all* inputs, which is what MFP growth measures.

p. 360 (1) An increase in the saving rate increases the level of per-person output and capital. (2) An increase in the saving rate has no effect on the growth rate of output per capita in the long run. (3) An increase in the rate of population growth reduces the level of per-person output and capital. (4) An increase in the rate of population growth has no long-run effect on the growth rate of output per capita.

p. 376 (1) Increases the growth rate of labor inputs relative to that of capital and other inputs, which reduces the growth of output relative to labor input and thus reduces the growth rate of productivity. (2) Reduces purchases of energy inputs, which makes labor less productive and reduces labor productivity growth. (3) The construction of the interstate highway system increased productivity growth by raising infrastructure capital, most obviously by allowing truck drivers to drive larger trucks at faster speeds.

p. 379 (1) More workers will be available at any given real wage rate, so the labor supply curve shifts to the right, representing an increase in labor supply. Real wages and labor productivity fall. (2) Fewer immigrant workers will be available at any given real wage rate, so the labor supply curve shifts to the left. Real wages and labor productivity rise. (3) With greater availability of energy resources, more workers will be demanded at any given real wage rate, so the labor demand curve shifts to the right. Labor productivity and real wages rise. (4) With less investment in new equipment, fewer workers will be demanded at any given real wage rate, so the labor demand curve shifts to the left. Labor productivity and real wages fall.

CHAPTER 12

The Government Budget, the Public Debt, and Social Security

In contrast to the original notion of activist fiscal stabilization policy, the budget decisions are now regarded as important because of their long-term effects on resource allocation.
—Martin S. Feldstein, 1988

12-1 Introduction: The Government Budget and Long-Run Economic Growth

This chapter is about the long-run aspects of fiscal policy. Should the government budget be balanced every year, on average over the business cycle, or not at all? The United States has run persistent government budget deficits year after year since 1980, except for the brief period between 1998 and 2001. What difference does it make if the government runs a surplus or deficit? What will be the long-run consequences of allowing the post–2001 deficits to continue? Will a persistent government budget deficit cause the public debt to explode without limit?

In addition to concern about the persistent deficit in basic government operations, in this decade increasing attention has been paid to the future problems of the Social Security transfer payment system. Social Security faces problems that stem from fluctuations in the U.S. birth rate over the postwar era. The birth rate was much higher during the "baby boom" years of 1947–63 than in any period before or after. The retirement of the baby boom generation, starting around the year 2012, will gradually raise the share of the retirement population receiving Social Security benefits and reduce the share of the working-age population paying the Social Security taxes that make those benefits possible. As benefits rise relative to tax revenues, the Social Security system is projected to run out of money at some point in the future, around 2050, and a great debate has begun about a range of possible solutions.

Most economists now agree that monetary policy is better suited than fiscal policy for controlling short-run fluctuations in real GDP, because the Federal Reserve is able to make decisions about monetary policy much faster than Congress and the administration can make decisions about fiscal policy. If monetary policy succeeds in stabilizing real GDP at the desired level of output—that is, at natural real GDP (Y^N)—then fiscal policy by default becomes responsible for the level of real interest rates. This is seen in the analysis of the mix of monetary and fiscal policy in Figure 4-10 on p. 117.

Stated another way, as we learned in Section 5-7, monetary policy has a *short-run orientation* toward the smoothing of business cycles in real GDP. In contrast, fiscal policy has a *long-run orientation* toward the level of real interest rates, which in turn have a major influence on the long-run growth rates of productivity and real output per person. This means that the government can use fiscal policy as a key tool to influence the economy's long-run growth rate.

This chapter begins by reviewing the relationship between the government budget deficit or surplus and the national saving rate, which influences the rate of economic growth. Then we examine the link between the government budget and the growth or shrinkage of the public debt. Does the debt impose a future burden on society? What is the history of the debt in the United States, and is it unusually high compared to that of other industrialized nations?

After discussing relations between the government budget surplus or deficit and the public debt, we examine some of the debates over whether large deficits are harmful and large surpluses should be encouraged, and then examine the Social Security debate and the pros and cons of possible solutions.

12-2 Long-Run Effects of Fiscal Policy on Economic Growth and Welfare

Already in Chapters 3 and 4 we have discussed the economy's *short-run* response to changes in fiscal policy, that is, in government expenditures and tax rates. Now we are ready to study the impact of fiscal policy on the rate of *long-run* economic growth. The key link between fiscal policy and long-run growth comes through the effect of the government budget on the national saving rate (data on the budget and national saving were discussed on pp. 138–46).

In Chapter 10 we concluded that an increase in the national saving rate is likely to stimulate economic growth, at least in the intermediate run of, say, the next decade or so. In this case, then, society must decide whether or not to save more, which requires the sacrifice of consumption *now* to obtain extra consumption *in the future*. This choice depends on society's **rate of time preference**, the extra amount people would be willing to pay to have consumption goods now instead of in the future. For instance, if people are willing to pay $1.05 to obtain a good today that they could have for $1.00 one year from now, then they are said to have a rate of time preference of 5 percent.

The **rate of time preference** is the extra amount a consumer would be willing to pay to be able to obtain a given quantity of consumption goods now rather than a year from now.

Raise Saving or Do Nothing?

Figure 12-1 illustrates two of the choices open to society, paths A and B. The green path A reflects a do-nothing policy that maintains the growth rate of per person consumption after time t_0 at the same rate as before. The red path B reflects a policy that deliberately raises the incentive to save and invest at time t_0 while reducing the incentive to consume. Initially, consumption along path B drops below path A by an amount shown by the blue shading. But then the higher rate of investment makes the capital stock grow faster, thus increasing future output and income. Consumption begins to grow faster along path B than path A, eventually catching up at time t_1 and moving ahead thereafter. The question for growth policy is: Which path is better, A or B?

If the rate of return on extra capital investment is greater than society's rate of time preference, then $1 shifted from present consumption to investment will yield enough future consumption to be worthwhile. For instance, if the rate of return is 10 percent, $1 less of consumption today will yield $1.10 next year. If the rate of time preference is less than 10 percent, say 5 percent, then people are equally happy with $1.05 next year and $1 this year, so that clearly they would prefer $1.10 next year to $1 this year. In this situation, with a rate of

Figure 12-1 Two Alternative Paths of Consumption per Person

Before time t_0, both paths involve exactly the same consumption per person. Along path A, consumption per person continues to grow at the same steady rate after time t_0. But along path B, a policy decision is made to consume less in order to save and invest more. At first, between time t_0 and t_1, consumption along path B drops below path A by an amount shown by the blue shading. Then, after t_1 (and forever thereafter), consumption along path B exceeds that along path A, as shown by the red shading.

return higher than the rate of time preference (sometimes called the rate at which individuals "discount" future consumption), society should save more and consume less, as along path B. This principle can be stated as follows: *The United States saves too little if the rate at which individuals discount future consumption is less than the rate of return on private investment.*

In recent years the real rate of return on private investment in the corporate sector has been about 12 percent, and the rate of time preference of individuals is less than that. How much less? The *real* interest rate on corporate bonds was roughly 4 percent in 2005. Many individuals have been willing to save despite the relatively low real interest rates available to them. Thus it is accurate to say that the United States now saves too little, because a dollar diverted from present consumption to present saving could earn a real return of about 12 percent, more than the real return after taxes now earned by most savers. People would want to save more if they were offered a real return of 12 percent than they save now at a real return of 4 percent or less.

National Saving, Economic Growth, and the Government Budget Deficit

To boost the growth rate of output and productivity, fiscal policy must raise the rate of national saving, which in turn would boost the growth rate of output. By definition, **national saving** is simply the sum of private saving and government saving. A government budget surplus is the same as government saving, while a government budget deficit is treated as *negative* government saving. Thus at any given amount of private saving, the larger the government budget deficit, *the more is subtracted from private saving—that is, the lower is the national saving rate.*

We have already learned to express national saving in the magic equation, originally introduced in Chapter 2 and used in equation (5.5) on p. 139 to examine national saving (NS). Using the familiar symbols:

$$S + (T - G) \equiv I + NX,$$
$$NS \equiv I + NX \qquad (12.1)$$

In words, this states that national saving on the left-hand side must be equal to the sum of domestic and foreign investment ($I + NX$) on the right-hand side.

National saving is the sum of private saving and government saving.

A reduction in national saving must reduce the sum of domestic and foreign investment. The only way that domestic investment can be maintained intact when national saving decreases is for the decline in national saving to be *completely offset* by a decline in foreign investment or increase in foreign borrowing. As we learned in Figure 5-7 on p. 143, this complete offset may occur in a small open economy but not in a large open economy like the United States. Instead, in a large open economy a decline in national saving caused by a higher government budget deficit must cause *both* a decline in domestic investment and an increase in foreign borrowing. Such an event will reduce the rate of economic growth for two reasons. First, less domestic investment implies a slower future growth rate (Path A instead of Path B in Figure 12-1). Second, higher foreign borrowing requires the nation's residents to make interest payments to foreigners in future years, thus reducing the growth of their own consumption expenditures.

To stimulate growth, the national saving rate needs to be raised, which means either that private saving or the government budget surplus must be increased. In choosing methods to raise the government budget surplus, policymakers should take care that the larger surplus is not accompanied by a reduction in private saving. For instance, attempting to raise the surplus by raising income tax rates will reduce the after-tax return to private saving. The beneficial boost to national saving caused by the higher budget surplus will be partly offset by a decline in private saving. To achieve an increase in national saving, a preferable method would be to raise taxes on consumption (rather than income) or reduce government expenditures in order to boost the government budget surplus.

The ultimate aim of policies to boost the rate of national saving is to increase the ratio of investment to real GDP. However, the types of investment that contribute to growth include not just private expenditures on machines and structures but also government investment, for instance on education or highways. Thus policymakers attempting to boost growth should either boost taxes on consumption or cut expenditures on government consumption rather than cutting government investment.

Self-Test

Would the following events raise or lower national saving as a percent of GDP?

1. An increase in federal spending on military aircraft without any change in tax rates.
2. An increase in sales taxes on food.
3. A reduction in income taxes.
4. An increase in the amount that can be contributed to tax-free retirement plans.

12-3 The Future Burden of the Government Debt

We have already learned that a higher government budget surplus raises national saving, holding other factors constant. Similarly, a higher government budget deficit reduces national saving, holding other factors constant. Each extra dollar of government deficit requires the government to issue one more dollar of government debt. We ask in this section whether the additional dollars of government debt are harmful. How do we assess the impact on the well-being of future generations implied by these extra dollars of government debt?

Government investment projects, such as the construction of hospitals, schools, and public universities, generate a future return, consisting of the benefits to future generations created by the project. Whether or not the government debt is a burden depends partly on whether the extra dollars of government debt pay for government expenditures on investment goods or for consumption goods. There is no burden if the government deficit finances productive government investment projects. In this case, the government acts just like a private corporation, say IBM, which pays for much of its new plant and equipment by selling bonds to the public.

But there is a burden if the extra dollars of government debt pay for consumption goods that yield no future benefits. Such expenditures would include, for instance, ammunition fired at target practice by soldiers or groceries purchased by recipients of Social Security benefits. These consumption expenditures have value for their recipients at the current time but not in the future.

The Burden of the IBM Debt

What is the difference between the "burden of the IBM debt" and the "burden of the government debt"? No one has ever accused IBM of creating a burden on future generations by issuing bonds, and for good reason. Like any other corporation, IBM is in business to make a profit for its stockholders. It attempts to estimate the future rate of return on each planned investment project, that is, the annual future profit likely to be contributed by each project divided by its cost. When each project is ranked in order of its rate of return, IBM is ready to make its investment decisions. Projects with rates of return greater than the interest rate that IBM must pay to sell bonds (IBM's borrowing rate, say r_0) are approved. Projects with a rate of return below the borrowing rate (r_0) are rejected.

The contribution to revenue and expenses of the marginal IBM project is summarized on the first line of Table 12-1. Net of all operating expenses (labor, materials, fuel, and so forth), the marginal project generates a rate of return (r_0) just equal to the borrowing rate (r_0), and thus contributes zero to net profit.[1] There is no burden on present or future generations. Individuals make voluntary purchases of IBM bonds without compulsion. Thus in the present generation everyone acts voluntarily in his or her own best interests, and there is no burden on anyone.

In future generations the bondholders receive the interest payments that induced them to purchase the bonds in the first place. Where does IBM obtain the money to pay the interest payments? By definition the marginal investment project creates exactly enough revenue (over and above operating costs) to pay the interest costs.

---

[1] This discussion neglects explicit consideration of corporation and personal income taxes. The IBM rate of return on line 1 can be calculated after payment of corporate income taxes. Although personal income taxes must be paid on interest payments to individuals by both IBM and the government, this factor makes no essential difference in the discussion.

Table 12-1 Comparison of Consequences of IBM Debt with Those of Public Debt

	(1) Rate of return	(2) Interest payment	(3) Net of interest return
1. IBM marginal investment project	r_0	r_0	0
2. Government marginal investment project	r_0	r_0	0
3. Government deficit-financed consumption expenditure	0	r_0	$-r_0$

If the government chooses to invest only in projects yielding future benefits to society that on an annual basis equal or exceed the government's borrowing rate, then the bonds floated to finance government investment projects are exactly analogous to IBM bonds. Stated another way, it is fair and equitable to finance government investment projects by deficit spending, since this will ensure that those who receive some of the benefits from the projects in the future help pay some of the costs (through their future tax payments). As illustrated on line 2 of Table 12-1, the marginal government investment project generates a rate of return in the form of future benefits to society that just suffice to pay the interest on the government bonds. If the interest rate on government bonds—like that on IBM bonds—is r_0, and the social rate of return of the government investment project is the same rate r_0, there are no future burdens on society. The IBM bond and the government bond are identical.

True Burdens of the Debt

The true burden on future generations is created by government spending that is financed by deficits rather than tax revenues and pays for goods that yield no future benefits, or benefits less than their social opportunity cost—for example, meals currently consumed by members of the armed forces. As illustrated on line 3 of Table 12-1, absolutely nothing is generated in the future as a rate of return; all benefits accrue in the present. The government must pay interest to keep bondholders happy, just as IBM must pay interest, yet in current government deficit-financed consumption there is no future benefit or income to pay the interest. Future taxpayers are forced to hand over extra payments to the government to cover the interest cost on the debt, and the taxpayers receive no benefit in return. Similarly, investment projects such as highways may impose a burden if their benefits are less than their social opportunity costs, such as for a little-used highway.

12-4 Will the Government Remain Solvent?

How can we tell if a government budget deficit in the United States or in some other country is too high? In this section we take a different approach to answer this question. What matters, according to this approach, is not whether the deficit is zero, but rather the criterion of stabilizing the ratio of the outstanding nominal federal debt (D) to nominal GDP (PY). The federal deficit can be quite large, yet the D/PY ratio can nevertheless remain stable instead of rise.

This paradox seems less mysterious when we recognize that the nominal government budget deficit is equal to the change in the debt (ΔD). How large can the deficit be and keep the debt-GDP ratio, D/PY, constant? It will remain constant as long as the *growth rate* of the debt-GDP ratio is zero.

Thus, our task is to determine what size deficit will keep the growth rate of the debt-GDP ratio equal to zero. We begin by noting that the growth rate of the debt-GDP ratio (D/PY) is the difference between the growth rate in debt (d) and the growth rate in nominal GDP ($p + y$):

$$\text{Growth of } \frac{D}{PY} = d - (p + y) \tag{12.2}$$

For stability in the debt-GDP ratio, we need the growth rate of debt (d) equal to the growth rate of nominal GDP ($p + y$):

$$d = p + y \tag{12.3}$$

When we multiply both sides of equation (12.3) by the size of the debt (D), we obtain the allowable deficit (that is, addition to debt) that is consistent with keeping the debt-GDP ratio constant:

$$\begin{array}{cc} \text{General Form} & \text{Numerical Example} \\ dD = (p + y)D & (0.05)(\$4{,}500 \text{ billion}) = \$225 \text{ billion} \end{array} \tag{12.4}$$

This simple expression (12.4) leads to a surprising conclusion: *The debt-GDP ratio remains constant if the deficit equals the outstanding debt times the growth rate of nominal GDP.* In the numerical example, federal government debt in the year 2005 is about $4,500 billion; that times an assumed growth rate of nominal GDP in 2005 of about 5 percent equals an "allowable deficit" of $225 billion.[2] Since the 2005 deficit was about $400 billion—well above the allowable amount of $225 billion—the implication is that the debt-GDP ratio was rising in 2005. Indeed, we will see in Figure 12-2 (p. 396) that the debt-GDP ratio declined from 1993 to 2001 and then increased in each year after 2001.[3]

But what is the optimum debt-GDP ratio? Should the ratio be stable? Is there any reason why the debt-GDP ratio should not be allowed to rise, as it did after 2001?

The Solvency Condition

Surely there is a limit to the size of the government debt, expressed as a percentage of GDP. The government must pay interest on the debt held by the public in the form of bonds. Some observers have pointed out that it is possible for the government to pay the interest on its outstanding debt by issuing more bonds. A typical bondholder holding $100,000 in bonds, let us call her

---

[2] The assumed 5.0 percent growth rate of nominal GDP ($p + y$) in this example is the sum of the rate of inflation (p) that seemed likely to occur in the 2004–05 period, assumed to be 2.0 percent, plus the growth rate of natural real GDP (y^N) of 3.0 percent. The debt of $4,500 billion in 2005 refers to the debt held by the public (excluding debt held by the Federal Reserve and government trust funds).

[3] Data in this chapter on the total debt refer to the federal government, but data on deficits in this book refer to the combined federal, state, and local governments. The combined budget and the federal budget both moved from deficit to surplus in 1998 and back to deficit in 2002 and thereafter. To find the latest data on government expenditures, revenue, and the government deficit, go to http://www.bea.gov/bea/dn/nipaweb/index.asp, then click on "list of all NIPA tables," then select section 3, then Table 3.1.

International Perspective

The Debt-GDP Ratio: How Does the United States Compare?

As shown in the accompanying figure, the debt-GDP ratio almost doubled in the United States between the mid-1970s and mid-1990s before it began to decline. How does this experience compare with other countries? The figure displays debt-GDP ratios for two European countries, Germany and Italy. The ratio for Germany became larger than in the United States after 1997.

In Italy, the ratio is much higher than in the United States. The rapidly growing ratio between 1970 and 1994 reflected persistent government deficits that were at least twice as large as those in the United States at that time. One reason for the large deficits in Italy is the political system; because political support is splintered among numerous parties, under the parliamentary system it is possible to form a government only through a coalition among several parties. The necessary political compromises tend to prevent tough action to raise taxes or cut spending.

Nevertheless, the high debt-GDP ratio in Italy is not as serious a problem as it might appear. Italy offsets its government deficit with a very high private saving rate, so that its national saving rate is more than double that in the United States. As a result, high private saving creates a large demand for the bonds that the government must constantly issue to cover its deficit.

A notable fact about Italy's debt-GDP ratio is that it increased rapidly from 1980 to 1994 but then turned around, falling after 1994. Like several other European nations, Italy sharply tightened its fiscal policy in order to reduce its deficit-GDP and debt-GDP ratios to meet the conditions to enter the euro single-currency block in early 1999 (see pp. 474–75).

Claudia R. Asset, would expect to earn $5,000 in interest each year when the overall economywide interest rate is 5 percent. Surely the government could simply issue $5,000 in extra bonds to meet its interest obligations without needing to levy taxes on future generations to pay this interest bill.

The government can meet its interest bill forever by issuing more bonds without increasing the debt-GDP ratio *only if the economy's real growth rate of output equals or exceeds its real interest rate.* Let us assume, unrealistically, that the real growth rate is 5 percent and the real interest rate is 5 percent. Then each year the government could issue 5 percent additional debt, raising Claudia's holdings from $100,000 to $105,000 without raising the ratio of outstanding debt to GDP (which also has grown 5 percent by assumption). In this case,

Claudia would receive the $5,000 payment that she expects, but the government would not have to levy additional taxes.

Clearly, if the real growth rate of output is less than the real interest rate, this method of financing the government debt is not available. If the real interest rate is 5 percent, Claudia expects to receive her $5,000, but with a real growth rate below 5 percent any issuance of $5,000 of extra debt *will raise the ratio of debt to GDP*. Next year, another $5,000 of interest will be due. To finance this interest obligation by printing more debt, the government will further raise the ratio of debt to GDP. Eventually, the ratio of debt to GDP will grow and grow, approaching infinity.

The Real-World Solvency Condition

The government faces the solvency condition whenever it runs a deficit and whenever the real interest rate exceeds the economy's real growth rate. Temporarily in 2002–04, the real interest rate on 10-year government bonds was in the range of 1 to 2 percent, lower than the economy's growth rate of 3 to 4 percent. But over a longer period of time, from 1987 to 2004, the real interest rate on 10-year government bonds was 4.2 percent, higher than the 3.0 average growth rate of real GDP over the same period. This longer-term average in which the real interest rate exceeded the growth rate of real GDP is a better guide for the future. Thus the government cannot escape from the inexorable logic of equation (12.4): The debt-GDP ratio will increase when the government deficit exceeds the current value of the debt times the growth rate of nominal GDP.

Self-Test

Calculate the allowable deficit that maintains a fixed debt to GDP ratio for the following situations:

	Real growth rate	Inflation rate	Existing debt
1.	0.01	0.10	$4,000 billion
2.	0.03	0.00	$4,000 billion
3.	0.03	0.00	$1,000 billion
4.	0.01	0.10	$1,000 billion

12-5 Case Study

Historical Behavior of the Debt-GDP Ratio Since 1790

We have now learned that the debt-GDP ratio increases when the government deficit exceeds the borderline value given by equation (12.4). And the debt-GDP ratio decreases when the government deficit is smaller than that borderline value. In the history of the United States, which events were responsible for causing the debt-GDP ratio to rise, and under which circumstances did the debt-GDP ratio decline?

Figure 12-2 exhibits the debt-GDP ratio of the U.S. federal government (excluding government bonds held by the Federal Reserve and other government

396 Chapter 12 • The Government Budget, the Public Debt, and Social Security

Figure 12-2 **The Ratio of U.S. Government Debt to GDP, 1790–2005**
The ratio of debt to GDP has ranged widely throughout U.S. history, rising during wartime and falling between wars. During peacetime periods, the debt-GDP ratio increased only during the Great Depression decade of the 1930s and during the high deficit period of 1981–93. The shift of the federal budget from deficit to surplus caused the debt-GDP ratio to decline sharply after 1995, but then a shift back to deficits caused the ratio to rise again after 2001.

agencies) since 1790. From this figure we can draw several significant generalizations.

Wars and Depressions

The most consistent feature of the historical record is the tendency of the debt ratio to jump during wars and to shrink during succeeding years until the next war breaks out. The Revolutionary War, the Civil War, World War I, and World War II all created major jumps in the debt ratio, while in most other periods the debt ratio fell. Less visible, but also important, is the effect of economic recessions and depressions in raising the public debt through the effect of automatic stabilization (which reduces government revenue automatically as the output ratio Y/Y^N falls, requiring an increase in the public debt to finance ongoing government expenditures). The most important example of this was the decade of the Great Depression, when the debt ratio rose from 17 percent in 1929 to 47 percent in 1939.

The 1980s and 1990s: The Ratio Rises and Then Declines

The bottom frame of Figure 12-2 magnifies the period since 1960 in order to exhibit the debt ratio more clearly over the past five decades. Until 1974 the debt ratio fell. From 1974 to 1976 the ratio rose, but then leveled off at about 26–28 percent until 1981. From 1981 to 1992 the ratio rose, indicating that the federal budget deficits were sizable enough to make the government debt grow much faster than nominal GDP.

After 1993 the deficit began to decline, and in 1998 the federal budget turned to surplus. As a result, the debt-GDP ratio stabilized in 1994–95 at about 50 percent and then fell sharply during 1998–2001. The return of deficits in 2002–05 ended the decline in the ratio and began a new period in which the ratio increased each year.

12-6 Why the Budget Deficit Disappeared Temporarily and then Reappeared

Viewed from the context of the 1980–2005 period of consistent government deficits, what was unusual about the brief period of government budget surpluses during 1998–2001? Were the persistent deficits due to an increase in expenditures, a drop in revenues, or both? Did the brief 1998–2001 period of surpluses reflect a surge in revenue, a cut in expenditures, or both?

The Budget Turnaround from Deficit to Surplus in the late 1990s

Figure 12-3 allows us to identify periods when there were significant changes in the ratio to natural GDP of federal government revenues and expenditures. The shaded red area between the expenditure and revenue lines identifies periods when the federal government was running a deficit, and the shaded green area identifies periods of a federal budget surplus. The interval 1998–2001 clearly was unusual, representing the first period of federal government budget surpluses since 1970. What caused this turnaround?

Figure 12-3 Federal Government Revenues and Expenditures as a Percent of Natural GDP, 1960–2005

The federal revenue share in GDP was amazingly stable at about 18 percent until 1995–2000, when it jumped rapidly to 21 percent, and then collapsed to below 16 percent. The expenditure share gradually increased until 1992, when it reached 22 percent. Then the expenditure share dropped back to 19 percent in 1999–2005.

Source: The Congressional Budget Office.

Revenues Surged and then Collapsed

Before 1980, large federal budget deficits were caused primarily by recessions, as in 1971 and 1975. But beginning around 1980, deficits persisted year after year and did not come close to disappearing, as they had in 1973–74 and 1979. We can identify the source of the persistent post-1980 deficits by looking at averages of revenues and expenditures as a percentage share of natural GDP.

	1968–80	1981–95
Expenditures	19.8	21.5
Revenues	18.3	18.0
Deficit	1.5	3.5

Thus the shift into persistent deficits after 1980 was almost entirely due to a higher share of expenditures in GDP. Despite the Reagan-era tax cuts, revenues as a share of GDP were almost as high in 1981–95 as in 1968–80.

The line for Federal revenues in Figure 12-3 prior to 1995 exhibits a zigzag pattern in which revenues creep up over the years, then fall sharply, then creep up again. This reflects "bracket creep," caused by an elasticity of tax revenues to increases of nominal GDP that is greater than unity. When bracket creep causes the share of government revenues in GDP to reach a relatively high level, Congress and the administration tend to institute periodic tax cuts that offset the creep, as in 1964, 1970–71, 1975, and 1982–84. The fact that the ratio of revenues to GDP remained so long in the range of 18 percent of natural GDP may reflect the "revealed preference" of the political process.

Categories of Spending

What caused the upward drift and then downturn in the percentage of expenditures in GDP? As illustrated in Figure 12-4, virtually all of the increased share of government spending in GDP can be attributed to transfer payments, mainly Social Security and Medicare, which went from 4.4 percent of GDP in

Figure 12-4 Components of Federal Government Expenditures as a Percent of Natural GDP, 1960–2004

The diagram has five "slices" corresponding to the shares in GDP of the five major types of federal government spending. The sum of the five slices is the share of total federal government spending in GDP. The increase in the share of federal government spending in GDP is mainly accounted for by transfer payments throughout the period and by net interest payments in the 1980s. The share of national defense declined until 2000 and then rose in 2001–04. Grants and subsidies rose until 1978 and then declined. Net interest declined after 1995 as the debt-GDP ratio began to decline, and it declined further in 2001–04 in response to low interest rates.

1960 to 8.7 percent in 2004. "Non-defense plus grants and subsidies programs" were cut somewhat, from 5.2 percent in 1980 to 4.2 percent in 2004, and the share of defense spending fell from 7.8 percent in 1960 to 3.3 percent in 2000, before rising to 4.1 percent in 2004. Also, the share of net interest declined from 4.2 percent in 1991 to 1.9 percent in 2004.

A central cause of U.S. fiscal deficits in the 1980–97 period was an unintended increase in the well-being of Social Security recipients in the 1970s that neither Congress nor the administration had the courage either to finance or to reverse. During the 1970s, Social Security benefits per retiree rose 50 percent after adjustment for inflation, while average real earnings per employee did not increase at all, amounting to a substantial redistribution of income from workers to the elderly. An important by-product was a marked reduction in the percentage of the elderly who have incomes below the official poverty line, from 35.2 percent of the over-65 population in 1959 to 10.2 percent in 2003.

The Tax Revenue Explosion and Collapse, 1995–2005

Besides the sharp reduction in the federal expenditure share between 1995 and 2000, the other most dramatic recent event depicted in Figure 12-3 is the sharp increase in the federal revenue share from 18 to 21 percent in 1993–2000 and then its subsequent collapse from 21 percent in 2000 to below 16 percent in

2003–04. The increase in the late 1990s reflected an increase in tax rates, particularly on higher-income individuals, legislated in 1993. Additional factors boosting federal tax revenues were overall prosperity and particularly the stock market boom that boosted revenue from the tax on capital gains made by investors in the stock market.

The collapse of federal tax revenues after 2000 reflected the reversal of all the factors that had boosted revenues in the late 1990s. Most important, the Bush administration cut tax rates in 2001 and 2003, not just on ordinary income but also on dividends and capital gains. Just as the 1993 tax rate increases had targeted higher-income individuals, the 2001 and 2003 tax rate cuts disproportionately benefited higher-income individuals, and in fact fully one-third of the tax reductions went to those in the top 1 percent of the income distribution. Another cause of the decline in federal tax revenue was the decline in stock market prices from 2000 to early 2003, since this caused revenue from the capital gains tax to dry up.

In summary, the temporary movement of the federal budget from deficit to surplus in 1998–2001 reflected in roughly equal parts an increase in the revenue share and a decrease in the expenditure share of about the same amount. But the return to deficits after 2001 was entirely due to a drop in the revenue share, with no further change in the expenditure share.

12-7 Alternative Views of Fiscal Policy: Supply-Side Economics

The period of persistent deficits began in the early 1980s with President Reagan's tax reductions enacted in 1981–83. This was the most dramatic shift in fiscal policy of the postwar era not related to the financing of wars. We have seen in this chapter that the period between 1980 and 1993 witnessed the most rapid increase in the debt-GDP ratio of the postwar period.

Supply-Side Argument for Reagan Tax Cuts

The Reagan program differed from previous episodes of fiscal policy stimulus, because its primary motive was *not* a belief that the economy was so weak, nor unemployment so high, nor monetary policy so impotent that the government needed to apply a fiscal stimulus. Instead, the Reagan administration believed that tax rates were simply too high and that the government sector was too large. According to the doctrine called **supply-side economics** embraced by the Reagan administration, high tax rates stifled individual initiative and saving.

The supply-side theory makes one uncontroversial statement and two controversial claims:

1. Income taxes reduce the after-tax reward to work and saving.
2. An increase in the after-tax reward to work and saving creates a *significant increase in the amount of work and saving*.
3. The resulting increase in work and saving is so significant that after the tax cuts the federal government would collect more revenue than before the tax cuts.

Supply-side economics predicts that a reduction in marginal income tax rates will create an increase in the supply of output, that is, in natural real GDP.

12-7 Alternative Views of Fiscal Policy: Supply-Side Economics

Response of work effort and saving. The first statement is uncontroversial, because everyone agrees that taxes reduce the after-tax reward to work and saving. In the second statement, the supply-siders argued that reductions in personal income taxes would lead people to work longer hours, would encourage more people to take second ("moonlighting") jobs, and would allow and encourage people to save more. Many economists were skeptical of these claims. At the time of the original 1981 debate about supply-side economics, Charles Schultze quipped that "There's nothing wrong with supply-side economics that division by ten couldn't cure."

As it turned out, even Schultze's skeptical assessment may have been too optimistic. When we compare the economy before the Reagan tax cuts to the economy after the tax cuts, we find that the amount of work effort, as measured by the labor-force participation rate, grew more slowly after 1981 than before, and the personal saving rate fell after rising during 1977–81. The only bit of support for supply-side doctrines is that hours per employee fell more slowly after 1981 than before.

Response of productivity growth. Some supply-side advocates also predicted a rebound in productivity growth. Everyone agreed in 1981 that the U.S. productivity growth record had been dismal since 1972—a slowdown that no one fully understood. If the supply-side advocates were correct, we would expect productivity growth to have been substantially more rapid after 1981 than before. But productivity growth was only moderately faster after 1981 in contrast to the larger acceleration that occurred after tax rates were raised in 1993.

	1948–72	1972–80	1980–93	1993–2004
Private nonfarm output per hour (annual growth rate in percent)	2.7	1.2	1.6	2.7

The Laffer curve. The third supply-side claim, that tax cuts raise government revenue, is even more controversial than the second. This claim was widely touted in 1981 during the debate about the Reagan tax cuts, because critics had claimed that such large tax cuts would create unprecedented government budget deficits. Supply-side proponents argued that the tax cuts would "pay for themselves."

The proponents' argument was illustrated by the famous Laffer curve, which Arthur Laffer of Yorktown University in California had drawn on a napkin in a Washington restaurant in an inspired moment in 1974. The Laffer curve, reproduced in Figure 12-5, starts from the obvious point that the government will raise no tax revenue at all if tax rates are zero, as at point A, and if tax rates are 100 percent, as at point E. In between, as the tax rate rises from zero to 100 percent, tax revenues will first rise and then fall. If the government introduces a tax cut (like the 1981 Reagan package) starting from point B, the economy would move leftward along the Laffer curve and government revenue would fall. But a tax cut starting from point D would cause a leftward movement that would raise government revenue.

Was the economy at point B or point D in 1981? Clearly, one can draw a Laffer curve with its peak at any tax rate—20, 50, or 80 percent. The peak at 70 percent in Figure 12-5 is completely arbitrary. The fact that the United States

Figure 12-5 The Laffer Curve

The curve shows that total government tax revenue depends on the tax rate. With either a zero or 100 percent tax rate, the government collects no revenue. Maximum revenue occurs at point C. If tax rates are cut starting from point B, government revenue declines, but if tax rates are cut starting from point D, government revenue increases.

Will a Tax Cut Reduce Government Revenues or Raise Them?

entered an era of persistent deficits after the Reagan tax cuts suggests that it moved from a point like C to B in the 1980s, not from D to C.

> **Self-Test**
>
> 1. Looking at the Laffer curve in Figure 12-5 and assuming that government spending is fixed, does a reduction in tax rates starting from point B raise or lower the government budget deficit? Starting from point D?
> 2. Which point, B or D, was believed to describe the position of the U.S. economy in 1981 by the following: Arthur Laffer? President Reagan? Critics of supply-side economics?

Robert J. Barro (1944–)

Barro's fame stems from his theory of fiscal policy, the Keynesian non-market-clearing model (Chapter 17), and his recent research on new models of economic growth (Section 10-7).

12-8 Alternative Views of Fiscal Policy: The Barro-Ricardo Equivalence Theorem

We have seen in the previous section that supply-siders depart from the traditional Keynesian analysis of fiscal policy by predicting a large effect on supply (Y^N), not just on demand. Another attack on the traditional Keynesian analysis of fiscal policy was launched in 1974 by Robert J. Barro of Harvard University.[4] Because Barro's approach echoed a theme originally proposed by the classical economist David Ricardo in the early nineteenth century, his point has become known as the "Barro-Ricardo equivalence theorem."

Barro's theory denies the efficacy of discretionary fiscal policy that takes the form of tax changes, because tax cuts are balanced by an increase in saving rather than an increase in consumption. Why? Barro points out that any tax cut is financed by deficit spending, which requires future tax payments to meet the interest on the public debt. People who see their taxes cut will tell themselves, "This just means lower taxes today and higher taxes in the future when the

---

[4] Robert J. Barro, "Are Government Bonds Net Wealth?" *Journal of Political Economy*, vol. 82 (November/December 1974), pp. 1095–1117.

government needs to pay the interest on the debt; I'll save today in order to build up a savings account that will be needed to meet those future taxes."

Bequests Imply Concern About Children

While economists had recognized that taxpayers might perceive their future obligation to meet government interest payments, most had not taken seriously the possibility that people would view higher future taxes as *completely equivalent* to lower current taxes (hence the name "equivalence theorem"). Economists had previously pointed out that much of the future interest burden of the higher public debt would occur after today's taxpayers are dead. Barro's contribution was to argue that people leave bequests to their children, implying that they care about their children and hence, indirectly, about the tax burden that they face. His striking deduction was that *today's taxpayers, reacting to a tax cut today, would raise their saving so as to increase their bequests to their children in order to pay for future taxes levied by the government.*

In other words, today's holdings of government bonds do not represent net wealth. When the government prints an additional one-dollar bond to pay for a tax cut, bondholders feel richer by one dollar, but taxpayers feel poorer by the same dollar, since they recognize that one dollar's worth of future taxes will have to be levied to pay the interest on the bonds.

Criticism of the Equivalence Proposition

Barro's ingenious argument let loose a torrent of criticism. The link between bequests and concern for children was doubted. Decision horizons of private individuals are often quite short. Some parents do not care about their descendants. Perhaps more important, the absence of "perfect" rental markets for consumer housing and household possessions means that almost every homeowner is likely to die with a significant positive net worth in the form of housing and furnishings, which will be bequeathed to charity or to some heir even if the deceased does not care about the exact standard of living that the heir achieves.

A separate criticism pointed out that most individuals pay a substantially higher interest rate to borrow than does the government (for example, 18 percent on credit cards compared to a long-term government bond rate in mid-2005 below 6 percent). This means that people apply a much higher discount rate to future government tax levies than the interest rate the government has to pay on its bonds. This point applies with special force when it is recognized that the typical adult consumer has an expected life span of about 35 years. If the government cuts taxes by raising the public debt, most of the burden of servicing or repaying the debt will be borne within that 35-year lifetime. Only a very small portion of the debt burden will be passed on to future generations, making moot the debate about the motives for bequests.

Evidence from the 1981 Tax Cuts

Most of the skepticism about the Barro-Ricardo equivalence theorem emerged immediately after the 1974 publication of Barro's article and was based on general principles. However, saving behavior after the 1981–83 tax cuts provided additional reason for doubt. If consumers had behaved in the forward-looking way postulated by the Barro proposition, consumption would have remained unaffected while saving would have jumped to pay for the future tax burden created by the extra federal debt. However, the personal saving rate *fell* after 1981, from 10.9 percent of disposable personal income in 1981 to an average of 9.6 percent in 1982–86. To set aside sufficient saving to pay for the future tax burden of the extra debt, households should have raised their saving rate from 10.9 percent in 1981 to roughly 14 percent in 1986, but *actual behavior went in the opposite direction.*

12-9 The Great Debate over Social Security

The reemergence of persistent government budget deficits after 2001 led to concerns about the immediate impact of the deficits. As shown earlier in equation (12.1) on p. 389, a shift of the government budget from surplus to deficit must reduce national saving and in turn this will cause a reduction in domestic investment and an increase in foreign borrowing. Immediate concerns, as we have learned in Chapter 6, focused on whether an increase in foreign borrowing was feasible and sustainable, and whether the indirect effect of the budget deficits would be a sharp decline in the foreign exchange rate of the dollar and an increase in domestic interest rates.

However, in addition to these immediate issues, the focus of politicians and economists in 2005 looked much further into the future at a potential crisis involving Social Security. Because of the retirement beginning in 2012 of the baby boom generation born in 1947–63, the benefits paid out by the Social Security system would soon soar above the revenues from Social Security tax collections. As a result, the Social Security system would run continuous deficits after 2019 and would run out of money after 2053.[5] The Bush administration placed top priority on reforming the Social Security system and ignited a heated political debate about the best way to achieve this. In this section we learn how the system currently operates and about the pros and cons of alternative proposals for reform.

How the Social Security System Works

The Social Security system is the basic source of retirement benefits for U.S. households. The system is not a pension fund that collects money from an individual, accrues interest, and then pays out the accumulated benefits over the years of retirement. Instead, the system is based on a "pay-as-you-go" principle; it collects taxes from workers and uses that current tax revenue to pay benefits to retired people and their spouses. The benefits that individuals receive during their retirement years comes from current taxpayers, not from the lifetime contributions of the retirees themselves.

Tax and benefit rates could be changed every year to make the Social Security system "break even" with tax revenues exactly equal to retirement benefits. However, tax rates are changed relatively seldom, while benefit rates are changed only to reflect changes in average real wage rates and in the rate of inflation. As a result, it is quite possible for the system to take in more revenues than it spends on benefits, and this has been the usual occurrence for the past two decades.

---

[5] Dates in this section involving the future of Social Security come from the U.S. Congressional Budget Office, *The Outlook for Social Security*, June 2004.

Dimensions of the "Crisis"

The excess revenues are held in the Social Security trust fund, which currently holds about $1.8 trillion and is projected to grow to a maximum size in the year 2019 and then to exhaust its assets in the year 2052. The rise and fall of the assets in the trust fund reflect the changing structure of the American population. As more and more baby boomers retire after 2012, the share of the population paying Social Security taxes will shrink and the share receiving benefits will increase, explaining why the trust fund is projected to shrink after 2019 and run out of money in 2053. The problem is caused by more than just the aging of baby boomers; increasing life expectancy of retirees due to better medical technology and improved personal health habits also increases the total of benefits that needs to be financed. One easy way to think about the population problem is that in 1950 there were 16 workers for every benefit recipient; by the year 2030 there will be only 2 workers per recipient.

The prospect that the fund will run large deficits after 2019 and "go broke" in 2053 gives rise to the phrase "Social Security crisis" and numerous proposals to "save Social Security." There has been so much publicity attached to the alleged crisis that many college-age young people respond to polls by saying that they do not believe they will ever receive any Social Security benefits, since they assume that the trust fund will have long since run out of money by the time they retire.

Why has the Social Security trust fund received no mention heretofore in this book? The standard data on the federal government budget combine two types of budgets, the so-called "on-budget" revenues and expenditures and the remaining Social Security revenues and expenditures. For instance, in 2004 the on-budget part of the federal government ran a deficit of $450 billion while the Social Security trust fund ran a surplus of $65 billion, accounting for the overall federal government budget deficit of $385 billion.

The Social Security trust fund is entirely invested in government bonds. When the on-budget part of the government runs a deficit and the Social Security trust fund runs a surplus, as in 2004, the on-budget part sells bonds to finance its deficit to the Social Security trust fund.

Is There a Problem?

How can we possibly forecast that the Social Security trust fund will run out of money at some exact moment almost 50 years in the future? The particular date when the trust fund runs out of money depends on numerous factors. Among these are the rate of population growth, since a higher rate of population growth implies more working people relative to retired benefit recipients. Forecasters must also predict growth of the real wage and the inflation rate, since growth in the real wage rate helps to determine both Social Security tax revenues and benefits while future inflation determines the growth rate of benefits.

The current forecast for the "exhaustion date" when the Social Security trust fund runs out of money is the year 2053. But this forecast is based on very pessimistic assumptions. The projected growth rate of productivity in the future is much slower than has occurred over the past ten years. And the official projections of the future population imply very slow growth. A major flaw in the projections is the assumption that the annual number of immigrants entering the United States will be a fixed number forever, with no growth, ignoring growth in the number of immigrants of almost 4 percent annually over the past four decades.

Faster growth in productivity improves the financial outlook for the trust fund, because it implies that real wages of the working population will grow relative to the benefits of the retired population, which are fixed in real terms at retirement age and not increased further in real terms even if retirees should live twenty or thirty years after retirement. Faster growth in population also improves the financial outlook, since it raises the ratio of people in the working age groups who pay taxes relative to the retired age groups who receive benefits.

How To "Save" the System As It Currently Operates

The problem, as shown in the top frame of Figure 12-6, is that the upcoming retirement of the baby boom generation causes a sharp increase in outlays relative to revenues after 2012, and after 2019 outlays exceed revenues forever into the future. The bottom frame shows that the Social Security trust fund grows until 2019, then begins to shrink and in 2053 runs out of money.

"So what?" say some defenders of the current system. If the problem is that outlays are greater than tax revenues, the solution is simple, they say. "Simply cut benefits or raise tax revenues." The Social Security payroll tax has been raised repeatedly during the history of the system since the 1930s, and the payroll tax could be raised again by enough to retain the solvency of the system.

A recent study provided a long menu of changes that would solve the problem. Here we list three of the most important possible solutions, together with the percent of the projected shortfall that would be covered by the change. For instance, the first solution on the list would eliminate 43 percent of the post–2019 gap between system outlays and revenues.[6]

1. Raise the ceiling on wages subject to the Social Security tax from the current $90,000 to $140,000 (eliminates 43 percent of the funding gap).
2. Gradually raise the retirement age from 67 to 70 by the year 2083 (38 percent).
3. Increase payroll taxes by 0.5 percent, divided between employers and employees (24 percent).

Together these three changes would be more than enough to solve the entire funding problem, and there are numerous other proposals that would move in the same direction, including minor changes in the way benefits are calculated, and a proposal to invest some of the Social Security trust fund in the stock market.

Should Social Security Funds Be Invested in the Stock Market?

Several reform proposals focus on raising the rate of return of the Social Security trust fund. Historically, stocks have returned more than bonds, and the Social Security trust fund is now required to invest only in government bonds. Much of the debate is between those who advocate the creation of private accounts that would allow individuals to invest in stocks and bonds and use the proceeds from these investments during retirement, versus those who oppose private accounts and believe that it is more efficient for the Social Security trust fund to invest in stocks and corporate bonds without giving individuals that responsibility.

---

[6] See Jackie Calmes, "On Social Security, It's Bush vs. AARP," *The Wall Street Journal,* January 21, 2005, p. A4.

Figure 12-6 Social Security Outlays, Revenues, and the Trust Fund, 1985–2080

The top frame shows that Social Security revenues have been higher than outlays for benefits continuously since 1985 and will continue to be higher until a crossover date in 2019. After that date, outlays will greatly exceed revenues. The bottom frame shows that the trust fund rises until 2019 and declines thereafter, reaching zero in approximately 2053.

Source: The Congressional Budget Office.

Most reform proposals agree that Social Security funds should be invested in the stock market, since historically the real return on stock market assets has been about three percentage points higher than the real return on government bonds. But there is a great split on the next question, "invested by whom?" Private accounts are supported by the Bush administration, using the analogy of current tax-free retirement accounts like IRAs and 401(k)s, by allowing everyone to make his or her own investment choices. Opponents of private accounts respond that the cost of setting up and administering 150 million separate retirement accounts would fritter away many of the extra returns, chewing up perhaps 20 percent of the accumulated value of the funds, and that all of the benefit of the extra stock market returns could be achieved by having the Social Security trust fund invest in the stock market by itself. Opponents of private accounts also point to endless complexity as Congress debates rules for these accounts. Should those making poor investment decisions and losing the entire value of their funds be bailed out by the government? Should Congress allow poverty-stricken or disabled workers to pull their money out before retirement?

Politics, Not Economics

This aspect of the debate is entirely political, not economic. Proponents of the private accounts fear direct investment by the Social Security trust fund, even though it would be more cost-effective, as socialism in disguise. They say "the Government would indirectly own huge parts of American companies, with the potential of political manipulation. Would Congress allow a Government fund to buy, say, shares of tobacco companies or of companies that are unfriendly to unions?"

For the trust fund to invest in stocks and bonds, no new money would be required. The fund would just sell some of its government bonds and buy stocks and corporate bonds and presumably earn a higher rate of return, allowing any of the following outcomes—putting off the date of the future "crisis," raising benefits, or reducing tax rates. The benefit of reducing tax rates is that some of the resulting extra after-tax income to individuals would be saved, thus raising the economy's capital stock and its future standard of living.

However, the Bush administration proposal of private accounts requires new money, because existing Social Security tax revenues would have to be paid into the current trust fund in order to provide benefits to current retirees (who are too old to accumulate benefits in private accounts). The extra money to fund the private accounts would have to come from additional Federal debt, thus exacerbating the problems of crowding out investment and increasing foreign borrowing.

A Debate Based on Dubious Assumptions

To conclude, the debate about "saving Social Security" rests on several dubious assumptions and arguments that are inherently political rather than economic. The dubious assumptions involve quite pessimistic projections of the attainable growth rate of the American economy in the future, falling well short of its performance over the past decade. Simply projecting out the performance of the past decade leads to the postponement of the Social Security "crisis" for more than a century. Another dubious assumption is that returns on the stock market will continue to exceed those on government bonds by as much as in the past.

This ignores the effect of the 1990s stock market boom in propelling the market to unparalleled heights relative to nominal GDP, profits, and other measures of economic activity (see Figure 15-7 on p. 506). When the stock market is unusually high, it is likely that returns on the stock market will be unusually low over the following few decades. Thus proponents of private accounts may exaggerate the benefits of setting up these accounts, and for the same reason the benefit for the trust fund in switching from bonds to stocks may be exaggerated.

Politics enters the debate in favor of private accounts because of the fear that investments in stocks by the Social Security trust fund would lead to the government owning substantial portions of private companies and trying to exert control for political purposes. Yet politics works against private accounts as well, since there would be a great political debate about how to protect individuals whose stock market investments are ill-chosen or who need the money in their funds before retirement.

12-10 Long-Run Economic Growth and the Fiscal Debate

The third basic macroeconomic concept introduced at the beginning of this book is the growth rate of productivity. Faster productivity growth raises the standard of living and is unambiguously desirable as a prime goal of economic policy. The more economic growth a nation can achieve, the better off will be the citizens of that nation in the future. Chapter 10 showed that a nation can raise its rate of economic growth temporarily, although not permanently, by increasing the ratio of its national saving to GDP. The only way to obtain a *permanent* increase in the rate of economic growth is for the rate of technological change to increase. The diffusion of new technological ideas, such as the Internet in the 1990s, is facilitated by having a high ratio of national saving to GDP, and indeed the post–1995 revival of U.S. productivity growth occurred simultaneously with an upsurge in private domestic investment as a share of GDP.

With only a brief interruption during the period of fiscal surpluses during 1998–2001, the debate over U.S. fiscal policy has returned to the harm done by persistent year-after-year deficits in the federal government budget. We are back to the era of the 1980s and early 1990s, when the "termites" debated the "pussycats." The termites viewed persistent deficits as insidious, slowly but steadily undermining the foundations of the U.S. economy by reducing the national saving rate and thus the funds available for domestic private investment. The pussycats believed that the deficits were benign and did no harm.

Looking back at the period of high fiscal deficits during 1980–97, the termites make an important point, because over much of this period the ratio of net investment to GDP was lower than at any point in the postwar period (see Figure 16-3 on p. 524). A much higher net investment ratio in the late 1990s went together with the temporary swing of the federal budget from deficit to surplus. But we should not deduce a one-way causation from the federal budget surplus to the investment boom. More likely, the fast pace of innovation in the late-1990s "New Economy" caused many good things to occur simultaneously, including the investment boom, the surge in stock prices that generated capital gains tax revenue for the federal government, and a strong inflow of foreign capital that boosted the dollar and helped to moderate U.S. inflation.

After the year 2000, all of this unraveled. Investment fell as a ratio to GDP, the federal budget moved back into deficit, and foreigners were less eager to invest in the United States, contributing to a decline in the value of the U.S. dollar after early 2002. A new element, as we learned in Chapter 6, is that the U.S. current account deficit is now much larger than the government budget deficit. Future growth in the U.S. standard of living may be limited not just by the crowding out of domestic private investment caused directly by government budget deficits, but also by interest and dividends paid out to foreign investors. In addition, if the dollar should decline further as a result of the large current account deficit, American consumers would have to pay more for imported goods, another form of subtraction from future growth in the standard of living. All these negative factors influencing future economic growth would be alleviated if the federal government budget were moved back into surplus by some combination of expenditure reductions and tax increases, particularly on the high-income households that benefited the most from the 2001 and 2003 tax cuts. But, as we learned at the beginning of this chapter, any expenditure reductions should avoid those government functions that contribute directly to growth and technological change, including support of education and research through such government programs as scholarship aid for college students and support for the National Science Foundation and National Institutes of Health.

Summary

1. A budget surplus raises national saving and raises the rate of economic growth. A budget deficit reduces national saving and lowers the rate of economic growth.
2. The two methods for stimulating national saving and hence economic growth are for policymakers to create incentives that raise private saving or to run a larger government surplus (or smaller deficit).
3. Deficits that raise the future level of the public debt create a burden on future generations if the deficits finance government consumption expenditures that yield no future benefits to balance the burden of taxes required to pay the interest on the debt.
4. The government faces a solvency condition, which states that it cannot perpetually run a deficit in the long run if the real interest rate exceeds the economy's growth rate of real output.
5. The U.S. ratio of public debt to GDP fell throughout the postwar period until 1974, rose between 1974 and 1993, fell between 1993 and 2001, and rose again after 2001. The deficits in the 1980s and 1990s were due to a higher ratio of government spending to GDP, not to a lower ratio of tax revenue to GDP. The shift to surplus after 1997 was mainly due to rapid increases in receipts from the personal income tax, and the shift to deficits after 2001 was due primarily to cuts in personal income tax rates.
6. The Laffer curve predicts that if initial tax rates are high enough, a cut in tax rates raises government tax revenue. Supply-side economists predicted in the early 1980s that tax rate cuts would not only raise government tax revenues but would also stimulate saving and work effort. The predicted effects did not occur.
7. The Barro-Ricardo equivalence theorem states that deficit-financed tax cuts will stimulate saving rather than consumption, because individuals will try to build up their savings accounts to pay the future taxes required to service the higher government debt.
8. The Social Security trust fund is projected to run out of money in the year 2053. This forecast is based on unrealistically pessimistic projections for real GDP and population growth. More realistic projections put off the Social Security crisis for several more decades.
9. Reformers of Social Security agree that funds should be invested in the stock market, not just (as at present) in government bonds. But there is a political disagreement as to whether individuals should be allowed to invest funds in their own retirement accounts or whether the trust fund should invest directly in the stock market without the extra costs or complications of individual accounts.

Concepts

rate of time preference   national saving   supply-side economics

Questions

1. Economic policymakers are concerned with both economic growth and economic stabilization. Explain the distinction between them. Are different policies used for the two purposes? Give some examples.
2. What is national saving? Under what circumstances would it be appropriate to increase the level of national saving?
3. Explain why a country saves too much if its rate of time preference equals 10 percent per year and the rate of return on private investment is 8 percent.
4. If the level of real GDP is held fixed by monetary policy, which of the following will provide the greatest stimulus to saving?
   (a) An increase in the personal income tax rates paid by the rich.
   (b) An increase in the personal income tax rates paid by the poor.
   (c) The introduction of a federal retail sales tax.
5. "An increase in national saving will increase economic growth. It follows, then, that deep cuts in government spending should be adopted to boost economic growth." Evaluate this argument.
6. "Unnecessary fears of the rising government deficit have restricted desirable government spending." Explain.
7. Explain why in a large open economy an increase in government consumption expenditures that is not offset by an increase in taxes or private saving must result in lower consumption expenditures in the future. Suppose that the increase in government spending is for an investment project, and again that there is no offsetting increase in either taxes or private saving. What must be true in terms of the return on the government investment project if future consumption expenditures are to remain unchanged?
8. We rarely hear concern about the "burden" of privately held debt, yet many people share a concern about the public debt. Why is this so? Is the concern about the public debt reasonable?
9. Many people are less concerned with the absolute size of the government debt than they are about its size relative to GDP. Such people would not worry about the size of government deficits if the ratio of government debt to GDP remained equal to some "appropriate" level.
   (a) Should people who hold this view worry about the solvency of the government?
   (b) Explain the conditions under which it is possible for the debt-GDP ratio to be a constant.
   (c) Don't people who hold the view that has just been described have to worry about the future solvency of the government?
10. (a) Was it a decrease in spending or a rise in tax revenues or some combination of the two that resulted in the temporary disappearance of budget deficits during the late 1990s?
    (b) Was it an increase in spending or a fall in tax revenues or some combination of the two that resulted in the re-emergence of budget deficits after 2001?
11. The supply-side argument for tax cuts is based on one uncontroversial claim and two controversial claims. What are they? Is the empirical record consistent or inconsistent with the controversial claims? Explain.
12. When analyzing the effects of price changes, microeconomists consider how consumers' behavior will respond to changes in relative prices (the "substitution" effect) and to changes in real purchasing power (the "income" effect). Substitution and income effects also occur when tax rates change. Not only do tax changes affect disposable income, but they also change the relative "prices" of certain types of behavior.
    (a) What is the opportunity cost of leisure? What happens to leisure's opportunity cost (its "price") following a tax rate cut? Describe the substitution and income effects on people's decision to consume leisure. Do these effects reinforce or offset one another?
    (b) Do the proponents of supply-side economics see the substitution effect or the income effect having the dominant impact on decisions to consume leisure following a tax rate cut? Explain.
13. Just as income tax rates affect the opportunity cost of leisure, they also affect the relative price of current versus future consumption. Describe the substitution and income effects of the following two proposals for raising national saving in order to determine which is likely to have the larger impact.
    (a) A cut in income tax rates that is offset by a decrease in government consumption expenditures, leaving the budget deficit unchanged.
    (b) A cut in income tax rates that is accompanied by an expansion of the income tax base, leaving income tax revenues unchanged. (This type of cut

in income tax rates is referred to as being revenue neutral.)
14. State and critique the Barro-Ricardo equivalence theorem.
15. Evaluate each of the following statements in terms of the Barro-Ricardo equivalence theorem's implications for saving.
    (a) "Retirement benefits promised by Social Security reduce workers' incentives to save and thus diminish private saving in the economy."
    (b) "Social Security is solvent now, but over the next 45–50 years it will likely go broke unless taxes are raised or benefits are reduced."
16. Projections that the Social Security system will run out of money sometime around 2053 have given rise to numerous proposals to reform Social Security.
    (a) How sensitive are the predictions of impending crisis in the Social Security system to projected growth rates of the labor force, labor productivity, and real GDP?
    (b) What are three proposals to "save" the Social Security system as a pay-as-you-go program? Do these proposals generate enough revenue and/or reduce benefits enough to do so?
    (c) What are the arguments for and against investing Social Security funds in the stock market, either through private accounts or having the government invest the funds?
17. What were the positions of the "termites" and the "pussycats" in the 1980s and early 1990s concerning the effect of persistent federal budget deficits on economic growth? Which one of these positions is supported by the behavior of the economy over the last 25 years?

Problems

1. The government has the opportunity to build two public recreational facilities, each of which costs $400,000 now and lasts for 10 years. The government can borrow the cost of each project at an interest rate of 5 percent. The benefits of the first project are $40,000 per year for the first 5 years, $60,000 per year for the next 2 years, and $80,000 per year for the last 3 years. The benefits of the second project are $70,000 per year for the first 4 years, $50,000 in the fifth year, $40,000 in the sixth year, and $30,000 per year for the last 4 years. Should the government borrow the money to build either one of these projects?

2. In 2005 a country had real GDP of $10,000 billion, a government debt of $5,000 billion, and a real interest rate of 3 percent. The country's growth rate of real GDP is 3 percent.
    (a) What is the value of the ratio of government debt to GDP for this country in 2005?
    (b) What is the amount of interest paid on the country's debt in 2005? What is the interest payment as a percentage of real GDP in 2005?
    (c) If the government issues new debt in 2006 to cover the interest charges on the 2005 debt, what is the new level of government debt in 2006? How much interest has to be paid in 2006 on the government debt, assuming the real interest rate is still 3 percent?
    (d) What was the level of real GDP in 2006? Compare the percentage of real GDP going for interest payments in 2006 to that for 2005. Compare the ratio of government debt to real GDP for the two years. Is the ratio of government debt to real GDP equal in the two years? If so, why? If not, why not?
    (e) Assume that the real interest rate was actually 5 percent, not 3 percent, for both years. How does this change affect your answers to (b)–(d)?

3. Assume that the current rate of inflation is 3 percent and that nominal GDP is $11,000 billion and growing at 1 percent per year. Suppose the current government deficit is $100 billion and the government wants to maintain the debt-GDP ratio at 20 percent. Should the government increase or decrease the budget deficit next year? By how much?

4. A country currently has a nominal GDP of $12 trillion and a debt of $4.8 trillion. The rate of inflation over the next 30 years will equal 2 percent per year and the growth rate of real GDP will equal 3 percent per year. For the last 2 decades of this period, the real government debt will grow by 4 percent per year due to the demands of an aging population. At the end of this 30-year period, the country would like to have the same debt-GDP ratio that it has now.
    (a) Calculate the country's nominal GDP at the end of 10 and 30 years.
    (b) Calculate the country's debt at the end of 30 years, given the country's desired debt-GDP ratio at the time.
    (c) Calculate the country's debt at the end of 10 years, given the country's desired debt-GDP ratio at the end of 30 years.
    (d) For the country to achieve its desired debt-GDP ratio at the end of 30 years, calculate the annual growth rate of its debt over the next 10 years.

5. The Laffer curve expresses tax revenue, T, as a function of the tax rate, t. The value of T clearly equals zero when t is 0 or 1. For at least one intermediate value of t, the value of T is positive. Hence, the Laffer curve must be an increasing function of t initially, and a decreasing values of t for higher values of t. Assume T is found by multiplying t and the tax base, T_B (taxable income):

$$T = tT_B.$$

The phenomenon of the Laffer curve arises because T_B is, by hypothesis, a decreasing function of the tax rate t. Assume:

$$T_B = 8{,}000 - 8{,}000t.$$

(a) For values of $t = 0.25, 0.4, 0.5, 0.6,$ and 0.75, find T and T_B.
(b) Note that for small changes, $\Delta T/T = (\Delta t/t) + (\Delta T_B/T_B)$. (This is analogous to the case of demand growth in Chapter 8—when $X = PY$, percentage rates of change are given by $x = p + y$.) The tax-rate elasticity of any variable Z is defined to be $\eta = (\Delta Z/Z)/(\Delta t/t)$. Let η_1 be the tax-rate elasticity of tax revenue and η_2 be the tax-rate elasticity of the tax base. Find η_1 in terms of η_2.
(c) Find η_1 for the values of t in part (a). On the basis of your calculations for this particular Laffer curve, over what range of t are tax revenues increasing in t? Decreasing in t?

Self-Test Answers

p. 390 By looking at the impact on national saving as a percent of GDP, we are able to ignore the multiplier effects of these fiscal policies. Since national saving is the sum of government saving and private saving, for each item we must determine the effect on each. (1) Government saving declines (deficit rises) with no impact on private saving, so national saving declines. (2) Government saving increases (deficit falls) while private saving may also increase due to the higher price of food, so national saving increases. (3) Government saving declines (deficit rises), while the increase in personal disposable income is split between higher private saving and higher consumption; thus national saving declines because government saving declines more than private saving increases. (4) Government tax revenue falls but private saving does not necessarily rise since money can be switched from taxable saving accounts to tax-free retirement accounts. National saving may rise or decline.

p. 396 (1) $440 billion; (2) $120 billion; (3) $30 billion; (4) $110 billion.

p. 402 (1) A reduction in tax rates moves the economy to the left in Figure 12-5, the Laffer curve diagram. Thus, starting from point B, tax revenues fall as we move to the left, raising the government deficit if government expenditures are fixed. Starting from point D, tax revenues rise and the government deficit declines. (2) Arthur Laffer and President Reagan believed that the 1981 economy was at point D, and critics of the supply-side economists believed that the 1981 economy was at point B.

PART FIVE

Stabilization Policy in an Open Economy

CHAPTER 13 Money and Financial Markets

CHAPTER 14 Stabilization Policy in the Closed and Open Economy

CHAPTER 13

Money and Financial Markets

Money is what the state says it is. The state claims the right not only to enforce the dictionary, but also to write the dictionary.
—John Maynard Keynes, 1925

13-1 Money in a World of Many Financial Assets and Liabilities

Over the past several decades monetary policy has emerged as the major tool of stabilization policy. Policymakers realize that discretionary fiscal policy is severely flawed as a means of controlling the economy over the short run (a year or two). These flaws include the time delay required for extensive debate over tax changes in Congress, political disagreements about whether to change tax rates or expenditures, and the small multiplier impact of temporary tax changes. In contrast, monetary policy can be changed promptly in response to new information about the economy, and as a result monetary policy has become the primary tool of short-run stabilization policy.

In this chapter we study money—the definition of the money supply, the determinants of the money supply, and the determinants of money demand. We discuss the components of the two most common definitions of the money supply, M1 and M2. Earlier in this book (Chapters 3 and 4) we developed the *IS-LM* model and assumed that the Federal Reserve could control the nominal money supply precisely. In this chapter we learn that, in practice, the Fed's control is not exact. We shall see that the process of **financial deregulation** has allowed more and more types of assets to serve as money. This has made it difficult to find a definition of "money" for which demand is reliably related to income and interest rates.

Financial deregulation of U.S. markets began in the 1970s and continues today. One of the first changes was permitting banks to pay interest on checking accounts.

We will learn that a reliable, or stable, demand for money is required for changes in the money supply to lead to predictable changes in the aggregate demand (*AD*) curve, and thus in nominal GDP. We will see that, unless the demand for money is stable, the *LM* curve will shift unpredictably, which in turn will translate into unpredictable shifts in the *AD* curve and therefore in nominal GDP.

Many different assets and liabilities are part of the financial markets. We learn which of them are included in the money supply, and which are not. We also learn how the Fed controls the money supply through its instruments of monetary control, and why its control over the money supply is not precise.

Next we turn to the major theories of the demand for money. These theories explain why the demand for money is related to income, to the interest rate, and to other variables, and why the demand for money appears to be stable at some times and unstable at others. We use these theories to show how the deregulation of financial markets contributed to the volatility of interest rates and of the velocity of money since 1980. And we conclude this chapter by learning why the instability of the demand for money has led the Fed to focus on interest rates rather than the money supply in its attempt to stabilize the economy.

13-2 Financial Institutions, Markets, and Instruments

Some economic units currently spend more than they earn and need to borrow funds. Others currently earn more than they spend and need a place to keep their savings. Financial markets and financial intermediaries perform the essential function of channeling funds from those with surplus funds (savers) to those in need of funds (borrowers).

Reasons for Saving and Borrowing

On balance, businesses are borrowers and households are savers (or lenders). A newly opened Burger King needs funds for its building and equipment before it can earn a single dollar selling hamburgers. Even long-established businesses like Boeing Aircraft Company may borrow when a surge of orders creates a temporary need for cash to buy materials and components. And farmers frequently borrow money in the spring in order to purchase seed and fertilizer, repaying the loans when their crops are sold in the fall. Because businesses need to borrow funds, financial markets that allow the efficient exchange of funds between savers and borrowers are essential.

Individuals save for many reasons: for their retirement, for their children's education, or simply for a rainy day such as an adverse health event. Many people save and borrow at the same time, setting funds aside for long-term needs like retirement while borrowing funds to purchase a car, a home, and other goods and services. The total saving of the household sector, however, greatly exceeds its borrowing.

What about the other two major economic units, the government and the foreign sector? Since 2001 both the government and foreign sectors have been large net borrowers.

Because borrowers have profitable uses for borrowed funds, they are willing to pay interest on them. And savers are happy to save when the interest they receive exceeds the benefit they would receive by spending the funds immediately. Thus fluctuations in the interest rate help create an equilibrium between the funds available from savers and those demanded by borrowers. And the Fed, through its control of monetary policy, can influence interest rates by its control over the money supply.

Financial Institutions and Financial Markets

Financial markets are organized exchanges where securities and financial instruments are bought and sold.

Funds are channeled from savers to borrowers, either directly or indirectly. The direct channel is through **financial markets**, exchanges where securities or financial instruments are bought and sold. Financial markets provide direct finance when borrowers issue securities directly to savers. The securities, such as General Motors stock or bonds, are a liability or debt of the borrower (General Motors) and an asset of the saver.

The indirect channel operates through **financial intermediaries**, such as Citibank, which issue liabilities in their own name. The intermediaries balance their liabilities (for example, savings accounts) with assets (for example, loans).

What determines whether savers channel their funds through financial markets or through intermediaries? The simple answer is that savers are only willing to purchase securities through the direct channel—that is, via financial markets—from borrowers *large enough* to have established a reputation for paying back borrowed money. Most large business firms and units of government issue securities directly through financial markets. But most individuals and small businesses cannot do so because they do not have established reputations: Individuals may be willing to entrust their savings to Citibank, but they are unlikely to accept IOUs issued by other individuals like themselves.

Financial intermediaries *spread risk* and *collect information efficiently*. Thus Citibank makes loans to many borrowers, only a small fraction of whom will fail to repay their loans. To cover the losses from borrowers who do not repay, Citibank sets aside a contingency fund and adds the cost of this fund to the rates charged to borrowers. Because Citibank is large enough to hire specialists to assess credit risks, it is less risky for it to lend to individuals than it is for individuals to lend to each other.

Figure 13-1 illustrates the role of financial markets and institutions. The blue box on the left represents savers, and the red box on the right represents

Financial intermediaries make loans to borrowers and obtain funds from savers, often by accepting deposits.

Figure 13-1 The Role of Financial Intermediaries and Financial Markets

Shown on the left are the savers—any economic unit with surplus funds. The arrows show where savers send their funds—they can be held as currency, deposited in a financial intermediary, or used to purchase a money market instrument, stocks, or bonds directly from the financial markets. Financial intermediaries both purchase financial market instruments and also lend to borrowers. So borrowers have two sources of funds, shown by the two red arrows pointing to the "borrowers" box: loans from intermediaries and funds that come from issuing financial market instruments.

borrowers. The green box represents the financial intermediaries, and the purple box represents the financial markets. The lines connecting the boxes indicate the flows of funds from savers to borrowers. Notice that financial intermediaries not only provide funds directly to borrowers (loans to individuals) but also purchase financial market instruments. Banks and other intermediaries hold billions of dollars worth of bonds, mostly issued by the government, in addition to loans granted directly to borrowers.

Categories of Financial Institutions and Instruments

Table 13-1 displays some of the breadth and size of U.S. financial intermediaries and instruments issued. Shown in the top half of the table are the three main categories of intermediaries, which correspond to the three categories indicated in the green box in Figure 13-1. Shown in the bottom half are financial market instruments corresponding to the purple box in Figure 13-1.

Depository institutions. Commercial banks comprise by far the largest category of depository financial intermediary. Commercial banks issue deposit accounts, both checkable and savings, hold government securities (or bonds), and grant a wide variety of loans. Savings and loan institutions (S&Ls), notorious for their many failures in the 1980s, historically were required by regulation primarily to make home mortgage loans. Credit union loans and deposits are limited to the members of the credit union. Together, savings institutions and credit unions are called **thrift institutions**. Financial deregulation has allowed thrift institutions to issue a far wider range of loans and deposits than they used to. Now, like commercial banks, they have checking accounts and real estate and business loans.

Thrift institutions include two types of financial intermediaries, savings and loan institutions and savings banks, that used to obtain most of their funds from savings deposits and make most of their loans in the form of mortgages. Credit unions historically accepted household deposits and made consumer loans. In recent years thrifts have been allowed to become more like commercial banks.

Contractual savings institutions. A primary form of saving for many households consists of contributions to retirement plans. Usually these contributions are deducted from the paycheck in a fixed amount previously determined as part of a written or unwritten contract between employer and employee.

Thus retirement contributions and other similar forms of saving are called "contractual savings." Contractual savings institutions are classed as financial intermediaries and include insurance companies, private pension funds, and state and local government retirement funds. These institutions receive contributions and pay out benefits upon retirement. Many retirement funds are managed by investment firms (like Fidelity Investments) that also manage mutual funds.

Investment intermediaries. These intermediaries differ from banks in the types of assets they hold, the types of liabilities they owe, or both. Finance companies make consumer loans but raise funds they lend not from depositors but from the financial markets, especially through the issuance of commercial paper. Mutual funds raise funds from investors and invest these funds in corporate stocks and bonds. Closest to banks are money market mutual funds, whose shareholders, like bank depositors, can write checks. Balances in these funds are not deposits but rather shares in the pool of money market instruments purchased by the fund.

Table 13-1 The Main Financial Intermediaries and Instruments in 2004

Type of financial intermediary	Value of assets, December 2004 ($ billions)
Depository institutions	
Commercial banks	8,487.0
Savings institutions	1,691.2
Credit unions	654.7
Contractual savings institutions	
Insurance companies	5,342.8
Private pension funds	4,444.4
State and local government retirement funds	2,072.4
Investment intermediaries	
Finance companies	1,458.0
Mutual funds (bonds and stocks)	5,435.3
Money market mutual funds	1,879.9

Type of financial market instruments	Amount outstanding, end of 2004 ($ billions)
Money market instruments	
Large-denomination negotiable certificates of deposit	1,065.5
Commercial paper	1,402.6
Repurchase agreements	512.7
Eurodollars	355.6
Banker's acceptances	4.4
U.S. Treasury bills	961.5
Capital market instruments	
Corporate bonds	2,947.4
U.S. Treasury notes and bonds	4,371.8
U.S. government agency securities	2,693.6
State and local government bonds	1,665.3
Corporate stocks (market value)	17,204.4
Consumer loans	2,151.4
Mortgages	10,507.5

Sources: Federal Reserve Board Flow of Funds Accounts and *2005 Economic Report of the President*.

Financial Market Instruments

As shown in Figure 13-1, savers can purchase financial market instruments not only directly but also indirectly through financial intermediaries like banks and money market mutual funds. Financial market instruments fall into two categories, **money market instruments** and **capital market instruments**. Money market instruments have short maturities, usually less than one year,

Sold in financial markets, **money market instruments** are assets that have short maturities, usually less than one year, small fluctuations in price, and minimal risk of default.

Sold in financial markets, **capital market instruments** are assets that have relatively long maturities, can experience large fluctuations in price, and often expose investors to more risk of default.

small fluctuations in price, and minimal risk of default. Capital market instruments have longer maturities, larger fluctuations in price, and often greater risk of default.

Money market instruments. Negotiable large-denomination (at least $100,000) certificates of deposit are issued by depository institutions and are called "negotiable" because, once issued, they can be traded like shares of stock. They are held by other financial institutions and by households. Commercial paper is a type of short-term, fixed-interest-rate, uncollateralized but high-quality bond that is usually issued by banks and large corporations. Repurchase agreements are equivalent to very short-term loans from corporations to banks. Eurodollars are dollar deposits in foreign banks. Finally, Treasury bills are short-term securities issued by the U.S. government, similar to the commercial paper issued by private corporations. They are the most actively traded and safest of all money market instruments.

Capital market instruments. More familiar are long-term capital market instruments, including stocks and bonds. Bonds are typically issued by large corporations and by the government. Because they generally offer a fixed nominal payment, called a coupon, bond prices move in the opposite direction of interest rates. Stocks are claims on the dividends of private corporations. They are riskier than bonds because bondholder interest is paid first and stockholders have a claim only on what is left over. Loans to consumers and mortgages are also considered capital market instruments.

> **Self-Test**
>
> Without looking at Table 13-1, answer the following questions:
> 1. Which is the largest single type of financial intermediary?
> 2. For each of the following, state whether it is classified as a financial intermediary, money market instrument, or capital market instrument: money market mutual funds, state government bonds, state government retirement funds, corporate bonds, and commercial paper.

13-3 Definitions of Money

In Chapter 4 we learned that households and firms value money for its usefulness in carrying out transactions and that they value bonds for the interest they pay. In the previous section we were introduced to a wide range of assets that pay interest. These assets differ in their time to maturity, in their risk of default, and in many other dimensions. Deciding whether a financial asset should be considered a bond or a part of the money supply is not always easy because the asset may pay interest and may also be used to carry out transactions. Faced with this practical difficulty, the Federal Reserve compiles several measures of the money supply. The two most important of these are **M1**, which corresponds roughly to the medium-of-exchange function of money, and **M2**, which adds to M1 some but not all assets that can be used solely as a store of value. Financial deregulation has blurred the former distinction between M1 and M2, the distinction between the medium-of-exchange and store-of-value functions of

M1 is the U.S. definition of the money supply that includes only currency, transactions accounts, and traveler's checks.

M2 is the U.S. definition of the money supply that includes M1; savings deposits, including money market deposit accounts; small time deposits; and money market mutual funds.

money, by allowing interest to be paid on some checkable deposits and allowing checks to be written on some non-M1 categories of M2.

The M1 Definition of Money

Table 13-2 shows the various components of the Fed's M1 and M2 definitions of the money supply. Each of the categories of assets in M1 can be used directly for transactions.

1. **Currency** (cash) includes coins and paper currency, consisting of notes ranging in denomination from $1.00 to $100.00, that is held outside the Fed and vaults of depository institutions.
2. **Transactions accounts** include demand deposits and other deposits on which checks can be written.
3. **Traveler's checks** outstanding have been purchased from a bank or other financial institution but have not yet been used for purchases.

The M2 Definition of Money

The major components of M2 are:

1. **M1.** Everything included in M1 is also included in M2.
2. **Savings deposits** include passbook savings accounts, as well as savings accounts that allow deposits and withdrawals to be made by mail or on the Internet. Included in this category are *money market deposit accounts* that allow the writing of a limited number of checks per month, pay a rate of interest comparable to money market mutual funds (category 4 that follows), and because they are deposits, qualify for deposit insurance.
3. **Time deposits** with balances under $100,000 are included in M2. These are more commonly called "certificates of deposit" and they have maturities ranging from six months to several years.

Table 13-2 Components of the M1 and M2 Measures of the Money Supply, February 2005 ($ billions)

	Component of M1	Component of M2
Currency	702.0	
Transactions accounts		
Demand deposits	335.6	
Other checkable deposits	321.8	
Traveler's checks	7.5	$1,366.9
Equals M1		
Savings deposits, including money market deposit accounts		3,546.9
Small-denomination time deposits		835.7
Money market mutual funds (retail only)		706.8
Equals M2		$5,089.4

Source: http://www.federalreserve.gov/releases/H6/Current/

4. **Money market mutual funds** allow an unlimited number of checks over a certain minimum value to be written.

Which financial market instruments are excluded from the M2 definition of the money supply? Comparing Tables 13-1 and 13-2 we can see that M2 mainly consists of liabilities of depository institutions and investment intermediaries (money market mutual funds but not stock or bond mutual funds). None of the money market or capital market instruments are included in M2.

Money Supply Definitions and the Instability of Money Demand

Because M2 omits several financial assets, for example stock and bond mutual funds, the demand for M2 may shift unpredictably when these omitted assets become more attractive relative to the assets that are included in M2. The demand for M1 is even more likely to be unstable, because some of the checkable deposits that are included in M1 are very similar to some of the assets, like money market deposit accounts, that are excluded from M1.

The availability of these close substitutes creates severe difficulties for *monetarists*, who endorse a constant growth rate rule (CGRR) for "*the* money supply." To implement the CGRR, they have to decide which money supply measure should have its growth rate held constant. The notion of a stable money demand function that links "money" to "income" is a central theme of the theories of the demand for money that we shall survey later in this chapter.

Self-Test

For each of the following, state whether the event raises or lowers the demand for M1 and whether it raises or lowers the demand for M2:

1. The introduction of money market mutual funds.
2. The invention of credit cards.
3. The introduction of money market deposit accounts.
4. Increased demand for equity mutual funds resulting from a boom in the stock market.

13-4 High-Powered Money and Determinants of the Money Supply

Regardless of what definition of the money supply we select, the basic mechanism for "creating" the money supply is the same. In this section we show how the Fed and depository institutions "create" money and learn that the Fed's actions have a multiplier effect on the money supply. Though the Fed can control the longer-run average growth rate of the money supply, we will see that in practice the Fed cannot always control the money supply precisely over shorter periods.

Money Creation on a Desert Island

The role of the Fed in the money supply process is best understood by starting with a simple banking system where there is no Fed. We begin with the First

Desert Island Bank, which is started by a banker who receives a deposit of 100 gold coins. Initially the bank holds the gold as an asset and has deposits of 100. However, the banker is missing an opportunity to make a profit: 100 gold coins earn no interest sitting in the vault. Because the depositor rarely withdraws more than 10 coins, the banker decides to keep "reserves" equal to just 10 percent of total deposits and to grant loans equal to the remaining 90 percent of total deposits.

Required Conditions for Money Creation

Depositing and lending the coins start the process of money creation. Suppose the loan of 90 coins is redeposited in the bank by a merchant, say, a used-raft dealer, who sold a raft to the person who borrowed the 90 coins. This raises total deposits to 190, consisting of the initial deposit of 100 and the new deposit of 90. Because the used-raft dealer has redeposited the 90 gold coins that were borrowed to pay for the raft, the bank again has the original 100 gold coins. At this point, the banker again decides to hold as reserves 10 percent of "total" deposits. Since the banker decides to hold only 10 percent of 190 for reserves, the remaining "excess" reserves of 81 gold coins can be loaned out.

The banker can continue making loans of excess reserves until total deposits equal 1,000. At that point, the banker's actual reserves (100) equal required reserves (100 = 10 percent of 1,000) and excess reserves equal zero. Thus the original deposit of 100 gold coins leads to the creation of 1,000 units of money, all in the form of bank deposits. The First Desert Island Bank has succeeded in creating an additional nine units of money for every gold coin that it initially received.

How has this magic occurred? Four conditions are necessary for the banker to turn 100 gold coins into a money supply of 1,000.

1. **Equivalence of coins and deposits.** Paper receipts representing ownership of bank deposits, that is, checks, must be accepted as a means of payment on a one-for-one basis. In other words, checks must be treated as equivalent to payment of gold coins.
2. **Redeposit of proceeds from loans.** Any consumer or business firm receiving a cash or check payment must deposit it into an account at the same bank. We assumed in the example that the used-raft dealer redeposited the 90 gold coins received as the proceeds of the first loan.
3. **Holding of cash reserves.** The bank must hold some fraction of its reserves in the form of cash (10 percent in gold coins in this example).
4. **Willing borrowers.** Someone must be willing to borrow from the bank at an interest rate that covers the bank's cost of operation. If the First Desert Island Bank stopped lending its excess reserves, the process of money creation would stop.

The Money-Creation Multiplier

When these four conditions are met, then the entire process of money creation can be summed up in a simple equation. We let the symbol H denote **high-powered money**, that is, the type of money that is held by banks as reserves. In the example, H consists of the 100 gold coins, which are high-powered because

High-powered money is the sum of currency held outside depository institutions and the reserves held inside them.

they generate the multiple expansion of money by the First Desert Island Bank. The symbol D represents the total bank deposits. The symbol e represents the fraction of deposits that banks hold as reserves. In equilibrium, the *demand* for high-powered money to be held as reserves (eD) equals the *supply* of high-powered money (H):

General Form   Numerical Example

$$eD = H \qquad\qquad 0.1(1{,}000) = 100 \tag{13.1}$$

The same equation can be rearranged (dividing both sides by e) to determine the amount of deposits (D) relative to the quantity of high-powered money (H) and the bank reserve-holding ratio (e):

General Form   Numerical Example

$$D = \frac{H}{e} \qquad\qquad 1{,}000 = \frac{100}{0.1} \tag{13.2}$$

Comparison with income-determination multiplier. The money-creation multiplier is $1/e$, or $1/0.1 = 10$ in the numerical example. This is the second usage of the word *multiplier* in this book. In Chapter 3 we examined the factors that determined the income-determination multiplier. In its simplest version, that multiplier in Chapter 3 was

$$\frac{\text{income-determination multiplier }(k)}{} = \frac{\text{autonomous planned spending }(A_p)}{\text{marginal propensity to save }(s)}$$

An increase in autonomous planned spending (A_p) is "multiplied" because spending creates income, a fraction of which *leaks out* into saving and taxes and the remainder of which goes into additional spending. The multiplier process ends only when the total of extra induced leakages equals the original increase in A_p.

The intuition behind the money-creation multiplier is the same. An increase in high-powered money (H) is multiplied in equation (13.2) because the initial deposit of H becomes reserves, a fraction of which *leaks out* into required reserves and the remainder of which is lent out and comes back as additional deposits of the households and business firms that receive the loan proceeds. The money-creation multiplier process continues until the extra induced leakages into required reserves equal the original increase in H.

Comparison with real-world conditions. In reality, some of the four conditions required to obtain the simple money-creation multiplier may not hold.

Condition (2) required that any seller receiving a payment from the proceeds of a loan redeposit it into the bank. If not, the multiplier process of money creation cannot occur at that bank. If the cash is redeposited at another depository institution, then the second institution will find itself with excess reserves, allowing the multiplier process to proceed. Thus condition (2) can be revised to apply to, say, all the banks within the United States. As long as sellers who receive loan proceeds in the form of either cash or checks redeposit the funds in a U.S. bank, the money-creation multiplier in equation (13.2) remains valid for the U.S. banking system as a whole.

Cash holding. The money-creation multiplier is changed, however, if households or businesses want to hold not only checkable deposits but some pocket cash as well. Imagine that everyone wants to hold a fixed fraction (c) of his or her deposits, say 15 percent, in the form of cash.[1] This demand for currency adds an extra amount (cD) to the total demand for high-powered money. In a revised desert island example, the demand for gold coins, the only form of high-powered money, might be 10 percent of deposits for bank reserves ($eD = 0.1D$), plus 15 percent of deposits for pocket cash ($cD = 0.15D$).

The total demand for high-powered money ($eD + cD$) can be equated to the total supply (H):

General Form	Numerical Example
Demand = Supply	Demand = Supply
$eD + cD = H$	$0.1D + 0.15D = 100$

or

$$(e + c)D = H \qquad 0.25D = 100 \qquad (13.3)$$

Dividing both sides by ($e + c$), we can solve for deposits:

$$D = \frac{H}{e + c} \qquad D = \frac{100}{0.25} = 400 \qquad (13.4)$$

In words, total deposits equal the supply of high-powered money (H) divided by the fraction of deposits that leaks into reserves (e) plus the fraction that leaks into cash (c).

Remember that the total money supply (M) includes not only deposits (D) but also currency:

$$M = D + cD = (1 + c)D \qquad (13.5)$$

Substituting for D in (13.5) from (13.4), we obtain

$$M = (1 + c)D = \frac{(1 + c)H}{e + c} = \frac{1.15(100)}{0.25} = 460 \qquad (13.6)$$

The ratio of the money supply (M) to high-powered money (H) is called the **money multiplier** (M/H). In equation (13.6), the money multiplier is equal to $(1 + c)/(e + c)$. In the next two sections we will learn that the money multiplier is volatile due to additional factors omitted from (13.6).

> **The money multiplier** is the ratio of the money supply to high-powered money, that is, M/H. There is a separate money multiplier for each definition of the money supply.

Gold Discoveries and Bank Panics

The supply of money depends only on the three terms that appear in equation (13.6): the supply of high-powered money (H), the cash-holding ratio (c), and the ratio of reserves to deposits (e). When only gold can serve as high-powered money (H), the total supply of money depends on the demand for and supply of gold. Because a sustained increase in monetary growth causes higher inflation in the long run, gold discoveries have caused some episodes of inflation.

---

[1] The cash fraction c has nothing whatsoever to do with the marginal propensity to consume (c) of Chapter 3. Nor does the reserve holding ratio (e) have anything to do with the foreign exchange rate (e) of Chapter 5. At this stage we have run through the alphabet and are asking some letters to perform double duty. See the guide to symbols provided on the inside back cover.

For instance, inflation was higher immediately following the gold discoveries in California in 1848 and in Alaska in 1898.

Before the establishment of the Federal Reserve in 1913 and the introduction of federal deposit insurance in 1934, the U.S. economy was at the mercy of capricious changes in the money supply, stemming not only from the influence of gold discoveries on the growth of H but also from episodes in which the cash-holding ratio (c) and the reserve ratio (e) fluctuated dramatically. During banking panics, which occurred about once a decade and culminated in the serious panic of 1907, depositors feared for the safety of their deposits and withdrew their deposits as cash. This raised the cash-holding ratio (c) and thereby lowered the money supply. To deal with the tide of withdrawals, banks began to bolster their reserves by raising the reserve ratio (e), which further reduced the money supply.[2] In the pre–Federal Reserve era, there was no way for the government to raise H to offset panic-induced increases in c and e. Panics caused a drop in the money supply and in aggregate demand, cutting both output and prices. It was the panic of 1907 that led directly to the formation of the Federal Reserve in 1914. The Fed was established to control directly two components of equation (13.6), namely high-powered money (H) and the reserves ratio (e) to offset both undesired changes in the cash-holding ratio (c) as well as any adverse events in the economy as a whole.

Self-Test

Assume that high-powered money is 500, the fraction of deposits held as currency is 0.25, and the fraction of deposits held as reserves is 0.15. Answer the following:

1. Calculate the value of deposits and the money supply.
2. Calculate the new value of deposits and the money supply if the currency-holding fraction changes from 0.25 to 0.35.
3. Calculate the new value of deposits and the money supply if the reserve-holding fraction changes from 0.15 to 0.25 (while the currency-holding fraction remains at the original 0.25).

13-5 The Fed's Three Tools for Changing the Money Supply

Suppose the Federal Reserve wants the economy to have a given money supply M. The Fed must predict the public's desired cash-holding ratio (c), over which the Fed has no control. Then the Fed can adjust the two remaining variables in equation (13.6), H and e, to make its desired M consistent with the public's chosen c. The Fed uses three tools to accomplish this task; the first two control H and the last influences e. This section helps us understand which real-world events change H and e.

---

[2] Notice in equation (13.6) that any increase in e reduces the quantity of money (M). Although c appears in both the numerator and denominator, an increase in c reduces the money supply as long as the reserve-holding ratio (e) is less than 1.0.

First Tool: Open-Market Operations

The first tool is by far the most important. The Fed can change H by purchasing and selling government securities like Treasury bills. When it buys Treasury bills in the open market, the Fed (electronically) receives the Treasury bills from the seller and pays for them with high-powered money. The Fed pays for the Treasury bills it has bought simply by raising (electronically) the account balance of the seller at the seller's bank and the reserve balance of the seller's bank at the seller's bank's Federal Reserve Bank. This addition to H, brought about by the Fed's **open-market operations**, leads to an even larger increase in M through the money multiplier.

Federal Reserve monetary policy is decided by the Federal Open Market Committee at meetings scheduled eight times each year. The meetings of the FOMC are held in a large and imposing room at the Federal Reserve Board in Washington, D.C., and are attended by the seven governors of the Federal Reserve Board and the twelve presidents of the regional Federal Reserve banks.[3] After its meetings, the FOMC often issues a statement indicating generally what policy it has decided to follow. The FOMC also issues a directive to the Fed's open-market manager at the Federal Reserve Bank of New York, a position held in 2005 by Dino Kos.

Open-market operations are purchases and sales of government securities made by the Federal Reserve in order to change high-powered money.

***H* is created out of thin air.** Let us say that Mr. Kos's directive from the FOMC calls for continued moderate growth in the money supply, and that he has decided that the time has come for a $100 million increase in high-powered money (H). All Mr. Kos has to do is pick up the phone and buy $100 million in U.S. Treasury bills from a government bond dealer, say Salomon Smith Barney. H is created out of thin air when the Fed electronically gives a credit of $100 million to the reserve account at the bank, say Citibank, where Salomon Smith Barney has a checking account. At the same time, the Fed notifies Citibank that it should give a $100 million credit to the Salomon Smith Barney checking account.

This transaction has given Citibank an additional liability of $100 million of deposits and an additional asset of $100 million of reserves, which earn no interest. Suppose that Citibank chooses to hold $10 million of reserves against the additional $100 million deposit. It then has $90 million of excess reserves that it can use to make interest-bearing loans. Borrowers usually get loans so that they can spend the funds. When the proceeds of the loans are spent, some will be redeposited in a depository institution someplace. That institution will then have excess reserves that it can lend out, just as Citibank did. Note that depository institutions no longer have excess reserves once all the funds have been loaned out and they are withdrawn to be spent. Thus another way to view the money-creation process is that it continues until no depository institution has excess reserves it is willing to lend out.

By buying Treasury bills with electronic credits, Mr. Kos has "created" more high-powered money, H. Salomon Smith Barney transferred Treasury bills to the Fed, but Fed regulations do not permit Treasury bills to be counted toward reserves. Thus, the transfer of Treasury bills did not lower H or reserves, but the Fed's paying for the Treasury bills did raise reserves. That is why the Fed's open-market purchase produced an increase in H. Mr. Kos also

---

[3] All twelve regional presidents attend, but only five may vote. The New York Fed president always has a vote and the other four votes are rotated. All governors are entitled to vote at every FOMC meeting.

created a multiple increase in the money supply. The total money supply rises each time funds are deposited. As the money-creation multiplier showed us, the money supply is likely to rise by a sizable multiple of the original value of Treasury bills purchased by the Fed on the open market.

Effect on interest rates. Mr. Kos's purchase influences not only the total supply of money but also the interest rate. When he demands $100 million of Treasury bills, the price of Treasury bills rises, thereby lowering the return, or interest rate, they pay.

Sometimes the Fed must engage in open-market operations even when it has no desire to raise or lower the money supply. For instance, during the Christmas shopping season, the public needs more cash for transactions and raises its desired cash-holding ratio (c). Without action by the Federal Reserve, this increase in the denominator of the money-supply equation (13.6) would reduce the money supply by a multiple of the public's cash withdrawals from deposit accounts. The Fed can prevent this decline in the money supply and the associated leftward shift of the *LM* curve by conducting a "defensive" open-market purchase of Treasury bills. To prevent a decline in the money supply, the Fed would raise H enough to offset the effect of the higher c.

Second Tool: Discount Rate

Depository institutions' incentives to borrow from the Fed increase when market interest rates rise relative to the **discount rate**, the interest rate that the Fed charges them when they borrow reserves. Depository institutions' so-called discount-window borrowings tend to be high when the interest rates they can earn on money market instruments, like Treasury bills, are substantially above the discount rate that the Fed has set.

Because $100 million in Fed loans provides banks with the same $100 million in bank reserves as a $100 million open-market purchase, the Fed can control high-powered money (H) either by varying the discount rate or by conducting open-market operations. Monetary control can be achieved with either instrument and does not require both. The primary justification for allowing discount-window borrowing at the Fed is the need for immediate help by individual banks suffering from an unexpected rush of withdrawals. Such cases are rare and can be handled individually. Many economists have criticized the Fed for keeping the discount rate low enough to induce banks to borrow substantially. The unpredictability of this borrowing reduces the Fed's day-to-day control over H.

Third Tool: Reserve Requirements

Unlike the desert island, where the banker chose *voluntarily* to keep 10 percent of the bank's deposits on hand in the form of gold coin reserves, in the United States all depository institutions must hold reserves equal to 10 percent of transactions balances as **required reserves**. Reserves can be held in reserve accounts at the Fed or as vault cash (currency and coin). **Reserve requirements** apply only to transactions accounts.

The main reason that the Fed retains reserve requirements is that they help the Fed control the money supply. Even without reserve requirements, depository institutions would hold some reserves. Institutions hold vault cash because customers control the depositing and withdrawing of cash and their deposits and withdrawals are somewhat unpredictable. Because the 10

The **discount rate** is the interest rate the Federal Reserve charges depository institutions when they borrow reserves.

Required reserves are the reserves that Federal Reserve regulations require depository institutions to hold.

Reserve requirements are the rules that stipulate the minimum fraction of deposits that must be held as reserves.

percent required reserve ratio is considerably higher than most depository institutions need to satisfy their customers' cash withdrawals, depository institutions typically hold no more reserves than they are required to hold. That is, depository institutions typically face a binding reserve ratio constraint and hold few, if any, excess reserves when the required reserve ratio is high. A high required reserve ratio then means that the reserve ratio, e, stays close to it. In the absence of binding reserve requirements, however, depository institutions would have lower and less predictable (excess) reserve ratios. As we can see from equation (13.6), low and unpredictable reserve ratios unpredictably change the money-creation multiplier and the money supply by sizable amounts.[4]

Self-Test

Be sure you can answer the following questions without looking back at the preceding text:

1. If the Fed wants to reduce the money supply, does it conduct an open-market purchase of bonds or sale of bonds?
2. Why might lowering the discount rate lead to a larger money supply?
3. If the Fed wants to raise the money supply, does it raise or reduce the reserve requirement ratio (e)?

Why the Fed Can't Control the Money Supply Precisely

This chapter focuses on two problems faced by the Fed: Why it can't control the money supply precisely, and why an unstable demand for money can break the link between changes in the money supply and changes in nominal GDP. We have now learned that the Fed can use its three instruments—open-market operations, the discount rate, and changes in reserve requirements—to achieve control of the money supply (as in equation 13.6 on p. 427). Why, then, is its control imprecise?

Multiple definitions of money. There are many types of financial assets included in M2 that are not included in M1, as we learned in Table 13-2 on p. 423. Both savings deposits and time deposits are included in M2 but excluded from M1. An increase in the attractiveness of these deposits relative to transactions accounts, for example, would raise the level of M2 relative to M1. In that case, the Fed will not be able to precisely control M1 and M2 simultaneously.

The public chooses the amount of currency. The Fed controls two elements in the money supply equation (13.6): high-powered money (H) and the reserve ratio (e). It does not control the ratio of currency to deposits (c), which is controlled by firms and households. If the Fed cannot predict precisely when c

---

[4] The Fed's control of reserve requirements was also useful during World War II. The Fed needed to expand H rapidly to buy up the huge federal government deficit caused by wartime expenditures, and to minimize the impact on the money supply, the Fed raised the reserve ratio e to offset some (but not all) of the increase in H.

will change, it cannot control the money supply precisely. As we will see later in this chapter, shifts in the demand for U.S. currency by foreigners further complicate attempts to control the money supply in the United States.

Other factors. Equation (13.6) simplifies the money supply process, omitting other factors that can interfere with precise Fed control. The equation does not take into account that transactions accounts have reserve requirements, while other accounts do not. And since money market mutual funds are not actually deposits, they are also free from reserve requirements. A consequence of these differing reserve requirement ratios is that shifts of funds across accounts will change the average reserve ratio, e.

Taken together, these factors make the money multiplier hard to predict and thus make it hard to control precisely the *LM* curve. These **money-multiplier shocks** play a central role in our discussion of monetary policy later in this chapter.

A **money-multiplier shock** is any event that causes the money multiplier to change, such as a change in the public's demand for currency relative to deposits or a shift between deposits having different reserve requirements.

13-6 Theories of the Demand for Money

Now we turn from the determinants of the supply of money to the determinants of the demand for money. Our first aim is to understand why the demand for money depends on the interest rates available on assets that are alternatives to money. This is a central assumption in our *IS-LM* model of Chapters 3 and 4, and we need to examine the theories that explain the dependence of money demand on the interest rate. Our second aim is to understand why the demand for money might shift in response to financial deregulation or other events.

Interest Responsiveness of the Transactions Demand for Money

In the early 1950s, William J. Baumol of Princeton and New York University and James Tobin of Yale demonstrated that the transactions (that is, medium-of-exchange) demand for money depends on the interest rate.[5] The funds that individuals hold for transactions, to "bridge the interval between the receipt of income and its disbursement," can be placed either in M1 (currency and transactions accounts, which are assumed by Baumol and Tobin to pay no interest) or in savings deposits (which do pay interest but cannot be used for transactions). The higher the interest rate, the more individuals shift their transactions balances into interest-bearing savings deposits and other components of M2 that do not serve as a medium of exchange.

James Tobin (1918–2002)

Tobin, 1981 Nobel Prize winner, was one of the most articulate advocates of policy activism and the inventor of the theories of the transactions and portfolio demands for money.

Baumol analyzes the money-holding decision of a hypothetical individual who receives income at specified intervals but spends it steadily between paydays. An example is given in the left frame of Figure 13-2, where the person is assumed to be paid $900 per month ($Y$) on the first of each month. How will the

---

[5] William J. Baumol, "The Transactions Demand for Cash: An Inventory Theoretic Approach," *Quarterly Journal of Economics* (November 1952), pp. 545–56; James Tobin, "The Interest-Elasticity of the Transactions Demand for Cash," *Review of Economics and Statistics* (August 1956), pp. 241–47.

Figure 13-2 Alternative Allocations of an Individual's Monthly Paycheck Between Cash and Savings Deposits

In the left frame, the individual holds the entire paycheck in the form of cash, indicated by the green triangle, which shrinks as the paycheck is spent on consumption purchases. In the middle frame only half as much cash is held, initially and on average, because the individual finds it advantageous to hold half the paycheck in a savings account for half the month. In the right frame, even less cash is held because initially two-thirds of the paycheck is deposited in a savings account.

person decide whether to convert all of the paycheck into currency and transactions accounts (M1), which bear no interest, or to deposit part of the paycheck in a savings deposit that pays a monthly interest rate r?[6]

Costs and benefits of holding money. The individual compares the costs and benefits of holding M1 instead of the savings deposit. The cost of M1 is its opportunity cost, the interest forgone on savings (r) when M1 is held instead of savings deposits. The main benefit of holding M1 is the avoidance of what Baumol calls the "broker's fee" of b dollars charged every time (T) cash is obtained, either by cashing the original paycheck or by obtaining cash at the depository institution. The broker's fee in real life includes the time and transportation expense required to make an extra trip to the bank to obtain cash from a savings account.

The number of times the broker's fee is incurred equals the size of the paycheck (Y) divided by the average amount of cash (C) obtained on each trip. For

---

[6] Throughout this section we assume that no interest is paid on transactions accounts, in contrast to the real world, where interest is paid on some components of M1 and M2 that can be used for transactions. Our analysis remains valid as long as a higher interest rate on nonmoney assets raises the average interest rate paid on M1 less than proportionately, thus reducing the demand for M1.

instance, the left frame of Figure 13-2 involves no savings account; the paycheck of $900 ($Y$) is cashed at the beginning of the month ($C = 900$), and the broker's fee is incurred only one time ($T = Y/C = 1.0$). The amount of cash held dwindles as money is spent on consumption, as shown by the green triangle in the left frame.

In the middle frame half the paycheck is cashed on the first of the month ($C = 450$); the other half is deposited in a savings deposit, shown by the blue rectangle. Interest forgone equals the interest rate times the value of the average amount held in cash, which is half the value of the cash withdrawal ($rC/2$). Why? In the first half of the month the individual starts with $450 in cash, winding up with zero on the fifteenth of the month, for an average holding of $225. Then the person converts the remaining savings deposit into cash, incurring a second broker's fee. The $450 of cash dwindles again to zero on the last day of the month. The average cash holding during the last half of the month is again $225. Total interest forgone is the interest rate times $C/2$, where $C/2$ is $225 in this example.[7]

In the right frame, only one-third of the paycheck is initially cashed ($C = 300$), while the other two-thirds are deposited in the savings deposit. On the tenth and on the twentieth, withdrawals are again made, so that the broker's fee is incurred three times ($T = Y/C = 900/300 = 3$). The interest income forgone by holding cash is once again $rC/2$, or r times $150.

How many trips to the bank? How should the individual behave—as in the left frame, the middle frame, or the right frame, or should even more trips be made to the bank? The answer is that the combined cost of broker's fees (bT) and interest income foregone ($rC/2$) should be minimized:

$$\text{cost} = bT + \frac{rC}{2} \tag{13.7}$$

or

$$= b\frac{Y}{C} + \frac{rC}{2}$$

It can be shown that the average value of the cash withdrawal (C) that minimizes cost is[8]

$$C = \sqrt{\frac{2bY}{r}} \tag{13.8}$$

This equation says that the average cash withdrawal equals the square root of the following: two times the broker's fee, times income, divided by the interest

---

[7] What is the area of the green triangle in the left frame? The formula for the area of a triangle is one-half times the height, times the length, or 1/2(900)(1), where the length is expressed in months. This equals 450. In the middle are two green triangles, each with an area 1/2(450)(1/2), or 1/2(450)(1) for both triangles. This equals 225. On the right are three triangles, each with an area 1/2(300)(1/3), or 1/2(300)(1) for the three triangles. This equals 150.

[8] Here elementary calculus is required. Cost is minimized by choosing C to make the derivative of cost with respect to C equal to zero:

$$\frac{\partial(\text{cost})}{\partial C} = \frac{-bY}{C^2} + \frac{r}{2} = 0$$

When this is solved for C, we obtain the square-root expression shown as equation (13.8).

rate. A higher broker's fee (*b*) raises cash holdings by discouraging trips to the bank, each of which incurs the broker's fee.

Conversely, as equation (13.8) indicates, a higher interest rate on savings deposits lowers average cash holdings. The higher interest rate makes it optimal to go to the bank more frequently and make smaller withdrawals, thereby leaving more on average in the interest-earning savings accounts. The smaller withdrawals mean that, on average, cash holdings are smaller. The extra broker's fees incurred by going to the bank more frequently are compensated for by the extra interest earned on the larger savings account balances at the higher interest rate. Equation (13.8) also shows that the transactions demand for money rises with increases in income. Just as with interest rates, the Baumol model implies specifically that the transactions demand for money is related to the square root of income.[9]

> **Summary:** The Baumol-Tobin contributions are of major importance. They show that the interest sensitivity of the demand for money is based on a transactions motive that is shared by almost everyone. Their theories underpin the positive slope of the *LM* curve, which implies that changes either in private spending desires or in fiscal policy will change both real output and the interest rate, at least in the short run.

The Portfolio Approach

At about the same time as the Baumol-Tobin contributions, several articles highlighted another source of the demand for money, as a store of value. In particular, James Tobin, in another classic article, showed that people diversify their portfolios by holding several categories of assets.[10]

Tobin's contribution. Some assets, particularly those in M1 and M2, have nominal values that do not change when interest rates change and thus are "safe" or "riskless."[11] The prices of other financial assets, like those of stocks or long-term bonds, vary all the time and thus are "risky" assets. If investors dislike the risk that the prices of the assets they own will fluctuate, they will hold risky assets only when those assets are expected to provide higher returns than riskless assets do. Without this risk premium on risky assets, risk-averse investors would not hold them.

Faced with various safe and risky assets, with the former paying less interest than the latter, most investors compromise, diversifying their portfolios of assets. Holding only risky assets yields a high average interest return but

---

[9] The Baumol theory's "square root hypothesis" of money holding can be tested against the data. In that case, both the output elasticity and the interest rate elasticity of real money demand should be one-half. Why? Let us rewrite (13.8) in exponential form:

$$C = (2bY)^{1/2}(r)^{-1/2}$$

Thus a 1 percentage point change in *Y* raises *C* by 1/2 percent. For a more advanced treatment that allows the theoretical elasticities to differ from 1/2, see Edi Karni, "The Transactions Demand for Cash: Incorporation of the Value of Time into the Inventory Approach," *Journal of Political Economy*, vol. 81 (September/October 1973), pp. 1216–25.

[10] James Tobin, "Liquidity Preference as Behavior Towards Risk," *Review of Economic Studies*, vol. 25 (February 1958), pp. 65–86.

[11] "Riskless" is placed in quotes because M1 is not free of risk when prices are flexible, since inflation reduces the real value of nominal holdings of M1. This is one of the costs of inflation emphasized in Chapter 9.

International Perspective

Cash Fades Out as Plastic Takes Over

In 2003, the United States passed a watershed. For the first time American households used plastic cards—both debit and credit—to pay for more retail goods and services than they used or cash or checks. Much of the growth in plastic card use has been in debit cards, not credit cards. The share of debit cards in total retail transactions in 2003 was 31 percent, which when added to the 21 percent share held by credit cards totaled a 52 percent share for plastic. The remaining 48 percent share was made up of a 15 percent share for checks and the a 32 percent share for cash.[a]

The explosion of card use occurred because more people carry cards and because more retail outlets accept them. Even some taxis, soft drink machines, and airport luggage cart machines accept credit cards. Many transactions, from magazine subscriptions to a plumber's bill, can be paid by credit cards, by mail invoice, or over the Web instead of the "old-fashioned way" of putting a handwritten check in an envelope. The development of "affinity cards" that provide additional benefits such as airline miles or charitable contributions has also speeded the transition from cash and checks to card purchases. Why send checks to the local plumber and electrician if they accept cards that can earn you airline miles and eventual free trips? The spread of cards has also been hastened by card-verifying machines at every checkout counter, often built into computerized cash registers that eliminate the need for the cashier to telephone the credit card company.

A novel example of a completely cashless society is the aircraft carrier U.S.S. *Harry S Truman*, which eliminated cash transactions early in 2004. The Navy issued MasterCards to all 5,000 sailors aboard. Each card is loaded with a credit amount on a sailor's payday and then debited for transactions during the following month. Records show that sailors on the ship buy 250,000 soft drinks monthly. Allowing the sailors to purchase these drinks with plastic saves the effort of collecting half a ton of quarters from vending machines each month. Even contributions at Sunday chapel services can be made by swiping the card at the door of the chapel.

The increasing use of debit cards relative to credit cards reflects the high interest rates charged on credit cards and the fear that many Americans rightly have of running up excessive debt on credit cards. Banks issuing credit cards make large profits from customers who "roll over balances" at high interest rates, and these customers in effect subsidize convenience and zero fees for the customers who pay their bills in full each month. While banks prefer that their customers use credit cards instead of debit cards, these banks nevertheless collect fees from merchants for every plastic transaction, whether made with a credit or debit card. So eager are banks to solicit new card customers that they sent out 4.9 billion solicitations in 2004, or almost one per week for every American household, which on average already held eight credit cards each! The largest card issuer is Citigroup, parent company of Citibank, which issues 145 million cards and brings in $19 billion in revenue each year.

As the use of credit cards spreads, life gets harder for the 60 million Americans who do not have bank accounts, typically the poor and the young. It is difficult to rent a car or stay in a hotel without having a credit card, and the growing world of electronic-commerce has been built almost entirely around the ease of entering a credit card number on a computer hooked up to the Internet. Buying books from Amazon or computers from Dell over the Internet would be impossible if retailers had to wait for a week or two for their checks to arrive by mail and be cleared.

The first credit card was issued in 1950 by Francis X. McNamara, who had been embarrassed to find that he lacked enough cash to pay the bill in a restaurant. Initially, he started a network of restaurant charge accounts in which customers identified themselves with a card. This network soon became Diners Club, the first

Total In-Store Purchases by Type

1995
- Debit cards 2%
- Credit cards 8%
- Checks 30%
- Cash 60%

2003
- Debit cards 31%
- Cash 32%
- Credit cards 21%
- Checks 15%
- Prepaid cards 1%

credit card company. The mass use of credit cards began in 1958 with the BankAmericard, which became an association of many banks issuing cards with the same name. Its name was changed in 1976 to the familiar "Visa."

The gradual disappearance of cash has proceeded faster in some countries than others. Cash hangs on in Japan, which has almost $4,000 of currency per person, twice that of the United States. Cash is used in Japan for many transactions that in the United States would be handled by checks or plastic cards. The surprisingly large amount of U.S. currency outstanding, about $2,300 per U.S. resident, is not used mainly for legitimate retail transactions within U.S. borders. Some of it is used within U.S. borders by drug dealers and for cash transactions in the "underground economy" by people trying to avoid paying income taxes. And at least two-thirds of the cash in the United States is believed to be outside U.S. borders, used for transactions in many countries with a history of rapid inflation, now or in the past. In these nations, the dollar is valued for its stable purchasing power.

Credit cards facilitate transactions but are not considered to be "money" and are not part of any of the definitions of the money supply listed in Table 13-2 on p. 423. Credit cards are simply a very convenient and fast way of taking out a bank loan, even for $1.00 at a soft drink machine. To the extent that credit cards allow households to reduce their use of currency and checking accounts, credit cards increase the velocity of money, that is, the ratio of nominal GDP to the money supply.

Are debit cards money? With a debit card, your bank account is instantly debited when you make a transaction. In the old days you might start the month with $900 in cash, gradually spending down the $900 to $0 by the end of the month, as shown by the green triangle in the left frame of Figure 13-2 on p. 433. If all transactions can now be made with debit cards instead of cash, then you start the month with $900 in your checking account and gradually spend down the $900 to $0 through use of your debit card. In this example, the invention of debit cards has no effect at all on the demand for money. In contrast, credit cards reduce the demand for cash and also reduce the demand for checking accounts for those who choose not to pay their full balances each month.

[a] Data from American Bankers Association. Some of the details in this box come from Jathon Sapsford, "Paper Losses," *The Wall Street Journal*, July 23, 2004, p. A1; and Katrina Brooker, "Just One Word: Plastic," *Fortune*, February 23, 2004, pp. 125–38.

exposes investors to much risk. Holding only safe assets eliminates risk completely but yields a low average return. A mixed, or diversified, portfolio is usually the best approach.

Although the Tobin approach gives a very appealing reason for diversifying portfolios, it does not explain why anyone holds currency or non-interest-bearing checking accounts when safe, interest-bearing assets are available. The major contribution of the portfolio approach is to explain why most households hold both safe, interest-bearing components of M1 and M2 and risky stocks and bonds.

Friedman's version. At roughly the same time that Tobin was writing, Milton Friedman developed a similar approach to the demand for money.[12] Friedman's theory was a generalization of the older quantity theory of money, in which he treated money as one among several assets, including bonds, equities (stocks), and goods. Friedman emphasized that, in principle, any category of spending on GDP could be a substitute for money and might be stimulated by an expansion of the real money supply. Because he viewed a wider range of assets as being substitutes for money than did Tobin, Friedman viewed monetary policy as having more potent effects on spending.

The portfolio approach pioneered by both Tobin and Friedman makes the demand for money a function of both income and wealth, not just income. The response of the demand for money to wealth has an implication for the efficacy of fiscal policy. A stimulative fiscal policy financed by deficit spending raises real wealth if people treat government bonds as part of their wealth (see Chapter 12, pp. 402–04). The increase in wealth, in turn, raises the demand for money and shifts the *LM* curve to the left, reducing the fiscal policy multipliers below those we calculated in Chapter 4, where the wealth effect on the demand for money was ignored.[13]

> **Self-Test**
>
> Answer the following questions according to the Tobin and Friedman versions of the portfolio theory:
>
> 1. Would an increase in the supply of M1 tend to raise or lower prices in the bond market?
>
> 2. Would an increase in the supply of M1 tend to raise or lower prices in the stock market?
>
> 3. Would an increase in stock market prices raise or reduce the demand for money?

---

[12] Friedman's approach is explained in more detail in his "The Quantity Theory of Money—A Restatement," in Friedman, ed., *Studies in the Quantity Theory of Money* (Chicago: University of Chicago Press, 1956), pp. 3–21.

[13] A formal analysis of the wealth effect in the demand-for-money function is the subject of Alan S. Blinder and Robert M. Solow, "Analytical Foundations of Fiscal Policy," in *The Economics of Public Finance* (Washington, D.C.: Brookings Institution, 1974), pp. 45–57. See also Benjamin M. Friedman, "Crowding Out or Crowding In? Economic Consequences of Financing Government Deficits," *Brookings Papers on Economic Activity*, vol 9. (1978), pp. 593–641.

13-7 Case Study

Why Interest Rates Were More Volatile in the 1980s and Less Volatile in the 1990s

This chapter began by introducing the wide variety of financial instruments that are available. We showed which assets are included in the major definitions of the money supply. It can be difficult to decide whether a particular type of asset should be included in M2, for example. Before the 1980s money market mutual funds were not included in M2. Now they are, because they are regarded as being close substitutes for other types of assets in M2, like money market deposit accounts and other interest-bearing checkable deposits. The definitions of the money supply can also change because deregulation and innovations alter the menu of assets that are available for households and businesses to hold. Next we show how the deregulation of financial markets can increase the volatility of interest rates.

Effects of regulations. Until 1986 federal regulations put ceilings on the interest rates that could be paid on various categories of deposits at banks and thrift institutions. When interest rates on money market instruments, like Treasury bills, increased, either because of a rightward shift of the *IS* curve or a leftward shift of the *LM* curve, a substantial gap could open up between the interest rates on money market instruments and the deposit interest rates that were *held down by regulations*.

Large gaps between the interest rates on Treasury bills and on passbook savings accounts caused massive withdrawals of funds from commercial banks and thrift institutions, each of which are depository institutions. The resulting reduction in loans made by thrifts had a disproportionately depressing effect on the housing market, because thrifts were required by law to hold almost all their assets in the form of mortgages. The supply of mortgage finance declined for purchasers of both new and used homes. The shift toward bonds, Treasury bills, and money market mutual funds and away from depository institutions was called **disintermediation**. An outflow of funds from the thrifts, a drop in mortgage finance, and a decline in housing expenditure occurred in every postwar episode of high interest rates before 1983.

Financial Deregulation and the *IS* Curve

Financial deregulation and innovation beginning in the late 1970s, including the introduction of new interest-sensitive deposits at the thrifts, the removal of deposit-rate and loan-rate ceilings, and the development of mortgage-backed securities, largely eliminated the incentive for disintermediation and its effects on mortgage finance. Another innovation was the **adjustable-rate mortgage** (ARM). Interest rates on ARMs tend to adjust to the interest rates in the open market, rising and falling about the same amount as interest rates on Treasury bills, for example.

Prior to financial deregulation and innovation, purchases of new homes and of consumer durables declined sharply when interest rates in the open market rose. They declined because disintermediation reduced the funds that depository institutions had available to lend. At the same time, regulations prevented some loan and mortgage rates from rising as much as other rates rose.

> **Disintermediation** was the withdrawal of funds from financial intermediaries like thrift institutions when market interest rates rose above the interest rate ceilings on savings and time deposit accounts.

> An **adjustable-rate mortgage** has an interest rate that can change frequently in response to changes in short-term interest rates, in contrast to a fixed-interest mortgage.

Thus construction of new houses declined dramatically even though mortgage rates rose relatively little when disintermediation reduced the funds that depository institutions had available to lend out. With the removal of virtually all ceilings on deposit and loan interest rates, depository institutions are free to raise deposit rates to prevent disintermediation and keep mortgage rates in line with other interest rates. Because disintermediation no longer stymies spending, larger increases in interest rates are now required to reduce spending by the same amount.

Recall that the *IS* curve displays all the combinations of real output (*Y*) and the market real interest rate (*r*) that are consistent with equilibrium in the commodity market. The slope of the *IS* curve indicates how much an increase in the interest rate reduces interest-sensitive spending, and thus reduces real output. Changes in financial markets made the *IS* curve steeper, shown in the left frame of Figure 13-3, because a larger increase in the interest rate on financial assets is required to reduce spending by the same amount.

Why the *LM* Curve Became Steeper

Chapter 4 showed that the *LM* curve normally slopes up because the demand for M1 responds to the interest rate paid on bonds and other nonmonetary assets. That interest rate (*r*) is plotted on the vertical axis in Figure 13-3. Our previous analysis, and the curve in Figure 13-3 labeled "old *LM* curve," assumed that the interest rate paid on M1 (r_m) was zero. Thus an increase in *r* raised

Financial Deregulation Tilts the *IS* and *LM* Curves

Figure 13-3 The Effect of Financial Deregulation in the Commodity and Money Markets

In the left frame, deregulation caused the *IS* curve to become the steeper line, *IS'*. This was the result not only of deregulation, but also of the introduction of new types of deposits at depository institutions with flexible interest rates, the development of mortgage-backed securities, and the introduction of adjustable-rate mortgages. In the right frame, the *LM* curve became the steeper line *LM'*, because a given increase in the interest rate in financial markets does not cause as much of a reduction of the demand for M1 as previously, since depository institutions are now able to raise the rates they pay for deposits.

$r - r_m$ by the same amount and increased the incentive for individuals to reduce their holdings of M1.

This analysis is still valid for holdings of currency, which pays no interest. But financial reforms have allowed banks to offer interest-bearing checking accounts. The interest rate on these accounts is variable, tending to rise and fall with the interest rate paid on nonmonetary assets (r). Thus r_m, which is an average of the zero interest rate on currency and the positive interest rate paid on some types of checking accounts, responds partially to changes in r. Thus the difference, $r - r_m$, now rises by less than the amount of any increase in r, providing less of an incentive than previously for individuals to reduce their checking account balances. As a result, the demand for money function, and thus the *LM* curve, has become steeper in the right frame of Figure 13-3.

Effects on Interest Rates

Now we can put our analysis into action and learn why the main effect of deregulation is likely to be increased volatility of interest rates. In Figure 13-4 both frames show the *LM* curve shifting to the left by the same horizontal distance, as the result of a decision by the Fed to tighten monetary policy. The difference between the frames is that the left-hand frame shows the economy before deregulation, with the flatter "old *IS* curve" and "old *LM* curve" copied

Why Deregulation Makes Interest Rates More Volatile

(a) Before deregulation

(b) After deregulation

Figure 13-4 The Effect of a Lower Money Supply on Interest Rates and Output

Both frames show the effect of the same leftward horizontal shift in the *LM* curve as the result of a decision by the Fed to tighten monetary policy. In both frames, the *IS* curve remains fixed. The difference is that the left frame uses the flatter *IS* and *LM* curves from the period before deregulation of financial markets, copied from Figure 13-3. The right frame uses the new steeper *IS'* and *LM'* curves, also copied from Figure 13-3. As a result of the steeper curves, a given leftward shift in the *LM* curve creates a much larger increase in the interest rate in the right frame than in the left frame. We cannot tell whether output fell more in the right frame than in the left frame.

from Figure 13-3. The right-hand frame shows the economy after deregulation, with the new curves *IS'* and *LM'*, also copied from Figure 13-3. The economy moves from point *A* to *B* in the left frame and from point *A* to *B'* in the right frame, with a much greater increase in the interest rate under the new deregulated environment.

This analysis helps us to understand why the short-term interest rate was so volatile in the 1980s, as shown in Figure 14-4 on p. 464. Interest rates became less volatile in the 1990s, because the Fed placed a higher priority on maintaining stability in the interest rate. The Fed achieved this stability by active open-market operations to offset shifts in the *IS* and *LM* curves. The following section examines the conditions under which the Fed finds it desirable to stabilize interest rates.

13-8 Why the Federal Reserve "Sets" Interest Rates

We have just seen how financial deregulation and innovation can alter the slopes of the *IS* and *LM* curves. The effects, and even the occurrence, of financial deregulation and innovation will not always be predictable. In addition, the *IS* and *LM* curves will sometimes shift unpredictably for reasons unrelated to financial deregulation and innovation.

Pervasive deregulation and innovation in financial markets were major contributors to the frequent instability of the demand for money after the mid-1970s. In this section we use the *IS-LM* model of Chapter 4 to explain why the unpredictability, or instability, of the demand for money led the Federal Reserve to shift its policies toward setting interest rates. Reports in the media and announcements from the Fed that the FOMC has decided to change interest rates often give the (incorrect) impression that the Fed sets interest rates directly. It is important to remember that the Fed can only affect the nominal federal funds interest rate indirectly. When the Fed wants to raise short-term interest rates, it undertakes open-market sales of bonds, which reduce reserves and thus the money supply. When the Fed sells the right amount of bonds, the *LM* curve shifts leftward and intersects the *IS* curve at the higher interest rate that the Fed seeks.

As in Chapter 4, Figure 13-5 illustrates the working of the *IS-LM* model. We assume that the expected inflation rate is zero, so that the nominal and real interest rates are the same; both are labeled simply as the "interest rate" on the vertical axis. A constant price level is an acceptable assumption when long-term wage and price contracts in the real world limit the flexibility of the price level in the short run. In such a case, the shifts in the *IS* or *LM* curves of Figure 13-5 mainly influence the level of real output in the first few months or quarters after the shift.

The position of the *IS* curve can be shifted by changes in business and consumer optimism, by changes in net exports, and by changes in government spending, autonomous net taxes, and tax rates. When *commodity demand is unstable* because of swings in optimism, net exports, or government policy, the *IS* curve shifts back and forth as shown in the left-hand frame of Figure 13-5. The position of the *LM* curve can be shifted by a change in the real money supply; the LM_0 curve in the left-hand frame assumes that the real money supply is fixed.[14] The *LM* curve will also be shifted when the demand for money is unstable. A sudden increase in the demand for money brought on by a financial panic would shift the *LM* curve leftward.

Implications of unstable commodity demand. William Poole, then of Brown University and in 2005 the president of the Federal Reserve Bank of St. Louis, first popularized the use of the *IS-LM* model to compare targeting of the money supply with the alternative of targeting the interest rate.[15] Unstable commodity demand, shown by the shifting *IS* curve in the left-hand frame of Figure 13-5, calls into question the wisdom of targeting the interest rate. When the real money supply is held constant and the *LM* curve remains fixed at LM_0, the economy moves back and forth between positions B_0 and B_1, and real output moves over the limited range between Y'_0 and Y'_1.

With unstable commodity demand, fixing the *LM* curve by targeting the money supply is superior to a policy of maintaining stable interest rates. When commodity demand is high (as along IS_1), a stable interest rate policy means that the real money supply must be allowed to rise to prevent the interest rate from increasing. The Federal Reserve must increase the money supply to accommodate the additional demand for money that occurs when commodity demand is high. The stable interest rate policy causes the economy to fluctuate between points A_0 and A_1, and it allows real output to vary over the wide range between Y_0 and Y_1.

Instead of targeting interest rates or the money supply, an alternative approach for the Fed would be to target real GDP itself. The policy of targeting real output is illustrated in the left-hand frame of Figure 13-5 by the points C_0 and C_1. Fluctuations in commodity demand would have to be offset by fluctuations in the supply of money in the *opposite* direction. If the *LM* curve can be promptly moved in the opposite direction of the shift in the *IS* curve, then the economy could remain at its natural real GDP (Y^N). And, as we learned in Chapter 8, keeping the economy at Y^N is consistent with steady inflation in the absence of supply shocks.

The analysis with unstable money demand. The right-hand frame of Figure 13-5 assumes that commodity demand is fixed, so that the *IS* curve remains fixed at IS_0. But here the demand for money is assumed to be unstable. When the real money supply is fixed, *an unstable demand for money causes the* LM *curve to move about unpredictably between* LM_1 *and* LM_2. A constant money supply policy leads to fluctuations in the economy between points B_0 and B_1, with output varying between Y'_0 and Y'_1. A superior policy is to change the money supply in order to maintain a constant interest rate. When the demand for money rises, the interest rate is prevented from rising by raising the money supply. This constant interest rate policy keeps the economy pinned to point C, with a fixed interest rate $\bar{r}$ and a fixed output level Y^N. In this diagram, an interest rate target and a natural real GDP (Y^N) target amount to the same thing.

---

[14] A fixed real money supply (M/P) and a fixed *LM* curve can be achieved either with a constant nominal money supply (M) and a fixed price level (P), or with the money supply growing at the same rate as the price level ($m = p$).

[15] William Poole, "Optimal Choice of Monetary Policy Instruments in a Simple Stochastic Macro Model," *Quarterly Journal of Economics*, vol. 84 (May 1970), pp. 197–216. A little-known earlier reference is M. L. Burstein, *Economic Theory* (New York: Wiley, 1966), Chapter 13.

Figure 13-5 Effects on Real Output of Policies That Either Stabilize the Interest Rate or Stabilize the Real Money Supply When Either Commodity Demand or Money Demand Is Unstable

In the left frame, the demand for commodities is unstable, fluctuating unpredictably between IS_0 and IS_1. A policy that maintains a fixed real money supply and a fixed LM_0 curve leads to smaller fluctuations of output than an alternative policy that stabilizes the interest rate at r by shifting LM. A third policy, which stabilizes real GDP at Y^N, causes interest rate instability between points C_0 and C_1. In the right frame, the demand for money is unstable. In this case, a policy of stabilizing the interest rate at $\bar{r}$ will stabilize real GDP. When the real money supply is held fixed, unstable money demand shifts the LM curve from LM_1 to LM_2 and causes output to fluctuate between Y'_0 and Y'_1.

The Choice of Targets

In the left-hand frame of Figure 13-5, an unstable demand for commodities makes a real GDP target superior to a money supply target, which in turn is superior to an interest rate target. In the right-hand frame, with an unstable demand for money, a real GDP and interest rate target are the same, and both are superior to a money supply target. If, as is likely, there is instability in both commodity and money demand, a real GDP target is superior to an interest rate target.

However, the choice of the best variable to target differs when we drop the unrealistic assumption that the price level is fixed. If there are shocks to the price level, such as the supply shocks that we studied in Chapter 8, then a real GDP target runs the risk that the price level and inflation rate could rise without limit. We return in Chapter 14 to the choice of target variables by the Fed. Two of those that avoid an unlimited acceleration of inflation are a target for the growth in nominal GDP, and a rule that targets a weighted average of the inflation rate and the ratio of actual to natural real GDP. A rule of the latter type, as we shall learn, is often called a "Taylor Rule."

> **Self-Test**
>
> Using the *IS-LM* model analysis of Figure 13-5, which neglects both lags and inflation, rank three types of policies (money supply rule, interest rate rule, real GDP rule) under two sets of circumstances:
>
> 1. If commodity demand is unstable, take the three policies and rank first the policy that minimizes the fluctuations in real output, rank second the policy that is next best, and rank third the policy that is worst.
>
> 2. If the demand for money is unstable, take the three policies and rank first the policy that minimizes the fluctuations in real output, rank second the policy that is next best, and rank third the policy that is worst.

Summary

1. Surplus funds from savers are channeled to borrowers by way of financial intermediaries and financial markets. The main types of financial intermediaries are depository institutions, contractual savings institutions, and investment intermediaries. The main types of financial market instruments are money market and capital market instruments.

2. The United States has two major definitions of the money supply. M1 includes currency, balances in transactions accounts, and traveler's checks. M2 comprises M1 plus other assets, including savings deposits, small time deposits, and retail money market mutual funds.

3. A set of banks in a closed economy—one with no transfers of funds to the outside—can "create money" by a multiple of each dollar of cash that is initially received. This is true for a single bank on a desert island or for all banks in the United States taken together.

4. The deposit-creation multiplier is 1.0 divided by the fraction of the initial cash receipt that is held as reserves or currency. The money multiplier is then the deposit multiplier times 1.0 plus the currency-holding fraction. The money supply is equal to high-powered money times the money multiplier.

5. The Fed uses three tools for changing the money supply: open-market operations, the discount rate, and reserve requirements.

6. Several theories have been developed to explain the relation between the demand for money, income, wealth, and the interest rate. The transactions demand for money depends on the interest rate; people will take the trouble to make extra trips to the bank and keep more of their income in savings accounts (and other interest-earning assets) when the interest rate is higher.

7. The portfolio approach emphasizes the household decision to allocate its wealth among money, savings accounts, bonds, and other assets. Any event that raises wealth, such as a stimulative fiscal policy, will tend to raise the demand for money.

8. Deregulation and innovation in financial markets have made both the *IS* and *LM* curves steeper, so that a given change in the supply of money now has a larger effect on interest rates.

9. In earlier chapters we assumed that the growth of aggregate demand could be controlled precisely by policymakers. We now recognize that in the real-world economy, policy shifts cannot instantly or precisely offset the effects on aggregate demand of shocks to *IS* or *LM* curves.

10. When commodity demand is unstable and money demand is stable, a money supply target is superior to an interest rate target, but a real GDP target is superior to both. When money demand is unstable and commodity demand is stable, both real GDP and interest rate targets are superior to a money supply target.

11. The ongoing instability of the demand for money has led the Fed to target interest rates rather than the money supply.

Concepts

financial deregulation
financial markets
financial intermediaries
thrift institutions
money market instruments
capital market instruments

M1
M2
high-powered money
money multiplier
open-market operations
discount rate

required reserves
reserve requirements
money-multiplier shock
disintermediation
adjustable-rate mortgage

Questions

1. What is meant by the term *financial markets*? Given the existence of financial markets, why do we have financial intermediaries? Explain which type of borrowers are most likely to obtain funds in financial markets and which type of borrowers most likely use financial intermediaries to obtain loans.
2. Distinguish among the three types of financial intermediaries in terms of from whom they obtain funds and what they do with those funds: depository institutions, contractual savings institutions, and investment intermediaries.
3. Distinguish between money market instruments and capital market instruments.
4. What are the two most important functions of money? Give examples of assets that perform both of these functions. Give examples of assets that perform one of the functions but not the other.
5. What is the main distinction between the M1 and M2 definitions of money?
6. Explain why there is a different money multiplier for each definition of the money supply.
7. What is high-powered money? Explain why *both* reserves and cash held by the public are considered to be high-powered money.
8. What are the conditions required for money creation? In the Great Depression of the 1930s, many bank failures occurred in part because one or more of these conditions was no longer met. Which are the most likely candidates to explain the failure of the banking system to operate properly in the depths of the Great Depression?
9. Explain what happens when the Fed conducts an open-market purchase of $200 billion in bonds. How do the banks get involved? What is the ultimate effect on the level of high-powered money and on the money supply?
10. Explain how the money-creation multiplier is similar to the income-determination multiplier of Chapter 3.
11. Explain how each of the following events affects the money supply.
    (a) An increase in income tax rates induces the public to conduct more of its business in currency to hide earnings.
    (b) An increase in interest rates encourages the public to hold less currency.
    (c) Banks obtain discount loans from the Fed.
    (d) Increasing uncertainty about deposit withdrawals leads banks to hold on to excess reserves.
12. What are the major ways in which the supply of money can change? If it is that simple, why couldn't the Fed effectively control the money supply in the past?
13. Explain the significance of the Baumol-Tobin analysis of the transactions demand for money.
14. In what ways are the portfolio approaches developed by Tobin and Friedman similar? In what ways do they differ?
15. What is meant by the term *disintermediation*? What impact did deregulation of financial markets have on the process and the volatility of the housing market?
16. Explain how financial deregulation and innovation since the early 1980s: (i) affected the slope of the *IS* and *LM* curves; (ii) contributed to increased volatility of interest rates in the 1980s; and (iii) affected the impact of monetary and fiscal policy on real GDP.
17. Money-multiplier shocks can be a source of instability in the economy. Suppose such a shock produces a decrease in the money supply. Use the *IS-LM* and *SP-LP* models to predict what will happen to real GDP, the real interest rate, the inflation rate, and the output ratio, in both the short run and the long run, if the Fed takes no action to offset the multiplier shock.
18. Many people advocate the supremacy of rules over discretion in the Fed's conduct of monetary policy, but there is less agreement as to what kind of rule the Fed should follow. A money supply rule, an interest rate rule, and a real GDP rule have all been suggested. Discuss the advantages and disadvantages of each type of rule.
19. Suppose that the Fed is able to target real GDP when there is instability in either commodity demand or the demand for money. Explain how the Fed must conduct open market operations, that is either buy or sell government bonds, as (a) commodity demand rises and falls or (b) the demand for money increases and decreases.

20. Explain why American households have moved away from the use of cash and checks to debit and credit cards to purchase retail goods and services. Explain what effect, if any, the increased use of debit and credit cards has on the demand for money.

Note: Asterisks designate Problems that require the Appendix to Chapter 4.

Problems

1. Given the following information for July 2004, calculate the amounts of M1 and M2 in July 2004. The amounts are in billions of dollars.

Currency	$684.6
Demand deposits	307.3
Money market mutual funds (retail only)	740.7
Other checkable deposits	325.9
Savings deposits, including money market deposit accounts	3,414.7
Small-denomination time deposits	796.6
Traveler's checks	7.6

2. Suppose the ratio of deposits that banks hold in the form of reserves is 7 percent. Suppose further that people want to hold 8 percent of their deposits in the form of cash. Then, if the Fed wants the money supply to be $6,228 billion, what is the necessary level of high-powered money?

3. Assume an economy in which the reserve ratio is 15 percent, people hold 10 percent of their deposits in the form of cash, and there are no other leakages.
   (a) Compute the value of the money multiplier.
   (b) If the current level of high-powered money is $1,500 billion, what is the money supply in this economy?
   (c) How much does the money supply change if the Fed buys $30 billion of U.S. government Treasury bills from a government bond dealer? How about if banks' borrowings of reserves from the Fed decline by $6 billion?
   (d) If the Fed set a target money supply of $6,424 billion, what would it have to do to achieve that target?

4. Suppose you earn and spend $2,400 per month. You receive your paycheck on the first day of the month and must decide how much of it to hold as cash or in a non-interest-earning checking account and how much to deposit in your savings account. The savings account pays 5 percent interest; however, the bank charges you $2 for each withdrawal you make during the month.
   (a) What will be your average demand for money over the month?
   (b) If the interest rate rose to 10 percent, what would be your average demand for money over the month? Is this change consistent with your expectations about the demand for money?

*5. The following equations summarize the structure of the commodity market before and after deregulation of the financial system.

$$C = C_a + 0.75(Y - T) \quad G = 1{,}950$$
$$C_a = 950 - 35r \quad T = 200 + 0.2Y$$
$$I_p = 2{,}250 - 90r \quad NX = 1{,}000 - 0.1Y$$

The demand for money before deregulation is $(M/P)^d = 0.2Y - 50r$, and the demand for money after deregulation is $(M/P)^d = 0.19Y - 28.5r$. The money supply both before and after deregulation is 1,900. Using the preceding information, answer the following questions:

(a) What is the equation of the IS curve?
(b) What is the equation of the LM curve before deregulation?
(c) What is the equation of the LM curve after deregulation?
(d) What are the equilibrium levels of Y and r before deregulation?
(e) What are the equilibrium levels of Y and r after deregulation?
(f) How do your answers to (b) through (e) differ before and after deregulation?
(g) Before deregulation, if the money supply increased to 2,000 from 1,900, what would Y and r be?
(h) After deregulation, if the money supply increased to 2,000 from 1,900, what would Y and r be?
(i) Are these results consistent with the text's explanation of the effect of deregulation on the variability of interest rates?

*6. Suppose that the IS and LM curves for an economy are given by:

$$IS: Y = 4A'_p - 300r$$
$$LM: Y = 3(M^s/P) + 300r$$

where M^s is initially 3,400 and $P = 1$. Because of unstable commodity demand, A'_p fluctuates between 3,000 and 3,300.

(a) What are equilibrium Y and r when A'_p is 3,000? 3,300?
(b) Suppose that the Fed sets an interest rate target of 4 percent. Between what values will Y fluctuate?

Compare this range of Y with the range of Y in part a.

(c) Suppose that the Fed is able to target real GDP itself and that Y^N is 11,400. Between what values will r fluctuate? Compare this range of r with the range of r in part a.

*7. Suppose that that the equation for an economy's IS curve is $Y = 12,600 - 300r$. Due to unstable money demand, the demand for money fluctuates between $(M/P)^d = 0.25Y - 50r$ and $(M/P)^d = 0.2Y - 40r$. The real money supply, M^s/P, equals 2,400.

(a) Derive the equation for the LM curve when the demand for money is $(M/P)^d = 0.25Y - 50r$ and when it is $(M/P)^d = 0.2Y - 40r$.

(b) What are equilibrium Y and r when the demand for money is $(M/P)^d = 0.25Y - 50r$ and when it is $(M/P)^d = 0.2Y - 40r$?

(c) Suppose that the Fed wants to target the interest rate in order to keep real GDP equal to natural real GDP. Given Y^N is 11,400, what is the interest rate that the Fed must target? In order to reach this target, what must the real money supply equal when the demand for money is $(M/P)^d = 0.25Y - 50r$ and when it is $(M/P)^d = 0.2Y - 40r$?

Self-Test Answers

p. 422 (1) Commercial banks are the largest single type of financial intermediary. (2) Money market mutual funds are financial intermediaries; state government bonds are capital market instruments; state government retirement funds are financial intermediaries; corporate bonds are capital market instruments; and commercial paper is a money market instrument.

p. 424 (1) This new type of account, which allows interest to be earned and checks to be written, is part of M2, and so its invention raises the demand for M2 and lowers the demand for M1. (2) As discussed on pp. 436–37, credit cards are not part of the money supply. Rather they are a quick and convenient way of obtaining a bank loan. Credit cards reduce the demand for M1 in two ways, first by reducing the need to carry currency, and second by reducing the size of checking accounts for those who choose not to pay off their entire credit card balances every month. Because M1 is part of M2, credit cards also reduce the demand for M2, including some components of M2 that are not in M1 like money market mutual funds. (3) Same as (1). (4) Equity mutual funds are in neither M1 nor M2, so the demand for both M1 and M2 will decline.

p. 428 (1) $D = H/(e + c) = 500/0.4 = 1,250$
$M = (1 + c)D = (1.25)1,250 = 1,562.5$
(2) $D = 500/0.5 = 1,000$
$M = (1.35)1,000 = 1,350$
(3) $D = 500/0.5 = 1,000$
$M = (1.25)1,000 = 1,250$

p. 431 (1) The short answer is that the Fed sells bonds when it wants to reduce high-powered money [and hence the money supply through equation (13.6)], and it buys bonds when it wants to raise the money supply. To pay for the bonds they bought, the purchasers send high-powered money to the Fed, thereby reducing the amount of H remaining in the economy. (2) Lowering the discount rate, the interest rate that they pay on their discount window borrowings, makes it more attractive for depository institutions to borrow H from the Fed. An increased stock of H in the economy raises the money supply. (3) It reduces the reserve requirement ratio (e), which appears in the denominator of equation (13.6).

p. 438 (1) and (2) Starting from an initial equilibrium, an increase in the supply of M1 creates an excess supply of M1. According to Tobin and Friedman, M1 is a substitute for both bonds and stocks, and so some of the M1 that is in excess of the initial demand will be used to purchase bonds and stocks, causing prices to rise in both markets. (Strictly speaking, the Tobin version makes stocks and bonds a substitute only for the interest-bearing part of M1, not non-interest-bearing currency and checking deposits.) (3) The effect is ambiguous in both the Tobin and Friedman models. Since money is a substitute for stocks, an increase in the return on stocks (as occurs when stock prices go up) will reduce the demand for money. But the demand for money also depends on wealth, and an increase in wealth caused by an increase in stock market prices will raise the demand for money. The two effects go in opposite directions, and so the net effect is uncertain.

p. 445 (1) With unstable commodity demand, a real GDP rule is most capable of maintaining stable real GDP, a money supply rule comes next, and an interest rate rule is least likely to maintain stable real GDP. (2) With unstable money demand, the real GDP and interest rate rules are equally capable of maintaining stable real GDP, while the money supply rule will result in unstable real GDP.

CHAPTER 14

Stabilization Policy in the Closed and Open Economy

Economic forecasting is the occupation that makes astrology respectable.[1]
—David Dremas, 1982

14-1 The Central Role of Demand Shocks

Unrealistic Precision of Policy Control in Previous Chapters

In earlier chapters we assumed that aggregate demand could be controlled exactly. But in the real world, life is more difficult for policymakers. Exogenous **demand shocks** can shift the *AD* curve and thus the level of nominal GDP, but policymakers cannot neutralize these shocks totally because nominal GDP reacts to policy changes with a lag and by an uncertain amount. As a result, many economists argue against **policy activism**, that is, the use of monetary and fiscal policy to offset exogenous demand shocks.

In this chapter we take into account those aspects of the real-world economy that make successful policy activism elusive. We contrast the real world with the idealized world of the simple *IS-LM* model (Chapter 4), where policymakers could compute the exact policy response needed to offset fully any shift in the *IS* or *LM* curves.

Demand shocks include unexpected changes in business and consumer optimism, changes in net exports, and changes in government spending or tax rates (for example, in wartime) not related to stabilization policy.

Policy activism purposefully changes the settings of the instruments of monetary and fiscal policy to offset changes in private sector spending.

The Economy as Supertanker

Unfortunately, policymakers cannot steer the economy back and forth as easily as a driver steers an automobile. Changing aggregate demand is much more like steering a giant supertanker. Even if the captain gives the signal for a hard turn, it takes a mile or so to see a change in the supertanker's direction, and ten miles before the supertanker completes the turn. In the same way, the real-world economy has a momentum of its own, and policy shifts cannot control aggregate demand precisely.

Chapter 13 on money demand and supply introduced several of the reasons why monetary control is so difficult. The Fed does not control the money supply precisely. Rather, money-multiplier shocks occur because the link between the Fed's instruments and the money supply depends in part on factors over which the Fed has no direct control, such as the public's demand for currency. Furthermore, shifts in the demand for money loosen the links between the money supply and nominal GDP.

---

[1] David Dremas, "The Madness of Crowds," *Forbes,* September 27, 1982, p. 201.

In this chapter we contrast policy activism with an alternative approach based on **policy rules**. These rules call for the Fed to use its tools of monetary control, introduced in Chapter 13, to maintain a fixed growth rate of a particular macroeconomic variable. Early proposals called for rules to fix the growth rate of high-powered money or some measure of the money supply. Subsequent proposals for rules have focused on the inflation rate, a so-called "inflation target." Some advocate a mixed rule that targets both the inflation rate and the output ratio or gap, the so-called Taylor Rule.

A major theme of this chapter is that both activist policy and policy rules face similar pitfalls, including lags, forecasting errors, uncertainty about responses of the economy to Fed actions, and the need to maintain credibility. The modern policy debate is less about the general merits of rules than about *which of several alternative rules should be implemented*. We also look into another monetary policy rule that has been much discussed internationally, targeting the exchange rate, and another that has been implemented in reality, namely the single European currency called the euro.

A **policy rule** can call for a fixed path of a policy instrument like the discount rate, of an intermediate variable like the money supply, or a target variable like inflation or unemployment. A rule can also call for a specified response of a policy instrument in response to a given change in a target variable.

14-2 Stabilization Targets and Instruments in the Activists' Paradise

This section sets forth the traditional analysis of stabilization policy favored by the proponents of policy activism. We then focus on the concerns of those who advocate policy rules and oppose activism.

The Need for Multiple Instruments

Just as driving a car requires a steering wheel, accelerator pedal, and brake, so hitting two policy targets requires at least two instruments of stabilization policy. For instance, Chapter 4 showed that changes in the real money supply could not simultaneously achieve both a target level of real GDP and a target interest rate. Both monetary and fiscal policy must be manipulated to achieve an intersection of the *IS* and *LM* curves at a given combination of the interest rate and real GDP (see Figure 4-10 on p. 117).

The *IS-LM* analysis assumed that the price level was fixed. Now that we have learned to allow for inflation, we recognize that monetary policy involves control of the growth rate of a nominal variable (like high-powered money or the money supply). In the long run, when actual and natural real GDP growth are equal to each other ($y = y^N$) and the output ratio (Y/Y^N) is at 100 percent, monetary policy controls the inflation rate (nominal minus real GDP growth, $x - y^N$) and fiscal policy controls the growth rate of natural real GDP, y^N.

Monetary, fiscal, and structural employment policies. The natural rate of unemployment is beyond the control of monetary and fiscal policy. A permanent reduction in unemployment requires a permanent drop in the natural rate of unemployment, which in turn requires a separate policy instrument. That instrument is the mixture of structural employment policy tools discussed in Chapter 9—training subsidies, unemployment benefits, and so on.

But we have not finished adding to our list of policy instruments. Fiscal policy really consists of two types of **policy instruments**: government spending and tax rates. A given government deficit can be achieved with high

Policy instruments for monetary policy are high-powered money and the Fed's discount rate; for fiscal policy they are government spending and tax rates.

spending and high tax rates or low spending and low tax rates. Thus another target of policy is the size of government spending and revenue relative to natural real GDP.

So far we are up to four instruments and four targets:

Instruments	Targets
Structural employment policy	Unemployment rate
High-powered money	Inflation rate
Government spending	Size of government
Tax rates	Long-run growth in real GDP per person

Figure 14-1 gives a more complete illustration of the principles of economic policy. The goal of economic policy is economic welfare, represented by the red box in the upper right corner. Economic welfare can be thought of simply as happiness, the things that individual members of society want—stable prices, full employment, and a high standard of living.

The Theory of Economic Policy

POLICY INSTRUMENTS

Fiscal instruments:
  Government spending
  Tax rates
Monetary instruments:
  High-powered money
  Discount rate
Structural employment policy

STRUCTURAL RELATIONS CONNECTING ALL THE VARIABLES

Consumption function
Investment function
Demand for money
Short-run Phillips Curve (SP)
Long-run Phillips Curve (LP)

TARGET VARIABLES

Unemployment rate
Inflation rate
Natural real GDP
Balance of payments or foreign exchange rate
Share of public vs. private spending
Distribution of income

ECONOMIC WELFARE

EXOGENOUS NONPOLICY VARIABLES

Business optimism
Consumer optimism
Wars
Foreign demand
Supply shocks

IRRELEVANT SIDE EFFECTS

Nominal GDP
Reelection of incumbent political party
Victory of monetarism
Consulting opportunities for activist economists
National debt

Figure 14-1 A Flowchart Showing the Relationship Between Policy Instruments, Policy Targets, and Economic Welfare

Both policy instruments and exogenous nonpolicy variables are fed into the structural relations that connect the exogenous (policy and nonpolicy) variables with the endogenous (target and nontarget) variables. Total economic welfare at the upper right depends on the achieved values of the target variables, and thus it depends on policymakers' decisions about the settings of policy instruments.

Targets, Instruments, and Structural Relations

Target variables are the economic aggregates whose values society cares most about—society's goals.

Directly to the left of the economic welfare box in Figure 14-1 we find a light red box that lists the main policy **target variables** that influence economic welfare. Some are more important than others. The distribution of income is quite different from the other targets; any policy shift that raises the income of one group at the expense of others (rich versus poor; creditors versus debtors) is bound to be controversial and lead to political conflict.

In the upper left corner of Figure 14-1 is a list of some of the policy instruments that the government can use to try to achieve its targets. Linking the green instrument box with the upper right red target box is the large blue central box, which contains the structural relations that link the variables. The *IS* and *LM* curves of Chapter 4 and *SP* and *LP* curves of Chapter 8 summarize the main relations that link money, taxes, and government spending to unemployment and inflation. But as shown in the lower left orange box, those curves can also be shifted by several exogenous factors not under the direct control of policymakers, such as a burst of business or consumer optimism or higher export sales (shifting the *IS* curve upward) or an adverse supply shock (shifting the *SP* curve upward).

When the values of the exogenous and instrument variables are fed into the structural economic relations in the middle box, they produce the values of the target variables—unemployment, inflation, and the others. Other variables, shown in the lower right purple box, are also affected, but these are called irrelevant variables because they are not major determinants of economic welfare.

Rules Advocates and the Activists' Paradise

The framework supporting activist policy intervention, as set out in Figure 14-1, evokes a skeptical response from economists who advocate policy rules. Rules advocates feel that activists are unrealistically optimistic about how successful their policies are likely to be. By contrast, policy rules advocates believe that activist stabilization policy may actually do more harm than good. "Activist economists," they claim, "require a utopian set of assumptions about the economy for activist stabilization policy to do more good than harm."

The utopian "activists' paradise" is a hypothetical world in which activist policy achieves almost perfect control over aggregate demand. It dramatizes the optimistic set of assumptions required for policy activism to be accepted without question. The activists' paradise has these main characteristics.[2]

1. Policymakers forecast accurately future changes in the private demand for and supply of goods and services.
2. Policymakers forecast accurately the future effect of current changes in monetary and fiscal policy.
3. Policymakers possess policy instruments that powerfully affect aggregate demand.

---

[2] The term *activists' paradise* and its major characteristics originate in Arthur M. Okun, "Fiscal-Monetary Activism: Some Analytical Issues," *Brookings Papers on Economic Activity*, vol. 3 (1972), pp. 123–163. In this, as in many other areas of economics (see Okun's Law, pp. 264-66), Okun had the unique ability to capture an issue in clear and vivid language. The author's tribute to the unique talents of Okun appears in *Brookings Papers on Economic Activity*, vol. 11 (1980), pp. 1–5.

Rules Versus Activism in a Nutshell: The Optimism-Pessimism Grid

The table in this box sorts out a wide variety of issues in debate between the policy activists and rules advocates. Activists' beliefs are presented in the top line. Activists are relatively pessimistic about the stability of the private economy. This pessimism stems from their concern that the private (that is, nongovernment) economy is subject to substantial business fluctuation. Such fluctuations are sometimes the result of a wave of business and consumer pessimism, as in the 1930s, or of a collapse of business investment, as in 2000–02. Business fluctuations may result also from government actions, as when military spending exploded during wartime.

While the activists are pessimistic about the stability of the private economy, they are optimistic about the feasibility of stabilizing the economy through government policy. This reflects their belief that the activists' paradise, while a caricature designed to exaggerate the conditions needed for successful policy activism, nevertheless contains a kernel of truth.

As shown in the table, the activists' position is disputed on both counts by policy rules advocates. This group optimistically views the private economy as inherently self-correcting, due in part to the belief that demand disturbances are partly or largely absorbed by changes in private saving. And policy rules advocates are pessimistic about stabilization policy, believing it can do more harm than good, due to lags, forecasting errors, uncertainty, and the other problems discussed in this chapter.

	Belief regarding automatic self-correcting properties of private economy?	Belief regarding efficacy of government stabilization policy?
Activists	Pessimistic	Optimistic
Rules advocates	Optimistic	Pessimistic

---

4. Policymakers can change policy instruments without incurring any costs, economic or social.
5. No political constraints affect the use of the policy instruments.

The activists' paradise is an extreme set of positions that no economist actually believes, but those positions rather set the stage for the debate over activism versus rules. *The core of the activists' paradise is a deep faith in the power of macroeconomics as a science. The activists' paradise requires policymakers to be able to forecast accurately not just future changes in demand, but also the future effects of current changes in policy.*

As shown in the box above, one easy way to think about the rules-versus-activism debate is to note the contrast between where the two groups place their optimism and pessimism. Policy activists are pessimistic about the self-correcting powers of the private economy and optimistic about the efficacy of stabilization policy. In contrast, rules advocates are optimistic about the underlying stability of the private economy but pessimistic about the efficacy of stabilization policy.[3]

> **Self-Test**
>
> Classify the following as policy instruments or target variables:
> 1. The inflation rate
> 2. The personal income tax rate
> 3. The Federal Reserve discount rate
> 4. The unemployment rate
> 5. High-powered money

14-3 Policy Rules

The great debate over policy rules primarily concerns monetary policy. In the 1930s University of Chicago economist Henry Simons posed a stark contrast between a totally discretionary monetary policy and a fixed rule that takes away all discretion from the central bank.[4] In reality, there is a continuum in monetary policy between completely **discretionary policy** at one extreme and a **rigid rule** at the other extreme.

The most extreme form of rigid rule would be for the Fed to carry out a specified set of open-market operations, for example, to buy exactly enough securities to make high-powered money (H, the sum of currency and reserves) grow by, say, 5 percent per year. However, as we learned in the last chapter (see equation [13.6] on p. 427), such an action would not lead to steady growth in the money supply, since the money supply depends not only on H but also on the reserve ratio and the public's currency-holding ratio. Even if growth in H is kept absolutely rigid, choices by the public to raise or lower its holdings of currency could lead to major swings in the money supply. Another form of rigid rule would be for the Fed to conduct whatever open-market operations are required to maintain absolutely constant a short-term interest rate like the federal funds rate.

The best-known early proposal for a policy rule, a **constant growth rate rule (CGRR)** for the money supply, was made in the late 1950s by Milton Friedman, then at the University of Chicago. Just as maintaining a fixed growth rate for H does not ensure a fixed growth rate for the money supply, due to variations in the money multiplier (M/H), the reverse is true as well. Maintaining a CGRR for the money supply would require the Fed to manipulate H actively in order to offset changes in the money multiplier.

Discretionary policy treats each macroeconomic episode as a unique event, without any attempt to respond in the same way from one episode to another.

A **rigid rule** for policy sets a key policy instrument at a fixed value, as in a constant growth rate rule for the money supply.

A **constant growth rate rule (CGRR)** stipulates a fixed percentage growth rate for the money supply, in contrast to the variable growth rate recommended by policy activists.

---

[3] Traditionally, macroeconomics textbooks interpreted the rules-versus-activism debate as about the strength of policy multipliers. An extended statement that attempted to reorient the monetarist debate is Franco Modigliani, "The Monetarist Controversy, or Should We Forsake Stabilization Policy?" *American Economic Review,* vol. 67 (March 1977), pp. 1–19. An earlier paper is Milton Friedman, "Why Economists Disagree," in *Dollars and Deficits* (Englewood Cliffs, NJ: Prentice-Hall, 1968), pp. 1–16. Friedman on pp. 6–9 shares the same orientation as this chapter, although on pp. 10–16 he places considerably more weight than we do here on the influence of money on inflation.

[4] Henry C. Simons, *Economic Policy for a Free Society* (Chicago: University of Chicago Press, 1948). Simons originally wrote on rules versus discretion in the mid-1930s.

In addition to rules calling for a fixed growth rate of H or the money supply, many other types of rules have been proposed. Some involve not a monetary variable like H or the money supply, but rather a target variable like the price level or output. Other rules fall under the category of **feedback rules**, which systematically change monetary variables like the money supply or interest rates in response to actual or forecasted changes in target variables like inflation or unemployment. The leading example of such a feedback rule is called the "Taylor" Rule, discussed in section 14-7.

The early school of thought advocating a rule for monetary policy was called **monetarism**.[5] This approach combined the key elements in the box on p. 453—optimism regarding the stability of the private economy and pessimism regarding the efficacy of discretionary policy—with a specific policy proposal advocating a CGRR for the money supply.[6] Subsequently, monetarism faded in popularity and was replaced by advocacy of rules that target the inflation rate, so called "inflation targeting," and mixed feedback rules such as the Taylor Rule.

A **feedback rule** sets stabilization policy to respond in a systematic way to a macroeconomic event, such as an increase in unemployment or inflation.

Monetarism is a school of thought that opposes activist or discretionary monetary policy and instead favors a fixed rule for the growth rate of high-powered money or of the money supply.

The Positive Case for Rules

The case for rules takes two forms. One is a positive case based on the advantages of rules themselves, and the other is a negative case based on the defects of a completely discretionary policy.

The main arguments for rules as set forth by Milton Friedman are three.[7] First, a rule insulates the central bank from political pressure, which might, for instance, take the form of pushing the central bank to overstimulate the economy in the year before an election. Second, a rule allows the performance of the central bank to be judged by the government and the public. For instance, a central bank charged with a CGRR for the money supply would be judged to be a failure if in reality the money supply gyrated wildly or grew at an average rate different from the one specified in the rule. Third, a rule reduces uncertainty since firms, workers, and consumers are able to gauge accurately what the central bank will be doing over the next several years.

However, as suggested by Stanley Fischer, formerly of MIT and now the Governor of the Central Bank of Israel, there are weaknesses in each of these arguments.[8] First, it is not necessarily desirable for the central bank to operate independently of political pressure; a central bank, in its attempts to achieve or maintain low inflation, might be more willing to sacrifice jobs in the short run than the general public is. The merits of the second and third arguments fail as a general support for rules, since their validity depends on what variable the central bank chooses to target. For instance, the public has no reason to care directly about the quantity of high-powered money or the money supply, since the target variables that concern the public are inflation, unemployment, and productivity growth.

---

[5] The term *monetarism* was introduced in Karl Brunner, "The Role of Money and Monetary Policy," *Federal Reserve Bank of St. Louis Review*, no. 50 (1968), pp. 9–24.

[6] See Milton Friedman, *A Program for Monetary Stability* (New York: Fordham University Press, 1959).

[7] Ibid.

[8] Stanley Fischer, "Rules versus Discretion in Monetary Policy," in Benjamin Friedman and Frank Hahn, eds., *Handbook of Monetary Economics*, vol. 2 (Amsterdam: Elsevier Science Publishers, 1990), pp. 1156–84.

In short, it is hard to make a general case for rules without specifying the exact nature of the rule. As in the saying "there are many slips between cup and lip," there are many sources of slippage between the Fed's policy instruments, particularly open-market operations, and the most important target variables, that is, inflation, unemployment, and productivity growth. These slippages include money-multiplier shocks (Chapter 13), money demand shocks (Chapter 13), commodity demand shocks (anything discussed in Chapters 3 or 4 that can shift the *IS* curve), and supply shocks (Chapter 8).

The Negative Case for Rules

The negative case for rules consists of a criticism of activism. As shown in the box on p. 453, rules advocates are pessimistic about activist (discretionary) policy, believing that such measures can do more harm than good. Much of the rest of this chapter looks in detail at their case by examining the many reasons why the activists' paradise is unrealistic—lags, uncertainty, forecasting errors, and other issues.

However, just as the merits of the positive case for rules depend on the particular type of rule being considered, so does the negative case for rules. For instance, lags and uncertainty may create so much slippage between the Fed's policy instruments and the economy's target variables that it becomes infeasible for the Fed to carry out a rule involving a target, such as the proposal that the Fed adhere to a fixed target for the inflation rate.

14-4 Policy Pitfalls: Lags and Uncertain Multipliers

The core of Milton Friedman's case against policy activism and in favor of a monetary rule has always been that there are what he called "long and variable" lags between changes in monetary policy instruments and the ultimate response of target variables like inflation and unemployment. In this section we distinguish five types of lags for monetary policy and attempt to estimate the length of these lags.

The Five Types of Lags

Lags prevent either monetary or fiscal policy from immediately offsetting an unexpected shift in the demand for commodities or in the demand for money. There are five main types of lags. Some are common to both monetary and fiscal policy; others are more important for one policy than the other:

1. The data lag
2. The recognition lag
3. The legislative lag
4. The transmission lag
5. The effectiveness lag

To explain the meaning of each lag and to estimate its length, let us take as an example the end of the 2001 recession.

1. **The data lag.** Policymakers do not know what is going on in the economy the moment it happens. The index of industrial production exhibited its first significant increase during January 2002. But this news did not arrive

until mid-February 2002. Typically, an economic change that starts at the beginning of one month, say January, is not fully evident in the data until the middle of the next month, so that the data lag is about 1.5 months.

2. **The recognition lag.** Policymakers do not pay much attention to changes in data that occur only for one month. The subsequent month might exhibit a reversal in the opposite direction, and frequently data are revised to change small increases into small decreases, or vice versa. Thus it was necessary to wait for the February data to confirm that industrial production had increased for two months in a row, and these data series were not released until March 2002.

3. **The legislative lag.** Although most changes in fiscal policy must be legislated by Congress, an important advantage of monetary policy is the short legislative lag. Once a majority of the Federal Open Market Committee (FOMC) decides that a monetary policy stimulus is needed, only a short wait is necessary, since the FOMC has eight regularly scheduled meetings annually and can meet by phone anytime. This brings us to April 2002.

4. **The transmission lag.** The transmission lag is the time interval between the policy decision and the subsequent change in policy instruments. Like the legislative lag, this lag is a more serious obstacle for fiscal policy. Once the FOMC has given its order for the open-market manager to make open-market purchases, the short-term (federal funds) interest rate declines immediately. Often the Fed signals that it has shifted policy by changing the discount rate; there is no transmission lag at all for such an action.

5. **The effectiveness lag.** Most of the controversy about the lags of monetary policy concerns the length of time required for an acceleration or deceleration in the money supply to influence real output. As we have seen, Milton Friedman has argued that the effectiveness lag is long and variable.

Evidence on the Effectiveness Lag

The most difficult lag to measure, as well as the longest, is the effectiveness lag between the change in monetary policy and the response of the economy. Estimates of this lag differ for numerous reasons, including the use of different measures of monetary policy (for example, money supply versus interest rates) and different indicators of the economy's response (for example, a monthly index of production or employment or a quarterly index of real GDP).

In determining the length of the effectiveness lag, it is useful to measure the monetary policy action by the change in short-term interest rates, since the Fed can change those interest rates almost immediately after a meeting of the FOMC (thus eliminating the transmission lag). One set of estimates of the effectiveness lag is presented in Figure 14-2. This figure plots for three alternative intervals the response of real GDP to a change in the short-term interest rate, specifically the Treasury bill rate.[9]

---

[9] For those readers trained in econometrics, the details lying behind Figure 14-2 are as follows. The annualized percentage change in quarterly real GDP over the indicated intervals was regressed on a constant and lags 2 through 8 of the quarterly changes in the nominal Treasury bill rate. Lag lengths of 9 quarters or greater were statistically insignificant and were omitted. The current change and the first lag were omitted because their coefficients are positive, indicating the presence of feedback from real GDP to the interest rate.

458 Chapter 14 • Stabilization Policy in the Closed and Open Economy

Figure 14-2 The Percent Change in Real GDP Following a 1 Percentage Point Change in the Treasury Bill Rate, Three Intervals, 1961–2004

Following a 1 percentage point change in the short-term (Treasury bill) interest rate, real GDP changes in the opposite direction by the percentages shown by the plotted lines drawn for each of three intervals, 1961–73, 1974–87, and 1988–2004. The lines show, for instance, that after 18 months real GDP would have dropped by about 1.2 percent during the 1961–73 and 1974–87 interval, but only by about 0.2 percent during 1988–2004. The boxed labels show how many months were required for half of the ultimate impact on real GDP to occur.

As shown by Figure 14-2, in all three intervals (1961–73, 1974–87, and 1988–2004) real GDP declined following an increase in the short-term interest rate. But the change in GDP is very spread out over time, distributed over more than two years. Because the economy's response is so spread out, the best measure of the effectiveness lag is not obvious. One sensible measure of this lag is the length of time necessary for *half of the ultimate effect* to be felt. As shown by the small boxes in the figure, this lag was 11.8, 11.1, and 21.6 months respectively. Notable also is the fact that the total responses in the more recent intervals were much smaller than in the first; we explain this shift in a subsequent section.

Another measure of the policy lag, one that does not rely on interest rate data, can be extracted from earlier research by David and Christina Romer of the University of California, Berkeley. They read the minutes of the FOMC to identify the months when the Fed "made a decision to try to cause a recession to reduce inflation,"[10] identifying six such episodes between 1947 and 1979. They ran a statistical test similar to that in Figure 14-2 to examine the response of industrial production in the three years after the Fed's policy shift. For their six episodes, their estimated effectiveness lag averages 19 months, consistent with the lags of 11 to 21 months shown in Figure 14-2.[11]

Adding the Lags Together

To summarize this section on lags, let us add up the total delay between an unexpected economic event and the economy's reaction to a monetary policy action taken in response to such an economic event.

Type of lag	Estimated length (months)
1. Data	1.5
2. Recognition	2.0
3. Legislative	0.5
4. Transmission	0.0
5. Effectiveness	19.0
Total	23.0

Thus the first half of the economy's reaction to the Fed's policy response to the economic recovery that began in January 2002 would not have been felt until December 2003 (plus or minus a few months, reflecting the variability of the effectiveness lag).

Multiplier Uncertainty

Chapters 3 and 4 developed a set of multiplier formulas indicating the size of the change in real GDP that would result from a change in a policy instrument, such as tax rates, government spending, or the money supply. But the *IS-LM* model summarized in those chapters was very simple. This section shows that we do not know nearly as much about the values of the multipliers as the simple *IS-LM* model initially led us to believe.

Figure 14-2 illustrates **dynamic multipliers** that show the response of real GDP to a change in the interest rate over several intervals. We noted that the multipliers were much smaller in 1988–2004 than before 1988. Also, even for a given time period economists differ widely regarding the size of the monetary and fiscal multipliers. This **multiplier uncertainty** creates a dilemma for policymakers. Even if they could forecast perfectly that the economy needs a policy stimulus now to add 2.0 percent to real GDP four quarters from now, there remains the question as to what exact policy action should be taken. Should the

Dynamic multipliers are the amount by which output is raised during each of several time periods after a given change in the policy instrument.

Multiplier uncertainty concerns the lack of firm knowledge regarding the change in output caused by a change in a policy instrument.

---

[10] Christina D. Romer and David H. Romer, "Does Monetary Policy Matter? A New Test in the Spirit of Friedman and Schwartz," in O. J. Blanchard and S. Fischer, *NBER Macroeconomics Annual 1989* (Cambridge, MA: MIT Press), p. 152.

[11] Romer and Romer, ibid., Table 1, p. 153. The maximum effect of their monetary policy variable (defined as unity in one of the six months when the Fed changed policy and zero otherwise) is reached 32 months after the policy change. Half of the total effect occurs after 18.8 months. This estimate is approximate, as it omits the impact of the lagged dependent variable in their equation.

interest rate be dropped today by 0.5, 1.0, or 2.0 percentage points? Any of these numbers might be correct, depending on the policy multiplier.[12]

Why Have Monetary Policy Multipliers Changed?

Three aspects of Figure 14-2 make life especially difficult for policymakers—these are the length of the lag, the change in the lag, and the change in the multiplier (that is, the total effect of an interest rate change on real GDP). We have already noted the fact that the effectiveness lag is long, with half of the effect taking 21 months during 1988–2004. Why is this lag longer now than it was before 1988?

Three changes in the structure of the economy since the 1960s help explain why lags are now longer and multipliers are now smaller than they were in the 1960s. The first change concerns thrift institutions and housing. In earlier decades housing expenditures took the brunt of tight monetary policy, declining quickly in response to upward movements in interest rates. After the late 1970s this channel of influence on housing became less important, because deregulation lifted the ceilings on interest rates paid to depositors by thrifts. Also, other types of financial institutions that were not subject to interest rate ceilings began to participate more in mortgage markets, further insulating the housing sector from the impact of tightened monetary policy (see pp. 437–40).

The second major change is the reduced impact of changing interest rates on consumer spending. More consumer borrowing now occurs on credit cards, but interest rates on credit cards are very insensitive to monetary policy.

The third major change was the adoption of flexible exchange rates in 1973, previously examined in Chapter 6. This added a major channel of influence of monetary policy, as changing interest rates cause changes in the foreign exchange rate and, after a long lag, changes in net exports. It takes two years or more for net exports to respond fully to changes in the foreign exchange rate, which helps to explain the longer effectiveness lag observed since the 1970s.

Summary: The effectiveness lag of monetary policy has become longer, and the multiplier of real GDP response to a change in interest rates has become smaller, because the prompt channel working through housing finance has become weaker, while the time-consuming channel working through exchange rates and net exports has become stronger.

Self-Test

For each of the following statements, indicate whether it relates to multiplier uncertainty or lags, and if your answer is "lags," indicate which of the five types of lags is most closely related to the statement:

1. Congress debated President Johnson's proposal for an income tax surcharge for 18 months, from late 1966 to mid-1968.
2. Interest rate ceilings on savings accounts were eliminated by financial deregulation.

---

[12] See William Brainard, "Uncertainty and the Effectiveness of Policy," *American Economic Review*, vol. 57 (May 1967), pp. 411–25. Brainard's formula suggests that the expected gap between actual and target GDP should be closed by only a fraction of the gap, but that fraction depends on correlations that we are most unlikely to know. An earlier analysis is Milton Friedman, "The Effects of a Full-Employment Policy on Economic Stability: A Formal Analysis," *Essays in Positive Economics* (Chicago: University of Chicago Press, 1953), pp. 117–32.

3. A record-setting snowstorm in Washington delays publication of the Consumer Price Index by two weeks.
4. Flexible exchange rates were adopted in 1973.

14-5 Case Study

Was the Fed Responsible for the Decline in Economic Volatility?

The U.S. economy has been considerably more stable since the mid-1980s than it was previously. Our task in this section is to explain the apparently paradoxical stability of the economy in view of the difficulties of managing monetary policy. One possibility is that the performance of monetary policy has improved substantially; another complementary hypothesis is that the economy's stability has improved for reasons unrelated to monetary policy. Both explanations could be true at the same time.

One way to appreciate the improved stability of the economy is to examine Figure 14-3, which in the top frame plots the log output ratio (the log ratio of actual to natural output, Y/Y^N) since 1960.[13] Clearly visible are the large positive output ratios of the late 1960s and the large negative ratios created by the 1973–75 and 1981–82 recessions. In contrast, since 1982 the log output ratio has been much closer to its desired value of zero. Shown in the bottom frame of Figure 14-3 is one way of summarizing the decreased volatility of the ratio, a 20-quarter moving average of the absolute value of the ratio.[14] If the ratio was always either +2 or −2 percent, the moving average of its absolute value would be 2.0. If the ratio followed the pattern 2, 0, −2, 0, averaging those numbers together would give an average of 1.0. As shown in the bottom frame, this measure of volatility was 3.7 in 1970:Q1, fell and then rose to a peak of 4.0 in 1985:Q2, and then declined to values of 2.0 percent or below from 1988:Q2 to 2004.[15]

Causes of Decreased Volatility: Smaller Shocks

One hypothesis is that demand and/or supply shocks became less important or less harmful after the mid-1980s. Demand shocks were the primary cause of volatility in the 1950s and 1960s. The Korean War (1950–53) and the Vietnam War (1965–75) caused sharp increases followed by decreases in government spending, a component of GDP. The positive output ratio of the 1960s was also caused by ill-timed tax decreases in 1964–65 that pushed up consumption and business investment.

Then as the Vietnam War was winding down in the 1970s, the economy was hit by several adverse supply shocks, consisting of the oil price shocks of

---

[13] The log output ratio is zero when actual real GDP equals natural real GDP. This concept was introduced in the Appendix to Chapter 8, p. 272.

[14] The absolute value of any number is its actual value with any negative signs converted to positive.

[15] A slightly different measure of decreased volatility is considered in Olivier Blanchard and John Simon, "The Long and Large Decline in U.S. Output Volatility," *Brookings Papers on Economic Activity*, vol. 32, no. 1 (2001), pp. 135–64.

Figure 14-3 The Log Output Ratio and the Moving Average of its Absolute Value, 1960–2004

The top frame shows the log output ratio in percent, that is, the log of the ratio of actual to natural real GDP (Y/Y^N). After 1985 the ratio never exceeded 3 percent or fell below −3 percent, in contrast to the period before 1985 when the range extended from +5.7 to −8.6 percent. This decrease in volatility is summarized by the 20-quarter moving average of the ratio's absolute value, as shown in the bottom frame. This moving average reached peaks of 3.7 in 1970 and 4.0 in 1985, in contrast to the period after 1989 when the moving average never exceeded 1.9 and fell as low as 0.9 in 1998.

1974–75, farm price shocks in 1972–73, higher non-oil import prices in 1973–74 due to the depreciation of the U.S. dollar, and, finally, the termination of Nixon-era price controls in 1974–75. All these shocks caused inflation to shoot up, and a side effect (as we learned in Chapter 8 on pp. 254–58) was a sharp decline in the output ratio.

What changed after 1982? There were no more disruptions caused by wars; the Gulf War of early 1991 and the Iraq War of 2003 and afterward were largely fought by using existing equipment and ground forces and did not cause a sharp increase in government spending as had the Korean and Vietnam wars. But the biggest difference was in the reversal of supply shocks, from primarily adverse shocks in 1974–75 and 1979–81 to primarily beneficial (or "benign") shocks in 1986 and again in 1996–99.

The Role of the Fed

The shift from adverse supply shocks during 1973–82 to beneficial supply shocks after 1982 made life much easier for the Fed. When adverse supply shocks strike, the Fed is forced to choose between faster inflation, lower output, or a combination of the two (see Figure 8-10 on p. 255). But with beneficial supply shocks, as when the price of oil fell sharply in 1986, and again in the late 1990s when there was a combination of several beneficial supply shocks, the Fed has the pleasant task of choosing between lower inflation and higher output. In making this choice, the Fed can contribute to reducing economic volatility by adjusting interest rates to boost the log output ratio if it is below zero (as in 2002–03) and to reduce the log output ratio if it is above zero (as in 1998–2000).

As shown in the left portion of Figure 14-4, the log output ratio first went above zero in 1988, and the Fed reacted almost immediately by raising the federal funds rate, with a delay of only about six months. Then when the output ratio fell below zero in late 1990, the Fed dropped the federal funds rate in a series of steps that lasted until early 1993. The Fed's actions in 1988–93 were prompt and represented movements in the right direction.

Perhaps trying to improve on its performance, the Fed took dramatic action to raise the federal funds rate in 1994, about a year before the log output ratio rose above zero. This move, called at the time a "preemptive strike," reflected imperfect knowledge of the log output ratio, which was thought at the time to be higher than it actually was, due to an underestimate of the economy's natural output (Y^N). But then the Fed reversed its preemptive strike and left the federal funds rate virtually constant as the log output ratio inched up from zero to +3 percent in 1998–2000, actually *reducing* the federal funds rate in late 1998 and early 1999.

The Fed's failure to raise the federal funds rate in 1997–99 appears to be a radical departure from its past policies aimed at stabilizing the log output ratio. Why did the Fed avoid the monetary tightening that it had successfully pursued a decade earlier in 1988–89? By far the most important reason was the behavior of inflation. As we learned from Figure 8-14 on p. 267, the inflation rate did not accelerate in 1996–98 in response to the rising log output ratio and declining unemployment rate and instead decelerated. The reasons for this unusual behavior were explored on pp. 258–60.

Additional factors weighed on the Fed's decision not to raise interest rates in 1997–98 and then actually to reduce rates. Most important was the Asian financial crisis, which began in Thailand in July 1997 and spread to Russia in

464 Chapter 14 • Stabilization Policy in the Closed and Open Economy

Figure 14-4 The Federal Funds Interest Rate and the Log Output Ratio, 1980–2005

Since the 1980s the Fed has tended to raise and lower interest rates in anticipation of the economy's overheating or stalling out. In the late 1980s the Fed began to raise interest rates as the economy neared a log output ratio of zero. When signals began to suggest in 1989 that the log output ratio would be falling appreciably below zero in the near future, the Fed began lowering interest rates. The Fed raised interest rates in 1994 as the log output ratio again seemed headed above zero. But after 1996 the Fed changed its behavior for reasons discussed in the text.

August 1998 and then to Latin America. To help stem the flow of international capital from these countries to the United States, the Fed reduced interest rates in the fall of 1998. Many observers think, in retrospect, that it was a mistake for the Fed to lower interest rates at this time when the log output ratio was well above zero. While inflation accelerated only modestly in 1999–2000, the low level of interest rates encouraged excess optimism in the stock market and excessive high-tech fixed investment and thus aggravated the instability of the economy when the stock market and high-tech fixed investment collapsed after mid-2000.

Only in early 2000 did the Fed respond to the excessively high output ratio by raising interest rates, and then by much less than in 1988–89. Starting in mid-2000, the output ratio began to plummet, and in this case the Fed also acted preemptively, reducing the federal funds rate before the output ratio reached zero (which occurred at about the time as the terrorist attacks on the United States on September 11, 2001).

Overall Rating of the Fed

The Fed deserves credit for its preemptive moves, timed in advance of movements of the output ratio above and below zero, which occurred in 1994 and in 2001. The Fed was only a few months late in acting to restrain the economy in 1988–89 although it acted too slowly to stimulate it in 1991–92. The real debate regards the wisdom of keeping interest rates constant for so long in 1997–99, when the economy had expanded so far. Supporters of the Fed say that the Fed's inaction was justified by the tame behavior of inflation. Opponents of the Fed point out that inflation finally did accelerate in 1999–2001, doubling in the case of the Consumer Price Index. Opponents also argue that if the Fed had acted earlier to restrain the economy, some of the excessive boom and subsequent collapse in high-tech investment and stock prices might have been avoided.

Clearly the improved stability and reduced volatility of the economy, as displayed in Figure 14-3, reflects both an improved environment and the effective performance of the Fed. There is no doubt that the atmosphere in which the Fed operated, with primarily beneficial supply shocks after 1982, accounts for much of the improved economic performance. But the Fed also deserves credit for its well-timed tightening moves in 1988–89 and 1994, as well as its rapid moves toward monetary in 2001–02 and to a lesser extent ease in 1991–92.

Is there any systematic way of describing the Fed's policy actions? Did the Fed's action represent discretionary policy or some sort of sophisticated rule? Subsequently in Section 14-7 we will compare the Fed's actual policy with the Taylor Rule that calls for the Fed to raise interest rates whenever inflation speeds up or whenever the log output ratio rises above zero.

14-6 Time Inconsistency, Credibility, and Reputation

We have already seen that one of the advantages that Milton Friedman claimed for policy rules was that firms, workers, and consumers would be able to form accurate expectations of future policy actions. Proponents of activism saw no merit in this claim, since any good rule could be adopted by a discretionary policymaker.

Time Inconsistency

In 1977, Finn Kydland of Carnegie-Mellon University and his colleague Edward Prescott (now at the University of Minnesota) introduced the concept of **time inconsistency**.[16] The basic idea is that discretionary policymakers decide on policy A because it is optimal at that time, and private decisionmakers make consumption, investment, and labor supply decisions based on that policy. However, once private decisionmakers have done so, it may be optimal for

Time inconsistency describes the temptations of policymakers to deviate from a policy after it is announced and private decisionmakers have reacted to it.

---

[16] Kydland and Prescott won the Nobel Prize in economics in 2004. The original reference is Finn E. Kydland and Edward C. Prescott, "Rules Rather Than Discretion: The Inconsistency of Optimal Plans," *Journal of Political Economy*, vol. 85 (June 1977), pp. 473–92. The most influential subsequent article was Robert J. Barro and David B. Gordon, "A Positive Theory of Monetary Policy in a Natural Rate Model," *Journal of Political Economy*, vol. 91 (August 1983), pp. 589–610.

policymakers to shift to policy B, thus invalidating the expectations on which private decisionmakers acted.

The simplest example arises in the classroom. Professors want their students to learn but hate to make up tests and grade them. Time inconsistency occurs when a professor announces that there will be a tough final exam. The students respond to policy A by studying hard, but then, just before the scheduled exam time, the professor announces policy B, that the exam has been canceled.

In macroeconomics the prominent example of time inconsistency involves the Phillips Curve trade-off between inflation and unemployment. For any given unemployment rate, the actual inflation rate will be low if expectations of future inflation are low. This gives the Fed an incentive to pursue policy A, vowing to achieve low inflation. But once inflation expectations have shifted down, the Fed is tempted to shift to policy B by a monetary stimulus that reduces unemployment, even though policy B will raise inflation and invalidate the low expectations of inflation held by workers and firms.

The implication of the time inconsistency argument is that economic performance may be better, on average, if private decisionmakers know that the central bank will adhere to a rigid rule to target the inflation rate. Knowing that there is no discretion and thus no chance of a surprise monetary stimulus (policy B), expectations of future inflation will subside, making possible a lower actual inflation rate for any given unemployment rate.

Credibility and Reputation

In order to achieve the best possible economic performance, with low or even zero inflation combined with unemployment at the natural rate (U^N), it may pay a central bank to invest in its reputation. If the central bank succeeds year after year in avoiding the temptation to boost monetary growth in order to reduce unemployment (policy B), it will convince private decisionmakers that a future upsurge of inflation is unlikely. Once the actions of policymakers create this type of reputation, they are said to gain **policy credibility**.[17]

Policy credibility is the belief by the public that the policymakers will actually carry out an announced policy.

Over the past decade economists have built sophisticated models of "reputational equilibrium."[18] These lead to the conclusion that *if* the policymaker has a long time horizon and *if* the policymaker has a low discount rate, then an equilibrium with zero inflation is possible. That is, the policymaker has an incentive to produce a time-consistent policy, and private decisionmakers adjust their expectations accordingly. However, such theoretical models are not very practical for real-world situations in which governments and central bankers do not last forever and in which governments face regular election campaigns.

In order to reduce the influence of the vagaries of government political motives, many nations like the United Kingdom have granted freedom to the central bank to operate independently of the elected economic officials of the government. And many central banks in foreign countries, but not the Federal Reserve in the United States, have used their independence to adopt

---

[17] A useful introduction is Benjamin M. Friedman, "The Use and Meaning of Words in Central Banking: Inflation Targeting, Credibility, and Transparency," NBER Working Paper 8972, June 2002.

[18] See Fischer, "Rules versus Discretion," pp. 1175–78.

rules that rigidly target the inflation rate without any concern for the performance of real output.[19]

Implications for Rules Versus Discretion

The debate over time inconsistency focuses on the process by which private decisionmakers form expectations concerning the inflation rate. Other target variables, such as the unemployment rate, are ignored on the assumption that the natural rate hypothesis is valid, so in the long run policymakers have no power to make the actual unemployment rate deviate from the natural rate.

Like many other aspects of the rules versus discretion debate, much of the literature on time inconsistency ignores the variety of different rules that are possible. It ignores as well the many slippages that occur between the policy instrument most directly under the Fed's control and the target variable of central concern in the debate, that is, the inflation rate.

Because of these slippages, no monetary policy based on rigid control of high-powered money is likely to produce a steady inflation rate. Only a policy rule that targets the inflation rate is likely to establish policy credibility, but all the problems with activism examined in this chapter apply as well to such a policy rule. We return to inflation targeting in Section 14-8 below.

> **Self-Test**
>
> Are the following statements true, false, or uncertain?
>
> 1. For any given deceleration of nominal GDP growth created by a tight monetary policy, the recession will be shorter and less severe if the central bank possesses policy credibility with the public.
> 2. For any given deceleration of nominal GDP growth created by tight monetary policy, the recession will be shorter and less severe if the public believes that the central bank's policy is subject to time inconsistency.
> 3. Policy credibility increases the merits of a "cold turkey" disinflation as compared to a policy of "living with inflation."
> 4. The possibility of time inconsistency strengthens the case of discretionary policy against a policy rule that targets the growth rate of high-powered money.

14-7 Case Study

The Taylor Rule and the Changing Fed Attitude Toward Inflation and Output

No matter what type of rule the Fed attempts to achieve, its short-term instrument of control is the federal funds rate, plotted as the green line in Figures 14-4 on p. 464 and in Figure 14-5 in this section. If the Fed attempts to achieve a rule

---

[19] An important reference on the concept and implementation of inflation targeting, and a set of papers on the experience of several countries is Ben S. Bernanke et al., *Inflation Targeting: Lessons from the International Experience* (Princeton, NJ: Princeton University Press, 1999).

for growth in the money supply, then the federal funds rate must be raised when the money supply exceeds the desired growth rate. Similarly, if the Fed wants to target the inflation rate, the federal funds rate must rise when the inflation rate exceeds the desired inflation rate.

A problem with targeting the inflation rate is that there are very long lags between an increase in the federal funds rate and a subsequent reduction in the inflation rate. Continuing increases in the federal funds rate, while the Fed waits for inflation to subside, may cause economic activity to falter, the output ratio to decline, and the unemployment rate to increase. The Fed may prefer to pursue two objectives at the same time, responding to *both* excessive inflation and insufficient output.

John Taylor, of Stanford University and formerly undersecretary of the Treasury, has proposed a simple rule for the Fed (or any other central bank) to follow in setting the real federal funds rate (r^{FF}).[20] The Fed would raise the real interest rate above its desired long-term value whenever inflation exceeded the desired rate and also whenever actual output exceeded natural output:

$$r^{FF} = r^{FF*} + a(p - p^*) + b\hat{Y} \qquad (14.1)$$

The terms on the right-hand side are the desired real federal funds rate (r^{FF*}), a parameter (*a*) times the deviation of the actual rate of inflation from the desired rate of inflation ($p - p^*$), and another parameter (*b*) times the log output ratio ($\hat{Y}$).[21] The more the Fed cares about avoiding an acceleration of inflation, the higher would be the parameter *a*. The more the Fed cares about avoiding recessions and high unemployment, the higher would be the parameter *b*. If the Fed cares equally about 1 percent of excess inflation and 1 percent of insufficient output, then it would set *a* and *b* equal to each other, for instance, $a = b = 0.5$. No matter what the values of *a* and *b* are, the formula written as equation (14.1) has become known as the **Taylor Rule**. The special case of a Taylor Rule with a zero weight on output ($b = 0$) is called an "inflation targeting rule."[22]

The **Taylor Rule** calls for the central bank to move the real short-term interest rate away from its desired long-term value in response to any deviation of actual inflation from desired inflation and in response to any deviation of real GDP from natural real GDP.

How closely did the Fed follow a Taylor Rule? To answer this question, we need to assume a value for the desired real interest rate (3.4 percent) and for the desired inflation rate (2 percent per year). Let us also assume that the Fed places equal weights on inflation and output and assign values of $a = b = 0.5$. Then we can calculate the nominal federal funds rate (the real rate plus the actual inflation rate) called for by the Taylor Rule. Figure 14-5 compares the actual federal funds rate as the green line with the calculated "fixed Taylor Rule" using fixed values of the parameters assumed in this paragraph.[23]

Compared with the green actual rate line, the blue fixed Taylor Rule line reveals interesting differences. First, the Fed did not cut the actual rate in 1981–86

---

[20] John B. Taylor, "How Should Monetary Policy Respond to Stocks While Maintaining Long-Term Price Stability? Conceptual Issues," in *Achieving Price Stability*, Federal Reserve Bank of Kansas City, 1996, pp. 181–95.

[21] *Review:* The symbol $\hat{Y}$ stands for the logarithm of the ratio of actual real GDP (*Y*) to natural real GDP (Y^N). Whenever $\hat{Y}$ equals zero, then actual real GDP is equal to natural real GDP. This notation was introduced at the beginning of the Appendix to Chapter 8, see p. 272.

[22] On inflation targeting, see Lars E. O. Svensson, "Inflation Targeting: Should It be Modeled as an Instrument Rule or a Targeting Rule?" *European Economic Review*, vol. 46 (2002), pp. 771–80.

[23] The inflation rate is the percent change in the quarterly GDP deflator from one year earlier, the log output ratio is the same as that plotted in Figure 14-4, and the desired real interest rate is chosen to minimize the mean difference between the actual rate and the calculated fixed Taylor Rule rate.

14-7 Case Study: The Taylor Rule and the Changing Fed Attitude Toward Inflation and Output **469**

A Variable Taylor Rule Tracks the Fed's Actual Policy Better than a Fixed Taylor Rule

Figure 14-5 The Actual Federal Funds Rate and Interest Rates Calculated by Two Versions of the Taylor Rule, 1980–2004

The green line plots the actual federal funds rate. The blue line plots the interest rate forecast by a Taylor Rule with equal weights of 0.5 on inflation and output ($a = b = 0.5$). The red line plots the interest rate forecast by a Taylor Rule that shifts the weights toward less concern about inflation and more concern about output after 1990. Comparing the actual green line with the variable red line, the surprises in the Fed's behavior were keeping interest rates so high in 1984–86, raising them preemptively in 1994, increasing them so little in 1998–99, and reducing them so much in 2001–03.

by nearly as much as the Taylor Rule would have required, that is, the Fed did not care enough about the large negative output ratio that occurred in the early 1980s. The blue Taylor Rule line tracks the actual rate remarkably well in the late 1980s but does not decline enough in 1993–94 nor increase at all in 1994. Most interestingly, the blue line fails to decline nearly as much as the actual green line in 2001–04.

The errors made by the blue line suggest that the Fed cared more about inflation and less about the output ratio during the disinflation period of the early 1980s. But the errors after 1990 suggest that the Fed cared more about low output in 1992–93 and 2001–04 than the Taylor Rule. To implement this idea, we can recalculate the Taylor Rule line *by assuming that the Fed changed its preferences, from caring so much about inflation to caring much more about output.* The red line in Figure 14-5 is calculated in just the same way as the blue line, but it assumes that the Fed's weight on inflation (a) is not 0.5 throughout, but rather changes from 0.9 to 0.1 after 1990. The red line also assumes that the Fed's weight on the output ratio (b) changes in the opposite direction from 0.1 before 1990 to 0.9 after 1990. The red line comes closer to the actual green line, especially in tracking the disinflation of 1981–84, the stimulative reduction of interest rates in 1991–93, and the reduction of interest rates in 2001–03.

The differences between the actual green line and the alternative red "variable Taylor Rule" highlights several periods when the Fed deviated from the Taylor Rule. The Fed's "preemptive" increase in interest rates in 1994 deviated from the Taylor Rule, because inflation was not accelerating and output was still below natural output. In this case the Fed was forecasting an ominous future of higher inflation that did not actually happen. Both the red and blue Taylor Rule lines indicate that the Fed should have raised interest rates more than it did in the late 1990s, a period when the Fed has been criticized for excessive monetary ease. Finally, neither of the Taylor Rule lines comes close to tracking the aggressiveness of the Fed's interest rate reductions in 2001–03.

14-8 Rules Versus Discretion: An Assessment

A central theme of this chapter is that money-multiplier shocks, money demand shocks, commodity demand shocks, and supply shocks loosen the links between the Fed's policy instruments and its targets for the economy. These shocks imply that a rigid rule for setting the growth rate of the supply of high-powered money (the only policy rule that the Fed is capable of achieving directly) may not achieve the nation's unemployment, inflation, and other targets. Similarly, these shocks may make a rule for a target variable like the inflation rate difficult to achieve.

A second theme is that some policy rules provide a **nominal anchor** for the economy. That is, these rules target a nominal variable (high-powered money, the money supply, nominal GDP, or the inflation rate) and thus automatically place a limit on the ability of inflation to accelerate. A nominal anchor is inherently desirable because it increases the chance that inflation expectations will turn out to be accurate, thus facilitating financial planning by households and firms.

A **nominal anchor** is a rule that sets a limit on the growth rate of a nominal variable, for instance, high-powered money, the money supply, the price level, or nominal GDP. A nominal anchor prevents inflation from accelerating without limit.

Rules for Policy Instruments

Table 14-1 assesses seven policy rules. The first two rules set the values of the Fed's policy instruments, either high-powered money or the federal funds interest rate. A rule for high-powered money growth provides a nominal anchor but allows shocks to carry the economy away from its target. A nominal interest rate target does not provide a nominal anchor, and either a fiscal stimulus or other positive IS shock, or a positive commodity demand shock, can lead to explosive inflation under a nominal interest rate rule.[24]

---

[24] This defect of a nominal interest rate rule was a major theme of Milton Friedman's 1967 address to the American Economic Association. A positive commodity demand shift boosts the nominal interest rate; to maintain its target, the Fed must raise the money supply; this raises inflationary expectations and boosts the nominal interest rate again; again, the Fed must raise the money supply. Soon the Fed has caused a spiral of accelerating money growth and inflation. This phenomenon occurred when the Fed accommodated the fiscal stimulus of the Vietnam War during 1967–68.

Table 14-1 Assessing Alternative Policy Rules

Variable to be fixed by policy rule	Main advantages	Main disadvantages
Growth rate of high-powered money	Feasible for Fed to achieve; provides nominal anchor	May lead to variable inflation and unemployment rates
Nominal interest rate	Feasible for Fed to achieve (in short run)	*IS* curve shocks or unstable commodity demand may lead to variable unemployment rate. Does not provide nominal anchor; hence inflation can increase without bound
Growth rate of the money supply (monetarist CGRR)	Provides nominal anchor	Money supply hard to control; money demand instability may lead to variable inflation and unemployment rates
Inflation rate or price level	Provides nominal anchor; if successful, most likely to stabilize inflation expectations and avoid time inconsistency	Hard to control; requires extinguishing reaction to supply shocks, creating highly variable unemployment rate
Unemployment rate or output ratio	Avoids welfare cost of variable unemployment; allows households and firms to carry through on plans without making mistakes	Hard to control; requires accommodating reaction to supply shocks, creating highly variable inflation rate; does not provide nominal anchor
Growth rate of nominal GDP	Provides nominal anchor; splits supply shock effect between output and inflation	Hard to control
Taylor Rule (combines inflation and output targeting)	Provides the advantages of inflation targeting and a nominal anchor while reducing the variance of output and unemployment	Hard to control

A Rule for the Money Supply

The money supply is neither directly under the control of the Fed nor is it a target variable. For this reason it is sometimes called an "intermediate variable." A money supply rule (like the monetarist CGRR) has only two advantages. In the first place, it provides a nominal anchor; in the second (as in Figure 13-5 on p. 463), it is superior to an interest rate rule when commodity demand is unstable but money demand is stable. Otherwise, it combines the weakness of rules for targets (they are difficult to control) with the weakness of a high-powered money rule.

Rules for Target Variables

The main target variables are inflation and unemployment. Unemployment moves inversely with the ratio of actual to natural output, so a rule that targets unemployment is similar to a rule that targets the output ratio.[25] Because inflation plus real GDP growth equals nominal GDP growth, a nominal GDP growth rule has some of the characteristics of other rules for target variables, even though nominal GDP itself is not a target variable.

Rules for target variables avoid slippage between the instruments and the targets. In particular, all target rules (if successful) prevent instability in either commodity or money demand from causing undesirable fluctuations in target variables. These rules also suffer from a common disadvantage: It is difficult to control target variables because of policy lags, forecasting errors, and multiplier uncertainty. As shown in Table 14-1, rules for target variables differ. Rules for nominal GDP growth or inflation provide a nominal anchor; rules for unemployment or the output ratio do not.

The main advantage of a nominal GDP rule is that it requires no policy response to a supply shock (defined in Chapter 8 as a "neutral policy" response). In contrast, an inflation rule requires that the effect of supply shocks on the price level be extinguished, which raises the variability of output; whereas a real GDP or unemployment rule requires that the effect of supply shocks be "accommodated," which raises the variability of inflation. Because a nominal GDP rule represents a compromise response to supply shocks and provides a nominal anchor, numerous prominent economists over the past decade have come to advocate that the Fed adopt such a rule.

By placing weight both on inflation and output, a Taylor Rule (as examined above on pp. 467–70) is similar to a nominal GDP rule. A nominal GDP rule is the same as a Taylor Rule that places equal weights on inflation and real GDP *growth* (relative to desired values), in contrast to the traditional Taylor Rule, which targets inflation and the *level* of real GDP relative to natural real GDP (that is, the output ratio). What is the difference? Consider a deep recession like that of 1981–82. The growth rate of real GDP was rapid after early 1983, but the previous recession had created a large negative output ratio that did not return to zero until 1987. In the intervening period of 1983–87, a Taylor Rule based on the output ratio would have caused a lower interest rate than a rule based on the growth rate of output and thus would have helped to make output less variable. *This distinction suggests that a traditional Taylor Rule is superior to a nominal GDP growth rule.*

---

[25] The negative "Okun's Law" line describing the close inverse relation of the unemployment rate and the output ratio is displayed in Figure 8-13 on p. 265.

Implementing a Nominal GDP Rule or a Taylor Rule

Either a nominal GDP growth rule or a Taylor Rule that responds both to excess inflation and insufficient output avoid some of the flaws of other rules listed in Table 14-1. But both approaches are still subject to the difficulties of forecasting and long lags between changes in the instruments controlled by the Fed and the ultimate response of inflation and output. One approach that attempts to circumvent the problem of long lags is for the central bank to target its best *forecast* of inflation and output. Thus, if the average lag between a monetary policy action and the response of inflation is two years, the central bank would respond to changes in its best forecast of inflation two years from now, rather than of inflation today.[26] Indeed, it is clear in analyzing Figure 14-5 on p. 469, that in at least two episodes the Fed relied on forecasts in implementing a policy that resembled a Taylor Rule. In 1994, the Fed's "preemptive strike" raised the federal funds rate sharply in anticipation of accelerating inflation and a positive log output ratio that did not actually occur for several years. And, in 2001, the sharpness of the Fed's interest rate reductions reflected its forecast of a recession that was deeper than actually occurred.

In the end, we may conclude that the distinction between policy discretion and rules may have been exaggerated in the literature on macroeconomic policy. As it implements a policy that seems similar to a Taylor Rule, the Fed has shown that it can change the weights on inflation and output within that rule. And in order to implement that rule, it still must choose a desired long-term real interest rate, a desired inflation rate, and it must determine the current value of natural real GDP in order to calculate the output ratio. Even in implementing a rule, there is plenty of discretion for the Fed and other central banks in deciding exactly how to implement that rule.

14-9 Case Study

Should Monetary Policy Target the Exchange Rate?

In Chapter 6 we learned that when a country has flexible exchange rates, its central bank is free to set policy to attain its objectives for the domestic economy. The more expansionary the monetary policy is, the more the exchange rate is likely to depreciate. The weaker currency stimulates exports and restrains domestic purchases of imported goods and services. Thus the easier monetary policy is likely to raise that country's net exports, thereby shifting its *IS* curve to the right. By contrast, when a country chooses to fix its exchange rate in relation to some other currency or some other group of countries, its central bank surrenders the freedom to pursue domestic objectives; its central bank must use monetary policy to keep the exchange rate fixed. It cannot independently operate to

---

[26] See Lars E. O. Svensson and Michael Woodford, "Implementing Optimal Policy through Inflation-Forecast Targeting," in Ben S. Bernanke and Michael Woodford, *The Inflation Targeting Debate* (Chicago and London: University of Chicago Press, 2005), pp. 19–83. The same book contains numerous other assessments and critiques of inflation targeting. A much earlier assessment of nominal GDP targeting and recommendation that it also be based on targeting the forecast value is Robert J. Gordon, "The Conduct of Monetary Policy," in A. Ando, H. Eguchi, R. Farmer, and Y. Suzuki, eds., *Monetary Policy in Our Times* (Cambridge MA: MIT Press, 1985, pp. 45–81.)

International Perspective

The Debate About the Euro

Ever since the end of World War II, the nations of western Europe have been moving toward closer relations. The formation of the NATO security alliance in 1949 was followed by the formation of an economic alliance, the European Economic Community, in the 1950s. During the 1960s and 1970s, a "single market" was created to permit the unfettered movement across national borders of goods and services, financial capital, and people. During the 1980s, economic policies were coordinated even more when the European Monetary System was formed to stabilize the exchange rates of its member nations. The 1992 Maastricht Treaty called for much greater economic integration in its proposal for a monetary union that would replace each member nation's currency with a single European currency.

The Euro Arrives

Finally, on January 1, 1999, the euro was created, while the franc, mark, and nine other European currencies disappeared from the computer screens of currency traders. Euro coins and currency began to circulate in January 2002, and the colorful French franc, German mark, and other European currencies disappeared from the purses and wallets of citizens in twelve different European countries.

The euro is the third stage of the Economic and Monetary Union (EMU), which has been controversial. Interestingly, the most ardent group of supporters has been politicians. Politicians across Europe have sought greater economic cooperation because, in general, such cooperation seems to enhance the chances of having Europe remain prosperous and at peace. Economists as a group have been among the most vocal detractors of the EMU and the euro.

For the Euro

Some have argued that international trade within Europe would be enhanced by having a single currency, which would eliminate the costs and risks associated with exchange rates. The irony is that advances in financial markets now make it easier and cheaper than before for firms and financial institutions to manage risks associated with exchange rate fluctuations. In spite of that, it may still be expensive, especially for smaller firms and tourists, to deal with the numerous European currencies and the risks and uncertainties that they entail.

Since World War II, Germany has kept its inflation rate low. Some supported the EMU as a vehicle for other countries to "free-ride" on the German resolve and reputation for low inflation. The European Central Bank (ECB), seems to carry out monetary policy the way the German Bundesbank did, with a single goal of low inflation and the low interest rates that accompany it. Thus the euro is favored by some as a vehicle for achieving the low inflation rates that Germany achieved.

The euro is a common currency, but it may also provide fiscal discipline. Countries that have very high inflation rates sometimes adopt fixed exchange rates in order to discipline both their monetary and their fiscal policies. Among the criteria for countries to qualify for inclusion in the euro were that government deficits not exceed 3 percent of GDP and that government debt not exceed 60 percent of GDP. Other entrance criteria stipulated that inflation and interest rates not diverge too widely from those of the other countries entering the euro.

The figure shows the ratio of fiscal deficits to GDP for several member countries of the euro, compared to the 3 percent goal. Countries like Italy and Spain struggled to implement sharp fiscal contractions to achieve admission into the euro club.

Against the Euro

In Chapter 6 we learned about some of the important *economic* costs and benefits of a fixed exchange rate regime like the euro or its predecessor, the EMU. Recall that when a nation chooses to fix its exchange rate, it surrenders the independence of its central bank. Its central bank is committed to use its one policy instrument, the money supply, to achieve its one goal, the exchange rate. In the case of the euro, each member gives up its national currency and any independent monetary policy.

To the extent that the macroeconomic shocks that strike Europe have similar effects on all euro members and that the members have similar preferences about how best to respond to such shocks, the ECB can apply a European monetary policy to the entire group of euro countries and that policy would also be appropriate to each member nation. On the other hand, to the extent that the effects or preferences tend to be more nation-specific, nations will probably have misgivings about the single European monetary policy.

Over the period of 1999–2004, substantial evidence has been accumulated to support the case against the euro. Economic conditions have evolved very differently in the different members of the euro. The largest member, Germany, has suffered from even slower economic growth than Japan and is now strangled by the lack of an independent monetary authority that would give it an ability to stimulate its economy. Germany suffers more than any other euro member from the expansion of the European Union in 2004 to twenty-five members, including Poland, Hungary, the Czech Republic, and other nearby nations that have lower wages and offer German firms an incentive to create jobs in those nations instead of at home in Germany. At the opposite extreme is Ireland, a euro member with such rapid economic growth that inflation accelerated without the ability to use an independent monetary policy to dampen inflation.

A final important qualifier about the euro is that the prohibition on fiscal deficits above 3 percent (as shown in the figure in this box) eliminates the possibility of automatic stabilization. No longer can the euro nations run higher fiscal deficits during recessions to balance lower deficits during booms. Thus, euro nations such as Germany that suffer from high unemployment rates have lost the capability to use any macroeconomic policy, monetary or fiscal, to fight high unemployment.

Source: OECD Economic Outlook, December 2004.

attain other domestic objectives, like stimulating aggregate demand. This is a fundamental lesson of the Chapter 6 trilemma.

In the previous section we saw that a country's average inflation rate would be lower if the central bank were committed to a rigid rule for the inflation rate. One way for the central bank to convey its commitment to a rigid inflation rule is to fix the exchange rate. Fixing the exchange rate commits the central bank to keeping domestic interest rates in line with that of the country to which its currency is fixed, thereby precluding the possibility of the central bank adopting a more stimulative monetary policy.

Countries do not casually inflate their economies. More often they print money out of desperation. Hyperinflations have almost always occurred among the vanquished following an international or civil war or other major calamity (Germany, Hungary, the Soviet Union, China, Nicaragua). The very high inflations in Latin America (Brazil, Argentina, Bolivia) occurred after the prices of commodities they exported collapsed, and energy prices and the interest rates they paid to foreigners soared. The very high inflations in eastern Europe and the countries of the former Soviet Union occurred during the difficult transition to market economies, when their needs for public outlays were high and their ability to generate tax revenue was low (Poland, Russia). (For more on hyperinflation and rapid inflation, see Section 9-6 on pp. 299–302).

During the 1990s many of the countries of western Europe pledged to keep their exchange rates fixed relative to each other (but not relative to the United States or Japan). This system was the precursor to the ultimate fixed exchange rate system, a single currency (the euro), discussed in the International Perspective box on pp. 474–75.

Summary

1. In earlier chapters we assumed that the growth of aggregate demand could be controlled precisely by policymakers. We now recognize that in the real world economy, policy shifts cannot control aggregate demand instantly or precisely.

2. Hitting several targets of stabilization policy, such as unemployment and inflation, requires several policy instruments. The conditions required for activist policy intervention to be effective (the "activists' paradise") are quite stringent, including accurate forecasting, possession of powerful tools, absence of costs of changing policy instruments, and absence of political constraints.

3. The general case put forth by advocates of policy rules is that rules insulate a central bank from political pressure, allow the performance of the central bank to be judged, and help private decisionmakers form correct expectations. However, the strength of this case depends on which variable is being targeted by a rule.

4. Policy activists are pessimistic about the stability of the private economy, while they are optimistic about the feasibility of discretionary policy. Advocates of rules reverse the locus of their optimism and pessimism.

5. Five lags (data, recognition, legislative, transmission, and effectiveness) limit the speed at which policy can respond to a demand or supply shock. By far the longest for monetary policy is the effectiveness lag. Additional obstacles to effective activist policy, or to policy rules based on targets, are multiplier uncertainty and forecasting errors.

6. Time inconsistency suggests that discretionary policymakers may have an incentive to alter policies after private decisionmakers have reacted to previous policy announcements. To encourage decisionmakers to form low expectations of inflation, it may pay the central bank to target the inflation rate and achieve a reputation for succeeding in keeping the inflation rate low, thus establishing policy credibility.

7. The economy's actual real GDP has been close to natural real GDP since the mid-1980s. Long lags suggest that rather than waiting until output deviates appreciably from its natural level, the Fed should be forward-looking, changing interest rates when the economy is forecasted to overheat or stall out, as it did in 1994 and 2001.

8. Proposed policy rules differ in the variables they propose to target. Rules targeting policy instruments

may be successful but irrelevant for the achievement of desirable outcomes for target variables like inflation and unemployment, due to slippages coming from money-multiplier shocks, money demand shocks, commodity demand shocks, and supply shocks. Rules for target variables may lead to better outcomes in principle, but may be difficult to implement successfully.

9. Fixing its exchange rate deprives a nation's central bank of discretionary monetary policy. In practice, that sometimes leads nations to redress their fiscal imbalances, as well as prevent the money growth that leads to inflation. Member nations of the euro have achieved fixed exchange rates with each other but have lost any control over monetary policy, which they have ceded to the European Central Bank.

Concepts

demand shocks
policy activism
policy rule
policy instruments
target variables
discretionary policy

rigid rule
constant growth rate rule (CGRR)
feedback rule
monetarism
dynamic multipliers
multiplier uncertainty

time inconsistency
policy credibility
Taylor Rule
nominal anchor

Questions

1. In the Appendix to Chapter 4, the equations of the IS and LM curves are given as follows:

   $$IS: Y = k(A'_p - br)$$

   $$LM: Y = [(M^S/P) + fr]/h.$$

   Here, $k = 1/[s(1 - t) + t + nx]$.
   Let $A'_p = C'_a - T_a + I'_p + G + NX_a$, where C'_a is that part of consumption spending that is independent of both Y and r, I'_p is similarly defined, and the other terms are as defined in the Appendix to Chapter 3.
   (a) List the exogenous variables (and parameters) in this model. (See Chapter 3 to review the definition of this term.)
   (b) List the endogenous variables in this model. (See Chapter 3 to review the definition of this term.)
   (c) List the target variables in this model.
   (d) List the variables that make up the policy instruments in this model.
   (e) What is the relationship, if any, between endogenous variables and target variables in this model?
   (f) What is the relationship, if any, between exogenous variables and policy instruments in this model?

   Note: In answering this question, use only the variables in the IS and LM equations and the variables defining k and A'_p. For example, don't include a variable such as structural employment policy as a policy instrument or the unemployment rate as a target variable; they are not variables in the preceding model, even though they are listed in Figure 14-1 as a policy instrument and target variable, respectively.

2. In the IS-LM model of the preceding question, what are the monetary policy variables? What are the fiscal policy variables?

3. In the model of question 1, how many policy instruments are there? How many target variables? Is this consistent with the text's statement that you need as many policy instruments as target variables to achieve the desired values of the target variables?

4. The case for activist intervention in the economy would work best in the activists' paradise. What are the characteristics of the activists' paradise?

5. What do advocates of policy rules think are the main objections to countercyclical activism?

6. Distinguish between a rigid rule and a feedback rule. Give an example of each.

7. One way of describing the rules-versus-activism debate is to compare the beliefs of each side regarding the self-correcting powers of the economy and the efficacy of stabilization policy. What does each side believe about these issues?

8. Under the constant growth rate rule (CGRR), the single target for the policymaker becomes the growth rate of the money supply. Does this statement suggest that those advocating the CGRR are not concerned with the level of real output and employment?

9. Explain why stability of the demand for money is so important to those advocating a constant growth rate rule for the money supply. What happens to the argument in favor of this rule if money demand is unstable?

10. Identify and describe the five main types of lags that affect the timeliness of monetary and fiscal policy.

11. What problems do long and variable lags present to the policymaker? If lags are long and fixed (rather than long and variable), do any problems remain?

12. Why does multiplier uncertainty create a dilemma for policymakers?

13. Figure 14-2 shows that the effectiveness lag of monetary policy increased during the period 1988–2004, as compared to earlier periods, and that the interest-rate multiplier declined in each of the successive periods 1961–73, 1974–87, and 1988–2004. What caused this trend toward diminished effectiveness of monetary policy?

14. Discuss the evidence that the economy's output has become more stable since the mid-1980s. Discuss how changes in the nature of shocks to the economy contributed to the increased stability as well as the role that the Fed played in reducing volatility.

15. During the period 1986–96 the Fed's use of its policy instruments produced a positive relationship between the output ratio and the federal funds interest rate. When the output ratio rose, the Fed increased the federal funds rate, and it did the opposite when the output ratio fell. What was the rationale for this, and why did the Fed discontinue it in 1996? Would the economy have performed better after 1996 if the Fed had acted to maintain the previous relationship between the output ratio and the federal funds rate?

16. Suppose policymakers announce their intentions to lower the inflation rate and adopt policy changes to slow nominal GDP growth. Describe, in terms of the SP model, the effects on the economy's output ratio, unemployment rate, and inflation rate under each of the following cases.
    (a) The public finds this announcement credible, and policymakers stick to their announced policies.
    (b) The public finds this announcement credible, but policymakers abandon their announced policies and leave the growth rate of nominal GDP unchanged.
    (c) The public does not find this announcement credible, but policymakers do stick to the announced policies.
    (d) The public does not find this announcement credible, and policymakers abandon their announced policies and do not lower the growth rate of nominal GDP.

17. Chapter 8 described three alternative policy responses by the Fed to a supply shock: neutral, accommodating, and extinguishing. In terms of how the Fed weighs inflation against output, that is, the parameters a and b of equation (14.1), explain how each of the Fed's policy responses to a supply shock would fit into a Taylor Rule.

18. Suppose the output ratio is 100 and the inflation rate is 5 percent. Given these conditions, why will policymakers be more likely to pursue a zero inflation target if they have a long time horizon and a low discount rate rather than a short time horizon and a high discount rate?

19. What is a nominal anchor for the economy and what is the advantage of using a nominal anchor in choosing a target variable to be fixed by a policy instrument? Explain why a nominal GDP growth rate rule and a Taylor Rule that places equal weight on inflation and output growth each has a nominal anchor. Finally, compare a Taylor Rule that places equal weight on inflation and output growth with one that places equal weight on inflation and the output ratio.

20. If effectiveness lags are long and variable, should policymakers use the current values or their best forecasts of target variables to determine policy? In evaluating the behavior of the Fed between 1994 and 2001, does it seem more likely that current or forecasted values of inflation and output determined their policies?

21. What are the arguments for and against using monetary policy to target a currency's exchange rate?

22. What are the arguments for and against the euro? Discuss which side of the argument is supported by the evidence from the period 1999–2004.

Problems

1. You are given the following two IS curves that show how real GDP (Y_t) in the current time period t depends on the current interest rate and interest rates in previous periods, where r_t is the interest rate in time period t. Furthermore each time period corresponds to a quarter or three months.

    I. $Y_t = 8{,}800 - 25r_t - 25r_{t-1}$
    $- 25r_{t-2} - 25r_{t-3} - 20r_{t-4} - 20r_{t-5}$
    $- 20r_{t-6} - 15r_{t-7} - 15r_{t-8} - 10r_{t-9}$

    II. $Y_t = 8{,}400 - 5r_t - 5r_{t-1}$
    $- 5r_{t-2} - 5r_{t-3} - 5r_{t-4} - 10r_{t-5}$
    $- 15r_{t-6} - 15r_{t-7} - 15r_{t-8} - 20r_{t-9}$

    Suppose that the Fed can set the interest rate and that for the last 10 quarters, the interest rate has been 4 percent.
    (a) Verify that initially real GDP equals 8,000 for both IS curves.
    (b) Suppose that the Fed lowers the interest rate to 3 percent and keeps it there for the next 10 quarters. Calculate real GDP for the next 10 quarters for each IS curve.
    (c) For each IS curve, what is the total increase in real GDP?
    (d) For each IS curve, how many quarters does it take for the increase in real GDP to equal one-half of the total increase?

(e) Using Figure 14-2, explain which one of the *IS* curves resembles the economy's response to a change in the interest rate prior to 1988 and which one resembles its response since 1988? Explain how your answer is related to the interest-rate parameters in each *IS* equation.

2. Suppose that natural real GDP (Y^N) equals 9,500, the Fed's desired real federal funds rate (r^{FF*}) equals 2.5 percent, and its desired inflation rate (p^*) equals 2 percent. You are given the following combinations of actual inflation and real GDP: (0.8, 8,930); (1.4, 9,215); (2.0, 9,500); (2.4, 9,690); (3.0, 9,975).
   (a) For each level of real GDP, compute $\hat{Y} = 100(\log(Y/Y^N))$.
   (b) Explain what each of the following pairs of values for the parameters *a* and *b* in equation (14.1), the equation for the Taylor Rule, means in terms of how the Fed weighs inflation against output: (0.5, 0.5), (2/3, 1/3), (1/3, 2/3).
   (c) Using the Taylor Rule as given by equation (14.1), calculate the real federal funds rate for the given combinations of inflation and real GDP when $a = b = 0.5$.
   (d) Using the Taylor Rule as given by equation (14.1), calculate the real federal funds rate (r^{FF}) for the given combinations of inflation and real GDP when $a = 2/3$ and $b = 1/3$.
   (e) Using the Taylor Rule as given by equation (14.1), calculate the real federal funds rate for the given combinations of inflation and real GDP when $a = 1/3$ and $b = 2/3$.
   (f) Compare your answers to parts c–e in terms of your answer to part b concerning how the Fed weighs inflation against output and how much variation there is in the log output ratio versus the inflation rate.

3. (a) Using the information given in problem 2, compute the real federal funds rate if the Fed sets it by targeting inflation, that is, if $a = 1$ and $b = 0$ in equation (14.1).
   (b) Explain why the real federal funds rate is less volatile if the Fed is targeting inflation as compared to when it is putting equal weight on inflation and output.

Self-Test Answers

p. 454 (1) target, (2) instrument, (3) instrument, (4) target, (5) instrument.

p. 460 (1) Legislative lag. (2) Multiplier uncertainty. (3) Data lag. (4) Both the effectiveness lag and multiplier uncertainty.

p. 467 (1) True; the public will believe that the central bank will maintain low rates of growth of the money supply and the price level. (2) False; opposite of (1). (3) True; same as (1). (4) False; time inconsistency strengthens advocates of rules involving nominal variables such as the growth of high-powered money or the inflation rate.

PART SIX

Sources of Instability in the Private Economy

CHAPTER 15 Instability in the Private Economy: Consumption Behavior

CHAPTER 16 Instability in the Private Economy: Investment Behavior

CHAPTER 15

Instability in the Private Economy: Consumption Behavior

Economists become upset when they learn that we aren't spending money as they've planned for us.
—Eliot Marshall

15-1 Consumption and Economic Stability

In Part Five (Chapters 13–14), we studied the role of stabilization policy, which consists of monetary and fiscal policy. The most basic question about stabilization policy is whether "activist" policy intervention should be attempted or whether policy rules are preferable. If policy rules are preferable, what variable should be targeted by such rules? A central issue in making these choices is the set of shocks that can cause target variables to be unstable even if a policy instrument is successfully targeted by a rigid rule. These shocks include money multiplier and money demand shocks (Chapter 13), supply shocks (Chapter 8), and commodity demand, or spending, shocks (Chapters 3 and 4).

We now turn to the nature of the shocks that destabilize consumption and investment demand. This chapter deals with the subject of consumption spending; the following chapter is devoted to investment spending. We start with consumption spending because it is by far the largest component of total spending, comprising two-thirds of GDP.

Consumption Spending and Shifts in the *IS* Curve

How did consumption spending enter into the basic theory of income determination earlier in the book? Chapter 3 introduced the simple Keynesian consumption function, which makes the level of consumption expenditures depend on disposable income and on an autonomous component. Shifts in this autonomous component, due to changes in consumer confidence or optimism and in household wealth, were cited among the factors that could shift the economy's *IS* curve. These shifts in the *IS* curve, amplified by the multiplier, cause fluctuations in real GDP as long as the *LM* curve is not completely vertical and the aggregate price level is not perfectly flexible. Further, the size of the multiplier is importantly affected by the size of the response of consumption to a change in disposable income, the marginal propensity to consume.

Forward-Looking Theories of Consumer Behavior

In this chapter we examine the determinants of consumption spending. The focus is a theory of consumer behavior that incorporates much more sophisticated consumer behavior than the Keynesian theory of Chapter 3. This theory states that consumers have **forward-looking expectations**. Because consumers

Forward-looking expectations are estimates of the future values of economic variables. They are generally based on the current and past values of several variables and an economic model that accounts for their behavior.

prefer stable as opposed to highly variable patterns of consumption, they assess whether changes in their incomes are likely to persist when deciding how much to change their consumption. Consumers behave quite differently in response to a change in disposable income that is expected to be *temporary* than they do in response to a change in disposable income that is expected to be *permanent*. Consumers can maintain their consumption when income changes temporarily by drawing down their accumulated savings. By contrast, if income is reduced permanently, consumption will fall more dramatically.

Introducing the PIH and LCH. The hypothesis that consumption depends on forward-looking expectations was developed independently in the 1950s by two economists who have since won the Nobel Prize, Milton Friedman and the late Franco Modigliani. Friedman's version is called the **permanent-income hypothesis (PIH)**. It predicts that consumption responds only to permanent changes in income, not to transitory ones. The PIH suggests that temporary changes in income will have minor effects on permanent income and, therefore, on consumption. As a result, the multiplier effect of a temporary change in autonomous spending is much smaller than the effect calculated in Chapter 3. In that case, the shifts in the *IS* curve are also much smaller than suggested in Chapter 4. The resulting stability of consumption spending supports the view of those who advocate policy rules that the economy can be trusted to remain fairly close to natural output.

Modigliani's version, called the **life-cycle hypothesis (LCH)**, holds that consumers attempt to smooth out their consumption spending over their lifetimes. This version also implies that transitory blips of income will cause only a small response in consumption. The LCH also implies that consumption spending depends not just on disposable income but on the real wealth of consumers as well. It implies, for instance, that major movements in stock market and housing prices affect consumption.

The **permanent-income hypothesis (PIH)** holds that consumption spending depends on the long-run average (or permanent) income that people expect to receive.

The **life-cycle hypothesis (LCH)** implies that households base their current consumption on their expected total lifetime incomes and their wealth.

15-2 Case Study

Main Features of U.S. Consumption Data

Before we study these two forward-looking theories of consumption behavior, we will examine data on aggregate consumption in the United States. Plotted in Figure 15-1 are total real consumption expenditures over the period 1960–2004, as well as the behavior of the three main components of consumption: durable goods, nondurable goods, and services.

Note that the growth of total consumption spending, shown by the top line, has not been perfectly steady. Particularly sharp slowdowns in the growth of total consumption spending took place in 1974–75, 1980–82, and 1990–91. In contrast, consumption spending never declined for even a single quarter in the recession of 2001. As we will see, the forward-looking theories emphasize that because consumers consider their permanent or lifetime incomes, they react to temporary declines in income (such as occur in a recession) primarily by reducing saving rather than consumption. Clearly, some consumers cut their consumption during recessions. They may not, for example, have enough savings to absorb the blow of losing a job. Also, banks typically will not lend to unemployed people, even though they may have good prospects of regaining their jobs and making an impressive total lifetime income.

Consumption Does Not Always Grow Steadily

Figure 15-1 Real Consumer Expenditure and Its Three Components, 1960–2004

The top line plots consumer expenditure and shows a marked pause in growth in 1974–75, 1980–82, and 1990–91, but not in the recession of 2001. Consumption of durable goods is both the most volatile and fastest-growing component on average over this period. Consumption of services also has grown rapidly but is much less volatile than expenditures on durable goods. Consumption of nondurable goods is the slowest-growing component and has moderate volatility.

Of the three components of consumption expenditures, spending on durable goods is by far the most volatile. Consumer durable expenditures, like the fixed-investment expenditures studied in the next chapter, are often made for big-ticket items that can be postponed. Many households buy new automobiles or TV sets simply because they want improved quality or new features; they can often postpone such purchases if income declines temporarily. Consumption of nondurable goods displays moderate cyclical volatility, while consumption of services tends to grow more smoothly.

Both durable goods and services spending grew much faster than spending on nondurable goods over the period shown in Figure 15-1. Percentages of total consumption for the three major categories of real consumption expenditures at the beginning and end of the period depicted are as follows:

	1960:Q1	2004:Q4
Durable goods	5.9	14.6
Nondurable goods	41.2	28.9
Services	52.9	56.5

The basic reason for the slow growth in nondurable goods purchases is that many such goods, particularly food and clothing, are necessities. Many types of durable goods (such as computers, DVD players, and cell phones) and services (airline trips to Florida) are luxuries, which experience disproportionately fast growth in demand when incomes rise.

Have these trends made total consumption more or less stable? The shrinking segment, nondurable goods, has moderate cyclical volatility. The increases in the shares of high-volatility durable goods spending and low-volatility services spending have roughly cancelled out, implying that the overall volatility of total consumption spending did not change appreciably between 1960 and 2004.

15-3 Background: The Conflict Between the Time-Series and Cross-Section Evidence

One of the major innovations in Keynes's *General Theory* was the multiplier, which followed directly from the assumptions that consumption responds to income and that the marginal propensity to consume is less than unity: "The fundamental psychological law ... is that men are disposed, as a rule and on the average, to increase their consumption as their income increases, but not by as much as the increase in their income."[1]

Keynes's second innovative idea was that there is a given amount, a, that individuals will consume no matter what their income, so that it is possible for saving to be negative if disposable income is very low. Denoting consumption

Figure 15-2 The Relation Between Disposable Income (Y_D), Consumption Spending (C), and the Ratio of Saving to Income (S/Y_D)

The top frame repeats the consumption function introduced in Chapter 3. At levels of disposable income below (to the left of) Y_{D0}, people consume more than their income and saving is negative, as shown by the shaded red area. To the right of Y_{D0} consumption is less than income, and the shaded blue area, which represents the difference between income and consumption, that is, the amount of saving, is a steadily growing fraction of disposable income. In the middle frame, the share of saving in disposable income is plotted as a negative fraction to the left of Y_{D0} and a positive and growing fraction to the right. The bottom frame plots actual data on the relation of saving to disposable income from a survey of consumers. Notice the close correspondence between the theoretical diagram in the middle frame and the actual data in the bottom frame.

---

[1] See John Maynard Keynes, *The General Theory of Employment, Interest and Money* (New York: Macmillan, 1936), Book III. The idea of the multiplier was first introduced by R. F. Kahn, "The Relation of Home Investment to Unemployment," *Economic Journal* (June 1931), but Keynes was the first to fit the multiplier into a general economic model of commodity and money markets.

15-3 Background: The Conflict Between the Time-Series and Cross-Section Evidence

People with Higher Incomes Have Higher Saving Rates

as C and disposable income as Y_D, the Keynesian consumption function can be written:

$$C = C_a + cY_D \qquad (15.1)$$

This is identical to equation (3.3) on p. 61.

The hypothetical Keynesian consumption function and saving ratio are plotted in the top two frames of Figure 15-2. In the top frame, consumption (C) rises less rapidly than disposable income (Y_D), since the marginal propensity to consume (c) is less than 1.0. Consumption starts out greater than Y_D, equals Y_D at the income level Y_{D0}, and then is less than Y_D. Everywhere to the right of Y_{D0} the shortfall of consumption below disposable income allows room for a positive amount of saving. For instance, the income level Y_{D1} is divided into the consumption level C_1 and the saving level S_1.

Moving down to the middle frame of Figure 15-2, we find plotted the saving/income ratio, S/Y_D. To the left of the income level Y_{D0}, saving is negative; to the right of Y_{D0}, saving is positive. As income rises, according to the hypothetical Keynesian relation in the middle frame, a larger share of disposable income is saved.

The actual data plotted in the bottom frame of Figure 15-2 confirm Keynes's hypothesis for a **cross section** of Americans who were polled on their income, saving, and consumption behavior. Most people with low incomes do not save at all, but instead "dissave," consuming more than they earn by borrowing or by drawing on accumulated assets in savings accounts. As we move rightward from the poor to the rich, we find that the saving/income ratio increases, just as in the hypothetical relationship of the middle frame.

A **cross section** consists of data for numerous units (for instance, households, firms, cities, or states) observed over a single period of time.

The Saving Rate: Short-Run Variability, Long-Run Constancy

Implicit in Figure 15-2 is a potentially serious problem for the economy. If individuals save more as their incomes rise, then consumption spending may be inadequate to maintain actual real GDP at the desired level of natural real GDP. Keynes's concern that the saving rate would rise as the years passed seemed particularly relevant during the Great Depression of the 1930s, when the world's actual real GDP was far below its natural level for many years and investment spending was very weak. The weakness of investment spending during the Great Depression led some to argue that government spending must be used to raise output to its natural level.

But, has the saving rate, in fact, risen over time as natural real GDP has risen? Look now at Figure 15-3, which plots the actual historical **time-series** data for the average saving ratio for each major business cycle of the twentieth century. Between 1898 and 1899, the first observation plotted, and 1991–2001, the last observation plotted, real income per person increased by a factor of seven.[2] Yet there is little indication that the saving ratio trended upward over the twentieth century. Instead, the saving ratio did not change dramatically over the twentieth century. In fact, in the 1990s the saving ratio was *lower* than it was before World War I. The main longer-term variations in the saving ratio were the low saving ratio during the Great Depression of the 1930s and the high saving ratio during World War I and World War II, and more recently the low saving ratio of the 1990s that we discuss later in this chapter.

A **time series** consists of data covering a span of time for one or more measures (for instance, disposable income or consumption spending).

---

[2] Data for 1991–2001 were used for the last observation because the years after 2001 have not yet comprised a complete business cycle.

Figure 15-3 Ratio of Personal Saving to Disposable Personal Income (S/Y_D), Averages over Business Cycles, 1898–2001

The low level of saving during the Great Depression is consistent with our theory (compare Figure 3-3 on p. 65). The high level of saving during World War I and World War II were caused by the shortages of civilian goods and services. Leaving out these two extreme periods, the ratio of saving to disposable income was fairly constant until after 1990. Observations plotted are averages over complete business cycles.

Sources: 1897–99: Paul David and John Scadding, "Private Savings: Ultrarationality, Aggregation, and 'Denison's Law,'" *Journal of Political Economy* (March/April 1974). 1900–32: Historical Statistics of the United States, Series F 639 and F 9. 1933–2001: National Income and Product Accounts.

Keynes's consumption function implies that the saving ratio will decline in recessions and that in cross-section data those with higher incomes will tend to have higher saving rates. The data confirm both of these implications. Keynes's consumption function, however, does not explain why over the longer run the saving ratio is constant or even declining instead of rising as predicted. The two most important hypotheses about consumption (and thus about saving) that can account for the long-run near-constancy of the saving ratio, as well as the short-run variability and the cross-section pattern of saving, are Friedman's permanent-income hypothesis and Modigliani's life-cycle hypothesis.

15-4 Forward-Looking Behavior: The Permanent-Income Hypothesis

A Theory of Steady Consumption

Imagine that you have a job and receive your take-home pay of $1,000 on the first day of each month. Suppose you regard your income on the first day of each month as $1,000, and your income on each of the remaining days of the month as zero. If you spend based on the simple Keynesian consumption function with a high marginal propensity to consume and a small autonomous component, you will do almost all your consumption spending on the first day of the month and consume very little over the rest of the month!

Of course people consume more steadily than that, setting aside part of their pay to buy groceries and other items during the rest of the month. Individuals who have variable income will be happier if they consume about the same amount each day rather than allowing their consumption to change each day with their changing income.

Permanent income is the annual average income that people expect to receive over a period of years in the future.

Milton Friedman first proposed the hypothesis that individuals consume a constant fraction (k) of their expected income, which Friedman called permanent income (Y^P).[3]

General Form | Numerical Example
$$C = kY^P \qquad C = 0.9(\$10{,}000) = \$9{,}000 \qquad (15.2)$$

The marginal propensity to consume out of permanent income (k) depends on individual tastes and on the variability of income (farmers, salespeople, and others with variable income need higher saving to support themselves during bad years). In addition, k may depend on the interest rate. People may be willing to save more (and spend less) when interest rates are higher.[4]

Revising the estimate of permanent income. The permanent-income hypothesis summarized in equation (15.2) does not say that individuals consume exactly the same amount year after year. Every year new events occur that are likely to change individuals' guesses about their permanent income. For instance, an individual might find that in good years income has increased. Gradually the individual will revise his or her estimate of average expected income upward and will increase his or her stable-consumption level.

Friedman's permanent-income hypothesis consists of the assumption in equation (15.2) that individuals consume a constant portion of their permanent income. But this is not enough, because an additional assumption is required to indicate how individuals estimate the size of their permanent income. Friedman proposed that individual estimates of permanent income for this year (Y^P) be revised from last year's estimate (Y^P_{-1}) by some fraction (j) of the amount by which actual income (Y) differs from (Y^P_{-1}):

General Form | Numerical Example
$$Y^P = Y^P_{-1} + j(Y - Y^P_{-1}) \qquad Y^P = 10{,}000 + 0.2(15{,}000 - 10{,}000) \quad (15.3)$$
$$= 11{,}000$$

Adaptive expectations. The behavior described in equation (15.3) is sometimes called the "error-learning" or "adaptive" hypothesis of expectation formation. This hypothesis implies that individuals will allow their consumption to respond modestly to changes in actual income because consumption depends on permanent income, and in turn permanent income in equation (15.3) depends only in part on this period's actual income. When we substitute (15.3) into (15.2), we obtain the following relationship between an individual's current consumption (C), this period's actual income (Y), and last period's estimate of permanent income (Y^P_{-1}):

General Form | Numerical Example
$$C = kY^P_{-1} + kj(Y - Y^P_{-1}) \qquad C = 0.9Y^P_{-1} + 0.18(Y - Y^P_{-1}) \qquad (15.4)$$

Exactly the same hypothesis for the formation of expectations was introduced in the Appendix to Chapter 8 in the discussion of inflation expecta-

---

[3] Milton Friedman, *A Theory of the Consumption Function* (Princeton, NJ: Princeton University Press, 1957). Milton Friedman's photo appears on p. 549.

[4] Because of the limitations of the alphabet we are once again forced to duplicate the use of letters. The k here is completely unrelated to the k used in Chapters 3 and 4 represent the multiplier.

tions (see equation (2) on p. 273). Equation (15.3) can be rewritten in the form used there.

$$Y^P = jY + (1 - j)Y^P_{-1}$$

This says that permanent income in this period is a weighted average of actual income and last period's permanent income.

Two marginal propensities to consume. Equation (15.4) helps us see that Friedman's theory is based on a distinction between two concepts of the marginal propensity to consume (MPC). The *long-run* MPC is simply the coefficient (k) of permanent income in the original consumption function (15.2), and indeed k is the coefficient of the first term in (15.4). In our numerical example, the long-term MPC (k) is 0.9. The *short-run* MPC is the coefficient of a change in actual income, the coefficient kj (or $0.18 = 0.9$ times 0.2) in the second term in (15.4). When today's actual income (Y) increases, the second term in (15.4) shows that today's consumption goes up by the short-run MPC (kj, or 0.18).

The portion of today's income change that is not expected to be permanent is called **transitory income** in Friedman's theory. Transitory income (Y^t) is simply actual income minus permanent income:

Transitory income is the difference between actual and permanent income and is not expected to recur.

General Form

$$\begin{aligned} Y^t &= Y - Y^P \\ &= Y - Y^P_{-1} - j(Y - Y^P_{-1}) \\ &= (1 - j)(Y - Y^P_{-1}) \end{aligned}$$

Numerical Example

$$\begin{aligned} Y^t &= Y - Y^P \\ &= 0.8(Y - Y^P_{-1}) \end{aligned} \quad (15.5)$$

Friedman achieves his sharp distinction between the long-run and short-run MPC by assuming that the MPC out of transitory income is zero. Thus his consumption function (15.2) could be rewritten as:

$$C = 0Y^t + kY^P \quad (15.6)$$

Reconciling the Conflict Between Cross-Section and Time-Series Data

The motivation for Friedman's PIH was the apparent conflict between the cross-section data in Figure 15-2, where high-income people were shown to have higher saving ratios than low-income people, and the long-run near-constancy of the saving ratio shown in Figure 15-3. The PIH contends that the high saving ratios of high-income people are due to their having atypically large, positive, transitory incomes (for example, executives who received large bonuses after a good year; movie stars after the release of unusually popular films; or professional athletes, who have short-lived, high-income careers). Similarly, the PIH contends that low-income people dissave or have low saving ratios (as in Figure 15-2) because they are more likely than the average person to have actual incomes that are temporarily below their permanent incomes. (Examples of people with negative transitory income include farmers whose crops were ruined by drought, floods, or disease; executives who have just been fired; and college students who believe that their incomes will be higher in the future.) Thus, the PIH explains how, even when the longer-run savings ratio is constant across individuals and across time, cross-section data will record that high-income people have higher saving ratios.

The two consumption functions illustrated. Figure 15-4 illustrates the distinction between the long-run and short-run consumption functions. The solid orange line running through points A and F is the long-run consumption function; its slope is the long-run MPC (k, or 0.9 in our example). It is called the long-run consumption function because it indicates the level of consumption only when actual income has remained long enough at a particular level for individuals to fully adjust their estimated permanent income to the actual level.

What happens in the short run, when actual income can differ from permanent income? The flatter dashed red schedule running between A and B is the short-run schedule and plots equation (15.4). When current income (Y) is exactly equal to last period's permanent income Y^P_{-1}, the short-run schedule intersects the long-run schedule at point A. But during an unusually good year, when an individual's income is at the high level Y_0, the current estimate of permanent income (Y^P) rises above last period's estimate Y^P_{-1} by a fraction (j) of the excess of actual income over last period's estimate. And the higher value of Y^P raises consumption by k times the increase in permanent income.

Thus consumption at point B lies vertically above point A by the fraction kj (18 percent in the numerical example) times the horizontal distance between Y^P_{-1} and Y_0. With the short-run marginal propensity to consume (kj) so far below the long-run propensity (k), any short-run increase in income goes disproportionately into saving. If Y_0 comes to be regarded as permanent, the short-run consumption function will go through F.

To summarize, estimates of permanent income are continually raised as actual income outstrips previous levels, causing the relationship between consumption and income to follow the long-run schedule, as marked by the arrows in Figure 15-4. Thus in the long run the saving ratio is roughly constant. But in the short run a temporary increase in income raises the saving ratio and a temporary decrease in income reduces the saving ratio, because permanent income does not adjust completely to changes in actual income.

Figure 15-4 The Permanent-Income Hypothesis of Consumption and Saving

The long-run schedule shows that consumption is a fixed fraction of income in the long run, when actual and permanent income are equal. But short-run gains in actual income, as at point B, are not fully incorporated into permanent income. Thus consumption increases only a small amount (compare points B and A), and at B most of the short-run increase in income is saved. When the same gain in income is maintained permanently, the short-run schedule shifts upward along the long-run schedule to point F.

The Long-Run Consumption Function Is Much Steeper Than the Short-Run Function

Self-Test

Determine whether actual income is above or below permanent income in each of the following situations and how consumption and saving compare to the values predicted by Friedman's theory if the income changes were permanent:

1. A stockbroker enjoying the best year of his or her career.
2. A North Dakota wheat farmer suffering from a severe drought.
3. The U.S. economy in a recession.
4. The U.S. economy in a period of unusually high real GDP, such as 1999–2000.

15-5 Forward-Looking Behavior: The Life-Cycle Hypothesis

About the same time that Friedman wrote his book on the permanent-income hypothesis, Franco Modigliani of MIT and collaborators devised a somewhat different way of reconciling the positive relation between the saving ratio and income observed in cross-section data and the constancy of the saving ratio observed over long periods in the historical time-series data.[5] Modigliani and Friedman both began with the perspective that individuals prefer to maintain a stable consumption pattern rather than allow consumption to rise or fall with every transitory oscillation of their income. But Modigliani carried the stable-consumption argument further than Friedman and suggested that people *would try to stabilize their consumption over their entire lifetimes.*

Because of its emphasis on the lifetime horizon of consumers, the Modigliani theory is called the life-cycle hypothesis (LCH). Since it stresses the way consumers smooth consumption over their lifetimes and save in preparation for their retirement years, the LCH falls into the category of theories based on *forward-looking expectations*. It shares with Friedman's theory the ability to reconcile a low short-run MPC with a high and stable long-run MPC. But the LCH adds a "lifetime budget constraint" to Friedman's theory, which is the condition that the consumption of households over their lifetimes equals their income plus their holdings of assets coming from sources other than work (for example, gifts from parents). This feature of the LCH provides a rigorous connection between consumption expenditures and the value of the assets held by consumers. As a result, the LCH *predicts that a stock market crash, like the one in 1987, will reduce consumption expenditures and a stock market boom, like that of the 1990s, will raise consumption expenditures.*

Franco Modigliani (1918–2003)

The 1985 Nobel Prize winner is best known for the life-cycle model of consumption behavior and for his articulate advocacy of policy activism.

Lifetime Asset Holding: Modigliani's Asset Pyramid Illustrated

We now examine Figure 15-5, which shows how a simple version of Modigliani's theory predicts how income, consumption, saving, and asset accumulation will behave over the lifetime of the typical consumer. The horizontal

---

[5] Franco Modigliani and R. E. Brumberg, "Utility Analysis and the Consumption Function," in K. K. Kurihara, ed., *Post-Keynesian Economics* (New Brunswick, NJ: Rutgers University Press, 1954). Also A. Ando and F. Modigliani, "The 'Life Cycle' Hypothesis of Saving: Aggregate Implications and Tests," *American Economic Review*, vol. 53 (March 1963), pp. 55–84.

494 Chapter 15 • Instability in the Private Economy: Consumption Behavior

Figure 15-5 The Behavior of Consumption, Saving, and Assets under the Life-Cycle Hypothesis

Under the life-cycle hypothesis particular attention is paid to the relation between the length of the lifetime (L) and an individual's age at retirement (R). The length of the retirement period is $L - R$. In the upper frame, a constant amount (C_0) is consumed every year of one's life, as indicated by the red line. A constant amount of income Y_0 is earned each year until retirement. During the working years until R, income exceeds consumption, as shown by the saving that occurs in the blue area. Then consumption exceeds the zero income during retirement and is financed by dissaving, as shown by the red area. In the bottom frame, the green line shows the growth of assets from the initial level (A_0) to the maximum level at retirement (A_R), followed by a decline in assets back to zero at death.

The Young Save During Their Working Years, and the Old Dissave During Retirement

axis shows various ages, with the age at retirement marked by R and the age at death marked by L. An individual is assumed to maintain a constant level of consumption (C_0) throughout life. Income, however, is earned only during the R working years. If there are no assets initially, as shown by the zero level of initial assets (A_0) in the bottom frame, then the only way individuals can manage to consume without any income during their retirement is to save during their working years. The amount saved, income minus consumption, is shown by the blue area during the period up to time R, and then the dissaving that occurs when consumption exceeds income during retirement is shown by the red area from time R through time L. In the bottom frame, the accumulation of assets occurs steadily during the working years through time R, when assets reach their maximum level A_R. Assets decline thereafter and are zero at time L.

No initial assets. How are consumption and income related when there are no initial assets? Total lifetime consumption of C_0 per year for L years is constrained to equal total income Y_0 per year for R years:

$$C_0 L = Y_0 R \quad \text{or} \quad C_0 = \left(\frac{R}{L}\right) Y_0 \qquad (15.7)$$

As Figure 15-5 is drawn, R is four-fifths of L, so consumption per year is limited to four-fifths of Y_0.[6]

The simple version of the life-cycle hypothesis can explain the positive association of saving and income, since the upward trend in per capita, natural real GDP raises both the saving and income of those of working age relative to those who are retired. The long-run constancy of the saving ratio can be explained by the fact that if the population in each historical era is divided into the same proportions of working and retired people, and each age group has the same saving behavior in generation after generation, then the long-run saving ratio will be constant.

The life-cycle hypothesis shares with Friedman's permanent-income hypothesis the implication that the saving ratio should rise in economic boom years and fall in recession years. A temporary increase in income today will be consumed over one's entire lifetime. For instance, imagine a person who believes he has 40 years left to live and receives an unexpected increase in income this year of $4,000 that he does not expect to receive again. His total lifetime consumption goes up by the $4,000 and his actual consumption this year goes up by only 1/40 of that amount, a mere $100. In each succeeding year, an additional $100 would be spent, for a total of $4,000 over the remaining 40 years of life.

Thus, in an economic boom widely expected to be temporary, an unexpected bonus of $4,000 would lead to only $100 extra of current consumption and $3,900 extra of saving. The short-run propensity to consume would be just 0.025, or 100/4,000. By contrast, if the $4,000 income increase is expected to be maintained for each of the next 40 years, then $4,000 extra can be consumed this year and again in each of the next 39 years and the saving ratio will not rise.

The role of assets. The Modigliani theory provides an important role for assets as a determinant of consumption behavior. Let us assume that initially a person has an endowment of assets of A_1, but plans to use these assets to raise consumption through his or her lifetime rather than to leave the assets to heirs. Then, as shown in Figure 15-6, consumption can be higher for a given level of income (Y_0), and saving can be lower, since the initial asset endowment provides more spending power. Now total lifetime consumption equals total lifetime income from work plus the available assets:

$$C_1 L = A_1 + Y_0 R$$

or

$$C_1 = \frac{A_1}{L} + \frac{R}{L} Y_0 \qquad (15.8)$$

---

[6] There are several simplifications in Figure 15-5 and equation (15.7) involving the treatment of interest income. Assuming that interest is earned on asset holdings at the nominal interest rate i, then total income is equal to wage income in real terms (W/P) plus real interest income (rA), where r is the real interest rate. Then (15.7) becomes

$$C_0 L = (W/P)_0 R + \sum_{t=0}^{L} r A_t$$

Thus total income increases gradually through time R and then decreases to zero, but is nevertheless positive during the retirement period. To reflect the fact that consumption depends on total income, including both wage income and earnings from the holding of assets, the symbol Y (for total real income) rather than W/P is used in (15.7) in the text. The official definition of income overstates Y, since it includes the entire income from assets, including that portion of the nominal return $(i - r)$ needed to maintain intact the real value of assets.

Figure 15-6 Consumption, Saving, and Assets under the Life-Cycle Hypothesis When There Is an Initial Stock of Assets

This diagram is identical to Figure 15-5, but here there is an initial stock of assets, A_1, in contrast to the initial stock of zero in the previous diagram. If we continue to assume that dissaving during retirement runs the stock of assets down to zero, then the existence of A_1 makes more total consumption possible with a smaller amount of saving. This is shown by an upward shift from the previous level of consumption (C_0) to a new higher level (C_1). The blue saving area is now smaller, as is the blue area in the bottom frame, which shows the increase in assets due to saving.

An Initial Endowment of Assets Raises Consumption and Reduces Saving

The right-hand expression shows that consumption per year (C_1) depends not just on income (Y_0); it also depends on the ratio of available assets per year of life.

Figure 15-6 is oversimplified because it assumes that the initial endowment of assets is received at the beginning of the working life. In reality, however, increases in the value of assets occur throughout one's life, so one would expect the response of annual consumption to a change in asset value to be larger than is assumed in equation (15.8). Modigliani's empirical research has estimated that a $1 increase in real asset values raised annual real consumption by about $0.06, which would indicate that people use a 15-year horizon over which to spend an increase in real assets.

In Chapter 7 we learned that the economy's self-correcting forces are enhanced when real consumption spending depends on real assets or real wealth. If a drop in spending cuts the price level, the level of real wealth is raised, which helps arrest the decline in spending.[7] In the other direction, if an increase in spending raises the price level, the level of real wealth declines, which helps dampen the original stimulus to spending. We return to the relationship between real wealth and consumption behavior in Section 15-8.

Thus, ironically, Modigliani's life-cycle hypothesis supports the optimism of rules advocates regarding the stability of the private economy, even though Modigliani was a prominent critic of policy rules. Private spending is stabilized because transitory increases in disposable income, those that are

---

[7] Review the Pigou, or real balance, effect discussed in Section 7-9 on pp. 218–19.

not expected to last very long, have only a modest influence on current consumption. In addition, the real-asset effect stabilizes the economy because higher prices cut the real value of assets and dampen spending. Overall, life-cycle considerations reduce the current marginal propensity to consume, cut the multiplier, and insulate the economy from unexpected changes in investment, net exports, or other types of spending.

> **Self-Test**
>
> Assume that an adult is making a consumption plan and anticipates a life of 40 more years, 30 of which will be spent in work and 10 in retirement.
> 1. If income during the working years is $50,000, and the endowment of initial assets is zero, what will annual consumption expenditures be during the working years? During the retirement years?
> 2. What will be the average propensity to consume (C/Y) during the working years?
> 3. Now, assume instead that initial assets are $200,000. What will annual consumption expenditures be during the working years? During the retirement years?
> 4. What will be the average propensity to consume during the working years?

15-6 Rational Expectations and Other Amendments to the Simple Forward-Looking Theories

In recent years consumption behavior has been one of the most active areas of research in macroeconomics. Much attention has been directed toward the implications of households using more sophisticated methods of forming their expectations about their future incomes than the simple adaptive expectations method shown in equation (15.3). The contrast between the predictions of the resulting theory and the actual cyclical behavior of consumption has highlighted the role of several additional factors that are not part of the pure PIH or LCH theories: liquidity constraints, consumer durables, bequests, and uncertainty.

Rational Expectations

Recall from equation (15.3) that in its original Friedman formulation, the PIH is combined with the adaptive or error-learning method of calculating permanent income. Thus when actual income increases, people only *gradually* revise upward their estimate of permanent income. Though it provides a simple and convenient approximation to how households might form their expectations about their future incomes, the adaptive expectations hypothesis may be too simple. Among its drawbacks are that it mechanically extrapolates the past and that it does not explicitly allow for the effects of variables other than income on expectations of future income.

The **rational expectations** hypothesis suggests that people use a more sophisticated method of forming their expectations about their future incomes. Rational expectations assume that expectations of future events are formed using *all* the information available. Thus rational expectations imply that all

Rational expectations are forecasts of future economic magnitudes based on information currently available about the structure and past performance of the economy and future government policies.

the information that can be gleaned from the past and even from credible announcements about the future, like tax cuts that have been enacted but that have not yet taken effect, will be used to form estimates of permanent income. As a result, only *new* information will change estimated permanent incomes, which implies that consumption will change only if *unanticipated* events occur. Previously expected events provide no news and therefore no revisions to permanent income and no change in consumption.

Is consumption too volatile or too smooth? A controversy has developed over the empirical implications of the rational expectations version of the PIH. Everything depends on how consumers view the nature of new information about income. If a change in current income provides no information about income in the future, then estimates of permanent income change very little, and the marginal propensity to consume out of this change in current income should be close to zero.[8] However, our case study (Section 15-2) showed that consumption displayed visible responses to the decline of income in the 1974–75, 1980–82, and 1990–91 recessions. This points toward the conclusion that actual consumption responds too strongly to changes in actual income, that is, it is *excessively volatile* relative to the prediction of the theory.[9]

However, another possibility is that changes in current income provide a good prediction of changes in future income. For instance, a person who loses a high-paying job may have very good reason to predict that future income will be lower, perhaps for many years. In the extreme case, if it were true that estimates of permanent income always responded by one dollar to any change in current income of one dollar (that is, $j = 1$ in equations 15.3 and 15.4), then the marginal propensity to consume out of current income would be k (simply because the marginal propensity to consume out of permanent income is k). But the data show clearly that consumption is smoother than current income. So by this contrasting approach, actual consumption is *too smooth* relative to the prediction of the theory.[10]

Thus far the debate over the cyclical behavior of consumption has not been settled. However, the initial conclusion that consumption was too volatile led to the realization that the simple versions of the PIH and LCH we have just reviewed, as well as the rational expectations updating of these theories, omit several important aspects of consumption behavior. Until these issues are adequately integrated into the theory, it is unlikely that the question of whether consumption is too volatile or too smooth will be resolved.

---

[8] In this case it can be shown in a specific mathematical model that the MPC would be $r/(1 + r)$, where r is the real rate of interest. Thus, depending on the asset used to measure r, the MPC would be between zero and 0.07. This result is developed in the excellent but mathematically advanced survey by Andrew B. Abel, "Consumption and Investment," in B.M. Friedman and F. Hahn, eds., *Handbook of Monetary Economics* (Amsterdam: Elsevier Science Publishers, 1990), pp. 725–78.

[9] The rational expectations approach to the study of consumption behavior was introduced in Robert E. Hall, "Stochastic Implications of the Life Cycle-Permanent Income Hypothesis: Theory and Evidence," *Journal of Political Economy*, vol. 86 (December 1978), pp. 971–87. The excess volatility argument is usually credited to Marjorie Flavin, "The Adjustment of Consumption to Changing Expectations about Future Income," *Journal of Political Economy*, vol. 89 (October 1981), pp. 974–1009.

[10] See Angus Deaton, "Life-Cycle Models of Consumption: Is the Evidence Consistent with the Theory?" in T. F. Bewley, ed., *Advances in Econometrics Fifth World Congress* (New York: Cambridge University Press, 1987), pp. 121–48.

Did Households Spend or Save the 2001 Tax Rebate?

After a long period of disuse, the role of fiscal policy for stabilization purposes was revived on June 7, 2001, when President Bush signed the Economic Growth and Tax Relief Reconciliation Act of 2001. Under the bill, taxpayers were entitled to receive an immediate check in the mail as a credit on their 2001 taxes, up to $300 for single taxpayers and up to $600 for married couples. The checks themselves were mailed during the period between late July and late September. These payments were commonly referred to as "tax rebates."

The theories of consumer behavior examined in this chapter predict that households will spend more of a change in disposable income if it is expected in advance rather than unexpected, and if it is permanent rather than temporary. Since the tax rebate was a first installment on tax reductions that had been legislated to be in effect for at least ten years, and since they were well publicized in advance, they can be considered both "expected" and "permanent." Thus economic theory would have predicted that most of the rebates would have been spent, that is, that the marginal propensity to spend would have been almost unity.

To assess this prediction, Matthew Shapiro and Joel Slemrod of the University of Michigan conducted a survey to determine how the receipt of the rebate checks would change behavior.[a] Much to their surprise, they found that only 22 percent of those receiving the rebate reported that it would mainly lead them to increase spending. Of those who did not plan to spend the rebates, 59 percent said they would repay debt and 41 percent said they would save the rebate. The implication of this low propensity to spend the rebate is that this type of fiscal policy intervention has a very lower multiplier effect on aggregate demand in relation to its budgetary cost to the government.

How do the authors explain the low spending response? Most important, survey respondents did not believe that the legislated tax cuts would occur. The authors also found that it would not have helped to target the tax rebate entirely at low-income households, since these households were no more likely to spend the rebates than high-income households. Skeptics might consider the authors' study flawed by its timing in the middle of the recession of 2001, for perhaps households were unusually likely to save the rebates (or pay off debts) because they feared they might lose their jobs in the recession. Perhaps other households were feeling financial pain from the decline in the stock market over the previous year and were anxious to rebuild their assets. However, these factors just amplify the bad news for fiscal policymakers that is implied by the survey, for if you choose not to introduce a stabilizing tax cut during a recession, at what other time would you want to implement it?

[a] Matthew D. Shapiro and Joel Slemrod, "Consumer Response to Tax Rebates," *American Economic Review*, vol. 93 (March 2003), pp. 381–96.

Consumer Durables

Both the permanent-income hypothesis and the life-cycle hypothesis are based on the desirability of maintaining a roughly constant level of enjoyment over time from consumption goods and services. If there is an increase in permanent income, people will not only want to increase their expenditures on services and nondurable goods, but will also want to increase their enjoyment of the services of durable goods. For consumer services and nondurable goods, such as haircuts and doughnuts, the enjoyment and the consumer spending occur at about the same time. Consumer durable goods are different. A television set is purchased at a single instant in time but produces enjoyment for many years thereafter. Thus the PIH and LCH suggest that it is not purchases of consumer durable goods that are kept equal to a fixed fraction of permanent income, but rather the flow of services (enjoyment) received from consumer durables. Consumers can keep the service flow at the same fixed fraction of permanent income by keeping the *stock* of consumer durable goods at the same fixed fraction of permanent income.

The essence of a durable good is that it provides service for many periods. New cars, for example, have service lives of ten years or more. Like any long-term asset, a durable good costs far more to purchase than the service it provides each period. A new car that sells for $25,000, for example, may provide only $2,500 worth of service each year. Thus, when a household decides that its higher permanent income warrants its annually consuming another $2,500 of car services, expenditure initially rises by $25,000. As a result, expenditures for durables may surge temporarily as consumers raise their stocks of durables in proportion to the increase in their permanent incomes.

As a result of the upsurge in purchases of consumer durables, total consumption expenditures may *rise* as a fraction of income when actual income rises, even though the PIH and LCH predict that consumption should *fall* as a fraction of income when actual income rises. Both the PIH and LCH predict that the saving ratio *falls* with higher income when consumer durables are counted as consumption expenditure but *rises* with higher income when consumer durables are counted as saving. Realization of the procyclical nature of consumer durable expenditures limits research on the validity of the PIH and LCH to consumer expenditures *excluding* durables—that is, including just services (haircuts) and nondurables (doughnuts).

Behavior of consumer durable expenditures in recessions. Both the PIH and LCH predict that in a recession, when income exhibits a transitory decline, households should maintain their consumption expenditures *by cutting back on the ratio of saving to disposable income* (S/Y^D). Data for postwar recessions confirm that the saving ratio declined slightly between the peak quarter and the trough quarters in nine recessions between 1953–54 and 2001. This tendency of the saving rate to decline is augmented considerably when we take account of the procyclical nature of expenditures on consumer durables. In the following table, the household saving rate, the ratio of consumer durables expenditure to disposable income, and the ratio of the sum of saving and consumer durables expenditure to disposable income $[(S + C^D)/Y^D]$ all decline in recessions.

Averages for Nine Recessions, 1953–54 to 2001, in percent

Ratio to disposable income	Peak	Trough	Peak to trough change
Personal saving	8.2	7.8	−0.4
Consumer durable expenditures	11.8	10.9	−0.9
Sum of personal saving and consumer durable expenditures	20.0	18.7	−1.3

Liquidity Constraints

The simple version of the LCH in Figure 15-5 assumes that consumption is constant over the lifetime and that labor income is constant until the date of retirement. Actually, however, labor income tends to rise with age, peaking a bit after age 50. To achieve a constant level of consumption throughout their lifetimes, young people would need to borrow during their low-income years and repay the loans later in high-income years. But banks generally will not allow young people to borrow all they would like, which implies that the consumption expenditures of young people are subject to a **liquidity constraint**. A liquidity constraint may afflict people of any age who are suffering from a transitory loss of income; for instance, banks may be unwilling to lend to a farmer who is close to bankruptcy after a year of poor growing weather, even though the weather can be expected to be better in the future.

People whose consumption can go no higher than their *current income* because of the unavailability of loans will have a much higher marginal propensity to consume in response to temporary changes in income than is predicted by the PIH or LCH theories. Economists have attempted to measure the importance of this so-called excess sensitivity of consumption to current changes in income. The consensus is that households whose consumption is subject to liquidity constraints account for about 15 percent of aggregate income. These households have MPCs out of transitory income of about 1. The remaining unconstrained households behave roughly as predicted by the LCH: They have negligible MPCs out of transitory income.[11] Thus liquidity constraints do not seem to be prevalent enough to seriously weaken the implication of the LCH (and PIH) that the short-run MPC will be much lower than the long-run MPC.

> A **liquidity constraint** prevents households from borrowing as much as they wish, even though there is sufficient expected future income to repay the loans.

15-7 Bequests and Uncertainty

In both of our diagrams of the LCH (Figures 15-5 and 15-6), individuals are assumed *to consume all of their lifetime savings during retirement*. Their assets dwindle to zero on the date of death, and nothing is left in the form of bequests to heirs. In fact, however, people do leave bequests. It has been claimed that about 80 percent of asset accumulation by U.S. households is transmitted to heirs rather than used for consumption during retirement.[12] This evidence seems to deny that the appropriate horizon to describe consumer behavior is the lifetime.

The Role of Bequests

As we learned in Section 12-8 on pp. 402–04, the existence of bequests has been interpreted as support for a striking theory of fiscal policy, often called the Barro-Ricardo equivalence theorem. People are expected to leave bequests because they care about their children. Any event that leaves their children worse

---

[11] Estimates that the share of aggregate income accruing to liquidity-constrained households has been as high as 50 percent can be found in John Y. Campbell and N. Gregory Mankiw, "Consumption, Income, and Interest Rates: Reinterpreting the Time Series Evidence," *NBER Macroeconomics Annual 1989* (Cambridge, MA: The MIT Press), pp. 185–216.

[12] Laurence J. Kotlikoff and Lawrence H. Summers, "The Role of Intergenerational Transfers in Aggregate Capital Accumulation," *Journal of Political Economy*, vol. 89 (August 1981), pp. 706–32. This finding is very controversial. A lengthy scholarly debate on the Kotlikoff-Summers findings is contained in Franco Modigliani, "The Role of Intergenerational Transfers and Life Cycle Saving in the Accumulation of Wealth," and Laurence J. Kotlikoff, "Intergenerational Transfers and Savings," both in *Journal of Economic Perspectives*, vol. 2 (Spring 1988), pp. 15–40 and 41–58, respectively.

International Perspective

Why Do Some Countries Save So Much?

While the world saving rate has remained relatively stable over the past few decades, saving rates differ by large amounts across countries and have fluctuated greatly within many countries. In general, saving rates in industrialized countries have been both lower and more stable than they have been in developing countries. National saving rates for industrialized countries have averaged about 20 percent since 1970, but they have averaged more than 25 percent in developing countries. In individual industrial countries, the national saving rate has typically fluctuated within a 10 percentage point range.

The Life-Cycle Model and Dependency Ratios

We have learned that consumption, and thus saving, responds to a number of factors: the stage of the life cycle, interest rates, wealth, and expectations about future income. The life-cycle model suggests that saving rates are lower for the young, who have recently embarked on their working lives and for the retired, who have left the labor force. Workers, especially those near their peak earnings years, have considerably higher saving rates. That means that countries with higher dependency ratios, that is, with larger fractions of the population not working, would save less.

Over the next few decades, dependency ratios are expected to rise in developed countries (especially Japan), where the number of retired people will increase markedly as life expectancy continues to rise and the huge baby-boom generation retires. By contrast, dependency ratios are expected to fall in developing countries, which now have populations with low average ages. Over the next few decades, large numbers of young people in developing countries will move from being students to being workers, but relatively few people in those countries will attain retirement age.

Saving and Economic Growth

In Chapter 10 we learned that an increase in the private saving rate can increase the rate of economic growth temporarily. But much of the causality runs in the opposite direction, from growth to saving rather than from saving to growth. Sustained increases in growth are associated with permanent increases in the rate of saving; in fact, an increase in the growth rate of 1 percent per annum can raise the private saving rate by as much as 1 percent.

Why does a higher growth rate tend to raise the saving rate? Look back at the top frame of Figure 15-5 on p. 494, which shows the lifetime pattern for a household that saves during the working years and spends all that saving during retirement. If a country has no economic growth, then there is no difference between the income of working people, say aged 40 today, and the income that today's 70-year-old retired people earned 30 years ago when they were aged 40. But if a country is growing rapidly, as in the case of Korea, then today's 40-year-old workers have much higher incomes than today's retired people had 30 years ago, and so the saving by people of working age is much greater than the dissaving of today's retired people, who were saving out of much smaller incomes 30 years ago.

Government Deficits and Private Saving

Do increased government deficits lead to increased private saving? If the Barro-Ricardo equivalence theorem holds (see pp. 402–04), then an increase in the government deficit would generate an equal increase in private saving, which would offset the expected future tax burden associated with the increased deficit. The very low level of U.S. private saving in 2002–04 accompanying large government deficits provides evidence that deficits do not boost private saving.

Interest Rates and Consumer Credit

Higher interest rates may either raise saving by providing people with a higher income level (some of which will be saved) or may lower saving by making less saving necessary to achieve a target level of saving for purposes such as retirement. There is no consensus in the economic literature on which effect is stronger. In the United States, the saving rate was lower in the 1990s than in the 1980s, which may have been partly due to a decline in the real interest rate over that period. However, as we shall see later in the chapter, the biggest reason for the decline in the U.S. saving rate were the large capital gains earned by American households on their holdings of equities on the stock market and on their ownership stake in their homes.

Forward-looking consumers will raise their current spending, and thus reduce their saving out of current income, in response to an increase in their expected future incomes. One reason why consumers might raise their spending less than their permanent or life-cycle incomes justify, and thus may raise their saving by more, is the inability to borrow on the basis of expected future incomes. Today's college students are experts on this phenomenon. An economics major may expect a relatively high income after graduation, but few financial institutions will lend today's student more than just a small fraction of that expected future income. In the same way, the household saving rate will tend to be low in countries like the United States where consumer credit is relatively easy to obtain and high in countries like Italy where consumer credit is harder to obtain.

Cross-Country Differences in Saving

The bar chart displays the 2005 household saving rate for seven countries, ranging from 10.9 percent for Italy down to −1.4 percent for Australia. How can these differences be explained? In this chapter we explore several explanations of differences across nations in their household saving rates. The LCH suggests that countries with faster economic growth will save more, because they have more households in the high-saving working age groups and fewer retirees. Yet in the bar chart Korea has a relatively low household saving rate despite achieving rapid economic growth.

The most notable aspect of the bar chart is the low saving rates of the United States, Canada, and Australia. The experience of these three countries supports the view that capital gains on the stock market and housing raise consumption and depress saving. These three nations have enjoyed substantial gains in stock market and housing wealth over the past decade, whereas in high-saving nations such as Italy and France, there has been much less accumulation of household wealth in the form of capital gains on stocks and housing equity, so Italian and French households need to save more by abstaining from consumption. We return subsequently in this chapter to discussing alternative measures of U.S. household saving that take account of wealth accumulation.

The relatively low saving rate of Japan, only 5.0 percent, is surprising in light of Japan's history as a high-saving country. Part of the decline in saving directly results from Japan's economic slump since the early 1990s (see pp. 118–19). As suggested by the permanent income hypothesis, households reduce their saving in response to higher unemployment or lower incomes that they believe to be temporary. Young Japanese, unable to afford their own housing, are returning to live with their parents and are able to consume all of their income without the need to save up for their own houses. Formerly many Japanese received semiannual bonuses, which they put into savings accounts, but economic hard times have caused firms to cut these bonuses drastically. Finally, interest rates on saving accounts in Japan are in many cases below 1 percent, providing no incentive to save.

Source: OECD Economic Outlook, December 2004, Annex Table 23.

off will lead members of the present generation to increase saving in order to leave a larger bequest to their children. A prime example of such an event would be a deficit-financed tax cut that raises the taxes that must be paid by future generations (to pay the interest and principal on the bonds issued to finance the debt). According to the Barro-Ricardo theorem, such a tax cut would not stimulate consumption because people would save all of the increase in their after-tax income in order to raise their bequests.

In Chapter 12 and in the International Perspective box, we reviewed some of the criticisms of the Barro-Ricardo theorem. Most important, the U.S. household saving rate did not increase at all following the Reagan tax cuts of the 1980s or the Bush tax cuts of 2001–03, as the theorem would have predicted. In fact, as we shall see in Figure 15-7 on p. 506, the saving rate in 2004 fell to its lowest level since the Great Depression. Thus it seems likely that the mere existence of bequests does not validate the kind of behavior postulated by the theorem—specifically the refusal of current households to raise their consumption in response to a tax cut.

Motives for Bequests

If parents do not adjust their bequests for every current event that changes their heirs' future tax liabilities, why does a large fraction of personal saving eventually flow to children in the form of bequests? Many think that the central issue is the uncertainty of the age of death. Benjamin Franklin's observation that "in this world nothing can be said to be certain, except death and taxes" omits the fact that the *timing* of death is quite uncertain. Contrary to the assumption of Figures 15-5 and 15-6, households cannot know the lengths of their lifetimes.

By this interpretation, *much saving is life cycle in nature, but only for a part of the lifetime and for medical care that does not occur for everyone*. Many people die before expensive nursing care treatment becomes necessary and thus have substantial wealth "left over" that goes as bequests to the children. By this interpretation, bequests are primarily involuntary and are made because parents do not want to lose control of their assets and their living conditions prior to death.

Implications for the LCH theory. The interpretation of bequests as primarily involuntary leaves the main predictions of the LCH intact. The only adjustment to the LCH is that the relevant horizon for most households extends beyond the actual age of death (as assumed in Figures 15-5 and 15-6) to the *oldest conceivable age of death*. For instance, a 25-year-old may have a future life expectancy of 50 years, with 75 the most probable age of death, but may base consumption and saving decisions on the outside chance of living until age 90.

This amended version of the LCH would operate just like the version depicted in Figure 15-6, except the extended lifetime (L^*, say 90) replaces the most probable lifetime (L, say 75). Use of L^* instead of the lower L would imply an even lower MPC for temporary changes in income, and would imply that increases in wealth from the stock market would be consumed over the extended period until L^*. If parents are unwilling to move out of their homes (and are also unwilling to sell their homes to their children and pay them rent), then the gains parents make from higher housing prices may not be consumed over the lifetime but may be largely ignored and lead to a larger bequest.

Why Retirees Cut Their Consumption So Much

Looking back at Figure 15-5 on p. 494, the LCH predicts that consumption is maintained at a fixed level throughout a person's working life and retirement years. But a growing body of evidence suggests that retirees consume much less than working people who are otherwise the same in terms of income and family characteristics.

Why do people cut their consumption after they retire? First, many people react to retirement by moving, because they are no longer tied to the location of their job, and they often move into smaller dwellings. Second, many retirees have paid off the mortgages on their homes, even if they do not move. Third, retirees can eliminate consumption expenses previously required by work, including job-related clothing, automobile and fuel expenses required by commuting, and business-related meals eaten outside the home. Fourth—perhaps a minor factor—retirees have more leisure time and can spend more time searching for bargains, thus reducing the cost of everyday household necessities.[13]

Does the decline in consumption after retirement, in contrast to the steady retirement depicted in Figure 15-5, invalidate the LCH? Not at all, because all of the reasons for lower consumption after retirement are anticipated by households long in advance of retirement. All the predictions of the LCH, including the effect of higher stock market or housing wealth in raising consumption and reducing saving, and the lack of response of consumption by working-age households to temporary changes of income, are still valid for households that plan their retirement consumption in advance, no matter whether that consumption is planned to equal working-age consumption or whether it is planned in advance to be lower.

> **Self-Test**
>
> Imagine that, in order to reduce the federal budget deficit, the government institutes a $1,000 increase in the yearly personal income tax paid by every household. The tax increase is announced to be permanent. What would the following theories predict to be the effects on consumption?
>
> 1. Permanent-income hypothesis
> 2. Life-cycle hypothesis with certain lifetime
> 3. Life-cycle hypothesis that explains bequests as resulting from uncertain lifetimes
> 4. Barro-Ricardo equivalence theory

---

[13] Two papers provide an illuminating analysis of the drop in consumption after retirement. See Michael Hurd and Susann Rohwedder, "The Retirement-Consumption Puzzle: Anticipated and Actual Declines in Spending at Retirement," NBER working paper 9586, March 2003, and John Ameriks, Andrew Caplin, and John Leahy, "Retirement Consumption: Insights from a Survey," NBER working paper 8735, January 2002.

15-8 Case Study

Did Soaring Household Assets Cause the Collapse in the Household Saving Rate?

Early in this book (Figure 3-3 on p. 65) we saw that since the late 1990s, household saving as a percentage of disposable income in the United States has been at its lowest level since the Great Depression of the 1930s. Figure 15-7 plots as a blue line the annual household saving rate since 1970. The rate was above 10 percent as recently as 1984 and was almost 8 percent in 1992, but since then has declined steadily to a record low rate of merely 1.0 percent in 2004.

What do the theories of this chapter predict as possible causes of a low or negative saving rate? The prediction of the Friedman permanent-income hypothesis goes in the opposite direction of the late 1990s' outcome, that unusually rapid income growth should cause the saving rate to be well above normal, not below normal. The Modigliani life-cycle hypothesis is more successful in predicting a decline in the household saving rate in the late 1990s. As we learned on p. 494, the Modigliani theory makes consumption depend not only on lifetime income but also on real assets. The extraordinary boom in the stock market that occurred in the late 1990s created huge gains in real household wealth and substantially boosted consumption relative to income, thus (by definition) depressing the percentage of disposable income saved by households.

Figure 15-7 The Household Saving Rate and the Ratio of Household Net Worth to Personal Disposable Income, 1970–2004

The Household Wealth Explosion

The most relevant measure of wealth for explaining household consumption and saving behavior is a series on household net worth, compiled by government statisticians at the Fed.[14] Figure 15-7 shows the ratio of net worth to disposable income as the green line that is compared to the household saving rate shown as the blue line. There is a clear negative correlation between the two lines, with low wealth and a high saving rate between 1974 and 1985, followed by an initial upward jump in wealth and decline in the saving rate between 1985 and 1989, and then a second larger jump in wealth and decline in the saving rate between 1995 and 2000.

What triggered the two big jumps in household net worth? Clearly the cause was the behavior of the stock market, which enjoyed a long boom over almost twenty years starting in August 1982, at the depths of the 1981–82 period of high unemployment, high inflation, and very high interest rates, and ending in mid-2000. The S&P 500 index of stock prices more than doubled from 160 to 335 between 1984 and 1989, and then it tripled from 460 in 1994 to 1,427 in 2000.[15] As of June 2005, the S&P 500 index still hovered around 1,200, more than 15 percent below its annual average for the year 2000.

Up to 2000, the close negative relationship between household net worth and the household saving rate, as shown in Figure 15-7, supports the Modigliani LCH reviewed in Section 15-5. Households with a lifetime perspective react to capital gains on the stock market by consuming some of these gains and thus reducing their saving. But there is an apparent problem with the theory—why did household saving remain so low in 2001 to 2004 despite the sharp decline in the stock market? The stock market caused household financial assets to decline by more than $4 trillion between 2000 and 2002. Shouldn't lower household wealth have caused the saving rate to *increase*?

Capital Gains on Houses and Low Interest Rates Keep the Saving Rate Low

There are two answers to the failure of the saving rate to revive after 2000. First, as we learned in the box on p. 106 and in Section 14-7 on pp. 467–70, the Fed pushed interest rates down rapidly to very low levels in 2002–03, stimulating a boom in automobile sales and the new phenomenon of housing refinance that boosted consumption on goods and services of all types. A second factor driving consumption and reducing saving were the capital gains that people made on their houses, boosting their housing wealth and partly offsetting their stock market losses.

Household net worth as shown in Figure 15-7 consists of total household assets minus total household liabilities. In 2004, total assets were 644 percent of disposable income and total liabilities were 116 percent. Subtracting the liabilities from the assets yields the 528 percent ratio of net wealth to disposable income shown in Figure 15-7.

---

[14] The data can be found at www.econstats.com/FOF/foftata.htm. The data displayed in Figures 15-7 and 15-8 come from table B.100, which can be selected from this Web site. The data include not just households but also nonprofit institutions such as hospitals and universities.

[15] S&P index values are averages of daily closing prices for each year.

Figure 15-8 Components of Household Assets as a Ratio to Personal Disposable Income, 1970–2004, in Percent

The red section shows the ratio of household tangible assets, primarily consisting of the value of owner-occupied homes, to disposable income. This ratio rose in the late 1970s, in the late 1980s, and especially during 2000–04. The green section shows the ratio of household financial wealth, including direct holdings of stocks and stock mutual funds, to disposable income. This ratio rose in the late 1980s and especially during 1994–2000. The total ratio shown by the top of the green area fell sharply from 2000 to 2002 and recovered from 2002 to 2004, but not enough to regain the 2000 peak.

In order to understand what happened after the year 2000, we display in Figure 15-8 the ratio of total household assets to disposable income, divided between financial assets (including volatile stocks and stock mutual funds) and "tangible assets" consisting mainly of the value of household ownership of houses and condominiums. The red area representing tangible assets grew from 2000 to 2004, because this was a period of record-setting year-after-year increases in house prices. This partly offset the shrinkage in the green area representing financial assets such as stocks. While the increase in the red area helped to offset the effect of stock market losses, it did not rise enough to offset the decline in the total ratio of household assets to disposable income, as shown by the fact that the top of the green area was still lower in 2004 than it was in 2000.

Besides the effects of low interest rates, what then explains the continued low household saving rate in 2002–04? An important hypothesis has been suggested by Karl Case of Wellesley College, John Quigley of the University of California at Berkeley, and Robert Shiller of Yale. Using data that vary across countries and across states within the United States, they find that the effect of housing wealth on consumption is much stronger than the effect of stock market wealth.[16] This result makes sense, since almost 70 percent of American households own their own homes and most of these have at least some equity in their houses, that is, the market value of the house or condominium is larger than the mortgage debt owed. While many households have stock mutual funds and retirement funds that are invested in stocks, more than 75 percent of the value of all stocks is owned by the top 10 percent of households, and the bottom 50 percent of households own virtually no stocks. Thus fewer people were affected by the decline of the stock market in 2000–02 than by the increase in house prices and home equity that occurred in 2000–04. This analysis helps us to understand why consumption spending was so strong during this period and why the household saving rate remained so low.

15-9 Why the Official Household Saving Data Are Misleading

When we say the household saving rate was only 1.0 percent in 2004, as in Figure 15-7, we are referring to the measure of saving used in the national income and product accounts (NIPA, reviewed in Chapter 2), namely personal disposable income minus consumption expenditures minus personal interest payments. However, the NIPA measure understates the true household saving rate. The most notable feature of the NIPA saving concept is that capital gains on stocks, bonds, houses, and other assets are excluded because these gains do not reflect returns from the current production of goods and services. A second flaw is that the NIPA saving measure does not include purchases of consumer durable goods, even though these goods provide a stream of benefits in the future, for example, the benefit of being able to use a large-screen color TV set or automobile over a number of years. A third flaw is that inflation influences the real significance of the household saving rate. Households receive nominal interest returns from corporations, and the nominal interest rate rises with the inflation rate. Thus when inflation is rapid, as in the period between 1974 and 1982, household saving is overstated by receipt of nominal interest earnings, which are simply a compensation for inflation, not real income. Conversely, when inflation declines as it has since 1990, household saving is understated because households receive lower nominal income but not lower real income.

Alternative Measures of Saving

Fortunately, alternative data sources are available to provide a more accurate impression of household saving behavior than the NIPA saving rate. Shown in Figure 15-9 are the NIPA series on the household saving rate compared with the equivalent saving rate from the "Flow of Fund Accounts" (FFA), which differ by including net investment in consumer durables. Here we see that the FFA measure is more than quadruple the NIPA measure in 2004, 4.4 percent rather than 1.0 percent. However, use of the FFA measure does not change the

---

[16] Karl E. Case, John M. Quigley, and Robert J. Shiller, "Comparing Wealth Effects: The Stock Market versus the Housing Market," NBER working paper 8606, November 2001.

Figure 15-9 Household Saving in the NIPA and Flow of Funds Accounts, 1960–2004

Source: National Income and Product Accounts and Flow of Funds Accounts.

conclusion that household saving has declined sharply in the 1990s. The NIPA declined from an average of 7.7 percent in 1985–89 to 1.0 percent in 2004, whereas the FFA measure declined from 13.1 percent to 4.4 percent, an even larger decline. However, the decline in both measures is misleading, because the FFA measure like the NIPA measure excludes the effect of capital gains.

Figure 15-10 shows an alternative measure of saving defined in terms of increases in household wealth (including financial assets and housing equity) relative to total income including capital gains. Clearly the adjustment makes an enormous difference. First, the alternative "gains-inclusive saving rate" is much more volatile than either the FFA or NIPA measures; for instance, it jumped from 11.8 percent in 1994 to 34.9 percent in 1995, and it collapsed from 44.1 percent in 1999 to −25.2 percent in 2002. Second, the broader measure contradicts the implication of the NIPA that household saving nearly disappeared in recent years; its average value was 19.2 percent in 1995–2004, a substantial value albeit lower than the average value of 33.0 percent in 1976–85.[17]

---

[17] For a comprehensive analysis of differences in saving rate concepts, see Marshall B. Reinsdorf, "Alternative Measures of Personal Saving," *Survey of Current Business* (September 2004), pp. 17–27. This article can also be found at www.bea.gov/bea/ARTICLES/2004/09September/PersonalSavingWEB.pdf.

The Gains-Inclusive Saving Rate Soared in the Late 1990s but Collapsed in 2000–02

Figure 15-10 Flow of Funds Accounts and Gains-Inclusive Saving Rates, 1976–2004
Source: National Income and Product Accounts and Flow of Funds Accounts.

15-10 Conclusion: Consumption and the Case For and Against Activism

If all consumption spending consisted of nondurable goods and services, the permanent-income hypothesis and life-cycle hypothesis both would strengthen the case of those who advocate policy rules and are optimistic that the private economy is basically stable if left alone by the government. Consumption would respond only partially to temporary bursts of nonconsumption spending, so that the economy's true short-run multipliers would be smaller than those calculated in Chapters 3 and 4.

On the other hand, the case for policy activism is strengthened by the procyclical fluctuations in consumer durable purchases, because this source of instability in the private economy may need to be offset by countercyclical government policy. The importance of erratic fluctuations in consumer spending is summarized by movements in the ratio of personal saving plus consumer durable expenditures to personal income. This ratio has fluctuated over a wide range during the postwar years. Part of these swings may reflect movements in consumer confidence, which are an important source of shifts in the *IS* curve.

As we learned in Chapter 14, there is little difference between an activist policy and one that operates by a Taylor Rule, targeting both the inflation rate and the output ratio. The Fed's aggressive easing of monetary policy in

2001–02 proved that monetary policy is capable of stabilizing consumer expenditures and residential housing investment. And we have now learned in this chapter that consumption spending is further stabilized by the indirect effects of low interest rates that boost housing prices, raising household wealth held in the form of housing equity and reducing the household saving rate. The ability of the Fed to keep consumption from declining significantly during the 2001 recession helps to explain why the economy has been much more stable since 1984, as shown in Figure 14-3 on p. 462.

Summary

1. A major area of dispute between policy activists and advocates of policy rules concerns the stability of private spending decisions. Friedman's permanent-income hypothesis (PIH) and Modigliani's life-cycle hypothesis (LCH) are based on the assumption that individuals achieve a higher level of total utility (enjoyment) when they maintain a stable consumption pattern than when they allow consumption to rise or fall with every transitory fluctuation in their actual income. Individuals can achieve the desired stable consumption pattern by consuming a stable fraction of their permanent or lifetime income.

2. If all consumption consisted of nondurable goods and services, both the PIH and the LCH would strengthen the case of those who advocate policy rules, who claim that the private economy is basically stable if left alone by the government. Consumption would respond only partially to temporary fluctuations of nonconsumption spending, so that the economy's short-run multipliers would be smaller than the simple theoretical multipliers of Chapters 3 and 4.

3. Both the PIH and the LCH can reconcile the observed cross-section increase in the saving ratio for higher incomes with the observed long-run historical constancy of the aggregate saving ratio.

4. Both hypotheses have important implications for fiscal policy. For example, a tax change announced as permanent should cause a bigger change in permanent income, and hence in consumption expenditures, than another equal-sized tax change announced as temporary. Thus temporary tax changes introduced to implement an activist fiscal policy may be rendered ineffective by offsetting movements in the saving ratio.

5. Numerous criticisms of the PIH and LCH have emerged in recent years. A large share of saving seems to be used not for consumption during retirement, but for bequests to children. Households may save more than they need, because they are uncertain about the date of death. People cut their consumption spending when they retire conflicting with the LCH assumption that consumption is stable over the lifetime. Liquidity constraints imply that perhaps 15 percent of income is earned by households for whom the short-run marginal propensity to consume is much higher than implied by the PIH or LCH.

6. An additional consideration in explaining observed consumption and saving behavior is that consumer durable expenditures should be treated as a form of saving, not as current consumption. Sharp increases in income tend to go mainly into saving, which means that consumer durable expenditures treated as a form of saving may be very responsive to transitory income changes. Thus the PIH and LCH may be valid, but consumer durable purchases are still a source of instability in the private economy.

7. The puzzle of the decline in the U.S. household saving rate during the 1992–2004 period can be traced partly to the stock market boom of this period, as well as steady increases in housing prices. The National Income and Product Accounts concept of the saving rate excludes capital gains and adjustments for inflation and thus greatly understates increases in household wealth during the 1990s and most earlier decades.

Concepts

forward-looking expectations
permanent-income hypothesis (PIH)
life-cycle hypothesis (LCH)
cross section
time series
permanent income
transitory income
rational expectations
liquidity constraint

Questions

1. The saving ratio has been remarkably stable since 1900. When we examine cross-section data, however, we find that the saving ratio tends to rise as incomes rise. How can these two observations be reconciled?
2. Why is a distinction made between a short-run marginal propensity to consume and a long-run marginal propensity to consume in the permanent-income hypothesis (PIH)?
3. Is permanent income permanent? If not, what causes it to change?
4. Is it true that both the adaptive expectations and rational expectations forms of the PIH give identical predictions concerning the effect of the 2001 tax rebate on consumption?
5. How does the existence of assets affect consumption and income in the life-cycle hypothesis (LCH)?
6. What is likely to happen to the household saving rate in the United States and other industrialized economies as the proportion of the population that is retired rises? What are some ways that this effect on the saving rate could be reversed?
7. In each of the following cases, explain whether permanent income would change and if so, how much it would change initially if permanent income is calculated using adaptive expectations or rational expectations.
    (a) Due to increased health care costs, Food-2-Go reduces its work force by 10 percent. In order to maintain its output, it requires the employees it retains to work overtime on a regular basis. (Answer this question for both the workers retained and the workers let go by Food-2-Go. Assume that when workers let go by Food-2-Go get new jobs, they will earn less than they earned at Food-2-Go.)
    (b) An unusually snowy winter forces a ski resort to offer its help overtime pay in order to provide the extra services demanded by the extra skiers it has that season.
    (c) A person receives a promotion that she was expecting. However, the salary that she earns in her new job is much more than she was expecting.
8. Does the fact that many individuals leave bequests (i.e., do not consume their entire income over their lifetimes) invalidate the LCH?
9. Both the LCH and the PIH predict that the marginal propensity to consume out of transitory income is quite small (perhaps, even zero). Nevertheless, we observe many younger families spending a fairly large percentage of their transitory incomes. Is this observation consistent with the two hypotheses?
10. The PIH and LCH suggest that consumer durable expenditures should be considered separately from expenditures on nondurables and services. Why? How does this distinction alter the appearance of saving and consumption behavior? Why do some economists argue that consumer durable expenditures should be treated as saving rather than consumption?
11. Both the PIH and the LCH predict that consumers react differently to tax changes that are perceived to be permanent rather than temporary. Explain why this is so. Has the empirical record of the past twenty years supported this prediction?
12. Explain why a rapid increase in economic growth can cause an increase in the savings rate.
13. Use the LCH to explain how differences in capital gains from the stock market and housing can be used to explain the differences between the household saving rates of Italy and France compared to those of the United States, Canada, and Australia.
14. Does a decline in consumption by retirees invalidate the LCH? Explain why retirees can reduce their consumption when compared to groups that are similar in terms of income.
15. The national income and product accounts (NIPA) measure of the personal saving rate fell dramatically during the late 1990s to 1.0 percent in 2004. Why did this happen? Does it accurately portray actual household saving behavior during this time period?
16. Just like the FFA and NIPA measures of the saving rate, even the "gains-inclusive saving rate" eventually declined and turned negative in 2000–02. Is it true, therefore, that even the results of the "gains-inclusive saving rate" support the predictions of the LCH by suggesting that the stock market boom of the late 1990s lowered the saving rate?
17. Explain why the household saving rate remained low during 2002–04 despite the fact that during those years, the stock market remained well below the peak it reached in 2000.
18. Do forward-looking theories of consumption such as the PIH and the LCH strengthen or weaken the case for the superiority of policy rules over activism?

Problems

1. Assume that consumption and permanent income are derived as shown in equations (15.2) and (15.3). In those equations, let $k = 0.8$ and $j = 0.5$. Assume that 2004 actual income of $30,000 equals permanent income.
   (a) What would be the permanent income for 2005, 2006, and 2007 if actual income for those three years were $36,000, $45,000, and $30,000, respectively?
   (b) What would be consumption spending in those three years?
   (c) What would be the short-run marginal propensity to consume in each of those three years?
   (d) Using the distinction between permanent income and transitory income, explain why the short-run marginal propensity to consume would differ from the long-run marginal propensity to consume in 2005.

2. You are given the following information concerning income, transitory income, and permanent consumption:

Income	Transitory income	Permanent consumption
6,000	0	4,500
6,880	−120	5,250
8,020	20	6,000
8,955	−45	6,750
10,200	200	7,500

   (a) Calculate the amount of permanent income at each level of income.
   (b) Calculate the long-run marginal propensity to consume, k.
   (c) Assuming that the marginal propensity to consume out of transitory income equals 0, compute the short-run marginal propensities to consume at income levels of 6,000, 6,880, 8,020, 8,955, and 10,200.
   (d) Explain how the short-run marginal propensities to consume differ from the long-run marginal propensity to consume.

3. Assume that Gina's consumption decisions are consistent with the LCH. In 2005, Gina is 25 years old, expects to earn income until she is 65, and expects to consume until she dies at age 85.
   (a) If Gina earns $30,000 per year and wishes to consume an equal amount each year, how much will she consume each year?
   (b) What is Gina's ratio of consumption to income? What is her saving ratio?
   (c) Assume that Gina has assets equal to $120,000 in 2005. Recalculate your answers for a and b.
   (d) Assume that in 2025, Gina inherits $40,000. Now what are your answers to c?

4. A recent medical school graduate age 26 will intern for 7 years, making $30,000 a year. Thereafter, she will make $250,000 a year for 30 years. At age 26, she also has assets of $570,000.
   (a) In the absence of liquidity constraints, how much will she consume per year if she expects to live to age 83?
   (b) Suppose that a collapse in the stock market reduces the value of her assets at age 26 to $285,000. How much will she now consume per year if she expects to live to age 83?

5. Suppose that Jim goes to work at age 25, earns on average $40,000 a year for 40 years. He inherits $320,000 when he starts working. He expects to live to be 75.
   (a) Calculate on average how much Jim consumes per year, the ratio of his annual consumption to annual income, and his annual savings rate.
   (b) Suppose now that Jim learns that he can expect to live to be 85. If Jim does not change his retirement age, compute Jim's new annual consumption, as well as the new ratio of annual consumption to annual income, and his new annual saving rate.

6. Suppose that Alan goes to work at age 22, earns on average $60,000 a year for 43 years, and inherits $300,000 the year he starts working. He expects to live to be 82.
   (a) Calculate on average how much Alan consumes per year, the ratio of his annual consumption to annual income, and his savings rate.
   (b) Suppose that a rise in housing prices causes Alan's inheritance to increase to $480,000. If Alan does not change his retirement age, calculate Alan's new annual consumption, as well as the new ratio of annual consumption to annual income, and his annual savings rate.
   (c) Given the increase in his inheritance listed in part b, suppose that Alan decides to use the increased inheritance to finance an earlier retirement age. He does this by maintaining the same average annual consumption as in part a. At what age will Alan be able to retire?

Self-Test Answers

p. 493 (1) A stockbroker enjoying his or her best year has actual income above permanent income and consumes less and saves more than he or she would if that income were permanent. (2) A wheat farmer suffering from a drought will have actual income below permanent income and will consume more and save less than he or she would if that income were permanent. (3) When the U.S. economy is in recession, an unusually large number of people will experience below-permanent income and will consume more and save less than they would if they considered their recession-level income permanent. (4) When the U.S. economy is in a period of unusually high real GDP, a large number of people will experience above-permanent income and will consume less and save more than they would if they considered their exceptionally high income permanent.

p. 497 (1) Use the right-hand part of equation (15.7). If $A_1 = 0$, and $R/L = 30/40$, then consumption expenditures per year will be 30/40 times $50,000, or $37,500 during both the working and retirement years. (2) C/Y during working years will be $37,500/50,000, or 0.75, which of course equals R/L. (3) With initial assets of 200,000, $A_1/L = 200,000/40 = 5,000$. Consumption expenditures by equation (15.8) will then be $5,000 plus $37,500 = $42,500 during both the working and retirement years. (4) C/Y during working years will be $42,500/50,000 = 0.85$.

p. 505 (1) Since the tax increase is assumed to be permanent, it will reduce permanent income by $1,000. Consumption will fall by k times $1,000 per year. (2) According to the life-cycle hypothesis as set forth in equation (15.7), Y per year will fall by $1,000, and consumption per year will fall by R/L times $1,000. (3) According to the life-cycle hypothesis, with an uncertain lifetime L, consumption per year will fall by R/L^* times $1,000. (4) According to the Barro-Ricardo equivalence theorem, consumption will not change at all, since saving will decline by the full amount of the tax increase (reflecting the lower anticipated future tax liabilities).

CHAPTER 16

Instability in the Private Economy: Investment Behavior

Whatever cannot go on forever must come to an end.
—Herbert Stein

If consumers purchased only nondurable goods and services, the permanent-income and life-cycle hypotheses predict that consumer behavior would stabilize the economy. An offsetting factor is the procyclical movement of consumer durable purchases. Although consistent with the PIH and LCH, such movement tends to aggravate booms and recessions. In this chapter we find that business fixed investment also fluctuates procyclically. Thus both durable purchases by consumers and investment purchases by businesses introduce instability into the private economy, leading policy activists to claim that an activist stabilization policy is justified.

The instability of private investment gains new relevance after the wild oscillations of the past decade. Compared to its average annual growth rate over the period 1960–2004 of 4.9 percent, nonresidential private fixed investment grew at a much faster average rate of 9.8 percent during 1996–2000 and then *declined*, exhibiting an average growth rate of –6.8 percent during 2000–02, followed by a bounce-back annual growth rate of 6.6 percent during 2002–04.

16-1 Investment and Economic Stability

In Chapter 15 we found that the permanent-income and life-cycle hypotheses of individual consumption behavior explain the partial insulation of aggregate consumption spending from changes in other types of spending in the short run. But what are the sources of changes in these other types of spending? Nominal GDP in 2004 was divided among the major types of expenditures as follows:

Personal consumption expenditures	70.4%
Gross private domestic investment	17.0
Government purchases of goods and services	18.0
Net exports	−5.4
	100.0

Having already considered consumer expenditures in Chapter 15, government spending and other aspects of fiscal policy in Chapters 5 and 12, and net exports in Chapter 6, we concentrate here on private investment.

We will review a very simple theory that explains why investment spending is likely to exhibit more pronounced fluctuations than other types of spending. According to the permanent-income hypothesis, introduced in the last chapter to explain consumer expenditures, households try to maintain a constant ratio of their consumer durable stock to permanent income. This creates sudden bursts of durable purchases when an upward revision of permanent income causes the desired durable stock to increase. In this chapter we will see that investment spending on plant, equipment, inventories, and housing is driven by the same principle and therefore is also subject to sudden bursts of purchases.[1]

16-2 Case Study

The Historical Instability of Investment

Total Investment Rises and Falls Dramatically and Procyclically

We begin by examining the historical record of investment spending since 1960. Figure 16-1 clearly shows that investment spending is far more variable than consumption spending (compare with Figure 15-1 on p. 485). The top line in the figure shows total real gross private domestic investment (GPDI). By any standard, the fluctuations in total investment are huge.

The following table shows how real GPDI has fluctuated since 1960.

Quarters			Percentage change (in lags)	
Peak	Trough	Peak	Peak to trough	Trough to peak
1960:Q1	1961:Q1	1969:Q4	−22	+61
1969:Q4	1970:Q4	1973:Q4	−7	+39
1973:Q4	1975:Q1	1980:Q1	−31	+46
1980:Q1	1980:Q3	1981:Q3	−17	+21
1981:Q3	1982:Q4	1990:Q3	−26	+47
1990:Q3	1991:Q1	2001:Q1	−11	+73
2001:Q1	2001:Q4	—	−11	—

Shown in the left part of the table are the dates of each successive business cycle peak and trough. We can see, for instance, that in the 1973–75 recession, GPDI fell 31 percent. Then GPDI more than recovered, growing 46 percent by the next peak in 1980:Q1. In the 1981–82 recession, GPDI also fell sharply, but by less than in 1973–75. After the 1991 trough, GPDI rose dramatically. Over

---

[1] Examples of plant and equipment investment include:

Nonresidential Plant (Structures)	Equipment
Factories	Computers
Oil refineries	Jet airplanes
Office buildings	Trucks
Shopping centers	Bar-code scanners
Private hospitals	Internet switching equipment
Private universities	Tractors

The principles developed in this chapter apply also to residential investment, construction of both single-family homes and apartment buildings.

518 Chapter 16 • Instability in the Private Economy: Investment Behavior

All Types of Investments Are Volatile over the Business Cycle

Figure 16-1 Real Gross Private Domestic Investment and Its Three Components, 1960–2004

The top line plots real gross private domestic investment and shows substantial declines in recessions. All three components contribute to this volatility, but their timing is different. There is a marked tendency for residential investment to turn down earlier than nonresidential investment and to recover earlier. Fluctuations in inventory investment are shorter-lived than fluctuations in either of the other two components The investment downturn of 2000–01 was severe by historical standards but left residential investment totally unaffected. By late 2004 total investment had surpassed the previous 2000 peak.

the record-breaking ten-year expansion that ended in 2001:Q1, total real GPDI increased by 73 percent. The decline of GPDI in the recessions of 1990–91 and of 2001 were relatively mild in historical perspective.

Behavior of the Components of GPDI

GPDI is divided into two main parts: fixed investment and inventory changes. Fixed investment is further divided into residential and nonresidential, and in turn nonresidential is divided into nonresidential structures and producers' durable equipment. For simplicity, Figure 16-1 distinguishes only fixed residential, fixed nonresidential, and inventory investment. Clearly all three of the major components contribute to the high volatility of GPDI.

Examining the three components more carefully, we note several differences among them:

1. **Residential investment turns early**. Comparing the plotted lines for residential and nonresidential investment, we note that in almost every business cycle the downturn begins earlier for residential investment, as does the subsequent upturn. For instance, residential investment peaked about a year before fixed nonresidential investment in the 1973–75, 1981–82, and 1990–91 recessions. However, in the 2001 recession, residential investment did not decline at all, responding to the Fed's aggressive easing of monetary policy (see pp. 106 and 467–70).

2. **Inventory change exhibits sharp but short-lived swings**. Inventory change appears as a series of small, jagged mountain peaks, with an occasional deep valley. In the mid-1970s, the early 1980s, and in 2001–02, the level of inventories changed by over $100 billion over periods of a year or less. Since changes in inventory investment are usually unpredictable and short-lived, it is difficult for the Federal Reserve Board to offset their effects.

3. **Fixed nonresidential investment** was slightly larger than residential investment in 1960; by 2000 it was more than three times as large as investment in housing. Business purchases of equipment in particular soared during the 1990s. Because nonresidential investment constituted over 60 percent of GPDI during the past two decades, this chapter concentrates primarily on this component.

16-3 The Accelerator Hypothesis of Net Investment

Businesses must continually evaluate whether their buildings are the right size and have the right amount of equipment. Will they have too little capacity to produce the output they expect to be able to sell in the forthcoming year, causing lost sales and dissatisfied customers? Or will capacity be excessive in relation to expected sales, wasting expenses on maintenance workers and interest costs on unneeded plants and equipment? The **accelerator hypothesis** of investment relies on the simple idea that firms attempt to maintain a fixed ratio of their stock of capital (plants and equipment) to their expected sales.

The **accelerator hypothesis** states that the level of net investment depends on the *change* in expected output.

Table 16-1 Workings of the Accelerator Hypothesis of Investment for the Hypothetical Mammoth Electric Company

Variable	0	1	2	3	4	5
1. Actual sales (Y)	10.0	12.0	12.0	12.0	12.0	12.0
2. Expected sales ($Y^e = 0.5Y_{-1} + 0.5Y^e_{-1}$)	10.0	10.0	11.0	11.5	11.75	11.87
3. Desired stock of electric generating stations ($K^* = 4Y^e$)	40.0	40.0	44.0	46.0	47.0	47.5
4. Net investment in electric generating stations ($I^n = K^* - K^*_{-1}$)	0.0	0.0	4.0	2.0	1.0	0.5
5. Replacement investment ($D = 0.10K_{-1}$)	4.0	4.0	4.0	4.4	4.6	4.7
6. Gross investment ($I = I^n + D$)	4.0	4.0	8.0	6.4	5.6	5.2

*Note: All figures in billions of dollars.

Estimating Expected Sales

Clearly, the first key ingredient in a business firm's decision about plant investment is an educated guess about the likely level of sales. Table 16-1 provides an example of how a hypothetical firm, the Mammoth Electric Company, estimates expected output and determines its desired stock of electric generating stations. The estimate of expected sales (Y^e) is revised from the estimate of the previous year (Y^e_{-1}) by some proportion, j, of any difference between last year's actual sales outcome (Y_{-1}) and what was expected:

$$Y^e = Y^e_{-1} + j(Y_{-1} - Y^e_{-1}) \qquad (16.1)$$
$$= jY_{-1} + (1 - j)Y^e_{-1}$$

This so-called adaptive or error-learning method of estimating sales expectations is exactly the same one that we encountered earlier in the formation of expectations of inflation and of permanent income.[2]

The error-learning method is illustrated in Table 16-1, where j is assumed equal to 0.5. In period 1, sales (Y^e) were expected to be $10 billion but actually turned out to be $12 billion ($Y$). The revision of expected sales in period 2 can be calculated from equation (16.1):

$$Y^e = 0.5(Y_{-1}) + 0.5(Y^e_{-1})$$
$$= 0.5(12) + 0.5(10)$$
$$= 11$$

---

[2] The formation of expectations of inflation was the subject of Section 8-3. The calculation of permanent income was discussed in Section 15-4.

Thus in period 2 expected sales are $11 billion, as recorded on line 2. But then another mistake is made, because in period 2 actual sales turn out to be $12 billion again instead of the expected $11 billion. Once again, expectations for the next period are revised, and they continue to be revised as long as actual sales differ from expected sales.

The Level of Investment Depends on the Change in Output

The next step in the accelerator hypothesis is the assumption that the stock of physical capital—that is, plant and equipment—that a firm desires (K^*) is a multiple of its expected sales:

General Form $\qquad$ Numerical Example

$$K^* = v^* Y^e \qquad K^* = 4.0 Y^e \qquad (16.2)$$

For example, Mammoth Electric in Table 16-1 wants a capital stock that is always four times as large as its expected sales. Notice that the desired capital stock on line 3 of the table is always exactly 4.0 times the level of expected sales on line 2. What determines the multiple v^*, which relates desired capital to expected sales? As we will see, in calculating v^*, firms pay attention to the interest rate and tax rates. Their chosen value of the multiple v^* reflects all available knowledge about government policies and the likely profitability of investment.

Net investment (I^n) is the change in the capital stock (ΔK) that occurs each period.[3]

$$I^n = \Delta K = K - K_{-1} \qquad (16.3)$$

In the example in Table 16-1, we assume that Mammoth Electric always manages to acquire new capital quickly enough to keep its actual capital stock (K) equal to its desired capital stock (K^*) in each period:

$$I^n = K - K_{-1} = K^* - K^*_{-1} \qquad (16.4)$$

Equation (16.4) implies that net investment (I^n) is always equal to the change in the desired capital stock in each period, which from equation (16.2) is 4.0 times the change in expected sales:

$$I^n = K^* - K^*_{-1}$$
$$= v^*(Y^e - Y^e_{-1}) = v^* \Delta Y^e \qquad (16.5)$$

The accelerator hypothesis says that the *level* of net investment (I^n) depends on the *change* in expected output (ΔY^e). When there is an acceleration in business and expected output increases, net investment is positive. If expected output stops increasing, net investment falls to zero. And if expected output were ever to decline, net investment would become negative as businesses undertook less gross investment than the amount by which their capital stocks depreciated.

Adding replacement investment. Total business spending on plant and equipment includes not only net investment—purchases that add to the capital stock—but also replacement purchases, which simply replace plant and equipment that has become worn out or obsolete. Line 5 of Table 16-1 assumes that

---

[3] This is an alternative but equivalent definition to the one we learned in Chapter 2, where net investment was defined as gross investment minus capital consumption allowances.

Figure 16-2 The Behavior of Actual Sales, Expected Sales, Gross Investment, Net Investment, and Replacement Investment for the Mammoth Electric Company Described in Table 16-1

In period 1 actual sales increase, but expected sales are not revised until period 2. Net investment shoots up in period 2, as Mammoth Electric purchases equipment needed to service the higher expected level of sales. Expected sales continue to grow in periods 3, 4, and 5, but more slowly, so net investment actually declines from its peak in period 2.

The Accelerator Theory Shows How a Permanent Increase in Sales Can Cause a Temporary Burst of Investment

each year 10 percent of the previous year's capital stock needs to be replaced. The total or gross investment (I) of Mammoth Electric, the amount recorded in the national income accounts of Chapter 2, is the sum of net investment (I^n) and replacement investment (D), and is written on line 6 of the table.

Figure 16-2 illustrates the Mammoth Electric example from Table 16-1. The level of actual sales is plotted as the top red line. Underneath, total gross investment is shown as the zigzag purple line that rises from $4 billion to $8 billion, only to fall in period 3 and afterward back toward the original level. Replacement investment is initially at the level of $4 billion, rising gradually as the capital stock increases. Net investment is the purple shaded area, which first increases in size and then shrinks. Overall, the accelerator theory explains why a firm's gross investment is so unstable, at first rising and then falling, even when actual sales increase permanently.

Self-Test

1. Which is likely to be most stable from year to year—gross investment, net investment, or replacement investment? Least stable?
2. Would gross investment in long-lived types of capital (like office buildings) be more or less stable than in short-lived capital (like computers)?

16-4 Case Study

The Simple Accelerator and the Postwar U.S. Economy

The relation between gross investment (I) and GDP (Y) for the economy as a whole is, according to the accelerator hypothesis, the same as for an individual firm. In the special case when expected sales are always set exactly equal to last period's actual sales and therefore $j = 1$, $Y^e = Y_{-1}$, so that $\Delta Y^e = \Delta Y_{-1}$. This allows us to rewrite equation (16.5) as

$$I^n = v^* \Delta Y_{-1} \qquad (16.6)$$

Net investment (I^n) equals a multiple of last period's change in sales (ΔY_{-1}). Equation (16.6) is the simplest form of the accelerator theory and was invented when J.M. Clark in 1917 noticed a regular relationship between the *level* of boxcar production and the previous *change* in railroad traffic.[4] *This equation summarizes succinctly the inherent instability of the private economy. Any random event—an export boom, an irregularity in the timing of government spending, or a revision of consumer estimates of permanent income—can change the growth of real sales and temporarily (but significantly) change the level of net investment in the same direction.*

Assessing the Simple Accelerator

Figure 16-3 compares real net nonresidential investment (I^n) with the annual change in real output (ΔY) in the U.S. economy since 1960.[5] Unfortunately, equation (16.6) is much too simple a theory to explain completely all historical movements in net investment in the United States. True, most peak years in net investment coincided with (or followed by one year) peak years in real GDP growth. And trough years in net investment coincided with (or followed by one year) trough years in real GDP growth, including the most recent episode in 2000–01. Furthermore, ten years of high net investment (1965–74) followed thirteen years (1961–73) in which real GDP growth rarely dipped below average.[6] Finally, low net investment in 1986–95 followed periods during which real GDP growth fell well below average. Overall, however, Figure 16-3 reveals quite an imperfect relationship.

There are three main problems with the simple accelerator theory of equation (16.6), judging from the historical U.S. data plotted in Figure 16-3:

1. Net investment does not respond instantaneously to changes in output growth, as in equation (16.6), but rather displays noticeable lags in response. These lags can be seen clearly in several episodes.

2. The lag, however, is not of uniform length, nor does net investment respond to accelerations and decelerations in real GDP growth with uniform speed. It is as if an automobile's engine responded in a split second

---

[4] J. M. Clark, "Business Acceleration and the Law of Demand," *Journal of Political Economy*, vol. 25 (March 1917), pp. 217–35.

[5] To adjust for the steady growth in the size of the economy, both I^n and ΔY are divided by real GDP (Y). Thus the actual variables plotted are the ratio of real net nonresidential fixed investment to real GDP (I^n/Y) and the percentage growth rate of real GDP ($\Delta Y/Y$) over the previous four quarters.

[6] Average real GDP growth over the 1960–2004 period plotted in Figure 16-3 is 3.3 percent.

The Ups and Downs of Net Investment Are Not Perfectly Related to Changes in Real GDP

Figure 16-3 The Relation of the Net Investment Ratio (I^n/Y) to the Growth Rate of Real GDP ($\Delta Y/Y$) in the U.S. Economy, 1960–2004

The net investment ratio does not have a perfect or simple relationship with the growth rate of real GDP. But net investment was high during 1965–74 following a long period of relatively rapid real GDP growth (1961–73). And the net investment ratio was low (1960–63, 1975–76, 1981–83, and 1990–92) following periods of relatively slow real GDP growth. During the 1990s net investment, particularly purchases of information processing equipment, soared, but then collapsed in 2000–03.

to some movements of the accelerator but took minutes to respond to other movements.

3. The overall level of net nonresidential fixed investment relative to real GDP (I^n/Y) does not have a consistent long-term relationship to real GDP growth ($\Delta Y/Y$). Although average real GDP growth was slower in the 1970s than it was in the 1960s, the ratio of net investment to GDP was higher in the 1970s than the 1960s. Further, the net investment ratio soared in the late 1990s, as shown in Figure 16-3, even though real GDP growth did not.

	Average	
Period	$\Delta Y/Y$	I^n/Y
1960s	4.3	2.1
1970s	3.2	2.4
1980s	3.0	2.6
1990s	3.0	2.5
2000–04	2.7	2.6

Prominent Features of Postwar Investment Behavior

Figure 16-3 allows us to reach some general conclusions about the behavior of investment spending, beyond its relationship with the change in output. What do we learn from a visual inspection of the net investment ratio (I^n/Y), the purple line in Figure 16-3? Two main facts stand out in the figure:

1. **Variability.** As we saw earlier, total GPDI is highly variable, as is the net investment ratio. The past three decades have shown that the net investment ratio can shift by as much as 3 percentage points of GDP within a short period, as between 2000:Q2 and 2002:Q4. This represents a large potential shock for the economy.

2. **Persistence.** The net investment ratio does not zigzag up and down each year but often stays relatively high or relatively low for several years in a row. The period of high net investment between 1965 and 1970 is a good example of this tendency: In every quarter from 1965 through 1970, the net investment ratio exceeded its 1960–2004 average. The persistence of low investment in the Great Depression decade was even more pronounced: The net investment ratio was negative for the entire decade 1931–40.

16-5 The Flexible Accelerator

Defects of the Simple Accelerator

The simple accelerator theory of equation (16.6) depends on several restrictive and unrealistic assumptions. A more realistic version of the theory, called the **flexible accelerator**, loosens several of these assumptions.

1. The simple accelerator assumes that this period's expected output equaled last period's actual output. But the error-learning, or adaptive, hypothesis states that in general expected output is based partially on last period's actual output and partially on last period's expected output.

2. The simple accelerator assumes that the desired capital stock (K^*) equals a constant (v^*) times expected output (Y^e). But actually the desired capital-output ratio (v^*) may vary substantially, depending on the cost of borrowing, the taxation of capital, and other factors; we will postpone until the next section a detailed consideration of the factors that change v^*.

3. The simple accelerator also assumes that firms can instantly put in place any desired amount of investment in plant and equipment needed to make actual capital this period (K) equal to desired capital (K^*). Actually, some kinds of capital take a substantial length of time to construct. Buildings sometimes take two or three years between conception and completion. Some types of electricity generating stations can take as long as eight years to complete.[7] Furthermore, investing very rapidly would be excessively costly because firms supplying capital goods might raise their prices. Also, rapid installation of new buildings and equipment might disrupt normal business activities.

The **flexible accelerator** theory of investment allows for gradual adjustment of sales expectations and of the capital stock. It also allows for variation in the optimal capital-output ratio.

---

[7] At the other extreme, a shop that opens for business today in a large city could probably obtain delivery of needed equipment—cash register, computers, mobile phones, and furniture—in a day or two.

Thus, in the real world, net investment does not always close the whole gap between desired capital and last year's capital stock; more often it closes only a fraction of it.

Determinants of Gross Investment

To summarize, the relationship between economywide gross investment and output depends on at least four major factors.

1. *The fraction of the gap between desired capital and last period's actual capital that can be closed in a single period.* The higher this fraction, the more current investment responds to the change in last period's output.
2. *The response of expected output to last period's error in estimating actual output.* The higher this response, the more expected output and hence investment respond to any unexpected change in last period's actual output.
3. *The proportion of the capital stock that is replaced each year.* For long-lived types of capital, such as office buildings, only a small fraction of the stock is replaced each year. In contrast, because equipment depreciates more quickly, a larger amount of equipment investment is required annually per dollar of equipment capital to maintain the same size equipment capital stock. Firms are not forced to replace old capital on a fixed schedule. If firms delay replacement investment until expected sales are strong, total investment will respond even more than the simple accelerator model suggests.[8]
4. *The desired ratio of capital to expected output (v^*).* Investment responds more to changes in expected output in capital-intensive industries (those with a high v^*, such as electric utilities, oil refining, and chemicals) than in labor-intensive industries (those with a low v^*, such as textiles, apparel, and barber shops). Thus faster growth expected in more capital-intensive industries will spur more investment.

In the next section we investigate the determinants of the desired capital-output ratio and the policy instruments with which the government can affect the size of v^*.

16-6 The Neoclassical Theory of Investment Behavior

One of the most important contributions to the theory of investment behavior was made in the early 1960s by Dale Jorgenson of Harvard University.[9] Jorgenson's insight was to show that the user cost of capital could be derived from neoclassical microeconomic theory by examining the decision of a profit-maximizing firm. Jorgenson then demonstrated that tax policies affected how much firms invest.

---

[8] A study that confirms the procyclical behavior of replacement investment is Martin S. Feldstein and David Foot, "The Other Half of Gross Investment: Replacement and Modernization Expenditures," *The Review of Economics and Statistics*, vol. 53, no. 1 (February 1971), pp. 49–58.

[9] Dale Jorgenson, "Capital Theory and Investment Behavior," *American Economic Review*, vol. 53 (May 1963), pp. 247–57. A comprehensive review of recent theories of investment is Ricardo Caballero, "Aggregate Investment," in J. B. Taylor and M. Woodford, eds., *Handbook of Macroeconomics* (North Holland, 1999), pp. 813–62.

The User Cost of Capital

Jorgenson's theory assumes that a business firm is willing to undertake an investment project only when it expects that a profit can be made. Chapter 7 showed that an extra unit of labor will not be hired unless its marginal product—the extra output it produces—equals or exceeds its real wage. Similarly, an extra unit of capital will not be purchased unless the expected **marginal product of capital (MPK)** is at least equal to the real **user cost of capital** (u):

> The **marginal product of capital (MPK)** is the extra output that a firm can produce by adding an extra unit of capital.
>
> The **user cost of capital** is the cost to the firm of using a piece of capital for a specified period.

$$\begin{array}{cc} \text{General Form} & \text{Numerical Example} \\ \text{MPK} \geq u & \text{MPK} \geq 14 \end{array} \qquad (16.7)$$

Both the marginal product and the real user cost can be expressed as percentages. The marginal product of capital consists of the amount of extra output produced each year by an extra piece of plant or equipment, divided by the cost of the plant or equipment. If the purchase of an extra machine costing $100,000 allows a firm to produce $14,000 of extra output each year, then MPK would be 14 percent.[10] *The user cost of capital is the cost to the business firm of using a piece of capital for a period of time, expressed as a fraction of its purchase price.* The user cost might be 14 percent, consisting perhaps of a 4 percent annual real interest rate and a 10 percent depreciation rate.[11]

What does equation (16.7) have to do with the profitability of a business firm? When MPK is 15 percent and user cost is only 14 percent, then the extra revenue generated by a new machine exceeds its cost, and the firm's profits are increased. On the other hand, when MPK is only 13 percent and user cost is the same 14 percent, the extra revenue is insufficient to pay the costs of the new machine, and profits go down if the machine is purchased. Only if user cost falls to 13 percent or lower will the new machine be purchased.[12]

The effect of a reduction in user cost on the desired capital-output ratio is illustrated in Figure 16-4. The diminishing MPK means that each extra machine adds less output than the machine added before it, implying that the MPK curve slopes downward. Suppose each business initially faces a constant user cost u_0. Each business will then maximize its profits by choosing the capital-output ratio v_0^*, at which point the marginal benefit of the machine, its MPK, equals its marginal cost, u_0. Why? A smaller amount of capital, to the left of E_0, would mean giving up some of the profits indicated by the lighter green area that measures the difference between the marginal product of capital and the user cost. But to purchase a larger amount of capital, to the right of E_0, would cause losses. These extra units of capital have an insufficient MPK to pay for their user cost.

Tax Incentives and Investment Behavior

The user cost of capital depends not only on the depreciation rate of capital and the real interest rate that must be paid on the funds borrowed to purchase the equipment. As derived by Jorgenson, the user cost also depends on three

---

[10] As is always true in economics, the marginal product of a single input measures the extra output produced by an extra unit of that input if the quantity of other inputs is held constant.

[11] Depreciation is part of user cost, because using a machine reduces its ability to produce and thus its value.

[12] If this analysis seems familiar, in Section 3-9 on pp. 79–81 you learned that firms make investment decisions by comparing the rate of return to the interest rate. As we learn in this section, the user cost contains several components in addition to the interest rate.

Figure 16-4 The Effect of a Drop in the User Cost of Capital (*u*) on the Desired Capital-Output Ratio (*v**)

Initially the economy is at point E_0: Firms are making a profit on their capital stock indicated by the light green area in the upper left. If the user cost falls from u_0 to u_1, the desired capital-output ratio will rise to v_1^*, the economy will move from E_0 to E_1, and the darker green area of extra profit is gained.

aspects of the tax system discussed in the next section. Thus both monetary and fiscal policy can influence the user cost—monetary policy by changing the real interest rate, and fiscal policy by affecting real interest rates and by altering tax rates and the rules of the tax system.

We can use Figure 16-4 to illustrate the effect of a change in government tax policy designed to stimulate investment. Let us assume that the government changes tax rates or rules in order to cut the user cost. For instance, the tax rate that corporations pay on their profits might be cut in half, and this reduces user cost to the firm. Additional units of capital will now be purchased to bring the capital-output ratio rightward to v_1^*. Increased investment is required to raise the capital-output ratio to its new, higher desired level, v_1^*. The reduction in user cost has made available extra profits, indicated by the darker green area. Increased investment is required to raise the capital-output ratio to its new, higher desired level, v_1^*. By using monetary and fiscal policy instruments, the user cost of capital can be changed. Firms can thus be induced to adopt more capital-intensive methods of production, and the opposite is true as well. Just as an increase in the wage rate can cause firms to replace marginal workers with extra machines, an increase in capital's user cost can cause firms to substitute away from elaborate machines toward more labor-intensive techniques of production.

16-7 User Cost and the Role of Monetary and Fiscal Policy

How can government policymakers affect the user cost of capital (*u*)? The user cost of capital depends on several factors, which can be introduced in two steps. First, let us neglect the effect of taxation. In the absence of taxation, a capital good that is purchased at a given real price imposes three types of cost on its user.

1. *An interest cost is involved in buying a capital good.* If funds are borrowed, interest at the nominal rate (*i*) must be paid. Alternatively, the investor loses

the interest (*i*) that would have been received had the funds used to buy the capital good been used instead to purchase a financial asset.

2. *Physical deterioration lessens the production ability of every capital good; in addition, some capital goods become obsolete.* The **depreciation rate** indicates the annual percentage decline in value of the capital good due to physical deterioration and obsolescence.

3. *The interest and depreciation cost are adjusted by price changes for capital goods.* Rapid price increases mean that used capital goods can sometimes be resold for more than their cost when new. These price increases reduce the user cost and imply that it is a *real* interest rate that matters (the nominal interest rate minus the rate of price changes for capital goods). Conversely, declines in the prices of computers, for example, raise their user costs.

> The **depreciation rate** is the annual percentage decline in the value of a capital good due to physical deterioration and obsolescence.

Policymakers cannot easily alter the relative price of capital goods. Similarly, they cannot change the rate of physical decay and economic obsolescence summarized in the depreciation rate. But the real interest rate can be influenced by policymakers. As we learned in Chapter 4, a fiscal policy stimulus raises the real interest rate and hence crowds out investment. A monetary policy stimulus, on the other hand, reduces the real interest rate and raises investment. A change in the monetary-fiscal policy mix toward easier monetary policy and tighter fiscal policy cuts the real interest rate and user cost and thus raises investment, as shown in Figure 16-4.

Taxation and Investment Behavior

So far taxation has been ignored. But fiscal policy can have a major effect on investment by altering the user cost. Three basic fiscal tools are available:

1. *Firms invest up to the point where the marginal product of the capital stock is just sufficient to cover the user cost of capital.* Imposing a tax on a firm's income effectively adds another element to user cost, the cost of taxes. The higher the firm's income tax rate is, the greater the effective user cost it faces. Thus a higher tax rate is likely to reduce the firm's desired capital stock, and thus investment, because only with a smaller capital stock will the firm have a larger MPK.

2. *Firms can cut their corporate income tax by deducting the value of depreciation of plants and equipment.* The amount of depreciation they can deduct depends on tax laws and how the IRS implements them. Though the government cannot change the rate of physical depreciation or obsolescence directly it can change the accounting rules used to calculate corporate income taxes. Liberalizing the tax rules regarding depreciation, for example, effectively reduces the corporate income tax rate. Whenever the depreciation tax rules are liberalized, corporate profits are protected from taxation, thus cutting the user cost of capital. The reverse happened in years when the rules were tightened.

3. *During most of the period 1962–86, a substantial part of investment in the United States was eligible for an investment tax credit.* This credit often allowed business firms to deduct 10 percent of the value of their equipment investment from their corporation income tax. Naturally this reduced the effective user cost of capital for firms making profits. The investment tax credit was rescinded in 1986 but could be reinstated if the government desired to stimulate investment.

Tobin's *q*: Does It Explain Investment Better Than the Accelerator or Neoclassical Theories?

Both the accelerator theory of Sections 16-3 and 16-5, as well as the neoclassical theory of Section 16-6, define a desired level of the capital stock (K^*), and then assume a gradual adjustment of the actual capital stock toward the desired level. The alternative *q* theory was developed by the late Nobel Prize winner James Tobin (who also did groundbreaking work on the demand for money and whose picture appears on p. 432). Tobin's *q* theory, instead of positing a desired level of capital and a *separate* process of adjustment, merges adjustment costs directly into the firm's single calculation of the desired rate of investment at each moment of time.[a]

Tobin's theory develops an idea of Keynes's that the attractiveness of purchasing new capital equipment depends on the market value of capital in the stock market as compared with the cost of purchasing the capital. For instance, if purchasing a new Boeing 757 airplane would raise the market value of American Airlines stock by $80 million, while the cost of the plane is $60 million, then the plane should be purchased. But if the new plane would raise the market value of American Airlines stock by only $50 million, then the plane should not be purchased. To create a quantitative measure that reflects changes in market value relative to the purchase cost, Tobin defined his variable *q* as the ratio of the firm's market value on the stock market to the replacement cost of its capital stock. Investment, then, is an increasing function of the *q* ratio.

An example of an investment equation in the *q* theory would be the following relation between gross investment relative to the capital stock (I/K), the *q* ratio (q), and the ratio of replacement investment to the capital stock (d):

$$\frac{I}{K} = j(q - 1) + d \qquad (16.8)$$

In words, this says that the I/K ratio is equal to d when Tobin's *q* ratio is unity. If $d = 0.1$ and $j = 0.2$, then I/K would be 0.1 when *q* equals unity; I/K would rise to 0.2 when *q* equals 1.5, and I/K would fall to zero when *q* equals 0.5.

In practice, the most important source of movement in *q* is the change in the price of a firm's shares on the stock market. During 1994–2000, for example, the change in stock prices was at an annual rate of 19 percent, whereas in 2000–02 stock prices *declined* at an annual rate of 18 percent. Since stock prices are part of the numerator in *q*, such changes could change *q* by large amounts. As we have noted before, households' consumption spending might be affected by the stock mar-

---

These three fiscal tools provide much more flexibility in conducting stabilization policy than would be available if the government were limited to controlling the economy by varying the level of government spending and the personal income tax rate. For instance, government spending can be restrained and the personal income tax rate raised to slow down an economy that is experiencing too much aggregate demand. At the same time, any of the investment-related fiscal instruments can be liberalized if it is believed that the economy has too little investment and too much consumption.

Studies by economists suggest that changes in tax incentives probably have at least a modest effect on investment. However, such changes have numerous limitations and are not a promising instrument for an activist fiscal policy. First, changes in tax incentives are almost always subject to lengthy debate in ket; higher stock prices might raise consumption by increasing households' wealth. Higher stock prices might also increase the amount of investment that firms undertake. Thus Tobin's q also suggests another channel through which changes in the stock market might affect aggregate demand.

Tobin's q theory of investment incorporates how the economic environment affects business firms' expectations of their future profitability. In addition to its theoretical appeal as a way to explain and forecast investment spending by firms, q has great practical appeal because it summarizes expectations about the level and riskiness of future profitability and thus makes unnecessary the exceedingly difficult job of estimating those expectations. Instead, Tobin's q theory states that we can simply look to the stock and bond markets for the valuation of the firm's expected future profitability, which is the numerator of q.

How does q fare in an empirical "horse race" with the accelerator and neoclassical models that we developed in Sections 16-3 and 16-6? A number of studies have tested the abilities of these three models to explain spending on fixed investment after the fact and also to forecast it.[b]

Empirical models have all been much better at explaining and forecasting business investment spending on *equipment*—so-called producers' durable equipment—than they have been at explaining and forecasting investment in nonresidential *structures*. The Oliner, Rudebusch, and Sichel study, for example, shows that investment spending on producers' durable equipment can be fairly well tracked by some of the models. They find that despite the theoretical and practical appeal of the q model of investment, both the accelerator and neoclassical models explain and forecast more accurately than do models based on q, with the accelerator model performing about as well as the neoclassical model. That is one reason why we presented both the accelerator and neoclassical models in this chapter—in practice neither is a clear-cut winner. (Findings similar to those reported by Oliner, Rudebusch, and Sichel emerge from the earlier time periods examined in other studies.)

Business investment in structures has proven more difficult to explain and forecast. In general, none of the models have demonstrated any significant ability to forecast movements in construction spending by business, although again, the accelerator and neoclassical models tend to outperform the q model. An example of the shortcomings of all the models was their inability to forecast, or even account for after the fact, the enormous surge in commercial real estate construction during the 1980s. The large variations in business investment in structures suggest that aggregate demand for GDP may shift importantly over time. The inability to forecast those shifts suggests that it may be difficult for policymakers to anticipate and take timely action to offset them.[c]

---

[a]Most of the references on Tobin's q theory are quite technical. For the original presentation, see James Tobin, "A General Equilibrium Approach to Monetary Theory," *Journal of Money, Credit and Banking*, vol. 1 (February 1969), pp. 15–29. More recent interpretations are Fumio Hayashi, "Tobin's Marginal and Average q: A Neoclassical Interpretation," *Econometrica*, vol. 50 (January 1982), pp. 213–24; and Andrew B. Abel, "A Stochastic Model of Investment, Marginal q, and the Market Value of the Firm," *International Economic Review*, vol. 26 (June 1985), pp. 305–22.

[b]See, for example, Stephen Oliner, Glenn Rudebusch, and Daniel Sichel, "New and Old Models of Business Investment: A Comparison of Forecasting Performance," *Journal of Money, Credit and Banking*, vol. 27 (August 1995), pp. 806–26, and the references cited there.

[c]A recent reinterpretation of Tobin's q theory is Andrew B. Abel and Janice C. Eberly, "Q Theory Without Adjustment Costs and Cash Flow Effects Without Financing Constraints," University of Pennsylvania, Wharton School working paper, June 2004.

Congress. Second, there is a substantial time lag between the passage of tax legislation and the resulting investment spending. Third, we are far from being able to estimate confidently how much investment will respond to tax incentives.

Self-Test

1. How may tools of fiscal policy potentially affect the user cost of capital?
2. If the government wants to stimulate investment, how should it change these tools?
3. Does monetary policy also have an effect on the user cost?

16-8 Business Confidence and Speculation

Confidence and the Flexible Accelerator

In Chapters 3 and 4 the terms *business* and *consumer confidence* were used as a convenient, shorthand way to refer to factors that could change output when government spending and the money supply were fixed at a given level. In the flexible accelerator theory of investment summarized here, the confidence of business firms may influence investment spending in three ways:

1. Investment depends on what fraction of the increase in last period's actual output is incorporated into expected output, and hence into desired capital and investment. When businesspeople lack confidence in the future, they may refuse to extrapolate a quarter or a year of increasing output, believing instead that any increase in output is temporary.

2. The user cost of capital (u) includes the borrowing costs that business firms *expect* to have to pay if they undertake an investment project. If businesses are pessimistic, they may underestimate how much the prices of capital goods will rise and therefore overestimate the real borrowing cost they are likely to face, making their estimate of u too high and their desired capital stock too low.

3. Perhaps most important, business firms can only guess the likely marginal product of new investment projects. It is the expected marginal product that matters. If business has recently been bad, a condition experienced by many business firms in 1930–33, or as recently as 2001, firms may already have more capital than they may desire. Some present capital may be underutilized, and future capital investments may appear unprofitable, with their expected marginal products being close to zero.

Investment and the Great Depression

Any event, whether political or economic, that causes a drop in business confidence can cause a sharp drop in the level of investment. In the extreme case of the Great Depression of the 1930s, a collapse in business confidence dropped the desired capital stock far below the actual inherited capital stock. Not only did businesses refuse to add to their capital stock, but they allowed net investment to become negative by refusing to replace worn-out and obsolete equipment. Gross private domestic investment plummeted more than 80 percent from 1929 to 1933. But, despite the low levels of gross investment in the 1930s, much capital remained underutilized. The overhang of too much inherited capital depressed investment for a full decade.

Cycles of Overbuilding

Periods of business overoptimism in U.S. history have led to overbuilding, underutilized capital, and extensive pessimism. This recurring sequence played out in the years surrounding 1970 and the years surrounding 1990, leaving the United States with billions of dollars' worth of empty apartments, office buildings, and stores. In 1996–2000 there was a new type of overbuilding consisting of excess investment in computers and telecommunications equipment. Excess capacity resulted in a collapse of this "high-tech" investment in 2000–01, as we will learn in Section 16-9.

Keynes placed major emphasis on the role of business confidence in determining the level of investment. In the following passage he stresses that investment decisions are based on estimates of the future yield (or marginal product) of extra capital, estimates that may be little better than a guess. Faced with identical information and uncertainty, businesspeople may go ahead with an investment project when they feel optimistic but postpone the same project when they feel pessimistic:

> The outstanding fact is the extreme precariousness of the basis of knowledge on which our estimates of prospective yield have to be made. Our knowledge of the factors which will govern the yield of an investment some years hence is usually very slight and often negligible. If we speak frankly, we have to admit that our basis of knowledge for estimating the yield ten years hence of a railway, a copper mine, a textile factory, the goodwill of a patent medicine, an Atlantic liner, a building in the City of London amounts to little and sometimes to nothing; or even five years hence. In fact, those who seriously attempt to make any such estimates are often so much in the minority that their behavior does not govern the market.[13]

Throughout this book we have treated such shifts in business confidence (as well as consumer confidence) as sources of important and unpredictable shifts in the *IS*, and thus *AD*, curves.

16-9 Case Study

The Boom and Bust in "New Economy" Investment

In the late 1990s the U.S. economy achieved a miracle—the lowest unemployment rate in 30 years combined with continued relatively low inflation that allowed the Fed to hold interest rates relatively low. Previously we have examined key components of the economic miracle, including the reasons for low inflation (pp. 258–60), the Fed's monetary policy response (pp. 467–70), the revival of productivity growth (pp. 372–73), and the role of the stock market in reducing household saving, thus allowing consumption to grow faster than household income (pp. 506–09). The economic miracle can be thought of as a simultaneous rightward shift in aggregate supply and aggregate demand that made possible higher output without extra inflation. Sources of the aggregate supply shift were the productivity revival and the beneficial supply shocks that held down inflation. One source of the aggregate demand shift was the surge in consumption spending, which was in part a response to the stock market boom. The other source of the aggregate demand shift was the explosion of investment spending, particularly on information technology equipment.

Dimensions of the New Economy Investment Boom

While the economic expansion of the 1990s started off slowly, everything seemed to accelerate beginning in 1995. Many commentators trace the source to an accelerating decline in the prices of computer equipment; this is displayed as the orange line in the bottom part of Figure 16-5. After declining at an average rate of 13 percent per year from 1987 to 1995, the rate of price decline accelerated to 28 percent per year from 1995 to 1999. The faster decline in

---

[13] Keynes, *General Theory*, pp. 149–50.

534 Chapter 16 • Instability in the Private Economy: Investment Behavior

Figure 16-5 Change in Real Investment in Computers and Peripherals and in the Computer Deflator, 1988–2004

The data shown are two-quarter average changes at an annual rate. In the bottom frame, the accelerated rate of price decline is clearly visible between 1996 and 1999, followed by a reversal in 2000–04. The top frame shows that, after erratic up-and-down movements from 1988 to 1994, the growth rate of real computer investment "took off" in 1995, registering an average growth rate of 35 percent per year from 1995 to 1999. Then came the collapse to an annual growth rate of *minus* 6 percent per year in 2001. Over the period 2000–04, real computer investment grew at 16 percent per year, substantially less than from 1987 to 1995.

computer prices was caused, in turn, by an acceleration in the rate of technological change in the manufacture of computers and their most important component, the semiconductors called processors. The entire history of computers over the past 50 years had been described by "Moore's Law," named after Gordon Moore, one of the founders of the Intel Corporation. Several decades ago, Moore predicted with uncanny accuracy that the number of transistors on a processor chip would double every 18 months, making possible great increases in computation speed. Between 1995 and 1999, Moore's law seemed to have accelerated as the number of transistors doubled every 12 months.

When a product becomes cheaper, people buy more of it. This happened after 1995, when the faster decline in computer prices stimulated an acceleration in real purchases. After averaging about 21 percent per year during 1987–95, the growth rate of real computer investment accelerated to a rate of about 35 percent per year during 1996–99, as shown in the top frame of Figure 16-5. Purchases of computers and peripherals are the most dynamic components of fixed nonresidential investment and this explosion of computer investment helps us to understand why real fixed nonresidential investment increased by 79 percent between 1994 and 2000, as is clearly visible in Figure 16-1 on p. 518.

The World Wide Web and the High-Tech Stock Market Bubble

The rapid decline in computer prices would not have caused such a burst of real investment in computers if people had no good uses for all of those computers. But at the same time in 1995 that computer prices began to decline faster, the World Wide Web was invented, and Web browsers became pervasive, initially in business firms and soon in homes and student dormitories. Whereas students in the mid-1990s relied heavily on campus computer labs, by 2000 most students had computers in their dorm rooms or apartments, and students had become expert in using the Web for researching papers, playing games, and downloading music.

The invention of the Web browser led to a frenzy of investment in computer hardware—not just the computers needed in homes and offices to access the Web, but also the servers and routers that are often called the Web's "infrastructure." Along with the hardware came the software, as every business firm rushed to hire programmers to build its first Web site and make subsequent refinements. Everything seemed to explode together, including the stock prices of equipment providers and e-commerce firms, the share of investment in GDP, and the willingness of the stock market and venture capital firms to provide ever-more finance for start-up firms.

The Collapse of the New Economy Investment Boom

Although some analysts claimed that it was a "new world" in which corporate profits were no longer relevant, eventually stock market investors refused to accept this story. When the crash came, it came rapidly. The value of the NASDAQ stock market index that specialized in high-tech stocks crashed, losing two-thirds of its value between March 2000 and March 2001. As shown in Figure 16-5, computer investment also crashed, with its growth rate suddenly dropping from an annual rate of +33 percent in the two quarters ending 2000:Q2 to −28 percent in the two quarters ending in 2001:Q3.

In retrospect, the high-tech investment boom was supported by numerous temporary factors that could not continue. First, the Web could only be invented once. It took much more investment in computer software and hardware to develop a firm's first Web site than to refine it and add new features in subsequent years. Second, some of the 1999–2000 boom in computer investment was due to the "Y2K problem," which was inherently temporary. Third, computer columnists began to suggest in 2000–01 that the industry was no longer developing "killer applications" like the Web that would drive the next wave of computer investments. Fourth, many of the e-commerce companies went bust; not only did they no longer need to buy new computers, but their now unneeded computers flooded the market. Finally, the late

International Perspective

The Level and Variability of Investment Around the World

For many years, investment was much lower in the United States than in Japan or Germany. And from the mid-1980s through the early 1990s, the investment gap between the United States and Japan and Germany widened. The accompanying figure shows the share of each country's GDP that is devoted to gross investment (net investment plus depreciation) for the years 1980–2004.

However, over the period 1992 to 2000, the investment ratio in the United States soared from 17.2 to 20.8 percent, and exceeding Germany's ratio in 2002–04. Japan remained ahead, but the gap between Japan and the United States fell from 15 percentage points in 1991 to 5 percentage points in 2004.

National saving, the sum of private and government saving, always equals national investment. One reason why the investment ratio was relatively low in the United States during most of the 1970–2000 period was the low rate of U.S. national saving. During the period 1980–96 and again in 2002–05, large U.S. government deficits meant that the government surplus was negative and national saving was low. The upsurge in the U.S. investment ratio shown in the graph was made possible by heavy borrowing from foreigners, not by domestic saving.

Firms finance their investment spending in a number of ways. In most countries the primary source of funds for business investment in plant and equipment is retained earnings, that is, the profits that firms have not paid out in dividends but have retained inside the firms. Especially in France, Italy, and Japan, firms also rely heavily on loans from banks to finance purchases of plant and equipment. Firms in Germany, the United Kingdom, and the United States are less dependent on bank loans, obtaining relatively more of the funds they use to finance investment expenditures by issuing stocks, long-term bonds, and short-term instruments like commercial paper.

In Chapter 15 we learned that consumers sometimes face liquidity constraints, which prevent them from borrowing the full amount of funds that they would be expected to be able to repay from permanent incomes. Business firms too sometimes face liquidity constraints. Young firms, like young households, may find it difficult to borrow the amount of funds justified by their longer-term prospects. And smaller firms may find that they must reduce investment when current profits or retained earnings decline, in much the same way that individuals who temporarily lose their jobs reduce consumption because they are unable to borrow the amounts justified by permanent income. Thus, for both households and firms, constraints on borrowing and therefore on spending may be more severe during recessions or when higher interest rates raise loan payments. These effects on investment have been noted particularly in Italy, the United Kingdom, and the United States. By stifling investment spending even more when the economy is weak, these borrowing constraints can exacerbate the variability of investment spending.

One way for firms to loosen these financing constraints may be to ally themselves with other firms. Firms in Korea sometimes belong to a *chaebol*; in Italy firms are sometimes linked by family connections; in Japan some firms belong to a group of firms called a *keiretsu*; businesses in Canada and in the United States may be owned by conglomerates; and some firms in

---

1990s had witnessed an additional boom in telecommunications equipment and especially in the laying of thousands of miles of fiber-optic cable intended to tie together all the office and home computers in a vast broadband network. However, like many speculative booms in the past, too many people laid too much fiber-optic cable, and by 2001 it was estimated that 97 percent of the fiber-optic capacity was not being utilized.

In summary, the new economy investment boom and collapse had some similarities with previous booms and collapses, such as the 1929–33 collapse that was led by both residential and nonresidential construction, and the 1989–92 collapse in commercial building of hotels and office buildings. The decline of investment spending in 2000–01 put substantial downward pressure on

Japan and in Germany have bankers on their boards of directors. Because the other firms in such alliances often are not in closely allied areas of business, the alliance is more likely to remain strong when one of its members may need financial support. Belonging to one of these business groups seems to provide some insulation from financing constraints, perhaps because the other firms in the group can either provide the funds needed for investment directly to a constrained firm, or can provide some assurance to an outside lender like a bank that the other firms will help repay a bank loan to the constrained firm.

the economy, which as we have seen was resisted by an easing of monetary policy by the Fed that was unprecedented in its speed of response.[14]

---

[14] Three references on the high-tech investment boom are Robert J. Gordon, "Does the New Economy Measure Up to the Great Inventions of the Past?" *Journal of Economic Perspectives*, vol. 14 (Fall 2000), pp. 49–74; Dale W. Jorgenson and Kevin J. Stiroh, "Raising the Speed Limit: U.S. Economic Growth in the Information Age," *Brooking Papers on Economic Activity*, vol. 31, no. 1 (2000), pp. 125–211; and Stephen D. Oliner and Daniel F. Sichel, "The Resurgence of Growth in the Late 1990s: Is Information Technology the Story?" *Journal of Economic Perspectives*, vol. 14 (Fall 2000), pp. 3–23. A more recent assessment is Susanto Basu et al., "The Case of the Missing Productivity Growth, or Does Information Technology Explain Why Productivity Accelerated in the United States but Not in the United Kingdom?" *NBER Macroeconomics Annual 2003*, pp. 9–63.

Finally, in 2003–04 computer investment began to revive, as shown in Figure 16-5, but not to the ebullient growth rates registered year after year in 1995–99. Furthermore, the rate of decline of computer prices slacked to less than 10 percent per year in 2004. The post-2000 "hangover" of the New Economy continued to be prolonged and difficult.

16-10 Investment as a Source of Instability of Output and Interest Rates

The accelerator theory resolves a favorite paradox of macroeconomics teachers. We became accustomed in Chapter 3 to associating low interest rates with high investment and high interest rates with low investment. This negative relationship between investment and interest rates has been confirmed in this chapter, because a low level of the real interest rate reduces the user cost of capital, which in turn raises the desired capital stock and hence the level of gross investment.

Yet a predominant feature of business cycles in almost every nation is a positive correlation between business investment and interest rates. U.S. business investment fluctuates procyclically, reaching peaks in years of high output and troughs during recessions or soon afterward. But, since interest rates also fluctuate procyclically, years of low interest rates are usually associated with low investment, not high investment.

How can the positive correlation between investment and interest rates be explained? The accelerator theory provides the answer. Figure 16-6 repeats the IS-LM analysis of Chapter 4. The LM curve maintains an unchanged position whenever the real money supply (M/P) and real demand for money function are fixed. The IS curve fluctuates whenever there is a change in the investment purchases that business firms make at a constant real interest rate.

Figure 16-6 Effect on Output and the Interest Rate of a Shift in the Level of Investment Relative to the Interest Rate

Shifts in business confidence or in user cost (apart from those due to changes in the real interest rate) can shift the red IS curve back and forth between IS_0 and IS_1. The real interest rate and investment will rise and fall together. This conclusion assumes that the real money supply, which fixes the position of the LM curve, remains unchanged.

Why the Interest Rate and Investment Often Are Positively Correlated

Causes of IS Shifts

We have seen that many factors can make the level of gross investment, and hence the *IS* curve, shift for a given interest rate. Among them are (1) a change in the expected growth rate of output and thus sales, (2) a previous episode of overbuilding that makes the actual capital stock high relative to the current desired stock, (3) a shift in demand toward shorter-lived equipment, (4) a change in the relative price of capital goods, and, finally, (5) a change in fiscal incentives that alters the effective user cost of capital. A change in any of these elements shifts the level of investment that occurs at a given interest rate and, through the multiplier, shifts the *IS* curve and the level of total output.

Figure 16-6 illustrates two *IS* curves, IS_0 and IS_1. The shifts back and forth between the two *IS* curves reflect any one of the factors in the previous paragraph that cause an increase or decrease in gross investment. The positive relationship between investment and interest rates is explained in Figure 16-6 by the *IS* shifting along LM_0, which is held fixed by the fixed real money supply. That positive relationship suggests that the depressing effect of low output on investment, working through the accelerator, dominates the stimulative effect of low interest rates on investment, at least in the short run.

16-11 Conclusion: Investment and the Case For and Against Activism

We concluded in Chapter 15 that consumption spending on nondurable goods and services is not likely to be very volatile. Both the permanent-income and life-cycle hypotheses suggested that spending on nondurable goods and services tends to fluctuate less than disposable income. This stability bolsters the case for following a policy rule.

But this chapter tilts the balance in the opposite direction, toward the proposition of policy activists that the private economy contains sources of instability that tend to make equality of actual and natural output an infrequent coincidence rather than a frequent occurrence. The problem is epitomized by the accelerator theory of investment. Any event that causes a *permanent* increase in the desired capital stock—whether an increase in expected output or a reduction in the user cost of capital—causes only a *temporary* burst of investment spending. After the temporary burst, when net investment falls, economic instability is aggravated by the multiplier effect of Chapter 3.

Until the 1980s, the tendency for fixed investment to undergo multiyear booms and slumps formed the core of the activist case. It then became apparent, however, that net exports can be an equally important source of fluctuations in aggregate demand, as we learned in Chapters 3 and 6. The decline in net exports in the mid-1980s provided as much of a challenge for policymakers as the investment slumps of 1973–75, 1980–82, 1990–92, and 2000–02.

Investment Volatility and the Taylor Rule

The multiyear cycles in fixed investment and in net exports support the activist contention that private spending is unstable. But this does not by itself mean that policy should be entirely discretionary without any tie to a rule. On the contrary, the Taylor Rule studied in Chapter 14 is based on a formula that calls for the Fed to shift to an easier monetary policy *either* when the inflation rate drops below the Fed's target for inflation, or when the log output ratio becomes negative. Thus, under the Taylor Rule, the Fed is still able to ease policy in response to severe slumps of investment, as occurred in 2000–02, and indeed we have learned (pp. 467–70) that the Fed reduced interest rates during this period even more than is called for by a Taylor Rule. The Fed's actions in 2000–02 pleased adherents of policy activism who stress the need for the Fed to respond to volatile swings of investment.

Summary

1. The major source of instability in consumption spending is consumer expenditures on durables, which can exhibit large fluctuations in response to income changes. This chapter adds private investment spending as an additional source of instability, with the potential of causing major changes in GDP in response to small shocks.
2. The simple accelerator theory of investment relies on the idea that firms attempt to maintain a fixed relation between their stock of capital and their expected sales. Thus the level of net investment—the change in the capital stock—depends on the change in expected output. The accelerator theory explains why the gross investment of most firms is relatively unstable, at first rising and then falling in response to a permanent increase in actual sales.
3. The flexible accelerator theory recognizes that net investment in the real world usually closes only a portion of any gap between the desired and actual capital stocks. Furthermore, the desired capital-output ratio may change, altering investment with a powerful accelerator effect.
4. The accelerator theory suggests that any event that causes a permanent increase in the desired capital stock, whether arising from an increase in expected output or from a reduction in the user cost of capital, causes only a temporary rise in investment spending.
5. Government policymakers can directly alter the user cost of capital. Fiscal and monetary policy can change the real interest rate component of user cost. Taxation can affect the user cost of capital through changes in the corporation income tax, depreciation deductions, and the investment tax credit. But the use of these policy instruments cannot eliminate all fluctuations in investment expenditures, because most policy measures operate only with lagged effects.
6. Spending on commercial construction has historically been quite variable, in part because the capital-output ratio for buildings is larger than that for other, shorter-lived types of physical capital. Because the lags between conception and completion of office buildings are long, booms and busts in spending for commercial real estate may last for several years. Changes in user costs and expected output also help explain this variability, but some of the fluctuations in construction still seem inexplicable and unpredictable.
7. Some firms face the same kinds of constraints on financing their spending that households face. Young and small firms seem particularly subject to constraints on how much investment they can undertake. In other countries around the world, firms sometimes are allied with other firms or with banks, which helps to reduce these constraints.
8. Shifts in the demand for investment spending tend to produce a positive correlation between investment and interest rates, even though the effect of higher interest rates, *ceteris paribus*, is to reduce investment spending. The former results from a shift of the *IS* curve; the latter from sliding along the *IS* curve.
9. The unpredictability of investment spending bolsters the case for policy activism. It also supports the Taylor Rule for monetary policy that reacts to booms and slumps of the output ratio caused by volatile swings of investment.

Concepts

accelerator hypothesis
flexible accelerator
marginal product of capital (MPK)
user cost of capital
depreciation rate

Questions

1. Distinguish between gross investment and net investment. Can gross investment ever be negative? Can net investment ever be negative?
2. Assume that output in the economy is growing. Does the simple accelerator model predict that net investment will also grow?
3. Discuss the role of lags in the accelerator theory. How does the existence of lags change the results of the simple accelerator model?
4. In summarizing the behavior of investment spending, the net investment ratio (I^n/Y) was described as volatile and persistent. Explain what is meant by these terms.
5. Business confidence and consumer confidence are often cited as playing a key role in the investment decision. How does business confidence enter the flexible accelerator model?
6. A capital good purchased at a given real price imposes three types of costs on its user. What are these costs? Which of these costs are subject to manipulation by policymakers?
7. What are the three tools of fiscal policy that can be used to influence the level of investment? According to the accelerator theory, are changes in these tools likely to lead to a permanent increase in the rate of investment?
8. What are the limitations to using tax incentives as a tool of activist fiscal policy?
9. If Congress and the president agree to government spending increases, while the Fed enacts open market sales of government securities, what is likely to happen to user cost, the desired ratio of capital to expected output, and the level of net investment?
10. What are the major factors that determine the relationship between gross investment and output in the economy? Briefly summarize the relationship involved.
11. Two of the functions of an economic model are to explain the behavior of economic variables and to forecast their future behavior. Using the information contained in the box on Tobin's q model, discuss how well each of the accelerator, neoclassical and q models have explained or forecast the behavior of business spending on construction. What is the implication of this for the use of either rules-based policies or discretionary policy in efforts to stabilize the economy?
12. Figure 16-5 shows that deflation in computer prices was much greater in the period 1996–99 than it was before and after those years. Simultaneously the amount of investment in computer equipment accelerated. Explain what the more rapid deflation in computer prices did to the real user cost of computer investment. Does that change in the real user cost of computer investment at the same time that investment in computer equipment accelerated invalidate the neoclassical theory of investment?
13. Are there other periods in the history of the U.S. economy that are similar to the collapse of the New Economy investment boom? What are some of the factors that contributed to the collapse in the boom? Finally, go to the Bureau of Economic Analysis Web site (www.bea.gov) to see if there has been a revival in investment spending on producers' durable equipment and software since the beginning of 2003.
14. According to the theory first presented in Chapter 3 and developed further in this chapter, the interest rate and investment are negatively related. Yet both business investment and interest rates tend to fluctuate procyclically, that is, are at their highest levels when the economy is at a high output level. Can you explain the paradox?
15. Using Tobin's q theory, explain what you would expect to happen to the construction of new houses as the prices of existing houses rise.
16. The procyclical nature of much investment spending tends to reduce the stability of the private economy. Suppose an investment tax credit plan is put in place under which the percentage tax credit granted to firms is negatively related to the output ratio. Would such a plan work to stabilize or destabilize the economy? Explain.
17. How does the existence of liquidity constraints affect the volatility of investment? Why might liquidity constraints be more binding on smaller firms than on larger ones and on U.S. firms than on firms in such countries as Germany and Japan?
18. Discuss how the behavior of investment described in this chapter strengthens or weakens the cases for discretionary policy and rules-based policy.

Problems

1. (a) Using the data contained in Table A-2 of Appendix A, calculate the percentage change (in logs) in real GDP from peak to trough and from trough to peak for the business cycles listed in the table at the beginning of Section 16-2's case study of the historical instability of investment.
   (b) Using your answer to part a and the data contained in the table at the beginning of the case study of the historical instability of investment, compare the volatility of real GDP with that of investment expenditures. Furthermore discuss whether the data show that the volatility of investment spending has varied over business cycles since 1960.

2. This problem uses the example in Table 16-1 (p. 520).
   (a) The economy will reach an equilibrium when expected sales no longer increase. What will net investment be at that point? What will gross investment be?
   (b) Assume that because of a new investment tax credit, the desired capital–expected sales ratio changes to 5. What would net investment be in periods 1–5?
   (c) When the economy reaches its new equilibrium, what will be the ultimate effect of the tax credits on investment?

3. This problem also uses the data in Table 16-1.
   (a) What would expected sales have to be in periods 3 to 5 for net investment to be constant at 4.0?
   (b) What would actual sales have to be in periods 3 to 5 to achieve a constant level of net investment?
   (c) What would actual sales have to be in periods 2 to 4 to achieve a steady 20 percent increase in gross investment in each of the periods 3 to 5?
   (d) At what rate do actual sales increase in part c?

4. This problem also uses the example in Table 16-1 (p. 520), except where noted. The flexible accelerator model states that net investment, I^n, equals a fraction, f, of the gap between the desired capital stock, K^*, and last period's capital stock, K_{-1}. The capital stock in any period equals last period's capital stock plus last period's net investment. The equations that describe these relationships are

   $$I^n = f(K^* - K_{-1}) \text{ and } K = K_{-1} + I^n_{-1}.$$

   (a) Assume that f equals 0.5. Calculate the amounts of the capital stock, net investment, and gross investment in periods 1–5.
   (b) Using the example in Table 16-1 and your answer to part a, discuss how net and gross investment differ between the simple and flexible accelerator models.

5. The problem also uses the example in Table 16-1 (p. 520) and the flexible accelerator from problem 4. Assume that f equals 0.5. Suppose that the desired capital-expected sales ratio, v^*, depends on the real user cost of capital, u. In particular, $v^* = 5.5 - 10u$.
   (a) Suppose that the real interest rate equals 5 percent (0.05) and that the capital stock lasts for 10 years, so that d equals 0.1. Calculate the real user cost of capital and the desired capital stock in periods 1–5. Explain why the amounts of the capital stock, net investment, and gross investment in periods 1–5 are the same as in part a of problem 4.
   (b) Suppose that in period 1, the real interest rate falls to 3 percent (0.03) and stays at that level for periods 2–5. Given no change in the depreciation rate, compute the new real user cost of capital, and the new amounts of the desired capital stock, the actual capital stock, net investment, and gross investment in periods 1–5.
   (c) Suppose that the real interest rate equals 5 percent (0.05), but that the capital stock depreciates more quickly, so that d equals 0.2. Calculate the new real user cost of capital, and the new amounts of the desired capital stock, the capital stock, net investment, and gross investment in periods 1–5.
   (d) Use your answers from parts b and c to discuss the effect of changes in the real interest rate and the depreciation rate on the amounts of net and gross investment.

6. This problem uses the Tobin q model of investment. (See the box on pp. 530–31.) Suppose that the adjustment rate, j, equals 0.2 and that the depreciation rate equals 0.1. The replacement value of the AB Corporation's capital equals 10 million dollars and the market value of its stock for the next 10 periods is listed in the table below. (The market value is listed in millions of dollars.)

Period	1	2	3	4	5	6	7	8	9	10
Market value	11	12	12	11	10	9	8	8	9	10

   (a) Calculate the value of Tobin's q for the AB Corporation in periods 1–10.
   (b) Calculate the AB Corporation's investment-to-capital stock ratio in periods 1–10.
   (c) Suppose that the Tobin q's and the investment-to-capital stock ratios for all businesses behave like that of the AB Corporation during periods 1–10. Other things being equal, explain how the economy's IS curves shift during periods 2–10.

Self-Test Answers

***p*. 522** (1) Assuming, as in this section, that replacement investment is a fixed fraction of the previous year's capital stock, replacement investment is the most stable. Net investment, which depends on the *change* in expected output, is the least stable. Gross investment, the sum of net investment and replacement investment, is in-between. (2) The longer-lived is capital, the smaller is the fraction of the previous year's capital stock that needs to be replaced; hence, the smaller is stable replacement investment relative to unstable net investment. Thus we would expect gross investment in office buildings to be less stable than gross investment in computers.

***p*. 531** (1) The three potential tools are the corporation income tax, the value of depreciation deductions, and the investment tax credit. (2) If the government wants to stimulate investment, it can reduce the corporation income tax rate, or raise the value of depreciation deductions (by allowing business firms to take depreciation deductions earlier), or raise the percentage rate of the investment tax credit. If there is no investment tax credit, as in the United States after 1986, the government can introduce such a credit. (3) Monetary policy affects the user cost through its ability to change the real interest rate.

PART SEVEN

Debates at the Macroeconomic Frontier

CHAPTER 17 New Classical Macro Confronts New Keynesian Macro

CHAPTER 18 Conclusion: Where We Stand

CHAPTER 17

New Classical Macro Confronts New Keynesian Macro

The chief cause of depressions is a want of confidence. The greater part of it could be removed almost in an instant if confidence could return, touch all industries with her magic wand, and make them continue their production, and their demand for the wares of others.
—Alfred Marshall, 1879

17-1 Introduction: Classical and Keynesian Economics, Old and New

The development of new theories in macroeconomics and the abandonment of old theories often occur in response to major macroeconomic developments. In Chapter 7 we were introduced to the classical economists whose ideas dominated macroeconomics prior to the 1930s; they believed that the price level was flexible and would shift by the amount necessary to eliminate any inadequacies in aggregate demand. We described this approach as assuming that the economy possesses strong self-correcting properties, in the form of price flexibility, that would automatically correct any tendency for real aggregate demand to be too high or too low.

In the 1930s a calamitous macroeconomic event, the Great Depression, brought a decade-long economic slump accompanied by double-digit unemployment rates. The Great Depression discredited the old classical approach based on flexible prices and self-correction. This epochal event created among economists, journalists, policymakers, and laypeople a receptive audience for the Keynesian revolution, based on John Maynard Keynes's influential book, *The General Theory of Employment, Interest, and Income*.[1]

However, the old Keynesian approach was not without its own problems. Only a few years after the publication of *The General Theory*, economists questioned Keynes's assumption that (as in Figure 7-7 on p. 209) real wages vary countercyclically, rising in recessions and falling in expansions. They pointed to data indicating that real wages do not change systematically during the business cycle. Nevertheless, the old Keynesian approach dominated macroeconomics until the late 1960s. The big event that undermined its dominance was the emergence at that time of significant inflation. The old Keynesian theory based on rigid nominal wages had little to say about the causes of inflation.

---

[1] The late Harry Johnson examined the reasons for the success of the Keynesian revolution and developed a parallel set of reasons for the late 1960s' monetarist "counterrevolution." See his article "The Keynesian Revolution and the Monetarist Counter-Revolution," *American Economic Review*, vol. 61 (May 1971), pp. 1–14.

New Classical Macroeconomics Versus New Keynesian Economics

Since the early 1970s, macroeconomics has been split between two basic explanations of business cycles. First to emerge as a challenge to the old Keynesian orthodoxy was the new classical approach originated by Milton Friedman, then at the University of Chicago, and Edmund S. Phelps of Columbia University. It was subsequently more fully developed by Robert E. Lucas, Jr., of the University of Chicago. This first approach was based on the idea that households and firms lack the full set of information needed to make their economic decisions. Later, a second strand of new classical macroeconomics emerged, based not on imperfect information but on shocks to technology and supply conditions. The second approach, the "real business cycle" model, was developed primarily by Edward Prescott of Arizona State University.

Common to all new classical models is the assumption of continuous equilibrium in labor and product markets. These markets "clear," in the sense that each worker and firm is acting as desired at the price and wage level that is expected to prevail during the period of employment or production. For Friedman, Phelps, and Lucas, business cycles emerge because workers and/or firms, while acting as desired, are doing so on the basis of incorrect information. If workers and firms had complete access to information on such macro variables as the aggregate price level and money supply, there would be no business cycles. In contrast, Prescott theorizes that business cycles emerge because a given amount of labor and capital input produces varying amounts of real GDP due to changes in the efficiency of production.

New classical macro contrasts with another recent set of theories intended in part to remedy weaknesses in the old Keynesian approach. These new theories are grouped together under the general heading of "new Keynesian" macro. Such models, examined in the second part of this chapter, accept Keynes's insight that prices and wages do not change fast enough for classical self-correction to occur. But they go beyond Keynes to examine the *reasons* why slow price and wage adjustment is often in the self-interest of workers and is consistent with profit maximization for firms. The implications of new Keynesian macro differ radically from those of new classical macro. For if prices and wages adjust slowly, no matter what the reasons, then markets do not always clear; workers are sometimes unable to obtain as many jobs as they want at the prevailing wages and prices, and firms are sometimes unable to sell as much as they would like to produce at those wages and prices.

17-2 Imperfect Information and the "Fooling Model"

One of two related theories to introduce the new classical approach was Milton Friedman's "fooling model," developed as part of his Presidential Address to the American Economic Association in 1967.[2]

---

[2] Milton Friedman, "The Role of Monetary Policy," *American Economic Review,* vol. 58 (March 1968), pp. 1–17.

Distinctive Features: Market Clearing and Imperfect Information

The first distinctive feature of Friedman's model is that (unlike some new Keynesian models) firms and workers are never required to operate off the labor demand and supply curves. Such models are often called classical, equilibrium, or market-clearing models. The second distinctive feature is that business cycles can occur only if workers *inaccurately perceive the price level*, hence the label "fooling model." This feature of the Friedman model is often called "imperfect information" and is a characteristic of many modern models of the market-clearing variety.

The fooling model is illustrated in Figure 17-1, which in the left frame copies the labor supply and demand curves of Figure 7-11 (p. 220), and in the right frame copies the short-run aggregate supply curve and one of the aggregate demand curves (AD_0) from the same figure. Friedman's treatment of the labor demand curve is identical to the Keynesian model in Figure 7-11; he assumes that the labor demand (N^d) curve depends on the actual real wage (W/P). Thus the *countercyclical* movement of the real wage occurs along the N^d line in Figure 17-1, just as in Figure 7-11. But Friedman adds one important new element. In his interpretation, the labor supply curve depends on the *expected real wage* (W/P^e), that is, the nominal wage rate (W) divided by the price level expected by workers (P^e).

Milton Friedman (1912–)

Friedman, a 1976 Nobel Prize winner, is the most famous proponent of policy rules (Chapter 14) and the inventor of the permanent-income hypothesis of consumption (Chapter 15).

A Business Expansion in the "Fooling Model"

Figure 17-1 Effects on the Price Index and Real Income of an Increase in the Nominal Money Supply While the Expected Price Level Is Fixed at P_0^e

The position of the short-run aggregate supply curve (SAS_0) in the right frame is fixed by the assumed constancy of the price level expected by workers (P_0^e). A higher nominal money supply shifts the aggregate demand curve upward from AD_0 to AD_1, and the economy moves from point E_0 to C in both the left frame and the right frame. Because the actual price level has risen from P_0 to P_1 the firms are happy to hire additional labor input at point C in the left frame, but the workers think that their real wage has increased to point D and are happy to provide more labor input for as long as W/P^e remains high.

Friedman's theory of the business cycle argues that an increase in aggregate demand raises the actual price level (P) and reduces the actual real wage (W/P), encouraging firms to hire more workers along their labor demand curve. For instance, in the right frame of Figure 17-1, an upward shift of the aggregate demand curve from AD_0 to AD_1 shifts the economy's short-run equilibrium from point E_0 to point C, raises real GDP from Y^N to Y_1, and raises the price level from P_0 to P_1. At point C in the left frame of Figure 17-1, N_1 workers are hired as the higher price level pushes the real wage down.

Yet only the firms know that the price level has increased; the *workers do not*. They still think the expected price level is P_0^e. If the firms raise the nominal wage rate from W_0 to W_1, workers will think that the expected real wage has increased from W_0/P_0^e to W_1/P_0^e and will happily work harder, moving up their labor supply curve to point D.

To explain business cycles, the Friedman model requires that the price level (P) differs from the expected price level (P^e). Thus, in the right frame of Figure 17-1, output can differ from Y^N along the SAS_0 supply curve only if P differs from the expected price level P_0^e. What happens when the workers catch on to the fact that they have been fooled? Their expected price level will rise, and workers will demand a nominal wage increase sufficient to regain the original real wage level. As a result, the supply curve will shift up and to the left. This process will continue until output has returned to Y^N along the vertical LAS line at a point like E_1.

Because the level of output is always equal to natural real GDP (Y^N) when expectations are accurate, the vertical LAS line is labeled "accurate expectations" in the right frame of Figure 17-1. Sooner or later any expectational errors will be corrected, so output cannot remain away from natural real GDP (Y^N) for long. As a result, Friedman's model is sometimes called a "natural rate" model, and in fact it is Friedman who is responsible for the terms "natural real GDP" and "natural rate of unemployment." It is common to describe a model with a vertical long-run supply curve (like LAS in Figure 17-1) as obeying the **natural rate hypothesis**.

A model obeys the **natural rate hypothesis** when shifts in aggregate demand have no long-run effect on real GDP.

The Phelps Version of the Fooling Model

Simultaneously with the publication of Friedman's fooling model, Edmund S. Phelps of Columbia University developed a slightly different model in the same spirit, and he deserves equal credit for the invention of the natural rate hypothesis. In contrast to Friedman's distinction between the smart firms and the fooled workers, in Phelps's world everyone is equally fooled. Both firms and workers see the price rise in their industry and produce more, not realizing that the general price level has risen in the rest of the economy. Phelps developed one model in which firms are fooled while the workers are not. Firms see that the price of their product has increased, and they offer to hire more workers, not realizing that all other firms in the economy are experiencing the same increase in prices.

In another model, workers are isolated from information about the rest of the economy. Normally there is turnover unemployment (see Section 9-9 on pp. 307–09), as workers regularly quit one firm to go look for more highly paid work at other firms. But in a situation in which their own firm raises the wage, they stay with that firm instead of quitting. Thus the unemployment rate decreases even though, without their knowledge, all other firms in the economy have raised the wage by the same amount at the same time. The workers are fooled into a reduction in turnover unemployment, and the macroeconomic data register a decline in the unemployment rate.[3]

Criticisms of the Friedman and Phelps Versions of the Fooling Model

How do Friedman and Phelps justify their claim that workers will hold incorrect expectations for any significant period of time? Friedman's answer was that *firms have more accurate information than is available to workers.* Firms have this informational advantage, because they have a concentrated interest in a small number of prices of particular products and monitor them continuously. Workers, on the other hand, are interested in a wide variety of prices of the things they buy and have insufficient time to keep careful track. The workers do not immediately notice when the price level rises.

The Phelps version of the fooling model does not assume any particular informational advantage of firms over workers. *Everyone* is ignorant of what is happening in the general economy, as if they were stranded on small islands completely cut off from the rest of the world. Three telling criticisms have been directed against the assumption of imperfect information that drives both the Friedman and Phelps models. First, there is no reason to single out any particular ignorance of workers, as does Friedman and one of the Phelps models. Workers and their families buy many goods, particularly food, gasoline, and drug items, on a weekly or even daily basis, and they would discover almost immediately if the general price level had risen. Second, news about the level of prices and wages is published by the government and repeated on television newscasts every month, so any ignorance could last no longer than one month, far too short to explain multiyear business cycles. Third, if periods of high real GDP and a prosperous period of economic activity were *always* accompanied by an increase in the aggregate price level, workers and firms would learn from past episodes and realize that any period of current prosperity is doubtless accompanied by higher prices.

With realistic intelligence on the part of workers and firms, there is no room in macroeconomics for any model that bases its entire explanation of business cycles on ignorance and fooling. Any change in aggregate demand will move wages and prices up or down simultaneously and the economy will remain at its natural level of output, with no business cycles at all, just as in the classical self-correcting model of Figure 7-9 on p. 215.

Edmund S. Phelps (1933–)

Phelps co-invented the natural rate hypothesis, pioneered the concept of the "golden rule" of economic growth, introduced the concept of imperfect information into many branches of economics, and helped to invent the analysis of supply shocks as summarized in Chapter 8.

Robert E. Lucas, Jr. (1937–)

Lucas, a 1995 Nobel Prize winner, is the leading developer of the new classical macroeconomics; he merged the concept of rational expectations with the assumptions of market clearing and imperfect information.

17-3 The Lucas Model and the Policy Ineffectiveness Proposition

The Assumption of Rational Expectations

Despite its limitations, the Friedman and Phelps models, with their twin assumptions of market clearing and imperfect information, appealed to many economists. Preeminent among these was Robert E. Lucas, Jr., who took Friedman's

---

[3] Phelps's contributions appear in two important articles. See "Phillips Curves, Expectations of Inflation and Optimal Unemployment over Time," *Economica,* vol. 34 (August 1967), and "Money-Wage Dynamics and Labor-Market Equilibrium," *Journal of Political Economy,* vol. 76 (August 1968, Part II).

model one step further by introducing an improved treatment of the way workers form their view of the expected price level (P^e). Instead of following Friedman's rather unsatisfactory assumption that workers only gradually adapted their expectations of the price level (P^e) to the actual value of the price level, allowing themselves to be fooled for weeks or even months, Lucas introduced the theory of **rational expectations**. Thus the **Lucas model** contains three basic assumptions: market clearing, imperfect information, and rational expectations.[4]

Rational expectations need not be correct but must make the best use of available information, avoiding errors that could have been foreseen by knowledge of history.

The **Lucas model** is based on the three assumptions of market clearing, imperfect information, and rational expectations.

Expectations are rational *when people make the best forecasts they can with the available data*. It is important to recognize that these forecasts do not have to be correct, and so observing forecasting errors by individuals or professional economists does not constitute evidence against rational expectations. Instead, the theory of rational expectations argues that people do not consistently make the same forecasting errors.

For instance, the errors (or fooling) of the Friedman-Phelps model are not rational. If the observance of past history suggested that any increase in employment had always been accompanied by a reduction in the actual real wage to a point below the expected real wage, then workers should anticipate that such *a reduction in the real wage would always accompany offers by employers of higher employment* and the workers would refuse such job offers. Workers would not provide more employment, since in Figure 17-1 employment cannot rise above N_0 along the workers' labor supply curve (N^s) unless the actual real wage rises above the original level W_0/P_0. More generally, individuals should not make errors in the same direction week after week, especially in circumstances similar to those that have occurred before. The errors should be random, that is, independent of previous forecasting errors.

The Friedman-Phelps-Lucas Supply Function and the "Price Surprise"

The Friedman-Phelps model implies a positively sloped aggregate supply curve, as in the right frame of Figure 17-1. This supply curve is drawn again in Figure 17-2 and labeled $SAS_0(P_0^e)$, with the term in parentheses indicating that the position of the SAS curve is shifted whenever workers change their expectations of the price level. For instance, a higher expected price level (P_1^e) would shift the SAS curve up from SAS_0 to SAS_1.

Note that we have drawn the supply curve in Figure 17-2 as a straight, positively sloped line rather than as a curved line; this allows us to use a simple equation to represent the supply curve:

$$Y = Y^N + h(P - P^e) \qquad (17.1)$$

This states that real GDP (Y) is equal to natural real GDP (Y^N), plus an amount that equals a coefficient (h) times the excess of the actual price level over the expected price level. This excess of P over P^e is sometimes called the price sur-

---

[4] Robert Lucas did not invent the idea of rational expectations, but rather receives credit for applying it to macroeconomics. The original idea was applied to microeconomic issues and was set forth in John Muth, "Rational Expectations and the Theory of Price Movements," *Econometrica*, vol. 29 (July 1961), pp. 315–35. Lucas's seminal contribution is contained in two articles. The more accessible of these is Robert E. Lucas, Jr., "Some International Evidence on Output-Inflation Tradeoffs," *American Economic Review*, vol. 63 (June 1973), pp. 326–34. A more technical article that motivates some of the assumed underlying microeconomic behavior is "Expectations and the Neutrality of Money," *Journal of Economic Theory*, vol. 4 (April 1972), pp. 103–24.

Figure 17-2 The Short-Run Aggregate Supply Curve Drawn for Two Alternative Values of the Expected Price Level

The Friedman-Phelps-Lucas supply curve is fixed in position by the price expectations of workers. Real GDP can rise above Y^N in the light red region only when the actual price level (P) rises above the expected price level (P^e). An increase in the expected price level from P_0^e to P_1^e shifts the curve up from SAS_0 to SAS_1.

prise. For instance, if $P = 1.1$ and $P^e = 1.0$, while $Y^N = 10,000$ and $h = 4,000$, then the price surprise is 0.1 and actual real GDP will be

$$Y = 10,000 + 4,000(1.1 - 1.0) = 10,400$$

Although equation (17.1) or the equivalent SAS curve in Figure 17-2 is now usually called the Lucas supply function, such a function is also implied by the Friedman-Phelps model. As a compromise, we describe it as the Friedman-Phelps-Lucas supply function. What Lucas contributed was to take the Friedman-Phelps two assumptions of market clearing and imperfect information, assumed in equation (17.1), and add the third assumption that expectations are formed rationally.

Why does a positive price surprise make firms produce more output, as assumed by the Friedman-Phelps-Lucas supply function? Unlike the Friedman version of the model, which emphasizes fooling workers, the Lucas version emphasizes (with Phelps) an information barrier shared by workers and firms alike. Firms sell in competitive markets and have no control over their own prices, which rise and fall in response to demand. Lucas's firms are like small farmers who produce wheat or corn and whose sales prices are determined at the Chicago Board of Trade. For firms to produce more, the price of their product must rise relative to marginal cost, which depends on the cost of raw materials and other goods purchased from suppliers. Firms know their own price, but information barriers prevent firms from knowing about prices charged in other markets.

Self-Test

Answer the following questions according to the Friedman-Phelps-Lucas supply function:

1. Does a recession in which Y falls below Y^N require a price surprise? In which direction?

2. Does a boom in which Y rises above Y^N require a price surprise? In which direction?
3. What happens to the output gap $(Y - Y^N)$ when people learn the true price level and the price surprise vanishes?

Slope of the supply function: Local versus aggregate price shocks. To overcome these barriers, firms use rational expectations to form the best possible estimate of the prices charged in other markets (P^e). If the price of their own product (P) rises relative to P^e, and thus relative to marginal cost, firms will anticipate higher profits and increase production. Hence Y rises above Y^N, as shown in equation (17.1). Thus the Lucas explanation of the business cycle hinges entirely on whether or not business firms believe that an increase in the price of their own product *will be experienced equally* by other firms.

How do firms make this prediction? They apply rational expectations to their knowledge of past price behavior. If past movements in their own *prices have always been accompanied by similar movements in prices of suppliers*, then firms should expect that this will happen again. P^e will be assumed to rise in proportion to P, and output will not increase. But if the firm's price has often exhibited unique movements in response to "local conditions," for example, changes in weather altering the supply of wheat, then P may have risen without any accompanying increase in suppliers' prices. In this case, firms may guess that P^e has not risen as much as P and that this is a good time to produce.

In short, for products that in the past have experienced unique price movements in response to local conditions, firms may raise production substantially in response to a demand increase that raises the price of their own products. In contrast, for products that typically have experienced price movements that mimic those in the rest of the economy, firms will predict that their own price increase will be duplicated by increases in the costs of raw materials purchased from suppliers, and they will refuse to raise production.

A major contribution of Lucas's analysis is the conclusion that the supply response (h in equation 17.1) will be high for firms that have previously experienced unique price movements and low for firms that have experienced price movements mimicking those in the aggregate economy. Lucas also predicted that the supply response would be high in countries like the United States, where the inflation rate has been relatively stable (making unique movements in individual prices more important). In contrast, the supply response would be small in countries like Brazil and Argentina, where the inflation rate has ranged from zero to 1,000 percent per year over the past few decades, and where movements in the aggregate price level *shared by all firms* completely swamp the influence of price movements for particular products.

Lucas's key insight helps explain how countries like Brazil can have huge price movements with relatively small business cycles in real GDP. Stated another way, it explains why countries like Brazil can have a much steeper *SAS* curve than countries like the United States. Prior to Lucas, economists had assumed that the *SAS* curve in all countries would have roughly the same slope.

The Policy Ineffectiveness Proposition

The concept of rational expectations, which states that individuals use all available information in forming their expectations, leads to a startling prediction by Lucas and his followers. In a modern version of monetary impotence, Lucas argues that *anticipated monetary policy cannot change real GDP in a regular or predictable way.* Usually called the **policy ineffectiveness proposition** (PIP), Lucas's argument for monetary impotence startled the economics profession when it was developed in the early 1970s.[5]

PIP can be understood in terms of equation (17.1), which states that the monetary authority (the Fed) can change output only if it can find some method of creating a price surprise. That is, the Fed must move P while not simultaneously moving P^e by the same amount. Yet if the public *knows* that an increase in the money supply raises the price level, and if the Fed's monetary stimulus is announced or can be *predicted* from the Fed's past behavior, then the public will boost the expected price level P^e along with the increase in the actual price level. Real GDP will not budge from natural real GDP (Y^N).

> **Summary:** The policy ineffectiveness proposition states only that fully anticipated changes in the money supply cannot affect real GDP. It does not deny that a money surprise (an unanticipated change in the money supply) can alter the level of real GDP. But it implies that the Fed faces a considerable problem in creating such a money surprise, since the Fed cannot respond to economic events in the same way it has in the past.

The **policy ineffectiveness proposition** asserts that predictable changes in monetary policy cannot affect real output.

Problem: The Prompt Availability of Information

Although PIP created a revolution that dominated macroeconomic discussion in the late 1970s, by the end of the decade several weaknesses of PIP had been pointed out. The problem was not the Lucas contribution of rational expectations. Rather, the weakness was in the twin assumptions inherited from Friedman and Phelps, continuous market clearing and imperfect information, which made deviations of the current actual price from the expected price the *only* source of business cycle movements in real GDP. The assumption of imperfect information implies that business cycles would be eliminated if we had accurate current information about the aggregate price level.

This imperfect information aspect of the Friedman, Phelps, and Lucas models has been widely criticized. Aggregate price information is easily available with short lags of a month or two. With aggregate price information easily available, why should firms or workers take any action that might move them away from labor market equilibrium?

17-4 The Real Business Cycle Model

There now appears to be general agreement that the imperfect information theory of the business cycle is unsatisfactory, since information lags are too short

---

[5] While Lucas receives the main credit for the basic ideas underlying the Lucas model, the formal case for PIP was made by Thomas J. Sargent and Neil Wallace in " 'Rational' Expectations, the Optimal Monetary Instrument, and the Optimal Money Supply Rule," *Journal of Political Economy*, vol. 83 (April 1975), pp. 241–54.

to be a plausible source of multiyear business cycles.[6] New Keynesian economists favor abandoning new classical economics and the assumption of continuous market clearing. Instead, they concentrate on the underlying sources of wage and price rigidity, as shown later in this chapter. Meanwhile, new classical macroeconomists have turned to an alternative theory of the business cycle, one that still assumes continuous market clearing. Their new theory is the **real business cycle (RBC) model** of economic fluctuations.

The RBC model assumes that the origins of the business cycle lie in real (or supply) shocks rather than monetary (or demand) shocks. In terms of our graphical analysis, the main source of shifts in output lies in swings in the aggregate supply curve (both long-run and short-run), not the aggregate demand curve. Contrast this with the Lucas imperfect information approach, in which unanticipated monetary shocks lead to cycles in real output and employment (because information barriers prevent business firms from accurately anticipating movements in prices charged in markets other than their own). In terms of the Friedman-Phelps-Lucas supply function (equation 17.1), the RBC approach is not based on price surprises, that is, deviations of P from P^e. Instead, the RBC approach states that fluctuations in Y are caused entirely by fluctuations in natural real GDP itself, Y^N.

What are these real (or supply) shocks that cause business cycles and account for the term "real" business cycle model? Shocks can include new production techniques, new products, bad weather, new sources of raw materials, and price changes in raw materials. Recall that the Lucas model failed to consider that information barriers are too short-lived to explain the *length* and *persistence* of actual business cycles. In contrast, the RBC approach assumes that these supply shocks are highly persistent, meaning that a favorable shock lasts several years, dies away smoothly, and is replaced by an adverse shock that lasts several years. It is important to note that the RBC theory simply *assumes* and does not explain the persistence of business cycles that undermined the Lucas approach.

In the RBC model, the economy responds to these persistent supply shocks according to the new classical assumption of continuous equilibrium. Firms produce the amount they desire at prices and wages that respond flexibly to changing economic conditions, and hire the number of workers they want; workers obtain exactly the number of hours of work that they desire at the market-determined real wage.[7] Our aggregate supply curve diagram introduced in Chapter 7 illustrates these aspects of the RBC model.

The **real business cycle (RBC)** model explains business cycles in output and employment as being caused by technology or supply shocks.

---

[6] For instance, Robert Barro, who made important contributions to the development of the Lucas approach and PIP, was convinced by the problems addressed in the previous section that "the upshot of these arguments is that the new classical approach does not do very well in accounting for an important role of money in business fluctuations." See Robert J. Barro, "New Classicals and Keynesians, or the Good Guys and the Bad Guys," *Schweiz, Zeitschrift für Volkswirtschaft und Statistik*, Heft 3, 1989. More recently, Robert Lucas has admitted that "Monetary shocks just aren't that important. That's the view I've been driven to. There's no question that's a retreat in my views." See John Cassidy, "The Decline of Economics," *The New Yorker* (December 2, 1996), p. 55.

[7] Two of the most influential papers in the development of the RBC approach are Finn E. Kydland and Edward C. Prescott, "Time to Build and Aggregate Fluctuations," *Econometrica*, vol. 50 (November 1982), pp. 1345–70; and Robert G. King and Charles I. Plosser, "Money, Credit, and Prices in a Real Business Cycle," *American Economic Review*, vol. 74 (June 1984), pp. 363–80. A sympathetic exposition is Bennett T. McCallum, "Real Business Cycle Models," in Robert J. Barro, ed., *Modern Business Cycle Theory* (Cambridge, MA: Harvard University Press, 1989), pp. 16–50. A less technical introduction is Charles I. Plosser, "Understanding Real Business Cycles," *Journal of Economic Perspectives*, vol. 3 (Summer 1989), pp. 51–77.

Figure 17-3 Effect of an Adverse Supply Shock on Output and Employment in the Real Business Cycle Model

In the top frame, F_0 is the normal production function. N_0^d is the normal labor demand curve. An adverse movement in supply conditions, like bad weather for growing crops, shifts the production function down to F_1 and the labor demand curve down to N_1^d. In normal times the economy operates at point B in the upper and lower frames, and in bad times at point V. The decline in employment depends on the slope of the labor supply curve; if the labor supply curve were a vertical line instead of a positively sloped line like N_0^s, the economy would move to Z instead of V. Employment would remain fixed and output would fall only from Y_0 to Y_0'.

The Labor Market in the RBC Model

The top frame of Figure 17-3 exhibits the production function (F), which shows how much output can be produced by each additional worker.[8] An adverse supply shock leads to a downward shift in the production function, for instance from the normal curve F_0 to the bad shock curve F_1, implying a decline in the productivity of each worker. In the lower frame the labor demand curve, which shows the marginal product of labor, shifts down in response to the adverse supply shock from the line labeled N_0^d to the line N_1^d.

The effect of the adverse supply shock on both output and employment depends on the slope of the labor supply curve. If this slope is positive, as along the line labeled N_0^s, then a lower real wage induces workers to supply less labor (working fewer hours or leaving the labor force). Since the economy is always in equilibrium in the RBC model, the demand for labor shifts as a result of the supply shock from point B to point V. Employment falls from N_0 to N_1, while output falls from Y_0 to Y_1, seen in the upper frame.

---

[8] We were first introduced to the production function in Figure 10-1 on p. 325. That production function related output per worker (Y/N) to capital per worker (K/N). In contrast, the production function in Figure 17-3 relates output (Y) to the number of workers (N).

A different slope of the labor supply curve would lead to a different conclusion. Imagine that the labor supply curve, instead of being N_0^s, is a vertical line rising above N_0 through points Z and B. Then the economy's equilibrium point would be shifted downward by the adverse supply shock from B to Z. The shock would cause no change in employment, and in the upper frame there would be a much smaller decline in output, from Y_0 to Y_0'. Thus the RBC model's ability to explain why employment declines in real-world recessions requires a positive slope of the labor supply schedule, as shown by the line N_0^s.[9]

> ### Self-Test
> Answer the following questions according to the RBC theory:
> 1. Why does output increase in a business expansion?
> 2. What are examples of events that would raise output in a business expansion?
> 3. What are examples of events that would reduce output in a business contractor?

Labor Supply Behavior and Intertemporal Substitution

As we have seen, it is critical for the RBC model that the labor supply curve have a positive slope, as drawn in the bottom frame of Figure 17-3. If the labor supply curve were vertical, the model would be able to explain business cycles of output (as from point B to Z in the upper frame) but would not be able to explain fluctuations of employment over the business cycle. Thus an explanation of the positive slope of the labor supply curve is an important component of RBC analysis.

The traditional microeconomic analysis of labor supply decisions stresses two conflicting effects of an increase in the real wage. A higher real wage increases the reward for work as compared to leisure (the substitution effect). But a higher real wage also raises real income and makes people want to consume more of all normal goods, including leisure, which means reducing work (the income effect). In drawing a positively sloped labor supply curve in Figure 17-3, we simply assume that the substitution effect dominates the income effect.

The RBC approach also assumes that the substitution effect is dominant, but stresses a particular dimension of substitution that takes place over time. This type of substitution is called **intertemporal substitution**. It occurs when workers reallocate the amount of working time in response to changes in the real wage. In good times, when the real wage is high, workers choose to work more. And they take more leisure in bad times, when the real wage is low.

Students face such choices during their college years. Many students want to take one summer off to go to Europe, while planning to work in the other summers. A sophomore has two summers left before graduation. Which summer should he or she choose to go to Europe? Obviously, the summer with the best opportunities to earn relatively high wages should be chosen for work, and the European trip should be taken in the summer when high-paying jobs are scarce.

Intertemporal substitution occurs when workers work more in periods of high real wages and less in periods of low real wages. It also occurs when producers raise output in periods of high prices and reduce output in periods of low prices.

---

[9] The effect of an adverse supply shock in shifting the labor demand curve downward was previously shown in the upper frame of Figure 11-6 on p. 378, but there the labor supply was not shown explicitly.

Variations in the interest rate introduce another element into the choice. If the real interest rate is high enough, it would pay to work in the first summer and postpone the trip to the second summer. Even if the wages earned in the first summer are somewhat lower than they are expected to be in the second summer, the extra interest earned on the savings account containing the earnings from the first summer would make that a better choice. In short, labor supply increases in response *either* to a high real wage or a high real interest rate.

This example highlights a problem in applying the theory of intertemporal substitution to the real world—how can students predict which future summer is likely to provide the most high-paying job opportunities? If even financial experts make major mistakes in predicting interest rates, are students any more likely to be able to predict whether interest rates will be higher or lower in future summers?

17-5 New Classical Macroeconomics: Limitations and Positive Contributions

Assessment of the Real Business Cycle Model

Both the RBC model and the conventional *AD-SAS* graphical analysis of Chapter 7 agree that supply shocks can cause business cycles. Why, then, is the RBC model so controversial? The criticisms concern the unique components of the RBC analysis: the emphasis on technological shocks as the *primary* cause of business cycles, the failure to include prices or money, and the RBC interpretation of what happens in labor markets during business cycles.

Nature of technology shocks. Critics focus on two aspects of the RBC model's treatment of technology shocks. While it is plausible that *advances* in technology may occur at an irregular pace, causing cycles in the growth rate of output, the implication that recessions are caused by *retreats* in technology ("forgetfulness") strikes some critics as implausible. Defenders of the RBC model respond that there are several types of events that have the same effect as a decay in technology, even if people do not literally forget how to produce efficiently. These include bad harvests, oil price shocks, and government regulations that require heavy investment and extra workers to reduce air and water pollution.[10]

Perhaps a more serious charge distinguishes between the aggregate economy and the behavior of individual industries. Unlike the *IS-LM* model of Chapter 4, the RBC model does not incorporate a multiplier effect that can magnify the impact of shocks on the economy. Therefore, to explain big recessions, the model needs big shocks. But technology is unique to particular industries. Highly distinctive technological innovations that, for instance, increase the speed of a Windows desktop computer have little impact on the

---

[10] The Great Depression is a major embarrassment for the advocates of the RBC model, since their approach forces them to interpret the massive unemployment of the 1930s as entirely voluntary, and the cause of the 27 percent decline in real GDP between 1929 and 1933 as a massive adverse supply shock, an implausible episode of "forgetfulness" in which firms and workers forgot one-quarter of the technological knowledge they had in 1929. For a contrary view that the 1930s were a period of unusually rapid technical progress, and that implicitly the Great Depression was caused by a decline in aggregate demand rather than aggregate supply, see Alexander J. Field, "The Most Technologically Progressive Decade of the Century," *American Economic Review*, vol. 93, no. 4 (September 2003), pp. 1399–1413.

International Perspective

Productivity Fluctuations in the United States and Japan

Productivity is simply the ratio of output to inputs and measures the efficiency with which inputs are used. Labor productivity is output per unit of labor input. As we learned in Chapter 11, a more general concept, called multifactor productivity (MFP), is output per unit of total input, including not just labor but also capital, energy, and imported materials.

Interest in the RBC model is motivated by productivity shocks that vary procyclically, that is, in the same direction as the business cycle. How important are procyclical fluctuations of MFP, that is, the ratio of output to total input? The charts on the facing page show the growth rate of output and input for the United States and Japan. Whenever output grows more rapidly than input, MFP growth is positive, as shown by the red-shaded area. Whenever output grows more slowly than input, MFP growth is negative, as shown by the blue-shaded area.

In the top frame of the figure, the data for the United States show that in booms, output growth consistently rises more than input growth (defined here as an average of growth in labor and capital input); during recessions, output growth consistently falls more than input growth. As a result, MFP growth is negative in such recession periods as 1970, 1974–75, 1980–82, and 1991. MFP growth is most strongly positive when output itself is growing most rapidly, as in 1966, 1973, 1976, 1984, 1992, 1998, and 2004.

In the bottom frame of the figure, the data for Japan show some striking differences. First, input growth is much smoother from year to year, with fewer cycles, particularly between 1975 and 1990. Because input growth was so remarkably stable, Japan was largely able to avoid the periodic episodes of massive layoffs that plagued the United States during recession periods.

And, because input growth was so stable, Japanese MFP growth was even more strongly procyclical than in the United States.

The stability of Japanese input growth was very different after 1990. Input growth dropped almost to zero in 1992–94 and was negative in 1999 and 2001–02. The ups and downs of Japanese input growth after 1998 mirror output growth, much more like the U.S. pattern than in Japan before 1990.

A second difference is that output growth in Japan never fell below zero in any year between 1965 and 1998, except for 1974. This contrasts with the United States where output growth turned negative in 1974–75, 1980, 1982, and 1991. A third difference is that the pattern of MFP growth (the difference between output and input growth) is quite different in Japan from that in the United States. MFP growth in Japan was positive in every year after 1975, except by very small amounts in 1980, 1983, and 1998. In contrast, MFP growth was negative in numerous periods in the United States, especially during the two oil shocks of 1974 and 1979–82. Overall, however, the pattern of input and MFP growth in Japan has grown more similar to that in the United States since 1990.

The procyclical behavior of MFP growth illustrated here is consistent with the procyclical technology shocks that drive the RBC model. However, it is also consistent with other theories, such as the idea that it is costly to hire and fire workers, with the result that firms adjust labor input only partially in response to changes in output.

---

productivity of coal miners. At an industry level, one would expect technological shocks (good and bad) to occur randomly, so that favorable shocks in some industries would largely cancel out adverse shocks in other industries. Any bad shock large enough to cause an economywide recession (considering that it would be partly canceled by good shocks in other industries) would be highly visible in industry data. Yet the proponents of the RBC model have as yet failed to identify any such shocks, particularly negative ones, other than the two OPEC oil price shocks.

Price and output changes. Although recently there has been some attention to real demand shocks, particularly those associated with government

17-5 New Classical Macroeconomics: Limitations and Positive Contributions

[Figure: United States and Japan output and input growth, 1965–2005. Shaded regions indicate: Output grows faster than input; MFP growth is positive. Output grows slower than input; MFP growth is negative.]

Sources: United States output and input from Bureau of Labor Statistics multifactor productivity database. Japan output and labor input from Groningen Growth and Development Center; Japan capital input from Japan Industry Productivity (JIP) database.

spending, the basic RBC model is based on an alternation of good and bad supply shocks, each persisting by about as long as an average U.S. business cycle. But this leads to a troublesome implication: If business cycles occur when the aggregate supply curve shifts back and forth but the aggregate demand curve remains fixed, then prices should rise in recessions and fall in booms. The business cycle should look much like the market for wheat, with low prices and high output in years of good harvests, and with high prices and low output in years with bad harvests.

The key problem is that prices are sometimes positively related to output changes, as in the Great Depression, and sometimes negatively related to output changes, as in the supply shock episodes of the 1970s and early 1980s. This suggests that business cycles are caused both by demand and supply shocks, not just by supply shocks, just as in the *AD-SAS* model of Chapter 7 and the inflation-output model developed above in Chapter 8.

Real wages and employment. As we have seen, both the RBC model and the graphical *AD-SAS* analysis can easily explain why, due to shifts in the production function, output changes in response to supply shocks. But in order to explain why employment fluctuates in the same direction as output over the business cycle, the labor supply curve must be positively sloped, as in Figure 17-3. To support this interpretation, we should observe that real wages move *procyclically*, that is, in the same direction as output. Note that this is the opposite prediction of the Friedman fooling model, which depicts the economy as operating continuously along the labor demand curve, so that the real wage rate must fluctuate *countercyclically*.

However, most of the statistical evidence shows that (with the exception of the big oil shocks of the 1970s and early 1980s) there is no systematic movement of real wages. If anything, there is a slight tendency of prices to rise more than wages in economic booms, implying countercyclical real wages. As we saw in Table 7-1 on p. 223, real wages actually rose during the Great Depression from 1929 to 1933, even while the unemployment rate was rising from 3 to 25 percent. Thus the central mechanism that drives employment fluctuations in the RBC model is absent in most U.S. business cycles other than the oil shock episodes of the 1973–82 period.

Positive Contributions of New Classical Macroeconomics

Despite their limitations, both the Lucas and RBC versions of new classical theory have a strong appeal to a broad range of economists. What are the attractions of new classical theory?

Rational expectations: linking micro- and macroeconomics. The assumption of rational expectations appeals to economists, since it requires that people do not repeat their mistakes. Instead, people make the best use of all available information to guide their economic behavior. Such an approach is much more appealing than the alternative assumption that people make repeated mistakes in the same direction, period after period. The rational expectations hypothesis also has appeal because of its grounding in microeconomics. This means that the assumption of rational expectations in macroeconomics parallels the basic microeconomic assumptions of profit maximization and utility maximization.

The theory of efficient financial markets. Many of the ideas developed by the new classical economists have been applied successfully to markets where continuous market clearing is a reasonable assumption. This is particularly true of financial markets, including the stock market, bond market, foreign exchange market, and the markets for agricultural and crude commodities, like sugar and gold. The theory of efficient markets incorporates the assumption of rational expectations. Expectations are assumed to incorporate all available information, implying that stock prices jump the instant new information is received and that there are no opportunities to make extraordinary profits on the stock market without access to inside information.

Greater understanding of economic policy. The idea that individuals in the private part of the economy have rational expectations has improved our understanding of economic policy. Even if long-term wage and price contracts impede the flexibility of wages and prices, as discussed later in this chapter, those who negotiate contracts attempt to do so with full information on what policymakers are likely to do. For instance, wage negotiators who suspect that the government will allow rapid inflation after a supply shock are likely to demand full cost-of-living adjustments in their contracts. In contrast, past refusal of a government to allow rapid inflation following a supply shock, as in the case of the German Bundesbank in the 1970s, will increase wage negotiators' confidence that full cost-of-living protection is not necessary.

Recall that the policy ineffectiveness proposition (PIP) developed as part of the Lucas information-barrier approach implies that fully anticipated monetary policy changes have no effect at all on output. While PIP does not appear to be valid in U.S. history, a milder and more acceptable proposition is that fully anticipated policy changes have *smaller* effects than unanticipated changes. The expansionary policies pursued in the United States in the 1960s caused the output ratio to exceed 100 percent for a few years, but not permanently. In contrast, in extreme inflationary episodes (hyperinflation), radical changes in government policy seemed to halt inflation without a major decline in output.[11]

Pervasive effect on economic research. Even if the new classical theories of the business cycle are subject to substantial skepticism, new techniques of analysis introduced by these theories have had a major influence on the way economists study variables such as consumption, investment, and the foreign exchange rate. The understanding of extreme episodes of inflation in places like Argentina and Brazil, as well as Turkey, is just one contribution of techniques introduced by new classical economists. The distinction between anticipated policy changes and policy "surprises" has improved our understanding of policy changes.

17-6 Essential Features of the New Keynesian Economics

Common Elements of the Original and New Keynesian Approaches

The adjective *new* distinguishes modern developments in Keynesian theory from the original Keynesian model developed during the Great Depression by Keynes and his followers and reviewed in Section 7-9 on pp. 216–21. The original Keynesian model combines a theory of shifts in aggregate demand (based on the *IS-LM* model of Chapter 4) with a theory of aggregate supply (based on the arbitrary assumption of a fixed nominal wage). Unlike the old and new classical models, with their assumptions of continuous equilibrium or market

---

[11] See Thomas J. Sargent, "The Ends of Four Big Inflations," Chapter 3 in his *Rational Expectations and Inflation* (New York: Harper & Row, 1986).

clearing, the Keynesian approach assumes that markets do not clear continuously. Hence the Keynesian model, either the original or the new variety, is often dubbed a **non-market-clearing model**, conveying the failure of prices to adjust rapidly enough to clear markets within a relatively short interval after a demand or supply shock. If slow price adjustment makes the return of the economy to natural output a long, drawn-out process, markets can fail to clear for years, as in 1929–41 or 1980–86.

In a **non-market-clearing model**, workers and firms are not continuously on their respective demand and supply schedules, but rather are pushed off these schedules by the gradual adjustment of prices.

The appeal of Keynesian economics stems from the evident unhappiness of workers and firms during recessions and depressions. Workers and firms *do not act as if they were making a voluntary choice to cut production and hours worked.* A simple thought experiment is enough. Ask yourself these questions about the real world: Can each worker during every day of a recession sell all the labor desired at the going wage and price? Would every worker in a recession refuse a job offer at the going wage and price? Then ask these related questions about business firms: Can each business firm sell all the output desired at today's prices? Would each business firm turn away customers at today's prices? The history of business cycles is punctuated by recessions and depressions lasting several years, during which workers and firms could not sell all the labor and output desired at the going wages and prices. Thus a theory of business cycles based on the failure of markets to clear, the new Keynesians believe, is more realistic than the new classical approach based on continuous market clearing.

In new classical models, business firms base their output level on news regarding their own price level, obtained from auction markets like the Chicago Board of Trade. In contrast, Keynesian non-market-clearing models turn the role of prices and output upside down. New Keynesian business firms base their choice of the price level on news regarding their own sales obtained by watching the ebb and flow of customers coming through the front door.

The New Keynesian Model

The **new Keynesian economics** explains rigidity in prices and wages as consistent with the self-interest of firms and workers, all of which are assumed to have rational expectations.

A **nominal rigidity** is a factor that inhibits the flexibility of the nominal price level due to some factor, such as menu costs and staggered contracts. Such factors make it costly for firms to change the nominal price or wage level.

A **real rigidity** is a factor that makes firms reluctant to change the real wage, the relative wage, or the relative price.

A **menu cost** is any expense associated with changing prices, including the costs of printing new menus or distributing new catalogs.

Staggered contracts are wage contracts that have different expiration dates for different groups of firms or workers.

What, then, is the difference between the original and **new Keynesian economics**? Both assume that prices adjust slowly. But unlike the original model, which assumed a fixed nominal wage, the new Keynesian approach *attempts to explain the microeconomic foundations of slow adjustment of both wages and prices.* The new Keynesian approach borrows—some would say steals—the concept of rational expectations from new classical economics. From traditional microeconomics, the new Keynesian approach borrows the core assumptions that firms maximize profits and workers maximize their own well-being or utility. The achievement of new Keynesian economics is to show how firms and workers make choices that maximize business profits and worker well-being at the microeconomic level, but that have adverse social consequences at the macroeconomic level.

Two distinctions are essential to the new Keynesian model. The first is between wage setting in labor markets and price setting in product markets. The second distinction is between **nominal rigidity** and **real rigidity**. Markets will not clear if something prevents the full adjustment of nominal prices, that is, prevents movements in nominal prices (P) proportionate to movements in nominal demand (X). The first group of new Keynesian theories explains wage or price stickiness as the result of factors that make prices costly to adjust. Included in this category are **menu costs** and overlapping **staggered contracts**, which limit the flexibility of both prices and wages. These factors are said to explain *nominal rigidity,* because they deal with barriers to the adjustment of nominal prices.

New Keynesian theories also explain *real rigidities*, the stickiness of a wage relative to another wage, of a wage relative to a price, or of a price relative to another price. Theories that explain real rigidities in labor markets include the efficiency wage model, which we will examine later in the chapter. Critics note that theories of real rigidities do not explain nominal rigidity, since nothing prevents each individual agent from indexing its nominal price to nominal aggregate demand, that is, automatically changing P by the same percentage change as X, thus leaving real output (Y) unaffected. We will be particularly interested in the arguments given by new Keynesians for the absence of such full indexation, which in turn would suggest that theories of real rigidities *are* relevant to the explanation of sticky prices and wages.[12]

17-7 Why Small Nominal Rigidities Have Large Macroeconomic Effects

A basic insight of Keynesian theory, both old and new, is that decisions of individual business firms do not always serve the best interests of society. The original Keynesian model argued that stimulative fiscal policy might be needed to avoid an economic slump resulting from some combination of monetary impotence, a failure of self-correction, and fixed wages. The new Keynesian model does not place any special emphasis on fiscal policy as opposed to monetary policy. Instead, it shows how rational profit-maximizing decisions by business firms may have adverse consequences for society.

Price Setting by a Monopolistic Firm

The new classical and new Keynesian approaches view business firm behavior from different perspectives. In the new classical model, firms are assumed to be perfectly competitive "price takers," with no control over the price. This approach may describe farmers producing goods sold on an **auction market**, like wheat or corn sold on the Chicago Board of Trade. Such farmers choose how much to produce but have no control over price. However, the assumption of perfect competition does not apply to firms in most other sectors of the economy. Imperfect competition describes a market in which the number of sellers is sufficiently small that each firm is a price setter rather than a price taker. For instance, manufacturing firms, airlines, and many other firms can choose exactly what price to set, but they have no control over the amount sold.

The new Keynesian approach assumes that small menu costs will deter imperfectly competitive firms from constantly changing their prices and shows that menu costs do not have to be large to explain price stickiness. To see why, look at the left frame of Figure 17-4, where we review the elementary theory of

An **auction market** is a centralized location where professional traders buy and sell a commodity or a financial security.

---

[12] The best source of accessible articles on the new Keynesian version of macroeconomics can be found in a symposium in the *Journal of Economic Perspectives,* Winter 1993, vol. 7, no. 1. David Romer provides an introduction to several of the models reviewed in this chapter; Bruce Greenwald and Joseph Stiglitz contrast the "new" and "old" Keynesians; James Tobin provides new insights on the old Keynesian model; and finally Robert G. King provides an insightful bridge between the new Keynesians and the *IS-LM* model.

Figure 17-4 The Price-Setting Decision of a Monopolist

In the left frame the red slanted line is the initial demand curve and the orange MR_0 line is the marginal revenue curve. The horizontal blue line is the initial marginal cost schedule MC_0. Output is chosen where MR equals MC. Price (P_0) is shown at point E_0, the intersection of the demand curve with the quantity produced. In the right frame the purple area shows the consumer surplus, the area below the demand curve and above the price level P_0. Profit is the green rectangle, the area to the left of Y_0 between P_0 and C_0.

price setting by a monopolist.[13] Our diagrams are particularly simple, since they assume that marginal cost is constant along the horizontal line labeled initial MC_0. There are no fixed costs, so marginal cost and average cost are the same. The quantity produced (Y_0) is determined at the point where the marginal revenue line (MR_0) intersects the marginal cost curve. The price is determined at point E_0, where the chosen quantity Y_0 intersects the initial demand curve. The right frame of Figure 17-4 shows exactly the same situation but identifies the areas that indicate the business firm's profit and the consumer surplus enjoyed by the purchasers of the product.[14]

The Firm's Response to a Decline in Demand

To understand how recessions in real output may occur, let us now examine the effects of a decline in the demand for the product. The decline is shown in the left frame of Figure 17-5 by the downward shift from the dashed red ini-

---

[13] The presentation in this section is a simplified version of the first half of N. Gregory Mankiw, "Small Menu Costs and Large Business Cycles: A Macroeconomic Model of Monopoly," *Quarterly Journal of Economics*, vol. 100 (May 1985), pp. 529–37.

[14] **Review:** When the demand curve is a straight line, the marginal revenue curve is always drawn so that it lies halfway between the demand curve and the vertical axis. The demand curve shows how much each purchaser is willing to pay for the product. At the price P_0, any purchaser whose willingness to pay is greater than P_0 enjoys a consumer surplus, reflecting the fact that the price charged is less than the willingness to pay.

17-7 Why Small Nominal Rigidities Have Large Macroeconomics Effects

Figure 17-5 The Price-Setting Choice of a Monopolist Facing a Decline in Demand

In the left frame a decline in demand shifts the demand curve down from the initial demand line to the new demand line. To maintain fixed output at Y_0, the price must fall from P_0 to P_1 and marginal cost must fall to required MC_1. To decide whether or not to reduce price to the profit-maximizing level P_1, the firm weighs the gain in profit (area B minus area A in the right frame) against any menu cost that may be involved in changing price. If the firm fails to cut price below P_0, the level of output falls from Y_0 to Y_1, and society loses the area D plus B, which is much larger than B minus A.

tial demand curve to the solid red new demand curve. To avoid a recession, the firm must produce the same amount as before, Y_0, which intersects the new demand curve at E_1. For unchanged output to be chosen by the profit-maximizing firm at point E_1, it is necessary that marginal cost decline by the amount shown between the initial MC_0 and required MC_1 lines. The lower blue line is called "required" because a decline in MC is needed to avoid a recession.

Will the firm avoid cutting output by reducing price from P_0 to P_1? Perhaps not, if there are menu costs, because the gain in profit by cutting price may not be sufficient to cover the menu costs. Recall from the right frame of Figure 17-4 that the profit box is a rectangle lying above the MC line with its upper right corner at the equilibrium point E_0 or E_1. Comparing the two profit boxes, by lowering the price from P_0 to P_1 the firm gains the profit area marked B and loses the profit area marked A.

Self-Test

1. Why does area A measure the profit lost?
2. Why does area B measure the profit gained?
3. Why must the area B be greater than A?
4. What does area F represent and how does it differ from area B?

Despite the gain in profit from cutting price, the firm may choose not to cut price if the menu cost, which we can call z, is large enough. The firm cuts price if the gain in profit $(B - A)$ exceeds z, but not if z exceeds $B - A$. As drawn in Figure 17-5, the area B minus the area A is only 23 percent of the total profit that would be earned at the lower price (P_1). So a menu cost greater than 23 percent of profit would deter the firm from cutting price.

But society loses much more if the firm decides not to cut price. Output drops from Y_0 to Y_1, and society loses the consumer surplus area D and the profit area B. In the diagram, the area $D + B$ is 66 percent of the total profit that would be earned at the lower price P_1. Thus the firm's decision not to cut price can cause society to lose more than triple the amount lost by the firm.

The Macroeconomic Externality and the Effects of Sticky Marginal Cost

Society's loss from the firm's profit-maximizing decision not to cut price is called a **macroeconomic externality**. The firm does not pay the costs its decision imposes on society, just as a firm causing air pollution or water pollution may not pay the costs imposed on the victims of dirty air and water. In the case of air and water pollution, society is better off if the government reduces the output of the polluting firm, for instance, by imposing a tax on smoke. Similarly, society would be better off if all firms cut price together. Their failure to do so, even though such price cuts are in society's best interest, is called a **coordination failure** because there is no guiding invisible hand to return to the firms some portion of the amount society as a whole would gain if they were to cut their price.

The analysis of Figure 17-5 assumes that the marginal cost declines instantly in proportion to the decline in demand. This is required to maintain output unchanged at the profit-maximizing price. Now let us look back at the left frame of Figure 17-5 and consider the case in which marginal cost does not decline at all and remains at the dashed blue line labeled initial MC_0. Why might marginal cost be sticky, failing to decline at all? There are many reasons, some of them discussed later in this chapter. Among these are contracts that fix wages and contracts that fix the prices of materials purchased from suppliers. If the wage paid to labor and the price paid to all suppliers remain fixed, then the MC line would stay fixed as well. In this case, the profit-maximizing price is at E_2, not E_1.[15]

The most important implication is that *with sticky marginal cost, menu costs are not needed at all to explain how recessions occur.* Any factor that prevents supplying firms from cutting the price of materials, or even delays such price reductions, will tend to make marginal costs sticky, implying that E_2 is the point that maximizes profit for the firm in Figure 17-5, not point E_1.

A **macroeconomic externality** is a cost incurred by society as a result of a decision by an individual economic agent (worker or business firm).

A **coordination failure** occurs when there is no private incentive for firms to act together to avoid actions that impose social costs on society.

17-8 Coordination Failures and Indexation

Our discussion of the new Keynesian model has now covered a variety of factors that may inhibit the prompt adjustment of prices in response to a change in nominal GDP, thus automatically implying a response in real GDP. Leaving aside

---

[15] To simplify Figure 17-5, the marginal revenue line is not shown. To draw it in, find the point halfway along the horizontal axis between the vertical axis and the demand curve. Then draw a slanted line going up and to the left; it intersects the lower required MC_1 line directly above Y_0. Point E_2 lies directly above the intersection of this marginal revenue line and the higher initial MC_0 line.

menu costs, the full adjustment of prices to a demand shock as depicted in Figure 17-5 depends on the instantaneous response of marginal cost. Following a negative demand shock, output must fall if marginal cost declines less than marginal revenue. There are two reasons why firms may rationally expect marginal cost to move differently than marginal revenue. First, marginal revenue may move with aggregate nominal demand but marginal costs may not. This would occur if a firm believes that its costs depend on many specific factors other than the perceived level of aggregate nominal demand (for example, volatile supply conditions, price changes for imported materials, changes in cost created by exchange rate movements). Second, with a fixed nominal aggregate demand, marginal cost would also remain fixed, while a local shift in demand (for example, a decline in smoking in response to new laws banning smoking in restaurants and bars) could reduce marginal revenue, providing another reason why marginal cost may move differently than marginal revenue.

The Input-Output Approach and the Absence of Full Indexation to Nominal Demand

To explain real price rigidity, the local-versus-aggregate cost distinction must apply to a world with many different firms purchasing supplies from each other. The automaker buys headlights from a firm that buys filament from a firm that buys copper from a firm that may mine copper using trucks purchased from the automaker. The input-output model emphasizes the importance of multiple buyer-supplier relations; each firm is simultaneously a buyer and a seller.[16] With only two firms, each supplying the other, firms could easily disentangle the local-versus-aggregate components of their costs. But with thousands of firms buying thousands of components, containing ingredients from many other firms, the typical firm has no idea of the identity of its full set of suppliers. Since the informational problem of trying to guess the effect of a demand shift on the average marginal cost of all these suppliers is probably impossible to solve, the sensible firm just "waits for the next e-mail" for news of cost increases and then passes them on as price increases.

The input-output approach provides a critical contribution to understanding not just real price rigidity, but also nominal rigidity. The standard argument against the theories of real rigidity suggested above is that they are consistent with nominal flexibility achieved through indexation to nominal demand. Yet the input-output approach emphasizes how high a fraction of a firm's costs are attributable to suppliers of unknown identity, with some unknown fraction produced in foreign countries under differing aggregate demand conditions. This environment would give pause to any firm considering nominal-demand indexation of the product price, since the failure of all suppliers to adopt similar indexation could lead to bankruptcy.

There is nothing to guarantee any confidence that supplier firms will adopt any aggregate indexation formula, for no single supplier acting alone has any incentive to do so. The rewards are too small and the penalties of acting alone are too great, *for a firm's viability depends on the relation of price to cost, not price to nominal GDP.* No individual firm has an incentive to take the risk posed by nominal GDP indexation, which would take away from the firm the required essential control of the relation of price to cost.

---

[16] The input-output approach is developed in Robert J. Gordon, "What Is New-Keynesian Economics?" *Journal of Economic Literature*, vol. 28 (September 1990), see especially pp. 1150–52.

Coordination Failures and Daylight Saving Time

The failure of marginal cost to decline instantly and fully in response to nominal demand reflects a coordination failure. Marginal cost would drop if all workers and firms cut wages and prices together by the same percentage as nominal demand. But each is afraid to act first, since they would lose out if other workers and firms failed to act also. Daylight saving time provides a simple example of government intervention in the face of a coordination failure. All firms may want to open and close earlier in the summer to allow more time in the late afternoon for recreational activities, but none does so because each store wants to keep the same hours as other stores. By simply decreeing a shift in the clock, the government solves the failure of individual stores to coordinate their actions.

17-9 Long-Term Labor Contracts as a Source of the Business Cycle

Long-term labor contracts are agreements between firms and workers that set the level of nominal wage rates for a year or more.

Long-term labor contracts are an important source of sticky marginal cost faced by business firms. Just as monopolistic firms impose social costs on society while maximizing profits, so too do firms and workers that enter into long-term labor contracts. Nevertheless, as the new Keynesian model emphasizes, there are good reasons why workers and firms desire such contracts. In this section, we study the features of long-term labor contracts.

Characteristics of Labor Contracts

In the United States, with few exceptions, formal labor contracts are negotiated in the union sector, which covers about 10 percent of the labor force. Industries that are heavily unionized include much of the manufacturing sector (especially autos, electrical machinery, rubber, and steel), as well as substantial parts of the construction and transportation industries (especially airlines, railroads, and trucking). Industries that tend to be nonunion include fast food and other services, retailing, and parts of manufacturing (especially apparel and textiles).

The behavior of wage rates in the union sector of the economy is more important than this 10 percent figure would suggest, since the wage rates that are negotiated in the union sector set a pattern that is imitated (although not copied exactly) by nonunion workers. The leading role of unions in moderating the flexibility of nonunion wages is evidenced by the evolution of union and nonunion wages. Nonunion wages are only moderately more flexible than union wages over the business cycle, and they exhibit a substantial degree of stickiness. One reason that unions set a pattern for nonunion wages is that nonunionized firms (such as Delta Airlines) do not want their employees to quit and join a rival unionized firm (such as American Airlines) or to vote to become unionized, and so they tend to pay wage rates similar to those in unionized firms.

Wage rigidity at colleges and universities. Academic institutions provide ample evidence that wages and salaries can be very rigid without unionization, because few staff or faculty members are members of unions.

Professors typically receive a salary that is fixed for the entire academic year, for example, from September to August, and it is typically determined in the previous spring without regard to macroeconomic conditions. Professors who are relatively young and tempted by offers from other universities receive relatively large salary increases, but only once per year, and older or less "marketable" faculty members receive small salary increases, also once per year. In some institutions the hourly rate paid to graduate student teaching and research assistants remains unchanged for several years. Macroeconomic conditions may affect university salaries only with a long lag, as when the recession of 2001 caused fiscal deficits for many state governments and they cut back budgets at state-financed universities in 2003 and 2004.

Scheduled wage changes and COLAs. Wages negotiated under labor contracts are not completely rigid or fixed. Rather they change when a new contract is negotiated. With labor contracts, the nominal wage rate is set at the time of negotiation for the duration of the contract. Wage changes during the lifetime of the contract are allowed, but they are set in advance at the time of the negotiation. There are two types of prenegotiated changes. First, there is usually a scheduled change that takes effect in each year of multiyear contracts. Second, there is sometimes a **cost-of-living agreement (COLA)** that sets in advance the change in the nominal wage that will be allowed for each percentage point of future inflation. For instance, a contract might specify that a worker will receive a 3.0 percent increase in each of the three years of a three-year contract, plus 100 percent of the inflation that occurs in each of the three years. Thus, if the actual inflation rate turned out to be 0.0 percent in a particular year, the wage increase would be 3.0 percent. Alternatively, with an actual inflation rate of 10.0 percent, the wage increase would be 13.0 percent. A COLA contract that gives workers a fixed increase, plus 100 percent of the inflation rate, is called "full COLA protection," whereas a fixed increase plus 50 percent of the inflation rate would be "half COLA protection."

Cost-of-living agreements (COLAs) provide for an automatic increase in the wage rate in response to an increase in the price level.

COLAs are intended to help workers maintain their real wage. Without COLAs, the real wage rate is reduced by inflation. The following example shows that a sudden change of the inflation rate from zero to 10 percent would cause a sharp decline in the real wage if the worker had no COLA protection. With full COLA protection (a nominal wage change equal to 3.0 percent plus the inflation rate), the real wage change is unaffected by inflation. With half COLA protection, the nominal wage change in the example is equal to 3.0 percent plus 0.5 times the inflation rate.

	Nominal wage change with COLA protection			Real wage change with COLA protection		
	None	Half	Full	None	Half	Full
Inflation of zero	3.0	3.0	3.0	3.0	3.0	3.0
Inflation of 10 percent	3.0	8.0	13.0	−7.0	−2.0	3.0

In this example each of the figures for real wage change is equal to the corresponding figure for nominal wage change minus the assumed inflation rate.

Self-Test

Under each of the following circumstances, tell whether or not the growth rate of the real wage is rigid, showing no response at all to a change in the rate of inflation.

1. With no COLA protection?
2. Half COLA protection?
3. Full COLA protection?

17-10 "Real" Sources of Wage Stickiness

Thus far, our discussion of the new Keynesian approach has emphasized nominal rigidities, particularly the menu costs of changing nominal prices and long-term contracts for both wages and prices that are incompletely indexed. These contracts imply that a business firm's marginal cost does not respond instantly to a decline in demand. Consequently, the contracts reinforce the role of menu costs in dissuading firms from changing their prices by the full amount needed to avoid changes in output and hence recessions. Now we turn to theories that attempt to explain real rigidities, that is, the slow adjustment of wages relative to prices or to other wages. The most prominent of these is the efficiency wage theory.

The Efficiency Wage Model

This theory explains real rigidities by stressing the reasons why firms would not want to cut the wage that they pay *relative to the wage paid by other firms*. A firm believes that the productivity of its workers will increase if the firm pays a higher wage. There will be greater effort by workers, reduced shirking or goofing off on the job, lower turnover (which reduces training costs), the ability to attract higher-quality workers, and improved morale and loyalty.

The efficiency wage result is obtained in a simple model with identical, perfectly competitive firms. Each firm has a production function in which labor input is multiplied by an efficiency factor (e) that depends on the wage rate paid relative to that paid by other firms (W), as shown in the left frame of Figure 17-6. Raising W raises labor cost by making firms pay more to workers, but reduces labor cost per unit of output by making workers more efficient. As shown in the left frame, initially a 1 percent increase in W raises e by more than 1 percent, so labor cost declines, as shown in the right frame. Firms continue raising W until it reaches the equilibrium value W^*, which occurs at the point where raising W by 1 percent raises efficiency by exactly 1 percent, thus leaving labor cost per unit of efficiency unchanged. Firms will refuse to raise W any further, since this would raise wage payments more than it would boost efficiency. The value W^* is called the efficiency wage.

Because W^* is completely fixed by whatever technological and institutional factors determine the e function, the firm's reaction to any change in demand for its product is to cut employment while maintaining the wage rate at W^*. Firms have no incentive to cut wages, since this would actually increase their wage bill per unit of output. The efficiency wage approach seems to explain numerous

Figure 17-6 The Relationship Between the Relative Wage Rate and Worker Efficiency

In the left frame, worker efficiency increases faster than the relative wage up to point W^* and more slowly thereafter. As a result, labor cost per unit of efficiency reaches a minimum at W^*, as shown in the right frame.

aspects of microeconomic labor market behavior, once we allow different groups of workers to have different levels of efficiency at any given relative wage rate. For example, the theory predicts the widely observed phenomenon that workers line up eagerly for high-paying jobs but firms hire only a few of them, maintaining the high wage in order to be able to pick and choose rather than reduce the wage rate in the face of the abundant supply of workers.

Self-Test

1. According to the efficiency wage theory, how is unemployment explained?
2. Assuming that the unemployed are willing to work at a lower wage rate than existing workers, why does the firm not simply fire the existing workers and hire the unemployed in their place at a lower wage?
3. What can the unemployed workers do to obtain jobs in light of the refusal of firms to hire them?

As a theoretical underpinning of the new Keynesian approach to wage and price rigidity, the efficiency wage model explains why firms resist cutting their wage rates in response to a decline in demand, and why they do not hire unemployed workers who may be willing to work for a lower wage. This approach is still subject to the same criticism as long-term wage contracts, that full wage indexation would allow firms simultaneously to maintain worker effort by paying the optimal relative wage W^* while maintaining a flexible nominal wage rate. However, for the reasons discussed in Section 17-8, firms and workers are unwilling to risk full wage indexation.

17-11 Assessment of the New Keynesian Model

The new Keynesian model introduces two improvements to the graphical short-run supply (*SAS*) analysis of Chapter 7. First, Chapter 7 simply assumed that shifts in the *SAS* curve would occur gradually. In contrast, the new Keynesian model provides the missing reasoning for wage and price adjustment to be gradual, not instantaneous. Second, Chapter 7 suffered from *asymmetry*, in assuming that firms were always on their labor demand curve but workers were forced off their labor supply curve. In contrast, the new Keynesian model allows *both* firms and workers to operate in disequilibrium.

Contrast with other theories. The new Keynesian model seems to solve the main dilemma of the other business cycle theories examined in Chapter 7 and the first part of this chapter, that is, how to explain observed business cycles without unrealistically assuming away output fluctuations (as does classical economics), assuming complete wage rigidity (as does the original Keynesian model), assuming unrealistic fooling of firms and workers (the Friedman-Phelps model), failing to explain persistent unemployment in the presence of easily available information on prices and the money supply (the Lucas information-barrier model), or requiring procyclical real wage movements and continuous labor market equilibrium (the real business cycle model).

Workers and firms in the new Keynesian model are rational, finding it *privately advantageous* to enter into long-term agreements that may have a *macroeconomic externality*, imposing employment and output losses on other workers and firms. The other approaches fail to provide an adequate theory of the business cycle, partly because they do not distinguish between the *private interest* (for instance, signing contracts) and the *collective interest* in avoiding business cycles.

Criticisms of the New Keynesian Approach

The new Keynesian model has been criticized for suggesting *too many* reasons why wages and prices are sticky. Some of these reasons, like staggered overlapping wage and price contracts, have been criticized on the grounds that business cycles were common before the rise of labor unions in the United States in the 1930s and 1940s. To explain business cycles in eras or industries where unions are not strong, we must rely on other new Keynesian explanations that do not require written contracts. Several of these, including the input-output approach and the efficiency wage model, do not depend on the existence of organized labor unions.

Testing of the new Keynesian approach is in its infancy. There is as yet no agreement on which of the various sources of nominal and real rigidity have been most important. The degree of wage and price rigidity differs greatly across countries and in different historical eras. For instance, prices were more flexible before World War II in Japan and France than in the United Kingdom and United States. Prices are clearly more flexible in countries like Argentina and Brazil that have experienced high and variable inflation than in countries like the United States. Research that would explain why this is true has barely begun.

One reason that prices may be more flexible in some countries than in others can be linked to rational expectations. When firms and workers expect the government to pursue inflationary policies, they are more likely to insist on full cost-of-living protection and to invest time in trying to predict changes in government policy. They may also be unwilling to enter into long-term staggered contracts.

Summary

1. Initially the new classical macroeconomics attempted to build a theory of the business cycle based on continuous market clearing and imperfect information. One of these theories was Milton Friedman's fooling model, in which workers are "fooled" into providing extra labor input because they do not have as prompt or complete information on the aggregate price level as do firms. Edmund S. Phelps at the same time developed theories in which *both* firms and workers have imperfect information.
2. Robert Lucas added rational expectations to the Friedman-Phelps assumptions of continuous market clearing and imperfect information. The central tool of the new classical model is the Friedman-Phelps-Lucas supply curve, which attributes business cycles in real output to expectational errors, also called "price surprises."
3. The central implication of the Lucas model is the policy ineffectiveness proposition, which states that monetary policy cannot affect output either through an *announced* policy change or through a change that reacts to past events in a consistent and predictable way.
4. The second new classical approach is called the real business cycle (RBC) model. It explains business cycles in output as the result of slowly changing (persistent) shocks to supply conditions and technology. It explains cycles in employment as the result of intertemporal substitution by workers, who choose to work harder in periods of high real wages and enjoy more leisure in periods of low real wages.
5. The RBC model has been criticized because no one has yet identified specific technology shocks at the industry level that are large enough to explain actual recessions and depressions, except for the oil price shocks of the 1970s and 1980s. It has also been criticized for two unrealistic implications, that prices and output always move in opposite directions and that real wages vary procyclically.
6. The new Keynesian approach shares with the original Keynesian approach an explanation of business cycles based on the failure of prices to adjust sufficiently to maintain a continuous equilibrium in the labor market. The new Keynesian model differs by developing microeconomic explanations of wage and price rigidity based on rational expectations and profit-maximizing behavior.
7. Small menu costs can cause large social costs of recessions by giving profit-maximizing firms a reason not to adjust the price level to every change in demand. Sticky marginal costs imply that firms will reduce output in response to a reduction in demand, even in the absence of menu costs.
8. One source of sticky marginal costs is the role of long-term labor contracts in preventing the prompt adjustment of the nominal wage rate to changes in demand.
9. One source of real rigidity is the efficiency wage. In the efficiency wage model, firms are reluctant to cut wages for fear of reducing the efficiency of their employees and of causing their best employees to quit.

Concepts

natural rate hypothesis
rational expectations
Lucas model
policy ineffectiveness proposition (PIP)
real business cycle (RBC) model
intertemporal substitution
non-market-clearing model
new Keynesian economics
nominal rigidity
real rigidity
menu cost
staggered contracts
auction market
macroeconomic externality
coordination failure
long-term labor contracts
cost-of-living agreement (COLA)

Questions

1. How does the Friedman-Phelps "fooling" model differ in terms of who misperceives changes in prices and/or wages and how the labor market clears?
2. Explain how the Friedman-Phelps "fooling" model predicts that an expansionary monetary policy can lead to increased output in the short run, while the Lucas model suggests that such a policy would have no effect on real output.
3. In what ways are the Friedman-Phelps "fooling" model and the Keynesian model similar? In what ways do they differ?
4. In what ways are the Friedman-Phelps "fooling" model and the Lucas model similar? In what ways do they differ?
5. What is meant by the term "price surprise"? What role does it play in determining the slope of the supply function in Lucas's "local" explanation of business cycles? Exposit Lucas's explanation for why the supply function in Brazil is likely to be steeper than that in the United States.
6. A firm has the choice of hiring either permanent or temporary employees when it needs to expand its output. If the firm hires temporary workers, it does not have to pay severance costs if it lets the workers go, which it will have to pay if it lays off anyone hired on a permanent basis. On the other hand, the wage rate paid to temporary workers exceeds the wage rate paid to permanent workers. The firm knows that the Fed follows a Taylor Rule and weighs equally the inflation rate and the output ratio. Given that the firm has rational expectations, discuss what the firm must consider in deciding whether to hire temporary or permanent workers when it sees its sales rise as the economy expands. How will its decision be affected if (a) the unemployment rate has just started falling or (b) the economy has been expanding for a number of years?
7. The policy ineffectiveness proposition (PIP) asserts that anticipated monetary policy cannot change real GDP in a regular or predictable way. Suppose that a monetary policymaker not only accepts the PIP, but is interested in adopting monetary policies that stabilize the economy. Explain what monetary polices this policymaker would advocate.
8. Explain why critics of the Friedman-Phelps and Lucas models argue that those models fail to provide a satisfactory explanation of business cycles.
9. How does an adverse supply shock affect the production function? What is the effect of an adverse supply shock on the demand for labor?
10. What does the real business cycle model predict will happen to prices, real wages, and employment in response to an adverse supply shock? Is this prediction matched by real-world experience? What explanation(s) for the real-world behavior of prices and real wages do real business cycle theorists offer?
11. What is meant by intertemporal substitution? How is the slope of the labor supply curve related to the ability of a real business cycle model to explain the real-world behavior of the real wage rate and employment over the course of the business cycle?
12. How does the real business cycle model differ from the Lucas model? Does it explain the persistence of business cycles?
13. What was the important assumption made with respect to wage rates in the original Keynesian model? How does the new Keynesian model differ in its approach to that assumption?
14. "Classical and new classical firms choose output, but new Keynesian firms choose price." Explain.
15. Explain why it is believed that greater pressure is placed on employment and output in response to shifts in aggregate demand under a situation of long-term staggered labor contracts than would be the case under shorter-term, uniform-expiration-date contracts.
16. What is a macroeconomic externality? How do long-term agreements impose a macroeconomic externality on the economy? What other sources of macroeconomic externalities are identified in this chapter?
17. In what ways are the original Keynesian model and the new Keynesian model similar? In what ways do they differ?
18. What is meant by the terms *nominal* and *real rigidities?* If nominal rigidities could be completely removed from the U.S. economy, would that solve the problem of output and employment fluctuations during business cycles?
19. Is it possible for there to be a business cycle without fluctuations in employment and output? Which, if any, school(s) of thought suggested that this would be the normal case?
20. What insights into the economy's adjustment to aggregate demand fluctuations does efficiency wage theory suggest? Is this theory consistent with new Keynesians' explanations of business cycles?
21. What are the similarities and differences between the new Keynesian model and the new classical and real business cycle models?
22. The new Keynesian model relies on the concept of coordination failure to explain why demand and supply shocks lead to undesirable output and employment fluctuations. What role does this suggest for government stabilization policy? Is this a point with which the new classical model agrees? Why?
23. Suppose there is a substantial drop in U.S. autonomous net exports. How would this affect output, employment, and the price level according to the following business cycle models: classical, Keynesian, Friedman-Phelps, Lucas, real business cycle, and new Keynesian? Why?

Problems

1. You are given the following two forecasts of the price levels by persons A and B, as well as the actual price level for the next ten periods. Initially, the price level is 100.

Period	1	2	3	4	5	6	7	8	9	10
Person A	102	104	106	109	112	116	119	122	122	127
Person B	103	103	106	112	114	118	120	121	126	126
Actual	102	104	107	110	114	117	120	123	125	128

   (a) For each person, calculate the difference between the actual price level and that person's forecast of the price level.
   (b) In terms of how rational expectations are described in this chapter and your answer to part a, which person's forecasts are most consistent with the concept of rational expectations?

2. Suppose that the following Friedman-Phelps-Lucas short-run aggregate supply function describes how real GDP responds to "price surprises" for countries I and II:

   $$Y = Y^N + h(P - P^e)$$

   where $Y^N = 9{,}000$ and $P^e = 1.5$. In country I, $h = 1{,}000$ and in country II, $h = 2{,}500$.
   (a) Calculate the levels of real output (Y) in countries I and II when the price level equals 1.00, 1.25, 1.50, 1.75, and 2.00.
   (b) According to Lucas, which country has the greater price stability?

3. Given the Friedman-Phelps-Lucas supply function in problem 2, what would be the equilibrium real income in both countries if people accurately expected that the price level were 1.00? 1.50? 2.00?

4. Suppose that the equation for the aggregate demand is $Y = 7{,}000 + 2{,}400/P$. In this real business cycle model, the equation for natural real GDP is $Y^N = 9{,}000 +$ technology shock. The technology shocks for periods 1–6 are given below.

Period	1	2	3	4	5	6
Technology shock	−400	−80	0	1,000	400	0

   (a) Calculate the points on the aggregate demand curve when the price level equals 0.75, 0.80, 1.00, 1.20, 1.25, and 1.50.
   (b) Compute the price level and real GDP in periods 1–6. Describe the cyclical behavior of real GDP and the price level in this real business cycle model.

5. Using Figures 17-4 and 17-5 as a guide, assume a price-setting monopolist firm with no fixed costs and constant marginal cost (MC_0) of $3.00 faces an original demand curve $P = 10 - 0.1Y$.

   (a) What is the equation of the firm's marginal revenue curve MR_0? (Recall that for a linear demand curve, MR is twice as steep as demand.)
   (b) What quantity will the firm produce to maximize profits? What price will it set to ensure that it sells all that it produces? (*Hint:* Recall that profit is maximized when $MC_0 = MR_0$.)
   (c) At the profit-maximizing price, what is the firm's total revenue? Total cost? Profit?
   (d) What is the value of consumer surplus? (*Hint:* Recall that the area of a triangle equals one half the area of the rectangle formed by its two sides.)

6. Now assume that the firm described in problem 5 faces a fall in demand such that the new demand curve is $P = 8 - 0.08Y$.
   (a) What is the equation for the firm's new marginal revenue curve (MR_1)?
   (b) If the firm is to maintain its original level of output (Y_0), what must happen to its marginal cost of production? What is the "*required*" marginal cost (MC_1)? (*Hint:* Set Y in MR_1 equal to Y_0.)
   (c) At what price on the new demand curve can the firm sell the original quantity of output?
   (d) If MC remains at $3.00, and there are no *menu costs*, what output would the firm choose to produce to maximize profits? What price will it set? (*Hint:* Find the quantity and price associated with point E_2 in Figure 17-5.)
   (e) If the firm maintains the original price, what is the maximum quantity that it can sell, given the new lower level of demand? (*Hint:* Find Y_1 in Figure 17-5.)
   (f) Calculate the profits lost and gained if the firm chooses to reduce the price from the original price to the new lower price associated with the original quantity. (*Hint:* Calculate the values for area A and area B in Figure 17-5 as they apply to this problem.)
   (g) What is the maximum value for *menu costs* under which we could expect this firm to maintain its original output (assuming that it could reduce its marginal costs to the required level)?
   (h) If *menu costs* are greater than $22.00, and marginal costs cannot be reduced below $3.00 due to contractual input prices, would the firm seek to maximize profits by choosing the solution found in problem 6(d) above (that is, where $MC_0 = MR_1$)?

Self-Test Answers

pp. 553–54 (1) Yes, there must be a price surprise when Y falls below Y^N in a recession. When the price level is surprisingly low, firms conclude that the current period is a bad time to produce (since they receive an unrewardingly low price for their product). Hence, they reduce production voluntarily. (2) Yes, there must be a price surprise and the price level must be surprisingly high. (3) The output gap must vanish when the price surprise disappears.

p. 559 (1) A business expansion is explained by RBC theory as the result of a favorable or beneficial supply shock, which makes factors of production unusually productive. Employment increases as workers add more hours and accept more jobs in the belief that the higher real wage, paid out by firms as a result of high productivity, makes the period an attractive one in which to expend extra work effort. (2) Examples are new inventions or discoveries of new oil reserves. (3) Examples are a drought that reduces agricultural output of an adverse energy supply shock.

p. 567 (1) and (2) If a price P_0 is charged, profit is the area between P_0, the new demand curve, and the "Required MC_1" line, that is, the sum of the rectangles A and F. If a price P_1 is charged, then profit is the area between P_1, the new demand curve, and the "Required MC_1" line, that is, the sum of the rectangles F and B. Since F is in common to both situations, shifting from a price of P_0 to a price of P_1 means losing the profit rectangle A and gaining the profit rectangle B. (3) Why is B greater than A? Because E_1 is the position that maximizes profit with the new demand curve and the required MC_1 line. Thus total profits must be greater when producing at E_1 than at E_0 (given the reduction in demand), so the amount of profit gained by cutting the price from P_0 to P_1 must be positive. (4) F represents the profit earned in both situations, whereas B represents the extra profit earned when the price is reduced.

p. 572 (1) With no COLA protection, the growth rate of the real wage will be reduced by an increase in the rate of inflation, especially when the faster inflation is caused by an adverse supply shock. (2) With half COLA protection, the growth rate of the real wage will be reduced less than with no COLA protection. (3) With full COLA protection, the growth rate in the real wage is completely unaffected by inflation. This makes the growth rate of the nominal wage rate change fully in response to the change in the inflation rate.

p. 573 (1) Unemployment is explained because the firm refuses to hire the unemployed, even at a wage rate lower than is being paid to current workers, because the firm does not believe that it would thereby lower its labor cost. (2) It believes that the unemployed workers, if hired at a lower wage, will be less productive than current workers. (3) The unemployed workers are condemned to low-skill jobs unless a rising tide of aggregate demand creates a shortage of workers and induces firms to hire them.

CHAPTER 18

Conclusion: Where We Stand

Experience, some people say, is like a light on a caboose, illuminating only where we aren't going. But we scrutinize the past for its elements of prologue, and consolation.
—George F. Will

We have now finished the formal task of learning macroeconomic theory. We have also found through the Case Study text sections and International Perspective boxes that macroeconomics is a subject with close ties to the real world. Many events in U.S. history illustrate important themes in macroeconomic theory. And differences between the economic performance of the United States and other nations help to clarify theory and to highlight the differences among nations that are easy to explain and those that are difficult. For instance, we learned in Chapter 9 that it is relatively easy to explain why some countries experience hyperinflation—their governments have allowed very rapid growth in the money supply; that growth in turn results from their need to finance large budget deficits. But it is relatively hard to explain why high unemployment in Europe has persisted since the early 1980s; this provides an example of an unsettled issue in macroeconomics.

18-1 The Evolution of Events and Ideas

Events and ideas evolve together.[1] The Case Studies in this book show how theoretical ideas can be directly applied to the understanding of historical events. But the process also works in reverse—the outcome of historical events often challenges theorists and overturns theories, leading to the evolution of new theories. Some of the central ideas of macroeconomics, including those proposed by the old Keynesians, the new classicals, and the new Keynesians, can be understood as a reaction to events. In some cases, the evolution of the economy helped to resolve a debate between different schools of thought. In other cases, events occurred that could not be understood until new theories were formulated.

In the rest of this chapter we will review some of the events that were sufficiently important to cause a change in ideas, starting in the next section with the Great Depression. The following sections treat the post–World War II period (the postwar era), dividing it in two parts, before 1970 and after 1970, and emphasizing the performance of the domestic U.S. economy. Then we examine

---

[1] The title of this section and the analysis in this chapter are in part an updated version of Robert J. Gordon, "Postwar Macroeconomics: The Evolution of Events and Ideas," in Martin S. Feldstein, ed., *The American Economy in Transition* (Chicago: University of Chicago Press, 1980), pp. 101–62.

the effect of events in the world economy, focusing primarily on the debate between advocates of fixed and flexible exchange rates. Two final sections summarize what we know, and what we still don't know—a remaining set of macro mysteries that are the focus of continuing debate, disagreement, and research in macroeconomics.

18-2 The Reaction of Ideas to Events, 1923–47

The most dramatic and unexpected event in the macroeconomic history of the United States was the Great Depression of the 1930s, consisting of the Great Contraction of 1929–33, followed by a weak recovery that failed to bring the unemployment rate below 10 percent until the outbreak of World War II. In plotting the behavior of central macroeconomic variables in Figure 18-1, we begin in 1923, in order to contrast the highly volatile 1930s and 1940s with the placid 1920s.

The Economy's Behavior in the 1920s and 1930s

The four-frame format of Figure 18-1 is identical to that used subsequently to examine the postwar era. The top frame plots nominal GDP growth and M1 growth, indicating changes in the velocity of M1 by shading. The second frame plots nominal GDP growth and the inflation rate, so that the shaded areas indicate real GDP growth. The third frame plots the output ratio and the unemployment rate, and the bottom frame plots the long-term and short-term interest rates.

Prior to the Great Depression, the dominant idea in macroeconomics was the old classical approach, based on the quantity theory of money—a theory that emphasized the strong self-correcting properties of the private economy and the tendency for changes in the money supply to influence mainly the price level rather than output (Section 7-8 on pp. 214–16). The placid 1923–29 period seemed consistent with the old classical approach. As shown in Figure 18-1, the inflation rate was almost zero, unemployment remained below 5 percent, and the output ratio remained near 100 percent. There were minor variations in the growth rate of nominal and real GDP and minor recessions in 1924 and 1927.

Everything changed in the 1930s. Growth in everything became negative during 1930–33, including M1, nominal and real GDP, and the price level. The output ratio fell to 67 percent, and the unemployment rate soared to 25 percent. As shown in the bottom frame, the corporate bond rate jumped in 1929–32 as increasing bankruptcies made investors shy away from financing corporations.

The most notable facts about the Great Depression were not only its severity but its length. The unemployment rate was still above 10 percent in 1940.[2] While real GDP growth was rapid during the 1933–37 recovery, that growth

---

[2] There is an ongoing debate as to whether the unemployment rate in the last half of the 1930s is exaggerated, due to the counting of workers on government relief programs as unemployed rather than employed. The original critique of the official statistics is in Michael Darby, "Three and a Half Million U.S. Employees Have Been Mislaid: Or, An Explanation of Unemployment, 1934–41," *Journal of Political Economy*, vol. 84 (February 1976), pp. 1–16. A balanced assessment of the debate is contained in Robert Margo, "Interwar Unemployment in the United States: Evidence from the 1940 Census Sample," in Barry Eichengreen and T. J. Hatton, eds., *Interwar Unemployment in International Perspective* (Dordrecht, Boston, and London: Kluwer Academic Publishers, 1988), pp. 325–52.

Figure 18-1 Key Macroeconomic Variables, 1923–47

These plots of annual data show the growth rates of nominal and real GDP, M1, and the GDP deflator. Also shown are the output ratio, the unemployment rate, the long-term interest rate, and the short-term interest rate. Notable features are the collapse of everything between 1929 and 1933, the weak 1933–37 recovery, the 1938 recession, and the takeoff of the economy as wartime spending began in 1940. Persistent unemployment and a continued low output ratio are the main features of the Great Depression.

was sufficient only to bring the output ratio back to 84 percent, far below the normal level of 100 percent. And despite very low short-term interest rates, a sharp setback occurred in the 1938 recession.

The Keynesian Revolution

Events cause the evolution of ideas. The Great Depression killed the old classical approach, stimulated John Maynard Keynes to develop his *General Theory*, and fostered the immediate worldwide acceptance of the Keynesian revolution (Section 7-9 on pp. 216–21). Rendered obsolete was the classical idea that a decline in the money supply would mainly reduce the price level, because in 1929–33 output fell so far and recovered so slowly. Also rendered obsolete was the quantity theory idea that velocity was stable, because it depended mainly on transaction practices; in 1929–33 the economy's collapse was caused as much by a drop in velocity as a drop in the money supply.

The underpinning of the Keynesian revolution was the concept of aggregate demand. Because the price level is sticky (that is, not sufficiently flexible to respond fully and completely to each change in nominal GDP), any change in aggregate demand would cause a change in output and employment. Unlike the old classicals, with their sole emphasis on the money supply, the Keynesians stressed other factors that could cause shifts in aggregate demand, including fiscal policy and changes in business and consumer confidence.

The old Keynesian school of thought was heavily influenced by the behavior of the economy in the late 1930s, the time when Keynes's *General Theory* was being avidly discussed and absorbed at academic seminars throughout the United States. As shown in Figure 18-1, the money supply soared in 1939 and 1940, yet velocity growth was negative and unemployment remained high. Short-term interest rates were near zero, so that the economy could not be stimulated by further reductions in short-term interest rates. This led to the expression that monetary policy was like "pushing on a string," or "You can lead a horse to water but you can't make it drink." The only answer was stimulative fiscal policy, and the economy's prompt recovery in response to higher defense spending in 1941–42 reinforced the supremacy of fiscal policy for a whole generation of economists.[3]

World War II

Macroeconomists usually omit from their analyses economic events during World War II, because government regulations skewed the normal operation of the economy. Output soared and unemployment fell almost to zero, but there was virtually no inflation, a feat made possible only because of stringent legal price controls. By 1944, government spending amounted to fully half of GDP, shifting the *IS* curve far to the right, but interest rates did not rise because the

---

[3] The stimulus of World War II began long before Pearl Harbor, due initially to military purchases by foreign countries and investment in factories producing military goods. Exports and domestic investment began to grow soon after the European war began in September 1939, and especially after the fall of France in June 1940. The United States introduced the military draft in September 1940, and as early as November 1940, there were 400,000 construction workers building military training camps for 1.4 million newly drafted soldiers.

government required the Fed to "peg" the long-term government bond interest rate, printing the money to purchase any bonds that the government issued to cover its massive fiscal deficit. After the war, in 1946–47, when the price controls were lifted, inflation soared (thus reducing the real wealth of those who had patriotically purchased government bonds during the war), but interest rates remained steady, as the Fed maintained its agreement to peg long-term government bond interest rates through 1951.

> **Summary** The big event of the interwar period was the Great Depression. This event spawned a big idea, the Keynesian revolution, with its emphasis on aggregate demand, sticky prices, and fiscal policy. The behavior of the economy during World War II seemed to support the main themes of the Keynesian revolution.

18-3 The Reaction of Ideas to Events, 1947–69

We now turn to the postwar U.S. economy, the main focus of this book. Macroeconomic behavior in the first part of the postwar period, 1948–69, is shown in Figure 18-2. Each of the four frames corresponds to Figure 18-1.

The Economy in the 1950s

The economy's performance in the 1950s looks much better in retrospect than it did at the time. The period 1950–53 was dominated by the economic effects of the Korean War, including a brief surge of inflation in 1950–51 and very low unemployment during 1951–53. Huge increases in government spending in 1950–53 and a subsequent decrease in 1953–54 caused wide swings in the *IS* curve. The 1953–54 recession was very mild and, in retrospect, exhibits the potency of easy monetary policy. A small reduction in the short-term interest rate (the federal funds rate) was sufficient to let loose a torrent of spending on housing and automobiles, causing 1955 to be a vintage year in economic annals.[4] With both the Korean War and the threat of a renewal of the Great Depression behind them, American businesses and consumers were eager to stock up on housing and durable goods to match their newly elevated estimate of their "permanent income" (Section 15-4 on pp. 489–93).

The short-term Phillips Curve trade-off became evident in 1956–57, when inflation increased even though unemployment remained above Korean War levels.[5] In response, the Fed allowed interest rates to creep up, and this ultimately choked off the boom and brought on the sharp recession of 1957–58. Unemployment rose to the highest level yet seen in the postwar period. After a brief recovery, the economy promptly fell into another recession in 1960–61.

---

[4] Nobel Prize winner Paul A. Samuelson of M.I.T. once announced to a graduate class that he would "flunk any student who could explain why auto sales in 1955 were so high." The auto boom was caused by the combination of attractive new models and new V-8 engines for the low-priced "Big Three" cars, by an easing of terms on installment loans, and by the normal accelerator effect that occurs in a period of rapid income growth (Section 16-3).

[5] There were price controls in effect during the Korean War, albeit milder than the draconian controls of World War II.

Figure 18-2 Key Macroeconomic Variables, 1948–69

The variables are the same as in Figure 18-1. Notable are the recessions of 1949, 1953–54, 1957–58, and 1960–61. Nominal and real GDP variations seem more closely related to velocity changes than changes in the money supply. Both inflation and interest rates began an uptrend after 1965.

Changes in Economic Ideas Through 1960

The old Keynesian school of thought held sway throughout this period. Wide swings in nominal GDP growth were mainly accounted for by changes in velocity, not by changes in the money supply. Changes in military spending during and after the Korean War were the main source of instability. Ironically, despite the new commitment to fiscal stabilization policy brought about by the Keynesian revolution and the Employment Act of 1946, government military spending was the most important single destabilizer of aggregate demand.

However, leaving aside the political forces that caused the Korean War, fiscal policy managed well in this period. In 1950, tax rates were raised immediately to finance the war, helping to dampen the surge of consumer buying and moderate the 1950–51 inflation. Further, taxes were cut in early 1954, moderating the 1953–54 recession and setting the stage for the 1955 boom. The monetary policy record is mixed; money was tightened too much in early 1957, helping set off the 1957–58 recession, but at least monetary easing was prompt once the 1953–54 and 1957–58 recessions had begun.

The main shift in ideas concerned the aggregate supply curve. Unlike the 1930s or the recession of 1949, prices did not decline at all in the recessions of 1953–54 and 1957–58. Just as U.S. economists were puzzling over the seeming inflexibility of prices, in 1958 A. W. Phillips published his famous article on the Phillips Curve, based on historical data for the United Kingdom (see Section 8-2 on pp. 235–38).

The Economy in the 1960s

Prior to the 1990s, the longest economic expansion in U.S. economic history occurred between 1961 and 1969, shown in the third frame of Figure 18-2 by the long period of low and stable unemployment and the high output ratio. In its early phases the expansion responded to easy monetary policy, and then to massive fiscal stimulus in the form of income tax reductions in 1964–65 and, beginning in 1965, spending for the Vietnam War. While unemployment fell to the lowest rates since the Korean War, inflation steadily accelerated.

Stabilization policy in the 1960s went too far in stimulating the economy. The tax cuts of 1964–65 occurred when the output ratio had already reached 100 percent, and these cuts had a particularly potent effect, since they were accommodated by stimulative monetary policy. Although monetary policy initially did not accommodate Vietnam spending (note the spike in the federal funds rate in 1966–67), monetary growth was allowed to accelerate in 1968. The great failure of fiscal policy was the long delay in raising taxes to finance the Vietnam War.

Intellectual Revolutions of the 1960s

Three new ideas dominated economic discussions in the 1960s: the new economics of Walter Heller, the monetarism of Milton Friedman and others, and the natural rate hypothesis, reflecting the influence of both Milton Friedman and Edmund S. Phelps.

Of these, the new economics occurred earliest and fell out of favor fastest. When President Kennedy was inaugurated in early 1961, the economy was in recession, with unemployment at almost 7 percent. Believing that monetary stimulus was a weak tool, Kennedy's chief economic advisers (including Walter Heller, Arthur Okun, and future Nobel Prize winners Robert Solow and

James Tobin) insisted that a new type of fiscal activism was necessary, consisting of changes in personal income taxes.[6] To stimulate the economy, they recommended a tax cut, which was implemented in early 1964 (with a second stage in 1965). To pay for the Vietnam War, they urged President Johnson in 1966 to enact an income tax surcharge.

Two events caused fiscal activism, later derided as "fiscal fine tuning," to fall out of favor. First was the legislative lag (Section 14-4 on pp. 456–59), which lasted 18 months, before enactment of the 1968 tax surcharge. Second was the permanent income hypothesis (Section 15-4 on pp. 489–93), which predicted that temporary tax changes would have a small multiplier effect. This prediction proved to be the case. By 1969–70, fiscal activism was discredited, and with it an underpinning of the old Keynesian school of thought.[7]

Another important weakness of Heller's new economics was the failure to understand the role of the monetary-fiscal policy mix (Section 4-11 on pp. 116–21). Heller's complaint that the 1959–60 full-employment budget surplus was too high would today be translated as fiscal policy being too tight. However, if accompanied by a sufficiently easy monetary policy, a tight fiscal policy is no obstacle to achieving the highest feasible level of output and employment.

Milton Friedman's approach was the exact opposite of the new economics; he favored rules over activism and monetary policy over fiscal policy. His approach, christened "monetarism" in 1968, advocated a constant growth rate rule for the money supply and no use at all of fiscal policy for stabilization purposes. As we learned in Section 14-2 on pp. 450–54, this approach reflected optimism that the private economy would remain stable and a pessimistic belief that activist policy would do more harm than good. Friedman's pessimism was reinforced by events of the 1960s, including long legislative lags for fiscal policy and the Fed's accommodative policy of 1964–65 and 1968, when aggregate demand was already growing too rapidly. Another event, the failure of the income-tax surcharge to slow the economy in the face of monetary stimulus in 1968, together with the impact of tight money in 1969 in ending the expansion, placed a final nail in the coffin of activist fiscal policy and left the stage open for the dominance of monetary policy over the following three decades. Only in 2001–03 was fiscal policy revived as a recession-fighting tool.

The third new idea was the most influential and long-lasting: the 1968 natural rate hypothesis, developed concurrently by Milton Friedman and Edmund S. Phelps of Columbia University. The natural rate hypothesis took the Phillips Curve (then barely ten years old) one step further by developing the distinction between the short-run and long-run Phillips Curves (the *SP* and *LP* curves of Chapter 8). No longer could policy activists choose any arbitrary level for the unemployment rate; the microeconomic structure of labor markets decreed a particular natural rate of unemployment, and any attempt to push the actual unemployment rate below this natural rate would cause accelerating inflation.

Lo and behold, accelerating inflation was exactly what was occurring at the time the Friedman-Phelps hypothesis was unveiled in 1968. So strong was the

---

[6] Kennedy's advisers viewed earlier attempts at fiscal stabilization as special events rather than as representative of a commitment to fiscal activism. The big tax increases of 1950–51, however successful, were viewed as a special event connected with the Korean War, and the 1954 tax cuts represented the expiration of temporary wartime tax increases, rather than a deliberate act of stabilization policy.

[7] Among the first to make this case was my late colleague Robert Eisner. See his "Fiscal and Monetary Policy Reconsidered," *American Economic Review*, vol. 59 (December 1969), pp. 897–905.

influence of unfolding events that by 1970–71 the natural rate hypothesis had been widely accepted.

Summary The big events of the 1947–69 period were the instability of aggregate demand, due in part to the Korean and Vietnam wars, the overstimulation of the economy after 1964 by both monetary and fiscal policy, and the ensuing acceleration of inflation. Spawned in part by these events were several new ideas, including the Phillips Curve, the new economics, monetarism, and the natural rate hypothesis.

18-4 The Reaction of Ideas to Events, 1970–2004

Our summary of macroeconomic events and ideas since 1970 is based on Figure 18-3, which is arranged exactly like Figure 18-2.

Economic Behavior, 1971–82

Figure 18-3 shows that everything in the economy seemed to get worse after 1970. Notable in the diagram are the twin peaks of inflation in 1974–75 and 1980–81, and the twin peaks of unemployment in 1975 and 1982–83. The federal funds rate also exhibits twin peaks in 1974 and 1982–83.

In the 1970s fiscal policy continued to be out of favor. Ironically, a relatively prompt fiscal stimulus in early 1975, with a much shorter legislative lag than in 1966–68, helped to end the 1974–75 recession. Monetary policy played a passive role in 1975–79, allowing rapid M1 growth, which encouraged a further acceleration of inflation. But in October 1979, the Fed changed its policy and adopted a policy close to the monetarist rule (although based on targeting bank reserves rather than the money supply). The Fed's shift toward a money-based target explains why interest rates were so volatile in 1979–82; the Fed abandoned any attempt to smooth interest rates during this three-year interval.

Reaction of Ideas to Events

Two major ideas were developed during the 1970s: the Lucas new classical macroeconomics (Section 17-3 on pp. 551–55) and the supply-shock analysis of inflation adjustment (Section 8-10 on pp. 254–58). We have seen in Section 17-3 that the Lucas model combined market clearing, imperfect information, and rational expectations, and as such represented a further development of the Friedman-Phelps natural rate hypothesis. The core of this approach was market clearing, which was the antithesis of Keynesian economics (based on sticky prices and nonmarket clearing).

A macro event, namely the sharp increase in food and oil prices in 1973–75, played an important role in helping to build support for new classical macroeconomics. As is clearly visible in Figure 18-3, in the mid-1970s inflation and unemployment were positively correlated, not negatively correlated. The food-oil price shock appeared to put another nail in the coffin of the Phillips Curve that assumed a negative correlation between inflation and unemployment, which Friedman and Phelps had already reduced from a universal phenomenon to a short-run phenomenon. Lucas and Thomas Sargent, now of New York University, declared that this positive correlation implied that not only the short-run Phillips Curve but also Keynesian economics as a whole were dead: "The task which faces contemporary students of the business cycle is that of

Figure 18-3 Key Macroeconomic Variables, 1970–2004

This figure duplicates the format of Figure 18-2. Evident are the positive correlation of the inflation rate in the second frame and the unemployment rate in the third frame, due largely to the supply shocks of 1973–74, 1979–81, and 1997–99. This diagram exhibits the puzzles of the twin peaks of inflation, unemployment, and interest rates in the mid-1970s and early 1980s, as well as the "twin valley" of low inflation and unemployment in 1998. Also visible are the disinflation of the early 1980s and the relatively mild recessions of 1990–91 and 2001.

sorting through the wreckage ... of that remarkable intellectual event called the Keynesian Revolution."[8]

The second idea of the 1970s was the integration of supply shocks into the Phillips Curve analysis, as in Chapter 8. This approach combines the natural rate hypothesis (in the form of a vertical long-run Phillips Curve) with a short-run analysis in which demand and supply shocks are of equal importance. A demand stimulus can cause inflation to increase and unemployment to decrease in the short run, as in 1965–69 or 1987–90. An adverse supply shock can cause both inflation and unemployment to increase at the same time, as in 1974–75 and 1980–81. The idea that demand and supply shocks affect macroeconomic variables symmetrically helped to revive Keynesian economics. The empirical basis of new Keynesian economics has been called the "triangle model," where the triangle refers to the three features of the *SP-DG* model of Chapter 8, namely demand shocks, supply shocks, and inflation inertia (that is, slow adjustment of inflation).

Economic Behavior, 1982–91

After a decade (1972–82) when everything seemed to get worse, everything seemed to get better for the rest of the 1980s. The unemployment rate fell from 10.5 percent in late 1982 to 5.0 percent in early 1989. The inflation rate fell from double digits in 1981 to just 3 percent in mid-1986. Both short-term and long-run interest rates fell from their peaks of early 1981 (see the bottom frame in Figure 18-3).

A major theme of this book has been the displacement of fiscal policy by monetary policy as the central tool of stabilization policy. The Reagan-era tax cuts of 1981–83 led to 15 years of persistent natural employment deficits. A political stalemate over the solution to the deficit problem left policymakers unable to discuss short-term fiscal policy changes and added to the skepticism about activist fiscal policy built up during the events of the late 1960s.

As we have seen, from 1979 to 1982 monetary policy attempted to target monetary growth and abandoned any attempt to stabilize interest rates, contributing to the unprecedented high level and volatility of interest rates during that period. An important legacy of high interest rates in 1979–82 was the "Volcker disinflation" (Section 8-8 on pp. 249–52), which helped to return the United States from the double-digit inflation of the late 1970s and early 1980s to a more moderate inflation rate that remained below 5 percent after 1984.

However in August 1982, surprised at the depth of the 1981–82 recession, the Fed abandoned its brief flirtation with monetarism. It announced that it would no longer hold short-term interest rates at high levels; short-term interest rates promptly fell and the stock market soared. For the rest of the decade of the 1980s, the Fed appeared to follow a Taylor Rule, responding to both inflation and the output ratio, as displayed in Figure 14-5 on pp. 467–70.[9]

---

[8] Robert E. Lucas, Jr., and Thomas J. Sargent, "After Keynesian Macroeconomics," in *After the Phillips Curve: Persistence of High Inflation and High Unemployment* (Boston: Federal Reserve Bank of Boston, 1978), pp. 49–50.

[9] A readable and comprehensive review of changes in monetary policy in the 1980s and 1990s, with an extensive list of references to the related literature, is Marvin Goodfriend, "Monetary Policy Comes of Age: A 20th Century Odyssey," *Federal Reserve Bank of Richmond Economic Quarterly*, vol. 83/1 (Winter 1997), pp. 1–22. An assessment of monetary policy in the 1990s is Alan S. Blinder, "What Central Bankers Could Learn from Academics—and Vice Versa," *Journal of Economic Perspectives*, vol. 11/2 (Spring 1997), pp. 3–19.

New Ideas of the 1980s and Early 1990s

The real business cycle (RBC) theory, that is, the second and more recent version of new classical macroeconomics (Section 17-4 on pp. 555–59), was not directly a response to events. But its introduction in the early 1980s found more ready acceptance against the background of the 1973–82 period, when supply shocks seemed a more dominant source of business cycles than demand shocks. The main debate about the RBC approach does not concern the realism of supply shocks, but rather the one-sided assumption that only supply shocks matter, while demand shocks do not.

As the 1990s began, two new strains emerged in macroeconomics, although they had not yet developed into a named "theory." First was the debate over the twin deficits (Chapters 6 and 12), which reflected a belief that fiscal policy now had more of an impact on long-term economic growth and on slow productivity growth than on the business cycle. In a sense, here the usual pattern of events-cause-ideas was reversed, since supply-side economics (Section 12-7 on pp. 400–02) was an idea that caused an event, namely, persistent budget deficits.

The second new idea of the late 1980s and early 1990s was to discredit any role for monetary aggregates (like M1) in the conduct of monetary policy by the Fed. As shown in the top frame of Figure 18-3, after 1980 there was almost no connection between the growth rate of M1 and the growth rate of nominal GDP. This continued in the 1990s, when wild fluctuations in M1 growth had no counterpart in nominal GDP growth. When M1 growth exceeds that of nominal GDP, it follows that the growth rate of velocity is negative. And the top frame of Figure 18-3 shows that velocity plummeted in 1985–87 and 1991–93, but soared in 1988–89 and 1995–2001. The wild gyrations of M1 growth did not make the economy unstable; on the contrary, the growth rate of nominal GDP was much more stable than that of M1, and this was particularly true in the years 1992–2000.

Economic Behavior, 1991–2004

The economic expansion of the 1990s began in March 1991, the official date for the trough of the 1990–91 recession. The expansion was unusual in at least three ways. First, the early part of the expansion was very weak. Employment barely grew in the first year, leading to the label "the jobless recovery." The unemployment rate peaked at 7.7 percent in July 1992, fully 16 months after the trough of the recession. Responding to the weak growth of jobs and to high unemployment, the Federal Reserve allowed short-term interest rates to remain low well into the expansion, with the federal funds rate remaining at 3 percent from the autumn of 1992 until early 1994.

The second unusual aspect of the expansion was the behavior of inflation. Instead of accelerating as it had in 1987–90, inflation exhibited a slight deceleration from 1993 to 1998. While many economists had previously believed that the natural rate of unemployment was 6 percent or above, no acceleration of inflation occurred when the unemployment rate declined below 6 percent in late 1994. As explained in Section 8-11 on pp. 258–60, beneficial supply shocks allowed inflation to decelerate through 1998, but we can see in Figure 18-3 that during 1999–2000 inflation accelerated again, propelled both by the normal Phillips Curve mechanism related to low unemployment and also because oil prices went into reverse, converting a beneficial supply shock into an adverse shock.

One of these beneficial shocks was the post-1995 revival of productivity growth, ending the dismal record of slow productivity growth in the previous period 1973–95. This productivity growth revival constitutes the third unusual aspect of the expansion of the 1990s. Initially, the causes of the productivity growth revival seemed to be the invention of the Internet and explosion of high-tech investment in computers, software, and telecommunications equipment. But after high-tech investment collapsed during 2000–02, productivity growth soared again in 2002–04 to a rate even faster than in 1995–2000, as we learned in Section 11-6 on pp. 372–76. Rapid productivity growth helped inflation remain low but raised questions about how long the rapid growth rate could be sustained.

The fourth unusual aspect of the expansion and the subsequent 2001 recession and recovery was the behavior of monetary policy. In Section 14-7 on pp. 467–70 we were introduced to the concept of the Taylor Rule, which calls for monetary policy to set the federal funds rate based on a double target, both avoiding an acceleration of inflation and also avoiding deviations of the output ratio away from 100 percent. Compared to the hypothetical predictions of the Taylor Rule, three aspects of monetary policy stand out as unusual over the 1994–2004 period. The first was the sharp increase in the federal funds rate from 3 to 6 percent in 1994, intended by the Fed as a "preemptive strike" to avoid an acceleration of inflation as had occurred in the late 1980s. The second was the Fed's response to the 2001 recession, when it cut the federal funds rate from 6.5 to 1.0 percent in little more than a year, lowering the interest rate to a level far below that called for by the Taylor Rule. The third unusual feature was the Fed's failure to boost interest rates in 1998–2000, when the peak interest rate of 6.5 percent was virtually the same as the 6.0 percent rate of late 1994. If the Fed had raised rates more in 1998–2000, the high-tech investment boom and bust, as well as the bubble in the stock market, might have been moderated and the subsequent recession less severe.

New Ideas of the 1991–2004 Period

The first big puzzle involving the domestic U.S. economy was the productivity growth revival cited in the previous section. Just as economists had failed to reach a consensus about the causes of the 1973–95 productivity growth slowdown, so they had failed to converge on an explanation of the post-1995 revival and the further productivity growth explosion of 2001–04. Thus the behavior of productivity growth did not spawn any big new idea, although it motivated economists to look to the experience of other countries, for example, the failure of Europe to match the U.S. productivity achievement, in a search for explanations.

The second big puzzle was why inflation had remained so low during the expansion of the late 1990s, despite the decline in the unemployment rate to 3.9 percent, the lowest rate achieved since the 1960s. Why had the negative Phillips Curve tradeoff stopped working, in the sense that record-low unemployment rates failed to trigger the expected acceleration of inflation? What explained the even-tempered "Goldilocks economy," which was neither "too hot" nor "too cold" but rather "just right"?

The "Goldilocks" puzzle led to a new idea—that there could be regular changes in the natural rate of unemployment, often called the NAIRU (Non-Accelerating Inflation Rate of Unemployment). Macroeconomic research in the late 1990s centered on the so-called "time-varying NAIRU" or TV-NAIRU, an idea that was entirely an attempt to explain an empirical puzzle with no theoretical content.[10] Explanations of the decline in the TV-NAIRU during the 1990s relied on specific factual aspects of the economy, including the declining share of teenagers and the rising share of the young male population that was in prison. This led to an ironic or even cynical explanation for the Goldilocks economy, that "we had put many of our unemployed in prison."[11]

An important new idea that developed in the 1980s and spread in the 1990s was the primacy of an inflation target as the optimal rule for central bank behavior. An inflation target was adopted in the 1990s by the Bank of England and by the European Central Bank. An inflation target is a special form of the Taylor Rule in which the short-term interest rate is set entirely to keep inflation at a particular target rate; the real interest rate is raised when inflation exceeds the target and is lowered when inflation is below the target. With inflation targeting, *a zero weight* is placed on deviations of the output ratio from 100 percent.

As we learned in Section 14-7 on pp. 467–70, the Fed went in the opposite direction, away from inflation targeting. The path of the federal funds rate (shown in the bottom frame of Figure 18-3 on p. 588) demonstrated that the Fed shifted from a primary concern in the early 1980s with reducing the inflation rate, to a primary concern in the 1990s with stabilizing the output ratio as close as possible to 100 percent. The failure of the Fed to boost interest rates in 1999–2000 reflected a lack of concern with the acceleration of inflation evident in the second panel of Figure 18-3 during those two years. The aggressive decline in interest rates in 2001–02 and maintenance of low interest rates in 2003–04 were consistent with the view that the Fed placed almost the entire weight of its policymaking on stimulus sufficient to bring the output ratio back up to 100 percent after the 2001 recession.

By 2005 another new idea, or rather a new theme, had emerged, and this was the revival of interest in fiscal policy, especially long-run issues such as the future solvency of Social Security and alternative proposals to "fix" Social Security (see Section 12-9 on pp. 404–09). Part of the Social Security debate involved a conflict between optimistic and pessimistic assumptions about future population growth, and this helped to stimulate interest in national policies about immigration as well as the fundamental causes of the post-1995 productivity growth revival.[12] Another part of the Social Security debate revolved around proposals for individual accounts that would allow younger workers to accumulate funds for their own retirement through investments in the stock market, and the alternative proposal that the current system be maintained but that the Social Security trust fund be allowed to invest partly in the stock market instead of entirely in government bonds.

An Omitted Idea

No mention has yet been made of the new Keynesian approach (Chapter 17). Almost alone among the other major macro theories covered in this book, the

---

[10] See Robert J. Gordon, "The Time-Varying NAIRU and Its Implications for Economic Policy," *Journal of Economic Perspectives*, vol. 11 (February 1997), pp. 11–32, and other articles on the natural rate of unemployment (or NAIRU) in the same issue.

[11] See Lawrence F. Katz and Alan B. Krueger, "The High-Pressure U.S. Labor Market of the 1990s," *Brookings Papers on Economic Activity*, vol. 30, no 1 (1999), pp. 1–65.

[12] The 2005 *Economic Report of the President* devoted an entire chapter to the effects of immigration and the debate over immigration policy.

new Keynesians' ideas did *not* emerge as a response to an event in the economy. Rather, the development of the new Keynesian theory seems to be mainly an intellectual event. Convinced of the continuing relevance of the original Keynesian paradigm based on sticky prices and non-market clearing, while impressed by Lucas's idea of rational expectations yet unconvinced of his reliance on continuous market clearing, the new Keynesians decided that it was time to recombine the same ingredients with a different recipe. Thus, the essential ingredient of each type of new Keynesian theory is some obstacle to instantaneous price flexibility (that is, price stickiness), justified by an analysis based on the assumptions of profit maximization and rational expectations at the level of the individual firm.

> **Summary:** The main events of the 1971–2001 period were the two adverse supply shocks of 1974–75 and 1979–81, which created twin peaks of inflation, unemployment, and interest rates, and the beneficial supply shocks of 1996–2000, which created a "valley" of inflation and unemployment in 1997–99. Monetary policy shifted from the accommodation of supply shocks in the 1970s, to a restrictive policy that created the Volcker disinflation of 1980–84, and finally to a policy of output ratio targeting that helped make possible a long economic expansion, from 1982 to 1990, and another long expansion from 1991 to 2001. New ideas spawned by these events included the real business cycle theory, concern over the twin deficits, discrediting of monetary aggregates, the notion of a natural rate of unemployment that varies over time, and a renewed interest in long-run issues concerning fiscal policy and Social Security. The new Keynesian theory developed during this period cannot be linked to any specific event but rather was a natural intellectual outgrowth of preceding theories.

18-5 The Reaction of Ideas to Events in the World Economy

Between the 1930s and mid-1960s, the United States was virtually a closed economy. In 1965 nominal exports and imports were barely 5 percent of GDP. But by 1999, foreign trade had become much more important, with nominal exports and imports of about 13 percent of GDP. In most other countries trade is an even larger share of GDP.

Interactions Between the World and U.S. Economies

After the Allied victory in World War II, the United States loomed large in the world economy. Its per-person GDP was far ahead of any other nation (see pp. 322–23). Interactions between the world and the United States primarily flowed out from the United States in the form of aid programs such as the Marshall Plan (1948–53). Interactions that flowed in toward the U.S. economy consisted primarily of political events such as the Korean War, which (as we saw in Figure 18-2) destabilized the U.S. economy during the 1950–54 period.

We have just described overexpansionary fiscal and monetary policies as a principal legacy of the 1960s, endowing the U.S. economy after 1970 with a higher inflation rate than would have occurred under a different policy environment. Another legacy of the 1960s was the breakdown of the fixed exchange rate Bretton Woods system, as the United States exported its inflation to other countries.

International Events Spawn Ideas: The Grass Is Greener

A simple way to summarize the international economy since the late 1960s is that the "grass is greener on the other side of the fence." This refers to the widespread enthusiasm for flexible exchange rates when the fixed (Bretton Woods) exchange rate system was breaking down, then the more recent longing for a return to fixed exchange rates, once observers noted that since 1973 flexible exchange rates were much more volatile and disruptive than had been predicted.

Flexible exchange rates had been expected to enable each country to attain monetary independence and choose the particular inflation rate that it desired. However, exchange rates turned out to be highly volatile and disruptive of the real economy, most notably when the dollar appreciated by 50 percent between 1980 and 1985, and then depreciated by the same amount between 1985 and 1987. The appreciation decimated the export markets of U.S. farms and factories. There was no doubt that businesses, jobs, and lives were disrupted by the volatility of exchange rates.

Since the late 1970s economists and politicians have been searching for a way to return partially or completely to fixed exchange rates. The notable example is the European Monetary System, which surprised almost everyone by achieving a convergence of inflation rates within Europe (pp. 250–51). Some European countries, however, still have much higher unemployment rates than others, leading to a debate about whether the unified European currency (the euro) has now robbed individual countries of the freedom to devalue in order to revive their economies, as the United Kingdom, Italy, and other countries chose to do in 1992. Since 1999 the exchange rates of the members of the euro have been fixed against each other. As we learned from the trilemma of Chapter 6 (pp. 155, 189), these nations have now lost any use of domestic monetary policy and have lost the ability (enjoyed by the U.S. Fed) to stimulate their economies when output growth is slow and the output ratio is 100 percent. A particular economic "basket case" handicapped by its membership in the euro is Germany, which in 1993–2004 registered a rate of real GDP growth even slower than Japan.

International economics in the United States in the 1991–2005 period was dominated by the questions of competitiveness with Asia and the desirability of free trade, particularly with China and other East Asian countries. Questions of trade policy involve relative prices and fall within the province of microeconomics, but there is an inevitable overlap with macroeconomics. For instance, a nation with a large trade deficit faces the alternatives of a depreciation of its foreign exchange rate or protectionist measures to reduce imports. The huge U.S. current account deficit of 2004–05 was widely expected to cause a further depreciation of the U.S. dollar beyond that which had already occurred in 2002–05. It was universally recognized that the dollar had been propped up by the seemingly unlimited appetite of the Chinese and Japanese central banks to buy up dollars in order to keep their own currencies from appreciating. The future willingness of these central banks (and others in Asia) to buy up even more hundreds of billions of dollars was a major puzzle looming over international macroeconomics in the middle of the decade.

However, a currency depreciation and protection are not the only alternatives when a nation faces a major current account deficit, as we learned at the beginning of the book with the magic equation (also called the leakages–injections identity, see p. 35) showing that the current account balance is linked to domestic saving and investment and the government budget. An improvement in the current account deficit can be achieved by any measure that increases national saving, especially measures that reduce the government budget deficit.

Summary: The main international events affecting the U.S. economy were the transition to flexible exchange rates in the early 1970s and the dislocations caused by the ups and downs of the dollar in the 1980s, its further appreciation during 1995–2002, and its subsequent depreciation during 2002–05. The unexpected volatility of exchange rates and the resulting dislocation of trade patterns led to a desire by many observers to return to some version of fixed exchange rates, as had occurred in Europe, with its adoption of the euro.

18-6 Macro Mysteries: Unsettled Issues and Debates

In their professional research papers, economists (micro and macro alike) often conclude with a section called unsettled issues or agenda for future research. This macro text also concludes by reviewing six issues where the debate is still most open and lively in macroeconomics.

How Can Poor Countries Achieve Economic Growth?

As we learned in Chapter 11, many barriers prevent low-income countries from joining the rich countries in achieving high levels of per-capita income. The barriers holding back the poor countries are not the simple matters of physical and human capital investment, which are emphasized in Chapter 10. Many impoverished countries remain poor because their geography is unfavorable, their governments are corrupt, their legal systems do not protect property rights, and they do not encourage foreign trade. Some of the most fundamental barriers to economic growth are political, not a matter of simple economics.

Why Productivity Growth Ebbs and Flows

A few years ago American economists were distressed about slow productivity growth, and Europeans are still puzzled as to why their productivity growth failed to duplicate the U.S. productivity revival after 1995 and particularly after 2001. The European failure raises questions about the role of high-tech investment as a cause of the U.S. post-1995 revival, since European firms use the same types of computers and software as do American firms, and Europe is generally ahead of the United States in its use of mobile phone technology. The reasons why Europe lagged behind and the United States experienced a 2002–04 productivity growth explosion remain leading puzzles for future research and debate. Many other questions, including future U.S. economic growth and the solvency of Social Security, hinge in part on a better understanding of the productivity growth process.

Why Did the Natural Rate of Unemployment Decline?

In 1996–2000 the United States experienced a "Goldilocks" economy, with sustained real income growth, the lowest unemployment rate since 1973, and relatively low inflation. Despite low unemployment, inflation did not accelerate in response, leading economists and the Fed governors to conclude that the natural rate of unemployment had fallen substantially since the late 1980s. But

International Perspective

How Does Macroeconomics Differ in the United States and Europe?

Europe consists of a large number of economies that in the aggregate have a larger economy than the United States, but that taken individually are smaller. Five main features differentiate European from U.S. macroeconomics; these are (1) the greater emphasis on international macroeconomic issues, (2) the continuing puzzle of high European unemployment, (3) the failure of Europe to duplicate the U.S. productivity growth revival, (4) the reversed roles of monetary and fiscal policy, and (5) the greater dominance of the Keynesian school of thought.

International Emphasis

Since foreign trade in countries such as Belgium and the Netherlands accounts for more than half of GDP, it is natural that international issues that address the interaction of different economies play a greater role in European macroeconomics, while questions of stabilization policy at the national level play a lesser role. In the 1990s, European macroeconomics was dominated by debates over the desirability of moving toward a single European currency. The 1992 Maastricht Treaty set down criteria for the maximum inflation rates and deficit–GDP and debt–GDP ratios allowed for countries to enter the new European common currency (the euro) in 1999. The transition to the euro was complete in early 2002 when euro currency and coins replaced French francs and German marks.

Unemployment Puzzle

Europeans are envious of the United States for achieving lower unemployment rates over the past 25 years. The restrictive monetary and fiscal policies adopted by many European countries attempting to meet the Maastricht criteria for joining the euro are a partial explanation of high European unemployment. Also, Europeans worry that they may have gone too far in regulating business through such devices as penalties for closing factories, restrictions on shop-opening hours on week-

---

why did the natural rate decline after 1990? Many suggestions were offered, including weak labor unions, worker anxiety over the fear of losing jobs, competition for jobs from immigrants, and the strong dollar, and the competition of foreign workers and markets operating through imports and global competition. The invention of the Internet and the development of Web-based job search sites may have reduced the time and expense previously required for unemployed workers to find new jobs.

Should We Go for Zero Inflation?

One of the fuzziest debates in macroeconomics is over the costs of inflation and the output costs of stopping inflation. Canada and New Zealand are two nations that have made a commitment to achieving zero inflation, and so far they have nights and weekends, legislation of high minimum wage levels, and the encouragement of strong unions. In contrast, many in the United States believe that our lack of regulations has pushed down the incomes of a large number of low-income workers, who might have done better under the European system.

The Productivity Growth Puzzle

Europeans are also envious of the U.S. productivity growth revival since 1995 and especially during 2002–04. Europe has not enjoyed the same type of revival and in fact productivity growth in Europe since 2000 has been *lower* than in the early 1990s. Europe had almost caught up to the *level* of U.S. productivity in 1995, but by one measure Europe slipped back from 97 percent of the U.S. level in 1993 to 89 percent in 2004. Explanations of this center on some of the same factors that help to explain high European unemployment, including an excess of regulation. For instance, the U.S. has surged ahead in retailing productivity thanks to big-box firms such as Wal-Mart and Home Depot, but regulations in Europe make it much more difficult for similar stores to be established, partly because of land scarcity and regulations on land use.

Reversed Roles for Monetary and Fiscal Policy

A theme of this book has been the replacement of fiscal policy by monetary policy as the U.S. government's main tool to tame the business cycle. Fiscal policy is now thought to be important mainly for discussions about foreign indebtedness and long-run economic growth. But in Europe the roles of monetary and fiscal policy are reversed. Those nations that have joined the euro have lost their monetary independence. This leaves fiscal policy as the only available tool for short-run stabilization. In most European nations the parliamentary form of government allows fiscal policy to act with a much shorter legislative lag than in the United States. Yet even fiscal policy has been handcuffed in recent years as nations struggle to reduce their deficits to meet the Maastricht criteria for joining the euro. In particular, Germany is prevented from using a fiscal policy expansion, in contrast to the aggressive U.S. tax cuts of 2001 and 2003, because to do so would push its fiscal deficit up beyond the Maastricht limit of 3 percent of GDP. Despite its slow growth since 1993, Germany is handcuffed, unable to use either monetary or fiscal policy to boost its growth rate or reduce its unemployment rate.

Keynesian Slant

As we learned in Chapter 17, the new classical macroeconomics consists both of Lucas's original version (combining market clearing, imperfect information, and rational expectations) and the real business cycle version (combining market clearing with an exclusion of demand shocks, thus relying entirely on supply shocks to explain business cycles). A notable difference in European macroeconomics in recent decades has been near-total lack of interest in new classical economics and common reliance on the Keynesian approach based on sticky prices of goods and services. The reason for this difference is not entirely clear; perhaps the emergence of persistent European unemployment since the 1980s prevented European macroeconomists from paying much attention to the new classicals. Perhaps the difference is political, since American new classicals tend to be more politically conservative than many Europeans. Or perhaps the answer is simpler: Lucas, Prescott, and other inventors of the new classical macroeconomics live in the United States, while Keynes lived on the other side of the Atlantic!

been successful in achieving low inflation rates, but at the cost of persistent high unemployment. Does society reap a large benefit from, say, zero inflation as compared to 2 percent inflation? Is that benefit great enough to offset the costs of high unemployment? There is as yet no consensus on these questions.

Inflation Targeting Versus the Taylor Rule

Over the past two decades, the analysis of monetary policy has shifted from a debate between "rules versus activism" to a debate over the merits of alternative rules. A rule that targets the inflation rate has become the standard point of departure for debate and is used by the Bank of England and the European Central Bank. An alternative approach called the Taylor Rule targets *both* the inflation rate and the output ratio. Our analysis on pp. 467–70 suggests that the

Fed uses a Taylor Rule rather than an inflation target and indeed has shifted to less emphasis on inflation and more on stabilizing the output ratio since the 1980s. Research continues on the merits of the Fed's approach compared to that in Europe, and over whether the difference in approach can explain part of the faster output and productivity growth experienced in the United States than in Europe since 2001.

Differences Among Countries

The science of comparative macroeconomics is only beginning to address the many differences among countries. Why did productivity growth in the United States accelerate after 2001 while that in Europe slowed down? Why do individuals in Italy and Japan save so much? Why is unemployment so high in France and Spain? Why do some countries such as Chile and Argentina suffer from hyperinflations for a time but then enter a period of economic stability, whereas other nations cannot make the same transition, even if they implement similar policies? All these questions will remain the subject of active debate among macroeconomists for years, if not decades.

A Final Word

We have learned in this chapter about the evolution of events and ideas. Many important economic ideas respond to events, changes in economic behavior that are not compatible with previous economic theories. Virtually every theory discussed in this book has evolved in some way in response to changing macroeconomic behavior.

This book has emphasized that the United States does not stand alone. Macroeconomics makes no sense if it applies to one country but cannot explain events in other countries or differences in behavior among countries. The International Perspective boxes in this book help to introduce readers to important differences between the United States and other advanced countries. Some differences can be explained by our theories; others cannot. A careful study of these differences reveals some that are explained by macroeconomic theory but others that require knowledge of microeconomic theory and institutions to reach a full understanding.

As we end this book, one thing is sure. While there are many things we do not understand, there are many things that we do. Any reader of this book now qualifies as an instant critic of popular and media discussions of macroeconomics. Any reader is now equipped to dissect the many misleading journalistic statements about the economy appearing almost every day, and also to recognize those statements that reflect the remaining puzzles that truly qualify as macro mysteries.

Summary

1. Just as real-world events illustrate how theories work, sometimes real-world events make some theories obsolete and spur the invention of new theories. Many of the important theories discussed in this book evolved from an attempt to understand surprising events.

2. The big event of the interwar period was the Great Depression. This event spawned a big idea, the Keynesian revolution, with its emphasis on aggregate demand, sticky prices, and fiscal policy.

3. The big events of the 1947–69 period were the instability of aggregate demand due in part to the Korean and Vietnam wars, the overstimulation of the economy after 1964 by both monetary and fiscal policy, and the ensuing acceleration of inflation. Spawned in part by these events were several new ideas, including the Phillips Curve, the new economics, monetarism, and the natural rate hypothesis.

4. The main events of the 1970–2004 period were the two supply shocks of 1974–75 and 1979–81, which created twin peaks of inflation, unemployment, and interest rates. Also important were the Volcker disinflation, persistent budget deficits, and the Goldilocks economy of the late 1990s, which combined low unemployment with low inflation. New ideas spawned by these events included the real business cycle theory, concern over the twin deficits, and the suggestion that the natural rate of unemployment varies over time.

5. The main international events affecting the U.S. economy were the transition to flexible exchange rates in the early 1970s and the dislocations caused by the ups and downs of the dollar in the 1980s. The unexpected volatility of exchange rates and the resulting dislocation of trade patterns led many observers to desire a return to some version of fixed exchange rates.

6. The average level of unemployment includes frictional and structural unemployment. Cycles in unemployment, together with the volatility of inflation and interest rates, reflect the combined influence of demand shocks, supply shocks, and inflation inertia. The slowdown in productivity growth during 1973–95 and the subsequent revival since 1995 remain partly unexplained. Volatile interest rates reflect demand and supply shocks, as well as the Fed's policy in 1979–82 of attempting to target money and ignore interest rates.

7. Remaining macro mysteries still under active research and debate include the causes of the productivity slowdown and subsequent post-1995 productivity growth revival, why productivity growth in Europe slowed while that in the United States accelerated, why the natural rate of unemployment declined after 1990, the costs and benefits of zero inflation, the merits of inflation targeting for monetary policy versus a Taylor Rule, and, finally, why macroeconomic behavior differs so much among countries.

Questions

1. Explain how the period 1923–29 was consistent with the old classical approach and how the period 1930–33 was not.
2. How did the economy in the late 1930s seem to reinforce the old Keynesian school?
3. How did the behavior of the economy during World War II support the main themes of the Keynesian revolution?
4. What events caused fiscal activism to fall out of favor by the end of the 1960s?
5. Explain how the events of the late 1960s gave rise to monetarism and the natural rate hypothesis.
6. What caused the twin peaks of unemployment and inflation in 1974–75 and 1980–82? What theoretical innovations developed to explain the twin peaks?
7. Why did both unemployment and inflation decline after 1982?
8. What is meant by the "Goldilocks economy" of the late 1990s? How do you explain its main features?
9. The ideas of the Taylor Rule and inflation targeting were developed in the 1980s. Inflation targeting is a special case of a Taylor Rule. Evaluate the Fed's conduct of monetary policy during 1991–2004 in terms of whether the Fed appears to have been targeting inflation or the output ratio or a weighted average of the two as implied by the Taylor Rule.
10. Which macroeconomic theories were responses to events and which were not?
11. Discuss how macroeconomic policy in the United States differs from Europe.
12. What events have led to increased interest in a return to fixed exchange rates?
13. Discuss how the view of the proper role of fiscal policy in the United States has evolved since the end of World War II.
14. Discuss how events have contributed to the unresolved issues and debates about the sources of business cycles.

APPENDIX A

Time Series Data for the U.S. Economy: 1875–2004

Table A-1 Annual Data, 1875–2004

	Nominal GDP(X) (B $)	GDP Deflator (2000 = 100)	Real GDP (Y) (B 2000 $)	Natural Real GDP (Y^N) (B 2000 $)	Unemploy. Rate (U) (Percent)	Natural Unemploy. Rate (U^N) (Percent)	Money Supply (M1) (B $)	Money Supply (M2) (B $)	Labor Productivity (Y/N) (1992 = 100)	Nominal Interest Rate (i) (Percent)	S&P Stock Price Index (1941–43 = 10)
1875	8.9	7.3	122.9	122.9	—	—	—	2.4	11.1	4.8	—
1876	8.6	6.9	124.4	130.8	—	—	—	2.4	11.4	4.6	—
1877	8.8	6.9	128.3	139.3	—	—	—	2.3	11.6	4.6	—
1878	8.6	6.4	133.7	148.2	—	—	—	2.2	11.8	4.5	—
1879	9.4	6.3	150.1	157.8	—	—	—	2.3	12.0	4.3	—
1880	11.0	6.6	167.9	167.9	—	—	—	2.8	12.1	4.2	—
1881	11.3	6.5	173.8	172.9	—	—	—	3.3	12.1	4.0	—
1882	12.4	6.7	184.8	178.0	—	—	—	3.6	12.2	4.0	—
1883	12.2	6.4	189.5	183.3	—	—	—	3.8	12.3	4.0	—
1884	11.9	6.2	192.9	188.7	—	—	—	3.8	12.3	4.0	—
1885	11.7	6.0	194.3	194.3	—	—	—	3.9	12.4	3.9	—
1886	12.0	6.0	200.2	200.1	—	—	—	4.2	12.5	3.7	—
1887	12.6	6.0	209.2	206.0	—	—	—	4.5	12.5	3.7	—
1888	12.7	6.1	208.2	212.1	—	—	—	4.7	12.6	3.7	—
1889	13.5	6.1	221.2	218.4	—	—	—	4.9	12.7	3.6	—
1890	13.4	6.0	224.3	224.9	4.0	4.3	—	5.4	12.4	3.7	—
1891	13.8	6.0	231.6	231.6	5.4	4.3	—	5.6	12.5	3.8	—
1892	14.3	5.9	242.5	240.3	3.0	4.3	—	6.1	12.6	3.7	—
1893	14.3	5.9	242.4	249.4	11.7	4.3	—	5.9	12.8	3.8	—
1894	13.1	5.6	235.3	258.9	18.4	4.3	—	5.9	12.9	3.6	—
1895	14.5	5.5	262.8	268.7	13.7	4.3	—	6.1	13.6	3.6	—
1896	14.2	5.5	256.8	278.9	14.4	4.3	—	6.0	13.3	3.6	—
1897	15.1	5.5	277.8	289.5	14.5	4.3	—	6.4	13.9	3.5	—
1898	15.7	5.5	284.5	300.4	12.4	4.3	—	7.3	14.1	3.4	—
1899	17.8	5.6	317.5	311.8	6.5	4.3	—	8.4	14.7	3.4	—
1900	18.5	5.7	323.6	323.7	5.0	4.3	—	9.1	14.9	3.4	6.1
1901	20.9	5.8	363.2	336.2	4.0	4.3	—	10.3	15.9	3.4	7.8
1902	21.6	5.8	369.5	349.3	3.7	4.3	—	11.3	15.5	3.4	8.4
1903	22.8	6.0	380.1	362.8	3.9	4.3	—	12.0	15.5	3.6	7.2
1904	23.9	6.0	394.6	376.9	5.4	4.3	—	12.7	16.4	3.6	7.0
1905	26.1	6.1	430.6	391.5	4.3	4.4	—	14.1	17.0	3.6	9.0
1906	28.0	6.2	448.4	406.7	1.7	4.4	—	15.3	17.0	3.6	9.6
1907	28.8	6.5	441.5	422.5	2.8	4.4	—	16.0	16.5	3.7	8.1
1908	26.6	6.4	417.3	438.9	8.0	4.4	—	15.8	16.2	3.7	7.8
1909	29.8	6.4	466.0	455.9	5.1	4.4	—	17.5	17.2	3.7	9.7
1910	31.1	6.7	468.0	473.6	5.9	4.4	—	18.3	16.8	3.8	9.4
1911	32.0	6.6	482.9	492.0	6.7	4.4	—	19.4	17.0	3.8	9.2
1912	34.7	6.8	510.8	511.1	4.6	4.4	—	20.8	17.5	3.8	9.5
1913	36.4	6.9	530.9	530.9	4.3	4.4	—	21.7	18.0	3.9	8.5
1914	34.1	7.0	490.7	546.7	7.9	4.4	—	22.6	16.9	1.9	4.1
1915	36.2	7.1	508.9	562.9	8.5	4.4	12.2	24.2	17.8	4.0	8.3
1916	45.9	7.8	591.5	579.6	5.1	4.4	14.3	28.9	19.2	3.9	9.5
1917	54.9	9.3	591.3	596.8	4.6	4.4	16.7	33.7	18.8	4.1	8.5

Continued

A-1

	Nominal GDP(X) (B $)	GDP Deflator (2000 = 100)	Real GDP (Y) (B 2000 $)	Natural Real GDP (Y^N) (B 2000 $)	Unemploy. Rate (U) (Percent)	Natural Unemploy. Rate (U^N) (Percent)	Money Supply (M1) (B $)	Money Supply (M2) (B $)	Labor Productivity (Y/N) (1992 = 100)	Nominal Interest Rate (i) (Percent)	S&P Stock Price Index (1941–43 = 10)
1918	69.5	10.9	636.8	614.5	1.4	4.5	18.5	36.8	20.4	4.3	7.5
1919	77.0	12.4	618.4	632.7	1.4	4.5	21.3	42.7	20.5	4.3	9.2
1920	86.9	14.4	605.2	651.5	5.2	4.5	23.2	48.0	19.9	4.9	8.3
1921	73.0	12.5	583.9	670.8	11.7	4.5	21.0	45.2	21.3	5.1	7.2
1922	72.7	11.6	625.7	690.7	6.7	4.5	21.2	46.5	21.2	4.3	8.7
1923	85.3	12.0	713.4	711.2	2.4	4.5	22.4	50.4	22.4	4.3	8.9
1924	87.6	12.0	732.3	732.3	5.0	4.5	23.2	53.2	23.5	4.1	9.4
1925	91.1	12.2	748.7	751.7	3.2	4.5	25.1	57.9	23.2	3.8	11.6
1926	97.2	12.2	793.7	771.6	1.8	4.6	25.6	60.3	23.8	3.5	13.0
1927	96.0	12.0	798.2	792.0	3.3	4.6	25.5	61.6	24.1	3.3	15.3
1928	97.0	11.9	812.9	813.0	4.2	4.6	25.8	63.9	24.3	3.3	19.4
1929	103.6	12.0	865.2	842.3	3.2	4.6	26.0	64.2	25.3	3.5	24.7
1930	91.2	11.5	790.8	872.7	8.9	4.6	25.2	63.0	24.7	3.5	19.4
1931	76.5	10.3	740.3	904.1	16.3	4.6	23.6	58.9	24.6	4.4	12.2
1932	58.7	9.1	643.4	936.3	24.1	4.8	20.7	49.6	24.1	5.7	6.3
1933	56.3	8.9	634.8	970.6	25.2	4.8	19.5	44.4	23.8	4.7	8.2
1934	66.0	9.4	704.0	1006.9	22.0	4.8	21.4	47.5	26.1	3.8	9.4
1935	73.3	9.6	767.4	1043.6	20.3	4.8	25.3	53.9	26.7	3.5	10.2
1936	83.7	9.7	866.1	1080.6	17.0	4.8	28.8	60.0	28.3	2.9	14.4
1937	92.0	10.1	912.2	1120.3	14.3	4.9	30.2	63.0	28.0	3.0	14.4
1938	86.1	9.8	879.3	1159.3	19.1	4.9	29.8	62.7	29.3	3.5	10.8
1939	92.0	9.7	951.2	1201.7	17.2	4.9	33.4	67.9	30.0	3.0	11.6
1940	101.5	9.8	1031.9	1244.5	14.6	4.9	38.8	76.1	31.1	2.8	10.8
1941	126.8	10.5	1211.4	1292.2	9.9	4.9	45.4	86.2	33.5	2.8	9.8
1942	161.8	11.3	1433.8	1338.6	4.7	4.9	54.1	98.2	37.0	2.8	8.7
1943	198.5	11.9	1671.5	1388.5	1.9	5.0	70.6	123.9	42.1	2.7	11.5
1944	219.9	12.2	1808.5	1438.2	1.2	5.0	83.3	147.2	46.2	2.7	12.5
1945	223.1	12.5	1784.6	1488.5	1.9	5.0	97.0	174.5	47.9	2.6	15.2
1946	222.4	14.0	1588.2	1543.8	3.9	5.0	104.1	191.1	38.5	2.5	17.1
1947	244.4	15.5	1578.4	1600.8	3.9	5.0	109.2	201.3	36.7	2.6	15.2
1948	269.4	16.4	1642.8	1654.5	3.8	5.1	109.7	204.1	37.7	2.8	15.5
1949	267.3	16.4	1633.6	1714.6	6.0	5.2	108.6	203.2	39.0	2.7	15.2
1950	293.9	16.5	1777.6	1758.2	5.3	5.3	111.5	207.9	41.7	2.6	18.4
1951	338.9	17.7	1912.7	1795.6	3.3	5.4	116.5	215.7	42.7	2.9	22.3
1952	358.4	18.0	1991.2	1914.1	3.0	5.6	122.3	227.4	43.6	3.0	24.5
1953	379.6	18.3	2079.5	1988.3	2.9	5.7	125.4	235.9	44.6	3.2	24.7
1954	380.6	18.4	2065.4	2059.1	5.5	5.9	127.3	244.2	45.5	2.9	29.7
1955	414.4	18.7	2211.8	2125.7	4.4	6.0	131.4	253.3	47.4	3.1	40.5
1956	437.6	19.4	2256.6	2204.0	4.1	6.0	133.0	257.6	47.0	3.4	46.6
1957	461.0	20.0	2300.9	2280.5	4.3	5.8	133.7	264.4	48.2	3.9	44.4
1958	467.5	20.5	2278.9	2361.1	6.8	5.6	135.2	277.3	49.3	3.8	46.2
1959	506.6	20.7	2443.8	2446.9	5.5	5.5	140.4	293.3	51.3	4.4	57.4
1960	526.6	21.0	2502.0	2534.1	5.5	5.6	140.3	304.3	51.9	4.4	55.9
1961	544.7	21.3	2560.0	2629.9	6.7	5.8	143.1	324.8	53.7	4.4	66.3
1962	585.4	21.6	2714.6	2734.2	5.6	5.9	146.5	350.1	56.1	4.3	62.4
1963	617.8	21.8	2832.6	2846.4	5.7	5.9	150.9	379.6	58.1	4.3	69.9
1964	663.3	22.1	2998.4	2977.7	5.2	5.9	156.8	409.4	60.6	4.4	81.4
1965	719.2	22.5	3190.3	3105.6	4.5	6.0	163.5	442.5	62.4	4.5	88.2
1966	788.2	23.2	3400.8	3236.8	3.8	6.2	171.0	471.4	64.6	5.1	85.3
1967	832.5	23.9	3484.2	3368.2	3.9	6.3	177.7	503.6	65.8	5.5	91.9
1968	909.9	24.9	3650.8	3504.3	3.6	6.4	190.1	545.3	67.8	6.2	98.7
1969	983.7	26.1	3763.7	3645.0	3.5	6.3	201.4	578.7	67.9	7.0	97.8
1970	1039.0	27.5	3772.4	3787.9	5.0	6.3	209.1	601.4	68.9	8.0	83.2
1971	1127.3	28.9	3898.1	3932.5	6.0	6.2	223.2	674.4	71.8	7.4	98.3

Continued

Appendix A **A-3**

	Nominal GDP(X) (B $)	GDP Deflator (2000 = 100)	Real GDP (Y) (B 2000 $)	Natural Real GDP (Y^N) (B 2000 $)	Unemploy. Rate (U) (Percent)	Natural Unemploy. Rate (U^N) (Percent)	Money Supply (M1) (B $)	Money Supply (M2) (B $)	Labor Productivity (Y/N) (1992 = 100)	Nominal Interest Rate (i) (Percent)	S&P Stock Price Index (1941–43 = 10)
1972	1238.8	30.1	4110.2	4076.8	5.6	6.2	239.1	758.1	74.2	7.2	109.2
1973	1383.2	31.9	4341.9	4203.1	4.9	6.2	256.3	831.8	76.6	7.4	107.4
1974	1498.0	34.7	4315.8	4349.2	5.6	6.2	269.2	880.7	75.3	8.6	82.9
1975	1634.1	38.0	4304.2	4504.1	8.5	6.1	281.4	963.7	77.4	8.8	86.2
1976	1827.4	40.2	4551.1	4666.8	7.7	6.2	297.2	1086.6	80.3	8.4	102.0
1977	2033.0	42.8	4751.6	4810.6	7.1	6.2	320.0	1221.4	81.5	8.0	98.2
1978	2295.3	45.8	5012.5	4963.3	6.1	6.3	346.3	1322.4	82.6	8.7	96.0
1979	2565.1	49.6	5174.6	5092.2	5.8	6.3	372.7	1425.8	82.2	9.6	103.0
1980	2792.2	54.1	5161.6	5229.8	7.2	6.3	395.7	1540.4	82.0	11.9	118.8
1981	3124.5	59.1	5288.2	5391.6	7.6	6.2	424.9	1679.6	83.0	14.2	128.1
1982	3256.2	62.8	5184.5	5561.7	9.7	6.3	453.0	1833.4	82.5	13.8	119.7
1983	3530.3	65.2	5414.0	5737.3	9.6	6.3	503.2	2057.7	86.3	12.0	160.4
1984	3934.7	67.6	5817.9	5923.1	7.5	6.3	538.6	2222.2	88.1	12.7	160.5
1985	4213.5	69.8	6037.4	6092.4	7.2	6.4	586.9	2419.8	89.3	11.4	186.8
1986	4460.6	71.3	6260.5	6286.7	7.0	6.4	666.3	2616.4	92.0	9.0	236.3
1987	4753.0	73.4	6476.4	6469.7	6.2	6.4	743.4	2786.5	92.3	9.4	286.8
1988	5105.1	75.7	6745.3	6651.8	5.5	6.3	774.8	2936.7	93.5	9.7	265.8
1989	5484.3	78.6	6979.2	6835.5	5.3	6.3	782.2	3059.9	94.2	9.3	322.8
1990	5798.2	81.6	7104.4	7027.1	5.6	6.2	810.6	3228.4	95.3	9.3	334.6
1991	5986.1	84.6	7079.1	7229.5	6.9	6.1	859.0	3349.4	96.4	8.8	376.2
1992	6329.1	86.5	7317.0	7451.7	7.5	5.9	965.9	3412.1	100.0	8.1	415.7
1993	6662.1	88.5	7531.3	7678.9	6.9	5.7	1078.5	3448.9	100.5	7.2	451.4
1994	7070.3	90.2	7836.8	7892.5	6.1	5.6	1145.0	3495.4	101.8	8.0	460.3
1995	7419.3	92.2	8044.6	8113.6	5.6	5.4	1142.6	3566.1	102.8	7.6	541.7
1996	7810.2	93.9	8318.5	8383.9	5.4	5.4	1105.7	3738.6	105.4	7.4	670.5
1997	8322.3	95.7	8698.1	8683.7	5.0	5.3	1069.2	3922.6	107.5	7.3	873.4
1998	8766.6	96.6	9076.2	8970.6	4.5	5.2	1079.7	4207.6	110.3	6.5	1085.5
1999	9232.2	97.8	9437.3	9260.3	4.2	5.1	1101.5	4525.5	112.9	7.0	1327.3
2000	9872.7	100.1	9863.3	9607.7	4.0	5.0	1103.5	4801.6	116.2	7.6	1427.2
2001	10150.3	102.2	9933.9	9931.9	4.7	5.0	1137.0	5219.4	117.7	7.1	1194.2
2002	10487.0	104.1	10074.8	10270.3	5.8	5.0	1192.0	5614.6	123.5	6.5	993.9
2003	11004.0	106.0	10381.3	10690.7	6.0	5.0	1268.5	6004.4	128.9	5.7	965.2
2004	11735.0	108.2	10841.9	11064.8	5.5	5.0	1338.5	6276.1	134.1	5.6	1130.7

Table A-2 Quarterly Data, 1947:Q1 to 2004:Q4

	Nominal GDP(X) (B $)	GDP Deflator (2000 = 100)	Real GDP (Y) (B 2000 $)	Natural Real GDP (Y^N) (B 2000 $)	Unemploy. Rate (U) (Percent)	Natural Unemploy. Rate (U^N) (Percent)	Money Supply (M1) (B $)	Money Supply (M2) (B $)	Labor Productivity (Y/N) (1992 = 100)	Nominal Interest Rate (i) (Percent)	Real Federal Budget Surplus (B 2000 $)	Trade-Weighted Exchange Rate (Mar 1973 = 100)
1947:Q1	237.2	15.1	1570.5	1575.2	3.9	5.1	107.8	198.0	36.5	2.6	39.1	—
1947:Q2	240.5	15.3	1568.7	1585.0	3.9	5.1	109.5	200.9	37.4	2.5	33.9	—
1947:Q3	244.6	15.6	1568.0	1595.0	3.9	5.1	110.5	203.1	36.3	2.6	12.8	—
1947:Q4	254.4	16.0	1590.9	1605.0	3.9	5.2	111.0	204.9	37.8	2.8	49.4	—
1948:Q1	260.4	16.1	1616.1	1615.0	4.4	5.2	111.0	205.5	37.9	2.8	47.8	—
1948:Q2	267.3	16.3	1644.6	1625.1	3.8	5.2	110.0	204.4	37.9	2.8	31.4	—
1948:Q3	273.9	16.6	1654.1	1638.6	3.6	5.2	110.1	204.7	38.0	2.8	8.5	—
1948:Q4	275.2	16.6	1658.0	1652.3	3.3	5.2	109.7	204.2	38.2	2.8	1.2	—

Continued

Appendix A

	Nominal GDP(X) (B $)	GDP Deflator (2000 = 100)	Real GDP (Y) (B 2000 $)	Natural Real GDP (Y^N) (B 2000 $)	Unemploy. Rate (U) (Percent)	Natural Unemploy. Rate (U^N) (Percent)	Money Supply (M1) (B $)	Money Supply (M2) (B $)	Labor Productivity (Y/N) (1992 = 100)	Nominal Interest Rate (i) (Percent)	Real Federal Budget Surplus (B 2000 $)	Trade-Weighted Exchange Rate (Mar 1973 = 100)
1949:Q1	270.0	16.5	1633.2	1666.1	5.5	5.2	109.2	203.6	38.6	2.7	−20.6	—
1949:Q2	266.2	16.4	1628.4	1680.0	5.9	5.2	109.3	204.1	39.0	2.7	−39.8	—
1949:Q3	267.7	16.3	1646.7	1693.8	6.4	5.3	109.0	203.7	39.9	2.6	−40.0	—
1949:Q4	265.2	16.3	1629.9	1707.6	6.0	5.3	109.0	203.7	39.7	2.6	−38.1	—
1950:Q1	275.2	16.2	1696.8	1721.2	7.5	5.3	109.9	205.3	41.0	2.6	−51.8	—
1950:Q2	284.6	16.3	1747.3	1734.7	5.6	5.4	111.6	208.0	41.5	2.6	17.2	—
1950:Q3	302.0	16.6	1815.8	1751.9	4.4	5.4	112.8	209.5	42.4	2.6	81.2	—
1950:Q4	313.4	17.0	1848.9	1769.1	3.6	5.4	113.7	210.7	42.5	2.7	83.8	—
1951:Q1	329.0	17.6	1871.3	1786.3	4.1	5.5	115.0	212.5	42.6	2.7	97.8	—
1951:Q2	336.7	17.7	1903.1	1803.7	3.1	5.5	116.1	214.2	42.5	2.9	56.5	—
1951:Q3	343.6	17.7	1941.1	1821.3	3.1	5.6	117.6	217.1	43.5	2.9	29.9	—
1951:Q4	348.0	17.9	1944.4	1839.1	3.0	5.6	119.7	220.9	43.5	3.0	33.5	—
1952:Q1	351.3	17.9	1964.7	1857.1	3.6	5.6	121.3	224.1	43.7	3.0	38.6	—
1952:Q2	352.2	17.9	1966.0	1875.4	3.0	5.7	122.2	226.3	43.6	2.9	19.0	—
1952:Q3	358.5	18.1	1978.8	1894.0	3.0	5.7	123.5	229.1	43.4	2.9	6.1	—
1952:Q4	371.4	18.2	2043.8	1913.0	2.5	5.7	124.8	232.0	44.3	3.0	19.3	—
1953:Q1	378.4	18.2	2082.3	1932.1	3.2	5.8	125.3	233.7	44.6	3.1	23.7	—
1953:Q2	382.0	18.2	2098.1	1951.4	2.7	5.8	126.1	236.0	44.7	3.3	14.3	—
1953:Q3	381.1	18.3	2085.4	1970.8	2.5	5.9	126.3	237.4	44.9	3.3	19.2	—
1953:Q4	375.9	18.3	2052.5	1990.5	3.3	5.9	126.4	238.9	44.8	3.1	−17.5	—
1954:Q1	375.3	18.4	2042.4	2010.5	6.1	5.9	126.7	240.9	44.8	3.0	−18.0	—
1954:Q2	376.0	18.4	2044.3	2030.6	5.8	6.0	127.0	243.1	45.1	2.9	−10.3	—
1954:Q3	380.8	18.4	2066.9	2050.8	5.5	6.0	128.2	246.4	45.9	2.9	−7.1	—
1954:Q4	389.5	18.5	2107.8	2071.0	4.7	6.1	129.6	249.0	46.4	2.9	0.0	—
1955:Q1	402.6	18.6	2168.5	2090.9	5.6	6.1	131.0	251.8	47.4	3.0	19.4	—
1955:Q2	410.9	18.6	2204.0	2110.8	4.5	6.1	131.8	253.4	47.5	3.0	35.9	—
1955:Q3	419.5	18.8	2233.4	2130.7	3.8	6.1	132.4	254.7	47.6	3.1	26.1	—
1955:Q4	426.0	19.0	2245.3	2150.7	3.7	6.2	132.6	255.6	47.4	3.1	41.1	—
1956:Q1	428.3	19.2	2234.8	2170.9	4.7	6.1	133.1	256.3	46.9	3.1	44.4	—
1956:Q2	434.2	19.3	2252.5	2191.4	4.3	6.2	133.4	257.6	47.1	3.3	34.8	—
1956:Q3	439.3	19.5	2249.8	2212.2	3.8	6.0	133.5	258.7	47.0	3.4	40.0	—
1956:Q4	448.1	19.6	2286.5	2233.3	3.7	6.0	134.1	260.3	47.5	3.7	37.2	—
1957:Q1	457.2	19.9	2300.3	2254.7	4.6	5.9	134.4	262.5	48.1	3.7	30.7	—
1957:Q2	459.2	20.0	2294.6	2276.5	4.2	5.9	134.4	264.4	47.9	3.8	21.5	—
1957:Q3	466.4	20.1	2317.0	2298.4	3.9	5.8	134.6	266.2	48.6	4.1	21.9	—
1957:Q4	461.5	20.1	2292.5	2320.6	4.4	5.8	133.7	266.9	48.8	4.0	−7.5	—
1958:Q1	454.0	20.4	2230.2	2343.2	7.4	5.8	133.6	269.7	48.0	3.6	−15.7	—
1958:Q2	458.1	20.4	2243.4	2366.0	7.4	5.7	135.1	276.3	48.9	3.6	−40.6	—
1958:Q3	471.7	20.6	2295.2	2389.0	6.7	5.7	136.5	281.2	49.9	3.9	−31.1	—
1958:Q4	485.0	20.7	2348.0	2412.1	5.7	5.6	138.2	284.5	50.7	4.1	−16.9	—
1959:Q1	495.4	20.7	2392.9	2435.2	6.8	5.6	140.0	288.5	50.7	4.1	15.5	—
1959:Q2	508.4	20.7	2455.8	2458.4	5.2	5.6	139.3	291.0	51.4	4.4	25.1	—
1959:Q3	509.3	20.8	2453.9	2481.8	4.9	5.6	140.2	295.1	51.4	4.5	14.0	—
1959:Q4	513.2	20.8	2462.6	2505.5	5.0	5.6	142.0	298.5	51.3	4.6	10.1	—
1960:Q1	526.9	20.9	2517.4	2529.5	6.0	5.6	140.5	299.4	52.5	4.6	55.9	—
1960:Q2	526.1	21.0	2504.8	2553.8	5.3	5.7	138.4	300.0	51.7	4.5	39.0	—
1960:Q3	528.9	21.1	2508.7	2578.3	5.1	5.7	139.6	305.5	51.9	4.3	31.3	—
1960:Q4	523.6	21.1	2476.2	2603.3	5.7	5.7	142.7	312.3	51.2	4.3	10.4	—
1961:Q1	527.9	21.2	2491.2	2628.6	7.9	5.8	142.2	317.1	51.8	4.3	11.8	117.1
1961:Q2	539.0	21.2	2538.0	2654.2	7.0	5.8	141.4	321.0	53.3	4.3	3.8	116.8
1961:Q3	549.4	21.3	2579.1	2679.9	6.3	5.9	142.0	326.5	54.0	4.4	11.7	117.7
1961:Q4	562.5	21.4	2631.8	2705.8	5.6	5.9	146.6	334.7	54.5	4.4	22.0	117.8
1962:Q1	576.0	21.5	2679.1	2731.7	6.5	5.9	146.4	341.2	55.5	4.4	11.2	118.0

Continued

Appendix A **A-5**

	Nominal GDP(X) (B $)	GDP Deflator (2000 = 100)	Real GDP (Y) (B 2000 $)	Natural Real GDP (Y^N) (B 2000 $)	Unemploy. Rate (U) (Percent)	Natural Unemploy. Rate (U^N) (Percent)	Money Supply (M1) (B $)	Money Supply (M2) (B $)	Labor Productivity (Y/N) (1992 = 100)	Nominal Interest Rate (i) (Percent)	Real Federal Budget Surplus (B 2000 $)	Trade-Weighted Exchange Rate (Mar 1973 = 100)
1962:Q2	583.2	21.5	2708.4	2757.8	5.5	5.9	145.4	346.2	55.4	4.3	10.2	118.6
1962:Q3	590.0	21.6	2733.3	2784.2	5.2	5.9	145.0	351.6	56.1	4.3	14.4	118.7
1962:Q4	593.3	21.7	2740.0	2810.9	5.1	5.9	149.2	361.3	56.4	4.3	11.1	118.5
1963:Q1	602.4	21.7	2775.9	2837.8	6.6	5.9	149.5	369.0	56.8	4.2	19.4	118.6
1963:Q2	611.2	21.7	2810.6	2865.1	5.8	5.9	148.9	374.6	57.3	4.2	29.0	118.8
1963:Q3	623.9	21.8	2863.5	2892.6	5.2	5.9	150.1	382.2	58.5	4.3	27.1	118.8
1963:Q4	633.5	22.0	2885.8	2920.3	5.1	5.9	155.2	392.5	58.5	4.3	23.7	118.8
1964:Q1	649.6	22.0	2950.5	2948.2	6.2	5.9	155.0	398.7	59.1	4.4	9.1	118.8
1964:Q2	658.8	22.1	2984.8	2976.2	5.3	5.9	153.9	403.0	59.5	4.4	−11.8	118.8
1964:Q3	670.5	22.2	3025.5	3004.4	4.7	5.9	156.3	412.0	60.0	4.4	5.9	118.8
1964:Q4	675.6	22.3	3033.6	3032.9	4.5	6.0	162.0	423.7	59.4	4.4	14.8	118.6
1965:Q1	695.7	22.4	3108.2	3061.7	5.4	6.0	161.8	431.6	60.2	4.4	34.0	118.6
1965:Q2	708.1	22.5	3150.2	3090.8	4.8	6.0	160.6	436.1	60.6	4.4	30.2	118.8
1965:Q3	725.2	22.6	3214.1	3120.3	4.2	6.0	162.3	444.6	61.7	4.5	−1.8	118.9
1965:Q4	747.5	22.7	3291.8	3150.1	3.7	6.1	169.1	457.8	62.8	4.6	−2.6	118.8
1966:Q1	770.8	22.9	3372.3	3180.0	4.2	6.1	170.4	465.6	63.7	4.8	21.9	118.8
1966:Q2	779.9	23.0	3384.0	3210.3	4.0	6.2	170.1	468.6	63.3	5.0	15.2	118.9
1966:Q3	793.4	23.3	3406.3	3240.9	3.6	6.2	169.5	471.7	63.3	5.3	6.0	118.8
1966:Q4	807.1	23.5	3433.7	3271.8	3.4	6.2	173.8	479.6	63.8	5.4	−3.8	119.0
1967:Q1	817.9	23.6	3464.1	3303.2	4.1	6.3	173.7	486.0	64.3	5.1	−41.1	118.9
1967:Q2	822.5	23.7	3464.3	3334.9	3.8	6.3	174.2	495.7	64.5	5.3	−43.8	118.8
1967:Q3	837.1	24.0	3491.8	3367.1	3.8	6.4	178.1	509.7	64.7	5.6	−35.5	118.8
1967:Q4	852.8	24.2	3518.2	3399.8	3.7	6.4	184.7	523.0	64.9	6.0	−36.3	119.7
1968:Q1	879.9	24.5	3590.7	3432.9	4.0	6.4	185.2	530.5	66.4	6.1	−24.5	121.1
1968:Q2	904.2	24.8	3651.6	3466.3	3.6	6.4	186.7	538.2	67.0	6.3	−29.9	121.2
1968:Q3	919.4	25.0	3676.5	3500.0	3.6	6.4	190.4	549.0	66.9	6.1	6.0	121.2
1968:Q4	936.3	25.4	3692.0	3534.2	3.2	6.4	198.2	563.6	66.8	6.2	10.6	121.1
1969:Q1	961.0	25.6	3750.2	3568.8	3.6	6.4	199.6	571.8	67.4	6.7	57.0	121.3
1969:Q2	976.3	26.0	3760.9	3603.9	3.4	6.3	199.7	576.5	66.8	6.9	44.3	121.4
1969:Q3	996.5	26.3	3784.2	3639.3	3.7	6.3	200.6	580.1	66.8	7.1	21.3	122.3
1969:Q4	1004.6	26.7	3766.3	3675.2	3.3	6.3	205.8	586.2	66.5	7.5	12.0	121.0
1970:Q1	1017.3	27.1	3760.0	3711.5	4.5	6.3	205.5	587.6	66.7	7.9	−8.5	120.8
1970:Q2	1033.2	27.4	3767.1	3748.3	4.7	6.3	206.4	593.7	67.7	8.1	−57.6	120.3
1970:Q3	1050.7	27.6	3800.5	3785.3	5.2	6.3	209.0	604.3	68.8	8.2	−70.2	119.8
1970:Q4	1052.9	28.0	3759.8	3822.6	5.4	6.3	215.6	620.0	68.3	7.9	−82.5	119.7
1971:Q1	1098.3	28.4	3864.1	3859.9	6.5	6.2	217.0	641.2	70.3	7.2	−83.0	119.4
1971:Q2	1119.1	28.8	3885.9	3897.2	5.8	6.2	221.0	668.5	70.6	7.5	−104.5	118.8
1971:Q3	1139.3	29.1	3916.7	3934.3	6.0	6.2	224.7	685.2	71.2	7.6	−100.0	116.7
1971:Q4	1151.7	29.3	3927.9	3971.5	5.5	6.2	230.0	702.7	70.6	7.3	−104.4	113.0
1972:Q1	1190.6	29.8	3997.7	4008.9	6.3	6.2	231.9	725.3	71.6	7.2	−75.9	108.4
1972:Q2	1225.9	30.0	4092.1	4046.3	5.6	6.2	235.1	746.5	73.0	7.3	−92.5	107.6
1972:Q3	1249.7	30.3	4131.1	4083.5	5.6	6.2	239.9	768.4	73.4	7.2	−54.9	108.1
1972:Q4	1287.0	30.7	4198.7	4120.8	4.9	6.2	249.4	792.3	74.0	7.1	−100.2	109.0
1973:Q1	1335.5	31.0	4305.3	4158.4	5.4	6.2	251.2	812.7	75.7	7.2	−47.4	104.1
1973:Q2	1371.9	31.5	4355.1	4196.1	4.9	6.2	253.7	829.5	75.7	7.3	−46.7	99.7
1973:Q3	1391.2	32.1	4331.9	4234.1	4.8	6.2	256.7	838.0	75.1	7.6	−31.5	97.4
1973:Q4	1432.3	32.8	4373.3	4272.4	4.4	6.2	263.7	847.1	74.6	7.7	−17.4	100.0
1974:Q1	1447.0	33.4	4335.4	4311.2	5.6	6.2	264.4	863.7	74.5	7.9	−24.9	103.5
1974:Q2	1485.3	34.2	4347.9	4350.4	5.1	6.2	266.7	878.0	74.3	8.4	−31.6	99.8
1974:Q3	1514.2	35.2	4305.8	4390.0	5.6	6.2	269.3	884.5	73.6	9.0	−29.9	102.6
1974:Q4	1553.4	36.2	4288.9	4429.9	6.2	6.2	276.4	896.4	74.3	9.0	−70.1	102.4
1975:Q1	1570.0	37.1	4237.6	4470.1	9.1	6.2	273.8	913.7	74.8	8.7	−127.4	99.5
1975:Q2	1605.6	37.6	4268.6	4510.2	8.7	6.1	278.1	951.4	76.0	8.9	−277.0	100.2

Continued

A-6 Appendix A

	Nominal GDP(X) (B $)	GDP Deflator (2000 = 100)	Real GDP (Y) (B 2000 $)	Natural Real GDP (Y^N) (B 2000 $)	Unemploy. Rate (U) (Percent)	Natural Unemploy. Rate (U^N) (Percent)	Money Supply (M1) (B $)	Money Supply (M2) (B $)	Labor Productivity (Y/N) (1992 = 100)	Nominal Interest Rate (i) (Percent)	Real Federal Budget Surplus (B 2000 $)	Trade-Weighted Exchange Rate (Mar 1973 = 100)
1975:Q3	1663.1	38.3	4340.9	4549.8	8.3	6.1	283.8	983.5	76.9	8.9	−161.8	104.3
1975:Q4	1714.6	39.0	4397.8	4589.0	7.8	6.2	290.1	1006.0	76.9	8.8	−161.1	105.4
1976:Q1	1772.6	39.4	4496.8	4627.7	8.5	6.2	288.7	1036.7	78.0	8.6	−132.9	105.4
1976:Q2	1804.9	39.8	4530.3	4665.9	7.4	6.2	294.3	1072.7	78.8	8.5	−120.7	106.3
1976:Q3	1838.3	40.4	4552.0	4703.8	7.6	6.2	298.0	1099.1	78.9	8.5	−128.0	105.7
1976:Q4	1885.3	41.1	4584.6	4741.6	7.3	6.2	307.7	1137.9	79.1	8.2	−133.3	106.4
1977:Q1	1939.3	41.8	4640.0	4779.2	8.2	6.2	308.9	1174.2	79.5	8.0	−108.4	106.9
1977:Q2	2006.0	42.4	4731.1	4816.7	6.9	6.2	315.9	1210.6	79.9	8.0	−92.9	106.4
1977:Q3	2066.8	42.9	4815.8	4854.1	6.8	6.2	322.0	1237.6	80.7	7.9	−105.3	105.6
1977:Q4	2111.6	43.9	4815.3	4891.5	6.3	6.2	333.1	1263.1	79.6	8.1	−106.0	103.1
1978:Q1	2150.0	44.5	4830.8	4929.3	6.9	6.3	332.7	1282.4	79.7	8.5	−104.0	100.0
1978:Q2	2275.6	45.3	5021.2	4967.7	5.9	6.3	342.2	1310.4	81.2	8.7	−56.3	98.8
1978:Q3	2336.2	46.1	5070.7	5006.3	6.0	6.3	349.9	1335.4	81.2	8.8	−42.1	93.8
1978:Q4	2417.0	47.0	5137.4	5046.0	5.6	6.3	360.5	1361.4	81.7	9.0	−31.2	92.7
1979:Q1	2464.4	47.9	5147.4	5086.0	6.3	6.3	357.1	1376.2	81.0	9.3	−12.7	94.1
1979:Q2	2527.6	49.1	5152.3	5126.7	5.6	6.3	368.5	1411.2	80.8	9.4	−12.6	95.6
1979:Q3	2600.7	50.1	5189.4	5168.1	5.8	6.3	378.6	1446.0	80.7	9.3	−23.7	94.1
1979:Q4	2660.5	51.1	5204.7	5210.0	5.6	6.3	386.7	1469.7	80.6	10.5	−40.7	96.0
1980:Q1	2725.3	52.2	5221.3	5252.5	6.8	6.3	384.5	1489.9	80.9	12.1	−59.2	96.1
1980:Q2	2729.3	53.3	5115.9	5295.6	7.2	6.3	384.0	1513.1	80.0	11.2	−102.5	95.6
1980:Q3	2786.6	54.6	5107.4	5339.3	7.5	6.3	399.2	1561.0	80.3	11.6	−125.9	93.0
1980:Q4	2916.9	56.1	5202.1	5383.5	7.1	6.3	415.3	1597.5	81.2	12.8	−107.4	94.7
1981:Q1	3052.7	57.5	5307.5	5427.9	8.0	6.3	411.4	1618.1	82.4	13.2	−68.3	97.5
1981:Q2	3085.9	58.6	5266.1	5472.2	7.3	6.2	424.1	1662.3	81.3	14.0	−74.1	103.4
1981:Q3	3178.7	59.6	5329.8	5516.6	7.3	6.3	426.9	1695.4	82.1	14.9	−85.7	108.4
1981:Q4	3196.4	60.7	5263.4	5560.9	7.9	6.2	437.2	1742.6	81.0	14.6	−130.7	104.9
1982:Q1	3186.8	61.6	5177.1	5605.3	9.5	6.2	438.8	1773.3	80.5	15.0	−163.1	108.5
1982:Q2	3242.7	62.3	5204.9	5649.6	9.3	6.2	446.1	1811.8	80.7	14.5	−170.0	112.6
1982:Q3	3276.2	63.2	5185.2	5693.5	9.7	6.3	451.8	1850.7	80.8	13.8	−227.6	117.3
1982:Q4	3314.4	63.9	5189.8	5737.0	10.3	6.3	475.3	1897.9	81.5	11.9	−277.6	118.4
1983:Q1	3382.9	64.4	5253.8	5779.7	11.2	6.3	479.9	1990.1	82.6	11.8	−269.0	114.9
1983:Q2	3484.1	64.9	5372.3	5821.7	10.0	6.3	498.7	2042.3	84.5	11.6	−261.2	117.1
1983:Q3	3589.3	65.5	5478.4	5862.9	9.1	6.3	510.1	2077.4	85.3	12.3	−283.4	120.3
1983:Q4	3690.4	66.0	5590.5	5903.4	8.2	6.3	524.1	2120.9	85.7	12.4	−248.1	120.2
1984:Q1	3809.6	66.8	5699.8	5943.5	8.4	6.3	523.4	2157.0	85.7	12.3	−230.3	120.8
1984:Q2	3908.6	67.4	5797.9	5983.4	7.4	6.3	537.3	2203.9	86.2	13.2	−243.3	122.2
1984:Q3	3978.2	68.0	5854.3	6023.3	7.3	6.3	541.6	2236.4	86.5	13.0	−252.7	128.8
1984:Q4	4036.3	68.4	5902.4	6063.3	7.0	6.3	552.2	2291.6	86.6	12.4	−267.3	131.6
1985:Q1	4119.5	69.2	5956.9	6103.5	7.8	6.4	557.1	2351.3	86.8	12.3	−212.6	138.5
1985:Q2	4178.4	69.6	6007.8	6143.9	7.2	6.4	576.5	2393.4	87.0	11.6	−283.7	135.0
1985:Q3	4261.3	69.8	6101.7	6184.5	7.1	6.4	596.3	2446.8	88.1	11.0	−249.6	128.6
1985:Q4	4321.8	70.3	6148.6	6225.2	6.7	6.4	617.9	2487.7	88.5	10.6	−257.9	120.1
1986:Q1	4385.6	70.7	6207.4	6266.0	7.5	6.4	621.2	2516.8	89.6	9.6	−255.8	113.8
1986:Q2	4425.7	71.0	6232.0	6306.9	7.1	6.4	651.8	2583.9	90.3	9.0	−284.6	108.2
1986:Q3	4493.9	71.4	6291.7	6347.9	6.8	6.4	678.8	2650.6	90.7	8.8	−290.0	103.5
1986:Q4	4546.1	71.9	6323.4	6389.0	6.5	6.4	713.6	2714.5	90.4	8.7	−241.1	103.6
1987:Q1	4613.8	72.5	6365.0	6430.4	7.1	6.4	725.8	2749.7	90.0	8.4	−249.0	98.1
1987:Q2	4690.0	72.9	6435.0	6472.1	6.2	6.4	745.0	2774.9	90.6	9.2	−172.9	94.6
1987:Q3	4767.8	73.4	6493.4	6514.2	5.9	6.4	744.9	2792.8	90.6	9.8	−183.0	96.0
1987:Q4	4886.3	74.0	6606.8	6557.6	5.6	6.4	758.0	2828.5	91.5	10.2	−188.1	90.7
1988:Q1	4951.9	74.6	6639.1	6601.4	6.2	6.3	753.4	2872.6	91.6	9.6	−190.9	87.6
1988:Q2	5062.8	75.3	6723.5	6645.8	5.4	6.3	773.3	2928.9	92.0	9.8	−174.0	86.6
1988:Q3	5146.6	76.1	6759.4	6690.9	5.4	6.3	782.0	2957.1	92.2	10.0	−168.1	91.2
1988:Q4	5253.7	76.7	6848.6	6736.6	5.1	6.3	790.3	2988.0	92.7	9.5	−177.8	87.2

Continued

Appendix A A-7

	Nominal GDP(X) (B $)	GDP Deflator (2000 = 100)	Real GDP (Y) (B 2000 $)	Natural Real GDP (Y^N) (B 2000 $)	Unemploy. Rate (U) (Percent)	Natural Unemploy. Rate (U^N) (Percent)	Money Supply (M1) (B $)	Money Supply (M2) (B $)	Labor Productivity (Y/N) (1992 = 100)	Nominal Interest Rate (i) (Percent)	Real Federal Budget Surplus (B 2000 $)	Trade-Weighted Exchange Rate (Mar 1973 = 100)
1989:Q1	5367.1	77.6	6918.1	6783.0	5.6	6.3	779.4	2999.5	92.4	9.7	−143.6	88.9
1989:Q2	5454.1	78.3	6963.5	6830.2	5.2	6.3	776.4	3019.8	92.6	9.5	−164.2	92.9
1989:Q3	5531.9	78.9	7013.1	6878.1	5.2	6.2	778.3	3077.0	93.0	9.0	−176.9	93.5
1989:Q4	5584.3	79.4	7030.9	6926.9	5.1	6.2	794.7	3143.1	93.2	8.9	−177.4	91.9
1990:Q1	5716.4	80.4	7112.1	6976.4	5.5	6.2	793.9	3184.3	94.1	9.2	−209.8	90.9
1990:Q2	5797.7	81.3	7130.3	7026.5	5.3	6.2	806.9	3211.8	94.7	9.4	−210.8	91.3
1990:Q3	5849.4	82.0	7130.8	7077.2	5.6	6.2	813.6	3243.0	95.1	9.4	−201.0	86.6
1990:Q4	5848.8	82.6	7076.9	7128.5	5.8	6.2	827.8	3274.6	94.4	9.3	−221.5	82.5
1991:Q1	5888.0	83.6	7040.8	7180.5	7.2	6.1	829.2	3311.4	94.6	8.9	−189.4	83.7
1991:Q2	5964.3	84.2	7086.5	7233.0	6.8	6.1	849.6	3350.8	96.0	8.9	−251.5	88.6
1991:Q3	6035.6	84.8	7120.7	7285.9	6.7	6.1	863.4	3358.1	96.7	8.8	−274.5	88.4
1991:Q4	6095.8	85.2	7154.1	7339.0	6.7	6.1	894.0	3377.4	97.3	8.4	−295.9	84.7
1992:Q1	6196.1	85.7	7228.2	7392.2	8.0	6.0	920.3	3399.6	98.8	8.3	−336.6	85.4
1992:Q2	6290.1	86.2	7297.9	7445.5	7.5	6.0	949.2	3405.6	99.5	8.3	−338.4	85.8
1992:Q3	6380.5	86.6	7369.5	7498.5	7.5	5.9	971.6	3404.4	100.4	8.0	−365.1	82.0
1992:Q4	6484.3	87.0	7450.7	7551.2	7.0	5.9	1022.6	3438.7	101.2	8.0	−337.1	86.3
1993:Q1	6542.7	87.7	7459.7	7603.7	7.7	5.8	1030.7	3419.7	100.4	7.7	−342.7	88.4
1993:Q2	6612.1	88.2	7497.5	7656.3	6.7	5.8	1062.0	3440.0	99.8	7.4	−303.9	85.5
1993:Q3	6674.6	88.6	7536.0	7709.2	6.7	5.7	1090.0	3451.9	100.2	6.9	−309.4	86.6
1993:Q4	6800.2	89.0	7637.4	7762.5	6.3	5.7	1131.3	3483.8	100.9	6.8	−282.2	88.0
1994:Q1	6911.0	89.6	7715.1	7816.3	7.1	5.6	1132.2	3483.2	101.6	7.2	−259.2	88.3
1994:Q2	7030.6	90.0	7815.7	7870.3	6.1	5.6	1141.9	3499.9	101.5	7.9	−211.6	86.9
1994:Q3	7115.1	90.5	7859.5	7924.9	5.9	5.6	1146.7	3494.6	101.1	8.2	−233.4	83.9
1994:Q4	7232.2	91.0	7951.6	7980.0	5.3	5.5	1159.3	3504.0	101.9	8.6	−236.9	83.4
1995:Q1	7298.3	91.5	7973.7	8037.1	5.9	5.5	1144.3	3497.6	101.7	8.3	−235.1	82.7
1995:Q2	7337.7	91.9	7988.0	8095.2	5.6	5.5	1144.6	3535.1	101.7	7.7	−212.6	78.0
1995:Q3	7432.1	92.3	8053.1	8154.2	5.6	5.4	1140.7	3594.6	102.0	7.4	−215.3	80.5
1995:Q4	7522.5	92.7	8112.0	8214.1	5.2	5.4	1140.8	3637.3	102.8	7.0	−192.7	82.0
1996:Q1	7624.1	93.3	8169.2	8274.9	6.0	5.4	1117.3	3675.6	103.7	7.1	−195.1	83.9
1996:Q2	7776.6	93.7	8303.1	8336.6	5.4	5.4	1116.8	3722.4	104.8	7.6	−152.8	84.8
1996:Q3	7866.2	94.0	8372.7	8399.1	5.2	5.3	1099.4	3754.4	105.1	7.6	−141.7	84.6
1996:Q4	8000.4	94.5	8470.6	8462.5	5.0	5.3	1089.6	3802.0	105.4	7.2	−115.1	85.2
1997:Q1	8113.8	95.1	8536.1	8526.7	5.7	5.3	1073.0	3844.6	104.9	7.4	−93.8	89.4
1997:Q2	8250.4	95.2	8665.8	8591.9	4.9	5.3	1063.6	3888.9	106.2	7.6	−72.6	90.7
1997:Q3	8381.9	95.5	8773.7	8657.9	4.8	5.2	1064.3	3942.7	107.2	7.2	−36.6	91.9
1997:Q4	8471.2	95.8	8838.4	8724.9	4.4	5.2	1075.9	4014.3	107.5	6.9	−31.3	92.9
1998:Q1	8586.7	96.1	8936.2	8793.0	5.1	5.2	1073.4	4090.7	108.4	6.7	13.5	95.2
1998:Q2	8657.9	96.2	8995.3	8862.3	4.4	5.2	1077.1	4162.5	108.7	6.6	30.0	96.6
1998:Q3	8789.5	96.6	9098.9	8932.8	4.5	5.2	1070.6	4225.2	109.8	6.5	62.5	98.2
1998:Q4	8953.8	96.9	9237.1	9004.6	4.1	5.1	1097.7	4352.0	110.4	6.3	54.7	93.0
1999:Q1	9066.6	97.3	9315.5	9077.5	4.7	5.1	1094.5	4436.2	111.3	6.4	81.6	93.4
1999:Q2	9174.1	97.7	9392.6	9151.8	4.2	5.1	1101.6	4495.8	111.5	6.9	107.1	95.5
1999:Q3	9313.5	98.0	9502.2	9227.5	4.2	5.1	1091.4	4544.7	112.3	7.3	110.0	94.5
1999:Q4	9519.5	98.4	9671.1	9304.5	3.8	5.1	1118.4	4625.5	114.2	7.5	124.7	92.7
2000:Q1	9629.4	99.3	9695.6	9382.8	4.4	5.0	1110.1	4706.3	113.7	7.7	214.2	94.7
2000:Q2	9822.8	99.7	9847.9	9462.5	3.9	5.0	1108.7	4774.5	115.8	7.8	181.9	97.4
2000:Q3	9862.1	100.3	9836.6	9543.6	4.0	5.0	1095.9	4817.7	115.5	7.6	190.7	99.1
2000:Q4	9953.6	100.7	9887.7	9626.1	3.7	5.0	1099.2	4908.1	116.6	7.4	171.4	102.2
2001:Q1	10021.5	101.5	9875.6	9710.1	4.6	5.0	1097.8	5041.7	116.4	7.1	154.3	101.9
2001:Q2	10128.9	102.3	9905.9	9795.6	4.3	5.0	1118.4	5161.5	118.1	7.2	120.9	105.3
2001:Q3	10135.1	102.7	9871.1	9879.7	4.8	5.0	1156.1	5265.9	118.5	7.1	−86.3	104.4
2001:Q4	10226.3	103.2	9910.0	9965.0	5.2	5.0	1175.7	5408.6	120.4	6.9	−4.6	105.4
2002:Q1	10338.2	103.5	9993.5	10051.0	6.2	5.0	1183.4	5500.8	122.4	6.6	−201.5	108.2
2002:Q2	10445.7	103.9	10052.6	10137.599	5.7	5.0	1186.1	5543.6	122.8	6.7	−242.1	107.2

Continued

A-8 Appendix A

	Nominal GDP(X) (B $)	GDP Deflator (2000 = 100)	Real GDP (Y) (B 2000 $)	Natural Real GDP (Y^N) (B 2000 $)	Unemploy. Rate (U) (Percent)	Natural Unemploy. Rate (U^N) (Percent)	Money Supply (M1) (B $)	Money Supply (M2) (B $)	Labor Productivity (Y/N) (1992 = 100)	Nominal Interest Rate (i) (Percent)	Real Federal Budget Surplus (B 2000 $)	Trade-Weighted Exchange Rate (Mar 1973 = 100)
2002:Q3	10546.5	104.2	10117.3	10224.52	5.7	5.0	1185.5	5638.7	124.1	6.4	−244.7	102.8
2002:Q4	10617.5	104.8	10135.9	10311.965	5.6	5.0	1213.1	5775.1	124.6	6.3	−289.0	102.6
2003:Q1	10744.6	105.5	10184.4	10400.072	6.3	5.0	1228.0	5857.2	125.8	6.0	−266.9	97.8
2003:Q2	10884.0	105.8	10287.4	10488.958	6.1	5.0	1264.7	5980.1	127.9	5.3	−344.4	93.3
2003:Q3	11116.7	106.1	10472.8	10578.284	6.0	5.0	1282.5	6088.9	130.5	5.7	−407.9	93.1
2003:Q4	11270.9	106.5	10580.7	10668.229	5.5	5.0	1298.7	6091.1	131.5	5.7	−356.0	87.8
2004:Q1	11472.6	107.2	10697.5	10758.815	6.1	5.0	1309.0	6114.6	132.7	5.5	−364.6	85.2
2004:Q2	11657.5	108.1	10784.7	10856.852	5.5	5.0	1335.9	6265.7	134.0	5.9	−351.5	88.0
2004:Q3	11814.9	108.5	10891.0	10927.4	5.4	5.0	1341.3	6316.2	134.4	5.6	−345.7	86.4
2004:Q4	11994.8	109.1	10994.3	10998.406	5.1	5.0	1367.9	6407.9	135.1	5.5	−326.5	81.8

APPENDIX B

International Annual Time Series Data for Selected Countries: 1960–2004

Table B-1 Canada, 1960–2004

	Nominal GDP (X) (B C$)	GDP Deflator	Real GDP (Y) (B 2000 C$)	Labor Productivity (Y/N) (C$/Hr)	Unemploy. Rate (U) (Percent)	Investment Share (Percent)	Consumer Price Index (CPI) (1995=100)	Long-Term Interest Rate (i) Percent	Labor Share (wN/X) (Percent)
1960	39.1	16.1	242.8	19.9	6.6	21.1	17.7	5.2	50.7
1961	40.5	16.2	250.2	20.0	6.8	20.6	17.9	5.1	51.4
1962	43.9	16.4	267.3	20.8	5.6	20.5	18.0	5.1	50.9
1963	47.2	16.8	280.9	21.5	5.3	20.2	18.4	5.1	50.6
1964	51.7	17.3	299.3	22.2	4.5	20.8	18.8	5.2	50.5
1965	57.0	17.9	318.7	23.0	3.8	22.6	19.2	5.2	51.0
1966	63.7	18.8	339.6	23.6	3.5	23.1	19.9	5.7	51.6
1967	68.5	19.6	349.7	23.8	4.0	21.1	20.6	5.9	53.1
1968	74.9	20.3	368.4	25.0	4.6	20.7	21.4	6.7	52.8
1969	82.4	21.2	388.0	25.7	4.6	21.6	22.4	7.6	53.6
1970	88.7	22.3	398.2	26.4	5.8	19.6	23.1	8.0	54.1
1971	96.8	23.0	420.2	27.4	6.3	20.1	23.9	6.9	54.3
1972	108.1	24.4	442.7	28.2	6.4	20.4	25.0	7.2	54.6
1973	126.8	26.7	474.5	28.9	5.7	21.7	26.9	7.5	53.6
1974	151.4	30.6	494.2	29.0	5.5	23.7	29.8	8.9	53.5
1975	170.7	33.8	505.1	29.5	7.1	22.6	33.1	9.0	55.4
1976	196.6	36.9	532.9	30.0	7.2	22.9	35.6	9.2	55.6
1977	217.2	39.4	551.3	30.6	8.1	21.2	38.4	8.7	55.7
1978	240.9	42.0	573.8	30.6	8.4	21.2	41.8	9.2	54.7
1979	275.1	46.0	597.9	30.5	7.5	23.9	45.6	10.2	53.8
1980	309.4	51.0	606.2	30.6	7.5	23.0	50.3	12.3	54.1
1981	354.6	56.8	624.7	31.0	7.6	25.9	56.6	15.0	54.4
1982	373.7	61.6	606.9	31.3	11.1	19.7	62.7	14.4	55.2
1983	404.7	64.9	623.4	31.8	11.9	20.2	66.3	11.8	53.4
1984	442.3	67.1	659.7	32.8	11.3	21.0	69.2	12.7	52.6
1985	477.8	69.2	690.8	33.2	10.5	21.4	71.9	11.1	52.5
1986	504.2	71.3	707.6	33.0	9.6	21.0	74.9	9.5	53.1
1987	549.9	74.6	737.6	33.6	8.8	22.1	78.2	9.9	52.9
1988	603.1	77.9	774.1	33.6	7.8	23.6	81.3	10.2	52.9
1989	647.0	81.5	794.1	33.2	7.5	23.4	85.4	9.9	53.2
1990	669.0	84.1	795.6	33.5	8.1	21.2	89.5	10.8	54.1
1991	674.2	86.6	778.6	34.0	10.3	20.1	94.5	9.8	55.2
1992	689.3	87.8	785.3	35.2	11.2	17.3	95.9	8.8	55.2
1993	716.0	89.0	804.1	35.2	11.4	17.8	97.7	7.9	54.1
1994	758.0	90.1	841.6	35.7	10.3	18.4	97.9	8.6	52.4
1995	798.0	92.1	866.1	36.3	9.4	18.7	100.0	8.4	51.6
1996	824.4	93.8	879.4	36.3	9.6	18.3	101.6	7.5	51.1
1997	869.1	94.7	917.5	36.9	9.1	20.5	103.2	6.5	51.2
1998	899.3	94.4	953.1	37.8	8.3	20.1	104.2	5.5	51.8
1999	958.7	95.6	1003.0	38.3	7.6	20.1	106.0	5.7	51.5
2000	1047.6	99.5	1052.8	38.9	6.8	20.9	108.9	5.9	50.8
2001	1089.2	101.2	1076.8	40.1	7.3	19.1	111.7	5.6	51.9
2002	1140.4	102.1	1117.0	41.2	7.6	19.6	114.2	5.3	53.2
2003	1200.1	105.3	1139.3	41.4	7.6	20.1	117.4	4.8	52.1
2004	1278.1	108.9	1173.5	41.9	7.2	19.8	119.7	4.7	52.0

Table B-2 Japan, 1960–2004

	Nominal GDP (X) (TR ¥)	GDP Deflator	Real GDP (Y) (TR 2000 ¥)	Labor Productivity (Y/N) (¥/Hr)	Unemploy. Rate (U) (Percent)	Investment Share (Percent)	Consumer Price Index (CPI) (1995=100)	Long-Term Interest Rate (i) Percent	Labor Share (wN/X) (Percent)
1960	16.0	23.9	66.7	724.7	1.6	25.2	18.4	7.5	41.0
1961	19.3	25.8	74.6	798.6	1.4	28.5	19.5	7.3	40.2
1962	21.9	26.9	81.4	870.8	1.3	27.1	20.8	7.5	42.3
1963	25.1	28.4	88.3	939.3	1.3	28.1	22.4	7.1	43.0
1964	29.4	29.9	98.6	1029.9	1.2	29.1	23.2	7.2	42.9
1965	32.8	31.5	104.3	1082.5	1.2	28.1	24.8	7.2	44.7
1966	38.1	33.0	115.5	1168.7	1.3	28.6	26.0	6.8	44.6
1967	44.6	34.8	128.2	1263.4	1.3	31.1	27.0	6.9	43.9
1968	52.9	36.6	144.7	1396.9	1.2	32.7	28.5	7.0	43.1
1969	62.1	38.1	162.8	1565.8	1.1	33.9	30.0	7.0	43.2
1970	73.2	40.6	180.3	1722.0	1.2	36.2	32.4	7.0	44.2
1971	80.5	42.8	188.2	1792.1	1.2	34.4	34.4	7.1	47.6
1972	92.2	45.2	204.0	1936.5	1.4	34.6	36.0	6.9	48.5
1973	112.2	50.9	220.4	2052.5	1.3	36.1	40.2	7.1	49.8
1974	133.9	61.5	217.7	2094.0	1.4	35.3	49.5	8.2	53.1
1975	148.0	65.9	224.4	2194.9	1.9	32.9	55.4	8.5	56.2
1976	166.2	71.2	233.3	2231.4	2.0	32.6	60.6	8.6	56.2
1977	185.2	76.0	243.6	2291.2	2.0	32.0	65.5	7.5	56.4
1978	203.9	79.5	256.4	2377.9	2.2	32.4	68.3	6.4	55.3
1979	221.0	81.7	270.5	2470.2	2.1	33.2	70.8	8.3	55.1
1980	242.1	81.6	296.6	2679.1	2.0	32.6	76.3	8.9	54.6
1981	260.3	85.1	306.0	2748.1	2.2	32.0	80.1	8.4	54.9
1982	273.3	86.6	315.5	2805.2	2.4	30.9	82.2	8.3	55.3
1983	284.8	88.3	322.7	2813.8	2.7	28.5	83.8	7.8	55.8
1984	303.9	90.8	334.9	2883.2	2.7	27.9	85.7	7.3	55.2
1985	324.7	93.0	349.2	3002.7	2.6	28.4	87.4	6.5	54.1
1986	340.2	94.5	359.9	3067.8	2.8	28.3	88.0	5.1	53.9
1987	355.0	94.4	376.1	3166.5	2.8	29.2	88.1	5.0	53.3
1988	380.4	95.0	400.4	3320.8	2.5	30.7	88.7	4.8	52.5
1989	408.2	96.8	421.9	3463.7	2.3	32.0	90.7	5.1	52.5
1990	440.8	99.2	444.3	3635.1	2.1	32.6	93.5	7.0	52.2
1991	467.8	102.2	457.8	3707.3	2.1	32.9	96.5	6.3	53.0
1992	480.5	104.0	462.0	3794.1	2.2	30.2	98.2	5.3	53.4
1993	485.5	104.5	464.4	3875.6	2.5	29.7	99.4	4.3	54.0
1994	489.4	104.6	467.8	3938.5	2.9	28.4	100.1	4.4	54.4
1995	495.6	104.3	475.0	3959.4	3.1	28.3	100.0	3.4	54.8
1996	510.6	103.3	494.2	4120.4	3.4	29.2	100.1	3.1	54.2
1997	520.9	103.6	502.5	4205.2	3.4	28.8	101.9	2.4	54.5
1998	515.0	103.5	497.4	4241.9	4.1	26.8	102.5	1.5	54.6
1999	510.9	102.1	500.3	4375.6	4.7	25.7	102.2	1.7	54.1
2000	508.6	100.0	508.4	4430.9	4.7	26.7	101.5	1.7	54.3
2001	501.9	98.5	509.7	4495.7	5.0	25.7	100.8	1.3	55.1
2002	498.1	97.3	511.9	4601.8	5.4	23.9	99.5	1.3	52.4
2003	498.6	94.9	525.5	4726.6	5.3	24.0	99.3	1.1	54.0
2004	506.6	92.7	546.5	4901.0	4.8	24.2	99.1	1.5	53.9

Table B-3 France, 1960–2004

	Nominal GDP (X) (B euro)	GDP Deflator	Real GDP (Y) (B 2000 euro)	Labor Productivity (Y/N) (euro/Hr)	Unemploy. Rate (U) (Percent)	Investment Share (Percent)	Consumer Price Index (CPI) (1995=100)	Long-Term Interest Rate (i) Percent	Labor Share (wN/X) (Percent)
1960	47.0	12.0	392.7	10.6	1.5	24.2	13.1	5.7	45.2
1961	51.3	12.4	414.3	11.1	1.2	24.3	13.3	5.5	46.4
1962	57.3	13.0	442.0	11.7	1.4	24.4	14.0	5.4	46.5
1963	64.2	13.8	465.6	12.3	1.6	24.5	14.8	5.3	47.4
1964	71.2	14.4	496.0	12.8	1.2	25.9	15.2	5.4	47.7
1965	76.7	14.8	519.7	13.4	1.5	25.6	15.7	6.2	47.8
1966	83.0	15.2	546.8	14.0	1.6	26.3	16.0	6.6	47.6
1967	89.7	15.7	572.4	14.6	2.1	26.1	16.5	6.7	47.5
1968	97.5	16.3	596.8	15.4	2.7	26.2	17.3	7.0	48.9
1969	111.2	17.4	638.5	16.4	2.3	27.3	18.3	8.2	49.1
1970	124.1	18.4	675.1	17.4	2.5	26.9	19.3	8.6	49.7
1971	138.3	19.6	707.4	18.3	2.7	26.4	20.4	8.4	50.3
1972	154.6	20.9	738.7	19.1	2.8	26.2	21.7	8.0	50.3
1973	176.8	22.7	778.9	20.2	2.7	27.3	23.3	9.0	50.6
1974	203.9	25.4	803.1	21.0	2.9	28.9	26.4	11.0	52.5
1975	229.6	28.7	800.9	21.5	4.0	24.6	29.5	10.3	55.1
1976	266.1	31.9	834.9	22.8	4.4	25.7	32.4	10.5	55.3
1977	300.0	34.8	861.7	23.5	4.9	24.8	35.4	11.0	55.8
1978	341.5	38.3	890.6	24.4	5.2	21.6	38.7	10.6	55.5
1979	388.2	42.2	919.5	25.2	5.8	24.2	42.8	10.8	55.5
1980	439.4	46.9	936.2	25.7	6.2	25.1	48.6	13.8	56.3
1981	493.8	52.2	946.2	26.5	7.4	23.7	55.1	16.3	56.9
1982	565.1	58.3	969.8	28.4	8.0	22.9	61.7	16.0	57.1
1983	625.1	63.7	980.9	28.9	8.3	22.2	67.6	14.4	56.7
1984	680.8	68.3	996.2	29.6	9.7	20.8	72.7	13.4	55.9
1985	728.8	72.1	1011.3	30.5	10.2	20.3	77.0	11.9	55.3
1986	783.8	75.8	1034.4	31.2	10.4	19.7	78.9	9.1	54.0
1987	826.3	77.9	1060.3	31.8	10.5	22.0	81.5	10.2	53.4
1988	889.1	80.5	1105.1	32.7	10.0	22.8	83.7	9.2	52.5
1989	957.6	83.1	1152.6	33.7	9.3	22.7	86.7	9.2	51.9
1990	1010.8	85.5	1182.5	34.4	8.9	23.4	89.6	10.3	52.5
1991	1051.9	88.0	1194.8	34.7	9.4	22.4	92.5	9.0	52.7
1992	1086.3	89.8	1209.9	35.4	10.4	20.3	94.7	8.6	52.9
1993	1102.8	92.0	1199.1	35.9	11.7	18.6	96.6	6.8	52.9
1994	1141.8	93.5	1220.9	36.6	12.1	18.8	98.3	7.2	52.1
1995	1184.4	95.0	1246.7	36.9	11.4	19.6	100.0	7.5	52.0
1996	1211.6	96.3	1257.6	36.9	12.1	18.3	102.0	6.3	52.1
1997	1250.5	97.5	1281.9	37.4	12.2	17.8	103.2	5.6	51.9
1998	1306.1	98.4	1326.8	38.1	11.6	18.8	103.9	4.7	51.5
1999	1349.6	98.9	1365.3	39.8	10.9	19.1	104.5	4.6	52.0
2000	1413.5	99.8	1415.8	41.4	9.5	20.7	106.3	5.4	52.1
2001	1472.6	101.6	1449.9	42.3	8.9	20.4	108.0	5.0	52.3
2002	1526.8	104.1	1467.1	43.1	9.0	19.6	110.6	4.9	52.3
2003	1557.2	105.7	1473.9	43.4	9.7	19.0	113.0	4.1	52.6
2004	1619.5	107.6	1504.9	44.3	9.8	19.9	115.7	4.1	52.3

Table B-4 Germany, 1960–2004

	Nominal GDP (X) (B euro)	GDP Deflator	Real GDP (Y) (B 2000 euro)	Labor Productivity (Y/N) (euro/Hr)	Unemploy. Rate (U) (Percent)	Investment Share (Percent)	Consumer Price Index (CPI) (1995=100)	Long-Term Interest Rate (i) Percent	Labor Share (wN/X) (Percent)
1960	133.2	20.0	666.0	8.8	1.0	—	31.3	6.3	56.6
1961	145.3	20.8	696.8	9.2	0.6	—	32.0	5.9	58.6
1962	162.2	22.2	729.3	9.7	0.6	—	32.9	6.0	58.0
1963	181.8	24.3	749.8	10.2	0.7	—	33.9	6.1	55.5
1964	201.7	25.2	799.8	10.7	0.6	—	34.7	6.2	54.7
1965	217.1	25.8	842.6	11.3	0.5	—	35.8	6.8	56.3
1966	235.0	27.1	866.1	12.1	0.6	—	37.2	7.8	56.0
1967	253.9	29.4	863.5	12.8	1.8	—	37.7	7.0	51.8
1968	276.0	30.3	910.6	13.5	1.2	—	38.3	6.7	51.2
1969	305.2	31.2	978.5	14.5	0.7	—	39.0	7.0	52.0
1970	345.3	33.6	1027.8	15.1	0.6	28.9	40.4	8.2	54.6
1971	383.3	36.2	1059.2	15.7	0.7	27.6	42.5	8.2	55.7
1972	420.8	38.1	1104.2	16.5	0.9	26.9	44.8	8.2	56.2
1973	468.9	40.5	1156.8	17.4	1.0	26.9	47.9	9.4	57.3
1974	503.1	43.4	1159.1	18.0	2.1	24.2	51.3	10.6	59.1
1975	524.9	45.9	1144.5	18.6	4.0	22.5	54.3	8.8	59.1
1976	572.9	47.5	1205.5	19.3	3.9	24.1	56.7	8.2	58.4
1977	611.1	49.3	1239.8	20.2	3.8	23.1	58.8	6.7	58.8
1978	656.2	51.4	1277.0	20.9	3.7	23.0	60.3	6.3	58.5
1979	709.9	53.3	1330.9	21.0	3.2	24.8	62.8	7.7	58.5
1980	752.6	56.0	1344.0	21.7	3.2	24.0	66.2	8.6	60.0
1981	784.8	58.3	1345.3	21.9	4.5	22.4	70.4	10.2	60.3
1982	812.0	60.9	1332.6	22.0	6.4	20.9	74.1	9.1	60.1
1983	853.1	62.9	1356.1	22.5	7.9	20.9	76.6	8.2	58.4
1984	895.2	64.2	1394.2	23.5	7.9	20.9	78.4	8.1	57.7
1985	932.2	65.5	1422.5	24.1	8.0	20.5	80.1	7.2	57.5
1986	984.4	67.6	1455.9	24.4	7.7	19.9	80.0	6.3	57.3
1987	1017.7	68.9	1477.4	24.8	7.6	19.8	80.2	6.4	57.7
1988	1071.6	69.9	1532.5	25.5	7.6	20.5	81.2	6.6	57.0
1989	1137.3	71.6	1588.0	26.5	6.9	21.3	83.5	7.1	56.1
1990	1240.4	73.9	1679.1	27.8	6.2	21.4	85.7	8.7	55.5
1991	1502.1	85.2	1763.3	29.8	5.4	23.9	87.2	8.5	56.2
1992	1613.2	89.5	1802.8	31.6	6.4	23.2	91.6	7.9	56.7
1993	1654.2	92.8	1783.2	32.6	7.6	22.8	95.7	6.5	56.7
1994	1735.5	95.1	1825.0	33.7	8.1	23.0	98.3	6.9	55.4
1995	1801.3	97.0	1856.6	34.8	7.9	22.9	100.0	6.9	55.3
1996	1833.8	98.0	1870.8	35.8	8.5	21.7	101.4	6.2	54.9
1997	1871.6	98.7	1897.0	36.5	9.4	21.4	103.3	5.7	54.0
1998	1929.4	99.8	1934.0	37.1	8.9	21.7	104.3	4.6	53.5
1999	1974.2	100.2	1969.7	36.9	8.2	21.4	104.9	4.5	53.7
2000	2030.0	99.9	2032.9	38.3	7.5	22.6	107.0	5.3	53.8
2001	2069.7	101.4	2041.1	38.7	7.5	19.4	109.6	4.8	53.9
2002	2107.3	102.9	2048.7	39.4	8.2	17.3	108.9	4.8	54.1
2003	2128.2	104.0	2046.2	39.7	9.2	17.5	110.1	4.1	53.6
2004	2172.9	104.9	2070.8	40.1	9.3	16.9	112.0	4.1	53.9

Table B-5 Italy, 1960–2004

	Nominal GDP (X) (B euro)	GDP Deflator	Real GDP (Y) (B 2000 euro)	Labor Productivity (Y/N) (euro/Hr)	Unemploy. Rate (U) (Percent)	Investment Share (Percent)	Consumer Price Index (CPI) (1995=100)	Long-Term Interest Rate (i) Percent	Labor Share (wN/X) (Percent)
1960	12.8	4.0	318.6	7.6	4.2	36.6	5.8	5.3	41.4
1961	14.2	4.1	344.8	8.2	3.8	37.3	5.9	5.0	41.5
1962	16.0	4.4	366.1	8.9	3.3	37.0	6.2	5.0	43.0
1963	18.3	4.7	386.7	9.7	2.8	36.9	6.7	5.2	45.7
1964	20.0	5.0	397.5	10.0	3.2	33.0	7.0	5.7	46.7
1965	21.6	5.3	410.5	10.9	4.0	29.7	7.4	5.4	45.9
1966	23.4	5.4	435.1	11.6	4.3	29.3	7.6	5.5	45.3
1967	25.7	5.5	466.3	12.2	4.0	30.6	7.8	5.6	45.4
1968	27.9	5.6	496.8	13.0	4.2	29.9	8.0	5.6	45.5
1969	30.8	5.8	527.1	13.9	4.2	31.3	8.1	5.8	45.4
1970	34.6	6.2	555.1	14.7	4.0	31.7	8.5	7.7	47.2
1971	37.7	6.7	564.0	15.4	4.0	29.0	9.0	7.0	49.7
1972	41.4	7.1	579.2	16.0	4.7	28.4	9.5	6.6	50.5
1973	50.0	8.1	620.4	17.0	4.7	30.8	10.5	6.9	50.3
1974	63.2	9.7	654.1	17.9	3.9	33.2	12.5	9.6	49.7
1975	71.7	11.3	636.7	17.6	4.3	28.0	14.6	10.0	52.9
1976	90.5	13.3	678.6	18.6	4.9	29.6	17.1	12.7	51.4
1977	110.9	15.8	701.5	19.5	5.3	26.8	20.0	14.7	51.3
1978	131.3	18.0	727.4	20.3	5.3	26.6	22.5	13.1	50.2
1979	160.4	20.8	770.9	21.6	5.7	27.1	25.8	13.0	49.9
1980	200.7	25.0	803.6	21.8	5.6	28.4	31.2	15.3	49.1
1981	240.3	29.7	808.0	22.0	6.3	25.8	36.8	19.4	49.9
1982	280.8	34.8	807.4	22.1	6.9	25.4	42.8	20.2	49.7
1983	327.1	40.0	817.4	22.4	7.7	22.5	49.1	18.3	49.0
1984	374.8	44.6	840.0	23.7	8.5	23.1	54.4	15.6	47.7
1985	420.3	48.6	865.0	24.0	8.6	23.9	59.4	13.7	47.5
1986	465.1	52.4	886.8	24.4	9.9	22.6	62.8	11.5	46.4
1987	508.6	55.7	913.3	25.2	10.2	22.2	65.8	10.6	46.0
1988	564.4	59.5	949.3	25.6	10.5	21.9	69.2	10.9	45.5
1989	618.1	63.3	976.6	26.2	10.2	22.8	73.5	12.8	45.5
1990	682.2	68.5	995.9	26.3	9.1	22.4	78.3	13.5	46.1
1991	744.1	73.7	1009.7	26.3	8.6	22.0	83.2	13.3	46.3
1992	783.8	77.0	1017.4	27.2	8.8	20.5	87.4	13.3	46.2
1993	807.4	80.1	1008.4	27.6	10.2	18.3	91.3	11.2	45.8
1994	854.0	82.9	1030.7	28.6	11.2	18.8	95.0	10.5	44.3
1995	923.0	87.0	1060.8	29.5	11.7	19.2	100.0	12.2	42.6
1996	982.5	91.6	1072.4	29.6	11.7	18.7	104.0	9.4	42.5
1997	1026.2	93.8	1094.1	30.0	11.8	18.9	106.1	6.9	42.7
1998	1072.9	96.3	1113.9	30.3	11.9	19.1	108.2	4.9	40.6
1999	1107.9	97.9	1131.7	30.9	11.5	19.8	110.0	4.7	40.8
2000	1165.9	100.1	1165.3	31.3	10.7	20.3	112.8	5.6	40.4
2001	1219.5	102.6	1188.1	31.5	10.0	19.7	115.9	5.2	40.3
2002	1260.4	105.8	1191.4	31.1	9.1	20.0	118.3	5.0	41.7
2003	1300.9	108.9	1194.5	30.9	8.8	19.6	121.6	4.3	42.3
2004	1354.2	111.9	1210.0	30.8	8.1	19.7	124.2	4.3	41.2

Table B-6 United Kingdom, 1960-2004

	Nominal GDP (X) (B £)	GDP Deflator	Real GDP (Y) (B 2000 £)	Labor Productivity (Y/N) (£/Hr)	Unemploy. Rate (U) (Percent)	Investment Share (Percent)	Consumer Price Index (CPI) (1995=100)	Long-Term Interest Rate (i) Percent	Labor Share (wN/X) (Percent)
1960	25.7	7.2	358.0	7.1	1.5	21.6	8.4	5.9	58.9
1961	27.2	7.4	367.2	7.3	1.4	21.7	8.6	6.3	60.1
1962	28.6	7.7	372.0	7.4	1.9	20.2	9.0	5.8	60.3
1963	30.4	7.8	386.8	7.7	2.1	20.2	9.2	5.2	59.8
1964	33.2	8.2	406.3	7.9	1.5	23.8	9.5	5.7	59.4
1965	35.7	8.6	417.6	8.2	1.4	23.4	10.0	6.6	59.6
1966	38.0	8.9	426.2	8.5	1.5	22.9	10.3	6.9	60.0
1967	40.0	9.2	436.0	8.8	2.2	24.1	10.6	6.7	59.4
1968	43.4	9.6	453.4	9.3	2.3	24.7	11.1	7.5	58.6
1969	46.7	10.1	462.7	9.5	2.3	24.0	11.7	8.8	58.2
1970	51.3	10.8	473.6	9.9	2.4	23.5	12.5	8.6	59.5
1971	57.3	11.9	483.0	10.4	3.1	21.9	13.6	7.9	58.4
1972	64.1	12.8	499.9	10.8	3.1	21.3	14.6	8.4	59.0
1973	73.7	13.7	536.7	11.4	2.1	23.8	15.9	10.6	59.5
1974	83.2	15.8	527.5	11.4	2.2	22.7	18.5	14.2	62.9
1975	104.9	20.0	523.9	11.6	3.6	19.5	22.9	13.2	65.2
1976	124.2	23.1	538.5	12.1	4.9	20.5	26.7	13.6	62.8
1977	144.7	26.3	551.2	12.4	5.2	21.7	31.0	12.0	59.8
1978	167.0	29.3	569.9	12.8	5.0	21.1	33.5	12.1	59.2
1979	196.5	33.5	585.7	13.2	4.6	21.4	38.0	12.9	58.9
1980	229.5	40.1	572.9	13.2	6.1	17.6	46.6	13.9	60.0
1981	252.1	44.6	565.5	13.7	9.0	15.3	52.2	14.9	59.4
1982	275.8	47.9	575.7	14.1	10.4	18.3	56.7	13.1	57.6
1983	301.4	50.5	597.3	14.7	11.2	17.5	59.6	11.3	56.4
1984	322.9	52.8	611.7	14.7	11.4	18.6	62.3	11.1	56.2
1985	354.0	55.8	635.0	15.1	11.6	18.4	65.5	11.0	55.6
1986	380.4	57.5	661.9	15.7	11.8	18.0	67.9	10.1	55.8
1987	418.0	60.5	691.2	16.2	10.2	19.1	70.6	9.6	55.0
1988	466.3	64.1	727.0	16.3	7.8	21.8	73.9	9.7	55.1
1989	511.6	68.9	742.6	16.3	6.1	21.7	77.7	10.2	55.9
1990	557.0	74.5	748.1	16.5	5.9	20.0	83.1	11.8	56.7
1991	585.8	79.4	737.8	16.7	8.2	18.2	89.3	10.1	57.3
1992	610.6	82.6	739.5	17.5	10.2	16.8	93.1	9.1	56.9
1993	642.0	84.7	757.9	18.2	10.3	16.2	95.5	7.5	55.7
1994	680.7	85.9	792.0	18.8	9.4	16.5	97.4	8.2	54.2
1995	718.2	88.3	813.3	19.0	8.5	16.5	100.0	8.2	53.7
1996	761.4	91.3	834.0	19.4	7.9	16.7	102.5	7.8	53.2
1997	811.5	93.9	864.6	19.8	6.5	17.3	104.3	7.0	53.4
1998	858.7	99.7	861.1	19.4	5.9	18.3	105.9	5.5	54.0
1999	900.0	99.0	908.7	20.2	6.0	17.5	107.4	5.1	54.9
2000	945.4	100.4	941.5	20.8	5.5	18.0	108.2	5.3	55.3
2001	987.9	101.6	972.1	21.3	5.1	17.3	109.5	4.9	56.2
2002	1044.1	105.5	989.6	21.8	5.2	16.7	111.0	4.9	55.5
2003	1099.9	108.7	1011.7	22.3	5.0	16.5	112.5	4.5	54.9
2004	1159.3	111.0	1044.1	22.8	4.7	16.9	114.2	5.0	55.5

APPENDIX C

Data Sources and Methods

C-1 Annual Variables (Sources and Methods for Table A-1)

1. Nominal GDP (X):
   1875–1928: Data from Nathan S. Balke and Robert J. Gordon, "The Estimation of Prewar GNP: Methodology and New Results," *Journal of Political Economy*, vol. 97 (February 1989), pp. 38–92, Table 10. Linked in 1929 to:
   1929–2004: Data from U.S. Department of Commerce, Bureau of Economic Analysis. National Income and Product Accounts: Table 1.1.5 on the BEA Web site: www.bea.doc.gov

2. Implicit GDP Deflator (P):
   Same as Nominal GDP (X), except Table 1.1.9 for 1929–2004.

3. Real GDP (Y):
   Same as Nominal GDP (X), except Table 1.1.6 for 1929–2004.

4. Natural Real GDP (Y^N):
   1875–1955: Y^N is the geometric interpolation between real GDP for the benchmark years 1869, 1873, 1884, 1891, 1900, 1910, 1924, and 1949 and the value of natural real GDP in 1955 (see below).
   1955–2004: Average annual values of the natural real GDP series described in Appendix C-2.

5. Unemployment Rate (U):
   1890–1899: Lebergott's series copied from Christina Romer, "Spurious Volatility in Historical Unemployment Data," *Journal of Political Economy*, vol. 94 (February 1986).
   1900–1946: Series B1 in *Long-Term Economic Growth, 1860–1970* (Washington, D.C.: U.S. Department of Commerce, 1973).
   1947–2004: Series LNU04000000Q from http://stats.bls.gov, Bureau of Labor Statistics, Department of Labor. Average of quarterly values.

6. Natural Unemployment Rate (U^N):
   1890–1901: Assumed to be the same level as in 1902, 4.1 percent.
   1902–1954: U^N is the linear interpolation between the U^N values of the benchmark years of 1902, 1907, 1913, 1929, and 1949 is calculated as $U^N = B*(U/UA)$ where UA is the published unemployment rate that adjusts for self-employment. UA equals the number of unemployed divided by the civilian labor force net of self-employed persons. The long-run equilibrium rate for UA ("B") reflects the value of UA observed in late 1954 when the economy was operating at its natural rate of unemployment. Changes in U^N before 1954 reflect only changes in the U/UA ratio.
   1955–2004: Time-varying NAIRU for chain-weighted GDP price index-based deflator with standard deviation = 0.2 from Robert J. Gordon, "Time-Varying NAIRU," *Journal of Economic Perspective*, vol. 11, pp. 11–34, extended to 2004 using unpublished research. For recent unpublished research papers on time-varying NAIRU, see http://faculty-web.at.northwestern.edu/economics/gordon/researchhome.html

7. Money Supply (M1):
   1915–1946: *Historical Statistics of the United States: Colonial Times to 1970* (Washington, D.C.: U.S. Department of Commerce, 1975), series 414. Linked in 1947 to:
   1947–1958: *Federal Reserve Bulletin* (Washington, D.C.: Board of Governors of the Federal Reserve System), various issues. Linked in 1959 to
   1959–2004: Data from FRED, Federal Reserve Bank of St. Louis.

8. Money Supply (M2):
   1875–1907: Milton Friedman and Anna J. Schwartz, *Monetary Statistics of the United States* (New York: National Bureau of Economic Research, 1970), pp. 61–65. Linked in 1907 to:
   1908–1946: *Historical Statistics*, series 415. Linked in 1947 to:
   1947–1958: *Federal Reserve Bulletin* (Washington, D.C.: Board of Governors of the Federal Reserve System), various issues. Linked in 1959 to:
   1959–2004: Data From FRED, Federal Reserve Bank of St. Louis.

9. Labor Productivity (Y/N):
   1875–1946: Data computed by dividing real output from item 3 above by series A173 from *Long Term Economic Growth, 1860–1970*. Linked in 1947 to:
   1947–2004: Series PRS85006093 from http://stats.bls.gov, Bureau of Labor Statistics, Department of Labor. Average of quarterly values.

10. Nominal Interest Rate (r):
    1875–1939: The yield on corporate bonds from Robert J. Gordon, ed., *The American Business Cycle* (Chicago: University of Chicago, 1986), Appendix B.
    1940–2004: Corporate bonds (Moody's Aaa) from the *2004 Economic Report of the President* (Washington, D.C.: United States Government Printing Office, 2005) and *Federal Reserve Bulletin* (Washington, D.C.: Board of Governors of the Federal Reserve System).

11. S&P Stock Price Index:
    1875–1939: The index of all common stocks from Gordon, *The American Business Cycle*, Appendix B. Linked in 1940 to:
    1940–2004: Standard and Poor's Composite Index (1941–43 = 10) from the *2004 Economic Report of the President* (Washington D.C.: United States Government Printing Office, 2005) and *Federal Reserve Bulletin* (Washington, D.C.: Board Of Governors of the Federal Reserve System).

C-2 Quarterly Variables (Sources and Methods for Table A-2)

1. Nominal GDP (X):
   1947:Q1–2004:Q4: Data from U.S. Department of Commerce, Bureau of Economic Analysis. National Income and Product Accounts: Table 1.1.5 on the BEA Web site: www.bea.gov.
2. Implicit GDP Deflator (P):
   Same as Nominal GDP (X) except Table 1.1.9.
3. Real GDP (Y):
   Same as Nominal GDP (X) except Table 1.1.6.
4. Natural GDP (Y^N):
   1947:Q1–2004:Q4: Data from Robert J. Gordon, "Exploding Productivity Growth: Context, Causes, and Implications," *Brookings Papers on Economic Activity*, 2003, no. 3, data underlying Figure 3, p. 227, updated in unpublished research.
5. Unemployment Rate (U):
   1947:Q1–2001:Q1: Series LNU04000000Q from http://stats.bls.gov, Bureau of Labor Statistics, Department of Labor.
6. Natural Unemployment Rate (U^N): See Appendix C-1, line 6.
7. Money Supply (M1):
   1947:Q1–1958:Q4: *Federal Reserve Bulletin* (Washington, D.C.: Board of Governors of the Federal Reserve System), various issues. Linked in 1959 to:
   1959:Q1–2004:Q4: Data from FRED, Federal Reserve Bank of St. Louis.
8. Money Supply (M2):
   1947:Q1–1958:Q4: *Federal Reserve Bulletin* (Washington, D.C.: Board of Governors of the Federal Reserve System), various issues. Linked in 1959 to:
   1959:Q1–2004:Q4: Data from FRED, Federal Reserve Bank of St. Louis.
9. Labor Productivity (Y/N):
   1947:Q1–2004:Q4: Series PRS85006093 from http://stats.bls.gov, Bureau of Labor Statistics, Department of Labor.
10. Nominal Interest Rate (r):
    1947:Q1–2004:Q4: Corporate bonds (Moody's Aaa) from the *2004 Economic Report of the President* (Washington, D.C.: United States Government Printing Office, 2005) and *Federal Reserve Bulletin* (Washington, D.C.: Board of Governors of the Federal Reserve System).
11. Real Federal Budget Surplus in 2000 Dollars:
    1947:Q1–2004:Q4: Calculated by dividing the nominal federal government surplus from the U.S. Department of Commerce by the implicit price deflator. Updated using the *Economic Report of the President* (2004) and the BEA Web site: www.bea.gov
12. Trade-Weighted Exchange Rate:
    1961:Q1–1966:Q4: Effective exchange rate (MERM) from various issues of *International Financial Statistics* (Washington, D.C.: International Monetary Fund). Linked in 1967:Q1 to:
    1967:Q1–2004:Q4: Trade-weighted exchange value of U.S. dollar versus Major Currencies from FRED, Federal Reserve Bank of St. Louis. Updated using the *Economic Report of the President* (2004) and the FRED, Federal Reserve bank of St. Louis.

C-3 International Variables (Sources and Methods for Appendix B, same sources for all countries)

1. Nominal GDP (X):
   Gross domestic product (expenditures) from *Organization for Economic Cooperation and Development, National Accounts, Volume 1: Main Aggregates*, 1992–2003, Line 27 (Paris: OECD Publications April, 2005). Linked with 1960–2001 data from same source. Updated to 2004 using OECD growth rates from OECD *Economic Outlook*, December 2004.
2. Implicit GDP Deflator (P):
   Calculated by diving nominal GDP by real GDP
3. Real GDP (Y)
   Gross domestic product (expenditures, 2000 prices) from *OECD National Accounts, Volume 1: Main*

Aggregates, 1992–2003, Line 54. Linked with 1960–2001 data from same source. Updated to 2004 using OECD growth rates from OECD *Economic Outlook*, December 2004.

4. Labor Productivity (Y/N):

   Real output (real GDP, Y) divided by total manhours, N (the product of total Employment E, and hours worked per employee, H). Real output is from *OECD National Accounts*, Employment and Total manhours is from *Groningen Total Economy Database* http://www.ggdc.net/index-dseries.html.

5. Unemployment Rate (U):

   Unemployment rate from http://stats.bls.gov, Bureau of Labor Statistics, Department of Labor. Average of quarterly values.

6. Investment Share:

   Penn World Table Version 6.1, Center for International Comparisons at the University of Pennsylvania (CICUP), October 2002 and IMF World Economic Outlook, April 2005.

7. Consumer Price Index (CPI):

   International Financial Statistics Yearbook, 2001 (Washington, D.C.: International Monetary Fund, 2001). Updated using IMF World Economic Outlook, April 2005.

8. Long-term Interest Rate (r):

   Interest rate, long-term from *OECD Economic Outlook*, December, 2004.

   Labor Share (wN/X):

   Calculated by dividing "compensation of employees" by "national income" from *OECD National Accounts, Volume I: Main Aggregates*, 1960–2004, Lines 1 and 5.

Glossary

Accelerator hypothesis (16-3) Theory that the level of net investment depends on the *change* in expected output.

Accommodating policy (8-10) Attempt by government or central bank, following a supply shock, to raise **nominal GDP** growth so as to maintain the original **output ratio**.

Actual real GDP (1-3) The value of total output corrected for any changes in prices.

Actual real interest rate (9-3) The **nominal interest rate** minus the actual inflation rate.

Adaptive expectations (8-6) Prediction for next period's economic values based on an average of actual values during previous periods.

Adjustable-rate mortgage (13-7) An interest rate that can change frequently in response to changes in short-term interest rates, in contrast to a fixed-rate mortgage.

Aggregate (1-2) Total amount of an economic magnitude for the economy as a whole.

Aggregate demand (AD) curve (7-1) The graphical schedule showing different combinations of the price level and real output at which the money and commodity markets are both in equilibrium.

Aggregate demand (3-1) The total amount of desired spending expressed in current (nominal) dollars.

Aggregate supply (3-2) The amount that firms are willing to produce at any given price level.

Appreciation (6-3) A rise in the value of one nation's currency relative to another nation's currency. When the dollar can buy more units of a foreign currency, say, the euro, the dollar is said to appreciate relative to that foreign currency.

Auction market (17-7) A centralized location where professional traders buy and sell a commodity or a financial security.

Automatic stabilization (5-4) The effect (on the government budget deficit or surplus) of the **leakage** of tax revenues when income rises or falls.

Autonomous magnitude (3-3) An amount independent of the level of income.

Backward-looking expectations (8-6) Predictions for next period's values based only on information on the past behavior of economic variables.

Balance of payments (6-2) The record of a nation's international transactions, both credits (which arise from sales of exports and sales of assets) and debits (which arise from purchases of imports and purchases of assets).

Budget line (5-4) The graphical schedule showing the **government budget surplus** or **deficit** at different levels of real income.

Business cycles (1-4) Expansions occurring at about the same time in many economic activities, followed by similarly general recessions and recoveries that merge into the **expansion** phase of the next cycle.

Capital account (6-2) The part of the balance of payments that records capital flows, which consist of purchases and sales of foreign assets by domestic residents, and purchases and sales of domestic assets by foreign residents.

Capital market instruments (13-2) Assets, sold in financial markets, that have relatively long maturities, can experience large fluctuations in price, and often expose investors to the risk of capital loss and default.

Chain-weighted GDP deflator (2-8) Calculated by weighting price changes by the average of quantities sold at the beginning and end of the period of change.

Chain-weighted real GDP (2-8) Calculated by valuing changes in quantities by the average of prices charged at the beginning and end of the period of change.

Closed economy (1-8) A nation that has no trade in goods, services, or financial assets with any other nation.

Cold turkey (8-7) An approach to disinflation that implements a sudden and permanent slowdown in **nominal GDP** growth.

Comparative statics (7-4) A technique of economic analysis in which a comparison is made between two equilibrium positions but ignoring the behavior of the economy between the two equilibrium positions—either the length of time required or the route followed during the transition between the initial and final positions.

Constant growth rate rule (CGRR) (14-3) The rule advocating a fixed percentage growth rate for the money supply, in contrast to the variable growth rate recommended by policy activists.

Consumption expenditures (2-2) Purchases of goods and services by households for their own use.

Contractionary monetary policy (4-7) Government monetary policy that has the effect of lowering GDP and raising interest rates.

Coordination failure (17-7) Result of firms neglecting to act together, due to lack of private incentive, to avoid actions that impose social costs on society.

Cost-of-living agreements (COLAs) (17-9) Contracts that provide for an automatic increase in the wage rate in response to an increase in the price level.

Countercyclical variable (7-7) A variable (such as the real wage) that moves over the **business cycle** in the opposite direction from **real GDP**.

Credibility (9-6) The extent to which households and firms believe that an announced **monetary** or fiscal policy will actually be implemented and maintained as announced.

Cross section (15-3) Data for numerous units (e.g., households, firms, cities, or states) observed at a single period of time.

Crowding out effect (4-8) Reduction of one or more components of private expenditures due to an increase in government spending or a reduction of tax rates.

Current account (6-2) The part of the balance of payments that includes **exports**, **imports**, investment income, and **transfer payments** to and from foreigners.

Cyclical deficit (5-4) The amount by which the actual **government budget deficit** exceeds the **structural deficit**.

Cyclical surplus (5-4) The amount by which the actual **government budget surplus** exceeds the **structural surplus**.

Cyclical unemployment (9-7) The difference between the actual unemployment rate and the natural rate of unemployment.

Demand inflation (8-9) A sustained increase in prices that is preceded by a permanent acceleration of **nominal GDP** growth.

Demand shocks (3-1, 8-1, 14-1) Unexpected changes in business and consumer optimism, changes in **net exports**, and changes in government spending or tax rates (for example, in wartime) not related to **stabilization policy**.

Depreciation (consumption of fixed capital) (2-6) The part of the capital stock used up due to obsolescence and physical wear.

Depreciation (of currency) (6-3) A decline in the value of one nation's currency relative to another nation's currency. When the dollar can buy fewer units of a foreign currency, say, the British pound, the dollar is said to depreciate relative to that foreign currency.

Depreciation rate (16-7) The annual percentage decline in the value of a capital good due to physical deterioration and obsolescence.

Devaluation (6-6) Under the **fixed exchange rate system**, a nation's reduction of the value of its money in terms of foreign money.

Discount rate (13-5) The interest rate the Federal Reserve charges depository institutions when they borrow reserves.

Discretionary fiscal policy (5-4) Alteration of tax rates and/or government expenditures in a deliberate attempt to influence real output and the **unemployment rate**.

Discretionary policy (14-3) Approach that treats each macroeconomic episode as a unique event, without any attempt to respond in the same way from one episode to another.

Disinflation (8-7) A marked deceleration in the **inflation rate**.

Disintermediation (13-7) The withdrawal of funds from financial intermediaries like thrift institutions when market interest rates rose above the interest rate ceilings on savings and time deposit accounts.

Domestic income (2-6) The earnings of domestic factors of production, computed as **net domestic product** minus indirect business taxes, which are taxes levied on business sales.

Dynamic multipliers (14-4) The amount by which output is raised during each of several time periods after a given change in a policy instrument.

Economic growth (1-4, 10-2) Topic area of **macroeconomics** that studies the causes and consequences of sustained growth in natural real GDP over periods of a decade or more.

Endogenous variables (3-2) Variables explained by an economic theory.

Equilibrium (3-5) A state in which there exists no pressure for change.

Equilibrium real wage rate (7-6) The real wage rate at which the labor supply and demand curves intersect, so there is no pressure for change in the real wage.

Exogenous variables (3-2) Variables that are relevant but whose behavior economic theory does not attempt to explain and whose values are taken as given.

Expansion (1-4) Period in the business cycle between the trough and the peak.

Expansionary monetary policy (4-7) Government monetary policy that has the effect of lowering interest rates and raising GDP.

Expectations effect (7-9) The decline in **aggregate demand** caused by the postponement of purchases when consumers expect prices to decline in the future.

Expectations-augmented Phillips Curve (*SP* curve) (8-2) A schedule relating the **inflation rate** to the output ratio (or **unemployment rate**) that shifts its position whenever there is a change in the **expected rate of inflation**.

Expected rate of inflation (8-2) Rate of inflation that is expected to occur in the future.

Expected real interest rate (9-3) The **nominal interest rate** minus the **expected rate of inflation**.

Exports (2-4) Goods produced within one country and shipped to another.

Extinguishing policy (8-10) Attempt by government or central bank, following a supply shock, to reduce **nominal GDP** growth so as to maintain the original **inflation rate**.

Glossary **G-3**

Extra convenience services (9-3) The services provided by holding one extra dollar of money instead of bonds.

Factor inputs (10-3) The economic elements that directly produce real GDP.

Feedback rule (14-3) A rule of stabilization policy that systematically changes a monetary variable like the money supply or interest rates in response to actual or forecasted changes in target variables like inflation or employment.

Final good (2-3) Part of final product.

Final product (2-3) All currently produced goods and services that are sold through the market but are not resold.

Financial deregulation (13-1) Change of rules for U.S. financial markets, begun in the 1970s and continuing today, that has allowed more and more types of assets to serve as money. One of the first changes was permitting banks to pay interest on checking accounts.

Financial intermediaries (13-2) Institutions, such as banks, that make loans to borrowers and obtain funds from savers, usually by accepting deposits.

Financial markets (13-2) Organized exchanges where securities and financial instruments are bought and sold.

Fiscal policy (1-7) Manipulations of government expenditures and tax rates in order to try to influence **target variables**.

Fisher Effect (9-3) Prediction that a one percentage point increase in the expected inflation rate will raise the nominal real interest rate by one percentage point, leaving the expected real interest rate unaffected.

Fisher equation (9-3) Statement that the nominal interest rate equals the expected inflation rate plus the expected real interest rate.

Fixed exchange rate system (6-6) System in which the **foreign exchange rate** is fixed for long periods of time.

Fixed investment (2-4) All final goods purchased by business that are not intended for resale.

Flexible accelerator theory (16-5) Theory of investment that allows for gradual adjustment of sales expectations and of the capital stock. It also allows for variation in the optimal capital-output ratio.

Flexible exchange rate system (6-6) System in which the **foreign exchange rate** is free to change every day, to establish an equilibrium between the quantities supplied and demanded of a nation's currency.

Flow magnitude (2-2) An economic magnitude that moves from one economic unit to another at a specified rate per unit of time.

Foreign exchange rate (6-3) The amount of another nation's money that residents of a country can obtain in exchange for a unit of their own money.

Foreign exchange reserves (6-6) Government holdings of foreign money used under a **fixed exchange rate system** to respond to changes in the foreign demand for and supply of a particular nation's money. Such reserves are also used for intervention under a **flexible exchange rate system**.

Foreign trade deficit (6-8) The excess of the nation's imports of goods and services over its exports of goods and services.

Foreign trade surplus (6-8) Net exports.

Forward-looking expectations (8-6, 15-1) Predictions of future behavior of an economic variable, using an economic model that specifies the interrelationship of that variable with other variables.

General equilibrium (4-6) A situation of simultaneous equilibrium in all the markets of the economy.

Government budget (1-1) Records government tax revenues and expenditures on goods, services, and transfer payments. Statements about the government budget may apply just to the federal government or to all branches of government (federal, state, and local) together.

Government budget constraint (9-5) Limitation of government spending to the three sources available to finance that spending: tax revenue, creation of bonds, and creation of money.

Government budget deficit (1-1) The excess of government expenditures (on goods, services, and transfer payments) over tax revenue.

Government budget surplus (1-1) The excess of government tax revenues over government expenditures.

Gross (2-6) Economic aggregate that includes capital consumption allowances.

Gross domestic product (GDP) (1-3) The value of all currently produced goods and services sold on the market during a particular time interval.

Gross national product (GNP) (2-4) Goods and services produced by labor and capital supplied by U.S. residents, whether the actual production takes place within the borders of the United States or in a foreign country.

High-powered money (13-4) The sum of currency held outside depository institutions and the reserves held inside them.

Household wealth (3-3) is the total value of household assets, including the market value of homes, possessions such as automobiles, and financial assets such as **stocks**, bonds, and bank accounts, minus any liabilities, including outstanding mortgage and credit card debt, automobile loans, and other loans.

Human capital (10-7) The value, for a person or for society in general, of the extra earnings made possible by education.

Hyperinflation (9-1) A very rapid inflation, sometimes defined as a rate of more than 22 percent per month or 1,000 percent per year, experienced over a year or more.

Implicit GDP deflator (2-7) The economy's aggregate price index, defined as the ratio of **nominal GDP** to **chain-weighted real GDP**.

Imports (2-4) Goods consumed within one country but produced in another country.

Incomes policy (9-6) An attempt by policymakers to moderate increases in wages and other income, either by persuasion or by legal rules.

Indexed bond (9-4) A bond that pays a fixed real interest rate; its nominal interest rate is equal to this real interest rate plus the actual inflation rate.

Induced consumption (3-3) The portion of consumption spending that responds to changes in income.

Induced saving (3-5) The portion of saving that responds to changes in income.

Inflation (8-1) A sustained upward movement in the aggregate price level that is shared by most products.

Inflation differential (6-5) Foreign inflation minus domestic inflation.

Inflation rate (1-1) The percentage rate of increase in the economy's average level of prices.

Inflation tax (9-5) The revenue the government receives from **inflation**, the same as seignorage (the **inflation rate** times real high-powered money), but viewed from the perspective of households.

Infrastructure (11-1) Types of capital that benefit society as a whole, including highways, airports, trains, waterways, ports, telephone networks, and electricity grids.

Injections (2-5) Nonconsumption expenditures.

Interest rate (1-1) The percentage rate that is paid by borrowers to lenders.

Interest rate differential (6-9) The average U.S. interest rate minus the average foreign interest rate.

Intermediate good (2-3) A product resold by its purchaser either in its present form or in an altered form.

Intertemporal substitution (17-4) Workers work more in periods of high real wages and less in periods of low real wages. Also occurs when producers raise output in periods of high prices and reduce output in periods of low prices.

Intervention (6-6) Under the **flexible exchange rate system**, the buying or selling of a nation's money by domestic or foreign central banks in order to prevent unwanted variations in the **foreign exchange rate**.

Inventory investment (2-4) All changes in the stock of raw materials, parts, and finished goods held by business.

Investment (2-4) Portion of final product that adds to the nation's stock of income-yielding physical assets or that replaces old, worn-out physical assets.

IS curve (3-10) The schedule that identifies the combinations of income and the **interest rate** at which the commodity market is in equilibrium; everywhere along the *IS* curve the demand for commodities equals the supply.

Keynes Effect (7-9) The stimulus to **aggregate demand** caused by a decline in the **interest rate**.

Labor force (2-9) Total of persons employed and unemployed.

Labor productivity (11-2) Real GDP per hour of work, or output per hour of work.

Large open economy (6-9) An economy that can influence its domestic interest rate. A high domestic interest rate generates a steady stream of capital inflows that are not great enough to eliminate an **interest rate differential** between the domestic and foreign interest rate; a low domestic interest rate generates a steady stream of capital outflows.

Leakages (2-5) The portion of total income that flows to taxes or saving rather than into purchases of consumer goods.

Life-cycle hypothesis (LCH) (15-1) Conjecture that households base their current consumption on their total lifetime incomes and their wealth.

Liquidity constraint (15-6) Occurs when households cannot borrow as much as they wish, even though there is sufficient expected future income to repay the loans.

Liquidity trap (4-9) Situation in which the central bank loses its ability to reduce the interest rate.

LM curve (4-5) The schedule that identifies the combinations of income and the interest rate at which the money market is in equilibrium; on the *LM* curve the demand for money equals the supply of money.

Long-run aggregate supply curve (LAS) (7-1) A vertical line drawn at the natural level of **real GDP**; it shows the amount that business firms are willing to produce when the nominal wage rate has fully adjusted to any changes in the price level.

Long-run equilibrium (7-7) A situation in which labor input is the amount voluntarily supplied and demanded at the **equilibrium real wage rate**.

Long-term labor contracts (17-9) Agreements between firms and workers that set the level of nominal wage rates for a year or more.

Lucas model (17-3) Economic model based on the three assumptions of market clearing, imperfect information, and rational expectations.

M1 (13-3) The U.S. definition of the money supply that includes only currency, transactions accounts, and traveler's checks.

M2 (13-3) The U.S. definition of the money supply that includes M1; savings deposits, including money market deposit accounts; small time deposits; and money market mutual funds.

Macroeconomic externality (17-7) A cost incurred by society as a result of a decision by an individual economic agent (worker or business firm).

Macroeconomics (1-1) The study of the major economic totals, or aggregates.

Magic equation (2-5) Private saving plus net tax revenue must by definition equal the sum of private domestic investment, government spending on goods and services, and **net export**.

Marginal product of capital (MPK) (16-6) The extra output that a firm can produce by adding an extra unit of capital.

Marginal propensity to consume (3-3) The dollar change in consumption expenditures induced by a dollar change in disposable income.

Marginal propensity to save (3-3) The change in personal saving induced by a dollar change in disposable income.

Market-clearing model (7-9) Theory that the economy is always in equilibrium at the intersection of supply and demand curves, particularly in the labor market.

Medium of exchange (4-2) Units used for buying and selling goods and services; a universal alternative to the barter system.

Menu cost (17-6) Any expense associated with changing prices, including the costs of printing new menus or distributing new catalogs.

Mismatch unemployment (9-7) Structural unemployment; one of the two components of the natural rate of unemployment (the other being turnover, or frictional unemployment); it occurs when the present location or skills of members of the labor force do not match location or skill requirements of job vacancies.

Monetarism (14-3) A school of thought that opposes activist or discretionary monetary policy and instead favors a fixed rule for the growth rate of high-powered money or of the money supply.

Monetary impotence (7-9) Failure of **real GDP** to respond to an increase in the real **money supply**.

Monetary policy (1-7) Changes made in the money supply or interest rates or both in order to try to influence target variables.

Money market instruments (13-2) Assets sold in financial markets that have short maturities, usually less than one year, small fluctuations in price, and minimal risk of default.

Money multiplier (13-4) The ratio (M/H) of the money supply to high-powered money. There is a separate money multiplier for each definition of the money supply, e.g., $M1/H$ and $M2/H$.

Money-multiplier shock (13-5) Any event that causes the money multiplier to change, such as a change in the public's demand for currency relative to deposits, or a shift between deposits having different reserve requirements.

Money supply (4-2) Currency and transactions accounts, including checking accounts at banks and **thrift institutions**.

Multifactor productivity (10-5) The growth in multifactor productivity is the growth rate of output per hour of work, minus the contribution to output of the growth in the quantity of other factors of production per hour of work, notably capital but sometimes including energy, raw materials, or other factors of production.

Multiplier (3-6) The ratio of the change in output to the change in autonomous planned spending that causes it; also 1.0 divided by the **marginal propensity to save** (the fraction of an extra dollar of income that is not spent on consumption).

Multiplier uncertainty (14-4) The lack of firm knowledge regarding the change in output caused by a change in a policy instrument.

National Income and Product Accounts (2-3) Official U.S. government economic accounting system that keeps track of **GDP** and its subcomponents.

National saving (5-5, 12-2) The sum of private saving (by both households and business firms) and government saving (the **government budget surplus**).

Natural employment surplus (NES) or **deficit (NED)** (5-4) The government budget surplus or deficit at the **natural level of real GDP**.

Natural rate hypothesis (17-2) The hypothesis that shifts in aggregate demand have no long-run effect on real GDP.

Natural rate of unemployment (1-3) The level of unemployment at which the **inflation rate** is constant, with no tendency to accelerate or decelerate.

Natural real GDP (1-3) The level of **real GDP** at which the **inflation rate** is constant, with no tendency to accelerate or decelerate.

Net (2-6) Economic aggregate excluding capital consumption allowances.

Net domestic product (2-6) **GDP** minus depreciation.

Net exports (2-4) Exports minus imports.

Net foreign investment (2-4) Equal to exports minus imports.

Net international investment position (6-2) The difference between all foreign assets owned by a nation's citizens and domestic assets owned by foreign citizens.

Neutral policy (8-10) Attempt by government or central bank, following a supply shock, to maintain **nominal GDP** growth so as to allow a decline in the **output ratio** equal to the increase of the **inflation rate**.

New Keynesian economics (17-6) Approach that explains rigidity in prices and wages as consistent with the self-interest of firms and workers, all of which are assumed to have rational expectations.

Nominal (2-7) An adjective that modifies any economic magnitude measured in current prices.

Nominal anchor (14-8) A rule that sets a limit on the growth rate of a nominal variable, for instance, high-powered money, the money supply, the price level, or nominal GDP, to prevent inflation from accelerating without limit.

Nominal GDP (2-7) The value of **gross domestic product** in current (actual) prices.

Nominal interest rate (9-3) The market interest rate actually charged by financial institutions and earned by bondholders.

Nominal rigidity (17-6) A factor that inhibits the flexibility of the nominal price level due to some factor, such as menu costs and staggered contracts. Such factors make it costly for firms to change the nominal price or wage level.

Non–market-clearing model (7-9, 17-6) Workers and firms are not continuously on their respective demand and supply schedules, but rather are pushed off these schedules by the gradual adjustment of prices.

Okun's Law (8-13) A regular negative relationship between the **output ratio** (Y/Y^N) and the gap between the actual **unemployment rate** and the average rate of unemployment.

Open economy (1-8, 5-5) An economy that exports (sells) goods and services to other nations, buys imports from them, and has financial flows (capital flows) to and from foreign nations.

Open-market operations (13-5) Purchases and sales of government securities made by the Federal Reserve in order to change high-powered money.

Output ratio (8-1) The ratio of **actual real GDP** to **natural real GDP**. In the absence of supply shocks, the inflation rate remains constant when the output ratio is 100 percent, accelerates when the output ratio is above 100 percent, and decelerates when the output ratio is below 100 percent.

Parameter (3-5) A value taken as given or known within a particular analysis.

Peak (1-4) The highest point reached by real output in each **business cycle**.

Perfect capital mobility (6-9) A condition that occurs when investors regard foreign financial assets as a perfect substitute for domestic assets, and when investors respond instantaneously to an **interest rate differential** between domestic and foreign assets by moving sufficient assets to eliminate that differential.

Permanent income (15-4) The average income that people expect to receive over a period of years in the future.

Permanent-income hypothesis (PIH) (15-1) Conjecture that consumption spending depends on the long-run average (or permanent) income that people expect to receive.

Persistent unemployment (7-9) A situation in which a high level of unemployment can last for many years, as in the United States from 1929–41 and from 1980–85.

Personal consumption deflator (2-8) The price deflator for the personal consumption expenditures component of GDP.

Personal disposable income (2-6) Personal income minus personal income tax payments.

Personal income (2-6) Income received by households from all sources, including earnings and transfer payments.

Personal saving (2-4) That part of personal income that is neither consumed nor paid out in taxes.

Pigou Effect (real balance effect) (7-9) The direct stimulus to **aggregate demand** caused by an increase in the real **money supply**; does not require a decline in the **interest rate**.

Policy activism (14-1) Active use of instruments of monetary and fiscal policy to offset changes in private sector spending.

Policy credibility (14-6) The belief by the public that the policymakers will actually carry out an announced policy.

Policy ineffectiveness proposition (17-3) Assertion that predictable changes in monetary policy cannot affect real output.

Policy instruments (1-7, 14-2) Elements that government policymakers can manipulate directly to influence target variables.

Policy mix (4-11) The combination of **monetary** and **fiscal policy** in effect in a given situation.

Policy rule (14-1) Requirement of a fixed path of a policy instrument like the short-term interest rate, of an intermediate variable like the money supply, or a target variable like inflation or unemployment. Also requirement of a specified response of a policy instrument to a given change in a target variable.

Price index (2-8) Weighted average of prices at any given time, divided by the prices of the same goods in a base year.

Private investment (2-4) The portion of **final product** that adds to the nation's stock of income-yielding physical assets or that replaces old, worn-out physical assets.

Production function (10-3) A relationship, usually written algebraically, that shows how much output can be produced by a given quantity of factor inputs.

Productivity (1-1) Average output produced per hour.

Purchasing power parity (PPP) theory (6-5) Theory that the prices of identical goods should be the same in all countries, differing only by the cost of transport and any import (or customs) duties.

Quantity theory of money (7-8) Theory that actual output tends to grow steadily, while velocity is determined by payment practices such as the use of cash vs. checks, and that as a result a change in the **money supply** mainly affects the price level and has little or no effect on velocity or output.

Rate of return (3-9) Annual earnings of an investment project divided by its total cost.

Rate of time preference (12-2) The extra amount a consumer would be willing to pay to be able to obtain a given quantity of consumption goods now rather than a year from now.

Rational expectations (15-6, 17-3) Forecasts of future economic magnitudes based on information currently available about the past performance of the economy and future government policies.

Real balance effect (Pigou Effect) (7-9) The direct stimulus to aggregate demand caused by an increase in the real money supply; does not require a decline in the interest rate.

Real business cycle (RBC) model (17-4) Explanation attributing business cycles in output and employment to technology or supply shocks.

Real consumption wage (10-2) The nominal wage rate divided by the price deflator for personal consumption expenditures.

Real exchange rate (6-5) The average nominal **foreign exchange rate** between a country and its trading partners, adjusted for the difference in **inflation rates** between that country and its trading partners.

Real GDP (2-7) Value of gross domestic product in constant prices.

Real GDP gap (output gap) (1-4) The percentage difference between actual and natural real GDP.

Real interest rate (1-6) The nominal interest rate minus the inflation rate.

Real money balances (4-4) Total **money supply** divided by the price level.

Real product wage (10-2) The nominal wage rate divided by the price index for total output, such as the GDP deflator.

Real rigidity (17-6) A factor that makes firms reluctant to change the real wage, the relative wage, or the relative price.

Recession (1-4) The interval in the business cycle between the peak and the trough.

Redistribution effect (7-9) The decline in **aggregate demand** caused by the effect of falling prices in redistributing income from high-spending debtors to low-spending savers.

Required reserves (13-5) The reserves that Federal Reserve regulations require depository institutions to hold.

Reserve requirements (13-5) Rules, which apply only to transactions accounts, that stipulate the minimum fraction of deposits that must be held as reserves.

Residual (10-5) The amount that remains after subtracting from the rate of real GDP growth all of the identifiable sources of economic growth.

Revaluation (6-6) A nation's raising of the value of its money when its **foreign exchange reserves** become so excessive that they cause domestic inflation.

Rigid rule (14-3) A rule for policy that sets a key policy instrument at a fixed value as in a constant growth rate rule for the money supply.

Rigid wages (7-9) The failure of the nominal wage rate to adjust by the amount needed to maintain equilibrium in the labor market.

Sacrifice ratio (8-7) The cumulative loss of output incurred during a **disinflation** divided by the permanent reduction in the **inflation rate**.

Seignorage (9-5) The revenue the government receives from inflation; equal to the **inflation rate** times real high-powered money.

Self-correcting forces (7-8) The role of flexible prices in stabilizing **real GDP** under some conditions.

Short-run aggregate supply (SAS) curve (7-1) Graph of the amount of output that business firms are willing to produce at different price levels, holding constant the nominal wage rate.

Short-run equilibrium (7-7) The point where the **aggregate demand curve** crosses the **short-run aggregate supply curve**.

Short-run Phillips (SP) Curve (8-2) The schedule relating **real GDP** to the **inflation rate** achievable given a fixed **expected rate of inflation**.

Small open economy (6-9) An economy with perfect capital mobility but with no power to set its domestic interest rate at a level that differs from foreign interest rates.

Solow's residual (10-5) Growth in multifactor productivity.

Stabilization policy (1-7) Any policy that seeks to influence the level of **aggregate** demand.

Staggered contracts (17-6) Wage contracts that have different expiration dates for different groups of firms or workers.

Standard of living (11-2) Real GDP per member of the population, or output per capita.

Steady state (10-3) A situation in which output and capital input grow at the same rate, implying a fixed ratio of output to capital input.

Stock (2-2) An economic magnitude in the possession of a given economic unit at a particular point in time.

Store of value (4-2) A method of storing purchasing power when receipts and expenditures are not perfectly synchronized.

Structural deficit (5-4) What the **government budget deficit** would be if the economy were operating at **natural real GDP**.

Structural surplus (5-4) What the **government budget surplus** would be if the economy were operating at **natural real GDP**.

Supply inflation (8-9) An increase in prices that stems from an increase in business costs not directly related to a prior acceleration of **nominal GDP** growth.

Supply shock (8-1) Caused by a sharp change in the price of an important commodity.

Supply-side economics (12-7) Theory predicting that a reduction in marginal income tax rates will create an increase in the supply of output, that is, in natural real GDP.

Target variables (1-7, 14-2) Economic **aggregates** whose values society cares about—society's goals.

Taylor Rule (14-7) This rule calls for the central bank to move the real short-term interest rate away from its desired long-term value in response to any deviation of actual inflation from desired inflation and in response to any deviation of real GDP from natural real GDP.

Thrift institutions (13-2) Financial intermediaries such as savings and loan institutions, mutual savings banks, and credit unions.

Time inconsistency (14-6) Policymakers' deviation from a policy after it is announced and private decisionmakers have reacted to it.

Time series (15-3) Data covering a span of time of one or more series (e.g., disposable income or consumption spending).

Total factor productivity (10-5) The growth rate of output per hour of work, minus the contribution to output of the growth in the quantity of other factors of production per hour of work, notably capital but sometimes including energy, raw materials, or other factors of production.

Total labor force (2-9) The total of the civilian employed, the armed forces, and the **unemployed**.

Transfer payments (2-3) Payments for which no goods or services are produced in return.

Transitory income (15-4) The difference between actual income and permanent income; it is not expected to recur.

Trilemma (6-1) The impossibility for any nation of maintaining simultaneously (1) independent control of domestic monetary policy, (2) fixed exchange rates, and (3) free flows of capital with other nations.

Trough (1-4) The lowest point reached by real output in each **business cycle**.

Turnover unemployment (frictional unemployment) (9-7) One of the two components of the natural rate of unemployment (the other being mismatch, or structural unemployment), it occurs in the normal process of job search.

Unanticipated inflation (9-3) Situation in which the actual inflation rate (p) differs from the expected (or anticipated) inflation rate (p^e).

Unemployed (2-9) Persons without jobs who either are on temporary layoff or have taken specific actions to look for work.

Unemployment rate (1-1, 2-9) A percentage that expresses the ratio of the number of jobless individuals actively looking for work or on temporary layoff divided by the total employed and **unemployed** in the labor force.

Unintended inventory investment (3-5) The amount business firms are forced to accumulate when planned expenditures are less than income.

Unit of account (4-2) A way of recording receipts, expenditures, assets, and liabilities.

User cost of capital (16-6) The cost to the firm of using a piece of capital for a specified period.

Value added (2-3) The value of the labor and capital services that take place at a particular stage of the production process.

Wage indexation (cost-of-living agreements) (9-6) An automatic increase in the wage rate in response to an increase in a price index.

Index

401 (k)s, 408

Abel, Andrew B., 498n, 531n
Absolute value, 461n
Accelerator
   flexible, 525–526, 532
   postwar U.S. economy and, 523–525
Accelerator hypothesis, 519–522
Accommodating policy, 256
Acemoglu, Daron, 363–364, 366
Activists' paradise
   policy rules advocates and, 452–454
   stabilization targets and instruments in, 450–454
Actual employment deficit, historical behavior of, 138–139
Actual real GDP, 6–8, 14
   in Great Depression, 226
   unemployment and, 13, 265
Actual real interest rate, 286
Actual unemployment, 7–8
   rate of, 302–303
Adaptive expectations, 245–246, 490–491
Adaptive (error-learning) method, of estimating sales, 520–521
AD curve. *See* Aggregate demand *(AD)* curve
Adjustable-rate mortgage (ARM), 439
Adjustment, to long-run equilibrium, 248, 249
Adjustment loops, 247–248
AD-SAS model, 232. *See also* Aggregate demand *(AD)* curve; Short-run aggregate supply *(SAS)* curve
Adverse supply shocks, 254, 285
   in 1970s, 257, 258
   beneficial shock turned into, 590
   and RBC model, 556–557
Affinity cards, 436
Africa, 349
Aggregate, 5
Aggregate demand
   aggregate supply and, 197–198
   defined, 59
   increases in, 213, 236–237
   weak, 222–224
Aggregate demand *(AD)* curve, 417
   alternative *SAS* curves and shift in, 204
   autonomous spending change and, 201–202
   defined, 198
   flexible prices and, 198–200
   inflation and, 232
   nominal GDP growth, inflation, and, 241n

   nominal money supply and, 200–201
   shifts in, 200–202, 203
Aggregate demand shift. *See also* Aggregate demand *(AD)* curve
   consumption spending and, 533
   investment spending and, 533
Aggregate demand-supply model, self-correction in, 214–215
Aggregate price information, 555
Aggregate supply, 59
   aggregate demand and, 197–198
Aggregate supply curve, 585. *See also* Long-run aggregate supply *(LAS)* curve; Short-run aggregate supply *(SAS)* curve
Aggregate supply shift, productivity, beneficial supply shocks, and, 533
Agriculture, in tropics, 365, 366
AIDS, 366
Airline industry
   investment decision in, 79, 80
   multiplier effect in, 71–72
American Airlines, investment by, 79, 80
Ameriks, John, 505n
Ando, A., 473n
Anti-convergence, 358
Appreciation, 161–162
Argentina, 357, 358
Aschauer, David A., 371n
Asia. *See also* specific countries
   codependent relationship with, 189
   competitiveness with, 594
   economic growth in, 319–320
   financial crisis in, 463–464
   Four Tigers of, 349, 350
   productivity growth in, 17–19
   U.S. dollar and, 174–177
Assets, under life-cycle hypothesis, 493–497
Auction market, 565
Australia, saving in, 503
Automatic stabilization, 92, 134–135
Autonomous consumption, 63–64, 197
Autonomous growth factor, 325–326
Autonomous magnitude, 61
Autonomous net exports, 92–93
Autonomous planned spending, 66–67, 71
   business/consumer confidence and, 81
   change in, 201–202
   components of, 72–73
   demand for, 82
   effects of increase on price level and real income, 211
   interest rate and, 79–82

Baby boom generation, retirement of, 387, 404
Backward-looking expectations, 245
Baily, Martin N., 223n
Balanced budget multiplier, 76, 93
Balance of payments
   BP line in small and large open economy, 187
   defined, 156
   exchange rate systems and, 170
   schedule of, 183
   surplus and deficit in, 156–158
Balance of payments deficit, flexible exchange rate system and, 171–172
Balance sheet, of Fed, 97
Bangladesh, 349
BankAmericard, 437
Banker's acceptances, 421
Bank of England, 597
Bank panics, money supply and, 428
Bank reserves, 97
Barnett, W. A., 340n
Barro, Robert J., 336n, 402, 403, 465n, 556n
Barro-Ricardo equivalence theorem, 402–404, 501–504
Basic deficit, 296
Basu, Susanto, 376n, 537n
Baum, L. Frank, 290
Baumol, William J., 432–433
BEA. *See* Bureau of Economic Analysis (BEA)
Beneficial supply shocks, 254, 463
   in 1990s, 257, 258–260, 590, 591
   unemployment and inflation created by, 267–268
Bequests
   Barro-Ricardo equivalence theorem and, 403
   motives for, 504–505
   uncertainty and, 501–505
Bernanke, Ben S., 467n, 473n
Bettman, Otto, 374, 375n
Big boxes (large stores), U.S. productivity revival and, 382
Big Mac standard, 169, 170, 171
Blanchard, Olivier, 459n, 461n
Blinder, Alan S., 438n, 589n
BLS. *See* Bureau of Labor Statistics (BLS)
Bluestone, Barry, 309n
Boeing, multiplier effect and, 71–72
Bond creation, vs. money creation, 296–297
Bond rate, 106, 107
Bonds, 293, 294, 421, 422

I-1

Borrowing, 158–159, 418
Botswana, economic growth in, 366
BP. *See* Balance of payments
Brainard, William, 460n
Bretton Woods system, 593, 594
Brewley, T. F., 498n
Bribes, 362
Brooker, Katrina, 437n
Brumberg, R. E., 493n
Brunner, Karl, 222n, 455n
Bruno, Michael, 370
"Brute force labor," 367
Bryan, William Jennings, 290
Bubbles, high-tech stocks and, 535, 591
Budget. *See* Government budget
Budget deficit. *See* Government budget deficit
Budget line, 136–137
Bullard, James B., 292n
Bureau of Economic Analysis (BEA), 28
Bureau of Labor Statistics (BLS), 28, 47–49
Bureau of the Census
  statistics from, 28
  unemployment survey and, 45–47
Burstein, M. L., 443n
Bush, George H. W., 5
Bush, George W., 5, 47, 499
  tax cuts and, 147, 400, 504
Business. *See also* Firm
  income flow to, 36–38
  investment of personal savings in, 30
Business confidence, speculation and, 532–533
Business cycles. *See also* Fooling model; Real business cycle (RBC) model
  concepts of, 9–10, 11
  defined, 9
  economic change and, 323, 351
  emergence of, 548
  imperfect information and, 549
  income determination and, 57–59
  interpretations of, 213–214
  investment and interest rates correlation in, 538
  real GDP and, 12–14
  in short run, 9
  stabilization policy and, 19–20
  theories of, 574
Business groups, financing constraints and, 536–537
Business optimism, 81

Cagan, Phillip, 16n, 245n
Calmes, Jackie, 406n
Cameroon, 357, 358
Campbell, John Y., 501n
Canada, 537
  economic growth in, 323
  saving in, 503
Capital
  intangible, 376
  marginal product of, 527
  user cost of, 526, 527
Capital account, 156
Capital deepening, 353n
Capital gains, on housing, 507
Capital good, 528–529
Capital growth, per person, 326
Capital-labor ratio, and output per person, 324–326
Capital losses, in Asia, 176–177
Capital market, government surplus or deficit and, 33
Capital market instruments, 421–422
Capital mobility
  interest rates and, 181–182
  in large open economy, 187–189
  perfect, 181
Capital stock
  fixed ratio of, 519
  sales expectations and, 521
Caplin, Andrew, 505n
Case, Karl E., 508–509
Cash, credit card use vs. use of (international comparison), 436–437
Cash holding, 432–433
  costs and benefits of, 433–434
  money-creation multiplier and, 427
Cash-holding ratio, 428
Cashless society, 436
Cassidy, John, 556n
Census Bureau. *See* Bureau of the Census
Census of Population, 28
Central bank
  buying of U.S. dollar by, 594
  exchange rate and, 473–476
  foreign, 172–173
  inflation target and, 592
  monetary growth and, 283–285
  operating independently, 466–467
  policy credibility and, 466
  policy rules and, 454
Certificates of deposit, 423
Chad, 365
Chaebol, 537
Chain-weighted GDP deflator, 45
Chain-weighted real GDP, 42, 43
Checking deposits, Fed and, 97–98
Chicago Board of Trade, 106
Children, Barro-Ricardo equivalence theorem and, 403
China
  economic growth in, 320
  exchange rates in, 175
  foreign investment in, 361
  free trade with, 594
Churchill, Winston, 216
Circular flow, 36
  saving and investment in, 31
  taxation, government spending, and foreign sector in, 33
Citibank, 419, 429, 436

Citigroup, 436
Clark, J. M., 523
Classical economics. *See also* New classical macroeconomics
  Keynesian revolution and, 216–223
  quantity theory of money and, 214
  self-correction in aggregate demand-supply model and, 214–215
  view of unemployment and output fluctuations in, 215–216
Classical models, 549
Clinton, Bill, 5
Closed economy, 20
  crowding out in, 140–142
  fiscal expansion in, 141
Cobb, Charles W., 347n
Cobb-Douglas production function, 335n, 338, 347–348
Cold turkey approach, 289
  defined, 247
  to disinflation, 249
Colonialism, economic growth and, 365
Commercial banks, 420
Commercial paper, 421, 422
Commodity demand, unstable, 439–440, 443
Commodity demand shocks, 456, 470, 483
Commodity markets, financial deregulation and, 440
Computers
  decline in real prices of, 260
  investment in, 532, 533–534, 535
  productivity growth revival and, 373
Conglomerates, 537
Congress, fiscal policy and, 387
Constant growth rate rule (CGRR), 424, 454, 455
Constant returns to scale, 347
Construction industry, productivity growth slowdown and, 371
Consumer(s)
  in 1950s, 585
  2001 tax rebate and, 499
Consumer confidence, 532
Consumer credit, interest rates and, 502–503
Consumer expenditure. *See also* Consumption expenditures
  changing interest rates and, 460
  components of (1960–2004), 485
Consumer loans, 421
Consumer optimism, 81
Consumption
  alternative paths of, 388–389
  behavior in, 62
  circular flow of, 26
  economic stability and, 483–484
  forward-looking theories of, 483–484
  housing wealth and stock market wealth and, 509
  income changes and, 501
  induced, 61

Index **I-3**

interest rate and, 82
  marginal propensity and, 61
  permanent-income hypothesis of saving and, 492
  policy activism and, 511–512
  during retirement, 505
  saving, disposable income, and, 65
Consumption behavior, 483–512
  assets as determinant of, 495–497
  forward-looking theories of, 483–484
  under life-cycle hypothesis, 494
Consumption expenditures, 26–27
  components of, 484–486
  disposable income, ratio of saving to income, and, 486
  future benefits and, 391
  IS curve shifts and, 483
Consumption function, 61–62
  Keynesian, 488
Continuous inflation, 236–237
Contractionary monetary policy, 105
Contracts
  long-term labor, 570–571
  staggered, 564
Contractual savings institutions, 420, 421
Convergence, 354–360
  among industrialized countries, 337
  in neoclassical growth model, 336–337
  rich and poor countries displaying, 358
  Solow model and, 354–355, 359–360
Coordination failure
  daylight saving time and, 570
  defined, 568
  indexation and, 568–570
Corporate bonds, 421
Corporate income tax, depreciation and, 529
Corporate stocks, 421
"Correct expectations" line. *See* Long-run Phillips *(LP)* Curve
Costa Rica, infrastructure of, 364
Cost-of-living agreements (COLAs)
  defined, 571
  inflation and, 256–257
Council of Economic Advisers, 264
Countercyclical fiscal policy, 77
Countercyclical variable, 213
Coupon, 422
Credibility
  defined, 302
  policy, 466
  and reputation, 466–467
Credit, interest rates and consumer, 502–503
Credit cards
  as alternative to currency, 291n
  international comparison of cash use and, 436–437
Credit unions, 420, 421
Cross-country differences. *See* International comparisons

Cross section
  defined, 488
  vs. time series, 486–489
Crowding-out effect, 110–111, 115
  in closed economy, 140–142
  fiscal expansion and, 186
  net exports and, 131–132
Currency, 97, 423. *See also* Foreign exchange entries; specific currencies
  devaluation in Europe, 594
  euro, 474–475, 594, 596
Currency to deposits ratio *(c)*, 431–432
Current account, 155–161
  capital account and, 156
  defined, 155
Current account balance, net international investment position and, 159
Current account deficit, 157, 159, 175
  national saving and, 594–595
  of United States (2004–05), 594
Curves. *See IS* curve; *LM* curve; specific curves
Cyclical deficit, 134
Cyclical surplus, 134
Cyclical unemployment, 303–304

Darby, Michael, 580n
Data lag, 456–457
David, Paul, 372, 489n
Daylight saving time, coordination failure and, 570
Deaton, Angus, 498n
Debit cards, 436, 437
Debt. *See also* Government debt
  foreign, 158–159
  monetizing, 119
Debt-GDP ratio, 393–395, 396
  historical behavior of, 395–397
  international comparisons of, 394
  in U.S., 395–397
Debtors, deflation and, 287–288
Deficit(s). *See also* Government budget deficit
  balance of payments, 156–158
  basic, 296
  current account, 157
  cyclical, 134
  financing of, 131–132, 285, 392
  foreign trade, 145–146, 155
  government, 33, 387
  natural employment, 137
  private saving and government, 502
  stalemate over, 589
  structural, 134
Deficit financing, hyperinflation and, 301
Deflation, 198
  debtors and, 287–288
  in Great Depression, 219
  rigid nominal wages and, 220
Delay hypothesis, 372
DeLong, Brad, 374

Demand. *See also* specific types
  aggregate, 59
  for autonomous planned spending, 82
  firm's response to decline in, 566–568
  inflation and acceleration of growth, 246
  for money, 109, 417–418, 424, 432–443
Demand curve, 566
  for currencies, 163–164
Demand for money, income, interest rate, and, 98–101
Demand inflation, defined, 252
Demand-pull inflation, 235
Demand schedule
  IS curve and, 83–84
  shifts in, 82
Demand shocks, 197, 232, 470
  in 1950s and 1960s, 584
  adjustment to, 569
  defined, 59, 234, 449
  SAS curve and, 205
  unemployment and inflation from, 267
  volatility and, 461
Demographics, of unemployment rates, 307–308
Dependency ratios, LCH and, 502
Depletion hypothesis, for U.S. productivity growth slowdown, 371
Depository institutions, 420, 421
Depreciation, 36, 162
  corporate income tax and, 529
  interest and, 529
  of U.S. dollar, 594
  user cost and, 527n
Depreciation rate, 529
Depressions. *See also* Great Depression
  debt-GDP ratio and, 397
Deregulation, financial, 293, 417, 420, 439–442
Deutsche Bundesbank, 250
Devaluation, 172
Developing nations. *See* Newly industrializing countries; Poor countries (developing nations)
DG line. *See also SP-DG* model
  equation for, 273
  shifting, 276
Diagrams
  AD curve, 203
  SAS curve, 207
  short-run *(SP)* and long-run *(LP)* Phillips Curves, 240
Diners Club, 437
Discount rate, 430
Discretionary policy, 135, 136–137, 454
  vs. policy rules, 467, 470–473
Discrimination, unemployment and, 306
Disease, in tropics, 365, 366
Disinflation
  1970–2001, 588
  1982–91, 589
  defined, 247

Disinflation *(continued)*
  in Europe and United States, 250–251
  Fed and, 469
  output cost of, 249
Disintermediation, 439
Disposable income
  consumption and, 64, 65, 486
  household assets as ratio to (1970–2004), 508
  personal, 38, 489
Dissaving, 488
Diversion, economic growth and, 363–364
Dollar (U.S.). *See also* Foreign exchange rate
  flexible exchange rates with Asian currencies, 174–177
  foreign exchange market and, 163–164
  foreign exchange rate of, 154, 173–174
  foreign holdings of, 175–176
  real and nominal exchange rates of, 173–174
  real corporate bond and real exchange rates of, 181
Domar, Evsey, 328
Domestic income, 37
Domestic investment
  in closed economy, 140
  national saving and, 389–390
Dornbusch, R., 281n, 300n
Douglas, Paul H., 347n
Draxe, Thomas, 154
Dremas, David, 449
Durable goods expenditures, 484, 485–486
Dynamic multipliers, 459

East Asia, economic growth in, 342
Easterly, William, 364n
Eberly, Janice C., 531n
E-commerce, 372, 436, 535
Economic and Monetary Union (EMU), 474
Economic growth, 9, 12, 319–348, 349–383. *See also* Solow's economic growth theory
  comparison of seven countries, 322–323
  conclusions on, 382–383
  convergence and, 354–360
  defined, 321
  diversion and, 363–364
  endogenous theory of, 339–341
  exogenous factors integrated in, 367–368
  fiscal debate and long-run, 409–410
  geography and, 365–367
  government budget and, 387–388
  growth miracle and, 350
  Harrod-Domar model of, 328
  human capital and, 360
  immigration puzzle and, 368
  importance of, 319–321
  international comparisons of, 355–359
  inventions and, 374–375
  in long run, 11
  long-run effects of fiscal policy on, 388–390
  mechanism of, 350–351
  national saving, budget deficit, and, 389–390
  physical infrastructure and, 364–365
  political capital and, 362–364
  political environment and, 350
  in poor countries, 595
  production function and, 323–327
  productivity and, 351–354
  real wage and, 353–354
  saving and, 502
  secrets of, 342
  in short run, 9
  slowdown and revival of, 351
  Solow's theory of, 327–331
  standard of living and, 320, 321–322, 351–352
  technology and, 360–362
  U.S. growth across eras, 368–370
Economic model, 127
Economic policy
  real business cycle model and, 563
  theory of, 451
Economic research, real business cycle model and, 563
Economics. *See also* Classic economics; New classical macroeconomics; New Keynesian economics
  changes in thinking through 1960, 585
  Keynesian, 221, 587, 597
  Social Security reform and, 408–409
  supply-side, 400–402, 590
Economic stability. *See also* Stabilization policy
  investment and, 516–540
Economic theory, 5
Economic volatility, decline in, 461–465
Economic welfare, policy instruments, policy targets, and, 451
Economy. *See also* Large open economy; New Economy; Small open economy
  in 1950s, 583
  in 1960s, 585
  in 1972–82, 587
  in 1982–91, 589
  in 1991–2004, 590–591
  in 2001, 3
  adjustment with shift in *SP* and *DG*, 276–277
  "always true" and equilibrium situations, 69
  closed, 20
  election of 2004 and, 47
  equilibrium and, 65–70
  general equilibrium of, 105
  Goldilocks, 258–260, 591
  in Great Depression, 580–582
  instability through investment in, 516–540
  in Japan, 118–119
  open, 20
  puzzles in 1991–2004 period, 591–592
  self-correcting forces in, 214
  simple accelerator and postwar United States, 523–525
  stability of, 461
  supply shocks and, 558
  world-U.S. interactions and, 593
  World War II and, 582–583
Edison, Thomas A., 375
Education
  economic growth and, 360, 361
  human capital and, 337
Effectiveness lag, 457–459
Efficiency wage model, 572–573
Efficient financial market theory, 562
Eguchi, H., 473n
Eichengreen, Barry, 223n, 580n
Eisner, Robert, 586n
Elasticity, 347n. *See also* Price elasticity of demand
Elderly, income redistribution between workers and, 399
Electric utility industries, productivity growth slowdown and, 371
Electronic commerce. *See* E-commerce
Electronic credits, 429
Employment
  in 1990s, 590
  adverse supply shock and, 557
  from Household and Payroll Survey, 48
  NAIRU of, 591–592
  payroll survey measure of, 376
  real wages and, 562
  relationship between real GDP and, 206–207
Employment Act (1946), 585
Employment policy, 451
Endogenous growth theory, 360, 362
  empirical studies and policy implications of, 341
  production of ideas and, 340–341
  technological change and, 339–341
Endogenous variables, 60
Energy prices
  in 1990s, 259, 260
  productivity growth slowdown and, 372
Engles, Friedrich, 216
Enron, corruption scandal at, 376
Equilibrium, 65–67
  defined, 67
  economy and, 67–69
  general, 105
  in labor and product markets, 548
  long-run, 212–213
  models of, 549
  money market, 109–110

reputational, 466
of saving/investment in Solow growth model, 330
short-run, 212
Equilibrium income, 84
autonomous planned spending and, 71
determining, 67
interest rate and, 126
Equilibrium real GDP, determining, 69–70
Equilibrium real wage rate, 208–210
Equivalence, Barro-Ricardo theorem of, 402–404
Error-learning method, of estimating sales, 520–521
Euro, 251, 594, 596
debate over, 474–475
dollar and, 175
United States, trilemma, and, 189–190
Eurodollars, 421, 422
Europe
disinflation in, 250–251
economic performance of, 21
fiscal and monetary policies in, 597
Great Depression in, 224–225
macroeconomics in, 596–597
productivity in, 379–382, 595, 597
unemployment in, 596
U.S. labor market policies and institutions compared with, 381
European Central Bank (ECB), 474, 475, 597
European Economic Community (EEC), 474
European Monetary System (EMS), 250, 474, 594
European Union (EU), expansion of, 475
Events
evolution of, 579–580
reaction of ideas to (1923–47), 580–583
reaction of ideas to (1947–69), 583–587
reaction of ideas to (1970–2004), 587–593
reaction of ideas to events in world economy, 593–595
Exchange rate. *See* Foreign exchange rate
Exogenous factors, in economic growth, 367–368
Exogenous variables, 60
Expansion, 10, 11
fiscal, 74, 141
recovery period in, 10n
Expansionary monetary policy, 105
Expectations
adaptive, 245–246, 490–491
backward-looking, 245–246
forward-looking, 245, 483–484
inflation and, 238–239
rational, 497–498
Expectations-augmented Phillips Curve, 237
Expectations effect, 219

Expected rate of inflation
defined, 237
10-year Treasury bond rate and, 289
Expected real interest rate, 286–287
Expenditures. *See also* Consumption expenditures; Spending
circular flow of, 25–27
components of, 29–32
on durable goods, 484, 485–486
equilibrium and, 65–66
income and, 34
on nondurable goods, 484, 485–486
planned, 61–64
on services, 484, 485–486
Exports, 32, 92–93, 594. *See also* Net exports
Extinguishing policy, 256
Extra convenience services, 291

Factor inputs, 323
Falling prices, destabilizing effects of, 219
Farmer, R., 473n
Fed. *See* Federal Reserve (the Fed)
Federal deposit insurance, 428
Federal funds rate
in 1970s and early 1980s, 587
increase in, 591
output ratio and, 463–465
as short-term instrument of control, 467–468
Taylor Rule and, 468–470
Federal Open Market Committee (FOMC), 106, 429, 457
Federal Reserve (Fed), 28, 428, 429
in 1994–2004 period, 591
balance sheet of, 97
bank reserves interest and, 291
control of, 417
discount rate of, 430
economic volatility decline and, 461–465
electronic credits and, 429
Great Depression and monetary policy of, 223
interest rates and, 430, 442–444
monetary policy and, 106, 387
money supply and, 97–98, 428–432
open-market operations of, 429–430
policy rules and, 456
reserve requirements of, 430–431
supply shocks and, 463–464
Taylor Rule and, 467–470, 598
unemployment rate and, 266
value of dollar and, 20–22
Federal Reserve Bank of New York, 429
Feedback rule, 455
Feldstein, Martin S., 387, 526n
FFA. *See* Flow of Funds Accounts (FFA)
Field, Alexander J., 559n
Final good, 29
Final product, 27
Finance companies, 420, 421

Financial crisis, in Asia, 463–464
Financial deregulation, 293
defined, 417
interest rates and, 439–442
IS curve and, 439–440
LM curve and, 440–441
of thrift institutions, 420
Financial intermediaries (institutions)
categories of, 420–421
defined, 419
deregulation of, 293
disintermediation and, 439
markets, instruments, and, 418–422
role of, 419–420
Financial market instruments, 418–422
Financial markets, 417
defined, 418
efficient, 562
role of, 419–420
Financing
government budget deficit and, 74–75
of investment spending, 537
Firm. *See also* Business
decline in demand and, 566–568
price setting by monopolist, 565–566
Fiscal activism, 586
Fiscal expansion, 74
in closed economy, 141
crowding-out effect and, 110
initial short-run effect of, 210–211
IS curve and, 108–110
IS-LM model in small open economy and, 184–186
in open economy, 143
in short and long run, 210–214
Fiscal multiplier, monetary response and, 116–120
Fiscal policy, 19, 130–131
in 1950s, 585
in 1960s, 585–587
in 1970s, 587
in 2005, 592
Barro-Ricardo equivalence theorem and, 402–404
business cycles, volatility, and, 59
demand shocks and, 197
discretionary, 135, 136–137
displacement by monetary policy, 589
economic control and, 417
in Europe and United States, 597
with fixed and flexible exchange rates, 185–186, 188–189
Great Depression and, 582
in Japan, 117–120
in large open economy, 144
long-run effects on economic growth and welfare, 388–390
long-run orientation of, 387–388
monetary policy used with, 116–121
national saving and, 139
natural rate of unemployment and, 450

Fiscal Policy (continued)
  in open economy, 142–144
  and persistent deficits, 409
  policy instrument types of, 450–451
  policy mix and, 120–121
  real balance effect and, 218–219
  real GDP fluctuations and, 387
  real income and, 117
  shifting aggregate demand curve with, 200–202
  stimulus in, 120, 144, 184
  strong and weak effects of, 114–115
  supply-side economics and, 400–402
  in United States and Japan, 77
  user cost and, 528–531
Fischer, Stanley, 455, 459n, 466n
Fisher, Irving, 237n, 288
Fisher Effect, 288–289
Fisher equation, 288
Fixed exchange rate, 182, 473–476, 593, 594
  and expansion in small open economy, 183–185
  fiscal policy and, 184, 186, 188
  monetary policy and, 188
Fixed exchange rate system, 172
Fixed investment, 30, 519, 523, 524
  Great Depression and collapse of, 222
Fixed-investment expenditures, 485
Fixed nonresidential investment, 519, 523, 524
Fixed wages, 565
Fixed-weight real GDP and GDP deflators, 42
Flavin, Marjorie, 498n
Flexible accelerator, 525–526, 532
Flexible exchange rate, 182, 473, 594
  between dollar and Asian currencies, 174–177
  fiscal policy and, 185–186, 188
  monetary policy and, 185–186, 188
Flexible exchange rate system, 171–174
Flexible prices, *AD* curve and, 198–200
Flow magnitude, 27
Flow of Funds Accounts (FFA), 509–510
FOMC. *See* Federal Open Market Committee (FOMC)
Food price shocks, 587
Fooling model
  criticisms of, 551
  of Friedman, 548–550
  Lucas model and, 551–555
  of Phelps, 550–551
Foot, David, 526n
Ford, Robert, 371n
Foreign central banks. *See also* Central bank
  dollars purchased by, 176
  flexible exchange rate systems and, 173
Foreign exchange, market for, 163–166
Foreign exchange rate, 154, 155, 161–162, 197. *See also* Purchasing power parity (PPP) theory

Asia, U.S. current account deficit, and, 174–177
  changes in, 161–162
  daily quotations of, 162
  defined, 161
  of dollar, 164, 173–174
  fixed, 182
  flexible, 171–172, 182, 460
  government influence on, 166
  in large open economy, 187–189
  monetary policy and, 473–476
  net exports and, 178–179
  supply and demand for dollar, 165
  systems of, 170–174
Foreign exchange reserves, 172
Foreign investment. *See also* Investment
  national saving and, 389–390
  political and legal determinants of, 362–364
  technological change and, 361–362
Foreign sector, 32
Foreign trade, 154–155, 163, 596
  balance of payments and, 157–158
  euro and, 474
  international economics and, 594
Foreign trade deficit, 145–146, 155
Forward-looking expectations
  defined, 245, 483–484
  life-cycle hypothesis and, 493–497
  permanent-income hypothesis and, 489–493
Four Tigers, 349, 350, 356, 357, 358, 361
France, 349
  economic growth in, 323
  infrastructure of, 364
  investment in, 537
  saving in, 503
FRED (database), 28
Free trade
  with Asia, 594
  foreign business start-ups and, 363
Friedman, Benjamin M., 438n, 455n, 466n, 498n
Friedman, Milton, 223n, 245n, 460n
  on demand for money, 438
  fooling model of, 548–550
  marginal propensity to consume and, 491
  on market clearing and imperfect information, 549–550
  monetarism of, 585, 586
  on monetary rule, 456
  natural rate hypothesis of, 586–587
  new classical approach of, 548
  on nominal interest rate rule defect, 470n
  on permanent income, 490
  permanent-income hypothesis of, 484, 489–492, 493, 495, 497–498, 506
  on policy rules, 454, 455
Friedman-Phelps-Lucas supply function, 552–554

Gains-inclusive saving rate, 510, 511
Garraty, John A., 216n
GDP. *See* Gross domestic product (GDP)
GDP deflator, 42, 43–45, 197, 198. *See also* Inflation rate
  chain-weighted, 42, 43, 45
  growth rate of (1970–2004), 253
  implicit, 40
  inflation rate measurement by, 232–233
  price level measurement and, 232
General equilibrium, 105
General functional form, 348
General Theory of Employment, Interest, and Money, The (Keynes), 216, 486, 547, 582
Geography, economic growth and, 365–367
Germany
  debt-GDP ratio of, 394
  economic growth in, 323
  euro and, 474
  Great Depression in, 16, 224–225
  hyperinflation in, 16–17
  indexed contracts and, 575
  investment in, 536
  slowed economic growth in, 475
Ghana, 357, 358, 366
GNP. *See* Gross national product (GNP)
Goethe, Johann Wolfgang, 25
Gold, money supply and discoveries of, 427–428
Goldilocks economy, 258–260, 591, 592, 595
Goodfriend, Marvin, 589n
Goods, intermediate, 29
Gordon, David B., 465n
Gordon, Robert J., 10n, 222n, 257n, 259n, 373n, 473n, 537n, 579n, 592n
Gore, Al, 5
Government(s)
  benefits from inflation, 298–299
  diversion and, 363–364
  as economic sector, 32
  foreign investment and, 362–368
  inflation and, 297–298
  wars and, 132–134
Government budget, 92. *See also* Deficit; Government budget deficit
  economic growth and, 387–388
  effects of, 131–132
  history of, 132–134
  international comparisons of, 148, 149
  twin deficits and, 35–36
Government budget constraint
  defined, 295
  equation, 296
  inflation tax and, 295–299
Government budget deficit, 390–391, 409–410
  financing and, 74–75
  foreign trade deficit and, 145–146
  growth and disappearance of, 397–400

international comparisons of, 148, 149
national saving, economic growth, and, 389–390
recessions and, 134
revenue and expenditures and, 398–399
solvency of government and, 392–395
to surplus (late 1990s), 397–398
wars and, 132–134
Government budget deficits
persistent, 590
Government budget surplus
deficit and, 397–398
government saving and, 389
methods for raising, 390
real income and, 135
Government debt
burden of IBM debt and, 391–392
future burden of, 390–392
ratio of United States to GDP (1790–2005), 396
true burdens of, 392
Government expenditures
budget line and, 136–137
categories of, 398–399
financed by deficits, 392
as percent of natural GDP, 398, 399
during persistent deficits, 398
real income, interest rate, and, 109
revenues, budget deficit, and, 133
taxation and, 73–74
Government investment projects, 391
Government revenues
as percent of natural GDP (1960–2005), 398
during persistent deficits, 389
Reagan tax cuts and, 401–402
Government saving, rate of, 147
GPDI. *See* Gross private domestic investment (GPDI)
Great Depression
causes of, 221–227
deflation during, 219
economy in, 580–582
international comparison during, 224–225
investment and, 532
Keynesian revolution and, 547, 582
money, output, unemployment, prices, and wages in, 223
price level and GDP during, 226
prices and output ratio in, 224–227
RBC model advocates and, 559n
real GDP and unemployment during, 13
real wages and unemployment in, 562
unemployment in, 15–16
Greenspan, Alan, 372
Greenwald, Bruce, 565n
Gross, 36
Gross domestic product (GDP), 6, 31–32. *See also* GDP deflator; Real income
actual and natural real, 5–8

current account and, 155
nominal, 38
ratio of U.S. government debt to (1790–2005), 396
real GDP and, 39
total expenditure and, 29
Gross investment, determinants of, 526
Gross national product (GNP), 31–32, 156
Gross private domestic investment (GPDI), 517–519, 525
"Group of Five" inventions, 375
Growth miracle, 350
Growth puzzles, 367–368
Growth rate, 168–169, 240–242, 393

Hahn, Frank, 455n, 498n
Hall, Robert E., 362n, 498n
Harrison, Bennett, 309n
Harrod, Roy, 328
Harrod-Domar model, 328
Harrod-neutral technical change, 332n
Harry S. Truman (aircraft carrier), cashless society on, 436
Hatton, T. J., 580n
Hayashi, Fumio, 531n
Heller, Walter, 585
Heston, Alan, 321n, 355, 356n, 357n, 358n
Hicks, John, 85n, 216
High-powered money *(H)*, 425–426, 427, 428, 470
creation of, 429–430
discount rate and, 430
Fed and, 431–432
High-tech investment
boom and bust in, 591
collapse of, 373–376, 532, 591
productivity growth revival and, 373
High-tech stocks, bubble and, 535, 591
Hitler, Adolf, Great Depression and, 16, 17
Hong Kong, 349, 356, 365, 366
Horizontal *LM* curve, 217–218
Households
assets and personal disposable income, 508
consumption expenditures and, 26
income flow from, 36–38
personal saving by, 30
remains after leakages, 37
tax rebate of 2001 and, 499
Household saving rate
FFA measure of, 509–510, 511
household net worth and, 506, 507
NIPA measure of, 509, 510
stock market and, 506–509
Household survey. *See* Households
Household wealth, 63–64
Housing. *See also* Residential investment
capital gains on, 507
investment spending on, 517
refinance of, 507
thrift institutions and, 460

Human capital, 350
defined, 337
economic growth and, 360
immigration puzzle and, 339
Solow puzzles and, 338–339
technological change and, 361
total output raised by, 338
Hurd, Michael, 505n
Hyperinflation, 476
costs of anticipated, 300
defined, 281
ending, 301–302
factors causing, 300–301
in Germany (1922–23), 16–17
starting and stopping, 299–302

IBM, burden of debt and, 391–392
Ideas
in endogenous growth theory, 340–341
evolution of, 579–580
productivity growth and, 371
reaction to events (1923–47), 580–583
reaction to events (1947–69), 583–587
reaction to events (1970–2004), 587–593
in world economy, 593–595
Immigration, neoclassical model and, 339
Immigration puzzle, 368
Imperfect information, 548–551, 555
Friedman on, 549–550
in Lucas model, 552
Phelps and, 550–551
Implicit GDP deflator, 40, 43
Imports, 31, 32, 259–260. *See also* Exports
Income, 25. *See also* Net investment income; Real income
circular flow of, 25–27
demand for money and, 99–100
disposable, 65
domestic, 37
economic growth and, 349–350
expenditures and, 34
fiscal policy stimulus and, 116
flow from business to households, 36–38
under life-cycle hypothesis, 494–495
permanent, 490
personal, 37–38
ratio of saving to, 486
redistribution between workers and elderly, 399
saving and, 64–65
transitory, 491
variation across countries, 334–335
wages and, 26
Income determination
business cycles and, 57–59
price level and, 59–60
Income-determination multiplier, money-creation multiplier and, 426
Incomes policy, 301
Income tax, 91–92
cuts in 2001, 77

I-8 Index

Income tax *(continued)*
    indexation of, 293–295
    multiplier and, 92
Indexation
    coordination failures and, 568–570
    inflation costs and, 293–295
    nominal demand and, 569
Indexed bond, 293, 294
India, 349
Individual accounts, Social Security debate and, 592
Induced consumption, 61
Induced net exports, 92–93
Induced saving, 69
    marginal propensity to save and, 62–63
Industrialized countries, convergence and, 337
Industrial Revolution, second, 374–375
Industries, U.S. productivity growth slowdown and, 371
Inflation, 198, 232–268. *See also* Disinflation; Federal Reserve Board (Fed); Hyperinflation
    in 1970s and early 1980s, 587
    in 1982–91, 589
    in 1990s, 590
    in 1991–2004 period, 591
    acceleration of demand growth and, 246
    adjustment path of, 243, 249
    annual rates in high inflation countries (1975–2005), 299
    calculating, 44
    causes of, 281
    COLAs and, 256–257
    "cold turkey" remedy for, 247
    conditions for harmlessness of, 287–293
    continuous, 236–237
    costs of, 280–281
    cures for, 263
    defined, 232
    demand, 252
    demand-pull, 235
    effects of, 297
    exchange rate and, 476
    expectations about, 238–239
    expected rate of, 237
    Fed and, 463, 464, 465
    Fisher Effect and expected, 288–289
    gold discoveries and, 427–428
    in Goldilocks economy, 595–596
    governments tempted by, 297–299
    indexation and, 293–295
    interest rates and, 286–292
    in late 1990s, 258–260
    in medical care, 260
    money and, 281–285
    nominal GDP growth and, 240–242, 242–244, 248
    and output fluctuations, 261–263
    output ratio and, 234
    and postwar unemployment, 266–267
    real exchange rate and, 167
    real wage growth and, 285–286
    recession as cure for, 247–248
    "shoe-leather cost" of, 291
    slowdown in nominal GDP growth and, 248
    solutions to, 311
    stabilization policy goals and, 280–311
    supply, 252
    supply shocks and, 254–258, 463
    Taylor Rule and Fed attitude toward output and, 467–470
    unanticipated, 287–288
    velocity, output, money, and, 281–283
Inflation cycle, expectations and, 245–247
Inflation differential, 169
Inflation rate, 4, 450. *See also* Hyperinflation
    1970–2001, 588
    actual and natural real GDP and, 6
    constant, 7
    in Great Depression, 580
    measurement of, 39–45, 232–233
    output and, 5
    output ratio and, 233, 251
    real GDP, short-run Phillips Curve, and, 235–238
    shifts in nominal GDP growth and, 262
    SP curve and increase in expected, 238
    targeting, 445, 467, 468
    unemployment rate and, 263–268
Inflation target, 450, 455
    in 1990s, 592
    rule, 468
    vs. Taylor Rule, 597–598
Inflation tax
    defined, 298
    government budget constraint and, 295–299
Information, availability of, 555
Infrastructure
    defined, 350
    economic growth and, 350, 364–365
    productivity growth slowdown in United States and, 370–371
Injections, 34, 36
Innovation, financial deregulation, interest rates, and, 439–442
Input(s), productivity growth slowdown and, 370–371
Input-output approach, 569
Instability
    investment, output, interest rates, and, 538–539
    investment and, 516–540
    Korean War and, 585
    in private economy, 483–512
Instruments. *See also* Policy instruments
    of stabilization policy, 450–451
Insurance companies, 420, 421
Intangible capital, 376
Intel Corporation, Moore and, 534
Intellectual revolutions, of 1960s, 585–587
Interest rate(s), 199
    in 1970–2004, 588
    in 1990s, 590
    in 1998–2000, 591
    in 2001–04, 592
    actual real, 286
    autonomous consumption, stock market, and, 63–64
    autonomous planned spending and, 79
    capital mobility and, 181–182
    comparison of targeting money supply with targeting, 440–445
    consumer credit and, 502–503
    consumer spending and changing, 460
    on credit cards, 436
    demand for money and, 100–101
    deregulation and, 439–440
    effects of low, 507–508
    equilibrium level of income and, 126
    equilibrium real income and, 84
    expected real, 286
    Fed and, 430, 442–445, 463–465
    financial deregulation, innovation, and, 439–442
    functions of, 78
    government spending and, 109
    inflation and, 286–292
    investment, output rate, and, 538–539
    in Japan and United States, 118
    market rate not paid on money, 289–291
    monetary policy and, 106–107
    money supply, income, and, 98–100
    money supply and, 442–443
    money supply increase and, 114n
    nominal, 286
    pegging of, 583
    real exchange rate and, 180–182
    real income and, 86
    regulation of, 439
    in surprise inflation, 287–288
    targeting of, 587
    taxation and, 292
    types of, 78–79
Interest rate differential, 180
Interest responsiveness of transactions demand for money theory, 432–435
Intermediate good, 29
International comparisons
    of Big Mac and PPP, 170, 171
    of cash and credit card use, 436–437
    of debt-GDP ratio, 395
    of disinflation in Europe and United States, 250–251
    of economic growth, 322–323, 355–359
    of economic performance, 21
    euro and, 474–475
    of fiscal policy in United States and Japan, 77

Great Depression in United States, 224, 225
of growth success and failure in tropics, 366
of indexed bonds, 294
of macroeconomics in United States and Europe, 596–597
of monetary and fiscal policy in Japan, 118–119
of money growth and inflation, 284
of national saving rates, 502–503
of per capita income, 334–335
of productivity in Europe and United States, 379–382
of productivity in Japan and United States, 560–561
of saving, investment, and government budgets, 148, 149
of worldwide investment, 536–537
International economy, 594–595
International investment position, U.S. standard of living and, 160–161
Internet
 credit card use on, 436
 economic data from, 28
 international Web sites and, 28
 rates in 1982–91, 589
Intertemporal substitution, 558
Intervention, 172–173
Inventions
 economic growth and, 351, 374–375
 productivity growth and, 371
 standard of living and, 382–383
Inventory changes, GPDI and, 519
Inventory investment, 29
Investment
 accelerator hypothesis of, 519–522
 by airline, 79, 80
 boom and bust in New Economy, 533–538
 business confidence, speculation, and, 532–533
 in circular flow, 31
 in closed economy, 140
 components of, 146
 economic growth and, 321, 326–327
 equilibrium in Solow growth model, 330
 fixed, 30, 519
 fluctuations in, 517–519
 foreign, 361–362
 Great Depression and, 532
 gross, 526
 gross private domestic (GPDI), 517–519
 in human capital, 337
 instability and, 516–540
 interest rate and, 82
 international comparisons of, 148, 149
 inventory, 29, 519
 national saving and, 389–390
 neoclassical theory of, 527–528

 net foreign, 31
 output change and, 521–522
 policy activism and, 539–540
 postwar behavior in, 525
 private, 29
 q theory of, 530–531
 saving and, 30–31
 taxation and, 529–531
 Taylor Rule and volatility of, 539–540
 types of, 29–30
 unintended inventory and, 68
 worldwide, 536–537
Investment firms, retirement fund management by, 420
Investment intermediaries, 420, 421
Investment rate, economic growth and, 359–360
IRAs, 408
Ireland, economic growth in, 475
IS curve, 83–86
 autonomous spending decline and, 201–202
 consumption spending and, 483
 defined, 83
 derivation of, 83
 expansionary fiscal policy and, 108–110
 financial deregulation and, 437–438
 information shown on, 85–86
 investment, saving, and, 86n
 LM curve and, 104–105
 nominal money supply and, 200, 201
 points off the curve, 85
 reasons for name, 85n
 shifts in, 85, 539
 slope of, 85
 steep, 113
 vertical, 217
IS-LM model, 94–129, 198, 417, 432, 538
 algebra of, 126–129
 comparison of targeting money supply with targeting interest rates, 444–445
 deficits and, 285
 Japanese fiscal policy and, 119
 real income, interest rate, and, 111
 real interest rate and, 288n
 real-world economy and, 449
 schedules in, 105
 in small open economy, 182–186
Italy
 debt-GDP ratio of, 395
 economic growth in, 323
 investment in, 537
 saving in, 503

Japan, 357, 358
 convergence by, 337
 dollar reserves of, 175
 economic growth in, 323, 356
 economic performance of, 21, 118–119
 fiscal policy in, 77, 117–120

 foreign exchange rate of yen, 161
 Great Depression in, 224, 225
 investment in, 536
 keiretsu in, 537
 productivity fluctuations in, 560–561
 saving in, 503
 use of cash in, 437
Jobless recovery, 376, 590
Job loss. *See also* Unemployment
 demographics of, 307–308
 fear of, 284–285
Job refusal, 308
Job search theory, 308
Job training, mismatch unemployment and, 306
Johnson, Harry, 547n
Johnson, Lyndon, 586
Johnson, Simon, 364n
Jones, Charles I., 358n, 362n
Jorgenson, Dale, 526–528, 537n

Kahn, R. F., 486n
Karni, Edi, 435n
Katz, Lawrence F., 310n, 592n
Keiretsu, 537
Kennedy, John F., 585
Kerry, John, 47
Keynes, John Maynard, 214, 417, 582, 597
 on business confidence and investment levels, 533
 consumption function and saving ratio of, 488–489
 on multiplier, 486
 Tobin's q theory and, 530
Keynes Effect, 218
Keynesian economics, 587
 Europe and, 597
 Germany and, 225
Keynesian revolution, 216–221, 582, 589
Keynesian theory
 weak aggregate demand and, 222–224
 after World War II, 585
King, Robert G., 556n, 565n
Kipling, Rudyard, 374
Kirkland, Lane, 130
Korea, 349, 350
 chaebol in, 537
 economic growth in, 319–320, 356
 per-capita real GDP in South Korea, 18–19
 saving in, 503
Korean War, 593
 demand shocks and, 461
 economic effects of, 583
 price controls during, 583n
 recession after, 583
Kos, Dino, 429
Kotlikoff, Laurence, 501n
Krueger, Alan B., 310n, 592n
Krugman, Paul, 118

I-10 Index

Kuttner, Kenneth N., 119n
Kydland, Finn E., 465, 556n

Labor and labor force, 352n
   "brute force labor," 367
   economy measured by participation rate, 401
   income redistribution between elderly and, 399
   total, 46
Labor-augmenting technological change, 332
Labor contracts
   characteristics of, 570–571
   long-term, 570–571
   wage rates and, 210
Labor demand curve, 377, 378, 379
   equilibrium real wage rate and, 209–210
   SAS curve and, 205, 206–207, 208
   shifting of, 558n
Labor input, economic growth and, 360
Labor market
   equilibrium in, 221
   in RBC model, 557–558
Labor market diagram, for labor supply shifts as source of faster/slower productivity growth, 377–379
Labor market policies, Europe/U.S. comparison, 381
Labor productivity. *See also* Productivity
   adverse productivity shocks or labor supply shocks and, 377–379
   defined, 352
   in Europe and United States (1970–2004), 380
   growth rate of (U.S. 1960–2004), 369
   multifactor productivity and, 353
   standard of living and, 351–352
Labor productivity shock, real wage decline and, 377–379
Labor quality, productivity growth slowdown and decline in, 370
Labor supply
   intertemporal substitution and, 558
   shifts as source of faster/slower productivity growth, 377–379
Labor supply curve, equilibrium real wage rate and, 209–210
Labor supply shock hypothesis, real wage rates, productivity rates, and, 377–379
Laffer, Arthur, 401
Laffer curve, government revenues, tax cuts, and, 401–402
Lags
   estimated lengths of, 459
   fiscal activism and, 586
   policy and, 456–460
   targeting inflation rate and, 468
   types of, 456–457
Landes, David, 349, 349n, 367n

Landlocked nations, economic development and, 365, 366
Large open economy
   capital mobility and exchange rates in, 187–189
   defined, 182
   fiscal policy in, 144
LAS curve. *See* Long-run aggregate supply *(LAS)* curve
Latin America, 349, 464
   hyperinflation in, 301–302
   inflation in, 41
Leahy, John, 505n
Leakages, 34, 37, 94n
Leakages-injections identity, 594
Legal environment, foreign investment and, 363
Legislative lag, 457
Leijonhufvud, Axel, 219n
Liabilities, of Fed, 97
Life-cycle hypothesis (LCH), 493–497, 504–505, 506, 507
   defined, 484
   dependency ratios and, 502
Lifetime budget constraint, of LCH, 493
Lifetime consumption, and lifetime income, 495
Liquidity constraint, 500–501
Liquidity trap, 114, 217–218
LM curve, 95, 100–104, 417, 538. *See also* IS-LM model
   change in nominal money supply and, 200, 201
   changing prices and, 198–200
   defined, 102
   derivation of, 101, 102
   financial deregulation and, 438–439
   flat, 113–114
   horizontal, 217–218
   IS curve and, 104–105
   money supply and, 106–108, 111, 114n
   slope of, 103
Loans, consumer, 421, 422
Local government retirement funds, 420, 421
Log output ratio, 461, 463, 464
Long run
   economic growth in, 11
   fiscal and monetary expansion in, 210–214
   macroeconomics in, 9
   saving rate in, 488–489
Long-run aggregate supply *(LAS)* curve, 205, 212
   defined, 198
   inflation and, 235, 236
Long-run consumption function, 492
Long-run equilibrium, 212–213, 244
   adjustment to, 248, 249
   defined, 212
   economic growth and, 354–355
Long-run MPC, 491, 493

Long-run orientation, of fiscal policy, 387
Long-run Phillips *(LP)* Curve, 239, 240
Long-term labor contracts, 570–571
LP curve. *See* Long-run Phillips *(LP)* Curve
Lucas, Robert E., Jr., 319, 340, 551–552, 556n, 589n, 597
   on monetary impotence, 555
   new classical approach and, 548
Lucas model, 551–555, 587, 597
Lucas supply function. *See* Friedman-Phelps-Lucas supply function; Lucas model

M1 definition of money, 417, 422, 423, 431, 432, 435, 580, 590
M2 definition of money, 283n, 417, 422, 423–424, 431, 435
Maastricht Treaty (1992), 474, 596
Macroeconomic data, sources of, 28
Macroeconomic externality, 568
Macroeconomics
   comparative, 598
   defined, 3, 5
   inflation rate and, 4
   internationalization of, 20–22
   New Economy in, 372
   productivity and, 4
   unemployment in Great Depression and, 15–16
   unemployment rate and, 3–4
   in United States and Europe, 596–597
Macroeconomic variables
   1923–47, 581
   in 1948–69, 584
   of 1970–2004, 588
Magic equation, 33–36
Malaysia, 320
   economic growth in, 366
Mali, 357, 358, 365, 366
Manchester, William, 16n
Mankiw, N. Gregory, 336n, 338n, 501n, 566n
Marginal cost
   and marginal revenue, 569
   sticky, 568
Marginal leakage rate, 91–92
Marginal product of capital (MPK), 527
Marginal propensity to consume (MPC), 61, 71–72, 491, 493
Marginal propensity to save, 62–63, 69
Marginal revenue curve, 566
Margo, Robert, 580n
Market(s)
   equilibrium in labor and product, 548
   financial institutions, instruments, and, 418–422
Market clearing, 555, 587
   Friedman on, 549–550
   in Lucas model, 552
Market-clearing model, 221
Marshall, Alfred, 214, 547
Marshall, Eliot, 483

Marshall Plan, 593
Marx, Karl, 216
MasterCard, 436
McCallum, Bennett T., 556n
McNamara, Francis X., credit cards and, 436–437
Measured capital per labor hour, productivity growth slowdown and, 370
Medical care, inflation in 1990s, 260
Medium of exchange, money as, 96
Menu costs
 defined, 564
  imperfectly competitive firms and, 565–566
  sticky marginal cost and, 568
Mill, John Stuart, 214
Mining industry, productivity growth slowdown and, 371
Minorities, employment discrimination against, 306
Miracle economy. *See* Goldilocks economy
Mismatch unemployment
 causes and cures for, 305–306
 compared to turnover unemployment, 307
 defined, 304
 location and, 306
 skills and, 305–306
 sources of, 304–306
 vacancies and unemployment in imaginary economy, 304–305
Mitchell, Kristen B., 310n
Mitchell, Wesley, 349
Modigliani, Franco, 454n, 501n
 life-cycle hypothesis of, 484, 489, 493–497, 504–505, 507
Monetarism
 abandonment of, 589
 counterrevolution by, 547n
 defined, 455
 of Friedman, 585, 586
Monetarists, 424
Monetary expansion
 IS-LM model in small open economy and, 184–186
 in short and long run, 210–214
 strong effects of, 112
 weak effects of, 112–114
Monetary factors, in Great Depression, 221–222
Monetary-fiscal policy mix, 586
Monetary growth, central banks and excessive growth, 283–285
Monetary impotence, 216–218, 565
 defined, 216
 Lucas on, 555
Monetary policy, 19, 105–108
 in 1950s, 585
 in 1960s, 585
 in 1970s, 587
 in 1994-2004 period, 591

 in 2001–04, 106–107
 business cycles, volatility, and, 59
 contractionary, 105
 demand shocks and, 197
 euro and, 474–475
 in Europe and United States, 597
 exchange rates and, 183, 185–186, 188–189, 473–476
 expansionary, 105
 failures of (1929–33), 227
 fiscal policy and, 116–121, 589
 Great Depression and, 223–224, 582
 in Japan, 118–119
 lags in, 456–459
 monetary aggregates and, 590
 natural rate of unemployment and, 450
 planned spending and, 78–79
 policy mix and, 120–121
 real GDP fluctuations and, 387
 shifting aggregate demand curve with, 200–202
 short-run orientation of, 387
 as stabilization tool, 417
 strong and weak effects of, 111–114
 user cost and, 528–531
Monetary policy multipliers, 460
Monetary shocks, 556n, 557
Monetization of debt, 119
Money, 417–418. *See also* M1 definition of money; M2 definition of money
 credit cards and, 436–437
 definitions of, 422–424
 demand for, 98–101, 109
 in Great Depression, 223
 high-powered, 425–426, 427, 428
 holding, 432–433, 433–434
 inflation and, 281–285
 market rate of interest and, 289–291
 as medium of exchange, 96
 quantity theory of, 214
 as store of value, 96
 as unit of account, 96–97
 uses of, 95–97
 velocity, inflation, output, and, 281–283
Money creation, 424–427
Money demand
 debit cards and, 437
 instability of, 424
 interest responsiveness of, 115
 portfolio approach to, 435–438
 shifts in, 449
 theories of, 417–418, 432–438
 transactions demand for money theory, 432–435
 unstable, 443–444
Money demand shocks, 456, 470, 483
Money market, 86
 financial deregulation and, 440
Money market deposit accounts, 423, 439
Money market equilibrium, 109–110

Money market instruments, 421–422
Money market mutual funds, 420, 421, 423, 424, 439
Money multiplier, 98n, 427, 454
Money multiplier shocks, 432, 449, 456, 470, 483
Money supply, 197
 credit cards and, 436
 definitions of, 95, 97, 424
 determinants of, 424–428
 Fed and, 97–98, 428–432
 increases in, 105–108, 113
 interest rates and, 114n, 441–442
 LM curves and, 108, 111
 rule for, 472
 targeting interest rates vs. targeting, 444–445
Monopolist, price setting by, 565–566, 567
Moore, Gordon, 534
Moore's Law, 534
Mortgage interest rates, refinancing of, 106
Mortgages, 421, 422, 437–438
MPC. *See* Marginal propensity to consume (MPC)
Multifactor productivity (MFP)
 defined, 333
 economic growth and, 352–353
 fluctuations of, 560–561
 labor productivity and, 353
Multiplier, 486n
 balanced budget, 76, 93
 calculating, 70–71
 changes in, 460
 defined, 70
 dynamic, 459
 fiscal, 116–120
 income taxes and, 92
 leakages and, 94n
Multiplier effect, 70–72, 197
Multiplier uncertainty, 459–460
Mundell, Robert, 288n
Mundell effect, 288n
Muth, John, 552n
Mutual funds, 420, 421

Nasar, Sylvia, 310n
NASDAQ stock market index, 535
National Income and Product Accounts (NIPAs), 27, 28, 30n, 509
National Industrial Recovery Act (NIRA), 227
National saving, 138–144, 536
 budget deficit, economic growth, and, 389–390
 current account deficit and, 594–595
 defined, 139, 389
 solutions to squeeze in, 147–150
National saving rates, 502–503
NATO (North Atlantic Treaty Organization), 474
Natural employment deficit (NED), 137, 138–139

Natural employment surplus (NES), 137
Natural GDP
    government revenues and expenditures as percent of, 398, 399
    unemployment and, 13
Natural rate hypothesis, 585, 586–587, 589
    defined, 550
Natural rate model, 550
Natural rate of unemployment, 7–8, 302–303, 550, 590
    decline in, 310, 595–596
    defined, 8
    regular changes in, 591–592
Natural real GDP, 6–8, 14, 550
    in Great Depression, 225, 226
    unemployment rate and, 265
Navy, credit cards issued by, 436
NDP. *See* Net domestic product (NDP)
NED. *See* Natural employment deficit (NED)
Negative unemployment-inflation tradeoff, 267–268
Negotiable large-denomination certificates of deposit, 421, 422
Neoclassical growth model. *See* Solow's economic growth theory
Neoclassical theory
    of economic growth, 323–324
    of investment behavior, 527–528
NES. *See* Natural employment surplus (NES)
Net. *See* Internet; World Wide Web (WWW)
Net (economic), 36
Net domestic product (NDP), 36
Net exports, 31, 131, 155, 157
    determinants of, 178–179
    fiscal policy stimulus and, 144
Net foreign investment, 31
Net international investment position, 158, 159
Net international transfers, 156
Net investment, accelerator hypothesis and, 519–522
Net investment income, U.S. generation of, 160
Net investment ratio, 524, 525
Net saving, components of, 146
Neutral policy, 255–256
Neutral technological change, 332
New classical macroeconomics, 587–589
    Europe and, 597
    limitations and positive contributions of, 560–563
    Lucas model and, 551–555
    New Keynesian macroeconomics and, 547–548
    real business cycle model and, 555–560, 590
New economics, of Heller, 585–586
New Economy, 372, 373, 409–410
    benefits of, 383
    collapse of, 383, 535–538
    high-tech stock market bubble and, 535
    investment boom and bust in, 533–538
New Keynesian economics
    assessment of, 574–575
    coordination failures and indexation of, 568–570
    defined, 564
    efficiency wage theory and, 572–573
    features of, 563–564
    as intellectual event, 592–593
    long-term labor contracts and, 570–572
    model of, 564–565
    new classical macroeconomics and, 547–548
    small nominal rigidities and large macroeconomics effects, 565–568
    triangle model of, 589
Newly industrializing countries, 319–320
New Zealand, 357, 358
NIPAs. *See* National Income and Product Accounts (NIPAs)
Nominal, 38
Nominal anchor, 470
Nominal exchange rate
    of dollar, 173–174
    real exchange rate and, 168
Nominal GDP, 38, 40, 516, 580
Nominal GDP growth
    acceleration in, 242–244
    inflation and, 240–242
    inflation and real GDP growth, 242
    inflation rate, output ratio, and, 262
    slowdown in, 248
Nominal GDP rule, 472, 473
Nominal interest rate, 286
    rule, 470
    taxes and, 292
Nominal money supply
    AD curve and, 200–201
    LM curve and, 198–199
Nominal rigidity
    defined, 564
    input-output approach and, 569
    small, 565–568
Nominal wage rates
    in Great Depression, 226–227
    long-run equilibrium and, 212
    and real wage rate, 205
    rigidity in, 220–221
    rising, 208–209
    SAS curve and constant, 205–207
Non-Accelerating Inflation Rate of Unemployment (NAIRU), 591–592
Nondurable goods expenditures, 484, 485–486
Non-market-clearing model, 221, 564
Nonresidential fixed investment, 519, 523, 524
Nordhaus, William D., depletion hypothesis of, 370, 371
North, Douglas, 363
Oil prices
    GDP deflator and nominal and real oil prices, 253
    supply inflation and, 251
Oil price shocks, 251, 587
Okun, Arthur M., 264, 309–310, 452n, 585
Okun's Law, 472n
    defined, 264
    unemployment rate, output ratio, and, 264–266
Oliner, Stephen D., 531, 537n
Open economy, 20. *See also* Large open economy; Small open economy
    defined, 142
    economic policy in, 189–190
    fiscal policy in, 142–144, 188
    monetary policy effects in, 188
Open-market operations, of Fed, 429–430
Optimism-pessimism grid, in rules vs. activism debate, 453
Output
    adverse supply shock and, 557
    classical view of fluctuations in, 215–216
    in Great Depression, 223
    growth in, 323–324
    human capital and, 338
    inflation and, 5, 261–263
    investment level and change in, 521–522
    money, velocity, inflation, and, 281–283
    per hour, 356
    per person, 324–326, 329, 336, 357, 359
    real, 39
    Taylor Rule, Fed, and, 467–470
    during World War II, 582
Output changes, price and, 560–562
Output rate, investment, interest rate, and, 538–539
Output ratio
    defined, 234
    federal funds and, 463–465
    in Great Depression, 580
    inflation and, 233, 252, 253–258
    and moving average of its absolute value, 461, 462
    and prices in Great Depression, 224–227
    and shifts in nominal GDP growth, 262
    unemployment rate, Okun's law, and, 264–266
Overbuilding cycles, 532–533

Parameter, 66, 128n
Payroll employment survey, 47–49, 376
Peak, 10, 11, 254
Pegging, during World War II, 583

Penn project, 321n
Per capita income, variation across countries, 334–335
Per capita real GDP
　in seven countries, 323
　in South Korea and Philippines, 18–19
Perfect capital mobility, 181–182
Perfect competition, 565
Perfectly competitive price takers, 565
Permanent income, 490, 492
Permanent income hypothesis (PIH), 493, 495, 497–498, 506, 586
　bursts of purchases and, 517
　defined, 484
　forward-looking behavior and, 489–493
Persistence, in postwar investment behavior, 525
Persistent unemployment, 221
Personal disposable income, 38
Personal income, 37–38
Personal income tax, 32, 400, 401
Personal saving, 30
　ratio to disposable personal income, 489
Peru, business start-up costs in, 362–363
Peter, Laurence J., 280
Phelps, Edmund S., 257n, 548
　fooling model of, 550–551
　natural rate hypothesis of, 586–587
Philippines, 350
　economic growth in, 319–320
　per-capita real GDP in, 18–19
Phillips, A. W. H., 237, 585
Phillips Curve, 585. *See also* Short-run Phillips *(SP)* Curve
　expectations-augmented, 237
　long-run, 239, 240
　mechanism, 590
　tradeoff, 466, 591
Pigou, Arthur C., 214, 216, 218
Pigou (real balance) Effect, 218, 496n
Planned autonomous spending. *See* Autonomous planned spending
Planned spending, 61–64
　autonomous, 66–67
　decline in, 215, 220
　monetary policy and, 78–79
　sources of shifts in, 72–76
Plant and equipment investment, 517n
Plosser, Charles I., 556n
Policy. *See also* Fiscal policy; Monetary policy
　inflation cures and, 263
Policy activism
　consumption and, 511–512
　defined, 449
　investment and, 539–540
Policy credibility, 466
Policy dilemma, COLAs, supply shock, and, 257

Policy ineffectiveness proposition (PIP), 555
Policy instruments, 19
　defined, 450
　policy targets, economic welfare, and, 451
　rules for, 470–471
　targets, structural relations, and, 452
Policy mix, 120–121
Policy responses, to supply shocks, 254–256
Policy rules, 454–456
　activists' paradise and advocates of, 452–454
　alternative, 471
　vs. assessment of alternative, 467, 470–473
　constant growth rate, 454
　defined, 450
　discretionary, 454
　vs. discretion debate, 467
　feedback, 455
　Modigliani and, 495
　monetarism and, 455
　for money supply, 472
　negative case for, 456
　nominal GDP, 472, 473
　for policy instruments, 470
　positive case for, 455–456
　rigid, 454
　for target variables, 472
　Taylor Rule, 473
Policy targets, 451, 452
Political capital, economic growth and, 362–364
Political environment, economic growth and, 350, 363–364
Politics, 4–5
　Social Security reform and, 408–409
Poole, William, 443
Poor countries (developing nations)
　economic growth in, 365, 383, 595
　neoclassical growth model and, 336–337
　rate of return on capital for, 335–336
　saving, investment, and capital per hour in long-run equilibrium for, 355
　Solow model, convergence, and, 354–360
　standards of living in, 320
　technology for, 361
Population growth
　economic growth and, 359
　optimistic vs. pessimistic assumptions about, 592
Poret, Pierre, 371n
Portfolio approach, to demand for money, 435–438
Posen, Adam S., 119n
Poverty, predictors of, 365
Preemptive strike, Fed and, 463, 591

Prescott, Edward C., 465n, 548, 556n, 597
Price(s)
　falling, 219
　in Great Depression, 223, 224–227
　and output changes, 560–562
Price controls
　during Korean War, 583n
　during World War II, 582
Price elasticity of demand, 165n
Price flexibility, 575–576
Price index, nominal money supply increase and, 549
Price level, 197, 198. *See also* GDP deflator
　actual vs. natural real GDP during Great Depression and, 226
　effects on real income of different values of, 199–200
　failure in self-correction of, 217
　GDP deflator measurement of, 232
　in Great Depression, 580, 582
　income determination and, 59–60
　planned autonomous spending and, 211
　in short run, 59–60
Price setting, by monopolist firm, 565–566
Price shocks, local vs. aggregate, 554
Price surprises, 552–553
Private accounts, for Social Security, 408, 409
Private investment, 29, 517–519
Private pension funds, 420
Private saving, 33, 389, 390
　fiscal policy stimulus and, 144
　government deficits and, 502
　rate of, 147
Production function
　adverse supply shock and, 557
　Cobb-Douglas, 335n
　defined, 324
　economic growth and, 323–327
　general functional forms and, 347–348
　per person output and input and, 325, 336
Productivity, 4
　in Asia, 17–19
　in Europe and United States, 379–382
　goal of, 19
　multifactor (Solow's residual), 352–353
　real wage and, 353–354
　standard of living and labor, 351–352
　in United States and Japan, 560–561
Productivity growth, 409
　in 1990s, 591
　in 1991–2004 period, 591
　debate over, 598
　ebbs and flows in, 595
　in Europe and United States, 597
　factor inputs and, 370–371
　high-tech investment and, 373–376
　labor supply shifts and, 377–379
　New Economy, delay hypothesis, and, 372

Productivity growth *(continued)*
    Reagan tax cuts and, 401
    revival of, 368–376
    slowdown in, 370–372
    in United States, 351
Productivity shock, 377–379
Property trap, 362
Public debt. *See* Government debt
Purchasing power parity (PPP) theory, 167–170
Pussycats, budget deficits and, 409

q theory (Tobin), 530–531
Quantity theory of money, 214
Quigley, John M., 508–509

Rand, Ayn, 57
Rate of return, 79
    for poor countries, 335–336
Rate of time preference, 388
Rational expectations, 497–498, 551–552, 593
    defined, 497, 552
    new classical macroeconomics and, 562
    price flexibility and, 574–575
Ratio of reserves to deposits (*e*). *See* Reserve ratio (*e*)
Ratios
    capital-labor, 324–326
    net investment, 524
    of personal saving to disposable personal income, 489
    sacrifice, 249
Raw materials, 372
Reagan, Ronald, tax cuts of, 400–402, 504, 589
Real balance effect, fiscal policy and, 218–219
Real business cycle (RBC) model, 548, 555–561, 590, 597
    assessment of, 559–562
    defined, 556
    labor market in, 557–558
Real corporate bond rate, 181
Real exchange rate, 167–170
    defined, 167
    of dollar, 173–174
    interest rate and, 180–182
    U.S. real corporate bond rate and, 181
Real GDP, 39, 40, 197, 198. *See also* Actual real GDP; Natural real GDP
    accelerator and, 523–524
    actual and natural, 6
    adjustment path of, 249
    aggregate demand and supply and, 59–60
    business cycles and, 12–14
    calculating changes in, 41–43
    equilibrium, 69–70
    fluctuations in, 387–388
    growth in U.S. (1950–2004), 58
    importance of, 41
    inflation and, 233, 234, 248
    inflation rate, short-run Phillips Curve, and, 235–238
    interest rate changes and, 459–460
    international comparison of, 224–225
    LM curve and, 95
    macroeconomic concepts and, 8
    measurement of, 39–44
    net investment ratio and, 524
    shifts in planned spending and, 72–73
    targeting of, 444
    unemployment rate changes and, 264
    in United Kingdom and United States, 321
    volatility and, 57–59
Real GDP gap, 9
Real GDP growth, 242
    calculating rate of, 44
Real gross private domestic investment. *See* Gross private domestic investment (GPDI)
Real income
    fiscal stimulus and, 117
    government budget surplus and, 135
    government spending and, 109
    increase in planned autonomous spending and, 211
    interest rate and, 86
    net exports and, 178, 179
    nominal money supply increase and, 549
    price level values and, 199
Real interest
    actual rate, 286
    expected rate, 286–287
    taxation and, 292
Real money balances, 99
Real money supply, 538
    LM curve and, 198, 199
Real output, 39
Real prices, of computers, 260
Real rate of return, on private investment, 389
Real rigidity, 565
Real wage(s)
    adverse productivity shock and, 377–379
    employment and, 562
    fooling model and, 549–550
    in Great Depression, 224–227
    increase in, 558–559
    productivity and, 353–354
    rational expectations and, 552
Real wage growth, inflation and, 285–286
Real wage rate
    decline in U.S., 370
    in Great Depression, 226–227
    vs. nominal wage rate, 205, 206
Recession, 11, 583
    1970–2004, 588
    in 1981–82, 589
    in 1990–91, 590
    in 2001, 3, 130, 373–376, 591, 592
    consumer durables in, 500
    defined, 10
    effect of, 134
    fear of, 284–285
    federal budget deficits and, 398
    Fed's restrictive policies and, 267
    human costs of, 309–310
    as inflation cure, 247–248
Recognition lag, 457
Recovery
    during expansion, 10n
    measurements in 2002–04, 47–49
Redistribution effect, 219
Refinancing, of mortgage interest rates, 106
Regulation, of interest rates, 437
Reinsdorf, Marshall B., 510n
Relative wage(s)
    unemployment and, 306
    worker efficiency and, 573
Replacement investment, 521–522
Repurchase agreements, 421, 422
Reputational equilibrium, 466
Required reserves, 430
Research and development, 361
Reserve ratio (*e*), 427, 428, 431, 432
Reserve requirements, 430–431
Residential investment, 519
Residual, 333
Retailing industry, Europe/U.S. productivity growth and, 382
Retirement
    assets used during, 501
    consumption during, 505
Retirement plans, as form of saving, 420
Revaluation, 172
Revenues. *See also* Government revenues
    government expenditures, deficit, and, 133
Ricardo, David, 214
Rich countries
    output per hour during convergence, 356
    standards of living in, 320
Rigidity
    nominal, 564, 565–568
    real, 564, 565
    wage, 216, 570–571
Rigid rule, 454, 470, 483
"Riskless" assets, 435n
"Risky" assets, 435
Robinson, James A., 363–364
Rockoff, Hugh, 290n
Rohwedder, Susann, 505n
Romer, Christina D., 223n, 458–459
Romer, David, 336n, 338n, 458–459, 565n
Romer, Paul M., 340, 341n
Rudebusch, Glenn, 531
Rules. *See* Policy rules
Rules vs. activism debate, 453–454, 597

Rules vs. discretion debate, 467, 470–473
Russell, Steven, 292n
Russia, 362, 463–464

Sachs, Jeffrey D., 364n, 365, 366, 367, 370
   on geography and economic growth, 365–367
Sacrifice ratio, 249–252
Sales, investment and, 520–522
Salomon Smith Barney, 429
Samuelson, Paul A., 583n
Sapsford, Jathon, 443n
Sargent, Thomas J., 555n, 563n, 587, 589n
SAS curve. *See* Short-run aggregate supply *(SAS)* curve
Savers, 419
Saving. *See also* Personal saving
   alternative measures of, 509–511
   Barro-Ricardo equivalence theorem and, 403–404
   bequests and, 501–505
   capital and income per person and, 331
   cross-country differences in, 503
   disappearance in 2004, 64–65
   economic growth and, 321, 326–327, 502
   equilibrium in Solow growth model, 330
   higher rate of, 329–331
   induced, 69
   international comparisons of, 148, 149
   investment and, 30
   under life-cycle hypothesis, 494–495
   marginal propensity and, 62–63
   national, 139–144, 389–390, 502–503, 537
   permanent-income hypothesis of consumption and, 492
   per person, 329
   personal, 30
   private, 33
   vs. process of saving, 64n
   raising incentive for, 388, 389
   Reagan tax cuts and, 401
   reasons for, 418
   of tax rebate (2001), 499
   in United States, 389
Saving function, 63
Saving rate, 147–150
   economic growth and, 359
   short-run variability and long-run constancy in, 488–489
Saving ratio, Keynesian, 488
Savings and loan institutions (S&Ls), 420, 421
Savings deposits, 423
   vs. cash holdings, 433–434
Saving to income ratio, 488
   disposable income, consumption spending, and, 486
Scadding, John, 489n

Schultze, Charles, 401
Schwartz, Anna J., 223n
"Search" unemployment theory (job search theory), 308
Second World War. *See* World War II
Securities industry, 373
Segert, Alice, 300n
Seignorage, 298
Self-correcting forces
   defined, 214
   in Great Depression, 226
   Keynes on, 216–221
Self-correction
   in aggregate demand-supply model, 214–215
   failure of, 565
Services expenditures, 484, 485–486
Shapiro, Matthew D., 499
Shiller, Robert J., 508–509
Shocks. *See* Commodity demand (spending) shocks; Demand shocks; Money demand shocks; Money-multiplier shock; Oil price shocks; Supply shocks; Technology shocks
"Shoe-leather cost," of inflation, 291
Short run
   business cycles in, 9
   fiscal and monetary expansion in, 210–214
   saving rate in, 488–489
Short-run aggregate supply *(SAS)* curve, 202, 232, 552, 553
   alternative shapes of, 203–205
   constant nominal wage rate and, 205–207
   defined, 198
   effect of rightward shift in *AD* curve and, 204
   labor demand curve and, 205, 206–207
   new Keynesian economics and, 574
   shifts of, 207
   short-run Phillips Curve and, 235
   slope of, 206–207, 236
   for values of wage rate, 208
Short-run consumption function, 492
Short-run equilibrium, 212
Short-run MPC, 491, 493
Short-run orientation, of monetary policy, 387
Short-run Phillips *(SP)* Curve, 587
   defined, 237
   equation for, 272–273
   inflation expectations and, 237, 238–239
   real GDP, inflation rate, and, 235–238
   SAS curve and, 235
   shifts of, 240, 275–276
   slope of, 240
   supply shocks and, 255
Short-term Phillips Curve trade-off, in 1950s, 583

Sichel, Daniel, 531n, 537n
Siegert, Alice, 17n
Simon, John, 461n
Simons, Henry C., 454
Simple accelerator
   assessing, 523–524
   defects of, 525–526
Singapore, 349, 356, 361, 365, 366
Single market, in Europe, 474
Skills
   mismatch unemployment and, 305–306
   structural unemployment and, 305
Slemrod, Joel, 499
Slope
   of *AD* curve, 203
   of *IS* curve, 85
   of *LM* curve, 103
   of *LP* curve, 240
   of *SP* curve, 240
Small open economy
   defined, 182
   expansion with fixed exchange rates, 183–185
   fiscal policy in, 142–144
   IS-LM model in, 182–186
Smith, Adam, 214
Social Security, 404–409
   baby boomer retirement and, 404, 406
   debate over, 592
   forecasts for, 405–406
   future problems of, 387
   outlays, revenues, and trust fund (1985–2080), 407
   political vs. economic arguments over, 408–409
   reform proposals for, 406–408
   rise in benefits, 399
   saving current system, 406
   trust fund of, 405, 406–408
Solow, Robert M., 232, 324n, 333–334, 341n, 352, 353, 372, 438n, 585
Solow's economic growth theory, 327–331, 341
   convergence in, 336–337
   human capital and, 338–339, 360
   immigration and, 339
   income and, 349–350
   miracle economies and, 350
   puzzles not explained by, 334–337
   technological change and, 331–334
Solow's paradox, 371
Solow's residual, 333–334, 352–353
Solvency, 392–395
South Korea, per-capita real GDP in, 18–19
SP curve. *See* Short-run Phillips *(SP)* Curve
SP-DG model, 589
   algebra of, 272–279
Speculation, business confidence and, 532–533

Spending, 38. *See also* Expenditures
  autonomous planned, 66–67
  governmental, 33
  of tax rebate (2001), 499
Spending stream, leakages from, 91–92
Square root hypothesis, of money holding, 435n
Stabilization
  automatic, 92, 134–136
  strategy to end hyperinflation, 301
  targets of, 450–454
Stabilization policy, 19–20, 483, 589
  in 1960s, 585
  in closed and open economy, 449–476
  fiscal policy and, 417
  fiscal tools and, 530
  low inflation and unemployment goals of, 280–311
  monetary policy and, 417
Stable-consumption argument, 493
Staggered contracts, 564
Standard & Poor's (S&P) 500 index, 507
Standard of living
  defined, 352
  economic growth and, 320, 321–322
  Europe/U.S. comparison, 381–382
  international investment position and, 160–161
  inventions and, 382–383
  labor productivity and, 351–352
  Penn project and, 321n
  U.S. productivity and, 383
State government retirement funds, 420, 421
Steady state
  defined, 326
  saving and investment in, 326–327
Stein, Herbert, 516
Sticky marginal cost, 568
Sticky prices, 565
Sticky wages, 565, 572–573
Stiglitz, Joseph, 342, 565n
Stiroh, Kevin J., 537n
Stock, 27, 421, 422
  high-tech, 535
Stock market
  in 1980s, 589
  autonomous consumption, interest rate, and, 63–64
  boom in, 400
  collapse in 2000, 373
  high-tech bubble and, 535
  household saving rate and, 506–509
  individual accounts and, 592
  monetary policy and, 107
  price explosion of late 1990s, 507
  Social Security funds investment in, 406–408
Stock of physical capital. *See* Capital stock
Stock prices, in 2001 recession, 376
Store of value, money as, 96
Structural budget, 134–138

Structural deficit, 134
Structural employment policy, 450
Structural surplus, 134
Structural unemployment, 305
Sub-Saharan Africa, economic growth and, 366
Substitution effect, in RBC approach, 560
Summers, Lawrence H., 501n
Summers, Robert, 321n, 355, 356n, 357n, 358n
Supply, aggregate, 59
Supply curve
  aggregate, 203–205
  for currencies, 163–164
Supply function
  Friedman-Phelps-Lucas, 552–554
  slope of, 554
Supply inflation, 252
Supply-shock analysis, of inflation adjustment, 587
Supply shocks, 232, 456, 470, 483
  of 1970–2004, 588
  in 1990s, 590
  adverse, 257, 258, 285, 463
  beneficial, 257, 258–260, 463
  business cycles and, 559–562
  consequences of, 277–278
  debate over RBC approach and, 590
  defined, 234–235
  economy's response to, 558
  Fed and, 463–464
  graphical summary of role, 257–258
  importance of, 252–254
  inflation, output ratio, and, 254–258
  peaks and valleys in, 254
  Phillips curve analysis and, 589
  policy responses to, 255–256
  RBC model and, 557, 558
  real GDP and, 444
  shifts in, 255
  SP curve and, 255
  types of, 254
  unemployment, inflation, and, 266–267
  volatility and, 461–463
Supply-side economics, 400–402, 590
Surplus
  balance of payments, 156–158
  cyclical, 134
  government, 33
  natural employment, 137
  structural, 134
Suzuki, Y., 473n
Svensson, Lars E. O., 468n, 473n
Swan, Joseph W., 375
Swiss franc, foreign exchange market and, 163–164

Taiwan, 349, 356
Targeting, 587. *See also* Policy targets
  inflation, 455
  money supply vs. interest rates, 442–445

  of policy, 451
  of real GDP, 444
Target variables, 19
  defined, 452
  rules for, 473
Taxation, 32, 33. *See also* Fiscal policy
  in 1950s, 585
  Barro-Ricardo equivalence theorem and, 402–404
  budget line and, 367
  Bush tax cuts, 400, 504
  financing cuts in, 75–76
  fiscal policy stimulus and, 144
  government saving rate and, 147–150
  government spending and, 73–74
  increase and collapse of revenues, 399–400
  interest rates and, 292
  investment and, 526
  investment behavior and, 529–531
  Johnson tax cut, 586
  personal income and, 38
  Reagan tax cuts, 400–402, 504, 589
  value-added tax, 301
Tax credits, 529
Tax incentives
  activist fiscal policy and, 530–531
  investment behavior and, 527–528
Tax multiplier, 75
Tax rebate (2001), household spending or saving of, 499
Tax surcharge, 586
Taylor, John B., 468–469, 526n
Taylor Rule, 445, 455, 472
  defined, 468
  Fed and, 467–470, 589
  federal funds and interest rates calculated by, 469
  implementing, 473
  inflation targeting vs., 597–598
  investment volatility and, 539–540
  monetary policy, double target, and, 591
Technological change, 331
  economic growth rate increase and, 409
  endogenous growth theory and, 339–341
  foreign investment and, 361–362
  human capital and, 361
  importing, 361
  labor-augmenting, 332
  neutral, 332
Technology
  economic growth and, 350–351
  human capital and, 360–361
  methods for obtaining, 361
  productivity growth revival and, 372, 373
  Solow model and, 331–334, 355
  in tropics, 365
Technology shocks, 559

Teenagers
  employment discrimination against, 306
  in labor force, 370
Telecommunications
  equipment investment and, 532
  speculative boom in, 536
Termites, budget deficits and, 409
Thailand, 320, 366, 463
Thornton, Henry, 197
Thrift institutions, 420, 439, 460
Time deposits, 423
Time inconsistency, 465–466
Time series
  vs. cross section, 486–489
  defined, 488
Time-varying NAIRU (TV-NAIRU), 591–592
TIPS (Treasury Inflation-Protection Securities), 293, 294
Tobin, James, 219n, 280, 319, 432, 435, 438, 565n, 586
  q theory of, 530–531
Total factor productivity, 333
Total labor force, 46
Trade. *See* Foreign trade entries; Free trade
Transactions accounts, 423, 430
Transfer payments, 29, 32, 74n, 398–399
Transitory income, 491
Transmission lag, 457
Traveler's checks, 423
Treasury bills, 421, 422, 429–430, 439
Treasury notes and bonds, 421
Triangle model, of new Keynesian economics, 589
Trilemma
  defined, 155
  United States, euro, and, 189–190
Tropics, growth and development in, 365–367, 366
Trough, 10, 11
Trust fund, Social Security, 405, 406–408
Turnover unemployment, 304, 307–310
Twin deficits, 35–36, 590
Tyco, corruption scandal at, 376

Unanticipated inflation, 287–288
Uncertainty, bequests and, 501–505
Unemployment, 14, 46
  1970–2001, 588
  in 1970s and early 1980s, 587
  1982–91, 589
  in 1990s, 590
  in 2001, 3
  actual and natural, 7–8
  actual and natural GDP and, 13
  classical view of, 215–216
  cyclical, 303–304
  in Europe and United States, 595, 596–597
  fluctuations in, 59
  in Great Depression, 15–16, 221–222, 223, 580–582
  in Keynesian model, 221
  measurement of, 45–47
  mismatch, 304–306, 307
  natural rate of, 450, 590
  persistent, 221
  and postwar inflation, 266–267
  rate of change of wage rates and, 237n
  solutions to, 311
  stabilization policy goals and, 280–311
  structural, 305
  survey of, 45–47
  turnover, 304, 307–310
  during World War II, 582
Unemployment (Pigou), 216n
Unemployment compensation, 308–309
Unemployment-inflation tradeoff, 267–268
Unemployment insurance, 216
Unemployment rate, 3–4, 46–47
  in 1920s and 1930s, 580
  actual and natural, 302–303
  actual and natural real GDP and, 265
  behavior of, 278–279
  decline in natural rate (1990s), 310
  defined, 46
  inflation rate and, 263–268, 463
  output ratio, Okun's law, and, 264–266
  in Phelps' fooling model, 550–551
  real GDP changes and, 264
  by reason, gender, and age (2004), 308
  reasons for not reducing, 302–304
Unintended inventory investments, 68
United Kingdom, 349
  economic growth in, 323
  Great Depression in, 224, 225
  investment in, 537
  standard of living in, 321
United States, 349
  consumer credit in, 503
  consumption data of, 484–486
  credit use in, 436–437
  current account deficit (2004–05), 594
  debt-GDP ratio international comparison for, 394
  delay hypothesis and, 372
  disinflation in, 250–251
  economic growth in, 323, 324, 351, 357
  economic performance of, 20–22
  Europe policy/institutions compared with, 381
  fiscal policy in, 77, 597
  Great Depression in, 16, 224–225
  inflation in, 41
  infrastructure of, 364
  investment in, 536
  macroeconomics in, 596–597
  monetary policy in, 597
  New Economy and, 372
  productivity compared with Europe, 379–382
  productivity growth in, 320, 368–376, 381, 382, 560–561, 595, 597
  productivity growth slowdown in (1975–95), 370–372
  revival of productivity growth in (post-1995), 372
  saving in, 502, 503
  simple accelerator and postwar economy in, 523–525
  standard of living in, 321
  trilemma, euro, and, 189–190
  unemployment in, 596–597
  world economy and, 593
Unit of account, money as, 96–97
User cost of capital, 526, 532
  defined, 527
  drop in, 528
  monetary and fiscal policy and, 528–531

Valleys, supply shocks and, 254
Value-added tax, 301
Variables
  countercyclical, 213
  exogenous and endogenous, 60
  target, 19, 452, 493
Vault cash, 430
Velocity, money, inflation, output, and, 281–283
Venezuela, 357, 358
Vertical *IS* curve, 217
Vietnam War
  demand shocks and, 461
  spending on, 585, 586
Volatility
  of business cycles, 57–59
  of consumption, 497
  decline in, 461–465
  Taylor Rule and investment, 539–540
  between wars, 581
Volcker disinflation, 589

Wage(s), 26
  in Great Depression, 224
  sticky nature of, 565, 572–573
Wage indexation, 300–301
Wage rate(s). *See also* Nominal wage rates; Real wage rate
  equilibrium real, 208–210
  job vacancies and, 305
  labor contracts and, 210, 570
  rate of change and unemployment, 237n
  SAS curve and, 205–207, 208
  setting of, 208–210
Wallace, Neil, 555n
Warner, Andrew, 364n
Wars
  debt-GDP ratio and, 397
  government size and, 132–134
  reserve requirements and, 431n

Wealth
   household, 63–64, 506, 507
   housing, 509
Wealth effect, on demand for money, 435
Web sites, 28
Weil, David N., 336n, 338n
Welfare, long-run effects of fiscal policy on, 388–390
Welfare gains, from economic growth, 319–320
Wilcox, James A., 222n
Wilde, Oscar, 374
Will, George F., 579
Wizard of Oz, as monetary allegory, 290
Wolfe, Kathy, 177n
Women
   employment discrimination against, 306
   in labor force, 370
Woodford, Michael, 473n, 526n
Work effort, Reagan tax cuts and, 401
Worker efficiency, relative wage rate and, 573
Worldcom, corruption scandal at, 376
World economy, ideas and events in, 593–595
World War II
   economy and, 582–583
   Great Depression and, 16
Worldwide investment, 537
World Wide Web (WWW), 372, 373, 535

Yen. *See* Japan
Y2k problem, 535

Zero-rate financing, 106

Guide to Symbols

[*Note:* For most variables, the level is indicated by an uppercase letter (X) while the growth rate is indicated by a lowercase letter (x). Each such variable is listed only once in this list by the appropriate uppercase letter (X).]

Symbol	Chapter Where Introduced	Definition
Δ	3	The change in a magnitude
A	3	Real autonomous expenditure
A	10	Autonomous growth factor; multifactor productivity
A	15	Assets held in life-cycle hypothesis
b	4–Appendix	Dollar change of A_p in response to a one percentage-point change in the interest rate
b	10	Elasticity of output with respect to capital input
b	13	Broker's fee in Baumol's theory of money demand
B	9	Dollar amount of government bonds outstanding
c	3	Marginal propensity to consume
c	13	Fraction of bank deposits held as currency by the public
C	2	Real personal consumption expenditures
C	13	Currency held by the public
d	10	Depreciation rate
D	12	Nominal government debt (ΔD = nominal government deficit)
D	13	Demand deposits (accounts at banks or thrift institutions that allow checks to be written)
e	6	Real foreign exchange rate
e'	6	Nominal foreign exchange rate
e	13	Fraction of deposits that banks hold as reserves
E	2	Real expenditures ($E = C + I + G + NX$)
f	4–Appendix	Dollar change of the demand for real money in response to a one percentage-point change in the interest rate
F	2	Real government transfer payments
g	8–Appendix	Slope of the short-run Phillips curve (*SP*)
G	2	Real government purchases of goods and services
h	8–Appendix	Response of unemployment to the output ratio
h	4–Appendix	Dollar change of the demand for real money in response to a one-dollar change in real income, holding the interest rate constant
h	17	Response of output to a price surprise in the Friedman-Lucas supply function
H	9	High-powered money (same as the monetary base; consists of currency plus bank reserves)
i	9	Nominal or market interest rate
I	2	Real gross private investment
j	8–Appendix	Coefficient of adjustment of expectations
k	3	Spending multiplier
k_1	4–Appendix	Multiplier for autonomous spending in *IS-LM* model
k_2	4–Appendix	Multiplier for real money supply in *IS-LM* model
k	15	Marginal propensity to consume out of permanent income
K	10	Capital stock
L	4	Money demand function
L	15	Age at death in life-cycle hypothesis
M	4	Nominal money supply